Communications in Computer and Information Science   1129

Commenced Publication in 2007
Founding and Former Series Editors:
Phoebe Chen, Alfredo Cuzzocrea, Xiaoyong Du, Orhun Kara, Ting Liu,
Krishna M. Sivalingam, Dominik Ślęzak, Takashi Washio, Xiaokang Yang,
and Junsong Yuan

T0171904

More information about this series at http://www.springer.com/series/7899

Vladimir Voevodin · Sergey Sobolev (Eds.)

Supercomputing

5th Russian Supercomputing Days, RuSCDays 2019
Moscow, Russia, September 23–24, 2019
Revised Selected Papers

 Springer

Editors
Vladimir Voevodin ⓘ
Research Computing Center
Moscow State University
Moscow, Russia

Sergey Sobolev ⓘ
Research Computing Center
Moscow State University
Moscow, Russia

ISSN 1865-0929   ISSN 1865-0937 (electronic)
Communications in Computer and Information Science
ISBN 978-3-030-36591-2   ISBN 978-3-030-36592-9 (eBook)
https://doi.org/10.1007/978-3-030-36592-9

This Springer imprint is published by the registered company Springer Nature Switzerland AG
The registered company address is: Gewerbestrasse 11, 6330 Cham, Switzerland

Preface

The 5th Russian Supercomputing Days Conference (RuSCDays 2019) was held September 23–24, 2019, in Moscow, Russia. It was was dedicated to the 85th anniversary of academician V.V. Voevodin, the outstanding Russian mathematician who made a valuable contribution to the parallel computing theory and supercomputing technologies. The conference was organized by the Supercomputing Consortium of Russian Universities and the Russian Academy of Sciences. The conference organization coordinator was Moscow State University Research Computing Center.

The conference was supported by the Russian Foundation for Basic Research and our respected platinum educational partner (IBM), platinum sponsors (NVIDIA, T-Platforms, Lenovo), gold sponsors (Mellanox, Xilinx, AMD, RSC, Intel, Dell), and silver sponsors (NEC, EAS, DDN). The conference was organized in a partnership with the ISC High Performance conference series.

The RuSCDays conference series was born in 2015 as a union of several supercomputing event series in Russia and quickly became one of the most notable Russian supercomputing international meetings. The conference caters to the interests of a wide range of representatives from science, industry, business, education, government, and students – anyone connected to the development or the use of supercomputing technologies. The conference topics cover all aspects of supercomputing technologies: software and hardware design, solving large tasks, application of supercomputing technologies in industry, exaflops-scale computing issues, supercomputing co-design technologies, supercomputing education, and others.

All papers submitted to the conference were reviewed by three referees in the first review round. The papers were evaluated according to their relevance to the conference topics, scientific contribution, presentation, approbation, and related works description. After notification of conditional acceptance, the second review round was arranged which aimed at the final polishing of papers and also at the evaluating of authors' work based on the referees' comments. After the conference, the 60 best papers were carefully selected to be included in this volume.

The proceedings editors would like to thank all the conference committees members, especially the Organizing and Program Committee members as well as the referees and reviewers for their contributions. We also thank Springer for producing these high-quality proceedings of RuSCDays 2019.

October 2019

Vladimir Voevodin
Sergey Sobolev

Organization

Steering Committee

V. A. Sadovnichiy (Chair)	Moscow State University, Russia
V. B. Betelin (Co-chair)	Russian Academy of Sciences, Russia
A. V. Tikhonravov (Co-chair)	Moscow State University, Russia
J. Dongarra (Co-chair)	University of Tennessee, USA
A. I. Borovkov	Peter the Great Saint-Petersburg Polytechnic University, Russia
Vl. V. Voevodin	Moscow State University, Russia
V. P. Gergel	Lobachevsky State University of Nizhni Novgorod, Russia
G. S. Elizarov	NII Kvant, Russia
V. V. Elagin	Hewlett Packard Enterprise, Russia
A. K. Kim	MCST, Russia
E. V. Kudryashova	Northern (Arctic) Federal University, Russia
N. S. Mester	Intel, Russia
E. I. Moiseev	Moscow State University, Russia
A. A. Moskovskiy	RSC Group, Russia
V. Yu. Opanasenko	T-Platforms, Russia
G. I. Savin	Joint Supercomputer Center, Russian Academy of Sciences, Russia
A. S. Simonov	NICEVT, Russia
V. A. Soyfer	Samara University, Russia
L. B. Sokolinskiy	South Ural State University, Russia
I. A. Sokolov	Russian Academy of Sciences, Russia
R. G. Strongin	Lobachevsky State University of Nizhni Novgorod, Russia
A. N. Tomilin	Institute for System Programming of the Russian Academy of Sciences, Russia
A. R. Khokhlov	Moscow State University, Russia
B. N. Chetverushkin	Keldysh Institutes of Applied Mathematics, Russian Academy of Sciences, Russia
E. V. Chuprunov	Lobachevsky State University of Nizhni Novgorod, Russia
A. L. Shestakov	South Ural State University, Russia

Program Committee

Vl. V. Voevodin (Chair)	Moscow State University, Russia
R. M. Shagaliev (Co-chair)	Russian Federal Nuclear Center, Russia

V. N. Lykosov	Institute of Numerical Mathematics, Russian Academy of Sciences, Russia
I. B. Meerov	Lobachevsky State University of Nizhni Novgorod, Russia
M. Michalewicz	University of Warsaw, Poland
L. Mirtaheri	Kharazmi University, Iran
S. G. Mosin	Kazan Federal University, Russia
A. V. Nemukhin	Moscow State University, Russia
G. V. Osipov	Lobachevsky State University of Nizhni Novgorod, Russia
A. V. Semyanov	Lobachevsky State University of Nizhni Novgorod, Russia
Ya. D. Sergeev	Lobachevsky State University of Nizhni Novgorod, Russia
H. Sithole	Centre for High Performance Computing, South Africa
A. V. Smirnov	Moscow State University, Russia
R. G. Strongin	Lobachevsky State University of Nizhni Novgorod, Russia
H. Takizawa	Tohoku University, Japan
M. Taufer	University of Delaware, USA
V. E. Turlapov	Lobachevsky State University of Nizhni Novgorod, Russia
E. E. Tyrtyshnikov	Institute of Numerical Mathematics, Russian Academy of Sciences, Russia
V. A. Fursov	Samara University, Russia
L. E. Khaymina	Northern (Arctic) Federal University, Russia
T. Hoefler	Eidgenössische Technische Hochschule Zürich, Switzerland
B. M. Shabanov	Joint Supercomputer Center, Russian Academy of Sciences, Russia
L. N. Shchur	Higher School of Economics, Russia
R. Wyrzykowski	Czestochowa University of Technology, Poland
M. Yokokawa	Kobe University, Japan

Industrial Committee

A. A. Aksenov (Co-chair)	Tesis, Russia
V. E. Velikhov (Co-chair)	National Research Center "Kurchatov Institute", Russia
A. V. Murashov (Co-chair)	T-Platforms, Russia
Yu. Ya. Boldyrev	Peter the Great Saint-Petersburg Polytechnic University, Russia
M. A. Bolshukhin	Afrikantov Experimental Design Bureau for Mechanical Engineering, Russia
R. K. Gazizov	Ufa State Aviation Technical University, Russia

M. P. Lobachev	Krylov State Research Centre, Russia
V. Ya. Modorskiy	Perm National Research Polytechnic University, Russia
A. P. Skibin	Gidropress, Podolsk, Russia
S. Stoyanov	T-Services, Russia
A. B. Shmelev	RSC Group, Russia
S. V. Strizhak	Hewlett-Packard, Russia

Educational Committee

V. P. Gergel (Co-chair)	Lobachevsky State University of Nizhni Novgorod, Russia
Vl. V. Voevodin (Co-chair)	Moscow State University, Russia
L. B. Sokolinskiy (Co-chair)	South Ural State University, Russia
Yu. Ya. Boldyrev	Peter the Great Saint-Petersburg Polytechnic University, Russia
A. V. Bukhanovskiy	ITMO University, Russia
R. K. Gazizov	Ufa State Aviation Technical University, Russia
S. A. Ivanov	Hewlett-Packard, Russia
I. B. Meerov	Lobachevsky State University of Nizhni Novgorod, Russia
V. Ya. Modorskiy	Perm National Research Polytechnic University, Russia
S. G. Mosin	Kazan Federal University, Russia
I. O. Odintsov	RSC Group, Russia
N. N. Popova	Moscow State University, Russia
O. A. Yufryakova	Northern (Arctic) Federal University, Russia

Organizing Committee

Vl. V. Voevodin (Chair)	Moscow State University, Russia
V. P. Gergel (Co-chair)	Lobachevsky State University of Nizhni Novgorod, Russia
B. M. Shabanov (Co-chair)	Joint Supercomputer Center, Russian Academy of Sciences, Russia
S. I. Sobolev (Scientific Secretary)	Moscow State University, Russia
A. A. Aksenov	Tesis, Russia
A. P. Antonova	Moscow State University, Russia
A. S. Antonov	Moscow State University, Russia
K. A. Barkalov	Lobachevsky State University of Nizhni Novgorod, Russia
M. R. Biktimirov	Russian Academy of Sciences, Russia
Vad. V. Voevodin	Moscow State University, Russia
T. A. Gamayunova	Moscow State University, Russia
O. A. Gorbachev	RSC Group, Russia

Russian
Supercomputing
Days 2019

Contents

HPC, BigData, AI: Architectures, Technologies, Tools

Distributed and Cloud Computing

Parallel Algorithms

A Highly Parallel Approach for Solving Computationally Expensive Multicriteria Optimization Problems

Victor Gergel$^{(\boxtimes)}$ (iD) and Evgeny Kozinov (iD)

Lobachevsky State University of Nizhni Novgorod, Nizhni Novgorod, Russia
gergel@unn.ru, evgeny.kozinov@itmm.unn.ru

Abstract. In this paper, a highly parallel approach for solving multicriteria optimization problems is proposed. The considered approach is based on the reduction of the multicriterial problems to the global optimization ones using the minimax convolution of the partial criteria, the dimensionality reduction with the use of the Peano space-filling curves, and the application of the efficient parallel information-statistical global optimization methods. The required computations can be time-consuming since functions representing individual criteria can be multi-extremal and computationally expensive. The proposed approach comprises two different schemes for efficient parallel computations on high performance systems with shared and distributed memory and with a large number of computational units. The computational efficiency is achieved by storing all the computed criteria values and their intensive reuse for finding new solutions. The results of numerical experiments have demonstrated that this approach allows to reduce the computational costs of solving multicriteria optimization problems by a factor between 10 and 100.

Keywords: Multicriteria optimization · Parallel computing · Dimensionality reduction · Criteria convolution · Global optimization algorithm · Computational complexity

1 Introduction

The multicriteria optimization (MCO) problems arise in a general formulation of a decision making problem. Reviews of the state of the art in multicriteria optimization can be found in [1–3, 12] and reviews of relevant techniques and applications in [4–7, 13, 24].

At the same time, the MCO problems are some of the most complex ones. To solve an MCO problem compromise decisions need to be found and having to find a representative set of those increases the computational complexity of solving the MCO problems. Bearing in mind that finding even a single efficient solution may require a large amount of computations, obtaining the whole Pareto set or even a limited subset of efficient decisions becomes a problem of high

© Springer Nature Switzerland AG 2019
V. Voevodin and S. Sobolev (Eds.): RuSCDays 2019, CCIS 1129, pp. 3–14, 2019.
https://doi.org/10.1007/978-3-030-36592-9_1

computational complexity. In order to solve such problems huge computational capabilities of high-performance systems are required.

The structure of this paper is as follows. Section 2 presents a general statement of a multicriteria optimization problem. A scheme of parallel computations to simultaneously solve a set of multicriteria global optimization problems is proposed in Sect. 3. A parallel algorithm of multicriteria global search is presented in Sect. 4. To demonstrate the proposed techniques, Sect. 5 presents results of numerical experiments.

2 Statement of a Multicriteria Optimization Problem

The problem of multicriteria (or multi-objective) optimization (MCO) can be defined as follows:

$$f(y) = (f_1(y), f_2(y), \ldots, f_s(y)) \to min, y \in D, \tag{1}$$

where $y = (y_1, y_2, \ldots, y_N)$ is a vector of varied parameters describing a system being designed, N is the dimensionality of the optimization problem, and D is the search domain being an N-dimensional hyperinterval

$$D = \{y \in R^N : a_i \leq y_i \leq b_i, 1 \leq i \leq N\}$$

with given boundary vectors a and b. Without a loss of generality, the efficiency criteria values in the problem (1) are assumed to be non-negative, and the decrease of these ones corresponds to the increase of the efficiency of the considered solutions $y \in D$. In addition it is assumed the efficiency criteria $f_i(y)$, $1 \leq i \leq s$ can be multiextremal, and the obtaining of the criteria values at the points of the search domain $y \in D$ can require a large amount of computations. It is assumed that the efficiency criteria $f_i(y)$, $1 \leq i \leq s$ satisfy the Lipschitz condition

$$|f_i(y') - f_i(y'')| \leq L_i||y' - y''||, y', y'' \in D, 1 \leq i \leq s \tag{2}$$

where L_i, $1 \leq i \leq s$ are the Lipschitz constants for the corresponding efficiency criteria $f_i(y)$, $1 \leq i \leq s$, and $||.||$ denotes the norm in the R^N space.

As *a solution* of the MCO problem, any efficient decision is considered. In a general case, it is required to find the whole set of Pareto-optimal solutions $PD(f, D)$, i.e. *the complete solution of an MCO problem.*

A general approach to solving the MCO problem used in this paper consists in the replacement of solving the original MCO problems by solving a series of simpler optimization problems:

$$\min (\phi(x) = F(\lambda, y(x)), y(x) \in D, x \in [0, 1]),$$
$$F(\lambda, y(x)) = \max (\lambda_i f_i(y(x)), 1 \leq i \leq s),$$
$$\lambda = (\lambda_1, \lambda_2, \ldots, \lambda_s) \in \Lambda \subset R^s : \sum_{i=1}^{s} \lambda_i = 1, \lambda_i \geq 0, 1 \leq i \leq s \tag{3}$$

where $F(\lambda, y(x))$ is the minimax convolution of the efficiency criteria of the MCO problem [2, 6, 19] with the use of the vector of the convolution coefficients $\lambda \in \Lambda$ and $y(x)$ is a continuous and unambiguous mapping of the interval [0,1] onto an N-dimensional search domain D – see, for example, [7, 8].

The necessity and sufficiency of this approach for solving MCO problems is a key property of the minimax convolution. The result of the minimization of $F(\lambda, y)$ leads to obtaining an efficient variant[1] of the MCO problem and vice versa, any efficient variant of an MCO problem can be obtained as a result of the minimization of $F(\lambda, y)$ at corresponding values of the convolution coefficients λ_i, $1 \le i \le s$. In order to obtain several efficient decisions (or in order to evaluate the whole Pareto domain) the problem (3) should be solved for the corresponding set of values of the vector $\lambda \in \Lambda$.

The dimensionality reduction applied in (3) allows to replace solving multidimensional MCO problems by the optimization of one-dimensional functions $F(\lambda, y(x))$ which satisfy the uniform Hölder condition i.e.

$$|F(\lambda, y(x')) - F(\lambda, y(x''))| \le H|x' - x''|^{1/N}, x', x'' \in [0, 1], \tag{4}$$

where the constant H is defined as $H = 2L\sqrt{N + 3}$, L is the Lipschitz constant of the function $F(\lambda, y)$ and N is the dimensionality of the optimization problem (1).

3   Parallel Computations for Solving the Multicriteria Global Optimization Problems

The scalarization of the vector criterion allows reducing the solving of the MCO problem (1) to solving a series of the multiextremal problems (3). Therefore, the problem of development of the methods for solving the MCO problems is resolved by the possibility of an extensive use of efficient parallel global optimization algorithms.

Multiextremal optimization is a research area being actively developed – its state of the art is presented, for example, in [7, 9, 10, 26]. The information-statistical theory of global optimization is considered to be one of the promising approaches [7]. HPC systems are used widely for solving time-consuming global search problems [7, 11, 14, 15].

The proposed approach to the use of parallel computations for solving time-consuming global optimization problems is based on the following main statements:

– The parallelism of the performed computations is provided by means of simultaneous computing the values of the efficiency criteria $f_i(y)$, $1 \le i \le s$ at several points of the search domain D. Such an approach provides the parallelization of the most computation-costly part of global optimization and is a general one – it can be applied with many global optimization methods for various global optimization problems.

---

[1] More precisely, the minimization of $F(\lambda, y)$ can lead to the obtaining of the weakly-efficient variants (the set of the weakly-efficient decisions includes the Pareto domain).

- The parallel computations are provided by means of simultaneous solving of several global optimization problems (3) for varying values of the coefficients λ_i, $1 \leq i \leq s$. For solving the problems of the family (3), a set of computational nodes of the high performance systems with distributed memory can be applied.
- The optimization data obtained in the course of parallel computations is exchanged between all employed processors because of the information compatibility of the global optimization problems of the family (3).

All these statements will be considered in more details below.

3.1   General Scheme of Parallel Computations

As mentioned above, when solving a multicriteria optimization problem (1), solving a series of scalar problems (3) with varying coefficients of the minimax convolution of the efficiency criteria may be required in order to find several different efficient decisions:

$$\Phi(y) = \{\phi_1(y), \dots, \phi_q(y)\}, \phi_i(y) = F(\lambda_i, y), 1 \leq l \leq q. \tag{5}$$

Such problems can be solved sequentially by various global optimization methods. Alternatively, these problems can be solved simultaneously using several processors. It is important to note that the obtained family of the one-dimensional problems $\Phi(y)$ is an information-dependent one because the values of the optimized functions computed for any problem $\phi_l(y)$, $1 \leq l \leq q$ can be transformed to the values of all the remaining problems of the family without time-consuming recalculations of the efficiency criteria values $f_i(y)$, $1 \leq i \leq s$ (see Sect. 3.2).

The information compatibility of the problems from the family (5) allows to propose the following unified scheme of parallel computations:

1. The family of the information-linked problems $\Phi(y)$ in (5) is distributed among the processors of the computing system.
2. For solving the optimization problems (5), a global optimization method implemented on each processor should be updated following the following rules:
   (a) Upon completing the iteration for any problem $\phi_l(y)$, $1 \leq l \leq q$ at any point $y' \in D$, the point y' with the particular criteria values $f_i(y)$, $1 \leq i \leq s$ computed at this point should be transferred to all employed processors.
   (b) Prior to the start of the next global search iteration, the method should check the queue of the received messages; if there are any data in the queue, the received information should be included into the search information.

The possibility of the asynchronous data transfer is a key feature of such a scheme of the parallel computations. It is important to note that this scheme does not depend on any of the single control nodes, and the number of computational nodes can vary in the course of global optimization.

3.2 Accumulation and Reuse of Calculated Optimization Data

For solving the stated optimization problems, the values of the efficiency criteria $f^i = f(y^i)$ at the points y^i, $1 \leq i \leq k$ of the search domain D are computed. The search information obtained as a result of these computations can be represented in the form of the *Search Information Set* (SIS):

$$\Omega_k = \{(y^i, f^i = f(y^i))^T : 1 \leq i \leq k\}. \tag{6}$$

As a result of the dimensionality reduction, the search information Ω_k from (6) can be transformed into the *Matrix of the Search State* (MSS)

$$A_k = \{(x_i, z_i, l_i)^T : 1 \leq i \leq k\} \tag{7}$$

where x_i, $1 \leq i \leq k$ are the reduced points of the executed global search iterations,[2] z_i, $1 \leq i \leq k$ are the values of the scalar criterion of the current optimization problem (3), l_i, $1 \leq i \leq k$ are the indices of the optimization iterations where the points x_i, $1 \leq i \leq k$ were computed.

The matrix of the search state can be used by the optimization algorithms in order to improve the efficiency of the global search – selecting the points for the scheduled iterations can be performed taking into account the results of all previously executed computations.

3.3 Parallel Computations on Multiprocessors with Shared Memory

Within the proposed approach, for solving the reduced one-dimensional multiextremal optimization subproblems (3) it is proposed to use the well-known Parallel Algorithm of Global Search (PAGS) developed within the framework of the information-statistical theory of the multiextremal optimization [7,25]. This method has a good theoretical background and has demonstrated its efficiency as compared to other global search algorithms (see also the results of numerical experiments in Sect. 4).

For completeness, let us briefly discuss the general computational scheme of PAGS, which consists in the following.

Let p be the number of employed parallel computers (processors or cores) of a computational system with shared memory. The initial two iterations of the algorithm are performed at the boundaries of the interval $x^0 = 0$, $x^1 = 1$. Apart from these boundary points, the algorithm should perform additional iterations at the points x^i, $1 < i \leq p$ which can be defined *a priori* or computed by any auxiliary computational procedure. Then, let $(k > p)$ global search iterations be completed, at each of which the computation of the value of the minimized function $\phi(x)$ from (3) (hereafter called *a trial*) has been performed. The choice of the points for trials performed within the next iteration in parallel is determined by the following rules.

---

[2] The lower indices denote the increasing order of the coordinate values of the points x_i, $1 \leq i \leq k$.

Rule 1. Renumber the trial points of the completed search iterations with the lower indices in the order of increasing coordinate values

$$0 = x_0 < x_1 < \cdots < x_i < \cdots < x_k = 1. \tag{8}$$

Rule 2. Compute the current estimate of the Hölder constant of the function $\phi(x)$:

$$m = \begin{cases} rM, & M > 0 \\ 1, & M = 0 \end{cases}, M = \max_{1 \le i \le k} \frac{|z_i - z_{i-1}|}{\varrho_i} \tag{9}$$

where $z_i = \phi(x_i)$, $\varrho_i = \sqrt[N]{x_i - x_{i-1}}$, $1 \le i \le k$. The constant r, $r > 1$, is the *reliability parameter* of the algorithm.

Rule 3. Compute *the characteristic $R(i)$* for each interval (x_{i-1}, x_i), $1 \le i \le k$ according to the expression

$$R(i) = \varrho_i + \frac{(z_i - z_{i-1})^2}{m^2 \varrho_i} - 2\frac{(z_i + z_{i-1})}{m}, 1 \le i \le k. \tag{10}$$

Rule 4. Arrange the characteristics of the intervals (x_{i-1}, x_i), $1 \le i \le k$ obtained according to (10) in the decreasing order

$$R(t_1) \ge R(t_2) \ge \cdots \ge R(t_{k-1}) \ge R(t_k) \tag{11}$$

and select p intervals with the indices t_j, $1 \le j \le p$ having the maximum values of the characteristics.

Rule 5. Perform new trials at the points x^{k+j}, $1 \le j \le p$ placed in the intervals with the maximum characteristics from (11) according to the expressions

$$x^{k+j} = \frac{x_{t_j} + x_{t_j-1}}{2} - sign(z_{t_j} - z_{t_j-1})\frac{[\frac{|z_{t_j} - z_{t_j-1}|}{m}]^N}{2r}, 1 \le j \le p. \tag{12}$$

Termination condition for the algorithm, according to which the execution of the algorithm is terminated, consists of checking the lengths of the intervals in which the scheduled trials are performed with respect to a required *accuracy* of the problem solution, i. e.

$$\varrho_{t_j} \le \varepsilon, 1 \le t_j \le p. \tag{13}$$

As the current estimate of the optimization problem solution, the minimum computed value of the optimization function is accepted i. e.

$$z_k^* = \min\{z_i : 1 \le i \le k\}. \tag{14}$$

Within the framework of the proposed approach, PAGS is applied to solving the MCO problem (1) according to the scheme (3). The availability of SIS from (6) allows transforming the results of the previous computations to the values of a next optimization problem (3) without any time-consuming computations of the efficiency criteria values for new values of the convolution coefficients, i.e.

$$z_i' = \max\left(\lambda_j' f_i^j, 1 \le j \le s\right), 1 \le i \le k. \tag{15}$$

As a result, all the search information accumulated so far can be employed for continuing the computations. In general, the reuse of the search information will provide a smaller and smaller amount of computations for solving every successive optimization problem (see the results of numerical experiments in Sect. 4).

The method obtained as a result of such extension is called hereafter Parallel Multicriteria Global Algorithm (PMGA) for multiprocessors with shared memory. The PMGA algorithm in combination with a general scheme of the parallel computations presented in Sect. 3.1 will be referred to as the Multilevel Parallel Multicriteria Global Algorithm (MPMGA) for high-performance computational systems with shared and distributed memory.

Theoretical properties of MPMGA can be established by a theoretical analysis of the sequential one-dimensional variant of the method, i.e. the MGA algorithm. Here is a summary (without a proof) of the theoretical results from [16].

Theorem 1. When switching from solving the optimization subproblem (3) with the convolution coefficients $\lambda' \in \Lambda$ to solving the next subproblem (3) with the coefficients $\lambda'' \in \Lambda$, the value of the function $F(\lambda'', y(x))$ at the point of the global minimum differs from the estimated minimum value z_k^* from (14) obtained by minimizing the function $F(\lambda', y(x))$, by no more than the bounded value

$$|z_k^* - F(\lambda'', y(x^*))| \le \frac{\alpha H \varepsilon}{2} + \delta, \alpha > 1, \tag{16}$$

where δ is the maximum possible change of the function $\phi(x)$ (being minimized) from one subproblem (3) to the next:

$$\delta = \Delta\phi_{max} = \max\left\{\Delta\lambda_{max} f_i^{max}, 1 \le i \le s\right\},$$
$$\Delta\lambda_{max} = \max\left\{|\lambda_i' - \lambda_i''|, 1 \le i \le s\right\}, \tag{17}$$
$$f_i^{max} = \max\left\{f_i(y), y \in D\right\}, 1 \le i \le s.$$

and for the value m from (9) the following inequality is satisfied

$$m \ge H\left(1 + \sqrt{\frac{\alpha + 4\beta(1 + \beta)}{\alpha - 1}}\right), \beta = \frac{2r\delta}{H\varepsilon(r - 1)}$$

with z_k^* from (14), $\phi(x^*)$ from (3), ε from (13), r from (9) and H from (4).

This statement means that if the deviation $\Delta\phi_{max}$ from (17) of the estimates of the minimum values of $F(\lambda'', y(x))$ is acceptable, then solving the subproblem (3) with the new convolution coefficients $\lambda'' \in \Lambda$ does not require any additional optimization iterations because the estimates of the minimum value of the function $F(\lambda'', x)$ can be obtained according to (16) using the values z_i, $1 \leq i \leq k$, located within the search information A_k from (7).

As a result, two different schemes for selecting various convolution coefficients $\lambda \in \Lambda$ can be proposed, with whose use the required conditions of the Theorem 1 will be satisfied. In the first scheme, initially a sparse grid can be built on the set Λ, so that when setting new values of λ, the values that are close to the ones already established on the grid built in Λ earlier could always be found. In the second scheme, new values of λ could be chosen by small perturbations of the values used earlier (this method is often used in solving practical MCO problems when the decision maker wants to refine the estimates of the efficient solutions obtained earlier). It is worth noting that the reuse of the search information could be beneficial even with significant differences in the chosen values of the coefficients λ from the previously established ones, see the results of numerical experiments in Sect. 4.

4   Results of Numerical Experiments

The numerical experiments have been carried out on the *Lobachevsky* supercomputer at State University of Nizhni Novgorod. Each supercomputer node has 2 Intel Sandy Bridge E5-2660 2.2 GHz octa-core processors, 64 Gb RAM.

To evaluate the efficiency the proposed approach, the MGA[3] algorithm was compared with a number of other popular multicriteria optimization methods. In [20] MGA was tested against four multicriteria optimization methods: the Monte-Carlo (MC) method where the trial points are selected within the search domain D randomly and uniformly, the genetic algorithm SEMO from the PISA library [21], the Non-Uniform Coverage (NUC) method [17] and the Bi-objective Lipschitz Optimization (BLO) method [18].

In [16] a series of numerical experiments were executed to compare MGA with four other MCO methods considered in [22], namely the Linear Combination Method (LCM), the Multi-Objective Genetic Algorithm (MOGA), the Global Criterion Method (GCM), the ε-Constraint Method (ECM).

The results of the numerical experiments have demonstrated that MGA has a considerable advantage compared to the considered multicriteria optimization methods even when solving the relatively simple MCO problems.

In this paper, we present the results of computational experiments to evaluate the efficiency of the MPMGA algorithm. The computations have been carried out for 100 of four-dimensional MKO problems with ten criteria, i.e. $N = 4$, $s = 10$. The criteria in these problems were obtained by the GKLS generator [23] that generates multiextremal optimization problems with a priori known properties: the number of local minima, the size of their attraction domains, the point of the global minimum, etc.

---

[3] MGA is the sequential implementation of the parallel MPMGA method.

In these experiments 100 multicriteria problems has been solved. To obtain the Pareto domain approximation, each problem has been solved for 50 coefficients λ uniformly distributed in Λ from (3). The obtained results were averaged over the number of solved MCO problems. The accuracy ε from (13) was 0.025 and the reliability parameter r from (9) was 5.6.

The following approach was used to evaluate the accuracy of the Pareto domain approximation calculated for each of the 100 solved MCO problems. First of all, for the domain D from (1) a uniform grid D_δ was constructed with the step $\delta = 0.01$ for each coordinate. On this grid D_δ, the minimum values were found for all 50 subproblems $F(\lambda, y(x))$ from (3) generated in accordance with the chosen set of coefficients $\lambda \in \Lambda$ – the resulting set $y \in PD_\delta(f, D) \subset D_\delta$ was taken as the δ-approximation of the Pareto domain of the MCO problem being solved.

To solve each subproblems $F(\lambda, y(x))$ in (3), the termination condition (13) was replaced by the termination condition by the condition

$$F(\lambda, y(x^{k+j})) \leq F(\lambda, y^*) + \varepsilon, 1 \leq j \leq p, F(\lambda, y^*) = \min_{y \in D_\delta} F(\lambda, y).$$

After solving subproblems (3) for 50 values of λ a numerical approximation of the Pareto domain $PD_{\Omega_k}(f, D)$ is constructed using the search information accumulated in Ω_k from (6) as result of the solution of the MCO problem. The resulting estimation of the accuracy of the calculated approximation $PD_{\Omega_k}(f, D)$ is defined as the closeness to the δ-approximation $PD_\delta(f, D)$ of the Pareto domain of the MCO problem

$$\Delta = \frac{1}{M} \sum_{y \in PD_\delta(f,D)} d(y), d(y) = \min_{\overline{y} \in PD_{\Omega_k}(f,D)} \|y - \overline{y}\|, \tag{18}$$

where $\|.\|$ denotes the norm in the R^N space, and M is the number of points used in the approximation $PD_\delta(f, D)$.

Results of the numerical experiments are presented in Table 1. The first two columns in Table 1 show the numbers of the processors (P) and of the parallel computational cores on each processor (Q) employed. The third column ($P*Q$) contains the total number of cores employed. In the fourth (*Iters*) column the average numbers of iterations spent on solving the problems for the corresponding numbers of the different coefficients λ from (3) are given. In the fifth column (*Nums*) the average numbers of the calculated solutions used to establish the approximation $PD_{\Omega_k}(f, D)$ are shown. In the sixth column (*Approx*) the accuracy Δ of the δ-approximation $PD_\delta(f, D)$ is presented.

The last two columns show the speedup[4] of the parallel computations obtained with the use of the search information ($S1$) and without ($S2$).

The obtained results of experiments demonstrate that even simple reuse of the search information allows reducing the total amount of computations by the

---

[4] Due to the initial assumption that the computational complexity of multicriteria optimization problems is determined by the complexity of calculations of the criteria values, the speedup is defined as the reduction of the number of executed iterations.

Table 1. Numerical results for solving four-dimensional problems with ten criteria

P	Q	P*Q	Iters	Nums	Approx	S1	S2
1	1	1	82,244.11	26,014.27	0.05		1,0
1	1	1	23,791.81	8,185.07	0.08	1.00	3.5
5	1	5	4,977.63	8,077.38	0.08	4.78	16.5
1	20	20	1,223.45	8,452.35	0.08	19.45	67.2
25	1	25	1,063.22	8,704.86	0.08	22.38	77.4
1	40	40	616.37	8,416.06	0.07	38.60	133.4
50	1	50	594.46	9,561.09	0.07	40.02	138.4
5	20	100	252.65	8,510.26	0.07	94.17	325.5
5	40	200	131.68	8,914.21	0.07	180.68	624.6
25	20	500	66.54	11,022.32	0.07	357.56	1236.0
25	40	1000	36.81	12,226.82	0.07	646.34	2234.3
50	20	1000	37.94	12,552.88	0.07	627.09	2167.7
50	40	2000	20.98	14,399.94	0.07	1,134.02	3920.1

Computations without the reuse of the search information appears as a spanning subtitle row above the `1 1 1 82,244.11 ...` line, and *Computations with the reuse of the search information* appears above the `1 1 1 23,791.81 ...` line.

factor of 3.5 without the use of additional computational resources. When 1000 computational cores were used, the obtained speedup varied from 627 to 646. If 2000 computational cores are used, the speedup with the reuse of the search information reaches 1134. The overall speedup in this case relative to the initial algorithm without the reuse of the search information was 3920.

5 Conclusion

In this paper, a new computationally efficient approach is proposed that allows a parallel solution of time-consuming multicriteria optimization problems where individual criteria can be multiextremal and their evaluation may require a large computing effort. The main feature of this approach is its efficient handling of the computational complexity of solving such multicriteria optimization problems. Improvements of the efficiency resulting in a significant reduction of the required computations have been achieved by an intensive use of the search information obtained in the course of computations. Within the framework of this approach, methods for a reuse of the already available search information for a currently handled scalar nonlinear programming problem have been proposed. Such search information is then used by the optimization methods for the adaptive planning of the iterative process of global search.

Results of numerical experiments demonstrate that such an approach allows reducing the computation costs of solving multicriteria optimization problems by a factor between tens and hundreds.

In conclusion, it was shown that the developed approach is a promising one that needs a further investigation. It is important to continue numerical experiments of solving multicriteria optimization problems with a larger number of criteria and of a larger dimensionality.

Acknowledgements. This work has been supported by Russian Science Foundation, project No 16-11-10150 "Novel efficient methods and software tools for time-consuming decision making problems using superior-performance supercomputers."

References

1. Miettinen, K.: Nonlinear Multiobjective Optimization. Springer, New York (1999). https://doi.org/10.1007/978-1-4615-5563-6
2. Ehrgott, M.: Multicriteria Optimization, 2nd edn. Springer, Heidelberg (2010). https://doi.org/10.1007/3-540-27659-9
3. Collette, Y., Siarry, P.: Multiobjective Optimization: Principles and Case Studies (Decision Engineering). Springer, Heidelberg (2011). https://doi.org/10.1007/978-3-662-08883-8
4. Marler, R.T., Arora, J.S.: Survey of multi-objective optimization methods for engineering. Struct. Multidisciplinary Optim. **26**, 369–395 (2004)
5. Figueira, J., Greco, S., Ehrgott, M. (eds.): Multiple Criteria Decision Analysis: State of the Art Surveys. Springer, New York (2005). https://doi.org/10.1007/b100605
6. Eichfelder, G.: Scalarizations for adaptively solving multi-objective optimization problems. Comput. Optim. Appl. **44**, 249–273 (2009)
7. Strongin, R., Sergeyev, Ya.: Global Optimization with Non-Convex Constraints. Sequential and Parallel Algorithms. Kluwer Academic Publishers, Dordrecht (2000). (2nd ed. 2013, 3rd ed. 2014)
8. Sergeyev, Y.D., Strongin, R.G., Lera, D.: Introduction to Global Optimization Exploiting Space-Filling Curves. Springer, New York (2013). https://doi.org/10.1007/978-1-4614-8042-6
9. Floudas, C.A., Pardalos, M.P.: Recent Advances in Global Optimization. Princeton University Press, Princeton (2016)
10. Locatelli, M., Schoen, F.: Global optimization: theory, algorithms, and applications. In: SIAM (2013)
11. Sergeyev, Y.D., Grishagin, V.A.: Parallel asynchronous global search and the nested optimization scheme. J. Comput. Anal. Appl. **3**(2), 123–145 (2001)
12. Marler, R.T., Arora, J.S.: Multi-Objective Optimization: Concepts and Methods for Engineering. VDM Verlag, Saarbrücken (2009)
13. Hillermeier, C., Jahn, J.: Multiobjective optimization: survey of methods and industrial applications. Surv. Math. Ind. **11**, 1–42 (2005)
14. Gergel, V., Sidorov, S.: A two-level parallel global search algorithm for solution of computationally intensive multiextremal optimization problems. In: Malyshkin, V. (ed.) PaCT 2015. LNCS, vol. 9251, pp. 505–515. Springer, Cham (2015). https://doi.org/10.1007/978-3-319-21909-7_49
15. Barkalov, K., Gergel, V., Lebedev, I.: Solving global optimization problems on GPU cluster. In: AIP Conference Proceedings, vol. 1738, p. 400006 (2016) https://doi.org/10.1063/1.4952194

16. Gergel, V., Kozinov, E.: Efficient multicriteria optimization based on intensive reuse of search information. J. Glob. Optim. **71**(1), 73–90 (2018)
17. Evtushenko, Y.G., Posypkin, M.A.: A deterministic algorithm for global multi-objective optimization. Optim. Meth. Softw. **29**(5), 1005–1019 (2014)
18. Žilinskas, A., Žilinskas, J.: Adaptation of a one-step worst-case optimal univariate algorithm of bi-objective lipschitz optimization to multidimensional problems. Commun. Nonlinear Sci. Numer. Simul. **21**, 89–98 (2015)
19. Pardalos, P.M., Žilinskas, A., Žilinskas, J.: Non-Convex Multi-Objective Optimization. Springer, Heidelberg (2017)
20. Gergel, V., Kozinov, E.: Accelerating parallel multicriterial optimization methods based on intensive using of search information. Procedia Comput. Sci. **108**, 1463–1472 (2017)
21. Bleuler, S., Laumanns, M., Thiele, L., Zitzler, E.: PISA—a platform and programming language independent interface for search algorithms. In: Fonseca, C.M., Fleming, P.J., Zitzler, E., Thiele, L., Deb, K. (eds.) EMO 2003. LNCS, vol. 2632, pp. 494–508. Springer, Heidelberg (2003). https://doi.org/10.1007/3-540-36970-8_35
22. Chiandussi, G., Codegone, M., Ferrero, S., Varesio, F.E.: Comparison of multi-objective optimization methodologies for engineering applications. Comput. Math. Appl. **63**(5), 912–942 (2012)
23. Gaviano, M., Kvasov, D.E., Lera, D., Sergeyev, Ya.D.: Software for generation of classes of test functions with known local and global minima for global optimization. ACM Trans. Math. Softw. **29**(4), 469–480 (2003)
24. Borisenko, A., Gorlatch, S.: Parallelizing metaheuristics for optimal design of multiproduct batch plants on GPU. In: Malyshkin, V. (ed.) PaCT 2017. LNCS, vol. 10421, pp. 405–417. Springer, Cham (2017). https://doi.org/10.1007/978-3-319-62932-2_39
25. Gergel, V.P., Strongin, R.G.: Parallel computing for globally optimal decision making. In: Malyshkin, V.E. (ed.) PaCT 2003. LNCS, vol. 2763, pp. 76–88. Springer, Heidelberg (2003). https://doi.org/10.1007/978-3-540-45145-7_7
26. Sakharov, M.K., Karpenko, A.P.: Adaptive load balancing in the modified mind evolutionary computation algorithm. Supercomput. Front. Innov. **5**(4), 5–14 (2018)

Data-Parallel High-Precision Multiplication on Graphics Processing Units

Konstantin Isupov[1(✉)], Alexander Kuvaev[1], and Vladimir Knyazkov[2]

[1] Vyatka State University, Kirov 610000, Russia
ks_isupov@vyatsu.ru, kyvaevy@gmail.com
[2] Penza State University, Penza 440026, Russia
kniazkov@list.ru

Abstract. In this article, we consider parallel algorithms for high-precision floating-point multiplication on graphics processing units (GPUs). Our underlying high-precision format is based on the residue number system (RNS). In RNS, the number is represented as a tuple of residues obtained by dividing this number by a given set of moduli. The residues are mutually independent, which eliminates carry propagation delays and introduces parallelism in arithmetic operations. Firstly, we consider a basic algorithm for multiplying high-precision floating-point numbers. Next, we provide three parallel GPU implementations of this algorithm in the context of componentwise vector multiplication. Experiments indicate that our implementations are several times faster than existing high-precision libraries.

Keywords: High-precision arithmetic · Floating-point arithmetic · Multiplication · Parallel computations · GPGPU

1 Introduction

For most scientific and engineering computations, either IEEE 32-bit or 64-bit floating-point arithmetic provides sufficient accuracy. But for a rapidly expanding body of applications, even 64-bit floating-point arithmetic is not sufficient. Typical situations that may require higher-precision arithmetic (also called multiple-precision arithmetic) include [1]:

– ill-conditioned linear systems;
– large summations;
– long-time simulations;
– large-scale simulations;
– resolving small-scale phenomena;
– experimental mathematical computations.

V. Voevodin and S. Sobolev (Eds.): RuSCDays 2019, CCIS 1129, pp. 15–25, 2019.
https://doi.org/10.1007/978-3-030-36592-9_2

Examples of high-precision applications include satellite collision simulation without the availability of complete data about their trajectories [2], the use of complete elliptic integrals for solving the Hertzian elliptical contact problems [3], finite element-based structural analysis [4], and semidefinite programming [5].

Since high-precision data types are not natively supported by general-purpose hardware, emulation of high-precision arithmetic implemented in software libraries is used. Currently, many optimized open-source libraries are available that support efficient extended- or multiple-precision computations on central processing units (CPUs). These libraries include GMP, MPFR, ARPREC, MPFUN2015, Arb, FLINT, and mpdecimal.

However, many modern high-performance systems have a hybrid architecture, which involves the use of various hardware accelerators (together with the CPU), such as graphics processing units (GPUs). But for GPUs there are only a small number of high-precision libraries.

The GQD [6] and CAMPARY [7] libraries provide *extended* precision on the GPU. GQD implements two extended-precision data formats, double-double and quad-double, using the built-in vector types double2 and double4 available in CUDA. The double-double format represents a number as an unevaluated sum of two floating-point numbers, which provides 106 bits of significand (quadruple precision). The quad-double format in turn uses four native floating-point numbers and provides 212 bits of significand (octuple precision). GQD mainly uses the same algorithms as the QD library on the CPU [8]. CAMPARY uses floating-point expansion-based arithmetic that extends double-double and quad-double formats for an arbitrary number of terms. CAMPARY allows for extended precisions on the order of a few hundred bits.

The GARPREC [6] and CUMP [9] libraries support *arbitrary* precision on the GPU using the "multi-digit" format. This format stores a high-precision number with a sequence of digits, which are themselves machine-precision integers. The GARPREC algorithms are from the ARPREC library for CPUs [10]; CUMP is based on the GNU MP library (GMP) [11], and its functions have a GMP-like regular interface. In both GARPREC and CUMP, each high-precision operation is implemented as a single thread and an interval memory layout is used in order to exploit the coalesced access feature of the GPU.

In this article, we consider algorithms for high-precision floating-point multiplication on systems with CUDA-enabled GPUs. In binary arithmetic, high-precision multiplication is one of the most difficult basic operations (for instance, see [12]). However, we use a residue number system (RNS) [13] to represent multiple-precision numbers, which greatly simplifies the multiplication process and provides its effective parallel implementations.

2   Background

2.1   Residue Number System

An RNS is defined by a set of n moduli $\{m_0, m_1, \ldots, m_{n-1}\}$ that are coprime integers. In RNS, an integer X is represented by an n-tuple $(x_0, x_1, \ldots, x_{n-1})$, where x_i is the least non-negative remainder of X divided by m_i. The digit x_i is called *the residue* of X mod m_i. According to the Chinese remainder theorem (CRT) [13], such a representation is unique for any integer $X \in [0, M-1]$, where $M = \prod_{i=0}^{n-1} m_i$ is the dynamic range of an RNS. The binary number X corresponding to given residues $(x_0, x_1, \ldots, x_{n-1})$ can be derived using the CRT as

$$X = \left| \sum_{i=0}^{n-1} M_i \left| x_i \alpha_i \right|_{m_i} \right|_M ,$$

where M_i and α_i are the RNS constants, namely $M_i = M/m_i$ and α_i is the modulo m_i multiplicative inverse of M_i.

In RNS, high-precision integer operations such as addition, subtraction and multiplication are naturally divided into groups of reduced-precision operations on residues, performed in parallel and without carry propagation. That is, if $X = (x_0, x_1, \ldots, x_{n-1})$, $Y = (y_0, y_1, \ldots, y_{n-1})$, and $op \in \{+, -, \times\}$, then we have:

$$Z = X \; op \; Y \rightarrow \begin{cases} z_0 = (x_0 \; op \; y_0) \bmod m_0, \\ z_1 = (x_1 \; op \; y_1) \bmod m_1, \\ \ldots \\ z_{n-1} = (x_{n-1} \; op \; y_{n-1}) \bmod m_{n-1}, \end{cases}$$

and it is this high-speed parallel processing that makes the RNS attractive [14].

Unlike addition, subtraction, and multiplication, the operations of comparison, overflow detection, and sign identification are complex in the RNS. The classic technique to perform these operations is based on the CRT and consists in computing binary representations of numbers with their subsequent analysis. In large dynamic ranges this technique becomes slow. Other methods for evaluating the magnitude of residue numbers are based on the mixed-radix conversion (MRC) [15]. However, these methods are often ineffective since they require large amount of modulo-m_i operations or use of large lookup tables.

An alternative method, targeted at large dynamic ranges, is based on interval evaluation of residue numbers [16]. The idea lies in the fact that the majority of modern computing platforms, including CPU, GPU, FPGA and ASIC, enable very fast and effective standard IEEE 754 floating-point operations. For a given residue number $X = (x_0, x_1, \ldots, x_{n-1})$, the interval evaluation is denoted by $I(X/M) = [\underline{X/M}, \overline{X/M}]$ and represents an interval with machine-precision floating-point bounds, which localize the value of X, scaled with respect to the moduli product M, that is: $\underline{X/M} \leq X/M \leq \overline{X/M}$. Thus, $I(X/M)$ provides information about the range of changes in the relative value of residue number. Generally, this information is insufficient to restore the binary representation, but it can be effectively used to perform inter-modulo computations such as magnitude comparison, sign determination and overflow detection.

Computation of $I(X/M)$ based on the residues $(x_0, x_1, \ldots, x_{n-1})$ using Algorithm 3 from [16] requires only machine-precision integer and floating-point operations (no residue-to-binary conversion is required), and most calculations can be concurrently performed on the n residues.

When M is large (approximately more than 2^{1000}) and the range of standard floating-point formats may not be enough to avoid underflow in computing X/M and $\overline{X/M}$, a wider range must be simulated. To do this, the integer i is paired with a conventional floating-point number f, and this pair is considered as an extended-range number $f \times 2^i$. The main algorithms for extended-range arithmetic are easy to implement in software.

2.2   High-Precision Data Representation

In our high-precision format, a floating-point number x is represented as follows:

$$x = (-1)^s \times \left| \sum_{i=0}^{n-1} M_i \, |x_i \alpha_i|_{m_i} \right|_M \times 2^e, \tag{1}$$

where $s = sign(x)$, $x_0, x_1, \ldots, x_{n-1}$ is the digits (residues) of the significand X, and e is the integer exponent. In order to quickly obtain a magnitude order of the significand, the interval evaluation $I(X/M) = [\underline{X/M}, \overline{X/M}]$ is also included in the number representation. Each bound of $I(X/M)$ is represented as an extended-range number. For a number of the form (1), we will use the following notation:

$$x = \langle s, X, e, I(X/M) \rangle.$$

Under the presented number representation, the precision of arithmetic operations in bits is approximately equal to $p = \lfloor \log_2 \sqrt{M} \rfloor - 1$.

3   Parallel High-Precision Multiplication

3.1   Description of the Algorithm

Algorithm 1 performs multiplication of x and y, represented as $\langle s_x, X, e_x, I(X/M) \rangle$ and $\langle s_y, Y, e_y, I(Y/M) \rangle$, where $X = (x_0, x_1, \ldots, x_{n-1})$, $Y = (y_0, y_1, \ldots, y_{n-1})$, and $X, Y < \sqrt{M}$. It returns the result $z = xy$, represented as $\langle s_z, Z, e_z, I(Z/M) \rangle$ with $Z = (z_0, z_1, \ldots, z_{n-1})$, $Z < \sqrt{M}$.

Algorithm 1. FPmul — multiplying high-precision numbers x and y

---

1: **for** $i \leftarrow 0$ to $n-1$ **do**
2:      $z_i \leftarrow x_i y_i \bmod m_i$ ▷ this can be done in parallel for all i
3: **end for**
4: $e_z \leftarrow e_x + e_y$
5: $s_z \leftarrow (s_x + s_y) \bmod 2$
6: $I(Z/M) \leftarrow \left[\underline{X/M} \triangledown \underline{Y/M} \triangledown W, \ \overline{X/M} \triangle \overline{Y/M} \triangle V \right]$
7: $z \leftarrow \text{round}(s_z, Z, e_z, I(Z/M))$
8: **return** z

In the presented algorithm, the symbols $\triangledown$ and $\overline{\triangledown}$ denote, respectively, the multiplication and division of extended-range floats, performed with rounding downwards. In turn, $\triangle$ and $\overline{\triangle}$ denote the same operations but with rounding upwards. The constant V is the greatest extended-range number that is less than or equal to $1/M$, and W is the least extended-range number greater than or equal to $1/M$. The round routine rounds the multiplication result as follows:

1. Compare the exponent of $\overline{Z/M}$ (denoted as i_U) with the precomputed integer H, which is the largest power of two less than or equal to $\sqrt{M}/M$. If $i_U < H$, then rounding is not required, otherwise go to next step.
2. Evaluate $\underline{Z/M}$ and $\overline{Z/M}$ and compute the number of rounding bits, r.
3. In the RNS domain, find Z' such that $Z = 2^r Z' + R$ with $0 \leq R < 2^r$.
4. Compute $I(Z'/M)$ using Algorithm 3 from [16].
5. The returned result is $\langle s_z, Z', e_z + r, I(Z'/M) \rangle$.

In step 3, the significand is scaled by a power of two. In [17], a new algorithm for RNS power-of-two scaling is presented, which is well suited for software implementation. This algorithm eliminates residue-to-binary conversion and supports parallel computations with residues. Notice that, knowing the required computation precision, we can always reduce the number of roundings by choosing a larger size of the RNS moduli set.

3.2 Data-Parallel GPU Implementations

Various parallel implementations of Algorithm 1 using CUDA-capable GPUs are possible. To illustrate them, we consider high-precision componentwise (element-by-element) vector multiplication. For two given vectors $\mathbf{a} = (a_0, a_1, \ldots, a_{N-1})$ and $\mathbf{b} = (b_0, b_1, \ldots, b_{N-1})$, componentwise multiplication consists in calculating the vector $\mathbf{c} = (c_0, c_1, \ldots, c_{N-1})$, where $c_i = a_i b_i$.

In the algorithms below, *blockIdx* and *threadIdx* denote the block index and thread index, respectively. We assume that the input high-precision vectors are loaded into the GPU global memory.

Algorithm 2 is the straightforward GPU-based algorithm for computing $\mathbf{c} = \mathbf{a} \circ \mathbf{b}$. In this algorithm, *gridDim* thread blocks, each of which consists of *blockDim* threads, multiply the elements of vectors, and each high-precision multiplication is performed by a single thread.

Algorithm 2. Straightforward high-precision componentwise multiplication of $\mathbf{a}$ and $\mathbf{b}$ on the GPU.

1: $p \leftarrow N/(gridDim \times blockDim) + 1$
2: $i \leftarrow blockDim \times blockIdx + threadIdx$
3: $k \leftarrow 0$
4: **while** $k < p$ and $i < N$ **do**
5:     $c_i \leftarrow \text{FPmul}(a_i, b_i)$ ▷ Algorithm 1
6:         $i \leftarrow i + blockDim \times gridDim$
7:         $k \leftarrow k + 1$
8: **end while**

If the GPU has enough resources, then $gridDim \times blockDim$ entries will be computed concurrently in Algorithm 2.

Algorithm 3 is the digit-parallel GPU-based algorithm for computing $\mathbf{c} = \mathbf{a} \circ \mathbf{b}$. In this algorithm, $gridDim$ thread blocks, each of which consists of n threads (where n is the size of the RNS moduli set), multiply the elements of vectors. In each block, ith thread computes the ith digit of the significand, and the thread with index 0 additionally performs the sequential parts of the multiplication operation. Thus, if the GPU has enough resources, then $gridDim$ high-precision elements will be computed concurrently.

Algorithm 3. Digit-parallel high-precision componentwise multiplication of $\mathbf{a}$ and $\mathbf{b}$ on the GPU.

1: $p \leftarrow N/gridDim + 1$
2: $i \leftarrow blockIdx$
3: $k \leftarrow 0$
4: **while** $k < p$ and $i < N$ **do**
5:     $c_i \leftarrow \text{ParFPmul}(a_i, b_i)$ ▷ Algorithm 4
6:     $i \leftarrow i + gridDim$
7:     $k \leftarrow k + 1$
8: **end while**

The pseudo code of the ParFPmul routine is shown in Algorithm 4. This routine uses a parallel version of Algorithm 2 from [17] to round the result.

Algorithm 4. ParFPmul — part of the digit-parallel multiplication of x and y. The algorithm appears from a single thread's perspective and must be performed by n threads simultaneously within a single thread block.

1: $i \leftarrow threadIdx$
2: $z_i \leftarrow x_i y_i \bmod m_i$
3: **if** $i = 0$ **then**
4:     $e_z \leftarrow e_x + e_y$
5:     $s_z \leftarrow (s_x + s_y) \bmod 2$
6:     $I(Z/M) \leftarrow \left[\underline{X/M} \triangledown \underline{Y/M} \triangledown W, \overline{X/M} \triangle \overline{Y/M} \triangle V \right]$
7: **end if**
8: thread synchronization
9: $z \leftarrow \text{round}(s_z, Z, e_z, I(Z/M))$ ▷ Each thread performs its part of the rounding
10: **return** z

The drawback of Algorithms 2 and 3 is that divergent execution paths within a warp can lead to significant performance degradation (on current GPU architectures, warp is a group of 32 threads running in lockstep). In Algorithm 5, this drawback is eliminated by splitting the multiplication operation into three GPU kernels (*global* functions), executed separately.

Algorithm 5. High-precision componentwise multiplication of **a** and **b** on the GPU, separated into three kernel functions.

1: **Kernel 1** in *gridDim1* blocks of *blockDim1* threads concurrently computes the signs, exponents, and interval evaluations of the significands for *gridDim1* × *blockDim1* entries of the result vector.

2: **Kernel 2** multiplies high-precision significands in RNS. For multiplication, *gridDim2* blocks of *blockDim2* threads are used, where $blockDim2 \geq n$. In each block, n threads concurrently multiply all digits (residues) of significands, and each ith thread is assigned for modulo m_j computations, where $j = i \bmod n$.

3: **Kernel 3** in *gridDim1* blocks of *blockDim1* threads rounds the componentwise product. For each multiple-precision entry c_i, the rounding is performed as a single thread using an RNS power-of-two scaling algorithm.

---

4 Performance Results

We implemented the described high-precision multiplication algorithms in C language using CUDA and compared their performance with the CUMP [9] and GARPREC [6] libraries for GPU, and the MPFR [18] and ARPREC [10] libraries for CPU. The CPU-based codes were developed using OpenMP and executed on four cores. Table 1 summarizes the experimental setup employed in the performance tests.

Table 1. Experimental setup summary for the performance tests

Host	Device
Intel Core i5 4590 (3.30 GHz)	NVIDIA GeForce RTX 2060 (1.68 GHz)
16 GB DDR3 RAM	1920 CUDA Cores, CUDA Capability 7.5
Ubuntu 19.04	6 GB GDDR6
GCC 8.3.0 (*-O3 -fopenmp*)	CUDA 10.1.105

For Algorithm 5, we implemented and evaluated two memory layouts, Array-of-Structures (AoS) and Structure-of-Arrays (SoA). The AoS layout is a traditional method of arranging a vector of high-precision numbers in memory, with a structure for each number, as shown in Fig. 1(a). This layout is more intuitive, but it does not match the coalesced access pattern of GPUs. SoA is the opposite layout that uses multiple arrays to represent a high-precision vector, as shown in Fig. 1(b). For a vector of length N, all digits of the high-precision significands are stored as an integer array of length $n \times N$.

The CUMP and GARPREC libraries use an interval addressing scheme where the digits of the high-precision numbers are interleaved. Instead, for the SoA memory layout, we have adopted a sequential addressing scheme in which all n digits of the same high-precision number are arranged consecutively in the device

```
typedef struct {
    int residue[n];      // Digits
    er_float_t ifc[2];   // Interval evaluation
    int exp;             // Exponent
    int sign;            // Sign
} mp_float_t;
mp_float_t Vector[N];
```

```
typedef struct {
    int *residue;     // Digits               - an array of length n x N
    er_float_t *ifc;  // Interval evaluations  - an array of length 2N
    int *exp;         // Exponents             - an array of length N
    int *sign;        // Signs                 - an array of length N
    int4 *buf;        // Temporary buffer      - an array of length N
} mp_float_array_t;
mp_float_array_t Vector;
```

(a) Array-of-Structures   (b) Structure-of-Arrays

Fig. 1. Data layouts for high-precision vectors

memory. Since Kernel 2 computes all digits of the same number in parallel, the access pattern for the threads in a warp is coalesced.

In the experiments, we considered the 32-bit moduli sets of sizes from 8 to 160, which provide the precisions from 120 to 2400 bits, respectively. The parameters of the moduli sets are presented in Table 2.

Table 2. Parameters of the RNS moduli sets used in the experiments

Moduli set size, n	Dynamic range, M	Precision, p
8	7.37606×10^{72}	120
32	4.03751×10^{289}	480
64	3.86535×10^{578}	960
96	3.76183×10^{867}	1440
128	3.62408×10^{1156}	1920
160	3.54596×10^{1445}	2400

All vectors have length $N = 1,000,000$ and are composed of uniform random multiple-precision numbers. We have excluded the time of data transfer between the host and the GPU. For each test case, we selected kernel execution configurations (*gridDim*, *blockDim*, *gridDim1*, *blockDim1*, etc.) that provide better performance. The evaluation results are shown in Table 3.

Among the considered GPU-based implementations, Algorithm 5 employing three separated kernel functions with the SoA data layout for high-precision multiplication has the better performance. This algorithm is around 6x and 4x faster than Algorithms 2 and 3, respectively. It is also 8–18x and 48–130x faster than quad-core CPU implementations based on the MPFR and ARPREC libraries, respectively. The SoA memory layout outperforms the AoS memory layout with a speedup of about 3x.

Compared to the GARPREC multiple-precision library for GPU, Algorithm 5 gives a speedup of 9–40x. At 120-bit precision, the CUMP library is slightly faster than Algorithm 5. However, Algorithm 5 is less dependent on the precision than CUMP and at 2400-bit precision it is 4x faster than CUMP.

Table 3. Performance in Mflop/s of high-precision componentwise vector multiplication. A flop is one operation using high precision.

	Precision, p					
	120	480	960	1440	1920	2400
MPFR (4 cores)	65.2	36.6	15.6	19.0	15.5	12.9
ARPREC (4 cores)	23.2	9.9	3.8	2.1	1.2	0.8
CUMP	1290.6	372.8	130.4	62.6	37.9	25.2
GARPREC	133.1	46.2	13.0	7.1	3.9	2.7
Algorithm 2	224.2	153.0	54.7	30.3	20.6	16.2
Algorithm 3	95.7	96.7	98.4	88.9	80.1	50.5
Algorithm 5 (AoS)	226.8	142.3	112.3	86.7	74.9	59.7
Algorithm 5 (SoA)	1175.9	471.7	265.6	187.7	145.9	107.6

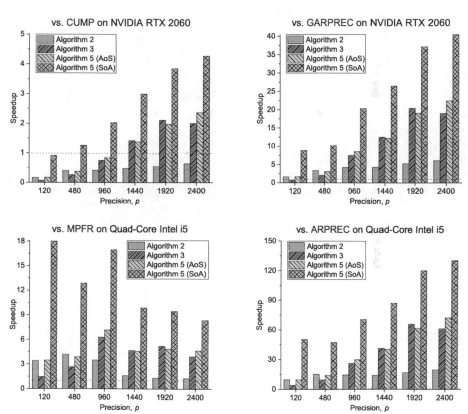

Fig. 2. Speedups of the parallel GPU implementations compared with existing high-precision libraries.

When $p = 120$, Algorithm 2 demonstrates better performance than Algorithm 3. This is because in Algorithm 2, each thread computes only 8 digits of the significands. However, there is a significant degradation in the performance of Algorithm 2 when a higher precision is employed. The opposite situation is observed in the case of Algorithm 3, where the sequential part of the multiplication operation results in a significant drop in performance when $p = 120$. However, the efficiency of Algorithm 3 is not as highly dependent on the precision as that seen for Algorithm 2.

Figure 2 has shown the speedup of our GPU-based implementations compared with CUMP, GARPREC, MPFR, and ARPREC.

5   Conclusion

Many scientific applications require calculations with numbers whose precision exceeds the standard double precision floating-point format. Since high-precision data types are not natively supported by general-purpose hardware, software emulation of high-precision arithmetic is used. In this paper, we have implemented and tested high-precision multiplication algorithms for parallel systems with CUDA-enabled GPUs. In these algorithms, a residue number system is used to represent multiple-precision floating-point numbers, which greatly simplifies the multiplication process and provides its various parallel implementations.

The algorithm that uses three separated kernel functions for high-precision data-parallel multiplication demonstrates better performance since it eliminates branch divergence and thus allows the efficient utilization of the GPU's resources. On the other hand, the Structure-of-Arrays memory layout, which matches the coalesced access pattern of GPUs, provides a significant performance improvement over the traditional Array-of-Structures memory layout.

The presented GPU implementations are part of MPRES, a new software library for parallel CPU+GPU systems. We plan to use the developed algorithms to implement high-precision BLAS operations on GPUs.

Acknowledgement. This work was supported by the Russian Science Foundation (grant number 18-71-00063).

References

1. Bailey, D., Barrio, R., Borwein, J.: High-precision computation: mathematical physics and dynamics. Appl. Math. Comput. **218**(20), 10106–10121 (2012). https://doi.org/10.1016/j.amc.2012.03.087
2. Hemenway, B., Lu, S., Ostrovsky, R., Welser IV, W.: High-precision secure computation of satellite collision probabilities. In: Zikas, V., De Prisco, R. (eds.) SCN 2016. LNCS, vol. 9841, pp. 169–187. Springer, Cham (2016). https://doi.org/10.1007/978-3-319-44618-9_9
3. He, K., Zhou, X., Lin, Q.: High accuracy complete elliptic integrals for solving the Hertzian elliptical contact problems. Comput. Math. Appl. **73**(1), 122–128 (2017). https://doi.org/10.1016/j.camwa.2016.11.003

4. Kannan, R., Hendry, S., Higham, N.J., Tisseur, F.: Detecting the causes of ill-conditioning in structural finite element models. Comput. Struct. **133**, 79–89 (2014). https://doi.org/10.1016/j.compstruc.2013.11.014

5. Simmons-Duffin, D.: A semidefinite program solver for the conformal bootstrap. J. High Energy Phys. **2015**(6), 174 (2015). https://doi.org/10.1007/JHEP06(2015)

6. Lu, M., He, B., Luo, Q.: Supporting extended precision on graphics processors. In: Sixth International Workshop on Data Management on New Hardware (DaMoN 2010), pp. 19–26. ACM, Indianapolis, Indiana, USA (2010). https://doi.org/10.1145/1869389.1869392

7. Joldes, M., Muller, J.-M., Popescu, V., Tucker, W.: CAMPARY: cuda multiple precision arithmetic library and applications. In: Greuel, G.-M., Koch, T., Paule, P., Sommese, A. (eds.) ICMS 2016. LNCS, vol. 9725, pp. 232–240. Springer, Cham (2016). https://doi.org/10.1007/978-3-319-42432-3_29

8. Hida, Y., Li, X.S., Bailey, D.H.: Algorithms for quad-double precision floating point arithmetic. In: Proceedings of 15th IEEE Symposium on Computer Arithmetic, pp. 155–162. Vail, CO, USA (2001). https://doi.org/10.1109/ARITH.2001.930115

9. Nakayama, T.: The CUDA multiple precision arithmetic library. https://github.com/skystar0227/CUMP. Accessed 09 June 2019

10. Bailey, D.H., Hida, Y., Li, X.S., Thompson, B.: ARPREC: an arbitrary precision computation package. Technical Report LBNL-53651, Lawrence Berkeley National Lab., Berkeley, CA, USA (2002). https://www.osti.gov/servlets/purl/817634

11. Granlund, T.: The GNU multiple precision arithmetic library. https://gmplib.org. Accessed 28 May 2019

12. Brent, R., Zimmermann, P.: Modern Computer Arithmetic. Cambridge University Press, New York (2010)

13. Omondi, A., Premkumar, B.: Residue Number Systems: Theory and Implementation. Imperial College Press, London (2007)

14. Kong, Y., Phillips, B.: Fast scaling in the residue number system. IEEE Trans. Very Large Scale Integr. Syst. **17**(3), 443–447 (2009). https://doi.org/10.1109/TVLSI.2008.2004550

15. Szabo, N.S., Tanaka, R.I.: Residue Arithmetic and its Application to Computer Technology. McGraw-Hill, New York (1967)

16. Isupov, K., Knyazkov, V.: Interval estimation of relative values in residue number system. J. Circ. Syst. Comput. **27**(1) (2018). https://doi.org/10.1142/S0218126618500044

17. Isupov, K., Knyazkov, V., Kuvaev, A.: Fast power-of-two RNS scaling algorithm for large dynamic ranges. In: Proceedings of IVth International Conference on Engineering and Telecommunication (EnT), pp. 135–139. Moscow, Russia (2017). https://doi.org/10.1109/ICEnT.2017.36

18. Fousse, L., Hanrot, G., Lefèvre, V., Pélissier, P., Zimmermann, P.: MPFR: a multiple-precision binary floating-point library with correct rounding. ACM Trans. Math. Softw. **33**(2) (2007). https://doi.org/10.1145/1236463.1236468. article no. 13

Efficiency of Basic Linear Algebra Operations on Parallel Computers

Igor Konshin[1,2,3,4]([✉])

[1] Marchuk Institute of Numerical Mathematics of the Russian
Academy of Sciences, Moscow 119333, Russia
[2] Dorodnicyn Computing Centre of FRC CSC RAS, Moscow 119333, Russia
[3] Moscow Institute of Physics and Technology (State University),
Dolgoprudny 141701, Moscow Region, Russia
[4] Sechenov University, Moscow 119991, Russia
igor.konshin@gmail.com

Abstract. The implementation of some linear algebra operations on parallel computers with shared and distributed memory is considered. A detailed analysis of the parallel efficiency for different operations is performed. Machine-dependent characteristics affecting the rate and efficiency of parallel computations are analyzed.

Keywords: Linear algebra · Parallel computing · Parallel efficiency estimation · Speedup

1 Introduction

During the last 30 years, an application of parallel computers has become widespread. Most of the modern numerical problems can be solved using parallel computing only. A great contribution to the development of parallel computing theory and practice was made by Valentin V. Voevodin. And now, commemorating his 85-th anniversary, we would like to represent a brief introduction to this paper based on his works.

The problem of algorithm mapping on the computer architecture in order to get the most efficient implementation [1] has always been relevant. With the development of computer technology, parallel computers became the most popular, and the theory of parallel computing [2–5] began to progress intensively. On the one hand, it includes the analysis and adaptation of existing algorithms to the features of parallel computing [1,6–9], and, on the other hand, the need to develop new methods and algorithms with given parallel properties [6,7]. Nowadays, there are a lot of information resources with an algorithms parallel properties description (see, e.g., [10]). There are also automatic tools for evaluation of the algorithms and programs information structure, the most developed among them is the V-ray technology [5].

The solution of the modern computational problems is based on exploiting linear algebra algorithms, while these algorithms use a set of some basic

© Springer Nature Switzerland AG 2019
V. Voevodin and S. Sobolev (Eds.): RuSCDays 2019, CCIS 1129, pp. 26–38, 2019.
https://doi.org/10.1007/978-3-030-36592-9_3

operations. The choice of such operations is an important and interesting task, that Voevodin had begun to develop [11,12] earlier than the works on the well-known LINPACK package and its subset BLAS (Basic Linear Algebra Sub-programs) [13] were started. This paper is devoted to an analysis of some BLAS operations. The work continues the research started in [14,15] taking into account the machine-dependent characteristics of parallel computers.

Section 2 discusses the computational models for the shared and distributed memory computers and provides a parallel efficiency estimation technology. Section 3 contains examples of some linear algebra operations and fragments of their implementation codes using the OpenMP and MPI technologies. Section 4 gives the numerical experiments results and provides a detailed analysis of these operations performance, as well as relations of parallel efficiency and machine-dependent characteristics. The final section sums up the key findings.

2 Computational Models and Efficiency Estimates

In this section we describe the computational model for both shared and distributed memory computers. The parallel efficiency estimates are presented as well.

2.1 Shared Memory Model

Let the parallel computations be performed on a shared memory computer and programming environment OpenMP is used for parallelization. In the most simple cases, OpenMP can be treated as an insertion of compiler directives for loops parallelization. At some intermediate parallelization stage or due to intrinsic algorithm properties some arithmetic operations can be performed in a serial mode.

Let the computations be sufficiently uniform by the set of arithmetic operations performed and the total numbers of parallel and serial operations can be calculated. Let the fraction of serial operation be $\sigma \in [0; 1]$ (from "serial" but to separate from designation "S" for speedup).

If the time T for the arithmetic operations is linear with respect to the number of arithmetic operations, then it is easy to estimate the maximum speedup, which can be obtained for some implementation of the considered algorithm.

Let denote by $T(p)$ the program execution time on p processors. The relative speedup can be expressed as

$$S(p) = T(1)/T(p). \qquad (1)$$

Using the fraction σ, it can be rewritten as

$$S(p) = T(1)/(\sigma T(1) + (1 - \sigma)T(1)/p)) = p/(1 + \sigma(p - 1)). \qquad (2)$$

The last formula expresses the well-known Amdahl's law [16], which is well fitted namely for implementation on shared memory computers.

One can specify the best conditions of the Amdahl's law applicability, i.e., when the algorithm actual speedup is close to the estimate (2). The most important conditions [14] are the load balance for all active threads and the scalability of threads usage, i.e., the performance of the threads does not depend on the threads number (or, in other words, the execution time for the parallel part of the code is actually p times reduced when running on p threads). The last one can be essentially affected by the memory access rate (see Sect. 4).

2.2 Parallel Computation Model for Distributed Memory Computers

We have supposed in Sect. 2.1 that some portion of computations is performed in serial. It is the reason to estimate the parallel efficiency for shared memory computing. In contrast, for the distributed memory computers it is more natural to consider that all computations are performed in parallel but the delays are due to communications.

To estimate the time spent by the data exchanges we can use the well-known formula (see, e.g., [14, 15]):

$$T_c = \tau_0 + \tau_c L_c,$$

where T_c is the time spent for the transmission of length L_c, τ_0 is the initialization time for the message transmission, τ_c is the rate of the data exchange (i.e., measured by the time of the unit length data exchange).

For algorithm with the "large-grained" parallelism with $L_c \gg 1$ we can set $\tau_0 = 0$, i.e., $T_c = \tau_c L_c$. The more general case $\tau_0 > 0$ is considered in [15].

If L_a is the total number of arithmetic operations of the algorithm and τ_a is the time spent per one namely such operation, then the total time for arithmetic operations can be expressed as $T_a = \tau_a L_a$. We assume that τ_a is a constant and skip considering of a cache effect.

In addition, we introduce two auxiliary parameters. The first one will describe the general characteristic of the parallel computer properties:

$$\tau = \tau_c/\tau_a.$$

(It should be noted, that communication-to-computation ratio τ was used not only in [14, 15] but much earlier in [17, 18].) The second important parameter specifies the algorithm parallel properties:

$$L = L_c/L_a.$$

Finally, we can estimate the speedup

$$S = S(p) = T(1)/T(p) = T_a/(T_a/p + T_c/p) = pT_a/(T_a + T_c) = p/(1 + T_c/T_a)$$
$$= p/(1 + (\tau_c L_c)/(\tau_a L_a)) = p/(1 + \tau L) \tag{3}$$

and the respective parallel efficiency

$$E = S/p = 1/(1 + \tau L).$$

```
// OpenMP:
#pragma omp parallel for
    for (i=0; i<N; i++)
        y[i] += a * x[i];

// MPI:
    for (i=0; i<N/p; i++)
        y[i] += a * x[i];
```

Fig. 1. AXPY $y = \alpha \cdot x + y$ implementation in OpenMP and MPI.

The above upper bound efficiency estimation iurns out to be quite simpl but fairly robust [14, 15].

In contrast to the Amdahl's law formula, we have assumed that all computations are performed completely in parallel and the serial part of the algorithm is absent ($\sigma = 0$). The other important assumptions are the independence of parameters τ_a and τ_c on the number of processors p. The complete set of assumptions can be found in [14].

3   Examples of Arithmetic Operations

As an example of parallel arithmetic operations, we consider several of the most frequently used linear algebra operations: a linear combination of vectors, the norm of a vector, and the multiplication of a dense matrix by a vector. All these operations are included in the BLAS (Basic Linear Algebra Subprograms) [13] subset of the LAPACK package (Linear Algebra PACKage) and are intensively used, for example, in the implementation of direct and iterative methods for linear systems solution.

Example 1 (operation AXPY (BLAS level 1, DAXPY)). Linear combination of vectors: $y = \alpha \cdot x + y$. This operation is completely parallelizable, it is easily implemented for both shared and distributed memory computers (see Fig. 1). Different processes operate with their own parts of the vectors x and y. In Fig. 1, N denotes the full length of the vector; in the MPI implementation, each process operates with its own part of the vectors of length N/p, where p is the number of computational cores used. For simplicity we suppose that N/p is integer.

Example 2 (operation NORM (BLAS level 1, DNRM2)). Vector norm calculation: $\|x\|$. This operation is well parallelizable. Different processes operate with their partial sums completely parallel, than the total sum is calculated and, finally, the square root is computed. This operation is also easily implemented using traditional tools with the "reduction" option in OpenMP directive "parallel for" or calling to MPI_Allreduce() function in MPI (see Fig. 2).

```
// OpenMP:
   sum = 0.0;
#pragma omp parallel for reduction (+:sum)
   for (i=0; i<N; i++)
       sum += x[i] * x[i];
   sum = sqrt(sum);

// MPI:
   sum = 0.0;
   for (i=0; i<N/p; i++)
       sum += x[i] * x[i];
   tmp = sum;
   MPI_Allreduce(&tmp, &sum, 1, MPI_DOUBLE, MPI_SUM,
       MPI_COMM_WORLD);
   sum = sqrt(sum);
```

Fig. 2. NORM $\|x\|$ implementation in OpenMP and MPI.

Example 3 (operation MVM (BLAS level 2, DGEMV)). Multiplication of a general type dense matrix by a vector: $y = A \cdot x$. This operation is quite well parallelizable. However, when implemented on distributed memory computers, the vector components exchange is required. To estimate the parallel efficiency of MVM operation relation (3) can be used [14].

Let N be a matrix dimension, and each processor owns a portion of N/p matrix rows and respective components of vector x are distributed to each processor. For MVM, it is necessary to collect on each processor the copy of vector X of full dimension N, and then to perform multiplication on the local part of the matrix A by a vector X. Then,

$$L_a = N^2/p, \quad L_c = (N/p)(p-1), \quad L = L_c/L_a = (p-1)/N,$$
$$S = p/(1 + (p-1)\tau/N), \quad E = 1/(1 + (p-1)\tau/N). \tag{4}$$

If $\tau = 30$ and $N = 3000$, then $E(p=10) \approx 0.9$, $E(p=100) \approx 0.5$, while if $N = 30000$, then $E(p=10) \approx 0.99$, $E(p=100) \approx 0.9$, $S(p=1000) \approx 0.5$.

The implementation of MVM by means of OpenMP [19] and MPI [20] is presented in Fig. 3. It should be noted that both the local vector x of local dimension $n = N/p$ and the global vector X of the full dimension N are present in the MPI implementation.

Note that the measurement of the execution time for a fragment of a parallel program is also easily implemented using both the OpenMP and MPI tools (see Fig. 4). Obviously, for the speedup analysis it is necessary to use namely wall-clock time to measure time. Barriers will not be required for OpenMP implementation, since time measurement is usually located outside the parallel program segment.

```
// OpenMP:
#pragma omp parallel for private (j)
   for (i=0; i<N; i++) {
       y[i] = 0.0;
       for (j=0; j<N; j++)
           y[i] += a[i][j] * x[j];
   }

// MPI:
   int i, j, n, id, p;
   double *a, *x, *y, *X, *ai;

   MPI_Comm_rank (MPI_COMM_WORLD, &id);
   MPI_Comm_size (MPI_COMM_WORLD, &p);

   n = N / p;
   a = (double *) malloc(sizeof(double) * n*N);
   x = (double *) malloc(sizeof(double) * n);
   y = (double *) malloc(sizeof(double) * n);
   X = (double *) malloc(sizeof(double) * N);

   // set x[] and a[] ...

   for (i=0; i<n; i++)
      X[i+id*n] = x[i];
   for (i=0; i<p; i++)
      MPI_Bcast(X+id*n, n, MPI_DOUBLE, i, MPI_COMM_WORLD);
   for (i=0; i<n; i++) {
      y[i] = 0.0;
      ai = a + i * N;
      for (j=0; j<N; j++)
         y[i] += ai[j] * X[j];
   }
```

Fig. 3. MVM $y = A \cdot x$ implementation in OpenMP and MPI.

```
// OpenMP:
#include <omp.h>
   double t;
   t = omp_get_wtime();
   .....
   t = omp_get_wtime() - t;

// MPI:
#include <mpi.h>
   double t;
   MPI_Barrier(MPI_COMM_WORLD);
   t = MPI_Wtime();
   .....
   MPI_Barrier(MPI_COMM_WORLD);
   t = MPI_Wtime() - t;
```

Fig. 4. Time measurement in OpenMP and MPI.

4   Numerical Experiments

The INM RAS cluster [21] was exploited for numerical experiments. It consists of the following computational segments:

- x6core: Compute Node Asus RS704D-E6, 12 cores (two 6-core Intel Xeon X5650@2.67 GHz processors), 24 GB RAM;
- x8core: Compute Node Arbyte Alkazar+ R2Q50, 16 cores (two 8-core Intel Xeon processors E5-2665@2.40 GHz), 64 GB RAM;
- x10core: Compute Node Arbyte Alkazar+ R2Q50, 20 cores (two 10-core Intel Xeon E5-2670v2@2.50 GHz processors), 64 GB RAM;
- x12core: Compute Node Arbyte Alkazar+ R2Q50, 24 cores (two 12-core Intel Xeon E5-2670v3@2.30 GHz processors), 64 GB RAM.

SUSE Linux Enterprise Server 11 SP1/SP3 (x86_64) operating system is installed on the above computing segments. Data transmissions were performed using the Mellanox Infiniband QDR 4x network.

A detailed analysis of the parallel efficiency for operations considered in Sect. 3 was performed for all computational segments of the INM RAS cluster.

In Fig. 5a the speedup for an OpenMP implementation of AXPY operation is shown for $N = 3 \cdot 10^6$. Linear speedup is marked as "ideal". It should be noted that when working on the x6core and x8core segments, there is a noticeable slowdown in the program execution time when the number of cores increases. This is probably due to the fact that for the insufficient memory access rate, there are delays in work of the computational cores, while for one combined multiplication-and-addition operation intensive memory access activity is required (it is necessary to read two numbers from and write one number to RAM).

Figure 5b shows the speedup for NORM operations in the OpenMP implementation for the same vector length N. In this case, a steady increase in speedup is observed on all computing segments. This is due to lower memory access rate requirements for this operation: with the same arithmetic costs, it is necessary to read only one number from memory, while there is no need to write data to RAM, since the results of the partial sum will be stored in the registers.

Figure 6a presents the speedup of AXPY operation for the MPI implementation. It is worth to note almost perfect speedup for the number of computational cores up to 32, inclusive, moreover, up to 64 cores for the vector dimension $N = 3 \cdot 10^7$.

Figure 6b demonstrates the speedup of NORM $\|x\|$ operation for the MPI implementation. In this case, the speedup is far from the linear one. This is probably due to the additional synchronization at the final stage of the algorithm. There is also a greater speedup for a vector of higher dimension, but this dependence is less noticeable.

Figure 7 shows a comparative speedups of MVM operation implemented in OpenMP and MPI. In addition, Fig. 7a contains plots of the above speedup estimates (4) for the specified values of N and $\tau = 30$ (see also [14]). It is easily seen that for this operation, greater speedup can be achieved using the OpenMP

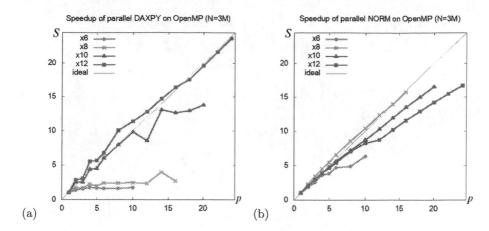

Fig. 5. Speedup for AXPY (a) and NORM (b) on OpenMP for $N = 3 \cdot 10^6$.

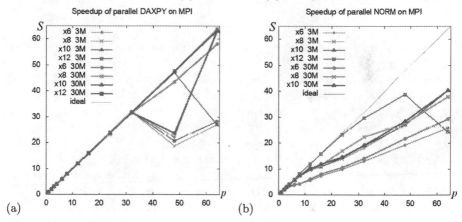

Fig. 6. Speedup for AXPY (a) and NORM (b) on MPI for $N = 3 \cdot 10^6$, $3 \cdot 10^7$.

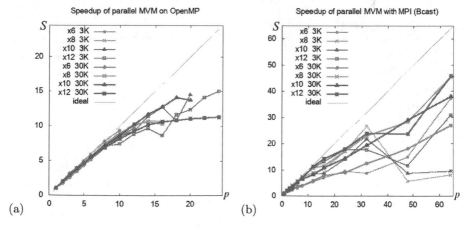

Fig. 7. Speedup for MVM on OpenMP (a) and MPI (b) for $N = 3 \cdot 10^3$, $3 \cdot 10^4$.

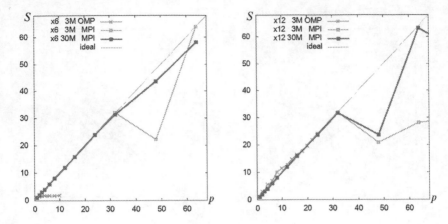

Fig. 8. Comparison of AXPY performance on OpenMP and MPI for x6core and x12core segments.

implementation. In most cases, it is worth noting greater speedup for a problem of higher dimension $N = 3 \cdot 10^4$.

The implementation efficiency for the considered operations can also being compared with respect to different segments of the INM RAS cluster to demonstrate the hardware dependencies. For this purpose, the segments with the least and most modern computing devices were selected, segments x6core and x12core, respectively. Figure 8 shows the comparative speedup of AXPY operation on two segments of the INM RAS cluster. It is worth noting the weak speedup of the OpenMP implementation on the x6core segment and, conversely, the superlinear speedup of the same operation on the x12core segment. This is caused by the insufficient memory access rate for x6core segment and the well matched RAM access rate and the rate of arithmetic devices for x12core segment. The MPI implementation of this operation shows a good speedup, with the exception of a special point, corresponding to 48 cores.

For the vector norm calculation (see Fig. 9), the behavior of various implementations is more uniform. Noticeable differences in performance are observed for MPI implementation for small and hight dimension runs only. Probably, this is due to the different processing of the cache memory for these runs on the x12core segment.

Figure 10 demonstrates the comparative speedup for MVM operation on two segments of the INM RAS cluster for problem dimensions $N = 3 \cdot 10^3$ and $N = 3 \cdot 10^4$. It is interesting to note that the OpenMP implementation demonstrates better performance on the x6core segment, and vice versa, the MPI implementation wins on the x12core segment. Actually, the same MPI implementation v.5.0.3 is installed on both computing segments. Therefore, the reason for this behavior for the OpenMP implementation can only be caused by memory conflicts for a large number of threads due to inconsistency of their processing. In the MPI implementation, the memory of each process is local and memory conflicts

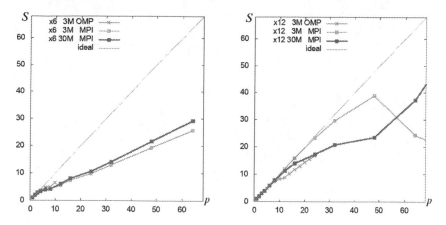

Fig. 9. Comparison of NORM performance on OpenMP and MPI for x6core and x12core segments.

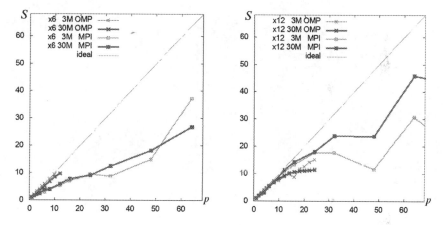

Fig. 10. Comparison of MVM performance on OpenMP and MPI for x6core and x12core segments.

occur much less frequently. In general, the behavior of speedup plots is quite expected, a little bit more stability is achieved by tasks of a higher dimension.

The most interesting is the performance comparison for all considered operations implemented in OpenMP on the same computing segments of the INM RAS cluster (see Fig. 11). For the x6core segment, the smallest speedup is indicated by AXPY operation, and the largest one by MVM operation. For x12core segment, the order of the parallel efficiency of operations becomes completely opposite. As before, this is due to the memory access rate, as well as the greater computational complexity of the MVM operation. It can be said that the ratio of the arithmetic devices and memory access rates for the x6core segment is

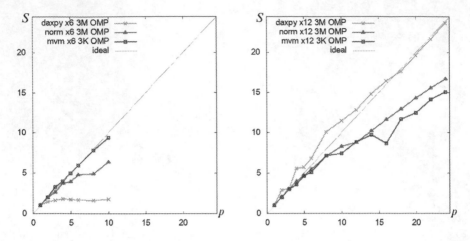

Fig. 11. Parallel performance of operations implemented in OpenMP for x6core and x12core segments.

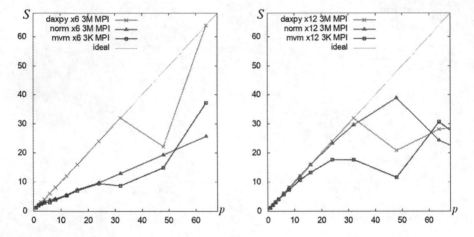

Fig. 12. Parallel performance of operations implemented in MPI for x6core and x12core segments for moderate values of N.

optimal for the AXPY operation, while on the x12core segment this is the case for MVM operation.

In general, the sequence of the least and most efficient operations for MPI implementation remains unchanged for both the x6core and x12core computing segments. This is the case for both moderate and large dimensions (see Figs. 12 and 13). The behavior of the speedup plots for problems of a higher dimension is more stable.

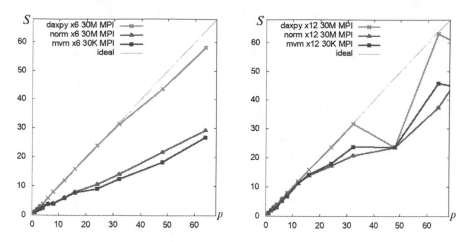

Fig. 13. Parallel performance of operations implemented in MPI for x6core and x12core segments for large values of N.

5   Conclusion

The paper presents parallel computational models for computers with shared and distributed memory. We consider the implementation of several linear algebra operations on parallel computers using OpenMP and MPI technology, respectively. The results of numerical experiments on a cluster consisting of processors of different types are presented. The focus of the paper is on the performance analysis for the set of linear algebra operations as well as on the dependencies of parallel efficiency on machine-dependent characteristics. Conclusions are drawn on the choice of the most efficient implementation in each of the cases considered.

Acknowledgements. This work has been supported by RFBR grant 17-01-00886.

References

1. Voevodin, V.V.: Mapping the problems of computational mathematics onto computer systems architecture. Russ. J. Numer. Anal. Math. Model. **15**(3–4), 349–359 (2000)
2. Voevodin, V.V.: Mathematical models and methods in parallel processes. Science, Moscow, 296 p (1986). (in Russian)
3. Voevodin, V.V.: Mathematical Foundations of Parallel Computing, p. 343. World Scientific Publ. Co, Singapore (1992)
4. Voevodin, V.V.: Parallel software from standpoint of mathematician. J. Numer. Linear Alg. Appl. **1**(2), 237–242 (1992)
5. Voevodin, V.V., Voevodin, V.V.: Parallel Computing. BHV-Petersburg, St. Petersburg (2002). (in Russian)
6. Voevodin, V.V.: Parallel computations and algorithm structure. Sov. J. Numer. Anal. Math. Model. **4**(4), 327–329 (1989)

7. Voevodin, V.V.: Parallelism in algorithms and programs. In: Computational Processes and Systems, Science, Moscow, no. 10, 26 p (1993). (in Russian)
8. Voevodin, V.V.: Macroparallelism and the decomposition of algorithms. Comput. Math. Math. Phys. **35**(6), 789–794 (1995)
9. Voevodin, V.V.: Graphs and algorithms. Russ. J. Numer. Anal. Math. Model. **11**(5), 411–419 (1996)
10. AlgoWiki: Open encyclopedia of algorithm properties. http://algowiki-project.org. Accessed 15 Apr 2019
11. Voevodin, V.V., Kim, G.D.: Principles of construction of a software package for solving of linear algebra problems. Numerical Analysis with Fortran, Moscow State University Press, no. 2, pp. 5–18 (1973). (in Russian)
12. Voevodin, V.V., Ismailova, N.A., Karysheva, L.I., Kim, G.D., Petrina, R.V., Chepurina, I.V.: Common macromodules generated by linear algebra problems. Numerical Analysis with Fortran, Moscow State University Press, no. 2, pp. 19–115 (1973). (in Russian)
13. BLAS (Basic Linear Algebra Subprograms). http://www.netlib.org/blas/. Accessed 15 Apr 2019
14. Konshin, I.: Parallel computational models to estimate an actual speedup of analyzed algorithm. Commun. Comput. Inf. Sci. **687**, 304–317 (2017)
15. Konshin, I.: Efficiency estimation for the mathematical physics algorithms for distributed memory computers. Commun. Comput. Inf. Sci. **965**, 63–75 (2019)
16. Amdahl, G.M.: Validity of the single-processor approach to achieving large scale computing capabilities. In: AFIPS Conference Proceedings, vol. 30 (Atlantic City, N.J., 18–20 April), pp. 483–485. AFIPS Press, Reston (1967). http://www-inst. eecs.berkeley.edu/~n252/paper/Amdahl.pdf. Accessed 15 Apr 2019
17. Li, X., Malek, M.: Analysis of speedup and communication/computation ratio in multiprocessor systems. In: Proceedings of Real-Time Systems Symposium, pp. 282–288 (1988)
18. Crovella, M., Bianchini, R., LeBlanc, T., Markatos, E., Wisniewski, R.: Using communication-to-computation ratio in parallel program design and performance prediction. In: Proceedings of the Fourth IEEE Symposium on Parallel and Distributed Processing, Arlington, TX, USA, pp. 238–245 (1992)
19. The OpenMP API specification for parallel programming. https://www.openmp. org. Accessed 15 Apr 2019
20. MPI: The Message Passing Interface standard. http://www.mcs.anl.gov/research/ projects/mpi/. Accessed 15 Apr 2019
21. INM RAS cluster. http://cluster2.inm.ras.ru. Accessed 15 Apr 2019

Explicit-Implicit Schemes for Parallel Solving of the Suspension Transport Problems in Coastal Systems

Alexander I. Sukhinov[1], Alexander E. Chistyakov[1(✉)],
Valentina V. Sidoryakina[2], and Elena A. Protsenko[2]

[1] Don State Technical University, Rostov-on-Don, Russia
sukhinov@gmail.com, cheese_05@mail.ru
[2] Taganrog University Named After A.P. Chehkov (Branch) of Rostov State University of Economics, Taganrog, Russia
cvv9@mail.ru, eapros@rambler.ru

Abstract. This paper is devoted to the parallel algorithms development for numerical simulation of 3D weighted suspension particles transport in coastal systems, using explicit-implicit difference schemes on multiprocessor systems. For the numerical solution of the initial-boundary value problem of suspension transport, explicit-implicit difference schemes are used. Decomposition of 3D grid region by vertical planes has been used for parallel algorithm constructing. Also second order time derivative with relatively small time-multiplier has been added for the permissible time step increasing in accordance of B. Chetverushkin method of regularization. Using these schemes allows to organize fully parallel computations. A set of independent one-dimensional three-point problems obtained as a result of implicit approximation (with optimal weight parameter) of the one-dimensional advection-diffusion and gravity sedimentation operator in the vertical direction may be solved in each processor independently without data exchanges between processors. Data exchanges requires only for the neighboring nodes in subdomains and they may be executed independently for each processor in horizontal spatial directions. The permissible value of time step is defined of stability requirements for the explicit difference scheme for grid equation of hyperbolic type and it is better in comparison of explicit schemes without regularization. Optimal value of weight parameter for this scheme has been defined. As the result the total time of parallel solution is also less in comparison of totally implicit schemes.

Keywords: Coastal zone · Mathematical model · Suspension transport · Difference scheme · Explicit-implicit scheme

---

The research is done with the financial support from Russian Foundation for Basic Research, Project No. 19-01-00701.

V. Voevodin and S. Sobolev (Eds.): RuSCDays 2019, CCIS 1129, pp. 39–50, 2019.
https://doi.org/10.1007/978-3-030-36592-9_4

1   Introduction

The transport of suspended matter is the most important factor that significantly affects the morphological and dynamic regime of the adjacent coastal zone of the reservoir, the construction and operation of port facilities, etc. [1–4]. Under the influence of waves and currents, the mass of alluvial material begins to move, undergoing chemical and mechanical changes. The processes arising at the same time find their expression in the emergence of benthic and coastal formations, which by their size can reach significant scales [5–7].

The paper presents parallel algorithm for numerical simulation of suspension transport processes based on an explicit-implicit scheme. The basic idea of constructing this scheme is to use difference equations containing explicit approximation of the diffusion-advection operator in horizontal directions with a regularized addition, the second-order difference derivative with a small multiplier and implicit approximation with weights, for the diffusion-advection and gravity sedimentation operator in the vertical direction. Restrictions on the time step are less stringent than the use of an explicit scheme that approximates a three-dimensional problem in the traditional way in the case of introducing a differential derivative of the second order [8]. This is due to the fact that in coastal systems like the Sea of Azov, the North Caspian Sea and others, typical grid cell sizes can be: few meters vertically, and tens of hundreds meters in horizontal directions. This makes it possible to choose a time step in the proposed scheme of the order of the characteristic time of propagation of disturbances in horizontal directions within one grid cell, which is significantly longer than the propagation time of disturbances in the vertical direction within a single grid cell. It is precisely this restriction that would have had to be oriented in approximating all the operators of a three-dimensional problem explicitly in the case of regularization. The use of such an explicit-implicit scheme allows to obtain a completely parallel algorithm for solving the problem, which boils down to solving a series of independent three-point difference problems using sweep method with exchanges at the border nodes when decomposing the three-dimensional grid area into equal vertical blocks according to the number of computers used in the multiprocessor system.

2   Continuous 3D Model of Diffusion-Convection-Aggregation of Suspensions

Consider a continuous mathematical model of suspended matter in the aquatic environment, taking into account the diffusion and convection of suspensions, sedimentation of suspended particles under the action of gravity, the presence of the bottom and the free surface [9–11].

We will use a rectangular Cartesian coordinate system $Oxyz$, where is the axis Ox passes on the surface of the undisturbed water surface and is directed towards the sea. Let be $h = H + \eta$ is the total water depth, [m]; H is the depth at undisturbed surface of the reservoir, [m]; η is the elevation of the free surface relative to the geoid (sea level), [m].

Let be $G \subset \mathbb{R}^3$ is the area where the process takes place, which is a parallelepiped beveled towards the shore, the upper base of which lies on the free surface $(z = \eta(x, y))$, and the bottom base is part of the bottom surface $(z = H(x, y))$. Let be Γ is the border area G, S, are the lateral boundary surface $\overline{G}$, S_{top}, S_{bottom} are the parts of the free surface and the bottom surface respectively, limited by conditions $\{0 \le x \le L_x,\ 0 \le y \le L_y\}$.

We believe that in the water volume $\overline{G}$ there are suspended particles that are at (x, y, z) and at the time t have a concentration $c = c(x, y, z, t)$, [mg/l]; t is the time in seconds (Fig. 1).

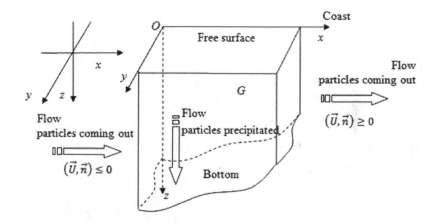

Fig. 1. Area of solving the problem of suspension transport

The equation describing the behavior of particles will be as follows:

$$\frac{\partial c}{\partial t} + \frac{\partial(uc)}{\partial x} + \frac{\partial(vc)}{\partial y} + \frac{\partial((w + w_g)c)}{\partial z} = \mu\left(\frac{\partial^2 c}{\partial x^2} + \frac{\partial^2 c}{\partial y^2}\right) + \frac{\partial}{\partial z}\left(\nu\frac{\partial c}{\partial z}\right) + F. \quad (1)$$

where u, v, w are the components of the velocity vector U of the fluid, [m/sec]; w_g is the hydraulic particle size or sedimentation rate, [m/sec]; μ, ν are the horizontal and vertical diffusion coefficients of particles, [m^2/sec]; F is the function describing the intensity of the distribution of suspended matter sources.

The area of the task of Eq. (1) is $\overline{Q}_T = G \times (0 < t \le T]$, $\overline{G}(x, y, z) = \{0 < x \le L_x,\ 0 \le y \le L_y,\ -\eta \le z \le H\}$, $\overline{G} = G \cup \Gamma$, where Γ is the border area G. Together with the boundary conditions for the particle concentration function, the solution of Eq. (1) allows determining the suspended matter fluxes both towards the coast and along the coast.

We add to the Eq. (1) the initial and boundary conditions (assuming that the deposition of particles on the bottom is irreversible):

– initial conditions at $t = 0$

$$c(x, y, z, 0) \equiv c_0(x, y, z); \tag{2}$$

– boundary conditions on the lateral boundary S at any time $0 < t \leq T$

$$\frac{\partial c}{\partial n} = 0, \quad \text{if } (\boldsymbol{U}_\Gamma, \boldsymbol{n}) \leq 0, \quad \frac{\partial c}{\partial n} = -\frac{u_\Gamma}{\mu} c, \text{ if } (\boldsymbol{U}_\Gamma, \boldsymbol{n}) \geq 0, \tag{3}$$

where $\boldsymbol{n}$ is the external normal to the region boundary S, $\boldsymbol{U}_\Gamma$ is the fluid velocity vector at the boundary S, u_Γ is the velocity vector projection $\boldsymbol{U}_\Gamma$ on the direction of the normal $\boldsymbol{n}$ on the border of the region S;
– boundary conditions on the surface of the water $S_{\text{top}} \times (0 < t \leq T)$

$$\frac{\partial c}{\partial z} = 0; \tag{4}$$

– boundary conditions at the bottom $S_{\text{bottom}} \times (0 < t \leq T)$

$$\frac{\partial c}{\partial n} = -\frac{w_g}{\nu} c. \tag{5}$$

The conditions for the correctness of the suspension transport problem in the case of multicomponent particle size distribution of particles, and therefore of problem (1)–(5), are investigated in [12], as its particular case under the conditions of smoothness of the solution function

$$c(x, y, z, t) \in C^2(Q_T) \cap C(\overline{Q}_T), \quad \operatorname{grad} c \in C(\overline{Q}_T)$$

and the required smoothness of the border area.

3 Constructing an Explicit-Implicit Scheme for the Suspension Transport Problem

The terms on the left side (except for the time derivative) of Eq. (1) describe the adjective transfer of suspended particles under the action of fluid flow and gravity. The terms on the right side describe the diffusion of suspensions. The behavior of the vertical microturbulent diffusion coefficient differs significantly from the almost constant diffusion coefficient in the horizontal direction for the processes-diffusion-convection of suspensions in coastal systems. The vertical coefficient of microturbulent diffusion can have several extremes depending on the vertical coordinate and varies in magnitude due to physical reasons. An additional complication that affects the significant change in the coefficient before the second difference derivative in the vertical coordinate is a significant change in depth for coastal systems, which quadratically affects the value of this coefficient. Thus, the one-dimensional discrete operator for diffusion-convection-sedimentation of suspensions in the vertical coordinate as a whole has poor conditioning (a large spread of eigenvalues). If we use an explicit scheme supplemented to increase the stability margin of a second-order differential derivative with a small factor, the admissible time step will be determined by the characteristic time of propagation of perturbations (concentrations of suspended matter) within one grid cell. For coastal systems, the time of propagation of disturbances in horizontal directions for practically used grids with cell sizes for many tens to hundreds of meters is tens to hundreds of seconds of physical time. For propagation of disturbances in the vertical direction, when the cell sizes in the vertical are tens of centimeters, the characteristic propagation time of the disturbances is several seconds, which will determine the allowable time step in an explicit scheme with the second time derivative. This circumstance is the main motive for constructing explicitly-implicit schemes considered below [13,14].

In our presentation, we focus on the use of an explicit-implicit scheme (Fig. 2), which allows you to build parallel algorithms that are economical in terms of total time costs for performing arithmetic operations and data exchange operations between processors.

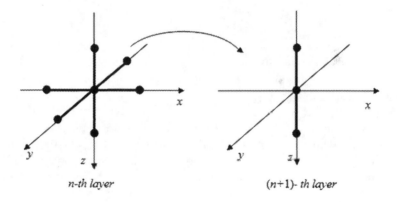

n-th layer   (n+1)- th layer

Fig. 2. Used nodes for explicit-implicit scheme

We write Eq. (1) in the form:

$$\frac{\partial c}{\partial t} + Ac = F(x, y, z, t), \quad (x, y, z) \in G, \quad t \in [0, T], \tag{6}$$

where A is the differential elliptic operator with respect to spatial variables with lower derivatives, for which the following representation is valid

$$Ac = \frac{\partial(uc)}{\partial x} + \frac{\partial(vc)}{\partial y} + \frac{\partial((w + w_g)c)}{\partial z}$$
$$- \mu \left(\frac{\partial^2 c}{\partial x^2} + \frac{\partial^2 c}{\partial y^2} \right) - \frac{\partial}{\partial z} \left(\nu \frac{\partial c}{\partial z} \right) = (A_{12} + A_3)c, \tag{7}$$

$$A_{12}c = \frac{\partial(uc)}{\partial x} + \frac{\partial(vc)}{\partial y} - \mu \left(\frac{\partial^2 c}{\partial x^2} + \frac{\partial^2 c}{\partial y^2} \right), \quad A_3c = \frac{\partial((w + w_g)c)}{\partial z} - \frac{\partial}{\partial z} \left(\nu \frac{\partial c}{\partial z} \right).$$

In the time span $0 \leqslant t \leqslant T$ build uniform grid ω_τ with step τ:

$$\omega_\tau = \{t_n = n\tau, \ n = 0, 1, \ldots, N, \ N\tau = T\}.$$

At each time step, the solution of problem (6), (2)–(5) will be represented as:

$$\frac{c^{n+1} - c^n}{\tau} + A_{12}c^n + A_3 c^{n+\sigma} = F, \quad n = 1, \ldots, N, \tag{8}$$

where $c^{n+\sigma} = \sigma c^{n+1} + (1 - \sigma)c^n$.

To increase the allowable time step in approximation of the two-dimensional problem (6), (7) by an explicit difference scheme, we add to the left-hand side of Eq. (8) a second-order time derivative with a small regularizer factor [15] not exceeding the characteristic time distribution of concentration perturbations in horizontal directions

$$\frac{\tau^*}{2} \frac{c^{n+1} - 2c^n + c^{n-1}}{\tau^2} + \frac{c^{n+1} - c^n}{\tau} + A_{12}c^n + A_3 c^{n+\sigma} = F, \quad n = 2, \ldots, N,$$

$$\tau^* \frac{c^{n+1} - c^n}{\tau^2} + \frac{c^{n+1} - c^n}{\tau} + A_{12}c^n + A_3 c^{n+\sigma} = F, \quad n = 1, \tag{9}$$

where $\tau^* \sim \dfrac{\tau}{\tilde{c}}$ is the coefficient, associated with characteristic spatial grid spacing τ and the characteristic speed of sound in the aquatic environment $\tilde{c}$.

It was shown [16] that with $\tau^* \to 0$, solution of problem (9) tends to solve problem (8).

To calculate the right side grid equation corresponding to the problem (9) you need $16N$ arithmetic operations. To solve problem (9) at the first time layer it is necessary $8N$, and for subsequent layers $5N$ arithmetic operations. Thus it is required $21N$ operations overall to calculate new time layer value. The calculation by the explicit scheme requires $16N$ arithmetic operations.

4 The Optimal Value of the Weight Parameter in the Scheme with Weights for the Diffusion-Convection Equation

For a difference scheme with weights approximating the initial-boundary value problem for the diffusion equation, convection, an algorithm is proposed for finding the optimal weight value providing the minimum approximation error for the specified values of the steps of the time grid. To find the value of the optimal parameter, the solution function and the approximation error are expanded depending on the time step along the trigonometric basis.

Consider the initial boundary value problem for a parabolic equation of the form

$$c'_t + uc'_x = \mu c''_{xx}, \quad u = const, \quad \mu = const, 0 < x < L, t > 0, \tag{10}$$

with initial condition

$$c(x, 0) = c_0(x) \tag{11}$$

and boundary conditions

$$c(0,t) = 0, c(L,t) = 0, t > 0. \tag{12}$$

It is required to find a solution to problem (10)–(12) class
$c(x,t) \in C^2 (0 < x < L) \cap C (0 \le x \le L) \cap C^1 (0 < t < +\infty) \cap C (0 \le t < +\infty)$.
Imagine the algorithm for finding the optimal parameter.

1. The models and parameters of all input functions are determined.
2. The initial and boundary conditions of the initial-boundary value problem corresponding to the model under consideration are specified.
3. The formal notation is written for the Fourier series on the orthogonal basis generated by the solution function of the problem using the formula:

$$c(x,0) = \sum_{m=-N}^{N} C_m (0) \exp (jwmx), w = \pi/L, j^2 = -1$$

4. Calculate the coefficients of the Fourier series using the expression:

$$C_m (0) = \frac{2}{L} \int_0^L q(x,0) \exp (jwmx) \, dx, m = 0..N.$$

5. Determine the eigenvalues by the formula:

$$\lambda_m = - \left(2\mu \frac{1 - \cos \left(\frac{\pi m}{N} \right)}{h^2} + ju \frac{\sin \left(\frac{\pi m}{N} \right)}{h} \right)$$

   and meaning $\lambda_{\max}$: $\lambda_{\max} = \max_m |\lambda_m|$, h is space step.
6. Calculate the value χ_m to determine the error at each time layer, using the formula:

$$\chi_m = \frac{\lambda_m}{\lambda_{\max}} \tau_0.$$

7. Find numbers $z_{1,m}, z_{2,m}$, using formulas

$$z_{1,m} = 1 - \exp (-\chi_m), \quad z_{2,m} = \frac{1 - \exp (-\chi_m) - \chi_m}{\chi_m}.$$

8. We determine the weight parameter σ at which the relative error is minimal, according to the formula:

$$\sigma = - \frac{\sum_{m=1}^{N} \max_{k=0,n-1} |C_m (t^k)|^2 (Re z_{1,m} Re z_{2,m} + Im z_{1,m} Im z_{2,m})}{\sum_{m-1}^{N} \max_{k=0,n-1} |C_m (t^k)|^2 \left((Re z_{1,m})^2 + (Im z_{1,m})^2 \right)}.$$

9. Based on the difference scheme with weights we find, we express the value of the function on the current time layer through the values on the previous layer:

$$\frac{c_i^{n+1} - c_i^n}{\tau} + u \frac{c_{i+1}^{n+\sigma} + c_{i-1}^{n+\sigma}}{2h} = \mu \cdot \frac{c_{i+1}^{n+\sigma} - 2c_i^{n+\sigma} + c_{i-1}^{n+\sigma}}{h^2}.$$

5   Description of the Parallel Algorithm

In parallel implementation, methods of decomposition of grid domains for computationally laborious diffusion-convection problems, taking into account the architecture and parameters of a multiprocessor computing system, were used. The decomposition of the computational two-dimensional domain is performed by two spatial variables (Fig. 3) and assumes that the number of vertical blocks of approximately the same number of grid nodes is equal to the number of calculators of a multiprocessor system.

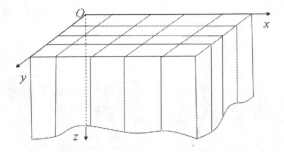

Fig. 3. Decomposition of a two-dimensional grid region

Table 1. Acceleration and performance of the parallel version of the explicit-implicit scheme

Number of cores	Acceleration			Efficiency		
	1000×1000	2000×2000	5000×5000	1000×1000	2000×2000	5000×5000
1	1	1	1	1	1	1
2	1.645	1.716	1.979	0.823	0.858	0.99
4	3.689	3.156	3.064	0.922	0.788	0.766
8	4.843	4.72	8.686	0.605	0.59	1.086
16	5.745	7.184	11.5	0.979	0.449	0.719
32	14.607	13.13	20.936	0.456	0.41	0.654
64	32.8	23.63	37.114	0.513	0.369	0.58
128	75.167	28.454	96.059	0.587	0.222	0.75
256	55.253	42.924	165.434	0.216	0.168	0.646
512	27.883	67.284	228.36	0.054	0.131	0.446

The maximum performance of a multiprocessor computing system is 18.8 teraflops. The compute nodes are 128 of the same type of HP ProLiant BL685c 16-core Blade servers, each of which is equipped with four AMD Opteron 8356

2.3 GHz four-core processors and 32 GB RAM. Table 1 shows the values of acceleration and efficiency for different numbers of computational cores for solving the model problem of suspended matter transport on the estimated grids of size 1000×1000, 2000×2000, 5000×5000 nodes.

6   The Results of a Numerical Experiment

As a model problem, the problem of convective-diffusive transfer and sedimentation of suspended matter during the dumping of the extracted bottom material onto the surface of a water body was considered. Baseline data are: reservoir depth 10 m; the volume of the substance discharged is 741 m³; flow rate 0.2 m/sec; deposition rate of 2.042 mm/sec (according to Stokes); soil density 1600 kg/m³; the percentage of dust particles (d less than 0.05 mm) in sandy soils is 26.83%. Parameters of the computational domain: length 3 km; 1.4 km wide; step in the horizontal spatial coordinate of 20 m; step in the vertical spatial coordinate of 1 m; settlement interval 2 h. It should be noted that the initial data are close to the real data, characteristic for the distribution of suspended matter in places of landfills of the extracted bottom material during dredging works in river mouths.

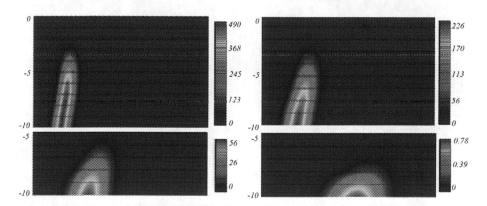

Fig. 4. The field values of suspended particles after 15 min; 30 min; 1 h; 2 h after the discharge of the suction pump hold

Figure 4 shows the dynamics of changes in the concentration of suspended particles (mg/l) over time. The values of the suspension concentration field are given in the cross section of the computational domain by a plane passing through the unloading point and formed by directional vectors: vertically and along the flow. The estimated interval was 15 min; 30 min; 1 h; 2 h respectively. Flows are directed from left to right. The results of numerical experiments are in good agreement with the field data [20].

The problems of the transfer of suspended particles were solved on the basis of an explicit scheme and an explicit implicit scheme to obtain the optimal values of the time steps for the (9). Figure 5 shows the values of the error of difference schemes (1 - the error function for the explicit scheme is indicated, 2 - the error for the scheme (9) is indicated). Along the vertical axis is indicated the value of the relative error $\psi = \sqrt{\sum_{i,j,k} \left(\tilde{c}_{i,j,k} - c_{i,j,k}\right)^2 / \sum_{i,j,k} c_{i,j,k}^2}$, $c_{i,j,k}$ is the exact value of solving the problem of transfer of suspended particles in a node (i, j, k), $\tilde{c}_{i,j,k}$ is the numerical solution depending on the size of the time step. Along the horizontal axis denotes the value of the time step, referred to the value $\tau_m = \left(2\mu \left(\frac{1}{h_x^2} + \frac{1}{h_y^2} + \frac{1}{h_z^2}\right)\right)^{-1}$. From the condition of stability of an explicit scheme, it follows that the quantity τ_m is a restriction from above to the time step [14]. Magnitude $\tau_0 = \tau/\tau_m$ [21] convenient to use to describe the error ψ, because when the grid size changes by spatial coordinates, there is practically no change in the function $\psi = \psi(\tau_0)$.

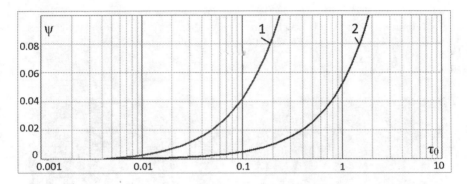

Fig. 5. The numerical study of the relative error as a function of the change in the time step according to explicit and explicit-implicit schemes

Figure 5 shows that the achievement error for an explicit scheme is that the restriction on the time step is significantly smaller than for the proposed explicit-implicit scheme (9). The relative error of the explicit scheme is 1% if the value is 0.10087, in the case of using the proposed explicit-implicit scheme (9), the parameter is 0.01348. Thus, to achieve the accuracy of 1% of the explicit-implicit scheme (9), it is necessary that the time step be greater by a factor of 7.483 than it is in the explicit scheme. This significantly improves the performance of the programs thanks to a better difference scheme. The proposed scheme (9) is effective if the step along one of the spatial directions is significantly smaller than the steps along the other spatial directions.

7 Conclusion

The construction and study of parallel algorithms for the numerical implementation of the problem of suspension transport in coastal marine systems is considered. The presented parallel algorithm is based on the use of an explicit-implicit scheme. Using this scheme allows you to organize fully parallel computing. The two-dimensional problem is solved on the basis of an explicit scheme. A set of independent one-dimensional three-point problems that approximate one-dimensional diffusion-convective problems along the vertical by implicit weighted schemes is solved independently of the others. The explicit-implicit scheme allows for efficient implementation on a high-performance computing system, which, in turn, allows us to repeatedly improve the accuracy of the operational forecast and the validity of engineering decisions made when creating coastal infrastructure facilities.

References

1. Pleiades Publishing, Moscow. https://doi.org/10.1134/S2070048218050125
2. Sidoryakina, V.V., Sukhinov, A.I.: Well-posedness analysis and numerical implementation of a linearized two-dimensional bottom sediment transport problem. J. Comp. Math. Math. Phys. **57**(6), 978–994 (2017). https://doi.org/10.7868/S0044466917060138
3. Alekseenko, E., Roux, B., Sukhinov, A., Kotarba, R., Fougere, D.: Nonlinear hydrodynamics in a mediterranean lagoon. J. Nonlinear Process. Geophys. **20**(2), 189–198 (2013). https://doi.org/10.5194/npg-20-189-2013
4. Chetverushkin, B.N.: Kinetic models for supercomputer simulation continuous mechanic problems. Math. Models Comput. Simul. **7**(6), 531–539 (2015). https://doi.org/10.1134/S2070048215060034
5. Alekseenko, E., Roux, B., Sukhinov, A., Kotarba, R., Fougere, D.: Coastal hydrodynamics in a windy lagoon. J. Comput. Fluids **77**, 24–35 (2013). https://doi.org/10.1016/j.compfluid.2013.02.003
6. Sukhinov, A.I., Chistyakov, A.E., Alekseenko, E.V.: Numerical realization of the three-dimensional model of hydrodynamics for shallow water basins on a high-performance system. J. Math. Models Comput. Simul. **3**(5), 562–574 (2011). https://doi.org/10.1134/S2070048211050115
7. Liu, X., Qi, S., Huang, Y., Chen, Y., Pengfei, D.: Predictive modeling in sediment transportation across multiple spatial scales in the Jialing river basin of China. Int. J. Sediment Res. **30**(3), 250–255 (2015)
8. Pleiades Publishing, Moscow. https://doi.org/10.1134/S0965542515080035
9. Nikitina, A.V., Semenyakina, A.A.: Mathematical modeling of eutrophication processes in azov sea on supercomputers. Comput. Math. Inf. Technol. **1**(1), 82–101 (2017)
10. Perianez, R.: Modelling the transport of suspended particulate matter by the Rhone River plume (France). Implic. Pollut. Dispers. Environ. Pollut. **133**(2), 351–364 (2005). https://doi.org/10.1016/j.envpol.2004.05.021
11. Sukhinov, A.I., Sukhinov, A.A.: Reconstruction of 2001 ecological disaster in the azov sea on the basis of precise hydrophysics models. In: Parallel Computational Fluid Dynamics, Mutidisciplinary Applications, Proceedings of Parallel CFD 2004 Conference, Las Palmas de Gran Canaria, Spain, pp. 231–238. Elsevier, Amsterdam-Berlin-London-New York-Tokyo (2005). https://doi.org/10.1016/B978-044452024-1/50030-0

12. Leipe, T., Knoppers, B., Marone, E., Camargo, R.: Suspended matter transport in coral reef waters of the Abrolhos Bank. Brazil. Geo-Marine Lett. **19**, 186–195 (1999). https://doi.org/10.1007/s003670050108
13. Samarskiy, A.A., Gulin, A.V.: Numerical Methods. Nauka, Moscow (1989). (in Russian)
14. Samarskiy, A.A. Vabishchevich, P.N.: Numerical Methods for Solving Convection-Diffusion Problems. URSS (2005). (in Russian)
15. Chetverushkin, B.N.: Resolution limits of continuous media models and their mathematical formulations. J. Math. Models Comput. Simul. **5**(3), 266–279 (2013). https://doi.org/10.1134/S2070048213030034
16. Pleiades Publishing, Moscow. https://doi.org/10.1134/S2070048217050039
17. Sukhinov, A.I.: Precise fluid dynamics models and their application in prediction and reconstruction of extreme events in the sea of Azov. J. Izv. Taganrog. Radiotech. Univ. **3**, 228–235 (2006). (in Russian)
18. Sukhinov, A., Chistyakov, A., Sidoryakina, V.: Investigation of nonlinear 2D bottom transportation dynamics in coastal zone on optimal curvilinear boundary adaptive grids. In: MATEC Web of Conf. XIII Int. Sci.-Tech. Conf. 'Dynamic of Technical Systems' (DTS-2017), vol. 132, Rostov-on-Don (2017). https://doi.org/10.1051/matecconf/201713204003
19. Samarskiy, A.A.: Theory of Difference Schemes. Nauka, Moscow (1989). (in Russian)
20. Kovtun, I.I., Protsenko, E.A., Sukhinov, A.I., Chistyakov, A.E.: Calculating the Impact on Aquatic Resources Dredging in the White Sea. J. Fundamentalnaya i prikladnaya gidrofizika **9**(2), 27–38 (2016). (in Russian)
21. Pleiades Publishing, Moscow. https://doi.org/10.1134/S2070048214030120

GPU Implementation of a Stencil Code with More Than 90% of the Peak Theoretical Performance

Ilya Pershin[1,2]([✉]), Vadim Levchenko[2], and Anastasia Perepelkina[2]

[1] Moscow Institute of Physics and Technology, Dolgoprudny, Russia
peshin2010@gmail.com
[2] Keldysh Institute of Applied Mathematics, Moscow, Russia
vadimlevchenko@mail.ru, mogmi@ya.ru

Abstract. The modern supercomputers come close to the sub-exaFLOPs scale performance, however, obtaining an adequate efficiency in applied codes remains a significant problem. The stencil codes, commonly known as memory-bound, may be made compute-bound with the use of advanced algorithms. We present an algorithm for 1D wave equation in which the data is localized in the on-chip register memory, while the L2 cache and the shared memory is used for the exchange between the domains. According to the Roofline model, the problem is compute-bound. To get more than 30% of the peak computing performance, more in depth considerations are required. We avoid the latency bottleneck with the use of overlapping domains - a halo of redundant computations. We have obtained more than 90% efficiency on nVidia V100 GPU after we found an efficient way of pairwise block synchronization, and a method of optimizing FLOP to FMA conversion of the compiler.

Keywords: Stencil · GPU · CUDA · Cache blocking · Domain decomposition · Latency hiding

1 Introduction

With the access to new supercomputers and computing architectures the topic of raising the efficiency of code implementations stays relevant [1,15,17]. Namely, the stencil simulation encompasses a wide range of scientific and engineering modeling, that is, wave modelling (seismic, electromagnetic, acoustic), plasma physics, computational fluid dynamics, filtering and image processing. By stencil computing we mean the simulation programs, where the data is defined on a discrete mesh, and the update of a value requires the data from neighboring cells. Such simulations commonly use a very small portion of the computing resources of the system. That is, data access takes time comparable and even much bigger that the arithmetic operations. This is the property of a memory bound problem.

© Springer Nature Switzerland AG 2019
V. Voevodin and S. Sobolev (Eds.): RuSCDays 2019, CCIS 1129, pp. 51–63, 2019.
https://doi.org/10.1007/978-3-030-36592-9_5

Specifically, on GPU, the search for the best algorithm implementation continues [2,3,5,14], and has led to a variety of high-performance implementations.

The CUDA framework [13] has been developed to ease the programming for the general purpose GPU computation, including scientific computation. It naturally provides a simple way to parallelize stencil computation. The classic way of stencil implementation is reported in [9], and it is a recommended way for beginner CUDA programmers [13]. The mesh cells are distributed among the CUDA threads, one cell per CUDA thread. The CUDA threads are grouped in CUDA-blocks, which are assigned for computing onto Streaming Multiprocessors (SMs). The 'memory access redundancy' metric is used to estimate the efficiency of the implementation. In [9] the optimum value is defined as 1.

The more modern method for performance estimation uses the 'operational intensity' metric, and the Roofline model, corresponding to it [16]. Operational intensity is the number of operations per byte of memory traffic. It increases with the decrease of the memory access redundancy, thus, the values may be easily converted to each other. The Roofline visually discerns two types of problems: memory bound problems are limited by the memory bandwidth, compute bound problems are limited by the peak computing performance. The classic stencil implementation is memory bound.

In this work our goal was an implementation with maximal efficiency, at least 90% of the computing performance limit. We take the most simple stencil problem for the test-bed: 1D finite difference solution of the Cauchy problem for wave equation. First, the memory-bound limit should be overcome. This is achieved by the increase of the operational intensity [7], which is impossible without the change of the algorithm. One method is introduction of temporal blocking, such as wavefront [11], overlapped regions [10], LRnLA algorithms [6].

The data access redundancy may be set to zero if all data is localized in the register file of the GPU, which is, in total, several MB on the modern GPU, and becomes larger on newer devices. It is 3.75 MB on Kepler, 6 MB on Maxwell, 14 MB on Pascal, 20 MB on Volta [12]. The number of cells that may be stored in it is about 10^6, we store all simulation data in the register file. Each thread is assigned with a localized portion of the cells in the domain. After the update, the synchronization and data exchange between threads take place. This is a common method of geometrical parallelization, we refer to it as domain decomposition (DD), or Recursive Domain Decomposition (RDD), since it happens at least on two levels: intra-block and intra-thread.

This alleviates the memory bound limit, since the data exchange is performed through L2 cache and shared memory. However, since the problem in question is 1D, the data portions that are to be exchanged are small. The limitation is not the memory throughput anymore, but the memory access latency. We estimate this value, and incorporate it into the performance model.

The latency overhead may be mitigated by the introduction of a halo of redundant compute [2,8]. Thus, we choose to improve the RDD algorithm to the RDD with Halo (RDDHalo) algorithm by introducing the overlapped region in the intra-thread and the intra-block interfaces. The key idea of halo is simple:

instead of the exchange of D data each step, the exchange of $\sim H \cdot D$ data each H steps takes place (Fig. 1). The domains are overlapped. In the region of the overlap (halo) on the interface of two threads or blocks, the cells are updated by both processes.

2   Algorithm

2.1   Recursive Domain Decomposition with Halo

Here we only describe the RDDHalo method for the interface between CUDA-blocks. The intra-thread parallelism is made identically. The use of 'heavy' CUDA-blocks is suggested: if larger number of cells is assigned to the block, the ration of the boundary cells number to the interior cells number is lower, and less data exchange and synchronization are required per whole domain. Thus, we assume one CUDA-block per SM. At the start, both SMs store the correct values for all cells, that are assigned to be updated on it, and r more values at each side which are required for the update (Fig. 1). The number of correct values is decreased by $2r$ each step between the synchronization events. Then, the data exchange takes place to reconstruct both domains. The size of the halo (domain overlap) is $2r(H - 1)$. The data to be exchanged are the cells of the half of the halo, and the r more values that are necessary for the stencil computation on the next step, $\frac{2r(H-1)}{2} + r$ values total. Since the stencil requires two time layers, $\frac{2r(H-1)}{2} - r$ more values are required from the previous time step. The data required for the exchange from the two time steps is outlined by the **exchange** boxes in Fig. 1.

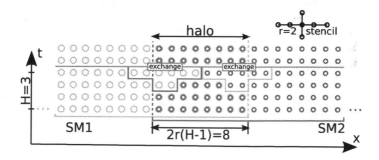

Fig. 1. DDHalo algorithms on the dependency graph. The cells that are computed correctly and stored on the two adjacent SMs are shown in two colors. The data that should be sent in the synchronization step is outlined in colored boxes. (Color figure online)

Two important remarks should be made here. First, in contrast to the RDD, the overhead for redundant computation appears, since some cells are computed twice. The size of the halo ($2r(H - 1)$) is smaller than the size of the domain

($\texttt{grp}\cdot\texttt{threads} \sim 15\div20\cdot10^3$) by several orders of magnitude. With the increase in H the overhead may become significant, however, the goal of hiding the latency by decreasing the number of synchronization events is achieved much earlier. Second, while some of the redundant computations may be skipped, it is better to perform these computations nonetheless. This is due to the SIMT architecture of GPU, which dictates the homogeneity of the thread computing. Thus, the conditional statements are not used in the implementation, and the incorrect cells continue to be updated until the synchronization event.

2.2   Performance Model

The Roofline is a visual performance model that provides an estimate of the performance limit from the two fundamental ceilings: peak computing performance and memory bandwidth, namely, $\Pi_{alg} \leq \min(\Pi_{peak}, \Theta \cdot I_{alg})$. Here Π_{alg} is the algorithm achievable performance and Π_{peak} is the maximum possible performance in the elementary operations per unit of time, Θ is the memory bandwidth, $I_{alg} = \frac{O_{alg}}{D_{alg}}$ is the arithmetic intensity of the algorithm, O_{alg} is the number of operations and D_{alg} is the memory traffic.

Π_{peak} and Θ can be estimated accurately enough as follows. Arithmetic instruction throughput τ is how many instructions may be executed per cycle. These values can be found in [4], and are determined by the GPU architecture. μ is the number of SM per GPU. To get the actual frequency of SM ν_{SM} the monitoring tools (such as $\texttt{nvidia-smi}$ or $\texttt{nvidia-settings}$) are run during the code execution, since the frequency may depend on many factors. Then, $\Pi_{peak} = \tau\mu\nu_{SM}$. Similarly, with the use of CUDA Runtime API the memory bus width β can be found out. With the use of monitoring tools the memory frequency ν_{mem} is measured during the code run. Thus, $\Theta = 2\beta\nu_{mem}$. The factor of 2 is explained by the Graphics Double Data Rate SDRAM (GDDR SDRAM) feature. All these values are collected in Table 1.

Table 1. GPU characteristics: arithmetic instruction throughput τ, number of SM μ, clock rate ν_{sm}, peak performance $\Pi_{peak} = \tau\mu\nu_{sm}$; β is the memory bus width, ν_{mem} is the memory clock rate, $\Theta = 2\beta\nu_{mem}$ is the memory bandwidth

GPU	Precision	τ $\left[\frac{FMA}{clock \cdot SM}\right]$	μ [SM]	ν_{sm} $\left[\frac{Gclock}{s}\right]$	Π_{peak} $\left[\frac{GFMA}{s}\right]$	β $\left[\frac{B}{clock}\right]$	ν_{mem} $\left[\frac{Gclock}{s}\right]$	Θ $\left[\frac{GB}{s}\right]$
GTX 1070	Single	128	15	1.860	3571	32	3.802	243.3
RTX 2070	Single	64	36	1.875	4320	32	6.801	435.3
Tesla V100	Single	64	80	1.380	7066	512	0.877	898.0
	Double	32	80	1.380	3533			

The unit for measurement of the performance is Fused Multiply Add (FMA), which may be 1 or 2 floating point operation (FLOP).

For one cell update $O_{alg} = (2r+1) \frac{\text{FMA}}{\text{cell·step}}$ operations are required. The operations are grouped manually into FMA as follows:

$$u_k^{n+1} = \alpha_{\pm r}\overbrace{(u_{k+r}^n + u_{k-r}^n)}^{\text{FMA}} + \ldots + \underbrace{\alpha_{\pm 1}\overbrace{(u_{k+1}^n + u_{k-1}^n)}^{\text{FMA}} + \overbrace{\alpha_0 u_k^n - u_k^{n-1}}^{\text{FMA}}}_{\text{FMA}} \tag{1}$$

In the classic implementation, to compute u_k^{n+1} $(2r+1)$ values are loaded from the u^n layer, one value is loaded from the u^{n-1} layer, and one value is saved: $(2r+3)$ values total. However, since the update is stepwise, the neighboring values which are updated by other threads may be found in the L1 cache. Each thread performs only three non-caching operations: load u_k^{n-1} and u_k^n, and write u_k^{n+1}. The L1 cache is much faster than the global memory, thus, the exchange with L1 may be neglected in the Roofline model. Data throughput is $D_{alg} = 3s \frac{\text{B}}{\text{cell·step}}$, where s is the size of floating point data type, namely 4B for single precision and 8B for double-precision. The operational intensity is

$$I_{alg} = \frac{O_{alg}}{D_{alg}} = \frac{2r+1}{3s} \frac{\text{FMA}}{\text{B}}. \tag{2}$$

In Fig. 2 we plot the Roofline for the classical implementation, mark the operational intensity for several values of r, and report the results of our implementation of this algorithm with markers.

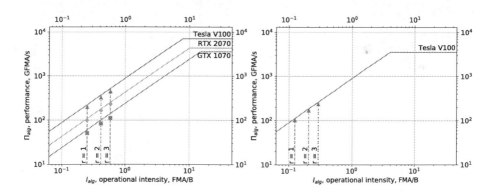

Fig. 2. Roofline for single and double precision implementation of the classical stencil algorithm on Tesla V100, RTX 2070, GTX1070 GPU

In the RDD algorithm, since the two memory levels are engaged, the two bandwidths are to be considered. Thus, the Roofline is defined by $\Pi_{alg} \leq \min(\Pi_{peak}, \Theta_{L2} I_{alg,L2}, \Theta_{sh} I_{alg,sh})$ The extra subscript denotes the type of memory (L2 cache or shared). As before, $O_{alg} = (2r+1) \frac{\text{FMA}}{\text{cell·step}}$. The data throughput is estimated as follows. In each block, there are `grp · threads` cells. Each block exchanges $4r$ values of s byte size. Thus, assuming `grp = 64` and `threads = 256`,

$$D_{alg,L2} = \frac{4r}{\texttt{grp} \cdot \texttt{threads}} \cdot s \frac{\text{B}}{\text{cell} \cdot \text{step}} = \frac{rs}{4096} \frac{\text{B}}{\text{cell} \cdot \text{step}}. \tag{3}$$

Similarly, each CUDA thread has `grp` cells and exchanges $4r$ values,

$$D_{alg,sh} = \frac{4r}{\texttt{grp}} \cdot s \frac{\text{B}}{\text{cell} \cdot \text{step}} = \frac{rs}{16} \frac{\text{B}}{\text{cell} \cdot \text{step}}. \tag{4}$$

The operational intensity is

$$I_{alg} = \frac{O_{alg}}{D_{alg}} = \begin{cases} 4096 \cdot \frac{2r+1}{rs} \frac{\text{FMA}}{\text{B}}, & \text{inter-block via L2 cache,} \\ 16 \cdot \frac{2r+1}{rs} \frac{\text{FMA}}{\text{B}}, & \text{inter-thread via shared memory.} \end{cases} \tag{5}$$

Both $I_{alg,L2}$ and $I_{alg,sh}$ are high enough, so the problem is in the compute-bound region of the Roofline against both types of synchronization.

In the RDDHalo algorithm, the latency overhead limits the performance, and we may write $\Pi_{alg} \leq \min(\Pi_{peak}, \Theta_{L2}I_{alg,L2}, \Theta_{sh}I_{alg,sh}, O_{\text{sync}}/\Lambda_{\text{sync}})$, where $O_{\text{sync}} = KHO_{alg}$ is the operation count between synchronizations, K is the number of cells, $\Lambda_{\text{sync}} = 1.3\mu s$ is the intra-block synchronization time (measured in Sect. 3.2). The Π_{peak} and $O_{\text{sync}}/\Lambda_{\text{sync}}$ limits are visualized as a Roofline in Fig. 3. The markers show the performance of our implementation for different values of `grp`, `halo_grid` (H) and `halo_block` (defined in Sect. 3). The graph confirms the attention to the latency overhead, and the fact that it is overcome with the introduction of halo.

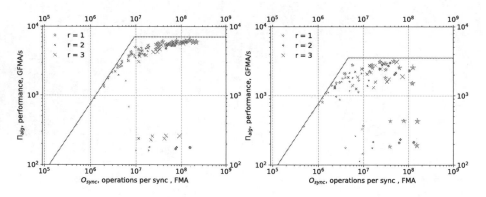

Fig. 3. Latency limits for single and double precision on Tesla V100 GPU. The markers show the results of the test runs with different halo and `grp` parameters. Larger marker correspond to larger halo.

The maximum performance we obtained with double-precision by varying the parameters is

- for $r = 1$, $\mathtt{grp} = 48$, $H = 16$, $\Pi = 90\%\Pi_{peak} \sim 1.05 \cdot 10^{12} \frac{\text{cell}\cdot\text{step}}{\text{s}}$;
- for $r = 2$, $\mathtt{grp} = 48$, $H = 8$, $\Pi = 86\%\Pi_{peak} \sim 0.60 \cdot 10^{12} \frac{\text{cell}\cdot\text{step}}{\text{s}}$;
- for $r = 3$, $\mathtt{grp} = 48$, $H = 8$, $\Pi = 88\%\Pi_{peak} \sim 0.44 \cdot 10^{12} \frac{\text{cell}\cdot\text{step}}{\text{s}}$.

3 Implementation

3.1 Computation Kernel

The simplified CUDA-kernel is presented in Fig. 4.

The `real` keyword implies float or double data type. The `layer`, `layer2` arrays contain the data of the u_k^n and u_k^{n-1} cells in the global memory. At the start of the kernel, the data is loaded from them into registers; at the finish it is saved into these arrays. Between the start and the finish, not one, but many time `iterations` take place. Additionally, these arrays are used for data exchange between CUDA-blocks at every iteration. Only the required data is sent in the data exchange moment, so only a small fraction of the cell data goes through the memory bus. The `volatile` specificator is necessary due to the compiler workflow [13]. The intra-block halo is denoted `halo_grid` (H), the intra-thread halo is denoted `halo_block`.

In each thread, the `center` and `prev` arrays are introduced to store the data of `grp` cells in the registers. The `center` array has a larger size, since the boundary cells need r cell data from each of the neighboring threads to apply the stencil. At the start, these arrays are filled from the global memory.

The `center_lefts` and `center_rights` arrays are defined for the data exchange between threads through the shared memory. The second pair `prev_lefts` and `prev_rights` are required for $H > 2$, since the data from two layers are necessary in this case. The `write_shared` function fills these arrays.

After this, the main loop in Δt takes place. In an iteration, the block data exchange occurs, and between the exchanges, the `halo_grid/halo_block` sub-iterations are started. Each sub-iteration, in turn, contains data exchange between threads, and `halo_block` stencil calculations. After the loop is finished, all data is saved from `center` and `prev` to the global memory arrays `layer` and `layer2`.

The loop in time is contained inside the kernel, so some means of inter-block and inter-thread synchronization is necessary. The common tool to synchronize threads is the `__syncthreads()` function. The `read_shared`, `write_shared`, `read_global` and `write_global` functions implement the data exchange and synchronization.

3.2 CUDA-Block Synchronization

In this section we show the synchronization method for Domain Decomposition without halo. RDDHalo synchronization is similar.

```
const int max_threads = 256;

template <int grp, int radius, int halo_grid, int halo_block>
__global__ void step(volatile real *layer, volatile real *layer2,
                     const real cour2, const int iterations) {
  const int node0 = //group size * thread number
                    //minus all prepending overlaps
  real center[grp + 2*radius], prev[grp];
  for(int g = 0; g < grp; ++g) {
    center[radius + g] = layer[node0 + g];
    prev[g] = layer2[node0 + g];
  }


  __shared__ real center_lefts[radius*halo_block][max_threads];
  __shared__ real center_rights[radius*halo_block][max_threads];

  //Only if halo_block > 2, otherwise these arrays are not needed
  __shared__ real prev_lefts[radius*(halo_block - 2)][max_threads];
  __shared__ real prev_rights[radius*(halo_block - 2)][max_threads];

  write_shared<grp, radius, halo_grid, halo_block>(
      center, prev, center_lefts, center_rights,
      prev_lefts, prev_rights);
  __syncthreads();
  for(int it = 0; it < iterations; ++it) {
    read_global<grp, radius, overlap_gr>(
        center, prev, node0, layer, layer2);

    for(int h_gr = 0; h_gr < halo_grid; h_gr += halo_block) {
      read_shared<grp, radius, halo_grid, halo_block>(
          center, prev, center_lefts, center_rights,
          prev_lefts, prev_rights);
      for(int h_bl = 0; h_bl < halo_block; ++h_bl) {
        for(int g = 0; g < grp; ++g)
          prev[g] = stencil<radius>(center + g, prev[g], cour2);
        for(int g = 0; g < grp; ++g)
          swap(prev[g], center[radius + g]);
      }
      __syncthreads();
      write_shared<grp, radius, halo_grid, halo_block>(
          center, prev, center_lefts, center_rights,
          prev_lefts, prev_rights);
      __syncthreads();
    }

    write_global<grp, radius, halo_grid, halo_block>(
        center, prev, node0, layer, layer2);
  }

  read_shared<grp, radius, halo_grid, halo_block>(
    center, prev, center_lefts, center_rights,
    prev_lefts, prev_rights);
  read_global<grp, radius, halo_grid, halo_block>(
    center, prev, node0, layer, layer2);
  for(int g = 0; g < grp; ++g) {
    layer[node0 + g] = center[radius + g];
    layer2[node0 + g] = prev[g];
  }
}
```

Fig. 4. Simplified code of the RDDHalo algorithm

CUDA Cooperative Groups. CUDA Cooperative Groups (CG) is an universal API for synchronization. It may be applied to a group of thread of arbitrary size, from one warp to all threads of several devices, situated on one node. This is a barrier synchronization, that is, a chosen group of threads is synchronized altogether. This mechanism seems convenient for our purposes, and we have applied it to our code.

The function read_global (Fig. 5) controls the exchange between neighboring blocks. This function is called in the step kernel (Fig. 4).

```
template <int grp, int radius>
inline __device__ void read_global(
    real center[grp + 2*radius], volatile real *layer) {
    grid_group grid = this_grid();
    grid.sync();

    if(first_in_block) {
        for(int g = -radius; g < 0; ++g)
            center[radius + g] = layer[node0 + g];    }
    else if(last_in_block) {
        for(int g = grp - 1 + radius; g > grp - 1; --g)
            center[radius + g] = layer[node0 + g];    }
}
```

Fig. 5. The CG synchronization function

First, we check if the thread is the first or the last in a block. Otherwise, it should not make any memory operations. If it is, this thread reads the global memory array layer and saves it to the register array center. In the beginning of the function, there are two instructions concerning the variable grid. They perform the synchronization, that is, they guarantee that after grid.sync all SMs are synchronized, and the data that is read is correct. The function write_shared is similar.

Unfortunately, CG synchronization appears to be inefficient for our problem (Fig. 6). The possible reason that the grid.sync is called for the whole grid of blocks at once, and all SMs are synchronized. This is superfluous for ensuring the correctness of the data read. Actually, it is sufficient to wait only for the two blocks (in 1D) to complete the work up to this point. If the synchronization of one block with only its neighbors was implemented, it would possibly lead to the acceleration of the memory access. Unfortunately, the current most recent CUDA version (10.1) does not provide such ability.

Semaphore Synchronization. We choose to manually implement and test the performance gain of the local block synchronization with a semaphore, the classic synchronization primitive (Fig. 7). The semaphore limits the number of parallel processes that can read and write the shared data. In this case two neighboring blocks work with the same data: one reads and the other writes. Thus, there are two states for the semaphore.

The semaph pointer array stores the semaphores, assigned to the data section which is subject to the racing condition. The length of the array is equal to twice the number of blocks, since each block has two regions, which are accessed by

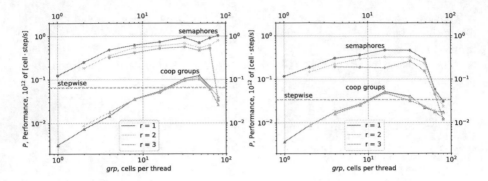

Fig. 6. Comparison of the synchronization methods on Tesla V100

```
const int READABLE = 0, WRITABLE = 1;

template <int grp, int radius> inline __device__ void read_global(
    real center[grp + 2*radius],
    volatile real *layer, volatile int *semaph) {
    if(first_in_block) {
        while(semaph[2*blockIdx.x - 1] != READABLE);
        for(int g = -radius; g < 0; ++g)
            center[radius + g] = layer[node0 + g];
        semaph[2*blockIdx.x - 1] = WRITABLE;      }
    else if(last_in_block) {
        while(semaph[2*blockIdx.x + 2] != READABLE);
        for(int g = grp - 1 + radius; g > grp - 1; --g)
            center[radius + g] = layer[node0 + g];
        semaph[2*blockIdx.x + 2] = WRITABLE;      }
}
```

Fig. 7. Manual implementation of semaphores for intra-block synchronization

other blocks: at the start and at the end. The semaphore data type is integer. Its two states are labeled READABLE and WRITABLE.

Before reading the data chunk from the other block, the corresponding semaphore is checked to be READABLE. The while loop clause is terminated by a semicolon, so it can not be escaped unless the state is changed externally. After the read from memory, the value WRITABLE is written into the semaphore, since no other block requires this data. The data can be overwritten by the adjacent block.

The write_global function is similar, except for one point. After the data is written from the center array into the layer array and before assigning the value READABLE to a corresponding semaphore, the __threadfence() instruction is called, since CUDA uses a weakly-ordered memory model [13]. The center and layer arrays are in the global memory. Thus, if the __threadfence() instruction is not called, from the point of view of the neighboring block the semaphore may be already READABLE, but the layer array still stores the old data. Note, that if the CG synchronization is used, this instruction is not necessary.

3.3 FMA Intrinsics

To estimate the operational intensity in Sect. 2.2 we assumed that operations are grouped as FMA wherever possible. However, the compiler does not always optimize the expressions in this way, and the performance may decrease. The decrease in performance is visible only after all other optimizations, when the problem reaches the compute-bound domain. In our case, before the manual control of FMA instructions, the performance was no greater $\sim$55% of Π_{peak}.

Here the `stencil` template code in the traditional `C++11` expressions:

```
template <> inline __device__ real
  stencil<1>(real u[], real p, real cour2) {
  return cour2*(u[0]+u[2]) + (2.0_r-cour2*2.0_r)*u[1] - p; }
```

We require this operation to take only $O_{alg}(1) = 3$ FMA, however it may take up to 5 FMA if the compiler does not use the FMA operations.

CUDA provides so-called FMA intrinsics [13], which directly translate to assembler instructions. The same function with FMA intrinsics is as follows:

```
template <> inline __device__ real
  stencil<1>(real u[], real p, real cour2) {
  return fma_r(cour2, u[0]+u[2], fma_r(2.0_r-cour2*2.0_r, u[1], -p));}
```

Here `fma_r(x, y, z)` is our wrapper for the FMA intrinsic, which guarantees the expression $xy+z$ to be computed in one cycle. The CUDA intrinsic notations differ for single and double precision:

```
inline __device__ float fma_r(float x, float y, float z){
  return __fmaf_rd(x, y, z);}
inline __device__ double fma_r(double x, double y, double z){
  return __fma_rd(x, y, z);}
```

The rounding mode may be controlled by changing the `_rd` suffix.

4 Conclusion

We have promoted the 1D stencil problem to compute-bound domain, and developed a CUDA GPU implementation of this problem with efficiency of up to 90% of the peak computing performance.

This was obtained by introduction of the RDDhalo algorithm. Its difference from the classic approach is the localization of data, and the fact that the synchronization is explicitly performed inside the CUDA-kernel.

In RDD the size of the problem is limited to the register file. This ($\sim 10^6$ cells) may be enough for some 1D problems. In other cases it may be supplemented by wavefront blocking to hide the communication with global memory, and also with the host memory, as was done in [7]. The formula of the operational intensity is verified by the performance tests for the classical implementation. For RDD and RDDHalo the operational intensity is high enough to make the algorithm compute-bound.

This 1D wave equation problem has little application in the modern simulation problems, nevertheless, the main findings of the paper are readily applied in future stencil implementations.

The obtained 1 GPU performance is $90\%\Pi_{peak} \sim 1.05 \cdot 10^{12} \frac{\text{cell}\cdot\text{step}}{\text{s}}$ for double precision finite difference solution of 1D wave equation. As the most simple and refined problem was taken as the example, this may be treated as a new ideal maximum for stencil computations. From the experience of the current implementation, we present two recommendations for stencil programming with CUDA. First, CG synchronization is still too inefficient when the problem requires only pairwise block synchronization, and we suggest a manual implementation of semaphores (Sect. 3.2). Second, to control the operation count in the code, FMA intrinsics may be used (Sect. 3.3).

References

1. Endo, T.: Applying recursive temporal blocking for stencil computations to deeper memory hierarchy. In: 2018 IEEE 7th Non-Volatile Memory Systems and Applications Symposium (NVMSA), Hakodate, Japan, 28–31 August 2018, pp. 19–24. IEEE (2018). https://ieeexplore.ieee.org/document/8537689/
2. Holewinski, J., Pouchet, L.N., Sadayappan, P.: High-performance code generation for stencil computations on GPU architectures. In: Proceedings of the 26th ACM International Conference on Supercomputing, pp. 311–320. ACM, San Servolo, June 2012
3. Hou, K., Wang, H., Feng, W.C.: GPU-unicache: automatic code generation of spatial blocking for stencils on GPUs. In: Proceedings of the Computing Frontiers Conference, 15–17 May, Siena, Italy, pp. 107–116. ACM (2017)
4. Jia, Z., Maggioni, M., Staiger, B., Scarpazza, D.P.: Dissecting the NVidia Volta GPU architecture via microbenchmarking. arXiv preprint arXiv:1804.06826 (2018)
5. Krotkiewski, M., Dabrowski, M.: Efficient 3D stencil computations using CUDA. Parallel Comput. **39**(10), 533–548 (2013)
6. Levchenko, V.D., Perepelkina, A.Y.: Locally recursive non-locally asynchronous algorithms for stencil computation. Lobachevskii J. Math. **39**(4), 552–561 (2018)
7. Levchenko, V., Perepelkina, A., Zakirov, A.: DiamondTorre algorithm for high-performance wave modeling. Computation **4**(3), 29 (2016)
8. Maruyama, N., Aoki, T.: Optimizing stencil computations for NVIDIA Kepler GPUs. In: Proceedings of the 1st International Workshop on High-Performance Stencil Computations, Vienna, Austria, pp. 89–95, January 2014
9. Micikevicius, P.: 3D finite difference computation on GPUs using CUDA. In: Proceedings of 2nd Workshop on General Purpose Processing on Graphics Processing Units, pp. 79–84. ACM, Washington, D.C., March 2009
10. Muranushi, T., Makino, J.: Optimal temporal blocking for stencil computation. Procedia Comput. Sci. **51**, 1303–1312 (2015)
11. Nguyen, A., Satish, N., Chhugani, J., Kim, C., Dubey, P.: 3.5-D blocking optimization for stencil computations on modern CPUs and GPUs. In: Proceedings of the 2010 ACM/IEEE International Conference for High Performance Computing, Networking, Storage and Analysis, New Orleans, Louisiana, 13–19 November, 2010, pp. 1–13. IEEE Computer Society (2010)

12. NVIDIA Corporation: NVIDIA Tesla V100 GPU architecture. The world's most advanced data center GPU, wp-08608-001_v1.1 edn, August 2017. https://images.nvidia.com/content/volta-architecture/pdf/volta-architecture-whitepaper.pdf
13. NVIDIA Corporation: CUDA C Programming Guide, pg-02829-001_v10.1 edn, May 2019. https://docs.nvidia.com/cuda/pdf/CUDA_C_Programming_Guide.pdf
14. Tabik, S., Peemen, M., Romero, L.F.: A tuning approach for iterative multiple 3D stencil pipeline on GPUS: Anisotropic nonlinear diffusion algorithm as case study. J. Supercomput. **74**(4), 1580–1608 (2018)
15. Treibig, J., Wellein, G., Hager, G.: Efficient multicore-aware parallelization strategies for iterative stencil computations. J. Comput. Sci. **2**(2), 130–137 (2011)
16. Williams, S., Waterman, A., Patterson, D.: Roofline: an insightful visual performance model for multicore architectures. Commun. ACM **52**(4), 65–76 (2009)
17. Yount, C., Tobin, J., Breuer, A., Duran, A.: YASK–yet another stencil kernel: a framework for HPC stencil code-generation and tuning. In: 2016 Sixth International Workshop on Domain-Specific Languages and High-Level Frameworks for High Performance Computing (WOLFHPC), pp. 30–39. IEEE (2016)

Memory-Optimized Tile Based Data Structure for Adaptive Mesh Refinement

Anton Ivanov[1]([✉]), Anastasia Perepelkina[1], Vadim Levchenko[1], and Ilya Pershin[1,2]

[1] Keldysh Institute of Applied Mathematics, Moscow, Russia
aiv.racs@gmail.com, mogmi@ya.ru, vadimlevchenko@mail.ru,
pershin2010@gmail.com
[2] Moscow Institute of Physics and Technology, Dolgoprudny, Russia

Abstract. Multi-scale simulation is relevant for many applications, such as modelling of fluids, electromagnetic or seismic waves, plasma physics, and it stands on the borderline of the supercomputer abilities. For this kind of problems, the Adaptive Mesh Refinement (AMR) methods aim to provide higher cell resolution only in areas, where it is necessary, while these domains may change in time. We propose a new framework for AMR data structure, with the goal to minimize the memory overhead for data storage, and, at the same time, to optimize the locality of data access. With higher locality, the performance gain of the computation is achieved by the use of the faster memory for each parallel processor. In the proposed framework, the cell data is combined in tiles. Two type of tiles (light and heavy) are used for minimizing the memory overhead in case a tile is sparsely filled. The interface allows implementation of various numerical methods. It provides a choice for a traversal rule with an iterator structure, which may be used for algorithms with higher operational intensity. The dynamic mesh adaptation works well for meshes that cover complex geometry.

Keywords: AMR · Grid refinement · Data structure · Z-curve

1 Introduction

Adaptive Mesh Refinement (AMR) [1] allows to significantly decrease the number of mesh nodes and the number of arithmetic operations for numerical simulation, without loss of precision. The area of applicability covers almost all of the mesh-based simulations. We have previously used the AMR technology for the approximation of wavefronts with a triangular mesh in seismic migration problems [11], micromagnetic modeling, construction of multidimensional distribution functions.

The implementation of AMR data structures may vary. The modern implementations are often graded for their ability of balanced parallel memory reallocation [2]. Indeed, the need for AMR arises for computationally heavy tasks,

© Springer Nature Switzerland AG 2019
V. Voevodin and S. Sobolev (Eds.): RuSCDays 2019, CCIS 1129, pp. 64–74, 2019.
https://doi.org/10.1007/978-3-030-36592-9_6

so the codes are necessarily parallel. Thus, good parallel scaling is important for AMR data structures. On the other hand, it would mean nothing if one process computation is not optimized. Most of the simulation codes in physics are memory-bound. That means that the performance efficiency is limited by memory bandwidth, and not the peak computing performance. The operational intensity [14] may be increased by using spatial and temporal blocking [5,10], and in this case the performance increases by an order of magnitude. Such algorithms were previously developed for uniform grids [6,15]. To enable such algorithms for AMR method, the data locality is crucial.

The parallel execution is used not only for higher performance, but, in case of GPU, due to the fact that one device can not store the data of the whole problem. Thus, another requirement for AMR data structure is low memory overhead. At the same time, in complex data structures, the integer memory offset computation may take an increased computational cost, comparable with the main floating point computation.

In total, we see these parameters as primary for efficient AMR data structure: the data locality, the complexity of access to the nearest neighbors, and memory overhead. The increase of the complexity of access to the nearest neighbors may be expressed by insufficient data locality, as well as by a large number of operations for computation of the memory offset of the required node. The memory overhead includes meta-data, such as information of the array index, neighbor indexes, information of the level of subdivision.

The traditional AMR implementation as a 2^D tree [8,12] (D is the dimensionality of the mesh), has low locality: only a half of the neighbors are situated close in the memory. It requires a large number of operations for access to the other neighbors and overhead of 8B per cell for pointer storage. In case two float values are stored in a cell, the memory overhead is twofold, and this may negate the advantages of AMR use in some cases. The tree traversal requires a long chain of pointer dereferencing. This is a highly inefficient operation, since it is essentially sequential, and may include many memory accesses with high latency. The tree nodes may include direct pointers to the cell neighbors to save on the pointer dereferencing for tree traversal. However, the memory overhead for pointer storage comes close to 100% even for data-heavy schemes. In extreme cases, all possible information for access to neighbors, parent and child cells of each cell is stored in the cell data structure [7]. In [4] the tree leaves use the free pointers that would be used to point at the child nodes to access the neighbors on the last subdivision level. This may save some computation during the mesh traversal at almost no cost.

To improve the locality and simplify the access to the nearest neighbors the number of cells in a tree node may be increased [13]. We suggest this number to be 2RD, where $R \geq 1$ defines the size of a so-called *tile*—D-dimensional cube of cells with linear size of 2^R. With an increase in R the data locality increases, and the complexity of neighbor cell access decreases. By choosing the power of two as a tile size the cell access is even more local, since the use of Z-curve [9] storage is possible. On the other side, memory overhead may be large since excessive numbers of refined cells can be created.

The solution we propose here is the use of 'light' tiles with indirect indexing. The usual tiles are called 'heavy' for contrast. The light tiles are used to store the cells, that are generated and allocated during the mesh adaptation but are unused in the numerical scheme. At the same time, the light tiles preserve the tree structure. As a result, with a small decrease in a locality of cell data access, the memory overhead may be significantly decreased, and it becomes possible to fully take advantage of the AMR approach.

2 Data Structure

The minimal element of the mesh is a cell. Its type T is defined by the user. In the initial, unsubdivided grid the cell size in h_0. For simplicity, we assume equal steps in all directions, however, it is not a constraint of the approach. The subdivision factor is set as 2, so that on the next level of subdivision the step is $h_1 = h_0/2$, and on the S-th step it is $h_S = h_{S-1}/2$.

Since the cell is subdivided into 2^D cells, it is reasonable to introduce the notion of a *chunk*—a cube with linear size of 2 cells. The introduction of the chunk provides good locality of access to some of the nearest neighbors, up to 50% of the neighbors, depending on the scheme stencil.

The next level of the data structure hierarchy is a *tile*—a cube with linear size of 2^R cells. The parameter $R \geq 1$ is fixed at the initialization of the data structure. The tile includes 2RD cells or $2^{(R-1)D}$ chunks. For the simplification of index computation the cells in a tile are in Z-order [9]. Due to the recursive construction of Z-array, chunks are in a Z-order as well.

Tiles form a 2^D tree (Fig. 1). All tiles on all levels of mesh subdivision have equal size in cells. This means, that at least 2RD sizeof(T) bytes of memory are allocated. However, the linear size of the cell on the next level of subdivision is twice smaller. This way, in theory, the domain is covered by cells of all levels of subdivision. Each cell of each level of subdivision has a place in this 2^D tree. In practice, at each geometrical position the data of no more than 2 levels of subdivision is required. Thus, the memory is allocated only for the tiles, in which at least one cell is required in the computation, and for all their parent tiles. If the tile is allocated, but some cells in it are not required for the computation, this memory is unused at this point.

Each tile additionally stores a pointer to the parent tile and 2^D pointers to the children tiles. In case the child tile does not exist (the memory is not allocated since no cells are required in the place on the corresponding subdivision level), the corresponding pointer is zero. The tiles of the initial unsubdivided mesh store the pointers to the nearest neighbors instead.

The introduction of tiles partially solves the problem of data locality. For large enough tiles, all nearest neighbors of the cell are likely to be in the same tile. Z-curve storage improves the locality even further. Some neighbors of the tile boundary cells are in the adjacent tiles, and the access to them may be more

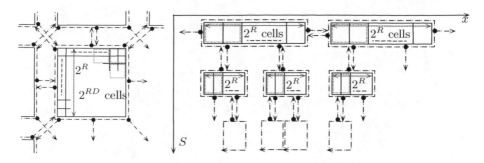

Fig. 1. Tiles of the uppermost level and the 2^D tree of tiles. The chunks of 2^D cells are outlined in green. (Color figure online)

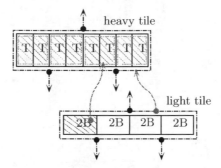

Fig. 2. The interaction of the light and the heavy tile. The chunk data of the light tile is stored in the free space of the heavy tile.

complex. With higher D and R we consider this event as rare, and the ratio of such accesses as small.

On the other hand, when more than half of the tile cells are unused, the memory is used inefficiently. To overcome this, a new type of tile is introduced: a *light* tile (Fig. 2). The tiles defined above are denoted as *heavy*. A light tile does not store data, and it uses indirect indexing in the following way. Instead of a cube with 2RD cells, a light tile stores a cube of $2^{(R-1)D}$ 2 byte numbers and a pointer to some heavy tile. This heavy tile should also be only partially filled with the relevant cells. In the free space in it, the chunks of cells of the light tile are stored. The 2-byte numbers of the light tile store a number of a chunk in the heavy tile, where its cells are stored. Several light tiles may use one heavy tile for data storage. If all heavy tiles in the domain are in use, additional heavy tiles may be allocated, so that they store only light tiles and no cell data.

In total, the memory overhead is $(1 + 2^D)$ pointers per tile, and additionally $2^{(R-1)D} \cdot 2B$ if the tile is a light tile. The latter is $2/2^D$ byte of memory per cell. The access to the cells of the light tiles may be slower due to the indirect addressing and low locality. However, since the overall efficiency of memory use is increased with the introduction of the light tiles, the use of light tile is justified.

```
template <typename T,  // cell type
          int D,       // dimension
          int R>       // tile size
class AdaptiveMesh{
    struct tile_t{ // base tile struct
        int S;                   // subdivision level
        tile_t *parent;          // parent tile pointer
        tile_t *childs[1<<D];    // chile tile pointer
        uint8_t flags[1<<(R-1)*D]; // chunk status
    };
    struct heavy_tile_t: public tile_t{
        T data[1<<R*D];   // data stored in the mesh
    };
    struct light_tile_t: public tile_t{
        heavy_tile_t *tile;       // tile for cell data
        uint16_t chunks[1<<(R-1)*D];   // chunk position
    };
    // uppermost tile
    struct up_tile_t: public heavy_tile_t{
        Ind<D> pos;   // tile position in the mesh
        Vec<D> a, b;  // tile corner coordinates
        // adjacent tile pointers; 3^D tiles
        CubicArr<up_tile_t*, D, 3> nb;
        std::list<heavy_tile_t> htiles;  // heavy tiles
        std::list<light_tile_t> ltiles;  // light tiles
    };
    Mesh<up_tile_t*, D> tiles;  // Mesh of pointers to the
                                // tiles of the uppermost level
    ...
};
```

Fig. 3. The simplified code of the AMR data structure.

Additionally, some data is required to store the chunk status. For example, whether or not it is marked for subdivision. Such flags may be packed into one byte.

The sample code of the data structure in C++11 is shown in Fig. 3. Ind<D> is a D–dimensional integer vector, Vec<D> is a D–dimensional vector of double data type.

3 Mesh Traversal and Access to Neighbors

The described structure is implemented in the template class AdaptiveMesh of the aiwlib [3] library with C++ programming language. The sample code for the interface of cell traversal is shown in Fig. 4.

Since the data structure is quite complex the iterators and the calc methods are used for the mesh traversal. The calc is a special method that updates the cells of the domain according to the correct application of the numerical scheme. There are at least two types of traversal.

1. Single data traversal of the cells of the smallest size may be used for data analysis and implementation of numerical schemes which do not require the Courant condition.
2. Recursive traversal with time step subdivision (subcycling), so that there are more cell updates for the smaller cells, and the subdivision factor for time step is equal to the subdivision factor of the spatial step.

The iterator with overloaded ++ operator implements the traversal of the smallest cells. It may be instanced for the whole mesh, or for some particular tiles. The iterator, instanced for a tile, provides the traversal only inside this tile.

The iterator behaves as a smart pointer, in a way that it provides access to the cell data to which it points to. Apart from this, it provides access to the cell neighbors. The operators [] and () are overloaded for this. The shift to the neighbor, in cells, is their argument. The iterator may return the subdivision level S, the coordinates of the cell center and cell corners, the cell size (mesh step in all directions at the current S) and it may provide the information whether or not the chunk of the smaller mesh corresponds to the cell, and whether the cell is at the boundary of the patch with subdivision S.

The iterator methods up() and down() return the iterator for the cell of the larger mesh or on the first cell of the chunk of the smaller size.

For the recursive traversal the calc method is used. Its argument is a callable object (a function or a functor) of a user defined numerical scheme. The object is called for each mesh cell in a correct order, taking subcycling into account. The arguments of the object call is the iterator and the simulation time value. For multiple stage numerical schemes, several objects are called.

The calc method may be called for the whole mesh, or for a particular tile.

4   Mesh Adaptation

The adaptation criteria and the interpolation method should be defined for mesh adaptation. The adaptation may be triggered during the numerical scheme iteration. However, at this point, the adaptation does not take place. The cells are flagged for subdivision (the split() method of the iterator) and chunks are flagged for fusion (the join() method). The changes are applied in an $S = 0$ tile when the tile method adapt() is called.

The data interpolation functions for fine-to-coarse and coarse-to-fine communication are implemented by a user and are taken as arguments of the adapt() method. Both functions take the iterator pointing to the cell of the coarse grid as an argument. First, for the fusing cells, the functions of the fine-to-coarse data transfer are called. Then the mesh is reconstructed, and then the functions of the coarse-to-fine data transfer for the subdivided cells are called.

The 'perfectly nested' [1] property of the subdivided patches is provided by the adapt() method. The level of subdivision S transitions are automatically matched. The cloud is an array of vector shifts that describes the stencil, and it is a parameter of the adapt() method. It performs the subdivision and merging of cells during the subdivision to ensure the 'perfectly nested' mesh structure.

If the conflict between heavy and light tile arises, for example, if the heavy tile requires the space of the chunks that are used by some light tile, the chunks of the light tile are easily shifted inside the heavy tile. In case the space is not enough, they are transferred to another heavy tile.

The interface of the methods for mesh adaptation is shown in Fig. 5.

```
template <typename T,  // cell type
          int D,       // dimension
          int R>       // tile size
class AdaptiveMesh{
    ...
public:
    class iterator{
        ...
    public:
        T* operator ->();  // access to the cell data
        T& operator *();   // access to the cell data
        int get_S();       // subdivision level

        // whether the cell is at the boundary of the
        // current subdivision level
        bool is_bound();

        // access to neighbor cells
        iterator operator + (Ind<D> offset);
        iterator operator - (Ind<D> offset);
        T& operator [](Ind<D> offset);

        // access to the next cell of the smallest
        // subdivision level
        iterator& operator ++();
        ...
    };
    iterator begin();
    iterator end();

    template <typename Funcs...>
    void calc(funcs...);
    ...
};
```

Fig. 4. Interface for mesh traversal and neighbor access

5   Data Serialization

The data structure should support serialization. It is required for data storage and data transfer through the network. In the current context, it is necessary for parallel execution on a cluster with a distributed memory. In the domain decomposition approach, the boundary cells should be transferred. When the mesh is subdivided in the domain on some node, for load balancing the larger portion of the domains should be exchanged. Data dump to disk is obviously required for diagnostics of the simulation results and creation of the control points that are used for the implementation of fault tolerance of the many-node runs.

In the current framework, each initial tile at $S = 0$ may list all its sub-tiles. When the data is saved to the disk, all tiles at $S = 0$ are saved sequentially. Inside such tile, first, its heavy tiles are saved, and then the light tiles. The pointers to the tile are replaced with a unique index (number) of the tile.

For parallel scheme implementation, each tile at $S = 0$ may be stored separately in a buffer, passed through the network, and then restored and implemented in an existing mesh. This kind of tile exchange between nodes allows

```
template <typename T,    // cell type
               int D,     // dimension
               int R>     // tile size
class AdaptiveMesh{
    ...
public:
    class iterator{
        ...
    public:
        ...
        bool splitted(); // if the cell is split
        bool marked2split(); // if the cell is marked for splitting
        bool marked2join(); // if the chunk is marked for fusion

        iterator up(); // get iterator of the cell with lower S

        // traversal of the chunk with higher S
        iterator begin();
        iterator end();

        void split(); // flag cell for subdivision
        void join();  // flag chunk with higher S for fusion
    };
    // apply mesh reconstruction
    template <typename IUp, typename IDown>
    void adapt(IUp up, IDown down, const std::vector<Ind<D> >& cloud);
    ...
};
```

Fig. 5. The interface for the methods of mesh adaptation.

different types of parallel algorithms and big problem decomposition on super-computers.

Moreover, a separate buffer may store the boundary of an $S = 0$ tile with a width of few cells. This buffer may have a structure of a light tile since the boundary represents a small portion of the tile cells. After the message passing through the network, this boundary may be stored in an $S = 0$ tile on another node.

The 2D slice visualization of the AMR mesh in the described format is supported by the `uplt` viewer of the `aiwlib` library.

6   Performance Benchmark

We test the framework prototype on a sample problem of function approximation on the grid (Fig. 6(a))

$$f(\mathbf{r}) = \exp\left(-\frac{(|\mathbf{r}| - r_0)^2}{\sigma^2}\right). \tag{1}$$

Here $\sigma = 0.5$, $r_0 = 4$. The function was approximated on a 2D and a 3D mesh. The subdivision criteria is as follows. The cell is subdivided until

$$S_{\max} \cdot f(\mathbf{r}) - \frac{1}{2} < S. \tag{2}$$

As an example, tracking of shockwaves in CFD may follow a similar subdivision pattern. Initially, there are 32^D cells with $h = 0.5$.

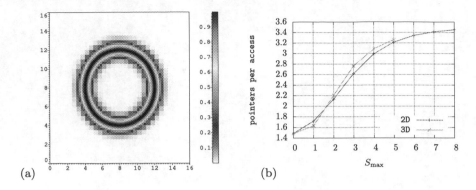

(a)   (b)

Fig. 6. (a) The function approximated on the $2D$ mesh, $S_{\max} = 3$. (b) Average number of pointers that have to be dereferenced for nearest neighbor access in a cross stencil.

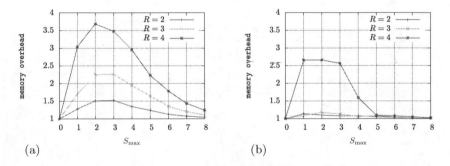

(a)   (b)

Fig. 7. Memory overhead for unused cell data in case light tiles are not introduced (a) and introduced (b) in 2D case.

Figure 6(b) shows the average number of pointers that are dereferenced per nearest neighbor access if $R = 1$. That is, in the traditional AMR 2^D tree without the introduction of tiles. At the relevant values of $S_{\max}$ (the last level of subdivision), it is higher than 3. This shows the relevance of the current work for such problems.

Further, we analyzed the memory overhead for the storage of the cells that are generated but unused. That means that they are overwritten in the visualization by the data of a mesh with the smaller size cells. In case all tiles of the domain are heavy (Fig. 7), the memory overhead reaches 150% even for a small size of tiles. For larger $S_{\max}$ the ratio of subdivided patch boundary becomes smaller, so the overhead decreases.

With the use of the light tiles (Fig. 8) the memory overhead decreases drastically. When $R = 4$ the $S = 0$ tile covers the whole domain. So this tile is too big for the current test problem. At $S_{max} < 5$ and $R = 4$ the size of the tile is $\geq \sigma$. So any tile is at the subdivision boundary, and the overhead is high. The size of the tile at the last subdivision level should be smaller than the characteristic scale of the solution.

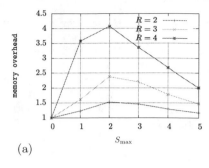 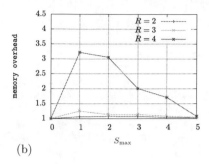

(a) (b)

Fig. 8. Memory overhead for unused cell data in case light tiles are not introduced (a) and introduced (b) in 3D case.

7 Conclusion

For the solution of a wide variety of multiscale problems in mathematical modeling we have developed the AMR data structure framework, and, in it, the methods of mesh traversal, neighbor access, user scheme application to every cell, and mesh adaptation. The tile structure provides an improvement in the locality of data retrieval and simplify the access to the neighbors compared to the traditional 2^D tree approach. The concept of light tiles allows minimizing the overhead for storage of the simulation data in the cells unused by the numerical scheme. The developed method of the data serialization allows to efficiently implement the parallel processing in the context of distributed memory, including the load balancing and fault tolerance.

References

1. Berger, M.J., Colella, P.: Local adaptive mesh refinement for shock hydrodynamics. J. Comput. Phys. **82**(1), 64–84 (1989)
2. Dubey, A., et al.: A survey of high level frameworks in block-structured adaptive mesh refinement packages. J. Parallel Distrib. Comput. **74**(12), 3217–3227 (2014)
3. Ivanov, A.V., Khilkov, S.A.: Aiwlib library as the instrument for creating numerical modeling applications. Sci. Vis. **10**(1), 110–127 (2018). https://doi.org/10.26583/sv.10.1.09
4. Khokhlov, A.M.: Fully threaded tree algorithms for adaptive refinement fluid dynamics simulations. J. Comput. Phys. **143**(2), 519–543 (1998)
5. Levchenko, V.D., Perepelkina, A.Y.: Locally recursive non-locally asynchronous algorithms for stencil computation. Lobachevskii J. Math. **39**(4), 552–561 (2018)
6. Levchenko, V., Perepelkina, A., Zakirov, A.: DiamondTorre algorithm for high-performance wave modeling. Computation **4**(3), 29 (2016)
7. Lutsky, A.E., Severin, A.V.: Numerical study of flow x–43 hypersonic aircraft using adaptive grids. Keldysh Institute preprints 102 (2016)
8. Menshov, I., Sheverdin, V.: A parallel locally-adaptive 3D model on cartesian nested-type grids. In: Malyshkin, V. (ed.) PaCT 2017. LNCS, vol. 10421, pp. 136–142. Springer, Cham (2017). https://doi.org/10.1007/978-3-319-62932-2_12

9. Morton, G.M.: A computer oriented geodetic data base and a new technique in file sequencing (1966)
10. Nguyen, A., Satish, N., Chhugani, J., Kim, C., Dubey, P.: 3.5-D blocking optimization for stencil computations on modern CPUs and GPUs. In: Proceedings of the 2010 ACM/IEEE International Conference for High Performance Computing, Networking, Storage and Analysis, pp. 1–13. IEEE Computer Society (2010)
11. Pleshkevich, A., Ivanov, A., Levchenko, V., Khilkov, S.: Multiarrival amplitude-preserving prestack 3D depth migration. Russ. Geophys. J. (0) 76–84 (2017). http://geofdb.com/en/articles/view?id=1905
12. Samet, H.: The quadtree and related hierarchical data structures. ACM Comput. Surv. (CSUR) **16**(2), 187–260 (1984)
13. Stout, Q.F., De Zeeuw, D.L., Gombosi, T.I., Groth, C.P.T., Marshall, H.G., Powell, K.G.: Adaptive blocks: a high performance data structure. In: Proceedings of the 1997 ACM/IEEE Conference on Supercomputing, SC 1997, pp. 1–10. ACM, New York (1997). https://doi.org/10.1145/509593.509650
14. Williams, S., Waterman, A., Patterson, D.: Roofline: an insightful visual performance model for multicore architectures. Commun. ACM **52**(4), 65–76 (2009)
15. Zakirov, A., Levchenko, V., Perepelkina, A., Zempo, Y.: High performance FDTD algorithm for GPGPU supercomputers. J. Phys: Conf. Ser. **759**, 012100 (2016)

Multithreaded Multifrontal Sparse Cholesky Factorization Using Threading Building Blocks

Rostislav Povelikin, Sergey Lebedev, and Iosif Meyerov$^{(\boxtimes)}$

Lobachevsky State University of Nizhni Novgorod, Nizhni Novgorod, Russia
povelikin.rostislav@gmail.com,
sergey.a.lebedev@gmail.com, iosif.meyerov@vmk.unn.ru

Abstract. The multifrontal method is a well-established approach to parallel sparse direct solvers of linear algebraic equations systems with sparse symmetric positive-definite matrices. This paper discusses the approaches and challenges of scalable parallel implementation of the numerical phase of the multifrontal method for shared memory systems based on high-end server CPUs with dozens of cores. The commonly used parallelization schemes are often guided by an elimination tree, containing information about dependencies between logical tasks in a computational loop of the method. We consider a dynamic two-level scheme for the organization of parallel computations. This scheme employs the task-based model with dynamic switching between solving relatively small tasks in parallel and using parallel functions of BLAS for relatively large tasks. There are several problems with the implementation of this scheme, including time-consuming synchronizations and the need for smart memory management. We found a way to improve performance and scaling efficiency using the model of parallelism and memory management tools from the Threading Building Blocks library. Experiments on large symmetric matrices from the SuiteSparse Matrix Collection show that our implementation is competitive with the commercial direct sparse solver Intel MKL PARDISO.

Keywords: Sparse direct methods · Multifrontal method · Parallel computing · High performance computing · Threading building blocks

1 Introduction

Direct methods for solving large sparse systems of linear algebraic equations (SLAEs) with a symmetric positive-definite (SPD) matrix are widely used in numerical simulations in different subject areas. During matrix factorization, the number of nonzero elements in the factor increases by several orders of magnitude compared to the original matrix, which significantly affects the memory requirements and the computation time. In this regard, a special reordering procedure [13] is applied to the original matrix, which rearranges the rows and columns of the matrix in order to reduce the number of nonzero elements in the factor. Next, a symbolic phase of the Cholesky decomposition is performed for the reordered SPD matrix. This numerical procedure analyses the matrix, creates special data structures and allocates necessary memory. The next stage of the solution is a numerical phase of the Cholesky decomposition. At

© Springer Nature Switzerland AG 2019
V. Voevodin and S. Sobolev (Eds.): RuSCDays 2019, CCIS 1129, pp. 75–86, 2019.
https://doi.org/10.1007/978-3-030-36592-9_7

this stage, non-zero elements of the factor are calculated. Next, the solution of two triangular SLAEs is performed and the inverse permutation of the components of the solution is applied [5, 6].

When solving state-of-the-art problems, each stage of the scheme described above is very computationally intensive and requires efficient parallelization for modern supercomputers. Appropriate algorithms have been under development over the past decades. The parallel algorithms for distributed and shared memory systems are implemented in Intel MKL PARDISO [12], MUMPS [2], SuperLU [19], CHOLMOD [4], HSL_MA57 [9], and in other solvers that are widely used in many research projects around the world. However, continuous improvement of multicore architectures motivates further development of high-performance scalable algorithms for such systems [1, 10, 11, 16, 22–25].

In this paper, we focus on achieving the efficiency of parallelization and using the memory subsystem on a high-end multicore computer when performing the numerical phase of the Cholesky decomposition. This phase is often very time-consuming, and its parallelization is a challenging problem. The MUMPS solver was originally developed for distributed memory systems, and then shared memory parallelism support was added to it [15]. For this, a modification of the Geist-Ng algorithm is used, in which prior to the start of the numerical phase the search for the layer of the elimination tree is performed, subtrees with the root belonging to the found layer are processed independently. Another widely used method of parallelization is the use of Direct Acyclic Graph, where the graph describes the dependencies between the nodes of the elimination tree and the sequence of operations inside the node which results in fine-grained parallelism. This approach is used in the HSL_MA57 solver [10]. Earlier, we proposed a dynamic two-level parallelization scheme for the multifrontal method that combines task-based parallelism at the lower levels of the elimination tree and the use of parallel BLAS functions at the upper levels when solving a limited number of large subtasks [18]. In this paper, we address two main problems encountered in the implementation of this scheme: moderate load balancing quality for dozens of computing cores, the need for adaptive selection of the switching point between two ways of parallelization. Further, it will be shown how a suitable usage of the TBB library allows us to overcome these problems, to improve the memory management scheme, and obtain competitive results with Intel MKL PARDISO outperforming it on several matrices.

The paper is organized as follows. Section 2 provides a general overview of the multifrontal method. In Sect. 3, the main ideas of two-level task-based parallelization of the multifrontal method for shared memory systems are described. In Sect. 4 we propose the new parallel scheme based on Threading Building Blocks. Section 5 presents numerical results and discussion. Section 6 concludes the paper.

2   Multifrontal Method Overview

The multifrontal method [7, 8] for the numerical phase of the Cholesky decomposition is commonly used in many sparse direct solvers, such as MUMPS, SuiteSparse and others. The advantages of this method include the efficient use of a hierarchical memory system, as well as simple and local dependencies between iterations, which creates good prospects for parallelization. The main idea of the method is to organize computations using high-performance implementations of operations on dense sub-matrices of the original matrix. The dependencies between operations are determined by an elimination tree [20] which is constructed during the analysis phase. The number of nodes in the tree corresponds to the dimension of the original matrix N, the nodes are numbered from 1 to N, each node is associated with a column of a factor L. Edges in the tree define the order of calculations of columns of L. The main principle is as follows: before calculating a column associated with some node of the tree we must calculate all columns corresponding to his child nodes. Therefore, the main computational loop of the multifrontal method performs calculations, examining the nodes of the elimination tree in order from leaves to root. In every node a set of operations with dense submatrices is performed (Fig. 1). First, the frontal matrix of the node is calculated using the elements of the column of the original matrix (the init_frontal_matrix procedure) and the updating matrices of the child nodes (the assembly_frontal_matrix procedure). Then, a partial dense factorization is performed for the frontal matrix (the factorize procedure) resulting in the column of the factor and in the update matrix (the form_update_matrix procedure), which will be used when building the frontal matrix for the parent node. A more detailed description of the method can be found in [14, 20].

```
1       foreach node i of elimination tree in topological order
2           init_frontal_matrix(F_i)
3           foreach child j of i do
4               U ← U ⊕ U_j
5           end for
6           assembly_frontal_matrix(F,U)
7           factorize(F)
8           form_update_matrix(U_i)
9           L_i←F_(1,*)
10      end for
```

Fig. 1. High-level overview of the multifrontal method

The multifrontal method can be easily parallelized using parallel implementations of the BLAS library functions to perform operations with frontal matrices. This approach does not scale well due to the lack of resources for parallelization in the lower levels of the elimination tree, where frontal matrices are usually too small. Another approach to parallelization is exploit task-based parallelism (Fig. 2), where the task is to calculate one column of the factor L. The order of calculations and the possibility of parallelization are determined by the elimination tree. This approach can be implemented using static or dynamic load balancing. In the case of static load balancing, tree nodes are assigned for processing to certain threads. When using dynamic balancing, the nodes of the elimination tree are assigned to be executed by threads during program execution. However, scaling efficiency is limited when processing the nodes of the tree close to the root. This is due to the fact that the number of parallel tasks decreases and some of the threads are not used while the dimension of frontal matrices for the upper part of the tree increases.

```
1     procedure process_node(node of elimination_tree)
2         foreach child of node in elimination_tree do
3             #spawn new task
4                 process_node(child)
5             end for
6         #wait for spawned tasks to complete
7             multifrontal_step(node)
8     end procedure

9     procedure multifrontal_step(node of elimination tree)
10        i←number of node in elimination tree
11            init_frontal_matrix(F_i)
12            foreach child j of i do
13                U ← U ⊕ U_j
14            end for
15            assembly_frontal_matrix(F,U)
16            factorize(F)
17            form_update_matrix(U_i)
18            L_i←F_(1,*)
19    end procedure
```

Fig. 2. The task-based parallel multifrontal method

3   Task-Based Two-Level Dynamic Parallel Algorithm

In [17, 18] we analyzed the task-based two-level algorithm. The algorithm employs task-based parallel load balancing, highly effective on lowest levels of the elimination tree, and switches to using parallel BLAS functions for computationally demanding tasks at the upper levels of the tree (Fig. 3). This approach greatly improves performance and scaling efficiency of the implementation.

```
1        procedure process_node(node i of elimination_tree)
2            init_frontal_matrix(F_i)
3            foreach child j of i do
4                U ← U ⊕ U_j
5            end for
6            assembly_frontal_matrix(F,U)
7            factorize(F)
8            form_update_matrix(U_i)
9            L_i←F_(1,*)
10       end procedure
11
12       procedure two-level_parallel_multifrontal
13           set_num_threads(MAX_SYSTEM_THREADS);
14           blas_set_num_threads(1);
15           #parallel section
16           while(there are enough independent tasks)
17               i ← nextTask()
18               process_node(i)
19           end while
20
21           set_num_threads(1);
22           blas_set_num_threads( MAX_SYSTEM_THREADS);
23           while(there is a task)
24               i← nextTask();
25               process_node(i)
26           end while
27       end procedure
```

Fig. 3. The parallel two-level multifrontal algorithm for shared memory systems

4 Exploiting Parallelism Using the Threading Building Blocks Library

Experiments have shown that the approach described above has two key problems. First, the approach assumes an explicit synchronization of the threads during the transition between levels. Such a scheme leads to the useless, from utilization of computing resources point of view, waiting for the completion of processing the nodes of the elimination tree. Taking into account that the second level of the described scheme assumes the absence of parallel processing of independent nodes, this leads to insufficient scalability when using dozens of CPU cores. Secondly, the approach requires the selection of the switching moment between two parallelization schemes, which intricately depends on the various characteristics of the original matrix.

In this paper, we propose a new scheme of parallelization based on the TBB library [27]. TBB was created to develop scalable parallel applications in terms of logical problems, not threads. In addition, Intel MKL implementation of BLAS functions also

```
1                procedure dynamic_parallel_multifrontal
2                  set_tbb_shared_thread_pool(MAX_SYSTEM_THREADS);
3
4                  parallel foreach leaf node i of elimination_tree do
5                      process_node(i)
6                      p ← getParentNode(i)
7                      while p has no left unprocessed children
8                          process_node(p)
9                          p ← getParentNode(p)
10                     end while
11                 end parallel foreach
12               end procedure
```

Fig. 4. The dynamic parallel multifrontal algorithm for shared memory systems

supports the use of the TBB library as a thread manager. Such support and the design of libraries allow the use of nested parallelism mechanisms for organizing the dynamic switching from parallel processing of the elimination tree nodes to parallel BLAS functions (Fig. 4).

The key difference of the proposed approach is the use of the TBB library parallelism model. A model is a dynamic distribution of logical tasks between a shared set of threads. Thus, the logical tasks of parallel processing of the tree nodes and parallel BLAS functions are distributed over the total set of threads. The organization of parallel logical tasks becomes the responsibility of the library's task scheduler. The work of the scheduler is decentralized and distributed among all threads. Each thread has its own local task queue. The thread accesses the queue to get a new task when it finishes executing the current one. If there are no tasks in the local queue, the thread searches for the task in the queue of another thread.

Consider the work of the task scheduler in the case of a new parallel scheme. The main thread puts all the available logical tasks of processing independent nodes in its local queue. Threads created by the TBB library when initializing a shared set of threads find a free logical task in the local queue of the main thread, steal and process it. When the local thread queue is empty, the thread looks for a task in the queues of other threads. Upon completion of the current task, the thread executes a new task for processing the node M, if the processing of the last child node of the node M has been completed. Parallel BLAS functions also generate new logical tasks. Thus, threads process tree nodes and auxiliary tasks of BLAS functions in parallel, dynamically switching between them. Thread finishes its work when it cannot find new tasks neither in its own queue nor in the queues of other threads. The described balancing process eliminates the need for explicit synchronization and the choice of its moment, and also allows us to process independent nodes of the tree in parallel throughout the whole computational loop. Also note that in the implementation of this scheme, we employed the Intel MKL BLAS version, using TBB for multithreading. In general, this scheme allows us to overcome two problems noted at the beginning of this section.

Note that previous versions of the method used the following memory management scheme for processing the elimination tree: each thread allocated the maximum required amount of memory for any node before processing the tree. The scheme assumed the exclusive use of previously allocated memory. The new task-based model of parallelism cannot exploit this scheme of working with memory producing the data race due to the task-stealing mechanism. The thread resets the memory when it takes the task of processing a new node, waiting for another thread to finish BLAS task of processing the actual node on the same memory, which raises the problem of data races. To solve this problem and also improve memory usage patterns, the following scheme of work with memory is proposed. We need logically bind the memory to the task but not to the thread. Standard memory managers will not cope effectively with such a scheme, as it involves frequent requests for memory allocation and deallocation. Therefore we propose to use the TBB library's scalable memory manager (`tbb::scalable_allocator`). One of the key features of this memory manager is caching freed memory for potential new allocations. This reduces the number of system calls, but increases the level of memory consumption by the application.

5   Numerical Results

5.1   Computational Infrastructure and Test Problems

The computational experiments were performed at a node of a supercomputer with 2x Intel Xeon Gold 6152 (Skylake, 22 cores each), 44 cores overall, 192 GB RAM, Ubuntu 18.04, Intel C++ Compiler, Intel MKL and TBB from the Intel Parallel Studio XE 2019 suite. For benchmarking purposes we used 8 large symmetric positive definite matrices from the SuiteSparse Matrix Collection [26]. All matrices were reordered using permutations computed using the Metis library [13] other libraries can be also used [21, 22]. The PARDISO solver was run with default settings. According to the documentation the `iparm(24)` value was set to 1 when a large number of threads was used.

Table 1. Matrices and their parameters

Matrix	Dimension	Nonzeros	Nonzeros in L
boneS10	914 898	28 191 660	266 173 272
Emilia_923	923 136	20 964 171	1 633 654 176
audikw_1	943 695	39 297 171	1 225 571 121
bone010_M	986 703	12 437 739	363 650 592
bone010	986 703	36 326 514	1 076 191 560
StocF-1465	1 465 137	11 235 263	1 039 392 123
Hook_1498	1 498 023	31 207 734	1 507 528 290
Flan_1565	1 564 794	59 485 419	1 451 334 747

5.2   Results and Discussion

First, we study performance of the two considered parallel schemes in the numerical phase of the Cholesky decomposition. To do this, we run these schemes on 8 large symmetric positive-definite matrices, the parameters of which are given in Table 1. In all experiments we use 44 cores of the Skylake processor (we also make sure that using such a large number of cores does not slow down the computations). We make each run 10 times and take the minimum time. For both schemes, we choose the appropriate strategy of padding the matrix columns with zeros in order to increase the size of the groups of columns with the same sparsity pattern under the upper triangle (the so-called supernodes). For the 'Old Scheme', based on OpenMP, in addition, we empirically choose a relevant moment of switching between parallel tasks solving and using parallel BLAS. Then we select the best results and compare them with the results of MKL PARDISO, also tested 10 times on each matrix.

Our first observation is that the strategy of padding supernodes with zeros on large matrices and huge number of threads affects performance of the considered algorithms. For example, on the matrix Emilia_923 with a largest factor, the computation time of the 'Old Scheme' varies from 33 s to 28 s, and the run time of the 'New Scheme' improves from 19 to 15 s, depending on the padding algorithm (Fig. 5).

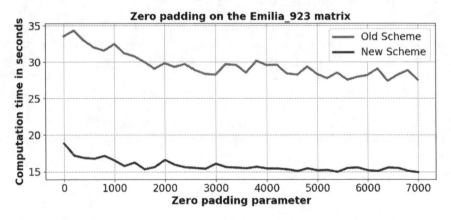

Fig. 5. Zero padding improves performance of the Cholesky decomposition. The parameter value on the x-axis corresponds to a maximum number of zeros added to a supernode.

Figure 6 presents a comparison of the best computation time of the considered algorithms and MKL PARDISO. Experiments have shown that the 'Old Scheme' loses PARDISO, whereas the 'New Scheme' is ahead on matrices with a large factor size, showing comparable or slightly worse results on the other matrices.

Further, we investigated how the considered algorithms are scaled with an increase in the number of threads involved in the computations. Figure 7 shows the performance results for the matrix Emilia_923. The results show that with the use of a small number of cores, the 'Old Scheme' works better due to the low overhead of the work of the scheduler. However, with an increase in the number of cores, the 'New Scheme' demonstrates its advantage and continues to scale, while the computation time of the 'Old Scheme' ceases to decrease. Note that all the algorithms do not show good scaling efficiency when using 44 cores, even on the large matrices from the SuiteSparse Collection.

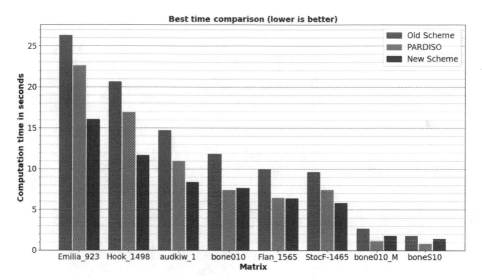

Fig. 6. Computation times of the numerical phase of the Cholesky decomposition. Three implementations are compared: Intel MKL PARDISO, the scheme based on OpenMP ('Old Scheme'), and the proposed scheme based on TBB ('New Scheme'). Time is given in seconds.

Let us make sure that the 'New Scheme' is significantly ahead of the 'Old Scheme' due to the decrease in the spin-time when using a large number of cores. To do this, we use the Intel Amplifier profiler. The results of the profiling of both implementations are shown in Figs. 8 and 9, respectively. The profiles contain basic hotspots and allow us to understand what the bottleneck of each algorithm is. Thus, in the 'Old Scheme', more than half of the time is spent waiting for the barrier to reach when synchronizing OpenMP threads. On the contrary, in the 'New Scheme', the vast majority of time is spent on calculations in several functions of BLAS, which indicates a more efficient implementation in terms of performance. It should be noted that the difference in the names of the BLAS functions used in the considered algorithms is likely caused by differences in the implementation of the parallel BLAS by means of OpenMP and TBB inside the MKL library.

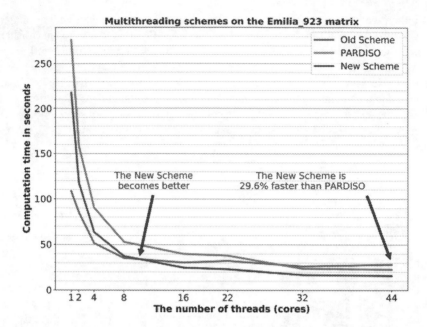

Fig. 7. Computation times of the scheme based on OpenMP ('Old Scheme'), MKL PARDISO, and the proposed scheme based on TBB ('New Scheme') when factorizing the Emilia_923 matrix. The number of threads (cores) varies from 1 to 44. Time is given in seconds.

Function	Module	CPU Time
__kmp_fork_barrier	libiomp5.so	658.379s ▶
[MKL BLAS]@dsyrk	libmkl_intel_thread.so	204.680s
__intel_avx_rep_memset	omp_solver	58.498s
[MKL LAPACK]@dpotrf	libmkl_intel_thread.so	54.043s
omp_driver_recursive	libmkl_intel_thread.so	47.210s
[Others]		142.479s

Fig. 8. Hotspots of the 'Old Scheme' collected by Intel Amplifier

Function	Module	CPU Time
[MKL BLAS]@avx512_dgemm_kernel_nocopy_NT_b1	libmkl_avx512.so	203.477s ▶
[MKL BLAS]@avx512_dgemm_kernel_0	libmkl_avx512.so	147.496s ▶
[vmlinux]	vmlinux	31.096s
cblas_daxpyi	libmkl_intel_lp64.so	24.258s
__intel_avx_rep_memcpy	tbb_solver	22.252s
[Others]		100.119s ▶

Fig. 9. Hotspots of the proposed 'New Scheme' collected by Intel Amplifier

6 Conclusion

In this paper, we presented a new scheme for the organization of parallelism when performing the numerical phase of the Cholesky decomposition for symmetric positive-definite sparse matrices. This scheme is based on the transparent creation of logical tasks that can encapsulate both the processing of the next node of the elimination tree, and individual BLAS operations. It results in a flexible load balancing scheme that allows us to dynamically assign tasks to threads, utilizing the available computational resources. The scheme is implemented using the TBB library and uses the library's scalable allocators for smart memory management. The results of experiments on the two 22-core Intel Skylake CPUs show that the performance and strong scaling efficiency of the described implementation is competitive to Intel MKL PARDISO.

References

1. Agullo, E., Buttari, A., Guermouche, A., Lopez, F.: Implementing multifrontal sparse solvers for multicore architectures with sequential task flow runtime systems. ACM Trans. Math. Softw. (TOMS) **43**(2), 13 (2016). https://doi.org/10.1145/2898348
2. Amestoy, P.R., Duff, I.S., L'Excellent, J.Y., Koster, J.: A fully asynchronous multifrontal solver using distributed dynamic scheduling. SIAM J. Matrix Anal. Appl. **23**(1), 15–41 (2001). https://doi.org/10.1137/s0895479899358194
3. Amestoy, P.R., Duff, I.S., L'excellent, J.Y.: Multifrontal parallel distributed symmetric and unsymmetric solvers. Comput. Methods Appl. Mech. Eng. **184**(2–4), 501–520 (2000). https://doi.org/10.1016/S0045-7825(99)00242-X
4. Chen, Y., Davis, T.A., Hager, W.W., Rajamanickam, S.: Algorithm 887: CHOLMOD, supernodal sparse Cholesky factorization and update/downdate. ACM Trans. Math. Softw. (TOMS) **35**(3), 22 (2008). https://doi.org/10.1145/1391989.1391995
5. Davis, T.A.: Direct Methods for Sparse Linear Systems, vol. 2. Siam, Philadelphia (2006)
6. Duff, I.S., Erisman, A.M., Reid, J.K.: Direct Methods for Sparse Matrices. Oxford University Press, Oxford (2017)
7. Duff, I.S., Reid, J.K.: The multifrontal solution of indefinite sparse symmetric linear. ACM Trans. Math. Softw. (TOMS) **9**(3), 302–325 (1983). https://doi.org/10.1145/356044.356047
8. Duff, I.S., Reid, J.K.: The multifrontal solution of unsymmetric sets of linear equations. SIAM J. Sci. Stat. Comput. **5**(3), 633–641 (1984). https://doi.org/10.1137/0905045
9. Duff, I., Hogg, J., Lopez, F.: A new sparse symmetric indefinite solver using A Posteriori Threshold Pivoting (2018)
10. Duff, I., Lopez, F.: Experiments with sparse Cholesky using a parametrized task graph implementation. In: Wyrzykowski, R., Dongarra, J., Deelman, E., Karczewski, K. (eds.) PPAM 2017. LNCS, vol. 10777, pp. 197–206. Springer, Cham (2018). https://doi.org/10.1007/978-3-319-78024-5_18
11. Hogg, J.D., Reid, J.K., Scott, J.A.: Design of a multicore sparse Cholesky factorization using DAGs. SIAM J. Sci. Comput. **32**(6), 3627–3649 (2010). https://doi.org/10.1137/090757216
12. Kalinkin, A., Anders, A., Anders, R.: Intel® math kernel library parallel direct sparse solver for clusters. In: EAGE Workshop on High Performance Computing for Upstream (2014). https://doi.org/10.3997/2214-4609.20141926

13. Karypis, G., Kumar, V.: A parallel algorithm for multilevel graph partitioning and sparse matrix ordering. J. Parallel Distrib. Comput. **48**(1), 71–95 (1998). https://doi.org/10.1006/jpdc.1997.1403
14. L'Excellent, J.Y.: Multifrontal Methods: Parallelism, Memory Usage and Numerical Aspects. Ph.D. thesis, Ecole normale superieure de lyon-ENS LYON (2012)
15. L'Excellent, J.Y., Sid-Lakhdar, W.M.: A study of shared-memory parallelism in a multifrontal solver. Parallel Comput. **40**(3–4), 34–46 (2014). https://doi.org/10.1016/j.parco.2014.02.003
16. LaSalle, D., Karypis, G.: Efficient nested dissection for multicore architectures. In: Träff, J. L., Hunold, S., Versaci, F. (eds.) Euro-Par 2015. LNCS, vol. 9233, pp. 467–478. Springer, Heidelberg (2015). https://doi.org/10.1007/978-3-662-48096-0_36
17. Lebedev, S., Akhmedzhanov, D., Kozinov, E., Meyerov, I., Pirova, A., Sysoyev, A.: Dynamic parallelization strategies for multifrontal sparse Cholesky factorization. In: Malyshkin, V. (ed.) International Conference on Parallel Computing Technologies, pp. 68–79. Springer, Cham (2015). https://doi.org/10.1007/978-3-319-21909-7_7
18. Lebedev, S., Meyerov, I., Kozinov, E., Akhmedzhanov, D., Pirova, A., Sysoyev, A.: Two-level parallel strategy for multifrontal sparse Cholesky factorization. Vestnik UGATU **19**(3 (69)), 178–189 (2015)
19. Li, X.S., Demmel, J.W.: SuperLU_DIST: a scalable distributed-memory sparse direct solver for unsymmetric linear systems. ACM Trans. Math. Softw. (TOMS) **29**(2), 110–140 (2003). https://doi.org/10.1145/779359.779361
20. Liu, J.W.: The multifrontal method for sparse matrix solution: theory and practice. SIAM Rev. **34**(1), 82–109 (1992). https://doi.org/10.1137/1034004
21. Pellegrini, F.: Scotch and libScotch 6.0 User's Guide. Technical report, LaBRI (2012)
22. Pirova, A., Meyerov, I., Kozinov, E., Lebedev, S.: PMORSy: parallel sparse matrix ordering software for fill-in minimization. Optim. Methods Softw. **32**(2), 274–289 (2017). https://doi.org/10.1080/10556788.2016.1193177
23. Schreiber, R.: A new implementation of sparse Gaussian elimination. ACM Trans. Math. Softw. (TOMS) **8**(3), 256–276 (1982). https://doi.org/10.1145/356004.356006
24. Sid-Lakhdar, W.M.: Scaling the solution of large sparse linear systems using multifrontal methods on hybrid shared-distributed memory architectures. PhD Thesis, prepared at ENS Lyon (2014)
25. Tang, M., Gadou, M., Rennich, S., Davis, T.A., Ranka, S.: Optimized sparse Cholesky factorization on hybrid multicore architectures. J. Comput. Sci. **26**, 246–253 (2018). https://doi.org/10.1016/j.jocs.2018.04.008
26. The SuiteSparse matrix collection. https://sparse.tamu.edu
27. The Threading Building Blocks library. https://www.threadingbuildingblocks.org

Optimal Packings of Congruent Circles on a Square Flat Torus as Mixed-Integer Nonlinear Optimization Problem

Vladimir Voloshinov[(✉)] and Sergey Smirnov

Center for Distributed Computing, Institute for Information Transmission Problems
(Kharkevich Institute), Moscow, Russia
vladimir.voloshinov@gmail.com, sasmir@gmail.com

Abstract. Hard problems of discrete geometry may be formulated as a global optimization problems, which may be solved by general purpose solvers implementing branch-and-bound (B&B) algorithm. A problem of densest packing of N equal circles in special geometrical object, so called Square Flat Torus, $\mathbb{R}^2/\mathbb{Z}^2$, with the induced metric, is considered. It is formulated as mixed-integer problem with linear and nonconvex quadratic constraints. The open-source B&B-solver SCIP and its parallel implementation ParaSCIP have been used to find optimal arrangements for $N \leqslant 9$. The main result is a confirmation of the conjecture on optimal packing for $N = 9$ that was published in 2012 by O. Musin and A. Nikitenko.

Keywords: Optimal packings · Square flat torus · Mixed-integer nonlinear optimization · Parallel branch-and-bound solver

1 Introduction

Densest packing problems appear in many areas of discrete geometry. Hereinafter Square Flat Torus (SFT) Packing Problem (SFTPP) is considered [10,11]. SFT is a factor–space $\mathbb{R}^2/\mathbb{Z}^2$ with metric induced by Euclidean metric ($\mathbb{Z}^2$ is an integer lattice in $\mathbb{R}^2$). As for the practical application, this problem is associated with obtaining aerial photographs (and satellite images) of super-high resolution. We paid attention to SFTPP in our researches on global and discrete optimization in distributed computing environment [14,15].

The problem is to find arrangement of N points in SFT maximizing minimal pairwise distance. A peculiar feature of the problem is a definition of distance between points of a torus, which are treated as equivalence classes of factor–space $\mathbb{R}^2/\mathbb{Z}^2$. The SFT–distance $d(x, y)$ (where $x = (x_1, x_2)$ and $y = (y_1, y_2)$) is the length of red segment in the Fig. 1, i.e. we have the following formula:

$$d(x, y)^2 \doteq \Big(\min \{ |x_1 - y_1|, 1 - |x_1 - y_1| \} \Big)^2 + \Big(\min \{ |x_2 - y_2|, 1 - |x_2 - y_2| \} \Big)^2 \tag{1}$$

© Springer Nature Switzerland AG 2019
V. Voevodin and S. Sobolev (Eds.): RuSCDays 2019, CCIS 1129, pp. 87–97, 2019.
https://doi.org/10.1007/978-3-030-36592-9_8

Musin and Nikitenko studied this problem for $N = 2{:}9$ in articles [10,11]. Their proof of optimality is based on a computer enumeration of irreducible contact graphs corresponding to potentially optimal arrangement of points at SFT. They proved optimal packings for N up to 8 and presented a conjecture on optimal arrangement for $N = 9$. The main advantage of combinatorial geometry is an explicit, analytic, expression for optimal "max-min" distance.

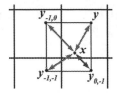

Fig. 1. Distance between **x** and **y** on SFT

Our approach is based on global optimization by solvers implementing branch-and-bound (B&B) algorithm. SFTPP is formulated as mixed-integer nonlinear programming problem (MINLP) with binary variables and nonconvex quadratic constraints. This approach is using in studies of packing problems, e.g. see [4]. The main advantage of global optimization is the ability to use general-purpose B&B-solver including parallel implementations for high-performance clusters. This approach for circles packing problems in a 2D-square (not flat torus!) has a long history (e.g. see [16]).

This paper is organised as follows. Formulation of SFTPP as mixed-integer nonlinear (with nonconvex quadratic constraints) mathematical programming problem is done in Sect. 2. The Sect. 3 presents results of computational experiments for $N = 4{:}8$ with SCIP global optimization solver [8]. The Sect. 4 shows results for $N = \{8, 9\}$ obtained by ParaSCIP solver [12] (parallel implementation of SCIP based on MPI). ParaSCIP solver has been built and used on three high-performance clusters from Russian Top50 list (edition #30, 02.04.2019). Finally, we present optimal arrangement found by ParaSCIP for $N = 9$, which confirmed conjecture made in [10,11]. Conclusion Sect. 4 is followed by Acknowledgements.

2   Formulation as Global Optimization MINLP

Let E be a set of unordered pairs of indices: $E \doteq \{(i,j) : 1 \leqslant i < j \leqslant N\}$. The problem is to maximize minimum of squared pairwise distances (1):

$$D \to \max_{x_{ik}} :$$

$$D \leqslant \sum_{k=1:2} \left(\min\left\{ |x_{ik} - x_{jk}|, 1 - |x_{ik} - x_{jk}| \right\} \right)^2 \; \Big((i,j) \in E \Big), \qquad (2)$$

$$0 \leqslant x_{ik} \leqslant 1 \Big(k = 1{:}2, \; i = 1{:}N \Big).$$

Formulation (2) has non-smooth and non-convex functions in constraints. Let's introduce auxiliary continuous and binary variables to avoid non-smoothness[1]:

$$y_{ijk} \doteq \min\{|x_{ik} - x_{jk}|, 1 - |x_{ik} - x_{jk}|\}, \ \left(k = 1{:}2, \ (i,j) \in E\right),$$

$$z_{ijk} \doteq -|x_{ik} - x_{jk}| = \min\{x_{jk} - x_{ik}, x_{ik} - x_{jk}\} \ \left(k = 1{:}2, \ (i,j) \in E\right), \quad (3)$$

$$\eta_{ijk} \in \{0,1\}, \ \zeta_{ijk} \in \{0,1\} \ \left(k = 1{:}2, \ (i,j) \in E\right).$$

The 1st equation of (3) is equivalent to the following system of inequalities:

$$y_{ijk} \leqslant |x_{ik} - x_{jk}|, \ y_{ijk} \leqslant 1 - |x_{ik} - x_{jk}|, \ y_{ijk} \geqslant |x_{ik} - x_{jk}| - \eta_{ijk}$$
$$y_{ijk} \geqslant 1 - |x_{ik} - x_{jk}| - 1 + \eta_{ijk} = -|x_{ik} - x_{jk}| + \eta_{ijk} \ (k = 1{:}2, \ (i,j) \in E). \quad (4)$$

Equivalence means that y_{ijk}, x_{ik}, x_{jk} satisfies first equation of (3) **iff** there exists some binary η_{ijk} that satisfies (4) with the same y_{ijk}, x_{ik}, x_{jk}. Easy proof may be done considering that 1 is the maximal difference between functions $|\Delta_{ijk}|$ and $1 - |\Delta_{ijk}|$ on the interval $|\Delta_{ijk}| \in [0,1]$ (inclusion $|\Delta_{ijk}| \in [0,1]$ follows from inclusions $x_{ik} \in [0,1]$ and $x_{jk} \in [0,1]$), see Fig. 2.

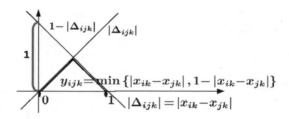

Fig. 2. Illustration for system of inequalities (4)

Continue transformation of (4). The 2nd and the 3d inequalities are equivalent to the following two-sided inequalities:

$$-y_{ijk} - \eta_{ijk} \leqslant x_{ik} - x_{jk} \leqslant 1 - y_{ijk},$$
$$-1 + y_{ijk} \leqslant x_{ik} - x_{jk} \leqslant y_{ijk} + \eta_{ijk}, \quad (5)$$

and the 1st and the 4th – to the following (see definition of z_{ijk} in (3)):

$$z_{ijk} + \eta_{ijk} \leqslant y_{ijk} \leqslant -z_{ijk}. \quad (6)$$

Note that definition of z_{ijk} is equivalent to the following linear inequalities:

$$z_{ijk} \leqslant x_{ik} - x_{jk} \leqslant z_{ijk} + 2\zeta_{ijk},$$
$$-z_{ijk} - 2\left(1 - \zeta_{ijk}\right) \leqslant x_{ik} - x_{jk} \leqslant -z_{ijk}. \quad (7)$$

---

[1] There is a lot of literature on reducing similar non-smooth problems to MINLP, but [5] seems to be one of the first.

The proof of that equivalence is the same as mentioned after system (4) considering that 2 is the maximal difference between functions Δ and $-\Delta$ on the interval $\Delta \in [-1, 1]$, see Fig. 3.

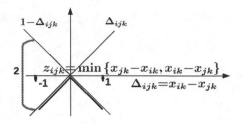

Fig. 3. Illustration for system of inequalities (7)

Finally, from definitions (3) and relations (4)–(7) it follows that the problem (2) is equivalent to the following mixed-integer nonlinear problem with nonconvex quadratic constraints ($k = 1{:}2$, $i = 1{:}N$, $(i, j) \in E$):

$$
\begin{aligned}
&D \to \max(\text{with variables } x_{ik}, y_{ijk}, z_{ijk}, \eta_{ijk}, \zeta_{ijk}), \text{s.t.} : \\
&D \leqslant \sum_{k=1:2} y_{ijk}^2, \\
&-y_{ijk} - \eta_{ijk} \leqslant x_{ik} - x_{jk} \leqslant 1 - y_{ijk}, \\
&-1 + y_{ijk} \leqslant x_{ik} - x_{jk} \leqslant y_{ijk} + \eta_{ijk}, \\
&z_{ijk} + \eta_{ijk} \leqslant y_{ijk} \leqslant -z_{ijk}, \\
&z_{ijk} \leqslant x_{ik} - x_{jk} \leqslant z_{ijk} + 2\zeta_{ijk}, \\
&-z_{ijk} - 2\left(1 - \zeta_{ijk}\right) \leqslant x_{ik} - x_{jk} \leqslant -z_{ijk}, \\
&0 \leqslant x_{ik} \leqslant 1, \ y_{ijk} \in \mathbb{R}, \ z_{ijk} \in \mathbb{R}, \ \eta_{ijk} \in \{0,1\}, \ \zeta_{ijk} \in \{0,1\}.
\end{aligned}
\tag{8}
$$

The problem has: $2N^2$ continuous variables x_{ik}, y_{ijk}, z_{ijk}; $2N(N-1)$ binary variables η_{ijk}, ζ_{ijk}; $5N(N-1)$ linear constraints with continuous variables and the same number of linear "mixed-integer" constraints; $\frac{N(N-1)}{2}$ nonconvex quadratic constraints with continuous variables. Moreover, auxiliary linear constraints (9) have been added to reduce a number of redundant solutions might be obtained by parallel shifting, renumbering of points and mirror-imaging:

$$
\begin{aligned}
&x_{11} = 0.5, x_{12} = 0 \text{ ("anti–shifting", the 1st point is fixed to } (\tfrac{1}{2}, 0)\text{)}, \\
&x_{i2} \geqslant x_{(i-1)2} \ (i = 2{:}N) \text{ ("anti–renumbering", 2nd coordinate increases)},
\end{aligned}
\tag{9a}
$$

$$
x_{11} \leqslant x_{21} \text{ (to prevent mirror-image w.r.t. vertical axis).}
\tag{9b}
$$

We note (see Table 1) that adding constraint (9b) to (8), (9a), reduces solving time almost twice (due to twice less volume of domain in multi–dimensional space of continuous variables). More explanation of increasing efficiency of BNB-algorithm after reducing volume of feasible domain may be found in [15].

3   Case Study: Solver SCIP, N ⩽ 8

We used SCIP (Solving Constrained Integer Programming) – an open-source solver freely available for research and educational purposes [8]. A short quotation from documentation: "SCIP is a framework for Constraint Integer Programming ... as a pure MIP and MINLP solver or as a framework for branch-cut-and-price. SCIP is implemented as C callable library and provides C++ wrapper classes for user plugins. It can also be used as a standalone program to solve MINLP given in various formats[2]".

In our studies we prefer another, so called NL-format from AMPL (A Mathematical Programming Language) [6], which has almost 35 years long history. SCIP supports NL-format by special `scipampl` build. Originally, usage of AMPL required special commercially licensed translator: to create NL-file that might be passed to any AMPL-compatible solvers; to parse solution SOL-files returned from solvers. In 2005 AMPL developers disclosed internal formats of NL-files [7]. Due to that, Pyomo (PYthon Optimization Modeling Objects)[3] [9], an open-source optimization modelling tool, now supports creation of NL-files. Thus, Python programming language may be used to generate optimization problems, which may be solved by a proper AMPL-compatible solver.

Important feature of SCIP is ability to solve optimization problems with polynomials in constraints (other nonlinearities are admitted also). Well–known problems of combinatorial geometry, e.g. Tammes and Thomson problems, may be formulated in such a way [15]. Details of implementations of B&B-algorithm in SCIP for the case of bilinear and nonconvex polynomial constraints may be found in the article [17]. For brevity we give the following citation: "SCIP uses convex envelopes for well-known univariate functions, linearization cuts for convex constraints, and ... McCormick "envelope" relaxation of bilinear terms...".

Returning to SFTPP, Pyomo is used to create NL-file from MINLP presented in (8) and (9). Then NL-file is processed by `scipampl` solver, which returns SOL-file with solution. Finally, SOL-file is imported by Python code via Pyomo package to analyse solution obtained, including plotting of figures below.

Solving times for cases $N = 4{:}8$ on different computers are presented in Table 1 desktop[4] for $N = 4{:}7$, standalone server[5] for $N = 8$ (with and without

Table 1. Solving times for $N = \{4, 5, 6, 7, 8\}$, seconds, one SCIP process

	$N = 4$	$N = 5$	$N = 6$	$N = 7$	$N = 8$
Problem (8) & (9a)	3, desk.	30, desk.	118, desk.	2552, desk.	70240, serv.
Problem (8) & (9)	–	–	66, lapt.	1940, lapt.	27230, serv.

---

[2] See all formats here https://scip.zib.de/doc/html/group__FILEREADERS.php.
[3] http://pyomo.org.
[4] CPU Intel®i7-6700 3.40 GHz, 32 Gb.
[5] CPU 2×Intel®Xeon®5620 2.4 GHz, 32 Gb.

constraint (9b)) and laptop[6] for $N = 6{:}7$ (with constraint (9b)). The presence
of constraint (9b) substantially reduces solving time. SCIP had been run with
default settings, except: relative gap had been set to 10^{-6} and memory limit -
to 28 Gb (actually the worst case $N = 8$ occupied about 8 Gb).

Results for N = 7 deserves more attention since, as shown in [10,11] (see
Fig. 3b–d there) there are three different (up to isometric transformation) optimal arrangements. We tried to find all of them in results of SCIP solving.

By default SCIP solver stores optimal solutions in a list that is available
by proper commands of SCIP-console. So, after successful completion of solving
user can retrieve a set of optimal solutions found. Results are presented in the
Figs. 4, 5 and 6. They have been selected manually (by "draw-and-compare")
from 11 optimal solutions found by standalone SCIP process. Because B&B-
algorithm inherently differs from "exact" combinatorial method (enumeration of
irreducible contact graphs) that has been used in [10,11], SCIP founds redundant
solutions (auxiliary constraints (9) are not enough to get rid of them all).

Every arrangement coincides with one of those found in [11] after some isometric transformation (see captions of the Figs. 4, 5 and 6). Pay attention to a
"free" position of the point number 7 on the Fig. 4, its circle can be freely moved
within area surrounded by other grey circles[7].

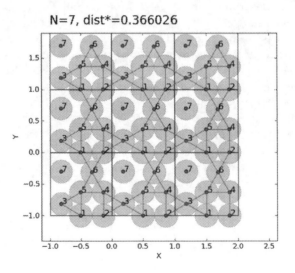

N=7, dist*=0.366026

Fig. 4. $N = 7$, the 1st optimal arrangement (see Fig. 3b [11], $d^* = \frac{1}{1+\sqrt{3}}$)

---

4   Case Study: Solver ParaSCIP, N = 8, 9

With the N value increase we see (in the Table 1) dramatic growth of solving time (and complexity of SFTPP). The article [11] presents only conjecture about optimal arrangement for $N = 9$. Our attempts to solve problem for $N = 9$ by "single–threaded" SCIP have failed. Computational efficiency of B&B algorithm

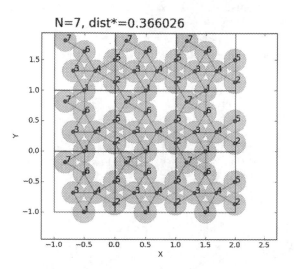

Fig. 5. $N = 7$, the 2nd optimal arrangement; to get Fig. 3c [11] rotate $90°$ ↻, $d^* = \frac{1}{1+\sqrt{3}}$

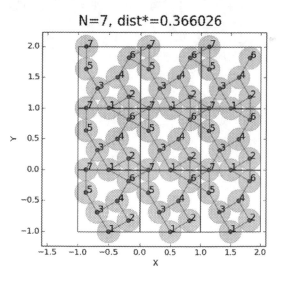

Fig. 6. $N = 7$, the 3d arrangement (to get Fig. 3d [11] flip ↕ and rotate $90°$ ↻, $d^* = \frac{1}{1+\sqrt{3}}$)

implemented in SCIP may be substantially increased by its parallel implementation as ParaSCIP solver does.

ParaSCIP – Parallel Implementation of B&B. ParaSCIP, [12], is a distributed memory massively parallel solver based on Ubiquity Generator (UG) framework, http://ug.zib.de. In the framework the solver and the communication mechanism are abstracted making it easier to parallelize different solvers. Two communication mechanisms are available in the UG: distributed memory MPI and shared memory POSIX-threads. SCIP, Xpress [1] and CPLEX [2] solvers are supported with MPI and only SCIP with both mechanisms. Only SCIP-based specializations of the framework (ParaSCIP for MPI-based and FiberSCIP for POSIX-threads based implementations) are publicly available. ParaSCIP can utilize quite big computing resources, e.g. it ran on 80000 cores in parallel while solving MIP instances from MIPLIB2010 [13] (Fig. 7).

ParaSCIP was compiled and tried by our team on the following clusters:

- "Lomonosov", MSU, https://users.parallel.ru/wiki/pages/22-config;
- "HPC4", NRC "Kurchatov Institute", http://computing.nrcki.ru;
- "Govorun", LIT JINR, http://hlit.jinr.ru/about_govorun/cpu_govorun.

Some technical details of used partitions are presented in the Table 2.

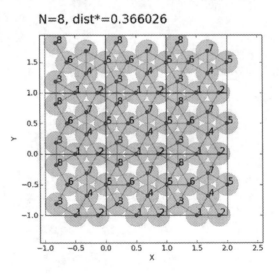

Fig. 7. $N = 8$, optimal arrangement found by SCIP (see [11], Fig. 3e, $d^* = \frac{1}{1+\sqrt{3}}$)

Table 2. Characteristics of partitions used on "Lomonosov", "HPC4" and "Govorun"

Cluster	Partition	CPU (Intel®Xeon®)	cores/node	mem/node
"Lomonosov"	regular4	X5570 2.93 GHz	8	12 Gb
"HPC4"	hpc4-3d	E5-2680 v3 2.50 GHz	24	128 Gb
"Govorun"	skylake	Gold 6154 3.70 GHz	36	192 Gb

Default ParaSCIP settings have been used. As to SCIP-solver, the only "depth-first search" priority parameter differs from default value (due to ParaSCIP team recommendations): `nodeselection/dfs/stdpriority = 300000`.

ParaSCIP vs SCIP for N = 8. This case has been used to compare performance of ParaSCIP and SCIP on "HPC4". Solving times are presented in the Table 3. Pay attention that solving with a single SCIP process on "HPC4" took almost twice more time than that on a standalone server (see last column of the Table 1). The reason is that the problem instance passed to the cluster did not have auxiliary constraint (9b).

Table 3. Solving times for $N = 8$, for SCIP and ParaSCIP ("HPC4", "Lomonosov")

	CPU cores	Solving time, min
SCIP, "HPC4"	1	780
ParaSCIP, "HPC4"	8 (7 solvers)	126
ParaSCIP, "HPC4", constraint (9b)	8 (7 solvers)	65
ParaSCIP, "Lomonosov", –"– (9b)	64 (63 solvers)	19

To evaluate efficiency of pallelization one should remember that one of ParaSCIP processes, MPI-master, plays role of Load Coordinator and, actually, does not solve sub-problems. So we have: efficiency (CPU): $780/126/8 = 0.77$; efficiency (solvers): $780/126/7 = 0.88$.

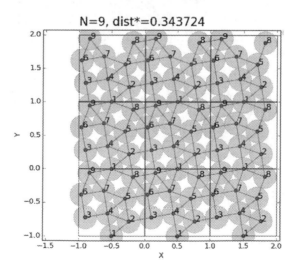

Fig. 8. $N = 9$, optimal arrangement by ParaSCIP (to get Fig. 3f [11] flip $\leftrightarrow$, $d^* = \frac{1}{\sqrt{5+2\sqrt{3}}}$)

Results of ParaSCIP for N = 9. ParaSCIP with 128 processes on 8 nodes (127 solvers) of cluster "HPC4" solved the problem (8), (9a) in 956 min and we can expect one-half as much, about 480 min., with (9b). The same problem with auxiliary constraint (9b) has been solved on 6 nodes (216 CPU cores, 215 solvers) of cluster "Govorun" in 108 min.

It is the main result presented in this work. Optimal arrangement found is shown in the Fig. 8 and coincides with conjecture presented in [10,11]. Taking into account load balancing between working processes the following evaluation of complexity may be done: $\approx 127 \times 480/60 = 1016$ CPU×hours on "HPC4"; $215 \times 108/60 \approx 388$ CPU × hours on "Govorun".

5   Conclusion

Obtained results confirmed the usefulness of global optimization in solving hard problems of combinatorial geometry. Formulation SFTPP as mixed-integer non-linear problem and use of global optimization solver SCIP have let to reproduce all known optimal arrangement for $N = 4{:}8$. Parallel SCIP version, ParaSCIP, gives "computer aided" proof of optimal arrangement for $N = 9$, confirming conjecture known since 2012. Rather moderate solving time of SFTPP with 9 circles (388 CPU × hours on "Govorun" cluster) gives hope for solving this problem for $N = 10$ not in far future.

There has been confirmed semi–empirical rule [15] that simple auxiliary constraints reducing the volume of feasible domain (e.g. (9b)) reduce solving time of nonlinear problems by B&B-algorithm that uses McCormik envelopes.

General purpose MINLP solver SCIP and its parallel implementation, ParaS-CIP, have been successfully built and used on three clusters from Russian Top50 list[8] (ed. #30, 02.04.2019). Work is currently in progress on integration of ParaS-CIP solver into optimization modelling toolset on the base of Everest distributed computing platform [14,15].

Acknowledgements. The work is supported by the Russian Science Foundation (project No. 16-11-10352). This work has been carried out using computing resources of the federal collective usage center Complex for Simulation and Data Processing for Mega-science Facilities at NRC "Kurchatov Institute". Also, computations were held on the basis of the HybriLIT heterogeneous computing platform (LIT, JINR) [3]. The research is carried out using the equipment of the shared research facilities of HPC computing resources at Lomonosov Moscow State University. Authors thank: Alexey Tarasov for the advice to try SFTPP as an example of global optimization problem; Yuji Shinano and Stefan Vigerske for consultations on the use of SCIP and ParaSCIP solvers.

---

[8]   http://top50.supercomputers.ru/list.

References

1. FICO Xpress Solver. https://www.fico.com/en/products/fico-xpress-solver
2. IBM ILOG CPLEX Optimization Studio. https://www.ibm.com/products/ilog-cplex-optimization-studio
3. Adam, G., et al.: IT-ecosystem of the HybriLIT heterogeneous platform for high-performance computing and training of IT-specialists. In: Selected Papers of the 8th International Conference "Distributed Computing and Grid-technologies in Science and Education" (GRID 2018), Dubna, Russia, vol. 2267, pp. 638–644 (2018). CEUR-WS.org
4. Castillo, I., Kampas, F.J., Pintér, J.D.: Solving circle packing problems by global optimization: numerical results and industrial applications. Eur. J. Oper. Res. **191**(3), 786–802 (2008)
5. Dantzig, G.B.: On the significance of solving linear programming problems with some integer variables. Econometrica J. Econ. Soc. **28**, 30–44 (1960)
6. Fourer, R., Gay, D., Kernighan, B.: AMPL: A Modeling Language for Mathematical Programming, 2nd edn. Duxbury Press/Brooks/Cole Publishing Company (2003). https://ampl.com/resources/the-ampl-book
7. Gay, D.M.: Writing.nl files. Technical report, No. 2005-7907P. Sandia National Laboratories (2005)
8. Gleixner, A., et al.: The SCIP Optimization Suite 6.0. Technical Report, 18–26, ZIB, Takustr. 7, 14195 Berlin (2018)
9. Hart, W.E., et al.: Pyomo-Optimization Modeling in Python, vol. 67, 2nd edn. Springer, Cham (2017). https://doi.org/10.1007/978-3-319-58821-6
10. Musin, O.R., Nikitenko, A.V.: Optimal packings of congruent circles on a square flat torus. ArXiv e-prints (2012)
11. Musin, O.R., Nikitenko, A.V.: Optimal packings of congruent circles on a square flat torus. Discrete Comput. Geom. **55**(1), 1–20 (2016)
12. Shinano, Y., Achterberg, T., Berthold, T., Heinz, S., Koch, T.: ParaSCIP: a parallel extension of SCIP. In: Bischof, C., Hegering, H.G., Nagel, W., Wittum, G. (eds.) Competence in High Performance Computing 2010, pp. 135–148. Springer, Heidelberg (2011). https://doi.org/10.1007/978-3-642-24025-6_12
13. Shinano, Y., Achterberg, T., Berthold, T., Heinz, S., Koch, T., Winkler, M.: Solving open MIP instances with ParaSCIP on supercomputers using up to 80,000 cores. In: 2016 IEEE International Symposium on Parallel and Distributed Processing, pp. 770–779. IEEE (2016)
14. Smirnov, S., Sukhoroslov, O., Voloshinov, V.: Using resources of supercomputing centers with everest platform. In: Voevodin, V., Sobolev, S. (eds.) RuSCDays 2018. CCIS, vol. 965, pp. 687–698. Springer, Cham (2019). https://doi.org/10.1007/978-3-030-05807-4_59
15. Smirnov, S., Voloshinov, V.: On domain decomposition strategies to parallelize branch-and-bound method for global optimization in Everest distributed environment. Procedia Comput. Sci. **136**, 128–135 (2018)
16. Szabó, P.G., Markót, M.C., Csendes, T., Specht, E., Casado, L.G., García, I.: New Approaches to Circle Packing in a Square: With Program Codes, vol. 6. Springer, Boston (2007). https://doi.org/10.1007/978-0-387-45676-8
17. Vigerske, S., Gleixner, A.: SCIP: global optimization of mixed-integer nonlinear programs in a branch-and-cut framework. Optim. Methods Softw. **33**, 1–31 (2017)

Parallel Global Optimization for Non-convex Mixed-Integer Problems

Konstantin Barkalov[✉] and Ilya Lebedev

Lobachevsky State University of Nizhni Novgorod, Nizhni Novgorod, Russia
{konstantin.barkalov,ilya.lebedev}@itmm.unn.ru

Abstract. The paper considers the mixed-integer global optimization problems. A novel parallel algorithm for solving the problems of this class based on the index algorithm for solving the continuous global optimization problems has been proposed. The comparison of this algorithm with known analogs demonstrates the efficiency of the developed approach. The proposed algorithm allows an efficient parallelization including the employment of the graphics accelerators. The results of performed numerical experiments (solving a series of 100 multiextremal mixed-integer problems) confirm a good speedup of the algorithm with the use of GPU.

Keywords: Global optimization · Non-convex constraints · Mixed-integer problems · Parallel algorithms

1 Introduction

In this paper the global optimization problems and the method of their solving are considered. The global optimization problems are the time-consuming ones since the global optimum is an integral characteristic of the problem being solved and requires the investigation of the whole search domain. As a result, the search of the global optimum is reduced to the construction of a coverage (in general, a nonuniform one) of the space of parameters; such problems are common in applications [1–3]. The problems, in which some parameters can take the discrete or integer values only (*mixed-integer global optimization problems*) are of special interest because for these problems it is more difficult to build the estimates of the optimum as compared to the continuous ones.

The situation when some parameters are featured by the discreteness or integerness is frequent in applied problems. As a rule, the integer parameters take a small number of values and may denote, for example, the trademarks of the materials used, the variant of typical layouts of components, etc.

A lot of publication have been devoted to the methods of solving the mixed-integer problems (see, for example, the reviews [4,5]). The well known deterministic methods of solving the problems of this class are based, as a rule, on the Branch-and-Bound [6] or on the Branch-and-Reduce approach [7]. Also, a

© Springer Nature Switzerland AG 2019
V. Voevodin and S. Sobolev (Eds.): RuSCDays 2019, CCIS 1129, pp. 98–109, 2019.
https://doi.org/10.1007/978-3-030-36592-9_9

number of the metaheuristic and genetic algorithms are known, which are based one way or another on the random search concept [8,9].

In the present study, we proposed a novel parallel method for solving the mixed-integer problems based on the index approach to solving the constrained global optimization problems [10,11]. Within the framework of this approach:

- the solving of the multidimensional problems is reduced to solving the equivalent one-dimensional problems; the corresponding reduction is based on the use of the space-filling curves;
- when solving the constrained optimization problems, each constraint is taken into account and processed separately, the penalty functions are not used;
- the parallelization of the search process is performed by means of the simultaneous computing of several objective function values at different points of the search domain within every iteration.

The paper text reflecting the results of the performed study is organized in the following way. In Sect. 2, a brief description of the dimensionality reduction scheme using the space-filling curves is given. Also, the index scheme of accounting for the constraints is described. Here the formulation of the parallel index algorithm for solving the continuous global optimization problems is given as well. In Sect. 3, the approach to the generalization of the parallel index algorithm with the purpose of solving the mixed-integer problems is presented. A method that allows to reduce solving of mixed-integer problem to solving a set of the continuous optimization problems, which can be performed in parallel, is given. Section 4 contains the results of numerical experiments. The comparison of the sequential version of the algorithm with the known analogs is conducted here. Also, the efficiency of the parallel CPU- and GPU-versions of the algorithm for solving a series of the multiextremal mixed-integer problem is demonstrated. Section 5 concludes the paper.

2 Global Optimization Algorithm and Dimension Reduction

A constrained global optimization problem can be formulated as follows

$$\varphi(y^*) = \min\{\varphi(y) : y \in D,\ g_i(y) \leq 0,\ 1 \leq i \leq m\}, \tag{1}$$
$$D = \{y \in R^N : a_j \leq y_j \leq b_j, 1 \leq j \leq N\}. \tag{2}$$

The objective function $\varphi(y)$ (hereafter denoted by $g_{m+1}(y)$) and the left-hand sides $g_i(y)$, $1 \leq i \leq m$, of the constraints satisfy the Lipschitz condition

$$|g_i(y_1) - g_i(y_2)| \leq L_i \|y_1 - y_2\|,\ 1 \leq i \leq m+1,\ y_1, y_2 \in D,$$

with a priori unknown constants L_i, $1 \leq i \leq m+1$, and may be multiextremal. It is assumed that the functions $g_i(y)$ are defined and computable only at the points $y \in D$ satisfying the conditions

$$g_k(y) \leq 0,\ 1 \leq k < i. \tag{3}$$

By employing the continuous single-valued Peano-Hilbert curve $y(x)$ mapping the unit interval $[0,1]$ on the x-axis onto the N-dimensional domain (2), it is possible to find the minimum in (1) by solving the one-dimensional problem

$$\varphi(y(x^*)) = \min\left\{\varphi(y(x)) : x \in [0,1], \ g_i(y(x)) \le 0, \ 1 \le i \le m\right\}.$$

Algorithms for numerical construction of Peano-Hilbert curve approximation (*evolvent*) are considered in [10,11]. These evolvents are fractals generated by an iterative process, that fill in the hypercube D with accuracy 2^{-m}, where integer $m > 0$ is the evolvent construction parameter. Examples of the evolvent with different m in two dimensions are given in Fig. 1.

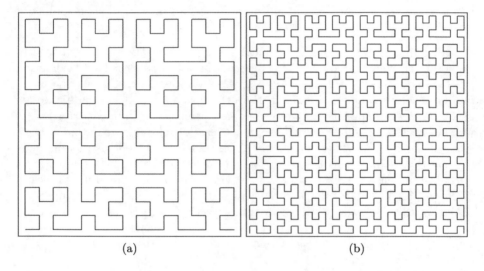

(a)   (b)

Fig. 1. Evolvents in two dimensions with (a) $m = 4$ and (b) $m = 5$

Due to (3) the functions $g_i(y(x))$ are defined and computable in the subranges

$$Q_1 = [0,1], \ Q_{i+1} = \{x \in Q_i : g_i(y(x)) \le 0\}, \ 1 \le i \le m.$$

These conditions allows us to introduce a classification of the points $x \in [0,1]$ according to the number $\nu(x)$ of the constraints computed at this point. The *index* $\nu(x)$ can also be defined by the conditions

$$g_i(y(x)) \le 0, \ 1 \le i < \nu, \ g_\nu(y(x)) > 0, \tag{4}$$

where the last inequality is inessential if $\nu = m + 1$.

In the dimensionality reduction scheme considered here, a multidimensional problem with Lipschitzian functions is juxtaposed with a one-dimensional problem, where the corresponding functions satisfy uniform Hölder condition (see [11]), i.e.,

$$|g_i(y(x_1)) - g_i(y(x_2))| \le H_i \, |x_1 - x_2|^{1/N}, \ x_1, x_2 \in [0,1], \ 1 \le i \le m+1.$$

Here, N is the dimensionality of the initial multidimensional problem and the coefficients H_i are related to the Lipschitz constant L_i of the initial problem as $H_i \leq 2L_i\sqrt{N+3}$.

Thus, *a trial* at a point $x^k \in [0,1]$ executed at the k-th iteration of the algorithm will consist of the following sequence of operations:

- Determine the *image* $y^k = y(x^k)$ in accordance with the mapping $y(x)$;
- Compute the values $g_1(y^k), ..., g_\nu(y^k)$, where $\nu = \nu(x^k)$ is from (4).

The dyad

$$\{\nu = \nu(x^k),\ z^k = g_\nu(y(x^k))\} \tag{5}$$

will be referred to as the *trial outcome*.

An efficient parallel index algorithm (PIA) for solving the constrained global optimization problem (1) has been developed at University of Nizhni Novgorod. The scheme of the algorithm is as follows.

Suppose we have $p \geq 1$ computational elements (e.g., processor cores), which can be used to run p trials simultaneously. In the first iteration of the method, p trials are run in parallel at various random points $x^i \in (0,1)$, $1 \leq i \leq p$. Suppose $n \geq 1$ iterations of the method have been completed, and as a result of which, trials were carried out in $k = k(n)$ points $x^i, 1 \leq i \leq k$. Then the points $x^{k+1}, ..., x^{k+p}$ of the search trials in the next $(n+1)$-th iteration will be determined according to the rules below.

1. Renumber the points $x^1, ..., x^k$ from previous iterations with lower indices, lowest to highest coordinate values, i.e.

$$0 = x_0 < x_1 < ... < x_i < ... < x_k < x_{k+1} = 1, \tag{6}$$

and match them with the values $z_i = g_\nu(y(x_i))$, $\nu = \nu(x_i)$, $1 \leq i \leq k$, from (5), calculated at these points; points $x_0 = 0$ and $x_{k+1} = 1$ are introduced additionally, the values z_0 and z_{k+1} are indeterminate.

2. Classify the numbers $i, 1 \leq i \leq k$, of the trial points from (6) by the number of problem constraints fulfilled at these points, by building the sets

$$I_\nu = \{i : 1 \leq i \leq k,\ \nu = \nu(x_i)\},\ 1 \leq \nu \leq m+1, \tag{7}$$

containing the numbers of all points $x_i, 1 \leq i \leq k$, with the same values of ν. The end points $x_0 = 0$ and $x_{k+1} = 1$ are interpreted as those with zero indices, and they are matched to an additional set $I_0 = \{0, k+1\}$. Identify the maximum current value of the index

$$M = \max\{\nu = \nu(x_i),\ 1 \leq i \leq k\}. \tag{8}$$

3. For all values of ν, $1 \leq \nu \leq m+1$, calculate the values

$$\mu_\nu = \max\left\{\frac{|z_i - z_j|}{(x_i - x_j)^{1/N}} : i, j \in I_\nu, j < i\right\}. \tag{9}$$

If the set I_ν contains less than two elements or μ_ν from (9) equals zero, then assume $\mu_\nu = 1$.

4. For all non-empty sets $I_\nu, 1 \leq \nu \leq m+1$, determine the values

$$z_\nu^* = \begin{cases} -\epsilon_\nu, \nu < M, \\ \min\{g_\nu(x_i) : i \in I_\nu\}, \nu = M, \end{cases} \tag{10}$$

where M is the maximum current value of the index, and the vector $\epsilon_R = (\epsilon_1, ..., \epsilon_m)$ with positive coordinates is called the *reserve vector* and is used as a parameter in the algorithm.

5. For each interval $(x_{i-1}, x_i), 1 \leq i \leq k+1$, calculate the *characteristic* $R(i)$:

$$R(i) = \Delta_i + \frac{(z_i - z_{i-1})^2}{(r_\nu \mu_\nu)^2 \Delta_i} - 2\frac{z_i + z_{i-1} - 2z_\nu^*}{r_\nu \mu_\nu}, \quad \nu = \nu(x_{i-1}) = \nu(x_i),$$

$$R(i) = 2\Delta_i - 4\frac{z_i - z_\nu^*}{r_\nu \mu_\nu}, \quad \nu(x_{i-1}) < \nu(x_i) = \nu,$$

$$R(i) = 2\Delta_i - 4\frac{z_{i-1} - z_\nu^*}{r_\nu \mu_\nu}, \quad \nu = \nu(x_{i-1}) > \nu(x_i).$$

where $\Delta_i = (x_i - x_{i-1})^{1/N}$, and the values $r_\nu > 1, 1 \leq \nu \leq m+1$, are used as parameters in the algorithm.

6. Reorder the characteristics $R(i), 1 \leq i \leq k+1$, from highest to lowest

$$R(t_1) \geq R(t_2) \geq ... \geq R(t_k) \geq R(t_{k+1}) \tag{11}$$

and choose p largest characteristics with interval numbers $t_j, 1 \leq j \leq p$.

7. Carry out p new trials in parallel at the points $x^{k+j}, 1 \leq j \leq p$, calculated by the formulae

$$x^{k+j} = \frac{x_{t_j} + x_{t_j-1}}{2}, \quad \nu(x_{t_j-1}) \neq \nu(x_{t_j}),$$

$$x^{k+j} = \frac{x_{t_j} + x_{t_j-1}}{2} - \frac{\text{sign}(z_{t_j} - z_{t_j-1})}{2r_\nu}\left[\frac{|z_{t_j} - z_{t_j-1}|}{\mu_\nu}\right]^N,$$

$$\nu(x_{t_j-1}) = \nu(x_{t_j}) = \nu.$$

The algorithm stops if the condition $\Delta_{t_j} \leq \epsilon$ becomes true for at least one number $t_j, 1 \leq j \leq p$; here $\epsilon > 0$ has an order of magnitude of the desired coordinate accuracy.

This method of organizing parallel computing has the following justification. The characteristics of intervals $R(i)$ used in the index algorithm can be considered as probability measures of the global minimum point location in these intervals. Inequalities (11) arrange intervals according to their characteristics, and trials are carried out in parallel in the first p intervals with the largest probabilities. A detailed description of the algorithm convergence theory is presented in [10]. The results of comparison of the algorithm with other sequential and parallel global optimization algorithms have been presented in [12].

3   Parallel Algorithm for Mixed-Integer Problems

Now let us consider the case when the argument of the problem functions consists of two components: the vector y from the hyperinterval D and the vector u taking a finite (and not too large) set of possible values, i.e.

$$\min\{g_{m+1}(y, u) : y \in D, \ g_i(y, u) \leq 0, \ 1 \leq i \leq m\}, \tag{12}$$
$$D = \{a_j \leq y_j \leq b_j, \ 1 \leq j \leq N\}.$$

Such finite sets can characterize, for example, the variant of material, which the object is made from, the geometric sizes, or other quantities, which can belong to a standard discrete series, etc.

Let us number by the integer values $s, 1 \leq s \leq S$, all possible values of the vector u, i.e. juxtapose each considered value s with the vector u_s. Then, the considered problem can be written in the form

$$\min_{s \in \{1, \dots, S\}} \{\min\{g_{m+1}(y, u_s) : y \in D, \ g_i(y, u_s) \leq 0, \ 1 \leq i \leq m\}\}, \tag{13}$$
$$D = \{a_j \leq y_j \leq b_j, \ 1 \leq j \leq N\}.$$

Using the dimensionality reduction scheme with the evolvent $y(x), x \in [0, 1]$, one can superimpose each nested minimization problem with respect to y to a one-dimensional problem

$$\min\{g_{m+1}(y(x), u_s) : x \in [0, 1], \ g_i(y(x), u_s) \leq 0, \ 1 \leq i \leq m\}, s \in \{1, \dots, S\}.$$

Now let us consider the relation

$$Y(x) = y(x - E(x)), \ x \in [0, S],$$

mapping any point of the interval $[0, S]$ onto the domain D (the notation $E(x)$ corresponds to the integer part of the number x) and define the functions

$$g_i(x) = g_i(Y(x), u_{E(x)+1}), x \in [0, S],$$

having, in general, the jump discontinuities at the integer points $x_k = i, 1 \leq i \leq S - 1$. The values $z_k = g_\nu(y(x_k))$ from (5) at these points will be considered to be undefined, and the values of the indices – to equal to 0, i.e. $\nu(x_k) = 0$.

Using the introduced notations, one can reformulate the original problem as

$$\min\{g_{m+1}(x) : x \in [0, S], \ g_i(x) \leq 0, \ 1 \leq i \leq m\}. \tag{14}$$

As an illustration, Fig. 2 presents the plots of the functions corresponding to a problem

$$\min\{u^2(\sin(x) + \sin(10x/3)) : x \in [2.7, 7.5], u \in \{1, 2\}\}$$

with one continuous parameter x and one integer parameter u.

Applying the parallel index algorithm to solving the problem (14), we will find the solution of the problem (12). In this case the major part of trials will

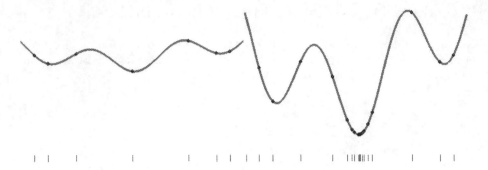

Fig. 2. Reduced mixed-integer global optimization problem

conducted in the subproblem, the solving of which corresponds to the solving of the initial problem (12). In the rest subproblems, only the minor part of trials will be performed since the solutions of these subproblems are the locally optimal ones. All the above is confirmed by Fig. 2, where the points of trials executed in the course of solving this problem are denoted by the dashes.

Thus, we have constructed the *Mixed-Integer Parallel Index Algorithm* (MIPIA) based on the reduction of the mixed-integer non-convex optimization problem to the non-convex optimization problem. The proposed computational scheme is based on the parallel index method for solving the continuous optimization problems and is not oriented onto any particular computational device. Here the parallel performing of several trials at different points of the search domain is one of key operations (see Step 7 of the algorithm), which can be implemented on CPU (with the use of OpenMP and/or MPI) as well as on GPU (with the use CUDA). The issues of the use of GPU for these purposes have been considered in details in [13,14]. This approach to the use of GPU has been applied in the implementation of the MIPIA algorithm as well.

4   Results of Experiments

The first series of experiments was conducted using the sequential version of the proposed algorithm in order to compare this one with well known methods of similar purpose.

Let us compare proposed MIPIA with a genetic algorithm for solving the mixed-integer global optimization problems implemented in Matlab Global Optimization Toolbox [15]. In Table 1, the numbers of trials required for solving the known test mixed-integer problems by these methods are presented. For both methods, the same accuracy of search 10^{-2} were used. These numerical experiments were conducted on a computer with Intel Core i5-7300 2.5 GHz processor and 8 Gb RAM under MS Windows 10. The results of experiments have demonstrated the advantage of MIPIA in the number of iterations as well as in the execution time.

Table 1. Comparison of MIPIA and GA

Test problem	GA		MIPIA	
	k	t	k	t
Problem 2 [16]	481	0.0601	417	0.04
Problem 3 [16]	1821	0.1130	3324	0.107
Problem 6 [16]	641	0.0510	118	0.001
Problem 1 [8]	481	0.1378	66	0.0007
Problem 2 [8]	481	0.0473	57	0.0006
Problem 7 [8]	841	0.0736	372	0.017

The next series of experiments were performed in order to evaluate the speedup of the parallel version of the proposed MIPIA algorithm with the use of CPU as well as GPU. In these experiments, a series of 100 mixed-integer test problems generated in a random way was solved. Computational experiments were carried out on Lobachevsky supercomputer. The node of supercomputer included two Intel Sandy Bridge E5-2660 2.2 GHz CPUs and 64 Gb RAM. The CPU had 8 cores, i.e. each node had a total of 16 cores and two NVIDIA Kepler K20X GPUs.

GKLS [17] is a well known generator of the test problems for the continuous multiextremal optimization. It allows generating the functions of arbitrary dimensionality with known properties (the number of local minima, the size of their domains of attraction, the global minimizer, etc.). This generator of multiextremal functions is often used for the investigations of the global optimization algorithms [18–22]. In Fig. 3(a) and (b), the contour plots of two-dimensional GKLS functions are presented. Figures also shows the points of the trials performed by the method until the required accuracy $\epsilon = 10^{-2}$ was achieved.

In the performed experiments, the GKLS generator was used as a base for the construction the mixed-integer problems. The rules allowing generating the test problems of this type consist in the following.

1. A continuous multiextremal function $\varphi(y), y \in D = \{a_j \leq y_j \leq b_j, 1 \leq j \leq N\}$ is generated with the use of the GKLS generator. The global minimum of this function is achieved at the known point $y' = (y'_1, ..., y'_N)$ and equals $\varphi(y') = -1$.
2. A concave mixed-integer function

$$h(y, u) = -2\left[\sum_{j=1}^{N}\left(\frac{y_j - y'_j}{b_j - a_j}\right)^2 + \sum_{j=1}^{M}\left(\frac{u_j - b_j}{b_j - a_j}\right)^2\right],$$

is generated where

$$y \in D = \{a_j \leq y_j \leq b_j, 1 \leq j \leq N\} \subset R^N,$$
$$u \in U = \{u_j \in \{a_j, ..., b_j\}, 1 \leq j \leq M\}.$$

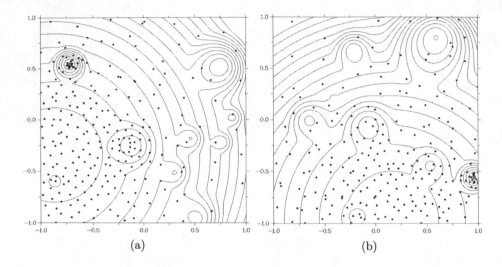

Fig. 3. Solving a two-dimensional problem using the index algorithm

This function has N continuous and M discrete parameters and achieves its minimum value at the point (y', b).

3. The coefficient

$$h_{max} = 4 - \min_{y,u} h(y, u), \ y \in D, u \in U.$$

is computed. It is obvious, that the minimum of a concave function $\mu(y, u)$ is located at one of the corner points of the search domain. Therefore, if the problem dimensionality is of the order of 10 it can be found by the brute force method.

4. A multiextremal mixed-integer function

$$f(y, u) = \left(\varphi(y) + \sum_{j=1}^{M} u_j \right) (h_{max} + h(y, u)).$$

is formed. By construction, $f(y, u)$ would take its minimum value at the point (y', b).

In the problems generated in our experiments, there were 5 discrete and 6 continuous parameters

$$y \in D = \{-1 \le y_j \le 1, 1 \le j \le 6\} \subset R^6,$$
$$u \in U = \{u_j \in \{-1, -1/3, 0, 1/3, 1\}, 1 \le j \le 5\}.$$

A hundred 11-dimensional mixed-integer problems of this type were generated in total. For the purpose of simulation of the computational complexity inherent to applied optimization problems, calculation of the objective function in all performed experiments was made more complex by additional calculations without changing the type of function and arrangement of its minima (series summation from 80 thousand elements). The accuracy of the search was equal to 10^{-2}.

In Table 2, the results of experiments on CPU with the use of OpenMP are presented subject to the number of employed threads p. Total 1, 8, and 16 threads were used. The average number of iterations K_{av} required to solve the problem, the average time of solving T_{av} (in seconds), the time speedup S, and iteration speedup s (with respect to the sequential run, i.e. for $p = 1$) are presented. In accordance with the parallelization scheme, the number of trials within a single iteration of the parallel algorithm was equal to the number of employed threads.

Table 2. The results of experiments on CPU

p	T_{av}	K_{av}	S	s
1	5520	3221023	...	...
8	1253	512314	4.4	6.3
16	717	209237	7.7	15.4

As one can see from Table 2, almost linear speedup in iterations and an significant speedup in the problem solving time have been observed. At that, the sequential algorithm spent almost 1.5 h in average to solve a problem.

In Table 3, the results of experiments on GPU with the use of CUDA are presented subject to the number of GPU threads employed. The average number of iterations K_{av} required to solve a problem, the average solving time T_{av} (in seconds), the time speedup S, and iteration speedup s (with respect to the full load of CPU on a cluster node) are presented.

Table 3. The results of experiments on GPU

p	T_{av}	K_{av}	S	s
256	33.6	1522	21.3	137
512	31.2	919	23.0	228
1024	30.2	412	23.7	508
2048	38.5	244	18.6	858

The results of experiments demonstrate almost the same time speedup and linear iteration speedup when using $p = 256, 512$, and 1024 threads. However, when using $p = 2048$ threads, the algorithm worktime increased but the number of iterations continued to decrease. This effect was explained by the fact that for parallel running of p trials GPU is used but for processing the results of the trials (which implies the processing of the whole search information accumulated during the preceding iterations) CPU is uses. And when employing $p = 2048$ GPU threads, the time, which is spent for the transfer and processing of the results of 2048 trials became comparable to the time of executing the trials that leads to the slowing down of the algorithm as a whole.

5   Conclusion

In the paper the results obtained in Lobachevsky State University of Nizhni Novgorod when developing and investigating the parallel global optimization algorithms for solving the multiextremal problems, in which some parameters are continuous and the others are the discrete ones are presented. An efficient parallel algorithm has been proposed for solving the problems of the specified class. In the sequential variant, this algorithm does not inferior to similar purpose algorithm implemented in Matlab Global Optimization Toolbox. In the parallel variant, the proposed algorithm allows the efficient implementations on CPU as well as on GPU. The numerical experiments on a series of 100 multiextremal mixed-integer test problems have been carried out convincingly demonstrating a good speedup of the algorithm with the use of GPU. Thus, the parallel algorithm with the use of GPU demonstrated the time speedup $S = 182$ relative to the sequential one and $S = 23.7$ relative to the algorithm fully employing two CPU on the cluster node.

Acknowledgments. This study was supported by the Russian Science Foundation, project No. 16-11-10150.

References

1. Anisimov, K.S., Savelyev, A.A., Kursakov, I.A., Lysenkov, A.V., Prakasha, P.S.: Optimization of BWB aircraft using parallel computing. Supercomputing Front. Innov. **5**(3), 93–97 (2018)
2. Romanov, S.Y.: Supercomputer simulations of nondestructive tomographic imaging with rotating transducers. Supercomputing Front. Innov. **5**(3), 98–102 (2018)
3. Kutov, D.C., Sulimov, A.V., Sulimov, V.B.: Supercomputer docking: investigation of low energy minima of protein-ligand complexes. Supercomputing Front. Innov. **5**(3), 134–137 (2018)
4. Burer, S., Letchford, A.N.: Non-convex mixed-integer nonlinear programming: a survey. Surv. Oper. Res. Manage. Sci. **17**, 97–106 (2012)
5. Boukouvala, F., Misener, R., Floudas, C.A.: Global optimization advances in mixed-integer nonlinear programming, MINLP, and constrained derivative-free optimization, CDFO. Eur. J. Oper. Res. **252**, 701–727 (2016)
6. Belotti, P., Lee, J., Liberti, L., Margot, F., Wächter, A.: Branching and bounds tightening techniques for non-convex MINLP. Optim. Methods Softw. **24**(4–5), 597–634 (2009)
7. Vigerske, S., Gleixner, A.: SCIP: global optimization of mixed-integer nonlinear programs in a branch-and-cut framework. Optim. Methods Softw. **33**(3), 563–593 (2018)

8. Deep, K., Singh, K.P., Kansal, M.L., Mohan, C.: A real coded genetic algorithm for solving integer and mixed integer optimization problems. Appl. Math. Comput. **212**(2), 505–518 (2009)

9. Schlüter, M., Egea, J.A., Banga, J.R.: Extended ant colony optimization for non-convex mixed integer nonlinear programming. Comput. Oper. Res. **36**(7), 2217–2229 (2009)

10. Strongin, R.G., Sergeyev, Y.D.: Global Optimization with Non-convex Constraints. Sequential and Parallel Algorithms. Kluwer Academic Publishers, Dordrecht (2000). ISBN: 978-1-4615-4677-1

11. Sergeyev, Y.D., Strongin, R.G., Lera, D.: Introduction to Global Optimization Exploiting Space-Filling Curves. Springer, New York (2013). https://doi.org/10.1007/978-1-4614-8042-6

12. Sovrasov, V.: Comparison of several stochastic and deterministic derivative-free global optimization algorithms. In: Khachay, M., Kochetov, Y., Pardalos, P. (eds.) MOTOR 2019. LNCS, vol. 11548, pp. 70–81. Springer, Cham (2019). https://doi.org/10.1007/978-3-030-22629-9_6

13. Barkalov, K., Gergel, V.: Parallel global optimization on GPU. J. Global Optim. **66**(1), 2–20 (2016)

14. Barkalov, K., Gergel, V., Lebedev, I.: Solving global optimization problems on GPU cluster. In: Simos, T.E. (ed.) ICNAAM 2015, AIP Conference Proceedings, vol. 1738, art. no. 400006 (2016)

15. https://www.mathworks.com/help/gads/mixed-integer-optimization.html

16. Floudas, C.A., Pardalos, P.M.: Handbook of Test Problems in Local and Global Optimization. Springer, Boston (1999). https://doi.org/10.1007/978-1-4757-3040-1

17. Gaviano, M., Kvasov, D.E., Lera, D., Sergeyev, Y.D.: Software for generation of classes of test functions with known local and global minima for global optimization. ACM Trans. Math. Softw. **29**(4), 469–480 (2003)

18. Paulavičius, R., Sergeyev, Y., Kvasov, D., Žilinskas, J.: Globally-biased DISIMPL algorithm for expensive global optimization. J. Global Optim. **59**(2–3), 545–567 (2014)

19. Sergeyev, Y.D., Kvasov, D.E.: A deterministic global optimization using smooth diagonal auxiliary functions. Commun. Nonlinear. Sci. Numer. Simul. **21**(1–3), 99–111 (2015)

20. Lebedev, I., Gergel, V.: Heterogeneous parallel computations for solving global optimization problems. Procedia Comput. Sci. **66**, 53–62 (2015)

21. Gergel, V., Sidorov, S.: A two-level parallel global search algorithm for solution of computationally intensive multiextremal optimization problems. In: Malyshkin, V. (ed.) PaCT 2015. LNCS, vol. 9251, pp. 505–515. Springer, Cham (2015). https://doi.org/10.1007/978-3-319-21909-7_49

22. Barkalov, K., Strongin, R.: Solving a set of global optimization problems by the parallel technique with uniform convergence. J. Global Optim. **71**(1), 21–36 (2018)

Parallel Ray Tracing Algorithm for Numerical Analysis of Laser Radiation Absorption in a Plasma

Alexey Kotelnikov$^{(\boxtimes)}$, Ilia Tsygvintsev, Mikhail Yakobovsky, and Vladimir Gasilov

Keldysh Institute of Applied Mathematics (Russian Academy of Sciences), Moscow 125047, Russia
kotelnikov@phystech.edu, iliatsygvintsev@gmail.com, lira@imamod.ru, dipm132013@gmail.com

Abstract. An original algorithm was developed for ray tracing across unstructured 3D grid. It is aimed at calculation of a laser energy deposition in plasma. A laser beam is represented as a set of individual rays whose path depends on a plasma density ratio per plasma critical density. A ray may be refracted while going through high density gradient regions. In general case rays approximating a laser beam have to be recalculated at every time step. Therefore calculation of a laser energy absorption in related plasma dynamics simulations require significant computational resources. We present a new ray-tracing algorithm for laser radiation modeling which can be implemented effective via HPC.

The set of rays built in a computational domain provides the base for the grid-characteristic computation of radiation transport in the plasma simulations using MPI parallel technique and grid decomposition. The algorithm is implemented as a C++ code and incorporated in 3D magnetohydrodynamic (MHD) Eulerian code [1]. Tracing of different rays within a single MPI-process is carried out in parallel with the use of OpenMP threads. The developed algorithm provides accounting for the anisotropy of the radiation field in complex multiscale 3D MHD simulations.

Keywords: 3D laser-produced plasma model · Plasma dynamics · Ray-tracing algorithm · Laser ray propagation and refraction · Rational arithmetic calculations

1 Introduction

Radiative energy transfer is an important part of high-temperature gas-dynamic processes. The thermal radiation begins to affect the heat exchange significantly, when the gas temperature is about $10^4 K$. At very high temperatures, the radiation of the substance affects its dynamics as well. Such phenomena are, for

© Springer Nature Switzerland AG 2019
V. Voevodin and S. Sobolev (Eds.): RuSCDays 2019, CCIS 1129, pp. 110–120, 2019.
https://doi.org/10.1007/978-3-030-36592-9_10

example, processes in stellar atmospheres, space vehicle reentry, high-current discharge, laser plasma [2]. A problem of today is the development of powerful ultraviolet and soft X-ray sources for nanotechnology, controlled fusion, laboratory astrophysics and fundamental studies of the matter properties under extreme conditions. All these tasks require high-precision predictive modeling with taking into account real-life the geometry and materials. This type of computations involves coupled radiation gas dynamic (RGD) problems, as gas-dynamic parameters are influenced by radiative heat transfer, and thermal radiation field depends on the emissivity and opacity of the gas. High-resolution computation of RGD fields by the grid method (the most widely used presently) is a very time-consuming computing process because of the large dimensions of the grid systems of equations solved. High-performance computing makes available mass calculations, and thus provides successful practical use of RGD models in the analysis of experimental data and the development of new technologies with the use of radiation sources.

1.1 Problem Statement

Radiation heat transfer processes in plasma dynamics are usually described by stationary transport equation [3] for the spectral intensity of the radiation

$$I_\nu(\mathbf{r}, \mathbf{\Omega})d\nu d\Omega = h\nu c f(\mathbf{r}, \nu, \mathbf{\Omega}, t)d\nu d\Omega \tag{1}$$

which can be written as:

$$(\mathbf{\Omega}, \mathbf{\nabla})I_\nu(\mathbf{r}, \mathbf{\Omega}) = k_\nu'(I_{\nu eq}(\mathbf{r}) - I_\nu(\mathbf{r})) \tag{2}$$

where f is the photon distribution function depending on the radius vector of the observation point $\mathbf{r}$, photon frequency ν, flight direction $\mathbf{\Omega}$, and time t; k_ν' is effective absorption factor corrected for the stimulated emission; and $I_{\nu eq}(\mathbf{r})$ is the specific emissivity of the material (the amount of energy emitted in unit volume per unit of time into one steradian).

Emissivity and opacity of the medium depends on its temperature and density as well as the frequency of the emitted and absorbed photons. The general solution of the transport Eq. (2) is given in [3]:

$$I_\nu(s) = \int_{s_0}^{s} k_\nu' I_{\nu eq} e^{-\int_{s'}^{s} k_\nu' ds''} ds' + I_{\nu 0} e^{-\int_{s_0}^{s} k_\nu' ds''} \tag{3}$$

Here $I_\nu(s)$ is the intensity $I_\nu(\mathbf{r}, \mathbf{\Omega})$ as a function of the coordinate s along the characteristic ("ray"), $I_{\nu 0}$ is an integration constant (the intensity of the incoming radiation at the border). Finding the radiation intensity at a point s is reduced to numerical quadrature (i.e. integration along the ray). If the emitting body is of a limited size, integration should be done from the boundary of the body s_0 to the point s. The direct numerical solution of Eq. (2) requires significant computing resources. It depends on three spatial coordinates, two angles, and the frequency of photons. Multigroup approximation is applied for spectral dependence of optical properties. The spectral range under study is divided into finite number of parts ("groups"), and Eq. (2) is solved for each group of this partition independently of all the others. Calculation formulas are identical for all the spectral groups and differ only in the values k_ν' and $I_{\nu eq}$, which are assumed to be independent of the photon energy within each group. The total intensity is calculated by summing over the spectral groups. Correct computation of the energy balance requires just a few dozens of spectral groups in the majority of applications. However, when the object of study is the radiation spectrum itself, it can take from several hundred to several thousand spectral groups for its accurate reproduction.

Plasma dynamic problems typically include modeling strongly nonlinear and non-stationary physical processes with very different characteristic scales in space and time. We use 3D irregular grids with variable cell size for the numerical solution of such problems. Grid-characteristic method for the radiation transport equation requires construction an additional grid of rays and data interpolation between the two grids. Both of these tasks are non-trivial, especially in the case of a distributed multiprocessor system, wherein a set of computational subdomains is stored and processed at different computing nodes. The process of energy transfer via radiation is essentially nonlocal (each point in the computational domain effects any other), thus a ray may cross several subdomains. Integration in Eq. (3) needs synchronization over the ray parts in different subdomains, and if possible, computational load balancing. This paper presents an original algorithm for efficient ray tracing, and radiation transport calculation when using distributed computational grid of large dimension on high-performance computers.

2   Ray Tracing Algorithm

2.1   State of the Art in Ray Tracing and Related Works

Ray tracing is widely used in computer graphics for scenes rendering, volume ray casting etc. A comprehensive discussion of appropriate algorithms can be found in [4]. In any case the aim is generating a 2D image of a 3D object based on its mathematical description and/or discretization. Thermal radiation of the matter is not considered in graphic applications. Quite the contrary, in RGD simulations we need essentially 3D ray – grid interaction with intensive data exchange, as well as detailed description of the radiation emission and absorption.

As for physical applications, the main up-to-date field of ray tracing is geometrical optics also referred to as ray optics. An example of well elaborated product of this kind is Ray Optics Module in COMSOL Multiphysics® Software Product Suite [5]. This module is designed for ray tracing simulations in optically large systems, including rich physics (e.g. absorbing media, aberration evaluation, circular and linear wave retarders, dielectric films, diffraction gratings, diffuse scattering, ideal depolarizers, linear polarizers, mueller matrices, reflection and refraction at material discontinuities, specular reflection, polarized and partially coherent radiation, etc). The application area of the product is rather wide; nevertheless ray model of thermal radiation (as described above) is not implemented, and coupled simulations involve only heat transfer, but not gas dynamics.

We also note the work [6] describing parallel ray tracing algorithm for laser light propagation. The algorithm was incorporated in arbitrary Lagrangian-Eulerian hydrocode with adaptive mesh refinement. The authors point out some computational problems. First, ambiguities may arise when solving quadratic and quartic equations for intersections of the parabolic ray trajectories with faces of hexahedral cells. If a ray passes close to edges and/or corners, incorrect selection of the exit face will result in a lost ray in the next cell as no valid exit points will be found. We overcome this obstacle by use of rational arithmetic providing exact solution. Another problem concerns load balancing issues. Some processors may hold subdomains that are traversed by few if any rays and may remain idle during a given laser ray tracing step.

2.2   Use of Rational Arithmetic

We consider an irregular 3D grid of non-degenerate star polyhedron (wherein an internal point exists, which can be connected to each vertex by a segment, completely lying inside the polyhedron). At the beginning each polyhedron is broken into a set of tetrahedrons, their union equal to the original polyhedron. Next we construct the intersection of a ray (straight line determined by two points or a point and a direction vector) with the set of tetrahedrons. Solving this problem with the standard machine floating-point arithmetic is attended with some difficulties. Firstly, it's impossible in the general case to detect exactly if a point or a segment belongs to the given triangle. Secondly, it is known that the result of calculation with finite precision depends on the order of operations. This complicates the algorithm for matching the coordinate values along the line for the adjacent segments of the ray.

Both types of rounding errors may lead to incorrect ray topology, namely wrong segment ordering, and/or shifted segments with gaps and overlaps. Inaccurate calculation of a segment length is also possible in the case of ill-conditioned linear system describing relative position of a line and a triangle. Because of this, simple mathematical expression defining the intersection of geometric primitives cannot be used directly. One has to treat a variety of special cases, resulting in expansion of the code and significant debugging troubles. For example, in [6] such ambiguities are removed by introducing a stochastic procedure slightly perturbing the ray entry point within the entry face.

Our solution is to use rational numbers of arbitrary precision instead of floating-point arithmetic. The exact rational calculations allow transfer of mathematical formulas into code without examining the accuracy of the calculation result and all the intermediate values. This radically reduces the size of the program, makes it trivial to debug, and practically ensure the code correctness. This is due to elimination of many additional check-ups. The result of linear system solution in rational numbers as well as the absence of solution are defined precisely and do not depend on the order of operations. A degenerate system is ignored, because it means that the line is parallel to the triangle under consideration, and the solution will be found for some other face. Digit capacity of long numbers required to store the exact solution of the system of three linear equations depends only on the digit capacity of the coefficients. The initial point coordinates are stored in double format, which determines the capacity of their rational representation. If the initial capacity of the numerator is n, and that of the denominator is m, then the capacity of the solution is $6 + 3n + 57m$. We used for the calculations the formula of a non-degenerate linear system solution via determinants. The coefficients of the matrix are calculated as the difference of two rational numbers, and this numbers are obtained directly from the initial data and have the above digital capacity.

The operations with the numerator and denominator of rational numbers are implemented with the use of the library for integers of unlimited range cbignum [7]. The rational arithmetic operations are more time consuming and requires a larger amount of RAM than the floating-point operations, but relevance and effectiveness of the proposed technique increases with the increase in available HPC resources.

2.3   Parallel Technique

The ray tracing algorithm works with distributed grids and independently process each pair (tetrahedron – ray). The result of one ray tracing at each MPI process is an unordered set of segments, which are the intersection of the given line with 3D computational grid cells in a subdomain related to the process. Tracing different rays within a single MPI process is carried out in parallel with the use of OpenMP threads by giving each thread its own set of lines.

Additional MARPLE3D ray-tracing solvers have been developed to implement calculations on distributed grids. These solvers perform splitting of a ray into some number of portions corresponding to the domains the ray passes through as well as building a one-dimensional grid along every splitted ray. A part of ray filled by ray-cell intersections with strict incidence between each serial intersections is called a segment. In fact, each segment is a sequence of intersections without information of their inner structure. That means any segment has no inlet, outlet or crossing a boundary between any domains of the distributed grid. Each ray includes an indefinite amount of segments depending on convexity of the external surface and mesh distribution topology. Generally the amount of segments is a single per mesh part or zero for some mesh parts aside the ray. To find out an order of all segments on the ray they are stored at a MPI process with zero rank by MPI routines blocking until the process has sent a sorted sequence of segments back. The described algorithm of segments ordering is non-optimal because of the usage of blocking MPI routines for each ray. Time losses caused by blocking MPI routines are partially compensated by information stored in a segment to be a very compact. The information includes two points at a ray represented by a distance from a start point at the ray and a pair of numbers for a mesh part and a ray.

When integrating Eq. (3) along a ray, we assume that the properties of the matter are constant within each segment. Then the solution in the n-th spectral group at the interval $[s_i, s_{i+1}]$ is given by

$$\begin{cases} I_n(s_{i+1}) = I_{neq} + (I_n(s_i) - I_{neq})e^{-k_n(s_{i+1}-s_i)}, \\ \quad I_n(s_0) = 0 \end{cases} \tag{4}$$

The values k_n and I_{neq} depend on the computed density and temperature of the matter (and via these on the time in non-stationary case).

Solver's work is to integrate the Eq. (4) for each segment belonged to a MPI process. When integrated from a start value to a final value the solver sends the final value for a next segment's owner to use it as a start value. At the 1D mesh preparation stage each MPI-process constructs an pipeline for the solver to send values as earlier as possible. The pipeline sequence of segments processing proceeds according to the following rules. First, the solver integrates segments without dependency of a previous neighbor. Then, segments with of both neighbors are integrated. Finally, the solver integrates other segments not needed for any MPI-process.

2.4 Scalability

A film of metal hydrogen is heated by laser in this series of numerical experiments. 26 laser radiation sources located around the plate to heat it at same time from different angles. An algorithm's total calculation time is made up of a 3D mesh preparation time, a time taken to build one-dimensional meshes being specific for each ray and a time of an required count of iterations.

The following Tables 1, 2 and 3 contain time measures of the algorithm for different numbers of 3D cells and 1D rays. These graphs show acceleration of ray mesh preparation part and solver iterations on the prepared mesh. This X axis shows MPI-processes amount p and the Y axis shows acceleration $S_p = \frac{T_1}{T_p}$ when T_p is a time of a considered stage of the algorithm. 12 MPI-processes are launched per each node [8] (Figs. 1 and 2).

Table 1. Time measures data, 4535920 3D cells, 25 ray per beam

Amount of MPI-processes	3D mesh preparation, min	1D meshes preparation, min	Solver work, min
1	75.9	17.9	33.8
12	31.3	2.7	8.3
24	17.0	1.8	4.4
48	9.0	1.3	2.2
96	3.1	0.8	1.1

Table 2. Time measures data, 4535920 3D cells, 961 ray per beam

Amount of MPI-processes	3D mesh preparation, min	1D meshes preparation, min	Solver work, min
1	518.3	502.0	78.9
12	110.6	84.3	8.7
48	68.8	61.8	2.3
96	54.8	53.6	1.2

Table 3. Time measures data, 36164352 3D cells, 25 ray per beam

Amount of MPI-processes	3D mesh preparation, min	1D meshes preparation, min	Solver work, min
1	245.0	115.7	604.5
12	756.1	11.6	57.1
48	179.0	4.2	18.8
96	64.4	3.4	10.1

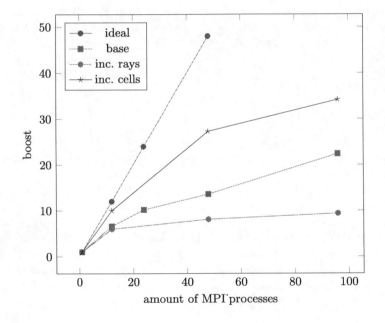

Fig. 1. Acceleration of ray mesh preparation part

The multigroup spectral approximation fits for the classical SIMD scheme: "single instruction – multiple data streams processing", which allows efficient use of pipeline accelerators.

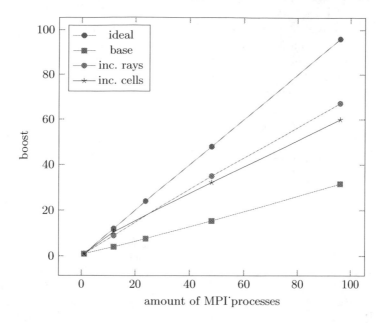

Fig. 2. Acceleration of solver's calculation part

3 Applications

3.1 Post-processing the Simulation Results, Allowing a Direct Comparison with Experimental Data

Computer simulation provides a three-dimensional spatial distribution of plasma density and temperature which are not directly measured in the experiments. In the same time the registration of plasma radiation is one of the major diagnostic methods [9] in state-of-the-art experimental physics. Thus comparison of simulation results versus experimental data is a challenge which can be mitigated by means of constructing special post-processing tools. Experimental studies of the spatial characteristics of ultraviolet and soft X-ray plasma radiation are performed using imaging systems based on a pinhole camera [9], which is a small diameter hole in an opaque to X-ray screen. Image is registered on X-ray film. Different filters are used to determine the spectral composition and the absolute intensity of the radiation. This method provides information about spatial variation of the plasma electron temperature. A numerical model of a pinhole camera has been created using the ray tracing algorithm described above. This tool is designed for the construction of two-dimensional image of a plasma object based on the computed temperature and density. This image can be directly compared with experimental pinhole images.

Another important post-processing technique is the estimation of the output radiation in different directions. It is carried out by means of ray tracing and calculating of the radiation field intensity with respect to the gas-dynamic parameters at prescribed time points. The obtained values are compared with the readings of vacuum X-ray diodes with different filters.

These post-processing tools were applied for theoretical support of the experiments with wire-array Z-pinches at the pulsed-power machine Angara-5-1 (TRINITY, Moscow region) [10].

3.2   Simulation of Laser Light Propagation

The results of the hydrogen plate explosion by laser ray energy is shown 3. We consider a model problem of a laser pre-pulse action on a thin film of a cryogenic hydrogen in experiments like that described in [11]. The initial density of the plate is $0.086\,\mathrm{g/cm^3}$. A centre of the plate is heated by a single thin laser impulse with total power as $0.2\,\mathrm{MW}$ distributed by Gauss with $D_{e^2} = 5\,\mu\mathrm{m}$ at an angle 45°. in a plane (Y, Z). Electron temperature distribution is shown at the moment 0.88 ns near before the end of the impulse. Calculating the laser radiation absorption concerns both fundamental and applied research: inertial confinement fusion, wakefield acceleration of particles, laser material processing, monochromatic short-wave radiation sources for nanotechnology (Fig. 3).

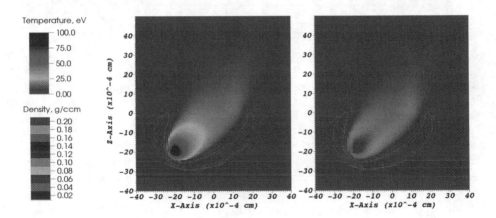

Fig. 3. Electron and ion temperature, KeV

The ray optics model for laser radiation propagation through the matter approximates the laser beam by a set of individual rays, each carrying a certain fraction of the beam energy [12]. When the laser light traverses the plasma, in general the rays can be refracted and lose some energy due to absorption in a matter. The equations defining the ray path and the change of its energy are the following:

$$\begin{cases} \frac{d\mathbf{r}}{d\tau} = n\mathbf{s}, \\ \frac{d(n\mathbf{s})}{d\tau} = \frac{1}{2}\nabla n^2, \\ \frac{dP}{d\tau} = -n\mu P \end{cases} \tag{5}$$

Here $\mathbf{r}$ is the radius vector along the ray, $\mathbf{s}$ is a unit vector in the direction of the beam propagation, $n = Re\sqrt{\epsilon}$ is the refractive index ($n > 0$), P is power in the ray, $\mu = \frac{\omega}{2c}Im\epsilon$ is the absorbtion coefficient, τ is the coordinate along the ray, ω is the circular frequency of the radiation, c is the velocity of light in free space, $\epsilon(\mathbf{r}, t, \omega)$ is the complex plasma permittivity.

Boundary conditions are imposed at each ray as consistent with the specific task. The essential difficulty for the solution of the system (5) by ray tracing method is due to refraction changing the ray path. Therefore the rays need dynamic adjustment. This can be overcome by using so-called short characteristics, when the ray path is constructed from segments of fixed lines in each cell is computation grid.

n^2 represented by a piecewise linear function with a constant gradient vector at each tetrahedron of the 3D grid so each ray path consists of parabolic and linear curves with common vertexes at surfaces. The gradient vector is completely defined by values at four vertexes of a tetrahedron.

$$\forall i \neq j \in [1 \dots 4] n^2(\mathbf{p_i}) = n^2(\mathbf{p_j}) + (\nabla n^2, \mathbf{p_i} - \mathbf{p_j}) \qquad (6)$$

Here p_i is a one of four different points of the tetrahedron. The system 6 has only a unique solution for ∇n^2 because of nonzero volume of the tetrahedron. Also coefficient $n\mu$ defining ray energy absorption is approximated by a piecewise linear function by the same way. In the "parabolic" case a ray tracing algorithm additionally incorporates a square root calculation for any rational number with a result also represented by a rational number.

4   Conclusion

An original algorithm for the ray tracing across distributed unstructured 3D grid has been developed. Accurate rational calculations using integers of arbitrary range were applied for the intersection of rays with tetrahedrons in order to avoid rounding problems. In contrast to other ray tracing approaches, it was applied not only to image processing but to radiative energy transfer in high-temperature gas dynamics. The resulting set of rays was used for the grid-characteristic scheme of radiative energy transfer calculation in the high-temperature plasma simulations using MPI technique and domain-decomposition approach for parallel computing. The algorithm was incorporated into the 3D Radiative - MHD code [12]. It is shown via numerical experiments that the algorithm provides a basis for building of effective parallel computation tool. The application fields are the following: post-processing the simulation results for the comparison with experimental data; modeling of laser light propagation with refraction and absorption in matter.

References

1. Olkhovskaya, O.G., Kotelnikov, A.M., Yakobovskiy, M.V., Gasilov, V.A.: Parallel ray tracing algorithm for numerical analysis in radiative media physics. Adv. Parallel Comput. **32**, 137–146 (2018). https://doi.org/10.3233/978-1-61499-843-3-137
2. Chetveruskin, B.N.: Dynamics of Radiative Gas, Moscow (1992). (in Russian)
3. Zel'dovich, Y.B., Raizer, Y.P.: Physics of Shock Waves and High-Temperature Hydrodynamic Phenomena. Academic Press, New York (1968). Dover Publication Inc., Mineola, New York 2002
4. Wald, I., et al.: State of the art in ray tracing animated scenes. Comput. Graph. Forum **28**(6), 1691–1722 (2009)
5. Simulate Ray Tracing in Optically Large Systems with the Ray Optics Module. http://www.comsol.com/ray-optics-module
6. Masters, N.D., et al.: Laser ray tracing in a parallel arbitrary Lagrangian-Eulerian adaptive mesh refinement hydrocode. J. Phys: Conf. Ser. **244**, 032022 (2010)
7. Shakirov, R.N.: C++ class for integers of unlimited range. http://www.imach.uran.ru/cbignum
8. K100 supercomputer resources. http://kiam.ru/MVS/resourses/k100.html
9. Pergament, M.I.: Research Methods in Experimental Physics: tutorial, Dolgopudnyi (2010). (in Russian)
10. Boldarev, A.S., et al.: Methods and results of studies of the radiation spectra of megampere Z-Pinches at the angara-5-1 facility. Plasma Phys. Rep. **41**(2), 178–181 (2015)
11. Liao, Q., et al.: Enhanced laser proton acceleration by target ablation on a femtosecond laser system. Phys. Plasmas **25**, 063109 (2018). https://doi.org/10.1063/1.5025239
12. Tsygvintsev, I.P., et al.: Mesh-ray model and method for calculating the laser radiation absorption. Math. Models Comput. Simul. **8**(4), 382–390 (2016)

Porting CUDA-Based Molecular Dynamics Algorithms to AMD ROCm Platform Using HIP Framework: Performance Analysis

Evgeny Kuznetsov[1] and Vladimir Stegailov[1,2,3]($\boxtimes$) (iD)

[1] National Research University Higher School of Economics, Moscow, Russia
`v.stegailov@hse.ru`
[2] Joint Institute for High Temperatures of RAS, Moscow, Russia
[3] Moscow Institute of Physics and Technology, Dolgoprudny, Russia

Abstract. The use of graphics processing units (GPU) in computer data processing tasks has long ceased to be an unusual event. However, now GPU computing is nearly synonymous with CUDA, a proprietary framework for developing applications for Nvidia's GPU devices. It provides comprehensive documentation and excellent development tools. Meanwhile, the main competitor of Nvidia in the market for the production of GPU devices, the AMD company is developing its own Radeon Open Compute (ROCm) platform that features an application programming interface compatible with CUDA. The primary objective of this work is to investigate whether ROCm provides a worthy alternative to CUDA in the field of GPU computing. The work has two sub-objectives: the description of the programmers experience investigation during porting classical molecular dynamics algorithms from CUDA to ROCm platform and performance benchmarking of initial and resulting programs on GPU devices with modern architectures (Pascal, Vega10, Vega20).

Keywords: GPU computing · Parallel computing · CUDA · ROCm · Molecular dynamics

1 Introduction

Parallelization of computationally intensive algorithms on graphics accelerators is an integral part of the development of high-performance software. There are quite a number of libraries for developing code for graphics processors, such as OpenMP, OpenCL, OpenACC. They allow using the same code to compile programs for both the GPU from different manufacturers and the CPU. However, for the most part, they provide too high-level abstractions, and in tasks where performance is critical, the only choice is specialized GPGPU language-based programming models, such as CUDA and ROCm. Only they, due to low-level optimizations and the use of features of each platform, allow achieving the highest possible performance.

© Springer Nature Switzerland AG 2019
V. Voevodin and S. Sobolev (Eds.): RuSCDays 2019, CCIS 1129, pp. 121–130, 2019.
https://doi.org/10.1007/978-3-030-36592-9_11

CUDA is a platform for writing applications for general-purpose computing on graphics processing units (GPGPU) designed by Nvidia. It was released about 11 years ago and made a long path. It has mature driver and runtime support, great debugging and profiling tools, detailed documentation and samples. Almost every algorithm that has high computational complexity and parallelization possibility was implemented in CUDA.

In contrast, ROCm is a part of the AMD's "Boltzmann Initiative" announced in 2015. At the moment, ROCm is barely known platform for developing GPGPU applications that may run only on the specific subset of AMD graphics processing units [1]. It has a limited operating system (OS) support too: only a few Linux based OS are supported [1]. Besides, it has insufficient documentation and debugging support. So, ROCm is just at the beginning of its path and is developing rather quickly (e.g., version 1.9 has been announced on 15 September 2018 and version 2.3 has been announced on 12 April 2019). However, already now AMD GPUs have enough computational power to compete on equal terms with Nvidia GPUs [2].

An appealing aspect of the ROCm platform is its open-source character that improves portability and corresponds to the best practices of community codes development.

Moreover, AMD's graphics accelerators have another important advantage. Scientific calculations mainly use double-precision floating point arithmetic, whose performance in graphics chips is artificially limited by manufacturers to encourage the purchase of much more expensive devices. For most AMD GPUs, this limitation is significantly lower than that of Nvidia, which makes it possible for enthusiasts to use devices of the middle price segment to develop high-tech software.

This work aims to perform a readiness review of the ROCm platform to production development by porting one real-world CUDA application on the ROCm platform and evaluating performance differences between them.

As an example of a real-world CUDA application CoMD-CUDA is taken. CoMD [3] is a mimi-application that represents a reference implementation of conventional classical molecular dynamics algorithms and workloads. CoMD-CUDA [4] is a CUDA implementation of this mini-application.

The choice of this mini-application is not accidental. The tasks of classical molecular dynamics provide about 20–30% of the load of the largest supercomputers in the world [5], a significant part of which have a heterogeneous architecture and use GPUs [6]. Therefore, this class of algorithms deserves a focused consideration.

2   Literature Review

According to Jon Peddie Research press release [7], discrete AMD GPUs occupy a significant market share (Table 1). However, they are mainly used only for games and for solving specific tasks, such as cryptocurrency mining and 3D rendering, while they have significant potential in the field of general-purpose computing.

Table 1. Discrete GPU market share

Supplier	Q2'18	Q3'18	Q3'17-Q3'18
AMD	25.7%	36.1%	27.2%
Nvidia	74.3%	63.9%	72.8%

The ROCm platform as a relatively new technology is a rare subject in the articles devoted to performance studies of parallel algorithms on GPU. No one has yet made a thorough comparison of the performance of the ROCm platform with the CUDA platform. Sometimes (e.g. see [8]) this tends to be caused by the complexity of the installation and testing processes.

When it comes to cross-platform analysis, most authors direct their attention to comparing the performance of the CUDA platform and the Open Computing Language (OpenCL) heterogeneous computing framework. A thorough research [9] was made to find out if OpenCL technology can provide efficiency comparable to CUDA. The answer is yes, but it will require the developer to make complex adjustments to the program execution parameters. Besides, the process of porting CUDA application to OpenCL may be even more complicated, but this aspect of the study was not reported.

Another limitation of the OpenCL technology is the inability to use architectural features such as AMD's global data share and Nvidia's inline PTX assembly. It is a fairly common practice to have independent, optimized for each platform implementation of bottlenecks in the program.

Interestingly enough for the purposes of this paper, the article [2] is devoted to comparing the performance of all three GPU programming frameworks supported by the ROCm platform: HIP, OpenCL, and HC++. According to it, the following conclusions can be drawn:

- HIP is the best performing high-level framework from choices that ROCm support.
- HIP does not add any noticeable overhead to the workloads and the execution times comparing to the corresponding CUDA implementation.

In addition, the authors compare the speed of the two vendor implementations of deep neural networks for the CUDA and ROCm architectures: cuDNN and MIOpen, respectively. The implementations of both manufacturers on devices similar in their reported single precision floating point calculation capabilities showed approximately equivalent timings. In this work we present similar results for hybrid MD algorithms.

3   Methods

A vast number of parallel algorithms and applications have been developed using the CUDA platform. To facilitate their porting process, ROCm provides a HIP framework [10], which provides CUDA-compatible API, as well as the *hipify* tool for semi-automatic translation of CUDA runtime library calls to ROCm calls. Moreover, the HIP platform allows executing the resulting code on both AMD devices and Nvidia graphics accelerators. In the latter case, the functions of the HIP library are simple wrappers over the corresponding functions of CUDA, which allows developing code for CUDA-compatible devices with near-zero overhead [2].

The first phase of this work is porting the CoMD-CUDA application to the ROCm platform using the HIP library. It includes several sub-steps:

1. Using the *hipify* tool to translate CUDA runtime library calls.
2. Revision of the GPU kernels under the architectural features of the ROCm platform.
3. Creation a cross-platform (AMD/Nvidia) CMake build project.

The second phase consists in analyzing the performance of the resulting application on several graphics accelerators from AMD and Nvidia manufacturers of the same class. The list of used video cards and their brief characteristics presented in Table 2.

Table 2. The comparison of main features of GPUs considered

	RX480	Vega 56	Radeon VII	GTX 1070
Manufacturer	AMD	AMD	AMD	Nvidia
Stream processors	2304	3584	3840	1920
Base frequency	1120 MHz	1156 MHz	1750 MHz	1506 MHz
Memory size	4 Gb	8 Gb	16 Gb	8 Gb
Memory type	GDDR5	HBM2	HBM2	GDDR5

In case the results have an inexplicable variation in execution time, a more thorough study of the performance drop-down by profiling is needed. Moreover, the CoMD-CUDA application is hard-wired for optimal performance for the GK110 graphics chip. Thus, the comparison will be incomplete without optimization for the architecture features of AMD GPUs. This step, in turn, requires some sophisticated register and shared memory usage analysis [11], which is supposed to be performed using the AMD architecture assembly code investigation.

ROCm uses Heterogeneous Compute Compiler (HCC) for compilation both host and device code. It is based on the open-source Clang C++ compiler and Low Level Virtual Machine (LLVM) framework [12] that provides powerful optimization possibilities. For the purposes of this study, it is interesting to compare HCC code generation quality with NVIDIA proprietary CUDA Compiler (NVCC). To accomplish this goal, a side by side examination of the generated NVCC and HCC codes are made.

The selected CoMD-CUDA application is best suited for all phases of work. It implements several different approaches to perform modeling in molecular dynamics problems [4]. The source code contains a wide range of operations, such as working with shared memory, double precision arithmetic, atomic operations, synchronization of threads, cross warp data exchange and asynchronous execution, which fully covers all typical scenarios of using GPU. Thus, a comparison of the performance of the two platforms using the CoMD-CUDA can be considered more relevant than when conducting synthetic tests.

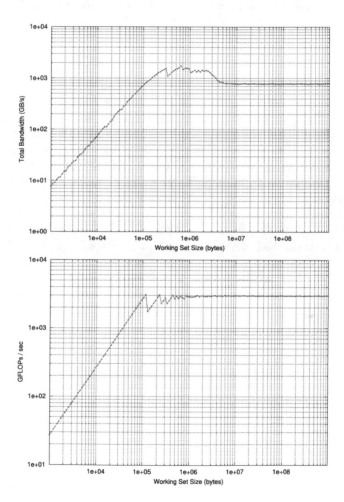

Fig. 1. ERT memory bandwidth and ERT FLOPS/sec for the case of 64 threads/640 blocks.

4   Results

Since the HPC community started to pay more attention not only to peak performance, but also to such parameters as memory throughput and caches, many other metrics and models became available to evaluate the performance effectiveness. In this paper we use the Berkeley lab's Empirical Roofline Toolkit [13]. This intuitive model bounds the floating point peak computation performance, the memory bandwidth and the arithmetic intensity, also taking into account such effects as caching, non-uniform memory access and instruction-level parallelism. The results for the newest Radeon VII GPU are presented on Figs. 1 and 2.

The CUDA-version of the ERT kernel has been hipified without any problems. However the current version of HCC compiler (ROCm version 2.2) can not properly detect FMA operation in the ERT kernel and only manual inclusion of these assembler instruction in the kernel allowed us getting full computational performance of Radeon VII (3 TFLOPS/sec). In this case the memory bandwidth is maximized as well and reaches 77% of the theoretical value of 1 TB/sec.

This paper addresses the gap in the area of developing high-performance GPGPU applications by comparing two modern GPGPU platforms: CUDA and ROCm. Due to the novelty and insufficient prevalence of the ROCm platform, this work also aims at examining the process of migrating existing CUDA applications to a new platform.

Despite the stated simplicity of porting CUDA applications to the ROCm platform, some problems have been met due to the lack of full-fledged examples, insufficient documentation and the presence of a large number of GPU kernels optimized for the Nvidia architecture as part of CoMD-CUDA.

The process of porting a CUDA application to the ROCm platform, as well as identification of the points that should be paid attention to, are illustrated on Fig. 3.

CoMD-CUDA contains two interatomic potential models for MD simulations: the standard Lennard-Jones pair potential and the EAM manybody potential. The thread_atom and cta_cell methods for neighbor search are considered for the LJ model, the wrap_atom method is considered for the EAM model as well.

The performance of CoMD algorithms on AMD video cards without corresponding optimizations is expected to be lower than on the Nvidia platform. When the optimal occupancy of all stream processors of the Vega 56 accelerator reached, its results can exceed those of GTX 1070. The results are summarized on Figs. 4 and 5.

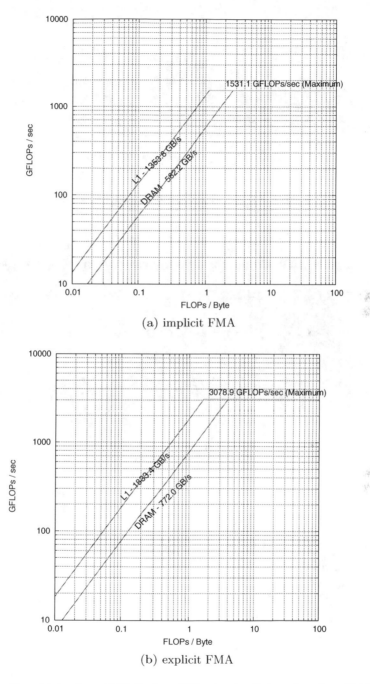

(a) implicit FMA

(b) explicit FMA

Fig. 2. Roofline obtained on AMD Radeon VII using implicit and explicit FMA operations.

```
grid = (s->n_boundary_cells + (block/WARP_SIZE)-1)/(block/WARP_SIZE);
UpdateBoundaryList<<<grid,block>>>(s->gpu, s->gpu.b_list, s->n_boundary_cells, cell_offsets1, s->boundary_cells);
hipLaunchKernelGGL((UpdateBoundaryList), dim3(grid), dim3(block), 0, 0, s->gpu, s->gpu.b_list, s->n_boundary_cells, cell_offsets1, s->boundary_cells);
CUDA_GET_LAST_ERROR

grid = (n_interior_cells + (block/WARP_SIZE)-1)/(block/WARP_SIZE);
UpdateBoundaryList<<<grid,block>>>(s->gpu, s->gpu.i_list, n_interior_cells, cell_offsets2, s->interior_cells);
hipLaunchKernelGGL((UpdateBoundaryList), dim3(grid), dim3(block), 0, 0, s->gpu, s->gpu.i_list, n_interior_cells, cell_offsets2, s->interior_cells);
CUDA_GET_LAST_ERROR

cudaMemcpy(&s->gpu.b_list.n, cell_offsets1 + s->n_boundary_cells, sizeof(int), cudaMemcpyDeviceToHost);
cudaMemcpy(&s->gpu.i_list.n, cell_offsets2 + n_interior_cells, sizeof(int), cudaMemcpyDeviceToHost);
hipMemcpy(&s->gpu.b_list.n, cell_offsets1 + s->n_boundary_cells, sizeof(int), hipMemcpyDeviceToHost);
hipMemcpy(&s->gpu.i_list.n, cell_offsets2 + n_interior_cells, sizeof(int), hipMemcpyDeviceToHost);

cudaFree(partial_sums);
cudaFree(cell_offsets1);
cudaFree(cell_offsets2);
hipFree(partial_sums);
hipFree(cell_offsets1);
hipFree(cell_offsets2);
```

```
        bool flag = r2 <= rCut2 && r2 > 0.0;
        unsigned int x;
        unsigned long long int x;
        int n;
        if(x = __ballot(flag))
        {
        //Scan
            x = x & mask2;
            n = __popc(x);
            n = __popcll(x);
            x = x & mask;
            const int p = __popc(x);
            const int p = __popcll(x);
            const int place = nNeighbors + p;
            if (flag) mytemp[(place/memoryPackSize) * 32 * memoryPackSize + (place & (memoryPackSize-1))] = jOff;
            if (flag) mytemp[(place/memoryPackSize) * WARP_SIZE * memoryPackSize + (place & (memoryPackSize-1))] = jOff;
            nNeighbors += n;
        }
```

Fig. 3. Examples of the CUDA to ROCm translations made by the hipify tool. Corrections of the GPU kernel due to different warp sizes of Nvidia and AMD GPUs.

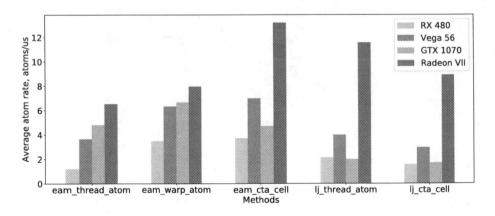

Fig. 4. Performance of different methods (problem size $50 \times 50 \times 50$)

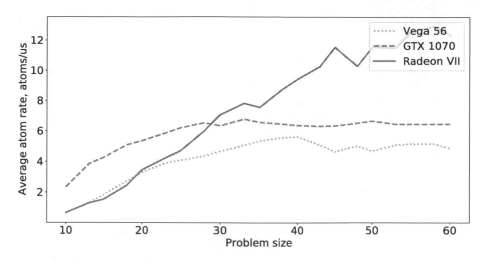

Fig. 5. Performance of the warp atom method on different problem sizes

5 Conclusion

New technologies require attention from software developers. It is essential to provide the necessary feedback, this allows to quickly correct occurring errors and develop the product.

AMD is the second-largest supplier of CPU and discrete GPU in the world. Its processors have considerable potential in the field of high performance computing. The significance of AMD's ROCm platform is hard to overestimate - it provides tools for developing cross-platform GPGPU applications that can run on both AMD video accelerators and Nvidia devices.

ROCm is still under development, so far there have been too few examples of its successful application. Therefore, it is necessary to discuss this technology, develop methods for and share experiences and results of its use, as well as track its production readiness.

To this aim, this work is going to start such a process by providing a comprehensive review of cross-platform ROCm framework and investigation of its performance in a real-world scenario.

Our results show that the transfer of a real-world application from CUDA to HIP does not requere major modifications of the code and gives the possibility to run the application considered on AMD GPUs without performance degradation.

References

1. ROCm Install. https://rocm.github.io/ROCmInstall.html#hardware-support. Accessed 15 Apr 2019
2. Sun, Y., et al.: Evaluating performance tradeoffs on the radeon open compute platform. In: 2018 IEEE International Symposium on Performance Analysis of Systems and Software (ISPASS) (2018)

3. Mohd-Yusof, J.: Codesign molecular dynamics (CoMD) proxy app. In: Los-Alamos National Lab, Technical report (2012)
4. Mohd-Yusof, J., Sakharnykh, N.: Optimizing CoMD: a molecular dynamics proxy application study. In: GPU Technology Conference (GTC) (2014). http://on-dem and.gputechconf.com/gtc/2014/presentations/S4465-optimizing-comd-molecular-dynamics.pdf. Accessed 15 Apr 2019
5. Norman, G., et al.: Why and what supercomputers of the exaflops class are needed in the natural sciences. Program Syst.: Theory Appl. **6**(4), 243–311 (2015)
6. November 2018 — TOP500 Supercomputer Sites. https://www.top500.org/lists/2018/11/. Accessed 15 Apr 2019
7. Peddie, J., Dow, R.: Jon Peddie Research releases its Q3, 2018 add-in board report. https://www.jonpeddie.com/press-releases/jon-peddie-research-releases-its-q3-2018-add-in-board-report. Accessed 15 Apr 2019
8. Turner, D., Andresen, D., Hutson, K., Tygart, A.: Application performance on the newest processors and GPUs. In: Proceedings of the Practice and Experience on Advanced Research Computing - PEARC (2018)
9. Fang, J., Varbanescu, A., Sips, H.: A comprehensive performance comparison of CUDA and OpenCL. In: International Conference on Parallel Processing (2011)
10. ROCm-Developer-Tools/HIP. https://github.com/ROCm-Developer-Tools/HIP. Accessed 15 Apr 2019
11. Aaltonen, S.: Optimizing GPU occupancy and resource usage with large thread groups. https://gpuopen.com/optimizing-gpu-occupancy-resource-usage-large-thr ead-groups/. Accessed 15 Apr 2019
12. The LLVM Compiler Infrastructure Project. https://llvm.org/. Accessed 15 Apr 2019
13. Lo, Y., et al.: Roofline model toolkit: a practical tool for architectural and program analysis. In: Jarvis, S.A., Wright, S.A., Hammond, S.D. (eds.) PMBS 2014. LNCS, vol. 8966, pp. 129–148. Springer, Cham (2015). https://doi.org/10.1007/978-3-319-17248-4_7

Solving of Eigenvalue and Singular Value Problems via Modified Householder Transformations on Shared Memory Parallel Computing Systems

Andrey Andreev and Vitaly Egunov[(✉)]

Volgograd State Technical University, Volgograd, Russia
andan2005@yandex.ru, vegunov@mail.ru

Abstract. Discusses the use of original modifications of Householder transformations for solving eigenvalue and singular value problems. Shared memory parallel computing systems are choosen as target computing systems. The proposed modifications allow to increase the computational performance due to the efficient use of cache memory and parallel execution of some transformation steps, which are traditionally performed serial. Mathematical descriptions of modified transformations are given, as well as software implementation issues and experimental results.

Keywords: Eigenvalues · Singular values · Householder transformation · Reflection transformation · Program performance · Cache memory · Shared memory system

1 Introduction

Finding eigenvalue and eigenvector systems, performing singular decomposition are widely used in solving a number of fundamental scientific and applied tasks. As an example, one can cite the problems of modeling various dynamic systems described by differential equations, specifically, when searching for the natural frequencies of oscillations of a dynamic system, the problem of determining the energy spectrum of quantum systems, image processing, etc.

The problems under consideration have a high computational complexity, which makes them the object of research for mathematicians and software engineers. The tasks themselves are well known. The task of finding its own decomposition is to find vectors and values that satisfy the condition (1).

$$Av = \lambda v \tag{1}$$

In this case, vector v is called the eigenvector of the linear operator A, the value λ is eigenvalue. In general, both λ and v can be complex even in the case of real A. Algorithms for solving the problem (1) can be divided into algorithms for finding all eigenvalues, as well as eigenvector systems, and algorithms for finding several (or probably the only one) eigenvalues. The most widely used are the iterative algorithms,

© Springer Nature Switzerland AG 2019
V. Voevodin and S. Sobolev (Eds.): RuSCDays 2019, CCIS 1129, pp. 131–151, 2019.
https://doi.org/10.1007/978-3-030-36592-9_12

that develop a sequence of transformations converging to the eigenvalues, as well as the development of a sequence of vectors converging to the eigenvectors of the linear operator.

$$A_{k+1} = U_k A_k U_k^* \qquad (2)$$

Here U_k - unitary matrix, U_k^* - conjugate transpose matrix. In the case of real matrices, orthogonal and transposed matrices are used. All matrices A_i are similar, i.e. their eigenvalues are equal. There are no relatively simple direct algorithms for finding eigenvalues and eigenvector systems, however, such algorithms are known for matrices of a special kind. As an example, triangular matrices with eigenvalues are located on the main diagonal.

The problem of finding a singular value decomposition is to find vectors and values that satisfy the condition (3).

$$A * u = \lambda v \qquad (3)$$

Vectors u and v are called the left and right singular vectors corresponding to the singular value λ, A* is the matrix, conjugate transpose to A. The singular value decomposition of the matrix is the decomposition of the form (4).

$$A = U \Sigma V^* \qquad (4)$$

Here A is the initial matrix, U and V areunitary matrices, Σ is the matrix which elements lying on the main diagonal are singular values. In the case of real matrices, orthogonal and transposed matrices are also used.

Most modern computing systems have a parallel architecture, as a result, currently there are many studies on the adaptation of known algorithms for use on parallel computing systems, as well as the study of the effectiveness of these algorithms when used on parallel systems with different characteristics, for example [1, 2]. In this work, we have optimized the modification of the known algorithms for solving the problems of finding a eigenvalues and singular values on parallel systems with shared memory, the result of these modifications reduces the time of solving these problems. The choice of this class of parallel systems is due to their wide prevalence. The choice of the object of research is determined by the demand for these tasks in solving various fundamental and applied problems. In many cases, these transformations are repeated many times, the calculations take a lot of time. Therefore, reducing the computation time seems to be an urgent task. One more reason for the paper is the fact that the authors have been engaged for several years in the study of issues related to the implementation of matrix transformations on heterogeneous computational systems, including the transformations mentioned above [3–6].

2   Used Methods

One of the methods of accelerating the process of calculating eigenvalues is to bring the original matrix of the general structure to the "almost triangular" structure, in which, in addition to the elements of the triangular matrix, the diagonal is stored under or above the main diagonal. Matrices of this type are called the upper or lower Hessenberg matrix, respectively. There is a finite sequence of transformations that leads a matrix of arbitrary structure to a Hessenberg structure with preservation of its eigenvalues. Such matrices, along with tridiagonal matrices, are the source for many eigenvalue search algorithms, such as, for example, the QR algorithm or the Jacobi method. Thus, it can be concluded that the reduction of the matrix of arbitrary structure to Hessenberg's one, and symmetric matrix – to the tridiagonal structure, is an integral part of a large number of algorithms for finding eigenvalues of the linear operator, and improving the efficiency of methods for solving this problem leads to a decrease in the time of solving the problem of finding eigenvalues as a whole.

In the case of singular value decomposition of matrices of General structure, one of the most effective methods is to reduce the matrix to a dual-diagonal structure by means of transformations (4), where in this case Σ is a dual-diagonal matrix, with further application of efficient algorithms for computing the singular value decomposition of a dual-diagonal matrix. Thus, improving the effectiveness of the methods of reduction of matrices to dual-diagonal structure leads to reduce the run-time of singular value decomposition in General.

Both (2) and (4) use unitary matrices as operators U and V, and orthogonal matrices in the case of real values computations. In this paper we consider the problem of reducing the matrix of General form to Hessenberg and dual-diagonal form in order to further calculate its eigenvalues or singular values. As a basic method will use Housholder reflections.

$$A = QRQ^{T} \tag{5}$$

Here A is initial matrix, R is Hessenberg or dual-diagonal matrix, Q is orthogonal matrix, representing a Housholder matrix multiplication, each matrix is uniquely determined by the reflection vector. In [4] examines the performance of the QR – decomposition by Householder reflections on parallel computing systems with shared memory. In particular, multiplication by the reflection matrix on the right (QR - decomposition) and on the left (LQ - decomposition) is considered. In the first case, the reflection vector is determined by the columns of the original matrix, the columns are also zeroed, in the second case, the reflection vector is determined by the rows of the original matrix, the rows are zeroed. The variant of LQ decomposition in this case is more preferable because of the lower probability of cache misses. A cache miss occurs when the microprocessor tries to access data that is not present in the cache memory. In this case, they must be loaded from the main memory. If the required data is in the cache, it is quickly retrieved. This event is called a cache hit. Improving the performance of the computer system is achieved when cache hits are implemented much more often than cache misses. The frequency of cache misses in this case can be estimated as the probability of missing the required data in the cache memory during the next iteration of the transformation applied to the column or row of the matrix. As the data in the cache memory is loaded from the lines, the more effective from the point of view of usage of the cache memory are algorithms in which the processing is performed along the rows of the matrix. This algorithm is a variant of LQ – decomposition, in contrast to the variant of QR – decomposition, in which data processing is carried out along the columns of the matrix.

In the case of a two-way transformation (2) or (4), the situation is not so clear, because it is necessary to multiply on both sides to preserve the eigenvalues or singular values. Consider the reduction of the matrix of dimension n*n to the upper Hessenberg structure. To do this, you need to perform (n − 2) steps within each:

- calculate the elements of the reflection vector on the elements of the next column of the original matrix;
- multiply the original matrix by the reflection matrix on the right;
- multiply the original matrix by the reflection matrix on the left.

The algorithm for performing the k-th conversion step can be written as follows (6).

$$s_k = -sign\left(a_{k+1,k}\right)\left(\sum_{i=k+1}^{n} a_{ik}^2\right)^{\frac{1}{2}}, \qquad \varphi_k = \left(s_k^2 - s_k a_{k+1,k}\right)^{-1}$$

$$\boldsymbol{u}_k^T = \left(0, \ldots, 0, a_{k+1,k} - s_k, a_{k+2,k}, \ldots, a_{nk}\right)$$

$$\begin{aligned} \lambda_j &= \varphi_k \boldsymbol{u}_k^T \boldsymbol{a}_j \\ \boldsymbol{a}_j &= \boldsymbol{a}_j - \lambda_j \boldsymbol{u}_k \end{aligned} \bigg|_{j=\overline{k,n}} \qquad (6)$$

$$\begin{aligned} \lambda_j' &= \varphi_k \boldsymbol{b}_j \boldsymbol{u}_k \\ \boldsymbol{b}_j &= \boldsymbol{b}_j - \lambda_j' \boldsymbol{u}_k^T \end{aligned} \bigg|_{j=\overline{k,n}}$$

Here $\boldsymbol{a}$ – columns of the original matrix, $\boldsymbol{b}$ – its rows, expression $j = \overline{k,n}$ indicates the range of indexes when processing rows and columns of the matrix in the current step of the transformation. The sequence of steps in this case is as follows:

- the reflection vector is determined from the values of the elements of the k-th column of the matrix under the main diagonal;
- multiplication by the Householder matrix on the right, which results in zero elements of k column, changes (n − 1) elements of all other columns, starting with (k + 1); the columns of the matrix can be processed in parallel;
- multiplication by the Householder matrix on the left, which changes (n − 1) elements of all matrix rows starting from k; the matrix rows can be processed in parallel.

To bring the matrix to a dual-diagonal structure, you need to perform more operations. This is due to the fact that the elements of the reflection vector are calculated at both stages of the transformation. The algorithm of matrix reduction in the upper dual-diagonal structure can be written as follows (7).

$$s_k = -sign(a_{k,k})\left(\sum_{i=k}^{n} a_{ik}^2\right)^{\frac{1}{2}}, \qquad \varphi_k = \left(s_k^2 - s_k a_{k,k}\right)^{-1}$$

$$\boldsymbol{u}_k^T = (0, \ldots, 0, a_{k,k} - s_k, a_{k+1,k}, \ldots, a_{nk})$$

$$\left.\begin{array}{l}\lambda_j = \varphi_k \boldsymbol{u}_k^T \boldsymbol{a}_j \\ \boldsymbol{a}_j = \boldsymbol{a}_j - \lambda_j \boldsymbol{u}_k\end{array}\right|_{j=\overline{k,n}} \qquad\qquad (7)$$

$$\left.\left.\begin{array}{c}s_k' = -sign(a_{k,k+1})\left(\sum_{i=k+1}^{n} a_{ki}^2\right)^{\frac{1}{2}}, \qquad \varphi_k' = \left(s_k'^2 - s_k' a_{k,k+1}\right)^{-1} \\ \boldsymbol{u}_k'^T = (0, \ldots, 0, a_{k,k+1} - s_k', a_{k,k+2}, \ldots, a_{kn}) \\ \left.\begin{array}{c}\lambda_j' = \varphi_k \boldsymbol{b}_j \boldsymbol{u}_k' \\ \boldsymbol{b}_j = \boldsymbol{b}_j - \lambda_j' \boldsymbol{u}_k'^T\end{array}\right|_{j=\overline{k,n}} \\ < n-1\end{array}\right|\right\| k$$

The sequence of actions is generally similar to the sequence of actions when reduced to the upper Hessenberg structure, except:

- when multiplying on the right for column calculations $\boldsymbol{a}_j$ in the formation of the reflection vector are used the elements of the column under the main diagonal together with the elements of the main diagonal;
- when multiplying on the left generates a new reflection vector based on the row elements to the right of the main diagonal;
- the total number of steps in this case is $(n-1)$;
- when multiplying on the left is done fewer steps $(n-2)$, what the symbol indicates $k < n-1$, indicates the number of steps within which you want to perform the conversions.

Since the transformations are generally similar, we focus on reducing the matrix to the Hessenberg structure, further extending the findings to the algorithm of reducing the matrix to the dual-diagonal form.

To reduce the matrix to the lower Hessenberg structure, perform the following steps at each step of the transformation (8).

$$s_k = -sign(a_{k,k+1})\left(\sum_{i=k+1}^{n} a_{ki}^2\right)^{\frac{1}{2}}, \qquad \varphi_k = \left(s_k^2 - s_k a_{k,k+1}\right)^{-1}$$

$$\boldsymbol{u}_k^T = (0, \ldots, 0, a_{k,k+1} - s_k, a_{k,k+2}, \ldots, a_{kn})$$

$$\lambda'_j = \varphi_k b_j u_k \Big|_{j = \overline{k, n}}$$
$$b_j = b_j - \lambda'_j u_k^T \Big|$$

$$(8)$$

$$\lambda_j = \varphi_k u_k^T a_j \Big|_{j = \overline{k, n}}$$
$$a_j = a_j - \lambda_j u_k \Big|$$

In General, the same actions are performed, taking into account the following comments:

– reflection vectors are formed on the basis of matrix row elements;
– is transformed first row, and then columns of the matrices.

All three of the above transformations (6)–(8) use the natural data parallelism inherent in these methods to write parallel programs:

– when multiplying to the right, the matrix columns can be processed in parallel;
– when multiplying from the left, matrix rows can be processed in parallel.

A large number of publications are devoted to the analysis of these transformations. Much attention of researchers is attracted by the solving of the eigenvalues problem for matrices of a special kind, for example [7–9], the use of singular value decomposition in solving various technical problems [10]. They Transformation of Hessenberg matrices, including to obtain eigenvalue and singular value decompositions are investigated [11, 12]. Traditionally, the attention of researchers is attracted by the Householder reflections [1, 2, 12–16]. The main publications are devoted to the application of this transformation to solving various problems of scientific and applied nature, often on computer systems of a certain type. A number of works are devoted to the effective use of cache memory when performing matrix operations [17]. In this article, we propose original modifications of the Householder reflections, designed to write programs for parallel computing systems with shared memory, effectively using cache memory, thereby significantly speeding up calculations compared to traditional computing schemes.

3 Proposed Solutions

In this section, we consider the proposed modifications of the methods described above, designed to speed up calculations on parallel computing systems with shared memory. In both algorithms (6) and (8) of matrix reduction to Hessenberg structure, the same transformations are performed over the columns and rows of the matrix, only the order of actions is changed, so these steps on parallel computing systems will be performed at the same time. A significant difference of the presented algorithms is the scheme of reflection vector formation. And from this point of view, the algorithm of bringing the matrix to the lower Hessenberg structure is more preferable (8). This is due to the fact that the formation of the reflection vector is based on the elements of the matrix rows, in contrast to the algorithm (6), where the reflection vector is formed on the basis of the column elements. The fact is that when using the elements of the columns of the matrix on parallel computing systems with shared memory will generate a greater number of cache misses. This effect has already been mentioned above. However, due to the fact that to determine the elements of the reflection vector in the total volume of calculations is small enough, both algorithms will have similar efficiency.

Consider these algorithms in terms of increasing their efficiency and reducing runtime on parallel systems with shared memory. There are several bottlenecks:

- in these algorithms, there are three serial stages at each step of the transformation, one of the stages is the calculation of the elements of the reflection vector, although there are implementations in which the elements of the reflection vector are pre-computed for the next step of the transformation, described, for example, in [4];
- when multiplied by the reflection matrix on the right, the columns of the matrix are processed, which significantly reduces the efficiency compared to the variant of calculations based on the processing of matrix rows.

First, we consider the modernization of these algorithms, aimed at improving the efficiency associated with the acceleration of processing columns of the original matrix.

In accordance with (6) in the process of reducing the original matrix to the upper Hessenberg structure when multiplied by the reflection matrix on the right, during which the next column of the original matrix is reset, the following actions are performed:

- the elements of the reflection vector are determined based on the values of the corresponding column of the original matrix;
- new values of matrix columns are calculated; columns can be processed in parallel, because in this case there are no information dependencies.

In this case, the following calculations are performed during the recalculation of the column values:

- the values of the inner products of the columns and the reflection vector are determined;
- new values of column elements are calculated based on the obtained values of inner products.

Both data stages are well parallelized, but due to the fact that the data is processed along the columns, a sufficiently large value of cache misses is generated, which greatly slows down the calculation process.

To eliminate the negative impact of cache misses, the following algorithm for calculating the new values of the matrix columns is proposed:

- at the first stage all necessary inner products are calculated;
- at the second stage, the new values of the column elements are calculated, but since the values of all inner products are known at this stage, the processing can be carried out line by line, for each element of the row, use its own value of the inner product.

This process can be written as follows (9). Here and in the future, the reflection vector formation algorithm is similar to (6) when reduced to the upper Hessenberg structure and similar to (8) when reduced to the lower Hessenberg structure. Therefore, except where it is really necessary, it will not be cited.

$$sc = \varphi_k u_k^T A$$

$$D = diag(sc_0, sc_1, \ldots, sc_n)$$

$$U[:j] = [u_k]$$

$$SCU = UD \tag{9}$$

$$b_j = b_j - scu_j \big| j = \overline{k, n}$$

$$\left. \begin{aligned} \lambda'_j &= \varphi_k b_j u_k \\ b_j &= b_j - \lambda'_j u_k^T \end{aligned} \right| j = \overline{k, n}$$

Before processing the columns, the vector of inner products of sc is calculated as the product of the reflection vector u_k^T on the original matrix A taking into account the scale factor φ_k. Next is calculation of new values of columns of the matrix, and the computation is carried out row by row, which is much more efficient from the point of view of using the cache memory. It should be noted that (9) uses the following symbols: D – a diagonal matrix containing the values of inner products sc on its main diagonal, U – a matrix whose columns are composed of a reflection vector, scu – rows of the matrix SCU, b - rows of the matrix A. As can be seen from (9), when multiplying the matrix both on the right and on the left, the processing is carried out row by row, which significantly increases the efficiency of the program implementation of the method, reducing the execution time of the program.

An algorithm for reducing the matrix to the lower Hessenberg structure using a row-oriented scheme of processing columns of the matrix is given in (10).

$$\left. \begin{aligned} \lambda'_j &= \varphi_k b_j u_k \\ b_j &= b_j - \lambda'_j u_k^T \end{aligned} \right| j = \overline{k, n}$$

$$sc = \varphi_k u_k^T A$$

$$D = diag(sc_0, sc_1, \ldots, sc_n) \tag{10}$$

$$U[:j] = [u_k]$$

$$SCU = UD$$

$$b_j = b_j - scu_j \big| j = \overline{k, n}$$

In (9) and (10) it is not shown the formation of the reflection vector, which is carried out similarly to (6) and (7), respectively, i.e. on the basis of columns and rows of the matrix, respectively.

Let us now consider the modernization of the computational process associated with the preliminary calculation of the reflection vector. In the basic version of the algorithm, as well as in the modifications discussed above, the elements of the reflection vector are formed in the serial part of the program. According to Amdahl's Law, it is serial computing that limits the acceleration of a program on parallel computing systems. Accordingly, one of the ways to improve the efficiency of programs, reduce the time of their execution, can be considered a reduction in the share of serial calculations in the total volume of calculations.

The idea is based on the transfer of the stage of determining the elements of the reflection vector from the serial part of the calculations to the parallel one. After analyzing the algorithm, we can conclude that in order to form the reflection vector for the step number $(k + 1)$ it is not necessary to wait for the end of all calculations associated with step number k. For a one-way transformation, this means that when you perform step k of the algorithm to bring the matrix to the upper triangular structure by multiplying the reflection matrix on the right, the reflection vector can be formed after the elements of the column number $(k + 1)$ are formed. Accordingly, when performing the step with number k of the matrix reduction algorithm to the lower triangular structure by multiplying the reflection matrix on the left, the reflection vector can be formed after the formation of the elements of the row with number $(k + 1)$. With parallel implementation of the algorithm, this leads to some acceleration of calculations, as the share of serial calculations in the total volume of calculations decreases.

When performing a two-way transformation, this strategy does not work, because when multiplying by the reflection matrix on the other hand, the elements on the basis of which the reflection vector is formed will change. Thus, when reduced to the upper Hessenberg structure, it would be erroneous to form a reflection vector based on the values of the column obtained at the next step when multiplying on the right, since the values of the elements of this column will change when multiplied by the reflection matrix on the left. The same situation will be observed when the matrix is reduced to the lower Hessenberg structure. In both cases, the reflection vector can be generated only after the second stage of the transformation is completed in this step. It looks like applying reflection transformations to bring the matrix to Hessenberg or dual-diagonal structure.

Consider a transformation algorithm that includes a preliminary computation of the reflection vector elements used to bring the matrix to the upper Hessenberg structure. The formation of the elements of the reflection vector in this case is based on the columns of the matrix, however, the final stage of the transformation at each step includes the processing of rows. Obviously, all elements of the target column will be known only after the whole step is completed. However, it is obvious that when processing the next row, the value of the next element of the target column becomes known, which is used to form the reflection vector in the next step. Thus, it is possible to form a reflection vector element by element, removing this stage from the serial part of the program, increasing its efficiency.

The formal definition of the process of bringing the matrix to the upper Hessenberg structure with a preliminary calculation of the elements of the reflection vector can be written as follows (11).

$$s_{k|j+1} = 0$$

$$\left. \begin{array}{l} \lambda_j = \varphi_k u_k^T a_j \\ a_j = a_j - \lambda_j u_k \end{array} \right| j = \overline{k,n}$$

$$\left. \begin{array}{l} \lambda_j' = \varphi_k b_j u_k \\ b_j = b_j - \lambda_j' u_k^T \\ u_{k+1}^T[j] = b_j[k+1] | j > k+2 \\ s_{k|j+1} = s_{k|j+1} + b_j[k+1]^2 | j \geq k+2 \end{array} \right| j = \overline{k,n} \qquad (11)$$

$$s_{k|j+1} = -sign\left(a_{k+2,k+1}\right) s_{k|j+1}^{\frac{1}{2}},$$

$$\varphi_{k|j+1} = \left(s_{k|j+1}^2 - s_{k|j+1} a_{k+2,k+1}\right)^{-1}$$

$$u_{k+1}^T[0 : (k+1)] = 0$$

$$u_{k+1}^T[k+2] = a_{k+2,k+1} - s_{k|j+1}$$

During the second stage of the next step of the transformation, the elements of the reflection vector are formed in the parallel part of the program, as well as the accumulation of the module $s_{k|j+1}$, necessary to calculate the scaling factor $\varphi_{k|j+1}$. A subscript indicates that this value will be used in step k to process column number j + 1. It should be noted that it was not possible to completely abandon the serial part of the calculations, because some compensation of the value of the module $s_{k|j+1}$ after processing all the rows is required. The code that would implement the algorithm given in (11) would look like this. This code snippet is written in the C programming language using OpenMP technology.

```
#pragma omp parallel for
    for(int row = step; row < N; row++)
    {
            double scalar = 0;
            for(int i = (step + shift); i < N; i++)
                    scalar += matr[row * N + i] * vect[i];
            scalar *= gamma;
            for(int i = (step + shift); i < N; i++)
            {
                    matr[row * N + i] -= scalar * vect[i];

                    if (i == (step + shift))
                    {
                            if (row > (step + 1 + shift))
                                    vectAdd[row] = matr[row * N + i];
                            if (row >= (step + 1 + shift))
#pragma omp atomic
                                    s += matr[row * N + i] * matr[row * N + i];
                    }
            }
    }
    s = sqrt(s);
    if (matr[(step + 1 + shift) * N + step + 1] > 0)
            s = -s;
    gamma = 1 / (s * s - matr[(step + 1 + shift) * N + step + 1] * s);
    for (int i = 0; i < (step + 1 + shift); i++)
            vectAdd[i] = 0;
    vectAdd[step + 1 + shift] = matr[(step + 1 + shift) * N + (step + 1)] - s;
```

Despite the fact that the reflection vector is formed almost entirely in the parallel part of the program, this code is inefficient because of the large number of checks carried out in each thread when processing each row. In addition, #pragma omp atomic synchronization can reduce the efficiency. The following code changes are made to improve efficiency:

– unroll the loop by performing its first iteration outside the loop; there is no need to check if (i == (step + shift));
– remove the check if (row > (step + 1 + shift)); the reflection vector will be corrected in the serial part of the program, zeroing the necessary elements;
– remove the check if (row > = (step + 1 + shift)); the value of the module is adjusted in the serial part of the program, subtracting from it the squares of unnecessary elements;
– remove #pragma omp atomic synchronization, each thread accumulates a module in its variable, their values are summed in the serial part of the program.

Get the following code.

```
#pragma omp parallel for
    for(int row = step; row < N; row++)
    {
                double scalar = 0;
                for(int i = (step + shift); i < N; i++)
                        scalar += matr[row * N + i] * vect[i];
                scalar *= gamma;
                matr[row * N + step + shift] -= scalar * vect[step + shift];
                vectAdd[row] = matr[row * N + step + shift];
                sAr[numT] += matr[row * N + step + shift] * matr[row * N + step +
shift];
                for(int i = (step + shift + 1); i < N; i++)
                        matr[row * N + i] -= scalar * vect[i];


    }
    s = 0;
    for(int ii = 0; ii < nT; ii++)
            s += sAr[ii];
    s -= matr[step * N + step + shift] * matr[step * N + step + shift];
    if (shift > 0)
            s -= matr[(step + shift) * N + step + shift] * matr[(step + shift) * N +
step + shift];
    s = sqrt(s);
    if (matr[(step + 1 + shift)  * N + step + 1] > 0)
            s = -s;
    gamma = 1 / (s * s - matr[(step + 1 + shift) * N + step + 1] * s);
    for (int i = 0; i < (step + 1 + shift); i++)
            vectAdd[i] = 0;
    vectAdd[step + 1 + shift] = matr[(step + 1 + shift) * N + (step + 1)] - s;
```

The shift parameter is assumed to be 1 when performing a two-way transformation to convert the matrix to Hessenberg structure and is assumed to be 0 when performing a one-way transformation to convert the matrix to triangular form. It is worth noting that before you start the transformation, you must calculate the elements of the reflection vector used to perform the first step of the transformation.

The transformation in this case will take the form (12).

$$s_{k|j+1} = 0$$

$$\begin{aligned} \lambda_j = \varphi_k u_k^T a_j \\ a_j = a_j - \lambda_j u_k \end{aligned} \bigg|_{j = \overline{k,n}} \qquad (12)$$

$$\lambda'_j = \varphi_k b_j u_k$$

$$b_j = b_j - \lambda'_j u_k^T \left. \vphantom{\begin{matrix} a \\ b \\ c \\ d \end{matrix}} \right| j = \overline{k,n}$$

$$u_{k+1}^T[j] = b_j[k+1]$$

$$s_{k|j+1} = s_{k|j+1} + b_j[k+1]^2$$

$$s_{k|j+1} = s_{k|j+1} - \mathbf{A}[k,k+1]^2 - \mathbf{A}[k+1,k+1]^2$$

$$s_{k|j+1} = -sign\left(a_{k+2,k+1}\right) s_{k|j+1}^{\frac{1}{2}},$$

$$\varphi_{k|j+1} = \left(s_{k|j+1}^2 - s_{k|j+1} a_{k+2,k+1} \right)^{-1}$$

$$u_{k+1}^T[0:(k+1)] = 0$$

$$u_{k+1}^T[k+2] = a_{k+2,k+1} - s_{k|j+1}$$

The reduction of the matrix to the lower Hessenberg structure with pre-calculated elements of the reflection vector will be as follows (13).

$$s_{k|j+1} = 0$$

$$\lambda'_j = \varphi_k b_j u_k \left. \vphantom{\begin{matrix} a \\ b \end{matrix}} \right| j = \overline{k,n}$$

$$b_j = b_j - \lambda'_j u_k^T$$

(13)

$$\lambda_j = \varphi_k u_k^T a_j$$

$$a_j = a_j - \lambda_j u_k \left. \vphantom{\begin{matrix} a \\ b \\ c \\ d \end{matrix}} \right|$$

$$u_{k+1}^T[j] = a_j[k+1] \quad j = \overline{k,n}$$

$$s_{k|j+1} = s_{k|j+1} + a_j[k+1]^2$$

$$s_{k|j+1} = s_{k|j+1} - \mathbf{A}[k+1,k]^2 - \mathbf{A}[k+1,k+1]^2$$

$$s_{k|j+1} = -sign\left(a_{k+1,k+2}\right) s_{k|j+1}^{\frac{1}{2}},$$

$$\varphi_{k|j+1} = \left(s_{k|j+1}^2 - s_{k|j+1} a_{k+1,k+2} \right)^{-1}$$

$$u_k^T[0:(k+1)] = 0$$

$$u_k^T[k+2] = a_{k+1,k+2} - s_{k|j+1}$$

Finally, both approaches can be combined, obtaining an effective implementation of the Householder transformation of to bring the matrix to Hessenberg structure in the framework of solving the eigenvalues problem.

The modification of the Householder reflection algorithm, consisting in the row-oriented scheme of processing of the matrix and the preliminary calculation of the elements of the reflection vector, applied to the problem of reducing the matrix to the upper Hessenberg structure, will be as follows (14).

$$s_{k|j+1} = 0$$

$$sc = \varphi_k u_k^T A$$

$$D = diag(sc_0, sc_1, \ldots, sc_n)$$

$$U[:j] = [u_k]$$

$$SCU = UD$$

$$b_j = b_j - scu_j \big| j = \overline{k,n}$$

$$\left. \begin{array}{l} \lambda'_j = \varphi_k b_j u_k \\ b_j = b_j - \lambda'_j u_k^T \\ u_{k+1}^T[j] = b_j[k+1] \\ s_{k|j+1} = s_{k|j+1} + b_j[k+1]^2 \end{array} \right| j = \overline{k,n} \tag{14}$$

$$s_{k|j+1} = s_{k|j+1} - A[k,k+1]^2 - A[k+1,k+1]^2$$

$$s_{k|j+1} = -sign(a_{k+2,k+1}) s_{k|j+1}^{\frac{1}{2}},$$

$$\varphi_{k|j+1} = \left(s_{k|j+1}^2 - s_{k|j+1} a_{k+2,k+1}\right)^{-1}$$

$$u_{k+1}^T[0:(k+1)] = 0$$

$$u_{k+1}^T[k+2] = a_{k+2,k+1} - s_{k|j+1}$$

(14) does not show the formation of the reflection vector for the first step of the transformation. Similarly, it is possible to obtain an algorithm for reducing the matrix to the lower Hessenberg structure, however, it will not give a tangible increase in efficiency compared to the algorithm (10), since in this case the elements of the reflection vector are determined in accordance with the elements of the matrix, i.e. quite effectively.

The resulting modification of the Householder reflection algorithm can be extended to an algorithm to bring the matrix to dual-diagonal form. Moreover, a significant increase in efficiency will be achieved both in the case of bringing the matrix to the upper dual - diagonal and to the lower dual - diagonal structure. This is due to the fact that in these algorithms, at each step, the calculation of the elements of the reflection vector is carried out twice – when multiplying on the right by the elements of the columns, when multiplying on the left by the elements of the rows. In (15), an algorithm for reducing the matrix to the upper dual – diagonal structure, taking into account the proposed modifications, in (16) - to the lower dual - diagonal structure is given.

$$s_{k|j+1} = 0$$

$$\mathbf{sc} = \varphi_k \mathbf{u}_k^T \mathbf{A}$$

$$\mathbf{D} = diag(sc_0, sc_1, \ldots, sc_n)$$

$$\mathbf{U}[:j] = [\mathbf{u}_k]$$

$$\mathbf{SCU} = \mathbf{UD} \tag{15}$$

$$\mathbf{b}_j = \mathbf{b}_j - \mathbf{scu}_j | j = \overline{k,n}$$

$$s_k' = -sign(a_{k,k+1}) \left(\sum_{i=k+1}^{n} a_{ki}^2 \right)^{\frac{1}{2}},$$

$$\varphi_k' = \left(s_k'^2 - s_k' a_{k,k+1} \right)^{-1}$$

$$\mathbf{u}_k'^T = (0, \ldots, 0, a_{k,k+1} - s_k', a_{k,k+2}, \ldots, a_{kn})$$

$$\lambda_j' = \varphi_k \mathbf{b}_j \mathbf{u}_k'$$

$$\mathbf{b}_j = \mathbf{b}_j - \lambda_j' \mathbf{u}_k'^T$$

$$\mathbf{u}_{k+1}^T[j] = \mathbf{b}_j[k+1] \quad \Bigg| j = \overline{k,n}$$

$$s_{k|j+1} = s_{k|j+1} + \mathbf{b}_j[k+1]^2 \Bigg|$$

$$\Bigg| k < n-1$$

$$s_{k|j+1} = s_{k|j+1} - \mathbf{A}[k,k+1]^2$$

$$s_{k|j+1} = -sign(a_{k+1,k+1}) s_{k|j+1}^{\frac{1}{2}},$$

$$\varphi_{k|j+1} = \left(s_{k|j+1}^2 - s_{k|j+1} a_{k+1,k+1} \right)^{-1}$$

$$\mathbf{u}_{k+1}^T[0:k)] = 0$$

$$\mathbf{u}_{k+1}^T[k+1] = a_{k+2,k+1} - s_{k|j+1}$$

$$s'_k = -sign(a_{k,k}) \left(\sum_{i=k}^{n} a_{ki}^2 \right)^{\frac{1}{2}}, \qquad \varphi'_k = \left(s'^2_k - s'_k a_{k,k} \right)^{-1}$$

$$u'^T_k = \left(0, \dots, 0, a_{k,k} - s'_k, a_{k,k+1}, \dots, a_{kn} \right)$$

$$s_k = 0$$

$$\left. \begin{aligned} \lambda'_j &= \varphi_k b_j u'_k \\ b_j &= b_j - \lambda'_j u'^T_k \\ u^T_{k+1}[j] &= b_j[k] \\ s_k &= s_k + b_j[k]^2 \end{aligned} \right| j = \overline{k,n}$$

$$s_k = s_k - \mathbf{A}[k,k]^2$$

$$s_k = -sign(a_{k+1,k}) s_k^{\frac{1}{2}}, \qquad \varphi_k = \left(s_k^2 - s_k a_{k+1,k} \right)^{-1}$$

$$u^T_k[0:\mathrm{k}] = 0 \tag{16}$$

$$u^T_k[\mathrm{k}+1] = a_{k+1,k} - s_k$$

$$\left. \begin{aligned} sc &= \varphi_k u^T_k A \\ D &= diag(sc_0, sc_1, \dots, sc_n) \\ U[:j] &= [u_k] \\ SCU &= UD \\ b_j &= b_j - scu_j \big| j = \overline{k,n} \end{aligned} \right\| k < n - 1$$

In (15) and (16), the calculation of the reflection vector based on the row elements can also be made in the parallel part of the program, however, this will not give a tangible increase in efficiency.

4 Results of Computational Experiments

The object of research was a parallel computer system with shared memory, built on the basis of multi-core microprocessors Xeon E5-2650v3(x2) 2.3 GHz. This system is a part of the computer cluster of Volgograd State Technical University.

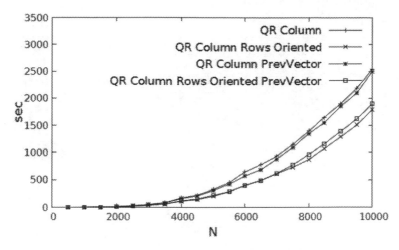

Fig. 1. Time of operation of serial variants of programs of matrix reduction to the upper Hessenberg structure.

Figure 1 shows the results of serial programs to bring matrices of arbitrary form to the upper Hessenberg structure. Programs were developed in the C programming language, the real type with double precision was used.

In Fig. 1, the following symbols are used:

- QR Column – traditional algorithm based on the classical Householder transformation (6);
- QR Column Rows Oriented – the algorithm based on the proposed row – oriented modifications of the Householder transformation (9);
- QR Column PrevVector– the algorithm based on the proposed modification of the Householder transformation with a preliminary calculation of the elements of the vector reflection (11);
- QR Column Rows Oriented PrevVector– an algorithm based on the simultaneous application of both proposed modifications of the Householder transformation (14).
- Analyzing the results presented in Fig. 1, we can draw the following conclusions:
- the least efficient is the implementation of the classical Householder transformation (6);
- despite the fact that the option with a preliminary calculation of the elements of the reflection vector (11) has a somewhat greater operating complexity of its serial software implementation is somewhat more rapid implementation of the classical transformation (6); the gain in execution time is about 5–6%; this is because in this case more effectively interacts with the cache memory in the formation of the elements of the vector reflection;
- the fastest is the variant with the use of row-oriented modification (9);
- the use of both modifications (14) works a little longer due to the greater operational complexity; at the same time, the gain due to the effective formation of the reflection vector elements in this case becomes insufficient, since the row – oriented scheme itself is effective in terms of interaction with cache memory.

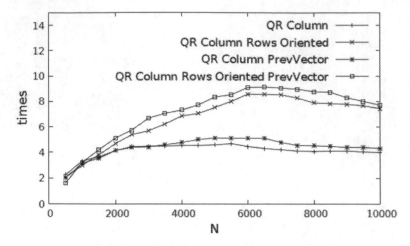

Fig. 2. Acceleration values of parallel variants of programs to bring the matrix to the upper Hessenberg structure in relation to the basic algorithm (6), five parallel threads.

Figure 2 shows the values of acceleration parallel implementations of the same algorithms against the baseline algorithm (6) – a serial algorithm based on the classical Householder transformation. The simulation was carried out on 5, 10 and 15 parallel threads. Figure 2 shows the simulation results on five threads.

In this case, the best option is the one in which both modifications were used:

- row-oriented computing optimize the operation of the microprocessor with cache memory;
- a preliminary calculation of the elements of a vector of reflection in the parallel implementations reduces their share of serial calculations, reducing the time of work of the program's General.

Analyzing the results presented in Fig. 2, we can conclude that all the assumptions made during the development of algorithms (9), (11) and (14) were justified and successfully confirmed by computational experiments. On 5 parallel threads, the operation of the basic version of the algorithm was accelerated by more than 9 times. In the resultant acceleration contributes not only to parallelize computations on multiple cores of the microprocessor, but also optimize the interaction with the cache memory.

Figure 3 shows the values of acceleration for parallel implementations of the same algorithms on ten parallel threads.

It can be observed from the Fig. 3, that the proposed modifications of the basic algorithm still have the best acceleration indicators, but their efficiency has decreased with the increase of the number of parallel threads.

When the matrix is reduced to a dual-diagonal structure while solving the problem of singular value decomposition, the same pattern is observed as in Figs. 1, 2 and 3.

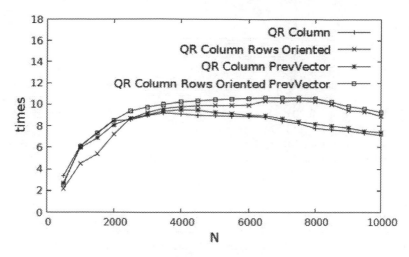

Fig. 3. Acceleration values of parallel programs to bring the matrix to the upper Hessenberg structure in relation to the basic algorithm (6), ten parallel threads.

5 Summary

According to the results of computational experiments we can conclude that the proposed modification of the custom Householder reflection transformations as applied to the solution of problems of a eigenvalues and singular values decompositions proved to be quite efficient on parallel computational systems with shared memory. It should also be noted that the proposed algorithms accelerate calculations not only for parallel but also for serial implementations. It can be stated that in the case of serial implementation it is advisable to use the proposed row-oriented reflection transformation, in the case of parallel – row-oriented transformation with the preliminary calculation of the elements of the reflection vector, i.e. the option in which both proposed modifications are used. The reduction of program execution time is achieved primarily due to the effective organization of work with cache memory, which significantly reduces the frequency of cache misses and as a consequence significantly speeds up the calculation process. Moreover, in the parallel implementations an additional increase in acceleration of calculations is achieved due to the reduction of the share of serial calculations. The results presented in this paper are original and obtained for the first time.

Acknowledgements. Work is performed with the financial support of the Russian Foundation for Basic Research - project#18-47-340010 r_a and the financial support of the Administration of Volgograd region.

References

1. Merchant, F., Vatwani, T., Chattopadhyay, A., Raha, S., Nandy, S.K., Narayan, R.: Efficient realization of householder transform through algorithm-architecture co-design for acceleration of QR Factorization. IEEE Trans. Parallel Distributed Syst. **29**(8), 1707–1720 (2018)
2. Tomas Dominguez, A.E., Quintana Orti, E.S.: Fast blocking of householder reflectors on graphics processors. In: Proceedings - 26th Euromicro International Conference on Parallel, Distributed, and Network-Based Processing, PDP 2018, pp. 385–393 (2018)
3. Andreev, A., Doukhnitch, E., Egunov, V., Zharikov, D., Shapovalov, O., Artuh, S.: Evaluation of hardware implementations of CORDIC-like algorithms in FPGA using OpenCL kernels. In: Kravets, A., Shcherbakov, M., Kultsova, M., Iijima, T. (eds.) JCKBSE 2014. CCIS, vol. 466, pp. 228–242. Springer, Cham (2014). https://doi.org/10.1007/978-3-319-11854-3_20
4. Egunov, V.A.: Implementation of QR and LQ decompositions on shared memory parallel computing systems. In: Egunov, V.A., Andreev, A.E. (eds.) 2016 2nd International Conference on Industrial Engineering, Applications and Manufacturing (ICIEAM), Chelyabinsk, Russia, 19–20 May 2016, 5 p. IEEE (2016)https://doi.org/10.1109/icieam.2016.7911607
5. Getmanskiy, V., Andreev, A.E., Alekseev, S., Gorobtsov, A.S., Egunov, V., Kharkov, E.: Optimization and parallelization of CAE software stress-strain solver for heterogeneous computing hardware. In: Kravets, A., Shcherbakov, M., Kultsova, M., Groumpos, P. (eds) CIT&DS 2017. CCIS, vol 754, pp. 562–674. Springer, Cham (2017). https://doi.org/10.1007/978-3-319-65551-2_41
6. Glinsky, B., et al.: The co-design of astrophysical code for massively parallel supercomputers. In: Carretero, J., et al. (eds.) ICA3PP 2016. LNCS, vol. 10049, pp. 342–353. Springer, Cham (2016). https://doi.org/10.1007/978-3-319-49956-7_27
7. Tian, Y.: Some results on the eigenvalue problem for a fractional elliptic equation. Boundary Value Problems **1**, 13 (2019)
8. Baker, C.G., Hetmaniuk, U.L., Lehoucq, R.B., Thornquist, H.K.: Anasazi software for the numerical solution of large-scale eigenvalue problems. ACM Trans. Math. Softw. **36**(3), art. no. 13 (2009). https://doi.org/10.1145/1527286.1527287
9. Polizzi, E.: Density-matrix-based algorithm for solving eigenvalue problems. Phys. Rev. B - Condensed Matter Mat. Phys. **79**(11), art. no. 115112 (2009). https://doi.org/10.1103/physrevb.79.115112
10. Bogoya, J.M., Grudsky, S.M., Malysheva, I.S.: Extreme individual eigenvalues for a class of large hessenberg toeplitz matrices. Operator Theory Adv. Appl. **271**, 119–143 (2018)
11. Vatankhah, S.: Large-scale inversion of magnetic data using golub-kahan bidiagonalization with truncated generalized cross validation for regularization parameter estimation. J. Earth Space Phys. **44**(4), 29–39 (2019)
12. Salam, A., Kahla, H.B.: An upper J-Hessenberg reduction of a matrix through symplectic Householder transformations. Computers and Mathematics with Applications (2019)
13. Liu, G., Liu, Y., Guo, M., Li, P., Li, M.: Variational inference with Gaussian mixture model and householder flow. Neural Networks **109**, 43–55 (2019)
14. Li, S., Cao, G., Wei, S.: Improved measurement matrix and reconstruction algorithm for compressed sensing. In: Proceedings of 2018 IEEE 8th International Conference on Electronics Information and Emergency Communication, ICEIEC 2018, 8473512, pp. 136–139 (2018)

15. Noble, J.H., Lubasch, M., Stevens, J., Jentschura, U.D.: Diagonalization of complex symmetric matrices: generalized Householder reflections, iterative deflation and implicit shifts. Comput. Phys. Commun. **221**, 304–316 (2017)
16. Bujanovic, Z., Karlsson, L., Kressner, D.: A householder-based algorithm for hessenberg-triangular reduction. SIAM J. Matrix Anal. Appl. **39**(3), 1270–1294 (2018)
17. Eljammaly, M., Karlsson, L., Kågström, B.: On the Tunability of a New Hessenberg Reduction Algorithm Using Parallel Cache Assignment. In: Wyrzykowski, R., Dongarra, J., Deelman, E., Karczewski, K. (eds.) PPAM 2017. LNCS, vol. 10777, pp. 579–589. Springer, Cham (2018). https://doi.org/10.1007/978-3-319-78024-5_50

Supercomputer Simulation

Analysis of the Influence of Changes in the Exterior Elements of the Car on the Drag Coefficient and the Problem of Its Optimization

Aleksei Maksimov[1,2]($\boxtimes$) (iD), Yury Boldyrev[1,2], Aleksei Borovkov[1,2],
Aleksei Tarasov[1,2], Oleg Klyavin[1,2], and Ilya Davydov[1,2]

[1] Peter the Great St. Petersburg Polytechnic University,
195251 Saint Petersburg, Russia
allevella@gmail.com, yyb150546@mail.ru,
{borovkov,tarasov,klyavin,davydov}@compmechlab.com
[2] SPbSTU "Center of Computer-Aided Engineering",
195220 Saint Petersburg, Russia

Abstract. The results of optimization of the external aerodynamic surface of the car in order to reduce the drag coefficient by making changes in its shape and do not affect the overall stylistic appearance are presented. The optimality criterion is the coefficient of longitudinal aerodynamic drag C_d, while the optimization parameters are the geometric characteristics and the appearance of the car, which was developed by stylists.

Computational procedure and an algorithm for solving an optimal problem are presented. We emphasize that the problem of calculating the aerodynamic drag coefficient C_d, taken separately, is a difficult and very computationally resource-intensive task of applied aerodynamics. Also note that the problem of optimizing (minimizing) the C_d coefficient includes the task of calculating one as a procedure, repeated at each step of the iterative optimization process, when the above-mentioned optimization parameters are changed.

Obviously, the considered optimal task is relevant, since, having solved it, it is possible to increase the driving distance of the car, reduce the generation of noise generated by its various parts and preserve the external aesthetic appearance developed by designers. The last point is particularly important, as usually when designing a car, its creation process is iterative in nature when interacting with groups of designers and development engineers. The approach presented in the paper will reduce the time and number of such iterations.

Keywords: High performance computing · Optimization · Car exterior · Aerodynamics · Drag coefficient

© Springer Nature Switzerland AG 2019
V. Voevodin and S. Sobolev (Eds.): RuSCDays 2019, CCIS 1129, pp. 155–165, 2019.
https://doi.org/10.1007/978-3-030-36592-9_13

1   Introduction

Recently, mathematical modelling plays a key role in the creation of aerodynamically perfect shape of the car. By aerodynamically perfect shape we mean a shape of the car that meets the requirements for the layout of the car, capacity, visibility, design requirements and many other requirements, but the drag coefficient of such a car should be as low as possible [1]. The requirement for the lowest possible drag coefficient (C_d) has always been a challenge in vehicle design. The problem is particularly acute now, when with the widespread development and appearance on the roads of electric vehicles, in which batteries are the weakest point due to the high cost, high weight and low energy intensity, decreasing the drag coefficient C_d is the main scientific and technical problem that helps to cope with such problems as increasing the range of the car and the noise generated by it.

To achieve the goal of a low drag coefficient, recent works use LES (Large Eddy Simulation) turbulence model to resolve the eddies in the turbulent flow with details over various parts of a car [2]. Approaches using LES turbulence model are still expensive computationally. However, approaches using Reynolds-averaged turbulence models provide good results in determining the aerodynamic parameters of cars [3–5]. One of the important components in solving the aerodynamic problem is the preparation of a high-quality finite-volume mesh [6]. This question is quite well covered in the literature and does not require additional research. At the same time, in the literature, approaches to designing an aerodynamically perfect shape of a car's exterior from scratch are poorly covered.

The most important element of the problem solution is the modelling of spatial three-dimensional turbulent flows behind the car, which fundamentally belongs to one of the most difficult areas in engineering calculations. This problem is associated with high computational costs and is usually used only at the last stage of the design of the car to determine the final C_d coefficient. Usually at the initial stage of the design, to estimate the drag coefficient it is sufficient to carry out a two-dimensional calculation of the turbulent flow around central section of the car. Note that the shape of the central section is created in compliance with the requirements for the placement in the cabin of people of different representativeness, reach and viewing angles, location of controls, dimensions of the engine and luggage compartments, placement of the fuel tank and spare wheel.

The process of designing a car, which is briefly described, for example, in [7], includes several steps. Sketch layout of the car starts with the placement of people in the cabin. Build the line of the internal boundaries of the floor and partitions of the engine compartment, then determined by the position of the seats. The driver's roof line is set taking into account the gap from the driver's head to the inner side of the skin, the thickness of the roof, the arrow of the transverse curvature of the roof and the fact that the seat is not located in the plane of symmetry of the car.

In the following stages, questions on the position of the steering wheel, pedal pads, instrument panel are being worked out. Then put the restrictive contour of the car, set the boundaries of the engine and luggage compartments. The engine layout begins with the application of the outer partition line of the engine compartment, the floor and its inclined part.

At the final design stage, the position of the wheel axles is determined. After approval of the outline layout, the design of the car begins. On the resulting sketch layout of the car superimposed various options for the external style, created by designers together with the engineers. As a result of such an iterative process, the external form of the various elements of the car, such as the hood, grille, bumper, and so on, may undergo changes until a consensus is reached between the design idea and the engineering thought. Since the shape of the car has a significant effect on the aerodynamic drag coefficient [8], design engineers and developers, as a rule, have to consider a significant number of vehicle parameters when optimizing C_d coefficient [9]. And here the issues of automating the process of finding the most important optimization parameters that determine the influence on the shape of a structure come to the forefront from the standpoint of finding the minimum of the C_d coefficient. Currently, for these purposes, they often resort to one or another software package that allows to automate the design optimization processes.

One of these software systems that uses the idea of moving elements - finite-volume meshes is the ANSYS Fluent software. The built-in tools of the Adjoint Solver available in the software allow to optimize the geometry of the external shape of the car. According to [10], the idea of the method is a sequential reconstruction of the finite-volume mesh space in the direction of reducing the optimality criterion, which we have is the drag coefficient C_d. Thus, choosing one or another fragment of the surface of the car exterior, we can change the geometric shape of the fragment of the car, and, consequently, change the aerodynamics of the car, and hence the corresponding aerodynamic coefficients.

The Adjoint Solver significantly speeds up the optimization process in comparison with the parametrisation of the geometry. Using this approach eliminates the need to manually rebuild the mesh at each step of the optimization process and re-assign the boundary and initial conditions.

2   Formulation of the Problem

We consider the flow of air flowing along the course of central section of the projected car, the length and height of which is limited, respectively, 2.5 m and 1.5 m. A rectangle with a length of 30 m and a height of 11 m is selected as the computational domain (see Fig. 1).

Considered medium: air with a density of 1.185 kg/m^3 and dynamic viscosity of $1.849 \cdot 10^{-5}$ kg/m·s, which corresponds to a temperature of 25 °C. Since Mach number does not exceed 0.3, when the car is moving, air can be considered as an incompressible medium. During the calculations, the air velocity at the inlet of computational domain varied from 10 to 120 km/h with a step of 10 km/h. For each velocity value, the drag force was calculated, which was converted into the drag coefficient by the formula 1:

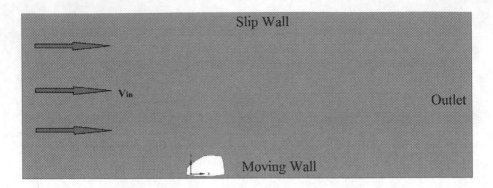

Fig. 1. Computational domain.

$$C_d = \frac{2F_d}{\rho \vartheta^2 A} \tag{1}$$

where A is the cross-sectional area, F_d is the drag force, ρ is the density of the medium, ϑ is the velocity of the incoming air flow.

The problem of air flow around the central section of the car was solved in the ANSYS Fluent software package, and the procedure for optimizing the shape of the car model, as mentioned, was carried out using the Adjoint Solver program module.

3   Calculation of the Aerodynamic Drag Coefficient

To simulate the air flow around the central section of the car, a high-quality quadrangular mesh was built. The entire mesh space was divided into 2 blocks, the first block was associated with the description of the movement of air at the far distance behind the car, while the second block was associated with the description of the air flow in close proximity to the surface of the car and had mesh of high density. The first block consists of rectangular cells, 150 mm in size. The second block, which includes the central section of the car, consists of cells 20 mm in size. Such a division of the mesh into 2 blocks allowed more efficient use of computational power.

By means of wall layers it is possible to resolve satisfactorily a boundary layer on a surface of the car. The height of the first wall cell $y = 1.6 \cdot 10^{-5}$, which corresponds to the value of $y+ = 1$ at an incoming flow speed of 90 km/h. Figure 2 shows the entire computational domain (left) and an enlarged fragment near the car surface (right). The total number of elements of the computational domain was about 200 thousand elements.

Determining the values of velocity, pressure, density in the cells of the computational mesh in ANSYS Fluent, an approximation of the averaged Reynolds equations is used by the method of control volumes. To complete the system of equations, the k-ω SST model of turbulence was used. The connection between

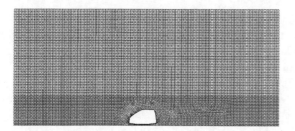 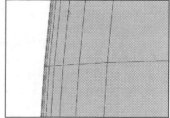

Fig. 2. Mesh of entire computational domain (left) and near car's surface (right).

the components of the velocity and pressure vector was carried out using a semi-implicit method for equations with a pressure coupling—SIMPLE. The mean square residuals of the required quantities were chosen as the convergence conditions of the problem. In this case, the calculations ended when an accuracy of the order of 10^{-6} was reached.

4   Optimization of the Car's Exterior Shape

The Adjoint Solver uses a discrete adjoint method to implement an optimization procedure, since this method provides greater stability than the continuous conjugate method [11].

Adjoint Solver requires the calculation results for a certain set of parameters to optimize the geometry of the original model. Next, we select the criterion of optimality we are interested in, in our case, the drag force, which we will minimize. Then the sensitivity of the considered system with respect to the selected criterion is calculated, i.e. the dependence of the optimality criterion on the selected range of parameters. Note that the transformation of the mesh area associated with the geometry of the optimized surface in the environment of the Adjoint Solver allows you to consistently improve the value of the optimality criterion. In other words, the Adjoint Solver sequentially modifies the mesh so that it continuously approaches the optimal value of the selected criterion.

This approach can be implemented for individual parts of the car, and for the entire car's shape [12]. In our work, the hood, grille, bumper, roof (its height), and the shape of the trunk lid were considered as elements of optimization.

5   Calculation Results

The results of aerodynamic calculations were the velocity fields for various solutions of the shape of the exterior of the car, obtained during the optimization procedure.

It took a lot of time to search through the exterior options of the car, with the parametric specification of the curves of its geometry, even when using the Polytechnic—RSC Tornado computer system containing 668 dual-processor nodes [13]. When one of the calculated optimized parameters is changed, the geometry of the calculated domain is rebuilt, and with it the entire finite-volume mesh. On the new mesh, boundary and initial conditions are reassigned, which entails a large time expenditure on the interaction between various component software systems. For example, we note that the optimization of the shape of only the front bumper took considerable time for the task calculators and the parameterization of the geometry. The calculation itself was performed using 20 nodes of the supercomputer.

Each node of the supercomputer consists of two processors with 14 cores each. When parallelizing calculations, one core is used for data exchange between nodes, in this way 27 cores per node are used for calculations.

On each of the nodes was calculated one version of the modified geometry. Busting through 400 options took about 15 h of computing. It was not possible to achieve the optimal value of the drag coefficient, as when using the Adjoint Solver tool.

Variants of the exterior of the car, obtained during the optimization, are shown in Fig. 3. For the designed car was taken into account that $A = 2\,m^2$. For the style variant in Fig. 3a, the drag coefficient is $C_d = 0.5$, which is a high indicator; the coefficient is higher than for the most popular car models produced on the market [11, 14]. The flow behind the car is highly turbulent and periodic. When designing a 3D style surface from a 2D optimized section, the final C_d will be higher, according to our estimates, the drag coefficient will increase to $C_d = 0.5 \div 0.55$. In Fig. 3 b, c, d, e for the obtained 2D style surfaces a decrease in the drag coefficient is observed, flow separation area is formed behind the car, but it does not have a periodic behavior as in Fig. 3a. On the Fig. 3f, car's style surface has the smallest drag coefficient among the considered style surfaces, was chosen optimal and served as the initial design point of the 3-D version as designers. On the basis of the selected shape of the central section, a three-dimensional model of the car was made, shown in Fig. 4.

The values of the drag coefficient C_d calculated for all variants are given in Table 1.

Table 1. The values of the drag coefficient for all style surfaces.

Style surface	1	2	3	4	5	6
C_d	0.5	0.236	0.231	0.184	0.209	0.174

Two-block mesh consisting of 100 million elements was used for aerodynamic calculation of the flow around the 3D model of optimal shape. The first block by analogy with the mesh for 2D calculation includes the air at far distance from the car. The second block describes the space near the car with smaller cells for qualitative resolution of the flow interaction with the car shape. First block consists of rectangular cells, the size of $125 \times 125 \times 125\,mm$. Second block, which

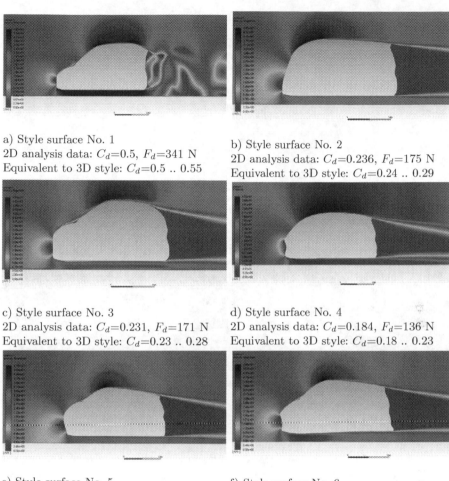

a) Style surface No. 1
2D analysis data: $C_d=0.5$, $F_d=341$ N
Equivalent to 3D style: $C_d=0.5 .. 0.55$

b) Style surface No. 2
2D analysis data: $C_d=0.236$, $F_d=175$ N
Equivalent to 3D style: $C_d=0.24 .. 0.29$

c) Style surface No. 3
2D analysis data: $C_d=0.231$, $F_d=171$ N
Equivalent to 3D style: $C_d=0.23 .. 0.28$

d) Style surface No. 4
2D analysis data: $C_d=0.184$, $F_d=136$ N
Equivalent to 3D style: $C_d=0.18 .. 0.23$

e) Style surface No. 5
2D analysis data: $C_d=0.209$, $F_d=155$ N
Equivalent to 3D style: $C_d=0.21 .. 0.26$

f) Style surface No. 6
2D analysis data: $C_d=0.174$, $F_d=129$ N
Equivalent to 3D style: $C_d=0.17 .. 0.22$

Fig. 3. Variants of style surfaces obtained as a result of optimization.

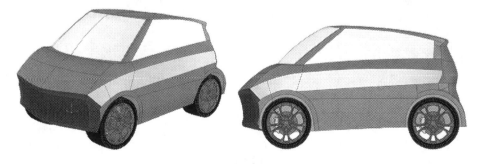

Fig. 4. 3D model created on the basis of style surface No. 6.

includes 3D model of the car, consists of cells, the size of $7.5 \times 7.5 \times 7.5 \, \text{mm}$. Boundary layer was resolved with a prism layers on a surface of the car. Example of such mesh is shown in Fig. 5.

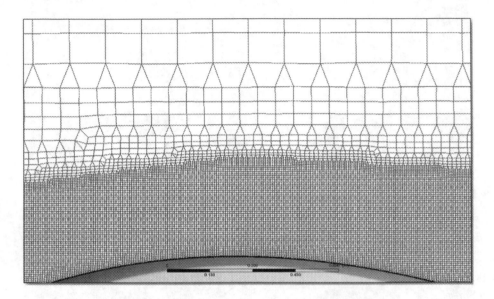

Fig. 5. Finite-volume mesh (central section) for 3D analysis.

By using mesh of 100 million elements, the optimal number of cores was chosen for calculation. Figure 6 shows how the speed up rate varies with the number of cores. This speed up rate is usually influenced by the mesh density, the mathematical formulation of the problem, the presence of interfaces between the meshes, the possibility of decomposition in the software itself, and the parameters of the supercomputer.

With presented mesh density, the calculation of the 3D model of the car is possible only on a supercomputer. The calculation using 810 cores (30 nodes) took, in a stationary formulation, about 2 h. No further increase in the number of cores was chosen, since the speed up rate of the parallel process is going far from linear.

Libraries of the MeTiS family are used for parallelization in ANSYS Fluent. Algorithms implemented in the library provide high-quality decomposition in accordance with the amount of data transferred between processes. Currently, the MeTiS package is used as the basis for data decomposition in the ANSYS package and is recommended for use. Additional algorithms such as Principal Axes and Cartesian Axes were tested, but did not give any increase in speed up rate or quality of decomposition. Parallelization occurs automatically from the moment when the method is selected and the calculation is started.

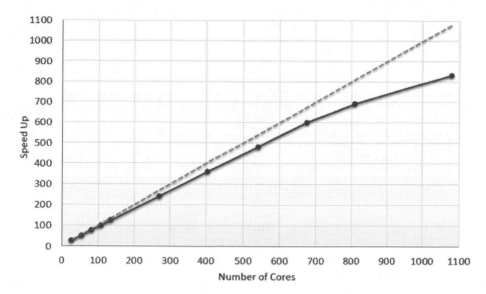

Fig. 6. Number of cores to speed up calculations.

However, the preparation of the geometry and the computational mesh for such an analysis by CFD engineers takes days, so it is not possible to do a full three-dimensional simulation of the car at the initial stage of design.

Calculated drag coefficient for the three-dimensional 3-D surface was $C_d = 0.17$. It should be understood that the created style surface belongs to the "class B". The style surface of the "class B" does not take into account gaps, door handles, the bottom of the car does not contain a fuel tank, transmission, suspension geometry, brake components and other subsystems, there is no grille. Only when creating "class A" surface are all visible external surfaces drawn (for example, body panels, bumpers, grilles, headlights, mudguards, etc.). In the article the style surface of "class A" was not considered because its development is carried out only at the final stage of the design of the car. We only note that in the calculation of the car's aerodynamic based on the stylistic surface "of A class" the drag coefficient increases.

Obtained dependences of the force and drag coefficient vs the car speed from 10 to 120 km/h are presented in Fig. 7. For comparison, the dependence was taken for the Mitsubishi Eclipse GS car [15] and according to the method described in the article, the force and C_d were calculated for the Smart ForTwo car [16,17], which is analogous to the dimensions developed in the article "Style No. 6". Drag force varies in a parabolic curve [18]. However, it is worth noting that the coefficient C_d (calculated by the formula 1) can remain constant, regardless of the car speed, as, for example, for Mitsubishi Eclipse. For the developed "style No. 6", the C_d coefficient decreases with increasing in speed, i.e. the faster the car moves, the more its aerodynamic shape is perfect. This form can be developed only using the optimization methods described in the article. For example, for electric vehicles such a form will increase the range.

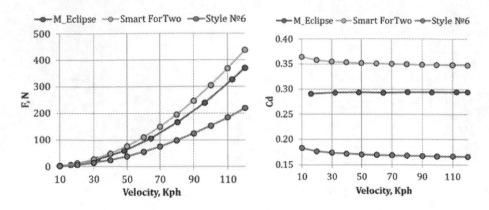

Fig. 7. Force (left) and C_d (right) versus car speed.

6   Conclusions

The results of two-dimensional calculation of the air flow around the central section of the car and optimization of its shape in order to reduce the drag coefficient of the C_d are presented.

6 variants of the external style of the car during optimization were developed, for each drag coefficient is calculated.

It is shown that the value of aerodynamic drag force for the optimized style surface No. 6 is lower than for other variants. The best option among the considered, after coordination with the designers is the last one with the lowest drag coefficient. Based on the selected shape of the central section, a three-dimensional style surface of "class B" was developed. The comparison of C_d coefficients for the developed and real cars is carried out. Thanks to the optimization tools and the technique described in the article, the developed style surface has a very low C_d coefficient, which will significantly increase the range of the car and reduce noise generated by car's shape.

The problem was solved using the "Polytechnic - RSC Tornado" supercomputer. The mesh of 100 million elements, in calculations, using the ANSYS Fluent software, were used and the problem was solved on 810 cores (30 nodes). The number of cores in parallelization is chosen based on the fact that with a further increase the process of parallelization moves away from the linear. In the ANSYS software, in parallelization, the MeTiS algorithm was used as the most efficient.

Acknowledgements. This work was financially supported from the project of the Ministry of Education and Science of the Russian Federation in the framework of the implementation of the Federal Target Program "Research and Development in Priority Directions for the Development of the Scientific and Technological Complex of Russia for 2014–2020". Agreement on the provision of subsidies from 20.12.2018.04.2014, No. 05.578.21.0269.

References

1. Przysowa, K., et al.: Shape optimisation method based on the surrogate models in the parallel asynchronous environment. Appl. Soft Comput. **71**, 1189–1203 (2018)
2. Krajnovic, S., Osth, J., Basara, B.: LES study of breakdown control of A-pillar vortex. Int. J. Flow Control. **2**(4), 237–258 (2010)
3. Daryakenari, B., Abdullah, S., Zulkifli, R., Sundararajan, E., Sood, A.B.: Mohd: reducing the aerodynamic forces through a rear spoiler. Int. Rev. Model. Simul. **5**(6), 2512–2517 (2012)
4. Bokser, V., Sudakov, G.: Aerodynamic drag of bodies in transonic flow. Theory and applications to computational aerodynamics. Fluid Dyn. **43**(4), 613–624 (2008). https://doi.org/10.1134/S0015462808040145
5. Sunny, S.A.: Effect of turbulence in modeling the reduction of local drag forces in a computational automotive model. Int. J. Energy Environ. **2**(6), 1079–1100 (2011)
6. Nor, E.A., Essam, A.-S., Adrian, G., Penerbit, A.B.: Mesh optimization for ground vehicle aerodynamics. CFD Lett. **2**(1), 54–65 (2010)
7. Karpouzas, G.K., et al.: Adjoint optimization for vehicle external aerodynamics. Int. J. Automot. Eng. **7**, 1–7 (2016)
8. He, P., et al.: An aerodynamic design optimization framework using a discrete adjoint approach with OpenFOAM. Comput. Fluids **168**, 285–303 (2018)
9. Wikipedia Homepage. https://en.wikipedia.org/wiki/Automobile_drag_coefficient
10. Katz, J.: Race Car Aerodynamics: Designing for Speed, 1st edn. Bentley Publishers, Cambridge (1995)
11. ANSYS ®, Release 17.2, Help System, Adjoint Solver Module Manual
12. Guo, Z., et al.: Optimization of the aerodynamic drag reduction of a passenger hatchback car. In: Proceedings of the Institution of Mechanical Engineers, Part G: Journal of Aerospace Engineering, pp. 1–18. SAGE Publications Ltd., London (2018). https://doi.org/10.1177/0954410018786619
13. RSC Group Homepage. http://scc.spbstu.ru/index.php/resources/polytechnik-rsk-tornado
14. ANSYS ®, Release 17.2, Help System, FLUENT Theory guide
15. Heft, A. et al.: Introduction of a new realistic generic car model for ANSYS Aerodynamic investigations. In: SAE 2012 world congress, Warrendale, Detroit, USA, pp. 1–14 (2012). https://doi.org/10.4271/2012-01-0168
16. Ecomodder Homepage, Vehicle Coefficient of Drag List. https://ecomodder.com/wiki/
17. AllesAuto Homepage. https://www.allesauto.at/smart-fortwo-mhd-passion/
18. Texas Tech University Homepage. http://www.phys.ttu.edu/ritlg/courses/p1401/drag_plt.html

Application of High-Performance Computing for Modeling the Hydrobiological Processes in Shallow Water

Alexander I. Sukhinov[1], Alexander E. Chistyakov[1], Alla V. Nikitina[2(✉)], Alena A. Filina[3], and Yulia V. Belova[1]

[1] Don State Technical University, Rostov-on-Don, Russia
sukhinov@gmail.com, cheese_05@mail.ru, yuliapershina@mail.ru
[2] Southern Federal University, Rostov-on-Don, Russia
nikitina.vm@gmail.com
[3] "Supercomputers and Neurocomputers Research Center" Co. Ltd, Taganrog, Russia
j.a.s.s.y@mail.ru

Abstract. The paper covers the development and research of a mathematical model for description hydrobiological processes using the modern information technologies and computational methods to improve the accuracy of predictive modeling the ecological situation in shallow waters. The model takes into account the following factors: movement of water flows; microturbulent diffusion; gravitational settling of pollutants; nonlinear interaction of phyto- and zooplankton populations; nutrient, temperature and oxygen regimes; and influence of salinity. A space splitting scheme taking into account the partial filling of cells was proposed for model discretization. This scheme significantly reduces both error and calculation time. The practical significance of the paper is determined by software implementation of the model and the determination of limits and prospects of its practical use. Experimental software is designed on the basis of a supercomputer for mathematical modeling of possible development scenarios of shallow water ecosystems taking into account the influence of environment. For this, we consider as an example the Azov Sea in summer. The parallel implementation involves decomposition methods for computationally laborious diffusion-convection problems taking into account the architecture and parameters of a multiprocessor computer system.

Keywords: Mathematical model · Hydrobiological process · Eutrophication · Field investigation · Algorithm · Supercomputer · Graphic accelerator

This paper was partially supported by grant No. 17-11-01286 of the Russian Science Foundation.

V. Voevodin and S. Sobolev (Eds.): RuSCDays 2019, CCIS 1129, pp. 166–181, 2019.
https://doi.org/10.1007/978-3-030-36592-9_14

1   Introduction

Hydrobiological processes significantly affect on the water quality, the reproduction and safety of commercial fish stocks. Many scientists researched mathematical modeling of hydrophysics and biological kinetics processes, which have a significant impact on the ecological situation and the water reproduction processes. Note the fundamental papers in the field of mathematical models, development of methods of diagnosis and prediction of changes in aquatic ecosystems, by authors such as Lotka [1], Volterra [2], Logofet [3], Hutchinson, Monod [4], Mitscherlich [5], Odum, Gause, Vinberg [6], Abakymov [7], Menshutkin [8], Ruhovetc [9], Vorovich, Gorstko [10], Boulion, Imberger, Jorgensen [11], Vollenweider [12]. They developed principles, mathematical models and approaches widely used at solving scientific and practical problems for water ecosystems. Fleishman was engaged in development and research of stochastic models of potential efficiency of ecosystems. The analytical model of "water blooming" was described in the papers of Krestin and Rosenberg, where the possible explanation of the phenomenon of outbreaks of blue-green algae abundance and the more complex process of "wave of flowering" on the water profile is given within the framework of interactions of the systems of species competition and "predator-prey". On the example of the plankton dynamics model of the North Sea, J. Steele described models of combining different hypotheses about food behavior, where a minimum attention was devoted to the peculiarities of spatial distribution of organisms.

John Dubo researched the causes of spatial heterogeneity in the North Sea taking into account two factors: the trophic relationship between phyto- and zooplankton, and the rate of water flow in a diffusion process. Later models of biota interaction with separate factors, including the solar radiation, temperature were developed and widely used, then – models of organism interaction with abstract "resources", developed by Abrosov, Bogolyubov. Detailed results and development of formalized representations on the examples of modeling the mouth of the Neva river and some lakes of the North-West of Russia are presented in the publications by Umnov, Alimov, Matishov, Ilyichev were researched of the optimal exploitation of water resources, the development of models of pollutant transport in waters [13]. Tyutyunov, Perevarukha were researched the interaction of populations, including taxis, interspecific competition, the lag effect [14,15]. Samarskiy [16], Tikhonov, Marchuk [17,18], Chetverushkin, Iakobovskiy [19], Ilyin developed supercomputer technologies to reseacrh the Hydrophysical processes.

In this regard, the construction of it mathematical models with predictive relevance is not only scientific, but also significance national economic importance. It's known that the eutrophication process is the enrichment of rivers, lakes and seas with biogens, accompanied by the increasing of the vegetation productivity in water, can be as a result of natural aging of water and anthropogenic influences. The main chemical nutrients, contributing to the water eutrophication, include the phosphorus and nitrogen. The relief and currents of sea are strongly interconnected with each other and have an impact on the biogenic regime of water. A spatially inhomogeneous, nonlinear 3D model was used for description the hydrobiological processes. It's numerical implementation is based on using the finite-difference approach. Due to the fact that calculations for different input data in a limited time interval are required for development the projects for sustainable development of water ecosystem, it's necessary to develop parallel algorithms for numerical solution of biological kinetics' problems, focused on systems with distributed memory.

In July 2017, members of the staffs of the Don State Technical University, Southern Federal University and Southern Scientific Center of the Russian Academy of Sciences (RAS) went on an expedition to the Azov Sea aboard the Scientific Research Vessel (SRV) "Deneb". The main purpose of the expedition was to carry out the comprehensive research of the current situation and spatial-temporal changes in the hydrobiological regime of the Azov Sea.

Various systems from the Unified State System of Information about the Situation in the World Ocean ("ESIMO"), "Analytical GIS" portal, developed by the Institute for Information Transmission Problems of RAS for complex geoinformational analysis of spatial-temporal processes and phenomena, were used along with expedition data and literature sources for modeling hydrophysical processes in shallow waters (Azov Sea).

2   Problem Statement

The papers by Matishov, Ilyichev, Yakushev, Sukhinov, Tyutyunov, Krukier devoted to the modeling of hydrochemical processes were used at construction of the eutrophication model of the Azov Sea and Taganrog Bay. The hydrobiological process, described the euthrophication process model of shallow water, has the form [20–24]:

$$\frac{\partial S_i}{\partial t} + \operatorname{div}\left(\mathbf{U}S_i\right) = \mu_i \Delta_{S_i} + \frac{\partial}{\partial z}\left(\nu_i \frac{\partial S_i}{\partial z}\right) + \psi_i, \qquad (1)$$

where S_i is the concentration of the i-th component, $i = \overline{1,17}$; $\mathbf{u}$ is the velocity vector of water flow, $\mathbf{u} = \{u, v, w\}$; $\mathbf{U} = \mathbf{u} + \mathbf{u}_{0i}$ represents the matter convective transport velocity, $\mathbf{U} = \{U, V, W\}$; $\mathbf{u}_{0i}$ stands for the velocity of the i-th component of sedimentation; ψ_i denotes the chemical-biological source, the index i corresponds to the next type: 1 is the hydrogen sulphide (H_2S); 2 is the elemental sulfur (S); 3 are sulfates (SO_4); 4 are thiosulfates (and sulfites); 5 is the total organic nitrogen (N); 6 is the ammonium (ammonia nitrogen) (NH_4); 7 are nitrits (NO_2); 8 are nitrates (NO_3); 9 is the dissolved manganese (DOMn); 10 is the weighted manganese (POMn); 11 is the dissolved oxygen (O_2); 12 are silicates (SiO_3 is the metasilicate; SiO_4 is the ortosilicate); 13 are phosphates (PO_4); 14 is the ferrum (Fe^{2+}); 15 is the silicic acid (H_2SiO_3 is the metasilicic; H_2SiO_4 is the ortosilicic); 16 is the phytoplankton; 17 is the zooplankton; μ_i, ν_i are diffusion coefficients in horizontal and vertical directions [25].

It is necessary to add initial conditions:

$$S_i(x, y, z, 0) = S_i^0(x, y, z), (x, y, z) \in \overline{G}, i = \overline{1,17}. \qquad (2)$$

Let the boundary Σ of the domain G be sectionally smooth, and suppose that $\Sigma = \Sigma_H \cup \Sigma_o \cup \sigma$, where Σ_H is the water bottom surface, Σ_o is the unperturbed surface of the aquatic medium, and σ is the lateral (cylindrical) surface. Let $\mathbf{n}$ be the outer normal vector to the boundary Σ; $\mathbf{u_n}$ be the normal component of the water flow velocity vector to the Σ surface. Assume that the concentrations S_i are:

on the lateral boundary $\sigma : S_i = 0$ if $\mathbf{u_n} < 0$; $\dfrac{\partial S_i}{\partial \mathbf{n}} = 0$ if $\mathbf{u_n} \geq 0$, $i = \overline{1,17}$;

at the bottom $\Sigma_H : \dfrac{\partial S_i}{\partial z} = \varepsilon_{1,i}S_i$, $i = \overline{1,15}$, $\dfrac{\partial S_i}{\partial z} = \varepsilon_{2,i}S_i$, $i = \overline{16,17}$; $\qquad$ (3)

on the unperturbed sugface $\Sigma_o : \dfrac{\partial S_i}{\partial z} = \varphi(S_i)$, $i = \overline{1,17}$,

where φ is a given function; $\varepsilon_{1,i}$ and $\varepsilon_{2,i}$ are nonnegative constants: $\varepsilon_{1,i}$, $i = \overline{1,15}$, account for absorption of nutrient by bottom sediments; $\varepsilon_{2,i}$, $i = \overline{16,17}$ account for the descent of phyto- and zooplankton to the bottom and their deposition.

We took into account the fact that anaerobic conditions occur arise in the bottom layers of the Azov Sea at calm and close to them wind situations. The reduction of surface water-saturated sludge entails the release of sulfates, bivalent manganese and iron, organic compounds, ammonium, silicates and phosphates into the solution (except hydrogen sulfide). The field of water flow velocities calculated in [26,27] was used as input data for the model (1)–(3).

3   Solution Method of Model Problems

Each equation of the proposed model in the form (1)–(3) after linearization in the two-dimensional case can be represent as a diffusion-convection problem in the form:

$$\frac{\partial S}{\partial t} + u\frac{\partial S}{\partial x} + v\frac{\partial S}{\partial y} = \frac{\partial}{\partial x}\left(\mu\frac{\partial S}{\partial x}\right) + \frac{\partial}{\partial y}\left(\mu\frac{\partial S}{\partial y}\right) + f \qquad (4)$$

with boundary conditions:

$$\frac{\partial S}{\partial \mathbf{n}}(x,y,t) = \alpha_n S + \beta_n, \qquad (5)$$

where u, v are water velocity components; μ is the turbulent exchange coefficient; f is the function, describing the intensity and distribution of sources; α_n, β_n are given coefficients.

We introduced a uniform rectangular grid:

$$\omega_h = \{t^n = n\tau, x_i = ih_x, y_j = jh_y; n = \overline{0,N_t}, i = \overline{0,N_x}, j = \overline{0,N_y},$$

$$N_t\tau = T, N_xh_x = l_x, N_yh_y = l_y\},$$

where τ is a time step; h_x, h_y are spatial steps; N_t is an upper time boundary; N_x, N_y are spatial boundaries; l_x, l_y are maximum dimensions of computational domain.

For discretization of euthrophication model we used the space splitting scheme, taking into account the partial filling of cells [28]. The discrete analogue of the diffusion-convection Eq. (4) has the form:

$$\frac{q_{i,j}^{n+1/2} - q_{i,j}^n}{\tau} + \psi_{xL}\frac{q_{i-1,j}^{n-1/2} - q_{i-1,j}^{n-1}}{2\tau} + \psi_{xR}\frac{q_{i+1,j}^{n-1/2} - q_{i+1,j}^{n-1}}{2\tau} + u\frac{q_{i+1,j}^n - q_{i-1,j}^n}{4h_x} +$$

$$+\psi_{xL}u\frac{q_{i,j}^n - q_{i-1,j}^n}{h_x} + \psi_{xR}u\frac{q_{i+1,j}^n - q_{i,j}^n}{h_x} = \frac{3}{2}\mu\frac{q_{i+1,j}^n - 2q_{i,j}^n + q_{i-1,j}^n}{h_x^2} + \frac{g(q_{i,j}^n) + \eta_{i,j}^n}{2};$$

$$\frac{q_{i,j}^{n+1} - q_{i,j}^{n+1/2}}{\tau} + \psi_{yL}\frac{q_{i,j-1}^n - q_{i,j-1}^{n-1/2}}{2\tau} + \psi_{yR}\frac{q_{i,j+1}^n - q_{i,j+1}^{n-1/2}}{2\tau} + v\frac{q_{i,j+1}^{n+1/2} - q_{i,j-1}^{n+1/2}}{4h_y} +$$

$$+\psi_{yL}v\frac{q_{i,j}^{n+1/2} - q_{i,j-1}^{n+1/2}}{h_y} + \psi_{yR}v\frac{q_{i,j+1}^{n+1/2} - q_{i,j}^{n+1/2}}{h_y} =$$

$$= 3/2\mu\frac{q_{i,j+1}^{n+1/2} - 2q_{i,j}^{n+1/2} + q_{i,j-1}^{n+1/2}}{h_y^2} + 1/2\big(g(q_{i,j}^n) + \eta_{i,j}^n\big), \tag{6}$$

where $\psi_{xL} = 1$, $\psi_{xR} = 0$ at $u > 0$, and $\psi_{xL} = 0$, $\psi_{xR} = 1$ at $u < 0$; $\psi_{yL} = 1$, $\psi_{yR} = 0$ at $v > 0$, and $\psi_{yL} = 0$, $\psi_{yR} = 1$ at $v < 0$.

The research of the scheme (6) showed that it is stable at the Courant numbers in the interval $[0; 0.75]$ and the large Peclet numbers ($Pe > 20$). In the limiting case (the diffusion coefficient is equal to zero) at large Peclet numbers, the maximum value of the numerical solution error of this problem (4), (5) on the basis of the proposed difference scheme (6) was equaled to the 0.125. The numerical solution error resulting at using the scheme (refeq:66) was less than the solution error of the problem (4), (5) with using the discretization of standard difference "cabaret" schemes.

The grid equations, obtained in the result of discretization, have been solved by the modified adaptive alternating-triangular method (MATM) [29–31].

4   Parallel Implementation

We describe some parallel algorithms with various types of domain decomposition for solving problems (1)–(3) on a multiprocessor computer system (MCS). Parallel algorithms for the MATM were implemented on MCS of the Southern Federal University (SFU). MCS technical parameters: the peak performance is 18.8 TFlops; 8 computational racks; the computational field of MCS is based on the HP BladeSystem c-class infrastructure with integrated communication modules, power supply and cooling systems; 512 single-type 16-core HP ProLiant BL685c Blade servers are used as computational nodes, each of which is equipped with four 4-core AMD Opteron 8356 2.3 GHz processors and 32 GB RAM; the total number of computational nodes is 2048; the total amount of RAM is 4 TB.

4.1   Algorithm 1

Each processor is assigned a computational domain after partition of the initial computational domain in two coordinate directions (see Fig. 1). Adjacent domains overlap over two layers of nodes in the direction perpendicularly to the plane of the partition.

The residual vector and it uniform norm are calculated after each processor receives information for its own part of the domain. Then each processor determines the maximum module element of the residual vector and transfer it value to all remaining calculators. For calculation the uniform norm of the residual vector, it is enough to define the maximum element on each processor.

The parallel algorithm for calculating the correction vector has the form:

$$(D + \omega_m R_1) D^{-1} (D + \omega_m R_2) w^m = r^m,$$

where R_1 is a lower-triangular matrix, and R_2 is a upper-triangular matrix. For calculation the correction vector, we should solve the two following equations simultaneously:

$$(D + \omega_m R_1) y^m = r^m, (D + \omega_m R_2) w^m = D y^m.$$

Initially, the vector y^m is calculated starting in the lower left corner. Then the correction vector w^m is calculated starting in the upper right corner. The calculation scheme for the vector y^m is given in Fig. 2 (the transference of elements after calculation of two layers by the first processor is shown).

At the first step, the first processor operates with the top layer. Then, the transfer of overlapping elements to the adjacent processors is occured. At the next step, the first processor operates with the second layer, while its neighbors operate with the first. The transfer of elements after calculation of two layers by the first processor is shown in Fig. 2. In the scheme for calculation of the vector y^m, only the first processor does not require additional information and can independently operate with its part of the domain. Other processors wait the results from the previous processor, while it transfers the calculated values of grid functions at the grid nodes located in the preceding positions of this line. The process continues until all layers are calculated. Similarly, we can solve systems of linear algebraic equations (SLAE) with the upper-triangular matrix for calculating the correction vector.

Further, scalar products are calculated, and the algorithm proceeds to the next iteration layer. We obtained the following theoretical estimates of the acceleration $S_{(1)}^t$ and efficiency $E_{(1)}^t$ of the parallel algorithm 1:

$$S_{(1)}^t = \frac{p}{1 + \left(\sqrt{p} - 1\right) \left(\frac{36}{50 N_z} + \frac{4p}{50 t_0} \left(t_p \left(\frac{1}{N_x} + \frac{1}{N_y}\right) + \frac{t_x \sqrt{p}}{N_x N_y}\right)\right)},$$

$$E_{(1)}^t = \frac{S_{(1)}^t}{p} = \frac{1}{1 + \left(\sqrt{p} - 1\right) \left(\frac{36}{50 N_z} + \frac{4p}{50 t_0} \left(t_p \left(\frac{1}{N_x} + \frac{1}{N_y}\right) + \frac{t_x \sqrt{p}}{N_x N_y}\right)\right)},$$

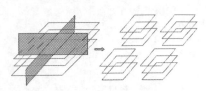

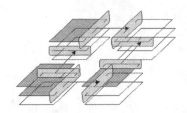

Fig. 1. Domain decomposition

Fig. 2. Scheme of calculation the vector y^m

where p is the total number of processors; t_0 is the execution time of an arithmetic operation; t_x is the latency; t_p is the time for transferring the flooating point numbers; N_x, N_y, N_z are the numbers of nodes in spatial directions.

Note that we considered the problem solution for a rectangular domain. In the case of a real water, the domain may have a complex shape. At the same time, the real acceleration is less than the theoretical estimation. The dependence obtained for the acceleration in theoretical estimates can be used as an upper estimate for the acceleration of parallel implementation of the MATM algorithm with a domain decomposition in two spatial directions.

4.2 Algorithm 2

The k-means method is used for the geometric partition of the computational domain so as to uniformly load a MCS calculators (processors). This method is based on the minimization of the functional $Q = Q^{(3)}$ of total variance of the element scatter (nodes of the computational grid) relative to the gravity center of subdomains. Let X_i be the set of computational grid nodes contained in the i-th subdomain, $i \in \{1, ..., m\}$, m is the given number of subdomains.

$$Q^{(3)} = \sum_i \frac{1}{|X_i|} \sum_{x \in X_i} d^2(x, c_i) \to \min, c_i = \frac{1}{|X_i|} \sum_{x \in X_i} x,$$

where c_i is the center of the subdomain X_i, and $d(x, c_i)$ is the distance between the computational node and the center of grid subdomain in the Euclidean metric. The k-means method converges only if all subdomain are approximately equal. The result of the k-means method for model domains is given in Fig. 3 (arrows indicate exchanges between subdomains).

All points on the boundary of each subdomains are required for data exchange during the computational process. The Jarvis's algorithm was used for this purpose (the problem of constructing the convex hull). A list of neighboring subdomains has been defined for each subdomain. An algorithm was designed for data transfer between subdomains.

Theoretical estimates for the acceleration and efficiency of algorithm 2 were obtained similarly to the corresponding estimates for the algorithm 1:

$$S_{(2)}^t = \frac{p \cdot \chi}{1 + \left(\sqrt{p} - 1\right) \left(\frac{36}{50N_z} + \frac{4p}{50t_0} \left(t_p \left(\frac{1}{N_x} + \frac{1}{N_y}\right) + \frac{t_x \sqrt{p}}{N_x N_y}\right)\right)},$$

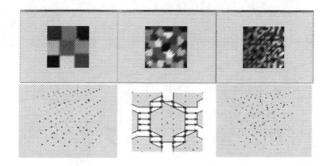

Fig. 3. Results of the k-means method for model domain decomposition into 9, 38, 150 (two-dimensional domain); into 6 and 10 subdomains (three-dimensional domain)

$$E_{(2)}^t = \frac{S_{(2)}^t}{p} = \frac{\chi}{1 + \left(\sqrt{p} - 1\right)\left(\frac{36}{50N_z} + \frac{4p}{50t_0}\left(t_p\left(\frac{1}{N_x} + \frac{1}{N_y}\right) + \frac{t_x\sqrt{p}}{N_xN_y}\right)\right)},$$

where χ is the ratio of the number of computational nodes to the total number of nodes (computational and fictitious).

Results of parallel implementation the algorithms 1 and 2 for solution the problem (1)–(3) were compared and presented in the Table 1.

Table 1. Comparison of acceleration and efficiency of algorithms

p	$t_{(1)}, s$	$S_{(1)}^t$	$S_{(1)}$	$E_{(1)}^t$	$E_{(1)}$	$t_{(2)}, s$	$S_{(2)}^t$	$S_{(2)}$	$E_{(2)}^t$	$E_{(2)}$
1	7.491	1.0	1.0	1	1	6.073	1.0	1.0	1	1
2	4.152	1.654	1.804	0.827	0.902	3.121	1.181	1.946	0.59	0.973
4	2.550	3.256	2.938	0.814	0.7345	1.811	2.326	3.354	0.582	0.839
8	1.450	6.318	5.165	0.7897	0.6456	0.997	4.513	6.093	0.654	0.762
16	0.882	11.928	8.489	0.7455	0.5306	0.619	8.520	9.805	0.533	0.613
32	0.458	21.482	16.352	0.6713	0.511	0.317	15.344	19.147	0.48	0.598
64	0.266	35.955	28.184	0.5618	0.4404	0.184	25.682	33.018	0.401	0.516
128	0.172	54.618	43.668	0.4267	0.3411	0.117	39.013	51.933	0.305	0.406

In the Table 1: $t_{(k)}, S_{(k)}, E_{(k)}$ are processing times, the acceleration and efficiency of the k-th algorithm; $S_{(k)}^t, E_{(k)}^t$ are theoretical estimates of the efficiency and acceleration of the k-th algorithm, $k = \{1, 2\}$. The acceleration graphs of the algorithms 1 and 2 for solution $(1) - (3)$, obtained theoretically and practically, are given in Fig. 4.

The practical estimation of the acceleration of the algorithm 1 (graph 3, Fig. 4) does not take into account the optimization of partitioning of all computational process between calculators in comparison with the practical estimation of acceleration of the algorithm 2 (graph 2). The theoretical estimate of

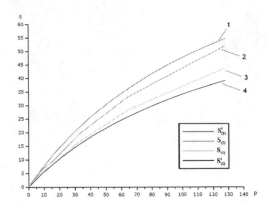

Fig. 4. Acceleration graphs of developed parallel algorithms

the acceleration (graph 4) does not take into account the ratio of the number of computational nodes to the total number of nodes, as opposed to the estimation presented in Fig. 4 (graph 1). The optimal partition of computational process between calculators is given in the theoretical estimation of acceleration of the algorithm 1 (graph 1). Thus, the graph 1 is the upper estimation of accelerations of calculation algorithms obtained practically (graphs 2, 3), and the graph 4 is the lower estimation of acceleration of the proposed algorithms.

The estimation for comparing the efficiency values of algorithms 1 and 2, was obtained experimentally according to the Teil criterion.

As a resullt, we obtained that the efficiency was increased on 10–20% using the algorithm 2 based on the *k-means* method. Therefore, the developed algorithms based on domain decomposition in two spatial directions and the *k-means* method can be effectively used for solving hydrodynamic problems for sufficiently large number of computational nodes.

4.3 Parallel Implementation on Graphic Accelerator

For numerical implementation of proposed interrelated mathematical models of biological kinetics, we developed parallel algorithms which will be adapted for hybrid computer systems using the NVIDIA CUDA architecture.

The NVIDIA Tesla K80 computing accelerator has the high computing performance and supports all modern both the closed (CUDA) and open (OpenCL, DirectCompute) technologies. The NVIDIA Tesla K80 specifications: the GPU frequency of 560 MHz, the GDDR5 video memory of 24 GB, the video memory frequency of 5000 MHz, the video memory bus digit capacity is equaled to 768 bits. The NVIDIA CUDA platform characteristics: Windows 10 (x64) operating system, CUDA Toolkit v10.0.130, Intel Core i5-6600 3.3 GHz processor, DDR4 of RAM 32 GB, the NVIDIA GeForce GTX 750 Ti video card of 2GB, 640 CUDA cores.

Using the GPU with the CUDA technology is required to address the effective resource distribution at solving the system of linear algebraic equations (SLAE).

The dependence of the SLAE solution time on the matrix dimension and the number of nonzero diagonals was obtained for implementation the corresponding algorithm (see Fig. 5). Due to it, in particular, we can choose the grid size and to determine the time for SLAE solution based on the amount of nonzero matrix diagonals.

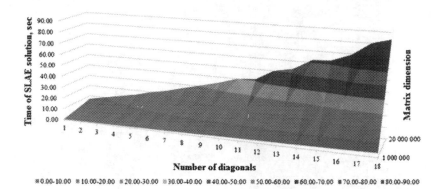

Fig. 5. The dependence of SLAE solution time on matrix dimension and the number of nonzero diagonals

Analysis of the CUDA architecture characteristics showed the algorithms for numerical implementation of the developed mathematical model of hydro-biological processes can be applied for designing high-performance information systems.

5 Program Complex Description

The SC was developed on MCS and intended for mathematical modeling of possible development scenarios of environmental situations in coastal systems (in this regard, we considered the Azov-Black Sea basin) [32]. The SC includes computational units allowing: to take into account factors influencing pollu-tant distribution in coastal systems (weather conditions, and bottom relief); to research the dependence of pollutant concentrations, the degree and size of affected water area on intensity of water flows, hydrophysical parameters, cli-matic and meteorological factors. The features of the SC are high performance, reliability, and high accuracy of simulation results.

New modules was developed and integrated into SC for solving the SLAE by methods: the Jacobi method; the minimum correction method; the steep-est descent method (gradient descent); the Seidel method; the upper relaxation method; the adaptive MATM of variational type.

We used sequentially condensed rectangular grids by dimensions $251 \times 351 \times 15$, $502 \times 702 \times 30$, $1004 \times 1404 \times 60$, etc., were used for mathematical modeling of hydrobiological and hydrodynamic processes in a three-dimensional domain of complex shape, namely the Azov Sea. The structure of the developed SC is shown in Fig. 6.

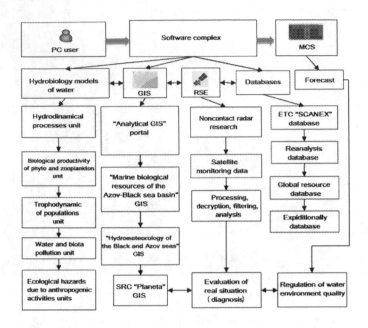

Fig. 6. Software complex

The SC includes: the control unit; the oceanological and meteorological databases; the program library for solving the hydrobiology grid problems; the integration with various geoinformation system (GIS), Global Resource Database (GRID) for binding to the geographic coordinates and access to the satellite data collection systems; the NCEP/NCAR Reanalysis database. Due to the application of satellite GIS information, we can perform more qualitative and complex spatial analysis; solutions, based on it, are more accurate. The high-performance computer system was used for solving such problems, which allows to perform a large amount of complex calculations and data processing in limited time. For development the SC we used the high-level programming language C++. Message Passing Interface technology (MPI) was employed for clusters.

6   Results of Numerical Experiments

Numerical experiments were performed for modeling hydrobiological euthrophication processes in shallow waters in summer taking into account the influence of environment [32].

The obtained results are shown in Fig. 7: the influence of the Azov Sea water flow structures on the distribution of phytoplankton concentration (Fig. 7(a));

calculation results of biogenic substances (nitrates) concentrations based on the model (1)–(3) (Fig. 7(b), initial distribution of water flow fields for the northern wind). The scenario shown in Fig. 7(a, b) allows to research the effect of ectocrine regulation of phytoplankton growth in case of excessive intake of nutrients, including nitrogen, phosphorus and silicon, into the water with river flow. In this case, biogens are no longer constraints on the growth of phytoplankton.

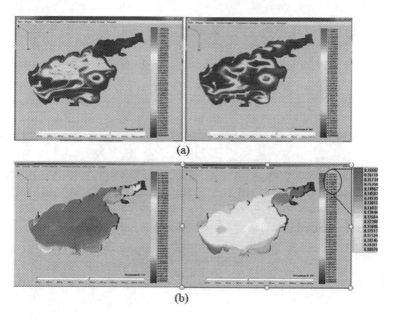

Fig. 7. Distribution of pollutant concentration: phytoplankton $(S_{16})(\mu_{16} = 5 \times 10^{-11};$ $\nu_{16} = 10^{-11})$ (a); nitrates $(S_8)(\mu_8 = 5 \times 10^{-10}; \nu_8 = 10^{-10})$ (b)

Actual data of the "ESIMO" portal (see Fig. 8(a)) and satellite data of the Scientific Research Center (SRC) "Planeta" [33] (phytoplankton spots are visible, revealing the structure of currents), were used for model verification (1)–(3) and the validation of SC result adequacy (Fig. 8(b)).

For checking the adequacy of mathematical model (1)–(3) the Earth satellite data were used. The data of SRC "Planeta" (imagery of the Azov Sea) are shown in Fig. 9, a (1, 2 are indicated areas of increased phytoplankton concentration, revealing the structure of the Azov Sea currents); results of SC are shown in Fig. 9, b (the variation of phytoplankton concentration). Calibration and validation of the complex of hydrological models in the perspective of the problem of assimilation of remote sensing data showed the qualitative correspondence of the fields of chlorophyll and biomass of phytoplankton, reconstructed from satellite data and calculated according to the models, as well as a high degree of spatial coherence as the hydrophysical and hydrobiology indicators (Fig. 9).

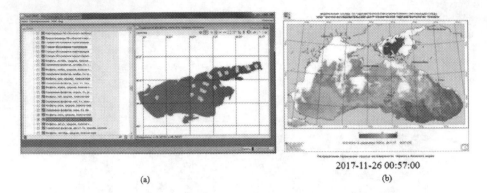

2017-11-26 00:57:00

(a)   (b)

Fig. 8. Simulation data: ecological data of the "ESIMO" portal (a); satellite image of the Azov Sea of the SRC "Planeta" (b)

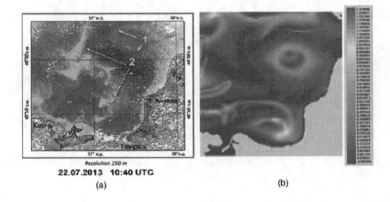

Resolution 250 m
22.07.2013 10:40 UTC

(a)   (b)

Fig. 9. Comparison of SC results with the satellite data

The developed SC implements the designed scenarios for changing ecological situation in the Azov Sea using the numerical implementation of plankton evolution problems of biological kinetics. We compared similar researches of mathematical modeling of hydrobiological processes in this paper [20–24].

As criteria for adequacy of the developed model (1)–(3) we used the error estimation according to the Teil criterion:

$$\delta = \sqrt{\sum_{k=1}^{n} (S_{k\ nat} - S_k)^2} \Big/ \sqrt{\sum_{k=1}^{n} S_{k\ nat}^2},$$

where $S_{k\ nat}$ is the value of concentration, obtained through field measurements; S_k is the value of concentration, calculated using the model (1)–(3). Concentrations of pollution, phyto- and zooplankton, calculated for various wind conditions, were taken into account if the relative error did not exceed 30%.

7   Conclusion

The three-dimensional mathematical model of euthrophication in shallow water was designed and researched taking into account the convective transport and diffusion transfer, absorption and release of nutrients by phytoplankton, as well as phosphorus, nitrogen and silicon cycles.

An analytical research of the continuous model developed in this paper allowed us to obtain inequalities ensuring the existence and uniqueness of the problem solution. The numerical implementation of model was performed on MCS with distributed memory. We obtained theoretical estimates for the velocity and efficiency of parallel algorithms. Experimental software was designed for mathematical modeling the possible development scenarios in shallow waters. In this regard, we considered the Azov Sea as an example. Decomposition methods of grid domains for computationally laborious diffusion-convection problems were employed for parallel implementation taking into account the architecture and parameters of MCS. Two parallel algorithms were developed for data distribution among processors. The algorithm based on the k-means method yielded the increase of efficiency from 10 to 20% in comparison with the algorithm based on standard partition of computational domain.

Due to the use of MCS and the NVIDIA Tesla K80 graphic accelerator, the calculation time for model problem solution was reduced, while maintaining the required accuracy for modeling hydrobiological processes in shallow waters. Note that this fact is one of primary importance in water ecology problems.

References

1. Lotka, A.J.: Contribution to the energetics of evolution. Proc. Natl. Acad. Sci. **8**, 147–150 (1922)
2. Volterra, V.: Variations and fluctuations of the number of individuals in animal species living together. Rapp. P. - V. Reun. Cons. Int. Explor. Mer. **3**, 3–51 (1928)
3. Logofet, D.O., Lesnaya, E.V.: The mathematics of Markov models: what Markov chains can really predict in forest successions. J. Ecol. Modell. **126**, 285–298 (2000)
4. Monod, J.: Recherches sur la croissance des cultures bacteriennes. Hermann, Paris (1942). 210 p
5. Mitscherlich, E.A.: Das Gesertz des Minimums und das Gesetz des Abnehmenden Bodenertrags. J. Landw. Jahrb **38**, 595 (1909)
6. Vinberg, G.G.: Some results of the practice of production- hydrobiological methods. In: Production of populations and communities of aquatic organisms and methods of its research. Sverdlovsk: UNC AN USSR, pp. 3–18 (1985)
7. Abakumov, A.I.: Signs of of water ccosystems stability in mathematical models. In: Proceedings of the Institute of System Analysis of RAS. System Analysis of the Problem of Sustainable Development. M: ISA RAS, vol. 54, pp. 49–60 (2010)
8. Menshutkin, V.V.: The skill of modeling (ecology, physiology, evolution). Petrozavodsk; St. Petersburg (2010). 419 p
9. Menshutkin, V.V., Rukhovets, L.A., Filatov, N.N.: Modeling of freshwater lake ecosystems (review). 2. Models of freshwater lake ecosystems. J. Water Resour. **41**(1), 24–38 (2014)

10. Vorovich, I.I., et al.: Rational use of water resources of the Azov Sea basin: mathematical models. Science (1981). 360 p
11. Jørgensen, S.E., Fu-Liu, X., Jorgensen, S.E., Tao, S., Li, B.-G.: J. Ecol. Model. **117**, 239–260 (1999)
12. Vollenweider, R.A.: Scientific fundamentals of the Eutrophication of lakes and flowing waters, with particular reference to nitrogen and phosphorus as factors in Eutrophication OECD. Paris. Tech Report DA 515C1168 27 (1968). 250 p
13. Matishov, G.G., Ilyichev, V.G.: On optimal exploitation of water resources. The concept of domestic prices. Rep. Acad. Sci. **406**(2), 249–251 (2006)
14. Tyutyunov, Y.V., Titova, L.I.: Simple models for studying complex spatiotemporal patterns of animal behavior. J. Deep-Sea Res. **II**(140), 193–202 (2017)
15. Perevaryukha, A.Y.: Hybrid model of bioresourses' dynamics: equilibrium, cycle, and transitional chaos. J. Autom. Control Comput. Sci. **45**(4), 223–232 (2011)
16. Samarskiy, A.A.: Theory of difference schemes. Science (1989). 616 p
17. Marchuk, G.I., Shutyaev, V.P.: Adjoint equations and iterative algorithms in problems of variational data assimilation. Proc. Steklov Inst. Math. (Suppl.) **276**(suppl. 1), 138–152 (2012)
18. Marchuk, G.I., Sarkisyan, A.S.: Mathematical modelling of ocean circulation. Science (1988). 297 p
19. Chetverushkin, B., et al.: Unstructured mesh processing in parallel CFD project GIMM. In: Parallel Computational Fluid Dynamics, Amsterdam, Elsevier, pp. 501–508 (2005). https://doi.org/10.1016/b978-044452206-1/50061-6
20. Yakushev, E.V., Mikhailovsky, G.E.: Mathematical modeling of the influence of marine biota on the carbon dioxide ocean-atmosphere exchange in high latitudes. In: Jaehne, B., Monahan, E.C. (eds.) Air-Water Gas Transfer, Sel. Papers, Third Int. Symp., Heidelberg University, AEON Verlag & Studio, Hanau, pp. 37–48 (1995)
21. Van Straten, G., Keesman, K.J.: Uncertainty propagation and speculation in projective forecasts of environmental change: a lake eutrophication example. J. Forecast. **10**, 163–190 (1991). https://doi.org/10.1002/for.3980100110
22. Sukhinov, A.I., Sukhinov, A.A.: Reconstruction of 2001 ecological disaster in the azov sea on the basis of precise hydrophysics models. In: Parallel Computational Fluid Dynamics, Multidisciplinary Applications, Proceedings of Parallel CFD 2004 Conference, Las Palmas de Gran Canaria, Spain, ELSEVIER, Amsterdam-Berlin-London-New York-Tokyo, pp. 231–238 (2005). https://doi.org/10.1016/B978-044452024-1/50030-0
23. Park, R.A.: A generalized model for simulating lake ecosystems. J. Simul. **23**(2), 33–50 (1974). https://doi.org/10.1177/003754977402300201
24. Bierman, V.J., Verho, F.H., Poulson, T.C., Tenney, M.W.: Multinutrient dynamic models of algal growth and species competition in eutrophic lakes. In: Modeling the Eutrophication Process. Ann Arbor: Ann Arbor Science (1974)
25. Monin, A.S.: Turbulence and microstructure in Ocean. J. Adv. Phys. Sci. **109**(2), 333–353 (1973)
26. Alekseenko, E., Roux, B., Sukhinov, A., Kotarba, R., Fougere, D.: Nonlinear hydrodynamics in a mediterranean lagoon. J. Nonlin. Process. Geophys. **20**(2), 189–198 (2013). https://doi.org/10.5194/npg-20-189-2013
27. Sidoryakina, V.V., Sukhinov, A.I.: Well-posedness analysis and numerical implementation of a linearized two-dimensional bottom sediment transport problem. J. Comput. Math. Math. Phys. **57**(6), 978–994 (2017). https://doi.org/10.1134/s0965542517060124

28. Sukhinov, A.I., Chistyakov, A.E., Alekseenko, E.V.: Numerical realization of the three-dimensional model of hydrodynamics for shallow water basins on a high-performance system. J. Math. Models Comput. Simul. **3**(5), 562–574 (2011). https://doi.org/10.1134/s2070048211050115
29. Samarsky, A.A., Nikolaev, E.S.: Methods of solving grid equations. Science (1978). 532 p
30. Konovalov, A.N.: The method of steepest descent with adaptive alternately-triangular preamplification. J. Diff. Equat. **40**(7), 953 (2004)
31. Sukhinov, A.I., Chistyakov, A.E.: Adaptive modified alternating triangular iterative method for solving grid equations with non-selfadjoint operator. J. Math. Models Comput. Simul. **24**(1), 3–20 (2012)
32. Sukhinov, A.I., Nikitina, A.V., Semenyakina, A.A., Chistyakov, A.E.: A set of models, explicit regularized schemes of high order of accuracy and programs for predictive modeling of consequences of emergency oil spill. In: Proceedings of 10th Annual International Scientific Conference on Parallel computational technologies (PCT 2016), Arkhangelsk. Chelyabinsk: Publishing center SUSU, pp. 308–319 (2016)
33. SRC "Planeta". http://planet.iitp.ru/english/index_eng.htm

Computer Simulation of Endothermic Decomposition of High-Energy Substances $C_xH_yN_mO_n$. Substance Composition Optimization

Vadim Volokhov, Alexander Volokhov, Dmitry Varlamov[✉],
Elena Amosova, Tatyana Zyubina, Pavel Toktaliev,
and Sergey Martynenko

Institute of Problems of Chemical Physics, Russian Academy of Sciences,
Chernogolovka, Russia
{vvm, vav, dima, aes, zyubina}@icp.ac.ru,
pavel_d_m@mail.ru, martyn_s@mail.ru

Abstract. Study of the thermochemical properties of energy-intensive substances $C_xH_yN_mO_n$ is of some interest in various fields of technology. There is a class of substances having high endothermic capacity of decomposition processes and high energy capacity of their decomposition products. A mathematical model of the decomposition of a multicomponent hydrocarbon fuel taking into account the energy content of the resulting combustible mixture has been developed and verified. The high-energy substance composition was optimized using two criteria (a) maximum endothermic effect of the decomposition process and (b) maximum energy content of the mixture resulting from the endothermic decomposition reaction. The results of quantum-chemical simulation of energy-intensive substances $C_xH_yN_mO_n$ are considered. Tasks considered have significant computational complexity (up to hundreds of thousands of core-hours). The article presents experience of using the Gaussian application package on computing resources with different types of Intel Xeon processors, the number of processor cores, available disk memory and RAM, combinations of CPU + GPU. The parallelism level and computational problems are assessed.

Keywords: Computer simulation · High-energy substance · Quantum chemistry · Gaussian · Thermochemical properties

1 Simulation of High-Energy Systems and Their Decomposition Processes

Now one of the most promising approaches to developing a direct-flow air-jet engine (ramjet engine) is the use of complex hydrocarbon fuels, which can also be decomposed into simpler hydrocarbon compounds at high temperatures. This process proceeds with the heat absorption i.e. it has an endothermic nature. Attractive features of these fuels are not only additional cooling capacity due to the endothermic effect, but

© Springer Nature Switzerland AG 2019
V. Voevodin and S. Sobolev (Eds.): RuSCDays 2019, CCIS 1129, pp. 182–192, 2019.
https://doi.org/10.1007/978-3-030-36592-9_15

also higher reactivity of their decomposition products. Experimental and theoretical methods are used for study of these endothermic fuels [1–8].

Chemists presented several tens of perspective high-energy substances in systems $C_xH_yN_mO_n$. The main part of them is rather difficult for fast synthesis and the experimental estimates of thermochemical characteristics. Quantum-chemical simulation allows to estimate quickly enough the potential of substances in terms of thermochemical effects and the prospect of their use.

1.1   Fuel in Ramjet

Figure 1 represents a block diagram of ramjet. Fuel from some source is supplied to a cooling system (CS) of the ramjet combustion chamber and cooled the upper wall of the combustion chamber using the physical and chemical capacities of the fuel. Air intake captures air for the ramjet operation, after the air-fuel-mixture is burned in the combustion chamber. The products of combustion through the ramjet nozzle flow out to the atmosphere creating engine thrust.

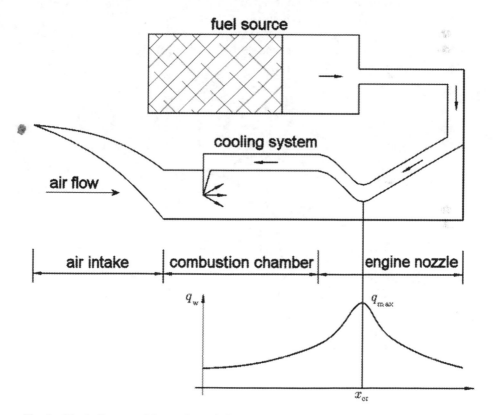

Fig. 1. Block diagram of the ramjet and distribution of the heat load: q_{max} is the maximum heat flux from the combustion chamber to the cooling system near the nozzle throat.

To create a ramjet, it is necessary to solve a number of scientific and technical problems, the most significant of which are:

1. optimal fuel from of thrust and cooling points of view,
2. stable fuel combustion in high-speed air flow,
3. thermal protection of thermally stressed elements of ramjet.

Solution of these coupled problems has complex nature.

1.2   Thermal Decomposition of Fuel

Thermal decomposition of hydrocarbon fuel containing dozens of components (alkanes, cycloalkanes, olefins, and aromatic hydrocarbons and others) is a complex multistage heterophase process [6–8]. In this case, the largest number of reaction paths with heat absorption under the conditions of the cooling system has linear molecules of saturated hydrocarbons. In general, reactions with a maximum endothermic effect at the hydrocarbons decomposition in the absence of oxygen are elementary reactions of the detachment of hydrogen atom from relatively short molecules of alkanes and the formation of alkyl radicals. Such reactions occur at the initial stage of decomposition of the original hydrocarbon compound, whereas the reverse exothermic recombination reactions proceed at the later stages of the decomposition process.

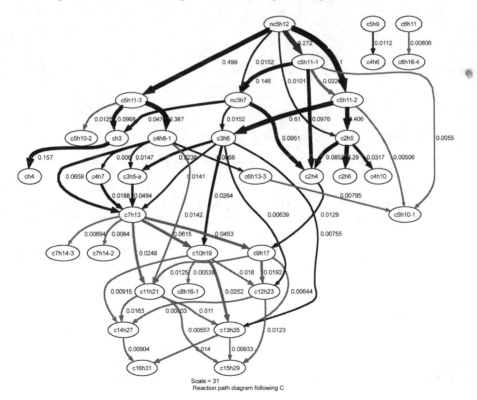

Fig. 2. Schematic representation of kinetics of *n-pentane* pyrolysis.

Figure 2 represents the highly simplified kinetic scheme of decomposition of the well-known and widely used high-energy substance – *n-pentane* $CH_3(CH_2)_3CH_3$. Light lines corresponds to the exothermic reactions on the scheme, dark lines corresponds to the endothermic reactions. Thickness of the lines is proportional to the mass flow from the source component. Because of the lack of space, the diagram represents approximately 10% of all chemical transformations occurring under these conditions.

One of the main goals of this work is the construction and verification of a mathematical model for the decomposition of a multicomponent hydrocarbon fuel taking into account the energy content of the resulting combustible mixture, the decomposition of the complex hydrocarbon mixture and the study of the endothermic ramjet effect [9–12].

The mathematical model is based on the kinetic mechanism of thermal decomposition of the hydrocarbons. Such models are constantly developed using theoretical calculations and experimental data. For example, model of the hexadecane decomposition includes 2102 components and 8056 elementary reactions and allows describe low and high temperature oxidation and alkane decomposition. Simplified model (up to an oxygen-free part) makes it possible to reduce the number of components down to 196 and the number of elementary reactions down to 1058.

Methods of the kinetic schemes simplifications and quantum chemical computations of the kinetic parameters play an important role due to the large number of non-linear kinetic equations (up to several thousand equations) [6, 8, 13–15].

The main result obtained with the model of physicochemical processes in the cooling system of the combustion chamber is development of a method for the composition optimization of the initial fuel from estimation of the thrust impulse from the thermodynamic principles without determination of the combustion chamber parameters. The following principle of the gas mixture optimization resulted from the thermal decomposition of the original fuel is used in this paper: the achievement of maximum thrust with the use of maximum endothermic effect.

Let us consider the following problem of optimization

$$\min_{Y}\left\{\overline{T_{out}(Y)}, \sup_{X} I^{-1}(X, Y)\right\},$$
$$Y \in S_1, X \in S_2, \tag{1}$$

where Y is a vector of the inlet mass concentration of the mixture in the cooling system, S_1 is a set of permissible values for inlet mass concentrations in the cooling system, $\overline{T_{out}(Y)} = H_1(Y)$ is a first objective function (mass-average mixture temperature in the cooling system outlet), X is a vector of problem parameters not related to inlet concentrations, these parameters are not variable in the problem as well as the similar parameters related to the combustion chamber. Thus X vector consists of the mode and geometric characteristics of the cooling system and the combustion chamber. Let $I(X, Y)$ be the specific impulse potentially achievable in the cooling system of the combustion chamber at fixed vector X, then when using equilibrium estimates for the flame temperature and no energy losses in the combustion chambers $\sup_X I^{-1}(X, Y) = H_2(Y)$ is the upper bound of the set $I(X, Y)$ and the second objective function. The definition of the mass concentrations also implies restrictions on the components of the vector Y:

$$Y_i \geq 0, \sum_{i=1}^{N} Y_i = 1, \tag{2}$$

In addition, only a class of alkanes with the carbonic number $0 < C < 9$ is considered as possible components of the inlet mixture in this problem. Thus, the vector Y consists of 8 elements corresponding to the concentrations of substances from the methane-octane series. We will look for such solutions of problem (1) Y * with constraints (2), for which we have:

$$H_i(Y*) \leq H_i(Y), i = 1, 2, Y \in S_1, \tag{3}$$

we will call such solutions as Pareto optimal solutions.

As the first series of the optimization computations, alkanes with carbonic numbers C from 1 to 8 were considered. The results of the optimization computations in axis «endothermic effect» – «specific impulse» form are shown on Fig. 3.

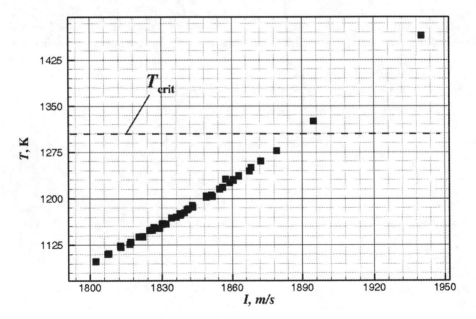

Fig. 3. Results of optimization of the alkanes mixture

The following example demonstrates meaning of the result obtained. If we choose as maximum allowable temperature for the ramjet construction 1305 K, then maximum specific impulse that can be achieved will be 1,890 m/s. Thus, the envelope line drawn through the points limits the set of points to the right that correspond to the suboptimal composition of the fuels, while the line itself contains the points corresponding to the maximum impulse at the given wall temperature of the cooling system.

2 Quantum Chemical Simulation

Now the leading scientific countries of the world are interested in quantum chemical simulation of the thermochemical properties of energy-intensive substances. The mechanisms of the kinetic processes accompanying combustion, detonation, etc. are also being studied. Supercomputer calculations for this purpose are performed using quantum-chemical packages GAUSSIAN, GAMESS, etc. [16–18].

The geometry of the system, local energy minima, and basic thermodynamic parameters are calculated in the simulation of high-energy substances. The adequacy of the calculated models assessed by comparison with the available experimental data.

A list of more than 40 substances of interest for creation of a new generation of solid fuels has been prepared based on preliminary expert assessment. The four most promising substances have been selected from the list at the initial stage of work (Fig. 4):

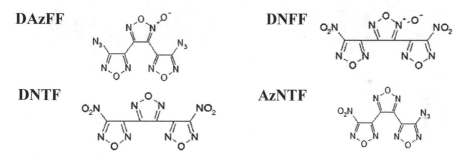

Fig. 4. Schematic structures of simulated energy-intensive components of endothermic hydrocarbon fuels

Quantum-chemical modeling was performed for isolated molecules using the B3LYP hybrid density functional well-proven in molecular calculations with an extended $6\text{-}311 + G$ (2d, p) basis [19, 20] using the GAUSSIAN software [17]. The results were refined within the framework of the G4 approach [18], where the data obtained in the framework of B3LYP are corrected for the basis expansion and more accurate allowance for electronic correlation. Thermochemical properties are calculated with high accuracy (up to 1 kcal/mol). The calculation results and comparison with experimental data are shown in Table 1. We took the experimental data and present them as 100%. The comparison value of settlement ΔH_{298} with an experiment was given in column Δ, %.

Table 1. Structures of substances, enthalpy of formation (ΔH_{298}), explosive transformation energy (Q_{max}), <u>relative</u> values (Δ) of calculated ΔH_{298} from the *experimental* data (taken as 100%).

Formula and structure	ΔH_{298}, kJ/mol	Δ, %	Q_{max}[3], кДж/кг	Calculation level
$C_6N_8O_8$ DNFF	634.5±1.2	100	7083	*experiment*
	749 [1]	118	7193	B3LYP/6-311+G(2d,p)
$C_6N_8O_7$ DNTF	661.1±2.6	100	6891	*experiment*
	701.9	106		G4
	721.2	109	7018.4	G4-M2
	762	115	6893	B3LYP/6-311+G(2d,p)
$C_6N_{12}O_4$ DAzFF	1305.1±4.5	100	6883	*experiment*
	1321	101	6414	B3LYP/6-311+G(2d,p)
			4612	B3LYP/6-31G*
$C_6N_{10}O_5$ AzNTF	958.0±4.6	100	6653	*experiment*
	1038	108	6452	B3LYP/6-311+G(2d,p)
			5740	B3LYP/6-31G*

3   Details of Computational Calculations

A number of computational configurations (Table 2) based on various Intel Xeon processors, provided pools of computational cores, RAM and disk memory, GPU availability, and versions of the Gaussian application package (https://gaussian.com) were used during the quantum chemical simulation.

The computational complexity of the tasks is rather high; the average calculation time for the indicated structures, depending on the basis used and the calculated temperatures, varies from 20 h to 10 days. The computation time is reduced when using more modern versions of processors. However, computation time for more complex systems (up to 50 atoms) on 24 physical core workstation in a pseudo-single-task mode reached a month.

The support of the **avx2** and **sse42** instructions by the used processors is critical to the speed of calculations, especially the former one that can benefit by 8-10 times on

Table 2. Computational combinations used

Computational resource	Processors/Cores/	Usage
Lomonosov-2 «compute»	Intel Xeon® E5-2697 v3@2.60 GHz, 14 cores, 64 Gb; Tesla K40s	Up to 14 cores, 64 Gb
Computational cluster of the IPCP RAS:	Intel Xeon® 5450| 5670@ 3 GHz, 4-6 cores, 8 and 12 GbRAM	1 to 50 CPU (up 200 cores), 1-12 Gb per node
RSC-Tornado-1	Intel Xeon® E5-2697Av4, 2x16 cores,	1 to 48 cores
RSC-Tornado-2	Intel Xeon® Gold 6148 CPU @ 2.40 GHz, 2x20 cores	Up to 40 cores
RSC-Tornado-3	Intel Xeon® Gold 6150 CPU @ 2.70 GHz, 4x18 cores	Up to 72 cores
Workstations IPCP RAS, GPU Tesla C2075	Intel Xeon® X5675@3.46 GHz, 2x6 cores, 48 Gb RAM, Nvidia Tesla C2075	Up to 12 cores
Workstation Godwin, IEM RAS	Intel Xeon® E5-2690v3, 2x12 cores, RAM 256 Gb, SSD	1-24 cores, 4-248 Gb RAM per task

note: the number of physical cores without threads is given

some tasks using the processors with a close clock rate [21]. Unfortunately, at the time of this writing we were not able to accurately assess the possibilities of using GPU accelerators. It is highly desirable to perform calculations on SSD disks or high-speed SAS disks with a large amount of allocated disk memory, since the package creates giant intermediate files up to 2 TB during the calculations. It can take up to 35–50 min to record them on an SSD disk and, of course, significantly longer on SATA arrays.

The different publications report that the speed of calculations is greatly influenced by the availability of the latest versions of the Gaussian package (as compared to g9 installed on the IPCP cluster), which fully realize the hardware capabilities of new series of processors, giving acceleration of calculations for most of the used bases up to 7–8 times. The authors did not intend to analyze in detail the degree of parallelization of the performed calculations (despite the fact that the Gaussian package usually uses its own "Linda" parallelization software). However, steady acceleration on pools up to 12 cores had been observed, while further this effect reduced (Fig. 5). It also depends on the amount of allocated memory task (but it should be not less than 4 GB per physical core).

The work was performed using the equipment of the Center for Collective Use of Super High Performance Computing Resources of the Lomonosov Moscow State University [22–24] (project "Enthalpy-2065"). We also thank the RSC group and the Institute of Experimental Mineralogy of the Russian Academy of Sciences for providing pools of computational resources for some of the calculations.

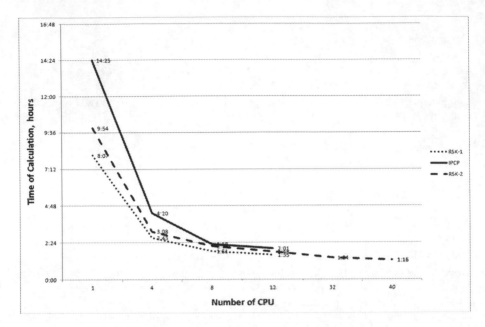

Fig. 5. The observed parallelization effect on different resources

4   Conclusion

Mixture of alkanes is optimized using the developed mathematical model of a turbulent reacting flow of hydrocarbons mixture in a flat channel coupled with the detailed kinetic mechanism. Average cross section of the outlet mixture temperature of the model cooling system and maximum specific impulse of the combustible mixture of decomposition products are taken as the objective functions. A set of Pareto optimal solutions has been obtained. It is shown that the greatest number of optimal solutions can be obtained using alkanes with carbonic numbers C = 4, 5.

Quantum-chemical simulation of high-energy substances of the $C_xH_yN_mO_n$ class was carried out using the Gaussian quantum-chemical package as part of a project to create or modify hydrocarbon fuels of new types for ramjets. For the presented substances, the calculation of thermochemical parameters was not previously performed or was made as an estimate. The calculations showed the prospects of these substances (and the classes they represent) as high-energy substances. The simulation showed good agreement with existing experimental data (not more 27 kcal/mol) and made it possible to calculate a number of energy parameters for previously non simulated substances. The majority of calculated thermochemical data for these classes of substances are received for the first time and also have no experimental analogs.

References

1. Edwards, T.: Cracking and deposition behavior of supercritical hydrocarbon aviation fuels. Combust. Sci. Technol. **178**, 307–334 (2006). https://doi.org/10.1080/00102200500294346
2. Vaccaro, S., Malangone, L.: Catalytic combustion for supplying energy for endothermic reaction. J. Adv. Chem. Eng. **4**(2), 1–16 (2014). https://doi.org/10.4172/2090-4568.1000107
3. Ning, W., Yu, P., Jin, Z.: Research status of active cooling of endothermic hydrocarbon fueled scramjet engine. Proc. Inst. Mech. Eng. Part G: J. Aeros. Eng. **227**(11), 1780–1794 (2012). https://doi.org/10.1177/0954410012463642
4. Pike, J.: The choice of propellants: a similarity analysis of scramjet second stages. Philosoph. Trans. Roy. Soc. London. Ser. A: Math. Phys. Eng. Sci. **357**, 2357–2378 (1999). https://doi.org/10.1098/rsta.1999.0435
5. Lewis, M.J.: Significance of fuel selection for hypersonic vehicle range. J. Propul. Power **17**(6), 1214–1221 (2001). https://doi.org/10.2514/2.5866
6. Mukhina, T.N., Barabanov, N.L., Babash, S.Ye., Menshikov, V.A., Avrekh, G.L.: Pyrolysis of hydrocarbons. Khimiya, Moscow (1987). (in Russian)
7. Shigabiev, T.N., Yanovskii, L.S., Galimov, F.M., Ivanov, V.F.: Endothermic fuels and working bodies of energetic and power plants. Kazan Science Center, Kazan (1996). (in Russian)
8. Westbrook, C.K., Pitz, W.J., Herbineta, O., Currana, H.J., Silke, E.J.: A comprehensive detailed chemical kinetic reaction mechanism for combustion of n-alkane hydrocarbons from n-octane to n-hexadecane. Combust. Flame **156**(1), 181–199 (2009). https://doi.org/10.1016/j.combustflame.2008.07.014
9. Volokhov, V., Toktaliev, P., Martynenko, S., Yanovskiy, L., Volokhov, A., Varlamov, D.: Supercomputer simulation of physicochemical processes in solid fuel ramjet design components for hypersonic flying vehicle. Commun. Comput. Inf. Sci. **687**, 236–248 (2016). https://doi.org/10.1007/978-3-319-55669-7_19
10. Volokhov, V.M., Toktaliev, P.D., Martynenko, S.I.: Numerical simulation of the conjugate heat transfer in the cooling system of the combustion chambers of the aviation ramjet on the endothermic fuels. In: Proceedings VII European Congress on Computational Methods in Applied Sciences and Engineering (ECCOMAS Congress 2016), vol. 1, pp. 979–991. https://doi.org/10.7712/100016.1865.6582
11. Toktaliev, P.D., Martynenko, S.I., Yanovskiy, L.S., Volokhov, V.M., Volokhov, A.V.: Features of model hydrocarbon fuel oxidation for channel flow in the presence of electrostatic field. Russ. Chem. Bull. **65**(8), 2011–2017 (2016). https://doi.org/10.1007/s11172-016-1545-2
12. Toktaliev, P.D., Babkin, V.I., Martynenko, S.I.: Simulation of coupled heat transfer in the structural elements of the cooling system of aircraft engines on endothermic fuels. Teplovye processy v tekhnike [Thermal processes in technology] **4**, 162–166 (2015). (in Russian)
13. Ertesvag, I.S., Magnussen, B.F.: The eddy dissipation turbulence energy cascade model. Combust. Sci. Technol. **159**(1), 213–235 (2000). https://doi.org/10.1080/00102200008935784
14. Lysenko, D.A., Ertesvåg, I.S., Rian, K.E., Lilleberg, B., Christ, D.: Numerical simulation of turbulent flames using the Eddy Dissipation Concept with detailed chemistry. In: Skallerud, B., Andersson, H.I. (eds.) Computational Mechanics, pp. 159–178. Tapir Academic Press, Trondheim (2013)
15. Herbinet, O., Marquaire, P.-M., Battin-Leclerc, F., Fournet, R.: Thermal stability of n-dodecane: experiments and kinetic modeling. J. Anal. Appl. Pyrol. **78**(2), 419–429 (2007). https://doi.org/10.1016/j.jaap.2006.10.010

16. Goodwin, D.G., Moffat, H.K., Speth, R.L.: Cantera: an object- oriented software toolkit for chemical kinetics, thermodynamics, and transport processes (2017). https://doi.org/10.5281/zenodo.170284, http://www.cantera.org. Accessed 20 Dec 2018

17. Frisch, M.J., Trucks, G.W., Schlegel, H.B., et al.: Gaussian 09, Revision B.01. Gaussian Inc., Wallingford (2010)

18. Curtiss, L.A., Redfern, P.C., Raghavachari, K.: Gaussian-4 theory. J. Chem. Phys. **126**(8), 084108 (2007). https://doi.org/10.1063/1.2436888

19. Becke, A.D.: Density functional thermochemistry. III. The role of exact exchange. J. Chem. Phys. **98**(7), 5648–5652 (1993). https://doi.org/10.1063/1.464913

20. Johnson, B.J., Gill, P.M.W., Pople, J.A.: The performance of a family of density functional methods. J. Chem. Phys. **98**(7), 5612–5626 (1993). https://doi.org/10.1063/1.464906

21. Grigorenko, B.L., Mironov, V., Polyakov, I., Nemukhin, A.: Benchmarking quantum chemistry methods in calculations of electronic excitations. Supercomput. Front. Innovations **5**(4), 62–66 (2019). https://doi.org/10.14529/jsfi180405

22. Voevodin, V.V., et al.: Practice of "Lomonosov" supercomputer. Otkrytye sistemy [Open Systems], **7**, 36–39 (2012). (in Russian)

23. Voevodin, V.V., et al.: Supercomputer Lomonosov-2: large scale, deep monitoring and fine analytics for the user community. Supercomput. Frontiers Innovations **6**(2), 4–11 (2019). https://doi.org/10.14529/jsfi190201

24. Nikitenko, D., Voevodin, V.V., Zhumatiy, S.: Deep analysis of job state statistics on Lomonosov-2 supercomputer. Supercomput. Frontiers Innovations **5**(2), 4–10 (2019). https://doi.org/10.14529/jsfi180201

Coupling of PDE and ODE Solvers in INMOST Parallel Platform: Application to Electrophysiology

Alexey Chernyshenko[1,2], Alexander Danilov[1,2,3], and Vasily Kramarenko[1,3(✉)]

[1] Marchuk Institute of Numerical Mathematics of the Russian Academy of Sciences, Moscow 119333, Russia
chernyshenko.a@gmail.com, a.a.danilov@gmail.com,
kramarenko.vasiliy@gmail.com
[2] Moscow Inistitute of Physics and Technology, Dolgoprudny 141701, Russia
[3] Sechenov University, Moscow 119991, Russia

Abstract. Mathematical modeling of cardiac electrophysiology is one of important and widely developing problems in personalized medicine. In this paper we present numerical simulations of electrophysiology in a human heart ventricles using high performance computing. For cardiac electrophysiology equations monodomain model is used. This PDE problem is discretized by P1 finite elements with the first order accurate implicit time scheme. Ionic currents are described by system of ODEs from O'Hara–Rudy model, provided by CellML model repository. The whole problem is solved using the CVODE solver, Ani3D and INMOST platforms. Efficiency in numerical simulations on high performance systems is almost 50% on 192 cores.

Keywords: Cardiac electrophysiology · High performance computing · O'Hara-Rudy model · Monodomain model

1 Introduction

Advanced methods of mathematical modeling coupled with the recent growth of the performance of supercomputers provide great opportunities in biomedical simulations. Recently, there has been a growing interest in developing and performing of high performance computer simulations of the cardiac and cardiovascular problems. According to the Russian Federal State Statistics Service, the circulatory system diseases remain the main cause for the population mortality, making about half of the total number of deaths. Moreover, among the deaths caused by the circulatory system diseases, nearly half of them are accounted for ischemic heart disease. The same holds true for other developed countries. Mathematical modeling of cardiac electrophysiology is one of important and widely developing problems in personalized medicine. It can be used in clinical applications, such as the prediction of the arrhythmias, defibrillation therapy

© Springer Nature Switzerland AG 2019
V. Voevodin and S. Sobolev (Eds.): RuSCDays 2019, CCIS 1129, pp. 193–202, 2019.
https://doi.org/10.1007/978-3-030-36592-9_16

optimization, study of the effects of drugs, determination of the most effective location for a pacemakers' electrodes and others.

Efficient computational frameworks for the treatment of heart diseases must provide simulations with the high performance, because the integration of a personalised model into a medical practice requires appropriate calculation times.

The most popular computational frameworks for cardiac simulations are Chaste (Cancer, Heart and Soft Tissue Environment) [3], developed in the University of Oxford, Alya Red CCM [5], created in the Barcelona Supercomputing Center, CMISS/openCMISS (Continuum Mechanics, Image analysis, Signal processing and System Identification), CardioSolv [6], CARPentry Modeling Environment, and FEniCS [7].

Inspirational results in numerical simulation of the cardiac electrophysiology are achieved in Computational Cardiology Lab in the Johns Hopkins University [4]. The laboratory implements personalised virtual heart and conducts both basic science and translational studies of heart dysfunction and therapies for heart disease. Current HPC simulations are performed on the Maryland Advanced Research Computing Center with 22,000 processors.

It is worth noting also the REO laboratory of INRIA, Research centers of IBM in conjunction with the Lawrence Livermore National Laboratory and team of researchers at the University of Oxford as primary researchers in this area.

Computational electrophysiology also being researched in Moscow Institute of Physics and Technology, the Institute of Immunology and Physiology of the Ural branch of the RAS, Lobachevsky State University of Nizhny Novgorod, Marchuk Institute of Numerical Mathematics of the RAS, and others Russian institutions. Major medicine universities and research centers such as Sechenov University are interested in developing and performing of high performance simulations of the cardiac problems.

Electrophysiology models are mainly based on system of PDEs coupled with systems of ODEs. The aim of our work is to couple two open-source PDE and ODE solvers in the open-source parallel platform INMOST. We use the resulting framework to develop our own electrophysiology solver for HPC systems. Our framework is built on the CVODE [1], Ani3D [10] and INMOST [11] platforms. Verification of the framework was conducted on a series of benchmarks proposed in the literature [8]. For cardiac electrophysiology equations we consider only monodomain model, but bidomain model is also available. This problem is discretized by P1 finite elements with the first order accurate implicit time scheme.

We describe our model and methods, the framework architecture and the parallel implementation using MPI technology. The remainder of the paper is organized as follows. Section 2 defines the electrophysiology model. Section 3 introduces numerical methods. Section 4 shows the results of several numerical experiments and the performance of the simulator. Section 5 concludes the paper with discussions.

2   Electrophysiology Model

The most common form of electrophysiology equations implemented in cardiac simulation are the monodomain and bidomain models. In this work we consider only the monodomain model. Let Ω represent a 3D domain with piecewise smooth boundary $\partial\Omega$ and v is membrane voltage. The monodomain equations for unknown v are given by

$$\chi\left(C_m\frac{\partial v}{\partial t} + I_{\text{ion}}\right) - \nabla\cdot(\sigma\nabla v) = I_{\text{stim}}, \tag{1}$$

$$I_{\text{ion}} = f(\mathbf{u}, t, v), \tag{2}$$

$$\frac{\partial\mathbf{u}}{\partial t} = \mathbf{g}(\mathbf{u}, t, v), \tag{3}$$

where C_m is the cell membrane capacitance, χ is the membrane surface-to-volume ratio, I_{stim} is the stimulus current, σ is the conductivity tensor. The current density in the ionic channels I_{ion} is defined by a function f of a vector of state variables $\mathbf{u}$ defined by a system of nonlinear ODEs $\mathbf{g}$. For the human heart we use the O'Hara-Rudy model [9].

The boundary condition represents zero flux across the boundary $\partial\Omega$:

$$\mathbf{n}\cdot(\sigma\nabla v) = 0.$$

The initial conditions defines starting voltage $v|_{t=0} = v_0$ and state variables.

3   Numerical Methods

Discretization in time is performed by the implicit scheme with the first order of accuracy. Spatial discretization is performed by the finite element method on unstructured tetrahedral grids. Let τ denote a time step and $\varkappa = \chi C_m/\tau$. In matrix notations the FEM formulation of (1) is as follows:

$$[\varkappa\mathbf{M} + \mathbf{K}]\mathbf{v}^{\mathbf{n+1}} = \mathbf{M}(\varkappa\mathbf{v}^{\mathbf{n}} - \chi\mathbf{i}_{\text{ion}}^{\mathbf{n}} + \mathbf{i}_{\text{stim}}) \tag{4}$$

where $\mathbf{M}$ is the FEM mass matrix, $\mathbf{K}$ is the FEM stiffness matrices with tensor σ, and $\mathbf{i}_{\text{ion}}$ and $\mathbf{i}_{\text{stim}}$ are the vectors of ionic current and stimulus current, respectively.

For the numerical solution of the system of nonlinear ODEs (3) in each mesh node we employ the CVODE solver [1]. CVODE is a numerical solver providing an efficient and stable method to solve ODEs. Ionic cell models are provided by biologically relevant cell models available from the CellML model repository [2]. The O'Hara-Rudy model has 49 unknowns. The CVODE solver employs Adams-Moulton multistep method with nonlinear iterations and adaptive timestep.

Numerical implementation of the discretization (4) is based on Ani3D [10] and INMOST [11] platforms. Ani3D provides numerical libraries for generation of unstructured tetrahedral meshes, sparse matrix assembly for finite element discretizations, and solution of sparse linear systems. We use AniFEM library from Ani3D package for mass and stiffness matrices generation.

INMOST platform is used for developing highly parallel applications. It is based on MPI library and provides common interface to optional third-party libraries for advanced parallel computations, e.g., PETSc [12] and ParMETIS [15]. In this work we utilized the Ani3D extension for INMOST platform introduced in [13]. This extension allows to use the AniFEM matrix assembly code with parallel environment.

The distributed stiffness matrix is assembled on each processor from local stiffness matrices generated by AniFEM library, taking into account the map between local indices and global indices. This mapping must be constructed before the matrix assembly and takes into account the type of finite elements and the degrees of freedom structure. In this paper we use P1 finite elements, therefore one degree of freedom for each mesh vertex is generated.

The basic numerical algorithm can be divided into three steps with substeps:

1. Preparing data for numerical experiment.
   (a) Loading and repartitioning a mesh. Repartition is provided by the ParMETIS library and INMOST interface.
   (b) Loading fiber orientation vectors and materials of mesh vertices.
   (c) Assembly matrices $\mathbf{M}$ and $[\varkappa\mathbf{M} + \mathbf{K}]$. Assembling is provided by Ani3D extension, presented above.
   (d) Preparing initial conditions and work arrays.
2. Numerical solving of (1)–(3) using first order time scheme. On the n-th time step:
   (a) Calculation of ionic current (2) in every mesh vertex. Calculation is independent for every vertex and provided by CVODE solver.
   (b) Calculation of vectors $(\varkappa\mathbf{v}^{\mathbf{n}} - \chi\mathbf{i}^{\mathbf{n}}_{\mathrm{ion}} + \mathbf{i}_{\mathrm{stim}})$ and $\mathbf{M}(\varkappa\mathbf{v}^{\mathbf{n}} - \chi\mathbf{i}^{\mathbf{n}}_{\mathrm{ion}} + \mathbf{i}_{\mathrm{stim}})$ using parallel built-in matrix-vector product. The calculation of first vector is carried out on each MPI process regardless of the rest. For second vector calculation INMOST built-in function is used.
   (c) Solving system (4).
   (d) Exchanging solution between processors and preparing local arrays for the next time step.
3. Saving resulting potentials.

4   Numerical Simulations

In this section the numerical experiments are described. For a mesh generation we use ceCT (contrast-enhanced computed tomography) segmented images provided by Sechenov University. We use the CGAL Mesh library [14] to generate an unstructured tetrahedral mesh of a human heart. The domain is defined implicitly by segmentated images. Mesh generation is based on Delaunay refinement, followed by global optimization, perturbation and sliver exudation. The mesh quality was also improved by the AniMBA library from the Ani3D package.

Figure 1 shows the tetrahedral mesh with 440857 vertices and 2469794 tetrahedra. The myocyte fibers orientation was generated by the rule-based algorithm from [17]. The anisotropic conductivity tensor σ was computed from the fiber orientation.

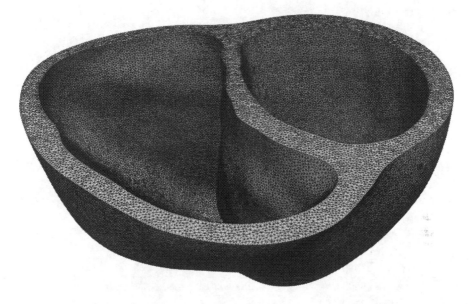

Fig. 1. Tetrahedral mesh of the human heart ventricles with 440857 vertices.

In the first set of experiments we consider the generated mesh with 440857 vertices and 2469794 tetrahedra. We consider two experiments with different simulation time. In the first experiment simulation time is equal to 30 ms. In the second experiment time is equal to 150 ms. These two times were chosen to investigate parallel properties of algorithm from Sect. 3 both at the beginning of the simulation and after a significant change in the wave front. For the CVODE solver we choose both relative tolerance and absolute tolerance equal to 10^{-7} and maximum time step parameter equals to 0.01 ms. For linear system solving we choose BiSGStab solver from PETSc library with additive Schwartz method for preconditioning. On each processor preconditioner ILU(k) with $k = 1$ is used. Stopping criterion for iterative process is residual fall into 10^9 times. Simulation time is measuring in seconds in all tables below.

Numerical experiments were performed on the INM RAS cluster [16] with 8 compute nodes:

- 24 cores (two 12-core processor Intel Xeon E5-2670v3@2.30 GHz);
- RAM: 64 Gb;
- operating system: SUSE Linux Enterprise Server 11 SP3 (x86_64);
- fast communication network: Mellanox Infiniband QDR 4x.

In the tables below we present the results, that show calculation times and speedups of iteration process, described in Sect. 3. The four main sections in all tables correspond to four substeps of part two in algorithm. We use the following notations for all tables:

- p denotes a number of processors;
- T_{total} is a whole calculation time, which includes preparation step;
- S_q is the speedup for calculation time for p processors with respect to q processors (in this work we use $S_3 = T_3/T_p$, in other words we compare all calculation times with respective time for three processors);
- T_{ion} is a time of a ionic current calculation (substep 2a–2b);
- T_{rhs} denotes a right hand side calculation time (substep 2c);
- T_{solve} is a time spent for linear system solve (substep 2d);
- T_{exch} denotes a data exchange time (substep 2e);
- $S_{q,ion}$ and $S_{q,solve}$ are speedups for T_{ion} and T_{solve}, respectively.

Table 1. Computation times and speedup for the first experiments set (mesh with 440857 vertices). Simulation time 30 ms.

p	T_{ion}	$S_{3,ion}$	T_{rhs}	T_{solve}	$S_{3,solve}$	T_{exch}	T_{total}	S_3
3	11889	1.00	241	3451	1.00	159	15740	1.00
6	6699	1.77	120	1491	2.31	80	8390	1.87
12	3777	3.14	67	885	3.89	43	4772	3.29
24	1915	6.20	47	403	8.56	29	2394	6.57
48	1370	8.67	24	258	13.37	17	1669	9.43
96	639	18.60	14	148	23.31	13	814	19.33
192	376	31.61	7	90	38.34	7	480	32.79

Numerical results from Tables 1 and 2 show that the main part of calculation time was spent on ionic currents calculation. The linear system solving step takes the second place in time spent. This step is more efficient, than ionic one. The exchange and right-hand side steps take much less time, than previous two. The results in Table 1 show higher efficiency, than in Table 2 because of increasing complexity of process modeling.

The speedup illustrations are presented on Fig. 2. These subfigures show speedup graphs in experiment with simulation time 30 ms (left) and 150 ms (right).

In the second set of experiments we consider the mesh created from the same data with 1945426 vertices and 11377363 tetrahedra. We provide two experiments with the same simulation time, as in the first set of experiments. All other parameters are the same too.

The results shown in Tables 3 and 4 are similar to that in the first set of experiments and present reasonable efficiency of the calculations (Fig. 3).

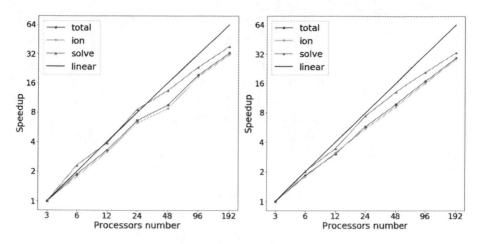

Fig. 2. Speedup for first experiment: simulation time 30 ms (left), and 150 ms (right).

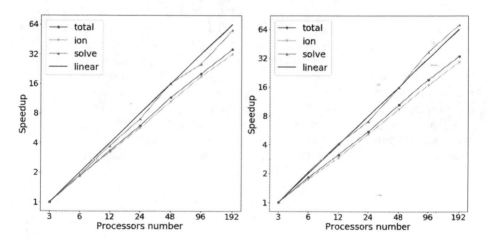

Fig. 3. Speedup for second experiment: simulation time 30 ms (left), and 150 ms (right).

Table 2. Computation times and speedup for the first experiments set (mesh with 440857 vertices). Simulation time 150 ms.

p	T_{ion}	$S_{3,\text{ion}}$	T_{rhs}	T_{solve}	$S_{3,\text{solve}}$	T_{exch}	T_{total}	S_3
3	56774	1.00	1039	14850	1.00	659	73322	1.00
6	31736	1.78	589	7330	2.02	356	40011	1.83
12	19240	3.11	337	4299	3.45	210	24086	3.04
24	10289	5.51	229	1993	7.45	143	12654	5.79
48	6146	9.23	143	1136	13.07	95	7520	9.75
96	3523	16.11	60	711	20.88	54	4348	16.86
192	1999	28.40	33	449	33.07	32	2513	29.17

Table 3. Computation times and speedup for the second experiments set (mesh with 1945426 vertices). Simulation time 30 ms.

p	T_{ion}	$S_{3,ion}$	T_{rhs}	T_{solve}	$S_{3,solve}$	T_{exch}	T_{total}	S_3
3	52915	1.00	1234	18827	1.00	729	73705	1.00
6	29000	1.82	713	9932	1.89	438	40083	1.83
12	16415	3.22	430	5047	3.73	256	22148	3.32
24	9271	5.70	229	2693	6.99	144	12337	5.97
48	5031	10.51	104	1167	16.13	65	6367	11.57
96	2792	18.95	67	743	25.33	42	3644	20.22
192	1650	32.06	38	337	55.86	29	2054	35.88

5   Discussions and Conclusions

As shown in all the above tables, the ionic current calculation part of our scheme has the biggest impact on a total calculation time. However, numerical algorithm of ionic current calculation can be applied independently at each vertex. We analyzed a computation time of this part for each MPI processor and measured the idle time caused by poor balancing of the vertices for each computed cardiac millisecond in the first experiment. Because of collective operations on each time step, in algorithm, described in Sect. 3, each substep is bounded by MPI Barrier function. It means, that after substep finished each MPI process waits other ones. We measured idle time for ionic substep for all timesteps for all MPI processes. The ratio of this idle time and execution time for the ionic timestep we call idle ratio. We also averaged idle ratio by MPI processes.

The average delay for 192 processors is shown in Fig. 4. One can observe that for 192 processors average idle ratio can be more than 60%. The idle ratio is caused by the inhomogeneity of ODE integration complexity in the CVODE solver. This space and time inhomogeneity is caused by the propagation of the electrical wave through the ventricles (Fig. 5). Since we used ParMETIS for redistribution of vertices across processors, the partitioner tends to keep adjacent vertices on the same processor, thus leading to poor balancing of the computation costs.

In order to reduce the inhomogeneity of the CVODE solver complexity across processors, we propose to use random redistribution of vertices across processors. This approach requires to include two extra communications in substep 2b. In our future work we will test this approach and analyze the idle ratios and decrease of the total computation times.

This work presents our computational framework for high performance simulations of heart electrophysiology. The framework is based on the open-source platforms Ani3D and INMOST and uses finite element method on unstructured tetrahedral meshes. The parallel implementation of the framework employs the MPI technology. Computational mesh can be constructed from segmented ceCT images of a human heart. We consider a monodomain model for electrophysiology equations.

Table 4. Computation times and speedup for the second experiments set (mesh with 1945426 vertices). Simulation time 150 ms.

p	T_{ion}	$S_{3,\text{ion}}$	T_{rhs}	T_{solve}	$S_{3,\text{solve}}$	T_{exch}	T_{total}	S_3
3	245742	1.00	7885	68094	1.00	4698	326419	1.00
6	140456	1.74	3947	32946	2.06	2400	179749	1.81
12	83770	2.93	2148	16596	4.10	1261	103775	3.14
24	47497	5.17	1306	9659	7.04	813	59275	5.5
48	26071	9.42	538	4304	15.82	338	31251	10.44
96	14656	16.76	324	1826	37.29	219	17025	19.17
192	8382	29.31	215	957	71.15	159	9713	33.60

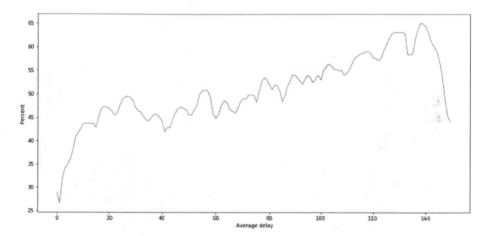

Fig. 4. The average idle ratio in ionic current calculation for 192 processors for each computed cardiac millisecond in the first experiment.

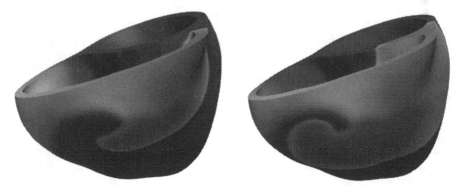

Fig. 5. Scroll wave on human ventricles: $t = 650\,\text{ms}$ (left), $t = 680\,\text{ms}$ (right).

Numerical simulations on INM RAS cluster show rather good efficiency: the speedup on 192 cores compared with 3 cores is 29× faster ideal one is 64× for the first experiment, and 33× faster for the second experiment. Higher efficiency is expected with above proposed implementation of vertex rebalancing.

Acknowledgements. The research was supported by RFBR grants 17-01-00886 and 18-00-01524 (18-00-01661).

References

1. Hindmarsh, A.C., et al.: SUNDIALS: suite of nonlinear and differential/algebraic equation solvers. ACM Trans. Math. Softw. **31**, 363–396 (2005)
2. Yu, T., et al.: The physiome model repository 2. Bioinformatics **27**, 743–744 (2011)
3. Mirams, G., et al.: Chaste: an open source C++ library for computational physiology and biology. PLOS Comput. Biol. **9**(3), e1002970 (2013)
4. Trayanova, N.A.: Whole-heart modeling. Circ. Res. **108**(1), 113–128 (2011)
5. Vázquez, M., et al.: Alya red CCM: HPC-based cardiac computational modelling. In: Klapp, J., Ruíz Chavarría, G., Medina Ovando, A., López Villa, A., Sigalotti, L. (eds.) Selected Topics of Computational and Experimental Fluid Mechanics. ESE, pp. 189–207. Springer, Cham (2015). https://doi.org/10.1007/978-3-319-11487-3_11
6. CardioSolv Ablation Technologies. https://www.cardiosolv.com/. Accessed 15 Apr 2019
7. A popular open-source (LGPLv3) computing platform for solving partial differential equations (PDEs). https://fenicsproject.org. Accessed 15 Apr 2019
8. Chernyshenko, A., Danilov, A., Vassilevski, Y.: Numerical simulations for cardiac electrophysiology problems. In: Mondaini, R. (ed.) BIOMAT 2018. Springer, Cham (2019). https://doi.org/10.1007/978-3-030-23433-1_21
9. O'Hara, T., Virág, L., Varró, A., Rudy, Y.: Simulation of the undiseased human cardiac ventricular action potential: model formulation and experimental validation. PLoS Comput. Biol. **7**, e1002061 (2011)
10. Ani3D (Advanced Numerical Instruments 3D). https://sourceforge.net/projects/ani3d/. Accessed 15 Apr 2019
11. INMOST (Integrated Numerical Modelling and Object-oriented Supercomputing Technologies). http://inmost.org/. Accessed 15 Apr 2019
12. PETSc – library for lineat system solving. https://www.mcs.anl.gov/petsc/. Accessed 15 Apr 2019
13. Kramarenko, V., Vassilevsky, Y., Konshin, I.: Ani3D extension of parallel platform Inmost and hydrodynamic applications. In: Voevodin, V., Sobolev, S. (eds.) RuSCDays 2017, vol. 793. Springer, Cham (2017). https://doi.org/10.1007/978-3-319-71255-0_17
14. CGAL – The Computational Geometry Algorithms Library. https://cgal.org/. Accessed 15 Apr 2019
15. ParMETIS – Parallel Graph Partitioning and Fill-reducing Matrix Ordering. http://glaros.dtc.umn.edu/gkhome/metis/parmetis/overview
16. INM RAS cluster. http://cluster2.inm.ras.ru/. Accessed 15 Apr 2019
17. Bayer, J., Blake, R., Plank, G., Trayanova, N.: A novel rule-based algorithm for assigning myocardial fiber orientation to computational heart models. Ann. Biomed. Eng. **40**(10), 2243–2254 (2012)

Digital Rock Modeling of a Terrigenous Oil and Gas Reservoirs for Predicting Rock Permeability with Its Fitting Using Machine Learning

Vladimir Berezovsky$^{(\boxtimes)}$ ⬤, Ivan Belozerov, Yungfeng Bai,
and Marsel Gubaydullin

M.V. Lomonosov Northern (Arctic) Federal University, Arkhangelsk, Russia
{v.berezovsky,i.belozerov,m.gubaidulin}@narfu.ru,
yumengleme@126.com

Abstract. In the process of mathematical modeling of the macroscopic properties of porous media, the problem of 3D-reconstruction of the core microstructure using machine learning apparatus was considered. The paper develops the process of modeling the pore space of the core and evaluating its permeability. The use of the LAMMPS molecular dynamics simulation package on a hybrid computing platform for solving problems of digital rock simulation is considered. A method has been developed for predicting rock permeability based on the methods of smoothed particles hydrodynamics. A technique has been developed for determining the total porosity of the rock, based on the analysis of images of lithologic-petrographic thin sections. Convolutional autoencoder were trained to extract feature of rock images, which can be applied to classify rock aimed to fit the digital rock model to available rock properties. The results of numerical calculations and their comparison with the results obtained in the course of laboratory research of the core are given.

Keywords: Digital rock · Molecular dynamics · Smoothed particle hydrodynamics · High-performance computing · Rocks classification · Image feature · Convolutional autoencoders · Artificial intelligence · GPU

1 Introduction

For today the technology of digital core modeling is demanded and developing area in assessing of the geological oil reserves in the World [1, 2]. Recently, significant advances in obtaining of pore space have been made, and the use of high-performance computing technologies has accelerated the development and use of digital core modelling in addition to physical laboratory experiments. The digital core model we offer represents a stochastic package, for the creation of which molecular dynamics methods can be used. In the initial stage of a digital core model creation, the geometric model of the pore space can be presented as the form of a close packing of balls, including dilation procedure, the size of which is selected based on the data obtained

© Springer Nature Switzerland AG 2019
V. Voevodin and S. Sobolev (Eds.): RuSCDays 2019, CCIS 1129, pp. 203–213, 2019.
https://doi.org/10.1007/978-3-030-36592-9_17

during determination of the granulometric size composition of samples, microtomography and other studies [3].

In the process of stochastic package creation for rocks modeling based on the size distribution of rock grains, the Monte-Carlo method can be applied. The size and other parameters of the grains in this case can be determined from the images of thin sections, according to the particle size analysis of rocks by laser diffraction method or other methods. In the digital core model we propose, the geometric parameters of the modeling particles are selected from thin section images by machine learning method, as well as according to the data of the particle size analysis of rocks by laser diffraction method.

The use of machine learning method to analyze petrographic thin sections in the process of digital core modelling requires big collection of images. To solve this problem, we have selected 176 images of petrographic thin sections of terrigenous rocks with depth reference to core samples. At the same time, according to these samples, the results of petrophysical studies conducted on them are known, including porosity and absolute permeability.

1.1 Method and Theory

Upon completion of stochastic package simulation in the creation of a digital core model, molecular dynamics methods can be used. Having made the transition from the representation of particle packing to the representation of the pore network model, the permeability of single channels can be calculated using molecular dynamics [4]. In order to estimate the absolute permeability of the simulated microstructure electrodynamic analogy can be used, and for each non-isolated pore (opened porosity), the law of conservation of mass is satisfied.

The process of fluid filtration in digital core model is "replaced" by the process of electricity current flow through a circuit with resistance and, accordingly, the task of finding the absolute permeability of rock in a network of microchannels of a porous medium is "replaced" with the task of finding the current in an electrical circuit. At the same time, filtration flows are represented as a network of connected electrical resistances. By solving the problem of finding the resistance, the overall absolute permeability of the model can be determined. In the course of conducting research on the application of the method of electrodynamic analogy for calculating the absolute permeability of a digital core model, we identified significant difficulties in determining of the electric circuit resistance of the model. In order to facilitate the solution of the problem of finding the resistance of an electrical circuit in digital core model, percolation theory can be applied.

In the study of inhomogeneous media by computer experiment methods, the percolation model (theory) is widely used [5]. The percolation theory is used to describe connected structures (pore space network) in random clusters consisting of individual elements. Representations of the percolation theory makes possible to describe the structure of the pore space, taking into consideration the individual conductive channels and combining them into clusters, thereby obtaining a micro-inhomogeneous capillary grid acting as a model of a porous medium [6].

1.2 Model Developing

While creating a digital core model of terrigenous rocks using the molecular dynamics method, percolation theory can be applied by separation of stochastic package into clusters and then determination of the total electrical resistance in of conducting channels in each of the clusters using the electrodynamic analogy method for determining permeability.

After the separation of stochastic package into clusters, the dependence of the percolation threshold of a network of pore channels on their volume in each of the clusters can be derived. After this, the electrical resistance of networks in clusters can be determined by analytical methods. Next, the current rate is calculated and the "translation" of values into absolute permeability obtains. As a result, based on the obtained values of absolute permeability in each cluster, the total absolute permeability of the model can be determined.

The application of the percolation theory in creating of a digital core model using the molecular dynamics method can significantly simplify the task of finding the total electrical resistance in digital core model using the electrodynamic analogy method and will allow to make more accurate determination of the total absolute permeability of the model.

An outline of an integrated digital rock framework is presented on Fig. 1. All models were simulated used high-performance facilities. Also, it has been noticed that rock classification is of one of time consuming process of rock core analysis. A convolutional autoencoder were trained with two platforms: multi-core CPU and general-purpose GPU to extract feature of rock images, which can be applied to classify rock in further research aimed to accelerate the processes of rock core analysis for petroleum industry. Experimental results on image dataset exhibit the promising value of convolutional autoencoder algorithm to extract feature of rock images with GPU platform.

A dependence of permeability on the temperature of the rock showed a good agreement in natural and simulated examinations. Permeabilities calculated for two types of simulated microstructures: microstructures obtained by stochastic packing, and microstructures from molecular dynamics simulations were close to one other. The permeability coefficient of clastic rocks is affected by: the granulometric composition of the rocks, sorting, the shape of the grains and packaging. A comparatively close direct relationship between permeability and granulometric composition is established in the investigated terrigenous rocks [4]. The correlation coefficient R is 0.467. The composition and content of the cementitious material is also reflected on the reservoir properties.

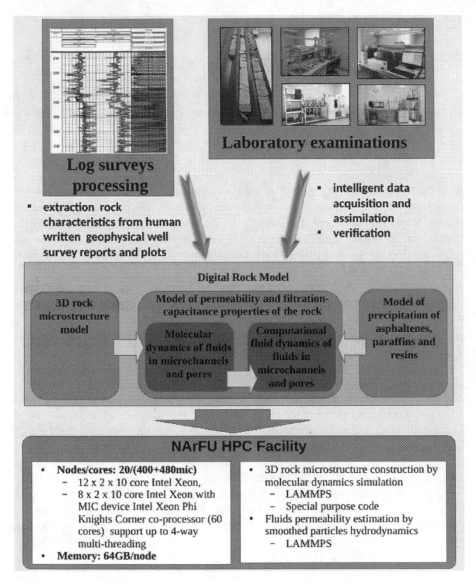

Fig. 1. Integrated digital rock framework at the Northern (Arctic) Federal University facilities.

2   Method

Rock core analysis has been widely used in petroleum industry. Convolutional autoencoder algorithm is proposed to extract feature of rock images, which can be applied to classify rock in further research aimed to accelerate the processes of rock core analysis for petroleum industry. Deep learning techniques have brought in revolutionary achievements for feature learning of images in plenty of fields [7–11].

Inspired by some successful image processing applications [12–16] of neural networks, we apply convolutional autoencoders algorithm in extracting features of rock core images. It can help to overcome challenges in the Digital Rock Modeling (DRM) to extract features of rock core images. As training of convolutional autoenconder networks with large data set of colorful rock core images becomes bottleneck of extraction features, we compare the performance of multicore CPU platforms and general-purpose GPU platforms to find the suitable platform and adjust the structure of neural network.

2.1 Related Works

In 2005, a generic 2-layer fully connected neural network GPU (graphic processing unit) implementation was proposed by Steinkraus, Buck, Simard. The implementation yielded over 3/spl times/speedup for both training and testing with respect to a 3 GHz P4 CPU [17].

In 2006, three novel approaches were presented by Kumar Chellapilla, Sidd Puri, Patrice Simard to speeding up Convolutional Neural Networks in their research using GPUs [12]. Results on character recognition problems indicated that the GPU implementation is even faster and produces a 3.1X-4.1X speedup [18].

In 2011, a fast, fully parameterizable GPU implementation of Convolutional Neural Network variants was presented by Ciresan, Meier, Masci, Gambardella, Schmidhuber [19]. Their feature extractors are neither carefully designed nor pre-wired, but rather learned in a supervised way. Their experiments were presented on GPUs. The result showed that for small nets the speedup was small (but still over 10) since they fit better inside the CPU cache, and GPU resources were underutilized. For huge nets the GPU implementation was more than 60 times faster than a compiler-optimized CPU version. Given the flexibility of their GPU version, this was a significant speedup. One epoch taked 35 GPU minutes but more than 35 CPU hours in their experiment [19].

2.2 Convolutional Neural Networks (CNN)

The CNN was first proposed by LeCun [20]. It simulates the processing system of human vision by using the local receptive field, shared weight, and subsampling [21]. Nowadays CNN is one of most popular artificial neural networks and widely used in computer vision, natural language processing, and speech recognition. A CNN is a multi-layered non-fully-connected neural network [21] composed by the input layers, the hidden layers and output layers. The hidden layer is of many neurons and connections between the input and output layers. The hidden layer can be composed of several convolutional layers, several pooling layers, and several full-connection layers in practice.

2.3 Convolutional Layer

A convolutional layer is parametrized by the size and the number of the maps, kernel sizes, skipping factors, and the connection table [19].

Each layer has M maps of equal size (Mx, My). A kernel of size (Kx, Ky) is shifted over the valid region of the input image. The skipping factors Sx and Sy define how many pixels the filter/kernel skips in x and y direction between subsequent convolutions. The size of the output map is then defined as:

$$M_x^n = \frac{M_x^{n-1} - K_x^n}{S_x^n + 1} + 1 \tag{1}$$

$$M_y^n = \frac{M_y^{n-1} - K_y^n}{S_y^n + 1} + 1 \tag{2}$$

Where index n indicates the layer. Each map in layer Ln is connected to at most Mn − 1 maps in layer Ln − 1. Neurons of a given map share their weights but have different receptive fields.

2.4   Pooling Layers

The purpose of the pooling layers is to achieve spatial invariance by reducing the resolution of the feature maps [22]. Each pooled feature map corresponds to one feature map of the previous layer [22]. There are two kinds of pooling layers: max pooling and subsampling.

The max pooling function

$$a_j = \max_{N*N}\left(\alpha_i^{n*n} u(n, n)\right) \tag{3}$$

applies a window function u(x; y) to the input patch, and computes the maximum in the neighborhood [22]. The subsampling function takes the average over the inputs, multiplies it with a trainable scalar β, adds a trainable bias b, and passes the result through the non-linearity [22].

In 2010, it has been found by Dominik Scherer, Adreas Muller and Sven Behnke that max-pooling can lead to faster convergence, select superior invariant features, and improve generalization [22].

2.5   Fully Connected Layers

The fully connected layer, as one of the important components of neural network, is mainly composed of two parts: linear operation and nonlinear operation. The linear transformation is a linear transformation from the perspective of the operation process. For an input vector $\mathbf{x} = [x_1, x_2, \cdots, x_n]^T$, it is transformed into $\mathbf{z} = [z_1, z_2, \cdots, z_n]^T$ by the matrix W, sometimes with an offset term $\mathbf{b} = [b_1, b_2, \cdots, b_n]^T$.

$$W\vec{x} + \vec{b} = \vec{z} \tag{4}$$

The linear part passes the summarized result to the nonlinear part, and the nonlinear part normalizes the obtained data. There will be problems when calculating from forward and reverse without the operation. Another important role of the nonlinear part is to break the previous linear mapping relationship. Suppose there is a two-layer fully connected neural network with no nonlinear layers, then for the first layer:

$$W^0 \vec{x^0} + \vec{b^0} = \vec{z^1} \tag{5}$$

For the second layer:

$$W^1 \vec{x^1} + \vec{b^1} = \vec{z^2} \tag{6}$$

Then:

$$W^1 W^0 \vec{x^0} + \vec{b^0} + \vec{b^1} = \vec{z^2} \tag{7}$$

$$W^1 W^2 \vec{x^0} + W^1 \vec{b^0} + \vec{b^1} = \vec{z^2} \tag{8}$$

It is clear that the role of multi-layer network is no different from the function of a layer of network if it is without nonlinear part [23].

2.6   Convolutional Autoencoder

Auto-Encoder (AE) was introduced by Rumelhart, Hinton, Williams [24]. AE is an unsupervised learning method which is designed to extract useful features from unlabeled data, to remove input redundancies and to realize dimensional data reduction [15]. AE can transform the input into a typically lower-dimensional space (encoder) and then reconstruct the code to reproduce the initial data [15].

Training an AE does not require label information of the input data [26]. It uses the back propagation algorithm to minimize the reconstruction error e between each input x_i and the corresponding output y_i, by adjusting the parameters of the encoder w and the decoder w' [26]. The equation of is:

$$e(x, y) = \frac{1}{2N} \sum_{i=1}^{N} \|x_i - y_i\|_2^2 \tag{9}$$

CAE (Convolutional Auto-Encoder) is composed of encoder part and decoder part. The encoder part is same with the CNN. CAE can span the entire visual field and force each feature to be global when extracting feature with 2D convolutional kernel [25]. Deconvolutional layers of decoder part are opposite with convolution, aim to reconstruct the initial input x. The equation of deconvolutional layers is:

$$e(x, y) = \sigma \left(\sum_{k \in H} h^k * \tilde{W}^k + c \right) \tag{10}$$

Where H denotes the number of the feature maps. $\tilde{W}$ denotes the flip operation over both dimensions of the W, c is the only one bias used to get the output y [15].

Up-Pooling Layers are used to expand the low dimensional representation into the size of initial input [15].

CAEs are similar to the ordinary AE, but the difference between them is the fact that in the CAE the weights are shared among all locations in the input, preserving the spatial locality, similar to CNN [27]. The loss function is similar to the AE [26]. The equation of is:

$$e(x, y, W) = \frac{1}{2N} \sum_{i=1}^{N} \|x_i - y_i\|_2^2 + \lambda \|W\|_2^2 \qquad (11)$$

2.7 TensorFlow

TensorFlow is Google's second-generation machine learning algorithm implementation framework and Google chose to open up TensorFlow on GitHub in 2015 and released TensorFlow 1.0 in January 2017 [28]. It is a machine learning system that operates at large scale and in heterogeneous environments [29]. The front end of TensorFlow supports Python, C++, Go, Java and other development languages, and the back end is written in C++, CUDA, etc. Dataflow graphs is used to represent computation, shared state, and the operations that mutate that state in TensorFlow. It gives flexibility to the application developer that TensorFlow maps the nodes of a dataflow graph across many machines in a cluster, multicore CPUs, general-purpose GPUs, and Tensor Processing Units (TPUs) [29]. TensorFlow enables developers to experiment with novel optimizations and training algorithms [29]. TensorFlow particularly strong support for training and inference on deep neural networks [29].

2.8 Proposed Methods

Motivated by the high performance of CAE applied in some applications [13–16], an method is proposed to extract feature of digital rock image via convolutional autoencoders. Our CAE is composed of 10 layers which are include 2 convolutional layers, 2 pooling layers, 2 full-connection layers, 2 deconvolutional layers, and 2 up-pooling layers.

The first convolutional layer of the CAE is composed of 16 filters with stride 5. It can make 16 feature maps with resolution of 52 * 52 pixels. The first pooling layer comes next to the first convolutional layer produces 16 feature maps with resolution of 26 * 26 pixels. The second layers have 32 filters. All pooling layers are realized by the max-pooling method 2 * 2 kernel. The decoder reconstructs the input by deconvolving and unpooling the input in reverse order. The output of final deconvolutional layer is the reconstructed version of the input. There is a conversion layer after the second pooling layer in order to reshape the matrix into row vector. In the decoder part of networks, the first layer is a conversion layer which reshapes row vector from encoder part to matrix. Two deconvolutional layers are lying after up-pooling layers.

In our experiments, TensorFlow is used as a framework to implement convolutional autoencoder mentioned above.

2.9   Machine Learning Experiment Results

The networks designed were training with two platforms: multicore CPU and general-purpose GPU. Then we compared the multicore CPU with the GPU implementation. The CPU used in the experiment is AMD FX-8320E Eight-Core Processor of CPU Cores, the threads of it is 8. Base Clock is 3.2 GHz and Max Boost Clock is 4 GHz. Total L1 Cache is 384 KB, Total L2 Cache is 8 MB, and Total L3 Cache is 8 MB. The GPU is GeForceGTX 1050 Ti. It has 768 NVIDIA CUDA Cores and 4G GDDR5 memory which is of 7 Gbps Speed. The GPU Architecture is Pascal.

The CAE model developed was applied to rock image dataset which includes 5000 pictures. In this section, encoder part of networks was used to extract feature and decoder part of networks was applied to rebuild the picture to show if encoder part works well as we need. The result of experiment demonstrates our model can extract the spatial information of rock pictures.

The execution time for execution of convolutional autoencoders for extracting feature of digital rock image is 151 s on GPU whereas 6770 s on the CPU. The speedup is 51.1. This is a significant speedup.

3   Conclusions

An approach to the solution of the problem of mathematical modeling of macroscopic properties porous media is proposed in which the molecular dynamics method is applied for 3D reconstruction of the core microstructure. The results of numerical calculations and their comparison with the full-scale experiment are presented in [4]. The conclusion that the main factor determining the porosity and permeability of terrigenous reservoirs-the dimension of the grains of rock-forming minerals is in good agreement with the initial assumptions of the model being developed: the construction of the microstructure of the rock by packing balls with the same size distribution as the grain size distribution of the simulated rocks. The conclusion that in the rocks studied quartz grains and rock fragments, which are irregular in shape and semi-entangled particles, and as a result they are less densely packed, which leads to an increase in porosity, suggests that for a more accurate modeling rock properties, the elements for constructing a microstructure, should be other than spheres, for example, spherical polyhedrons [30]. Despite the good agreement between numerical and natural results, it can be improved by more accurate construction of the rock microstructure and accounting of the shaliness impact.

From the experiments of extracting feature of digital rock image via convolutional autoencoders above we can say that the execution of this model on GPU is quite faster than on CPU. As the result demonstrates that TensorFlow GPU implementation can outperform multi-core CPUs, one of our future works is scale this GPU implementation into several GPUs, another is that we are going to train new models on GPUs using TensorFlow with a bigger dataset.

Acknowledgements. The research was carried out with the financial support of the Russian Foundation for Basic Research (RFBR) within the framework of the scientific project No. 16-29-15116. All models has been simulated used HPC facilities of Northern (Arctic) Federal University.

References

1. Renard, P., Genty, A., Stauffer, F.: Laboratory of the tensor. J. Geophys. Res. **106**, 443–452 (2001)
2. Carpenter, C.: Digital core analysis and pore-network modeling in mature-field project. J. Petrol. Technol. **67**(1), 97–99 (2015)
3. Belozerov, I.P.: Experimental determination of the digital core model. Arct. Environ. Res. **18** (4), 141–147 (2018)
4. Berezovsky, V., Belozerov, I., Yur'ev, A., Gubaydullin, M.: Examination of permeability clastic oil and gas reservoir's rock by molecular dynamics simulation using high-performance computing. In: Supercomputer Days in Russia. Proceedings of the International Conference. Supercomputer Consortium of Universities of Russia, Russian Academy of Sciences, pp. 195–205 (2018)
5. Tupitsyna, A.I., Fadin, Y.: Study of permeability and percolation properties of systems of solid rectangular particles by computer simulation. J. Tech. Phys. **86**(10), 25–31 (2016)
6. Galechan, A.M.: Percolation analysis of hysteresis of phase permeabilities in two-phase flow in oil reservoirs: dissertation for the degree of Candidate of Physical and Mathematical Sciences, Moscow (2018)
7. Neary, P.: Automatic hyperparameter tuning in deep convolutional neural networks using asynchronous reinforcement learning. In: 2018 IEEE International Conference on Cognitive Computing (ICCC), pp. 73–77 (2018)
8. Park, S., Yu, S., Kim, M., Park, K., Paik, J.: Dual autoencoder network for retinex-based low-light image enhancement. IEEE Access **6**, 22084–22093 (2018)
9. Li, Y., Pu, T., Cheng, J.A.: Biologically inspired neural network for image enhancement. In: 2010 International Symposium on Intelligent Signal Processing and Communication Systems, pp. 1–4 (2010)
10. Zhao, Y., Zan, Y., Wang, X., Li, G.: Fuzzy C-means clustering-based multilayer perceptron neural network for liver CT images automatic segmentation. In: 2010 Chinese Control and Decision Conference, pp. 3423–3427 (2010)
11. Kinattukara, T., Verma, B.: Clustering based neural network approach for classification of road images. In: 2013 International Conference on Soft Computing and Pattern Recognition (SoCPaR), pp. 172–177 (2013)
12. Joseph, S., Ujir, H., Hipin, I.: Unsupervised classification of Intrusive igneous rock thin section images using edge detection and colour analysis. In: 2017 IEEE International Conference on Signal and Image Processing Applications (ICSIPA), pp. 530–534 (2017)
13. Masci, J., Meier, U., Cireşan, D., Schmidhuber, J.: Stacked convolutional auto-encoders for hierarchical feature extraction. In: Honkela, T., Duch, W., Girolami, M., Kaski, S. (eds.) ICANN 2011. LNCS, vol. 6791, pp. 52–59. Springer, Heidelberg (2011). https://doi.org/10.1007/978-3-642-21735-7_7
14. Gong, J., Fan, J., Wang, H., Ma, X., Li, B., Chen, F.: High-resolution SAR image classification via deep convolutional autoencoders. IEEE Geosci. Remote Sens. Lett. **12**(11), 2351–2355 (2015)
15. Ke, M., Lin, C., Huang, Q.: Anomaly detection of Logo images in the mobile phone using convolutional autoencoder. In: 2017 4th International Conference on Systems and Informatics (ICSAI), pp. 1163–1168 (2017)
16. Ji, J., Mei, S., Hou, J., Li, X., Du, Q.: Learning sensor-specific features for hyperspectral images via 3-dimensional convolutional autoencoder. In: 2017 IEEE International Geoscience and Remote Sensing Symposium (IGARSS), pp. 1820–1823 (2017)

17. Steinkraus, D., Buck, I., Simard, P.Y.: Using GPUs for machine learning algorithms. In: Eighth International Conference on Document Analysis and Recognition, ICDAR 2005, pp. 1115–1120 (2005)
18. Chellapilla, K., Puri, S., Simard, P.: High performance convolutional neural networks for document processing. In: Tenth International Workshop on Frontiers in Handwriting Recognition. Suvisoft (2006)
19. Ciresan, D.C., Meier, U., Masci, J., Gambardella, L.M., Schmidhuber, J.: Flexible, high performance convolutional neural networks for image classification. In: Twenty-Second International Joint Conference on Artificial Intelligence (2011)
20. Lecun, Y., Bottou, L., Bengio, Y., Haffner, P.: Gradient-based learning applied to document recognition. Proc. IEEE **86**(11), 2278–2324 (1998)
21. Peng, M., Wang, C., Chen, T., Liu, G.: NIRFaceNet: a convolutional neural network for near-infrared face identification. Information **7**(4), 61 (2016)
22. Scherer, D., Müller, A., Behnke, S.: Evaluation of pooling operations in convolutional architectures for object recognition. In: Diamantaras, K., Duch, W., Iliadis, Lazaros S. (eds.) ICANN 2010. LNCS, vol. 6354, pp. 92–101. Springer, Heidelberg (2010). https://doi.org/10.1007/978-3-642-15825-4_10
23. Feng, C.: The basement of CNN: fully connected layer (2017). (in Chinese)
24. Rumelhart, D.E., Hinton, G.E., Williams, R.J.: Learning representations by back-propagating errors. Cogn. Model. **5**(3), 1 (1986)
25. Jarrett, K., Kavukcuoglu, K., Ranzato, M.A., Lecun, Y.: What is the best multi-stage architecture for object recognition? In: 2009 IEEE 12th International Conference on Computer Vision, pp. 2146–2153 (2010)
26. Ribeiro, M., Lazzaretti, A.E., Lopes, H.S.: A study of deep convolutional auto-encoders for anomaly detection in videos. Pattern Recognit. Lett. **105**, 13–22 (2018)
27. Krizhevsky, A., Hinton, G.E.: Using very deep autoencoders for content-based image retrieval. In: ESANN (2011)
28. Huang, W., Tang, Y.: TensorFlow Actual Combat. Publishing House of Electronics Industry, Beijing (2017). (in Chinese)
29. Abadi, M., Barham, P., Chen, J., Chen, Z., Davis, A., Dean, J., Kudlur, M.: Tensorflow: a system for large-scale machine learning. In: 12th {USENIX} Symposium on Operating Systems Design and Implementation, OSDI 2016, pp. 265–283 (2016)
30. Petrov, M., Gaidukov, V., Kadushnikov, R., Antonov, I., Nurkanov, E.: Numerical method for modelling the microstructure of granular materials. Powder Metall. Met. Ceram. **43**, 330–335 (2004)

Digital Twin of the Seismogeological Object: Building and Application

Vladimir Cheverda[1]([⊠]), Dmitry Kolyukhin[1], Vadim Lisitsa[1],
Maksim Protasov[1], Galina Reshetova[1,2], Anastasiya Merzlikina[3],
Victoriay Volyanskaya[4], Denis Petrov[5], Valery Shilikov[5],
Artjem Melnik[5], Boris Glinsky[2], Igor Chernykh[2], and Igor Kulikov[2]

[1] Institute of Petroleum Geology and Geophysics SB RAS, Novosibirsk, Russia
{CheverdaVA, LisitsaVV, ProtasovMI}@ipgg.sbras.ru,
kgv@nmsf.sscc.ru
[2] Institute of Computational Mathematics and Mathematical Geophysics,
Novosibirsk, Russia
gbm@opg.sscc.ru, Chernykh@parbz.sscc.ru
[3] IGIRGI, Vavilova 25, Bld.1, Moscow, Russia
MerzlikinaAS@igirgi.su
[4] PAO Rosneft, Moscow, Russia
v_volyanskaya@rosneft.ru
[5] RN KrasnoyarskNIPIneft Ltd., 9th May strt., 65d, Krasnoyarsk, Russia
{PetrovDA, ShilikovVV, MelnikAA}@knipi.rosneft.ru

Abstract. The current level of development of numerical methods and high-performance computer systems opens the way to obtain detailed information about the structure of geological objects using 3D seismic study. A universally recognized necessary component that ensures the successful development of modern high-tech technologies for acquiring, processing, and interpreting geophysical data is the complete digital models of geological objects - their digital counterparts. It is on this basis that a detailed assessment of the resolution and information content of the proposed methods and their comparison with the already known processing and interpretation algorithms using the example of a specific geological object becomes possible. Besides, the presence of such digital models allows you to determine the optimal acquisition system, focused on the study of specific features of the object being studied and the selection of the most appropriate graph for processing the data obtained.

In this paper, the primary attention is paid to the construction of a realistic three-dimensional geological model with a family of faults, as well as fracture corridors and clusters of cavities. After constructing such an inhomogeneous multi-scale model, we perform a finite-difference numerical simulation of 3D seismic waves' propagation. The data obtained are processed using the original procedures for extracting scattered/diffracted waves with the subsequent construction of images of the corresponding small-scale objects, which generate these waves.

The results obtained are using for verification of the algorithms of scattering and diffraction imaging as well as full waveform inversion.

Keywords: Digital twin · Discrete elements · Fault formation · Multiscale geological media · GPU parallelization · MPI+OpenMP parallelization · Scattering imaging · Full waveform inversion

© Springer Nature Switzerland AG 2019
V. Voevodin and S. Sobolev (Eds.): RuSCDays 2019, CCIS 1129, pp. 214–224, 2019.
https://doi.org/10.1007/978-3-030-36592-9_18

1 Introduction

Advances in supercomputing technology make it feasible for solving big data problems. Those seemed like impossible in the recent past but became a common practice today. In the geoscience, those have been opening new horizons for understanding the subsurface structures by getting 3D images and velocity models of high fidelity and microscale reservoir characterization. To keep up-to-date on front-end technologies, Oil and Gas companies spend huge budgets to buy, rent, and upgrade/maintain currently owned supercomputers (see, e.g. [1]). Forward modeling and inversion associated with field data processing and velocity estimation may require TBs of RAM and TFLOPs of computing power; this is why most of the arising algorithms have to be parallel.

One of the principal direction of High-Performance Computing application in the Oil and Gas industry is the development of specialized databases for understanding the main peculiarities of the wave field's propagation in 3D heterogeneous multiscale media and approbation and validation of new data processing techniques. This stage is becoming more and more confident using synthetic data sets, including large-scale seismic observations for multiscale 3D realistic geological media. Naturally, these data must correspond to some extent to real geological situations. The creation in the early 2000 s the specialized consortium SEAM (SEG Advanced Modeling) whose goal is to develop digital three-dimensional seismic models, followed by bids for full-scale numerical modeling, confirms the importance of this direction. The developed models and the synthesize data are available for purchase. To date, this consortium has developed several very complex and relevant models, for which full-scale 3D synthetic data have been simulated [2, 12]. Among them:

- Phase I. Subsalt imaging in Tertiary Basins;
- Phase II. Land Seismic Challenging;
- Pressure prediction and Hazard Avoidance;
- Time Lapse Pilot.

In this paper, we build a seismic, geological model containing the main features inherent in geological objects at some licensed sites of Rosneft PJSC in the North of Eastern Siberia. They are:

1. Three-dimensional faults with the damage zones;
2. The system of cracks confined to these zones;
3. Areas of high cavernosity;
4. Fracture corridors.

We took into account several scales:

(a) Macroscale, tens of meters, obtained by 3D seismic study (seismic interfaces forming the skeleton of the model);
(b) Mesoscale, first meters, obtained by various well log measurements;
(c) Microscale, tens of centimeters, obtained by sonic logs, FMI fullbore formation micro-imager, and analysis of core samples.

2 Model Building

2.1 Skeleton of the Model

The initial stage of building the model is definition of the skeleton, in other words, description of the totality of all interfaces known in the result of processing and interpretation three-dimensional seismic data. We have started with mapping of all interfaces known by regular 3D seismic study, including 3D geological faults.

A general view of these surfaces one can see in Fig. 1a,b. The first of them represents the geometry of all interfaces and the second looks of faults only.

The next step is to fill the layers with an elastic medium with the given parameters. In the Fig. 2 one can see three orthogonal 2D view of the model with parameters used to fill the skeleton.

So far, we consider these layers homogeneous, with parameters given in the Table 1. Nevertheless, we can introduce any given spatial dependence of elastic parameters within layers when necessary.

2.2 Simulation of 3D Geological Faults

At present, it is generally acceptable to understand a geological fault is not as a slip surface, but as a complex 3D geological body [9]. Therefore, we consider faults as volumetric entities consisting of deformed rocks formed in the process of destruction caused by tectonic movements [6]. The products of this process are closely linked to a wide range of parameters, such as tectonic regime, the magnitude of fault displacement, and mechanical properties of the host rock [8]. The reasonable way to perform a numerical simulation of these complicated processes is the application of discrete elements technique with parameters calibration by comparing real observations and simulation results [3, 4]. Recall that when using this method, the continuum medium is represented as a set of "discrete elements"/particles with a simple geometric shape. In particular, we use their representation in the form of balls of different radii interacting according to a particular set of physical laws. When modeling tectonic processes, one of the primary types of particle interactions is the friction, which determines the angle of internal friction of the rocks. Additionally, one can consider other effects, like moment of rotation of elements, but at our target scale the effects associated with them are minor [3, 7, 8], so we limited ourselves to the model of pure particle elastic interactions.

To describe the main aspects of the modeling let us consider interaction of two elements, that is two elastic balls with numbers i and j. Each element has what we call its radius R – the distance at which it begins to interact with other elements. Let us introduce the vectors $\vec{X}^{ij} = \vec{x}^i - \vec{x}^j$ and $\vec{n}^{ij} = \vec{X}^{ij}/\|\vec{X}^{ij}\|$. Then interaction along the normal direction is given as follows:

$$\vec{F}^{ij} = \begin{cases} K_r^-\left(R^i + R^j - \|\vec{X}^{ij}\|\right)\vec{n}^{ij}, & R^i + R^j - \|\vec{X}^{ij}\| > 0, \quad \text{repulsion} \\ K_r^-\left(R^i + R^j - \|\vec{X}^{ij}\|\right)\vec{n}^{ij}, & 0 < \|\vec{X}^{ij}\| - R^i - R^j < r_0, \quad \text{active interaction} \\ 0, & \|\vec{X}^{ij}\| - R^i - R^j > r_0, \quad \text{no interaction} \end{cases}$$

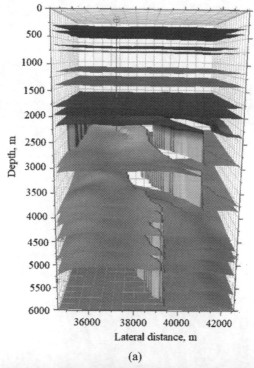

(a)

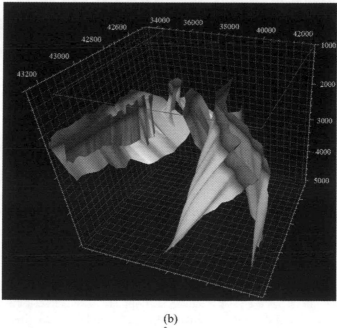

(b)

Fig. 1. Skeleton of the model. (a) Interfaces of the layers, (b) Geometry of faults

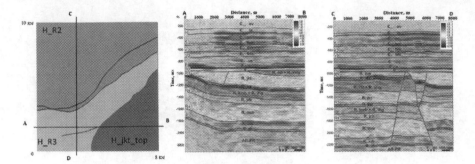

Fig. 2. 2D orthogonal slices of 3D field seismic images.

Table 1. Elastic parameters of the layers

Sequence	Vp, m/sec	Vs, m/sec	ρ, kg/m³	Structural intervals	
				Top	Bottom
E2-3_ev	3070		1400	0	H_E1_lit_top
E1-2_lit	5260	2940	2400	H_E1_lit_top	H_E1_an_top
E1_an	5740	3210	2600	H_E1_an_top	H_K
E1_bul	6680	3710	2800	H_K	H_E1_bul_bot
E1_bls2	4990	2720	2400	H_E1_bul_bot	H_K2
E1_bls1	5960	3190	2700	H_K2	H_E1_bls1_bot
E1_us	5240	2900	2400	H_E1_bls1_bot	H_B_top
V	5900	3310	2700	H_B_top	H_R0
R2_lrm1	5100	4020	2700	H_R0	H_R2
R2_rsl	6500	2800	2800	H_R0	H_jkt_top
R2_jkt	6680	3500	2840	H_jkt_top	H_R3
R2_kp	6100	2850	2700	H_R3	H_kp_top
R2_kmb	6550	3520	2800	H_kp_top	H_dlg_top
R2_dl	6480	3480	2800	H_dlg_top	H_jrb2_top
R2_jrb2	6570	3550	2800	H_jrb2_top	H_jrb1_top
R2_jrb1	7060	3620	2800	H_jrb1_top	H_mdr_top
R1_mdr	5550	3040	2700	H_mdr_top	H_R4
R1_vdr	3870	2280	2600	H_R4	H_vdr_bot
R1_zl	5420	2120	2500	H_vdr_bot	H_zl_bot
Basement	5390	3320	2800	H_zl_bot	Foundation_bot

Numerical experiments by discrete elements proved that the main mechanism determining the properties of the medium at the macro level is tangential forces, in particular friction [5]. The classical and most popular model, describing the internal friction in the model of discrete elements is the Coulomb law, according to which the static friction governs the interaction between particles, until it does not exceed a certain critical value, after which the sliding friction becomes responsible for the motion. In general, the friction force has the following form:

$$\vec{F}^{ij} = \begin{cases} -K_s\delta_t\vec{t}^{ij}, & K_s\delta_t \leq \mu^s||\vec{F}_n^{ij}|| \\ -\mu^d||\vec{F}_n^{ij}||\vec{t}^{ij}, & K_s\delta_t > \mu^s||\vec{F}_n^{ij}|| \end{cases}$$

where $\vec{t}^{ij}$ is the unit tangential vector parallel to the motion of the particle i with respect to the particle j. Parameter K is the shear modulus, δ_t is the displacement in tangential direction from the static point, $\mu^d < \mu^s$ are coefficients of dynamic and static friction respectively. For most geomaterials, the static friction coefficient is 0.9, so it is taken in our simulations. The coefficient of dynamic friction varies from 0 to 0.4 and determines the angle of internal friction of materials. Finally, taking into account the dissipative terms, the equations of motion of particles are written down as:

$$M^j\frac{d^2\vec{x}^j}{dt^2} = \sum_{i \in J(i)} \left(\vec{F}_n^{ji}(\vec{x}^i, \vec{x}^j) + \vec{F}_t^{ji}(\vec{x}^i, \vec{x}^j)\right) - v\frac{d\vec{x}^i}{dt}.$$

Here we assume the forces do not explicitly depend on the velocities of the particles, but only on their coordinates. Explicit dependence on speed is in the dissipative term only. It is also necessary to note that according to the above formulas, the interaction between the particles is local, in other words, they interact when the distance between them does not exceed some fixed value r_0. Consequently, the maximum number of particles $dim(J(i))$ interacting with the particle number i can be estimated by knowing the maximum and minimum radii of particles in the system:

$$dim(J(i)) \leq 4\left(\frac{R_M + R_m + r_0}{R_M}\right),$$

where R_M and R_m are maximal and minimal radius of the discrete elements.

To resolve the system of nonlinear ordinary differential equations we use the following finite difference scheme [11]:

$$\frac{(\vec{x}^j)^{n+1} - (\vec{x}^j)^n}{\tau} = (\vec{V}^j)^n + \frac{\tau}{2}(\vec{F}^j)^n/M^j$$

$$\frac{(\vec{V}^j)^{n+1} - (\vec{V}^j)^n}{\tau} = 0.5\left((\vec{F}^j)^{n+1} + (\vec{F}^j)^n\right)/M^j$$

The main goal of 3D modeling is to determine and analyze the distribution of deformations in the horizontal direction along the fault at the macroscale level, especially for scenarios with displacement. The computational area was chosen in the form of a parallelepiped with dimensions of 500 m vertically and 2000 m in each horizontal direction. The size of the elements ranged from 2.5 to 15 m with a uniform distribution. The modulus of stiffness of the elements was 16 GPa, regardless of which layer the element belonged to. To take into account the differences in the geomechanical properties of the layers, we varied the dynamic friction coefficient within them, which determines the intensity of tangential forces.

The numerical experiments provide the distribution of deformations near the fault. The next step is to transform these deformations to the variations of elastic parameters on the base of some experimental curve presented in the Fig. 3a. In the Fig. 3b we give the fine-scale distribution of elastic parameters describing the tectonic breccia which we use to fill 3D structure of the faults.

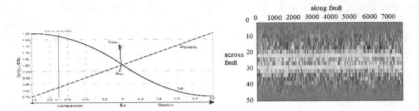

Fig. 3. Left: Experimental dependence of elastic parameters with respect to deformations. Right: "Tectonic breccia" used to fill the faults in the model.

We present the general view of the 3D synthetic model with faults and other small-scale heterogeneities in the Fig. 4.

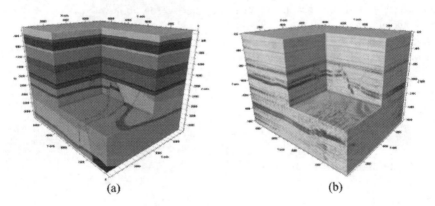

Fig. 4. 3D skeleton used for 3D seismic simulation (a) and its convolution with Ricker pulse (b).

3   3D Seismic Simulation

3.1   Presentation of the Model

For the first of all, let us present some formal parameters of the model and acquisition.

Model fills parallelepiped of 8 km × 10 km × 6 km with uniform cells with 5 m everywhere out of localization of small-scale heterogeneities. Within areas with this kind of heterogeneities (faults filled with tectonic breccia, clusters of caves and fracture corridors) we use the locally refined grid with cells of 0.5 m that allows us to describe the variability of elastic properties with reasonable accuracy.

Acquisition: is the rectangular of 8 km × 10 km with:

- 3C receivers placed uniformly with 25 m, 128000 receivers;
- Vertical force point sources placed with step of 50 m along lines which are 300 m from each other, 5280 sources;
- Recording length equal to 4 s with discretization of 2 ms;
- Source function is Ricker pulse with dominant frequency 40 Hz.
- The total volume of synthetic data is about 15 Tb.

In the Fig. 5a one can see distribution of the folds for this acquisition.

To simulate seismic wave propagation we use parallel (MPI+OpenMP) implementation of finite-difference technique with local grid refinement in time and space (see details in [10] and [15]). It is thanks to this approach that we manage to perform numerical simulations of seismic waves in this multiscale medium, ensuring description of small-scale heterogeneities on a fine grid.

The Fig. 5b presents some common shot seismogram together with amplitude-frequency response at its central point. As one can see the dominant frequency of this seismogram is equal to the dominant frequency of the impulse used in simulation, that characterizes reasonable accuracy of the synthetic data, in particular this indicates the absence of any significant numerical dispersion.

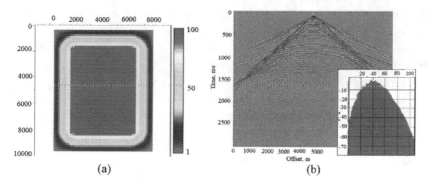

(a)   (b)

Fig. 5. Synthetic seismic wavefield. (a) CMP fold for the acquisition used. (b) Some common shot seismogram with amplitude-frequency response.

3.2 Hardware and Software Used for Simulation

To perform the simulation we used the equipment of Siberian Supercomputer Center (SSCC, Institute of Computational Mathematics and Mathematical Geophysics SB RAS) and Joint Supercomputer Center of Russian Academy of Sciences (JSCC RAS).

We used the following components of these centers:

20 Broadwell: CPU (2x) Intel Xeon E5-2697A v4 (16 2.6 GHz RAM 126 Gb
16 CPU Intel Xeon Phi 7290 KNL (72 1.5 GHz RAM 96 Gb + 16 Gb)
Cluster Interconnection Intel OmniPath 100 Gbps
Parallel file system Intel Lustre 200 Tb
Peak performance 81.9 Teraflops

JSCC RAS

10 Skylake: CPU (2x) Intel Xeon Gold 6154 (18 3 GHz RAM 192 Gb
Cluster Interconnect Intel OmniPath 100 Gbps
Peak performance 34 Teraflops.

Software Used: Intel Parallel Studio XE 2019 Update 3 with compiler Intel C ++/
Fortran Compiler 19.0.

3.3   Justification of Equipment Selection

As it turned out, the computational code possesses the best efficiency when using 2–3
computational nodes. With an increase in the nodes involved, there is a drop in performance due to an increase in the number of network data links. When testing the code
on alternative IBM Power9, AMD processors, we observed the performance reduction
in comparison with Intel ones due to the differences in the architecture. The highest
performance corresponds to the effective use of vectorization and possessing the
AVX2, AVX-512 instruction set. In this regard, there is a requirement for the optimal
amount of RAM per single processor core - 4 GB of RAM and more than 1 core. On
this base, we decided to use computing modules with two processors and a network for
transferring data with a capacity of 100 Gbps and higher when using processors with a
clock frequency higher than 2.5 GHz. The use of a segment with Intel Xeon Phi 7290
processors is reasonable as a backup when there is necessary to repeat/refine results in a
particular computational domain. 4 nodes with Intel Xeon Phi 7290 processors in terms
of performance on the author's code replace 3 nodes with Intel Xeon E5-2697A v4
processors. For these reasons, the most suitable computing equipment for performing
the calculations is located at Institute of Computational Mathematics and Mathematical
Geophysics SB RAS (Novosibirsk) and Joint Supercomputer Center RAS (Moscow).
These centers have the similar infrastructure (access to computing equipment, data
storage system, task queue, system software set), which reduced the time for preliminary data preparation and calculations.

4   Scattering Imaging of Microheterogeneities

In our previous studies [13, 14], we have developed numerical methods and software
for scattered waves imaging of singular objects like clusters of caves and fracture
corridors. The approach developed needed the depth velocity model to provide correct
positioning of these objects within the medium. However, usually this kind of model is
not available. Instead, they know time velocity model in the result of some standard set
of routine seismic data processing.

Based on these needs of practice, we performed a modification of the method to
ensure the possibility to use the time velocity model for scattered/diffracted waves
imaging. To this end, we continue to use Gaussian beams, but have significantly
changed the imaging conditions.

We use the aforementioned digital twin to validate the approach of scattered waves imaging. The Fig. 6 presents the model (left) and the corresponding image in scattered waves (right). As one can see, there is almost unambiguous correspondence between the model and the image.

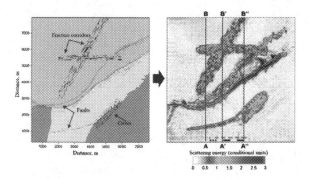

Fig. 6. Right: The model (digital twin). Left: its scattering image.

5   Conclusions

We have developed the 3D digital twin for some real test site on the base of all available geological information about the geometry of the existing faults, clusters of caves, and fracture corridors. To populate the faults with tectonic breccia, we performed geomechanical simulation of tectonic motions and interaction of blocks. Next, we performed a 3D seismic simulation to obtain multicomponent synthetic data. We used this data to validate the scattering imaging technique.

We want especially emphasize the importance of these digital twins of real geological objects, in particular, those inherent in the complex geological conditions of the East Siberia, for validating methods of the Full Waveform Inversion and seismic imaging. It is their use that ensures that proposed approaches provide the correct solution to the inverse problem and recovers the desired parameters with desired quality.

Author Contributions
Vladimir Cheverda proposed and together with Maksim Protasov justified the asymmetric summation with Gaussian beams to image small-scale heterogeneities. Dmitry Kolyukhin and Vadim Lisitsa applied discrete elements simulation to describe fault formation and calibrate parameters of tectonic breccia. Maksim Protasov developed asymmetric summation for 3D imaging and constructed 3D images of small-scale heterogeneities; Galina Reshetova applied finite-difference technique with local grid refinement in time and space and computed 3D synthetic seismic wave fields.

Anastasiya Merzlikina developed 3D skeleton of the model, Victoriya Volyanskaya supervised simulation of tectonic motions creating faults, Denis Petrov is responsible for filling the skeleton with seismic parameters (density and wave propagation velocities), Valery Shilikov did interpretation of the data processing, Arjem Melnik developed faults geometry and positioning.

Boris Glinsky dealt with optimization of parallel programming, Igor Chernykh determined the technology of the workflow of high performance computations and Igor Kulikov learned the processes within faults.

Acknowledgments. Vladimir Cheverda, Vadim Lisitsa, Maksim Protasov and Galina Reshetova have been supported by the Russian Science Foundation, project 17-17-01128.

Boris Glinsky, Igor Chernykh and Igor Kulikov have been supported by Russian Foundation of Basic Research, project 16-29-15120.

We thank Public Company Rosneft and KrasnoyarskNIPIneft Ltd. for permission to publish this work.

References

1. Albanese, C., Gilblom, K.: This oil major has a supercomputer the size of a soccer field, Bloomberg, 18 January 2018
2. Aminzadeh, F., Brac, J., Kuntz, T.: 3-D salt and overthrust models: SEG/EAGE modelling series, no. 1, SEG Book Series, Tulsa (1997)
3. Botter, C., Cardozo, N., Hardy, S., Lecomte, I., Escalona, A.: From mechanical modeling to seismic imaging of faults: a synthetic workflow to study the impact of faults on seismic. Mar. Pet. Geol. **57**, 187–207 (2014)
4. Botter, C., Cardozo, N., Lecomte, I., Rotevatn, A., Paton, G., Escalona, A.: Seismic characterization of fault damage in 3D using mechanical and seismic modeling. Mar. Pet. Geol. **77**, 973–990 (2016)
5. Duan, K., Kwok, C.Y., Ma, X.: DEM simulations of sandstone under true triaxial compressive tests. Acta Geotech. **12**(3), 495–510 (2017)
6. Faulkner, D.R., et al.: A review of recent developments concerning the structure, mechanics and fluid flow properties of fault zones. J. Struct. Geol. **32**, 1557–1575 (2010)
7. Hardy, S., Finch, E.: Discrete-element modelling of detachment folding. Basin Res. **17**(4), 507–520 (2005)
8. Hardy, S., Finch, E.: Mechanical stratigraphy and the transition from trishear to kink-band fault-propagation fold forms above blind basement thrust faults: a discrete-element study. Mar. Pet. Geol. **24**, 75–90 (2007)
9. Kolyukhin, D.R., et al.: Seismic imaging and statistical analysis of fault facies models. Interpretation **5**(4), 1–11 (2017)
10. Kostin, V.I., Lisitsa, V.V., Reshetova, G.V., Tcheverda, V.A.: Local time-space mesh refinement for simulation of elastic wave propagation in multi-scale media. J. Comput. Phys. **281**, 669–689 (2015)
11. Mora, P., Place, D.: Simulation of the frictional stick-slip instability. Pure. appl. Geophys. **143**, 61–97 (1994)
12. Pangman, P.: SEAM launched in March. Lead. Edge **26**(6), 718–720 (2007)
13. Protasov, M.I., Tcheverda, V.A.: True-amplitude elastic Gaussian beam imaging of multi-component walk-away VSP data. Geophys. Prospect. **60**(6), 1030–1042 (2012)
14. Protasov, M.I., Tcheverda, V.A., Reshetova, G.V.: Fracture detection by Gaussian beam imaging of seismic data and image spectrum analysis. Geophys. Prospect. **64**(1), 68–82 (2016)
15. Tcheverda, V., Kostin, V., Reshetova, G., Lisitsa, V.: Simulation of seismic waves propagation in multiscale media: impact of cavernous/fractured reservoirs. Commun. Comput. Inf. Sci. **793**, 183–193 (2017)

GPU-Based Discrete Element Modeling of Geological Faults

Vadim Lisitsa[1][(✉)], Dmitriy Kolyukhin[2], Vladimir Tcheverda[2],
Victoria Volianskaia[3], and Viatcheslav Priimenko[4]

[1] Institute of Petroleum Geology and Geophysics SB RAS,
Sobolev Institute of Mathematics SB RAS, Novosibirsk, Russia
lisitsavv@ipgg.sbras.ru
[2] Institute of Petroleum Geology and Geophysics SB RAS, Novosibirsk, Russia
{kolyukhindr,cheverdava}@ipgg.sbras.ru
[3] PAO RosNeft, Moscow, Russia
v_volyanskaya@rosneft.ru
[4] North Fluminense State University Darcy Ribeiro,
Campos dos Goytacazes, Brazil
slava@cana.lenep.uenf.br

Abstract. In this paper, we present an algorithm for numerical simulation of the tectonic movements leading to the formation of geological faults. We use the discrete element method, so that the media are presented as an agglomeration of elastic, visco-elastic, or elasto-plastic interacting particles. This approach can naturally handle finite deformations and can account for the structural discontinuities is the Earth crust. We implement the algorithm using CUDA technology to simulate single statistical realization of the model, whereas MPI is used to parallelize with respect to different statistical realizations. Obtained numerical results show that for low dip angles of the tectonic displacements relatively narrow faults form, whereas high dip angles of the tectonic displacements lead to a wide V-shaped deformation zones.

Keywords: Geomechanics · Discrete elements method · CUDA · MPI

1 Introduction

A classical definition of the geological faults is that they are discontinuities of sedimentary, metamorphic or magmatic rock bodies. Thus, no physical properties are assigned to a fault; however, real geological faults have a complex structure which includes main fault body ("fault core") and fractured or damage zones around [7,25]. In particular, damage zone may be highly fractured, thus, permeable especially for carbonates [16], or it can be an impermeable due to the presence of deformation bonds which is typical for the sandstones [10]. Such differences of the local permeability near faults may strongly affect the reservoir performance [3]. Thus a detailed representation of the fault and damage zone is required for efficient oil and gas exploration.

© Springer Nature Switzerland AG 2019
V. Voevodin and S. Sobolev (Eds.): RuSCDays 2019, CCIS 1129, pp. 225–236, 2019.
https://doi.org/10.1007/978-3-030-36592-9_19

Very often, to do field observations or laboratory studies of the real fault is difficult or impossible due to some natural reasons. Thus, numerical simulation is a reliable and efficient way to investigate the peculiarities of the structure's forming and tectonic movement process. There are numerous techniques to simulate finite deformations in geological formations either grid-based methods such as finite differences [11], finite elements [13], boundary elements [26] or by meshless approaches also known as discrete elements method (DEM) [12,22]. The letter is preferred because no predefined crack or fault geometry is needed for simulation. However, particle-based methods are more computationally intense and require calibration of the particle properties to match the mechanics of the whole body [22]. Despite this, the particle-based methods are incredibly flexible and can be used to generate multiple statistical realizations of the fault zones and study statistical features of the strongly deformed and highly-distorted zones. In our opinion, meshless methods of geological faults formation simulations can be used to generate faults geometries in realistic environments. After that simulated faults can be introduced in geological models which are used for seismic modeling and imaging [17,28], moreover use advanced simulation techniques such as local mesh refinement [18,21] allow studying seismic responses of the fine structure of near-fault damage zones.

In this paper, we present an algorithm based on the Discrete Elements Method (DEM). This approach is based on the media representation by a set of discrete particles. These particles interact as stiff elastic bodies according to the mechanical rules; i.e., elastic and frictional forces affect each particle, that leads to the particle movement according to the Newton mechanics [14]. Computation of the forces affecting a particle includes a high number of floating point and logical operations; thus it is computationally intense and hard to implement on CPU, using vectorization, etc. As a result, the efficiency of the CPU based realizations of DEM is low, and computation time to solve even a 2D problem may be as long as several thousand node-hours. On the contrary, GPU architecture is more appropriate for DEM implementation, because it can efficiently handle a big number of flops with a small amount of memory involved in computations.

2   Discrete Elements Method

To simulate the tectonic movements causing finite deformations and geological fault formation in the Earth's crust we use the discrete element method, following [14,23]. In this approach, the media is represented as an assembly of individual particles with a particular geometry and physical properties. Each particle is characterized by the coordinate of its center $\boldsymbol{x}^j$, radius R_j, repulsion and attraction bulk moduli K_r^+ and K_r^- respectively, tangential sliding stiffness K_s, and two friction coefficients μ_s is the static one and μ_d is the dynamic friction coefficient. Having set these parameters, one may define the interaction forces between two adjoint particles.

2.1 Forces Computation

Consider two particles with the numbers i and j, with the coordinates $\boldsymbol{x}^i$ and $\boldsymbol{x}^j$ and radii R^i and R^j respectively. Particle j acts on particle i with the normal elastic forces:

$$\boldsymbol{F}_n^{ji} = \begin{cases} K_r^-(R^i + R^j - \|\boldsymbol{X}^{ji}\|)\boldsymbol{n}^{ji}, & R^i + R^j - \|\boldsymbol{X}^{ji}\| > 0, & repulsion, \\ K_r^+(R^i + R^j - \|\boldsymbol{X}^{ji}\|)\boldsymbol{n}^{ji}, & 0 \leq R^i + R^j - \|\boldsymbol{X}^{ji}\| \leq r_0, & active\ \ bond, \\ 0, & R^i + R^j - \|\boldsymbol{X}^{ji}\| > r_0, & no\ \ bond, \end{cases} \tag{1}$$

where r_0 is the bond length, typically chosen equal to $0.05(R_i + R_j)$, vector $\boldsymbol{X}^{ji} = \boldsymbol{x}^i - \boldsymbol{x}^j$ connects the centers of the particles and directed from particle j to particle i, vector $\boldsymbol{n}^{ji} = \boldsymbol{X}^{ji}/\|\boldsymbol{X}^{ji}\|$ is the unit vector directed from the centers of particle j to the center of particle i or normal vector, because it is normal to the contact plane. Note, that we use the model of linear elastic particles interaction and assume that the repulsion and attraction bulk moduli coincide, which is mainly valid for geomaterials across a wide range of scales.

Additionally frictional forces are taken into account if two particles are in a contact [23]:

$$\boldsymbol{F}_t^{ji} = \begin{cases} -K_s\delta_t\boldsymbol{t}^{ji}, & K_s\delta_t \leq \mu^s\|\boldsymbol{F}_n^{ji}\|, & static\ \ friction, \\ -\mu^d\|\boldsymbol{F}_n^{ji}\|\boldsymbol{t}^{ji}, & K_s\delta_t > \mu^s\|\boldsymbol{F}_n^{ji}\|, & dynamic\ \ friction, \end{cases} \tag{2}$$

where K_s is the tangential sliding stiffness, usually considered to be equal to bulk modulus; i.e., $K_s = K_r$, vector $\boldsymbol{t}^{ji}$ is the unitary tangential vector directed along the projection of the relative velocity onto the contact plane of two particles; i.e.,

$$\boldsymbol{t}^{ji} = \frac{\boldsymbol{v}^{ji} - (\boldsymbol{v}^{ji}, \boldsymbol{n}^{ji})\boldsymbol{n}^{ji}}{\|\boldsymbol{v}^{ji} - (\boldsymbol{v}^{ji}, \boldsymbol{n}^{ji})\boldsymbol{n}^{ji}\|}, \ \boldsymbol{v}^{ji} = \boldsymbol{v}^i - \boldsymbol{v}^j. \tag{3}$$

In this notations $\boldsymbol{v}^{ji}$ is the relative velocity of the particle i with respect to particle j. Parameter δ^{ji} denotes the tangential displacement of the contact point from its initial position. Tangential forces provided by formula (2) satisfy the Coulombs law; i.e., the static friction governs the particles interaction if the forces as below a critical value. If the tangential forces exceed the critical dynamical friction proportional to normal force is applied. Typically the static friction is much higher than the dynamical one.

Additionally, an artificial dissipation is introduced in the system to prevent elastic waves from propagating through the model and ensuring the media to remain stable at infinite instants:

$$\boldsymbol{F}_d^i = -\nu\boldsymbol{v}^i, \tag{4}$$

where ν is an artificial viscosity.

The Earth's crust also remains under gravitational forces which are accounted as

$$\boldsymbol{F}_g^i = M_i g\boldsymbol{e}_3, \tag{5}$$

where $g = 9.8$ m/s is the gravitational constant, $\boldsymbol{e}_3 = (0, 0, 1)^T$, and M_i is the mass of the considered particle.

To compute the total forces acting at a particle one needs to account the forces due to interactions with all the neighbors, plus artificial dissipation, plus gravitational forces, as a result, one gets:

$$\boldsymbol{F}^i = \sum_{j \in J(i)} \left[\boldsymbol{F}_n^{ji} + \boldsymbol{F}_t^{ji} \right] + \boldsymbol{F}_d^i + \boldsymbol{F}_g^i, \tag{6}$$

where $J(i)$ is the set of indexes of the neighbors of i-th particle.

2.2   Time Integration

Having computed all external forces acting at j-th particle one may recompute its position using classical mechanics principles:

$$M^i \frac{d^2 \boldsymbol{x}^i}{dt^2} = \boldsymbol{F}^i \left(t, \boldsymbol{x}^i, \boldsymbol{x}^j, \frac{d\boldsymbol{x}^i}{dt}, \frac{d\boldsymbol{x}^j}{dt} \right), \tag{7}$$

where dissipative $\boldsymbol{F}_d^i$ and frictional forces $\boldsymbol{F}_t^{ji}$ explicitly depend on the particles velocities $\boldsymbol{v}^i = \frac{d\boldsymbol{x}^i}{dt}$.

To numerically resolve system of Eq. (7) we use the Verlet-like scheme with the velocity half-step [15]. Assume coordinates, velocities, and thus forces of all particles are known at instant $t = t^n = \tau \cdot n$, then they can be updated to the instant t^{n+1} by the rule:

$$
\begin{aligned}
&\frac{(\boldsymbol{v}^i)^{n+1/2} - (\boldsymbol{v}^i)^n}{\tau/2} = \frac{1}{M^i} \boldsymbol{F}^i \left(t^n, (\boldsymbol{x}^i)^n, (\boldsymbol{x}^j)^n, (\boldsymbol{v}^i)^n, (\boldsymbol{v}^j)^n \right), \\
&\frac{(\boldsymbol{x}^i)^{n+1} - (\boldsymbol{x}^i)^n}{\tau} = (\boldsymbol{v}^i)^{n+1/2}, \\
&\frac{(\boldsymbol{v}^i)^{n+1} - (\boldsymbol{v}^i)^{n+1/2}}{\tau/2} = \frac{1}{M^i} \boldsymbol{F}^i \left(t^{n+1}, (\boldsymbol{x}^i)^{n+1}, (\boldsymbol{x}^j)^{n+1}, (\boldsymbol{v}^i)^{n+1/2}, (\boldsymbol{v}^j)^{n+1/2} \right), \\
&j \in J(i).
\end{aligned}
\tag{8}
$$

In case of no explicit dependence of forces on the velocities the scheme is the second order accurate, however if applied to the equation of motion for DEM, this scheme possesses only the first order of approximation.

To ensure the stability of the finite-difference scheme we use the time step as suggested in [15]

$$\tau \le 0.2 \frac{D_{min}}{V_{max}}, \tag{9}$$

where R_{min} is the minimum diameter of the particles, and V_{max} is the maximal velocity of perturbation propagation in the system.

2.3   Boundary Conditions

Proper implementation of the boundary conditions is a challenging task for the particles-based methods. In our research, we deal with two types of boundary conditions. First, we impose the rigid boundary condition; i.e., the surface Γ_s is fixed, or its movement is prescribed. Moreover, it is stiff; thus the particles cannot penetrate through it. Formally, this type of boundary condition can be stated as follows. Assume a boundary $\Gamma_s = \{\boldsymbol{x}|x_2 = x_2^B\}$. If a particle is close enough to the boundary; i.e., if for the j-th particle $|x_2^j - x_2^b| \leq R^j$, then $F_2^{jB} = K_r^-(R^j - |x_2^j - x_2^b|)$.

However, numerical implementation of this condition requires extra conditional operators. Thus it is worth implementing stiff-boundary as a series of particles, to make the simulation uniform either in the interior of the domain or near the boundary. To do so, we introduced the "boundary" particles with the same physical properties as those of the interior particles. However, we do not compute the forces acting on the "boundary" particles but allow the "boundary" particles to move according to a prescribed law. We specify the particular movement laws in the Sect. 4.

The second type of the boundary conditions is $P_{over} = const$. This condition ensures the constant overburden pressure. Note that, condition P_{over} assumes that external forces act at the upper boundary of the domain $\Gamma_p(t)$ along the normal direction to the boundary. This boundary is flexible, and it evolves in time; thus, to impose the boundary condition we need to follow the elements which form the upper boundary. This can be done, for example, by computing Voronoi diagrams for upper elements. However, such procedures are computationally intense. To overcome this difficulty, we suggest using the flexible membrane at the upper boundary [4,29]. The idea of the approach is to introduce a layer of discrete elements so that the membrane elements are affected only by the normal forces.

If two adjoint membrane elements are interacting

$$\boldsymbol{F}_n^{m,m\pm1} - K_r(R^{m\pm1} + R^m - \|\boldsymbol{X}^{m,m\pm1}\|)\boldsymbol{n}^{m,m\pm1}, \tag{10}$$

if membrane element interacts with other elements

$$\boldsymbol{F}_n^{mi} = K_r(R^i + R^m - \|\boldsymbol{X}^{mi}\|)\boldsymbol{n}^{mi}, \; R^i + R^m - \|\boldsymbol{X}^{mi}\| > 0. \tag{11}$$

It means that the adjoint membrane elements are bonded, and these bonds never bake, however no bonds of friction are considered when membrane elements interact with elements of other types. The membrane elements are ordered; thus it is easy to approximate constant pressure condition. If a membrane element with number m is considered then additional force, due to the pressure is

$$\boldsymbol{F}_p^m = 2PR^m\boldsymbol{n}, \tag{12}$$

where $\boldsymbol{n}$ is the vector normal to the boundary, which can be computed as:

$$\boldsymbol{n} = (x_2^{m-1} - x_2^{m+1}, x_1^{m-1} - x_1^{m+1})^T,$$

the direction of the normal vector is defined uniquely due to the ordering of the membrane elements.

2.4   Output Parameters

Numerous parameters can be obtained as a result of discrete elements simulations. If rock properties are studied using uniaxial and triaxial stress tests, then the primary attention is paid to the distribution of the braked bonds [8,19], stresses, and normal forces distribution [9] However, at the scale of the geological bodies a reliable parameter to determine fault zones is the strains distribution [1,5,14,15,24]. These strains can be further translated to the changes of physical parameters of rocks using the experimental laboratory measurements.

3   Implementation of the Algorithm

According to the general formulation of the particle-based methods, one has to compute the forces affecting each particle due to the interaction with all other particles. However, in geomechanical modeling by the discrete element method, for each particle only a small number of neighboring particles directly contact the considered one. The adjacency matrix is sparse, but it can evolve. Thus, two related problems should be solved. First, organizing the process of adjacency matrix construction (approximation). Second, computing forces and applying time stepping.

To construct the adjacency matrix, we suggest using the lattice method [20]. As it follows from the Eqs. (1) and (2), only directly contacting particles affect each other; thus, for each particle, the domain of dependence does not exceed $2R_{max} + r_0$, where R_{max} is the maximal radius of the particles. Also, due to the stability criterion of the Verlet scheme, a single particle cannot move more than $0.1R_{min}$ per a single time step, where R_{min} is the minimal radius over all particles. Thus, we can introduce a grid with the lattice size equal to $2R_{max} + r_0$, so that each particle and all its neighbors belong to the same lattice of directly adjoint lattice. Now we can state the rule of adjacency matrix approximation - for each particle, all the particles belonging to the same or directly adjoint lattices are neighbors. In this case, we overestimate the number of connected particles but strictly simplify the process of the matrix construction.

The initial assignment of the particles to the lattices is performed by a sequential code by CPU. It is implemented particle-by-particle so that we determine the lattice number for considered particle and add the particle number to the list of particles for this lattice. This procedure is inapplicable under OMP of CUDA parallelization. Thus, the GPU implementation of the reassignment of the particles to the lattices is done lattice-by-lattice. The lattices are large enough, so that after one time step a particle may either stay in the same lattice or move to a directly adjoint lattice. Thus, to update the list of particles for each lattice, we need to check the particles which previously belonged to this lattice or the directly adjusted one. Similar ideas are used in the molecular dynamics and lattice Boltzmann methods but with different principles of lattices construction [2].

Computation of the forces and the numerical solution of the equation of motion is implemented on GPU. The parallelization is applied particle-by-particle so that a GPU core compute forces for one particle at a time.

4   Numerical Experiments

In this paper, we focus our attention on the effect of the direction and amplitude of tectonic movement on the geometry of the fault and damage zone. DEM-based simulations include uncertainties due to the particle's positions and radii distributions. It means that for each scenario of the tectonic movements we need to perform a series of numerical simulations for different statistical realizations of the particles geometry distribution.

In all the experiments presented below, we use the following set of parameters. The size of the computational domain is 4000 m in horizontal and 500 m in the vertical direction. The repulsion/attraction modulus is 16 GPa, and same value is used for the tangential sliding stiffness. The coefficient of static friction is 0.8, which is typical for the majority of geomaterials, whereas the dynamic friction coefficient is 0.3, which is close to that of sandstone and limestone. We consider the bonds length proportional to the radii of the adjoint particles; i.e., $r_0 = 0.05(R_j + R_i)$. We assume that the formation is buried at 3000 m; thus the overburden pressure of 10^7 Pa is applied at the top boundary of the model. The particles radii are homogeneously distributed from 1.25 to 2.5 m. So, the total number of elements is 390000.

We consider several scenarios of dipping normal tectonic movements with the dip angles equal to $90°$, $75°$, $60°$, $45°$, $30°$. Maximal vertical displacement is 100 m.

For each tectonic movement we simulate ten statistical realizations of the particles distributions; thus, 10 simulations are performed for each scenario. Also, we computed extra 20 realizations for the most common movement scenario with the dip angle equal to $60°$. Each simulation consists of two stages. First, the elements should be compacted under the overburden pressure and gravitational forces. This step takes about 60 % of the computational time. Second, the tectonic movements are applied. The total simulation time for one experiment (one realization) is about 8.7 h by a single GPU (NVIDIA Tesla M 2090).

We provide the strains distribution for each movement scenario in Figs. 1, 2 and 3. The main trend observed from the presented figures is that for big dip angles; i.e., for nearly vertical displacements no narrow fault cores are formed. When the dip angle gets smaller fault cores are formed (Fig. 1) and they are located within a narrow zone. Moreover, for low dip angles the form of the fault and its inclination is similar, thus might depend mainly on the medium properties rather than on the direction of tectonic movements. To verify this assumption, we perform clustering of the results and their statistical analysis in the following section.

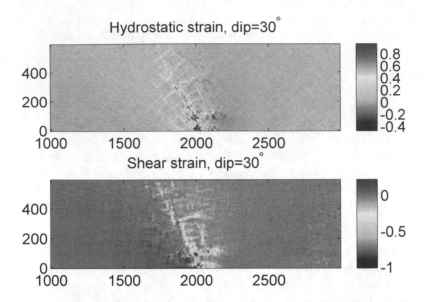

Fig. 1. A single realizaton of hydrostatic (top) and shear (bottom) strains distribution in the fault zone for the displacement dip equal to 30°.

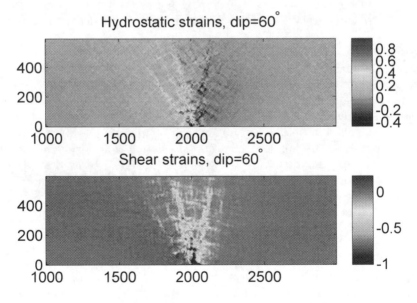

Fig. 2. A single realizaton of hydrostatic (top) and shear (bottom) strains distribution in the fault zone for the displacement dip equal to 60°.

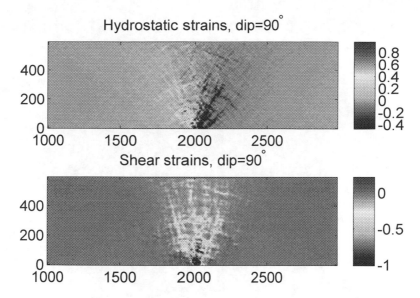

Fig. 3. A single realizaton of hydrostatic (top) and shear (bottom) strains distribution in the fault zone for the displacement dip equal to 90°.

4.1 Clustering of the Results

Results of the numerical simulation tend to form narrow inclined faults if the dipping angle is small, whereas high dipping angles cause a wide V-shape damage zone. To quantify this observation, we applied k-means clustering of the computed strains distribution. Before processing to the formal analysis, we need to point out, that we performed two additional series of simulations (9 realizations in each series) corresponding to the tectonic movement dip angle equal to 60°. In total we have 27 statistical realizations corresponding to this scenario; however, we will still consider them as three independent series in our statistical analysis.

According to the Calinski-Harabasz Index [6] and the silhouette criterion [27] the optimal number of clusters of the considered data is two. We applied the k-means clustering technique to our data. We constructed clusters for each component of the strain tensor separately, as well as for all of them together. The panels in Fig. 4 represent the clustering results in two clusters applied to all components of the strain tensor. One may note that the displacement scenarios with dip angles equal to 75° and 90° form one cluster. This confirms the assumption that direction of the tectonic movement strictly affects the structure of the fault and near fault damage zone.

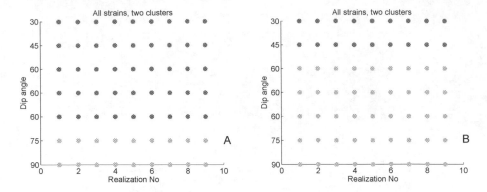

Fig. 4. Panels representing data clustering (two clusters) for all components of strain tensor. Left panel (A) corresponds to the optimal clustering with minimal distance, right panel (B) represents a case of local minimum of k-means functional. Different colors correspond to different clusters.

5   Conclusions

We presented an algorithm for simulation of the Earth's crust tectonic movements and formation of the geological faults and near-fault damage zones. The algorithms are based on the Discrete Elements Method, and it is implemented using CUDA technology. We used to simulate faults formation due to different scenarios of tectonic movements. We considered the displacements with dipping angles varied from 30 to 90 degrees; i.e., up to vertical throw. For each scenario, we performed simulations for some statistical realizations. According to clustering analysis shows that displacements with high (75° and 90°) and low (30° and 45°) dip angles form completely different geological structures. Nearly vertical displacements, high dip angles, form wide V-shaped deformation zones, whereas the flat displacements cause narrow fault-cores with rapidly decreasing strains apart from the fault core. Results of the presented simulations can be used to estimate mechanical and seismic properties of rocks in the vicinity of the faults and applied further to construct models for seismic modeling and interpretation, hydrodynamical simulations, history of matching simulation, etc.

Acknowledgements. Development of mathematical basis of the algorithm was done by V. Lisitsa in IPGG SB RAS under financial support of the grant of the Precedent of the Russian Federation for young researchers MD-20.2019.5. Parallel implementation of the algorithm was done by V. Lisitsa in IM SB RAS under support of Russian Science Foundation grant no. 19-77-20004. D. Kolyukhin performed the statistical analysis of the results under support of Russian Foundation for Basic Research grant no. 18-05-00031. Numerical experiments were carried out by V. Tcheverda under support of the Russian Science Foundation grant no. 17-17-01128. V. Priimenko applied the clustering analysis of the results. V. Volianskaia did the geological interpretation. The research is carried out using the equipment of the shared research facilities of HPC computing resources at Lomonosov Moscow State University and cluster NKS-30T+GPU of the Siberian supercomputer center.

References

1. Abe, S., Gent, H., Urai, J.: DEM simulation of normal faults in cohesive materials. Tectonophysics **512**, 12–21 (2011). https://doi.org/10.1016/j.tecto.2011.09.008
2. Alpak, F.O., Gray, F., Saxena, N., Dietderich, J., Hofmann, R., Berg, S.: A distributed parallel multiple-relaxation-time lattice-Boltzmann method on general-purpose graphics processing units for the rapid and scalable computation of absolute permeability from high-resolution 3D micro-CT images. Comput. Geosci. **22**(3), 815–832 (2018). https://doi.org/10.1007/s10596-018-9727-7
3. Bense, V.F., Gleeson, T., Loveless, S.E., Bour, O., Scibek, J.: Fault zone hydrogeology. Earth Sci. Rev. **127**, 171–192 (2013). https://doi.org/10.1016/j.earscirev.2013.09.008
4. de Bono, J., Mcdowell, G., Wanatowski, D.: Discrete element modelling of a flexible membrane for triaxial testing of granular material at high pressures. Géotechnique Lett. **2**(4), 199–203 (2012). https://doi.org/10.1680/geolett.12.00040
5. Botter, C., Cardozo, N., Hardy, S., Lecomte, I., Escalona, A.: From mechanical modeling to seismic imaging of faults: a synthetic workflow to study the impact of faults on seismic. Mar. Pet. Geol. **57**, 187–207 (2014). https://doi.org/10.1016/j.marpetgeo.2014.05.013
6. Calinski, T., Harabasz, J.: A dendrite method for cluster analysis. Commun. Stat. **3**(1), 1–27 (1974). https://doi.org/10.1080/03610927408827101
7. Choi, J.-H., Edwards, P., Ko, K., Kim, Y.-S.: Definition and classification of fault damage zones: a review and a new methodological approach. Earth Sci. Rev. **152**, 70–87 (2016). https://doi.org/10.1016/j.earscirev.2015.11.006
8. Cundall, P.A., Strack, O.D.L.: A discrete numerical model for granular assemblies. Géotechnique **29**(1), 47–65 (1979). https://doi.org/10.1680/geot.1979.29.1.47
9. Duan, K., Kwok, C.Y., Ma, X.: DEM simulations of sandstone under true triaxial compressive tests. Acta Geotechnica **12**(3), 495–510 (2017). https://doi.org/10.1007/s11440-016-0480-6
10. Fossen, H., Schultz, R.A., Shipton, Z.K., Mair, K.: Deformation bands in sandstone: a review. J. Geol. Soc. **164**(4), 755–769 (2007). https://doi.org/10.1144/0016-76492006-036
11. González, G., et al.: Crack formation on top of propagating reverse faults of the Chuc ulay fault system, northern Chile: Insights from field data and numerical modelling. J. Struct. Geol. **30**(6), 791–808 (2008). https://doi.org/10.1016/j.jsg.2008.02.008
12. Gray, G., Morgan, J., Sanz, P.: Overview of continuum and particle dynamics methods for mechanical modeling of contractional geologic structures. J. Struct. Geol. **59**(Suppl. C), 19–36 (2014). https://doi.org/10.1016/j.jsg.2013.11.009
13. Guiton, M.L.E., Sassi, W., Leroy, Y.M., Gauthier, B.: Mechanical constraints on the chronology of fracture activation in folded Devonian sandstone of the western Moroccan anti-atlas. J. Struct. Geol. **25**(8), 1317–1330 (2003). https://doi.org/10.1016/S0191-8141(02)00155-4
14. Hardy, S., Finch, E.: Discrete-element modelling of detachment folding. Basin Res. **17**(4), 507–520 (2005). https://doi.org/10.1111/j.1365-2117.2005.00280.x

15. Hardy, S., McClayc, K., Munozb, J.A.: Deformation and fault activity in space and time in high-resolution numerical models of doubly vergent thrust wedges. Mar. Pet. Geol. **26**, 232–248 (2009). https://doi.org/10.1016/j.marpetgeo.2007.12.003

16. Hausegger, S., Kurz, W., Rabitsch, R., Kiechl, E., Brosch, F.J.: Analysis of the internal structure of a carbonate damage zone: implications for the mechanisms of fault Breccia formation and fluid flow. J. Struct. Geol. **32**(9), 1349–1362 (2010). https://doi.org/10.1016/j.jsg.2009.04.014

17. Kolyukhin, D., et al.: Seismic imaging and statistical analysis of fault facies models. Interpretation **5**(4), SP71–SP82 (2017). https://doi.org/10.1190/int-2016-0202.1

18. Kostin, V., Lisitsa, V., Reshetova, G., Tcheverda, V.: Local time-space mesh refinement for simulation of elastic wave propagation in multi-scale media. J. Comput. Phys. **281**, 669–689 (2015). https://doi.org/10.1016/j.jcp.2014.10.047

19. Li, Z., Wang, Y.H., Ma, C.H., Mok, C.M.B.: Experimental characterization and 3D DEM simulation of bond breakages in artificially cemented sands with different bond strengths when subjected to triaxial shearing. Acta Geotechnica **12**(5), 987–1002 (2017). https://doi.org/10.1007/s11440-017-0593-6

20. Lisitsa, V., Tcheverda, V., Volianskaia, V.: GPU-based implementation of discrete element method for simulation of the geological fault geometry and position. Supercomput. Front. Innov. **5**(3), 46–50 (2018). https://doi.org/10.14529/jsfi180307

21. Lisitsa, V., Reshetova, G., Tcheverda, V.: Finite-difference algorithm with local time-space grid refinement for simulation of waves. Comput. Geosci. **16**(1), 39–54 (2012). https://doi.org/10.1007/s10596-011-9247-1

22. Lisjak, A., Grasselli, G.: A review of discrete modeling techniques for fracturing processes in discontinuous rock masses. J. Rock Mech. Geotech. Eng. **6**(4), 301–314 (2014). https://doi.org/10.1016/j.jrmge.2013.12.007

23. Luding, S.: Introduction to discrete element methods. Eur. J. Environ. Civil Eng. **12**(7–8), 785–826 (2008). https://doi.org/10.1080/19648189.2008.9693050

24. O'Sullivan, C., Bray, J.D., Li, S.: A new approach for calculating strain for particulate media. Int. J. Numer. Anal. Meth. Geomech. **27**(10), 859–877 (2003). https://doi.org/10.1002/nag.304

25. Peacock, D.C.P., Dimmen, V., Rotevatn, A., Sanderson, D.J.: A broader classification of damage zones. J. Struct. Geol. **102**, 179–192 (2017). https://doi.org/10.1016/j.jsg.2017.08.004

26. Resor, P.G., Pollard, D.D.: Reverse drag revisited: why footwall deformation may be the key to inferring Listric fault geometry. J. Struct. Geol. **41**, 98–109 (2012). https://doi.org/10.1016/j.jsg.2011.10.012

27. Rousseeuw, P.J.: Silhouettes: a graphical aid to the interpretation and validation of cluster analysis. J. Comput. Appl. Math. **20**, 53–65 (1987). https://doi.org/10.1016/0377-0427(87)90125-7

28. Vishnevsky, D., et al.: Correlation analysis of statistical facies fault models. Dokl. Earth Sci. **473**(2), 477–481 (2017). https://doi.org/10.1134/s1028334x17040249

29. Wang, Y., Tonon, F.: Modeling triaxial test on intact rock using discrete element method with membrane boundary. J. Eng. Mech. **135**(9), 1029–1037 (2009). https://doi.org/10.1061/(ASCE)EM.1943-7889.0000017

High Performance Parallel Simulations of Subsurface Radar Sounding of Celestial Bodies

Yaroslaw Ilyushin[1,2]([✉])

[1] Physical Faculty, Moscow State University, Moscow, Russia
ilyushin@phys.msu.ru
[2] Kotel'nikov Institute of Radio Engineering and Electronics,
Russian Academy of Sciences, Moscow, Russia

Abstract. Subsurface radar location currently is the only measurement technique which is able to provide valuable information about the interior structure of celestial bodies of the Solar system. Numerical simulations plays a key role in the whole subsurface radar experiment, from its development and planning to the final data interpretation and analysis. These simulations typically are time and resource consuming, so high performance parallel computing systems are suitable platform for them. This paper briefly summarizes the tools and approaches developed by the author during past one and a half decades. The radar echo simulation approach on the multiple phase screen basis, developed by the author, is formulated and discussed. Applications to the Martian subsurface radar experiments MARSIS and SHARAD are shown.

Keywords: Mars · Polar ice sheets · Ground penetrating radar · Climate record

1 Introduction

Obtaining information about the internal structure of celestial bodies of the Solar system is a vital problem of the space research. Answering this question plays the key role in many fields of investigation, including cosmology, planetary geology, astronomy, climatic history of the planets, astrobiology etc.

Subsurface radar location [1–6] is now practically the only plausible technique applicable for such investigations. Several experiments of such kind have been successfully implemented or are now discussed and planned.

Analysis and interpretation of the radar sounding data, as well as development of the instrument and planning of the observation strategy, require extensive computer simulations of the process of measurements, i.e. numerical solving of the problem of interaction of electromagnetic radiation with the object under investigation. Numerical solution of the electromagnetic equations in the large domain with the size, greatly exceeding the wave length, is a complicated

© Springer Nature Switzerland AG 2019
V. Voevodin and S. Sobolev (Eds.): RuSCDays 2019, CCIS 1129, pp. 237–248, 2019.
https://doi.org/10.1007/978-3-030-36592-9_20

and resource consuming problem. For this reason, on the other hand, special approaches to the solution should be developed, and on the other hand, high performance computing systems must be used for this.

This report summarizes the results of many years, spent for computer modeling of subsurface radar sounding, in particular MARSIS and SHARAD experiments on board Mars Express (MEX) and Mars Reconaissance Orbiter (MRO), and some perspective projects on icy moons of giant planets, including the Galilean satellites of Jupiter.

Reflection of the wide band radar signals from the planetary surface and subsurface terrain has been simulated, provided the scattering on the ionospheric disturbances has been accounted for. Diffuse reflection from layered geological structures has been also modeled. Besides, synthetic aperture radar echoes from particular planetary surface areas, for which digital elevation models (DEM) are available, have been calculated and analyzed. In addition, perspective experiments on active and passive radar sounding of Jovian icy moons have been considered. Necessary algorithms for high performance parallel computing systems have been developed and tested.

Typical simulation approach includes development of electrophysical model of the object under investigation using available information and data, and solution of the electromagnetic problem of scattering of the sounding wave on the object with further post-processing (aperture synthesis etc.) In the planetary problems, complicated three dimensional structure of the object and large size of the simulation domain makes the problem computationally expensive. This requires special simplifying assumptions, on the other hand, and making use of highly efficient computing equipment, on the other hand.

Selection of suitable approach for electromagnetic simulation and post-processing is dominated both by the specific problem statement (the object property or parameter, which is to be retrieved from the experiment) and the specific model formulation. It is worth saying here that the layered medium model (flat of spherical) is the basis for most models of upper layer of the planets and their moons. This is due to the vertical stratification caused by the gravity, which determines the layered structure of the object (see the Fig. 1).

Thus, theory of the wave propagation in layered medium is the basic theory applied to the numerical modeling of the subsurface radar sounding of the planets.

The rest of the paper is organized as follows. In the Sect. 2 the models of waves in layered media are applied to the radar sounding of the polar layered deposits on Mars. In the Sect. 3 formulation of the multiple phase screen algorithm for simulations of the wave propagation in random media is given. In the Sect. 4 the algorithm is applied to propagation of the subsurface radar signal through the inhomogeneous Martian ionosphere and rough surface of the planet. Some concluding remarks are drawn in the Sect. 5.

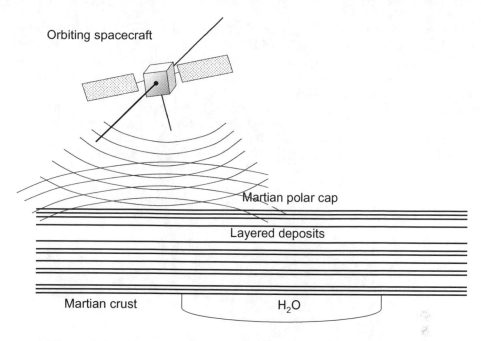

Fig. 1. Subsurface radar sounding of the Martian polar layered deposits

2 Simulations of Radar Pulses in Plane-Parallel Layered Media

Simulation algorithms for the wave propagation in inhomogeneous media are sufficiently well developed due to many applications in radio physics and optics. Medium boundary impedance, which plays the key role in the reflection from boundary, can be efficiently evaluated with the recurrent relation. Suppose a layered medium consists of a number of layers, provided the electrical properties of each layer is constant. Then in the case of normal wave incidence the impedance of it can be determined by recurrent formula which may be found [7]:

$$Z^{(n)} = \frac{Z^{(n-1)} - iZ_n \tan(k_n d_n)}{Z_n - iZ^{(n-1)} \tan(k_n d_n)} Z_n, \tag{1}$$

where $Z^{(n)}$ is the impedance of n-layers medium, $Z^{(n-1)}$ is the $(n-1)$-layers medium impedance, $Z_n = 1/\sqrt{\varepsilon_n}$ is the impedance of n-th layer itself, $k_n = \omega/c\sqrt{\varepsilon_n}$ is the wave number in the n-th layer, ε_n and d_n are the complex dielectric permittivity and thickness of n-th layer, respectively. From this formula, the recurrent formula for amplitude reflection coefficient can be derived:

$$\tilde{R}_n = \frac{(k_n - k_{n-1}) + \tilde{R}_{n-1} \exp(2ik_{n-1}d_{n-1})(k_n + k_{n-1})}{(k_n + k_{n-1}) + \tilde{R}_{n-1} \exp(2ik_{n-1}d_{n-1})(k_n - k_{n-1})}, \tag{2}$$

where $\tilde{R}_n = R_n \exp(2ik_n z_n)$, z_n is depth of the interface between $(n-1)$-th and n-th layers. Making use one of these relations, the amplitude reflection coefficient of the multilayered medium can be calculated for the given frequency.

Wide band radar signals, which are typically exploited in subsurface radar sounding, are simulated in the whole spectrum of frequencies. This allows effective parallelization for many processing cores. In real experiments, the digitized signal record length and respectively the number of frequencies in the discrete spectrum is about several hundred. Thus, the model spectrum of the medium impedance can be independently evaluated by several hundred of cores.

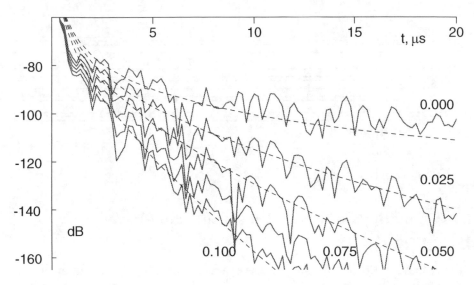

Fig. 2. Three-dimensional model of the monostatic sounding. Exact solutions of the EM wave equations (solid curves) and large time asymptotic solutions of radiative transfer theory (dashed curves). Numerical labels are the medium loss tangents. Radar chirp bandwidth 10–15 MHz.

Such approach allows evaluation of reflected waves from different types and configuration of sources with corresponding integral decompositions of electromagnetic fields like Weyl integral [8] in the spatial domain and conventional Fourier spectrum in the temporal domain, respectively. Partial components of these decompositions can be then independently processed in their usual way, with recursive evaluation of the partial reflection coefficients $R(\boldsymbol{k}, \omega)$. In the Fig. 2, amplitudes of the radar pulse reflected from the flat layered medium with different medium tangent $\tan\delta$ are plotted together with their asymptotic curves according the radiative transfer theory [8,9].

Because of very low memory requirements of these calculations, they can be effectively implemented using modern graphics processing units (GPU). The set of constants describing the medium (lists of permittivities and losses and thicknesses of individual layers) can be preloaded in the GPU constant memory.

After that, only algebraic operations and evaluation of trigonometric functions are needed, with very few memory transactions. In the papers [8–10], however, all the results were computed on the parallel cluster "Tschchebysheff" using MPI protocol.

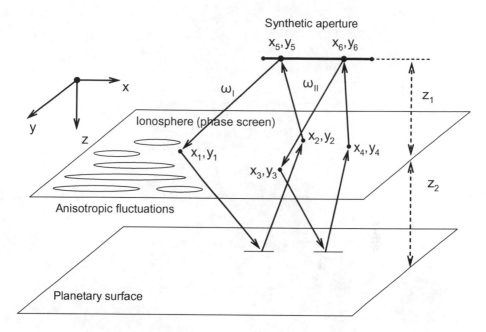

Fig. 3. Plane parallel model of the irregular ionosphere phase screen

When wave phase is perturbed across the front due to inhomogeneous medium, one of the most common approaches is the so called multiple phase screen method [11, 12]. If the irregularities are localized in specific particular layers of the medium (ionospheric layers, medium boundary interfaces), then a few phase screens are sufficient for the simulation, as it is shown in the Fig. 3.

If topography data for some portion of the planetary surface are available, the reflected signals can be immediately simulated with known physical optics algorithms [13–15] for the known DEM models used as input data. When the irregularities are random and described statistically, the wave field is also a random process. What is to be determined from the simulations are its statistical characteristics (mean field, mean intensity and higher statistical moments, the Stokes parameters, if the polarization is accounted for, etc.). In the paper [16], such and algorithm is developed for evaluation of correlation functions (statistical moments) of arbitrary order for the wave fields in random phase screen systems. Wave propagation from one phase screen to the other is simulated within the Kirchhoff approximation [17]. This algorithm has been applied to the radar sounding of Mars [18–21] and Ganymede [16, 22]. In addition, the same technique can be applied for estimates of radio channel scattering functions [23, 24].

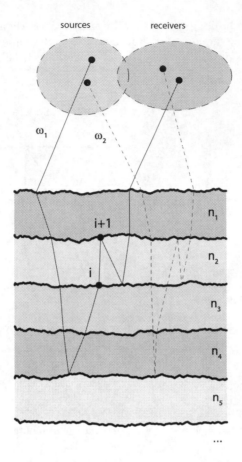

Fig. 4. General scheme of phase screen technique applied for the calculations.

3   Phase Screen Technique for Simulation of Wave Propagation

One of widely used approach to the numerical simulation of wave propagation in inhomogeneous media is the phase screen technique [18,24]. The geometry of general model of multi-layered medium is shown in the Fig. 4. Rough boundary surfaces, which separate the layers, are approximately modeled by random phase screens

$$\phi_i = -2kh(x_i, y_i) \tag{3}$$

and

$$\phi_i = 2\Delta kh(x_i, y_i) = 2\frac{\omega}{c}\Delta nh(x_i, y_i), \tag{4}$$

for transiting and reflected waves, respectively. Here Δk is the difference of wave numbers in two media, separated by the i-th surface.

Between the boundaries all the media are homogeneous, i.e. volume scattering is neglected. For nearly vertical wave propagation, in the paraxial approximation the complex amplitude of the transiting or reflected wave can be expressed in the form

$$E(x, y) = \int A_i \exp(i\phi_i) E(\mathbf{r}') G(\mathbf{r}', \mathbf{r}) dx' dy', \tag{5}$$

where $\mathbf{r} = (x, y, z)$ is an arbitrary point within the medium, $\mathbf{r}' = (x', y', z')$ is an integration point on the phase screen plane, A_i is the Fresnel amplitude reflection or transmission coefficient, respectively, ϕ_i – is the random phase shift (3) or (4), introduced by the phase screen. The Green function of the Helmholtz equation in the paraxial approximation equals to

$$G_{ij} = \frac{k}{2\pi i |z - z'|} \exp\left(ik|z - z'| + ik\frac{(x - x')^2}{2|z - z'|} + ik\frac{(y - y')^2}{2|z - z'|} \right). \tag{6}$$

In the point (x_0, y_0, z_0) a concentrated (point) source of the sounding radiation $E_0 \delta(\mathbf{r} - \mathbf{r}_0)$ is located. Within the paraxial approximation, adopted in this study, the field generated by the source in the medium is

$$E(\mathbf{r}) = E_0 \int \delta(\mathbf{r}' - \mathbf{r}_0) G(\mathbf{r}', \mathbf{r}) d^3 \mathbf{r}' = E_0 G(\mathbf{r}_0, \mathbf{r}). \tag{7}$$

Thus, complex amplitude of the wave field of frequency ω in the point $\mathbf{r}_{N+1}$ in the medium after N reflections from and transmissions through the rough boundary surfaces equals to

$$E_\omega(\mathbf{r}_{N+1}) = E_0 \int \ldots \int \prod_{i-1}^{N} A_i \exp(i\phi_i) G_{i,i+1} dx_i dy_i, \tag{8}$$

where $G_{i,i+1} \equiv G(\mathbf{r}_i, \mathbf{r}_{i+1})$. Taking an average of two fields (8) at different frequencies $\langle E_{\omega_1} E_{\omega_2}^* \rangle$, we obtain the two frequency correlation function of the field [25]

$$\Gamma_{\omega_1 \omega_2}(\mathbf{r}_{N+1}, \mathbf{r}_{2N+2}) = \langle E_{\omega_1} E_{\omega_2}^* \rangle \tag{9}$$

$$= E_0 E_0^* \int \ldots \int M\{\phi\} \prod_{i=1}^{N} A_i \exp(i\phi_i) G_{i,i+1} \prod_{i=N+2}^{2N} A_i^* G_{i,i+1}^* dx_i dy_i,$$

where

$$M\{\phi\} = \langle \exp(\sum_{i=1}^{N} i\phi_i(x_i, y_i) - \sum_{i=N+2}^{2N} i\phi_i(x_i, y_i)) \rangle \tag{10}$$

is the characteristic function of the joint distribution of all the random phases. In the case of multi-variable normal distribution of the phases, the characteristic function is [26]

$$M\{\phi\} = \langle \exp(\sum i\phi_i) \rangle = \exp\left(-\frac{1}{2} \sum_{i,j} \beta_{ij}(x_i, y_i, x_j, y_j) \right), \tag{11}$$

where β_{ij} are the random phase covariations $\phi_i(x_i, y_i)\phi_j(x_j, y_j)$, accounting their signs in the formula (10). If aperture synthesis of some another averaging procedure is applied to the observed fields, the expressions (8) and (9) should be integrated over corresponding variables with proper weighting (aperture) functions. Similarly, higher order field correlation functions can be evaluated.

After matched filtration, we get the temporal profile of the mean signal intensity

$$< |E(t)^2| >\propto \frac{1}{(2\pi)^2} \int\limits_{-\infty}^{+\infty} \int\limits_{-\infty}^{+\infty} H(\omega_1)H(\omega_2)\Gamma(\omega_1,\omega_2) \exp\left(i(\omega_1 - \omega_2)t\right) d\omega_1 d\omega_2.$$

(12)

An expression for the characteristic function $M\{\phi\}$ (11), which appears in the formula (9) for the two-frequency correlation function, can be expanded in power series of the random phase covariations β_{ij}. It the correlation functions of the random phases, i.e. random surface roughness [27], and the aperture functions [18–20] are gaussian, integration of these series term by term results in the sum of terms of general form

$$\int \exp\left(-A_{ij}x_i x_j + B_i x_i\right) d^n x = \sqrt{\frac{\pi^n}{det A_{ij}}} \exp\left(\frac{B^T A_{ij}^{-1} B}{4}\right).$$

(13)

Therefore, the approach accounts for diffractional effects and correctly treats aperture synthesis. It worth also noting that the wave paths shown in the Fig. 4 include both ladder and cyclic scattering diagrams [28], so that the coherent backscattering enhancement effect [29–32], which is essential in monostatic radar sounding configurations, is automatically accounted for.

This technique has been recently applied for computer simulation of the subsurface radar sounding through inhomogeneous ionospheric plasma [18–20], as well as sounding of rough subsurface horizon through surface terrain [21].

In the algorithm, similar mathematical operations of the same type are repeated many times, especially evaluation of the matrix determinants and matrix inversion. In fact, for evaluation of exponent in (13) the matrix inversion is not needed. Instead, it is sufficient to solve the matrix linear equation $Ax = B$, which is much less computationally expensive.

If the matrices are small and sparse enough (like in [16,18–21], where the integration variables can be partially separated), analytic expressions for the exponent and matrix determinant in (13) can be obtained, e.g., with Wolfram Mathematica and other applied software like that. These explicit expressions can be directly exported to C and Fortran source code format, appropriate for further incorporation into the source code for parallel cluster. In general, all the calculations in (13) can be performed numerically, e.g. with the Intel Math Kernel Library (Intel MKL) routines [33].

The calculations are essentially summation of large numbers of terms of similar structure (11). Memory consumption is also low, communication among process is not needed.

However, immediate parallelizing of the computations is prevented by the following. The matrix determinant in (13) is a complex-valued function of the frequency difference $\omega_2 - \omega_1$. In the particular case of second statistical moment of the field, it is a complex-valued function of the frequency difference $\Delta\omega = \omega_1 - \omega_2$. Within the operational bandwidth of the radar, its graph in the complex plane is a spiral-shaped curve centered around the zero point. It can intersect the branch cut of the square root function, which is in most realizations the negative real axis by default. To ensure continuity of the square root function, one can properly account for this. In practice, it can be done by incremental increase of the difference frequency step by step, with small increments. Thus, for effective parallelization with correct treatment of the branch cut, one should organize evaluation of partial sums of (11) in the whole frequency spectrum, with final summation at the end of program. This can be implemented both in MPI and Open MP code.

4   Discussion of the Results

Samples of the compressed signals distorted by isotropic ($\sigma_x = \sigma_y$) non-stationary ionospheric scintillations are shown in the Fig. 5 [18]. The following parameters were accepted for simulation: radar chirp signal bandwidth $B = 1\,\text{MHz}$, central frequency of the chirp $f_0 = 5\,\text{MHz}$ (LFM Band IV of the MARSIS radar), ionospheric plasma frequency $f_{p0} = 4\,\text{MHz}$ (constant throughout the ionosphere), the height of the ionosphere over the planetary surface $z_2 = 120\,\text{km}$, the height of the spacecraft over the surface $h = 250\,\text{km}$, the thickness of the ionospheric layer $H = 15\,\text{km}$, the synthetic aperture length $2L = 1500\,\text{m}$, plasma density perturbation $\Delta N/N = 0.4\%$, spatial correlation scales $\sigma_x = \sigma_y = \sigma$ are labeled near each pair of the curves in the Fig. 5. Solid curves correspond to the non-stationary correlations with $L_c = \tau v = 333\,\text{m}$, while dashed curves represent the case $L_c = 1669\,\text{m}$. The spatial correlation scale along the wave propagation direction everywhere is $\sigma_z = 1000\,\text{m}$.

One can see that the ionospheric fluctuations cause both temporal pulse broadening and degradation of the peak amplitude of the compressed radar pulse. Characteristic width of the pulse, however, depends mostly on the spatial scale σ alone, while the peak amplitude is governed by both spatial and temporal scales σ and τ, respectively.

The sample of undisturbed radar pulse (labeled as "Hann") is shown for comparison purposes in the left part of the figure. The low peak energy of the pulse (about $-10\,\text{dB}$ against the $-6\,\text{dB}$ value predicted by the theory) is due to the scallop loss [34] and other errors coming from the simplified chirp processing technique used in the simulations for the sake of the computational efficiency.

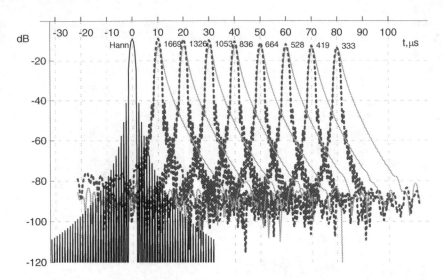

Fig. 5. Samples of the simulated GPR signals distorted by the ionospheric scintillations. MARSIS Band IV (4.5–5.5 MHz). Ionospheric layer thickness $H = 15$ km, ionospheric plasma frequency $f_{p0} = 4$ MHz.

5   Conclusions and Remarks

Computer simulations of the radar echoes became an essential part of the planetary subsurface radar experiments. Simulation software, elaborated during past years, with models of the radar targets developed from a priori known information (DEM models of the surface topography etc.) as input data proved to be of great help for data analysis and interpretation. Numerical modeling of MARSIS experiment, performed on parallel computing clusters, greatly helped to predict the results of radar sounding of Mars before the instrument was deployed in the orbit and radar measurements were started.

Acknowledgements. The research is carried out using the equipment of the shared research facilities of HPC computing resources at Lomonosov Moscow State University [35]. Support from Russian Science Foundation with the grant 17-77-20087 is kindly acknowledged.

References

1. Peeples, W.J., et al.: Orbital radar evidence for lunar subsurface layering in Maria Serenitatis and Crisium. J. Geophys. Res.: Solid Earth **83**(B7), 3459–3468 (1978)
2. Ilyushin, Y.A., Hagfors, T., Kunitsyn, V.E.: Cometary surface layer properties: possible approaches to radio sounding retrieval during the consert experiment-numerical simulation and discussion. Radio Sci. **38**(1), 8/1–8/9 (2003)
3. Picardi, G., et al.: Performance and surface scattering models for the Mars Advanced Radar for Subsurface and Ionosphere Sounding (MARSIS). Planet. Space Sci. **52**, 149–156 (2004)

4. Picardi, G., et al.: MARSIS: mars advanced radar for subsurface and ionosphere sounding. In: Mars Express: The Scientific Payload, pp. 51–69 (2004)
5. Seu, R., et al.: SHARAD: the MRO 2005 shallow radar. Planet. Space Sci. **52**(2004), 157–166 (2005)
6. Jordan, R., et al.: The mars express MARSIS sounder instrument. Planet. Space Sci. **57**(14–15), 1975–1986 (2009)
7. Born, M., Wolf, E.: Principles of Optics: Electromagnetic Theory of Propagation, Interference and Diffraction of Light, 7th edn. Cambridge University Press, Cambridge (1999)
8. Ilyushin, Y.A.: Radiative transfer in layered media: application to the radar sounding of Martian polar ices. II. Planet. Space Sci. **55**(1–2), 100–112 (2007)
9. Ilyushin, Y., Seu, R., Phillips, R.: Subsurface radar sounding of the martian polar cap: radiative transfer approach. Planet. Space Sci. **53**(14–15), 1427–1436 (2005)
10. Ilyushin, Y.A.: Martian northern polar cap: layering and possible implications for radar sounding. Planet. Space Sci. **52**(13), 1195–1207 (2004)
11. Gorbunov, M.E., Kirchengast, G.: Processing X/K band radio occultation data in the presence of turbulence. Radio Sci. **40**, RS6001 (2005)
12. Karayel, E.T., Hinson, D.P.: Sub-fresnel-scale vertical resolution in atmospheric profiles from radio occultation. Radio Sci. **32**(2), 411–423 (1997)
13. Nouvel, J.F., Herique, A., Kofman, W., Safaeinili, A.: Radar signal simulation: surface modeling with the facet method. Radio Sci. **39**(1) (2004)
14. Berquin, Y., Kofman, W., Herique, A., Alberti, G., Beck, P.: A study on ganymede's surface topography: perspectives for radar sounding. Planet. Space Sci. **77**, 40–44 (2013)
15. Ilyushin, Y.A., Orosei, R., Witasse, O., Sanchez-Cano, B.: CLUSIM: a synthetic aperture radar clutter simulator for planetary exploration. Radio Sci. **52**(9), 1200–1213 (2017)
16. Ilyushin, Y.: Subsurface radar location of the putative ocean on Ganymede: numerical simulation of the surface terrain impact. Planet. Space Sci. **92**, 121–126 (2014)
17. Goodman, J.: Introduction to Fourier Optics, 2nd edn. MaGraw-Hill, New York (1996)
18. Ilyushin, Y.: Impact of the plasma fluctuations in the martian ionosphere on the performance of the synthetic aperture ground-penetrating radar. Planet. Space Sci. **57**(12), 1458–1466 (2009)
19. Ilyushin, Y.: Influence of anisotropic fluctuations of the ionosphere plasma density on deep radio sounding by a ultra wide band radar with synthesized aperture. Cosm. Res. **48**(2), 157–164 (2010)
20. Ilyushin, Y.: Influence of the ionospheric plasma density fluctuations on the subsurface sounding of the martian soil by a synthetic aperture radar. Radiophys. Quantum Electron. **52**(5–6), 332–340 (2009)
21. Ilyushin, Y., Smirnov, V., Yushkova, O.: Deep subsurface radar sounding of rough extraterrestrial terrains: numerical simulations. In: 2012 6th International Conference on Ultrawideband and Ultrashort Impulse Signals, UWBUSIS 2012 - Conference Proceedings, pp. 112–114 (2012)
22. Hartogh, P., Ilyushin, Y.: A passive low frequency instrument for radio wave sounding the subsurface oceans of the Jovian icy moons: an instrument concept. Planet. Space Sci. **130**, 30–39 (2016). Atmospheres, Magnetospheres and Surfaces of the outer planets, their satellites and ring systems: Part XI
23. Cannon, P.S., Groves, K., Fraser, D.J., Donnelly, W.J., Perrier, K.: Signal distortion on VHF/UHF transionospheric paths: first results from the wideband ionospheric distortion experiment. Radio Sci. **41**(5) (2006)

24. van de Kamp, M., Cannon, P.S., Terkildsen, M.: Effect of the ionosphere on defocusing of space-based radars. Radio Sci. **44**(1) (2009)
25. Ishimaru, A.: Wave Propagation and Scattering in Random Media. Academic, New York (1978)
26. Davenport, W.B.J., Root, W.L.: An Introduction to the Theory of Random Signals and Noise. Lincoln Laboratory Publication (1958)
27. Ostro, S.J.: Planetary radar astronomy. Rev. Mod. Phys. **65**, 1235–1279 (1993)
28. Ilyushin, Y.A.: Backscattering effects in media with strongly elongated scattering indicatrices. Radiophys. Quantum Electron. **60**(4), 323–331 (2017)
29. Watson, K.M.: Multiple scattering of electromagnetic waves in an underdense plasma. J. Math. Phys. **10**(4), 688–702 (1969)
30. Barabanenkov, Y.: Wave corrections to the transfer equation for "back" scattering. Radiophys. Quantum Electron. **16**(1), 65–71 (1973)
31. Ilyushin, Y.A.: Coherent backscattering enhancement in highly anisotropically scattering media: numerical solution. J. Quant. Spectrosc. Radiat. Transfer **113**(5), 348–354 (2012)
32. Ilyushin, Y.A.: Coherent backscattering enhancement in refracting media: diffusion approximation. J. Opt. Soc. Am. A **30**(7), 1305–1309 (2013)
33. Intel Math Kernel Library. Reference Manual. Intel Corporation (2009)
34. Harris, F.J.: On the use of windows for harmonic analysis with the discrete fourier transform. Proc. IEEE **66**(1), 51–83 (1978)
35. Sadovnichy, V., Tikhonravov, A., Voevodin, V., Opanasenko, V.: "Lomonosov": supercomputing at Moscow State University. In: Contemporary High Performance Computing: From Petascale Toward Exascale, pp. 283–307. Chapman & Hall/CRC Computational Science, Boca Raton (2013)

High-Performance Hybrid Computing for Bioinformatic Analysis of Protein Superfamilies

Dmitry Suplatov[1($\boxtimes$)], Yana Sharapova[1], Maxim Shegay[1], Nina Popova[1],
Kateryna Fesko[2], Vladimir Voevodin[1], and Vytas Švedas[1]

[1] Lomonosov Moscow State University, Moscow, Russia
{d.a.suplatov,sharapova,vytas}@belozersky.msu.ru, max.shegai@gmail.com,
popova@cs.msu.su, voevodin@parallel.ru
[2] Institute of Organic Chemistry, Graz University of Technology, Graz, Austria
kateryna.lypetska@tugraz.at

Abstract. Construction of a multiple alignment of proteins that implement different functions within a common structural fold of a superfamily is a valuable tool in bioinformatics, but represents a challenge. The process can be seen as a pipeline of independent sequential steps of an equivalent computational complexity each performed by a different set of algorithms. In this work the overall productivity of the corresponding Mustguseal protocol was significantly improved by selecting an appropriate optimization strategy for each step of the pipeline. This HPC-installation was used to collect and superimpose within 12 h a representative set of 299'976 sequences and structures of the fold-type I PLP-dependent enzymes what appears to be the largest alignment of a protein superfamily ever constructed. The use of hybrid acceleration strategies provided a routine access to a sequence/structure comparison of evolutionarily related proteins at a scale that would previously have been intractable to study the structure-function relationship and solve practically relevant problems, thus promoting the value of bioinformatics and HPC in protein engineering and drug discovery.

Keywords: Bioinformatics · Protein superfamilies · Multiple alignment · Mustguseal · High-performance computing · Hybrid computing

1 Introduction

Comparative analysis of homologous proteins implementing diverse functions within a common structural framework can reveal the complex interplay between a protein structure, function, and regulation, but represents a methodological challenge [1–7]. Various algorithms and tools were proposed to study evolutionarily related proteins by constructing large alignments of protein families/superfamilies based on their structures and sequences available in public

© Springer Nature Switzerland AG 2019
V. Voevodin and S. Sobolev (Eds.): RuSCDays 2019, CCIS 1129, pp. 249–264, 2019.
https://doi.org/10.1007/978-3-030-36592-9_21

databases [8–13]. Identification of positions in such multiple alignments demonstrating a particular pattern of conservation or variability among homologs can help to study the molecular mechanisms of protein action and regulation, design improved variants of enzymes/proteins, and selective ligands to modulate their functional properties [14–20]. The most prominent superfamilies subjected to such a bioinformatic analysis include the industrially relevant fold-type I [3, 21–23], III [24], and IV [3, 25–27] PLP-dependent enzymes, α/β-hydrolases [28–33], Ntn-hydrolases [34, 35], neuraminidases/sialisases [36–40], serine/threonine kinases [41–44], and others.

The construction of a multiple alignment and its subsequent analysis become more time-consuming with the increase of the number of proteins to be compared, thus representing a growing computational challenge as the public databases depositing protein primary data (i.e., sequences and structures) continue to expand in a geometric progression. E.g., in the last two years the UniProtKB database [45] doubled in size—from 75 to 150 million sequences—and the number of entries in PDB database [46] increased by $\approx$22% to 150 thousand structures. The growing availability of protein primary data has created a demand for more powerful and faster versions of the software to align and study protein superfamilies.

The recently proposed Mustguseal protocol can automatically collect and align all available sequences and structures of proteins within a superfamily [13]. The procedure consists of a pipeline of independent sequential steps of an equivalent computational complexity performed by a different set of algorithms. Each step can benefit from a deep re-design of the algorithms and corresponding re-implementation of program source codes for compatibility with the state-of-the-art HPC-resources. However, optimization of the overall productivity and total running time of a such an integrated computational solution represents a significant challenge, as the complete re-implementation of all stages of such a pipeline would be very labor-intensive, and partial re-implementation of only some steps would provide a limited positive effect. In this work, the computational efficiency of the Mustguseal was significantly improved by selecting the most appropriate and the least labor-intensive optimization strategy for each step of the pipeline. The potential of the proposed HPC-based installation was evaluated at constructing a sequences/structure alignment of the fold-type I PLP-dependent enzymes.

The article is organized as follows. Section 2 provides an overview of the Mustguseal pipeline and describes the strategies used to optimize each step of the protocol. Section 3 presents the HPC-installation of the Mustguseal and evaluation of its potential at large-scale alignment of protein sequences and structures within a superfamily. In Sect. 4, we discuss the obtained results in a wider context of high-performance computing in computational biology and summarize the study.

2   Methods

The Mustguseal protocol represents a pipeline of independent sequential steps of an equivalent computational complexity each performed by a different set of bioinformatic algorithms. The overall productivity of the Mustguseal protocol was significantly improved by selecting an appropriate re-implementation strategy and a complementary hardware for each step of the pipeline. The details are provided below: Subsect. 2.1 presents the hardware used in this study; Subsect. 2.2 provides an overview of the Mustguseal protocol; Subsects. 2.3–2.6 discuss optimization of each step of the Mustguseal pipeline; finally, Subsect. 2.7 describes the setup used to evaluate the proposed HPC-installation.

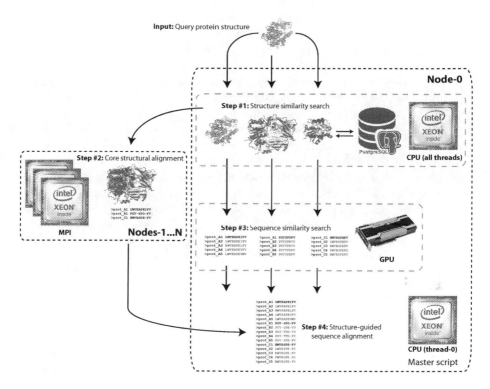

Fig. 1. Overview of hybrid acceleration strategies and hardware within the proposed HPC-installation of the Mustguseal bioinformatic protocol

2.1   The Hardware

The computations were carried out on the "Lomonosov-2" supercomputer [47] using nodes equipped with (1) one Tesla K40 GPU, one Intel Xeon E5-2697 v3 CPU, and 64 GB RAM (i.e., the partition "compute", 1487 nodes in total); and (2) two Tesla P100 GPUs, one Intel Xeon Gold 6126 CPU, and 96 GB RAM (i.e., the partition "pascal", 160 nodes in total). The System/Service/Management Networks were Infiniband FDR/Infiniband FDR/Gigabit Ethernet. The source codes were compiled with Intel collection v.15.0.3, GNU collection v.4.8.5, MKL v.11.1.3, CUDA v.8.0, and Open-MPI v.1.10.7.

2.2   Overview of the Mustguseal Protocol

The Mustguseal protocol for collection and subsequent structure-guided sequence alignment of evolutionarily close and distantly related proteins within a super-family was initiated from a query protein structure (i.e., a member of the corresponding superfamily) and consisted of four major steps (Fig. 1). (1) First, the structure similarity search was used to collect evolutionarily distantly related proteins that lost sequence similarity during natural selection and specialization from a common ancestor. These were expected to represent different protein families within the superfamily (i.e., the representative proteins). (2) A 3D-superimposition of the collected structures was performed to create the core structural alignment. Selection and 3D-alignment of the representative proteins sharing a common structural core defined the diversity and scope of the final structure-guided sequence superimposition of the protein superfamily. (3) Each representative protein was used as a query to run a sequence similarity search and collect close evolutionarily relatives—members of the corresponding families. (4) Finally, superimposition of all the collected sequences was performed by using the core structural 3D-alignment as a guide. Such a combination of sequence- and structure-based strategies for database search and subsequent alignment of the selected data was implemented in the Mustguseal to take into account a vast variability of the proteins within a superfamily—superimposition of the protein 3D-structures known to be more conserved among homologs throughout the evolution was implemented to match evolutionarily distant relatives, whereas alignment of amino acid sequences was used to match close homologues [13].

2.3   Step 1: Structure Similarity Search

On the first step, structure similarity search using the SSM algorithm [48] was implemented for the submitted query protein to collect similar structures from the PDB database based on the percentage of secondary structure equivalences [13]. The discovered proteins were filtered based on pairwise sequence identity by the CD-HIT tool [49] to select the non-redundant core collection of representative proteins. The computational complexity of this step was due to the fact that the query protein had to be matched with each of ≈330 thousand structures from the PDB database corresponding to individual protein chains to estimate the structural equivalences. The following three strategies were applied to accelerate this process within a single node.

Preprocessing of the Input Data. The PDB database was preprocessed to focus the structure similarity search only on a small subset of entries which were the most likely to share a common structural core with the query. All protein chains in the PDB were clustered at the 95% sequence similarity threshold by the CD-HIT tool [49]. In a separate development, the number of amino acid residues participating in secondary structure elements of each chain was estimated using the SSM [48]. Both characteristics were permanently stored in a flat-file database on the HDD. The PDB chain entries to be used for the structure similarity search were selected based on the threshold percentage of secondary structure equivalences requested by the user at the time of a task submission—i.e., at least $Q\%$ of the query protein had to make at least $T\%$ of the target from PDB to be selected for further consideration. First, all target protein chains were selected from the database that had $N_{target}^{SSE} \neq 0$ and $N_{query}^{SSE} \geq T\% \times N_{target}^{SSE}$ and $N_{target}^{SSE} \geq Q\% \times N_{query}^{SSE}$, where N denotes the number of amino acid residues participating in secondary structure elements (SSE) of the query or target proteins. Violation of any of these conditions made it impossible for the two proteins to share the requested degree of similarity. Second, only one representative chain was selected from those corresponding to one similarity cluster, and all pairwise superimpositions of the query with this initial subset of targets was performed. Then, all chains of a cluster whose representative member was successfully matched with the query were included into the second iteration of pairwise superimpositions. All obtained pairwise alignments were finally processed to select proteins from the PDB structurally similar to the query. Implementation of this strategy reduced the amount of bioinformatic calculations by $\approx 90\%$ when the default parameters were used so that $Q = 70\%$ and $T = 70\%$ [13].

Single Node Multitasking. The pairwise structure similarity matching of the user-submitted query protein with the selected subset of PDB entries is a computationally demanding task that can be divided into independent subtasks to be analyzed separately without interprocess communication. Such an algorithmic structure is common in bioinformatics, as recently discussed [50]. Accordingly, the SSM [48] routine was implemented using the Master-Worker pattern to utilize all CPU-cores of a single node. The Master process managed the subtasks, distributed them among Worker processes on demand, and stored the results. In such a parallel process there was no communication between the Workers and minimum overhead for communication with the Master leading to efficient scalability [50]. Further re-implementation of the program to utilize multiple nodes is possible given the simple Master-Worker communication pattern, but at this point does not seem practically useful as the current single-node version of the software took only ≈ 10–60 min to complete the majority of tasks on a 12-core Intel Xeon Gold 6126 CPU, and this expected operating time was comparable to that of the consequent steps of the Mustguseal pipeline (see detail below). In addition, the CD-HIT tool [49] used for database preprocessing and postprocessing of the results was compiled in the OpenMP mode and executed on all available CPU-cores.

Caching Results to a Database for Future Re-use. A pairwise super-imposition between two protein chains (i.e., of the query and the target) was computed only once and then permanently stored in the PostgreSQL-managed database [51] on the HDD to be re-used when the comparison of the corresponding structures was requested again. Such a caching of results to a database did not speed-up a single task, but helped to accelerate the processing of consequent submissions initiated by the same query protein. Retrieval of all pairwise super-impositions previously computed for the query took just a few seconds. Such a feature can be practically useful to compute several variations of a superfamily alignment starting from the same query protein but using different parameters to modulate the diversity and scope of proteins to be considered for a particular purpose.

2.4   Step 2: 3D-Alignment

The 3D-alignment of multiple proteins becomes more time-consuming with the increase of the number of input structures. To address this issue as the PDB database demonstrates a geometric growth the recently proposed parMATT program intended for large-scale 3D-alignment of protein superfamilies by running in a parallel environment of a classical cluster/supercomputer [52] was selected to perform the Step 2 in this HPC-installation of the Mustguseal protocol. The par-MATT is a MPI/pthreads/OpenMP parallel re-implementation of the popular MATT algorithm which searches for compatible pairs of fragments and permits structural allowances such as twists and translations [53], and thus demonstrates good performance in aligning distant relationships and length variations [54]. The most computationally demanding steps of the algorithm—the initial construction of pairwise alignments between all input structures and further iterative progression of the multiple alignment—were parallelized using the MPI and POSIX threads, and the concluding refinement step was accelerated by introducing the OpenMP support (i.e., the shared-memory multitasking). The temporary data were stored in the RAM and distributed across all allocated nodes to use the available resources efficiently (see [52] for details). The output alignment produced by parMATT was identical to that of MATT. The parMATT was tested on 1–256 nodes of the partition "compute" of the "Lomonosov-2" supercomputer (i.e., 14 computing cores per node, up to 3584 computing cores in total) and demonstrated a significant speedup compared to other methods. The observed computational efficiency and saturation point where performance growth stopped were proportional to the number of PDB structures in the input set and their size (i.e., the number of amino acid residues) with better performance on a larger number of nodes observed when aligning more populated sets of a bigger protein structures (see [52] for details). E.g., acceleration of up to ×31.7 was observed when superimposing a set of 2000 protein 3D-structures on 128 nodes compared to performance of the MATT on all cores of a single node, i.e., 4.08 h when running on a distributed-memory system compared to 5.39 days on one 14-core CPU. The parMATT is available as a standalone program and distributed under the GNU public license version 2.0 at https://biokinet. belozersky.msu.ru/parMATT.

2.5   Step 3: Sequence Similarity Search

Each representative protein was independently used as a query to run a sequence similarity search versus the UniProtKB/Swiss-Prot and UniProtKB/TrEMBL databases which together contained almost 150 million protein entries. The following two strategies were applied to accelerate this process within a single node.

Preprocessing of the Input Data. The UniProtKB database was preprocessed to remove redundant entries at the 95% sequence similarity threshold. The plain-text file of the database in the FASTA format was divided into chunks of at most 2 million randomly assigned protein sequences and further processed by the CD-HIT tool [49] in the OpenMP mode on a one-chunk-per-node basis. This routine removed all redundant entries within each file but not between files. Thus, these output files were merged and the procedure was repeated on the next iteration, unless the number of redundant sequences eliminated on the previous iteration was less than 2%. Implementation of preprocessing reduced the size of the database and computational complexity of the corresponding sequence similarity search by ≈25%.

Single-Node CPU+GPU Multitasking. The GPU-compatible version of the popular BLAST tool [55] was selected to perform the sequence similarity search in this HPC-installation of the Mustguseal protocol. The running time of the GPU-accelerated version of the algorithm was not significantly different compared to the CPU-only version. The practical benefit of the GPU-BLAST is that multiple tasks can be executed on the same GPU device. In this study, at most 12 sequence similarity searches using different representative proteins as queries were simultaneously processed on a single node in the CPU+GPU mode by a 12-core CPU and two Tesla GPUs (i.e., one task occupied one CPU core and shared one GPU device with five other tasks). Proteins within each set collected by such a search corresponded to evolutionarily close homologs and were further aligned using the MAFFT routine executed on a single core [56], and then filtered to remove too distant proteins (i.e., outliers) by the HHFilter routine of the HHpred package [57]. Such a parallel strategy was efficient as the tasks were fully independent and did not overlap across resources, in particular, the power of one Tesla P100 was more than sufficient to accommodate six simultaneous searches by the BLAST routine.

2.6   Step 4: Structure-Guided Sequence Alignment

During this step columns of gaps were inserted into individual sequence alignments built on Step 3 in a way that their total lengths became equal so that superposition of the representative proteins in the merged sequence alignments matched their superimposition in the core structural alignment built on Step 2. In practice, this led to a large number of low-information columns with a high number of gaps as a result of sequence and structural variability among evolutionary distantly related homologues, thus significantly increasing the RAM consumption and the size of the output file. To address this issue at constructing multiple alignments of large protein superfamilies the superimpositions of close homologues created at Step 3 were trimmed by the sequences of representative proteins, i.e., all columns which contained a gap in a representative protein were removed. Consequently, the final alignment contained the complete sequences of the representative proteins aligned with each other and subsequences of their homologues (Fig. 2). The trimming significantly reduced the RAM consumption and decreased by up to ≈99% the size of the final alignment file. In practice, the trimming does not lead to loss of information because further bioinformatic and statistical analysis of the final alignment is usually focused only on the columns which contain amino acid residues of the representative proteins, and this information is identical in the original and trimmed versions of the alignment.

```
>REP_A1  ----------YTKAIADIWAIGCIFAEMY-GK---     >REP_A1  --YTKAIADIWAIGCIFAEMYGK
>SEQ_A2  ----------YT-AV-DIWAVGCIYAEKCS-MFIL     >SEQ_A2  --YT-AV-DIWAVGCIYAEKC-M
>SEQ_A3  ----------YTPAI-D-WAIGCIYGEKCS-MF-L     >SEQ_A3  --YTPAI-D-WAIGCIYGEKC-M
>SEQ_A4  ----------YTPAV-DLWA-GCIFAEECS-MF--     >SEQ_A4  --YTPAV-DLWA-GCIFAEEC-M
>SEQ_A5  ----------YTTAV-DLWA-GCIFAEGTE-----     >SEQ_A5  --YTTAV-DLWA-GCIFAEGT--
>REP_B1  -------MSYNEKS~DIWSLGCLLYE~~~~~~~~~     >REP_B1  MSYNEKS~DIWSLGCLLYE~~~~
>SEQ_B2  ---LRMYRKFTTES-DVWSFG-VLWE--------     >SEQ_B2  RKFTTES-DVWSFG-VLWE----
>SEQ_B3  --A--FRT-SSAS-DVWSFG---WE---------     >SEQ_B3  RT-SSAS-DVWSFG---WE----
>SEQ_B4  ----HE-YNGYNFKS-DIWSLGCLLYE-------     >SEQ_B4  NGYNFKS-DIWSLGCLLYE----
>SEQ_B5  IPQE-YSGYNFKS-DLWSTGCLLYE--------     >SEQ_B5  SGYNFKS-DLWSTGCLLYE----
```

        a) Raw alignment   b) Trimmed alignment

Fig. 2. Trimming of the multiple alignment by the sequences of representative proteins (i.e. "REP_A1" and "REP_B1"). The alignment columns which contain a gap in all representative proteins are colored in red. (Color figure online)

2.7   Multiple Alignment of the PLP-Dependent Enzymes

The proposed HPC-installation of the Mustguseal protocol was used to build the alignment of the fold-type I PLP-dependent enzymes superfamily from the data publicly available in the PDB and Uniprot as of 28.10.2018. First, all proteins from the PDB that shared at least 30% secondary structure equivalences with L-allo-threonine aldolase from *Aeromonas jandaei* (PDB 3WGB, chain A) were collected. This initial set of structures was further processed to select the largest subset that shared at least 30% secondary structure equivalences with each other as recently described [52], and then filtered at the 40% pairwise sequence identity threshold. The finally selected non-redundant set of representative proteins contained 186 structures. Each representative protein was used to run the sequence similarity search versus UniProtKB/Swiss-Prot and

UniProtKB/TrEMBL databases and collect at most 10'000 proteins per search. The initially collected sets of sequences were further filtered to remove redundant entries and outliers: sequences which were too small or too large compared to the respective representative protein (i.e., differed by more than 20% in length) were dismissed; similar sequences were removed at the 95% sequence identity threshold; sequences sharing less than 0.25bit score per column with the query representative protein were removed to eliminate too distant proteins that could have caused errors during the sequence alignment [13,58].

3 Results

The computational efficiency of the Mustguseal protocol at constructing a protein superfamily alignment was significantly improved by selecting/developing an appropriate software with respect to a complementary hardware for each particular step of the bioinformatic pipeline (Fig. 1). The proposed HPC-implementation of the Mustguseal can utilize shared-memory, distributed-memory, and GPU-based parallel multitasking and was installed on the partition "pascal" of the "Lomonosov-2" supercomputer of the Lomonosov Moscow State University. The core of the bioinformatic protocol can be executed on a single node equipped with one 12-core Xeon CPU, two Tesla GPUs, 96 GB of RAM, and connected by Infiniband FDR with the data storage device (see Subsect. 2.1 for details). As an option, the computationally demanding Step 2 (i.e., the multiple 3D-alignment of protein structures) can be manually started on multiple CPU-nodes of the supercomputer, followed by a re-start on a single node for further processing. Such an installation of the Mustguseal engine potentially allows for tens-to-hundreds of different alignments to be constructed simultaneously using all available nodes of the supercomputer. The construction of a multiple alignment can be performed in a fully automated way; however, in practice, manual curation should be applied at the Step 1 of the protocol to select the evolutionarily remote homologs (i.e., the representative proteins) that are expected to represent different protein families, and at the Step 2 to check whether all representative proteins share a common structural core. Such an intervention of an expert bioinformatician at these two initial steps of the pipeline can improve the accuracy of the comparative analysis as the diversity of selected representative proteins defines the scope of the final structure-guided sequence superimposition. The running time of each step depends on the particular superfamily and the parameters setup, but should take no more than ≈1–4 h. Consequently, the total running time of automatically performed calculations excluding the manual curation should fit into the 12 h time-frame. For a comparison, a rough estimate of the total running time of un-optimized fully sequential version of the Mustguseal to automatically construct the alignment of a large superfamily on a regular Desktop CPU-only computer can exceed many weeks.

Multiple alignment of the fold-type I PLP-dependent enzymes was constructed to evaluate the potentials of the proposed HPC-installation of the Mustguseal (see Subsect. 2.7 for details). A non-redundant set of 186 evolutionarily

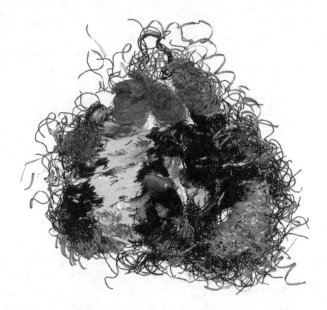

Fig. 3. A multiple 3D-superimposition of 186 representative proteins with high structural but low sequence similarity and corresponding to different families within the superfamily of fold-type I PLP-dependent enzymes. The legend for secondary structure types: α-helix (pink), β-sheet (yellow), loop (black). (Color figure online)

distantly related homologs was selected and superimposed to create the multiple 3D-alignment of representative proteins (Fig. 3). The common structural core (i.e., structural equivalences which were shared by all representative proteins) contained 187 amino acid residues or 34–56% of the length of the selected proteins. Each representative protein was used to run the sequence similarity search to collect the close homologs, i.e., members of the corresponding families. The initially collected set of 1'175'558 different protein sequences was further filtered to remove redundant entries and outliers. The finally created structure-guided sequence alignment of the fold-type I PLP-dependent enzymes contained a non-redundant set of 299'976 sequences and structures of homologs. The collection and subsequent alignment of proteins at such a scale using the publicly available conventional methods and web-servers [8,9,11,12] is implausible. The largest multiple alignment of the fold-type I PLP-dependent enzymes reported so far was created in 2015 by the 3DM tool [10] and contained 42'080 protein sequences and structures [23]. The description of software and hardware setup implemented in the 3DM has not been published as the service is available on a commercial basis, therefore a detailed analysis of the computational efficiency of that tool is not possible. The multiple structure-guided sequence superimposition of the fold-type I PLP-dependent enzymes constructed by the HPC-installation of Mustguseal is 613% larger than the one built by 3DM in 2015 for the same superfamily of proteins, although the growths of UniProtKB and PDB databases over the corresponding period of time was only 133% and 27%, respectively. To the best of our knowledge, the multiple alignment of a protein superfamily reported in this study is the largest ever constructed and incorporates ≈0.24% of the currently known variability of the protein Universe.

4   Discussion and Conclusions

High-performance computing is popular in computational biology in general [59,60], but is relatively new in the field of protein bioinformatics for sequence/structure analysis due to a significantly different algorithmic structure. Complex tasks in biology usually require multi-step solutions. E.g., analysis of proteins using the well-known methods of molecular dynamics or docking can be roughly divided into three major steps: preparation of the molecular models of the proteins/ligands of interest, the molecular dynamics/docking itself, and, finally, postprocessing of the raw output to facilitate its biological interpretation by an expert (e.g., see [38,44] for details). The first and last steps of such an integrated computational solution can require dozens of different algorithms and programs to be executed in a sequential order; however, only the middle step demands a huge amount of resources. I.e., the computational complexity of one step is superior compared to all other steps of such a multi-step procedure. As a result, the re-designed versions of software to accelerate these most resource-demanding routines—e.g., GPU re-implementations of the molecular dynamics [61–64] and parallel solutions for the molecular docking [50,65,66]—are practically useful and popular among biologists. On the contrast, complex solutions in protein bioinformatics are usually represented by a pipeline of independent sequential steps of an equivalent computational complexity performed by a different set of algorithms. Optimization of all steps of such a multi-step procedure is needed to improve the overall performance, and thus represents a significant challenge.

In this work the Mustguseal protocol to collect and align all available sequences and structures of proteins within a superfamily was re-implemented using hybrid acceleration strategies specifically selected for each step of the bioinformatic pipeline to improve its overall performance. The corresponding software was installed on the "Lomonosov-2" supercomputer of the Lomonosov Moscow State University currently ranked #72 in the world Top-500 list. It can be noted that construction of a multiple alignment is not the ultimate objective of bioinformatics and further analysis of the collected data is needed to establish the structure-function relationship—e.g., by statistical analysis of conserved and variable positions in structures of homologs [16,18,67] followed by molecular modeling to study the role of selected residues in protein function [21,32] or stability [7,35]. Therefore, the multi-step Mustguseal procedure is itself only the first phase of a larger computational biology pipeline. The proposed HPC-implementation of the Mustguseal provides a routine access to a sequence/structure comparison of hundreds of thousands of evolutionarily related proteins with different functional properties. Bioinformatic analysis of protein superfamilies on such a scale can significantly expand our capabilities to study common and specific patterns of local structure among functionally diverse homologs for a deeper understanding of the structure-function relationship in proteins and towards a more efficient solution of practically relevant problems in biotechnology and biomedicine, thus promoting the value of bioinformatics and high-performance computing in protein engineering and drug discovery.

Acknowledgements. This work was supported by the Russian Foundation for Basic Research grant #18-29-13060 and carried out using the equipment of the shared research facilities of HPC computing resources at Lomonosov Moscow State University supported by the project RFMEFI62117X0011 [47].

References

1. Beerens, K., et al.: Evolutionary analysis as a powerful complement to energy calculations for protein stabilization. ACS Catal. **8**(10), 9420–9428 (2018)
2. Bornscheuer, U.T.: The fourth wave of biocatalysis is approaching. Philos. Trans. Roy. Soc. A Math. Phys. Eng. Sci. **376**(2110), 20170063 (2017)
3. Buß, O., Buchholz, P.C., Gräff, M., Klausmann, P., Rudat, J., Pleiss, J.: The ω-transaminase engineering database (oTAED): a navigation tool in protein sequence and structure space. Proteins Struct. Funct. Bioinf. **86**(5), 566–580 (2018)
4. Hendrikse, N.M., Charpentier, G., Nordling, E., Syrén, P.O.: Ancestral diterpene cyclases show increased thermostability and substrate acceptance. FEBS J. **285**(24), 4660–4673 (2018)
5. Lutz, S., Iamurri, S.M.: Protein engineering: past, present, and future. In: Bornscheuer, U.T., Höhne, M. (eds.) Protein Engineering. MMB, vol. 1685, pp. 1–12. Springer, New York (2018). https://doi.org/10.1007/978-1-4939-7366-8_1
6. Pellis, A., Cantone, S., Ebert, C., Gardossi, L.: Evolving biocatalysis to meet bioeconomy challenges and opportunities. New Biotechnol. **40**, 154–169 (2018)
7. Suplatov, D., Voevodin, V., Švedas, V.: Robust enzyme design: bioinformatic tools for improved protein stability. Biotechnol. J. **10**(3), 344–355 (2015)
8. Armougom, F., et al.: Expresso: automatic incorporation of structural information in multiple sequence alignments using 3D-coffee. Nucleic Acids Res. **34**(suppl-2), W604–W608 (2006)
9. Krieger, E., Vriend, G.: YASARA view–molecular graphics for all devices–from smartphones to workstations. Bioinformatics **30**(20), 2981–2982 (2014)
10. Kuipers, R.K., et al.: 3DM: systematic analysis of heterogeneous superfamily data to discover protein functionalities. Proteins Struct. Funct. Bioinf. **78**(9), 2101–2113 (2010)
11. Papadopoulos, J.S., Agarwala, R.: COBALT: constraint-based alignment tool for multiple protein sequences. Bioinformatics **23**(9), 1073–1079 (2007)
12. Pie, J., Kim, B., Grishin, N.: PROMALS3D: a tool for multiple sequence and structure alignment. Nucleic Acids Res. **36**(7), 2295–2300 (2008)
13. Suplatov, D.A., Kopylov, K.E., Popova, N.N., Voevodin, V.V., Švedas, V.K.: Mustguseal: a server for multiple structure-guided sequence alignment of protein families. Bioinformatics **34**(9), 1583–1585 (2018)
14. Pleiss, J.: Systematic analysis of large enzyme families: identification of specificity- and selectivity-determining hotspots. ChemCatChem **6**(4), 944–950 (2014)

15. Sumbalova, L., Stourac, J., Martinek, T., Bednar, D., Damborsky, J.: Hotspot wizard 30: web server for automated design of mutations and smart libraries based on sequence input information. Nucleic Acids Res. **46**(W1), W356–W362 (2018)
16. Suplatov, D., Kirilin, E., Arbatsky, M., Takhaveev, V., Švedas, V.: pocketZebra: a web-server for automated selection and classification of subfamily-specific binding sites by bioinformatic analysis of diverse protein families. Nucleic Acids Res. **42**(W1), W344–W349 (2014)
17. Suplatov, D., Kirilin, E., Švedas, V.: Bioinformatic analysis of protein families to select function-related variable positions. In: Understanding Enzymes, pp. 375–410. Pan Stanford (2016)
18. Suplatov, D., Kirilin, E., Takhaveev, V., Švedas, V.: Zebra: a web server for bioinformatic analysis of diverse protein families. J. Biomol. Struct. Dyn. **32**(11), 1752–1758 (2014)
19. Suplatov, D., Shalaeva, D., Kirilin, E., Arzhanik, V., Švedas, V.: Bioinformatic analysis of protein families for identification of variable amino acid residues responsible for functional diversity. J. Biomol. Struct. Dyn. **32**(1), 75–87 (2014)
20. Suplatov, D., Sharapova, Y., Timonina, D., Kopylov, K., Švedas, V.: The visualcmat: a web-server to select and interpret correlated mutations/co-evolving residues in protein families. J. Bioinf. Comput. Biol. **16**(02), 1840005 (2018)
21. Fesko, K., Suplatov, D., Švedas, V.: Bioinformatic analysis of the fold type I PLP-dependent enzymes reveals determinants of reaction specificity in l-threonine aldolase from Aeromonas jandaei. FEBS Open Bio **8**(6), 1013–1028 (2018)
22. Genz, M., et al.: Engineering the Amine Transaminase from Vibrio fluvialis towards Branched-Chain substrates. ChemCatChem **8**(20), 3199–3202 (2016)
23. Steffen-Munsberg, F., et al.: Bioinformatic analysis of a PLP-dependent enzyme superfamily suitable for biocatalytic applications. Biotechnol. Adv. **33**(5), 566–604 (2015)
24. Knight, A.M., et al.: Bioinformatic analysis of fold-type III PLP-dependent enzymes discovers multimeric racemases. Appl. Microbiol. Biotcchnol. **101**(4), 1499–1507 (2017)
25. Bezsudnova, E.Y., et al.: Biochemical and structural insights into PLP fold type IV transaminase from thermobaculum terrenum. Biochimie **158**, 130–138 (2019)
26. Bezsudnova, E.Y., Dibrova, D.V., Nikolaeva, A.Y., Rakitina, T.V., Popov, V.O.: Identification of branched-chain amino acid aminotransferases active towards (R)-(+)-1-phenylethylamine among PLP fold type IV transaminases. J. Biotechnol. **271**, 26–28 (2018)
27. Bezsudnova, E.Y., Stekhanova, T.N., Suplatov, D.A., Mardanov, A.V., Ravin, N.V., Popov, V.O.: Experimental and computational studies on the unusual substrate specificity of branched-chain amino acid aminotransferase from thermoproteus uzoniensis. Arch. Biochem. Biophys. **607**, 27–36 (2016)
28. Jochens, H., Aerts, D., Bornscheuer, U.T.: Thermostabilization of an esterase by alignment-guided focussed directed evolution. Protein Eng. Des. Sel. **23**(12), 903–909 (2010)
29. Kourist, R., et al.: The α/β-hydrolase fold 3DM database (ABHDB) as a tool for protein engineering. ChemBioChem **11**(12), 1635–1643 (2010)
30. Pleiss, J., Fischer, M., Peiker, M., Thiele, C., Schmid, R.D.: Lipase engineering database: understanding and exploiting sequence-structure-function relationships. J. Mol. Catal. B Enzym. **10**(5), 491–508 (2000)
31. Rauwerdink, A., Kazlauskas, R.J.: How the same core catalytic machinery catalyzes 17 different reactions: the serine-histidine-aspartate catalytic triad of α/β-hydrolase fold enzymes. ACS Catal. **5**(10), 6153–6176 (2015)

32. Suplatov, D., Besenmatter, W., Švedas, V., Svendsen, A.: Bioinformatic analysis of alpha/beta-hydrolase fold enzymes reveals subfamily-specific positions responsible for discrimination of amidase and lipase activities. Protein Eng. Des. Sel. **25**(11), 689–697 (2012)
33. Widmann, M., Juhl, P.B., Pleiss, J.: Structural classification by the Lipase Engineering Database: a case study of Candida antarctica lipase A. BMC Genom. **11**(1), 123 (2010)
34. Deaguero, A.L., Blum, J.K., Bommarius, A.S.: Biocatalytic synthesis of β-lactam antibiotics. Encycl. Ind. Biotechnol. Bioprocess Bioseparation Cell Technol., 1–18 (2009)
35. Suplatov, D., Panin, N., Kirilin, E., Shcherbakova, T., Kudryavtsev, P., Švedas, V.: Computational design of a pH stable enzyme: understanding molecular mechanism of penicillin acylase's adaptation to alkaline conditions. PLoS ONE **9**(6), e100643 (2014)
36. Grienke, U., et al.: Discovery of prenylated flavonoids with dual activity against influenza virus and streptococcus pneumoniae. Sci. Rep. **6**, 27156 (2016)
37. Sharapova, Y.A., Švedas, V.: Molecular modeling of the binding of the allosteric inhibitor optactin at a new binding site in neuraminidase a from streptococcus pneumoniae. Mosc. Univ. Chem. Bull. **73**(5), 205–211 (2018)
38. Sharapova, Y., Suplatov, D., Švedas, V.: Neuraminidase a from streptococcus pneumoniae has a modular organization of catalytic and lectin domains separated by a flexible linker. FEBS J. **285**(13), 2428–2445 (2018)
39. Walther, E., et al.: Dual acting neuraminidase inhibitors open new opportunities to disrupt the lethal synergism between streptococcus pneumoniae and influenza virus. Frontiers Microbiol. **7**, 357 (2016)
40. Xu, Z., et al.: Sequence diversity of nana manifests in distinct enzyme kinetics and inhibitor susceptibility. Sci. Rep. **6**, 25169 (2016)
41. Karasev, D., Veselovsky, A., Lagunin, A., Filimonov, D., Sobolev, B.: Determination of amino acid residues responsible for specific interaction of protein kinases with small molecule inhibitors. Mol. Biol. **52**(3), 478–487 (2018)
42. Korbee, C.J., et al.: Combined chemical genetics and data-driven bioinformatics approach identifies receptor tyrosine kinase inhibitors as host-directed antimicrobials. Nat. Commun. **9**(1), 358 (2018)
43. Song, J., et al.: Phosphopredict: a bioinformatics tool for prediction of human kinase-specific phosphorylation substrates and sites by integrating heterogeneous feature selection. Sci. Rep. **7**(1), 6862 (2017)
44. Suplatov, D., Kopylov, K., Sharapova, Y., Švedas, V.: Human p38α mitogen-activated protein kinase in the Asp168-Phe169-Gly170-in (DFG-in) state can bind allosteric inhibitor doramapimod. J. Biomol. Struct. Dyn. **37**(8), 2049–2060 (2019)
45. Consortium, U.: UniProt: a worldwide hub of protein knowledge. Nucleic Acids Res. **47**(D1), D506–D515 (2018)
46. Burley, S.K., Berman, H.M., Kleywegt, G.J., Markley, J.L., Nakamura, H., Velankar, S.: Protein Data Bank (PDB): the single global macromolecular structure archive. In: Wlodawer, A., Dauter, Z., Jaskolski, M. (eds.) Protein Crystallography. MMB, vol. 1607, pp. 627–641. Springer, New York (2017). https://doi.org/10.1007/978-1-4939-7000-1_26
47. Sadovnichy, V., Tikhonravov, A., Voevodin, V., Opanasenko, V.I.: "Lomonosov": supercomputing at Moscow State University. Contemporary High Performance Computing: From Petascale toward Exascale (Chapman & Hall/CRC Computational Science), pp. 283–307 (2013)

48. Krissinel, E., Henrick, K.: Secondary-structure matching (SSM), a new tool for fast protein structure alignment in three dimensions. Acta Crystallogr. Sect. D: Biol. Crystallogr. **60**(12), 2256–2268 (2004)
49. Fu, L., Niu, B., Zhu, Z., Wu, S., Li, W.: CD-HIT: accelerated for clustering the next-generation sequencing data. Bioinformatics **28**(23), 3150–3152 (2012)
50. Suplatov, D., Popova, N., Zhumatiy, S., Voevodin, V., Švedas, V.: Parallel workflow manager for non-parallel bioinformatic applications to solve large-scale biological problems on a supercomputer. J. Bioinf. Comput. Biol. **14**(02), 1641008 (2016)
51. Obe, R.O., Hsu, L.S.: PostgreSQL: Up and Running: A Practical Guide to the Advanced Open Source Database. O'Reilly Media Inc., Sebastopol (2017)
52. Shegay, M.V., Suplatov, D.A., Popova, N.N., Švedas, V.K., Voevodin, V.V.: par-MATT: parallel multiple alignment of protein 3D-structures with translations and twists for distributed-memory systems. Bioinformatics **35**(21), 4456–4458 (2019)
53. Menke, M., Berger, B., Cowen, L.: Matt: local flexibility aids protein multiple structure alignment. PLoS Comput. Biol. **4**(1), e10 (2008)
54. Kalaimathy, S., Sowdhamini, R., Kanagarajadurai, K.: Critical assessment of structure-based sequence alignment methods at distant relationships. Briefings Bioinf. **12**(2), 163–175 (2011)
55. Vouzis, P.D., Sahinidis, N.V.: GPU-BLAST: using graphics processors to accelerate protein sequence alignment. Bioinformatics **27**(2), 182–188 (2010)
56. Katoh, K., Standley, D.M.: Mafft multiple sequence alignment software version 7: improvements in performance and usability. Mol. Biol. Evol. **30**(4), 772–780 (2013)
57. Söding, J., Biegert, A., Lupas, A.N.: The HHpred interactive server for protein homology detection and structure prediction. Nucleic Acids Res. **33**(suppl-2), W244–W248 (2005)
58. Fischer, J., Mayer, C.E., Söding, J.: Prediction of protein functional residues from sequence by probability density estimation. Bioinformatics **24**(5), 613–620 (2008)
59. Nobile, M.S., Cazzaniga, P., Tangherloni, A., Besozzi, D.: Graphics processing units in bioinformatics, computational biology and systems biology. Briefings Bioinf. **18**(5), 870–885 (2016)
60. Vega-Rodríguez, M.A., Rubio-Largo, A.: Parallelism in computational biology: a view from diverse high-performance computing applications. Int. J. High Perform. Comput. Appl. **32**(3), 317–320 (2018)
61. Götz, A.W., Williamson, M.J., Xu, D., Poole, D., Le Grand, S., Walker, R.C.: Routine microsecond molecular dynamics simulations with amber on GPUs. 1. Generalized born. J. Chem. Theor. Comput. **8**(5), 1542–1555 (2012)
62. Salomon-Ferrer, R., Götz, A.W., Poole, D., Le Grand, S., Walker, R.C.: Routine microsecond molecular dynamics simulations with AMBER on GPUs. 2. Explicit solvent particle mesh Ewald. J. Chem. Theor. Comput. **9**(9), 3878–3888 (2013)
63. Sharapova, Y.A., Suplatov, D.A., Švedas, V.K.: Simulating the long-timescale structural behavior of bacterial and influenza neuraminidases with different HPC resources. Supercomput. Frontiers Innovations **5**(3), 30–33 (2018)
64. Suplatov, D., Sharapova, Y., Popova, N., Kopylov, K., Voevodin, V., Švedas, V.: Molecular dynamics in the force field FF14SB in water TIP4P-EW, and in the force field FF15IPQ in water SPC/EB: a comparative analysis on GPU and CPU (in Russian). Bull. South Ural State University Ser. Comput. Math. Softw. Eng. **8**(1), 71–88 (2019)
65. Imbernón, B., Prades, J., Giménez, D., Cecilia, J.M., Silla, F.: Enhancing large-scale docking simulation on heterogeneous systems: an MPI vs rCUDA study. Future Gener. Comput. Syst. **79**, 26–37 (2018)

66. Prakhov, N.D., Chernorudskiy, A.L., Gainullin, M.R.: VSDocker: a tool for parallel high-throughput virtual screening using autodock on windows-based computer clusters. Bioinformatics **26**(10), 1374–1375 (2010)
67. Suplatov, D., Timonina, D., Sharapova, Y., Švedas, V.: Yosshi: a web-server for disulfide engineering by bioinformatic analysis of diverse protein families. Nucleic Acids Res. **47**(W1), 308–314 (2019)

Improving Parallel Efficiency
of a Complex Hydrogeological Problem
Simulation in GeRa

Dmitry Bagaev[1,2], Fedor Grigoriev[1,3(✉)], Ivan Kapyrin[1,3], Igor Konshin[1,3,4],
Vasily Kramarenko[1,3], and Andrey Plenkin[3]

[1] Marchuk Institute of Numerical Mathematics of RAS, Moscow 119333, Russia
bvdmitri@gmail.com, grig-fedor@ibrae.ac.ru, ivan.kapyrin@gmail.com,
igor.konshin@gmail.com, kramarenko.vasiliy@gmail.com
[2] Lomonosov Moscow State University, Moscow 119991, Russia
[3] Nuclear Safety Institute of RAS, Moscow 115191, Russia
[4] Dorodnicyn Computing Centre, FRC CSC RAS, Moscow 119333, Russia
golden_dragon_84@mail.ru

Abstract. The aspects of parallel efficiency of hydrogeological calculations in the GeRa code are considered. The scalability of computations is tested on a model of a real object. The methods of dynamic optimization of linear solver parameters are presented, which allow to accelerate the calculations.

Keywords: Parallel computing · Hydrogeological modeling · Linear solver parameters optimization

1 Introduction

Hydrogeological modeling is one of the main tools for safety assessment of radioactive waste (RW) disposal facilities and other objects affecting groundwater. It is also applied for sanitary protection zones and groundwater (GW) supplies calculations, drainage systems design, etc. The development of hydrogeological software allowing the computations of high precision for large time periods is an important task. The contemporary trends in hydrogeological modeling software development are calculations on unstructured locally refined grids, parallelization and coupling multiple physical processes. Recent advances in this field more or less following these common trends are:

- MODFLOW-USG (developed by USGS, [1]), which uses control volume finite difference discretizations and employs different types of unstructured grids;
- FEFLOW, which is a finite-element code using triangular prismatic grids [2];
- OpenGeoSys – an open-source scientific thermo-hydro-mechanical-chemical simulator for high-performance computations on unstructured grids [3].
- PFLOTRAN – an open-source reactive multiphase flow and transport simulator aimed at high-performance petascale computing on unstructured grids [4].

V. Voevodin and S. Sobolev (Eds.): RuSCDays 2019, CCIS 1129, pp. 265–277, 2019.
https://doi.org/10.1007/978-3-030-36592-9_22

One more contemporary hydrogeological software, the GeRa (Geotransport of Radionuclides) code, is being developed by Nuclear Safety Institute of RAS (IBRAE) and Marchuk Institute of Numerical Mathematics of RAS (INM RAS) on order of SC "Rosatom" for 3D groundwater flow and transport modeling in RW disposal facilities' safety assessment. GeRa provides tools for full modeling workflow: from geological modeling to radiation dose evaluation, including such specific models like radioactive chain decay, decay heat generation and heat transport. It also can be used outside the nuclear industry, for example, in the tasks of groundwater protection from contamination, for landfill design or water supply design. The first version of the code (GeRa / V1) was certified by the Russian regulatory authority (Rostechnadzor) in 2018 for use in nuclear facilities safety assessment and transferred to a number of organizations in the nuclear industry under license agreements. The code is based on finite volume methods including nonlinear monotone [5], runs on polyhedral unstructured grids [6] and utilizes MPI-based parallelization. The second version of the code is under development, which will have extended modeling abilities and enhanced computational performance [7–9].

The purpose of this work is to increase the efficiency of calculations in GeRa by means of parallelization and optimizing the choice of parameters for the parallel linear solver. Hydrogeological modeling of the site of the projected RW deep geological disposal (DGD) with realistic parameters is considered. To take into account the details of the DGD construction a computational mesh with 10 million cells is used. The acceleration of calculations with increasing number of processors is analyzed. Since the solution of systems of linear equations is one of the most computationally expensive procedures for hydrogeological modeling, methods for choosing optimal linear solver parameters are developed. The choice of parameters is based on the linear solver previous launches history and is used in the modeling process, which requires repeated solution of systems of linear equations with similar properties.

In Sect. 2 the mathematical model of the DGD site and its discretization are described. In Sect. 3 linear solvers parameters optimizing methods and experiments to determine the optimal parameters are described. In Sect. 4 the results of numerical experiments are shown, scalability of the calculation is studied. The final section summarizes the main findings.

2   The Model of Projected RW Deep Geological Disposal

The hydrogeological model used for numerical experiments in this work is being created within the studies on the long-term safety of RW deep geological disposal facility, which is planned to be constructed at the Yeniseisky site (Krasnoyarsk region). The model is aimed to correctly represent hydrogeological features in the far and near fields of the disposal, so it should include disposal construction details. This motivates us to use rather large grids and massively parallel computing.

Fig. 1. Prismatic grid of the DGD upper horizon. (Color figure online)

Fig. 2. Prismatic grid of the DGD lower horizon. (Color figure online)

The model is based on one of the concepts proposed for DGD [10]. According to this design, horizontal excavations used for RW of class 2 (intermediate-level waste with low heat output) emplacement and transport tunnels are built at two levels. RW of class 1 (vitrified heat-generating high level waste) is placed into vertical boreholes drilled between upper and lower levels. Figures 1 and 2 show the elements of the DGD grid cells (geological environment cells are hidden). RW of class 1 boreholes are shown in red, RW of class 2 disposal cells are shown in blue, transport tunnels are shown in gray, drilling chambers are shown in green.

To date, the DGD site's state of exploration corresponds to the stage of underground research laboratory (URL) allocation. The data to build a reliable hydrogeological model of the DGD far field and to verify it shall be available at the stage of URL construction and maintenance. Therefore, in this work the problem is formulated using some "typical" conditions for this object without taking into account fracture zones, which are likely to change the direction of the GW flow. The boundaries of the model with no-flow condition are drawn along the assumed watersheds. The upper boundary of the model is determined by the topography of the area and has boundary condition of rainfall recharge.

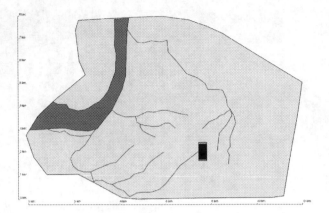

Fig. 3. The simulation area.

Four layers with different thickness are present in the area. They also have different hydraulic conductivities, which are decreasing with depth from 10^{-1} to 10^{-4} m/day following [11]. Surface watercourses are considered as boundary with Robin-type condition for GW flow model. The simulation area is shown in Fig. 3.

GW flow is simulated using a model of steady-state flow in unconfined regime developed in [7] and based on the stationary Richards' equation:

$$-\nabla \cdot (K_r(\theta)\mathbb{K}\nabla h) = Q \tag{1}$$

written in terms of hydraulic head h, $h = \Psi + z$. Here θ is volumetric water content; ϕ is porosity; Ψ is pressure head; $\mathbb{K}$ is hydraulic conductivity tensor; $K_r(\theta)$ is relative permeability; Q is specific sink and source terms. Water content θ is considered as a function of h, its formula can be found in [7], and $K_r(\theta)$ is equal to saturation S, namely, $K_r(\theta) = S = \theta/\phi$ here.

Transport is driven by advection and diffusion processes and governed by the transport equation

$$\theta\frac{\partial C}{\partial t} - \nabla \cdot SD\nabla C + \nabla \cdot (\boldsymbol{u}C) = 0. \tag{2}$$

The notations are: C – concentration of the contaminant; D – effective diffusion tensor; $\boldsymbol{u}$ – Darcy flux given by the formula

$$\boldsymbol{u} = -K_r(\theta)\mathbb{K}\nabla h. \tag{3}$$

Conservative tracer transport is modeled starting from unit concentration in the repository boreholes (without sorption and radioactive decay). The release of contamination beyond the engineering safety barriers was simulated by diffusion from RW of class 1 boreholes (contamination from RW of class 2 is not considered here).

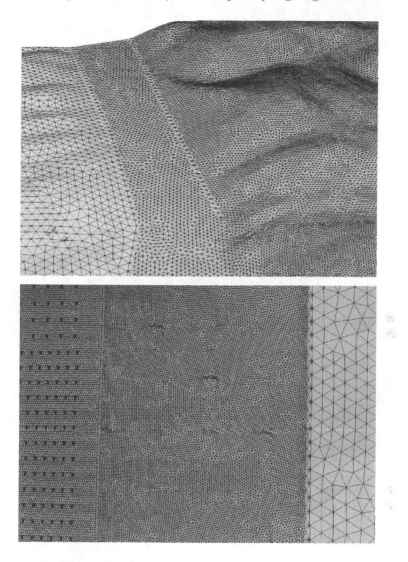

Fig. 4. Two fragments of the computational mesh.

The space discretization of the flow equation (1) and of the diffusion operator within the transport equation (2) is done using the linear two-point flux approximation finite volume (FV) method. Advection operator is discretized via the upwind first-order accurate FV method. In order to make sufficiently large time steps an implicit Euler scheme is applied for time stepping. The stationary problem (1) is solved using relaxation method, say, by iterative solution of unstationary problems till convergence to stationary solution is achieved. On each iteration of the relaxation method the nonlinear GW flow problem in unconfined regime is solved by Newton method. Numerical implementation of this algorithm in GeRa is described in [7].

The computational grid contains more than 10 million cells and is locally refined to the DGD construction details (shafts, tunnels, etc.). In Fig. 4 two fragments of the surface mesh are shown. On the first fragment the area of the far field with Yenisey river is shown. On the second fragment one can see the connection between far and near field meshes.

3   Optimization of Linear Solver Parameters

To reduce the runtime of a parallel application, it is necessary to correctly select the parameters for solving auxiliary tasks. The task, which takes up to 90% of the time of the whole modeling process, is the solution of linear systems arising from discretization. However, the use of traditional optimization methods to find the optimal parameters of linear solvers is difficult because of the uncertainty of a previously optimized function, as well as the fact that it may change during the simulation. Furthermore, additional calculation of the optimized function (i.e., re-solving the same linear system with different parameters) would be extremely inefficient. For such a class of non-stationary problems, automated optimization algorithms can be used, which allow one to further analyze the behavior of the function during the search for the minimum (maximum) and make assumptions about its properties.

To carry out the automatic optimization of the parameters of linear solvers, the additional module TTSP (Trace and Tuning of Solver Parameters or more generally Trace and Tuning Software Platform) [12] for the software platform INMOST [13,14] was developed at the INM RAS. Directly in the process of modeling, it allows to analyze the course of solving the problem and, without additional solutions of linear systems, select more optimal parameters of the linear solver, thereby reducing the total time to solve the non-stationary problem.

In the present paper, using the example of the above described model, the performance of the following three automatic optimization methods are analyzed.

1. *Alternating* – the main idea of this algorithm for optimizing the linear solver parameters for a non-stationary problem is to study the area near the current local minimum. The algorithm will remain close to the local minimum if it does not move very quickly during the simulation, and by examining a nearby area can find more and more optimal values up to the global minimum.
2. *Annealing* – the simulated annealing (see [15]) is a function optimization method based on simulating the physical process that occurs during the crystallization of a substance, including annealing of metals. By modeling this process, the algorithm searches for the minimum of a certain function $F(\overline{x})$, where $\overline{x} = (x_1, x_2, \ldots, x_n) \in S$. The elements of the set S are the states of an imaginary physical system, and the values of the function $F(\overline{x})$ at these points are interpreted as the energy of the system $E = F(\overline{x})$. It has been shown (see [16]) that the annealing method and its modifications are one of the most effective methods for randomly finding the optimal solution for a wide class of problems.

Table 1. Quasi-optimal values of parameter q for $\tau = 10^{-2}$.

p	6	12	24
gw	3	3	3
tr	2	2	2

Table 2. The quasi-optimal values of parameter τ for $q^*_{gw} = 3$ and $q^*_{tr} = 2$, respectively.

p	6	12	24
gw	0.07	0.07	0.07
tr	0.08	0.07	0.07

3. *Bayesian* – a family of optimization algorithms for unknown functions, the computation of which at a certain point can be computationally expensive. These algorithms from the previously calculated function values in the already known points try to reconstruct the objective function using regression methods. Using this reconstruction, they choose the next point that needs to be checked for optimality, after which the process of finding the minimum is restarted (see [17]).

When conducting numerical experiments for the model considered in Sect. 2, the linear solver BIILU2(τ, q) [18, 19] was chosen. This solver is a combination of the ILU2(τ) and BIILU(q) factorizations. Here, q is the overlap size parameter for the subdomains assigned to each of the parallel processes, and τ is the threshold parameter for the triangular factorization for each of these subdomains. Second-order factorization ILU2(τ) is used because of its greater reliability and efficiency as compared to the structural factorization ILU(k) or with the traditional threshold factorization ILU(τ). A more efficient parallelization scheme, BIILU(q), is used instead of the traditional Additive Schwarz scheme AS(q).

Table 1 shows the results of numerical experiments on finding the quasi-optimal parameter q when simulating the GW flow and transport stages using a different number of computing cores $p = 6, 12, 24$ for the fixed filtering threshold $\tau = 0.01$. The search for optimal parameter values was performed using the Alternating algorithm. The found quasi-optimal values of q completely coincided with the values used in GeRa by default $q^*_{gw} = 3$ and $q^*_{tr} = 2$ for the GW flow (gw) and transport (tr) stages, respectively.

Table 2 shows similar results for finding the optimal parameter τ while fixing the values of the parameter q obtained in Table 1. From the results of the experiments, it can be seen that the obtained quasi-optimal values of τ are almost independent of the number of computing cores p used. It should also be noted that the found quasi-optimal values $\tau^* = 0.07$ are slightly different from the default values $\tau^*_{gw} = 0.01$ and $\tau^*_{tr} = 0.02$. However, the differences in execution time are not very significant.

An example of the operation of all three considered parameters optimization algorithms is shown in Figs. 5, 6, 7 and 8. Figures 5 and 7 show the process of searching the quasi-optimal values of τ parameter for the GW flow and transport stages, respectively. Figures 6 and 8 show the cumulative time for solving linear

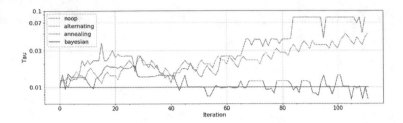

Fig. 5. Optimization of BIILU2 parameter τ for the GW flow modeling.

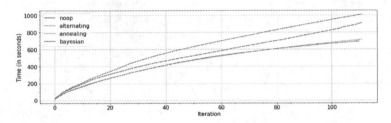

Fig. 6. The total simulation time for parameter optimization algorithms in comparison with the use of default parameters for the GW flow modeling.

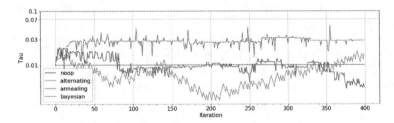

Fig. 7. Optimization of BIILU2 parameter τ for the transport process.

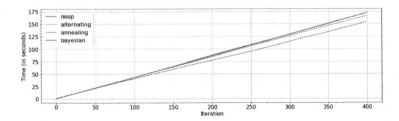

Fig. 8. The total simulation time for parameter optimization algorithms in comparison with the use of default parameters for the transport process.

systems during the entire modeling process. From these results it can be seen that the use of algorithms for optimizing the parameters of linear solvers in real time of simulation can reduce the total time for solving linear systems by 10–20%. In this case, for the GW flow stage, the Annealing and Alternating algorithms were able to find more optimal parameter values than those used by default. For the transport stage, it turned out that the region of the optimal parameters is quite large, and a change in the parameter τ does not greatly affect the total solution time for the linear systems under consideration.

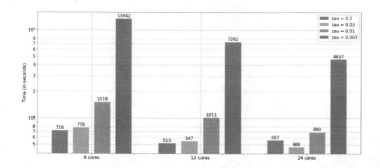

Fig. 9. Comparison of the solution time for different fixed values of parameter τ.

Figure 9 presents the results of an experiment comparing the efficiency of solving linear systems for the transport stage when specifying different fixed values of parameter τ. The data show that the choice of the non-optimal value of parameter τ can significantly, up to 10 times, slow down the total simulation time. The use of any optimization method is free from this drawback, because when choosing some initial value of parameter τ, it will change during the modeling process until the most optimal value is reached. Thus, in most cases, when the optimal values of the linear solver parameters are unknown in advance, their optimization during the modeling process is the only way to accelerate the solution of linear systems.

4   Parallel Efficiency Analysis

This section presents the results of parallel computations of the model described in Sect. 2. The calculation of the transport problem is carried out for a period of $10\,000$ years with a time step $\triangle t = 100$ years.

The linear systems obtained after discretization were solved by the BIILU2(τ, q) method [18,19] with parameters $\tau^*_{\text{gw}} = 0.01$ and $q^*_{\text{gw}} = 3$ for the GW flow problem and $\tau^*_{\text{tr}} = 0.02$ and $q^*_{\text{tr}} = 2$ for the transport problem parameters. As a stopping criterion, the 10^9 times of initial residual reduction was exploited. The distribution of cells among processors was carried out using the ParMetis [20] package, called via the INMOST [14] software platform.

Numerical experiments were performed on the INM RAS cluster [21] on the computing nodes of the x12core segment with the following parameters:

- Compute Node Arbyte Alkazar+ R2Q50;
- 24 cores (two 12-core Intel Xeon E5-2670v3@2.30GHz processors);
- RAM: 64 GB;
- Operating system: SUSE Linux Enterprise Server 11 SP3 (x86_64);
- Network: Mellanox Infiniband QDR 4x.

Table 3 shows the results of calculations using a different number of computing cores $p = 3, 6, ..., 192$. It was impossible to use a smaller number of cores due to limitations on the amount of memory and on the program execution time. The data are presented separately for GW flow modeling and transport subproblems, as well as the total solution time. In Table 3 the following notation is used: p is the number of computational cores on which the calculation was performed; T_{gw}, T_{tr}, and T_{total} are the times to solve the GW flow and transport subproblems, as well as the total time of the entire calculation; S_{gw}, S_{tr}, and S_{total} are the corresponding speedup values calculated with respect to the solution times for $p = 3$ computational cores.

The data presented in Table 3 shows a monotone decrease in the calculation time when the number of involved computational cores is increased. The maximum speedup of 18.8 was achieved when solving the GW flow problem.

Table 3. Calculation results on the x12core computing segment of the INM RAS cluster.

p	T_{gw}	S_{gw}	T_{tr}	S_{tr}	T_{total}	S_{total}
3	2995.2	1.00	3478.9	1.00	6474.1	1.00
6	2102.4	1.42	2213.7	1.57	4316.1	1.50
12	1570.4	1.90	1376.2	2.52	2946.6	2.19
24	807.9	3.70	737.2	4.71	1545.1	4.19
48	388.9	7.70	478.6	7.26	867.5	7.46
96	330.1	9.70	302.0	11.51	632.1	10.24
192	159.3	18.80	226.3	15.37	385.6	16.78

Fig. 10. Calculated GW head.

In Fig. 10 the calculated hydraulic head as a solution to the GW flow problem is shown. Figure 11 shows a calculated contamination plume forecast for time 8000 years against the background of the calculated head value. In addition, in Fig. 11 the vertical disposal wells are also made visible.

Fig. 11. The predicted pollution plume with a relative concentration above $5 \cdot 10^{-6}$ at a time point of 8000 years.

5   Conclusion

A detailed hydrogeological model of the far field of the projected RW deep geological disposal in the Nizhnekansky massif was created. The main design features of the disposal were taken into account. In comparison with the previous models it allows to assess the influence of the disposal on GW flow inside the excavations and its vicinity as well as to compare various layout solutions. The computational grid contains more than 10 million cells demanding the use of supercomputer for the computations of contamination transport forecast. The scalability of the problem was demonstrated by the results of calculations using from 3 to 192 cores. A more than 16 times speedup was achieved. The use of a fine grid allows to obtain a detailed contamination plume prediction for large time periods.

Application of optimization algorithms to dynamic linear solver parameters correction was proposed in order to accelerate this computationally expensive procedure. The optimization resulted in 10–20% reduction of the overall linear systems' solution time.

The presented numerical model of the disposal will be updated with new data characterizing the hydrogeological conditions of the DGD site and applied for its safety assessment.

References

1. Panday, S., Langevin, C.D., Niswonger, R.G., Ibaraki, M., Hughes, J.D.: MODFLOW-USG version 1.4.00: an unstructured grid version of MODFLOW for simulating groundwater flow and tightly coupled processes using a control volume finite-difference formulation: U.S. Geological Survey Software Release (2017)
2. Diersh, H.-J.G.: FEFLOW – Finite Element Modeling of Flow, Mass and Heat Transport in Porous and Fractured Media, XXXV, 996 p. Springer, Heidelberg (2014). https://doi.org/10.1007/978-3-642-38739-5
3. Kolditz, O., et al.: OpenGeoSys: an open-source initiative for numerical simulation of thermo-hydro-mechanical/chemical (THM/C) processes in porous media. Environ. Earth Sci. **67**(2), 589–599 (2012)
4. Hammond, G.E., Lichtner, P.C., Mills, R.T.: Evaluating the performance of parallel subsurface simulators: an illustrative example with PFLOTRAN. Water Resour. Res. **50**(1), 208–228 (2014)
5. Nikitin, K.D., Vassilevski, Y.V.: A monotone finite volume method for advection-diffusion equations on unstructured polyhedral meshes in 3D. Russ. J. Numer. Anal. Math. Model. **25**(4), 335–358 (2010)
6. Plenkin, A.V., Chernyshenko, A.Y., Chugunov, V.N., Kapyrin, I.V.: Adaptive unstructured mesh generation methods for hydrogeological problems. Vychislitel'nye Metody i Programmirovanie **6**(4), 518–533 (2015). (in Russian)
7. Anuprienko, D.V., Kapyrin, I.V.: Modeling groundwater flow in unconfined conditions: numerical model and solvers' efficiency. Lobachevskii J. Math. **39**(7), 867–873 (2018)
8. Kapyrin, I., Konshin, I., Kramarenko, V., Grigoriev, F.: Modeling groundwater flow in unconfined conditions of variable density solutions in dual-porosity media using the GeRa code. Commun. Comput. Inf. Sci. **965**, 266–278 (2019)
9. Konshin, I., Kapyrin, I.: Scalable computations of GeRa code on the base of software platform INMOST. In: Malyshkin, V. (ed.) PaCT 2017. LNCS, vol. 10421, pp. 433–445. Springer, Cham (2017). https://doi.org/10.1007/978-3-319-62932-2_42
10. Martynov, K.V., Zakharova, E.V.: The analysis of localization and the scenario of evolution of DGDF for RW at the Yeniseisky site (Krasnoyarsk region). Radioact. Waste **2**(3), 52–62 (2018). (in Russian)
11. Rumynin, V.G.: Experience of studying the clay masses and crystalline core-areas as geological environment for RW final isolation. Radioactive Waste (1), 42–53 (2017). (in Russian)
12. Bagaev, D.V., Konshin, I.N., Nikitin, K.D.: Dynamic optimization of linear solver parameters in mathematical modelling of unsteady processes. Commun. Comput. Inf. Sci. **793**, 54–66 (2017)
13. Vassilevski, Y., Konshin, I., Kopytov, G., Terekhov, K.: INMOST - a software platform and graphical environment for development of parallel numerical models on general meshes. Lomonosov Moscow State University Publ., Moscow, 144 p. (2013). (in Russian)
14. INMOST - a toolkit for distributed mathematical modeling. http://www.inmost.org/. Accessed 15 Apr 2019
15. Metropolis, N., Rosenbluth, A.W., Rosenbluth, M.N., Teller, A.H., Teller, E.: Equation of state calculations by fast computing machines. J. Chem. Phys. **21**(6), 1087–1092 (1953)
16. Ingber, L.: Very fast simulated re-annealing. Math. Comput. Model. **12**(8), 967–973 (1989)

17. Mockus, J.: Bayesian Approach to Global Optimization. Springer, Dordrecht (1989). https://doi.org/10.1007/978-94-009-0909-0
18. Kaporin, I.E., Konshin, I.N.: Parallel solution of large sparse SPD linear systems based on overlapping domain decomposition. In: Malyshkin, V. (ed.) PaCT 1999. LNCS, vol. 1662, pp. 436–446. Springer, Heidelberg (1999). https://doi.org/10.1007/3-540-48387-X_45
19. Kaporin, I.E., Konshin, I.N.: A parallel block overlap preconditioning with inexact submatrix inversion for linear elasticity problems. Numer. Linear Algebra Appl. **9**(2), 141–162 (2002)
20. ParMETIS - Parallel graph partitioning and fill-reducing matrix ordering. http://glaros.dtc.umn.edu/gkhome/metis/parmetis/overview. Accessed 15 Apr 2019
21. INM RAS cluster. http://cluster2.inm.ras.ru. Accessed 15 Apr 2019

Morphing and Wave Perturbations in Distinguishing Molecular Clouds' Collision

Boris Rybakin[1](✉) and Valery Goryachev[2]

[1] Department of Gas and Wave Dynamics, Moscow State University,
Moscow, Russia
rybakinl@mail.ru
[2] Department of Mathematics, Tver State Technical University, Tver, Russia
gdv.vdg@yandex.ru

Abstract. We use a gasdynamics approach to numerical modeling of Molecular Cloud-Cloud Collision that leads to formation conditions for triggering protostars in the interstellar medium. The calculations were performed according to different colliding scenarios between two dissimilar clouds. In numerical experiments non-identical oppositely moving molecular clouds collide with each other in head-on motion at relative velocity which could vary within the range of 5 to 25 km·s^{-1}. The post-collision clouds' shaping and the compression oscillation in bow-shock core depend on initial conditions of colliding. In situations with insufficiently smoothness of pressure/energy fields between clouds and interstellar medium, the energy disturbance in a compressed core with originated clumps leads to coherent perturbations both shock layer and in outside space. The paper gives a morphological analysis of inclusions in a bow-shock layer, perturbations and turbulization of matter, fragmentation and disruption of gas remnants. Waved stratum perturbations - density rarefactions in interstellar medium were interpreted as a new phenomenon of Rayleigh–Taylor and Nonlinear Thin Shell Instability aftereffect. A parallel Eulerian code based on high resolution grids is used to perform numerical experiment on high-performance computers.

Keywords: Parallel computing · Supersonic turbulence · Perturbations · Molecular Cloud-Cloud Collision

1 Introduction

Cloud-Cloud Collisions (CCC) between molecular clouds (MCs) as well as the interaction between MCs and a strong shock wave of remnants after supernova explosion is proposed as key mechanisms for triggering protostars originated in highly compressed zones of new formations.

Collisions between MCs within the interstellar medium (ISM) are widespread events in space. In these days a number of such experimentally observed space occurrences are constantly increasing [1, 2]. Authors of [3] have presented a comprehensive reference of such facts and modeling solutions for some (order twenty) cases of them. Among other things one can indicate a distinct molecular clouds' collision with a shock-compressed layer that serves a trigger of cluster formation in the starburst cluster NGC 3603 observed by the NANTEN2 collaboration telescope [4].

© Springer Nature Switzerland AG 2019
V. Voevodin and S. Sobolev (Eds.): RuSCDays 2019, CCIS 1129, pp. 278–289, 2019.
https://doi.org/10.1007/978-3-030-36592-9_23

Data treatment in the collaborated study revealed more two cases of massive star formation by CCC scenario in star cluster Westerlund 2 [5].

The Cloud–Cloud Collisions were studied using hydrodynamics and MHD simulations. Modeling of CCC on hydrodynamics basis continues to perfect using Smoothed Particle Hydrodynamics (SPH) and Adaptive Mesh Refinement (AMR) Eulerian methods since the pioneering work on two-dimension simulation of two clouds collision, developed in [6]. The authors [6, 7] indicate that direct MCs impact can induce the generation of high-compressed clumps inside the matter layer formed at the interface of the collision.

Recent simulation of dissimilar CCC performed in three-dimensional modeling [8] shows that morphological shaping of new formations is the aftereffect of initial cloud surface perturbations and the interplay between internal energy and pressure in highly compressed bow-shock layers. To improve the fine resolution of instabilities influence onto core/shells/filaments morphing, the Eulerian mesh resolution (or SPH particles number) could be increased radically. Gasdynamics-magnetic field simulation is accompanied by addition of gravitation influence. Supersonic matter motions and other properties of molecular clouds often have been interpreted in terms of possible acoustic and hydro-magnetic waves and other physical effects [9]. To study details of the way by which CCC forms dense filaments and clumps, the advanced solutions based on addition of heating and cooling functions to the models used were carried out in series of 3D/HD-MHD/AMR simulations. New model based on photo-dissociation approach was used for the explanation of atomic-to-molecular transition in clouds in a post compressing zone [10, 11]. This mechanism may be a major driver of star formation activity in galactic disks.

Numerical simulation of MCs collision presented in this article is a continuation of modeling of the similar shock processes occurring in interstellar medium [12, 13].

2   Problem Setup

We modeled a head-on MC_1/MC_2 collision with mutual penetration of dissimilar in size and density distribution molecular clouds of initially spherical forms, with the velocities of collision varied. The scheme of Cloud-Cloud Collision between MCs is shown in Fig. 1.

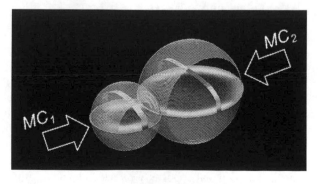

Fig. 1. Scheme of collision.

2.1   Eulerian Description and Numerical Realization

The problems being solved consider the impact of compressible gas flows coupling in nonsteady definition. Gas movement is described with a set of Euler equations which are conservation laws for mass, momentum, and energy

$$
\frac{\partial U}{\partial t} + \nabla \cdot T = 0, U = \begin{pmatrix} \rho \\ \rho u \\ e \end{pmatrix}, T = \begin{pmatrix} \rho u \\ \rho u u + p I \\ (e+p)u \end{pmatrix}^T, e = \frac{p}{\gamma - 1} + \frac{|u|^2}{2}, \quad (1)
$$

where ρ denote the gas density, $\mathbf{u} = (u, v, w)$ is the velocity vector. The total energy density e and gas pressure p are related through the ideal gas closure, where adiabatic index - $\gamma = c_p/c_v$ is equal to 5/3.

The computing area used for the problem under consideration is parallelepiped of $1.6 \times 0.8 \times 0.8$ pc dimensions. Lateral and outlet computational domain edges are determined as open boundary conditions for primitive variables.

Eulerian equations are solved on regular mesh with an adaptive Roe solver using the schemes of total variation diminishing (TVD) type. High-order accurate difference schemes have guaranteed monotonicity preservation of conservation laws. The non-linear, second-order accurate TVD approach provides a high resolution capturing of shocks and prevents unphysical oscillations.

Serial calculations were carried out using grids consisting of about two billion cells. An application programming interface OpenMP for parallelization is employed. The tuning with Intel VTune Amplifier XE is carried out for Xeon E2630 and Xeon E5 2650 Ivy Bridge processors. Some computations are done with graphics accelerators NVIDIA K40 and CUDA for PGI Fortran. To compute with graphical accelerators, the computation program has been retargeted so that some subprograms should be directed to GPU and the others – to CPU. To study the sensing mechanisms of instabilities growth and the formation of filament structures in post collision nebulae, calculations with a high resolution mesh are required.

Problems of parallel realization of authorized in-house code are discussed in [13]. An extensive set of solver utilities and postprocessing system HDVIS were used to analyze a big output data after a numerical experiment.

2.2   Modeling Assumptions and Parameters Used

In case of non-identical clouds colliding, main physical parameters of MCs/ISM matter and the initial setup are assumed as those used in [14–16]. The objective setting of simulation, numerical approach and code developed are given in [13].

Commonly accepted assumption about cold MCs embedded in warm interstellar medium was made in a simulation setup. The interstellar medium consists of relatively warm matter with $T_{ism} = 10^4$ K, the temperature of colder molecular clouds $T_{cl} = 10^2$ K. The ambient gas density of the outer cloud medium (ISM) $\rho_{ism} = 2.15–10^{-25}$ g·cm^{-3}, the gas density in the undisturbed cloud centers $\rho_{cl} = 1.075–10^{-22}$ g·cm^{-3}.

The simulation was performed according to different two-cloud impact scenarios. In numerical experiments non-identical oppositely directed clouds (of different mass, size and density distribution) collide with each other at relative velocities of 5–25 km·s^{-1}. Colliding velocities U_{cl} of each MC are assigned as 2.94, 5.88, 11.77 km·s^{-1}. Initial density contrast χ that is equal to ratio ρ_{cl}/ρ_{ism} prescribed for density between the cloud centers and the interstellar medium is assigned to each cloud as 25, 100, and 500 respectively. Velocities U_{cl} and density contrast χ for molecular clouds are varied in simulation. Molecular clouds' masses range from 0.3 to 1.2 $M_\odot$ respectively.

The initial distribution of matter density in clouds plays an important role in the mass impulse action. Initial relations of the overlapping gas layers in a smoothed density and the flux energy for conditional ISM/MCs boundaries are regulated by parameters of radial profile distribution taken from [14, 15]. The equation adopted in [14] tends to give a flatter density profile in radial direction within the center of the cloud, and a steeper profiles as the cloud merges into the ambient medium, then more smoothed profiles are obtained using the equation [15]. "Harshly outlined" profile is used to set the radial density description (Bonnor-Ebert density profile) for MC_1, more "indistinct" – for MC_2.

3 Morphological Peculiarities of MCs Head-on Collision

Numerical simulation has been performed to study morphology and redistribution of the compressed matter in a core of colliding MCs as a determinative factor of triggering pre-stellar space area originated in disbalanced regime of no equilibrium impulse action of two clouds.

3.1 Clouds Matter Interplay During Collision

The selected head-on collision scenario of CCC allows us to check the way to advance the most probable matter compressibility in new post-collision formations.

In numerical experiments non-identical oppositely moving MCs collide with each other in head-on motion at relative velocity which could vary within the range of 5 to 25 km·s^{-1}. Contrast density (appointed in cloud centers) relations χ 25/100/500 are combined in alternate solutions.

In general outline, the evolution of MCs formations simulated in numerical experiments contains conditionally allocated stages:

- Initial penetration of left (more heavy) cloud MC_1 into right MC_2 accompanied by sharp change of local pressure in a contact shock layer and the energy and density fields repartition, with allocation of slightly more compressed stratum near the spacer layer of rarefied ISM; formation of cavern accretion in the right area of this cloud accompanied by some decrease of initial outward cloud diameters;
- Generation of a bow-shock layer – highly compressed core with waved conditional boundary. It depends on counter gas streams and strong shock pulsations in bundle spatial associations and is accompanied by the clumpy fragmentation spread-out and the posterior stochastic pre-filaments overgrowth;

- At the stage of rupturing the MC_2 shell and the final intervention of MC_1 new compressed forms bundled in the back area of a target cloud transforms into more compressed clumps with maximum possible density;
- Then begin a recession of MCs remnants in their relative motion, filaments stretch morphing in a post-shock area accompanied by ripple gas turbulization on outer sheets; continuation of clump shaping with strengthening of Kelvin-Helmholtz instabilities (KHI), growth of finger structures, acceleration of clumps ablation into outer ISM and cloud clump fragments collapse.

Morphing evolution during the collision triggering, the generation of a bow-shock layer and the subsequent disaggregation of post-shock formations is shown in Fig. 2.

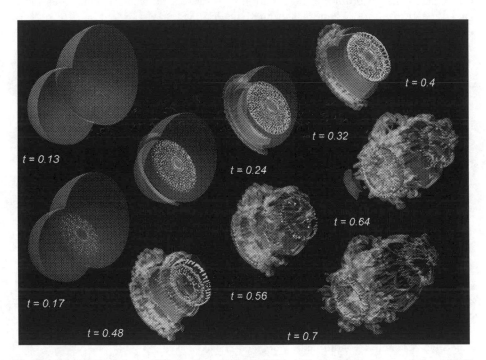

Fig. 2. Phases of head-on collision of two dissimilar MCs with density contrast χ relation 100/25 and cross-cloud velocities 5.885 km·s^{-1}. Time of interplay is 0.7 Myr.

The density contrast isosurfaces with $\chi = 1.4$ and 2000 illustrate the process of head-on cloud-cloud collision at a relevant post-collision stage, with local gas velocity distribution maps being shown on originated clumps.

The interplay between shearing layers of MCs and interstellar medium is provoked by Kelvin-Helmholtz instability. It accelerates the generation of vortex paths that can be manifested via the formation of ripples and rolls over outer cloud surfaces and inside a cavern shell. In the case of a bow-shock formation, normal stress accumulated between local stream jets on the contact spots is provoked by propagating of oblique shocks. The illustrations are shown in Fig. 3. Immediately on rupture transmission of the first cloud through the second one the compression in pre-clumps can reach maximal values. Contrast density in new formations can be hundred or thousand times higher than in a prescribed initial value. In the numerical experiment performed a density of clump matter amounts to 10^{-18} g·cm^{-3}, that corresponds to generally accepted pre-stellar conglomeration level. Revealed compressed locations and pre-stellar area formations generally agree with a data of the recent simulations announced in [6–10].

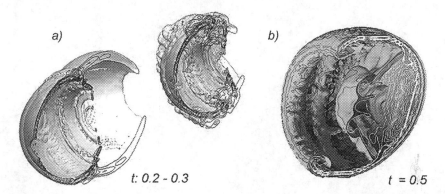

Fig. 3. Vortex distribution in core and shell of MCs (a) and density contrast layers $\chi = 2$, 10,100 (b) for density cloud relation 500/25 (a) and 500/500 (b) in the case of cross-cloud velocities 5.885 km·s^{-1}. Ripple vortex folds and pre-clumps are forming during MC$_2$ perforation at stage 0.3–0.38 Myr.

Morphology history of new gas formation in the presented simulation is in accordance with results cited in [7, 8]; they indicate that CCC incidents can induce the formation of condensed clumps inside the high compressed matter layer being formed at the interface of MCs during a collision.

3.2   Instabilities in a Bow-Shock Layer and Post-collision Shell Shaping

Density and velocity fields in a shock-compressed core of colliding clouds are quite intermittent. Perturbations initiated by extremely strong contractions of clouds' cores become clearly observable under the analysis of temporal pulsations of gas density field that accompany the penetration of the left small and heavier cloud into the right but a larger cloud.

During the central collision the main gas tensions are accumulated over the stag-nation surface of contrary gas flows. A compressed bow-shock layer stochastically changes its density structure compressing spatial blobs originated above stagnation points. Isosurfaces of density field inside the shock layer look like a sieve screen continuously morphing into a filament net. Fractal-replicable density filaments are shown in Fig. 4.

Figure 5 presents a comparison of U-component isosurfaces for different values of oscillating contrary flows in a colliding zone. One can see that the observed shock

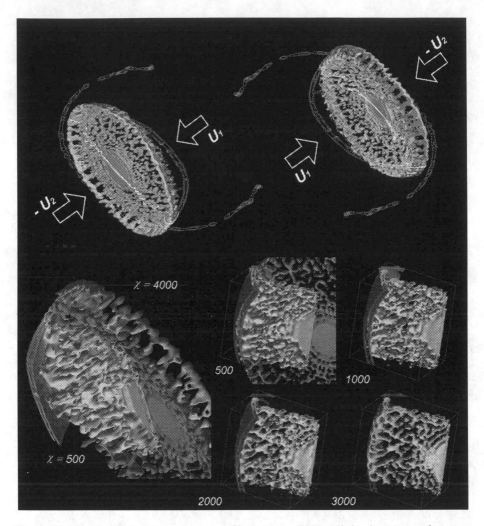

Fig. 4. Rendered velocity contours on core filaments $\chi = 3000$ and density contrast fragments with isosurfaces $\chi = 500, 1000, 2000, 3000$ in collision, with χ relation – 100/25 and cross-cloud velocity – 5.885 km·s^{-1} at stage 0.4 Myr.

surfaces have high level of intermittency depending on energy amplification on the impacted stream front. Definitely this process is accompanied by the intensive kinetic energy interchange through clumpy inclusions and concomitant nonlinear deformations along the bow-shock layer. The Nonlinear Thin Shell Instability (NTSI) [17] in shock compressed lence-like core can play a crucial role in triggering this process. Occurrence of the NTSI can be manifested in abruptly growth of oscillation amplitude comparable with the thickness of a shock layer.

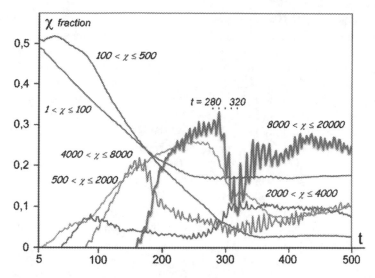

Fig. 5. Change of density contrast fractions in solution with χ relation 500/100, velocities $U_1 = 5.885$ km·s^{-1} and $U_2 = -2.943$ km·s^{-1}.

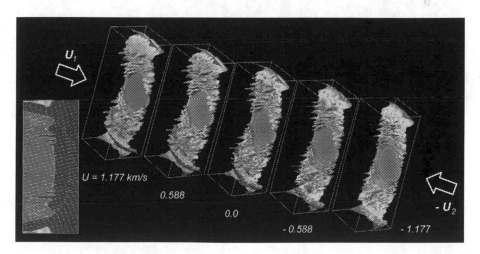

Fig. 6. Dendritic U-components of contrary gas flow velocities in highly compressed MCs layer near stagnation point-flow surface corresponding to the case of CCC with χ relation 100/25 and cross-cloud velocity 5.885 km·s^{-1} at stage 0.4 Myr. Surface $|U| = 0.0$ is a stagnation point-flow set.

This can be confirmed by the analysis of density fraction and time correlation. The gradient energy conversion in a shock layer leads to perturbation of density contrast fractions as a whole which is illustrated in Fig. 5.

Figure 5 shows the time plot of gas density contrast fractions during clouds' collision. One can define the areas of oscillated shaking in MCs shells and core filaments.

The largest amplitudes of oscillation can be specified in the range χ of 8000 to 20000 for originated pre-clump cluster at the beginning of cloud remnants rupturing.

Density contrast of clump cores can reach the largest values inherent in pre-stellar conglomeration. Observed in recent simulation, the amplitude values of subsonic/transonic fluctuations on a shock layer stagnation surface are in accord with the results of others authors who have analyzed the consequences of gas slab colliding in two and three-dimension simulations [18, 19].

Bow-shock layer configuration depends on the Kelvin-Helmholtz, Nonlinear Thin Shell Instability in a compressed core and the Rayleigh–Taylor Instability over remnant sheets with far different density of matter. Instabilities are ultimate factors auspicious to the formation of contiguous needle-shaped dendritic structures that are shown in Fig. 6. The gas kinetic energy is dissipated within a bow-shock layer via pulsated over-pressed extrusions. Eventually these formations reduce to the filament net and clamps in a stretched post-shock zone. Pre-stellar areas of these elongated objects are oriented along the collision axis.

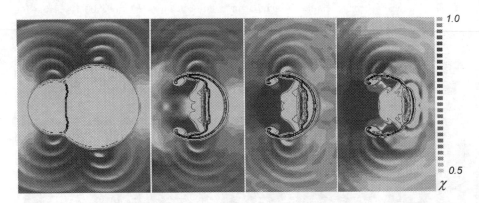

Fig. 7. Waved stratum perturbations of ISM matter above the post-collision formation with alternation of the reduced ($\chi < 0.8$) density zones as opposed to background value $\chi = 1$ ($\rho_{ism} = 2.15\text{--}10^{-25}$ g·cm^{-3}). Collision with χ relation: 500/500 and cross-cloud $\mathbf{U} = 5.885$ km·s^{-1}.

Presented numerical simulation of CCC in the head-on MCs motion revealed a few details of pressure amplification (or reducing) and spatial density perturbation in layers between MCs and ISM matter, which was overlooked in similar [7, 18, 19] simulations. At first stages of collision a spatial redistribution of clouds' matter can conduce to the local grow of density in superficial cloud layers, with two-or-more-fold increase being observed as opposed to values in more deep layers. Outer layers of clouds rapidly take a shape of convex-concave envelope that transmits a density perturbation as a "tympanic membrane" and leads to onset of acoustic interaction between clouds and interstellar medium. Revealed undulating perturbations of ISM matter over new formation have narrow stratums with the reduced density level in this area as compared to the background level.

Fig. 8. Perturbations of density field in interstellar medium above the post-collision clouds formation. Screenshot of stratums for CCC with parameters: χ relation 500/100, cross cloud velocities 5.885 km·s^{-1}. Stratums with χ over 0.5 - 1.0 - 10 correspond to time epoch 0.14 Myr.

Figures 7 and 8 show the perturbed density field in a symmetry plane of MCs colliding with stratus formations oscillated in conical space area and originated on outer surface spots of superficial layers. Arising pulsations are provoked by the joint Nonlinear Thin Shell (and most likely Rayleigh–Taylor) instabilities in the disturbed bow-shock layer. The gradient of energy stream transmitted through shell in the abovementioned spot (compressed two-three time more in comparison with average in a cloud) is not so high as in the over compressed shock layer of a core. The amplitude of density fluctuations in layers between ISM and MCs is greatly smaller than that in a bow-shock. Matter joggles over spots generates reverberated rarefaction waves with considerable attenuation and distortion.

Thin convex-concave shell fragments of the abovementioned superficial surface pulsate synchronously. This process reflects the change of the energy gradient value and the direction of this vector through shell spots.

Changes of local shape flection in MCs shock core/layer and on outer shells are accompanied by coherent pulsations: local strong compression in a bow-shock layer and rarefaction – in interstellar medium.

4 Conclusions

Molecular Cloud-Cloud Collisions in interstellar medium and the dynamic stability of the bow-shock layers on interface between clouds were studied by using different scenarios of colliding. The post-collision forming and crushing of new formation were simulated with the HPC parallelization based on in-house code. Morphology of a bow-shock layer generated during impact, perturbations and turbulization of MCs matter were compared by different CCC scenarios. Simulations revealed that the shock interplay between colliding MCs is provoked and magnified via Kelvin-Helmholtz and Nonlinear Thin Shell Instability in a compressed core and the Rayleigh–Taylor Instability over clouds superficial boundaries. The NTSI influence can increase vigorously. Last factors can play a crucial role in generation of bow-shock layer and pre-stellar area triggering. The stochastic shock concussion induces the occurrence of pre-filamentous structures in a bow-shock layer and their post-shock morphing. Modeling shows that the post-collision MCs morphing and generation of pre-stellar conglomerations is in a good accordance with recent studies of shock cloud-cloud collisions. Approach proposed in the simulation can be used as the most likely way to predict star triggering structures in new nebular formations. Revealed in modeling acoustic perturbations - density rarefactions, with a stratus extensional mode in interstellar medium, were analyzed and interpreted as a new phenomenon of above mentioned instabilities aftereffect.

Acknowledgements. The study is supported by the RAS Program of Fundamental Research.

References

1. Ferriere, K.M.: The interstellar environment of our galaxy. Rev. Mod. Phys. **73**, 1031–1066 (2001)
2. Truelove, J.K., et al.: Self-gravitational hydrodynamics with 3-D adaptive mesh refinement: methodology and applications to molecular cloud collapse and fragmentation. Astrophys. J. **495**, 821 (1998)
3. Dobbs, C.L., et al.: Formation of molecular clouds and global conditions for star formation. In: Beuther, H., Klessen, R., Dullemont, C., Henning, T. (eds.) Protostars & Planets VI, pp. 3–26. University of Arizona Press (2014)
4. Fukui, Y., Ohama, A., Hanaoka, N., et al.: Molecular clouds toward the super star cluster NGC 3603. Possible evidence for a cloud-cloud collision in triggering the cluster formation. Astrophys. J. **780**(36), 13 (2014)
5. Ohama, A., Dawson, J.R., Furukawa, N., et al.: Temperature and density distribution in the molecular gas toward Westurlund 2: further evidence for physical associations. Astrophys. J. **709**, 975–982 (2010)
6. Habe, A., Ohta, K.: Gravitational instability induced by a cloud-cloud collision: the case of head-on collision between clouds with different sizes and densities. Publ. Astron. Soc. Japan **44**, 203–226 (1992)
7. Anathpindika, S.V.: Collision between dissimilar clouds: stability of the bow-shock and the formation of pre-stellar cores. Mon. Not. R. Astron. Soc. **405**, 1431–1443 (2010)

8. Takahira, K., Shima, K., Tasker, E.J., Habe, A.: Formation of massive, dense cores by cloud-cloud collisions. PASJ **70**(SP2), 1–24 (2018)
9. Tritsis, A., Tassis, K.: Striations in molecular clouds: streamers or MHD waves? Mon. Not. R. Astron. Soc. **462**, 3602–3615 (2016)
10. Torii, K., et al.: Triggered O star formation in M20 via cloud-cloud collision: comparisons between high-resolution CO observations and simulations. Astrophys. J. **835**(142), 1–12 (2017)
11. Wu, B., Tan, J.C., Nakamura, F., Van Loo, S., Christie, D., Collins, D.: GMC collisions as triggers of star formation. II. 3D turbulent, magnetized simulations. Astrophys. J. **835**(137), 1–23 (2017)
12. Rybakin, B., Goryachev, V.: Modeling of density stratification and filamentous structure formation in molecular clouds after shock wave collision. Comput. Fluids **173**, 189–194 (2018)
13. Rybakin, B., Goryachev, V.: Parallel algorithms for astrophysics problems. Lobachevskii J. Math. **39**(4), 562–570 (2018)
14. Pittard, J.M., Falle, S.A.E.G., Hartquist, T.W., Dyson, J.E.: The turbulent destruction of clouds. MNRAS **394**, 1351–1378 (2009)
15. Nakamura, F., McKee, C.F., Klein, R.I., Fisher, R.T.: On the hydrodynamic interaction of shock waves with interstellar clouds. II. The effect of smooth cloud boundaries on cloud destruction and cloud turbulence. Astrophys. J. **164**, 477–505 (2006)
16. Melioli, C., de Gouveia Dal Pino, E.M., Raga, A.: Multidimensional hydro dynamical simulations of radiative cooling SNRs-clouds interactions: an application to starburst environments. Astron. Astrophys. **443**, 495–508 (2005)
17. Vishniac, E.T.: Nonlinear instabilities in shock-bounded slabs. Astrophys. J. **428**, 186–208 (1994)
18. Folini, D., Walder, R.: Supersonic turbulence in shock-bound interaction zones I. Symmetric settings. Astron. Astrophys. **459**, 1–19 (2006)
19. McLeod, A.D., Whitworth, A.P.: Simulations of the non-linear thin shell instability. MNRAS **431**, 710–721 (2013)

Numerical Experiments with Digital Twins of Core Samples for Estimating Effective Elastic Parameters

Galina Reshetova[1](✉), Vladimir Cheverda[2], and Tatyana Khachkova[2]

[1] The Institute of Computational Mathematics
and Mathematical Geophysics SB RAS, Novosibirsk, Russia
kgv@nmsf.sscc.ru

[2] The Trofimuk Institute of Petroleum Geology and Geophysics SB RAS,
Novosibirsk, Russia
{CheverdaVA,KhachkovaTS}@ipgg.sbras.ru

Abstract. The use of 3D Computed Tomography (CT) throws light on the interior structure of the core samples. That is why the 3D CT has become increasingly widespread in digital rock physics. However, the CT does not provide information about the elastic properties of the rocks. So far, the most common approach to recover these properties is static laboratory measurements, when a sample is subject to a variety of static loads, followed by the measurement of displacements. This way is rather expensive, time-consuming and sometimes result in the destruction of a sample. Instead, we propose to implement numerical experiments by solving a 3D elastic static problem to perform upscaling of the CT data and to compute effective elastic parameters. In fact, to find these parameters we need to resolve a huge system of linear algebraic equations, which is a troublesome task. We have decided not to use a direct solver, but to apply a new iterative relaxation technique by considering a dynamic elastic problem with a special choice of relaxation parameters. The approach proposed needs parallelization. We have come to the conclusion to use the new feature of the latest Fortran extension known as CoArray Fortran (CAF) and to compare the three ways of parallel implementation as applied to this problem: MPI, MPI+OpenMP and CAF. Our experiments have proved that CAF and MPI approximately demonstrate the same performance, but the CAF possesses a clearer structure and is easy for coding.

Keywords: Digital core · Virtual experiments · Elastic static stresses · 3d tomographic images · Coarray fortran · MPI

1 Introduction

Over the last two decades, the construction of digital core sample twins in digital rock physics has become increasingly widespread. This opens up a principally new possibility of replacing physical experiments by the numerical ones with

© Springer Nature Switzerland AG 2019
V. Voevodin and S. Sobolev (Eds.): RuSCDays 2019, CCIS 1129, pp. 290–301, 2019.
https://doi.org/10.1007/978-3-030-36592-9_24

digital twins. In this way, it becomes possible to reduce the time to perform experiments, to improve the quality of the results obtained and, with is important, to avoid damage and destruction of the samples in the course of laboratory experiments.

By now various algorithms have been proposed for estimating effective rock properties, such as elastic moduli, porosity, permeability, etc. Two popular methods for computing static elastic properties from digital rock images are the finite-difference and finite-element methods [2,19]. To simulate pore-scale fluid flow, the Lattice Boltzmann method is generally used [5,7]. The dynamic pulse propagation approach has been proposed for computing the elastic properties of the digital core samples [12]. A common feature of all the methods is the use of a regular Cartesian grid obtained from the segmented digital rock voxel image for the numerical discretization of a problem. The use of high-resolution CT images leads to a huge dimension of the problem and the necessity to use parallel computations.

Within the framework of these studies, there are a number of approaches to determining the effective heterogeneous elastic moduli, including the methods based on the analysis of inclusions [4,14,15], the use of a wide range of homogenization methods [1] and some other approaches. Since we do not impose any assumptions about the statistical homogeneity of the samples but work directly with their digital images, we exclude the theory of homogenization from our considerations. In this paper, we are concentrating on the development of a new efficient parallel numerical algorithm to determine the effective elastic parameters of core samples from their digital twins. Compared to homogenization methods, this approach is more computationally expensive because it uses all available digital information of the internal structure of a core and requires the development of new parallel computational approaches.

For solving the problem, we choose the method based on the energy equivalence principle proposed in [16] enabling the numerical parallelization with linear acceleration. The elastic moduli are determined by the parallel computation of potential energy of the elastic deformations in a sample under static homogeneous stresses applied to the boundary, thus simulating the effects occurring in laboratory measurements. To compute the potential energy of a core one needs to solve an elastic static problem for 3D multiscale (caves, pores, fractures, etc.) heterogeneous media. The straightforward way to solve this kind of problems results in the necessity to search for the solution of huge systems of linear algebraic equations. We have chosen another way by applying new iterative relaxation technique, which allows implementing parallel computations of the potential energy of elastic deformations arising in laboratory samples. The use of a combination of these techniques has allowed us to create an efficient parallel algorithm for computing the effective elastic parameters of core samples.

2   Statement of the Problem

The effective elastic properties of a sample are determined based on the generalized Hooke's law, which expresses the relationship between the averaged deformations and stresses over a representative volume:

$$\bar{\sigma}_{ij} = c^*_{ijkl}\bar{\varepsilon}_{kl} \quad or \quad \bar{\varepsilon}_{ij} = s^*_{ijkl}\bar{\sigma}_{kl}. \tag{1}$$

The components of the stiffness tensor c^*_{ijkl} and of the compliance tensor s^*_{ijkl} form the tensors of the fourth rank which, by definition, are the effective tensors of stiffness C^* and of compliance S^*. The average stresses and strains are determined by the formulas:

$$\bar{\sigma}_{ij} = \frac{1}{V}\int_V \sigma_{ij}dV, \quad \bar{\varepsilon}_{ij} = \frac{1}{V}\int_V \varepsilon_{ij}dV, \tag{2}$$

where σ_{ij} and ε_{ij} are the components of the stress and the strain tensors describing the stress-strain state of a sample in the representative volume V and satisfying the equilibrium equations and the Saint-Venant compatibility equations.

3   The Method

To find the effective tensors of stiffness C^* and of compliance S^* we use the energy equivalence principle method [11,16]. This approach is based on the theorem [1] asserting that the homogeneous static (kinematic) boundary conditions applied to the boundary S of a non-homogeneous representative volume V generate such a stress field σ_{ij} (strain ε_{ij}) that its averaging over volume (2) is equal to the value of the constant stress σ^0_{ij} (strain ε^0_{ij}) applied to the boundary S:

$$\bar{\sigma}_{ij} = \sigma^0_{ij}, \quad \bar{\varepsilon}_{ij} = \varepsilon^0_{ij}. \tag{3}$$

The potential energy of deformations in the heterogeneous elastic body V is expressed by the formula:

$$U = \frac{1}{2}\int_V \sigma_{ij}\varepsilon_{ij}dV. \tag{4}$$

We calculate the energy of deformations when homogeneous static boundary conditions are applied to a heterogeneous elastic body:

$$U = \frac{1}{2}\int_V \sigma_{ij}\varepsilon_{ij}dV = \frac{1}{2}\int_S \sigma_{ij}u_in_jdS = \frac{1}{2}\sigma^0_{ij}\int_S u_in_jdS = \frac{1}{2}\sigma^0_{ij}\int_V u_{i,j}dV = \frac{1}{2}\sigma^0_{ij}\int_V \varepsilon_{ij}dV = \\ = \frac{1}{2}\bar{\sigma}_{ij}\bar{\varepsilon}_{ij}V = \frac{1}{2}s^*_{ijkl}\sigma^0_{kl}\sigma^0_{ij}V. \tag{5}$$

Therefore it follows that the potential energy of a heterogeneous elastic body in the stress-strain state is represented in the following form:

$$U = \frac{1}{2}s^*_{ijkl}\sigma^0_{kl}\sigma^0_{ij}V. \tag{6}$$

Thus, if the value of the potential energy U of the stress-strain state of the elastic body, in which it has been transferred under the homogeneous boundary conditions (static stresses) σ_{ij}^0 is known, then Eq. (6) can be used to find the components of the effective compliance tensor s_{ijkl}^*.

4   The Algorithm for Determining the Components of the Tensor S^*

We assume the volume V to be fixed in space by a parallelepiped with the edges parallel to the coordinate axes. To find the components s_{ijkl}^*, we seek the solution of the boundary value problem of static linear elasticity theory

$$\sigma_{ij,j} = 0, \tag{7}$$

$$\sigma_{ij} = c_{ijkl}\varepsilon_{kl} = c_{ijkl}u_{k,l}, \quad i,j = 1,2 \tag{8}$$

with the corresponding homogeneous static boundary conditions applied to the faces of a sample.

In the case of a 3D sample, the tensor S^* is written down in the form:

$$
\begin{bmatrix} \varepsilon_{11} \\ \varepsilon_{22} \\ \varepsilon_{33} \\ 2\varepsilon_{23} \\ 2\varepsilon_{13} \\ 2\varepsilon_{12} \end{bmatrix} = S^* \begin{bmatrix} \sigma_{11} \\ \sigma_{22} \\ \sigma_{33} \\ \sigma_{23} \\ \sigma_{13} \\ \sigma_{12} \end{bmatrix}, \quad S^* = \begin{pmatrix} s_{1111}^* & s_{1122}^* & s_{1133}^* & s_{1123}^* & s_{1113}^* & s_{1112}^* \\ & s_{2222}^* & s_{2233}^* & s_{2223}^* & s_{2213}^* & s_{2212}^* \\ & & s_{3333}^* & s_{3323}^* & s_{3313}^* & s_{3312}^* \\ & & & s_{2323}^* & s_{2313}^* & s_{2312}^* \\ & sym & & & s_{1313}^* & s_{1312}^* \\ & & & & & s_{1212}^* \end{pmatrix}. \tag{9}
$$

When calculating s_{iiii}^*, $i = 1, 2, 3$ and s_{1212}^*, s_{1313}^*, s_{2323}^*, located on the main diagonal, according to (6) and to the static boundary conditions from Table 1, we obtain:

$$U^{(i)} = \frac{1}{2}s_{iiii}^* V, \quad s_{iiii}^* = 2U^{(i)}/V, i = 1,2,3, \tag{10}$$

$$U^{(4)} = \frac{1}{2}s_{2323}^* V, \quad s_{2323}^* = 2U^{(4)}/V, \tag{11}$$

$$U^{(5)} = \frac{1}{2}s_{1313}^* V, \quad s_{1313}^* = 2U^{(5)}/V, \tag{12}$$

$$U^{(6)} = \frac{1}{2}s_{1212}^* V, \quad s_{1212}^* = 2U^{(6)}/V. \tag{13}$$

Here the superscript in the notation indicates to number of the case under consideration. To determine the remaining components, we use the linearity property of the elasticity problem. In this case, the components of s_{ijkl}^* located above the

Table 1. The boundary conditions for finding the components s^*_{ijkl}.

U	Faces (0, 0, 1)	Faces (0, 1, 0)	Faces (1, 0, 0)	Value s^*_{ijkl}
1	$\sigma_{33} = \sigma_{13} = \sigma_{23} = 0$	$\sigma_{22} = \sigma_{12} = \sigma_{23} = 0$	$\sigma_{11} = 1, \sigma_{12} = \sigma_{13} = 0$	$s^*_{1111} = 2U^{(1)}/V$
2	$\sigma_{33} = \sigma_{13} = \sigma_{23} = 0$	$\sigma_{22} = 1, \sigma_{12} = \sigma_{23} = 0$	$\sigma_{11} = \sigma_{12} = \sigma_{13} = 0$	$s^*_{2222} = 2U^{(2)}/V$
3	$\sigma_{33} = 1, \sigma_{13} = \sigma_{23} = 0$	$\sigma_{22} = \sigma_{12} = \sigma_{23} = 0$	$\sigma_{11} = \sigma_{12} = \sigma_{13} = 0$	$s^*_{3333} = 2U^{(3)}/V$
4	$\sigma_{23} = 1, \sigma_{33} = \sigma_{13} = 0$	$\sigma_{23} = 1, \sigma_{22} = \sigma_{12} = 0$	$\sigma_{11} = \sigma_{12} = \sigma_{13} = 0$	$s^*_{2323} = 2U^{(4)}/V$
5	$\sigma_{13} = 1, \sigma_{33} = \sigma_{23} = 0$	$\sigma_{22} = \sigma_{12} = \sigma_{23} = 0$	$\sigma_{13} = 1, \sigma_{11} = \sigma_{12} = 0$	$s^*_{1313} = 2U^{(5)}/V$
6	$\sigma_{33} = \sigma_{13} = \sigma_{23} = 0$	$\sigma_{12} = 1, \sigma_{22} = \sigma_{23} = 0$	$\sigma_{12} = 1, \sigma_{11} = \sigma_{13} = 0$	$s^*_{1212} = 2U^{(6)}/V$

main diagonal, are calculated by the formulas from Table 2, where the values of $U^{(k,l)}$ are defined as:

$$
U^{(k,l)} = \frac{1}{2} \int_V (\sigma^{(k)}_{ij} \varepsilon^{(l)}_{ij} + \sigma^{(k)}_{ij} \varepsilon^{(l)}_{ij}) dV = \int_V \frac{1}{E} (\sigma^{(k)}_{11} \sigma^{(l)}_{11} + \sigma^{(k)}_{22} \sigma^{(l)}_{22} + \sigma^{(k)}_{33} \sigma^{(l)}_{33}) dV -
$$

$$
- \int_V \frac{\nu}{E} (\sigma^{(k)}_{11} \sigma^{(l)}_{22} + \sigma^{(l)}_{11} \sigma^{(k)}_{22} + \sigma^{(k)}_{22} \sigma^{(l)}_{33} + \sigma^{(l)}_{22} \sigma^{(k)}_{33} + \sigma^{(k)}_{11} \sigma^{(l)}_{33} + \sigma^{(l)}_{11} \sigma^{(k)}_{33}) dV +
$$

$$
+ \int_V \frac{2(\nu+1)}{E} (\sigma^{(k)}_{12} \sigma^{(l)}_{12} + \sigma^{(k)}_{23} \sigma^{(l)}_{23} + \sigma^{(k)}_{13} \sigma^{(l)}_{13}) dV.
$$

Table 2. The formulas for computing s^*_{ijkl}.

$s^*_{1122} = U^{(1,2)}/V$	$s^*_{1123} = U^{(1,4)}/V$	$s^*_{1113} = U^{(1,5)}/V$	$s^*_{2313} = U^{(4,5)}/V$	$s^*_{3312} = U^{(3,6)}/V$
$s^*_{1133} = U^{(1,3)}/V$	$s^*_{2223} = U^{(2,4)}/V$	$s^*_{2213} = U^{(2,5)}/V$	$s^*_{1112} = U^{(1,6)}/V$	$s^*_{2312} = U^{(4,6)}/V$
$s^*_{2233} = U^{(2,3)}/V$	$s^*_{3323} = U^{(3,4)}/V$	$s^*_{3313} = U^{(3,5)}/V$	$s^*_{2212} = U^{(2,6)}/V$	$s^*_{1312} = U^{(5,6)}/V$

5 Numerical Solution to the Static Elasticity Problem

The most time-consuming computations are connected with the solution of a series of static problems in the elasticity theory with external stresses given at the boundaries. In the final analysis, these problems are reduced to systems of linear algebraic equations, for which it is possible to apply both direct and iterative methods. The fact is, direct methods, having certain advantages, are in this case not suitable for solving three-dimensional problems due to excessive demands for computer resources. Therefore, we have chosen iterative methods for determining effective parameters.

We propose to find a solution of static problem (7), (8) with the static boundary conditions by finding the steady-state solution of the dynamic problem of the elasticity theory in the formulation of the stress/displacement velocity with additional dissipative terms to equations of motion (14):

$$
\rho \dot{v}_i + \alpha v_i = \sigma_{ij,j} \tag{14}
$$

$$
\dot{\sigma}_{ij} = C_{ijkl} \dot{\varepsilon}_{kl} = C_{ijkl} v_{k,l} \tag{15}
$$

with zero initial conditions for $t = 0$:

$$v_i = 0, \quad \sigma_{ij} = 0 \tag{16}$$

and constant in time boundary conditions on the boundary S. Here $v_i = \dot{u}_i$ is the displacement velocity of the i-th component of the displacement vector. It is possible to estimate the value of the parameter α by inserting an additional source within the computational domain and to evaluate the attenuation behavior of the excited wave amplitude.

In order to show the convergence of problem (14)–(16) to the static problem (7), (8), we use the virial theorem ([10], §10) asserting that the kinetic energy of the mechanical system T averaged over an infinite time interval is equal to the virial averaged over the same time interval. If the potential energy U is a homogeneous function of the first degree of inverse values of the radius vectors, then the relation

$$2T = -U \tag{17}$$

is satisfied.

Hence it follows that if the kinetic energy of the system is reduced through an artificially introduced damping mechanism in the equation, then the rigid connection between the kinetic and the potential energies provided by this theorem leads to a decrease in the potential energy up to its minimum. Then, based on the Lagrange-Dirichlet principle, for a statically stressed body (*of all possible stress-strain states of a deformable solid, the actual stress state corresponds to a minimum of the total deformation energy*), we can conclude that the solution of the dynamic problem (14)–(16) converges to the solution of the stationary problem (7), (8). For a numerical solution of the initial boundary value problem (14)–(16), we apply a finite-difference staggered scheme grids [18] with modified coefficients to provide approximation in heterogeneous media [8,17].

6   Parallel Implementation

6.1   MPI/OpenMP Parallelization

The most time-consuming part of the algorithm, which in the three-dimensional case requires the obligatory parallel implementation, consists in solving six stress-strain linear elasticity problems for calculating the potential energy of the elastic deformations in a sample under boundary static stresses. As these problems can be solved independently, the most natural way is to use the MPI parallelization to split the calculations to individual tasks. Further, the solution of an individual task can be parallelized with the MPI or the OpenMP, depending on the number of nodes and cores in the problem to be solved. This is the commonly used strategy of parallelization. Briefly, let us consider these versions.

MPI. Parallelization has two stages. At the first stage, using the MPI group constructor, the solution of the problem is divided into six independent tasks, as mentioned above. Each task is assigned to its independent MPI group. Each group solves the local problem (14)–(16) with the help of the finite-difference time domain staggered grid scheme combined with the domain decomposition method. The domain decomposition is applied in order to decompose the original computational domain to multiple elementary subdomains of lower dimensions, each one being handled by its individual Processor Unit (PU) and solves the system of equations within the subdomain. Updating unknown data while moving from a time layer to the next one requires the exchange of values in the grid nodes along the interface between the adjacent subdomains. The message passing library MPI is used to communicate data between the neighboring PU. The necessity of this exchange negatively impacts the scalability of the method. However, the impact is less distinct on the 3D domain decomposition than on one- and two-dimensional ones [9]. In the implementation in question, we choose the 3D domain decomposition. In order to reduce the idle time, the asynchronous computations based on the non-blocking MPI procedures are used. The non-blocking MPI functions Isend()/Irecv() allow us to overlap communications and computations, thus hiding communication latencies and improving the performance of the MPI application.

MPI+OpenMP. The choice of a specific method of parallelization depends on the number of resources allocated to solve the problem. If, for example, we are limited only by six nodes, a possible way to numerically solve the problem may be the use of a combination of the MPI with OpenMP. In this case, parallelization is also performed in two stages. At the first stage, the MPI is used in order to split the calculations to individual tasks. Then the solution of an individual task is parallelized with OpenMP, using the threads with shared memory in the node. This approach is simpler in terms of writing a code, but has a limitation on the number of nodes used.

In both cases, the MPI or MPI+OpenMP, after solving six stress-strain elasticity problems, each process sends the calculated values to the zero process, which saves them into a disk as binary files, containing the values of the stress components in the representative volume. After this, the zero process produces a sequential reading of information from files and calculates the result using the formulas from Table 2. The time required for the zero process for this operation is negligible as compared to the time needed for solving the static elasticity problems, therefore this amount of work is not taken into account in the theoretical evaluation of the efficiency of the algorithm we carry out below. In particular, from the MPI+OpenMP parallelization scheme, it follows, that the best architecture for calculating the problem: the choice of six nodes with a maximum number of cores per node.

In order to estimate the real acceleration and efficiency, a set of test calculations were performed and are discussed below.

6.2   Parallelization Approach with Coarray Fortran

The Coarray Fortran (CAF) is based on a modern Fortran extension and incorporates a Partitioned Global Address Space (PGAS) in order to improve the clarity of a parallel programming language. The CAF is a feature of Fortran 2008 standard published in 2010 [6] and, like the MPI is based on a Single Program, Multiple Data model. A parallel program with the use of Coarray can be interpreted as a set of replicated copies (*images* in the Coarray language) of the code executed asynchronously. The syntax of Fortran was extended by adding arrays with additional trailing subscripts in square brackets, which provide the concise representation of references to data that can be accessed from other images and distributed among them [3]. Using Coarrays, data can be directly accessed in the neighbor memory without using sending and receiving functions. Since the MPI uses the same SPMD model, the Fortran features allow the MPI and Coarray live together in a program. This fact is very convenient for a gradual conversion of the MPI program to Coarray language.

The MPI and OpenMP Fortran codes implementing the above-described algorithm were rewritten in the Coarray. The parts of the program responsible for the parallel input/output of big data have remained in the MPI, while the data exchanges between the neighbors in the domain decomposition method were rewritten in terms of the Coarray. The new version of the code has become more compact and clear, there is no need to write sending and receiving messages and to check the packing and unpacking data for beeing in correspondence. The advantage of the Coarray is in that a parallel algorithm is in a significantly simpler style than the MPI and less prone to the programmer's errors.

7   Numerical Experiments

7.1   Validation of the Numerical Algorithm

First, to validate the algorithm proposed, the homogeneous isotropic plexiglas, copper and steel material samples (Table 3) were considered, and the calculated effective stiffness parameters were compared with the elastic moduli of a material itself (Table 4). In the numerical experiments the attenuation parameter α was equal to 0.001. We observe a good match of the exact and the calculated values not exceeding 1%.

Second, to check the accuracy of the method, the elastic moduli for the samples of layered materials were calculated (Fig. 1a–b). The size of the models varied along the interlayers, across them, the number of layers and their incline being changed. The results of the method proposed were compared with the Schoenberg averaging method [13]. The difference decreased with increasing the size along the interlayer. For the digital core sample of 500 * 500 * 30 grid points along the interlayer this difference was about 4%.

Finally, representative series of calculations were done for a three-dimensional segmented digital carbonate core of 500 * 500 * 500 grid points (Fig. 1c). The seismic velocities recovered from the computed elastic moduli were compared with the results of laboratory measurements. The difference makes up less than 3%.

Table 3. The Lame parameters for some homogeneous materials.

Material	Density (kg/m³)	Velocities (m/s)		Lame parameters	
	ρ	V_p	V_s	λ, Pa	μ
Plexiglass	1180	2670	1121	5446429240	1482836380
Copper	8930	4660	2260	102353560000	45457640000
Steel	7800	5900	3260	105727440000	82895280000

Table 4. The comparison of exact and calculated effective stiffness parameters.

Material	Exact values	Calculated values
Plexiglass	$\lambda + 2\mu = c^*_{1111} = 8412102000$ $\mu = c^*_{1212} = 1482836380$	$\lambda + 2\mu = c^*_{1111} = 8412102000.07929$ $\mu = c^*_{1212} = 1482836379.99971$
Copper	$\lambda + 2\mu = c^*_{1111} = 193920308000$ $\mu = c^*_{1212} = 45610868000$	$\lambda + 2\mu = c^*_{1111} = 193920307998.550$ $\mu = c^*_{1212} = 45610868000.0077$
Steel	$\lambda + 2\mu = c^*_{1111} = 271518000000$ $\mu = 82895280000$	$\lambda + 2\mu = c^*_{1111} = 271518000633.164$ $\mu = 82895279858.3661$

7.2   Comparison of MPI, MPI+OpenMP and Coarray Fortran

To compare the performance of the MPI, MPI+OpenMP and Coarray Fortran communications in terms of the speedup, a three-dimensional segmented digital model of a carbonate core (Fig. 1c) from the previous section was considered as a validation test. To assess a strong scaling, the problem with digital core of $500 * 500 * 500$ grid points remains the same as the number of processors (cores) increases. This test was performed on the Siberian Supercomputer Center cluster, Novosibirsk, Russia, that includes 27 CPU Intel Xeon E5-2697A v4 with $16 * 2$ logical cores per node (32 threads). The Intel Fortran Compiler 2019.1.144 was used to create the executable file. For comparison we have chosen the performance on 96 cores as a baseline. The CPU number is scaled from 3 to 16. Figure 2 (left) presents the strong scaling results measured for MPI, MPI+OpenMP and Coarray. The measured values are compared with the ideal speedup (black). We observe the speedup of about 4.5 when scaling from 96 cores to 576 cores.

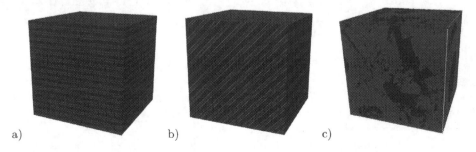

a)   b)   c)

Fig. 1. Different models of layered media (a–b) and a segmented digital model of a core sample (c).

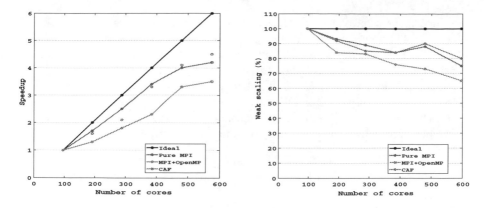

Fig. 2. Strong scaling speedup and weak scaling efficiency on CPU Intel Xeon E5-2697A v4.

To estimate a weak scaling, we have to increase the problem size at the same rate as the number of processors, keeping the amount of work per processor the same. To be able to make this comparison, we have chosen the problem of $500 * 500 * 100$ size as a baseline and have increased the size of the problem in the third dimension. In order to analyze the performance, we have limited computations to a constant number of iterations, because the numerical scheme is subject to the stability condition and may take longer to converge with a denser grid. Figure 2 (right) presents the week scaling efficiency results measured for the MPI, MPI+OpenMP and Coarray Fortran version of the code.

The results presented demonstrate that with an increase in the number of cores, the CAF implementation provides a comparable performance to an equivalent MPI version, while the MPI+OpenMP hybrid model is worse than a pure MPI model and CAF.

8 Conclusion

The results presented describe one of the most important components of research into the development of the promising and recently intensively developing direction of the digital rock physics, known as the digital core. This concept, in our opinion, should be understood as a set of methods and experimental data, which is possible to completely abandon laboratory measurements, replacing them with virtual numerical experiments. The undoubted advantages of this approach are the following:

– the safety of the core samples;
– the possibility of carring out multiple experiments with the same samples to analyze a variety of mechanical, hydrodynamic and other properties of the samples;
– testing various methods for determining the physical properties of a sample from 3D computer tomography scans.

The implementation of this methodology of the core analysis is impossible in practice without parallel algorithms. We have presented three of them, written in Fortran 90. The main essence of our approach is the use of the new relaxation iterative technique to resolve the large-scale 3D elastic static problems. Using this technique, we compute the potential energy of the elastic deformation, which arises in a core sample. The numerical experiments with synthetic data have proved the acceptable accuracy of the method proposed.

We have compared the three different approaches to perform parallelization:

- standard MPI based on the 3D domain decomposition;
- MPI+OpenMP, when within each MPI process we apply the multi-core based parallelization;
- the new feature of Fortran90 known as Coarrays.

These approaches were compared in terms of performance and ease of programming. We can conclude that for the large-scale computations the latter approach has some advantages, in particular, thanks to its simple implementation, and can be considered as an alternative to the MPI and MPI+OpenMP.

We are aware of the fact it is quite possible that the best implementation of the MPI+OpenMP among many possible implementations was not chosen. However, we did not intend to compare all alternative task distributions among the MPI processes and the OpenMP threads within them for choosing the best one. We were aimed at revealing whether the Coarray can be considered to be an alternative to the conventional parallel parallelizations. The analysis of acceleration and efficiency shows that Coarrays start to manifest superiority when using rather a large number of processes.

Acknowledgements. The reported study was funded by RFBR according to the research project №19-01-00347.

The research is carried out using the equipment of the shared research facilities of HPC computing resources at the Joint Supercomputer Center of RAS [20], the Siberian Supercomputer Center [21] and Irkutsk Supercomputer Center of SB RAS [22].

References

1. Aboudi, J.: Mechanics of Composite Materials: A Unified Micromechanical Approach. Elsevier Science, Amsterdam (1991)
2. Arns, C.H., Knackstedt, M.A., Pinczewski, W.V., Garboczi, E.J.: Computation of linear elastic properties from microtomographic images: methodology and agreement between theory and experiment. Geophysics **67**(5), P1395–P1405 (2002)
3. Chivers, I., Sleightholme, J.: Introduction to Programming with Fortran, 3rd edn. Springer, London (2015). https://doi.org/10.1007/b137984
4. Christensen, R.: Introduction to Mechanics of Composite Materials, 1st edn. Wiley, New York (1979)
5. Fredrich, J.T., DiGiovanni, A.A., Noble, D.R.: Predicting macroscopic transport properties using microscopic image data. J. Geophys. Res. **111**, B03201 (2006). https://doi.org/10.1029/2005JB003774

6. ISO/IEC 1539–1:2010, Fortran - Part 1: Base language, International Standard (2010)
7. Keehm, Y.: Computationa lrock physics: transport properties in porous media and applications. Ph.D. dissertation. Stanford University (2003)
8. Kostin, V., Lisitsa, V., Reshetova, G., Tcheverda, V.: Parallel algorithm with modulus structure for simulation of seismic wave propagation in 3D multiscale multiphysics media. In: Malyshkin, V. (ed.) PaCT 2017. LNCS, vol. 10421, pp. 42–57. Springer, Cham (2017). https://doi.org/10.1007/978-3-319-62932-2_4
9. Kostin, V., Lisitsa, V., Reshetova, G., Tcheverda, V.: Simulation of seismic waves propagation in multiscale media: impact of cavernous/fractured reservoirs. In: Jónasson, K. (ed.) PARA 2010. LNCS, vol. 7133, pp. 54–64. Springer, Heidelberg (2012). https://doi.org/10.1007/978-3-642-28151-8_6
10. Landau, L.D., Lifshitz, E.M.: Mechanics. Nauka, Moscow (1988)
11. Reshetova, G., Khachkova, T.: Parallel numerical method to estimate the effective elastic moduli of rock core samples from 3D tomographic images. In: Dimov, I., Faragó, I., Vulkov, L. (eds.) FDM 2018. LNCS, vol. 11386, pp. 452–460. Springer, Cham (2019). https://doi.org/10.1007/978-3-030-11539-5_52
12. Saenger, E.H.: Numerical methods to determine effective elastic properties. Int. J. Eng. Sci. **46**, 598–605 (2008)
13. Schoenberg, M., Muir, F.: A calculus for finely layered anisotropic media. Geophysics **54**(5), 581–589 (1989)
14. Sendetski, J. (ed.): Composition Materials, vol. 2. Mechanics of Composition Meterials [Russian translation]. Mir, Moscow (1978)
15. Shermergor, T.: The theory of elasticity of microinhomogeneous media [Russian translation]. Nauka, Moscow (1977)
16. Zhang, W., Dai, G., Wang, F., Sun, S., Bassir, H.: Using strain energy-based prediction of effective elastic properties in topology optimization of material microstructures. Acta. Mech. Sin. **23**(1), 77–89 (2007)
17. Vishnevsky, D., Lisitsa, V., Tcheverda, V., Reshetova, G.: Numerical study of the interface errors of finite-difference simulations of seismic waves. Geophysics **79**, T219–T232 (2014)
18. Virieux, J.: P-SV wave propagation in heterogeneous media: velocity-stress finite-difference method. Geophysics **51**, 889–901 (1986)
19. Zhan, X., Lawrence, M.S., Wave, S., Toksoz, M.N., Morgan, F.D.: Porescale modeling of electrical and fluid transport in Berea sandstone. Geophysics **75**(5), F135–F142 (2010)
20. Joint Supercomputer Center of RAS. http://old.jscc.ru/eng/index.shtml
21. Novosibirsk Supercomputer Center of SB RAS. http://www.sscc.icmmg.nsc.ru
22. Irkutsk Supercomputer Center of SB RAS. http://hpc.icc.ru

Orange Carotenoid Protein Absorption Spectra Simulation Using the Differential Evolution Algorithm

Roman Pishchalnikov[1](✉) [iD], Igor Yaroshevich[2] [iD],
Eugene Maksimov[2,3] [iD], Nikolai Sluchanko[2,3] [iD], Alexey Stepanov[4],
David Buhrke[5] [iD], and Thomas Friedrich[5] [iD]

[1] Prokhorov General Physics Institute of the Russian Academy of Sciences,
119991 Moscow, Russia
rpishchal@kapella.gpi.ru
[2] Department of Biophysics, Faculty of Biology, Lomonosov Moscow State
University, 119991 Moscow, Russia
iyapromo@gmail.com, emaksimoff@yandex.ru,
nikolai.sluchanko@mail.ru
[3] A.N Bach Institute of Biochemistry, Federal Research Center of Biotechnology
of the Russian Academy of Sciences, 119071 Moscow, Russia
[4] M.M. Shemyakin and Yu.A. Ovchinnikov Institute of Bioorganic Chemistry,
Russian Academy of Sciences, Moscow 117997, Russia
stepanov.aleksei.v@gmail.com
[5] Institute of Chemistry, Technical University of Berlin,
PC 14, 10623 Berlin, Germany
david.buhrke@campus.tu-berlin.de,
friedrich@chem.tu-berlin.de

Abstract. Linear optical response of the orange carotenoid protein (OCP) and its mutants was successfully simulated by applying the Differential evolution (DE) algorithm. OCP is a pigment-protein complex, which plays an important role in non-photochemical quenching of excitation energy in photosynthetic light-harvesting complexes in cyanobacteria. It contains a single carotenoid pigment molecule surrounded by protein matrix. This pigment is entirely responsible for OCP absorption in the region of 350–600 nm. To calculate the OCP absorption spectra, we used the Multimode Brownian oscillator model considering four high vibronic modes (v_1, v_2, v_3 and v_4) and one low frequency mode. The frequencies of these modes were estimated from the OCP Raman spectra; whereas the Huang-Rhys factors alongside the carotenoid electronic transition and the FWHM of inhomogeneous broadening and the low frequency mode were fitted by DE. It was show that characteristic features of OCP absorption spectra can be explained by mutual variations of Huang-Rhys factors of v_1 and v_2 that is corresponded to the in-phase stretching of C = C and C-C bonds.

Keywords: Orange carotenoid protein · Absorption spectrum · Cumulant expansion · Multimode Brownian oscillator model · Differential evolution

V. Voevodin and S. Sobolev (Eds.): RuSCDays 2019, CCIS 1129, pp. 302–312, 2019.
https://doi.org/10.1007/978-3-030-36592-9_25

1 Introduction

For the last two decades the application of supercomputer modeling and evolutionary computations has breathed a new life into theoretical investigations of the energy transfer and charge separation processes in photosynthesis. Photosynthesis is a complex of physical and chemical processes in nature that allows plants, algae and bacteria to convert the light energy into the energy of chemical bonds. Photosynthetic processes have a rather wide range of characteristic times: from femtoseconds needed for fast energy migration in the light-harvesting complexes, to milliseconds that scale the chemical reactions of carbohydrate synthesis.

The subject of our theoretical investigation is a water-soluble photosynthetic pigment-protein complex (PPC) called orange carotenoid protein (OCP). Wild type (WT) OCP consists of a single keto-carotenoid molecule enclosed from direct interactions with the solvent by C- and N- terminal domains [1]. Absorption of light by carotenoid in a compact dark-adapted protein state induces series of conformational rearrangements, which leads to 12 Å translocation of carotenoid into the N terminal domain, separation of domains and formation of so-called red active state [2, 3], which can interact with light-harvesting antennas and effectively quench their excitation [4]. In numerous works process of OCP photoactivation and consequent relaxation is monitored by absorption measurements in visible region [5, 6], however molecular mechanism of OCP photoactivation and the red shift of carotenoid S_0-S_2 absorption is far from being clear.

Since carotenoid is the only pigment responsible for OCP optical response at 350–600 nm, which is a rare case among photosynthetic PPCs, it may seem that to simulate absorption spectra of OCP and its mutants is more or less an easy task. However, there is no exact quantum solution, which could comprehensively describe broad absorption bands of carotenoid molecules, and in this case we are going to apply a semicalassical effective theory such as multimode Brownian oscillator model [7]. To fit the experimental data, some parameters of the model (the frequencies of vibronic modes) can be taken from other sources, for example, the Raman spectroscopy measurements, yet there are always those for which only empirical search is possible.

A search for free parameters of a system can be done most effectively by using the Differential evolution (DE) algorithm [8, 9]. DE is a multiparameter optimization routine, which is based on principles of natural selection [10]. It must be stressed that a real advantage of DE in comparison of genetic algorithms is a search over continuous space of parameters and a possibility to choose different strategies of selection.

The aim of our study is to find a proper set of parameters for the OCP (and its mutants) Brownian oscillator model. Taking into account our previous studies on absorption modeling of chlorophyll and bacteriochlorophyll in solution where DE has been used [11], we are going to apply the same DE strategies and the strategy settings for OCP absorption modeling.

2   Materials and Methods

2.1   Sample Preparation and Characterization

Holoforms of the His6-tagged wild type OCP (further WT OCP), OCP Y201A/W288A (OCP^{AA}) and C-terminal OCP-related carotenoid protein (C-terminal domain of Synechocystis OCP, amino acids 165–317, further COCP) were expressed in NEBt-urbo *E. coli* cells (New England Biolabs, Germany) employing the pAC-CAR25ΔcrtXZcrtO plasmid for synthesis of echinenone (ECN) and canthaxanthin (CAN) as described in Moldenhauer et al. [12]. All proteins were purified by immo-bilized metal-affinity and SEC to electrophoretic homogeneity and stored at 4 °C in the presence of sodium azide. Carotenoid content was analyzed by thin-layer chro-matography, which showed that WT OCP binds exclusively ECN, while holoprotein of and OCP^{AA} and COCP contain CAN. Absorption spectra were recorded using a Cary 1E Varian spectrophotometer (Agilent Technologies, USA) at 22 °C. Resonance Raman Spectra were recorded at −140 °C (Linkam cryostat, Resultec, Germany) using a Fourier Transform Raman spectrometer RFS-100/S (Bruker, Germany) equipped with a 1064 nm cw NdYAG laser (Compass 1064–1500 N, Coherent LaserSystems, Germany). To induce OCP^{O} → OCP^{R} photoconversion, a 900 mW blue LED (M455L3; Thorlabs, USA) with 455 nm maximum emission was used.

2.2   Differential Evolution

The DE algorithm includes the initialization part and the main cycle [8, 9]. In the main cycle three procedures: mutation, crossover and selection are sequentially repeated until the conditions of exit from the cycle are fulfilled. In particular, the exit conditions can be either reaching the limit value of the number of generations, or a proper fitting of the experimental data, which is determined by the objective function:

$$f(x_i^g) = \chi^2 = \frac{1}{N} \sum_{n=1}^{N} \left(\frac{I(\omega_n) - \sigma_{abs}(\omega_n, x_i^g)}{I(\omega_n)} \right)^2, \tag{1}$$

where $I(\omega_n)$ is the experimental absorption spectrum as a function of frequencies ω_n, $n = 1..N$, and $\sigma_{abs}(\omega_n, x_i^g)$ is the calculated absorption spectrum. x_i^g are free parameters of a model for the current generation g.

At the initial stage of DE, a set of vectors is created and initial values of objective function are calculated. The length of each vector, D, is the number of free system parameters. The number of vectors, Np, is the size of the population. The initial values of the vectors are randomly chosen considering the boundary conditions which is set taking into account the physical limits of parameters to search.

After initialization new vectors of mutant parameters are generated.

$$v_i^g = x_{r0}^g + F\left(x_{r1}^g - x_{r2}^g\right), \tag{2}$$

where x_{r0}^g, x_{r1}^g and x_{r2}^g are random vectors of the current population, $(i \neq r0 \neq r1 \neq r2)$ $\in [0, Np]$. F is a scaling factor. The crossover operation mixes parameters of two vectors from the current population increasing the diversity of a new generation. The probability to be crossed is determined by the crossover rate, Cr. In DE algorithm two types of crossover are implemented: exponential and binomial.

At the selection stage, the target vector is created comparing values of the objective function (1) of the current population with those of a newly created. If a new vector gives better value of the objective function, the corresponding old vector is substituted by the new one.

Totally, the standard realization of DE includes ten strategies based on two types of crossover and a way of mutant vector generation. In our previous studies we have performed a strategy test by fitting chlorophyll and bacteriochlorophyll absorption spectra calculated in terms of the Brownian oscillator model [11]. It turned out that the most effective strategies for modeling are DE/best/1/bin with $F = 0.6$ and $Cr = 0.9$. DE/best/exp with $F = 0.4$ and $Cr = 0.8$ has shown a bit slower convergence.

2.3 Programming Details

We used the 3.6 version of DE available online (basically de.c file) as a starting point to make the optimization routine suitable for our purposes. The main procedure of DE was modified applying the MPI library to be able to run it on several nodes of the cluster and to speed up calculations significantly. Among the available nodes, a one node is supposed to be a master one; DE routine runs on it as well as the absorption simulation procedures. All other nodes are used only for OCP absorption simulation. The master node opens data files and loads the setting parameters; it also saves the intermediate and the final results. When an initial vector of fitting parameters is generated on the master node, it sends this vector to all other nodes to simulate the absorption spectra. To run the program correctly, it is necessary that the population size is chosen by a multiple of the number of available nodes. When the simulations are ended on all nodes, the master node collects the values of objective functions and chooses the best one. Then a new trial vector is generated according to the selected strategy and a new DE cycle starts.

The strategy choice is crucial for getting proper fitting results. The number of free parameters can radically change the convergence rate for any strategy. A detailed description of the DE strategy test for the linear optical response of photosynthetic pigment molecules considering the cumulant expansion technique can be found in our previous paper [11]. Finally, for the OCP absorption modeling we are going to use DE/best/1/bin with $F = 0.6$ and $Cr = 0.9$. All programs were written in C++ and compiled with the MPI and MKL libraries.

3   Theory of the Multimode Brownian Oscillator Model

The observable lineshape of any electronic transition of a pigment molecule is a broad spectrum band. The reason of this broadening is the interaction of an optically allowed electron transition with surrounding molecules and with the bath. To simulate the effect of broadening, it is necessary to consider the surrounding of a system as an ensemble of Brownian oscillators. In this case the interaction between electronic transition and oscillators can be treated as a perturbation and the cumulant expansion can be applied [7]. If we have an electronic system with surrounding, which can be found in the ground $|g\rangle$ and the excited $|e\rangle$ states, the Hamiltonians of those states can be written as follows:

$$H_g = \frac{1}{2}\sum_j \hbar\omega_j \left(p_j^2 + q_j^2\right), \tag{3}$$

$$H_e = \hbar\Omega_{eg} + \frac{1}{2}\sum_j \hbar\omega_j \left[p_j^2 + \left(q_j + d_j\right)^2\right], \tag{4}$$

where Ω_{eg} is the frequency of an electronic transition, p_j, q_j, and d_j are the dimensionless momentum, coordinate and deviation parameter. Then the stochastic modulation of the electronic energy gap is

$$\omega_{eg} = \Omega_{eg} + \frac{1}{2}\sum_j d_j^2 \omega_j \tag{5}$$

Knowing the correlation functions of ω_{eg} modulations, we can simulate absorption spectrum of the system, which is described by (3) and (4). The correlation function $C(\tau) = \langle U(\tau)U(0)\rangle/\hbar$ is calculated from the equation for the interaction U between the electronic state and the oscillators considering Hamiltonians (3) and (4).

$$U = \hbar\sum_j \omega_j d_j q_j \tag{6}$$

$$U(\tau) = e^{\frac{iH_g t}{\hbar}} U e^{-\frac{iH_g t}{\hbar}} \tag{7}$$

Introducing the lineshape function of a system, $g(t) = \int_0^t d\tau_2 \int_0^{\tau_2} C(\tau_1)d\tau_1$, we can finally write the equation for the absorption spectrum:

$$\sigma_{abs}(\omega) = \frac{1}{\pi} Re \int_0^\infty dt e^{i(\omega - \Omega_{eg})t} e^{-g(t)}, \tag{8}$$

In order to simulate the OCP correlation function, first of all, the $\tilde{C}(\omega)$ spectral density of the Brownian oscillators has to be evaluated. In terms of spectral density the lineshape function can be rewritten as following:

$$\tilde{C}(\omega) = \sum_j \frac{2S_j \omega \omega_j^3 \gamma_j(\omega)}{\left(\omega_j^2 - \omega^2\right)^2 + \omega^2 \gamma_j^2(\omega)},$$ (9)

$$g(t) = \frac{1}{2\pi} \int_{-\infty}^{+\infty} d\omega \frac{1 - \cos \omega t}{\omega^2} \coth\left(\frac{\beta \hbar \omega}{2}\right) \tilde{C}(\omega) -$$

$$-\frac{i}{2\pi} \int_{-\infty}^{+\infty} d\omega \frac{\sin(\omega t)}{\omega^2} \tilde{C}(\omega),$$ (10)

where $\beta = 1/kT$, k is the Boltzmann constant, T is temperature. Thus, the lineshape function introduces the temperature effect into the absorption spectrum formula (8).

Summation in (9) is carried out over the number of vibronic modes specified in (3) and (4). Each mode is described by $\{\omega_j, S_j, \gamma_j\}$, where ω_j is frequency of a mode, S_j is a Huang-Rhys factor, and γ_j is a damping factor.

To simulate the effect of inhomogeneous broadening caused by the interaction with protein environment or solution, the Gaussian distribution of the electronic gap modulation $\Delta\Omega_{eg}$ with the standard deviation $SD_\Omega = FWHM_\Omega/2\sqrt{2\ln 2}$ was used [13, 14].

Finally, based on (8), the resulting equation for the OCP absorption spectrum in solution has to be recast in following form:

$$\sigma_{abs}(\omega) = \frac{1}{\pi} Re \int_0^\infty dt e^{i(\omega - \Omega_{eg})t} e^{-g(t)} e^{-\frac{1}{2}(SD_\Omega t)^2},$$ (11)

4 Results

The complete procedure of OCP absorption spectra simulation involves the numerical solutions of Eqs. (9), (10) and (11). To calculate the spectral density according (9), a full set of $\{\omega_j, S_j, \gamma_j\}$ for each modification of OCP has to be determined. ω_j and γ_j can be estimated from Raman spectroscopy, for example. We have measured OCP Raman spectra (Fig. 1) in the range of 900–1600 cm^{-1}. Carotenoids of OCP produce four pronounced bands in this region: v_1 is C = C in-phase stretching mode, v_2 is C-C in-phase stretching mode, v_3 is the methyl in-plane rocking vibrations (Table 1). The low intensity v_4 mode represents hydrogen out of the plane (HOOP) wagging mode.

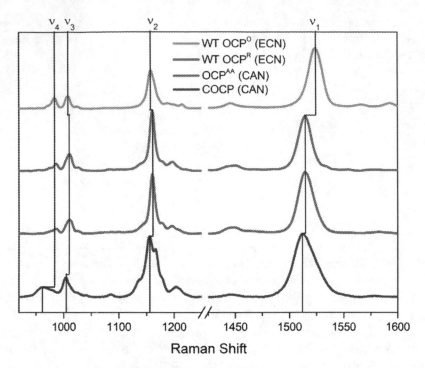

Fig. 1. Raman spectra of WT OCP in dark adapted (orange line) and photoactivated (red) states, OCP^{AA} (purple) and COCP (violet). (Color figure online)

The Huang-Rhys factors S_j cannot be estimated directly from Raman spectroscopy, however, ratio between Raman intensities for some types of carotenoids is proportional to ratio between Huang-Rhys factors [15]. Thus, in our modeling we consider S_j as free parameters. To describe the influence of solvent molecules on electronic transition of carotenoids in OCP and its mutants, the low frequency mode $\{\omega_{low}, S_{low}, \gamma_{low}\}$ is introduced [16]. So, as well as Huang-Rhys factors of ν_i, the free parameters of DE are Ω_{eg}, FWHM$_\Omega$, $\{\omega_{low}, S_{low}, \gamma_{low}\}$.

Table 1. Frequencies (ω_i) and intensities (I_i^{norm}) for four vibronic modes (ν_i) of normalized Raman spectra of OCP and its mutants.

OCP	ν_1		ν_2		ν_3		ν_4	
	ω_1	I_1^{norm}	ω_2	I_2^{norm}	ω_3	I_3^{norm}	ω_4	I_4^{norm}
WT O	1524	1.0	1158	0.6	1008	0.21	983	0.19
WT R	1515	0.9	1160	1.0	1010	0.28	986	0.12
AA	1515	1.0	1160	0.99	1012	0.23	986	0.08
COCP	1512	1.0	1155	0.96	1004	0.31	962	0.16

Equations (10) and (11) were integrated with a time step of 0.0024 ps, $2^{13} = 8192$ points of the time (frequency) array size, and $T = 300$ K.

Table 2. Fitting parameters of the orange and red OCP forms and its mutants absorption spectra obtained after DE optimization.

	Ω_{eg}	$FWHM_\Omega$	ω_{low}	S_{low}	γ_{low}	S_{v_1}	S_{v_2}	S_{v_3}	S_{v_4}
WT O	21402.0	1112.0	152.0	1.8	400.0	0.65	0.25	0.1	0.12
WT R	20310.0	1407.0	250.0	2.0	400.0	0.94	1.0	0.2	0.11
AA	19403.0	1420.0	260.0	1.8	400.0	0.9	0.1	0.1	0.04
COCP	18798.0	1506.0	260.0	1.8	400.0	0.88	0.2	0.1	0.05

Tuning of the DE optimization program was done in the same manner as it is describe in our previous publication [11]. The maximum number of generation was set to 100. However, after approximately 40 generations, no significant changes of χ^2 were observed.

The results of fitting procedure are show in Figs. 3, 4, 5 and 6 and in Table 2. It must be stressed that for OCP^{AA} and COCP mutants the ratio between S_{v_1} and S_{v_2} Huang-Rhys factors do not correspond to the ratio of Raman intensities. This effect is connected with the existence of two carbonyl groups in canthaxanthin molecules [16] which binds to OCP^{AA} and COCP mutants. In opposite, WT OCP binds echinenone with a single keto-group, thus for the dark adapted and photoactivated WT OCP the S_{v_1} and S_{v_2} values keep the ratio of intensities in the Raman spectrum (Table 2).

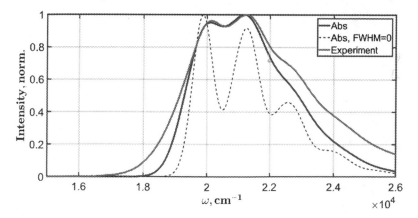

Fig. 3. Experimental (red line) and calculated (blue solid line and black dashed line) of dark adapted WT OCP^O (ECN). (Color figure online)

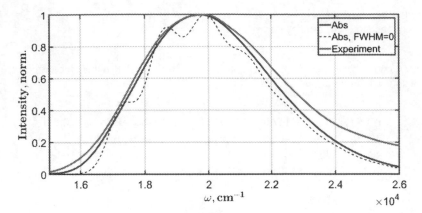

Fig. 4. Experimental (red line) and calculated (blue solid line and black dashed line) of photoactivated WT OCP^R (ECN) (Color figure online)

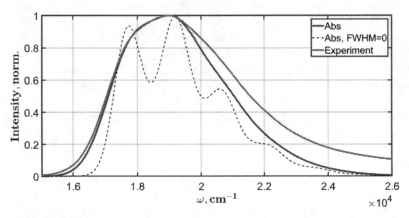

Fig. 5. Experimental (red line) and calculated (blue solid line and black dashed line) of OCP^{AA} (CAN) (Color figure online)

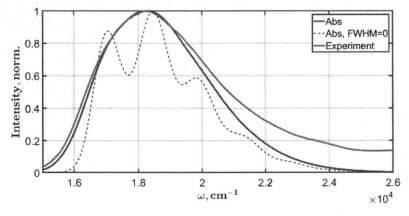

Fig. 6. Experimental (red line) and calculated (blue solid line and black dashed line) of COCP (CAN) (Color figure online)

5 Conclusions

Thus, we demonstrate that DE allows calculations of absorption spectra of carotenoids as a pigment of OCP and its mutants. The overall shape and position of all major peaks and minor shoulders of S_0-S_2 absorption could be predicted with good precision. We got the best congruence of experimental and calculated absorption for red species (OCP^R and OCP^{AA}), which both represent physiologically active quenching state, despite the fact that they bind different types of carotenoids. Although, existence of two keto groups in end-rings of CAN interrupts correlation between the intensity of bands in Raman spectrum and Huang-Rhys factors, DE allows estimation of bi-ketolated carotenoids absorption in COCP and OCP^{AA}. We found that accurate modeling of WT OCP absorption requires consideration of two distinct populations with different spectral characteristics, in other words such broad spectra cannot represent pure species. Thus, we found that $\sim 25\%$ of red form is present in a compact dark-adapted WT OCP. This observation indicates that there is a dynamic equilibrium between these two configurations of ECN molecule, and it spontaneously convert into the state which is spectrally indistinguishable from the red photoactivated state, while being present in a compact protein state. Considering the atomic structure of OCP, we postulate that appearance of the red spectral species in the compact state are due to isomerization of carotenoid, which leads to the increase of conjugation length. We assume that such isomerization requires conformational flexibility for the end-ring with keto-group in C-domain, which may appear if one (or both) hydrogen bonds between the carotenoid and Trp-288 and Tyr-201 may be spontaneously broken. We are aimed to test this hypothesis in our future works, which will rely on combination of experimental and theoretical approaches.

Acknowledgement. The authors acknowledge the support of the Russian Science Foundation (RSF grant no. 18-44-04002) and Russian Foundation of Basic Research (RFBR grant no. 19-01-00696). This study was carried out using equipment of the shared research facilities of HPC computing resources at Moscow State University.

References

1. Sluchanko, N.N., Slonimskiy, Y.B., Maksimov, E.G.: Features of protein-protein interactions in the cyanobacterial photoprotection mechanism. Biochemistry-Moscow **82**, 1592–1614 (2017). https://doi.org/10.1134/s000629791713003x
2. Sluchanko, N.N., Klementiev, K.E., Shirshin, E.A., Tsoraev, G.V., Friedrich, T., Maksimov, E.G.: The purple Trp288Ala mutant of Synechocystis OCP persistently quenches phycobilisome fluorescence and tightly interacts with FRP. BBA-Bioenergetics **1858**, 1–11 (2017). https://doi.org/10.1016/j.bbabio.2016.10.005
3. Maksimov, E.G., et al.: A comparative study of three signaling forms of the orange carotenoid protein. Photosynth. Res. **130**, 389–401 (2016). https://doi.org/10.1007/s11120-016-0272-8
4. Shirshin, E.A., et al.: Biophysical modeling of in vitro and in vivo processes underlying regulated photoprotective mechanism in cyanobacteria. Photosynth. Res. **133**, 261–271 (2017). https://doi.org/10.1007/s11120-017-0377-8

5. Maksimov, E.G., et al.: The photocycle of orange carotenoid protein conceals distinct intermediates and asynchronous changes in the carotenoid and protein components. Sci. Rep. **7**, 15548 (2017). https://doi.org/10.1038/s41598-017-15520-4
6. Maksimov, E.G., et al.: The signaling state of orange carotenoid protein. Biophys. J. **109**, 595–607 (2015). https://doi.org/10.1016/j.bpj.2015.06.052
7. Mukamel, S.: Principles of Nonlinear Optical Spectroscopy. Oxford University Press, New York, Oxford (1995)
8. Storn, R.: System design by constraint adaptation and differential evolution. IEEE Trans. Evol. Comput. **3**, 22–34 (1999). https://doi.org/10.1109/4235.752918
9. Storn, R., Price, K.: Differential evolution - A simple and efficient heuristic for global optimization over continuous spaces. J. Global Optim. **11**, 341–359 (1997). https://doi.org/10.1023/A:1008202821328
10. Das, S., Mullick, S.S., Suganthan, P.N.: Recent advances in differential evolution - an updated survey. Swarm Evol. Comput. **27**, 1–30 (2016). https://doi.org/10.1016/j.swevo.2016.01.004
11. Pishchalnikov, R.: Application of the differential evolution for simulation of the linear optical response of photosynthetic pigments. J. Comput. Phys. **372**, 603–615 (2018). https://doi.org/10.1016/j.jcp.2018.06.040
12. Moldenhauer, M., et al.: Assembly of photoactive orange carotenoid protein from its domains unravels a carotenoid shuttle mechanism. Photosynth. Res. **133**, 327–341 (2017). https://doi.org/10.1007/s11120-017-0353-3
13. Pishchalnikov, R., Shubin, V., Razjivin, A.: Single molecule fluorescence spectroscopy of psi trimers from arthrospira platensis: a computational approach. Molecules **24**(4), 822 (2019). https://doi.org/10.3390/molecules24040822
14. Pishchalnikov, R.Y., Shubin, V.V., Razjivin, A.P.: Spectral differences between monomers and trimers of photosystem I depend on the interaction between peripheral chlorophylls of neighboring monomers in trimer. Phys. Wave Phenom. **25**(3), 185–195 (2017). https://doi.org/10.3103/s1541308x17030050
15. Kelley, A.M.: Resonance raman overtone intensities and electron-phonon coupling strengths in semiconductor nanocrystals. J. Phys. Chem. A **117**, 6143–6149 (2013). https://doi.org/10.1021/jp400240y
16. Uragami, C., Saito, K., Yoshizawa, M., Molnar, P., Hashimoto, H.: Unified analysis of optical absorption spectra of carotenoids based on a stochastic model. Arch. Biochem. Biophys. **650**, 49–58 (2018). https://doi.org/10.1016/j.abb.2018.04.021

Parallel Dynamic Mesh Adaptation Within INMOST Platform

Kirill Terekhov[(✉)]

Marchuk Institute of Numerical Mathematics of the Russian Academy of Sciences,
Moscow 119333, Russia
kirill.terekhov@gmail.com

Abstract. The work is concerned with parallel dynamic mesh adaptation in INMOST software platform, a toolkit for mathematical modelling. The dynamic mesh adaptation functionality is in big demand in mathematical physics applications governed by approximate numerical solution of partial differential equations. The adaptation of computational mesh is required for two reasons: first, to better resolve the features of physical process by refining the mesh, second, to reduce computational costs by coarsening the mesh in regions away from zones of interest. This requires the mesh to be adapted and balanced along the simulation process based on the numerical solution. In this work the functionality of INMOST is extended to enable refinement of general polyhedral meshes in parallel.

Keywords: Open-source library · Parallel grid generation · Mesh adaptation · Mesh refinement

1 Introduction

Parallel modelling of complex multiphysics phenomena is a challenge for a programmer, who has to deal with numerical methods in parallel, manage the unstructured grid, data exchanges, assembly and solution of large distributed linear and nonlinear systems, and finally result post-processing. INMOST [13] is an open-source library that alleviates the most of the burden from the programmer providing a unified set of tools to address each of the aforementioned issues. We have used the INMOST platform to implement the fully implicit black-oil reservoir model and fully coupled blood coagulation model [8].

Parallel generation of huge computational meshes is primarily based on adaptation. Dynamic mesh adaptation through refinement and coarsening allows one to construct large meshes fine enough at regions of interest. In turn, such strategy reduces the computational work. Mesh operations needed for mesh adaptation and modification require very flexible and efficient data structure for storage of mesh elements, adjacency information, allowing for fast removal and addition of elements, as well as high level modification routines. Mesh libraries allowing for mesh modification, such as Dune [11], project DuMuX [3] based on Dune, STK mesh from Trilinos package [15], OpenFOAM [14], have attracted ever-growing

V. Voevodin and S. Sobolev (Eds.): RuSCDays 2019, CCIS 1129, pp. 313–326, 2019.
https://doi.org/10.1007/978-3-030-36592-9_26

attention. There are other notable packages for parallel mesh management, such as MOAB [6] and MSTK [4], they offer basic mesh modification functionality: delete and add mesh elements. INMOST platform provides high level mesh modification tools which are applicable to meshes composed of arbitrary polyhedral cells, these tools were previously reported in [9]. The algorithms and functionality that form the basis of the INMOST mesh operations module were previously reported in [1, 2, 7–10]. In the present work we extend the mesh modification functionality to support synchronization and balancing of general mesh after arbitrary modification in parallel. Both the synchronization and balancing preserve the layers of ghost cells (see Fig. 1 for illustration) requested by the user.

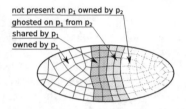

Fig. 1. Designation of the owned, shared and ghost elements for distributed mesh on processor p_1.

2   Internal Representation

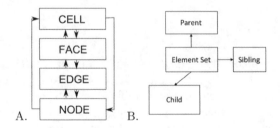

Fig. 2. Element zoo and adjacency connections (A). Organization of sets of elements into a tree structure (B).

The data structure of INMOST supports the full zoo of elements: nodes, edges, faces, cells as well as bidirectional adjacency connections between them as depicted in Fig. 2(A). The elements can be organized into sets of elements which in turn can be organized into a tree structure by three connections as depicted in Fig. 2(B). One of the extensions in the present work is the parallel handling of hierarchy of sets and their elements.

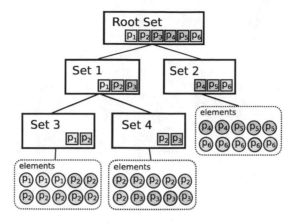

Fig. 3. Distribution of set hierarchy in parallel.

The parallel handling of set hierarchy follows the requirements:

- The sets are uniquely defined by names.
- The set belongs to the union of the processors of their elements.
- The processor with the lowest rank is declared to be the owner of the set (Fig. 3).
- The reconstruction of the set's connection to the parent is mandatory, *i.e.* when set is being exchanged to remote processor, its parent set is being exchanged as well, so that entire upwards hierarchy is reconstructed on remote processor (Fig. 3).
- On each processor a set is required to know only about elements and child sets that are present on the current processor (Fig. 4).

The requirements provide transparent logic on how the sets and their elements are shared and exchanged in parallel. When a set is being sent to another processor, then the sets in hierarchy upwards and the links to elements and child sets that are already present on remote processor are being sent as well. This information is serialized into a binary buffer; the set hierarchy and connections to elements are reconstructed from the buffer on remote processor.

Various scenarios of data usage imply a large variety of mesh data representations. Mesh data can be dense or sparse, *i.e.* given on all or some elements of various length and various data types. For parallel run of simulations INMOST reconstructs a predefined number of layers of ghost elements and organizes the exchange of data from processors-owners of elements to processors possessing the copy of elements [10]. It also allows for data reduction, when all processors that posses a ghost copy of element send the data to processor-owner of element, where the user-defined function accumulates multiple data. To enable the mesh adaptation algorithm, we implemented the exchange and reduction of data that represents references to elements.

Here and further we differentiate two terms for exchange of mesh elements: migration and ghosting. On migration the original copy of the element is deleted

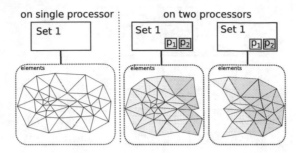

Fig. 4. Handling the elements of the set on single processor (left) and two processors (right) for the mesh with one layer of ghost elements. The same "Set 1" shared between both processors contains only elements present on each of the processors.

and the element is recreated at remote processor. The remote processor is assigned as the new owner of the element. On ghosting the copy of the element is created at remote processor. The owner of the element remains the same.

The main issue in the exchanging of data of type reference between mesh partitions is that we need to reconstruct the referenced element on remote processor. As a result, the referenced element is ghosted on a remote processor and then the link to the element can be established on remote processor. In turn, if the referenced element references some other elements, we may end up with the need to reconstruct the entire mesh on each processor in order to maintain all the references. To avoid this scenario, we adapt the following strategy for exchange of references to elements:

- When the user explicitly requests the exchange (or reduction) of references to elements, each processor packs and sends all the elements, referenced from shared (or ghost) elements. Since this results in conversion of owned elements into shared and addition of new ghost elements, multiple repetition of the procedure may reconstruct the entire mesh on each processor.
- When the data is passively exchanged during ghosting or migration, only links to the elements being sent to the remote processor or elements already owned by remote processor are being exchanged. If the element is not present on the remote processor, then an invalid link is sent. To reconstruct missing data, the user has to explicitly request the exchange.
- In load balancing algorithm, before mesh migration, we have to ensure that the references are not completely lost after migration. To achieve this, we enforce each referenced element to be present on the owner processor of the referencing element.

All the referenced elements that are to be reconstructed on remote processors are serialized into binary buffers. Elements are unpacked from the buffer in the same order as they were serialized. As a result, this allows us to serialize and restore the references to elements by using the order of serialization of elements into buffer. To avoid sending excessive information, *e.g.* when the element is already present on remote processor and we only need to send over the reference to it, we pack only global identificators. Then on the remote processor we use binary search of the element by global identificator among ghost or shared elements.

The method has many applications beyond the mesh adaptation example, One such application is precomputing and maintaining a stencil of discretization scheme, during mesh balancing.

3 Parallel Mesh Modification

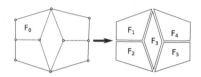

Fig. 5. Separation of a face F_0 by a set of edges into faces $F_1...F_5$.

The detailed description of sequential mesh modification capabilites in INMOST can be found in [9]. Here we note, that apart of trivial removal and addition of elements, INMOST provides a number of procedures facilitating the mesh modification by managing all the necessary reconnections in the mesh. Three types of high-level mesh modification procedures are available: functions for collapsing elements, functions uniting a set of elements into a single element and functions splitting an element into subelements. The algorithm of face splitting by a set of edges is depicted in Fig. 5. Controls of mesh topological correctness are provided within INMOST to prevent topologically inconsistent configurations during modification.

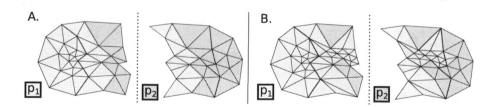

Fig. 6. Initial grid, the yellow and green color correspond to elements owned by processors p_1 and p_2, respectively (A). Local refinement of the grid and edge swap results in loss of ownership information for new elements, coloured in grey (B). (Color figure online)

In a general case, the mesh can be rebuilt by deleting part of the mesh and adding new elements, as shown in Fig. 6(B). We assume that the modifications are synchronized between processors, *i.e.* the modification on different processors should not produce geometrically non-matching meshes on different processors. Once the mesh was locally modified, the parallel consistency of the modified part of the mesh has to be established as illustrated in Fig. 7(A) for local mesh refinement of triangular mesh.

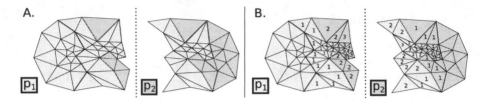

Fig. 7. Resolution of shared elements establishes ownership information, required for data exchange, but attributes all shared elements to processor p_1 (A). Assignment of element's owner processor by the minimal distance in the graph of shared and ghost elements connected by nodes (B).

3.1   Resolve Modified Elements

We have to resolve geometrical correspondence of new elements on one processor to elements on the other processors. First, to limit the communication volume and pattern, we build the bounding boxes around all the new nodes. Then each processor collects, sorts by coordinates and exchanges all its nodes that fall into other processor's bounding boxes. By comparing sorted lists of coordinates with their own, each processor determines for each node the list of processors that has a copy of the node. The processor with the lowest rank is determined to be the owner of the node. This allows us to establish communication of data between nodes of processors. Then we have to resolve shared edges, faces and cells. For those elements we determine a candidate set of shared elements based on processors list of lower adjacencies, *i.e.* if both nodes of an edge belong to processors 1 and 2, then we assume that an edge may belong to the same processors. Then the processors exchange the candidate sets to check if these elements are really present on remote processors. As a result we get processors list for edges, then faces and, finally, cells. The procedure is illustrated in Fig. 7(A).

3.2   Equilibrate Shared Elements

The ghost and shared elements are equilibrated between the processors by computing the graph distance to owned elements. The graph nodes are formed by shared and ghost elements, the graph edges are lower adjacency elements prescribed by user. Then we reassign the owner processor of the element by the one that has the minimal distance in the graph. If the distance is equal on all processors, then the owner is the processor with the lowest rank. To compute the minimal distance and the new owner processor, we first perform the data reduction operation from ghost elements to shared elements and then synchronize the reduced data among the processors. The result of the procedure is illustrated in Fig. 7(B).

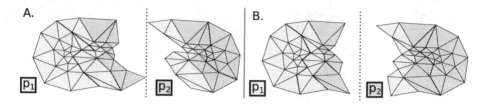

Fig. 8. Reconstruction of ghost layers leads to removal of unnecessary elements and addition of one element (A), the resulting mesh has 43 and 28 elements owned by processor p_1 and p_2, respectively. Load balancing results in 35 and 36 elements owned by processor p_1 and p_2, respectively (B).

3.3   Reconstruct Ghost Layers

The algorithm above only balances the number of ghost layers between processors. We have to add (or remove) ghost elements in places where there is insufficient (or excessive) number of layers. To achieve this, we compute a set of faces, that are located between elements owned by different processors. In Fig. 8(A) such set of edges (in 2D) for all elements is marked by red dotted line. Starting from a set of faces (or their adjacent elements requested by user), we collect a layer of owned and shared elements and, if necessary, exchange them with the processor sharing these faces. The procedure can be repeated for the outer adjacent elements of the collected layer until required number of layers is reached. Unvisited elements are the ones to be deleted. The result is illustrated in Fig. 8(A).

4   Data Transfer

Mesh modification is often accompanied by data transfer. To reduce the memory footprint we do not require to store the original mesh before modification. The approach is based on modification epochs. The user can switch the mesh into a modification state. In this state, the deleted elements are hidden from the mesh, but their data is still available for data transfer. All the added elements are marked as new. Then if the original mesh has to be recovered, the markers for new elements and hidden elements are swapped. The steps are presented in Algorithm 1.

The transfer of physical quantities is not provided automatically during mesh modification as their interpolation is problem-dependent. The user has to implement his own interpolation procedures on the basis of the above functions.

Algorithm 1. Mesh modification epoch.

1: *BeginModification* puts the mesh into modification state. From this point all deleted elements are only marked for deletion but remain in the mesh. Requests for adjacent elements skip elements marked for deletion.

2: Perform modification of the mesh. Delete old elements and create new elements.

3: *ResolveModification* performs the steps necessary for exchange of data in parallel on the new mesh.

4: (optional) *SwapModification* allows to fully recover the old mesh to transfer the mesh data.

5: *EndModification* exits the modification state. Links to removed mesh elements are replaced by invalid links. All the elements marked for deletion and their data are irreversibly destroyed.

5   Mesh Balancing

The local mesh refinement may result in significant disbalance in the number of mesh elements on each of the processors as demonstrated in Fig. 8(A). Balancing the mesh involves computation of a new mesh distribution and migration of mesh elements, Fig. 8(B). When local mesh modification is involved, large portion of the mesh may be changed during a single stage of modification.

The computation of the new distribution of mesh cells should reasonably depend on the former distribution of the mesh elements to minimize the communication volume and work required for mesh reconstruction when exchanging parts of the mesh between processors. We employ the K-means clustering algorithm [5]. On initialization step we reconstruct the location of clusters by initial mesh distribution. As a result, centers of clusters move smoothly with the mesh refinement. The downside of the algorithm is apparent absence of control of the number of cells assigned to each cluster. To slightly alleviate the problem, we introduce the fourth (third in 2D) coordinate to the centers of clusters as illustrated in Fig. 9. The larger the number of cells that were assigned to the cluster, the larger is the additional coordinate. The coordinate is proportional to the respective number of cells that were assigned to each cluster and the diagonal of the bounding box of the mesh. As a result the number of cells is better balanced between clusters, but is still not ideal. We plan to further address this problem.

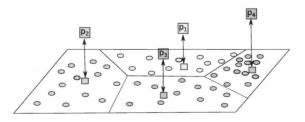

Fig. 9. The K-means clustering algorithm for a set of cells with the additional coordinate for cluster centers. The coordinate is proportional to the respective number of cells that were assigned to each cluster and the diagonal of the bounding box of the mesh.

Once the new distribution is computed, we determine, for each element, the set of processors that should possess each of the elements and element sets, as described in Algorithm 2.

Algorithm 2. Determining processors for redistribution of elements.

1: Compute partitioning for cells with K-means algorithm.
2: For faces, edges and nodes compute the set of processors, they should belong to, based on the union of processors of their upper adjacencies.
3: Compute the shared skin, *i.e.* the set of faces that appear on the boundary between parts owned by different processors.
4: Starting from these faces, layer by layer, determine which cells should be shared with remote processors to keep the number of ghost layers requested by user. Repeat step 2 to compute processors set for lower adjacencies in ghost layers.
5: For all the elements with references to other elements prescribe that referenced elements should be also present on processor that owns the element. Repeat step 2 to compute processors set for lower adjacencies of reffered elements.
6: For the sets of elements compute the list of processors, they should belong to, based on the union of processors of their elements and their children.
7: Request migration of elements to new owner processors.

The migration of elements is performed by serializing information into binary buffer. For elements we serialize their lower adjacency list and all their data. For sets we serialize their name, data, upwards graph tree structure and connections to child sets and set elements, that are sent to or present on the remote processor.

To reduced the memory footprint, we delete the elements and the sets that should not belong to the current processor anymore, *i.e* they do not have the current processor in their list of new processors. In turn, to reduce the message size, we do not pack the elements that already exist on remote processor. Once the buffers are transferred to remote processors, the mesh and all the data are reconstructed from binary buffers information on remote processors.

6   General Mesh Refinement and Coarsening

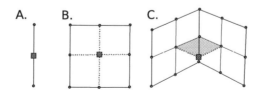

Fig. 10. Steps for splitting (A) edge, (B) face and (C) introduction of faces splitting a cell. Red color indicate new elements on each step. (Color figure online)

In the present work we employ the following strategy for local refinement:

- An edge is refined by splitting it into two edges by node, added in the middle of the edge as in Fig. 10(A). The new node becomes a hanging node of all adjacent faces.
- A face is refined only if all the edges are refined, *i.e.* it has the same number of hanging nodes as original edges. We introduce a new node in the middle of the face. The coordinate of this new node is the average of coordinates of hanging nodes of the face. This new node becomes the hanging node of all the adjacent cells. Then we introduce new edges, connecting the new node and hanging nodes of the face and request to split the face by the new edges. The process is illustrated in Fig. 10(B).
- A cell is refined only if all the faces are refined, *i.e.* it has the same number of hanging nodes as original faces. We introduce a new node in the middle of the cell. The coordinate of this new node is the average of coordinates of hanging nodes of the cell. Then we introduce new edges, connecting the new node and hanging nodes of the cell and finally create new faces as illustrated in Fig. 10(C). The new faces are not necessarily flat. We request the splitting of the cell by the set of new faces.

This algorithm requires to store the references to hanging nodes. We also need the information to coarsen the refined cells back. For this, we use hierarchy of sets.

Once one of the cells is refined, a new set that represent the coarse cell is attached to the parent set and all the new cells become the elements of this set as illustrated in Fig. 11. To make the set unique, we name the set by attaching the child number to the parent set name. The coarsening can be performed only on the leaf set. The coarsening for the cells follows these steps:

- For the cells that belong to the leaf set, we search for the node that is shared by all the cells. This node is connected by edges to the future hanging nodes of the cell, which we collect.
- We unite the cells into single coarse cell.
- We connect the coarse cell to the parent of the leaf set.
- We add the references of all the hanging nodes to the cell.

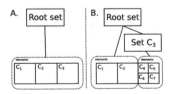

Fig. 11. Original unsplit mesh of three cells (A). After splitting of one of the cells a new set is attached to the root set (B). The set remembers all the fine cells that formed original cell.

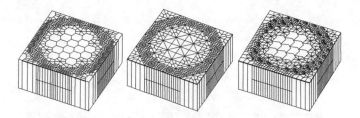

Fig. 12. Local refinement of three kinds of prismatic meshes, from left to right: hexagonal, triangular, non-convex squama. The middle cutaway of the grids is displayed.

If some face of the mesh has higher level of refinement than both adjacent cells, we have to coarsen the face. We collect all the faces shared by the two adjacent cells and unite them. To reconstruct the references to hanging nodes, we first find the node shared by all faces and use their connections to hanging nodes over edges. At last if some edge has higher level of refinement than all the adjacent faces, we unite the two edges shared by these faces. On a single sweep over the mesh we do not refine or coarsen by more than one level. As a result, we get the general mesh refinement method, the only requirement for the mesh is the star-shapeness of its elements. The application of the method to the three types of general grids is illustrated in Fig. 12.

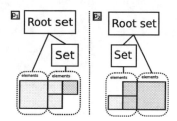

Fig. 13. A single cell, required for coarsening step, is missing on each of the processors. The situation requires synchronization of the elements of the sets.

In parallel implementation the following issues are worth mentioning:

- All the indicators for splitting and coarsening of elements should be synchronized to maintain geometric consistency of the distributed mesh, *i.e.* an edge should be simultaneously split by every processor.
- The references to hanging nodes and parent sets of cells should be synchronized between processors.
- We may encounter the situation that some cells to be coarsened, are missing on some processors, see Fig. 13. Thus, before coarsening, all the elements of the set are requested to be sent to the same processors the set belongs to.
- After refinement and coarsening we have to maintain load balancing and a number of ghost layers, requested by user.

The procedures described in previous sections allow us to address all these issues.

7 Numerical Tests

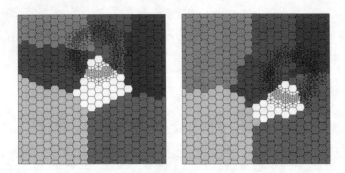

Fig. 14. Parallel mesh adaptation of $20 \times 20 \times 1$ hexagonal mesh, distributed between 8 processors, at steps $k = 1$ (left) and $k = 8$ (right).

For the numerical test we use a single layer hexagonal prismatic mesh of the unit cube $\Omega = [0,1]^3$, the mesh is adapted by two level refinement in a ring whose parameters are given by:

$$
\begin{aligned}
x &= \frac{1}{2} + \frac{1}{4}\sin\left(\frac{k\pi}{20}\right), \\
y &= \frac{1}{2} + \frac{1}{4}\sin\left(\frac{k\pi}{20}\right),
\end{aligned} \tag{1}
$$
$$
0.125 < \sqrt{(x_c - x)^2 + (y_c - y)^2} < 0.175,
$$

here (x_c, y_c) is the center of a cell to be refined and k is the step number. The application of the adaptive refinement method to the original $20 \times 20 \times 1$ hexagonal prismatic grid at $k = 1$ and $k = 8$ is illustrated in Fig. 14. During refinement the cells are split in z direction as well.

Table 1. Performance on different numbers of processors.

Processors	1	12	24	48	96
Refinement, s	699.409	319.795	243.311	152.678	120.228
Coarsening, s	1034.540	325.289	242.216	144.145	111.534
Balancing, s	0.000	47.404	40.089	29.773	28.001
Total, s	1734.661	692.512	525.647	326.646	259.852

For the test we use $120 \times 120 \times k$ hexagonal grid with the maximum $k = 80$ which corresponds to two revolutions of the center of refinement ring. During the step more than half ($\approx 77\%$) of the mesh elements are changed. The initial number of hexagonal prisms in the mesh is 14580. On refinement the number of cells of the mesh gets up to ≈ 115000 and on coarsening gets down to ≈ 83000. This indicates that ≈ 64000 cells are changed during single step. The results of the test on INM RAS cluster [12] are illustrated in Table 1. Note, that the refinement and coarsening work is not distributed equally between processors, thus the method demonstrates reduced scalability.

8   Conclusion

This work presents the new functionality of the open-source platform INMOST for parallel mathematical modelling. The platform allows the user to greatly facilitate programming of complex scenarios of mesh modification in parallel. Certain parts of the INMOST platform are still under active development. In the future we plan to advance the multiphysics tools for the solution of non-linear systems of equations and abstractions for seamless modular integration of independent physical models. One of the important tools required for multiphysics modelling is reinterpolation of physical fields which enables one to take full advantage of mesh adaptation and modification routines of the present work. A big effort should be also made to improve the balancing with the K-means clustering algorithm and optimization of the mesh adaptation routines.

Acknowledgment. The author would like to thank the Lomonosov Moscow State University student Andrey Burachkovsky for the help with implementation of some algorithms. This work was supported by the Russian Science Foundation grant 18-11-00111.

References

1. Bagaev, D.V., Burachkovski, A.I., Danilov, A.A., Konshin, I.N., Terekhov, K.M.: Development of INMOST software platform: dynamic grids, linear solvers and automatic differentiation. In: Proceedings of the International Conference on Russian Supercomputing Days, 26–27 September 2016, Moscow, Russia. Moscow State University, Moscow, pp. 543–555 (2016). (in Russian)
2. Danilov, A.A., Terekhov, K.M., Konshin, I.N., Vassilevski, Y.V.: Parallel software platform INMOST: a framework for numerical modeling. Supercomput. Front. Innovations **2**(4), 55–66 (2015)
3. Flemisch, B., et al.: DuMux: DUNE for multi-phase, component, scale, physics,... flow and transport in porous media. Adv. Water Res. **34**(9), 1102–1112 (2011)
4. Garimella, R.V.: MSTK-a flexible infrastructure library for developing mesh based applications. In: IMR, pp. 213–220 (2004)
5. Hartigan, J.A., Manchek, A.W.: Algorithm AS 136: a K-means clustering algorithm. J. Roy. Stat. Soc. Ser. C (Appl. Stat.) **28**(1), 100–108 (1979)
6. Tautges, T.J.: MOAB-SD: integrated structured and unstructured mesh representation. Eng. Comput. **20**(3), 286–293 (2004)

7. Terekhov, K.M.: Application of unstructured octree grid to the solution of filtration and hydrodynamics problems, Ph.D. Thesis, INM RAS (2013). (in Russian)

8. Terekhov, K., Vassilevski, Y.: INMOST parallel platform for mathematical modeling and applications. In: Voevodin, V., Sobolev, S. (eds.) RuSCDays 2018. CCIS, vol. 965, pp. 230–241. Springer, Cham (2019). https://doi.org/10.1007/978-3-030-05807-4_20

9. Terekhov, K., Vassilevski, Y.: Mesh modification and adaptation within INMOST programming platform. In: Garanzha, V.A., Kamenski, L., Si, H. (eds.) Numerical Geometry, Grid Generation and Scientific Computing. LNCSE, vol. 131, pp. 243–255. Springer, Cham (2019). https://doi.org/10.1007/978-3-030-23436-2_18

10. Vassilevski, Y.V., Konshin, I.N., Kopytov, G.V., Terekhov, K.M.: INMOST - programming platform and graphical environment for development of parallel numerical models on general grids. Moscow University Press, p. 144 (2013). (in Russian)

11. Distributed and Unified Numerics Environment. https://dune-project.org/. Accessed 10 Mar 2019

12. INM RAS cluster. http://cluster2.inm.ras.ru/. Accessed 15 Apr 2018

13. INMOST - a toolkit for distributed mathematical modeling. http://www.inmost.org/. Accessed 10 Mar 2019

14. OpenFOAM is the free, open source CFD software. http://www.openfoam.com/. Accessed 10 Mar 2019

15. Trilinos - platform for the solution of large-scale, complex multi-physics engineering and scientific problems. http://trilinos.org/. Accessed 10 Mar 2019

Parallel Implementation of Coupled Wave and Bottom Deposit Transportation Models to Simulate Surface Pollution Areas

Alexander Sukhinov[1], Alexander Chistyakov[1], Elena Protsenko[2],
Valentina Sidoryakina[2], and Sofya Protsenko[1(✉)]

[1] Don State Technical University, Rostov-on-Don, Russia
sukhinov@gmail.com, cheese_05@mail.ru, rab55555@rambler.ru
[2] Chekhov Taganrog Institute Taganrog branch of Rostov State University
of Economics (RSUE), Taganrog, Russia
eapros@rambler.ru, cvv9@mail.ru

Abstract. The requirements for models designed for calculating the volumes and areas of the contaminated sediment zones determine the quality of model calculations, which should take into account different-scale turbulence, sedimentation of suspensions, adhesion conditions for suspended particles at the water-bottom interface, jet effects, salvo discharge of soil. Estimation of the spatial distribution of concentrations of pollutants and the size of their areas of impact more accurately. This paper describes an improved software package that takes into account dynamic changes in the computational domain due to wave processes, jet effects, and multicomponent impurities. Dynamic rebuilding occurs not only due to rebuilding of the bottom, but also due to sedimentation of suspensions. The model has been developed for calculating suspended pollution zones in the presence of wave processes.

Keywords: Mlti-scale turbulence · Jet effects · Multicomponent impurities · Spatial distribution of pollutant concentrations

1 Introduction

According to the requirements for models designed to calculate the volumes and areas of contaminated suspension areas, the following processes and conditions should be taken into account in such models to adequately assess the scale and intensity of impacts on the aquatic environment:

- multi-scale turbulence, which determine the mixing parameters for different phases of the process;
- the speed of the explosion, for an adequate description of the transport suspension, a three-dimensional model is used, including the described characteristics of the explosion, the deposition rate of each of the components is calculated based on the Stokes law or from experimental data;

V. Voevodin and S. Sobolev (Eds.): RuSCDays 2019, CCIS 1129, pp. 327–338, 2019.
https://doi.org/10.1007/978-3-030-36592-9_27

- conditions of adhesion of suspended particles at the "water-bottom" boundary, sediments on the bottom surface are described in boundary conditions on the lower surface of the model of transport of pollutants;
- jet effects, including accelerated initial immersion of a "heavy" jet or salvo discharge of soil.

The development of modern mathematical models of hydrophysics, which should take into account the factors that affect the state of coastal systems when water is polluted one of the most pressing issues. The problem arises of solving systems of high-dimensional linear algebraic equations with ill-conditioned operators when solving problems of pollutant transport in coastal systems. They use direct (exact) and iterative methods to find an approximate solution of systems of linear algebraic equations. It is necessary to distinguish alternately-triangular method in the field of two-layer iterative methods among the most effective. In [1], this method, in the case of a non-self-adjoint operator (with an asymmetric matrix), was applied to solve problems of hydrodynamics.

2   Statement of Wave Hydrodynamics Problem

The initial equations of hydrodynamics of shallow water bodies are [2–4]:

- the Reynolds's equations:

$$u'_t + uu'_x + vu'_y + wu'_z = -\frac{1}{\rho}p'_x + (\mu u'_x)'_x + (\mu u'_y)'_y + (\nu u'_z)'_z,$$

$$v'_t + uv'_x + vv'_y + wv'_z = -\frac{1}{\rho}p'_y + (\mu v'_x)'_x + (\mu v'_y)'_y + (\nu v'_z)'_z, \tag{1}$$

$$w'_t + uw'_x + vw'_y + ww'_z = -\frac{1}{\rho}p'_z + (\mu w'_x)'_x + (\mu w'_y)'_y + (\nu w'_z)'_z + g,$$

- the equation of continuity in the case of variable density:

$$\rho'_t + (\rho u)'_x + (\rho v)'_y + (\rho w)'_z = 0, \tag{2}$$

where $\mathbf{V} = \{u, v, w\}$ are the components of the velocity vector, p is the pressure, ρ is the density, μ, ν are the horizontal and vertical components of the coefficient of turbulent exchange, g is the acceleration of gravity.

The system of Eqs. (1)–(2) is considered under the following boundary conditions:

- at the entrance $\mathbf{V} = \mathbf{V}_0$, $P'_n = 0$,
- the bottom border $\rho\mu\left(\mathbf{V}_\tau\right)'_n = -\tau$, $\mathbf{V}_n = 0$, $P'_n = 0$,
- the lateral border $\left(\mathbf{V}_\tau\right)'_n = 0$, $\mathbf{V}_n = 0$, $P'_n = 0$,
- the upper limit $\rho\mu\left(\mathbf{V}_\tau\right)'_n = -\tau$, $w = -\omega - P'_t/\rho g$, $P'_n = 0$,

where ω is mass evaporation rate of the liquid, which is equal to mass evaporated from free surface of unit area in percent, $\mathbf{V}_n$, $\mathbf{V}_\tau$ is the normal and tangential component of the speed of rotation, $\boldsymbol{\tau} = \{\tau_x, \tau_y, \tau_z\}$ is the vector of tangential stress [5,6].

The components of the tangential stress for the free surface: $\boldsymbol{\tau} = \rho_a Cd_p \boldsymbol{w} \, |\boldsymbol{w}|$, where $\boldsymbol{w}$ is the vector of the wind speed relative to the water, ρ_a is the density of the atmosphere, Cd_p is the dimensionless coefficient, which depends on the wind speed, was considered in the range 0.0016–0.0032.

The components of the tangential stress for the bottom, taking into account the water motion, may be written as follows [7]:

$$\boldsymbol{\tau} = \rho Cd_b \, |\mathbf{V}| \, \mathbf{V}, Cd_b = gn^2/h^{1/3}, \tag{3}$$

where $n = 0,04$ is the group coefficient of roughness in Manning's formula, 0,025 − 0.2; $h = H + \eta$ is the total depth of the water area, [m]; H is the depth at the unperturbed surface of the reservoir, [m]; η is the elevation of the free surface relative to the geoid (sea level), [m].

The approximation considered below makes it possible to build on the basis of the measured velocity pulsations the coefficient of vertical turbulent exchange, inhomogeneous in depth [5]:

$$\nu = C_s^2 \Delta^2 \frac{1}{2} \sqrt{\left(\frac{\partial \overline{U}}{\partial z}\right)^2 + \left(\frac{\partial \overline{V}}{\partial z}\right)^2} \tag{4}$$

where $\overline{U}, \overline{V}$ are the time-averaged pulsations of the horizontal velocity components, Δ is the characteristic scale of the grid, and C_s is Smagorinsky dimensionless empirical constant whose value is usually determined on the basis of calculating the decay process of homogeneous isotropic turbulence.

3 Discrete Model of Shallow Water Reservoirs Hydrodynamics

The computational domain inscribed in a parallelepiped. For the numerical implementation of the discrete mathematical model of the hydrodynamic problem posed, a uniform grid is introduced:

$$\bar{w}_h = \{t^n = n\tau, \; x_i = ih_x, \; y_j = jh_y, \; z_k = kh_z; \; n = \overline{0..N_t}, \; i = \overline{0..N_x},$$

$$j = \overline{0..N_y}, \; k = \overline{0..N_z}; \; N_t\tau = T, \; N_x h_x = L_x, \; N_y h_y = L_y, \; N_z h_z = L_z\},$$

where τ is the time step, h_x, h_y h_z are space steps, N_t is the number of time layers, T is the upper bound on the time coordinate, N_x, N_y N_z is the number of nodes by spatial coordinates, L_x, L_y L_z are boundaries along the parallelepiped in the direction of the axes Ox, Oy and Oz accordingly.

To solve the hydrodynamic problem, we used the method of correction to pressure. The variant of this method in the case of a variable density will take the form [8,9]:

$$\frac{\tilde{u} - u}{\tau} + u\bar{u}'_x + v\bar{u}'_y + w\bar{u}'_z = \left(\mu\bar{u}'_x\right)'_x + \left(\mu\bar{u}'_y\right)'_y + \left(\nu\bar{u}'_z\right)'_z,$$

$$\frac{\tilde{v} - v}{\tau} + u\bar{v}'_x + v\bar{v}'_y + w\bar{v}'_z = \left(\mu\bar{v}'_x\right)'_x + \left(\mu\bar{v}'_y\right)'_y + \left(\nu\bar{v}'_z\right)'_z,$$

$$\frac{\tilde{w} - w}{\tau} + u\bar{w}'_x + v\bar{w}'_y + w\bar{w}'_z = \left(\mu\bar{w}'_x\right)'_x + \left(\mu\bar{w}'_y\right)'_y + \left(\nu\bar{w}'_z\right)'_z + g, \qquad (5)$$

$$\hat{p}''_{xx} + \hat{p}''_{yy} + \hat{p}''_{zz} = \frac{\hat{\rho} - \rho}{\tau^2} + \frac{\left(\hat{\rho}\tilde{u}\right)'_x}{\tau} + \frac{\left(\hat{\rho}\tilde{v}\right)'_y}{\tau} + \frac{\left(\hat{\rho}\tilde{w}\right)'_z}{\tau},$$

$$\frac{\hat{u} - \tilde{u}}{\tau} = -\frac{1}{\hat{\rho}}\hat{p}'_x, \quad \frac{\hat{v} - \tilde{v}}{\tau} = -\frac{1}{\hat{\rho}}\hat{p}'_y, \quad \frac{\hat{w} - \tilde{w}}{\tau} = -\frac{1}{\hat{\rho}}\hat{p}'_z,$$

where $\mathbf{V} = \{u, v, w\}$ are the components of the velocity vector, $\{\hat{u}, \hat{v}, \hat{w}\}$, $\{\tilde{u}, \tilde{v}, \tilde{w}\}$ are the components of the velocity vector fields on the new and intermediate time layers, respectively, $\bar{u} = (\tilde{u} + u)/2$, $\hat{\rho}$ and ρ is the distribution of the density of the aqueous medium on the new and previous time layers, respectively.

In the construction of discrete mathematical models of hydrodynamics, the fullness of the control cells was taken into account, which makes it possible to increase the real accuracy of the solution in the case of a complex geometry of the investigated region by improving the approximation of the boundary.

Through $o_{i,j,k}$ marked fullness of the cell (i, j, k) [10]. The degree of fullness of the cell is determined by the pressure of the liquid column inside this cell. If the average pressure at the nodes that belong to the vertices of the cell in question is greater than the pressure of the liquid column inside the cell, then the cell is considered to be full $(o_{i,j,k} = 1)$. In the general case, the fullness of the cells can be calculated by the following formula [8]:

$$o_{i,j,k} = \frac{p_{i,j,k} + p_{i-1,j,k} + p_{i,j-1,k} + p_{i-1,j-1,k}}{4\rho g h_z}. \qquad (6)$$

In the case of boundary conditions of the third kind $c'_n(x, t) = \alpha_n c + \beta_n$, the discrete analogues of the convective uc'_x and diffusion $\left(\mu c'_x\right)'_x$ transfer operators, obtained with the help of the integro-interpolation method, taking into account the partial fullness of the cells, can be written in the following form:

$$uc'_x \simeq (q_1)_i\, u_{i+1/2}\frac{c_{i+1} - c_i}{2h_x} + (q_2)_i\, u_{i-1/2}\frac{c_i - c_{i-1}}{2h_x},$$

$$\left(\mu c'_x\right)'_x \simeq (q_1)_i\, \mu_{i+1/2}\frac{c_{i+1} - c_i}{h_x^2} - (q_2)_i\, \mu_{i-1/2}\frac{c_i - c_{i-1}}{h_x^2} - \left|(q_1)_i - (q_2)_i\right| \mu_i\frac{\alpha_x c_i + \beta_x}{h_x}.$$

Discrete analogs of the system of Eqs. (5) are solved by an adaptive modified alternating-triangular method of variational type.

4 Continuous 3D Model of Diffusion-Convection-Aggregation of Suspensions

Suppose that there are R types of particles in the water volume $V = \{0 \leq x \leq L_x,\ 0 \leq y \leq L_y, 0 \leq z \leq L_z\}$, which at the point (x, y, z) and at the time t have a concentration $c_r = c_r(x, y, z, t)$, [mg/l]; t is the time variable, [s]; $r = 1, 2, \ldots, R$.

The system of equations describing the behavior of particles will look like this [9, 10]:

$$
\begin{cases}
\dfrac{\partial c_r}{\partial t} + \dfrac{\partial(u c_r)}{\partial x} + \dfrac{\partial(v c_r)}{\partial y} + \dfrac{\partial((w + w_{g,r}) c_r)}{\partial z} \\
\qquad\qquad = \mu \left(\dfrac{\partial^2 c_r}{\partial x^2} + \dfrac{\partial^2 c_r}{\partial y^2} \right) + \dfrac{\partial}{\partial z}\left(\nu \dfrac{\partial c_r}{\partial z} \right) + F_r, \\
F_1 = (\alpha_2 c_2 - \beta_1 c_1) + \Phi_1(x, y, z, t), \\
\ldots \\
F_r = (\beta_{r-1} c_{r-1} - \alpha_r c_r) + (\alpha_{r+1} c_{r+1} - \beta_r c_r) + \Phi_r(x, y, z, t), \\
\ldots \\
F_R = (\beta_{R-1} c_{R-1} - \alpha_R c_R) + \Phi_R(x, y, z, t), \quad r = 2, \ldots, R-1,
\end{cases}
\tag{7}
$$

where u, v, w are the components of the velocity vector $\boldsymbol{U}$ of the fluid, [m/s]; $w_{g,r}$ is the hydraulic size or the rate of deposition of particles of the r-th type, [m/s]; μ, η are the coefficients of horizontal and vertical diffusion of particles of the r-th type, [m^2/s]; α_r, β_r are the particle conversion rates of the r-th type into $(r-1)$-th and $(r+1)$-th type, $\alpha_r \geq 0$, $\beta_r \geq 0$ [m/s]; Φ_r is the power of sources of particles of the r-th type, [mg/l s].

Add to the system (7) the initial and boundary conditions (assuming that the deposition of particles on the bottom is irreversible):

– initial conditions at time $t = 0$

$$
\begin{aligned}
c_1(x, y, z, 0) &\equiv c_{10}(x, y, z), \ \ldots, \ c_r(x, y, z, 0) \equiv c_{r0}(x, y, z), \ \ldots, \\
c_R(x, y, z, 0) &\equiv c_{R0}(x, y, z), \quad r = 2, \ldots, R-1;
\end{aligned}
\tag{8}
$$

– boundary conditions on the cylindrical (lateral) boundary of the region S cylinder C_T

$$
\frac{\partial c_1}{\partial n} = \ldots = \frac{\partial c_r}{\partial n} = \ldots = \frac{\partial c_R}{\partial n} = 0, \quad \text{if } (\boldsymbol{U}_\Gamma, \boldsymbol{n}) \leq 0,
\tag{9}
$$

$$
\frac{\partial c_1}{\partial n} = -\frac{u_\Gamma}{\mu} c_1, \ \ldots, \ \frac{\partial c_r}{\partial n} = -\frac{u_\Gamma}{\mu} c_r, \ \ldots, \ \frac{\partial c_R}{\partial n} = -\frac{u_\Gamma}{\mu} c_R, \text{ if } (\boldsymbol{U}_\Gamma, \boldsymbol{n}) \geq 0,
\tag{10}
$$

where $\boldsymbol{n}$ is the outer normal to the boundary of the domain S, $\boldsymbol{U}_\Gamma$ is the velocity vector of the fluid at the boundary S, u_Γ is the velocity vector projection $\boldsymbol{U}_\Gamma$ on the direction of the normal $\boldsymbol{n}$ on the border of the region S;

– boundary conditions on the water surface

$$
\frac{\partial c_1}{\partial z} = \cdots = \frac{\partial c_r}{\partial z} = \cdots = \frac{\partial c_R}{\partial z} = 0;
\tag{11}
$$

– boundary conditions at the bottom [9]

$$
\frac{\partial c_1}{\partial n} = -\frac{w_{g,1}}{\nu} c_1, \ \ldots, \ \frac{\partial c_r}{\partial n} = -\frac{w_{g,r}}{\nu} c_r, \ \ldots, \ \frac{\partial c_R}{\partial n} = -\frac{w_{g,R}}{\nu} c_R.
\tag{12}
$$

5   2D Model of Sediment Transport

The reformation of the coastal zone of the water areas due to the movement of water and solid particles will be described for the case when the sediment particles move in one direction (the side of the shore). In the work, the assumption is made that the sediments move only in one direction – the resultant transfer. The motion of the particles in the direction opposite to the direction of the resulting transfer will be neglected.

Let the sediments that participate in sediment transport consist Q of fractions, each of which has a relative fraction V_q in the total volume and density ρ_q, $q = 1, 2, \ldots, Q$.

The equation of sediment transport, which generalizes the known equation (see [1, 13, 14]) and takes into account the complex granulometric composition of the bottom material, will be written in the form

$$
(1 - \bar{\varepsilon}) \frac{\partial H}{\partial t} + \operatorname{div} \left(\sum_{q=1}^{Q} V_q k_q \boldsymbol{\tau}_b \right) = \operatorname{div} \left(\sum_{q=1}^{Q} V_q k_q \frac{\tau_{bc,q}}{\sin \varphi_0} \operatorname{grad} H \right)
$$
$$
+ \sum_{r=1}^{R} \frac{w_{g,r}}{\rho_r^*} c_r,
$$
(13)

where $\bar{\varepsilon} = \sum_{q=1}^{Q} V_q \varepsilon_q$ is the averaged over fractions porosity of bottom materials; ε_q is the porosity of q-type sediment fraction; $\boldsymbol{\tau}_b$ is the vector of tangential stress sat the water bottom; $\tau_{bc,q}$ is the critical value of the tangential stress for the q-th fraction; $\tau_{bc,q} = a_q \sin \varphi_0$, φ_0 is an angle of repose of soil in the water; ρ_r^* is density of particles of suspended matter of the r-th type, which move in accordance with Eqs. (7); $k_q = k_q(H, x, y, t)$ is the nonlinear coefficient, determined by the relation:

$$
k_q \equiv \frac{A \bar{\omega} d_q}{((\rho_q - \rho_0) g d_q)^{\beta}} \left| \boldsymbol{\tau}_b - \frac{\tau_{bc,q}}{\sin \varphi_0} \operatorname{grad} H \right|^{\beta - 1},
$$
(14)

(ρ_q, d_q are the density and characteristic particle size of the q-th fraction, respectively; ρ_0 is the density of the aquatic environment; g is the gravity acceleration; $\bar{\omega}$ is the averaged wave frequency; A and β are dimensionless constants).

We supplement Eq. (13) by the initial condition assuming that the function of the initial conditions belongs to the corresponding class of smoothness:

$$
H(x, y, 0) = H_0(x, y).
$$
(15)

Let us formulate the conditions on the boundary of the region, starting from physical considerations:

$$
H_n' = 0.
$$
(16)

The mathematical models of the transport of suspensions and sediments described above are also supplemented by models of the motion of the aquatic environment and turbulence, the equations of which are solved in the hydrodynamic block by the method of correction to pressure.

6   Parallel Version of Algorithm for Solving Grid Equations

Consider the parallel algorithm for calculating the correction vector [15]:

$$(D + \omega_m R_1)D^{-1}(D + \omega_m R_2)w^m = r^m,$$

where R_1 is the lower-triangular matrix, and R_2 is the upper-triangular matrix. To this end, we solve successively the systems:

$$(D + \omega_m R_1)y^m = r^m, \quad (D + \omega_m R_2)w^m = Dy^m.$$

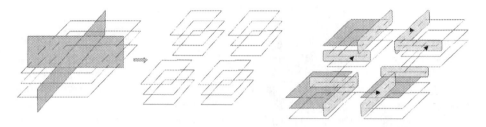

Fig. 1. The scheme for calculating the vector y^m

First, the vector y^m is calculated, and the calculation starts in the lower left corner. Then the calculation of the correction vector w^m begins from the upper right corner. Figure 1 shows the calculation of the vector y^m.

The results of calculating the acceleration and efficiency, depending on the number of processors for the parallel variant of the adaptive alternating-triangular method, are given in the Table 1.

Table 1. The dependence of acceleration and efficiency on the number of processors.

Number of processors	Time, s.	Acceleration	Efficiency
1	7,490639	1	1
2	4,151767	1,804	0,902
4	2,549591	2,938	0,734
8	1,450203	5,165	0,646
16	0,882420	8,489	0,531
32	0,458085	16,351	0,511
64	0,265781	28,192	0,44
128	0,171535	43,668	0,341

The decomposition techniques of grid areas for labor-consuming problems of diffusion convection considering architecture and parameters of a multiprocessor computer system at parallel implementation are used [16, 17]. Maximum capacity of a multiprocessor computer system is 18.8 TFLOPS. As computing nodes 128 same 16-core ProLiant BL685c HP Blade servers are used, each of which is equipped with four Opteron 8356 2.3 GHz AMD quad-core processors and random access memory of 32 GB.

The Table 1 shows that the algorithm of the alternating-triangular iterative method [18] and its parallel implementation on the basis of decomposition in two spatial directions can be effectively applied to solve hydrodynamic problems for a sufficiently large number of calculators ($p \leq 128$).

7 Results of Numerical Experiments

On the basis of full-scale data, a three-dimensional model of wave hydrody-namic processes has been developed that describes the motion of an aquatic environment taking into account wave propagation towards the shore. A mod-ern software package adapted for simulation of hydrodynamic wave processes is developed, the field of application of which is the construction of the velocity and pressure field of the aquatic environment, and the evaluation of the hydro-dynamic impact on the shore in the presence of surface waves. Based on the developed complex of programs, numerical simulation of hydrodynamic wave processes in the coastal zone of a shallow water body was carried out.

The practical significance of numerical algorithms and the complex of pro-grams that realize them consists in the possibility of their application in the study of hydrophysical processes in coastal water systems, as well as in the con-struction of the velocity and pressure field of the aquatic environment, and the evaluation of the hydrodynamic impact on the shore in the presence of surface waves [19].

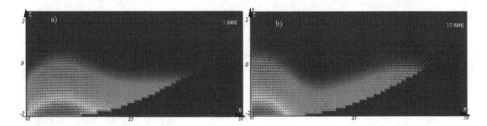

Fig. 2. The field of the velocity vector of the aquatic environment (XOZ plane cut)

The constructed program complex allows you to specify the shape and inten-sity of the oscillation source, as well as the geometry of the bottom of the reser-voir. The results of numerical experiments on the simulation of the propagation of wave hydrodynamic processes when the wave leaves the shore, taking into account the geometries of the bottom of the object located in the liquid and bottom of the reservoir, are shown in Fig. 3. As an example of the practical use of a problem-oriented program complex, the problem of calculating the velocity and pressure fields is solved. The selected modeling site measures 50 by 50 m and a depth of 2 m, the peak point rises above sea level by 2 m. The disturbance source is given at some distance from the shore line. At the initial time, the liquid is at rest. To solve this problem, a grid of $100 \times 100 \times 40$ dimensions was used, the time step is 0.01 s.

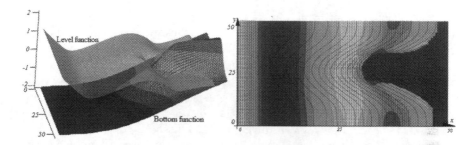

Fig. 3. Level and bottom elevation function

Figure 3 shows the field of velocity vector of the aquatic environment when the wave approaching the shore, while the function of elevating the level dynamically changes, zones of flooding and shallowing are formed.

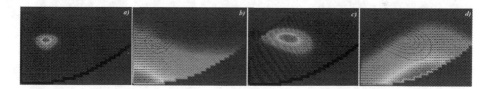

Fig. 4. Cross-section by the XOZ plane, corresponding through $y = ly/2$, suspension concentration after 2 (a, b) and 5 (c, d) sec after the moment of ejection (a, c show the concentration field, b, d show the pressure field)

Consider the distribution of suspended solids in the aquatic environment. Suspension occurs at time zero. The source of suspension is located 5 m from the source of oscillations along Ox (the left border of the region), in the center of the computational region along the Oy and 20 cm below the liquid level along the Oz. The fluid at the initial moment of time was at rest [20]. The density of the suspension coincides with the density of the liquid. Figure 4 shows the location of the suspension 2 and 5 s after the moment of ejection.

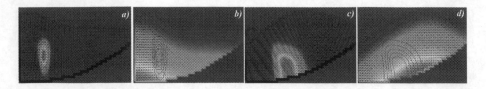

Fig. 5. Cross-section by the XOZ plane, corresponding through y = ly/2, suspension concentration after 2 (a, b) and 5 (c, d) sec after the moment of ejection (a, c show the concentration field, b, d show the pressure field)

Computational experiments simulate the propagation of suspended matter in an aqueous medium in the presence of surface waves, with a suspended density equal to the density of an aqueous medium, and study the effect of waves on the transfer of momentum in horizontal and vertical directions. Figure 4 shows the results of calculations of modeling the distribution of suspension with a density of 2700 kg/m^3. The location of the suspension source coincides with the previous case. Figure 5 shows the simulation of the "jet effect", accelerated by initial immersion of a "heavy" jet during a salvo discharge of soil occurs.

The initial data of the simulation for suspension transport modeling were: the maximum depth of the reservoir is 2 m; at the dump with dimensions 1 × 1 m the loading volume is 0.289 m^3 (Fig. 6a); at the dump with dimensions of 3.5 × 3.5 m, the loading volume is 5.729 m^3 (Fig. 6b); the deposition rate was in the range from 1 to 10 mm/s; soil density 2700 kg/m^3.

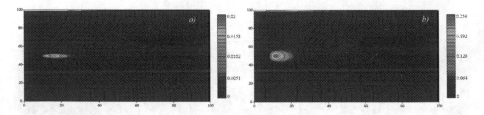

Fig. 6. Change of bottom relief function: (a) the dump with dimensions 1 × 1 m, (b) the dump with dimensions 3.5 × 3.5 m

The results of the numerical experiment allow us to analyze the dynamics of changes in the bottom geometry, the formation of structures and sediments, the transfer of suspensions in the water area, as well as the level of water pollution. This mathematical model and the developed problem-oriented set of programs make it possible to predict the appearance of sea ridges and streamers, their growth and transformation, to predict a change in the concentration field in the event of an emission from a source, to predict the siltation of approaching canals, and the record of hydraulic structures and structures.

8   Conclusion

The paper describes an improved software package that takes into account the effect of wave processes on dynamic changes in the computational domain not only due to the bottom rebuilding, but also due to sedimentation of suspensions, jet effects and multicomponent impurities, taking into account the requirements for models for calculating the volumes and areas of contaminated sediment and other impurities, to adequately assess the scale and intensity of impacts on the aquatic environment and its inhabitants. The model has been developed for calculating suspended pollution zones in the presence of wave processes. The following processes and conditions are taken into account: multi-scale turbulence, which determines the mixing parameters for different phases of the process; sedimentation of suspensions; a three-dimensional model was used to adequately describe suspension transport; adhesion conditions for suspended particles at the water-bottom interface; jet effects, including such an important effect as an accelerated initial immersion of a "heavy" jet or volley dumping of soil.

Acknowledgments. This work was supported by Russian Foundation for Basic Research, Project No. 19-07-00623.

References

1. Sukhinov, A.I., Chistyakov, A.E.: Adaptive modified alternating triangular iterative method for solving grid equations with a non-self-adjoint operator. Math. Models Comput. Simul. **4**(4), 398–409 (2012). https://doi.org/10.1134/S2070048212040084
2. Sukhinov, A.I., Sukhinov, A.A.: 3D model of diffusion-advection-aggregation suspensions in water basins and its parallel realization. In: Parallel Computational Fluid Dynamics, Mutidisciplinary Applications, Proceedings of Parallel CFD 2004 Conference, Las Palmas de Gran Canaria, Spain, pp. 223–230. Elsevier, Amsterdam (2005). https://doi.org/10.1016/B978-044452024-1/50029-4
3. Gushchin, V.A., Kostomarov, A.V., Matyushin, P.V., Pavlyukova, E.R.: Direct numerical simulation of the transi tional separated fluid flows around a sphere and a circular cylinder. J. Wind Eng. Ind. Aerodyn. **90**(4–5), 341–358 (2002). https://doi.org/10.1016/S0167-6105(01)00196-9
4. Sukhinov, A.I., Sukhinov, A.A.: Reconstruction of 2001 ecological disaster in the Azov Sea on the basis of precise hydrophysics models. In: Parallel Computational Fluid Dynamics, Multidisciplinary Applications, Proceedings of Parallel CFD 2004 Conference, Las Palmas de Gran Canaria, Spain, pp. 231–238. Elsevier, Amsterdam (2005). https://doi.org/10.1016/B978-044452024-1/50030-0
5. Gushchin, V.A., Kostomarov, A.V., Matyushin, P.V.: 3D visualization of the separated fluid flows. Visualization **7**(2), 143–150 (2004). https://doi.org/10.1007/BF03181587
6. Alekseenko, E., Roux, B., Sukhinov, A., Kotarba, R., Fougere, D.: Coastal hydrodynamics in a windy lagoon. Nonlinear Process. Geophys. **20**(2), 189–198 (2013). https://doi.org/10.1016/j.compfluid.2013.02.003

7. Alekseenko, E., Roux, B., Sukhinov, A., Kotarba, R., Fougere, D.: Nonlinear hydrodynamics in a mediterranean lagoon. Comput. Math. Math. Phys. **57**(6), 978–994 (2017). https://doi.org/10.5194/npg-20-189-2013

8. Sukhinov, A.I., Chistyakov, A.E., Alekseenko, E.V.: Numerical realization of the three-dimensional model of hydrodynamics for shallow water basins on a high-performance system. Mathe. Models Comput. Simul. **3**(5), 562–574 (2011). https://doi.org/10.1134/S2070048211050115

9. Belotserkovskii, O.M., Gushchin, V.A., Shchennikov, V.V.: Decomposition method applied to the solution of problems of viscous incompressible fluid dynamics. Comput. Math. Math. Phys. **15**, 197–207 (1975)

10. Sukhinov, A.I., Chistyakov, A.E., Protsenko, E.A.: Mathematical modeling of sediment transport in the coastal zone of shallow reservoirs. Math. Models Comput. Simul. **6**(4), 351–363 (2014). https://doi.org/10.1134/S2070048214040097

11. Sidoryakina, V.V., Sukhinov, A.I.: Well-posedness analysis and numerical implementation of a linearized two-dimensional bottom sediment transport problem. Comput. Math. Math. Phys. **57**(6), 978–994 (2017). https://doi.org/10.7868/S0044466917060138

12. Favorskaya, A.V., Petrov, I.B.: Numerical modeling of dynamic wave effects in rock masses. Doklady Math. **95**(3), 287–290 (2017). https://doi.org/10.1134/S1064562417030139

13. Kvasov, I.E., Leviant, V.B., Petrov, I.B.: Numerical study of wave propagation in porous media with the use of the grid-characteristic method. Comput. Math. Math. Phys. **56**(9), 1620–1630 (2016). https://doi.org/10.1134/S0965542516090116

14. Nikitina, A.V., et al.: Optimal control of sustainable development in the biological rehabilitation of the Azov Sea. Math. Models Comput. Simul. **9**(1), 101–107 (2017). https://doi.org/10.1134/S2070048217010112

15. Sukhinov, A., Chistyakov, A., Nikitina, A., Semenyakina, A., Korovin, I., Schaefer, G.: Modelling of oil spill spread. In: 5th International Conference on Informatics, Electronics and Vision, ICIEV 2016, 28 November 2016, pp. 1134–1139. https://doi.org/10.1109/ICIEV.2016.7760176

16. Chetverushkin, B.N., Shilnikov, E.V.: Software package for 3D viscous gas flow simulation on multiprocessor computer systems. Comput. Math. Math. Phys. **48**(2), 295–305 (2008). https://doi.org/10.1007/s11470-008-2012-4

17. Davydov, A.A., Chetverushkin, B.N., Shil'nikov, E.V.: Simulating flows of incompressible and weakly compressible fluids on multicore hybrid computer systems. Comput. Math. Math. Phys. **50**(12), 2157–2165 (2010). https://doi.org/10.1134/S096554251012016X

18. Sukhinov, A.I., Nikitina, A.V., Semenyakina, A.A., Chistyakov, A.E.: Complex of models, explicit regularized schemes of high-order of accuracy and applications for predictive modeling of after-math of emergency oil spill. In: CEUR Workshop Proceedings, vol. 1576, pp. 308–319 (2016)

19. Sukhinov, A., Chistyakov, A., Protsenko, S.: Three-dimensional mathematical model of wave propagation towards the shore. Commun. Comput. Inf. Sci. **910**, 322–335 (2018)

20. Sukhinov, A.I., Chistyakov, A.E., Sidoryakina, V.V.: Parallel solution of sediment and suspension transportation problems on the basis of explicit schemes. Commun. Comput. Inf. Sci. **910**, 322–335 (2018)

Recovery of the Permittivity
of an Anisotropic Inhomogeneous Body
in a Rectangular Waveguide

Medvedik Mikhail[✉], Moskaleva Marina, and Smirnov Yury

Penza State University, Penza, Russia
mmm@pnzgu.ru

Abstract. The main purpose of this paper is to study the mathematical model of the diffraction of the electromagnetic waves on the anisotropic inhomogeneous body located in a rectangular waveguide. The determination of the properties of the body placed in waveguide by measuring the electromagnetic field is an important direction in radio engineering. The direct problem of scattering the electromagnetic waves on an anisotropic inhomogeneous body placed in a waveguide is considered. This problem is reduced to solving an integrodifferential equation. We apply the Galerkin projection method for solving integrodifferential equation. The inverse problem of recovery of the permittivity of the inhomogeneous anisotropic body in a waveguide is formulated. The inverse problem is reduced to solving the first kind integral equation and the procedure of recalculating the permittivity through the polarization current. The numerical results are presented. We used a parallel algorithm.

Keywords: Boundary value problem · Inverse problem of diffraction · Permittivity tensor · Tensor Green's function · Integrodifferential equation

1 Introduction

The paper is devoted to determining the permittivity of a body, that has a composite structure, located in a waveguide using the two-step method.

Composite materials have a complex structure and are multicomponent. Substances with different types of components in various combinations form the material, the parameters of which are significantly different from the parameters of the substances forming it. We can change the parameters of the composite components to obtain a wide range of materials with a set of properties necessary for a specific problem in practice.

Due to its properties composite materials are widely used in various fields of science and technology. In this regard, it is relevant to determine the various parameters of the composites, such as permittivity and permeability. In certain cases, these parameters are extremely difficult to determine experimentally.

© Springer Nature Switzerland AG 2019
V. Voevodin and S. Sobolev (Eds.): RuSCDays 2019, CCIS 1129, pp. 339–349, 2019.
https://doi.org/10.1007/978-3-030-36592-9_28

Substances with different types of components in various form the different materials. The parameters of these materials can have significantly different from the parameters of the substances forming it. The desired parameters of composite materials can also be determined using mathematical modeling [1–5]. In such cases, the problem is solved by various numerical methods. Such methods are mainly based on solving hyperbolic systems of differential equations in the time domain using finite difference or finite element methods, with subsequent minimization of the corresponding functionals and Tikhonov regularization. Such approaches are described in [6, 7].

We solve the inverse boundary value problem to determine the tensor function of the permittivity of an inhomogeneous body located in a waveguide. We will consider the composite as the material with anisotropic properties. These changes will affect on the course of the experiment. We assume that the body is non-magnetic. The same problem for determining permeability of the material is solved similarly. For this we use the symmetry of Maxwell's equations for the electric and magnetic fields. In this case, the permittivity of a material is considered to be equal to ε_0. Therefore, we will consider only the problem of determining the permittivity of the body.

It is important that there is no need to choose initial approximations that are required when applying iteration methods. This advantage makes it possible to consider the proposed method as very promising.

2   Direct Diffraction Problem

Let a body Q located in a rectangular waveguide $P = \{\, x : 0 < x_1 < a, 0 < x_2 < b, -\infty < x_3 < +\infty \}$. The body has a composite structure with piecewise smooth boundary ∂Q. We assume that the permeability of the body Q is constant μ_0 and the permittivity of the body is positive (3×3)–matrix (tensor) $\hat{\varepsilon}(x)$. Components of $\hat{\varepsilon}(x)$ are bounded functions in $\overline{Q}$ and $\hat{\varepsilon} \in L_\infty(Q)$, $\hat{\varepsilon}^{-1} \in L_\infty(Q)$ [8].

Let the field $\mathbf{E}, \mathbf{H}$ is induced by the electric current $\mathbf{j}_E^0 \in L_{2,loc}(P)$. We assume that field $\mathbf{E}, \mathbf{H}$ is a monochromatic electromagnetic one. Let us consider the diffraction problem field $\mathbf{E}, \mathbf{H}$ on the body Q.

We seek weak (generalized) solutions to Maxwell's equations

$$\operatorname{rot} \mathbf{H} = -i\omega\hat{\varepsilon}\mathbf{E} + \mathbf{j}_E^0, \ \operatorname{rot} \mathbf{E} = i\omega\mu_0\mathbf{H}, \tag{1}$$

where ω is circular frequency. In this case if u is a quite smooth vector field in P, we denote by $u_\nu|_{\partial P}$ and $u_\tau|_{\partial P}$ the normal and the tangential component of u on ∂P, respectively. The following generalized boundary conditions on ∂P are true. If $\operatorname{div} u \in L_2(P)$, then $u_\nu|_{\partial P} = 0$ means that

$$(u, \operatorname{grad} \nu) = -(\operatorname{div} u, \nu) \quad \forall \nu \in H^1(P),$$

where $H^1(P)$ is the Sobolev space. If $\operatorname{rot} u \in L_2(P)$, then $u_\tau|_{\partial P} = 0$ means that

$$(u, \operatorname{rot} w) = -(\operatorname{rot} u, w) \quad \forall w \in L_2(P) : \operatorname{rot} w \in L_2(P).$$

In the sense of the theory of traces for $u \in H^1(P)$ there exist boundary values in the space $H^{1/2}(\partial P)$. The normal vector is defined almost everywhere on ∂P. Therefore, we can consider the equalities of traces $u_\nu|_{\partial P} = 0$ and $u_\tau|_{\partial P} = 0$, which are equivalent to the corresponding equalities in the sense of definitions given above.

On the walls of the waveguide the field $\mathbf{E}, \mathbf{H}$ must satisfy the following boundary conditions:

$$\mathbf{E}_\tau|_{\partial P} = 0, \quad \mathbf{H}_\nu|_{\partial P} = 0. \tag{2}$$

If Maxwell equations are satisfied, then the second condition in (2) results from the first one, and it can be omitted. However, if the Maxwell operator induced by the left-hand side (1) is considered, both boundary conditions must be used.

The field $\mathbf{E}, \mathbf{H}$ obtained as solutions to (1) must satisfy the conditions at infinity. Let $-\triangle$ be the two-dimensional Laplace operator in the rectangle $\Pi = \{(x_1, x_2) : 0 < x_1 < a, 0 < x_2 < b\}$. We introduce the following notations: $\lambda_p^{(1)}, \Pi(x_1, x_2)$ and $\lambda_p^{(2)}, \psi(x_1, x_2)$ is the complete system of eigenvalues and orthogonal normalized in $L_2(\Pi)$ eigenfunctions of the above mentioned Laplace operator with Dirichlet and Neumann conditions at the boundary of Π, respectively. The fields $\mathbf{E}$ and $\mathbf{H}$ have following representations for $|x_3| > C$ with sufficiently large $C > 0$

$$\begin{pmatrix} \mathbf{E} \\ \mathbf{H} \end{pmatrix} = \begin{pmatrix} \mathbf{E^0} \\ \mathbf{H^0} \end{pmatrix} + \sum_p R_p^{(\pm)} \exp(i\gamma_p^{(1)}|x_3|) \begin{pmatrix} \lambda_p^{(1)} \Pi_p \mathbf{e_3} - i\gamma_p^{(1)} \nabla_2 \Pi_p \\ -i\omega\varepsilon_0 (\nabla_2 \Pi_p) \times \mathbf{e_3} \end{pmatrix}$$

$$+ \sum_p Q_p^{(\pm)} \exp(i\gamma_p^{(2)}|x_3|) \begin{pmatrix} i\omega\mu_0 (\nabla_2 \psi_p) \times \mathbf{e_3} \\ \lambda_p^{(2)} \psi_p \mathbf{e_3} - i\gamma_p^{(2)} \nabla_2 \psi_p \end{pmatrix}, \tag{3}$$

where $\gamma_p^{(j)} = \sqrt{k_0^2 - \lambda_p^{(j)}}$, $\operatorname{Im}\gamma_p^{(j)} \geq 0$, $k\gamma_p^{(j)} \geq 0$, $k_0^2 = \omega^2\varepsilon_0\mu_0$, k_0 is the wave number of a free space and $\nabla_2 \equiv \mathbf{e_1}\partial/\partial x_1 + \mathbf{e_2}\partial/\partial x_2$. For the coefficients of series (3), the following estimates

$$R_p^{(\pm)}, \; Q_p^{(\pm)} = O(p^m), \; p \to \infty \tag{4}$$

are valid, for certain $m \in N$. From the physical viewpoint, conditions (3) mean that the scattered field is a superposition of normal waves that radiate off the dielectric body [9]. Conditions (4) allow one termwise differentiation with respect to x_j arbitrary number of times.

We also assume that $\mathbf{E_0}, \mathbf{H_0}$ is the known field (the incident wave), which is a solution of the equations

$$\operatorname{rot}\mathbf{H_0} = -i\omega\varepsilon_0\mathbf{E_0}, \; \operatorname{rot}\mathbf{E_0} = i\omega\mu_0\mathbf{H_0}, \tag{5}$$

with boundary conditions

$$\mathbf{E}_\tau^0|_{\partial P} = 0, \quad \mathbf{H}_\nu^0|_{\partial P} = 0, \tag{6}$$

in the absence of Q, that is, $\hat{\varepsilon}(x) = \varepsilon_0\hat{I}, x \in P$, where $\hat{I}$ is the identity tensor.

Solutions **E**, **H** to (1) can be represented in an analytical form in terms of $\mathbf{j}_E^0$ using Green's tensor

$$\hat{G} = \begin{pmatrix} G_E^1 & 0 & 0 \\ 0 & G_E^2 & 0 \\ 0 & 0 & G_E^3 \end{pmatrix},$$

where

$$G_E^1 = \frac{2}{ab} \sum_{n=0}^{\infty} \sum_{m=1}^{\infty} \frac{e^{-\gamma_{nm}|x_3-y_3|}}{\gamma_{nm}(1+\delta_{0n})} \cos\frac{\pi n}{a}x_1 \sin\frac{\pi m}{b}x_2 \cos\frac{\pi n}{a}y_1 \sin\frac{\pi m}{a}y_2,$$

$$G_E^2 = \frac{2}{ab} \sum_{n=1}^{\infty} \sum_{m=0}^{\infty} \frac{e^{-\gamma_{nm}|x_3-y_3|}}{\gamma_{nm}(1+\delta_{0m})} \sin\frac{\pi n}{a}x_1 \cos\frac{\pi m}{b}x_1 \sin\frac{\pi n}{a}y_1 \cos\frac{\pi m}{b}y_2,$$

$$G_E^3 = \frac{2}{ab} \sum_{n=1}^{\infty} \sum_{m=1}^{\infty} \frac{e^{-\gamma_{nm}|x_3-y_3|}}{\gamma_{nm}} \sin\frac{\pi n}{a}x_1 \sin\frac{\pi m}{b}x_1 \sin\frac{\pi n}{a}y_1 \sin\frac{\pi m}{b}y_2.$$

Here

$$\gamma_{nm} = \sqrt{\left(\frac{\pi n}{a}\right)^2 + \left(\frac{\pi m}{b}\right)^2 - k_0^2},$$

the branch of the square root is chosen so that $\operatorname{Im}\gamma_{nm} \geq 0$ and $\operatorname{Re}\gamma_{nm} \geq 0$ if $\operatorname{Im}\gamma_{nm} = 0$. The problem (1)–(6) is reduced to the integro-differential equation [10] with respect to the field **E**:

$$\mathbf{E} = \mathbf{E}^0(x) + k_0^2 \int_Q \hat{G}_E(x,y) \left(\frac{\hat{\varepsilon}(y)}{\varepsilon_0} - \hat{I}\right) \mathbf{E}(y)dy$$

$$+ \operatorname{grad} \operatorname{div} \int_Q \hat{G}_E(x,y) \left(\frac{\hat{\varepsilon}(y)}{\varepsilon_0} - \hat{I}\right) \mathbf{E}(y)dy. \tag{7}$$

3   Inverse Diffraction Problem

The inverse problem consists in determining the permittivity $\hat{\varepsilon}(x)$ of the body Q in the waveguide P by measuring the scattered field outside the body. The scattered field is measured at the observation points (x_c), which are disposed in a surface S. The surface S is parallel to the face of the body and it is perpendicular to the axis Ox_3. The surface S is located at some distance d from the face of the body Q. An example of the location of the observation points is shown in Fig. 1, where the body which is a rectangular parallelepiped. We can obtain more accurate results in reconstructing of inhomogeneity locating observation points in several parallel surfaces. Thus the observation points should be located in a bounded volume of space. An example of this is shown in Fig. 2. The proposed method allows one to reconstruct the permittivity of a body of arbitrary form.

Let us discretize the problem. We assume that the body Q is contained in the parallelepiped Θ,

$$\Theta = \{\, x : a_1 < x_1 < a_2, b_1 < x_2 < b_2, c_1 < x_3 < c_2 \},$$

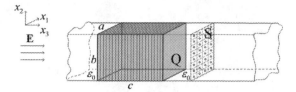

Fig. 1. An example of the location of observation points at the surface S inside the waveguide.

$$0 \le a_1 < a_2 \le a, 0 \le b_1 < b_2 \le b, c_1 < x_3 < c_2,$$

which is located in the waveguide, $Q \subset \Theta$. We choose a regular rectangular grid in Θ of the size $N_1 \times N_2 \times N_3$. The grid consists of parallelepipeds

$$\Theta_{klm} = \left\{ x : x_{1,k} < x_1 < x_{1,k+1}, \quad x_{2,l} < x_2 < x_{2,l+1}, \quad x_{3,m} < x_3 < x_{3,m+1} \right\}$$

with

$$x_{1,k} = a_1 + \frac{a_2 - a_1}{N_1}k, \quad x_{2,l} = b_1 + \frac{b_2 - b_1}{N_2}l, \quad x_{3,m} = c_1 + \frac{c_2 - c_1}{N_3}m,$$

where $k = 0, \ldots, N_1 - 1$, $l = 0, \ldots, N_2 - 1$, $m = 0, \ldots, N_3 - 1$.

We assume that the body Q consists of q subdomains Q_i: $Q = \bigcup_j Q_j$, $Q_i \cap Q_j = \varnothing$, $i \ne j$. In addition, the subdomains Q_i must consist of a union of elementary parallelepipeds (cells) of the grid $Q_j = \bigcup_\eta \Theta_\eta$, $\eta = 0, \ldots, N$, here N - general number of cells. Inside each cell, we assume that the permittivity is constant. The incident field is a plane wave (coming from infinity) of the form $\mathbf{E}^0(x) = \mathbf{e_2} A^{(+)} i\omega\mu_0 \frac{\pi}{a} \sin\left(\frac{\pi x_1}{a}\right) e^{-i\gamma_1^{(2)} x_3}$.

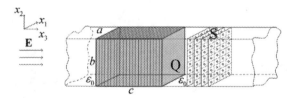

Fig. 2. An example of location of observation points x_c at several parallel surfaces S inside the waveguide.

We calculate the diffracted field at the observation points x_c. Thereto we solve the direct diffraction problem (1)–(6) and determine the field $\mathbf{E}(x)$ inside the body Q by solving Eq. (7) for $x \in Q$. Using the field calculated at the previous step, we compute the field $\mathbf{E}(x)$ at the observation points $x = x_c$ by the formula

$$\mathbf{E}(x_c) = \mathbf{E}^0(x_c) + k_0^2 \int\limits_Q \hat{G}_E(x_c, y) \left(\frac{\hat{\varepsilon}(y)}{\varepsilon_0} - \hat{I} \right) \mathbf{E}(y) dy$$

$$+ \text{grad div} \int\limits_Q \hat{G}_E(x_c, y) \left(\frac{\hat{\varepsilon}(y)}{\varepsilon_0} - \hat{I} \right) \mathbf{E}(y) dy, \quad x \notin Q, \quad (8)$$

where $E(y)$ is calculated before. Then we solve (7) with respect to the unknown function

$$\mathbf{J}(y) = \left(\frac{\hat{\varepsilon}(y)}{\varepsilon_0} - \hat{I} \right) \mathbf{E}(y).$$

Thus we have calculated the diffracted field at the observation points. This data will be used below. We note that the diffracted field can be measured experimentally. Now we pass to the second step in the solution, which is the determination of permittivity of the body Q. We solve the equation

$$\frac{\mathbf{J}(x_c)}{\left(\frac{\hat{\varepsilon}(y)}{\varepsilon_0} - \hat{I} \right)} - \mathbf{E}^0(x_c) = k_0^2 \int\limits_Q \hat{G}_E(x_c, y) \left(\frac{\hat{\varepsilon}(y)}{\varepsilon_0} - \hat{I} \right) \mathbf{E}(y) dy$$

$$+ \text{grad div} \int\limits_Q \hat{G}_E(x_c, y) \left(\frac{\hat{\varepsilon}(y)}{\varepsilon_0} - \hat{I} \right) \mathbf{E}(y) dy, \quad x \notin Q. \quad (9)$$

Equation (9) is an integral equation of the first kind. Solving this equation is the most complicated part in the permittivity reconstruction problem. In order to increase the efficiency, we apply the regularization or preconditioning method for solving problem of ill-conditionality of the matrix. From Eq. (9), we obtain $\mathbf{J}(x)$ and determine the permittivity of the body $\hat{\varepsilon}(y)$ in each cell, by solving the following equation

$$\frac{\mathbf{J}(x)}{\left(\frac{\hat{\varepsilon}(y)}{\varepsilon_0} - \hat{I} \right)} - k_0^2 \int\limits_Q \hat{G}_E(x, y) \mathbf{J}(y) dy - \text{grad div} \int\limits_Q \hat{G}_E(x, y) \mathbf{J}(y) dy = \mathbf{E}^0(x), \quad x \in Q,$$

with respect to the permittivity $\hat{\varepsilon}(y)$ of the body Q. As an example, we present a visualization of the results of determining the permittivity of the bodies Q_1, Q_2, Q_3 (Figs. 3, 4 and 5, respectively) in the waveguide. The bodies are rectangular parallelepipeds of sizes $a = 0.02$ m, $b = 0.01$ m, $c = 0.02$ m. The wave number outside the bodies is $k_0 = 250$ m^{-1}. The size of the computational grid is $16 \times 16 \times 16$. While solving the direct problem we determine the "initial" value of the permittivity $\hat{\varepsilon}$ of the bodies Q_1, Q_2, Q_3.

Figure 3 shows the reconstructed values of the real (Fig. 3(a)) and imaginary (Fig. 3(b)) parts of the permittivity of the body Q_1. The body consist of three parts. Each part has a unique permittivity and regular lattice structure. The noise is not introduced in the initial values of $\hat{\varepsilon}$. The maximum difference between absolute values of the initial and reconstructed permittivities is of order 10^{-9}.

Figure 4 shows the reconstructed values of the real (Fig. 4(a)) and imaginary (Fig. 4(b)) parts of the permittivity of the body Q_2. The composite Q_2 has a tubular structure. The noise is not introduced in the initial values of $\hat{\varepsilon}$. The maximum difference between absolute values of the initial and reconstructed permittivities is of order 10^{-9}.

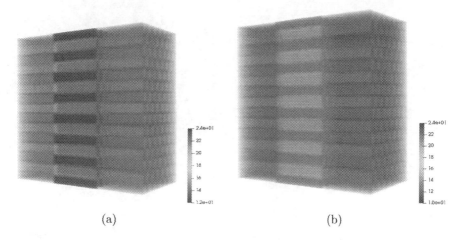

(a)   (b)

Fig. 3. The reconstructed values of the real and imaginary parts of the permittivity of Q_1.

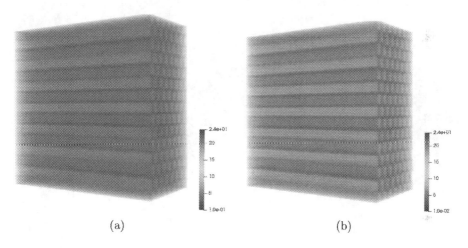

(a)   (b)

Fig. 4. The reconstructed values of the real and imaginary parts of the permittivity of Q_2.

Figure 5 shows the reconstructed values of the real (Fig. 5(a)) and imaginary (Fig. 5(b)) parts of the permittivity of the body Q_3. The composite body Q_3 has a layer-built structure. The noise is not introduced in the initial values of $\hat{\varepsilon}$. The maximum difference between absolute values of the initial and reconstructed permittivities is of order 10^{-9}.

Below we present one more example in which the permittivity is determined. The body Q_4 contains several inclusions with different permittivities. The body is a rectangular parallelepiped of sizes $a = 0.02$ m, $b = 0.01$ m, $c = 0.02$ m. The wave number outside the body is $k_0 = 250$ m^{-1}. The size of the computational grid is $16 \times 16 \times 16$. Solving the direct problem we determine the "inital" value of permittivity of Q_4, see Fig. 6.

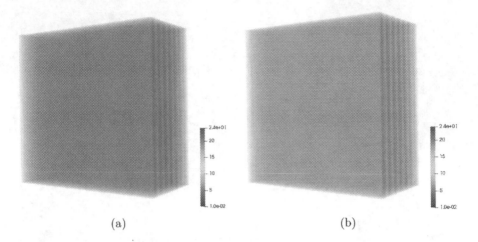

(a)   (b)

Fig. 5. The reconstructed values of the real and imaginary parts of the permittivity of Q_3.

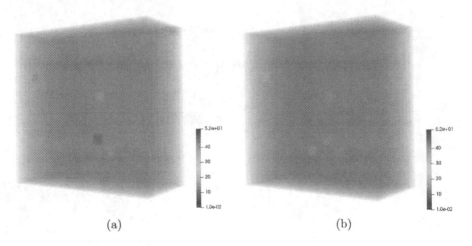

(a)   (b)

Fig. 6. The "inital" value of permittivity of Q_4.

Figure 7 shows the reconstructed values of the real (Fig. 7(a)) and imaginary (Fig. 7(b)) parts of the permittivity of the body Q_4. The problem was solved with noisy data. The noise level was 1%. The maximum difference between absolute values of the initial and reconstructed permittivities is about 0.015946.

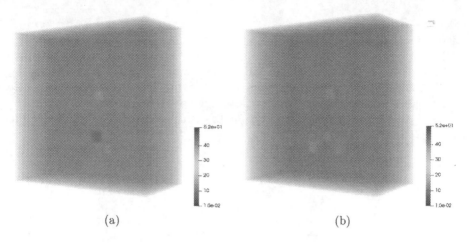

(a)   (b)

Fig. 7. The reconstructed values of the real and imaginary parts of the permittivity of Q_4.

4   Parallel Algorithm and Issue of Saving Matrix Coefficients

Let us consider the case when the body Q is a cuboid. The total number of matrix elements is described by the following formula

$$N = 9m^6,$$ (10)

where m is number of elementary cells of the calculation grid along one coordinate axis.

The volume of computation memory needed for save of matrix coefficients depends on the size of calculation grid. The results of calculation the necessary volume of memory for saving this coefficients for different m is shown in Table 1.

Table 1. The results of calculation the necessary volume of memory for saving matrix coefficients

m	MegaByte using formula (10)
4	0.5625
8	36
16	2304
32	147456

The Table 1 is shown that the volume of computation memory is a one of the main problems in solving such problems by numerical methods. Also we can not calculate these coefficients on the personal computer (PC) because it requires a lot of computation time.

For solving these problems we used MPI technology. On each computational multiprocessor complex was calculated one or several blocks of matrix elements.

We allocated memory as a one dimensional array for simplify the calculation process and process of transfer matrix coefficients between processors.

The total scheme of calculation algorithm is considered on Fig. 8, where p is the number of processors on one problem.

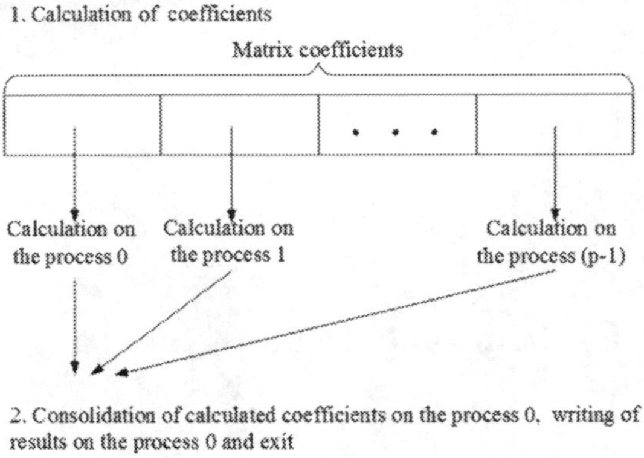

Fig. 8. The total scheme of calculation algorithm.

The following formula is described the number of coefficient on one processor.

$$C = \begin{cases} \left[\frac{N}{p}\right] + 1, & p < \{\frac{N}{p}\}, \\ \left[\frac{N}{p}\right], & p \geqslant \{\frac{N}{p}\}, \end{cases}$$

where N is the total number of coefficients, $\{\frac{N}{p}\}$ is remainder of integer division, $\left[\frac{N}{p}\right]$ is whole part of division, p is the process number.

We used 256 processors for calculation matrix coefficients for $m = 16$ and $n = 50$, where n is the number of terms in the components of Green's tensor. The calculation time was about 3 h. The total number of elements of matrix is 12288×12288. For PC the calculation time is about 120 h.

We tested our problem on the different number of the cores. Below we show results of speed gain for different number of cores:

1. with $p = 16$ the computational speed increases approximately 9 times;
2. with $p = 64$ the computational speed increases approximately 27 times;
3. with $p = 256$ the computational speed increases approximately 40 times.

The parallel algorithm is quite simple in use and allows reducing calculating time up to 40 times.

5   Conclusion

The nonlinear problem of the permittivity reconstruction of an inhomogeneous body placed in a waveguide is reduced to solving a linear problem and recalculating the permittivity function. The proposed algorithm is implemented in two steps. The advantage of this method is that the choice of the initial value is not required. This method also allows one to identify a big number of inhomogeneities (more than 1000 elements). The proposed method also allows one to reconstruct the permittivity of an anisotropic body and a body that has a complex permittivity. The method can be effectively used to determine permittivity of a body with arbitrary shape. This problem is quite difficult to calculating so we used a parallel algorithm.

Notes and Comments. This study is supported by the Russian Foundation for Basic Research [projects 18-31-00108, 18-01-00219]. The research is carried out using the equipment of the shared research facilities of HPC computing resources at Lomonosov Moscow State University.

References

1. Baena, J., Jelinek., L., Marques, R., Medina, F.: Near-perfect tunneling and amplification of evanescent electromagnetic waves in a wave guide filled by a metamaterial: Theory and experiments. Phys. Rev. B. **72**, 075–116 (2005)
2. Eves, E., Murphy, K., Yakovlev, V.: Reconstruction of complex permittivity with neural-network-controlled FDTD modelling. Power Electromag. Energy **4**(41), 22–34 (2007)
3. Pan, T., Guo-Ding, X., Zang, T.-C., Gao, L.: Study of a slab waveguide loaded with dispersive anisotropic. Appl. Phys. A **95**, 367–372 (2009)
4. Usanov, D., Skripal, A., Romanov, A.: Complex permettivity of composites based on dielectric matrices with carbon nanotrubes. Techn. Phys. **56**(1), 102–106 (2011)
5. Werner, P.: Resonance phenomena in local perturbations of parallel-plane waveguide Math. Methods Appl. Sci. **19**, 773–823 (1996)
6. Beilina, L., Klibanov, M.: Approximate Global Convergence and Adaptive for Coefficient Inverse Problems. Springer, New York (2012)
7. Romanov, V.G.: Inverse Problems of Mathematical Physics. VNU, Utrecht (1986)
8. Smirnov, Y.G.: Mathematical Methods for Electromagnetic Problems. Informacionno-izdatel'skij centr PenzGU, Penza (2009)
9. Ilinsky, A.S., Smirnov, Y.G.: Electromagnetic Wave Diffraction by Conducting Screens. VPS, Utrecht, The Netherlands (1998)
10. Medvedik, M.Y., Smirnov, Y.G.: Obratnye Zadachi Vosstanovlenija Dielektricheskoj Pronichaemosti Neodnorodnogo Tela v Volnovode. Izdatel'stvo PGU, Penza (2014)

Relativistic Hydrodynamics Modeling by Means Adaptive Nested Mesh on IBM Power 9

Igor Kulikov[⊠][iD], Igor Chernykh, Evgeny Berendeev, Dmitry Karavaev,
and Viktor Protasov

Institute of Computational Mathematics and Mathematical Geophysics SB RAS,
Novosibirsk, Russia
kulikov@ssd.sscc.ru, chernykh@parbz.sscc.ru, evgeny.berendeev@gmail.com,
kda@opg.sscc.ru, inc_13@mail.ru

Abstract. In this paper, the results of numerical simulations of relativistic hydrodynamics flows using the latest IBM Power 9 processors are presented. The numerical method implemented in the code is based on a combination of the Godunov method and Piecewise-Parabolic on Local Stencil method and extended for using nested adaptive mesh technologies. A relativistic hydrodynamic evolution of astronomical objects is performed on the node with IBM Power 9 on shared memory architecture. A new numerical method and parallel implementation for shared memory architectures are described in details. Studies of the code parallel implementation are presented. When using a regular mesh with an effective resolution of 512^3, 60x acceleration was obtained using 196 threads of IBM Power 9. When using a nested mesh with an effective resolution of 1024^3, 42x acceleration was obtained using 64 threads of IBM Power 9. When using a nested mesh with an effective resolution of 4096^3, 34x acceleration was obtained using 48 threads of IBM Power 9. The results of mathematical modeling of relativistic hydrodynamics of jet galaxy formation are presented in paper.

Keywords: Relativistic hydrodynamics · IBM Power 9 · Numerical methods

1 Introduction

Many astrophysical phenomena are associated with gas motion at relativistic velocities. The source of such currents are relativistic jets [1] in active galactic nuclei [2,3], microquasars [4], blazars [5,6], gamma bursts [7], extragalactic jets [8], core collapse [9] and stellar collapse in massive stars [10], black holes [11–14] and binary black holes [15], neutron stars [16–19], pulsars [20], and gravitational waves [21].

To study such phenomena, it is necessary to perform simulation within the scope of special relativistic hydrodynamics, for the solution of which a number of

© Springer Nature Switzerland AG 2019
V. Voevodin and S. Sobolev (Eds.): RuSCDays 2019, CCIS 1129, pp. 350–362, 2019.
https://doi.org/10.1007/978-3-030-36592-9_29

numerical methods have been created (see the review [22]). One of the difficulties of modeling relativistic flows is the different scale of processes, which requires the use of both parallel computing and adaptive meshes. On the basis of developed numerical methods, a number of program codes were developed for simulation of relativistic astrophysical flows, including that using adaptive grids.

CAFE [23]. The program code is intended to solve problems of relativistic ideal magnetic gas dynamics. The basis of the software package WENO is the fifth order accuracy scheme with the method of solving the Riemann problem HLLE. To ensure the divergenceless magnetic field, the Stokes theorem is used.

RAM [24]. The program code is intended for solving problems of special relativistic hydrodynamics. The program code is based on the WENO scheme and the piecewise parabolic method on adaptive grids. The testing of the program code in details and the presentation of equations of special relativistic hydrodynamics in cylindrical and spherical coordinates are presented in the paper.

PLUTO [25]. The program code is intended for all astrophysical flows, including relativistic ones. A solver is based on a combination of HLL and PPM methods. The code testing is described in details in the paper.

A powerful alternative to adaptive grids is an approach based on nested grids, when a complete problem with a sufficiently detailed grid is actually solved in a cell. In fact, the use of nested grids make it possible to reproduce any flows of multi-scale type. The development of such an approach would, for example, eliminate the GAP problem between modeling the evolution of galaxies and the star formation process, and also reproduce in some detail the turbulent flows and processes of nuclear collapse.

An original approach to the creation of a computational model of special relativistic hydrodynamics of astrophysical objects based on the technology of nested grids will be described in the paper. In the second section, the equations of special relativistic hydrodynamics are written in the form of conservation laws. The procedure for restoring primitive variables is described in details. A numerical method for solving equations of hyperbolic equations based on a combination of the Godunov method and the piecewise parabolic method on a local template is also described in this section. The third section is devoted to the architecture of the program code, where the structure of calculations using nested grids is described. In the fourth section the study of software implementation on nodes equipped with IBM Power 9 processors is presented in details. The fifth section is devoted to computational experiments to study formation and evolution processes of relativistic hydrodynamic jet. An analysis of characteristic times of instabilities evolution of Kelvin–Helmholtz type is also presented. The sixth section contains conclusion.

2   The Numerical Method

2.1   The Equations

In the paper the light speed is taken $c \equiv 1$. The equations of relativistic hydrodynamics in the form of conservation laws are written in the form:

$$\frac{\partial D}{\partial t} + \frac{\partial \left(Dv_k\right)}{\partial x_k} = 0, \tag{1}$$

$$\frac{\partial M_j}{\partial t} + \frac{\partial \left(M_j v_k + p\delta_{jk}\right)}{\partial x_k} = 0, \tag{2}$$

$$\frac{\partial E}{\partial t} + \frac{\partial \left(E + p\right) v_k}{\partial x_k} = 0, \tag{3}$$

or in compact vector form in the three-dimensional space:

$$\frac{\partial U}{\partial t} + \sum_{k=1}^{3} \frac{\partial F_k}{\partial x_k} = 0, \tag{4}$$

where the vector of conservative variables U and the vector of flows F_k are given in the form:

$$U = \begin{pmatrix} D \\ M_j \\ E \end{pmatrix} = \begin{pmatrix} \Gamma\rho \\ \Gamma^2\rho h v_j \\ \Gamma^2\rho h - p \end{pmatrix} \quad F_k = \begin{pmatrix} \rho\Gamma v_k \\ \rho h\Gamma^2 v_j v_k + p\delta_{jk} \\ \rho h\Gamma^2 v_k \end{pmatrix}, \tag{5}$$

where ρ is the density, v_k are the components of the velocity vector, δ_{jk} is the Kronecker symbol, p is the pressure and h is the special enthalpy:

$$h = 1 + \frac{\gamma}{\gamma - 1}\frac{p}{\rho}, \tag{6}$$

where γ is the adiabatic index. The Lorentz factor Γ is determined by the formula:

$$\Gamma = \frac{1}{\sqrt{1 - v^2}}. \tag{7}$$

The speed of sound is determined by the formula:

$$c_s^2 = \gamma\frac{p}{\rho h}. \tag{8}$$

It shall be noted that in the numerical method, calculations are carried out in conservative variables D, M_j, E. With respect to nonlinear relationship between conservative variables and primitive ρ, v, p, a special procedure for their recovery is required. Such procedure will be described in the next subsection.

2.2   The Primitive Variables Recovery

To recovery of primitive variables, we use the Newton method to determine the root of the equation:

$$f(p) = \Gamma^2 \rho h - p - E = 0, \tag{9}$$

according to the classical iterative scheme:

$$p_{m+1} = p_m - \frac{f(p_m)}{f'(p_m)}, \tag{10}$$

where

$$f'(p) = \frac{\gamma}{\gamma - 1}\Gamma^2 - \frac{M^2\Gamma^3}{(E+p)^3}\left(D + 2\frac{\gamma}{\gamma - 1}p\Gamma\right) - 1. \tag{11}$$

The procedure for primitive variables restoration is written as follows:

1. set $m = 0$,
2. choose the pressure at the previous step as the initial value of the pressure p_m,
3. use the value of p_m to calculate the components of the velocity $v_k = M_k/(E + p_m)$,
4. recalculate the value of the Lorentz factor Γ and the special enthalpy h,
5. recalculate the values of the function $f(p_m)$ and the derivative $f'(p_m)$ according to the Eqs. (9) and (11), respectively,
6. using the formula (10) we find the new pressure value p_{m+1},
7. if $|p_m - p_{m+1}| < \varepsilon$, then set the pressure $p = p_{m+1}$ and go to step 9,
8. increase m by one and go to step 3,
9. we find the components of the velocity $v_k = M_k/(E + p)$, the Lorentz factor Γ, the special enthalpy h and the density $\rho = D/\Gamma$.

2.3   The Relativistic Hydrodynamics Solver

We will consider a region in which a uniform rectangular grid is introduced with h steps. For the cell numbering, a fractional index will be used. For the node numbering, an integer index will be used. We write the one-dimensional analogue of the Godunov scheme for Eqs. (4):

$$\frac{U_{i+1/2}^{n+1} - U_{i+1/2}^{n}}{\tau} + \frac{F_{i+1}^{n+1/2} - F_{i}^{n+1/2}}{h} = 0, \tag{12}$$

where $F_i^{n+1/2}$ is the solution of the linearized Riemann problem for special relativistic hydrodynamics. Let us consider in detail the procedure for solving the linearized Riemann problem written for primitive variables:

$$\frac{\partial}{\partial t}\begin{pmatrix} \rho \\ v_x \\ v_y \\ v_z \\ p \end{pmatrix} + A\frac{\partial}{\partial x}\begin{pmatrix} \rho \\ v_x \\ v_y \\ v_z \\ p \end{pmatrix} = 0. \tag{13}$$

The matrix A can be decomposed in the form of $A = R\Lambda L$, where R and L are the matrix of right and left eigenvectors, Λ is the diagonal matrix of eigenvalues. The Eq. (13) can be written as:

$$\frac{\partial w}{\partial t} + R\Lambda L \frac{\partial w}{\partial x} = 0, \tag{14}$$

where $w = (\rho, v_x, v_y, v_z, p)^T$. We multiply the equations on the left by the matrix L. Using the equality $LR = I$ and making the substitution $q = Lw$, we obtain the independent transport equations:

$$\frac{\partial q}{\partial t} + \Lambda \frac{\partial q}{\partial x} = 0. \tag{15}$$

The solution of the last equation depends on the sign of the eigenvalue. The solution of the Riemann problem is restored by the formula $w = Rq$ using the piecewise-parabolic representation of the solution [26]. It is obvious that the one-dimensional scheme is naturally generalized to the multidimensional case.

To find the full spectral decomposition, we will use the approach partially described in [27]. Next, we present the solution of the spectral problem for the matrix A in the Eq. (13). The matrix A has the form:

$$A = \begin{pmatrix} v_x & a_{1,2} & 0 & 0 & a_{1,5} \\ 0 & a_{2,2} & 0 & 0 & a_{2,5} \\ 0 & a_{3,2} & v_x & 0 & a_{3,5} \\ 0 & a_{4,2} & 0 & v_x & a_{4,5} \\ 0 & a_{5,2} & 0 & 0 & a_{5,5} \end{pmatrix}, \tag{16}$$

where

$$a_{1,2} = \frac{\rho h \Gamma^2 (\rho \kappa - 1)}{N},$$

$$a_{1,5} = \frac{v_x (1 - \rho \kappa)}{N},$$

$$a_{2,2} = \frac{v_x \Gamma^2 (\rho h \kappa - h + \rho \xi)}{N},$$

$$a_{2,5} = \frac{\rho h \Gamma^2 \kappa \left(1 - v_x^2\right) - h - h \Gamma^2 \left(v_y^2 + v_z^2\right) + \rho \kappa \Gamma^2 \left(v_y^2 + v_z^2\right)}{\rho h \Gamma^2 N},$$

$$a_{3,2} = \frac{v_y \rho \xi}{N},$$

$$a_{3,5} = -\frac{v_x v_y (\rho \xi - h + \rho h \kappa)}{\rho h N},$$

$$a_{4,2} = \frac{v_z \rho \xi}{N},$$

$$a_{4,5} = -\frac{v_x v_z (\rho \xi - h + \rho h \kappa)}{\rho h N},$$

$$a_{5,2} = -\frac{\rho^2 h \Gamma^2 \xi}{N},$$

$$a_{5,5} = \frac{v_x \Gamma^2 \left(\rho\xi - h + \rho h\kappa\right)}{N},$$

where in turn

$$\kappa = \frac{\gamma}{\gamma - 1}\frac{1}{\rho},$$

$$\xi = -\frac{\gamma}{\gamma - 1}\frac{p}{\rho^2},$$

$$N = \Gamma^2 \left(h\rho\kappa - h + \rho\xi v^2\right).$$

Note that the Roe's scheme [26] for all hydrodynamic quantities f is used to calculate the average values between the left (L) and right (R) cells:

$$f = \frac{f_L \sqrt{\rho_L} + f_R \sqrt{\rho_R}}{\sqrt{\rho_L} + \sqrt{\rho_R}}. \tag{17}$$

The eigenvalues of the matrix A are written as:

$$\lambda_1 = v_x \frac{\left(1 - c_s^2\right) - c_s \Gamma^{-1}\omega}{1 - c_s^2 v^2}, \tag{18}$$

$$\lambda_{2,3,4} = v_x,$$

$$\lambda_5 = v_x \frac{\left(1 - c_s^2\right) + c_s \Gamma^{-1}\omega}{1 - c_s^2 v^2}.$$

The matrix of left eigenvectors of L is written in the form:

$$L = \begin{pmatrix} 0 & -\frac{\rho\Gamma}{2c_s\omega} & 0 & 0 & \frac{1}{2c_s^2 h} \\ 1 & 0 & 0 & 0 & -\frac{1}{c_s^2 h} \\ 0 & -\frac{v_x v_y}{1-v_x^2} & 1 & 0 & \frac{v_y}{\Gamma^2 \rho h(1-v_x^2)} \\ 0 & -\frac{v_x v_z}{1-v_x^2} & 0 & 1 & \frac{v_z}{\Gamma^2 \rho h(1-v_x^2)} \\ 0 & \frac{\rho\Gamma}{2c_s\omega} & 0 & 0 & \frac{1}{2c_s^2 h} \end{pmatrix}, \tag{19}$$

and the matrix of right eigenvectors R has the form:

$$R = \begin{pmatrix} 1 & 1 & 0 & 0 & 1 \\ -\frac{c_s\omega}{\rho\Gamma} & 0 & 0 & 0 & \frac{c_s\omega}{\rho\Gamma} \\ -\frac{v_y c_s (\Gamma\omega v_x + c_s)}{\rho\Gamma^2(1-v_x^2)} & 0 & 1 & 0 & \frac{v_y c_s (\Gamma\omega v_x + c_s)}{\rho\Gamma^2(1-v_x^2)} \\ -\frac{v_z c_s (\Gamma\omega v_x + c_s)}{\rho\Gamma^2(1-v_x^2)} & 0 & 0 & 1 & \frac{v_z c_s (\Gamma\omega v_x + c_s)}{\rho\Gamma^2(1-v_x^2)} \\ c_s^2 h & 0 & 0 & 0 & c_s^2 h \end{pmatrix}, \tag{20}$$

where

$$\omega = \sqrt{1 - v_x^2 - c_s \left(v_y^2 + v_z^2\right)}.$$

The time step is calculated from the Courant condition defined by the eigenvalues (18).

3   The Code Architecture

The main difficulty of the code architecture lies in the hierarchy of the discretization of the computational domain and the organization of calculations on such a hierarchical structure. To perform discretization using nested grids, we introduce in the three-dimensional domain of the solution a uniform cubic root grid with coordinates of the cell centers $x_i = i \times h - h/2$, $i = 1, .., I_{max}$, $y_k = k \times h - h/2$, $k = 1, .., K_{max}$, $z_l = l \times h - h/2$, $l = 1, .., L_{max}$, where h is the step of the root grid, I_{max}, K_{max}, L_{max} - the number of cells in the x, y, z directions. In the implementation, for convenience of organizing calculations and without losing the generality of the code, $I_{max} = K_{max} = L_{max} = N$ was used. In the cell with the number (i, k, l), we introduce a nested cubic grid with coordinates of the cell centers $x_{i,nested} = i \times h_{nested} - h_{nested}/2$, $i = 1, .., M$, $y_{k,nested} = k \times h_{nested} - h_{nested}/2$, $k = 1, .., M$, $z_{l,nested} = l \times h_{nested} - h_{nested}/2$, $l = 1, .., M$, where h_{nested} is the step of the nested grid of the grid, M is the number of cells of the nested grid by x, y, z directions. The equations of relativistic hydrodynamics will be calculated for the values placed in the cells of the root and nested grids. An important step is to find solution of the Riemann problem, which must be calculated on the interfaces of cells of different sizes. The Fig. 1 shows the code architecture. Gray color indicates work performed in parallel and implemented by means of OpenMP. Solving the equations of relativistic hydrodynamics (finding the solution of the Riemann problems) occurs in two stages: solving the Riemann problems on all boundaries of the embedded grid, solving the Riemann problems on all internal interfaces of the embedded grid. If the second part of finding a solution to the Riemann problem is rather trivial, then the first part requires a different method of calculation depending on the cell size

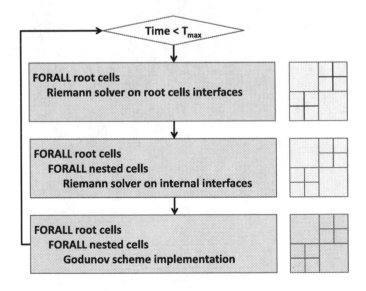

Fig. 1. The code architecture

of two adjacent nested grids. In the case of equal cell sizes, solving the Riemann problem is similar to solving the Riemann problems on the internal interfaces of the nested grid and is trivial. In the case when the cell of the neighboring nested grid is larger than the considered one, then the uniform distribution of values over the larger cell is assumed and the Riemann problem is resolved for the interface between the reduced neighboring cell and the considered cell. In the case when the considered cell borders with several cells of the adjacent nested grid, using the assumption of a uniform distribution of hydrodynamic quantities over the considered cell, the Riemann problem is solved on all interfaces, and then the flux values are averaged. This approach is similar to solving hydrodynamic equations [28].

4   The Research of Code on IBM Power 9 Nodes

IBM Power 9 is a superscalar multithread multiprocessor based on POWER architecture announced at Hot Chips conference in august 2016 [29]. The processor based on SMT8 cores is under consideration in the paper. The structure of processor's pipelines is divided into frontal component (responsible, for example, for dispatching) and execution units (EU) component. One layer of an EU, called Slice (S), has vector and scalar units (VSU) dealing with 64-bit data both integer and floating point. Two S forms SuperSlice (SS) dealing with 128-bit data. One core of SMT8 has four SS. For the most traditional in the field of HPC work with double precision numbers (DP), each SS could execute two scalar and one vector (two numbers length) instructions of "multiply and add" type, or 4 DP-results per cycle. Thus, SMT8 core with four SS gets 16 DP-results per cycle and IBM Power 9 entirely – 192 DP-results. Let us notice, that Intel Skylake could operate with more wide vectors than SMT8 and gets 32 DP-results per cycle, thus providing more vectorization. It should also be noted, that for the formation of a common L3 cache, data exchange between its regions is implemented through a common high-performance commutator. The cores used in IBM Power 9 microarchitecture have more specific functionality than in other common processors. For example, in Intel x86-architecture processors cores perform almost all functions of the entire processor. In Power9, SMT cores give some of the functionality to a common switch. Hence, IBM Power 9 quite comparable with Broadwell processors – the SMT8 core has 8 hardware threads but they process only 16 DP per cycle in total. It means that vectorization will not work as effectively as in Broadwell and even more so in KNL. It is confirmed by performance drop of the vectorized code on 512^3 grid, and not more than 60x acceleration on 192 cores. For computational experiments we use 2×12-core Typical 2.7 to 3.8 GHz (max) IBM Power 9 Processor, 32×32 GB DDR4 Memory, and one 300GB 15K RPM SAS SFF-3 Disk Drive (OS Linux).

In all configurations, the root mesh size of 128^3 was chosen as the base mesh. Three configurations of nested grids were considered:

1. All nested grids are size of 4^3 (uniform grid with an effective resolution of 512^3).

2. 75% of nested grids are size of 2^3 and 25% are size of 8^3 (effective resolution is 1024^3).
3. 75% nested grids are size of 2^3, 15% are size of 8^3 and 10% are size of 32^3 (effective resolution is 4096^3).

The results of the code performance study are presented in the Fig. 2. When using a regular grid with an effective resolution of 512^3, a 60-fold acceleration was obtained using 196 threads of IBM Power 9. A 42-fold acceleration was obtained using 64 threads of IBM Power 9 using a nested grid with an effective resolution of 1024^3. When using a nested grid with an effective resolution of 4096^3, a 34-fold acceleration was obtained using 48 threads of IBM Power 9. As can be seen from the results, the hyper-threading system works quite effectively with uniform loading of cores. In case of non-uniform loading the system has local optimum of number of used cores that is several times less than the total number of threads.

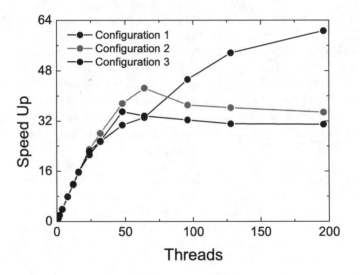

Fig. 2. The speed up research

5   The Numerical Expriments of Relativistic Hydrodynamics of Jet Galaxy Formation

As a model problem, we will explore relativistic hydrodynamics of a jet limited by a spherical region size of 10 pc at the initial time moment. Environment density is one particle per cm^3 and initial jet density is 10 particles per cm^3. Jet speed corresponds to $\Gamma = 10^4$. The Fig. 3 shows the results of simulation of relativistic jet dynamics. From the simulation results it can be seen that the forward front of the jet moving at light speed is formed. Jet shrinks along the axis of movement in time. A low-density region and the tail with unstable flow of Richtmyer–Meshkov Instability type are formed behind the jet. In the future it is planned to add the chemical dynamics of hydrogen occurring in the jet.

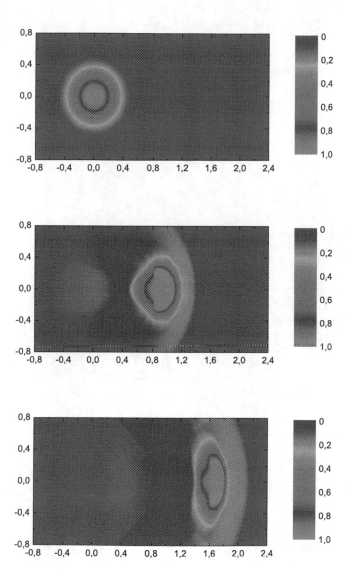

Fig. 3. The density of relativistic jet in $10 \times cm^{-3}$ in time 0 yr, 30 yr, 60 yr

6   Conclusion

The results of mathematical modeling of relativistic hydrodynamic flows using IBM Power 9 processors are presented in the paper. A 60-fold acceleration was obtained using 196 threads of IBM Power 9 using a regular grid with an effective resolution of 512^3. 42-fold acceleration was obtained using 64 threads of IBM Power 9 Using a nested grid with an effective resolution of 1024^3. A 34-fold acceleration was obtained using 48 threads using a nested grid with an effective resolution of 4096^3 IBM Power 9. In terms of computational experiments, the results of mathematical modeling of relativistic hydrodynamics of galactic jets are presented.

Acknowledgements. The research work was supported by the Grant of the Russian Science Foundation (project 18-11-00044).

References

1. Wang, P., Abel, T., Zhang, W.: Relativistic hydrodynamic flows using spatial and temporal adaptive structured mesh refinement. Astrophys. J. Suppl. Series **176**, 467–483 (2008). https://doi.org/10.1086/529434
2. Karen Yang, H.-Y., Reynolds, C.S.: How AGN jets heat the intracluster medium-insights from hydrodynamic simulations. Astrophys. J. **829**, 90 (2016). https://doi.org/10.3847/0004-637X/829/2/90
3. Khoperskov, S., Venichenko, Y., Khrapov, S., Vasiliev, E.: High performance computing of magnetized galactic disks. Supercomput. Front. Innov. **5**, 103–106 (2018). https://doi.org/10.14529/jsfi180412
4. Bosch-Ramon, V., Khangulyan, D.: Understanding the very-high-energy emission from microquasars. Int. J. Mod. Phys. D. **18**(3), 347–387 (2009). https://doi.org/10.1142/S0218271809014601
5. Fromm, C.M., Perucho, M., Mimica, P., Ros, E.: Spectral evolution of flaring blazars from numerical simulations. Astron. Astrophys. **588**, A101 (2016). https://doi.org/10.1051/0004-6361/201527139
6. Janiuk, A., Sapountzis, K., Mortier, J., Janiuk, I.: Numerical simulations of black hole accretion flows. Supercomput. Front. Innov. **5**, 86–102 (2018). https://doi.org/10.14529/jsfi180208
7. Nagakura, H., Ito, H., Kiuchi, K., Yamada, S.: Jet propagations, breakouts, and photospheric emissions in collapsing massive progenitors of long-duration gamma-ray bursts. Astrophys. J. **731**, 80 (2011). https://doi.org/10.1088/0004-637X/731/2/80
8. Hughes, P., Miller, M., Duncan, G.: Three-dimensional hydrodynamic simulations of relativistic extragalactic jets. Astrophys. J. **572**, 713–728 (2002). https://doi.org/10.1086/340382
9. Nagakura, H., Sumiyoshi, K., Yamada, S. Three-dimensional Boltzmann hydro code for core collapse in massive stars. I. Special relativistic treatments. Astrophys. J. Suppl. Ser. **214**, 16 (2014). https://doi.org/10.1088/0067-0049/214/2/16
10. O'Connor, E., Ott, C.: A new open-source code for spherically symmetric stellar collapse to neutron stars and black holes. Class. Quantum Gravity **27**, 114103 (2010). https://doi.org/10.1088/0264-9381/27/11/114103

11. Komissarov, S.: Electrodynamics of black hole magnetospheres. Mon. Not. R. Astron. Soc. **350**(2), 427–448 (2004). https://doi.org/10.1111/j.1365-2966.2004.07598.x

12. Komissarov, S.: Observations of the Blandford-Znajek process and the magnetohydrodynamic Penrose process in computer simulations of black hole magnetospheres. Mon. Not. R. Astron. Soc. **359**(3), 801–808 (2005). https://doi.org/10.1111/j.1365-2966.2005.08974.x

13. Palenzuela, C., Garrett, T., Lehner, L., Liebling, S.: Magnetospheres of black hole systems in force-free plasma. Phys. Rev. D. **82**, 044045 (2010). https://doi.org/10.1103/PhysRevD.82.044045

14. Palenzuela, C., Bona, C., Lehner, L., Reula, O.: Robustness of the blanford-znajek mechanism. Class. Quantum Gravity **28**, 4007 (2011). https://doi.org/10.1088/0264-9381/28/13/134007

15. Palenzuela, C., Lehner, L., Liebling, S.: Dual jets from binary black holes. Science **329**, 927–930 (2010). https://doi.org/10.1126/science.1191766

16. Komissarov, S.: Simulations of the axisymmetric magnetospheres of neutron stars. Mon. Not. R. Astron. Soc. **367**(1), 19–31 (2006). https://doi.org/10.1111/j.1365-2966.2005.09932.x

17. Duez, M.D., Liu, Y.T., Shapiro, S.L., Shibata, M., Stephens, B.C.: Collapse of magnetized hypermassive neutron stars in general relativity. Phys. Rev. Lett. **96**, 031101 (2006). https://doi.org/10.1103/PhysRevD.77.044001

18. Duez, M.D., Liu, Y.T., Shapiro, S.L., Shibata, M., Stephens, B.C.: Evolution of magnetized, differentially rotating neutron stars: simulations in full general relativity. Phys. Rev. D. **73**, 104015 (2006). https://doi.org/10.1103/PhysRevD.73.104015

19. Shibata, M., Duez, M.D., Liu, Y.T., Shapiro, S.L., Stephens, B.C.: Magnetized hypermassive neutron-star collapse: a central engine for short gamma-ray bursts. Phys. Rev. Lett. **96**, 031102 (2006). https://doi.org/10.1103/PhysRevLett.96.031102

20. Marsh, T., et al.: A radio-pulsing white dwarf binary star. Nature **537**, 374–377 (2016). https://doi.org/10.1038/nature18620

21. Coleman Miller, M., Yunes, N.: The new frontier of gravitational waves. Nature **568**, 469–476 (2019). https://doi.org/10.1038/s41586-019-1129-z

22. Marti, J.M., Muller, E.: Numerical hydrodynamics in special relativity. Living Rev. Relativ. **6**, 7 (2003). https://doi.org/10.12942/lrr-2003-7

23. Lora-Clavijo, F., Cruz-Osorio, A., Guzman, F.: CAFE: a new relativistic MHD code. Astrophys. J. Suppl. Ser. **218**, 24 (2015). https://doi.org/10.1088/0067-0049/218/2/24

24. Zhang, W., MacFadyen, A.: RAM: a relativistic adaptive mesh refinement hydrodynamics code. Astrophys. J. Suppl. Ser. **164**, 255–279 (2006). https://doi.org/10.1086/500792

25. Mignone, A., et al.: PLUTO: a numerical code for computational astrophysics. Astrophys. J. Suppl. Ser. **170**, 228–242 (2007). https://doi.org/10.1086/513316

26. Kulikov, I., Vorobyov, E.: Using the PPML approach for constructing a low-dissipation, operator-splitting scheme for numerical simulations of hydrodynamic flows. J. Comput. Phys. **317**, 318–346 (2016). https://doi.org/10.1016/j.jcp.2016.04.057

27. Lamberts, A., Fromang, S., Dubus, G., Teyssier, R.: Simulating gamma-ray binaries with a relativistic extension of RAMSES. Astron. Astrophys. **560**, A79 (2013). https://doi.org/10.1051/0004-6361/201322266

28. Kulikov, I.: The numerical modeling of the collapse of molecular cloud on adaptive nested mesh. J. Phys: Conf. Ser. **1103**, 012011 (2018). https://doi.org/10.1088/1742-6596/1103/1/012011
29. Sadasivam, S.K., et al.: IBM power 9 processor architecture. IEEE Micro. **37**(2), 40–51 (2017). https://doi.org/10.1109/MM.2017.40

Search for Approaches to Supercomputer Quantum-Chemical Docking

Alexey Sulimov[1,2], Danil Kutov[1,2], Anna Gribkova[1], Ivan Ilin[1,2],
Anna Tashchilova[1,2], and Vladimir Sulimov[1,2(✉)]

[1] Dimonta, Ltd., Moscow 117186, Russia
{as,dk,ilyin,at}@dimonta.com,
gribkova.anna.2013@post.bio.msu.ru,
vladimir.sulimov@gmail.com
[2] Research Computer Center, Lomonosov Moscow State University,
Moscow 119992, Russia

Abstract. The quasi-docking procedure with a combination of the classical MMFF94 force field and the PM7 quantum-chemical semiempirical method is applied for docking ligands into proteins with which they are co-crystallized. Main peculiarities of the test set of protein-ligand complexes are: a high resolution of the structures obtained from Protein Data Bank, no missed residues or atoms in the active sites of the proteins and the availability of experimentally measured protein-ligand binding free energies including separate contributions of the enthalpy and entropy terms. The goal of this work is to determine positioning accuracy of the quasi-docking by a comparison of best docked ligand poses with the respective ligand poses in the crystallized protein-ligand complexes, to estimate values of the protein-ligand binding enthalpy for the best ligand poses and to compare these values with the measured ones. The best ligand pose corresponds to the global energy minimum of the protein-ligand complex calculated with PM7 and with the COSMO continuum solvent model either in the old parameterization, COSMO, or in the recent one, COSMO2, in the quasi-docking procedure. It is found that the docking positioning accuracy is better in the case of PM7 with COSMO energy calculations than with COSMO2 calculations. The correlation between values of the calculated and experimentally measured binding enthalpy is also better, R = 0.74, for the PM7+COSMO energy.

Keywords: Generalized docking · Quasi-docking · PM7 quantum-chemical · Global energy minimum · Binding enthalpy · High-performance computing · Molecular modeling · Drug design

1 Introduction

The rational drug development mainly relies on the following paradigm: the drug molecule must selectively bind to a specific site of a macromolecule involved in the disease progression, and thereby affect the course of the disease. Most often, these target macromolecules are proteins, and biologically active molecules must bind to their active centers. These molecules can be either inhibitors blocking protein functioning upon binding or biologically active molecules of another nature. For brevity,

© Springer Nature Switzerland AG 2019
V. Voevodin and S. Sobolev (Eds.): RuSCDays 2019, CCIS 1129, pp. 363–378, 2019.
https://doi.org/10.1007/978-3-030-36592-9_30

we will call such biologically active molecules inhibitors, and molecules which are considered as candidates to become inhibitors will be referred as ligands. Docking is a molecular modeling method performing ligand positioning in the active site of a target protein and estimating the protein-ligand binding energy [1]. The latter defines the drug effectiveness: the more this energy is, the less concentration of the drug can be used to achieve the desired effect. Docking is a very popular computer modeling tool at the initial stage of the new drug development, and several dozen docking programs are now available [2]. However, despite their usefulness, these programs still do not have sufficiently high accuracy of estimating the protein-ligand binding energy to become the main driving force during the stage of the inhibitor optimization. Obviously, that the high accuracy of the binding energy estimation can be achieved only for the high accuracy of ligand positioning.

It has been shown recently that the best ligand positioning accuracy can be achieved by using the quasi-docking procedure [3, 4] when at first a sufficiently broad spectrum of low energy minima of the protein-ligand system in the frame of a force field is found, and then energies of these minima are recalculated by the quantum-chemical semiempirical PM7 method [5] with the COSMO solvent model [6], and the ligand pose with the lowest PM7+COSMO energy is the best approximation of the experimentally determined ligand position in the protein-ligand crystal according to the docking paradigm [3, 4, 7–9].

In the present investigation the quasi-docking procedure is applied to the test set of 25 protein-ligand complexes, the ligand positioning accuracy is determined, the best ligand poses are used for the estimation of the protein-ligand binding enthalpies and the latter are compared with the experimentally measured values of binding enthalpies.

2   Materials and Methods

2.1   Quasi-Docking

At the first stage of the quasi-docking procedure [3, 4] the MMFF94 force field is used and the search for low energy minima of the protein-ligand complex is performed by the FLM docking program [7, 10, 11]. Several thousand unique low energy minima are found for each test protein-ligand complex. At the second stage energies of all these minima are recalculated by the PM7 method with COSMO without further energy optimization using the MOPAC program [12], and the ligand pose with the lowest protein-ligand PM7+COSMO energy is determined. This ligand pose is considered to be the best one and it is compared with the ligand position in the crystallized protein-ligand complex taken form the Protein Data Bank (PDB) [13]. The comparison of ligand positions is made by calculating the standard deviation (RMSD) over respective ligand atoms.

2.2   FLM Program

The FLM generalized docking program performs a massive parallel search for a given number of low energy minima of a given protein-ligand complex [7, 10, 11].

The search for minima is carried out from random positions of various ligand conformations in the active center of the protein, and local optimizations are performed with the help of an accurate gradient method by varying the Cartesian coordinates of all ligand atoms. The ligand geometrical center (the center of gravity when all atomic masses are equal) is randomly moved in the search area which is defined as the sphere of a given radius centered at the native ligand geometrical center. The present investigations are conducted when the radius is equal to 8 Å and this sphere covers active sites of all protein-ligand complexes under consideration.

The energy is calculated in the frame of MMFF94 force field without taking into account the influence of water solvent in opposite to what has been done in the first works on quasi-docking [3, 4]. It has been shown recently [11] that the quasi-docking procedure is faster and the minima search is more effective when FLM without solvent (version 0.05) is used at the first step of quasi-docking. FLM finds a pool of a given number of unique low energy minima. This pool consists of the global minimum and every successive unique minimum above it. The uniqueness of minima is calculated during the FLM performance less accurately and after the end of FLM more accurately taking into account chemical symmetry: two minima, i.e. two ligand poses corresponding to two respective energy minima, are considered as different from each other if the RMSD value is larger than a given distance and the difference of their energies is larger than a given value, in the present work they are 0.001 Å and 0.001 kcal/mol, respectively. As a rule for each protein-ligand complex the search is made for 8192 minima with lowest MMFF94 energies. However for some complexes (see Table 2 in Sect. 3.1) we were forced to save much more low energy minima because there was no one minimum among 8192 low energy minima found at the first quasi-docking stage with a ligand pose near the crystallized ligand position. FLM can be used also for the search for low energy minima of an unbound ligand. More details about the performance of the FLM program can be found in [7, 10, 11].

The first stage of quasi-docking with FLM-0.05 consumes from 8 (for the 1C5P complex with a small ligand) to 23 (for the 1J84 complex with a large ligand) thousand CPU*hours (16 and 47 h at 504 computing cores) per protein-ligand complex depending mainly on the number of ligand atoms.

2.3 PM7 Method

It is still impossible to perform calculations of protein-ligand systems containing several thousand atoms by *ab initio* quantum-chemical methods, but this can be done by semiempirical quantum-chemical methods with the help of the MOZYME method [14] implemented in the MOPAC package [12]. In MOZYME, the usual LCAO (Linear Combination of Atomic Orbitals) approximation is replaced by the localized molecular orbitals (LMO) method, and this allows to increase the upper size limit for geometry optimization up to 15,000 atoms. However until recently all semiempirical quantum-chemical methods suffered from the bad description of intermolecular interactions including hydrogen bonds. Nevertheless novel semiempirical methods PM6-D3H4X [15, 16] and PM7 [5] have been developed and implemented in MOPAC. These methods describe noncovalent interactions including the dispersion term and hydrogen and halogen bonds on the ground of NDDO approximations and they demonstrate high accuracies [17] for such interactions which are better than or comparable with the accuracy of the B3LYP DFT method [5].

2.4 COSMO Solvent Model

The COSMO solvent model [6] describes polar part of the solute-solvent interaction. The solvent is represented by a homogeneous metal continuum (the dielectric constant $\varepsilon = \infty$) surrounding the solute molecule and it is applied to solvents with high dielectric constants, e.g. to water ($\varepsilon = 78.4$ at the room temperature). The respective COSMO equation describes Coulomb interactions between atomic charges of the solute molecule and the polarization charges induced the atomic charges at the surface (Solvent Accessible Surface or SAS) separating the solute from the solvent. The COSMO model was implemented in MOPAC long time ago, just after the COSMO model publication [6] and since then its main parameters were not changed. These parameters are Van der Waals radii of atoms composing the solute molecule and they were fitted to reproduce experimentally measured hydration energies of small molecules by quantum-chemical calculations with the AM1 semiempirical parameterization. Certainly, these parameters are not optimal for other quantum-chemical methods and reparameterizations of the COSMO model for methods PM6 and PM7 have been done recently [18]. These reparameterizations are made on a large set of small molecules and ions and in addition to the polar term they include the nonpolar term of the hydration energy in its simplest form as a product of the total SAS area and an effective surface tension coefficient ξ, the SAS area being calculated with MOPAC. In the present work we use old and new COSMO parameterizations both: for the former we perform MOPAC calculations with default COSMO parameters, for the latter (COSMO2) we use atomic radii, the value of ξ for PM7/COSMO2 from Table 1 of [18] and the effective radius of solvent molecule equals to 1.0 Å – the respective MOPAC parameter RSOLV = 1.0.

2.5 Protein-Ligand Binding Enthalpy

The protein-ligand binding free energy is estimated as follows. The next general equation defines this value:

$$\Delta G_{bind} = G(PL) - G(P) - G(L) \tag{1}$$

where $G(X)$ is the free energy of the protein-ligand complex (PL), the unbound protein (P) and the unbound ligand (L). Free energies of the protein, the ligand and their complex can be calculated through the configuration integrals over the respective phase space. The binding free energy consists of two terms:

$$\Delta G_{bind} = \Delta H_{bind} - T\Delta S_{bind} \tag{2}$$

where ΔH_{bind} and $T\Delta S_{bind}$ are the binding enthalpy and entropy, respectively, T is temperature in energy units. ΔH_{bind} expresses the energy gain when the ligand binds to the protein and its negative value shows that the protein-ligand bound state is energetically favorable comparing with their unbound state. The entropy contribution is connected with the restriction of the ligand conformation mobility in the bound state and with the entropy component of hydrophobic interactions. If low energy minima are separated by sufficiently high energy barriers the configuration integral transforms into a sum of configuration integrals over these separated minima [7, 19]. For the rigid protein with all atoms fixed $G(P)$ boils down to the energy of the protein $E_1(P)$ in its given configuration. It has been shown in [7] that as a first approximation the binding enthalpy could be calculated neglecting contributions from ligand vibrations and using only the global energy minima of the protein-ligand complex $E_1(PL)$ and of the unbound ligand $E_1(L)$:

$$\Delta H_{bind} = E_1(PL) - E_1(P) - E_1(L) \tag{3}$$

It has been shown previously that the best docking positioning accuracy is reached with PM7 energy calculations using the COSMO solvent model at the second stage of the quasi-docking procedure, and we decided that the binding enthalpy estimation should be calculated also by PM7 with the COSMO solvent. The best ligand pose in the protein corresponds to the global energy minimum of the complex calculated by the PM7 method with the COSMO solvent in the frame of the quasi-docking procedure (see Sect. 2.1). That is why the energy $E_1(PL)$ is calculated as follows. The PM7 energy of the protein-ligand complex is optimized with variations of Cartesian coordinates of all ligand atoms from the ligand initial position corresponding to the best ligand pose found in the quasi-docking procedure and the PM7 minimum is found; then, the energy of the complex in this minimum is recalculated by PM7 with the COSMO solvent.

The global energy minimum of the unbound ligand $E_1(L)$ is calculated in the procedure which is very similar to quasi-docking but at the second stage the ligand PM7 energy is optimized from each ligand conformation corresponding to every ligand MMFF94 energy minimum determined by the FLM program for the unbound ligand without solvent at the first stage of the quasi-docking procedure; the optimization is performed with variations of Cartesian coordinates of all ligand atoms. Then, ligand energy in each minimum is recalculated by PM7 with the COSMO solvent and the ligand global PM7+COSMO energy minimum is determined.

For the old COSMO parameterization the binding enthalpy is calculated by the Eq. (3) with $E_1(X)$ being the heat of formation of the X molecular system ($X = PL, P, L$) printed in the output of the MOPAC program executed with the COSMO solvent model. For the new COSMO parameterization Eq. (3) should be modified as follows:

$$\Delta H_{bind} = E_1(PL) - E_1(P) - E_1(L) + E_{np}^{DS} \tag{4}$$

where E_{np}^{DS} is the nonpolar part of the desolvation energy calculated using a simple relation (see Sect. 2.4):

$$E_{np}^{DS} = \xi \times \Delta S \tag{5}$$

where $\Delta S = S(PL) - S(P) - S(L)$ is the difference of SAS areas of the complex $S(PL)$, protein $S(P)$ and ligand $S(L)$, $\xi = 0.042$ kcal/mol/Å^2.

The binding enthalpy is also calculated for the ligand pose found by the SOL docking program as follows. The ligand pose with the lowest energy in the field of the protein found by SOL is used as the initial ligand position in the protein. Then the PM7 energy of the protein-ligand complex is optimized from this initial ligand position with variations of Cartesian coordinates of all ligand atoms, and the energy is recalculated in the minimum either with COSMO or with COSMO2. Further, the binding enthalpy is calculated with Eqs. (3) or (4) for COSMO or COSMO2, respectively, using the same values of the unbound protein $E_1(P)$ and the unbound ligand $E_1(L)$ energies obtained as described above.

Note that using the continuum solvent model in the calculation of the binding enthalpy, ΔH_{bind}, we include in this value some contribution from the entropy change upon binding and this contribution is partly included in the E_{np}^{DS} term.

2.6   Test Set of Protein-Ligand Complexes

The adequate estimation of any docking technique highly depends on quality of a test set of protein-ligand complexes. In this work, to assess positioning approach based on quasi-docking we created a test set of protein-ligand complexes from PDB which possessed high resolution and quality. The primary inclusion criteria are: good resolution (less than 2.0 Å), no gaps near an active site of a protein, the presence of experimentally determined thermodynamics (ΔG_{exp}, ΔH_{exp}, and ΔS_{exp}), no metal ions and any cofactors crystallized in an active site. From crystal complexes selected by these criteria native ligand molecules are extracted into separate files. The first step of protein structures preparation implies removing all rest "HETATM" records related to water molecules, ions, crystallization salts and, if present, redundant copies of complexes. Protonation of protein atoms (pH = 7.4) is then performed by the APLITE program [20]. Ligand molecules are protonated at pH 7.4 as well by using the Avogadro program [21].

Since the FLM program works relying upon MMFF94 force field, prior to quasi-docking we have applied the additional check of selected complexes by means of two programs also using this force field. Firstly, all prepared complexes were checked by our original LME program which performs optimization of a native ligand in the frame of MMFF94 force field and determines root-mean-square deviation of the optimized ligand pose relative to its crystallized pose (abbreviated as *RMSD LME*). When the *RMSD LME* is high (here, the threshold was set up to 2.0 Å), it is expected that even if FLM finds minima near the global minimum corresponding a native ligand pose, their local optimization in the frame of MMFF94, which is performed for each found minimum, causes them to "shift" too far from the global minimum. Quasi-docking for complexes with *RMSD LME* being larger than 2.0 Å therefore tends to fail and such complexes were excluded from the test set. Secondly, for all complexes a procedure of positioning a native ligand was carried out by the grid-based SOL docking program [20] with MMFF94-based energy assessing and the genetic algorithm-based conformational search. The purpose of this docking is to determine whether the simplified (comparing with FLM) grid-based SOL docking finds minima which are near the global minimum (RMSD < 2.0 Å). If SOL finds such minima, regardless of how it interprets them (as global minimum or not), high chances are that FLM finds them as well. The quantitative value related to checking complexes by this criterion is determined as *RMSD SOL* which corresponds to lowest found RMSD value for SOL docked poses relative to the crystallized native ligand position. Summing up, both tests, LME-based optimization of a native ligand and grid-based docking with the genetic algorithm conformational search, might be said to aim at preliminarily estimating success of quasi-docking that enables avoiding complexes prone to fail and saving computational resources.

By following these criteria (primary inclusion criteria and secondary criteria based on optimization in LME and docking with SOL) we have selected from the PDB [13] 25 protein-ligand complexes of 12 different proteins containing ligands of various sizes and flexibility with experimentally determined thermodynamics. Crystal features of these complexes, *RMSD LME*, *RMSD SOL* are listed in Table 1.

Table 1. Protein-ligand complexes selected for the test set and their characteristics: PDB ID is the identifier of the complex in Protein Data Bank, protein names, *Res* is the resolution of the complex, N_P, N_L are numbers of protein and ligand atoms, respectively, Q_P, Q_L are protein and ligand charges, respectively, N_{tor} is the number of ligand torsions, *RMSD LME* calculated in LME, and *RMSD SOL* calculated in SOL. All proteins have no gaps near the active site.

Protein	PDB ID	RES,Å	N_P	Q_P	N_L	N_{tor}	Q_L	$RMSD\ LME$,Å	$RMSD\ SOL$,Å
GNB/LNB-binding protein	2Z8D	1.85	5897	−21	51	6	0	0.64	0.98
	2Z8E	1.99	5897	−21	51	6	0	0.72	0.8
α-fucosidase	2XII	1.8	7042	2	51	4	1	0.74	0.64
KIV-10 module of Apo (a)	3KIV	1.8	1206	1	20	5	0	0.9	0.8
BET protein	4MR5	1.63	1860	2	42	3	0	0.44	1.08
	4MR6	1.67	1860	2	49	6	0	0.62	1.24
CRP	1HW5	1.82	3284	1	33	1	−1	0.57	0.72
Trypsin	1C5P	1.43	3220	6	18	1	1	0.4	1.1
	1K1J	2.2	3220	6	68	10	1	0.5	1.7
	2ZDM	1.93	3220	6	59	9	1	0.96	0.89
	2ZDN	1.98	3220	6	58	9	1	0.38	1.22
	2ZFS	1.51	3220	6	64	9	2	0.46	0.71
YKL-39	4P8V	1.64	5741	−1	57	8	0	1.06	1.12
Factor XIa	4CRC	1.6	3711	2	60	11	0	0.46	0.93
	4CRD	2.1	3692	2	57	11	0	0.86	1.25
EngF	1J84	2.02	2642	−7	87	10	0	1.54	2.15
Mp1p-LBD2	5CSD	1.45	2407	−4	53	14	−1	0.62	1.8
HIV-1 protease	1MRX	2	3140	6	74	11	0	0.96	1.51
	1MSM	2	3138	6	78	12	0	1.03	0.71
	2PYM	1.9	3100	2	86	12	1	0.8	0.9
	2PYN	1.85	3116	4	86	12	1	0.8	0.9
	3KDB	1.66	3138	6	86	13	0	1.63	1.71
	3NU3	1.02	3134	6	70	13	0	0.5	1.4
	4LL3	1.95	3134	4	75	13	0	0.9	2.0
Renin	2IKO	1.9	5144	−8	46	5	1	0.47	0.79

A special remark should be made on the protonation state and the charge of the native ligand from the 2IKO complex. On the one hand, the PoseView plugin utilized by {www.rcsb.org} shows the ligand from 2IKO to be neutral as presented at web page of the complex. On the other hand, diaminopyrimidine-based moiety of the ligand possesses a basic character and seems to be capable of accepting a proton from a cluster of aspartic acids and obtaining a positive charge while binding. Crystal orientation of the ligand in 2IKO complex in which diaminopyrimidine is placed towards this cluster confirms the hypothesis and we used +1 charge of the ligand from the 2IKO complex in our calculations.

2.7   Energy Indexes: INN

In the analysis of the docking positioning accuracy and the feasibility of the docking paradigm it is convenient to use special indexes of energy minima of protein-ligand complexes. All energy minima of a protein-ligand complex for a given energy function can be ranked in ascending order of their energies. Wherein every minimum gets its own integer index equal to the number of its position in this ranked list of minima. The index of the lowest energy minimum is equal to 1. We introduced special indexes [4, 7–9] to analyze the docking positioning accuracy and the feasibility of the docking paradigm as follows. The list of minima can include some minima corresponding to ligand positions located near the nonoptimized native (crystallized) ligand pose in the given crystallized protein-ligand complex structure taken from the PDB [13]. By our definition the ligand is near the non-optimized native ligand position if the RMSD, the root-mean-square deviation between equivalent atoms of the ligand in the two positions, is less than 2 Å. Let us designate the index of such minimum which is close to the native (crystallized) ligand position as INN. It is the abbreviation of the term "Index of Near Native". If there are several such minima, we attribute INN to the minimum with the lowest energy among all minima which are close to the native ligand pose. If INN is equal to 1, the docking paradigm is satisfied and the ligand pose in the protein corresponding to the global energy minimum is near the ligand position in the protein-ligand crystal.

3   Results

3.1   Positioning Accuracy

For all test protein-ligand complexes INN indexes for different methods of energy calculations used in docking or quasi-docking are presented in Table 2. These methods of the energy calculation are: the MMFF94 force field used at the first stage of the quasi-docking procedure, and the PM7 method with the old parameterization of the COSMO solvent model and the PM7 method with the new parameterization of the COSMO solvent model (COSMO2) used at the second stage of the quasi-docking procedure. The results of docking with the SOL program are also presented in Table 2: the RMSD distance of the crystallized ligand pose from the docked ligand pose with the lowest ligand energy in the field of the protein. Parameters describing reliability of

SOL docking results are also presented in Table 2: m is the occupation of the 1st cluster, l is the number of clusters for 50 independent runs of the genetic algorithm. The 1st cluster presented in the output of the SOL program contains ligand poses differing between one another in RMSD < 1 Å with lowest energies in the field of the protein. Standard docking parameters are used for most of complexes: population size 30000; number of generations 1000, otherwise: *high docking parameters population size 3000000, number of generations 1100, **very high docking parameters: population size 6000000, number of generations 2000. The high occupation of the 1st cluster, the small number of clusters for the given number of the independent runs of the genetic algorithm are indicators of high reliability of ligand position in the protein corresponding to the lowest energy of the ligand in the field of the target protein.

We see that values of INN indexes with energies calculated by PM7+COSMO or PM7+COSMO2 methods at the second stage of quasi-docking are much smaller than ones calculated by MMFF94 in vacuum at the first stage of quasi-docking. So, docking with FLM-0.05 in the frame of the MMFF94 force field without any solvent is very effective at the first stage of the quasi-docking procedure [11] followed by the second stage with the energy recalculation using PM7 and COSMO. Docking with FLM-0.05 by itself has much less positioning accuracy: too many complexes have INN ≠ 1. This confirms our previous observations made for another set of protein-ligand complexes and supports the usefulness of the quasi-docking procedure [3, 4]. The docking paradigm (INN = 1) is satisfied for 19 and 15 complexes (among 25 ones) for PM7 +COSMO and PM7+COSMO2 energy calculations, respectively. It can be seen in Table 2 that unfortunately the new COSMO parameterization works worse than old one: the number of complexes with INN = 1 is 19 for COSMO and it is equal only to 15 for COSMO2. In spite of the fact that in this paper new complexes are treated, the relative number (76%) of complexes with INN = 1 (when the docking paradigm is satisfied) is the same as in our previous investigations for another set of protein-ligand complexes for the same energy calculation with PM7 and the COSMO solvent model. It is interesting to note that even when INN = 2 RMSD of the ligand position corresponding to the global energy (PM7+COSMO) minimum from the crystallized ligand position is not very large, e.g. RMSD = 2.67 or 3.67 Å for 4CRC or 2Z8D.

More detailed analysis of the cases when INN ≠ 1 reveals following observations which can explain some bad results of positioning. The first peculiarity we found is related to symmetrical binding sites which enable ligands to bind in two alternative symmetric conformations. Taking only one native conformation when calculating RMSD values, the correct binding mode can be wrongly estimated as a false conformation, if neglect the symmetry. This problem might arise when dealing with homodimers, for example, with HIV-1 protease. We were faced with such case for 2PYM and 4LL3 complexes containing this protease. As seen from Table 2, at the primary calculation INN indexes and RMSD values for 2PYM turned out to be unsatisfactory in the cases of COSMO and COSMO2 both. Having identified symmetrically bound ligand in the calculated global minimum relative to the used native conformation, we retrieved an alternative conformation of a native ligand from PDB and performed RMSD calculation using this conformation. New RMSD values of the global minimum both in COSMO and in COSMO2 turned out to be 1.66 Å (global minima are totally the same in COSMO and COSMO2) that allows us to assign INN to

Table 2. INN indexes, and the RMSD deviation of the ligand position corresponding to the global energy minimum from the crystallized native ligand position in the protein for different energy functions: the MMFF94 force field, PM7 with the old COSMO and PM7 with new COSMO2; N_{min} is the number of unique energy minima found by the FLM program at the first stage of the quasi-docking procedure.

PDB ID	N_{min}	MMFF94		PM7 COSMO		PM7 COSMO2		SOL	
		INN	RMSD, Å	INN	RMSD, Å	INN	RMSD, Å	m/l	RMSD, Å
1C5P	5349	1	0.62	1	0.43	1	0.43	50/1	1.15
1HW5	6848	1	0.54	1	0.48	1	0.48	50/1	0.72
1J84	8192	538	5.43	1	1.97	3	2.12	1/25	2.15
1K1J	8101	1	1.96	1	0.33	7	9.43	22/17	6.04[**]
1MRX	2627	1	0.62	1	0.47	96	3.93	1/50	1.51
1MSM	6030	1	0.95	1	1.87	2	8.34	2/49	0.71[*]
2IKO	2622	1	0.55	1	0.49	1	0.49	43/5	0.86
2PYM	4340	2	9.57	9 (1)	1.66	5 (1)	1.66	1/50	0.95
2PYN	4953	2	9.61	1	1.22	1	1.22	5/43	0.86[*]
2XII	8192	3	6.59	1	0.58	1	0.58	44/2	7.03[**]
2Z8D	8192	1	0.73	2	3.67	1	0.68	46/4	7.38[**]
2Z8E	8192	1	1.09	1	1.11	1	1.11	2/21	2.00
2ZDM	5971	1	0.96	1	0.91	1	1.11	13/27	1.16
2ZDN	5645	1	0.59	1	0.68	1	0.68	20/20	1.98
2ZFS	5986	1	1.56	2	2.67	3	2.67	7/36	0.71
3KDB	4504	2	12.18	1	0.96	2	6.43	1/49	1.71[*]
3KIV	5363	1	1.25	1	0.75	1	0.75	17/5	1.59
3NU3	4935	1	1.34	1	0.44	2	4.16	5/44	0.97[*]
4CRC	11809	928	9.79	2	2.67	2	2.67	15/24	0.93
4CRD	20222	5237	5.46	1	1.00	1	1.00	8/23	0.50[*]
4LL3	5888	1	1.04	4	8.38	1	1.89	3/30	0.73[*]
4MR5	5002	1	0.45	5	8.05	3	8.05	50/1	9.24[**]
4MR6	4313	9	8.84	1	1.16	1	1.16	1/4	5.69[**]
4P8V	8193	232	8.1	1	0.58	2	4.13	6/7	1.13
5CSD	29528	14997	11.65	993	10.33	1	0.93	1/49	1.85[*]

be 1 both for COSMO and COSMO2 for 2PYM complex (INN = 1 in brackets in Table 2). The similar situation was also observed for 4LL3 in COSMO calculation. Accounting for an alternative conformation of a native ligand in RMSD calculation for 4LL3 enabled to obtain more reasonable estimation of positioning: 4.78 Å instead of 8.38 Å.

Secondly, we observed that some global minima, i.e. the respective ligand poses, differ from the native conformation only in the position of one moiety. This caused them to have INN not equal to 1, but in terms of pharmacology and drug design quasi-docking managed to reproduce the inhibition conformation of the ligand when access to catalytic triad is blocked. In other words, for such complexes quasi-docking succeeds in predicting activity of native ligands but finds global minima corresponding to ligand poses which are slightly different from crystallized ligand poses. These cases were observed for 2ZFS and 4CRC and, as can be seen in Table 2, RMSD values calculated for these complexes slightly differ from 2 Å.

The third peculiarity which can explain unsatisfactory positioning for two complexes is possible discrepancy between ligand charges during modeling and ligand charges taken place during crystallization. As described in Sect. 2.6, protonation of all molecules under consideration is performed at pH 7.4, although crystallization pH, as given from in-depth experimental data, was not 7.4 for some complexes and 2ZFS and 5CSD are among them. If consider the case of 2ZFS, the absence of the second positive charge on a nitrogen atom near a cycloheptane ring which could be possible at higher pH (crystallization pH for this complex is 8.0) might help in positioning the cycloheptyl moiety more accurately. In the case of 5CSD crystallization pH was 4.8 at which an arachidonic acid, a native ligand of 5CSD, exists in both (deprotonated and protonated) states since its pKa is 4.752. Hydrophobic character of the binding site in this complex favors binding the deprotonated and neutral form of the ligand over the protonated form. We studied the protonated form that could affect the results.

Additionally, relying upon Tables 1 and 2 one can infer that energy calculations based on COSMO2 for most of complexes containing HIV-1 protease turned out to fail in comparison to calculations based on COSMO. This is seemingly a consequence of an atypical value of E_{np}^{DS} which for complexes with HIV-1 protease is fewer than -20 kcal/mol while the mean of E_{np}^{DS} is about -16 kcal/mol if not account for these complexes. High negative values of E_{np}^{DS} can be explained by architecture of the active site of HIV-1 protease. It possesses a pipe-like shape and binding a ligand inside this "pipe" is accompanied by its almost total isolation from the solvent environment. This creates high E_{np}^{DS} during COSMO2 calculations which penalties conformations close to the native ligand pose. The possible improvement of positioning in the frame of COSMO2 parameterization for complexes with HIV-1 protease or with other proteins having deep narrow binding sites is application of another ξ coefficient in the equation for E_{np}^{DS}. Finally, some unsatisfactory results for a few complexes cannot be explained by the similar abovementioned observations. For such complexes (for example, 4MR5) entropic factors seem to be predominant over enthalpy during a binding process and, since we account for only part of these factors, we are not able to perform quasi-docking for them with total accuracy.

For four complexes (4MR6, 2Z8D, 2XII, and 1K1J) quasi-docking with either PM7 +COSMO or PM7+COSMO2 finds the global minimum near (RMSD $\lesssim 1$ Å) the crystallized native ligand position as opposed to SOL which could not find such ligand poses for these four complexes even for very high docking parameters. At first glance SOL demonstrates good ligand positioning results: for 19 test complexes RMSD of the ligand pose with a lowest energy from the crystallized ligand position is less than 2 Å. However for 8 of these complexes the occupation of the first cluster is only 1 or 2 and the respective global energy optimization cannot be considered as successful and positioning as reliable.

3.2   Binding Enthalpy

Experimental values of the binding enthalpy, ΔH_{exp}, are available for almost all test complexes (except 3KIV, 4CRC and 4CRD) in the relevant articles describing resolving the crystal structure, crystallization methods and measured thermodynamic properties of the protein-ligand complexes; the references can be found at the respective web-pages of each complex in www.rcsb.org [13]. Selecting complexes for the comparison of the calculated and measured binding enthalpies we take into account following considerations. Firstly, we choose only complexes for which quasi-docking or docking procedures give good positioning accuracy because *a priori* we cannot trust results of binding enthalpy calculations if positioning accuracy is low. So, only complexes for which INN = 1 (for quasi-docking) or RMSD < 2 kcal/mol (for SOL docking) are chosen for the comparison of the calculated and measured binding enthalpies. Secondly, we get rid of two complexes, 2PYM and 2PYN, for which the formation of the protein-ligand complex is entropy-driven and the binding enthalpy is positive.

Finally, we exclude complexes 1J84, 2Z8D, 2Z8E, 4P8V from the consideration in this section because we find that all carbohydrate ligand molecules of these complexes contain distorted pyranose rings in the global energy minimum for a bound ligand state and for an unbound one. This distortion is manifested by the presence of boat or twist-boat conformations instead of usual chair conformations that enables distorted molecules to form additional inner hydrogen bonds. It is possible that inclusion of solvation during the optimization process might help to reduce an energy weight of hydrogen bonding and preserve the proper conformations of pyranose rings.

Different protein-ligand complexes satisfy all these three conditions for different methods of the ligand positioning in the target protein. The results of the comparison of ΔH_{exp} with ΔH_{bind} calculated for ligand positioning by the quasi-docking procedure using PM7+COSMO or PM7+COSMO2 energy calculation method at the second stage of the quasi-docking procedure are presented in Table 3, respectively; the binding energies ΔH_{bind} calculated for ligand positioning with SOL are presented in the same table.

We see in Table 3 that all calculated binding enthalpies ΔH_{bind} are negative (the bound states of the protein-ligand complexes are more preferable than their unbound ones), but their absolute values are much larger than the measured binding enthalpies ΔH_{exp}. The coefficient of correlation R between calculated and measured binding enthalpy values is large (0.74) for quasi-docking with the PM7+COSMO energy but low (0.2) for quasi-docking with PM7+COSMO2. For ligand positioning with SOL docking the coefficient of correlation R is low for both methods of the energy calculation. The correlation between calculated and measured binding enthalpies for PM7 with COSMO2 energy calculations is worse than for PM7 and with the COSMO solvent model. Positioning accuracy of calculations with COSMO2 is also worse than with COSMO (see Table 2). The main difference between COSMO and COSMO2 models is the use in the latter the non-polar contribution into the solute-solvent interaction: the presence of the non-polar desolvation term in Eq. (4) comparing with (3). Values of this non-polar desolvation term amount to 25–50% of the total value of the binding enthalpy. The relatively large non-polar contribution points to the cause of the worse COSMO2 performance. It is possibly connected with the too simplified (but commonly used) approximation of the non-polar part of the solute-solvent interaction.

Table 3. Experimentally measured ΔH_{exp} and calculated ΔH_{bind} binding enthalpies.

The ligand pose is obtained by		Quasi-docking		SOL docking	
PDB ID	ΔH_{exp}, kcal/mol	ΔH_{bind}, COSMO, kcal/mol	ΔH_{bind}, COSMO2, kcal/mol	ΔH_{bind}, COSMO, kcal/mol	ΔH_{bind}, COSMO2, kcal/mol
1C5P	−4.52	−54.75	−44.70	−54.89	−44.86
1HW5	−0.97	−54.74	−52.12	−49.13	−46.13
1K1J	−9.46	−82.71	–	–	–
1MRX	−2.10	−54.89	–	−46.75	−47.23
1MSM	−7.60	−67.86	–	−54.29	−58.94
2IKO	−9.50	−81.19	−78.78	−81.30	−79.13
2XII	−9.80	−92.09	−86.41	–	–
2ZDM	−7.24	−82.20	−81.20	−83.67	−81.21
2ZDN	−5.09	−85.08	−79.37	−80.20	−73.17
2ZFS	−4.52	–	–	−85.38	−80.26
3KDB	−1.55	−54.68	–	−28.08	−31.95
3NU3	−7.30	−54.46	–	−53.54	−55.40
4LL3	−16.40	–	−52.87	−37.38	−43.83
4MR6	−4.04	−47.42	−54.41	–	–
5CSD	−14.20	–	−67.50	−32.95	−56.84
The coefficient of correlation R between ΔH_{exp} and ΔH_{bind}		0.74	0.20	−0.14	0.15

Better results should be obtained with the more keen model for the non-polar part taking into account specificity of interactions of each atom type with solvent, e.g. as in [22]. It is noteworthy that calculations of ΔH_{bind} with accounting for solvent during ligand pose optimization for both the bound state and the unbound form led to a slight increase of the coefficient of correlation between experimental binding enthalpies and enthalpies calculated by quasi-docking (for the COSMO method, R was increased from 0.74 to 0.77 and in the case of the COSMO2 method – from 0.2 to 0.29); absolute values of ΔH_{bind} differed from initial values by several kcal/mol.

3.3 Discussion of the Results

The high positioning accuracy of the quasi-docking procedure for most of the test complexes confirms our previous results obtained for another set of complexes. Almost in all cases when the docking paradigm is not satisfied (INN $\neq$ 1) we found some peculiarities explaining the reason of this and for some cases the bad positioning accuracy is illusory – for the symmetric binding sites. Relatively high correlation between the calculated and measured values of the protein-ligand binding enthalpy for the PM7+COSMO method of energy calculation is an encouraging result of the present research especially that the best ligand pose has been determined in the quasi-docking procedure with the same energy calculation method. The use of the new COSMO parameterization did not demonstrate an advantage over the old one, and we need more deep investigation to understand better particularity of the former. The large difference of the calculated and measured values of the protein-ligand binding enthalpy is the most disappointing result of the present research and more efforts are needed to overcome this problem.

In the present investigation we stroke on the problem of the determination of the global energy minimum of the unbound ligand. This problem in some sense is more complicated than the global energy minimum search of the protein-ligand complex. In the latter case the ligand has limited freedom of the conformation variation restricted by its presence in the active site of the target protein. In the unbound state of a flexible drug-like ligand having 5–15 torsions the ligand energy surface can be much more complicated than in the bound state due to larger freedom for unrestricted ligand distortions, and the chemically wrong ligand conformations can be found for the global energy minimum due to either inherent shortcomings of the force field or the quantum-chemical method or the unrealistic number of intra-molecular hydrogen bonds formation, π-stacking interactions, *etc.* arising due to absence or inadequate solvent accounting. The correctly determined global energy minimum of the unbound ligand defines the ligand strain energy contribution into the protein-ligand binding enthalpy (due to the last term in Eqs. (3) and (4)) and it can be as small as several kcal/mol or as large as several dozen kcal/mol for different complexes [10].

In connection with this we should also to point at the inherent quasi-docking shortcoming: the local energy optimizations in the frame of the MMFF94 force field performed at the first stage of the quasi-docking procedure by the FLM program can result in an unrealistic ligand distortion which cannot be corrected by the following PM7 local energy optimization. This shortcoming can be overcome only by direct quantum-chemical docking which can be realized in the close future using super-computer resources.

4 Conclusions

The effectiveness of the quasi-docking procedure on the base of the PM7 quantum-chemical semiempirical method with the continuum COSMO solvent model for ligand positioning is demonstrated for a set of protein-ligand complexes. This result supports the similar observation demonstrated previously [3, 4] for another set of protein-ligand complexes. The relatively high correlation (0.74) of measured and calculated values of the binding enthalpy is observed when the binding enthalpy is calculated by the PM7 method with the old COSMO parameterization. The performance of the new COSMO2 parameterization [18] is worse and this shortcoming is possibly connected with the too simplified model of the non-polar part of the solute solvent interaction. Further investigations of the peculiarities of the quasi-docking procedure and more detailed comparison of COSMO and COSMO2 models are needed.

The presented results demonstrate that quasi-docking procedure and the use of the PM7 semiempirical method with the COSMO solvent model are promising for the computer aided structure-based drug design.

Acknowledgements. The work was financially supported by the Russian Science Foundation, Agreement no. 15-11-00025-П. The research is carried out using the equipment of the shared research facilities of HPC computing resources at Lomonosov Moscow State University, including the Lomonosov supercomputer [23].

References

1. Sulimov, V.B., Sulimov, A.V.: Docking: molecular modeling for drug discovery. AINTELL, Moscow (2017). (in Russian)
2. Sulimov, V.B., Kutov, D.C., Sulimov, A.V.: Advances in Docking. Curr. Med. Chem. **26**, 1–25 (2019). https://doi.org/10.2174/0929867325666180904115000
3. Sulimov, A.V., Kutov, D.C., Katkova, E.V., Sulimov, V.B.: Combined docking with classical force field and quantum chemical semiempirical method PM7. Adv, Bioinform. **2017** (2017). Article ID: 7167691. https://doi.org/10.1155/2017/7167691
4. Sulimov, A.V., Kutov, D.C., Katkova, E.V., Ilin, I.S., Sulimov, V.B.: New generation of docking programs: supercomputer validation of force fields and quantum-chemical methods for docking. J. Mol. Graph. Model. **78**, 139–147 (2017). https://doi.org/10.1016/j.jmgm.2017.10.007
5. Stewart, J.J.: Optimization of parameters for semiempirical methods VI: more modifications to the NDDO approximations and re-optimization of parameters. J. Mol. Model. **19**(1), 1–32 (2013). https://doi.org/10.1007/s00894-012-1667-x
6. Klamt, A., Schuurmann, G.: COSMO: a new approach to dielectric screening in solvents with explicit expressions for the screening energy and its gradient. J. Chem. Soc. Perkin Trans. **2**(5), 799–805 (1993). https://doi.org/10.1039/P29930000799
7. Oferkin, I.V., et al.: Evaluation of docking target functions by the comprehensive investigation of protein-ligand energy minima. Adv. Bioinform. **2015** (2015). Article ID: 126858. https://doi.org/10.1155/2015/126858
8. Oferkin, I.V., Zheltkov, D.A., Tyrtyshnikov, E.E., Sulimov, A.V., Kutov, D.C., Sulimov, V.B.: Evaluation Of The Docking Algorithm Based On Tensor Train Global Optimization. Bull. South Ural State Univ. Ser. Math. Model. Program. Comput. Softw. **8**(4), 83–99 (2015)
9. Sulimov, A.V., et al.: Evaluation of the novel algorithm of flexible ligand docking with moveable target-protein atoms. Comput. Struct. Biotechnol. J. **15**, 275–285 (2017). https://doi.org/10.1016/j.csbj.2017.02.004
10. Sulimov, A., Kutov, D., Sulimov, V.: Parallel supercomputer docking program of the new generation: finding low energy minima spectrum. In: Voevodin, V., Sobolev, S. (eds.) RuSCDays 2018. CCIS, vol. 965, pp. 314–330. Springer, Cham (2019). https://doi.org/10.1007/978-3-030-05807-4_27
11. Kutov, D.C., Sulimov, A.V., Sulimov, V.B.: Supercomputer docking: investigation of low energy minima of protein-ligand complexes. Supercomput. Front. Innov. **5**(3), 134–137 (2018)
12. Stewart, J.J.P.: MOPAC2016: Stewart computational chemistry, colorado springs, CO, USA (2016). http://OpenMOPAC.net
13. Berman, H.M., et al.: The protein data bank. Nucleic Acids Res. **28**(1), 235–242 (2000)

14. Stewart, J.J.P.: Application of localized molecular orbitals to the solution of semiempirical self-consistent field equations. Int. J. Quantum Chem. **58**, 133–146 (1996)
15. Rezac, J., Hobza, P.: Advanced corrections of hydrogen bonding and dispersion for semiempirical quantum mechanical methods. J. Chem. Theory Comput. **8**(1), 141–151 (2012). https://doi.org/10.1021/ct200751e
16. Řezáč, J., Hobza, P.: A halogen-bonding correction for the semiempirical PM6 method. Chem. Phys. Lett. **506**(4), 286–289 (2011). https://doi.org/10.1016/j.cplett.2011.03.009
17. Hostaš, J., Řezáč, J., Hobza, P.: On the performance of the semiempirical quantum mechanical PM6 and PM7 methods for noncovalent interactions. Chem. Phys. Lett. **568–569** (Supplement C), 161–166 (2013). https://doi.org/10.1016/j.cplett.2013.02.069
18. Kříž, K., Řezáč, J.: Reparametrization of the COSMO solvent model for semiempirical methods PM6 and PM7. J. Chem. Inf. Model. **59**(1), 229–235 (2019). https://doi.org/10.1021/acs.jcim.8b00681
19. Chen, W., Gilson, M.K., Webb, S.P., Potter, M.J.: Modeling protein-ligand binding by mining minima. J. Chem. Theory Comput. **6**(11), 3540–3557 (2010)
20. Sulimov, A.V., Kutov, D.C., Oferkin, I.V., Katkova, E.V., Sulimov, V.B.: Application of the docking program SOL for CSAR benchmark. J. Chem. Inf. Model. **53**(8), 1946–1956 (2013). https://doi.org/10.1021/ci400094h
21. Hanwell, M.D., Curtis, D.E., Lonie, D.C., Vandermeersch, T., Zurek, E., Hutchison, G.R.: Avogadro: an advanced semantic chemical editor, visualization, and analysis platform. J. Cheminform. **4**(1), 17 (2012). https://doi.org/10.1186/1758-2946-4-17
22. Basilevsky, M.V., Leontyev, I.V., Luschekina, S.V., Kondakova, O.A., Sulimov, V.B.: Computation of hydration free energies of organic solutes with an implicit water model. J. Comput. Chem. **27**(5), 552–570 (2006)
23. Sadovnichy, V., Tikhonravov, A., Voevodin, V., Opanasenko, V.: "Lomonosov": super-computing at Moscow State University. In: Contemporary High Performance Computing: From Petascale Toward Exascale, Boca Raton, United States, pp. 283–307 (2013)

Simulation of "ExoMars" Spacecraft Landing on the Surface of Mars Using Supercomputer Technologies

Anuar Kagenov$^{(\boxtimes)}$, Sergey Prokhanov, Anatoliy Glazunov, Ivan Eremin,
Kirill Kostyushin, Konstantin Zhilcov, Iliya Tyryshkin, and Sergey Orlov

Tomsk State University, Tomsk 634050, Russia
{anuar,orlov}@ftf.tsu.ru, viking@math.tsu.ru,
{gla,iveremin,konstantin,tyryshkin}@niipmm.tsu.ru,
kostushink@hotmail.com

Abstract. This article presents the results of a three-dimensional simulation of the soft landing of the ExoMars spacecraft on the Mars surface. The interactions of multiple supersonic jets with surfaces are investigated. According to the obtained gas-dynamic parameters of the gas, lift loss effect, erosion and particle motion under Mars conditions are studied. It was obtained that the influence of lift loss effect on the thrust characteristics of the propulsion system affects no more than 6% of the thrust level. For erosion, the estimates show that when the propulsion system is operating at a minimum load, the force effect of the jets will not lead to the erosion of the surface of the landing site for all types of Martian soils considered. The trajectories for solid particles with sizes up to 100 mkm coincide with the gas streamlines. The calculations using the free Open-FOAM software was performed. Parallelization of the task using the Scotch computational domain decomposition method using MPI technologies on a tetrahedral computational mesh was carried out. The efficiency and acceleration of the modified dbnsTurbFoam of OpenFoam solver on the considered landing problem of the ExoMars decent module using Bare Metal, KVM and Docker was investigated. It is obtained that the use of Docker virtualization compared with KVM gives the most efficient acceleration when parallelizing the calculations.

Keywords: Mars · ExoMars · Parallel computing · Docker · KVM · MPI · 3D mathematical modeling · Supersonic multiple turbulent jets · Impact jets · Lift loss · Erosion · Particles · OpenFOAM

1 Introduction

At present, study of the planet Mars is carried out using artificial satellites launched into the orbit of Mars, landing platforms and rovers delivered to its surface. The development of the Martian programs dates back to the 1960s. A number of spacecraft were launched to the planet Mars. Total for the present

© Springer Nature Switzerland AG 2019
V. Voevodin and S. Sobolev (Eds.): RuSCDays 2019, CCIS 1129, pp. 379–391, 2019.
https://doi.org/10.1007/978-3-030-36592-9_31

time, 48 space programs have been developed for the study of the Mars plan, among which less than half successfully took place (22 missions). Therefore, it is necessary to improve the reliability of the structures of the landing modules and soft landing technology for the implementation of further space missions.

In continuation of the Martian missions, a joint project "ExoMars" between the Federal Space Agency and the European Space Agency is currently being implemented [1]. This paper discusses the landing of the ExoMars decent module on the surface of Mars. It is a platform on which are placed: rover, tanks with fuel and helium, landing supports, radar, thermal co-panels, solar panels, scientific equipment, various sensors, and the propulsion system, which consist of four liquid rocket engines. Final braking is performed at an altitude of less than 10 m. Due to the fact that the work of the engines at the final stage of the soft landing occurs at a small height (a few meters), the outflowing jets of combustion products interact with the surface of the planet Mars. Many experimental and theoretical studies are devoted to the interaction of supersonic jets with flat and inclined surfaces [2–4]. However, the interaction of jets with uneven surfaces is not enough. At the same time, at low altitudes, a negative effect of lift loss, which affects the propulsion system, is possible. This effect has been well studied for vertical take-off and landing aircraft [5–7]. Therefore, for landing platforms in the conditions of other planets, this effect has not been previously studied. The erosion of the surface of the landing site, the motion of dust particles and soil of Mars is also possible. Unlike the Soviet automatic stations, where there was instruments for measuring the properties of soil, the US Mars vehicles were not equipped with them. Therefore, there is not a lot of information on the Martian soil; the process of accumulation of the current Martian missions is underway. We note a number of papers that summarize main results of soils study. The work [8] provides data on the structure and characteristics of the soils at the landing sites of the Viking, Pathfinder and MER. It is also worth noting the work [9], in which a complete summary of data on the properties of various types of soils on the surface of Mars. In this work, almost all the information currently available on the characteristics and properties of dry, frozen, rocky and semi-rocky soil of Mars is systematized. Some groups of scientists imitate the properties of Mars soil with the use of terrestrial rocks similar in physical properties. This approach allows us to assess the strength properties of the soil [26,27].

2   Problem Statement

2.1   Mathematical Model for Gas Flow in Nozzles and Jets

The mathematical formulation for the gas flow in nozzles and jets consists of a system of Favrou averaged Navier-Stokes equations together with the $SST\ k-\omega$ turbulence model [10,11]. The system of equations in a rectangular Cartesian coordinate system x_1, x_2, x_3 for nonstationary gas flow has the form:

$$\frac{\partial \bar{\rho}}{\partial t} + \frac{\partial}{\partial x_j}\left[\bar{\rho}\tilde{u}_j\right] = 0 \tag{1}$$

$$\frac{\partial \left(\bar{\rho} \tilde{u}_i \right)}{\partial t} + \frac{\partial}{\partial x_j} \left[\bar{\rho} \tilde{u}_i \tilde{u}_j + \bar{p} \delta_{ij} - \tilde{\tau}_{ij} \right] = 0 \tag{2}$$

$$\frac{\partial \left(\bar{\rho} \tilde{E} \right)}{\partial t} + \frac{\partial}{\partial x_j} \left[\bar{\rho} \tilde{u}_j \tilde{E} + \tilde{u}_j \bar{p} + \tilde{q}_j - \tilde{u}_i \tilde{\tau}_{ij} \right] = 0. \tag{3}$$

The ideal gas equation:

$$\bar{p} = \bar{\rho} R \tilde{T}. \tag{4}$$

2.2   Lift Loss Effect

The lift loss effect is expressed by the following ratio [5–7]:

$$L_f = \frac{G - G_0}{P}, \tag{5}$$

where G and G_0 – pressure force integrals over the inner surface with and without opposite site, P – thrust of nozzle.

2.3   Erosion

To assess the possible erosion of the Mars soil, the pressure distribution on the surface of the landing site and the experimental characteristics of the Mars soil are used. Evaluation using the Coulomb-More criteria is performed [12,13]:

$$\tau = \sigma \, tan(\varphi) + c, \tag{6}$$

where τ – shear stresses; σ – normal stresses; φ – internal friction angle; c – specific cohesion.

2.4   Particle Motion

The equation of motion in the gas flow for each particle, taking into account resistance force and gravity in a rectangular Cartesian coordinate system x_1, x_2, x_3 has the form [14]:

$$m_p \frac{du_{pi}}{dt} = F_{Di} - m_p g_{Mars}, \tag{7}$$

where is the index p determines the belonging of variables to the particle, and the index $i = 1, 2, 3$.

The drag force has the following expression:

$$F_{Di} = C_D \pi D_p^2 \rho \frac{(u_i - u_{pi}) \, |u_i - u_{pi}|}{8}. \tag{8}$$

Here is the drag coefficient C_D determined by the following relationship:

$$C_D = \frac{24}{Re_p} f_D (M_p, Re_p),$$ (9)

where $f_D (M_p, Re_p)$ – drag function.

In the conditions of Mars, it is necessary to take into account rarefaction of the atmosphere of Mars and the compressibility of the medium of the carrier phase. So, taking into account rarefaction, compressibility and inertia, the drag function has the following form [15]:

$$f_D (M_p, Re_p) = \frac{\left(1 + 0.15 Re_p^{0.687}\right) \left[1 + e^{-\frac{0.427}{M_p^{4.63}} - \frac{3.0}{Re_p^{0.88}}}\right]}{1 + \frac{M_p}{Re_p} \left[3.82 + 1.28 e^{-1.25 \frac{Re_p}{M_p}}\right]}.$$ (10)

3   Numerical Implementation and Acceleration of Calculations

To implement the physical and mathematical model and conduct numerical research free software OpenFOAM was used [16]. Numerical method on finite volume method is based. Hexahedral numerical mesh using Salome Platform software was make. A difference scheme of MUSCL-Hancock type TVD of the second order of accuracy was used [17,18]. From the approximate solution of the Riemann problem according to the HLLC scheme, there were fluxes through the faces of the computational grid cells. System of linear of algebraic equations using the Gauss-Seidel methodwas solved. The time sampling was carried out by a four-step Runge-Kutta method of second-order accuracy [19].

Parallelization of the task is carried out using the Scotch computational domain decomposition method using MPI technologies [20]. The tetrahedral computational mesh, which is generated by the NetGen algorithm [21], is used; the number of cells is about 30 million. An example of a calculation mesh of one of the calculation variants is shown in Fig. 1. All calculations was performed on the supercomputer of TSU SKIF Cyberia [22]. The efficiency and acceleration of the modified dbnsTurbFoam OpenFoam solver on the landing task of the ExoMars landing platform using Bare Metal, KVM and Docker was investigated [23,24], the result are shown in Fig. 3. In the study compute nodes with processors Xeon 5670, 48 GB of RAM was used. For various virtualization technologies, data exchange using the QDR Infiniband network was organized.

Figure 2 shows the time spent on conditional iterations depending on the number of processors. It can be seen that the time sequential solution requires about 2000 s, and when using 192 cores, it takes from 16 to 20 s. In Fig. 3 the acceleration of the calculation depending on the number of processes for Bare Metal, Docker, and KVM is shown. Accelerated 120 times compared to the serial solution using 192 processors was obtained.

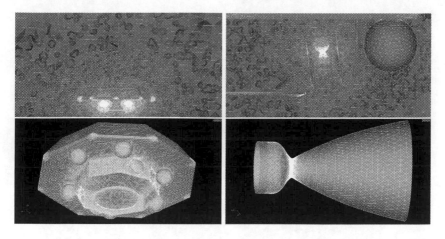

Fig. 1. Computational mesh in cross section of domain and of landing module and nozzle

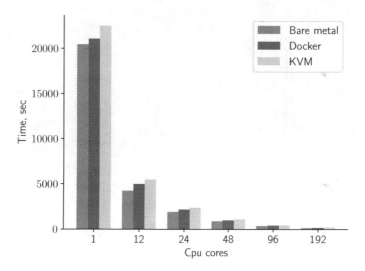

Fig. 2. Performance comparison

Test results show that using containers under Docker control allows achieving better performance than using the KVM hypervisor. The performance of Docker containers in most cases is slightly different from the Bare Metal.

4   Numerical Results and Discussion

In numerical experiments, a simplified configuration of the ExoMars landing module was used. The computational domain is presented in Fig. 4. The distance from the nozzle to the landing surface was: $h = 1$ m, $h = 0.5$ m, $h = 0.3$ m.

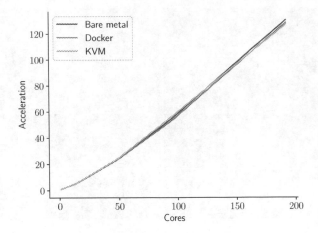

Fig. 3. Program acceleration

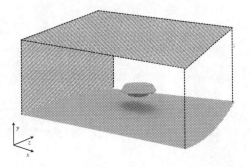

Fig. 4. Computational domain

The propulsion system contains four brake motors. The thrust of propulsion system corresponds to 13734 N at maximum operating mode, and at minimum 1962 N [25]. The nozzles of the propulsion system are angled 7° at a distance of 1.2 m from each other. The geometric characteristics of the nozzle were as follows: nozzle throat diameter 0.03613 m, nozzle diameter 0.19395 m, and the angle of the semi-solution of the nozzle is 10°. Parameters on the nozzle inlet section at minimum load: pressure – 0.28 MPa, temperature – 1180 K, adiabatic index – 1.33719; at maximum load: pressure – 1.962 MPa, temperature – 1336 K, adiabatic index – 1.29222. The Mach number at the nozzle exit at the minimum thrust corresponded to $M = 4.7$ and at the maximum thrust $M = 4.5$. The environment parameters was set as follows: pressure – 650 Pa, temperature – 250 K, components of the velocity vector – 0 m/s.

4.1   The Results of Jet Interaction with Surfaces

For the height $h = 1$ m, Fig. 5 shows the isosurfaces of the Mach numbers for the propulsion system to operate at the minimum and maximum modes.

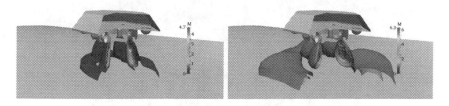

Fig. 5. Isosurfaces of Mach numbers for h = 1 m at the minimum and maximum thrust of the propulsion system

For a detailed representation of the gas-dynamic structure during the interaction of multiple jets with the surface, more detailed flow patterns are depicted in the plane passing through the symmetry axes of the opposite nozzles. It shows the distribution of Mach numbers and gas flow streamlines. In Fig. 6 shows the results of calculations when the remote control is operating at maximum load at heights $h = 1$, 0.5, 0.3 m.

The gas-dynamic picture under the apparatus is realized complicated. With a decrease in height from $h = 1$ m to $h = 0.5$ m, the single vortex stretched upward changes in shape. At a height of $h = 0.5$ m, it has a round shape, and at a height of $h = 0.3$ m, it is compressed due to the reverse flow, taking an "elliptical" shape and a weak second vortex appears at the boundary of the right jet. This is due to the fact that a radar is located in the interspin region, which blocks the flow of a portion of the gas of reflected jets into the bottom region of the apparatus. Therefore, in the bottom area of the landing module for the calculation options at heights $h = 1$ and $h = 0.5$ m, the environment is almost at rest. As a result, at the bottom of the landing module platform, behind the radar, the back flow of the jets basically does not affect. It is interesting to note that the qualitative picture of the change in the structure of the vortices during the operation of the propulsion system at the minimum thrust coincides with their changes at the maximum thrust.

4.2   The Results of Lift Loss Effect

Having integrated the pressure over the lower surface of the apparatus using Eq. 5, the effect of lift loss is determined. Table 1 shows the values of the force effect of the reflected supersonic jets of a propulsion system from the surface of Mars on the considered ExoMars landing platform.

At the minimum thrust of the propulsion system at the location of the lander on the height of 1 m lift loss effect does not occur, but rather the opposite occurs the force effect of 2%. With a further decrease in height, the effect begins to

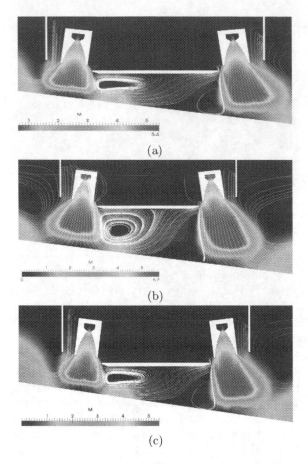

Fig. 6. Mach number distribution with gas flow streamlines, maximum propulsion mode (a) – h = 1 m, (b) – h = 0.5 m, (c) – h = 0.3 m

manifest itself and its greatest effect is 3.8%. At maximum thrust, the opposite behavior is observed when disposition of the vehicle at height of 1 m, the effect is 5.6%, while further reducing the height of force leads to the opposite effect on the bottom of the landing platform, and this effect is 22%.

4.3   The Results of Land Surface Erosion

Evaluation of the surface erosion of the landing site was carried out according to the Coulomb-More criterion (6) for dry cohesive soils. The following Martian soil types are considered: crusty to cloddy material τ_1 (internal friction angle 18°, cohesion 3 kPa), cloddy to crusty material τ_2 internal friction angle 35°, cohesion 3 kPa), blocky material τ_3 (internal friction angle 30°, cohesion 11 kPa), sand τ_4 (internal friction angle 30°, cohesion 1 kPa) and analogue of the Martian soil τ_5 (internal friction angle 32.5°, cohesion 0.718 kPa).

Table 1. The results of calculations of the force effect of the supersonic jets on the surface of the landing platform and the lift loss effect

Mode	Minumum			Maximum		
Height, m	1.0	0.5	0.3	1.0	0.5	0.3
G_0, N		5017			4635	
G, N	5055	4959	4941	3871	5657	7749
L_f	0.0192	−0.0296	−0.0384	−0.056	0.072	0.224

It is known for an analogue of the Martian soil Mojave Mars Simulant esti-mates of shear strength in the range of 3–20 kPa [26]. For another analogue of the Martian soil ES-1, ES-2 and ES-3, shear strength estimates are in the range of 5–20 kPa [27]. The properties (angle of internal friction and cohesion) are similar to ES-1, ES-2, ES-3, similar to Mojave Mars Simulant, loose ground and sand of Mars. Therefore, for these types of soils, if the limiting resistance of the soil to a shift of 20 kPa is exceeded, erosion of the landing site is possible. Since other types of soil have a greater specific cohesion, it can be assumed that for their destruction it is necessary to apply higher normal stresses. Table 2 presents the results of the calculation of tangential stresses for the soils described above.

Table 2. The values of the tangential stress of the soil of Mars

Mode	Height, m	τ_1, Pa	τ_2, Pa	τ_3, Pa	τ_4, Pa	τ_5, Pa
Minimum	1.0	3620	5330	12100	2100	1934
	0.5	4360	6930	13400	3420	3394
	0.3	4780	7840	14200	14200	4212
Maximum	1.0	5010	8330	14600	4570	4665
	0.5	8410	15700	20600	10600	11333
	0.3	13000	25500	28700	18700	20258

In the landing module control system, it is incorporated that, when carrying out the descent the real thrust of the propulsion system at the detuned heights will be close to the minimum thrust. When the control unit operates at minimum load and height h = 0.3 m, the limiting resistances of sand, analogue of Martian soil and cloddy to crusty material do not exceed 5 kPa, and for crusty to cloddy material 7 kPa. These values fall within the shear strength evaluation limit 3–20 kPa for Mojave Mars Simulant and 5–20 kPa for ES-1, ES-2 and ES-3. When the propulsion system works on the maximum load, according to the calculation results, it can be seen that when the landing platform is located at a height of h = 1 m and h = 0.5 m, the values of the tangent components for τ_1, τ_2, τ_4 and τ_5 do not exceed the value of 20 kPa. Consequently, at these altitudes, the power load of the flowing supersonic multiple jets will not lead to the erosion of these types of soils.

4.4   The Results of Particle Motion

The trajectories of solid particles are calculated from the obtained gas field. In the studied landing sites of Viking, Pathfinder and MER the surface of Mars consists of crusty to cloddy material (1–10 mkm), cloddy to crusty material (5–500 mkm), blocky material (50–3000 mkm) and sand (60–200 mkm), therefore the particle diameter in numerical calculations ranged from 10 to 1000 mkm. Two variants of their initial distribution are considered.

The first, when they are evenly located on the surface of the landing site and the second in the form of a cloud of dust. For the first case, it was found that for particles whose diameter does not exceed 100 mkm, they could be lifted from the surface to height of more than 0.5 m with the landing module at the height of 0.3 m. The trajectories of the behavior of the lightest particles are similar to the behavior of the gas streamlines. For several test particles, Fig. 7 shows their trajectories depending on the size and location in the computational domain.

Fig. 7. The gas flow streamline and the trajectories of the particles for minimum load of propulsion system

Heavier particles with diameter of more than 100 mkm showed more inert behavior in the gas field, and any increase from the surface depending on the height and load of operation of the propulsion system was not observed. For clarity, Fig. 8 shows the evolution of the particles motion of sizes 10 and 100 mkm at the same time point.

For the second variant of the distribution of particles, the smallest amount of particles settled on the landing platform with the maximum and minimum load conditions of the propulsion system is obtained – these are particles of diameter 10 and 50 mkm (Table 3).

Their values do not exceed 2% of the total number of particles. In addition, the greatest number of particles deposited on the surface of the landing platform is particles of 100 mkm diameter. With a minimum load of 1 m high, their content is about 3.5%. This character is explained by the fact that the lighter particles are less inert, and the heavy ones are more inert and not so actively entrained by the gas flow, while some of them are deposited by gravity.

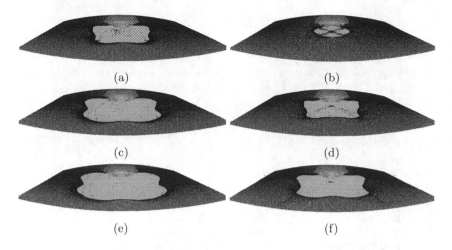

Fig. 8. The evolution of the movement of particles for minimum load and height 0.3 m (a, c, e) – 10 mkm, (b, d, f) – 100 mkm, (a, b) – 0.01 s, (c, d) – 0.03 s, (e, f) – 0.05 s

Table 3. The percentage of particles deposited on the landing platform

Mode	Minimum			Maximum		
Diameter, mkm	10	50	100	10	50	100
Height, m						
0.3	1.1%	1.2%	1.35%	1%	1.4%	2%
0.5	0,9%	1.2%	1.4%	1.1%	1.65%	2.6%
1	0.5%	1.5%	2.5%	1.9%	2.1%	3.5%

5   Conclusions

The three-dimensional mathematical modeling of the interaction of supersonic multiple jets of the propulsion system of the ExoMars landing platform with surfaces in Mars environment using high-performance computing systems has been carried out. The efficiency and acceleration of the modified dbnsTurbFoam OpenFoam solver on the landing task of the ExoMars landing platform using Bare Metal, KVM and Docker was investigated. It was obtained that the use of Docker virtualization compared with KVM gives the most efficient acceleration when parallelizing the calculations. The lift loss effect for the first time, for the given configuration of the landing platform was studied. It was obtained that the lift loss effect on the thrust characteristics of the propulsion system affects not more than 6% of the thrust level. Using the Coulomb-Mohr criterion, estimates of the soil erosion of Mars at the landing site of the ExoMars landing platform was done. Estimates show that when the propulsion system is operating at the minimum load, the force effect of the jets will not lead to erosion of the surface of the landing site for all the types of soils considered. In addition, particle motion was investigated.

Acknowledgements. This work was done with the financial support of the Ministry of Education and Science of the Russian Federation as part of a state task, the project N 9.9063.2017/8.9.

References

1. Space complex "ExoMars-2018". http://www.laspace.ru/projects/planets/exomars. Accessed 04 Mar 2019
2. Volkov, K.N., Emelyanov, V.N., Zazimko, V.A.: Turbulent Jets - Statistical Models and Large Vortex Modeling. FIZMATLIT, Moscow (2014)
3. Kagenov, A.M., Glazunov, A.A., Kostyushin, K.V., Eremin, I.V., Tyryshkin, I.M., Zhilcov, K.N.: Numerical investigation of the interaction of a single supersonic jet with a flat obstacle. In: AIP Conference Proceedings, vol. 2027, p. 030071 (2018)
4. Mehta, M., et al.: Thruster plume surface interactions: applications for spacecraft landings on planetary bodies. AIAA J. **51**(12), 2800–2818 (2013)
5. Wyatt, L.A.: Tests on the loss of vertical jet thrust due to ground effect on two simple VTOL platforms, with particular reference to the short SCI aircraft. Aeronaut. Res. Counc. Rep. Memoranda **3313**, 1–40 (1963)
6. Krothapalli, A., Rajkuperan, E., Alvi, F., Lourenco, L.M.: Flow field and noise characteristics of a supersonic impinging jet. J. Fluid Mech. **392**, 155–181 (1999)
7. Chotapalli, I.M., Krothapalli, A., Alkislar, M.B., Lourenco, L.M.: Flowfield and noise char-acteristics of twin supersonic impinging jets. AIAA J. **45**, 793–805 (2007)
8. Golombek, M.P., et al.: The Martian Surface: Composition, Mineralogy and Physical Properties. Cambridge Planetary Science, pp. 468–498. Cambridge University Press, Cambridge (2008)
9. Demidov, N.E., Bazilevsky, A.T., Kuzmin, R.O.: Martian soils: varieties, structure, composition, physical properties, drillability and risks for landers. Sol. Syst. Res. **49**(4), 243–261 (2015)
10. Wilcox, D.C.: Turbulence Modeling for CFD. DCW Industries Inc., California (1993)
11. Menter, F.R.: Two-equation eddy-viscosity turbulence models for engineering applications. AIAA J. **32**(8), 1598–1605 (1994)
12. Bartolomey, A.A.: Soil Mechanic. Publishing Association of Construction Universities, Moscow (2004)
13. Ter-Martirosyan, Z.G.: Soil Mechanic. Publishing Association of Construction Universities, Moscow (2005)
14. Vasenin, I.M., Arhipov, V.A., Butov, V.G., Glazunov, A.A., Trofimov, V.F.: Gas Dynamics of Two-Phase Flows in the Nozzles. Publishing house of Tomsk University, Tomsk (1986)
15. Sternin, L.E.: Basics of Gas Dynamics in Two-Phase Nozzles. Mashinostroenie, Moscow (1974)
16. OpenFOAM. http://openfoam.org. Accessed 29 Mar 2019
17. Toro, E.F.: Riemann Solvers and Numerical Methods for Fluid Dynamics. Springer, Heidelberg (2009). https://doi.org/10.1007/978-3-662-03915-1
18. Toro, E.F., Spruce, M., Speares, W.: Restoration of the contact surface in the HLL-Riemann solver. Shock Waves **4**, 25–34 (1994)

19. Lallemand, M.-H.: Dissipative properties of Runge-Kutta schemes with upwind spatial approximation for the Euler equations INRIA Reseach Report 1173 (1990)
20. MPI Forum. https://www.mpi-forum.org. Accessed 29 Mar 2019
21. NetGen/NGSolve. https://ngsolve.org. Accessed 29 Mar 2019
22. Supercomputer SKIF Cyberia. https://cyberia.tsu.ru. Accessed 29 Mar 2019
23. Kernel Virtual Machine. https://www.linux-kvm.org. Accessed 29 Mar 2019
24. Docker. https://docker.com. Accessed 29 Mar 2019
25. Aleksandrov, L.G., et al.: Propulsion system of descent module landing platform. Vestnik NPO imeni S.A. Lavochkina **23**(2), 116–120 (2014)
26. Hanley, J., Mellon, M.T., Arvidson, R.E.: Mechanical strength of Martian analog soil. In: 45th Lunar and Planetary Science, p. 2879 (2014)
27. Brunskill, C., et al.: Characterisation of martian soil simulants for the ExoMars rover testbed. J. Terramech. **48**, 419–438 (2010)

Solving Inverse Problems of Ultrasound Tomography in a Nondestructive Testing on a Supercomputer

Eugene Bazulin[1], Alexander Goncharsky[2],
and Sergey Romanov[2(✉)] ⓘ

[1] ECHO+ Ltd., Moscow, Russia
bazulin@echoplus.ru
[2] Lomonosov Moscow State University, Moscow, Russia
gonchar@srcc.msu.ru, romanov60@gmail.com

Abstract. This paper is concerned with the use of a supercomputer to solve tomographic inverse problems of ultrasonic nondestructive testing in the framework of a scalar wave model. The problem of recovering the velocity of a longitudinal wave in a solid is formulated as a coefficient inverse problem, which in this formulation is nonlinear. First, the algorithms were tested on real data obtained in experiments on a test bench for ultrasound tomography examinations. Ultrasound in the 2–8 MHz band was used for sounding. The experiment employed a rotating transducer system. A rotating transducer system substantially increases the number of emitters and detectors in a tomographic scheme and makes it possible to neutralize the image artifacts. An important result of this study is an experimental confirmation of the adequacy of the underlying mathematical model. The proposed scalable numerical algorithms can be efficiently parallelized on CPU– supercomputers. The computations were performed on 384 computing CPU cores of the "Lomonosov–2" supercomputer at Lomonosov Moscow State University.

Keywords: Supercomputer · Ultrasound tomography · Nondestructive testing · Inverse problems

1 Introduction

Applications of wave tomography methods include ultrasonic nondestructive testing (NDT). Typical NDT tasks include finding defects in solids [21, 24], ultrasonic inspection of welds, non–destructive testing of concrete structures and products made of plastics and composite materials [4, 8]. The ultrasonic methods widely used in nondestructive testing are not tomographic and they involve sounding of the object only on one side. There are many NDT methods, which allow detecting defect boundaries using ultrasonic waves in the reflection mode. Examples include the «topological imaging» techniques [1, 6, 9, 23, 26]. Also widely used is the Synthetic Aperture Focusing Technique (SAFT) [2, 19, 20, 25, 31].

Currently, ultrasonic tomography is making its first steps in the domain of non-destructive testing. One of the aims of this paper is to assess the potential of using

© Springer Nature Switzerland AG 2019
V. Voevodin and S. Sobolev (Eds.): RuSCDays 2019, CCIS 1129, pp. 392–402, 2019.
https://doi.org/10.1007/978-3-030-36592-9_32

ultrasonic tomography devices for examining the internal structure of solids in a real physical experiment. A distinctive feature of the propagation of ultrasonic waves in solids is the presence of several types of waves (longitudinal, transversal, and surface). Waves in solids can be most adequately described in terms of vector models [22]. The development of solution algorithms for inverse problems in vector and tensor models appears to be a very difficult task.

In this paper we analyze the inverse problem of tomography examinations in nondestructive testing tasks in terms of scalar wave model. The propagation velocities of longitudinal and transversal waves in most solids differ by several times allowing the longitudinal wave to be separated from transversal wave by the pulse arrival time to the detectors. In this case we can single out the inverse problem of the determination of the propagation velocity of the longitudinal wave in a nonuniform medium in terms of scalar wave model. This problem can be viewed as a coefficient inverse problem for scalar wave equation. Even in the simplest case of scalar wave model inverse problems of the tomography of solids are nonlinear and require a supercomputer to solve them.

A distinctive feature of nondestructive testing is that sounding is performed with high–frequency (1 MHz and higher) ultrasonic waves. Ultrasonic examinations of solids are mostly performed with multielement linear transducer arrays where each element operates both in the emission and receiver modes.

In this paper we for the first time validate our methods and algorithms [10, 13, 29] of solving inverse tomography problems aimed at nondestructive ultrasonic testing of solids by applying them to real data obtained in experiments performed on a test bench for ultrasonic tomography examinations (unlike work [29]). To obtain experimental data for tomographic examinations we made a sample phantom of a rexolite with a several mm large ebonite inset. To perform measurements, a bench was assembled for tomographic flaw detection with a rotating sounding system including two linear ultrasonic transducer antenna arrays. Sounding was performed with a 2–8 MHz ultrasonic pulse and the velocity structure of real phantoms was reconstructed using the algorithms developed.

The authors of [3] investigated NDT ultrasonic tomography methods for systems with incomplete range of sounding angles. In this paper we analyze an experiment with a rotating system for sounding the object at different viewing angles, which makes it possible to improve the quality of the reconstructed image. In addition, the use of a sounding system with rotation makes it possible to increase the number of source positions and compensates the insufficient number of receivers in linear antenna arrays of transducers. However, the amount of computations increases linearly with the increase of the number of sources. The scalable algorithms that we developed earlier made it possible to efficiently solve this problem on 384 CPU cores of Lomonosov–2 supercomputer. The issues of computational implementation of solving inverse problems of ultrasound tomography on CPU/GPU processors are considered in [3, 17].

2 Formulation of the Inverse Problem of Ultrasonic Tomography in Nondestructive Testing

In this paper we solve the inverse problem in terms of scalar wave equation for longitudinal waves $u(r, t)$ $r \in R^2$ for the given initial data

$$c(r)u_{tt}(r,t) - \Delta u(r,t) = \delta(r - r_0)g(t), \tag{1}$$

$$u(r, t = 0) = u_t(r, t = 0) = 0. \tag{2}$$

Here $c(r) = 1/v^2(r)$ and $v(r)$ is the longitudinal wave velocity in the medium. Computation of the wave field at given $c(r)$ from Eqs. (1)–(2) is a direct problem.

Let us now formulate the 2D inverse problem of ultrasonic testing in NDT in the scheme of the experiment with rotation shown in Fig. 1. The linear antenna arrays of transducers indicated by digit 1 in Fig. 1 are located at the lateral surface of square 2. Each transducer array consists of M piezoelectric transmit–and–receive cells. The velocity structure is reconstructed in circular area 3 made of the same material as area 2. Wave velocity in area 2 is known and equal to v_0. Area 3 under examination can turn around the center by arbitrary angle. We refer to such measurement scheme as the full–data scheme. If the scheme uses, e.g., only two turn angles equal to 0 and 90° we call it an incomplete–data scheme. Area 3 under examination contains irregularity domain denoted by digit 4. The inverse problem consists in reconstructing the velocity structure in area 3. In reality in the scheme of real experiment the 3D phantom is represented by cylinder 3, which contains cylindrical irregularity area 4 (Fig. 2). The inverse problem can be solved as a 2D problem because both the object and the insert have cylindrical shapes.

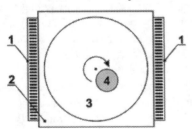

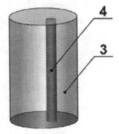

Fig. 1. The scheme of a tomographic examination.

Fig. 2. 3D model of the phantom.

The experiment was conducted as follows. Each of the 2M piezoelectric cells of both antenna arrays emits successively. All 2M piezoelectric cells of both antenna arrays are used as receivers. The object under control is then turned by angle α. Sounding is then repeated with all cells, etc. In our experiment the object is turned by angles β_i, allowing area 3 to be sounded from different angles.

The inverse problem of ultrasonic tomography in scalar model consists in recon- structing the unknown longitudinal–wave velocity $v(r)$ from Eq. (1) in area 3 under examination containing irregularity 4 based on experimentally measured wave field

$u(r, t)$ at transducers when the area is sounded at different turn angles. Let us write residual functional $\Phi(c)$ as a function of argument $c(r)$ for a single source

$$\Phi(c) = dt \sum_{j=1}^{2M} \frac{1}{2} \left(\int_0^T u(s_j, t; c) - U(s_j, t) \right)^2. \tag{3}$$

Here $U(s_j, t)$ are the experimental data measured at j-th ($j = 1, \ldots, 2M$) piezoelectric cell of the transducer during time $(0, T)$, and $u(s_j, t; c)$ is the wave field in the solution of direct problem (1)–(2) for the given coefficient $c(r) = 1/v^2(r)$. T is the time of measurements. Note that in the case where several sources are used the residual functional is equal to the sum of residuals (3) over all sources and turn angles. The inverse problem is formulated as the problem of finding longitudinal–wave velocity $v(r)$ that minimizes the residual functional [11, 15].

We consider the inverse problem as a coefficient inverse problem with respect to the propagation velocity of the longitudinal wave. Iterative algorithms for solving the inverse problem are based on representing the gradient of the residual functional between the experimentally measured and the theoretically computed wave fields, which depends on the longitudinal–wave propagation velocity. The principle of operation of the numerical algorithm is described in detail in [5, 12, 14, 16, 18, 27]. A distinctive feature of the numerical realization of the algorithms employed in this study is the use of high–frequency sources of ultrasonic radiation (above 1 MHz). It was shown in [28] that the use of second–order difference schemes for second–order differential equations is insufficient. The numerical methods developed are based on 4th–order schemes for approximating second–order differential equations [7]. In this study we use an explicit difference scheme, which proves to be highly efficient for parallel computations.

3 Numerical Tests of the Inverse Problem of Ultrasonic Tomography in Nondestructive Testing

To implement numerical algorithms, we used our C++ program for solving ultrasonic tomography problems developed to be run on high–performance computing systems operating under a Linux OS clone. We chose MPI interface for interprocessor data exchange. The computations were performed on "Lomonosov–2" supercomputer of Lomonosov Moscow University Supercomputing Center [30] on CPU Intel Haswell–EP E5–2697v3, 2.6 GHz, 14 cores, 64 GB, Infiniband FDR.

CPU supercomputer computations were parallelized by sources with computing cores distributed among the sources and each core performing the computations for its allocated source exclusively. This is natural parallelization because in the algorithms employed computations for each source are performed practically independently. This approach proved to be highly efficient and provide practically linear weak scalability for up to several hundred computing cores. In the used parallel approach of the task (1 computing core performs computations for 1 source), data transfer between the cores occurs only after the end of each iteration. Thus, it is easy to measure the transfer time using the C function time(). The data transfer time between the computing cores makes up for ~ 2% of the total amount of computations. We used 384 CPU cores, which is equal to the number of positions of ultrasonic radiation sources. Test computations were carried out on 192 CPU cores (for 192 source positions). In both cases, the computation time of 40 iterations was about 30 min.

Model calculations were made in accordance with the scheme shown in Fig. 1. First, the direct problem of the propagation of the wave in the entire square area 2 with irregularity 4 was solved (Fig. 1) for each of the 2M sources of antenna arrays 1 and for each turn of area 3 with irregularity 4 by angle β_i. The computed wave field at the detectors of both antenna arrays 1 for each turn angle was stored and used as model experimental data for solving the inverse problem.

The scheme and parameter values of the model experiment coincided with those of the physical experiments as far as it was possible. In our model experiment we used two antenna arrays of transducers each consisting of 24 emitting–and–receiving piezoelectric cells 0.6 mm apart. The wavelength of the central frequency of the sounding pulse was $\lambda = 0.466$ mm (the central pulse frequency was 5 MHz). The beam width of each piezoelectric cell was equal to 50°. The large step between the detectors (greater than the wavelength) and narrow beam of transducer elements are typical for NDT tasks.

The sound speed in area 2 was equal to $v_0 = 2.33$ km/s (rexolite), and that of circular irregularity $4 - v_1 = 2.45$ km/s (ebonite) – differs from v_0 by about 5%. The size of square computational domain 2 is 20×20 mm^2, that of the computational grid, 700×700 points. In our computations we used 384 source positions (including different turns). The computations were carried out on 384 CPU computing cores (1 core carried out computations for 1 source). In such a configuration, for one iteration on 1 core, it is necessary to perform 3 times the computation of wave propagation in time in the scalar wave model (1) on a grid of 700×700 points of spatial coordinates and 1500 time steps [5, 12, 14, 16, 27]. The computation time for 40 iterations on 384 CPU cores was about 30 min.

Figure 3a shows the image reconstructed from incomplete data in the experimental design where the domain under examination was turned by angles β_i equal to 0 and 90°. Figure 3b shows the image obtained after 40 iterations in the experimental design presented in Fig. 1 with complete set of data and turns by angle β_i ($0 \leq i \leq 7$, $\beta_i - \beta_{i-1} = \alpha = 22.5^0$, $\beta_0 = 0^0$). In both cases the initial approximation of the iterative process was chosen to be $v_0 = \text{const} = 2.33$ km/s.

As is evident from Figs. 3 a, b, in both experimental designs with incomplete and complete data the method employed makes it possible to precisely reconstruct not only the boundary of the object but also the velocity inside it. However, in the experimental design with complete data the reconstructed image contains no artifacts characteristic of reconstructions based on incomplete experimental data. The design with turns makes it possible to increase both the number of sounding nodes and that of the source positions. This compensates the incompleteness of experimental data when sounding is performed only from four directions and the incompleteness of the data due to large distance between the detectors and the narrow beams of the sources of transducer antenna arrays used NDT.

(a)   (b)

Fig. 3. Model computations: image reconstructed from incomplete (a), complete (b) set of data.

Model computations showed that the velocity structure inside irregularity 4 can be reconstructed in tomography schemes where both reflected and transmitted radiation is detected. The more complete are the data, the better is the quality of reconstruction of irregularity 4. Thus in NDT tasks the use if tomographic schemes involving the detection of both reflected and transmitted radiation makes it possible not only to reconstruct the boundaries of the irregularity but also to recover important information about its internal structure. Experimental designs involving the detection of only reflected radiation do not allow reconstructing the velocity structure inside the irregularity.

Computations for model problems showed that single–precision floating point arithmetic ensures sufficient accuracy of the resulting wave propagation for the problem parameters employed. It was difficult to find the differences in the recovered images visually. A comparison of the computation times in the cases of the use of single– and double–precision floating–point arithmetic on CPU cores showed no important differences. At the same time, test computations performed on Nvidia Tesla X2070 graphic–card devices demonstrated a threefold increase of computing speed when passing from double–precision to single–precision floating point arithmetic. This result demonstrates the potential of the use of small GPU clusters in tomography devices for nondestructive testing [17].

4 Reconstruction of the Velocity Structure from Experimental Data

We performed a dedicated experiment to validate the developed algorithms for solving inverse problems of nondestructive testing. To obtain the image in nondestructive testing problem, we used two ultrasonic antenna arrays operating at frequencies in the 2–8 MHz range. Each of the linear equidistant antenna arrays contains 32 identical receiving–and–radiating piezoelectric cells with the parameters listed above for the model experiment.

We used thee following simplest testing object for the physical experiment (see Fig. 4). As a control object we chose the bar denoted by digit 3 and having the shape of a cylinder elongated along the Z–axis with a diameter of $d \approx 15$ mm. A bigger parallelepiped–shaped bar with a square cross–section in the XY plane denoted by digit 2 with the size of $20 \times 20 \times 40$ mm^3 was made of the same material. A hole of diameter d was drilled inside parallelepiped 2 along the Z axis so that cylindrical bar 3 could be inserted into it and turned there.

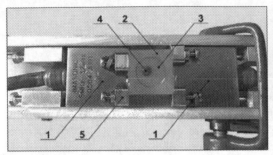

Fig. 4. Photo of the bench used to perform the measurements.

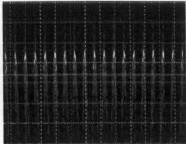

Fig. 5. Echo–signals in the raster form recorded during the experiment.

The square XY cross section of parallelepiped 4 has the size 20×20 mm^2. Such a choice allows accommodating all the active cells of the antenna array on a single side of the bar because the extreme cells of the array are ~ 19.2 mm apart.

A cylindrical hole is drilled along the Z–axis inside cylindrical bar 3, which serves as the control object. Cylindrical inset 4 with a diameter of 4 mm and made of a different material is inserted into this hole. Figure 2 shows an example of cylindrical bar 3 with inset 4.

To perform measurements, we assembled a bench (Fig. 4) for locking antenna arrays number 1 at the surface of parallelepiped 2 with locks 5. Control object 3 with inset 4 can be turned inside parallelepiped 2 by 360° with a step of 22.5° to sound the control object from different viewing angles.

Active cells of the antenna array were 0.5 mm wide and about 10 mm long and they had their long side aligned along the Z–axis. In the case of such a geometry of the experiment it is safe to assume that cells emit a cylindrical wave in the XY plane, which propagates through the cylindrical bar. This approximation allows using the 2D model of the problem of the reconstruction of the cross–section of the control object in the $z = z_0$ plane. Thus, in accordance with designations in Fig. 1, the computational domain is represented by the square denoted by digit 2 and the control object, by circle denoted by digit 3, whereas the inset has the shape of a small circle denoted by digit 4.

Bars and the inset were made of rexolite and ebonite, respectively. The velocity of the longitudinal wave in ebonite (2.45 km/s) is higher than in rexolite (2.33 km/s). The difference of velocity in the bar and in the inset did not exceed 5%. The choice of the materials was determined by the good matching of acoustic parameters with the antenna arrays, which allowed us to obtain close–to–ideal short pulses with the length of 2–3 periods in control objects. The acoustic parameters in these materials are such that the length of the emitted wave at 5 MHz is of about 0.5 mm. Thus the length of the side of the bar is of about 40 wavelengths. Model computations showed that at such a free path of the emitted pulse the fourth–order difference schemes employed ensure sufficient accuracy of the computation of the wave. The time for computing the propagation of the wave over such distances on a supercomputer is quite acceptable for performing numerous computations.

For experiments on nondestructive testing in solid bodies we used an ultrasonic multichannel flaw detector complete with a control computer for acquiring ultrasonic control data with antenna arrays. Figure 6 shows the block diagram of the device for measuring signals. Computer–controlled multichannel flaw detector can emit a sounding pulse by any cell of the antenna array and receive the signal by any cell of the same or the second antenna array. Such a configuration allows performing measurements both in the reflection and transmission modes.

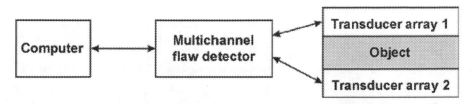

Fig. 6. Block diagram of the measurement facility.

We performed measurements 19 times with subsequent averaging of the results and frequency filtering in the 2–8 MHz band. Figure 5 shows the record of the signals emitted successively by piezoelectric cells of the same antenna array and recorded by the piezoelectric cells of the other antenna array in a sample without reflectors. Recorded signals, except for the extreme ones, differ little from each other.

Let us now present the results of the solution of the inverse problem of ultrasonic tomography for real data of a physical experiment and compare them with the results obtained in model computations from the numerical solution of the direct problem in Fig. 3. The scheme and parameter values of the physical experiments are very close to those of model computations described in Sect. 3.

The wavelength of the central frequency of the pulse was of about $\lambda = 0.5$ mm (the central frequency of the pulse is 5 MHz), the size of the computational domain was 20×20 mm^2, and the size of the difference grid was 700×700 points. Sources were arranged uniformly on the opposite sides of the square, 24 sources 0.6 mm apart on each side as shown in Fig. 1, and a total of 384 source positions (with 8 turns for each source) were used in the computations. The receivers were arranged in a similar way.

Figure 7a shows the image of a phantom. Figure 7b shows the reconstructed image of the velocity structure in a real physical experiment after 40 iterations. In the iteration process the initial approximation of velocity in the medium was set equal to $v_0 = \text{const} = 2.33$ km/s.

As is evident from Fig. 7, the quality of the reconstructed image obtained in a physical experiment using the scheme with rotation is very high. The reconstructed velocity of the longitudinal wave in the ebonite inset is equal to 2.42–2.45 km/s (in Fig. 7 the image of the inset is lighter than the background). The artefacts that show up

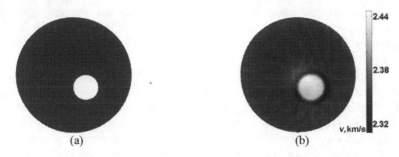

Fig. 7. Velocity structures: (a) – phantom and (b) – reconstructed velocity structure in the rexolite sample with an ebonite inset.

in Fig. 3a and arising in model computations for incomplete set of viewpoints turned by 90° are absent in Figs. 3b and 7 because in these cases the object was sounded within the framework of a scheme with turns by 22.5°.

Unlike the traditional NDT methods, the proposed method for solving the inverse problem of ultrasonic tomography in NDT and the proposed scheme of conducting the tomography experiments make it possible not only to locate the irregularity and find its boundary, but also determine the velocity value inside it to within 1% based on the transmission and reflection data. The knowledge of velocity inside the irregularity is of extreme importance in the tasks of nondestructive testing.

5 Conclusion

In this paper methods and algorithms are proposed for solving inverse problems of ultrasonic tomography in nondestructive testing tasks, which were first tested on real data obtained in experiments conducted on a test bench for ultrasonic tomography examinations. We showed that when used in nondestructive testing tasks in a real experiment performed within the framework of the reflection and transmission scheme the tomography methods developed make it possible not only to locate the boundaries of irregularities in the control object, but also to recover the velocity structure inside the object. An important result of this study is that it provides experimental evidence confirming the adequacy of the scalar wave model employed.

For our experiment we propose a test bench for ultrasonic tomography in NDT with a rotating sounding system. The rotating system allows eliminating artifacts on the reconstructed image that are due to the incompleteness of experimental data. The resulting reconstructed images of the internal structure of the control object have high resolution and demonstrate the great potential of tomography technologies in NDT.

The rotating system significantly increases the number of emitters and detectors in the tomography scheme, thereby increasing several times the amount of computations. The proposed scalable numerical algorithms can be efficiently parallelized on CPU supercomputers and efficiently solve the problem of the large amount of computations. We performed our computations on 384 CPU cores of «Lomonosov–2» supercomputer of Lomonosov Moscow State University.

Acknowledgement. This research was supported by Russian Science Foundation (project no. 17–11–01065). The research is carried out at the Lomonosov Moscow State University. The research uses the equipment of the shared research facilities of HPC computing resources at Lomonosov Moscow State University.

References

1. Bachmann, E., Jacob, X., Rodriguez, S., Gibiat, V.: Three–dimensional and real–time two–dimensional topological imaging using parallel computing. J. Acoust. Soc. Am. **138**(3), 1796 (2015)
2. Bazulin, E.G.: Comparison of systems for ultrasonic nondestructive testing using antenna arrays or phased antenna arrays. Russ. J. Nondestruct. Test. **49**(7), 404–423 (2013)
3. Bazulin, E.G., Goncharsky, A.V., Romanov, S.Y., Seryozhnikov, S.Y.: Parallel CPU– and GPU–algorithms for inverse problems in nondestructive testing. Lobachevskii J. Math. **39**(4), 486–493 (2018). https://doi.org/10.1134/S1995080218040030
4. Bazulin, E.G., Sadykov, M.S.: Determining the speed of longitudinal waves in anisotropic homogeneous welded joint using echo signals measured by two antenna arrays. Russ. J. Nondestruct. Test. **54**(5), 303–315 (2018)
5. Beilina, L., Klibanov, M.V., Kokurin, M.Y.: Adaptivity with relaxation for ill–posed problems and global convergence for a coefficient inverse problem. J. Math. Sci. **167**(3), 279–325 (2010). https://doi.org/10.1007/s10958-010-9921-1
6. Bellis, C., Bonnet, M.: Crack identification by 3D time–domain elastic or acoustic topological sensitivity. C. R. Mecanique **337**(3), 124–130 (2009)
7. Bilbao, S.: Numerical Sound Synthesis: Finite Difference Schemes and Simulation in Musical Acoustics. Wiley, Chichester (2009)
8. Blitz, J., Simpson, G.: Ultrasonic Methods of Non-destructive Testing. Springer, London (1995)
9. Dominguez, N., Gibiat, V.: Non–destructive imaging using the time domain topological energy. Ultrasonics **50**(3), 367–372 (2010)
10. Goncharsky, A.V., Romanov, S.Y.: Supercomputer technologies in inverse problems of ultrasound tomography. Inverse Probl. **29**(7), 075004 (2013). https://doi.org/10.1088/0266-5611/29/7/075004
11. Goncharsky, A.V., Romanov, S.Y.: Iterative methods for solving coefficient inverse problems of wave tomography in models with attenuation. Inverse Probl. **33**(2), 025003 (2017). https://doi.org/10.1088/1361-6420/33/2/025003
12. Goncharsky, A.V., Romanov, S.Y.: Inverse problems of ultrasound tomography in models with attenuation. Phys. Med. Biol. **59**(8), 1979–2004 (2014). https://doi.org/10.1088/0031-9155/59/8/1979
13. Goncharsky, A.V., Romanov, S.Y.: A method of solving the coefficient inverse problems of wave tomography. Comput. Math Appl. **77**, 967–980 (2019). https://doi.org/10.1016/j.camwa.2018.10.033
14. Goncharsky, A., Romanov, S., Seryozhnikov, S.: Inverse problems of 3D ultrasonic tomography with complete and incomplete range data. Wave Motion **51**(3), 389–404 (2014). https://doi.org/10.1016/j.wavemoti.2013.10.001
15. Goncharsky, A.V., Romanov, S.Y., Seryozhnikov, S.Y.: Low–frequency three–dimensional ultrasonic tomography. Doklady Phys. **61**(5), 211–214 (2016). https://doi.org/10.1134/s1028335816050086

16. Goncharsky, A.V., Romanov, S.Y., Seryozhnikov, S.Y.: Low-frequency ultrasonic tomography: mathematical methods and experimental results. Mosc. Univ. Phys. Bull. **74**(1), 43–51 (2019). https://doi.org/10.3103/S0027134919010090

17. Goncharsky, A.V., Seryozhnikov, S.Y.: The architecture of specialized GPU clusters used for solving the inverse problems of 3D low–frequency ultrasonic tomography. In: Voevodin, V., Sobolev, S. (eds.) Supercomputing. RuSCDays 2017. Communications in Computer and Information Science, vol. 793, pp. 363–395. Springer, Cham (2017). https://doi.org/10.1007/978-3-319-71255-0_29

18. Goncharsky, A., Romanov, S., Seryozhnikov, S.: Supercomputer technologies in tomographic imaging applications. Supercomput. Front. Innov. **3**(1), 41–66 (2016)

19. Hall, T.E., Doctor, S.R., Reid, L.D., Littlield, R.J., Gilber, R.W.: Implementation of real–time ultrasonic SAFT system for inspection of nuclear reactor components. Acoust. Imaging **15**, 253–266 (1987)

20. Jensen, J.A., Nikolov, S.I., Gammelmark, K.L., Pedersen, M.H.: Synthetic aperture ultrasound imaging. Ultrasonics **44**, 5–15 (2006)

21. Langenberg, K.-J., Marklein, R., Mayer, K.: Ultrasonic Nondestructive Testing. CRC Press, Boca Raton (2012)

22. Lechleiter, A., Schlasche, J.W.: Identifying Lame parameters from time–dependent elastic wave. Inverse Probl. Sci. Eng. **25**(1), 2–26 (2017)

23. Lubeigt, E., Mensah, S., Rakotonarivo, S., Chaix, J.-F., Baquè, F., Gobillot, G.: Topological imaging in bounded elastic media. Ultrasonics **76**, 145–153 (2017)

24. Maierhofer, C., Reinhardt, H.-W., Dobmann, G.: Non-destructive evaluation of reinforced concrete structures: non–destructive testing methods. Elsevier (2010)

25. Mayer, K., Markelein, R., Langenberg, K.J., Kreutter, T.: Three–dimensional imaging system based on Fourier transformation synthetic aperture focusing technique. Ultrasonics **28**, 241–255 (1990)

26. Metwally, K., et al.: Weld inspection by focused adjoint method. Ultrasonics **83**, 80–87 (2018)

27. Natterer, F.: Possibilities and limitations of time domain wave equation imaging. In: AMS vol. 559: Tomography and Inverse Transport Theory, pp. 151–162. American Mathematical Society (2011). https://doi.org/10.1090/conm/559

28. Romanov, S.: Optimization of numerical algorithms for solving inverse problems of ultrasonic tomography on a supercomputer. In: Voevodin, V., Sobolev, S. (eds.) Supercomputing. RuSCDays 2017. Communications in Computer and Information Science, vol. 793, pp. 67–79. Springer, Heidelberg (2017). https://doi.org/10.1007/978-3-319-71255-0_6

29. Romanov, S.Y.: Supercomputer simulations of nondestructive tomographic imaging with rotating transducers. Supercomput. Front. Innov. **5**(3), 98–102 (2018)

30. Voevodin, V.V., et al.: Supercomputer Lomonosov-2: large scale, deep monitoring and fine analytics for the user community. Supercomput. Front. Innov. **6**(2), 4–11 (2019)

31. Schmitz, V., Chakhlov, S., Müller, W.: Experiences with synthetic aperture focusing in the field. Ultrasonics **38**, 731–738 (2000)

Supercomputer Modelling
of Spatially-heterogeneous Coagulation
using MPI and CUDA

Rishat Zagidullin[1,2(✉)], Alexander Smirnov[1], Sergey Matveev[2,3],
and Eugene Tyrtyshnikov[1,3]

[1] Lomonosov Moscow State University, Moscow, Russia
sap@cs.msu.ru
[2] Skolkovo Institute of Science and Technology, Moscow, Russia
{r.zagidullin,s.matveev}@skoltech.ru
[3] Marchuk Institute of Numerical Mathematics, Moscow, Russia
eugene.tyrtyshnikov@gmail.com

Abstract. In this work we propose two parallel implementations of
numerical method for the two-dimensional advection-coagulation equation: pure CPU and hybrid CPU/GPU. We approximate the advection
component across the two dimensional space with use of unstructured
grid and finite volume method with flux limiters. Smoluchowski coalescence operator corresponds to the coagulation process. We evaluate
it within low complexity ($O(N \log N)$) via exploitation of the low-rank
skeleton decomposition of coagulation kernel. We decompose spatial grid
into the subdomains and solve the model equation in parallel using MPI.
Even though we exploit the fast methods for evaluation of coalescence
operator it is the most time-consuming part of numerical algorithm.
Hence, we test performance of GPU accelerators for corresponding Smolushowski integrals. All in all, we evaluate the efficiency of incorporating
MPI and Nvidia CuFFT library for speedup of calculations and obtain
almost linear scalability of MPI implementation of our algorithm. We
also find that hybrid exploitation of CPUs and GPUs leads to additional
speedup of computations by 2–4 times.

Keywords: Advection-coagulation · Unstructured grid · Hybrid
parallelism

1 Introduction

The main purpose of this article is to analyze scalability of two parallel implementations of numerical algorithm solving advection-coagulation equation in case
of two dimensional spatial heterogeneity. Coagulation equation is used for the
description of physical systems where big amounts of chaotically moving particles
collide with each other and upon collision with a certain probability, particles
merge forming a larger particle. For example, aerosol formation process [15] and

© Springer Nature Switzerland AG 2019
V. Voevodin and S. Sobolev (Eds.): RuSCDays 2019, CCIS 1129, pp. 403–414, 2019.
https://doi.org/10.1007/978-3-030-36592-9_33

synthesis of urea [16] are governed by coagulation. Time-evolution of particle sizes can be represented with the use of Smoluchowski coalescence equation [3]. In order to obtain a broader range of physical systems where coagulation might play an important role we include spatial heterogeneity and incorporate advection operator into the model [12,14].

In this work, we extend our previous results [1,2] which correspond to the simpler one-dimensional case of spatial heterogeneity. Even though there exist efficient parallel stochastic solvers for aggregation kinetics [13,17] we develop parallel implementation of the classical deterministic approach with easily tractable accuracy level as a natural alternative to Monte Carlo or particle-based methods. In the subsequent paragraphs we present the equation and the algorithm allowing to construct its numerical solution. In Sect. 2 we give information about the algorithm solving the advection-coagulation equation which we parallelize. In Sect. 3 we explain the parallelization scheme. Section 4 is devoted to presentation of the benchmarks of the proposed parallel algorithm.

2   Advection-Coagulation Equation and Numerical Method

2.1   Advection-Coagulation Equation

In our work we seek to solve the following equation:

$$\frac{\partial f(t,x,y,v)}{\partial t} + \nabla \cdot (c(x,y,v)f(t,x,y,v)) =$$

$$= \frac{1}{2}\int_0^v K(u,v-u)f(t,x,y,u)f(t,x,y,v-u)du -$$

$$-f(t,x,y,v)\int_0^\infty K(u,v)f(t,x,y,u)du,$$

where x, y are spatial coordinates, v is particle size coordinate, c corresponds to the velocity of advection (which is assumed to be given), $K(u,v)$ defines the coagulation kernel describing the intensities of collisions for particles of sizes u and v. Obviously, $f(x,y,v,t)$ is a mean concentration of particles per unit volume and we seek to find it for the given initial $f(x,y,v,t=0)$ and some boundary condition.

The coagulation kernel is usually dictated by physical properties of the system. The simplest model example is

$$K(u,v) = 1,$$

which indicates that particles coagulate with the same intensity and there is no matter what their sizes are. In this work, we use the ballistic coagulation kernel:

$$K(u,v) = (u^{\frac{1}{3}} + v^{\frac{1}{3}})^2\sqrt{\frac{1}{u} + \frac{1}{v}}.$$

2.2   Discretization and Algorithm

As we have mentioned above, the spatial coordinates are two-dimensional. We discretize spatial domain corresponding to x and y variables with use of the unstructured triangular grid. For the particle size coordinate v (which is one dimensional) we use uniform grid. In our work we consider rectangular spatial domain which is shown in Fig. 1 and allows us to proceed with well-tractable scalability analysis of our parallel algorithm. In case of problems related to physics the target domain may have more subtle form leading us to a certain need to exploit unstructured grids.

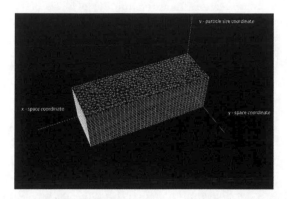

Fig. 1. Example of the domain for numerical simulations with use of the advection-coagulation equation.

Under assumption that coagulation does not impact the advection process, we can evaluate the advection and coagulation components separately. As a result, the numerical scheme for solving advection-coagulation equation can be represented in the following way:

$$\frac{f^{n+1} - f^n}{\Delta t} = A(f^n) + S(f^n),$$

where $A(f)$ is the advection component and $S(f)$ is the Smoluchowski coagulation operator. In terms of parallel implementation we can approximate the advection and coagulation components simultaneously. Then we have to collect data and evaluate the solution for the next time-step (f^{n+1}).

2.3   Numerical Scheme for Advection Process

In this work we use the finite volume method for the advection component. In order to exploit it we need the data from triangle elements of the grid which are shown in Fig. 2.

Values for the function f are located in the centers of triangles. For the finite volume method we need to interpolate those values at the interfaces (where

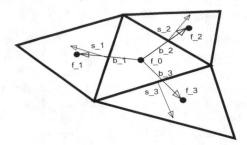

Fig. 2. b_1, b_2, b_3—distance vectors between the triangle centers, s_1, s_2, s_3—outward pointing normal vectors from the middle of each of the triangle's sides, f_1, f_2, f_3—values of the function f (stored at the center of a cell).

outward pointing normal vectors are located) [4–7]. Interpolation at the given interface is calculated with use of the values from the two triangles which share that face.

$$f^* = (1 - \frac{\phi(r)}{L})f_C + \frac{\phi(r)}{L}f_D,$$

where C is the upwind triangle, D is the downwind triangle, $L = \frac{|d_C| + |d_D|}{|d_C|}$ is the weight of the triangle C, $|d_C|, |d_D|$ is the distance from the triangle center to the interface, $\phi(r)$ is the flux limiter, which upholds the monotonicity condition, which depends on the r-factor. Now we can use the value f^* at the interface in the finite volume method.

Thus, at first, let us consider the advection equation separately from the whole model:

$$\frac{\partial f(t, x, y)}{\partial t} + \nabla \cdot (cf(t, x, y)) = 0.$$

Further we integrate the non-trivial parts of the equation over small domain R:

$$\iint_R \frac{\partial f(t, x, y)}{\partial t} dR + \iint_R \nabla \cdot \boldsymbol{F} dR = 0,$$

where $\boldsymbol{F} = cf(t, x, y)$. If the region is small enough we can replace first part of the equation with multiplication of the triangle area by value of the function. For the second part of the equation we use the divergence theorem:

$$A_R \frac{\partial f(t, x, y)}{\partial t} + \oint_S \boldsymbol{F} \cdot \boldsymbol{n} dS_R = 0.$$

Then we incorporate the triangular form of the region and approximate time derivative with the finite difference scheme:

$$\frac{f^{n+1} - f^n}{\Delta t} = -\frac{1}{A_R} \sum_{k=1}^{3} \boldsymbol{F_k} \cdot \boldsymbol{s_k},$$

where s_k is the outward pointing normal vector which length equals to the length of its corresponding interface, F_k is a flux of particles that passes through k-th interface of a triangle and the F_k is located at the interfaces. To calculate F_k we need to use the value f^*.

From the numerical scheme for the advection component we see that evaluation of the data for next time-step from neighbouring cells is needed (for calculation of the f^* at the every interface). Hence, parallel implementation of the scheme which uses domain decomposition across spatial axes would require message passing. All in all, the boundary cells require given values of f at the interface that has no neighbouring cell. In some cases the Perfectly Matched Layers are used to remove the reflection.

2.4   Numerical Approximation of Coagulation

For approximation of the coagulation component we use the skeleton decomposition of the coagulation kernel [9]. The algorithm of constructing the skeleton decomposition can be found in the work [8]. The skeleton decomposition allows to transform the Smoluchowski integrals into the form which makes the equation easier for numerical treatment:

$$K(u,v) = \sum_{\alpha=1}^{R} a_\alpha(u) b_\alpha(v).$$

First integral takes the form:

$$\int_0^v K(u, v-u) f(t,u) f(t, v-u) du =$$
$$= \sum_{\alpha=1}^{R} \int_0^v a_\alpha(u) f(t,u) b_\alpha(v-u) f(t, v-u) du.$$

The second integral takes the form:

$$\int_0^\infty K(u,v) f(t,u) du \approx \int_0^{V_{\max}} \sum_{\alpha=1}^{R} a_\alpha(u) b_\alpha(v) f(t,u) du =$$
$$= \sum_{\alpha=1}^{R} b_\alpha(v) \int_0^v a_\alpha(u) f(t,u) du.$$

Thus, the first integral is reduced to a sum of R convolutions, which means we can use FFT for its evaluation in $O(M \log M)$ operations (where M is a number of points in particle size axis dicretization). The second integral requires $O(MR)$ operations. If R is small enough, we obtain dramatic acceleration of computations. The ballistic coagulation kernel (which we exploit in this work) is an example of such low rank kernels.

2.5   Full Algorithm

Now we can present the complete algorithm.

1. Get the initial data $f^n(x, y, v)$;
2. Interpolate the values at the triangle interfaces for each given particle size;
3. Apply the advection operator using the interface values for each given particle size—find $A(f^n(x, y, v))$;
4. Find R convolutions from the first Smoluchowski integral for each triangle center in the two dimensional domain;
5. Evaluate the second integral for each triangle center and find $S(f^n(x, y, v))$;
6. Use $A(f^n(x, y, v))$ and $S(f^n(x, y, v))$ to find $f^{n+1}(x, y, v)$;
7. Use $f^{n+1}(x, y, v)$ as new initial data, go back to step 1.

In the following section we present the parallelization scheme of this algorithm.

3   Parallel Implementation

The computational process can be parallelized across subareas of the target domain. The domain is three dimensional, however it is shown in the work [9] that decomposition across particle size axis requires to many exchange operations for parallel FFT and has certain drawbacks in terms of the parallel scalability. This fact motivates us to provide decomposition across the spatial coordinates only. Evaluation of the coagulation integrals at the each grid point does not require additional data exchanges. At the same time local calculation of the advection operator requires only neighbouring cells for the data transfers. Example of a domain decomposition is shown in Fig. 3.

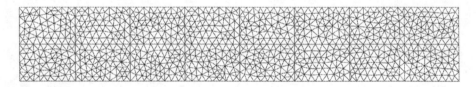

Fig. 3. Division of the space domain among 16 MPI processes. Triangulation was performed with use of Fade2D library (www.geom.at).

3.1   CPU Parallelization

Using MPI we can assign each subdomain to a separate process. Hence, each process calculates the advection and the coagulation components sequentially for corresponding subdomain. Before evaluation of the advection operator we need to interpolate the data across the interfaces f^*. Thus, the data exchange is necessary for the interpolation of values for the neighbouring interfaces. Then each process deals with the advection component, computes convolutions for the coagulation operator and prepares the coagulation component for the next time-step. All in all, we put this process into a loop allowing to solve the initial advection-coagulation equation numerically for an arbitrary number of time-steps. Fig. 4 illustrates the contents of that loop.

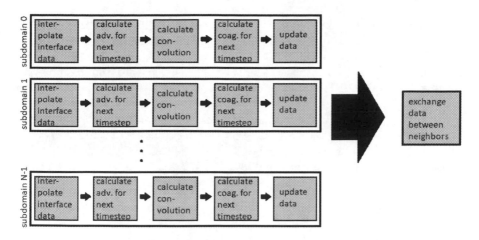

Fig. 4. Loop for the construction of the numerical solution. Calculation at CPU for each subdomain runs in parallel. Then processes provide the necessary data-exchanges and repeat the scheme for the updated data.

3.2 Adding GPU Parallelism

Considering the numerical scheme we find that calculation of the advection and coagulation components does not have to be sequential. Hence, we can introduce even more parallelism into the computational process. There are several possible ways for separate approximation of the advection and the coagulation compo-

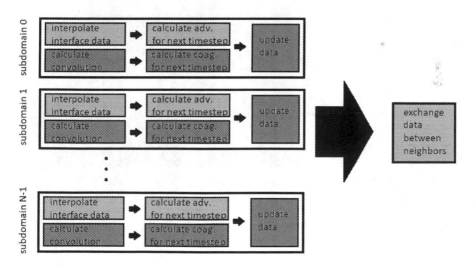

Fig. 5. Numerical solution loop. Calculation on CPU and GPU for each subdomain "runs" in parallel. The coagulation "runs" at GPU (green), the advection "runs" at CPU (blue). Data updates are provided by GPU. Then processes exchange the data and repeat the scheme with the new data. (Color figure online)

nents. They can either "run" in race-condition at the common CPU or they can "run" simultaneously at different CPUs. But they also can "run" simultaneously at GPU and CPU! The first option requires context changes which can be time-consuming in comparison with the other two options. Second option requires data exchanges between CPUs for entire subdomains, which leads to disproportional growth of volume of necessary data for exchanges and provokes an obvious performance degradation. Third option also requires data exchanges of entire subdomains but between GPU and CPU. Thus, we prefer to use the third listed option and note that Cuda libraries contain GPU-oriented implementations of FFT [10]. All in all, the parallel scheme incorporating GPU is shown in Fig. 5.

4   Results

In this section we demonstrate the scalability measurements and benchmarks of the pure MPI and the hybrid MPI/Cuda implementations of the numerical scheme for the advection-coagulation equation. Calculations were performed at Lomonosov supercomputer, Zhores supercomputer and a PC with Nvidia GPU.

In this work we model a source term in the upper left corner of the computational domain (Fig. 6). Velocities are constant and provoke transport of the particles from the source region toward the lower right part of the computational domain (Fig. 7). At the same time particles coagulate and larger particles move down faster. Performance of the parallel implementations can be seen in the Tables 1, 2, 3, 4 and 5.

Fig. 6. The initial condition and the computational domain of advection-coagulation equation at 1 CPU.

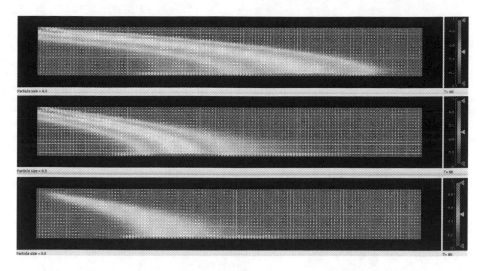

Fig. 7. Solution of the advection-coagulation equation at 800-th time-step.

Table 1. Computational times for 32 time-integration steps (in sec) for different grid sizes on PC using CPU cores (Intel Core i7-7700HQ) only. First number in the grid indicates amount of grid-nodes for spatial coordinate, second—along particle size axis.

P cores	8192 × 1024	4096 × 1024	2048 × 1024	1024 × 2048	1024 × 4096	1024 × 8192
1	381.868	203.763	89.0121	92.48	201.05	412
2	192.71	124.673	45.31	65.606	136.338	300.9
4	98.5735	75.0756	25.4674	35.0096	71.12	152.94

Table 2. Computational times of 2 time-integration steps (in sec) for the grid 5000×8192 at the student cluster (with 1 Gb/s Ethernet interconnect) of Marchuk Institute of Numerical Mathematics, RAS with use of CPU cores only.

P cores	Time, sec	Speedup
1	138.64	1.00
2	96.69	1.43
4	58.2	2.38
8	33.31	4.16
16	18.53	7.48
32	10.16	13.65

From our experiments we conclude that both parallel implementations are well-scalable. Unfortunately, we conclude that use of GPU accelerators leads to rather modest speedup of computations (about 2–4 times, see the Table 4) and

Table 3. Computational time (in sec) for the grid 7700×8192 and 2 time-integration steps at Lomonosov supercomputer *regular4* queue ($40\,\mathrm{Gb/s}$ QDR interconnect) with use of only CPU cores.

P cores	Time, sec	Speedup
1	159.312	1.0
2	74.6913	2.13
4	38.9939	4.08
8	21.54	7.4
16	10.5112	15.16
32	5.53312	28.79
64	2.94353	54.12
128	1.59911	99.63
256	0.931789	170.97
512	0.504464	315.8
1024	0.328353	485.19

Table 4. Computational time (in sec) for the grid $3830 \times 32\,768$ and 2 time-integration steps at Zhores supercomputer *GPU big* queue ($100\,\mathrm{Gb/s}$ EDR interconnect). For the hybrid version each MPI process corresponds to single GPU NVidia V100 device.

P cores	Without GPU, sec	Speedup without GPU	With GPU, sec	Speedup with GPU
1	396.512	1.00	186.47	2.13
2	219.966	1.8	101.12	3.92
4	123.606	3.2	65.33	6.07
8	73.52	5.39	35.32	11.22
16	42.51	9.33	18.53	21.4
32	36.06	11.0	12.18	32.6
64	17.86	22.2	5.93	66.87

Table 5. Computational time (in sec) for the different grid sizes and 32 time-integration steps on PC using CPU (Intel Core i7-7700HQ) and GPU cores (NVIDIA GeForce GTX 1050). The first number in the grid indicates amount of grid-nodes for the spatial coordinate, second—along the particle size axis.

P Cores	8192×1024	4096×1024	2048×1024	1024×2048	1024×4096	1024×8192
1	241.73	120.015	58.1369	54.15	106.46	226.809
2	142.204	97.5476	34.8797	40.5617	78.719	168.944
4	98.5735	65.3446	23.42	23.0669	46.69	90.57

simple growth of utilized CPU-cores in the pure MPI way might be better due to the economical or power consumption reasons (see Table 3). Tests of the hybrid version at PC (Intel Core i7-7700HQ and NVIDIA GeForce GTX 1050) show signs of long stalls in CPU as every CPU core assigns tasks to a single GPU device. It also happens for GPU-powered Zhores supercomputer: if we associate more than one MPI-process with single GPU accelerator we obtain performance stagnation or even degradation. We obtain good results in terms of the strong scalability which persist in both supercomputer tests and for PC. However, if node has single GPU-device and multiple CPU cores one can obtain CPU stalling because the assignments from the each CPU-core queue up. If it happens, better solution would be to give the device power only to a subset of CPU cores, while the rest of the cores perform computations in the "pure" MPI way.

Acknowledgements. We would like to thank Dmitry Zheltkov for valuable consultations during preparation of the numerical experiments. The research is carried out using the equipment of the shared research facilities of HPC computing resources at Lomonosov Moscow State University [11] and Zhores supercomputer of Skolkovo Institute of Science and Technology [18].

This article contains the results of the project performed in the framework of the implementation of the programs of the Central Competences of the National Technological Database "Center for Big Data Storage and Analysis" (project "Tensor methods for processing and analysis of Big Data") of Lomonosov MSU with the Project Support Funding of the National Technological Reporting dated December 11, 2018 No. 13/1251/2018.

References

1. Zagidullin, R.R., Smirnov, A.P., Matveev, S.A., Tyrtyshnikov, E.E.: An efficient numerical method for a mathematical model of a transport of coagulating particles. Moscow Univ. Comput. Math. Cybern. **41**, 179–186 (2017)
2. Matveev, S.A., Zagidullin, R.R., Smirnov, A.P., Tyrtyshnikov, E.E.: Parallel numerical algorithm for solving advection equation for coagulating particles. Supercomput. Frontiers Innovations **5**(2), 43–54 (2018)
3. Galkin, V.A.: Smoluchowski equation. Fizmatlit, Moscow, p. 336 (2001)
4. Darwish, M.S., Moukalled, F.: TVD schemes for unstructured grids. Int. J. Heat Mass Transf. **46**, 599–611 (2003)
5. Denner, F., van Wachem, B.G.M.: TVD differencing on three-dimensional unstructured meshes with monotonicity-preserving correction of mesh skewness. J. Comput. Phys. **298**, 466–479 (2015)
6. Syrakos, A., Varchanis, S., Dimakopoulos, Y., Goulas, A., Tsamopoulos, J.: A critical analysis of some popular methods for the discretisation of the gradient operator in finite volume methods. Phys. Fluids **29**, 127103 (2017)
7. Sozer, E., Brehm, C., Kiris, C.C.: Gradient Calculation Methods on Arbitrary Polyhedral Unstructured Meshes for Cell-Centered CFD Solvers. In: Science and Technology Forum and Exposition: Conference Paper (2014)
8. Tyrtyshnikov, E.E.: Incomplete cross approximation in the mosaic-skeleton methods. Computing **64**, 367–380 (2000)
9. Matveev, S.A.: A parallel implementation of a fast method for solving the smoluchowski-type kinetic equations of aggregation and fragmentation processes. Vychislitel'nye Metody i Programmirovanie **16**, 360–368 (2015)
10. Steinbach, P., Werner, M.: gearshifft - the FFT Benchmark Suite for Heterogeneous Platforms. arXiv:1702.00629 (2017)

11. Sadovnichy, V., Tikhonravov, A., Voevodin, Vl., Opanasenko, V.: "Lomonosov": supercomputing at Moscow State University. In: Contemporary High Performance Computing: From Petascale toward Exascale (Chapman & Hall/CRC Computational Science), pp. 283–307. CRC Press, Boca Raton (2013)
12. Betelin, V.B., Galkin, V.A.: On the formation of structures in nonlinear problems of physical kinetics. Doklady Math. **99**(1) (2019). Pleiades Publishing
13. Xu, Z., Zhao, H., Zheng, C.: Accelerating population balance-Monte Carlo simulation for coagulation dynamics from the Markov jump model, stochastic algorithm and GPU parallel computing. J. Comput. Phys. **281**, 844–863 (2015)
14. Volochuk, V.M., Sedunov, Y.: Coagulation Processes in Dispersed Systems. Gidrometeoizd, Leningrad (1975)
15. Aloyan, A.E., Arutyunyan, V.O., Lushnikov, A.A., Zagaynov, V.A.: Transport of coagulating aerosol in the atmosphere. J. Aerosol Sci. **28**(1), 67–85 (1997)
16. Hackbusch, W., John, V., Khachatryan, A., Suciu, C.: A numerical method for the simulation of an aggregation-driven population balance system. Int. J. Numer. Meth. Fluids **69**(10), 1646–1660 (2012)
17. Boje, A., Akroyd, J., Kraft, M.: A hybrid particle-number and particle model for efficient solution of population balance equations. J. Comput. Phys. **389**, 189–218 (2019)
18. Zacharov, I., et al.: 'Zhores'-Petaflops supercomputer for data-driven modeling, machine learning and artificial intelligence installed in Skolkovo Institute of Science and Technology. arXiv preprint arXiv:1902.07490 (2019)

Supercomputing the Seasonal Weather Prediction

Rostislav Fadeev[1,3]([✉]), Konstantin Ushakov[1,2,4], Mikhail Tolstykh[1,3],
Rashit Ibrayev[1,2,4], Vladimir Shashkin[1,3], and Gordey Goyman[1,3]

[1] Marchuk Institute of Numerical Mathematics Russian Academy of Sciences,
Moscow, Russia
rost.fadeev@gmail.com, ushakovkv@mail.ru, mtolstykh@mail.ru,
ibrayev@mail.ru, vvshashkin@gmail.com, gordeygoyman@gmail.com
[2] Shirshov Institute of Oceanology Russian Academy of Sciences, Moscow, Russia
[3] Hydrometeorological Centre of Russia, Moscow, Russia
[4] Marine Hydrophysical Institute of Russian Academy of Sciences, Sevastopol, Russia

Abstract. Most of the WMO Global Producing Centres for Long-Range
Forecasts use ensemble prediction systems together with an ensemble
re-forecast dataset, also called hindcast. Both ensembles usually come
from integrations of a global coupled atmosphere, ocean, land-surface
and sea ice model. This article describes SLAV–INMIO–CICE coupled model developed at Marchuk Institute of Numerical Mathematics
RAS, Shirshov Institute of Oceanology RAS and Hydrometeorological
Centre of Russia. The model components are coupled using the own-
developed Compact Modeling Framework. SLAV–INMIO–CICE model
requires several thousands of cores of CRAY XC40 system. The performance of the model is comparable to the latest European Centre for
Medium-Range Weather Forecasts SEAS5 operational model.

Keywords: Long–term forecast · Numerical weather prediction ·
Coupled model · High-performance computing

1 Introduction

According to the classification of the World Meteorological Organization (WMO)
[12], meteorological forecasts are called *long–term* if they have lead times between
30 days and two years. In particular, WMO's Global Producing Centres for Long-
Range Forecasts (GPCLRFs) should provide a weather forecast with lead time
between 0 and 4 months [22]. Hydrometeorological Centre of Russia is one of 13
Global Producing Centres. The goal of long–range forecasting is not to obtain
the instantaneous values of meteorological parameters, but the generalized statistical characteristics of the atmosphere state, averaged over a period of time.
Their deviations from the observed climate-average values are also of peculiar
interest. The necessity of this approach is caused by the dynamic instability of
atmospheric flows, which manifests in the possibility of a rapid increase in the

© Springer Nature Switzerland AG 2019
V. Voevodin and S. Sobolev (Eds.): RuSCDays 2019, CCIS 1129, pp. 415–426, 2019.
https://doi.org/10.1007/978-3-030-36592-9_34

amplitude of the initially small disturbances due to the internal energy of the system. In other words, a slight difference in the initial state of the atmospheric model can lead to a significant difference in the results of a direct long–term forecast based on the same hydrodynamic model. Thus, the perturbation of the atmosphere state at the beginning of the calculations is one of the possible methods for generating the ensemble of forecasts, by which the future averaged state of the atmosphere is predicted.

Sources of long–range predictability include slowly changing meteorological characteristics, such as sea surface temperature (SST), sea ice concentration, and deep soil parameters (temperature and moisture content). For example, due to the high thermal inertia of the ocean, the initial distribution of temperature anomalies in its upper mixed layer can significantly affect the evolution of atmospheric processes during the forecast period. SST anomalies can be a source of large–scale waves in the atmosphere, their breaking can lead to, for example, the blocking phenomena. Modern long–range forecast models are gradually refusing the inertial forecast of SST anomalies in favor of coupled models of the atmosphere and the ocean, often supplemented by models of sea waves, sea ice, land surface, rivers, etc. The possibility of creating such models is due to the growing power of available computing systems, particularly, due to the development of grid computing.

Table 1 lists the most high-performance systems from the Top500 list (November 2018) [18] installed at national meteorological centers over the world. Besides, the German DWD located at the 278'th place should be mentioned. The National Weather Service in USA uses IBM systems with combined processing power of 5.78 PFlops. Of course, the listed systems are also used to process observational data and other operations related to the forecast technology. For the long–term forecast, in the leading centers, mainly coupled models are used. In the European Centre for Medium-Range Weather Forecasts, it is SEAS5 [14]. The UK Met Office uses GloSea5 [11], in France it is SYSTEM5 [20]. CFSv2 [15] is used in the USA, and CanSIPS [16] in Canada. In the above-mentioned coupled models, the main components are models of the atmosphere, ocean and sea ice. At the same time, the SYSTEM5 model includes a description of rivers and river runoff, and the SEAS5 is supplemented by a model of sea waves WAM. For model coupling, the OASIS3 [19] system is mainly used (particularly, in GloSea5, SEAS5 and SYSTEM5). A detailed overview of the modern coupled models for long–term weather forecasting is given in [5].

The coupled model of the atmosphere SLAV [17], ocean INMIO [8] and soil [21] is developed at the Marchuk Institute of Numerical Mathematics, Shirshov Institute of Oceanology and Hydrometeorological Centre of Russia. Together with the third–party sea ice model CICE [7], these models are combined into the single software product SLAV–INMIO–CICE [5] by means of the Compact Modeling Framework (CMF) [9]. Currently, the coupled model is being tested in two versions that differ in horizontal resolution of the ocean and sea ice components: $0.5°$ and $0.25°$. Here, both components use the same grid, similar to the standard ocean grids of the European consortium NEMO [13] and [4].

Table 1. High-performance systems (from Top500 list) installed in national meteorological centers over the world.

Site, Country	System	Cores	Rmax, TFlops	Rank
United Kingdom Meteorological Office, UK	Cray XC40	241 920	7 038.9	23
Japan Meteorological Agency, Japan	Cray XC50	135 792	5 730.5	28, 29
ECMWF, UK	Cray XC40	126 468	3 944.7	42, 43
Indian Institute of Tropical Meteorology, India	Pratyush - Cray XC40	119 232	3 763.9	45
United Kingdom Meteorological Office, UK	Cray XC40	89 856	2 801.8	66, 67
National Centre for Medium Range Weather Forecasting, India	Mihir – Cray XC40	83 592	2 570.4	73
China Meteorological Administration, China	PAI-BSystem - Sugon TC4600LP/W740I	50 816	2 547.0	75
China Meteorological Administration, China	PAI-ASystem - Sugon TC4600	48 128	2 435.0	81
Korea Meteorological Administration, Korea	Nuri - Cray XC40	69 600	2 395.7	82, 83
Meteo France, France	Prolix2 - bullx DLC 720	72 000	2 168.0	89
Meteo France, France	Beaufix2 - bullx DLC 720	73 440	2 157.4	90
Main Computing Center of Roshydromet, Russia	Cray XC40	35 136	1 200.3	283

The resolution of the atmosphere model in both versions is $0.9°$ in longitude and $0.72°$ in latitude.

This article describes SLAV–INMIO–CICE design and some aspects related to the coupled model parallel performance tuning.

2 Why Supercomputing?

The technology of long–term forecasting relies on numerical models that allow one to predict the future state of the atmosphere and its near-surface layer. The ensemble approach allows to take into account the instability of the processes and phenomena being simulated with respect to small perturbations [10]. It is assumed that the statistics of prognostic outcomes obtained as a result of the ensemble modeling gives information on the most probable state of the system at the time of the forecast and on the degree of its uncertainty. There are several methods for generating an ensemble. One of the most common ways is the perturbation of the initial state of the atmosphere that is used as initial data for a model. Similarly to initial data, these perturbations can be introduced into the settings of the model and its physical parameterizations. Furthermore, a practical implementation of the uncertainty in the atmospheric model is the construction of multi-model ensembles of prognostic calculations. As worldwide practice shows, joint prognostic products usually turn out to be more successful than predictions of individual models participating in an ensemble.

The typical number of participants in an ensemble of a long–term weather forecast based on an individual model is from 30 to 50, depending on the meteorological center, complexity of the numerical model and its spatial resolution. In particular, this means that one 4–month long–term forecast using the SLAV–INMIO–CICE coupled model in the version with 0.5° ocean and sea ice resolution takes about 55 min. on 669 cores of the Cray XC40 system, installed in 2018 at the Main Computing Center of Roshydromet. Calculation of the ensemble forecast in this case will require at least 27 h. or 2/3 of the whole system for 55 min., if the ensemble members are calculated simultaneously. However, there is a need to correct simulation results taking into account the model systematic errors. To do this, preliminary *hindcasts* computations are performed that are quite time consuming.

Hindcasts are a series of historical ensemble long–range forecasts with the same lead time as the main forecast. The initial date of all hindcasts corresponds to the same calendar day, as for the basic forecast. In order to save computation time, the ensemble of each year includes 2–3 times less participants. Historical forecasts usually cover at least 10 years. Averaging over each day of each ensemble of historical forecasts and, then, averaging over all hindcasts allows one to obtain the average climate of the numerical model. Thus, systematic model errors can be identified, which arise, for example, as a result of inaccurate reproduction of large–scale atmospheric dynamics and/or of subgrid–scale processes. The model drift can also be caused by initially inconsistent states of the simulated media. The process of their mutual adaptation in a coupled model can be accompanied by large-scale phenomena, such as a spurious El Nino.

Taking the model climate into account can significantly improve the quality of the long–range forecast. Therefore, the hindcasts calculation is a necessary and, at the same time, resource–consuming part of the long–range forecasting technology. Indeed, one long–range forecast based on the coupled SLAV–IVMIO–CICE model with 0.5° resolution in the ocean and sea ice models and with 10 ensemble members requires about 550 min on 669 cores of Cray XC40. Ten historical forecasts require almost 4 days of continuous calculations, while 15 ensemble members with a coverage of 15 years will require more than 8 days. The increased spatial resolution in the models of ocean and sea ice commensurately increases the time required for calculating the hindcasts and, respectively, the long–range forecast.

The need to treat the systematic errors by calculating historical forecasts implies increased demands for the efficiency of both the coupled model and its components. The following section discusses the features of coupling in the SLAV–INMIO–CICE model.

3   Coupled Model Configuration

Our coupled model includes the SLAV atmosphere model, the INMIO ocean model and the third-party CICE sea ice model. To describe the processes of heat and moisture transfer in the deep soil, the INM RAS multi-layer soil model is incorporated directly into the atmospheric model.

The global atmospheric model SLAV [17] within the framework of the coupled model works at the regular latitudinal–longitudinal grid with a resolution of $0.9° \times 0.72°$, which corresponds to 400 points in longitude and 251 points in latitude (including the poles). The number of vertical levels – 96 with the top layer at a height corresponding to 0.03 hPa. Thus, the model of the atmosphere includes a description of the stratosphere dynamics. Model time step is 1440 s. It should be noted that a vertical coordinate with an uneven grid spacing is used in SLAV model: to describe the stratospheric dynamics, the grid step in the range from 100 to 10 hPa is about 500 m. Calculation of radiation transfer in the atmosphere occurs every model hour, all other parameterizations of subgrid–scale processes are calculated at each time step. Preliminary assessment of the climate characteristics of the SLAV model shows a good agreement of the average annual fields of heat flux on the surface, precipitation and pressure with the ERA–Interim reanalysis data [1]. SLAV reproduces well the semi–annual and quasi-two-year oscillations in the equatorial stratosphere with amplitude and period corresponding to observational data [3].

The ocean model INMIO [8] and the sea ice model CICE [7] operate on the same tripolar grid. Two grid configurations are available, with a nominal resolution of 0.5° and 0.25°, similar to the [13] and [4] grids, respectively. The atmosphere model is the same for both configurations. The ocean model in both cases has 49 levels with a vertical grid spacing from 6 m in the upper layer to 250 m at the depth. The time steps of the main cycle for solving model equations are the same for the ocean and the ice. In both cases, the model, within the restrictions of its resolution, implements the most eddy–permitting mode by not using the laplacian viscosity in the momentum equations. Horizontal turbulent mixing of heat and salt is parameterized with the diffusion coefficient equal to the nominal value at the equator and scaled towards the poles proportionally to the square root of the cell area. To ensure numerical stability in the equations of momentum transfer, a biharmonic filter is applied with a coefficient scaled proportionally to the cell area to the power 3/2. Additionally, in the 0.25° configuration, the Smagorinsky biharmonic scheme in [6] the formulation is used for stable simulation of sharp fronts. The differences in the main model parameters for the two grid resolutions are given in Table 2. It should be noted that most forecast studies are planned to be performed with the 0.25° resolution. Thus, only in this version the ocean and ice model timesteps have been tuned according to stability conditions.

The coupled model uses the sea ice model CICE of the version 5.1. We apply the simulation regime that includes calculation of five categories of ice and one of snow, the upwind transport scheme, and the description of melting ponds. The ice dynamics is parameterized with the elastic – viscous – plastic rheology model

Table 2. Main ocean and sea ice configuration parameters.

Configuration	Grid size	Main cycle step	Ocean barotropic subcycle step	Nominal tracer diffusion	Nominal biharmonic viscosity	Ice dynamic subcycle step
0.5°	720 × 360	720 s	30 s	2000 m²/s	$-8.5 \cdot 10^{11} \mathrm{m}^4/\mathrm{s}$	6 s
0.25°	1440 × 720	600 s	20 s	300 m²/s	$-1.5 \cdot 10^{11} \mathrm{m}^4/\mathrm{s}$	5 s

which requires the subcycle with small timesteps for explicit resolving of elastic waves. In the calculation of ice thermodynamics, the zero layer approximation is applied, similarly to the GloSea5 system [11].

The models of the atmosphere, ocean and sea ice are combined together in one program by means of the CMF [9] coupled modeling system, which is also responsible for synchronizing calculations and calendars of the components, providing data exchanges between them (including interpolation from one computational grid to another), and some file system operations. The coupling of the models is illustrated in Fig. 1 and is arranged as follows: data is transferred from SLAV to INMIO with the coupling interval of 2 h and includes two components of the wind stress, precipitation and evaporated water at the ocean surface (accumulated over the coupling interval), sensible and latent heat fluxes, short-wave solar radiation and total thermal radiation fluxes at the surface. The ocean model, in turn, sends three fields to the SLAV every 4 h: SST, sea ice concentration and its surface temperature.

As described in [5], for correct simulation of inertial oscillations in the Arctic Ocean, the models of ocean and sea ice should exchange data mutually with a coupling interval less than one hour. Therefore, in both configurations, ocean–ice exchanges occur at every second step (that is, once every 24 and 20 min for resolutions of 0.5° and 0.25°, respectively). The INMIO model sends seven fields to CICE (surface temperature, salinity and components of current velocity, components of the ocean surface slope and freezing–melting potential), getting back nine fields integrated over ice categories (ice thickness and concentration, penetrating solar radiation, surface stress components, sensible heat, salt and fresh water fluxes, ice surface temperature). Detailed features of the coupled model, in particular, the superimposition of grids and coastlines of INMIO and CICE models are discussed in [5].

The SLAV and CICE models do not exchange data directly, since information on the state of sea ice (concentration and surface temperature) required by SLAV is updated in INMIO much more frequently than it is necessary for the atmosphere model. Similarly, the fields from the SLAV (components of the wind stress, short-wave and total thermal radiation fluxes, sensible and latent heat, precipitation) are transmitted to CICE via INMIO. This approach not only reduces the number of data exchanges, but also greatly simplifies setting up the coupled model, which is necessary to synchronize performance speeds of its components. Features of the parallel configuration tuning and optimizing calculations of the coupled model are discussed in the next section.

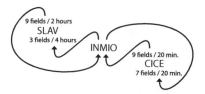

Fig. 1. The coupled model design: periods of data exchange between components and amount of fields transferred.

4   Computational Characteristics of the Coupled Model

One of the most important characteristics of the coupled model is its performance. Usually, a nondimensional quantity equal to the ratio of model time to the computer wall-clock time necessary to calculate the model up to this time is used as a performance measure. As an example, the ECMWF low-resolution model SEAS5 [14] can run a simulation for 1.9 years per astronomic day using 100 processor cores of Cray XC40 system that corresponds approximately to 11.56 h/min. A detailed comparison of the SLAV–INMIO–CICE coupled model with SEAS5 is considered in [2].

The performance of the coupled model depends on efficiency of each component but also on its parallel configuration that defines the amount of processor cores allocated for each component. In doing so, the speed of computation for each model is adjusted to synchronize them. The data exchanges in many coupled models for long–range forecasts are done by the coupler that also interpolates data between model grids. In the CMF coupler used in SLAV–INMIO–CICE, data exchanges between components are carried out in asynchronous mode: having sent data, the model does not wait for an acknowledgement of data receipt from the other model. However, a disbalance of the computation speed of the components becomes noticeable due to the bidirectional character of data exchange. Usually, this can be seen as a lag for one or more components while waiting for data from other model.

Figure 2a, b, c, and d show the wall-clock time for one time–step for each component of the coupled model SLAV–INMIO–CICE as a function of model time. Figure 2a and b correspond to the coupled model version with 0.25° resolution in the ocean and sea ice components, while c and d are for the version with 0.5° resolution. One can see that the components produce calculations with approximately the same speed. Note that the blue line is almost invisible because the wall-clock time for the ocean model is on average slightly less than that for the sea-ice model. The balanced configuration of the coupled model was selected so that there would be no peaks (i.e. waiting times) in the figures similar to Fig. 2a, b, c and d at the time moments of data exchanges. The coupled model performance depends not only on amount of processor cores allocated for each component but also on parallel data decomposition inside every model.

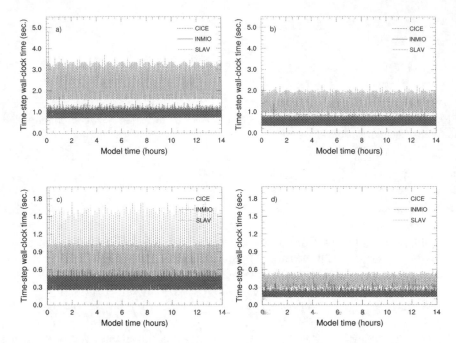

Fig. 2. Wall-clock time for one model step (s) as a function of model time (hours) for each component of the coupled model (atmosphere – green line, ocean – blue line, sea ice – red line). (*a*) and (*b*) correspond to the coupled model version with 0.25° resolution in the ocean and sea ice components, while *c* and *d* are for the version with 0.5° resolution. See the text for additional details. (Color figure online)

The optimal and near-optimal configurations of the coupled model are shown in Fig. 3 where the performance of SLAV–INMIO–CICE is depicted as a function of the number of processor cores used. One can see that the increase in the number of cores used by the components is accompanied by the coupled model per–core performance decrease even if each model component shows separately a better scalability.

The clusterization of points in Fig. 3 is explained by the details of data decomposition in the atmosphere model. The 1D data decomposition in latitude is supplemented by the OpenMP decomposition in longitude in the SLAV model. This means, in particular, that an optimal data decomposition in the SLAV model is achieved when the number of MPI processes is a divisor of the grid-point number in latitude. In our case, these numbers are 125 and 63. Table 3 shows some optimal configurations differing by the number of processor cores used. The last column shows the performance of the coupled model. One can see that for 0.5° resolution in the ocean and sea ice models, most of the cores are allocated to the atmosphere model. The situation is opposite in the case of the ocean and sea-ice models with 0.25° horizontal resolution when these components use much more cores than the atmosphere model.

The nonlinear growth of wall-clock time necessary to calculate 14 model days is explained mainly by difficulties in synchronization between the ocean and sea ice models. The data exchange between INMIO and CICE occurs every second time-step. The coupler work on mapping (gathering data from the sender component, interpolation and distribution to the receiver component) between theses components becomes essential in this case. One of these models has inevitably to wait for both forward and backward mapping, however, it is possible to tune the ratio of resources allocated to theses components so that the second model almost does not stand idle.

The example of computational resources allocation for the ocean and sea ice models is shown in Fig. 4 where they use 480 and 80 cores respectively, while the coupler uses one core. The amount of cores for CICE model is selected in a way that every time step in this model requires approximately 1.5 more wall-clock time than the INMIO model step. In doing so, the CICE sea ice model does not wait for the INMIO model. At the same time, the INMIO ocean model waits for results of coupler operations but not for sea ice model itself. The overhead of sending data to the coupler is low because this is an asynchronous operation. Further studies in this direction will assume multidimensional optimization for 4 model components – three models and the coupler. The problem of balancing all the component models is aggravated by the differences in data decomposition in the models, the presence land-sea mask, the variability in time-step wall-clock time due to changes in sea ice and the application of iterative procedures.

We have also studied the parallel structure of data exchange using the Intel Trace Analyzer tool. Unfortunately, we were not able to use this software for selecting an optimal configuration due to significant difference in the overhead of each component.

Table 3. The coupled model performance as a function of its configuration and total number of processor cores.

Configuration	Total number of processor cores	SLAV	INMIO	CICE	Performance (h/min)
0.25°	827	250	480	96	11.38
0.25°	430	125	240	64	18.86
0.25°	224	63	128	32	31.57
0.5°	661	500	128	32	5.53
0.5°	331	250	64	16	10.73

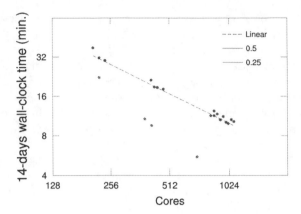

Fig. 3. Wall-clock time necessary to calculate 14 model days as a function of processor cores used by the coupled model.

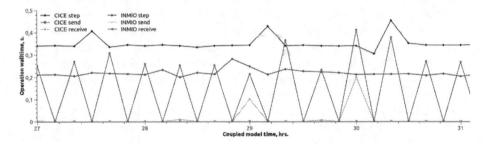

Fig. 4. Wall-clock times for computations and waiting for data in case of 480 cores for INMIO, 80 cores for CICE and 1 core for the coupler. The horizontal resolution of the ocean and sea ice models is $0.25°$.

5   Conclusion

Currently, the leading Global Producing Centres of the World Meteorological Organization (UK Met Office, European Centre for Medium-Range Weather Forecasts, USA NOAA, Meteo France, etc.) produce operational long–range weather forecasts using coupled models. In addition to the atmospheric component, such models include components of the World Ocean, sea ice and underlying surface. This allows to increase the accuracy of forecasts due to a more detailed description of the Earth system internal feedbacks and due to the use of long–range predictability sources from its slowly evolving components. The possibility of constructing and utilizing such models is provided by constantly increasing power of available computing systems, often already stepping over the petaflops threshold. At the same time, even at the scales of the most advanced supercomputers, the long–range forecast problem is extremely resource-consuming, primarily because of the increasing resolution of the models and the need for massive ensemble calculations to obtain the model climate and generalized statistical characteristics of the solution.

The resolution of SLAV–INMIO–CICE coupled model corresponds to the models applied by WMO's Global Producing Centres for Long-Range Forecasts (GPC LRFs) for operational long–term forecasting. The performance of a coupled model depends on many factors: the total number of processor cores used, the amount of cores allocated for each model component, periodicity and way to organize data exchange between the models, parallel data decomposition inside every model. That is why the work on determination of the coupled model optimal configuration allowing to use the computational resources most efficiently is a complex problem with non-trivial solution.

The development of SLAV model was partially supported with the RFBR grant No. 17-05-01227 at the Marchuk Institute of Numerical Mathematics, Russian Academy of Sciences. The development of INMIO–CICE coupled model with 0.25° horizontal resolution was supported by the Russian Science Foundation (project no. 17-77-30001) and performed at the Federal State Budget Scientific Institution "Marine Hydrophysical Institute of RAS". The work described in Sect. 4 was supported with the Russian Academy of Sciences Program for Basic Researches I.2P (2019).

References

1. Fadeev, R.Y., Tolstykh, M.A., Volodin, E.M.: Climate version of the SL-AV global atmospheric model: development and preliminary results. Russ. Meteorol. Hydrol. **44**, 13–22 (2019). https://doi.org/10.3103/S1068373919010023
2. Fadeev, R.Y., Ushakov, K.V., Tolstykh, M.A., et al.: Coupled SLAV-INMIO-CICE model: design and features of parallel realization. In: Proceedings of PCT 2019 (in press)
3. Shashkin, V.V., Tolstykh, M.A., Volodin, E.M.: Stratospheric circulation modeling with the SL-AV semi-Lagrangian atmospheric model. Russ. Meteorol. Hydrol. **44**, 1–12 (2019). https://doi.org/10.3103/S1068373919010011
4. Barnier, B., Madec, G., Penduff, T., et al.: Impact of partial steps and momentum advection schemes in a global ocean circulation model at eddy permitting resolution. Ocean Dyn. **56**, 543–567 (2006). https://doi.org/10.1007/s10236-006-0082-1
5. Fadeev, R.Y., Ushakov, K.V., Tolstykh, M.A., Ibrayev, R.A.: Design and development of the SLAV-INMIO-CICE coupled model for seasonal prediction and climate research. Russ. J. Numer. Anal. Math. Model. **33**, 333–340 (2018). https://doi.org/10.1515/rnam-2018-0028
6. Griffies, S.M., Hallberg, R.W.: Biharmonic friction with a Smagorinsky-like viscosity for use in large-scale eddy-permitting ocean models. Mon. Weather Rev. **128**, 2935–2946 (2000). https://doi.org/10.1175/1520-0493(2000)128⟨2935:BFWASL⟩2.0.CO;2
7. Hunke, E.C., Lipscomb, W.H., Turner, A.K., Jeffery, N., Elliott, S.: CICE: the Los Alamos Sea Ice Model documentation and software user's manual, version 5.1. Technical report LA-CC-06-012. Los Alamos National Laboratory, Los Alamos, NM (2015). http://www.ccpo.odu.edu/klinck/Reprints/PDF/cicedoc2015.pdf. Accessed 25 Feb 2015
8. Ibrayev, R.A., Ushakov, K.V., Khabeev, R.N.: Eddy-resolving 1/10° model of the world ocean. Izvestiya Atmos. Ocean Phys. **48**, 37–46 (2012)

9. Kalmykov, V.V., Ibrayev, R.A., Kaurkin, M.N., Ushakov, K.V.: Compact modeling framework v3.0 for high-resolution global ocean-ice-atmosphere models. Geosci. Model Dev. **11**, 3983–3997 (2018). https://doi.org/10.5194/gmd-11-3983-2018
10. About long-range forecasting. The North EurAsia Climate Centre (NEACC). http://seakc.meteoinfo.ru/training. Accessed 23 Apr 2019
11. MacLachlan, C., Arribas, A., Peterson, K.A., et al.: Global seasonal forecast system version 5 (GloSea5): a high-resolution seasonal forecast system. Q. J. Roy. Meteor. Soc. **141**, 1072–1084 (2015). https://doi.org/10.1002/qj.2396
12. Manual on the Global Data-processing and Forecasting System. Volume 1: Global aspects. WMO, no. 485 (2012). http://www.wmo.int/pages/prog/wcp/wcasp/gpc/gpc.php. Accessed 23 Apr 2019
13. Molines, J.M., Barnier, B., Penduff, T., et al.: Definition of the global $1/2°$ experiment with CORE interannual forcing, ORCA05-G50. LEGI report November 2006, reference: LEGI-DRA-1-11-2006. https://www.drakkar-ocean.eu/publications/reports/orca05-g50.pdf. Accessed 25 Feb 2019
14. Roberts, C.D., Senan, R., Molteni, F., et al.: Climate model configurations of the ECMWF integrated forecasting system (ECMWF-IFS cycle 43r1) for HighResMIP. Geosci. Model Dev. **11**, 3681–3712 (2018). https://doi.org/10.5194/gmd-11-3681-2018
15. Saha, S., Moorthi, S., Wu, X., et al.: The NCEP climate forecast system version 2. J. Clim. **27**, 2185–2208 (2014). https://doi.org/10.1175/JCLI-D-12-00823.1
16. von Salzen, K., McFarlane, N.A., Lazare, M., et al.: The Canadian fourth generation atmospheric global climate model (CanAM4). Part I: physical processes. Atmos. Ocean **51**, 104–125 (2013). https://doi.org/10.1080/07055900.2012.755610
17. Tolstykh, M.A., Volodin, E.M., Kostrykin, S.V., et al.: Development of the multi-scale version of the SL-AV global atmosphere model. Russ. Meteorol. Hydrol. **40**, 374–382 (2015). https://doi.org/10.3103/S1068373915060035
18. Top500 the list. www.top500.org/. Accessed 23 Apr 2019
19. Valcke, S.: The OASIS3 coupler: a European climate modelling community software. Geosci. Model Dev. **6**, 373–388 (2013). https://doi.org/10.5194/gmd-6-373-2013
20. Voldoire, A., Sanchez-Gomez, E., Salas y Melia, D., et al.: The CNRM-CM5.1 global climate model: description and basic evaluation. Clim. Dyn. **40**, 2091–2121 (2013). https://doi.org/10.1007/s00382-011-1259-y
21. Volodin, E.M., Lykosov, V.N.: Parameterization of heat and moisture transfer in the soil-vegetation system for use in atmospheric general circulation models: 1. Formulation and simulations based on local observational data. Izvestiya Atmos. Ocean Phys. **34**, 405–416 (1998)
22. World Meteorological Organization Global Producing Centres for Long-Range Forecasts. http://www.wmo.int/pages/prog/www/DPS/GDPS-Supplement5-AppI-4.html. Accessed 23 Apr 2019

The Creation of Intelligent Support Methods for Solving Mathematical Physics Problems on Supercomputers

Boris Glinskiy[1] , Yury Zagorulko[2] , Galina Zagorulko[2],
Igor Kulikov[1] , and Anna Sapetina[1(✉)]

[1] Institute of Computational Mathematics and Mathematical Geophysics
SB RAS, Novosibirsk, Russia
gbm@opg.sscc.ru, kulikov@ssd.sscc.ru,
afsapetina@gmail.com
[2] A.P. Ershov Institute of Informatics System SB RAS, Novosibirsk, Russia
{zagor,gal}@iis.nsk.su

Abstract. An approach to creating methods and means of intelligent support for solving compute-intensive problems (CI problems) of mathematical physics on modern peta- and future exaflops supercomputers, containing millions and, eventually, billions of simultaneously running computational cores and providing an enormous degree of parallelism, is proposed. The relevance of the intelligent support of the process of solving problems at all stages - from setting a problem, selecting a method of numerical solution to choosing a supercomputer architecture and software implementation is substantiated. The proposed system of intelligent support is based on the ontology of computational methods and algorithms, the ontology of parallel architectures and technologies and uses decision rules to find the best possible approach to parallel solving a problem specified by a user, at all stages of its solution, up to choosing the best planning strategy for the computational process. The paper describes the concept of creating intelligent support for solving CI problems, using ontologies and inference rules. An example demonstrating the use of the proposed approach for solving a problem of astrophysics is presented.

Keywords: Ontology · Knowledge base · Compute-intensive problems · Astrophysics · Decision support system · Co-design

1 Introduction

A researcher who applies the methods of mathematical modeling to solve a problem in his problem area faces several problems: (1) What computational method should be chosen to solve this problem? (2) On which computing platform should be conducted numerical experiments? In each subject area, where there is a set of methods for solving CI problems on modern multi-core computing systems, it is important to choose the method that most effectively solves the problem in a reasonable time with a given accuracy. On the other hand, the representation of knowledge in the form of ontologies and inference rules for solving specific problems is becoming increasingly popular [1, 2].

V. Voevodin and S. Sobolev (Eds.): RuSCDays 2019, CCIS 1129, pp. 427–438, 2019.
https://doi.org/10.1007/978-3-030-36592-9_35

Note that ontologies (a system of concepts and relationships linking them) are the foundation of knowledge bases in complex areas that require systematization. Their use facilitates the creation of generally available knowledge bases and the use of artificial intelligence methods thanks to a large set of freely available editors for creating ontologies and inference engines (reasoners) that make a logical conclusion.

The foreign authors have repeatedly put forward the need to create resources based on ontological descriptions in various fields of science (physics [3], geology [4], biology [5], astrophysics [6, 7], and others). There are web resources on astrophysics [8], on genomics [9], on geology [10]. It also explores approaches to the use of ontologies to improve the efficiency of using computational resources and support users who solve their problems with them.

Thus, in [11], it is proposed to use ontologies to describe Grid-resources in order to simplify and structure the construction of Grid-applications by composing and reusing existing software components and developing knowledge-based services and tools. For this purpose, an ontology of the Data Mining knowledge area has been developed, which makes it possible to simplify the development of Grid applications that focus on knowledge elicitation from data. In [12] the approach that uses the ontology describing the metadata of a Grid-resource and the inference mechanisms in the ontology for more effective management of Grid-resources is considered.

The paper [13] discusses the use of ontologies and inference mechanisms to assist users in solving CI problems on heterogeneous computing architectures, in particular on clusters equipped with NVIDIA GPGPUs and Intel Xeon Phi in addition to the traditional Intel processor. Here, ontology inference mechanisms help to find the best possible solution by combining hardware, software, and planning strategies. The application of the proposed approach to solving bioinformatics problems is also demonstrated. The described approaches to the use of ontologies are close to the approach proposed in this paper, but they are focused on other areas of knowledge and computational architectures.

The most significant Russian projects to support solving problems on supercomputers is AlgoWiki [14] – an open encyclopedia of algorithms properties and features of their implementations on different hardware and software platforms with the possibility of collective work of worldwide computing community. Unlike this work, AlgoWiki does not resort to ontologies and does not provide support for the selection of suitable methods and algorithms for solving specific problems.

Consider the need to develop a system of intelligent support for solving a problem of mathematical physics on the example of astrophysics. A large number of codes have been developed for solving astrophysical problems. They can be divided into three groups: codes based on the SPH method [15–17]; mesh codes [18–20] including codes on adaptive meshes [21–23]; codes based on moving meshes [24–26]. Each code and method implemented in it is focused on a specific class of problems and is often limited to the use of classical supercomputer architectures. A number of codes were developed for graphics accelerators [27–29] and for Intel Xeon Phi accelerators [30]. However, the use of any of these codes to solve a specific astrophysical problem requires substantial improvement. Using the new architecture of supercomputers further complicates the problem, not to mention the development of the code from scratch. Unfortunately, currently there are no universal systems for generating astrophysical codes. Although attempts to create such systems exist, such as [31] in the University of Costa Rica on the basis EXCALC packet. The MPI-AMRVAC code has some flexibility for solving the problems of stellar evolution [32], but nevertheless it has a number of limitations when going to problems of the galaxies evolution or supernova explosions. Similar researches are carried out in Russia. So, in the Institute of Astronomy RAS under the leadership of the corresponding member RAS D.V. Bisikalo the code generation system for the close binary stars evolution was created. However, an intelligent system for generating astrophysical has not yet been created. A similar situation exists in other areas of knowledge requiring high-performance computing, for example, geophysics, plasma physics, etc.

The current state of computer technology provides researchers with a wide range of computational architectures with the ability to use high-performance parallel computing to solve their problem. It should be noted that along with classical computational clusters with MPP (massive parallel processing) architectures, hybrid supercomputers, equipped with accelerators of computing, are becoming increasingly popular. In the TOP 500 of the world's most powerful computers [33] a supercomputer Summit with a capacity of 188 PFlops is in the first place. Note that this supercomputer is optimized for the analysis of big data; nevertheless, intensive work is underway on using the advantages of the V100 architecture for solving problems of plasma physics and accelerator physics. The performance of the most powerful Russian supercomputer Lomonosov-2 is 2.1 Pflops [34]. However, in Russia it is planned to build up national supercomputer centers with a capacity of dozens PFlops [35]. On such supercomputers, it is possible to solve problems of large computational complexity.

Thus, from the above example of astrophysics it is clear that there is a set of codes for solving problems on the one hand, and on the other hand there is a set of computational architectures, libraries and software tools that allow solving the set problem. Considering that it is difficult for a researcher to easily navigate simultaneously in computational methods and in existing tools for high-performance computing (architectures, parallel languages and software tools), it is necessary to create an intelligent support system (IS system) for solving CI problems on supercomputers taking into account user computing architecture.

2 Basic Principles of Building IS System

Consider the principles of building the IS system for solving CI problems and its main blocks. Figure 1 shows a conceptual scheme of the IS system. The core of such a system is a knowledge base, including a set of interconnected ontologies and inference rules that extend the logic of these ontologies. An important module of the IS system is an inference engine (a reasoner), which, using the knowledge base and the user specification of a problem, builds the optimal scheme for its solution.

An example of the application of such an approach based on the consideration of various schemes for solving a problem is given in [36]. This paper considered the simulation of seismic wave propagation in a complex heterogeneous media using the co-design methodology [37]. Within the framework of the dynamic elasticity, the problem has been solved in two statements: (1) in terms of displacement velocities and stress; (2) in terms of displacements. In the first case, it is necessary to solve a system of nine equations, in the other – of three, while the computation time in both approaches is comparable, but the second approach is significantly more efficient in terms of the memory usage.

Another component of IS system, the automated code generation module, supports the creation of parallel code that solves the problem set by user. This module inserts the corresponding code fragments from the software component library (SC library) into the problem solving scheme. If there is no suitable component in the SC library, the user can substitute the necessary component by taking it from the standard library or writing a new one.

The system also includes a simulation modeling unit that evaluates the scalability of the resulting code on a given architecture before carrying out final time-consuming calculations on a multi-core computing system. The main purpose of this unit is to select the optimal number of cores for the implementation of the algorithm by studying its behavior in model time. An example of simulation modeling usage with the help of AGNES simulation system [38] for problems of geophysics, astrophysics, and plasma physics to study the scalability of algorithms is given in [39].

In the authors' opinion, the proposed methods of intelligent support for solving CI problems will allow the user to create efficient parallel programs using modern computational methods, supercomputer architectures and libraries.

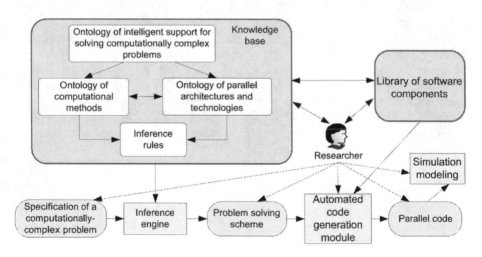

Fig. 1. A conceptual scheme of the IS system for solving CI problems.

3   Designing the Knowledge Base

The foundation of the knowledge base of IS system is the ontology of the problem domain (PD) "IS for solving CI problems of mathematical physics". To formulation this ontology, we proceed from the logic that we use when building a program for the simulation of a phenomenon. This ontology is multilevel and contains several linked ontologies, among which an important role is played by the ontology of computational methods and parallel algorithms and the ontology of parallel architectures and technologies. Consider the top-level of the ontology (see Fig. 2).

The main Study Objects in this area are Physical Objects and Physical Phenomena, which are studied in certain Branch of Science and are described by Physical laws, derived from Empirical Observations. Study Objects are described by an approximate Physical Model, formalized Mathematical Model which is given by an Equation System and is verified by Empirical Observations. Consequently, we have the Mathematical Model in the form of the Equation System satisfying the initial and boundary conditions containing all parameters (state equations, values of coefficients, etc.).

The Equation System is solved by a Computational Method, which, in turn, is implemented by certain Parallel Algorithm. The Parallel Algorithm is optimized for a Target Architecture and is represented by certain Parallel Programming Technologies. The final representation of the Parallel Algorithm is encoded by program Code containing a set of Program Components and is executed on the Target Architecture.

The described ontology contains the basic concepts of the considered PD and their interrelations. Since concepts such as the Computational Method, Parallel Algorithm, and Target Architecture are very important for this PD, and they define the specifics of solving CI problems, their descriptions are discussed in more detail and are presented in two separate ontologies.

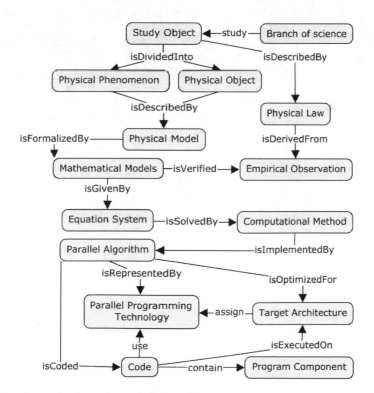

Fig. 2. The top-level ontology of IS for solving CI problems of mathematical physics.

Figure 3 shows a fragment of the ontology of computational methods and parallel algorithms. Each Computational Method is characterized by Computational complexity and Accuracy. It is implemented by a specific Parallel Algorithm, which is determined by a Decomposition of the computational domain and a Data Structure. The Parallel Algorithm is optimized for the Target Architecture and is encoded by software Code that contains Program Components written in the selected Program language. The Code is characterized by such interrelated properties as Performance, Computation time, Size of memory used, Precision, Scalability, Energy Efficiency, Utilization level (of memory and processor).

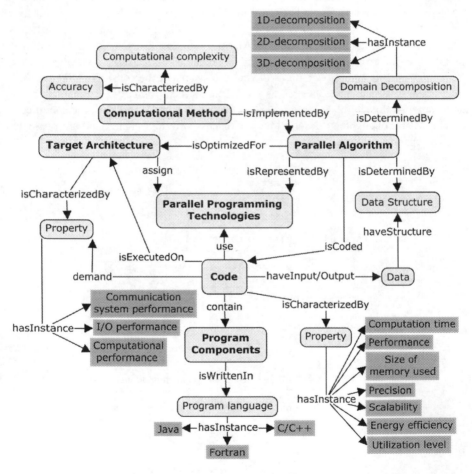

Fig. 3. The ontology of computational methods and parallel algorithms.

Figure 4 shows a fragment of the ontology of parallel architectures and technologies. Upon detailed consideration, the Target Architecture is determined by the Type of Computing System (the main type are MPP, SMP, NUMA) and contains Computing

Nodes connected by Interconnect. Computing Nodes also contain Computing Devices —the main CPUs and Computing Accelerators, and Memory, coupled with Computing Devices. As Computing Accelerators, we can consider both actual General-purpose Accelerators (for example, GPU, Xeon Phi, PEZY) and Specialized Accelerators for specific problems (for example, GRAVE or MPRACE boards for accelerating calculations of interactions of bodies and particles in astrophysics, chemistry, biology). The specific configuration of the Target Architecture is characterized by properties such as Computational performance, Communication and I/O system performance. At this fragment of the ontology, we do not consider the individual properties and technical features of Computing Devices and Memory, but they are included in a more detailed description.

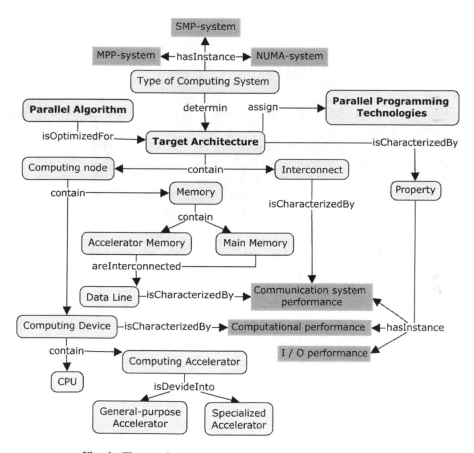

Fig. 4. The ontology of parallel architectures and technologies.

The ontologies discussed above are described in the OWL language [40] and include a description of classes and their properties, as well as instances of classes (individuals) that make up the knowledge base filled with specific methods, algorithms, software components and elements of parallel architectures. The logical conclusion in OWL-ontologies is made on the basis of the axioms specified in the ontology by means of one of the inference engine (Pellet, FaCT++, HermiT). To build ontologies and set axioms, the ontology editor Protégé 5.2 with the inference engine connected to it is used [41].

In addition to the ontology, knowledge base of IS system contains expert (inference) rules that allow one based on the specification of a CI problem to select program components for generating code and determine the architecture on which it will be executed. Such rules allow you to infer information that is not explicitly contained in the ontology. So, for example, using the Properties of the Computing Method and the Parallel Algorithm, you can define its bottleneck in terms of compute or memory-bound problem (the limiting factor is the speed of the processor or speed of access to memory, respectively). Further, guided by the inference rules, one can give qualitative and quantitative estimates of the Properties of the Code executed on the Target Architecture, focusing on its Properties. Also, inference rules may allow one to set the requirements that the Program Code imposes on the Properties of the Target Architecture (Fig. 3). For example, if the performance of the communication system of the Target Architecture is not high enough, then efforts to improve the performance of the Code will be in vain. Thus, the inference rules define implicit links between the Computational Method, the Parallel Algorithm, the Target Architecture, and the Code. Guided by them at different stages of problem solving, you can quickly find the optimal approach to the solution that satisfies the concept of co-design.

The SWRL (Semantic Web Rule Language) language [42] is used to represent the rules. Note that the rules written in the SWRL, in fact, are Horn clauses, which greatly simplifies their construction and understanding.

4   An Example of Using the Intelligent Support System for Solving Astrophysics Problems

To clarify the proposed approach, we give a detailed description of the process of solving a CI problem on a supercomputer using the example of astrophysics. Let us complement the basic concepts of the proposed ontologies with a finite set of objects of the selected branch of science (see Fig. 5).

Let us need to simulate the development of hydrodynamic turbulence of the interstellar medium at the early stage of evolution in the maximum resolution for the qualitative determination of gas fragmentation. To solve this problem, it is supposed to use computing nodes equipped with manycore Intel Xeon Phi processors (for example, nodes that are part of the Siberian Supercomputer Center of ICMMG SB RAS). This is an initial problem specification.

The inference rules of the developed knowledge base should suggest us that in this case we should apply the equations of magnetic isothermal hydrodynamics without gravity (since the early stage is considered, at which the velocity perturbation is significant, and not the pressure – gravity interaction), which are most correctly solved numerically by the Godunov method. Then you can choose the most accurate fifth order method WENO (for example, Intel Xeon Phi computational power allow you to effectively implement it) and the most optimal 3D decomposition of the computational domain. The fixed architecture of the Computing Device in this case uniquely identifies the Parallel Programming Technologies that need to be used: MPI for exchanges between nodes, OpenMP for multithreading, and the AVX extension for code vectorization. Thus, a scheme for solving the problem is defined. The automated code generation module will allow a scalable parallel code that solves the problem numerically on the chosen type of the Computing Device with a high order of accuracy.

Further, the problem is calculated on a small number of cluster computing nodes to determine the time delays for the simulation model. We enter the obtained data into the AGNES simulation system and in model time we determine the optimal number of computational cores for the final calculation of the problem on a given supercomputer architecture.

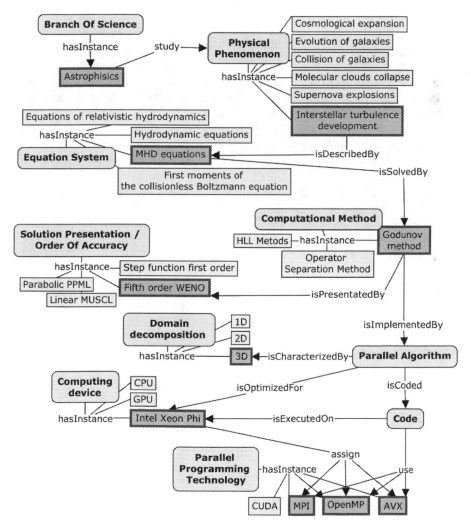

Fig. 5. The ontology of IS for solving CI astrophysics problems with a denoted scheme for solving a real problem.

This example illustrates the use of the ontological approach to the description of the logic for constructing computational models, which as well has been widely used in the development and implementation of the astrophysical codes PEGAS [43], GPUPEGAS [28], AstroPhi and its AVX-512 modification [30, 44]. In this regard, all the performance gains: 92% scalability of PEGAS code for 1024 cores of classical CPU, 55-fold acceleration for NVIDIA GPU in GPUPEGAS code, 27-fold in offload mode and 134-fold in native mode of Intel Xeon Phi MIC processors in AstroPhi code, and also 302 gigaflops performance gooPhi code for Intel Xeon Phi KNL, take place when using the proposed approach to the design of software implementation.

5   Conclusions

In this paper, we presented the concept of a IS system for solving CI problems of mathematical physics. The paper shows how, having, on the one hand, the ontology of computational methods and the corresponding parallel algorithms, and on the other hand, the ontology of parallel architectures and technologies, it is possible to create parallel programs for solving problems as soon as possible.

This system will be useful to ordinary users, who, as a rule, have little knowledge of multiprocessor system architectures and parallel technologies for creating parallel programs. On the other hand, it will also be useful for specialists in computational technologies, who fill at home in supercomputer architectures and parallel languages, but not know much about computational methods.

Acknowledgements. This research was conducted within the framework of the budget project No. 0315-2019-0009 for ICMMG SB RAS and supported in part by the Russian Foundation for Basic Research [grant No. 19-07-00085].

References

1. Compton, M., Barnaghi, P., Bermudez, L., et al.: The SSN ontology of the W3C semantic sensor network incubator group. Web Semant. Sci. Serv. Agents World Wide Web **17**, 25–32 (2012)
2. Keet, C.M., Ławrynowicz, A., d'Amato, C., et al.: The data mining optimization ontology. Web Semant. Sci. Serv. Agents World Wide Web **32**, 43–53 (2015)
3. Cvjetkovic, V.: Web physics ontology: online interactive symbolic computation in physics. In: 2017 4th Experiment@International Conference (Exp.at'17), Faro, pp. 52–57 (2017)
4. Ma, X.: Ontology Spectrum for Geological Data Interoperability. ITC, Netherlands (2011)
5. Cook, D., Neal, M., Bookstein, F., Gennari, J.: Ontology of physics for biology: representing physical dependencies as a basis for biological processes. J Biomed. Semant. **4**, 41 (2013)
6. Sarro, L.M., Martínez, R.: First steps towards an ontology for astrophysics. In: Palade, V., Howlett, R.J., Jain, L. (eds.) KES 2003. LNCS (LNAI), vol. 2774, pp. 1389–1395. Springer, Heidelberg (2003). https://doi.org/10.1007/978-3-540-45226-3_188
7. Louge, T., Karray, M.H., Archimède, B., Knödlseder, J.: Semantic interoperability in astrophysics for workflows extraction from heterogeneous services. In: van Sinderen, M., Chapurlat, V. (eds.) IWEI 2015. LNBIP, vol. 213, pp. 3–15. Springer, Heidelberg (2015). https://doi.org/10.1007/978-3-662-47157-9_1

8. ESPAS. https://www.espas-fp7.eu/portal/browse.html#ontology
9. SemGen. http://sbp.bhi.washington.edu/projects/semgen
10. Awesome geoscience semantics. http://www.geoscience-semantics.org
11. Cannataro, M., Comito, C.: A data mining ontology for grid programming. In: Proceedings of the 1st International Workshop on Semantic in Peer-to-Peer and Grid Computing, pp. 113–134 (2003)
12. Amarnath, B.R., Somasundaram, T.S., Ellappan, M., Buyya, R.: Ontology-based grid resource management. Softw. Pract. Exper. **39**, 1419–1438 (2009)
13. Faheem, H.M., König-Ries, B., Aslam, M.A., Aljohani, N.R., Katib, I.: Ontology design for solving computationally-intensive problems on heterogeneous architectures. Sustainability **10**(2), 441 (2018)
14. Antonov, A., Dongarra, J., Voevodin, V.: Algowiki project as an extension of the TOP500 methodology. JSFI **5**(1), 4–10 (2018)
15. Springel, V.: The cosmological simulation code GADGET-2. Mon. Not. R. Astron. Soc. **364**(4), 1105–1134 (2005)
16. Wadsley, J.W., Stadel, J., Quinn, T.: Gasoline: a flexible, parallel implementation of TreeSPH. New Astron. **9**(2), 137–158 (2004)
17. Steinmetz, M.: GRAPESPH: cosmological smoothed particle hydrodynamics simulations with the special-purpose hardware GRAPE. Mon. Not. R. Astron. Soc. **278**(4), 1005–1017 (1996)
18. The Pencil code. http://pencil-code.nordita.org/references.php
19. Stone, J.M., Norman, M.L.: ZEUS-2D: a radiation magnetohydrodynamics code for astrophysical flows in two space dimensions. I-The hydrodynamic algorithms and tests. ApJS **80**(2), 753–790 (1992)
20. Stone, J.M., Gardiner, T.A., Teuben, P., Hawley, J.F., Simon, J.B.: Athena: a new code for astrophysical MHD. ApJS **178**(1), 137–177 (2008)
21. Mignone, A., Bodo, G., Massaglia, S., et al.: PLUTO: a numerical code for computational astrophysics. ApJS **170**(1), 228 (2007)
22. Bryan, G.L., Norman, M.L., O'Shea, B.W., et al.: ENZO: an adaptive mesh refinement code for astrophysics. ApJS **211**, 19 (2014)
23. Teyssier, R.: Cosmological hydrodynamics with adaptive mesh refinement. A&A **385**, 337–364 (2002)
24. Hopkins, P.F.: GIZMO: a new class of accurate, mesh-free hydrodynamic simulation methods. Mon. Not. R. Astron. Soc. **450**(1), 53–110 (2015)
25. Springel, V.: E pur si muove: galilean-invariant cosmological hydrodynamical simulations on a moving mesh. Mon. Not. R. Astron. Soc. **401**(2), 791–851 (2010)
26. Murphy, J., Burrows, A.: BETHE-Hydro: an arbitrary Lagrangian-Eulerian multidimensional hydrodynamics code for astrophysical simulations. ApJS **179**, 209–241 (2008)
27. Schive, H.Y., Tsai, Y.C., Chiueh, T.: GAMER: a graphic processing unit accelerated adaptive-mesh-refinement code for astrophysics. Astrophys. J. Suppl. Ser. **186**(2), 457 (2010)
28. Kulikov, I.: GPUPEGAS: a new GPU-accelerated hydrodynamic code for numerical simulation of interacting galaxies. ApJS **214**, 12 (2014)
29. Schneider, E.E., Robertson, B.E.: CHOLLA: a new massively parallel hydrodynamics code for astrophysical simulations. ApJS **217**, 24 (2015)
30. Kulikov, I.M., Chernykh, I.G., Snytnikov, A.V., Glinskiy, B.M., Tutukov, A.V.: AstroPhi: a code for complex simulation of the dynamics of astrophysical objects using hybrid supercomputers. CPC **186**, 71–80 (2015)
31. Frutos-Alfaro, F., Carboni-Mendez, R.: MHD Generation Code. Revista de Matematicas: Teoria y Aplicaciones **23**(1) (2016)

32. Goedbloed, J., Keppens, R., Poedts, S.: Computer simulations of solar plasmas. Space Sci. Rev. **107**, 63 (2003)
33. TOP500. https://www.top500.org
34. Voevodin, V., Antonov, A., Nikitenko, D., et al.: Supercomputer Lomonosov-2: large scale, deep monitoring and fine analytics for the user community. JSFI **6**(2), 8–11 (2019)
35. TASS. Russian news agency. https://tass.ru/nauka/5327107
36. Glinskiy, B., Sapetina, A., Martynov, V., Weins, D., Chernykh, I.: The hybrid-cluster multilevel approach to solving the elastic wave propagation problem. In: Sokolinsky, L., Zymbler, M. (eds.) PCT 2017. CCIS, vol. 753, pp. 261–274. Springer, Cham (2017). https://doi.org/10.1007/978-3-319-67035-5_19
37. Glinskiy, B., Kulikov, I., Snytnikov, A., Romanenko, A., Chernykh, I., Vshivkov, V.: Co-design of parallel numerical methods for plasma physics and astrophysics. JSFI **1**(3), 88–98 (2014)
38. Podkorytov, D., Rodionov, A., Choo, H.: Agent-based simulation system AGNES for networks modeling: review and researching. In: Proceedings of the 6th International Conference on Ubiquitous Information Management and Communication (ACM ICUIMC 2012), p. 115. ACM (2012)
39. Glinskiy, B., Kulikov, I., Chernykh, I., Snytnikov, A., Sapetina, A., Weins, D.: The integrated approach to solving large-size physical problems on supercomputers. In: Voevodin, V., Sobolev, S. (eds.) RuSCDays 2017. CCIS, vol. 793, pp. 278–289. Springer, Cham (2017). https://doi.org/10.1007/978-3-319-71255-0_22
40. Antoniou, G., Harmelen, F.: Web ontology language: OWL. In: Staab, S., Studer, R. (eds.) Handbook on Ontologies, pp. 67–92. Springer, Heidelberg (2004). https://doi.org/10.1007/978-3-540-24750-0_4
41. Protege. https://protege.stanford.edu. Accessed 10 Jan 2018
42. SWRL. http://www.w3.org/Submission/SWRL/. Accessed 10 Jan 2018
43. Kulikov, I.: PEGAS: hydrodynamical code for numerical simulation of the gas components of interacting galaxies. Book Series of the Argentine Astronomical Society, vol. 4, pp. 91–95 (2013)
44. Kulikov, I.M., Chernykh, I.G., Glinskiy, B.M., Protasov, V.A.: An efficient optimization of HII method for the second generation of Intel Xeon Phi Processor. Lobachevskii J. Math. **39**(4), 543–551 (2018)

The Parallel Implementation of the Adaptive Mesh Technology in Poroelasticity Problems

Sergey Kalinin[1], Dmitry Karavaev[2] (iD), and Anna Sapetina[2]([⊠]) (iD)

[1] JSC Geologika, Novosibirsk, Russia
`sergey.kalinin@list.ru`
[2] Institute of Computational Mathematics and Mathematical
Geophysics SB RAS, Novosibirsk, Russia
`dimkaravaev@gmail.com`, `afsapetina@gmail.com`

Abstract. The actual process of oil and gas field development is associated with a large amount of numerical modeling. This is due to unreliable data used in modeling. For example, these are a small amount of reliable measurement information on a geological structure, reservoir and geomechanical properties of rocks forming a given field. There is a need to solve a large number of inverse problems to determine the structure and properties that satisfy the whole set of reliable measurement results, taking into account the interinfluence of physical processes occurring in the course of development.

The poroelasticity problem in question is of essential practical interest, when a value of the pore pressure is affected by the stress-strain state of a reservoir, depending on the same pressure. The process of solving the inverse problem is associated with solving a large number of direct problems, while a major challenge is in reducing the calculation time of each direct problem. A large amount of computation requires the usage of supercomputer technologies.

This paper discusses the adaptive mesh usage for building hydro-geomechanical proxy models and solving poroelasticity problems with an effective strategy for adapting the computational grid for parallelization. Parallelization is performed with the computing cluster of the Siberian Supercomputer Center.

Keywords: Proxy model · Poroelasticity · Adaptive mesh · Fluid filtration · Flow simulation · Geomechanical simulation

1 Introduction

Nowadays the numerical modeling of oil & gas reservoirs takes a big part of the whole reservoir development process. In particular, models are used by geologists to build a layered structure, reflecting a real reservoir to a certain amount. Every layer consists of relatively small cells extending tens of kilometers across the reservoir area. The total amount of cells may reach several millions. Every cell has certain properties such as permeability, porosity, saturation, etc. The accuracy of such models strictly depends on assumptions attracted. In particular, there is no unique technique to distribute properties among the cells located between the wells. The problem is the lack of measurement techniques capable of investigating media far beyond the radius of a borehole. In other

© Springer Nature Switzerland AG 2019
V. Voevodin and S. Sobolev (Eds.): RuSCDays 2019, CCIS 1129, pp. 439–450, 2019.
https://doi.org/10.1007/978-3-030-36592-9_36

words, one needs to attract the tools of geostatistics such as kriging or variograms. On the other hand, seismic models are only the tools to take an image of the ground structure between wells, but the vertical accuracy of a layer location may take up to 50 m, while the thickness of this layer may be about tens of centimeters or even smaller. Nevertheless, a geological model is the basis for building other models such as hydrodynamic models or geomechanical models. It is clear that the accuracy of such models cannot be higher than geological model. Moreover, due to a huge amount of cells, the time required to calculate a change in the reservoir pressure, across the whole reservoir or part of it, caused by the production of wells, become huge as well. Taking into account relatively a small significance of every particular calculation, the engineers need a tool capable of estimating a change in the reservoir characteristics (pressure, temperature, stress, strain, etc.) in a matter of minutes or even seconds for each particular calculation. By combining the results of several runs of slightly different models (different assumptions) one can estimate required characteristics with certain probability. This workflow has become a standard in the industries.

The frontier of modeling techniques is now shifting to the so-called proxy models [1]. These models are based on the reduced amount of cells using the so-called upscaling of the cells [2]. Nevertheless the accuracy of upscaled models may become too poor in some regions.

Even the most popular commercial software uses different tricks to overcome the problem of a low accuracy. In particular, the inflow into a certain well is calculated by sewing a numerical solution in far field zone (where the error between the numerical and the exact solutions is small) and the analytical solution near the borehole [3]. Such technique helps one to use relatively simple finite difference models (FDM) to calculate the pressure across a reservoir while blocks with the wells are treated separately.

Another problem comes to the foreground when one tries to estimate strains that are close to geological faults or fractures. In this case, a stress field may change dramatically leading to the risks of a wellbore instability as well as an unpredictable behavior of hydraulic fractures.

It is important to mention that a change in a stress filed may cause a change in the pore pressure and vice versa. This effect is known as poroelasticity. In other words, building separate models for hydrodynamics and geomechanics increases the risks to get negative impact in the development process or even in people.

A finally, it is worth to mention that there is no universal tool to solve poroelastic problems of sufficiently a large size. To efficiently solve the problems under consideration, it is necessary to choose such an approach to constructing numerical solutions, in which a computational grid would have the smallest size (by the number of grid nodes), and the accuracy of calculations would be maximum possible.

The commercial software tries to solve a problem of an accuracy by increasing the number of cells in the zones of a rapid change of a certain field (pressure, temperature etc.). At the same time, the total amount of cells is changed for certain problems, as well as the number of equations needed for a solution. It is difficult to find an optimum solution in terms of a number of cores in a supercomputer, as well as a memory volume required.

Of great practical interest are such algorithms of building a grid for which the total number of elements would remain constant. A constant number of elements allows one uniform loading of computational nodes in the course of parallel computing. The main difficulty here is to preserve the numbering of grids (nodes and elements): if all the nodes and grid elements, after a cycle of mesh adaptation retain their numbers, it is relatively easy to organize a uniform breakdown of a single computational domain into subdomains, thereby ensuring a uniform loading of cluster computing nodes. It is obvious that one can save the numbering of the grid only if the reduction in the size of some elements occurs due to an increase in the size of others. In a finite element method, such an approach is called r-adaptation technique. Moreover, in the case of the usage of high order polynomials for the shape functions, the hybrid technique can be called as rp-adaptaion.

Currently, there are relatively a few publications on the application of the rp-adaptation technique for solving problems of the oil and gas hydrodynamics, and in particular, problems of estimating the production of hydrocarbons. One of the main reasons for a low popularity of the method lies in the well-established methodology for the distribution of environmental properties in terms of computational volume. Standard grid algorithms with an increase in the total number of computational elements (nodes) and an analytical solution in the near-wellbore area mentioned above are already embedded to commercial simulators. With a simple increase in the number of elements, the error of the final result will only decrease if we assume that the initial distribution of properties on a coarse grid is close to a real one.

The idea of this research is to present a technique that is appropriate for solving large poroelastic problems with the help of a supercomputer with an effective strategy for adapting computational grid for parallelization.

2 Some Aspects of Using Adaptive Grids

Let us note that at any time step, an adaptive grid can be considered as an adaptive fixed grid with a non-uniform distribution of nodes. In the theory of the finite element method, it is proved that reducing the size of elements leads to an increase in the accuracy of the numerical solution. Based on this fact, we can conclude that the preservation of nodes of the original grid and the n-fold addition of intermediate nodes will not worsen the accuracy of a numerical solution.

Figure 1 shows the solution of the problem of a fluid inflow into the well with different step sizes of the computational grid and at different time instants. In this case, the one-dimensional problem of the non-stationary filtration of reservoir fluids through a non-deformable reservoir with specified properties has been solved. The direct problem has been solved by the finite element method, for which the so-called weak formulation of the boundary value problem has been obtained under given initial conditions.

$$\int_V \frac{\varphi \rho_f}{K} \frac{\partial p}{\partial t} \delta p \, dV + \int_V \rho_f \frac{k}{\mu} \nabla p \cdot \nabla \delta p \, dV = \int_{A^m} m \delta p \, dA, \tag{1}$$

where φ is the porosity, ρ_f is the fluid density, K is the compressibility of a reservoir fluid, k is the reservoir permeability, μ is the viscosity of the reservoir fluid, p is the desired pressure, m is the mass flow through the part A^m of the outer boundary A. From the analysis of the solution shown in Fig. 1, we can conclude that even with constant porosity and permeability properties for arbitrary finite element sizes, a computational error can be sufficiently significant (it is enough to estimate the error using the Euclidean L2 norm for solutions on a grid with a constant step and on an adaptive grid).

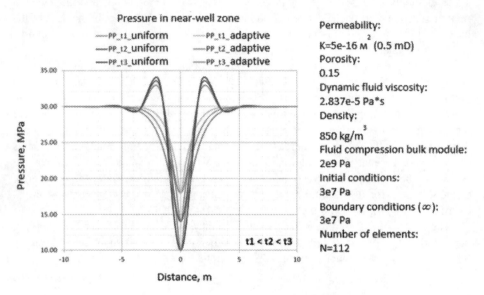

Fig. 1. The pressure distribution in a near-well zone for uniform and adaptive grids.

3   The Algorithm of Adaptive Mesh Construction

There are two main methods for constructing an adaptive mesh [4]. The first method is based on the principle of an equidistributing grid: the step of such a grid is chosen in such a way that the error in estimating a desired function (for example, pressure or temperature) is the same for each element, for which the so-called error density function is chosen (the grid density function). The second method is based on writing and finding a solution of the grid differential equation. Both methods lead to a system of related equations both for determining the position of nodes of a moving grid and for determining a sought for function reflecting the distribution of a certain physical quantity (for example, pressure). The second method can be used both with keeping equal-to-error principle, and without keeping this principle. In practice, strict keeping the principle of an equally distributed error leads to considerable difficulties in constructing a stable computational algorithm for solving multidimensional problems. For this reason, one of the most useful methods of formulating and solving the grid equation in the multidimensional case is the use of the variational method. In this case, the Euler-Lagrange equations are written down with a "grid" functional of a special form.

As an example, which is well suited for solving practical problems of hydrodynamics, we will consider the Euler-Lagrange differential equation used to form an
adaptive grid:

$$-\nabla \cdot \left(\frac{1}{w} \nabla \xi_i \right) = 0, \quad i = 1, 2 \ldots d, \tag{2}$$

where $w = w(x) > 0$ is the defined weight function.

Such a principle of forming the «grid» equation is called the «variable diffusion»
method [4, 5]. It should be noted that the first results with the use of adaptive moving
meshes were obtained by Godunov et al. [6], when considering a problem of impact a
certain volume of water against a rigid wall. In essence, formula (2) is a stationary
diffusion equation, in which the spatial-variable diffusion coefficient affects the concentration distribution (in this case, the «density» of the mesh lines).

The coefficient in Eq. (2) depends on the so-called «physical» solution and the
variable ξ depends on unknown coordinates x of nodes of the mesh on which a solution
to the «physical» differential equation is sought. There is no need a direct solution of
Eq. (2). Since in practice, it is required to find the distribution of $x = x(\xi)$, since it
changes the roles of the independent and dependent variable. If we set $w = 1$, then in a
two-dimensional case such a role changing in (2) leads to the «grid» equations:

$$\left(x_\eta^2 + y_\eta^2 \right) x_{\xi\xi} - 2 \left(x_\xi x_\eta + y_\xi y_\eta \right) x_{\xi\eta} + \left(x_\xi^2 + y_\xi^2 \right) x_{\eta\eta} = 0,$$
$$\left(x_\eta^2 + y_\eta^2 \right) y_{\xi\xi} - 2 \left(x_\xi x_\eta + y_\xi y_\eta \right) y_{\xi\eta} + \left(x_\xi^2 + y_\xi^2 \right) y_{\eta\eta} = 0.$$

If in formula (2), we accept that $w = w(x) > 0$, then we can obtain more cumbersome expressions given in [5].

In the case of a variation approach, the general form of the Euler-Lagrange equation
can be obtained in the following form:

$$-\nabla \cdot \left[\frac{\partial F}{\partial a^i} - J \frac{\partial F}{\partial J} a_i \right] = 0, \quad i = 1, 2, 3, \tag{3}$$

where the corresponding functional is as follows:

$$I[\xi] = \int_\Omega F\left(a^1, a^2, a^3, J, x \right) dx. \tag{4}$$

In Eqs. (3) and (4), it is assumed that J is the Jacobian of the transformation, and
the corresponding vectors a^i are the columns of the inverse Jacobi matrix:

$$J = \frac{\partial x}{\partial \xi} = \frac{\partial(x_1, x_2, x_3)}{\partial(\xi_1, \xi_2, \xi_3)} = [a_1, a_2, a_3]. \tag{5}$$

For practical purposes, the function F in the integral can be represented as follows:

$$F(a^1, a^2, a^3, J, x) = F_1(\rho, \beta) + F_2(\rho, J) \tag{6}$$

$$F_1(\rho, \beta) = \frac{1}{2} \sum_i (\nabla \xi_i)^T M^{-1} \nabla \xi_i = \frac{1}{2} \beta \tag{7}$$

$$F_2(\rho, J) = 0 \tag{8}$$

$$M = w(x)I \tag{9}$$

$$w = \sqrt{1 + |\nabla p|^2}. \tag{10}$$

It should be noted that in Eq. (9), $w(x)$ is the function that determines the «density» of grid lines used to solve the physical Eq. (1). In Eq. (10), the explicit form of the grid density function is shown, depending on the gradient of the unknown function. After performing rather a cumbersome chain of transformations aimed at changing the roles of the independent and dependent variables in Eq. (3), we can obtain a compact form of the «grid» differential equation for determining the function $x = x(\xi)$.

$$\sum_{i,j} A_{ij} \frac{\partial^2 x}{\partial \xi_i \partial \xi_j} + \sum_i B_i \frac{\partial x}{\partial \xi_i} = 0. \tag{11}$$

In this equation:

$$A_{ij} = \left((a^i)^T M^{-1} a^j \right) I \tag{12}$$

$$B_i = I \sum_k \left((a^k)^T \frac{\partial M^{-1}}{\partial \xi_k} a^i \right). \tag{13}$$

When solving Eq. (7) with a finite elements method, it is necessary to obtain a weak formulation of the boundary value problem

$$\sum_{i,j} \int_{\Omega_c} \frac{\partial x}{\partial \xi_i} \cdot \frac{\partial}{\partial \xi_j} (A_{ij} v) d\xi + \sum_i \int_{\Omega_c} \frac{\partial x}{\partial \xi_i} (B_i v) d\xi = 0. \tag{14}$$

Here it should be noted that as the boundary conditions for Eq. (11), it is often sufficient to set the immobility of the nodes on the boundary of the region.

4   Using an Adaptive Grid for Geomechanical Problems

Let us consider using the adaptive mesh method (Fig. 2) for a problem of subsurface fluids filtering. Figure 3 shows the pressure distribution field around a separate production well for an adaptive grid with the number of elements $N^2 = 2500$ and for a grid with constant mesh spacing $((3N)^2 = 22500)$. It is possible to note a change in the position of the nodes of the computational grid, as well as a characteristic change in the size and shape of the elements while preserving the total number of nodes. The calculations are performed with the use of the open-source FreeFem++ software package [7]. It should be noted that formula (10) depends on the derivative of an unknown function, which itself is numerically calculated, and, therefore, with a certain error. This error can be quite substantial. For this reason, the practical application of adaptive grids requires a suitable choice of function (10), and here the researcher is provided with a wide field for creativity. In this study we used an ordinary Gaussian function whose approach to the delta-function while the variance (in the Gaussian function definition) approach is close to zero. The numerical solution in the near-well zone using the such function is close to the analytical solution given in [8].

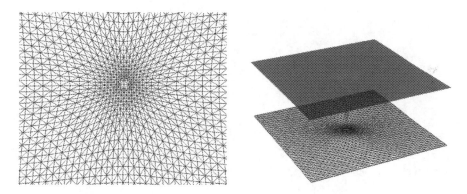

Fig. 2. An adapted grid (left) and a pressure distribution field (right).

5   The Statement of Poroelasticity Problem

The numerical solution of hydrodynamic problems has been carried out under the assumption of incompressibility of a rock. In most cases, this assumption was used to simplify the problem being solved and to reduce the calculation time, since the contribution of the compressibility of rocks to the estimation of the volume of a produced fluid was often insignificant. However in some cases it is necessary to take into account the deformability of rocks, since a change in a pore volume affects the pressure field and may lead to an underestimation of the level of production. In general, there is a reverse effect of the level of the reservoir pressure on the magnitude of the deformations, and an incorrect account of these deformations can lead to the collapse of the walls of a wellbore when performing various technological operations. Using the method of adaptive grids allows us not to separate the problems of hydrodynamics and geomechanics, since it suffices to use a single computational grid both for estimating the pressure fields and estimating the stress and strain fields.

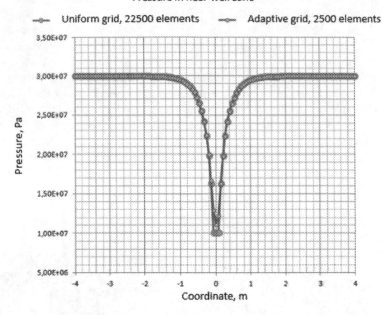

Fig. 3. The 2D pressure distribution for uniform and adaptive grids

The poroelasticity problem can be formulated by the following system of differential equations:

$$-G\nabla \cdot \left(\nabla u + (\nabla u)^T\right) - G\frac{2v}{(1-2v)}\nabla(\nabla \cdot u) + \alpha\nabla p = F \qquad \text{in } \Omega \times (0,T), \quad (15)$$

$$\frac{\partial}{\partial t}\left(Se\, p + \alpha\nabla \cdot u\right) - \nabla \cdot \left(\frac{k}{\mu}\nabla p\right) = Q \qquad \text{in } \Omega \times (0,T), \quad (16)$$

$$u = 0 \qquad \text{on } \Gamma_c, \quad (17)$$

$$\left[G\left(\nabla u + (\nabla u)^T\right) + G\frac{2v}{1-2v}\nabla \cdot uI\right]\widehat{n} - \beta\alpha p\widehat{n}\chi_{tf} = 0 \qquad \text{on } \Gamma_t, \quad (18)$$

$$p = 0 \qquad \text{on } \Gamma_d, \quad (19)$$

$$-\frac{\partial}{\partial t}((1-\beta)\alpha u \cdot \widehat{n})\chi + \frac{k}{\mu}\nabla p \cdot \widehat{n} = h_1\chi_{tf} \qquad \text{on } \Gamma_f, \quad (20)$$

$$e\, p + \alpha\nabla \cdot u = v_0 \qquad \text{in } \Omega \times \{0\}, \quad (21)$$

$$(1-\beta)\alpha u \cdot \widehat{n} = v_1 \qquad \text{on } \Gamma_{tf} \times \{0\}. \quad (22)$$

Equation (15) is responsible for determining the displacements u of points of a poroelastic medium given by the elastic constants G, v as well as the constants of the poroelasticity α (the Biot constant) and Se (the Skempton constant). The meaning of the remaining notation is presented in [9]. Equation (16) is responsible for determining the pressure in the process of the filtration of a fluid through a deformable poroelastic medium, taking into account the contribution of the compressibility of the rock matrix.

One needs to add (2) or (3) to the system of Eqs. (15, 16) with the corresponding boundary conditions for obtaining a complete system of equations for solving the poroelasticity problem using adaptive grids. As usual, it is assumed that a poroelastic medium is continuous, isotropic and homogeneous. To solve the poroelasticity problem numerically using the finite element method, it is necessary to write down a weak formulation of the boundary value problem:

$$
\int_{\Omega} \left[G\left(\nabla u^{n+1} + \left(\nabla u^{n+1}\right)^T\right) : \nabla v + G\frac{2v}{1-2v}\left(\nabla \cdot u^{n+1}\right)\left(\nabla \cdot v\right) \right] + \int_{\Omega} \alpha \nabla p^{n+1} v
$$
$$
= \int_{\Omega} F^{n+1} v + \int_{\Gamma_t} G\left(\nabla u^{n+1} + \left(\nabla u^{n+1}\right)^T\right) \cdot \widehat{n}v + \int_{\Gamma_t} G\frac{2v}{1-2v}\left(\nabla \cdot u^{n+1}\right)\widehat{n} \cdot v,
$$
$$\tag{23}$$

$$
-\int_{\Omega} \alpha u^{n+1} \cdot \nabla q + \int_{\Omega} \left(Se\, p^{n+1} q + \frac{k\tau}{\mu}\theta\nabla p^{n+1} \cdot \nabla q \right)
$$
$$
= \int_{\Omega} \left(\tau\left(\theta Q^{n+1} + (1-\theta)Q^n\right) + \alpha\nabla \cdot u^n + Se p^n \right) q - \int_{\Omega} \frac{k\tau}{\mu}(1-\theta)\nabla p^n \nabla q \tag{24}
$$
$$
-\int_{\Gamma_f} \alpha u^{n+1} \cdot \widehat{n}q + \int_{\Gamma_f} \frac{k}{\mu}\left(\theta\nabla p^{n+1} + (1-\theta)\nabla p^{n+1}\right) \cdot \widehat{n}q
$$

$$
\sum_{i,j} \int_{\Omega_C} \frac{\partial x^{n+1}}{\partial \xi_i} \cdot \frac{\partial}{\partial \xi_j}\left(A_{ij}\omega\right)d\xi + \sum_i \int_{\Omega_C} \frac{\partial x^{n+1}}{\partial \xi_i}\left(B_i\omega\right)d\xi = 0. \tag{25}
$$

Thus, system (23, 24) is a weak formulation of the boundary value problem of poroelasticity using adaptive grids. It should be noted that rebuilding the adaptive grid according to Eq. (25) is determined only by the fluid pressure gradient. In many cases, such a formulation will be sufficient, since the applied tasks of the oil and gas geomechanics relate to the effects occurring in the near-well zone, where large gradients of both pressures and displacements are observed in the first place.

6   The Parallel Implementation of a Finite Element Method

To speed up the computations of the 2D poroelasticity problem and to make possible large grid calculations, the parallelization of the numerical solution of the equation system with a finite element method was carried out using the FreeFem++ solver.

Let us note that an extended interface with MPI has been added to FreeFem++. The Schwarz algorithm [10] with overlapping and a coarse grid preconditioner is used to decompose the computational domain. The grid of triangles is adapted once before the calculations in the main time cycle. The Metis graph partitioner [11] is used for partitioning into an equal (according to the number of elements) subdomain among computational nodes (cores). At each time step, the problem is first solved on a coarse grid, and then this solution is used as an initial approximation in each subdomain of the partitioning. For the numerical solution of the coupled problem of poroelasticity, each of the equations, rewritten in a matrix form, is solved one after another iteratively in all subdomains at the same time.

The considered approach of grid adaptation is convenient because it keeps the number of grid elements unchanged and does not require additional solving the problem of load balancing between MPI processes during computing. With the initial selection of a regular grid of triangles, the problem of its optimal decomposition between computational nodes is solved trivially. With a more complex initial organization of the grid of triangles, the functions of the Metis package are used to divide it.

A strong scalability study has been conducted on a node of the Siberian Supercomputer Center (SSCC) cluster equipped with two 16-core Intel processors on Broadwell architecture. The calculations were carried out on a grid consisting of 240000 triangles.

The results (Fig. 4) show that acceleration has been reached about 14 times on 32 cores as compared to a single core.

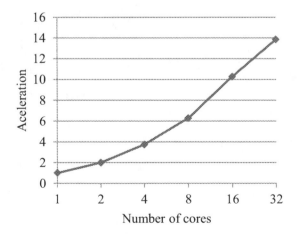

Fig. 4. The results of strong scalability research at Intel Broadwell

The possibility of using a node of SSCC equipped with Intel Memory Drive Technology (IMDT) called Optane was also investigated. Intel Optane is a new SSD product based on the novel 3D XPointTM technology, which can be used instead of DRAM, albeit as a slow memory [12]. It can be still an attractive solution given that Intel Optane is notably cheaper than the random access memory (RAM) per gigabyte. The novel Intel Memory Drive Technology (IMDT) allows one to use Intel Optane drives as a system memory. Various benchmarking results [13] for large dense tasks show different efficiencies. We have used two memory configurations (Table 1): hybrid IMDT DDR4/Optane and DDR4 only for systems of different sizes of a grid for the numerical solution of filtering problem (16) with our parallel implementation.

Table 1. The results of the two memory configurations usage: hybrid IMDT DDR4/Optane and DDR4 only systems for filtering problem.

Memory configurations	Number of triangles	Used memory, Gb	Execution time, s
DDR4	$12,5 \cdot 10^6$	51	941
DDR4	$32 \cdot 10^6$	125	5508
DDR4/Optane	$50 \cdot 10^6$	293	8373
DDR4/Optane	$72 \cdot 10^6$	466	19614

7 Conclusion

In this paper, the use of adaptive grids for solving geomechanical problems is discussed. An algorithm for constructing an adaptive grid with the Jacobian coordinate transformation is presented. The adaptation algorithm changes the grid density, which depends on the gradient of a desired function. The number of nodes of the adaptive mesh remains unchanged and is equal to the number of nodes of the initial grid. The results of the simulation by the finite elements method of the pressure distribution for the fluid filtration problem in the near-well zone using adaptive mesh are presented. The calculations were carried out using the freeware and open-source Freefem++ software package. The formulation of the poroelasticity problem in the integral form is presented. The studies of the parallel implementation for poroelasticity problems show the acceleration of about 14 times in 32 cores.

Acknowledgements. This research was supported by the Russian Foundation for Basic Research [grant No. 16-29-15120].

References

1. Filippov, D.D., Vasekin, B.V., Mitrushkin, D.A.: Multiphase filtration modeling of complex structure on dynamic adaptive PEBI-grid. PROneft. Professionals Oil **4**(6), 48–53 (2017)
2. Qi, D., Hesketh, T.: An analysis of upscaling techniques for reservoir simulation. Petrol. Sci. Technol. **23**(7–8), 827–842 (2005)

3. Peaceman, D.W.: Interpretation of well-block pressures in numerical reservoir simulation. SPEJ **23**(03), 183–194 (1978)
4. Huang, W., Russell, R.D.: Adaptive Moving Mesh Methods. Springer, New York (2011)
5. Winslow, A.M.: Adaptive mesh zoning by the equipotential method. Technical report UCID-19062. Lawrence Livemore Laboratory (1981)
6. Godunov, S.K., Prokopov, G.P.: The use of moving meshes in gas-dynamical computations. USSR Comput. Math. Math. Phys. **12**, 182 (1972)
7. Hecht, F.: New development in FreeFem++. J. Numer. Math. **20**(3–4), 251–265 (2012)
8. Basniev, K.S., Kochina, I.N., Maksimov, V.M.: Podzemnaya gidromekhanika: Uchebnik dlya vuzov. Nedra, Moscow (1993). (in Russian)
9. Aji, C.A.: Poroelasticity. Auburn, Alabama (2007)
10. Toselli, A., Widlund, O.: Domain Decomposition Methods - Algorithms and Theory. Computational Mathematics, vol. 34. Springer, Heidelberg (2004). https://doi.org/10.1007/b137868
11. Karypis, G., Kumar, V.: A fast and high quality multilevel scheme for partitioning irregular graphs. SIAM J. Sci. Comput. **20**(1), 359–392 (1998)
12. Shenoy, N.: What happens when your PC meets intel optane memory? (2018). https://newsroom.intel.com/editorials/what-happens-pc-meets-intel-optane-memory/
13. Mironov, V., Kudryavtsev, A., Alexeev, Y., Moskovsky, A., Kulikov, I., Chernykh, I.: Evaluation of Intel Memory Drive Technology performance for scientific applications. In: MCHPC 2018: Workshop on Memory Centric High Performance Computing (MCHPC 2018), pp. 14–21. ACM, New York (2018)

The Simulation of 3D Wave Fields in Complex Topography Media

Pavel Titov[1,2](✉)

[1] Institute of Computational Mathematics and Mathematical Geophysics SB RAS,
Novosibirsk, Russia
tapawel@gmail.com
[2] Trofimuk Institute of Petroleum Geology and Geophysics of SB RAS,
Novosibirsk, Russia

Abstract. A parallel algorithm for the simulation of wave field in 3D heterogeneous media with a curved free surface is proposed. In this paper we use a mapping method to transform the initial problem. It is based on the construction of a curvilinear mesh that conforms with the geometry of the free surface in the domain of interest. This domain is then to be mapped onto the "calculation" rectangular domain covered with a regular mesh. Therefore, now we have the initial problems restated in generalized coordinates but in the domain of simple geometry. To solve the transformed problem in the "calculation" domain, we use a finite difference method. Numerical tests were carried out on the SSCC cluster of SB RAS. The results of numerical simulation are presented.

Keywords: 3D · Wave field · Elasticity · Parallel algorithm ·
Simulation · Curvilinear mesh · Finite difference method

1 Introduction

The numerical simulation of elastic waves is actively used in studying the seismic-wave propagation in 3D complex media. There are several principal methods to compute a wave field: Finite differences [1–5], finite elements [6], spectral elements [7,8], discontinuous Galerkin [9,10], finite volumes [11], and combinations of these methods [12–14]. Finite elements, discontinuous Galerkin and spectral methods can provide a high accuracy by increasing the dimension of the functional space used. The methods in question can be applied on irregular meshes. However the generation of a mesh in this case is time consuming and is difficult to automate. Finite difference methods are universal when solving such problems in the Cartesian coordinate system. These methods are applied in this paper. Note that often the domain under study can have a complex geometry of the free surface (solid/air interface). For the consistency of the numerical model and the physical model a curvilinear mesh is used. The theory of curvilinear meshes construction and application for solving real problems is considered in detail within [15–17]. As applied to the problems of elastodynamics, curvilinear meshes were

© Springer Nature Switzerland AG 2019
V. Voevodin and S. Sobolev (Eds.): RuSCDays 2019, CCIS 1129, pp. 451–462, 2019.
https://doi.org/10.1007/978-3-030-36592-9_37

utilized in [18,19] for a 2D case, and in [20–22] for 2D and 3D case, respectively. A distinctive feature of this paper is the use of the original mesh generator that allows better accuracy of numerical realization for the free surface conditions. From [20–22] author has taken a balance technique idea to construct the finite difference scheme. Considering the size of the domain in solving real-scale problems (tens of kilometers in each coordinate direction), it is necessary to carry out the numerical simulation using high-performance systems. The use of a curvilinear mesh in the finite difference method implies the original problem to be solved in generalized coordinates. The author has developed and implemented a parallel 3D algorithm using the Fortran language and the MPI library.

Both the test for the simulation of wave fields in heterogeneous medium as well as the test for the algorithm scalability, were carried out on the cluster NKS-30T of SSCC SB RAS.

2   Statement of the Problem

The wave field simulation is carried out based on the numerical solution of the elasticity linear system, expressed via displacements in Cartesian coordinates. If perturbations occur in a medium, the particles of the medium deviate from the equilibrium position when a wave passes through them. The deviation is represented by the displacement vector $(u, v, w)^T$. The density ρ, longitudinal waves speed V_p, share wave speed V_s and the Lame coefficients $\lambda = \rho(V_p^2 - 2V_s^2), \mu = \rho V_s^2$ are the medium parameters, $(F_x, F_y, F_z)^T$ is the mass force vector that represents a source of perturbations. Physical domain geometry is also considered to be given.

By restoring the displacement vector at each point of the domain at each time instant, we can simulate the process of elastic waves propogation.

The sequence of steps to solve the problem can be represented as follows:

1. Statement of the problem and its mathematical formulation in Cartesian and generalized coordinate systems.
2. Construction of a curvilinear mesh consistent with physical domain geometry.
3. Development of the numerical parallel algorithms to solve the problem.
4. Software implementation of the parallel numerical algorithms.
5. Conducting experiments on a parallel architecture for the complex media models.

2.1   Mathematical Model in Cartesian Coordinates

We introduce the following notations: $\partial\Gamma$ is the boundary of the domain inside the ground, ∂S is the free curvilinear surface. In Cartesian system (x, y, z), the equations are:

$$\rho\frac{\partial^2 u}{\partial t^2} = \frac{\partial \sigma_{xx}}{\partial x} + \frac{\partial \sigma_{xy}}{\partial y} + \frac{\partial \sigma_{xz}}{\partial z} + F_x$$

$$\rho\frac{\partial^2 v}{\partial t^2} = \frac{\partial \sigma_{xy}}{\partial x} + \frac{\partial \sigma_{yy}}{\partial y} + \frac{\partial \sigma_{yz}}{\partial z} + F_y \qquad (1)$$

$$\rho\frac{\partial^2 w}{\partial t^2} = \frac{\partial \sigma_{xz}}{\partial x} + \frac{\partial \sigma_{yz}}{\partial y} + \frac{\partial \sigma_{zz}}{\partial z} + F_z$$

where

$$\sigma_{xx} = (\lambda + 2\mu)\frac{\partial u}{\partial x} + \lambda\frac{\partial v}{\partial y} + \lambda\frac{\partial w}{\partial z}, \; \sigma_{yy} = \lambda\frac{\partial u}{\partial x} + (\lambda + 2\mu)\frac{\partial v}{\partial y} + \lambda\frac{\partial w}{\partial z},$$

$$\sigma_{zz} = \lambda\frac{\partial u}{\partial x} + \lambda\frac{\partial v}{\partial y} + (\lambda + 2\mu)\frac{\partial w}{\partial z}, \; \sigma_{xy} = \mu\frac{\partial u}{\partial y} + \mu\frac{\partial v}{\partial x}, \; \sigma_{xz} = \mu\frac{\partial u}{\partial z} + \mu\frac{\partial w}{\partial x},$$

$$\sigma_{yz} = \mu\frac{\partial v}{\partial z} + \mu\frac{\partial w}{\partial y} \text{ are components of the stress tensor } \overline{\sigma}.$$

Condition on the free surface ∂S: $\overline{\sigma} \cdot \overline{n} = 0$, or in the scalar form,

$$n_x\left((\lambda + 2\mu)\frac{\partial u}{\partial x} + \lambda\frac{\partial v}{\partial y} + \lambda\frac{\partial w}{\partial z}\right) + n_y\left(\mu\frac{\partial u}{\partial y} + \mu\frac{\partial v}{\partial x}\right) + n_z\left(\mu\frac{\partial u}{\partial z} + \mu\frac{\partial w}{\partial x}\right) = 0$$

$$n_x\left(\mu\frac{\partial u}{\partial y} + \mu\frac{\partial v}{\partial x}\right) + n_y\left(\lambda\frac{\partial u}{\partial x} + (\lambda + 2\mu)\frac{\partial v}{\partial y} + \lambda\frac{\partial w}{\partial z}\right) + n_z\left(\mu\frac{\partial v}{\partial z} + \mu\frac{\partial w}{\partial y}\right) = 0$$

$$n_x\left(\mu\frac{\partial u}{\partial z} + \mu\frac{\partial w}{\partial y}\right) + n_y\left(\mu\frac{\partial v}{\partial z} + \mu\frac{\partial w}{\partial y}\right) + n_z\left(\lambda\frac{\partial u}{\partial x} + \lambda\frac{\partial v}{\partial y} + (\lambda + 2\mu)\frac{\partial w}{\partial z}\right) = 0 \quad (2)$$

where $(n_x, n_y, n_z)^T$ is the unit normal to the free surface.

The conditions on the inside boundary $\partial\Gamma$ are:

$$u|_{\partial\Gamma} = v|_{\partial\Gamma} = w|_{\partial\Gamma} = 0 \qquad (3)$$

The initial conditions:

$$u|_{t=0} = v|_{t=0} = w|_{t=0} = 0, \quad \left.\frac{\partial u}{\partial t}\right|_{t=0} = \left.\frac{\partial v}{\partial t}\right|_{t=0} = \left.\frac{\partial w}{\partial t}\right|_{t=0} = 0 \qquad (4)$$

2.2 Mathematical Model in Generalized Coordinates

We consider (q^1, q^2, q^3) to be the new generalized coordinates. System (1) must be accordingly transformed:

$$\rho\frac{\partial^2 u}{\partial t^2} = \frac{1}{J}\left(\frac{\partial \tilde{\sigma}_1}{\partial q^1} + \frac{\partial \tilde{\sigma}_2}{\partial q^2} + \frac{\partial \tilde{\sigma}_3}{\partial q^3}\right) + F_x$$

$$\rho\frac{\partial^2 v}{\partial t^2} = \frac{1}{J}\left(\frac{\partial \tilde{\sigma}_4}{\partial q^1} + \frac{\partial \tilde{\sigma}_5}{\partial q^2} + \frac{\partial \tilde{\sigma}_6}{\partial q^3}\right) + F_y \qquad (5)$$

$$\rho\frac{\partial^2 w}{\partial t^2} = \frac{1}{J}\left(\frac{\partial \tilde{\sigma}_7}{\partial q^1} + \frac{\partial \tilde{\sigma}_8}{\partial q^2} + \frac{\partial \tilde{\sigma}_9}{\partial q^3}\right) + F_z$$

where

$$\tilde{\sigma}_1 = J\left(\sigma_{xx}\frac{\partial q^1}{\partial x} + \sigma_{xy}\frac{\partial q^1}{\partial y} + \sigma_{xz}\frac{\partial q^1}{\partial z}\right), \; \tilde{\sigma}_2 = J\left(\sigma_{xx}\frac{\partial q^2}{\partial x} + \sigma_{xy}\frac{\partial q^2}{\partial y} + \sigma_{xz}\frac{\partial q^2}{\partial z}\right),$$

$$\tilde{\sigma}_3 = J\left(\sigma_{xx}\frac{\partial q^3}{\partial x} + \sigma_{xy}\frac{\partial q^3}{\partial y} + \sigma_{xz}\frac{\partial q^3}{\partial z}\right), \quad \tilde{\sigma}_4 = J\left(\sigma_{xy}\frac{\partial q^1}{\partial x} + \sigma_{yy}\frac{\partial q^1}{\partial y} + \sigma_{yz}\frac{\partial q^1}{\partial z}\right),$$

$$\tilde{\sigma}_5 = J\left(\sigma_{xy}\frac{\partial q^2}{\partial x} + \sigma_{yy}\frac{\partial q^2}{\partial y} + \sigma_{yz}\frac{\partial q^2}{\partial z}\right), \quad \tilde{\sigma}_6 = J\left(\sigma_{xy}\frac{\partial q^3}{\partial x} + \sigma_{yy}\frac{\partial q^3}{\partial y} + \sigma_{yz}\frac{\partial q^3}{\partial z}\right),$$

$$\tilde{\sigma}_7 = J\left(\sigma_{xz}\frac{\partial q^1}{\partial x} + \sigma_{yz}\frac{\partial q^1}{\partial y} + \sigma_{zz}\frac{\partial q^1}{\partial z}\right), \quad \tilde{\sigma}_8 = J\left(\sigma_{xz}\frac{\partial q^2}{\partial x} + \sigma_{yz}\frac{\partial q^2}{\partial y} + \sigma_{zz}\frac{\partial q^2}{\partial z}\right),$$

$$\tilde{\sigma}_9 = J\left(\sigma_{xz}\frac{\partial q^3}{\partial x} + \sigma_{yz}\frac{\partial q^3}{\partial y} + \sigma_{zz}\frac{\partial q^3}{\partial z}\right).$$

Components of the mass force vector are $F_x(t,\overline{x}) = F_x(t, x(\overline{q}), y(\overline{q}), z(\overline{q}))$, $F_y(t,\overline{x}) = F_y(t, x(\overline{q}), y(\overline{q}), z(\overline{q}))$, $F_z(t,\overline{x}) = F_z(t, x(\overline{q}), y(\overline{q}), z(\overline{q}))$

Here we offer only σ_{xx} in detail in order for reader to get a general idea of equations complexity and how it imposes additional difficulties for numerical solution: $\sigma_{xx} = (\lambda + 2\mu)\sum_{i=1}^{3}\frac{\partial q^i}{\partial x}\frac{\partial u}{\partial q^i} + \lambda\sum_{i=1}^{3}\frac{\partial q^i}{\partial y}\frac{\partial v}{\partial q^i} + \lambda\sum_{i=1}^{3}\frac{\partial q^i}{\partial z}\frac{\partial w}{\partial q^i}.$

The rest components of the stress tensor $\overline{\sigma}$ are to be transformed the same way. And as for the free surface condition (2), it transforms into:

$$n_x\left((\lambda + 2\mu)\sum_{i=1}^{3}\frac{\partial q^i}{\partial x}\frac{\partial u}{\partial q^i} + \lambda\sum_{i=1}^{3}\frac{\partial q^i}{\partial y}\frac{\partial v}{\partial q^i} + \lambda\sum_{i=1}^{3}\frac{\partial q^i}{\partial z}\frac{\partial w}{\partial q^i}\right) +$$

$$n_y\left(\mu\sum_{i=1}^{3}\frac{\partial q^i}{\partial y}\frac{\partial u}{\partial q^i} + \mu\sum_{i=1}^{3}\frac{\partial q^i}{\partial x}\frac{\partial v}{\partial q^i}\right) + n_z\left(\mu\sum_{i=1}^{3}\frac{\partial q^i}{\partial z}\frac{\partial u}{\partial q^i} + \mu\sum_{i=1}^{3}\frac{\partial q^i}{\partial x}\frac{\partial w}{\partial q^i}\right) = 0$$

$$n_x\left(\mu\sum_{i=1}^{3}\frac{\partial q^i}{\partial y}\frac{\partial u}{\partial q^i} + \mu\sum_{i=1}^{3}\frac{\partial q^i}{\partial x}\frac{\partial v}{\partial q^i}\right) +$$

$$n_y\left(\lambda\sum_{i=1}^{3}\frac{\partial q^i}{\partial x}\frac{\partial u}{\partial q^i} + (\lambda + 2\mu)\sum_{i=1}^{3}\frac{\partial q^i}{\partial y}\frac{\partial v}{\partial q^i} + \lambda\sum_{i=1}^{3}\frac{\partial q^i}{\partial z}\frac{\partial w}{\partial q^i}\right) +$$

$$n_z\left(\mu\sum_{i=1}^{3}\frac{\partial q^i}{\partial z}\frac{\partial v}{\partial q^i} + \mu\sum_{i=1}^{3}\frac{\partial q^i}{\partial y}\frac{\partial w}{\partial q^i}\right) = 0$$

$$n_x\left(\mu\sum_{i=1}^{3}\frac{\partial q^i}{\partial z}\frac{\partial u}{\partial q^i} + \mu\sum_{i=1}^{3}\frac{\partial q^i}{\partial x}\frac{\partial w}{\partial q^i}\right) + n_y\left(\mu\sum_{i=1}^{3}\frac{\partial q^i}{\partial z}\frac{\partial v}{\partial q^i} + \mu\sum_{i=1}^{3}\frac{\partial q^i}{\partial y}\frac{\partial w}{\partial q^i}\right) +$$

$$n_z\left(\lambda\sum_{i=1}^{3}\frac{\partial q^i}{\partial x}\frac{\partial u}{\partial q^i} + \lambda\sum_{i=1}^{3}\frac{\partial q^i}{\partial y}\frac{\partial v}{\partial q^i} + (\lambda + 2\mu)\sum_{i=1}^{3}\frac{\partial q^i}{\partial z}\frac{\partial w}{\partial q^i}\right) = 0$$

$$(6)$$

where $(x^1, x^2, x^3) = (x, y, z)$, $J = det\left(\frac{\partial x^i}{q^j}\right)$, and

$\frac{\partial q^i}{\partial x^j} = \frac{1}{J}\left(\frac{\partial x^{j+1}}{\partial q^{i+1}}\frac{\partial x^{j+2}}{\partial q^{i+2}} - \frac{\partial x^{j+1}}{\partial q^{i+2}}\frac{\partial x^{j+2}}{\partial q^{i+1}}\right)$ with the cyclic numeration $i, j = $

$1, 2, 3$. Components $\frac{\partial q^i}{\partial x^j}$ are a metrical coefficients. They are defined by proper-ties of the curvilinear mesh. The normal unit vector in generalized coordinates is

$$(n_x, n_y, n_z) = \frac{\left(\frac{D(y,z)}{D(q^1,q^2)}, \frac{D(z,x)}{D(q^1,q^2)}, \frac{D(x,y)}{D(q^1,q^2)} \right)}{\sqrt{\left(\frac{D(x,y)}{D(q^1,q^2)} \right)^2 + \left(\frac{D(y,z)}{D(q^1,q^2)} \right)^2 + \left(\frac{D(z,x)}{D(q^1,q^2)} \right)^2}}$$

with $\dfrac{D(x,y)}{D(q^1,q^2)} = \dfrac{\partial x}{\partial q^1} \dfrac{\partial y}{\partial q^2} - \dfrac{\partial x}{\partial q^2} \dfrac{\partial y}{\partial q^1}$, $\dfrac{D(y,z)}{D(q^1,q^2)} = \dfrac{\partial y}{\partial q^1} \dfrac{\partial z}{\partial q^2} - \dfrac{\partial y}{\partial q^2} \dfrac{\partial z}{\partial q^1}$,

$\dfrac{D(z,x)}{D(q^1,q^2)} = \dfrac{\partial z}{\partial q^1} \dfrac{\partial x}{\partial q^2} - \dfrac{\partial z}{\partial q^2} \dfrac{\partial x}{\partial q^1}$.

Boundary conditions (3) and initial conditions (4) remain the same.

Now the equations in generalized coordinates are to be solved within a domain of simple parallelepiped shape, that can be covered with regular 3D mesh.

3   Constructing a Curvilinear Mesh

The technique of constructing a 3D mesh is considered in [12]. The main advantage of building a mesh with the method described, is that the mesh nodes are calculated analytically which means good scalability potential for the numerical realization. In this study we will just note an important point: near the free surface, all the coordinate lines of a curvilinear mesh are mutually orthogonal. This way we can obtain better approximation accuracy of the free surface condition.

Also, we should mention, that due to specific features of the finite difference approximation of equations (5), (6), every cell unit for each discrete node of the displacement vector $(u, v, w)^T$ consists of eight cell units of a curvilinear mesh (Fig. 1). It allows better accuracy of metric coefficients and Jacobian approximation.

4   Finite Difference Approximation

According to the results obtained in [12], the finite difference method possesses a good scalability potential.

The factors ρ, λ, μ and u, v, w are positioned at the center of the cell unit. The metrical coefficients and Jacobian are positioned at the center as well as in the middle of every edge and side of the cell unit (Fig. 1). The indices (i, j, k) are consistent with the axes (Oq^1, Oq^2, Oq^3).

The position of u, v, w is explained by the complexity of equations (5). Unlike as it is in [3], there is no benefit of using a staggered mesh. It would widen the scheme template and, therefore, make worse the accuracy.

In order to develop a finite difference scheme, we have applied a balance technique to (5). It is considered in detail in [23] for the case of Cartesian coordinates.

V is the unit cell volume in Cartesian coordinates, V' is the corresponding unit cell volume in generalized coordinates, which in our case has a cubic shape. The length of V' edges in each direction is considered to be $h_{q^1} = h_{q^2} = h_{q^3} = h$,

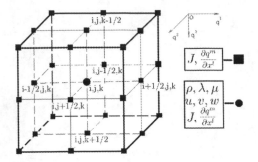

Fig. 1. A scheme of elements position in cell units

S' is the boundary of V'. Also, $S' = \sum\limits_{m=1}^{6} S'_m$, where S'_1 is the side that contains the node $(i-1/2, j, k)$, and S'_2 - $(i+1/2, j, k)$, S'_3 - $(i, j-1/2, k)$, S'_4 - $(i, j+1/2, k)$, S'_5 - $(i, j, k-1/2)$, S'_6 - $(i, j, k+1/2)$, respectively. Here we will only illustrate as an example how the balance technique is applied to the first equation of (1) and (5). Integrating over a unit cell volume V

$$\int_V \rho \frac{\partial^2 u}{\partial t^2} dV = \int_V \left(\frac{\partial \sigma_{xx}}{\partial x} + \frac{\partial \sigma_{xy}}{\partial y} + \frac{\partial \sigma_{xz}}{\partial z} \right) dV + \int_V F_x dV \tag{7}$$

and using the substitution of variables in (7) we come to:

$$\int_{V'} J\rho \frac{\partial^2 u}{\partial t^2} dV' = \int_{V'} \left(\frac{\partial \tilde\sigma_1}{\partial q^1} + \frac{\partial \tilde\sigma_2}{\partial q^2} + \frac{\partial \tilde\sigma_3}{\partial q^3} \right) dV' + \int_{V'} J F_x dV' \tag{8}$$

Applying the divergence theorem to (8) we have the following:

$$\int_{V'} J\rho \frac{\partial^2 u}{\partial t^2} dV' = \oint_{S'} (\tilde\sigma_1 n_1 + \tilde\sigma_2 n_2 + \tilde\sigma_3 n_3)\, dS' + \int_{V'} J F_x dV' \tag{9}$$

where (n_1, n_2, n_3) is a unit normal to $\partial S'$. Then (9) can be rewritten as:

$$\int_{V'} J\rho \frac{\partial^2 u}{\partial t^2} dV' = -\oint_{S'_1} \tilde\sigma_1 dS' + \oint_{S'_2} \tilde\sigma_1 dS' - \oint_{S'_3} \tilde\sigma_2 dS' + \oint_{S'_4} \tilde\sigma_2 dS' -$$
$$\oint_{S'_5} \tilde\sigma_3 dS' + \oint_{S'_6} \tilde\sigma_3 dS' + \int_{V'} J F_x dV' \tag{10}$$

For the convenience we will define finite-difference operators that are used for constructing the scheme. Here h is the discrete space step, τ is the discrete time step. $A^N_{i,j,k} = A(N\tau, ih, jh, kh)$, and for Jacobian and metrical coefficients $B_{i,j,k} = B(ih/2, jh/2, kh/2)$.

$$D_{tt}[f]^N_{i,j,k} = \frac{1}{\tau^2} \left(f^{N+1}_{i,j,k} - 2f^N_{i,j,k} + f^{N-1}_{i,j,k} \right) = \frac{\partial^2 f}{\partial t^2}(N\tau, ih, jh, kh) + O(\tau^2),$$

$$D_1[f]^N_{i-1/2,j,k} = \frac{1}{h}\left(f^N_{i,j,k} - f^N_{i-1,j,k}\right) = \frac{\partial f}{\partial q^1}(N\tau, ih - h/2, jh, kh) + O(q^1 q^1),$$

$$D_2[f]^N_{i,j-1/2,k} = \frac{1}{h}\left(f^N_{i,j,k} - f^N_{i,j-1,k}\right) = \frac{\partial f}{\partial q^2}(N\tau, ih, jh - h/2, kh) + O(q^2 q^2),$$

$$D_3[f]^N_{i,j,k-1/2} = \frac{1}{h}\left(f^N_{i,j,k} - f^N_{i,j,k-1}\right) = \frac{\partial f}{\partial q^3}(N\tau, ih, jh, kh - h/2) + O(q^3 q^3),$$

And

$$D_1[f]^N_{i,j-1/2,k} = \frac{1}{4}\left(D_1[f]^N_{i-1/2,j,k} + D_1[f]^N_{i+1/2,j,k} + \right.$$
$$\left. D_1[f]^N_{i-1/2,j-1,k} + D_1[f]^N_{i+1/2,j-1,k}\right),$$

$$D_1[f]^N_{i,j,k-1/2} = \frac{1}{4}\left(D_1[f]^N_{i-1/2,j,k} + D_1[f]^N_{i+1/2,j,k} + \right.$$
$$\left. D_1[f]^N_{i-1/2,j,k-1} + D_1[f]^N_{i+1/2,j,k-1}\right).$$

The rest operators $D_2[f]^N_{i-1/2,j,k}$, $D_2[f]^N_{i,j,k-1/2}$, $D_3[f]^N_{i-1/2,j,k}$, $D_2[f]^N_{i,j-1/2,k}$ are being defined in the same manner. Now the scheme for (10) in terms of the above-described operators with allowance for the mean value theorem, takes the form

$$\rho_{i,j,k}J_{2i,2j,2k}D_{tt}[u]^N_{i,j,k} = \frac{1}{h}\left(-\tilde\sigma 1^N_{i-1/2,j,k} + \tilde\sigma 1^N_{i+1/2,j,k} - \tilde\sigma 2^N_{i,j-1/2,k} + \right.$$
$$\left. \tilde\sigma 2^N_{i,j+1/2,k} - \tilde\sigma 3^N_{i,j,k-1/2} + \tilde\sigma 3^N_{i,j,k+1/2}\right) + J_{2i,2j,2k}F^N_{i,j,k} \tag{11}$$

The detailed scheme for the first component of the right-hand side in (11) is as follows:

$$\tilde\sigma 1^N_{i-1/2,j,k} = J_{2i-1,2j,2k}\left(\sigma_{xx}{}^N_{i-1/2,j,k}\left(\frac{\partial q^1}{\partial x}\right)_{2i-1,2j,2k} + \right.$$
$$\left. \sigma_{xy}{}^N_{i-1/2,j,k}\left(\frac{\partial q^1}{\partial y}\right)_{2i-1,2j,2k} + \sigma_{xz}{}^N_{i-1/2,j,k}\left(\frac{\partial q^1}{\partial z}\right)_{2i-1,2j,2k}\right) \tag{12}$$

The rest components of (11) are to be done in the same manner. And, finally, for $\sigma_{xy}{}^N_{i-1/2,j,k}$ in (12) the finite difference scheme is:

$$\sigma_{xy}{}^N_{i-1/2,j,k} = \frac{1}{2}(\mu_{i-1,j,k} + \mu_{i,j,k})\sum_{m=1}^{3}\left(\frac{\partial q^m}{\partial y}\right)_{2i-1,2j,2k}D_m[u]^N_{i-1/2,j,k} + $$
$$\frac{1}{2}(\mu_{i-1,j,k} + \mu_{i,j,k})\sum_{m=1}^{3}\left(\frac{\partial q^m}{\partial x}\right)_{2i-1,2j,2k}D_m[v]^N_{i-1/2,j,k}$$

where

$$\left(\frac{\partial q^m}{\partial x^l}\right)_{2i-1,2j,2k} = \frac{1}{J_{2i-1,2j,2k}}\left(D_{m+1}[x^{l+1}]_{2i-1,2j,2k}D_{m+2}[x^{l+2}]_{2i-1,2j,2k} - \right.$$
$$\left. D_{m+2}[x^{l+1}]_{2i-1,2j,2k}D_{m+1}[x^{l+2}]_{2i-1,2j,2k}\right).$$

The rest components of the stress tensor $\bar{\sigma}$ are to be approximated the same way. For the free surface condition, approximation does not differ from the one covered in [12]. Overall, the scheme proposed provides second accuracy order with respect to space and time, except for the interfaces between two layers with different media parameters. In this case, accuracy reduces to first order in space and to second order in time.

5   Parallel Algorithm and Its Realization

In this section we use the same technology as in [12]. In general, we decompose the domain to small 3D-cubes, every one of which is being assigned to a single process to realize the above finite difference scheme. After every time step, the neighboring processes conduct the data exchange via created 3D-cube topology. Each process has 26 neighbors. The parallel program was developed by means of the Fortran language and the MPI library.

6   Numerical Simulation and Scalability Tests

Numerical tests are carried out on the NKS-30T cluster of SSCC SB RAS, on SL390S G7 servers, each having 2×6 core Xeon X5670 2.93 GHz and 96 Gb RAM). In our case we have used CPUs exclusively.

For the simulation tests we have chosen the domain shown in Fig. 2, with corresponding mesh in Fig. 3. The medium parameters are: size $18.0 \times 18.0 \times 12.0$ km; for layers I and III: $\rho = 1.0$ g/cm^3, $V_p = 1.0$ km/s, $V_p = 0.5$ km/s; for layer II: $\rho = 0.81$ g/cm^3, $V_p = 0.888$ km/s, $V_s = 0.222$ km/s. The wave generator is of a "pressure center" type, located at $(x_0, y_0, z_0) = (5.5$ km, 9.0 km, 0.5 km$)$. For elements of $F = (F_x, F_y, F_z)$ we consider

$$
F_x = \begin{cases} \dfrac{\partial \delta(x - x_0, y - y_0, z - z_0)}{\partial x} F_1(t), & 0 \le t \le 2, \\ 0, & t > 2, \end{cases}
$$

$$
F_y = \begin{cases} \dfrac{\partial \delta(x - x_0, y - y_0, z - z_0)}{\partial y} F_1(t), & 0 \le t \le 2, \\ 0, & t > 2, \end{cases}
$$

$$
F_z = \begin{cases} \dfrac{\partial \delta(x - x_0, y - y_0, z - z_0)}{\partial z} F_1(t), & 0 \le t \le 2, \\ 0, & t > 2, \end{cases}
$$

where $F_1(t) = sin(\pi t - \pi) + 0.8 sin(2\pi t - 2\pi) + 0.2 sin(3\pi t - 3\pi)$ and $\delta(x, y, z)$ is the Dirac delta.

The discrete domain size is $900 \times 900 \times 600$ points, and the size of the curvilinear mesh is $1801 \times 1801 \times 1201$ points. The required amount of RAM for such a size of a problem is around 290 GB. In Fig. 4, the results of the wave field

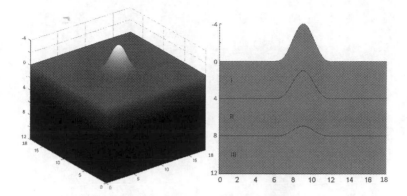

Fig. 2. The domain and its vertical slice with heterogeneous layers

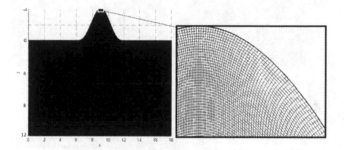

Fig. 3. Curvilinear mesh

simulation for the component W of the displacement vector are presented. The snapshots are taken from the cross-section that is parallel to the plane OXZ and contains the point of the source position (x_0, y_0, z_0). Also, in the Courant stability condition $V_p\tau/h \leq C/\sqrt{3}$, we have taken $C = 0.34$.

To study the strong scalability properties of the parallel program and algorithm developed, to each SL390S G7 server that has 12 cores, the cube with the size of $240 \times 240 \times 240$ points was assigned. The shape of the free surface or medium parameters do not matter for such a test. We proportionally increase the size of the domain and the number of cores. Thus, the amount of computation for each server remains the same, but the total number of data exchanges between processes increases. Each core conducts one thread of calculations. Ideally, the program execution time must not change, in which case the efficiency is considered to be unity. However the presence of data exchanges impacts the efficiency. Figure 5 shows the test results from which it can be seen that the algorithm and the program have good scalability properties. Within the range from 12 to 72 cores the efficiency drops to 0,946 and remains consistent through the increase from 72 to 120 cores.

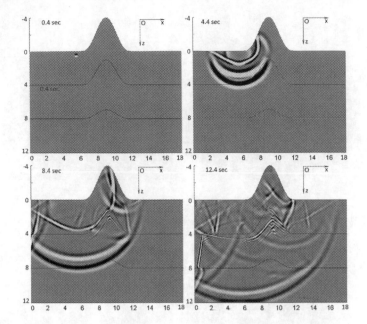

Fig. 4. Wave field at the time instants 0.4 s, 4.4 s, 8.4 s, 12.4 s

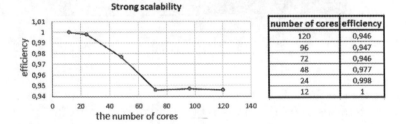

number of cores	efficiency
120	0,946
96	0,947
72	0,946
48	0,977
24	0,998
12	1

Fig. 5. The results of the strong scalability tests

7   Conclusion

This paper proposes the algorithm of 3D seismic waves simulation in elastic heterogeneous media for the domain with complex free surface geometry. The problem is formulated in terms of displacements in Cartesian and in generalized coordinates. Constructing a curvilinear mesh allows good consistency between physical domain and computational domain. The main result of this paper is the creation of the parallel 3D algorithm and its software implementations aimed at the numerical modeling of elastic waves in isotropic heterogeneous 3D media with complex free surface geometry. The algorithm was developed using the balance technique and finite difference method. The novelty of the scheme constructed is the positioning of metrical coefficients with respect to components of the displacement vector, which allows better accuracy. The algorithm developed shows good results in terms of strong scalability. Further, the algorithm improvement we see as: utilizing the CCPML method [24] to dispose of the side boundary reflections; to adapt the program for other architectures like Intel Xeon Phi; to increase the scalability and the energy efficiency of the algorithm by optimizing RAM usage and data exchange.

Acknowledgement. The theoretical part of this research (Sects. 1, 2) has been supported by the Russian Science Foundation, project 17-17-01128. Work on Sects. 3, 4 was conducted within the framework of the budget project 0315-2019-0009 for ICMMG SB RAS, and for the technical part, Sects. 5 and 6, were supported by the RFBR grants 19-07-00085 and 18-07-00757 respectively.

All simulations have been done using the equipment of the Siberian Supercomputer Center.

References

1. Lebedev, V.I.: Difference analogues of orthogonal decompositions of basic differential operators and some boundary value problems. Comput. Math. Math. Phys. **4**, 449–465 (1964)
2. Alford, R.M., Kelly, K.R., Boore, D.M.: Accuracy of finite-difference modeling of the acoustic wave equation. Geophysics **39**, 834–842 (1974)
3. Virieux, J.: P-SV wave propagation in heterogeneous media: velocitystress finite-difference method. Geophysics **51**, 889–901 (1986)
4. Levander, A.R.: Fourth-order finite-difference P-SV seismograms. Geophysics **53**, 1425–1436 (1988)
5. Saenger, E.H., Gold, N., Shapiro, S.A.: Modeling the propagation of the elastic waves using a modified finite-difference grid. Wave Motion **31**, 77–92 (2000)
6. Zhang, J., Verschuur, D.J.: Elastic wave propagation in heterogeneous anisotropic media using the lumped finite-element method. Geophysics **67**, 625–638 (2002)
7. Komatitsch, D., Vilotte, J.-P.: The spectral element method: an efficient tool to simulate the seismic response of 2D and 3D geological structures. Bull. Seismol. Soc. Am. **88**, 368–392 (1998)
8. Tromp, J., Komatitsch, D., Liu, Q.: Spectral-element and adjoint methods in seismology. Commun. Comput. Phys. **3**, 1–32 (2008)
9. Grote, M.J., Schneebeli, A., Schotzau, D.: Discontinuous Galerkin finite element method for the wave equation. SIAM J. Numer. Anal. **44**, 2408–2431 (2006)
10. Etienne, V., Chaljub, E., Virieux, J., Glinsky, N.: An hp-adaptive discontinuous Galerkin finite-element method for 3D elastic wave modelling. Geophys. J. Int. **183**, 941–962 (2010)
11. Zhang, J.: Quadrangle-grid velocity-stress finite-difference method for elastic-wave-propagation simulation. Geophys. J. Int. **131**, 127–134 (1997)
12. Dumbser, M., Kaser, M.: An arbitrary high-order discontinuous Galerkin method for elastic waves on unstructured meshes II. Three-dimensional isotropic case. Geophys. J. Int. **167**, 319–336 (2006)
13. Kaser, M., Dumbser, M.: An arbitrary high-order discontinuous Galerkin method for elastic waves on unstructured meshes - I. The two-dimensional isotropic case with external source terms. Geophys. J. Int. **166**, 855–877 (2006)

14. Zhang, L., Wei, L., Lixin, H., Xiaogang, D., Hanxin, Z.: A class of hybrid DG/FV methods for conservation laws II: two-dimensional cases. J. Comput. Phys. **231**, 1104–1120 (2012)

15. Liseykin, V.: Difference Meshes. Theory and Applications, p. 254. SB RAS Publishing, Novosibirsk (2014). (in Russian)

16. Khakimzyanov G., Shokin Yu.: Difference schemes on adaptive meshes. Editorial and Publishing Center of NSU SB RAS, 130 p. (2005). (in Russian)

17. Yu, S., Danaev, N., Khakimzyanov, G., Shokina, N.: Lectures on difference schemes on moving meshes. Editorial and Publishing Center of KazNU Named After Al-Farabi, 183 p. (2005). (in Russian)

18. Daniel Appelo, N., Petersson, N.A.: A stable finite difference method for the elastic wave equation on complex geometries with free surfaces. Commun. Comput. Phys. **5**(1), 84–107 (2009)

19. Jose, M., Carcione, J.M.: The wave equation in generalized coordinates. Geophysics **59**(12), 1911–1919 (1994)

20. Titov, P.: An algorithm and a program for simulation of 2D-wave fields in areas with a curved free surface. In: Materials of the Conference "Scientific Service on the Internet - 2014" Novorossiysk, Abrau-Dyurso, 21–26 September 2014, pp. 446–455. (in Russian)

21. Titov, P.: Modeling of elastic waves in media with a complex free surface topography. Vestnik of NSU: Inf. Technol. **164**, 153–166 (2018). (in Russian)

22. Titov, P.: A technology of modeling of elastic waves propagation in media with complex 3D geometry of the surface with the aid of high performance cluster. In: Proceedings of Russian Supercomputing Days, pp. 1020–1031 (2016)

23. Vishnevsky, D., Lisitsa, V., Tcheverda, V., Reshetova, G.: Numerical study of the interface errors of finite-difference simulations of seismic waves. Geophysics **79**(4), T219–T232 (2014)

24. Komatitsch, D., Martin, R.: An unsplit convolutional perfectly matched layer improved at grazing incidence for the seismic wave equation. Geophysics **72**(5), SM155–SM167 (2007)

Three-Dimensional Ultrasound Tomography: Mathematical Methods and Experimental Results

Alexander Goncharsky and Sergey Seryozhnikov[✉]

Lomonosov Moscow State University, Moscow, Russia
gonchar@srcc.msu.ru, s2110sj@gmail.com

Abstract. This paper is concerned with developing the methods for solving inverse problems of ultrasound tomography under the model that accounts for diffraction, refraction and absorption. The inverse problem is posed as a nonlinear coefficient inverse problem for the wave equation. Iterative numerical algorithms have been developed to solve this inverse problem using supercomputers. The paper presents the results of 3D tomographic imaging of a test sample with acoustic properties close to those of human soft tissues. The data used for imaging were collected in a physical experiment on a test bench for ultrasound tomographic studies. The frequency range of sounding pulses was 50–800 kHz. The acoustic field was registered on a cylindrical surface surrounding the test sample. The 3D sound speed image was reconstructed using multistage iterative algorithm with gradually increasing signal bandwidth. The results showed that the tomographic methods developed can achieve a high spatial resolution while the contrast of the object doesn't exceed 20%. The proposed algorithms are designed for compact GPU clusters. Such clusters can be used as computing devices in medical tomographic facilities.

Keywords: Ultrasound tomography · Coefficient inverse problem · Medical imaging · GPU cluster

1 Introduction

This paper is concerned with developing supercomputer methods for solving inverse problems of ultrasound tomography. The main applications of wave tomography are medical imaging and nondestructive testing [1]. The most interesting application is soft tissue imaging for early-stage breast cancer diagnosis. Numerous research groups from the USA, Germany, Russia [2–4] work in this field.

In this study, the inverse problem of 3D wave tomography is posed as a coefficient inverse problem, in which the unknown coefficient represents the three-dimensional pressure wave propagation velocity in the studied object [5–7]. The scalar wave model is based on a hyperbolic differential equation and accurately

© Springer Nature Switzerland AG 2019
V. Voevodin and S. Sobolev (Eds.): RuSCDays 2019, CCIS 1129, pp. 463–474, 2019.
https://doi.org/10.1007/978-3-030-36592-9_38

describes wave diffraction and absorption effects. The algorithms for solving the inverse problem of ultrasound tomography in three dimensions are much more computationally expensive than the algorithms for the 2D layer-wise image reconstruction [8–10].

The inverse problem of wave tomography is nonlinear. To solve this inverse problem, the authors propose iterative algorithms which are based on direct calculation of the residual functional gradient. The residual functional represents the discrepancy between the wave field measured by the detectors and the numerically computed wave field. Due to nonlinearity of this inverse problem, iterative gradient descent algorithms might not converge to the global minimum of the functional if started from an arbitrary initial approximation.

An efficient multi-stage iterative method for solving the inverse problem is proposed. The essence of the method is that at the first stage the inverse problem is solved using only the low-frequency part of the spectrum of the measured signals. The resulting approximate solution is used as an initial approximation for the next stage of the algorithm, which utilizes a higher signal bandwidth.

An important result of this study is that the algorithms developed were tested on actual experimental data obtained on the test bench for ultrasound tomographic studies [11]. The test samples (phantoms) used for imaging had the acoustic properties close to those of human soft tissues. The volume of data collected in the experiment amounts to ≈ 3 GB. The number of unknowns in the nonlinear inverse problem exceeds 10 million.

The proposed algorithms for solving inverse problems of wave tomography are designed for graphics processors and GPU clusters, which have proven to be the most efficient computing devices for this task. The architecture of a GPU cluster for image reconstruction in a ultrasound tomographic complex is discussed.

2   Formulation of the Inverse Problem of 3D Ultrasound Tomography and Its Solution Methods

The main result of this study is that for the first time the developed inverse problem solution algorithms were tested on actual experimental data obtained at the ultrasound tomographic test bench. The 3D model of the test bench is shown in Fig. 1a.

Ultrasound emitters 1 and receiver 2 are mounted on vertical consoles that can be moved vertically by means of linear drives 3. Each of the consoles can be rotated around the axis of a cylindrical water-filled acoustic bath 4 using rotary drives 5. Test sample 6 is positioned at the center of the acoustic bath. During the experiment the emitters are positioned on the cylindrical surface shown on Fig. 1b, and the acoustic field is measured on a smaller cylindrical surface shown on Fig. 1c. The measurements are performed for each source position. Let Ns be the number of source positions, and Nd—the number of detector positions. In tomographic imaging schemes, the product $Ns \cdot Nd$ should amount to hundreds of thousands or more. In our experiments, the number of source positions $Ns = 48$ and the number of detector positions $Nd \approx 20000$. This scheme has

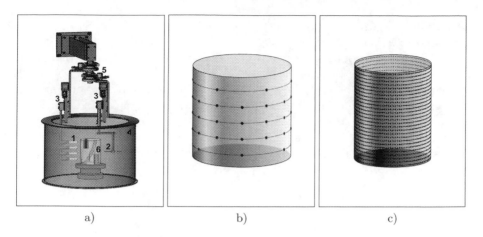

a)   b)   c)

Fig. 1. The test bench (a); scheme of emitters (b) and detectors (c) placement on cylindrical surfaces

a small number of sources and is simple to implement and to parallelize the computations.

A cylinder made of soft silicone was used as a test sample. The sample contains holes and inclusions to be imaged. Acoustic properties of the silicone are close to the properties of human soft tissues. The aim of the experiment is to reconstruct the three-dimensional sound speed image $c(r), r = \{x, y, z\}$ using the measured data. A scalar wave model was used to describe pressure waves in the medium. This model accounts for the effects of diffraction, refraction and absorption of ultrasound waves. Acoustic pressure $u(r, t)$ satisfies the equation:

$$c(r)u_{tt}(r, t) + a(r)u_t(r, t) - \Delta u(r, t) = 0; \tag{1}$$

$$u(r, t)|_{t=0} = F_0(r), \quad u_t(r, t)|_{t=0} = F_1(r). \tag{2}$$

Here, $c(r) = 1/v^2(r)$, $v(r)$ and $a(r)$ are the speed of sound and the absorption coefficient, respectively; Δ is the Laplace operator with respect to r. Initial conditions $F_0(r)$ and $F_1(r)$ represent the initial pulse emitted by the ultrasound source. Non-reflecting boundary condition [12] is applied at the boundary of the computational domain.

The inverse problem of reconstructing unknown coefficients of the wave equation is an ill-posed problem. The methods for solving ill-posed problems were developed in [13,14]. We formulate this inverse problem as a problem of minimizing the residual functional

$$\Phi(u(c, a)) = \frac{1}{2} \int_0^T \int_S (u(s, t) - U(s, t))^2 \, ds \, dt \tag{3}$$

with respect to its argument (c, a). Here, wavefield $u(s, t)$ is the solution of the direct problem (1)–(2) at detector points s with given $c(r) = 1/v^2(r)$ and $a(r)$. The exact solution of the inverse problem is a set of coefficients $c(r), a(r)$, which, when substituted into (1)–(2), produces the wave field $u(\boldsymbol{r}, t)$ equal to the measured wave field $U(\boldsymbol{s}, t)$ at detector points $\boldsymbol{s}$. Wavefield $U(\boldsymbol{s}, t)$ is measured for each source position, hence the total value of the residual functional is the sum of the residuals (3) for each source position.

Representations for the gradient $\Phi'(c, a)$ of the residual functional in various formulations were obtained in the authors' works [15–17]. The gradient $\Phi'(u(c, a)) = \{\Phi'_c(u), \Phi'_a(u)\}$ of the functional (3) represents the linear part of the increment of the functional with respect to the variation of the coefficients $\{dc, da\}$ and has the form:

$$\Phi'_c(u(c)) = \int_0^T w_t(\boldsymbol{r}, t) u_t(\boldsymbol{r}, t)\, \mathrm{d}t, \quad \Phi'_a(u(a)) = \int_0^T w_t(\boldsymbol{r}, t) u(\boldsymbol{r}, t)\, \mathrm{d}t. \tag{4}$$

Here, $u(\boldsymbol{r}, t)$ is the solution of the direct problem (1)–(2), and $w(\boldsymbol{r}, t)$ is the solution of the following "conjugate" problem with the given $c(\boldsymbol{r})$, $a(\boldsymbol{r})$ and $u(\boldsymbol{r}, t)$:

$$c(\boldsymbol{r}) w_{tt}(\boldsymbol{r}, t) - a(\boldsymbol{r}) w_t(\boldsymbol{r}, t) - \Delta w(\boldsymbol{r}, t) = E(\boldsymbol{r}, t); \tag{5}$$

$$w(\boldsymbol{r}, t = T) = 0, \quad w_t(\boldsymbol{r}, t = T) = 0; \tag{6}$$

At the points where the measured wavefield $U(\boldsymbol{r}, t)$ is known, $E(\boldsymbol{r}, t) = u(\boldsymbol{r}, t) - U(\boldsymbol{r}, t)$. Otherwise, $E(\boldsymbol{r}, t) = 0$. Non-reflecting boundary condition [12] is applied for $w(\boldsymbol{r}, t)$ at the boundary of the computational domain. In order to compute the gradient (4), we must solve direct problem (1)–(2) and "conjugate" problem (5)–(6). Then the residual functional can be minimized using iterative gradient descent method.

Finite Difference Time-Domain method (FDTD) [16] was used to implement the proposed method numerically. Finite-difference method can be efficiently implemented on graphics processors and GPU clusters [18].

3   GPU Algorithm for Solving the Inverse Problem of Wave Tomography Using Experimental Data

3.1   Flowchart of the Algorithm

The algorithm of reconstructing the 3D sound speed image from experimental data consists of the data processing algorithm and the iterative algorithm for solving the inverse problem. Figure 2 shows the flowchart of the algorithm.

The data processing algorithm executes only once before the iterative inverse problem solution algorithm starts. The data processing algorithm includes the following operations:

– Data collection. Two datasets are acquired in a physical experiment: measurements of the acoustic field scattered by the object (Object wavefield) and measurements of the acoustic field in the homogeneous medium (Reference wavefield).

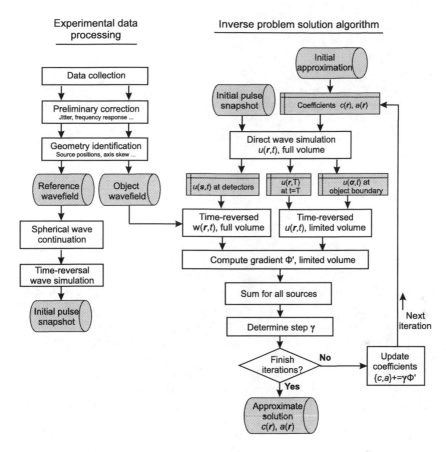

Fig. 2. The flowchart of the data processing algorithm and the inverse problem solution algorithm

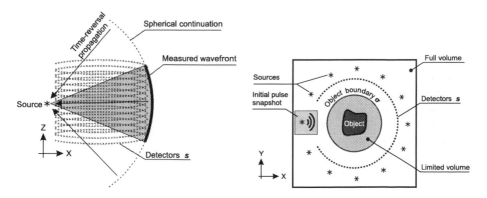

Fig. 3. Computing the initial conditions via spherical extrapolation of the wave

Fig. 4. Computational domains in the inverse problem solution algorithm

- Preliminary correction, which includes jitter correction, correction of frequency spectrum to account for the frequency responses of emitters and detector, and other factors.
- Geometry identification. At this stage the geometric parameters of the experimental setup, such as actual positions of sources and actual movement axis are determined via measurement of pulse arrival times and statistical regression.
- Computing the initial pulse from the reference wavefield via time-reversal method [19].

Unlike in numerical simulations [18], in a physical experiment the initial pulse emitted by the source is unknown and must be computed using the measured data. To this end, the data processing algorithm reconstructs the initial pulse using the data measured at a cylindrical surface $0 < z < H$ via the time-reversal method. The small size of the ultrasound emitters results in a wavefront that is very close to spherical. In order to compute the initial pulse, it is necessary to know the wavefield not only at the cylindrical surface where the measurements are taken, but also in the areas $z < 0$ and $z > H$. To obtain these data, we extrapolate the measured wavefront onto a larger area (Fig. 3) using the assumption that the emitted wave is a spherical wave. Using extrapolated data, the Eq. (1) is solved in reverse time to obtain initial conditions (2). The initial pulse is stored as a snapshot of the wavefield in some area around the emitter for two consecutive time steps of the finite-difference scheme.

The right-hand side of the flowchart describes the iterative algorithm for solving the inverse problem. This algorithm implements a gradient-descent method of minimizing the residual functional and relies on an important result obtained by the authors [7], in which a method to compute the gradient of the residual functional was formulated. The algorithms are designed for GPU clusters.

3.2   GPU Implementation of the Iterative Gradient Method of Minimizing the Residual Functional

Having the initial conditions (2) determined, we can solve equations (1)–(2) and (5)–(6), compute the gradient of the residual functional (4) and use this gradient to minimize the functional and obtain an approximate solution of the inverse problem.

One of the problems with the implementation of this method is that to calculate the gradient using formulas (4) the values of wave fields $u(\boldsymbol{r}, t)$ and $w(\boldsymbol{r}, t)$ at the same point are required, while equations (5)–(6) are solved in reverse time. Storing the values of $u(\boldsymbol{r}, t)$ obtained while solving equations (1)–(2) in order to use them later to compute the gradient would take an immense amount of memory.

The large volume of the computational domain, which is determined by the experimental setup, poses yet another problem, especially relevant to GPU devices with limited onboard memory. In the experiment, the ultrasound wave propagates inside the full volume of $380 \times 380 \times 380\,\mathrm{mm}$, as shown in Fig. 4.

The number of operations required to compute the wavefield is proportional to the fourth power of the domain size $(X \times Y \times Z \times T)$. The amount of memory required is proportional to the third power of the domain size $(X \times Y \times Z)$.

To overcome these difficulties, the proposed algorithm employs an artificial Object boundary (σ) as a temporary storage for the wavefield. The volume enclosed by the object boundary ("Limited volume") must be sufficient to contain the object being imaged. The gradient of the residual functional is computed only inside this limited volume. As the wavefield $u(r,t)$ is computed via solving equations (1)–(2), the values of $u(s,t)$ at detector points s and $u(\sigma,t)$ at the object boundary σ for each time step t are stored in system memory.

After that, conjugate problem (5)–(6) is solved in reverse time. Wavefield $w(r,t)$ is computed using previously stored values of $u(s,t)$ and the measured wavefield $U(s,t)$ (Object wavefield). Simultaneously, wavefield $u(r,t)$ is reconstructed from previously stored $u(\sigma,t)$ at the object boundary by solving Eq. (1) in reverse time and applying Dirichlet boundary condition at boundary σ. Having both $u(r,t)$ and $w(r,t)$ determined inside the limited volume, we compute the gradient of the residual functional by formula (4).

In the experiment, the size of limited volume amounted to $120 \times 120 \times 140$ mm, which constitutes less than 5% of the full volume. Thus, the computations over the full volume are the most resource-intensive. These computations include only one wavefield in forward time and one in reverse time. Further optimization of the algorithm can be achieved primarily by limiting the size of the computational domain. A 20% decrease of the domain size would yield a 2.5x speedup.

3.3 Multistage Algorithm for Solving Inverse Problem of Wave Tomography

One of the main difficulties in solving the inverse problem of wave tomography lies in its nonlinearity. As a consequence, the residual functional is not convex, and the gradient descent method might converge to a local minimum instead of the global minimum of the functional. Numerical simulations [20] showed that the convergence of the iterative gradient descent method is affected primarily by the pulse wavelength. The shorter the wavelength, the more local minimum points are encountered. For the iterative method to converge to the global minimum, an initial approximation that is sufficiently close to the global minimum must be provided.

To this end, the authors propose the following multistage iterative method for solving the inverse problem of wave tomography. At the first stage of the method, the spectrum of the measured signals is limited to 50–200 kHz band, thus limiting the minimal wavelength to 7.5 mm. Using these band-limited signals, we solve the inverse problem of sound speed image reconstruction using the iterative gradient descent method. A constant initial approximation $c(r) = const$ is used to start the gradient descent process at the first stage. The obtained sound speed image has very low resolution, but is much closer to the global minimum of the residual functional that an initial approximation of $c(r) = const$. We use this approximate solution as an initial approximation for the next stage.

At the second stage we use a wider band of 50–350 kHz and obtain a higher resolution image by solving the inverse problem via the same iterative gradient descent method. The result is used as an initial approximation for the next stage with even higher bandwidth, and so on. At the last stage a high-resolution image is obtained using all available bandwidth of 50–800 kHz. Small increase in bandwidth from one stage to the next, not exceeding 50%, and sufficiently large wavelength at the first stage ensure the convergence of the iterative gradient-descent method to the global minimum of the residual functional [20]. It takes 15–20 iterations to obtain an approximate solution at each stage.

Computing the three-dimensional wavefields is a very computationally expensive task. However, at first stages of the multistage method the image resolution is low and the signals are band-limited. Thus, the computations can be carried out on a coarse grid. As the signal bandwidth is increased from one stage to the next, so is the grid size.

The grid size is chosen so that the errors introduced by numerical dispersion are sufficiently small. At the first stage the grid step $dx = 1.5$ mm. According to the Courant stability condition for 3D FDTD schemes, $\sqrt{3}v_{max}dt < dx$. Assuming that the waves with a maximum velocity of $v_{max} = 2$ km·s^{-1} should be processed correctly, the time step should amount to $dt = 0.6$ μs. With this grid step we can use the signal bandwidth up to $\approx$250 kHz until the numerical dispersion becomes noticeable.

The computation time at each stage is proportional to the fourth power of the signal frequency limit. With a typical 30–40% bandwidth increase from one stage to the next, the computation time increases by 3–5 times. At the first stage the grid step is 1.5 mm and it takes 1–2 min to obtain an approximate solution. At the second stage the grid step is 1 mm and the computation time amounts to $\approx$5 min. The last stage takes over an hour. Figure 5a shows the computation time for one gradient descent iteration at each stage. This test was performed on a widely available AMD Radeon RX580 graphics card on a single ultrasound source. There are 48 source positions in the experimental setup; thus, a cluster of 48 such devices would be needed to reconstruct a high-resolution image in 1.5 h.

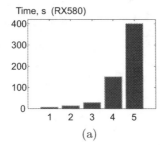 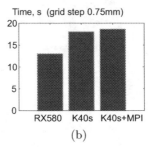

Fig. 5. Time per iteration: by stages (a), by devices (b)

The algorithms were tested on "Lomonosov-2" supercomputer [21] equipped with NVidia Tesla K40s devices. Figure 5b shows the performance test results for various GPU devices. The grid step in this test was fixed at 0.75 mm, which corresponds to stage 3. Supercomputer tests were carried out on a single K40s device ("K40s") and on 48 nodes of the supercomputer running in parallel ("K40s+MPI"). The tests showed very low communication overhead of 2%, as the communications are used only to sum the gradient for all sources at the end of each iteration [18] and the gradient is computed only inside the limited volume. Thus, a 48-node setup yielded a 47-fold acceleration compared to a single node.

The computations are carried out almost exclusively on graphics processors. Supercomputer tests showed less than 2% CPU load on the nodes equipped with 4 CPUs and one GPU. Taking into account these properties of the algorithm, a practically feasible computing solution could include compact GPU-clusters which typically contain two CPUs per 8–10 GPU devices.

New graphics processors equipped with High Bandwidth Memory (HBM) are beginning to emerge. The performance of HBM devices is approximately three times higher than that of the GDDR5-equipped devices tested in this study. With HBM devices, the number of devices in a cluster can be brought down to half the number of ultrasound sources, which amounts to $\approx$24 GPUs for a typical practical task. The computation time would amount to less than an hour, which is acceptable for medical examinations. Such GPU clusters could be used as computing devices in tomographic diagnostic facilities.

4   Results of 3D Sound Speed Image Reconstruction Using Experimental Data

The experiments were carried out on the test bench for ultrasound tomographic studies shown in Fig. 1a. The ultrasound emitters form sounding acoustic waves with a wavefront close to spherical and a wide frequency spectrum of 50–800 kHz. A precision piezoceramic hydrophone is used as a receiver. The receiving element has a diameter of 1.5 mm and a frequency range of 10 kHz–1 MHz.

Figure 6 shows the functional scheme of the experiment. Electrical pulses generated by the digital waveform generator are amplified and transmitted via a switch to each of the four emitters sequentially. The signal registered by the hydrophone is amplified, digitized and stored by the control computer. The computer also controls the motors, data collection process, and other processes. The duration of the experiment is about 1.5 h and the volume of data collected amounts to 3 GB.

Figure 7 shows the 3D model of the test sample used for imaging. The acoustic properties of the sample are close to that of human soft tissues. Low contrast is a distinctive characteristic of soft tissue imaging. The difference in the speed of sound between water and soft tissues does not exceed 10%. The test sample is a silicone cylinder 1 with inhomogeneities 2, 3, 4, 5. The cylinder is affixed to the mount with thin metal pins 6. The object is not cylindrically symmetrical,

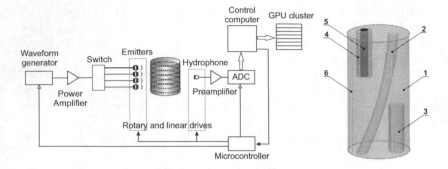

Fig. 6. Functional scheme of the experiment   **Fig. 7.** 3D model of the test sample

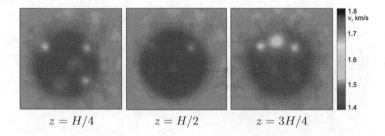

$$z = H/4 \qquad z = H/2 \qquad z = 3H/4$$

Fig. 8. Sound speed image reconstructed from experimental data using 50–250 kHz band

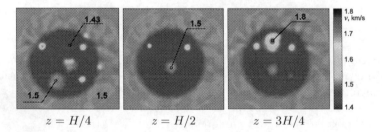

$$z = H/4 \qquad z = H/2 \qquad z = 3H/4$$

Fig. 9. Sound speed image reconstructed from experimental data using 50–400 kHz band. The numbers indicate the speed of sound

the cross-sections of the object in $z = const$ planes, parallel to the base of the cylinder, are different.

Figures 8 and 9 illustrate the multistage iterative inverse problem solution method developed in this study. Figure 8 shows the cross-sections of the reconstructed 3D sound speed image of the test sample in $z = H/4$, $z = H/2$ and $z = 3H/4$ planes, where H is the cylinder height equal to 130 mm. The diameter of the cylinder is 60 mm. This image was reconstructed from experimental data at the first stage of the multistage algorithm using 50–250 kHz band and an initial approximation of $c_0(r) = const$.

Figure 9 shows the cross-sections of the reconstructed 3D sound speed image of the test sample at the third stage of the algorithm using 50–400 kHz band. The spatial resolution has improved to $\approx$2.5 mm. The metal pins are 1 mm in diameter, so the images of the pins indicate the spatial resolution achieved. On the $z = H/2$ cross section only hole 2 is visible (see Fig. 7). On the $z = H/4$ cross-section holes 2 and 3 are visible, and on the $z = 3H/4$ cross-section holes 2, 4 and insert 5 with a higher speed of sound are present.

5   Conclusion and Discussion

The main result of this study is that the developed algorithms for solving inverse problems of 3D ultrasound tomography were tested on experimental data. The algorithms not only reconstruct the boundaries of inhomogeneities, but also precisely determine the speed of sound inside the object. Good correspondence between the reconstructed image and the actual speed of sound inside the test sample confirms that the scalar wave model accurately describes the physical processes. The algorithms developed are designed for GPU-supercomputers. The architecture of a GPU cluster which can be used as a computing device in a tomographic complex is proposed. The implementation with one GPU device per ultrasound source utilizes the internal parallelism of the problem most efficiently and delivers an acceptable level of performance using widely available hardware.

Acknowledgements. This work was supported by Russian Science Foundation [grant number 17-11-01065]. The research is carried out at Lomonosov Moscow State University. The research is carried out using the equipment of the shared research facilities of HPC computing resources at Lomonosov Moscow State University.

References

1. Bazulin, E.G., Goncharsky, A.V., Romanov, S.Y., Seryozhnikov, S.Y.: Parallel CPU- and GPU-algorithms for inverse problems in nondestructive testing. Lobachevskii J. Math. **39**(4), 486–493 (2018). https://doi.org/10.1134/S1995080218040030
2. Sak, M., et al.: Using speed of sound imaging to characterize breast density. Ultrasound Med. Biol. **43**(1), 91–103 (2017). https://doi.org/10.1016/j.ultrasmedbio.2016.08.021
3. Wiskin, J., et al.: Three-dimensional nonlinear inverse scattering: quantitative transmission algorithms, refraction corrected reflection, scanner design, and clinical results. J. Acoust. Soc. Am. **133**(5), 3229–3229 (2013). https://doi.org/10.1121/1.4805138
4. Birk, M., Dapp, R., Ruiter, N.V., Becker, J.: GPU-based iterative transmission reconstruction in 3D ultrasound computer tomography. J. Parallel Distrib. Comput. **74**, 1730–1743 (2014). https://doi.org/10.1016/j.jpdc.2013.09.007
5. Natterer, F.: Sonic imaging. Handbook of Mathematical Methods in Imaging, pp. 1–23. Springer, New York (2014). https://doi.org/10.1007/978-3-642-27795-5_37-2

6. Klibanov, M.V., Timonov, A.A.: Carleman estimates for coefficient inverse problems and numerical applications. Walter de Gruyter GmbH (2004). https://doi.org/10.1515/9783110915549
7. Goncharsky, A.V., Romanov, S.Y.: Iterative methods for solving coefficient inverse problems of wave tomography in models with attenuation. Inverse Probl. **33**(2), 025003 (2017). https://doi.org/10.1088/1361-6420/33/2/025003
8. Goncharsky, A., Seryozhnikov, S.: Supercomputer technology for ultrasound tomographic image reconstruction: mathematical methods and experimental results. In: Voevodin, V., Sobolev, S. (eds.) RuSCDays 2018. CCIS, vol. 965, pp. 401–413. Springer, Cham (2019). https://doi.org/10.1007/978-3-030-05807-4_34
9. Goncharsky, A.V., Romanov, S.Y., Seryozhnikov, S.Y.: Supercomputer technologies in tomographic imaging applications. Supercomput. Frontiers Innovations **3**(1), 41–66 (2016). https://doi.org/10.14529/jsfi160103
10. Goncharsky, A.V., Seryozhnikov, S.Y.: Supercomputer simulations in design of ultrasound tomography devices. Supercomput. Frontiers Innovations **5**(3), 111–115 (2018). https://doi.org/10.14529/jsfi180321
11. Goncharsky, A.V., Romanov, S.Y., Seryozhnikov, S.Y.: Low-frequency ultrasonic tomography: mathematical methods and experimental results. Moscow Univ. Phys. Bull. **74**(1), 43–51 (2019). https://doi.org/10.3103/S0027134919010090
12. Engquist, B., Majda, A.: Absorbing boundary conditions for the numerical simulation of waves. Math. Comput. **31**(139), 629–629 (1977). https://doi.org/10.1090/s0025-5718-1977-0436612-4
13. Tikhonov, A.N., Goncharsky, A.V., Stepanov, V.V., Yagola, A.G.: Numerical Methods for the Solution of Ill-Posed Problems. Springer, Netherlands (1995). https://doi.org/10.1007/978-94-015-8480-7
14. Bakushinsky, A., Goncharsky, A.: Ill-Posed Problems: Theory and Applications. Springer, Berlin (1994). https://doi.org/10.1007/978-94-011-1026-6
15. Goncharsky, A.V., Romanov, S.Y.: Supercomputer technologies in inverse problems of ultrasound tomography. Inverse Probl. **29**(7), 075004 (2013). https://doi.org/10.1088/0266-5611/29/7/075004
16. Goncharsky, A.V., Romanov, S.Y., Seryozhnikov, S.Y.: Low-frequency three-dimensional ultrasonic tomography. Dokl. Phys. **61**(5), 211–214 (2016). https://doi.org/10.1134/s1028335816050086
17. Goncharsky, A., Romanov, S., Seryozhnikov, S.: A computer simulation study of soft tissue characterization using low-frequency ultrasonic tomography. Ultrasonics **67**, 136–150 (2016). https://doi.org/10.1016/j.ultras.2016.01.008
18. Goncharsky, A.V., Seryozhnikov, S.V.: The architecture of specialized GPU clusters used for solving the inverse problems of 3D low-frequency ultrasonic tomography. In: Voevodin, V., Sobolev, S. (eds.) RuSCDays 2017. CCIS, pp. 363–375 (2017). https://doi.org/10.1007/978-3-319-71255-0_29
19. Fink, M.: Time reversal in acoustics. Contemp. Phys. **37**(2), 95–109 (1996). https://doi.org/10.1080/00107519608230338
20. Romanov, S.: Supercomputer simulation study of the convergence of iterative methods for solving inverse problems of 3D acoustic tomography with the data on a cylindrical surface. In: Voevodin, V., Sobolev, S. (eds.) RuSCDays 2018. CCIS, vol. 965, pp. 388–400. Springer, Cham (2019). https://doi.org/10.1007/978-3-030-05807-4_33
21. Voevodin, V.V., et al.: Supercomputer lomonosov-2: large scale, deep monitoring and fine analytics for the user community. Supercomput. Frontiers Innovations **6**(2). https://doi.org/10.14529/jsfi190201

Validation of the Regional Climate Model for the South of Russia

Alexander Titov[1], Alexander Khoperskov[1(✉)], Konstantin Firsov[1],
Sergey Khoperskov[2,3], and Tatiana Chesnokova[4]

[1] Volgograd State University, Volgograd, Russia
{alexandr.titov,khoperskov,fkm}@volsu.ru
[2] Institute of Astronomy, Russian Academy of Sciences, Moscow, Russia
[3] Max Planck Institute for Extraterrestrial Physics, Garching, Germany
sergey.khoperskov@gmail.com
[4] V.E. Zuev Institute of Atmospheric Optics of Siberian Branch of the Russian
Academy of Science, Tomsk, Russia
ches@iao.ru

Abstract. We present the results of the verification of the regional climate model (RCM) RegCM 4.5 for the territory of Southern Russia using NCEP/NCAR Reanalysis and GHCN + CAMS data. In this paper we aimed to explore the complexity of choosing of a computational domain, numerical grid parameters and their impact on the climate model prediction for models with hydrostatic and non-hydrostatic cores for the vertical coordinate. We upgraded the RegCM base code with a new module that allows splitting a territory into an arbitrary number of zones, each of which is characterized by its own set of physical parameters. In order to study the sensitivity of the simulations results we performed > 100 simulations varying the climatic conditions with terrain topography, surface roughness, soil, and vegetation properties, and the numerical grids. The features of numerical regional climate algorithm were discussed in case of the shared research facilities of high-performance computing at Lomonosov Moscow State University.

Keywords: Numerical simulation · Regional climate model ·
Reanalysis and big data · Radiation transfer · Parallel computing

1 Introduction

Regional climate models (RCMs) are the natural outcome of the global climate modelling with a possibility to expand the capabilities of global circulation models [1]. RCMs allow to increase the spatial resolution and to take into account smaller-scale features of the Earth's surface compare to the global climate models (GCMs). Validation of new models is an important issue for the climate modeling on small and large scales [2–4]. The quality of forecasts based on both GCM and RCM simulations is based on the fine-tuning of the model parameters and a careful selection of a large number of physical characteristics, including the

© Springer Nature Switzerland AG 2019
V. Voevodin and S. Sobolev (Eds.): RuSCDays 2019, CCIS 1129, pp. 475–486, 2019.
https://doi.org/10.1007/978-3-030-36592-9_39

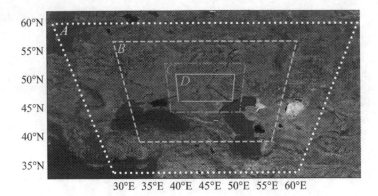

Fig. 1. The boundaries of computational domains with the center at the airport Gumrak (15 km west of Volgograd): A—3000 km × 3000 km, B—2000 km × 2000 km, C—1000 km × 1000 km. We compare the simulation results for zone D, which is embedded in the computational domains of three different sizes.

parameters of subgrid physics. There are additional problems for the regional climate models compare to the global ones. In particular, RCMs are quite sensitive to the boundary conditions and the choice of the computational domain [5]. The dynamical scalability of various climate models is being actively studied on the basis of RCMs for different territories [1,6]. These studies indicate the necessity of choice of the optimal configuration of the model parameters which depends on the specifics of the problem being solved. For example, the regional climate models are based on the integration of atmospheric hydrodynamics equations assuming the vertical hydrostatic equilibrium. In recent years, RCMs with non-hydrostatic cores along z-coordinates have been actively discussed in the literature [7,8]. One of the most common regional climate models is RegCM 4.5 which is developed by the International Center for Theoretical Physics (Trieste, Italy). The hydrostatic equilibrium condition imposes a natural limit on the numerical cell size on the Earth's plane $\Delta x, y > 10$ km. Meanwhile a typical cell size for RCM is $\Delta x = \Delta y = 20$ km. In numerical simulations the number of cells (N_σ in the vertical direction, or so-called σ-layers), is a free parameter, and we discuss the sensitivity of simulations to the choice of the parameter N_σ which in turn determines the detalization of the vertical structure of the atmosphere. Note that the ability to use models with a non-hydrostatic core with a cell size of $\Delta x \leq 10$ km is an important advantage of regional climate models compare to GCMs.

Validation of climate models is the major topic of the climate science [4,9] where the quality of climate models strongly depend on the adequacy of the radiation transfer description in the atmosphere of Earth [10–12]. Thereby the climate models validation issue is in the focus of our study. In this context, we study the impact of the choice of the computational domain size (Fig. 1) on the simulations results by comparing the simulation results for the three different

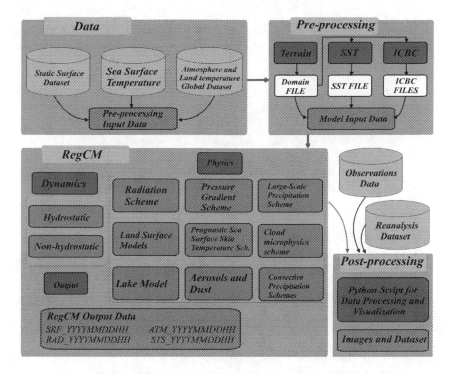

Fig. 2. Main components of the RegCM model

embedded areas (A, B and C). Our verification conception is based on two sets of reanalysis data: NCEP/NCAR, and GHCN+CAMS. We also analyze deeply a possibility for the most efficient parallel usage of supercomputer facilities of the Moscow State University (Lomonosov-1).

2   Components and Structure of RegCM 4.5

Figure 2 demonstrates the general structure of RCM RegCM 4.5. Prior to the simulation, it is necessary to prepare the input data for RCM which include the following components:

(1) "Static Surface Dataset" is a global archive with a horizontal resolution of 30 arcsec, containing the information about the surface topography and its type.
(2) "Sea Surface Temperature" is a global sea temperature dataset.
(3) "Atmosphere and Land Temperature Dataset" is the output of global climate models for defining the initial and boundary conditions.

The work cycle for the regional climate model RegCM can be divided into three main steps: Pre-processing, Modeling, Post-processing. The Pre-processing stage includes the localization of the computational domain, specification of the surface topography (Terrain module), sea temperatures (SST), as well as initial and boundary conditions (ICBC module) using the data mentioned above. RegCM software is designed to simulate the climate system and it already includes a set of approaches for various subgrid physics. Processing of the simulations results and their visualization are carried out in the Post-processing component. We have created an additional module for processing and visualization of the output of the simulation by using the Python programming language.

By using the topographic data from GTOPO (resolution 30″), hydrostatic core with a cell size of 20 km or non-hydrostatic core with $\Delta x = 10$ km we performed the numerical experiments for three different computational domains A, B, C with a number of cells of 150×150, 100×100, 50×50 cells in the Earth's plane respectively. The initial and boundary conditions were taken from the ERA-Interim GCM European Center for Medium-Range Weather Forecast's ERA-Interim (EIN15) where we also adopted the Indian Ocean Sea Surface Temperature (IOSST) data for the sea surface temperature.

3   Testing the RegCM 4.5 Radiative Code

Forecast quality of the climate models is closely related to the accuracy of the radiation transfer calculation in the atmosphere. It stimulates the spectroscopic investigations, development of new spectroscopic databases and regular updates of existing ones. For example, the latest version of the widely used HITRAN spectroscopic database was published in 2016. It includes 9133535 spectral lines [https://www.cfa.harvard.edu/hitran/]. However, the direct methods of the calculation, based on these databases are inapplicable due to the large computational costs. More detailed the equation of monochromatic radiation transfer can be written as:

$$Z(x) = \int_X k(x', x)\, Z(x')\, dx' + \Psi(x), \tag{1}$$

where $Z(x)$ is the collision density function which in tern connected to the radiation intensity by the following relation:

$$I(\boldsymbol{r}, \boldsymbol{n}) = |\mu_\Theta|\, S_\Theta \frac{Z(\boldsymbol{r}, \boldsymbol{n})}{\alpha(\boldsymbol{r})}, \tag{2}$$

where Θ is the phase space of coordinates and directions, $x = (\boldsymbol{r}, \boldsymbol{n})$.

The solution of the Eq. (1) is presented as a Neumann series:

$$Z = \sum_{i=1}^{\infty} K^i \Psi, \tag{3}$$

where K is an integral operator; in general case, $K\Psi$ is sixfold integral over the phase space, and $K^2\Psi$ is twelvefold, respectively. Then the solution (3) is necessary to integrate over the wavenumber, while the integration step is proportional to the absorption line width, $0.1\,\mathrm{cm}^{-1}$ at the Earth surface level.

This value decreases significantly at higher altitudes and the number of spectral lines up to 105 should be considered for the intensity calculation at each wavenumber. However, the information about the fine structure of absorption spectra is not required for the radiative-climatic problems because only integral characteristics matter for the model. The spectral resolution for the solution of such problems is affected by the absorption bandwidth, and it can reach the hundreds cm^{-1}. The most effective methods of the molecular absorption simulation in the radiative-climatic simulations are based on the usage of transmission function and its parameterization. At the early stage of climate models development, the absorption bands models suffered from the large uncertainty of the radiative fluxes calculation. These errors can lead to an artificial increase of CO_2 atmospheric concentration by a factor of two. The exponential expansion of the transmission function provides much higher accuracy of the parameterization, comparable to the direct calculation methods. By using the exponents series transformation we succeeded to resolve the problems in case of overlapping absorption bands. Our model allows us to determine the parameters of the expansion in exponents series on the basis of the direct calculation method. This approach decreases the computational size and speeds up the radiative calculations by several orders of magnitude. For example, the calculation with the line-by-line method requires 2×10^4 points in numerical integration in the $20 \, cm^{-1}$ spectral interval, whereas the approximation by the exponents series uses 5–10 computation points (terms of series) with the error of less than 1%.

The parameters, precomputed by the line-by-line method, were included in the radiative block that also improves significantly the performance of our simulations. It should be noted that the problem of approximation of the transmission function by exponents series can be described as a mean-square approximation, therefore it is easy to control the propagation of the error.

At a present time, the sources of significant uncertainties in the climate modeling problems are the water vapor and the aerosol abundance which play a key role in the radiative processes and phase transformation, including clouds formation. The radiative blocks in climate models are required to calculate the radiative characteristics with high accuracy. The climate models estimations show that the CO_2 atmospheric concentration doubling can increase the surface temperature of about 1.2 K. It corresponds to the change in the downward longwave fluxes of about 2 W/m^2 that is 1% of a total flux [13]. Our calculations of the longwave radiative fluxes with different versions of the spectroscopic database HITRAN have shown that the difference in downward fluxes at the atmosphere bottom for mid-latitude summer does not exceed 0.1 W/m^2, and 0.6 W/m^2 in upward fluxes at the top of the atmosphere [10]. By using the spectroscopic database HITRAN2012 we found that the upward flux at the top of the atmosphere calculated is 281.01 W/m^2, and the downward flux at the bottom of atmosphere bottom is 351.16 W/m^2. From these estimations, it can be concluded that modern spectroscopic databases provide the high accuracy of the broadband fluxes simulation.

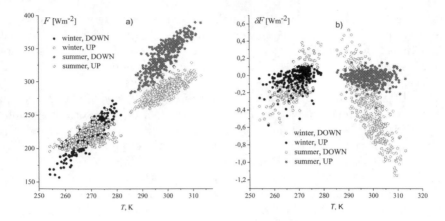

Fig. 3. (*a*) The dependence of the upward fluxes (UP) at the top of the atmosphere and the downward fluxes (DOWN) at the bottom of the atmosphere on surface air temperature. (*b*) Discrepancies in longwave radiative fluxes due to different water vapor continuum models.

The situation is different in the case of water vapor continuum absorption. The sensitivity of the radiative fluxes to errors of the continual absorption in macro and micro-windows of the atmospheric transparency is stronger in comparison to the selective absorption. It caused by the saturation effect observed in various absorption bands, whereas despite the continual absorption is relatively small it is not saturated and slowly varies with wavenumber, and contributes to the broad spectral intervals. New studies define more precisely the continuum models with progress in experimental technics. The radiative forcing of the water vapor continuum absorption in the visible and near-infrared spectral regions is considered in [11] for two continuum models: CKD, used in climate models, and CAVIAR, obtained on basis of recent experimental data. In particular, the global-mean clear-sky atmospheric absorption is enhanced by 1.5 W/m^2 (about 2%) for CKD and 2.8 W/m^2 (about 3.5%) for CAVIAR, relative to a no-continuum case.

The continuum absorption contribution in the longwave spectral region ($\lambda \geq 3\,\mu$m) is significantly larger than in the shortwave spectral region and it can reach several tens of W/m^2. By using the regional climatic model RegCM 4.5 we made an analysis of the CKD model but in the longwave spectral region. The calculations are carried out by means of a modern empirical continuum model MT_CKD2.5. This model is developed as an open source software [http://rtweb. aer.com], and it suits to the effective application for the line-by-line calculation. We found that the longwave continual absorption contributes more significantly in the atmospheric transparency macro-window of 8–12 μm. The detailed investigations of the continuum absorption were recently carried out in this spectral region, and it was shown that the MT_CKD model provides a significant difference of absorption coefficients in comparison to existing experimental data, and it has also stronger temperature dependence [12,14]. Therefore, we used MT_CKD

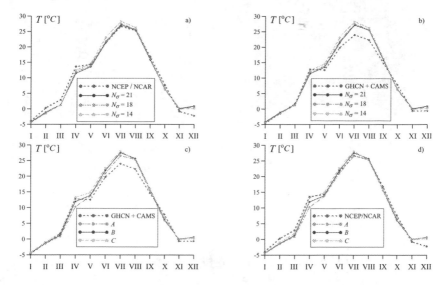

Fig. 4. The average monthly temperature at two meters high in the territory of the airport Gumrak for various models

in the whole longwave spectral region, with the exception for 8–12 μm regions, where it was replaced by our model based on the experimental data obtained by Baranov et al. [12,14].

Since a new continuum model could not be incorporated to the radiative code of the regional climatic model RegCM 4.5 our calculations were carried out by using of the radiative model which is based on the exponents series expansion of the transmission function in the spectral region of 0–$3000\,cm^{-1}$ with a spectral resolution of $20\ cm^{-1}$ for the atmospheric altitudes in the range of 0–$100\,km$ from the surface of Earth. Both continua were includes in this radiative model. In order to estimate a possible variation of the longwave upward fluxes at the atmosphere top and downward fluxes at the atmosphere bottom, and water vapor continuum contribution to the fluxes, we used two samplings of meteorological data for summer and winter periods of the Lower Volga region. The samplings were obtained from the reanalysis data and they contain also the vertical profiles of pressure, temperature, and humidity measured by the balloon sounding, and the vertical profiles of small gaseous constituents as well.

The dependence of upward fluxes at the atmosphere top and downward fluxes at the atmosphere bottom on surface air temperature is presented in Fig. 3a. The difference in the radiative fluxes, calculated for two models continua is shown in Fig. 3b. As follows from the presented data, the radiative block of the regional climatic model RegCM 4.5 provides, in general, high accuracy of the radiative fluxes calculations for the wide range of meteorological conditions, observed in the Lower Volga region. As follows from Fig. 3b, the difference in downward fluxes can reach 1 W/m^2 at the extremely high temperatures. These discrepancies can

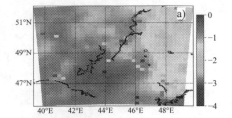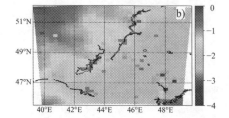

Fig. 5. Distribution of the average monthly temperature residuals for the region D: (a) $\Delta T_{AB} = \langle T_A^{(VI)} \rangle - \langle T_B^{(VI)} \rangle$, (b) $\Delta T_{AC} = \langle T_A^{(VI)} \rangle - \langle T_C^{(VI)} \rangle$

not impact significantly on the climatic characteristics of the Lower Volga region, but the difference in the models can be important for tropical latitudes.

4   Results and Experience of the Supercomputer Modeling

Climate modeling is one of the most computational expensive research fields where new powerful supercomputers are being created [15,16]. In this section we discuss some important features of parallel high-performance computing for RegCM on powerful computers, in particular on the Lomonosov-1 supercomputer (MSU).

Validation of simulation results is based on the high-resolution data sets ($0.5° \times 0.5°$) provided by the Climate Prediction Center (National Centers for Environmental Prediction) [17] and reanalysis data ($2.5° \times 2.5°$), which are the joint product of the National Centers for Environmental Prediction (NCEP) and National Center for Atmospheric Research (NCAR) [18].

Figure 4 shows the comparison of the average monthly air temperature in the atmospheric surface layer with reanalyses data. We argue that the structure of solutions do not dependent on the number of σ-layers (N_σ) for $N_\sigma \gtrsim 18$–21 and hence we restrict ourselves for $N_\sigma = 21$ for basic models. In general, the simulation results are in better agreement with NCEP/NCAR data than with GHCN + CAMS, especially during the warm period (May—September). However, the RCM results are closer to GHCN + SAMS during the November—April.

Figure 5 demonstrates the impact of a computational domain for the entire D zone (See Fig. 1). In order to measure the impact of the boundary conditions, we compare the results of various scale simulations (regions A, B è C) for a single common region D.

In Fig. 4 we demonstrate that in a given geographical location the simulated temperature can be different by a few degrees in some months for considered models. For example, it is seen that during June model A provides a lower temperature in comparison to models B and C. Note also that the temperature distribution is highly inhomogeneous and small-scale variations can locally reach $3\,°C$.

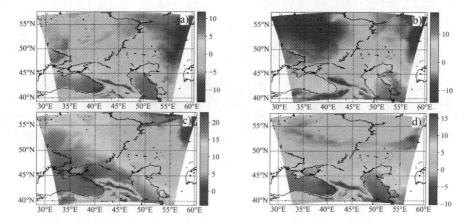

Fig. 6. The temperature distributions of T in the model for the computational domain B (See Fig. 1) at different times: (a) 15.02.2000, (b) 23.02.2000, (c) 03.10.2000, (d) 19.10.2000

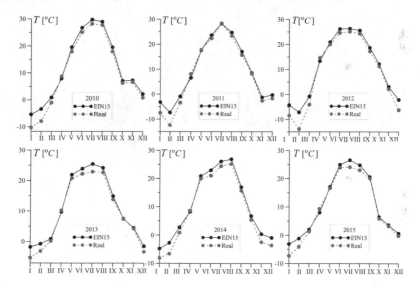

Fig. 7. Evolution of the meat temperature in various models (black) compared to the observational data (red) (Color figure online)

Figure 6 shows the temperature distribution for four different days. A strong warming impact from large water reservoires (Black and Caspian sea) is seen well. A similar contribution is detected from Tsimlyansk Reservoir which is of about 20 km width and it can be resolved even for hydrostatic core model. In Fig. 8 we compare the mean temperature with the observational data during 2010–2015 years (Fig. 7).

The numerical model is coded to use an MPI2 library to run in parallel mode using multiple cores/processors or run on a cluster. In the version 4.5 the model parallelizes execution dividing the work between the processors, with the minimum work per processor is 9 points or a box 3×3, but for the communication overhead, the optimal would be around 12 or a 10×10 patch per processor. In Fig. 8 shows the dependencies of calculation time on the number of cores n for a different number of cells n_c on supercomputer Lomonosov, and for a workstation with multicore, Xeon Processor E5-2650 V4 also (See the symbols of the cross) [19]. By looking in Fig. 8 we can conclude that for a small ($n_c \leq 100$) simulations it is more efficient to use multiprocessor workstations with modern processors.

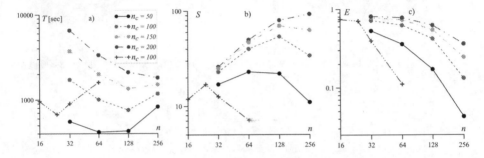

Fig. 8. (a) Calculation time T as a function of number of cores n for models with different number of cells n_c in one dimension, (b) parallel speedup $S = T(1)/T(n)$ and (c) parallelization efficiency $E = S/n$ for the same computing system

Table 1. Input and output data amount for models with different spatial resolution in a model A shown in Fig. 1

	5 km	10 km	20 km
Model input data	285 Gb/year	71 Gb/year	5.5 Gb/year
Model output data	1.2 Tb/year	290 Gb/year	28 Gb/year

Our simulations allow us to underline the following problem of climate simulations based on high-performance remote supercomputers. Increase of the number of computational cells n_c allows decreasing significantly the computational time however the communication costs tend to increase also. Moreover, the amount of simulations input/output data also increases for the high-resolution simulations which require a significant transfer of the data from/to supercomputer. In Table 1 we collect the information about the amount of input/output data for the regional models with different spatial resolution. Taking into account that climate model is reasonable to simulate for long periods of about tens of years, the amount of output data reaches very large numbers. An additional constraint in our case is the bandwidth of Lomonosov which allows as to use 10-15 Mb/sec for the data transfer.

5   Conclusion

In this section we briefly summarize our main results.

(1) Calculation time non-monotonically varies with a number of cores n and the location of the minimum $n_c^{(min)}$ depends strongly on the spatial resolution adopted in the model. The reason for such a puzzling characteristic is the features of parallelization adopted in RegCM.

(2) Main limiting factor for regional climate simulations is the amount of output data and the limits of the bandwidth for the data transfer from/to supercomputer.

(3) Our simulations demonstrate a clear dependence of results on a number of vertical layers for $N_\sigma \lesssim 20$, however for $N_\sigma \gtrsim 20$ our results converge. Data taken from NCEP/NCAR is in better agreement with RCM in comparison to GHCN+CAMS. This is a clearly seen for the warm summer period of Lower Volga however for cold winter period GHCN+CAMS shows a better agreement.

(4) We found that for small-scale features driven by the presence of large water bodies (Volgograd, Tsimlyansk reservoirs) and Volga-Akhtuba Floodplain (VAF) it is necessary to adopt an extra subgrid parametrization and hydrostatic equilibrium should be revisited by using high-resolution models of 1–5 km to further accommodate the climate model with a hydrological model of the VAF [20].

(5) We conclude that the radiation transfer routine in RegCM 4.5 provides a typical error of $1 \mathrm{W} \cdot \mathrm{m}^{-2}$ in climate conditions of the South of Russia, but for tropics, the error can be significantly larger.

Acknowledgments. AK has been supported by the Ministry of Science and Higher Education of the Russian Federation (government task No. 2.852.2017/4.6). AT is thankful RFBR and Volgograd Region Administration (grant No. 18-47-340003). The research is carried out using the equipment of the shared research facilities of HPC computing resources at Lomonosov Moscow State University. TC thanks for the support the Program of Fundamental Scientific Research of Russian Academy of Science (project no. AAAA-A17-117021310148-7).

References

1. Xue, Y., Janjic, J., Dudhia, J., Vasic, F.: A review on regional dynamical downscaling in intraseasonal to seasonal simulation/prediction and major factors that affect downscaling ability. Atmos. Res. **147**, 68–85 (2014)

2. Sen, B., Killinc, R., Sen, E., Sonuc, E.: Validation of daily precipitation estimates of the regional climate model RegCM4 over the domains in Turkey with NWP verification techniques. Fresenius Environ. Bull. **23**, 1892–1903 (2014)

3. Anisimov, A.E., Yarovaya, D.A., Barabanov, V.S.: Reanalysis of atmospheric circulation for the Black Sea-Caspian region. Phys. Oceanogr. **4**, 14–28 (2015)

4. Takane, Y., Kikegawa, Y., Hara, M., et al.: A climatological validation of urban air temperature and electricity demand simulated by a regional climate model coupled with an urban canopy model and a building energy model in an Asian megacity. Int. J. Climatol. **37**, 1035–1052 (2017)
5. Lagutin, A.A., Volkov, N.V., Mordvin, E.Y., Reznikov, A.N.: Modelling western siberia climate: results of the RegCM4 model. Izv. Altai State Univ. **73**, 182–190 (2012)
6. Meng, C., Ma, W., Xu, Y.: Modeling of a severe winter drought in eastern China using different initial and lateral boundary forcing datasets. Theoret. Appl. Climatol. **133**, 763–773 (2018)
7. Lyra, A., Tavares, S., Chou, G., et al.: Climate change projections over three metropolitan regions in Southeast Brazil using the non-hydrostatic Eta regional climate model at 5-km resolution. LitTitov-Niwano2018
8. Niwano, M., et al.: NHM-SMAP: spatially and temporally high resolution non-hydrostatic atmospheric model coupled with detailed snow process model for Greenland Ice Sheet. Cryosphere **12**, 625–655 (2017)
9. Makushev, K.M., Lagutin, A.A., Volkov, N.V., Mordvin, E.Y.: Validation of the RegCM4/CLM4.5 regional climate modeling system over the Western Siberia. In: Proceedings of the SPIE 10035, 22nd International Symposium on Atmospheric and Ocean Optics: Atmospheric Physics, p. 100356P (2016)
10. Firsov, K.M., Chesnokova, T.Y., Bobrov, E.V., Klitochenko, I.I.: Estimation of uncertainties in the longwave radiative fluxes simulation due to spectroscopic errors. In: Proceedings of the SPIE, p. 929205 (2014)
11. Radel, G., Shine, K.P., Ptashnik, I.V.: Global radiative and climate effect of the water vapour continuum at visible and near-infrared wavelengths. Q. J. R. Meteorol. Soc. **141**, 727–738 (2015)
12. Baranov, Y.I., Lafferty, W.J.: The water vapour self- and water-nitrogen continuum absorption in the 1000 and 2500 cm -1 atmospheric windows. Phil. Trans. R. Soc. A. **370**, 2578–2589 (2012)
13. Forster, P., Ramaswamy, V., Artaxo, P., et al.: Changes in atmospheric constituents and in radiative forcing. In: Climate Change 2007: The Physical Science Basis. Contribution of Working Group I to the Fourth Assessment Report of the Intergovernmental Panel on Climate Change. Cambridge University Press, Cambridge; New York (2007)
14. Baranov, Y.I., Lafferty, W.J., Ma, Q., Tipping, R.H.: Water-vapor continuum absorption in the 800–1250 cm-1 spectral region at temperatures from 311 to 363 K. JQSRT **109**, 2291–2302 (2008)
15. Kramer, D.: DOE acquiring new supercomputers and climate models. Phys. Today **67**(10), 27–28 (2014)
16. Denisova, N.Y., Gribanov, K.G., Werner, M., Zakharov, V.I.: Climate modeling for Yamal territory using supercomputer atmospheric circulation model ECHAM5-wiso. In: Proceedings of SPIE, vol. 9680 (2015)
17. Fan, Y.A., van den Dool, H.: Global monthly land surface air temperature analysis for 1948-present. J. Geophys. Res. **113**, Article ID D01103 (2008)
18. Kalnay, E., Kanamitsu, M., Kistler, R., et al.: The NCEP/NCAR 40-year reanalysis project. Bull. Amer. Meteor. Soc. **77**, 437–472 (1996)
19. Titov, A., Khoperskov, A.: Regional climate model for the lower volga: parallelization efficiency estimation. Supercomput. Front. Innov. **5**(4), 107–110 (2018)
20. Khrapov, S., et al.: The numerical simulation of shallow water: estimation of the roughness coefficient on the flood stage. Adv. Mech. Eng. **5**, 1–11 (2013). Article ID 787016

HPC, BigData, AI: Architectures, Technologies, Tools

An Experimental Study of Deep Neural Networks on HPC Clusters

Dmitry Buryak, Nina Popova[(⊠)], Vladimir Voevodin, Yuri Konkov, Oleg Ivanov, Denis Shaykhlislamov, and Ilya Fateev

Faculty of Computational Mathematics and Cybernetics, Lomonosov Moscow State University, Moscow, Russia
dyb04@yandex.ru, popova@cs.msu.su, voevodin@parallel.ru, konkov96@gmail.com, ivon_wrk@gmail.com, sdenis1995@gmail.com, bkmz12332@gmail.com

Abstract. Deep neural networks (DNN) offer great opportunities for solving many problems associated with processing large-scale data. Building and using deep neural networks requires large computational resources. In this regard, the question naturally arises about the possibility of using HPC-systems for the implementation of DNN. In order to better understand the performance implications of DNN on High Performance clusters we analyze the performance of several DNN-models over 2 HPC systems: the Lomonosov-2 supercomputer (the section with processors equipped with P100 GPUs) and the Polus high-performance cluster based on IBM Power8 processors with P100 GPUs. Comparing these frameworks is interesting as they represent different types of processors (Intel for Lomonosov-2 and IBM for Polus). Apart from different processor architectures, these systems feature different internode communications, which may affect the performance of the analysed algorithms in case of parallel and distributed implementation of neural network algorithms. The studies were carried out on the basis of the PyTorch framework.

Keywords: Deep neural networks · HPC cluster · GPU · Lomonosov-2 · Power8

1 Introduction

Deep neural networks (DNN) offer great opportunities for solving many problems associated with processing large-scale data. Building and using DNN requires large computational resources. In this regard, the question naturally arises about the possibility of using HPC-systems for the implementation of DNN-models. Recently, the direction in building a DNN-oriented high-performance systems based on an increasing number of GPU-processors has been actively developing. However, with all the attractiveness of this direction, such systems can be attributed to the number of specialized systems. A pressing question is the possibility of using existing high-performance clusters for neural network data processing. The goal of this work is to provide an experimental study of Deep Neural Networks on HPC clusters.

© Springer Nature Switzerland AG 2019
V. Voevodin and S. Sobolev (Eds.): RuSCDays 2019, CCIS 1129, pp. 489–504, 2019.
https://doi.org/10.1007/978-3-030-36592-9_40

This paper summarises the results produced in the testing of 4 neural networks within the two following HPC-systems: the Lomonosov-2 supercomputer (the section with processors equipped with P100 GPUs) [1] and the Polus high-performance cluster based on IBM Power8 processors with P100 GPUs [2]. Both systems are part of the supercomputer complex of Lomonosov Moscow State University. Comparing these frameworks is interesting as they represent different types of processors (Intel for Lomonosov-2 and IBM for Polus). Apart from different processor architectures, these systems feature different internode communications, which may affect the performance of the analysed algorithms in case of parallel and distributed implementation of neural algorithms. The studies were carried out on the basis of the PyTorch framework, one of the most popular neural network packages currently available, providing distributed data processing capabilities. In our study we do not address the issues of accuracy in machine learning. Accuracy and batch size, and, therefore, learning time, are interrelated. However, this problem requires more specific consideration.

1.1   Related Works

In the past few years, the topic of comparative analysis of various DNN frameworks has attracted more and more attention [3–6]. On the one hand, this is due to the need to choose the most appropriate framework for solving a problem on an existing computing system. On the other hand, this is due to the choice of the most suitable hardware platform for the chosen framework. A full-scale review of various aspects of the implementation of DNN was carried out in [3].

The comparison of open-source machine learning packages on edge devices (MacBook, FogNode, Jetson TX2, Raspberry Pi, Nexus 6P) is given in the paper [5]. Studies were conducted for such frameworks as Tensorflow, Caffe, MXNet, Pytorch and Tensorflow Lite. This works orientated to help in choosing appropriate combination of hardware and software, and also pointed out possible directions to optimize packages. In the paper [6] authors compared deep learning framework for HPC architectures and studied support of HPC-specific features provided by each framework. Authors observed some design problems between classical frameworks for deep learning and traditional HPC job's schedulers. It was also shown, that limited HPC-specific hardware support could lead to scalability issues and high communication overhead. In [7] conducted experiments on hybrid supercomputer Finis Terrae 2 are described. The study included scalability comparison of classical DL frameworks (Tensorflow, Caffe, CNTK, Theano), storage analysis and analysis of the influence of the batch size on speedup and accuracy. The report summarised the results of a benchmark of DL frameworks on HPC-systems. The authors also encountered the same problems of installing and applying HPC specific features, that were mentioned in the previous paper [6]. In all the above articles, an analysis of modern packages is carried out and their scalability is mainly studied. However, only in [7] influence of batch size on scalability was touched.

1.2   Scope

The rest of the paper is organized as follows. Section 2 provides a description of computing platforms. Section 3 gives an overview of the tested DNNs. Section 4 outlines results for Polus, and Sect. 5 outlines test results for Lomonosov-2. In conclusion, we provide research findings and recommendations on further developments.

2   Description of Computing Platforms

2.1   Cluster Polus Architecture

Polus high-performance computing cluster is a parallel computing system that consists of 5 IBM Power 8-based computer nodes [8]. The general cluster structure is shown in Fig. 1. General Parallel File System (GPFS) is installed on data nodes.

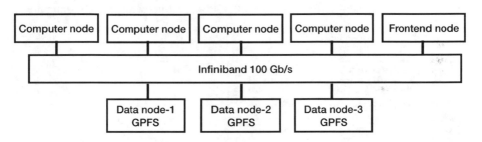

Fig. 1. Hardware configuration of polus cluster.

Parameters of Polus computer nodes are as following:

- two 10-core IBM Power 8 processors, 8 threads per core (160 threads overall),
- 256 GB ECC RAM (the fifth computer node features 1 TB of RAM),
- 2 NVIDIA Tesla P100 GPU accelerators with NVIDIA NVLink.

A high level of multithreading in the Power 8 processor is noteworthy. In general, the processor ensures running simultaneous operations on up to 160 threads per node. This feature of the processor architecture may be leveraged in neural algorithms as well. The computer nodes are interconnected with Infiniband SB7700EDR (100 Gb/s). Cluster performance (Tflop/s): 55.84 (peak); 40.39 (Linpack).

2.2   Hardware Configuration of the Lomonosov-2 Supercomputer Section

Node configuration in the tested section of the Lomonosov-2 supercomputer (Pascal Type):

- 2x Tesla P100, 16 GB
- 12-core Intel Xeon Xeon Gold 6126 2.60 GHz processors
- 64 GB RAM

The nodes are interconnected with Infiniband FDR. There are 2 parallel file systems: Panasas 97 TB and Lustre 360 TB. Access to the file system is also ensured with Infiniband FDR.

2.3 Software

The following software was used for this study: PyTorch 0.4 [9] (on Polus Cluster), PyTorch 0.5 (on Lomonosov-2), torchvision, cv2, numpy, and all associated libraries. The Polus cluster has several MPI versions installed, specifically IBM Spectrum MPI and OpenMPI. PyTorch was installed using Anaconda. Tasks are run on Polus Cluster via IBM's LSF Scheduler on Polus and via Slurm Scheduler on Lomonosov-2.

3 DNN Models and Experimental Methodology

Experimental study was performed on 4 different neural network models summarized in the Fig. 2.

Architecture	Input size	Parameters (millions)
Mobilenet V2 [8]	320x200	3.47
VGG16 [9]	320x200	9.73
VGG16 [9]	640x480	9.73
SqueezeNet [11]	640x480	0.42

Fig. 2. Characteristics of used neural networks.

VGG16 is a convolutional neural network model proposed by K. Simonyan and A. Zisserman [12], which is used in many deep learning image classification problems. The model achieves 92.7% top-5 test accuracy in ImageNet and it is the 1st runner-up of the ILSVRC 2014 in the classification task. Unfortunately, there are two disadvantages of VGGNet: it trains slow and the number of network's weights is quite large. This makes deploying VGGNet a hard task. SqueezeNet is a neural network with convolutional architecture. The authors' goal was to create a smaller neural network with fewer parameters for implementation on mobile platforms. SqueezeNet achieves AlexNet-level of accuracy on the ImageNet with 50x fewer parameters. The Mobile-NetV2 architecture is based on an inverted residual structure. MobileNetV2 uses lightweight depthwise convolutions that makes more possible to use MobileNetV2 on mobile devices. Authors also describe efficient ways of applying these models to object detection.

Images of 2 different sizes were used as input data. Images of different sizes are considered for estimating performance on batches with wide range of sizes. Particular image sizes were selected because of used image dataset. As can be seen from the table, the models differ in the number of parameters. The parameters of a neural network are the weights of the connections, that are need to be learned during the training stage.

The Adam algorithm [13] with learning rate equal to 0.001 was used as a training method for each model of neural network. The mean squared error was used as the error function. Original dataset consists of 71 images. To be able to conduct tests with a large batch size, a sample of 10,000,000 images was augmented using upper mentioned 71 images. Since the purpose of this work was not to study the issues of achieved accuracy, only a duplication and scaling of images were used for augmentation.

Testing was carried out by running the scripts developed on Python. Through the parameters of the scripts, it is possible to set the number of learning epochs, the number of processes on a single node, the total number of processes, the number of GPUs used, size of the batch on a single process. Execution time of every script is measures for different configurations. Mobilenet V2 model was tested on two modes: serial implementation on one node and parallel implementation on several nodes. To study the effect of the characteristics of the HPC systems under consideration on the models run time, we limited ourselves to the consideration of only one learning epoch.

4 Experimental Results on Polus

4.1 Serial Implementation of Mobilenet V2

The results produced on Polus are shown on Fig. 3. Tests on 1 GPU failed at batch size >7 due to the lack of GPU memory. Tests on 2 GPUs failed at batch size >14 due to the lack of GPU memory.

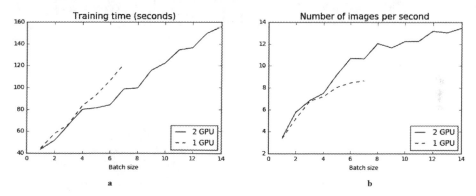

Fig. 3. a. Training time of the one epoch on one node of the cluster Polus with 1 and 2 GPUs depending on the batch size. **b.** Number of images processed per second on one Polus node with one or two GPUs depending on batch size.

It can be seen from the Fig. 3a that the training time grows as the batch size increases. At batch sizes of up to 4 the inclusion of a new GPU does not affect the run time. However, the batch size for one GPU is limited to 7. Such behaviour has been reported by other researches in their work on identifying the optimal batch size. It is worth keeping it in mind in further researches on learning parallelism.

Figure 3b shows the same results in terms of number of images processed per second.

4.2   Parallel Implementation of DNN-Models on Polus

The following remark should be made prior to reviewing the research results. The term "parallelism" will be always used hereinafter that, according to the supplied modules, should nevertheless be interpreted as distributed training.

Parallel implementation of Mobilenet V2. Figures 4a and b compare the run time per one learning epoch of Mobilenet V2 at a different number of processes for batch size 12 and 24. Figures 4c and d show the same results recalculated in terms of images processed per second. It should be specifically noted that we use a cumulative batch size value for all batches distributed on different nodes. Note that for both batch sizes (12 and 24) the best option for number of images per seconds is 4 processes with two GPUs (31 and 36, respectively).

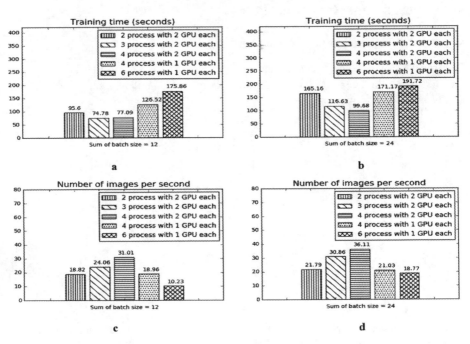

Fig. 4. Training time of Mobilenet V2 on different configurations **a.** batch size: 12. **b.** batch size: 24; Number of images processed per second for the Mobilenet V2 on different configurations **c.** batch size: 12. **d.** batch size: 24.

Parallel Implementation of VGG16. Figure 5a shows the run time per one learning epoch at a different number of processes for batch size 24. Figures 5b and c present the number of images processed per second at a different number of processes for batch sizes 12 and 24 respectively.

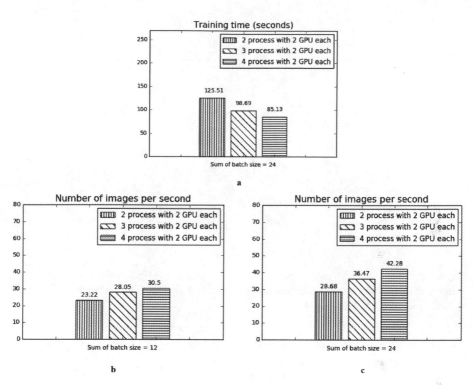

Fig. 5. Training time of VGG16 on different configurations **a.** batch size: 24; Number of images processed per second for the VGG16 on different configurations **b.** batch size: 12 **c.** batch size: 24

Parallel Implementation of VGG16 (640 × 480). Figure 6a compares the run time at a different number of processes for batch size 24. Figures 6b and c show the same results recalculated in terms of number of images processed per second for batch sizes of 12 and 24. Note that for this model the number of images processed per second increases with the number of processes used. Note that for this model, the number of images processed per second increases with an increase in the number of processes used, but at the same time it is less than the similar result obtained for the previous model. This effect can be explained by the greater complexity of the VGG16 model compared to Mobilenet V2.

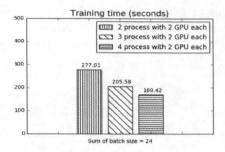

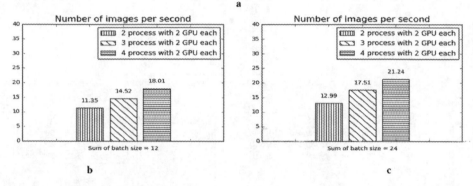

Fig. 6. Training time of VGG16 (640 × 480) on different configurations **a.** batch size: 24; Number of images processed per second for the VGG16 (640 × 480) on different configurations **b.** batch size: 12 **c.** batch size: 24

Parallel Implementation of SqueezeNet. SqueezeNet is the simplest in terms of the number of parameters of the models considered. Figure 7a compares the run time at different number of processes for batch size 24. Figures 7b and c show the same results recalculated in terms number of images processed per second for batch sizes of 12 and 24. As for the case of the VGG16 model, for this model the number of processed images per second increases with an increase in the number of processes used and an increase in the batch size.

Overall Comparison of Results for Polus Cluster. In all the performed tests, the best results were demonstrated in the parallel structure where we launch one process on each host and assign 2 GPUs to each process. The maximum run time was demonstrated by neural network VGG16 (640 × 480). Figure 8 shows the run time for the networks concerned.

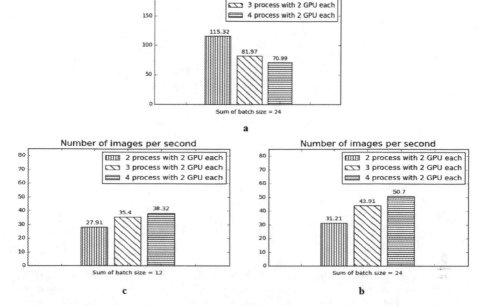

Fig. 7. Training time of SqueezeNet on different configurations **a.** batch size: 24; Number of images processed per second for the SqueezeNet on different configurations **b.** batch size: 12 **c.** batch size: 24

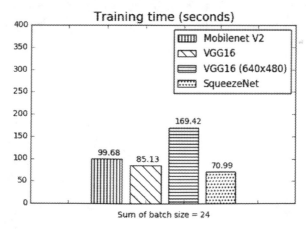

Fig. 8. Training time of considered networks at the batch size of 24 for 4 processes using 2 GPUs (1 Master + 3 Slaves).

5 Experiment Results on Lomonosov-2

5.1 Serial Implementation of Mobilenet V2

Test results are shown in Figs. 9a and b.

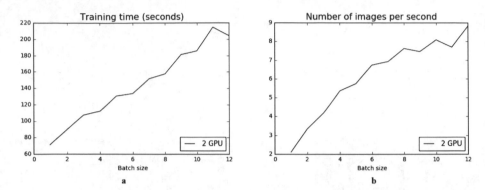

Fig. 9. a. Training time of the one epoch on one node of the Lomonosov-2 with 2 GPUs depending on the batch size. **b.** Number of images processed per second on one node of the Lomonosov-2 with 2 GPUs depending on batch size.

It can be seen from the figure that the training time grows as the batch size increases. For the batch size equal to 1 this time is approximately 71 s. A similar test for Polus resulted in about 44 s. Better time results (almost 2 times as much) may be due to NVLink communication between Power 8-based GPUs, despite the fact that the test was run using 2 similar accelerators.

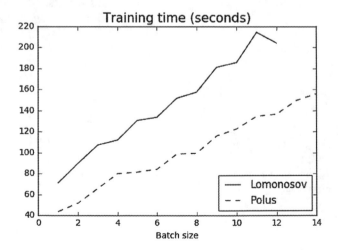

Fig. 10. Training time for Mobilenet V2 depending on batch size for Lomonosov-2 and Polus.

Note that on Lomonosov-2, the out_of_memory error occurred at batch size 13. This problem was not present on Polus. It should be noted that in a standard network, the correlation between time and batch size is different. As we have already seen, the time for a standard network goes down. Figure 10 shows charts of the run time for Mobilenet V2 depending on batch size for Lomonosov-2 and Polus. The figure shows that this time is consistently lower for Polus.

5.2   Parallel Implementation

Parallel Implementation of Mobilenet V2. Figures 11a and b show number of images processed per second for Mobilenet V2 at batch sizes 12 and 24 for different number of processes and GPUs. It can be seen from the figures that, in general, options with batch size 24 show better results in comparison with size 12. The best result (30 images per second) was obtained for 3 processes with 2 GPUs each. This is less than the similar result of 36, obtained for this model on the Polus.

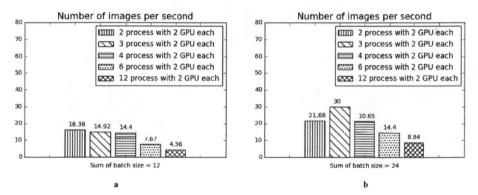

Fig. 11. a. Number of images per second for Mobilenet V2 at batch size 12. **b.** Number of images per second for Mobilenet V2 at batch size 24.

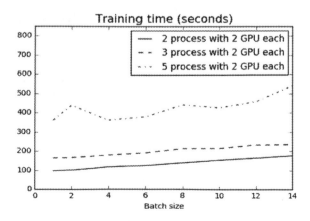

Fig. 12. Training time for VGG16 depending on batch size for a different number of processes.

Parallel Implementation of VGG16. Test results for VGG16 network are shown in Figs. 12 and 13. It can be seen from Fig. 12 that the training time for VGG16 is the best for the case of 2 processes (1 Master, 1 Slave).

Parallel Implementation of VGG16 (640 × 480). The test results for the VGG16 (640 × 480) model at Lomonosov-2 are shown in the Fig. 14. As in the previous case (VGG16 models), the number of processed images per second decreases with an increase in the number of processes used, which can be explained by the overhead associated with transferring data between processes. However, we did not observe this effect in the case of the Polus.

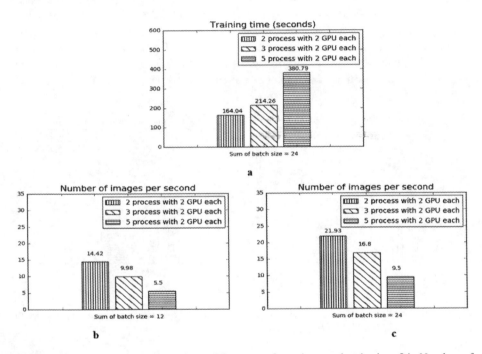

Fig. 13. Training time of VGG16 on different configurations **a.** batch size: 24; Number of images processed per second for the VGG16 on different configurations **b.** batch size: 12 **c.** batch size: 24

Parallel Implementation of SqueezeNet. Training time of the SqueezeNet model over batch size from 1 to 14 on one process is shown in the Fig. 15. As can be seen from the figure, the best option is 2 processes with a 2 GPU each.

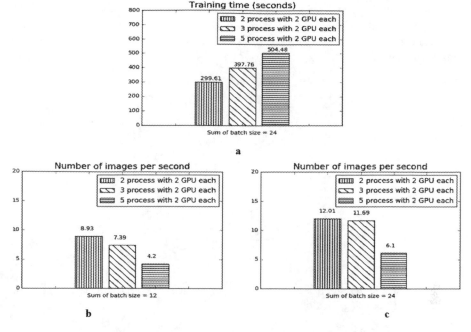

Fig. 14. Training time of VGG16 (640 × 480) on different configurations **a.** batch size: 24; Number of images processed per second for the VGG16 (640 × 480) on different configurations **b.** batch size: 12 **c.** batch size: 24

Number of images processed per second for the SqueezeNet model on different configurations of batch size (12 and 24) are shown in Fig. 16. The case of 2 processes with 2 GPU each is also the best, both for a batch size of 12 and 24.

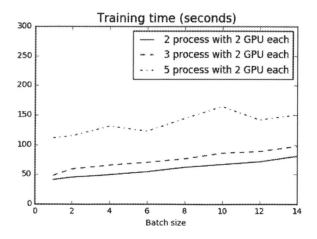

Fig. 15. Training time of the SqueezeNet over batch size on one process.

Overall Comparison of Various Architectures for 5 Processes on Lomonosov-2.
Training time of all models for a package size of 30 is presented in Fig. 17. As can be seen from the figure, the training time increases with an increase in the number of model parameters.

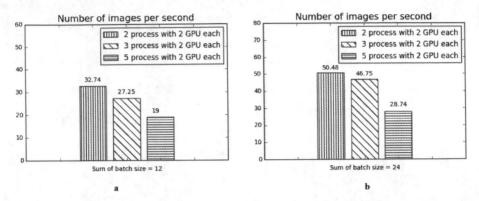

Fig. 16. Number of images processed per second for the SqueezeNet on different configurations **a**. batch size: 12 **b**. batch size: 24

5.3   Comparison of SqueezeNet for Batch Size 24: Lomonosov-2 – Polus

Training time of the SqueezeNet for the batch size of 24 on Lomonosov-2 and Polus is shown in Fig. 18a and b. The best case for the training time is the 4-process case for Polus (the training time is 71 s), which almost coincides with the 2-process version for Lomonosov-2. For the larger VGG16 model presented in Fig. 19a and b, the same trend persists, but the difference in training time becomes almost 2 times larger. Polus is better than Lomonosov-2 for this case.

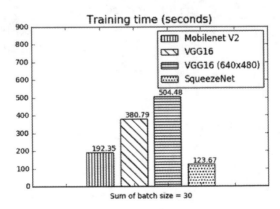

Fig. 17. Comparison of the execution time for different neural net architectures for 5 processes with 2 GPUs (1 Master + 4 Slaves).

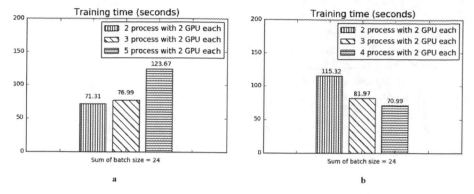

Fig. 18. a. Training time of the SqueezeNet for the batch size of 24 on Lomonosov-2. **b.** Training time of the SqueezeNet for the batch size of 24 on Polus.

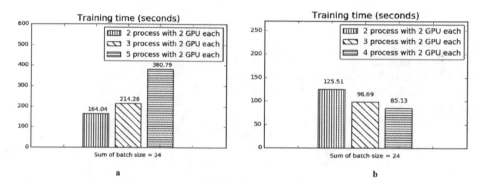

Fig. 19. a. Training time of the VGG16 for the batch size of 24 on Lomonosov-2. **b.** Training time of the VGG16 for the batch size of 24 on Polus.

6   Conclusion

Tested DNN architectures are widely used by researchers and engineers for solving image classification and detection problems. Selected image sizes are common for many practical tasks. So the obtained results could be directly used by science community for application of CNNs in image recognition area. The experimental study of performance for supercomputer Lomonosov-2 and high performance cluster Polus has been fulfilled on deep learning task. The obtained results allow us to make the following conclusions.

Cluster Polus demonstrates higher calculation performance on deep learning tasks. The advantage in the execution speed is experimentally proved both for serial implementation (training on one node) and for parallel implementation (distributed training). Performance gain becomes noticeable in case of deep neural networks of larger size. Cluster Polus executes training with larger batches. It is important for increasing training efficiency. In this regard, the use of cluster Polus for deep learning tasks is preferable to the supercomputer Lomonosov-2.

The optimal configuration of the cluster Polus for all tested deep architectures consists of four processes and two GPUs each.

The implementation of distributed training on high-performance clusters with the use of the supplied software modules will be feasible, provided that training sets are big. Configurations with one computer node and multiple GPU accelerators proved to be optimal in terms of time input. There is scaling potential as the number of GPUs per node grows. One of the explanations for the effect observed might be that the implemented training functions were initially meant to be used on multiple GPUs.

HPCs and supercomputers offer extensive capabilities for neural information processing, especially in the transition to big data operations. This requires effective parallel algorithms.

References

1. Specifications of supercomputer Lomonosov-2. https://parallel.ru/cluster/lomonosov2.html
2. Specifications of cluster Polus. http://hpc.cs.msu.su/polus
3. Ben-Nun, T., Hoefler, T.: Demystifying parallel and distributed deep learning: an in-depth concurrency analysis. arXiv:1802.09941 (2018)
4. Liu, L., Wu, Y., Wei, W., Cao, W., Sahin, S., Zhang, Q.: Benchmarking deep learning frameworks: design considerations, metrics and beyond. In: 2018 IEEE 38th International Conference on Distributed Computing Systems (ICDCS), Vienna, pp. 1258–1269 (2018). https://doi.org/10.1109/icdcs.2018.00125
5. Zhang, X., Wang, Y., Shi, W.: pCAMP: performance comparison of machine learning packages on the edges. In: USENIX Workshop on Hot Topics in Edge Computing (HotEdge 2018) (2018)
6. Asaadi, H., Chapman, B.: Comparative study of deep learning framework in HPC environments. In: 2017 New York Scientific Data Summit (NYSDS), pp. 1–7 (2017)
7. Tato, A.G.: Evaluation of machine learning fameworks on finis terrae II. arXiv:1801.04546 (2018)
8. Mericas, A., et al.: IBM POWER8 performance features and evaluation. IBM J. Res. Dev. **59**, 6:1–6:10 (2015)
9. PyTorch. https://pytorch.org
10. Sandler, M., Howard, A., Zhu, M., Zhmoginov, A.: MobileNetV2: inverted residuals and linear bottlenecks. In: 2018 IEEE Conference on Computer Vision and Pattern Recognition (CVPR), pp. 4510–4520 (2018). arXiv:1801.04381
11. Simonyan, K.: Very deep convolutional networks for large-scale image recognition. arXiv: 1409.1556 (2014)
12. Iandola, F.N., Han, S., Moskewicz, M.W., Ashraf, K., Dally, W.J.: SqueezeNet: AlexNet-level accuracy with 50x fewer parameters and <0.5 MB model size. arXiv:1602.07360 (2016)
13. Kingma, D., Jimmy, B.: Adam: a method for stochastic optimization. In: Contribution to International Conference on Learning Representations, San Diego, 7–9 May 2015 (2015)

Artificial Intelligence Problems in Mathematical Modeling

Valery Il'in[1,2]([✉])

[1] Institute of Computational Mathematics and Mathematical Geophysics SBRAS,
Novosibirsk, Russia
ilin@sscc.ru
[2] Novosibirsk State University, Novosibirsk, Russia

Abstract. The artificial intelligence problems in creating the integrated computational environment (ICE) for the mathematical modeling on the modern supercomputers are considered. The mathematical tasks to be solved present the direct and inverse interdisciplinary problems which are described by the systems of partial differential and/or integral equations in the multi-dimensional computational domains with real complicated multiscale geometry and contrast material properties. The conception of ICE consists in developing the instrumental media to support all main stages of large scale computational experiments, with a long life cycle of the products. The technical requirements for ICE include the flexible extension of the mathematical models and methods, the adaption to evolution of the computer platforms, the reusing external program products, and coordinated participation in the project of the different groups of developers. The objectives of intelligent tools consist in automatic construction of algorithms as well as generating and executing the applied software packages for the end users in particular domains.

Keywords: Artificial intelligence · Integrated computational environment · Mathematical modeling · Numerical methods · Ontology of designing · Knowledge base · Automatic construction of algorithms

1 Introduction

The dramatic quantitative and qualitative growth of supercomputers, which in the coming years should mark the emergence of exaflops machine, as well as the predicted breakthrough in the advanced countries in all kinds of scientific and technological spheres means not only the transition to a principally new level of obtaining fundamental and applied knowledge, but also their application in all areas of human activity. A special role in the progress is given to mathematical modeling, which, on the one hand, holds an intermediate position between theoretical and experimental scientific studies, and on the other - becomes an indispensable attribute of the study and/or control of production, natural, and

Supported by the RFBR grants N 16-29-15122 ofi-m and N 18-01-00295.

V. Voevodin and S. Sobolev (Eds.): RuSCDays 2019, CCIS 1129, pp. 505–516, 2019.
https://doi.org/10.1007/978-3-030-36592-9_41

social processes. The principal point here is to solve on a supercomputer such supertasks, which in terms of mathematical complexity and resource intensity could not be imagined a decade ago.

As is noted in [1] the key problem of the world computing community is the development in a short time of huge amounts of the new generation of software, whose creation is possible only with the extensive cooperation. With regard to scientific application software this means the transition from conventional problem-oriented software packages of the ANSYS, FeniCS [2,3] type, libraries of universally or method-oriented algorithms (see, for example, NETLIB [4] or MKL INTEL [5]) and specialized tools, to integrated computational environments (ICE) designed to support the computational stages of a large-scale supercomputer experiment. Such examples are the projects DUNE, INMOST and BSM, see [6–8].

In general, the models of the processes and phenomena under consideration are interdisciplinary direct and inverse multidimensional initial-boundary value problems (IBVPs) described by the systems of differential and/or integral equations of different types in classical or generalized formulations, for which the real source data are characterized by complex multi-scale geometry of computational domains with piecewise smooth multi-connected boundary surfaces and contrast material properties. The current requirements to the accuracy and resolution of the applied mathematical models impose strict conditions on the stability, convergence, conservative and robustness of rapidly developing computational methods.

With all the variety of mathematical problems and algorithms, the organization of large-scale computational experiments is carried out by clearly structured technological stages: geometric and functional modeling associated with the description of the initial data of the problem to be solved, the generation of spatial-temporal adaptive grids, i.e. discretization of continuous initial statements, approximation of given differential and/or integral equations, the solution of the resulting systems of linear or nonlinear algebraic grid problems, optimization approaches for the inverse problems with constrained minimization of objective functionals, post-processing and visualization of the results of calculation, computational process control and decision-making according to the results of modeling, [9]. All the described stages are implemented by the corresponding rather autonomous method-oriented software subsystems, which can be developed independently and interact through the formed data structure. (geometric, functional, grid, algebraic, etc.) in the coordinated formats, which can be converted and interact with the external word. Each subsystem present the integrated program environment in the own methodological domain and the whole their totally represent the functional content of BSM.

In the last decades, despite the active dynamics of development of multiprocessor computing systems (MPS), their architecture can be considered fairly stable and represent heterogeneous clusters of multifunctional nodes with distributed memory, each of which contains several multi-core processors (CPU) with a shared hierarchical memory, as well as graphics accelerators such as

GPGPU or INTEL Phi. The scalable parallelization of such MPS is achieved by means of hybrid programming with the passing of messages between different MPI - processes, organization of multithread computing using OpenMP systems, as well as operations vectorization by using AVX system. A typical situation is also the solution of problems in remote access via the Internet to a large general access supercomputer center based on the cloud computing.

It is important to note that now the world has a huge number of application and system products, both public and commercial, representing an invaluable intellectual potential that can and should be effectively used in new developments which should save many hundreds of man-years of programming. The creation of the ICE is of multi-purpose insignificance, and its architecture is defined from the following conceptual technological requirements: flexible expansion of a set of considered models and the applied algorithms, adaptation to evolution of supercomputer platforms, effective reusing of external software products, high modern mathematical characteristics and performance of computing methods and technologies, the coordinated participation of various groups of developers, intelligent output and output interfaces for the comfortable work of the end users with various professional backgrounds.

These characteristics of the development are designed for a long life cycle of ICE and its reasonable for demand various industries, which in general should ensure its competitiveness and economic success, which is an important factor, because of the global nature of the project.

The use of ICE is oriented in two directions. The first one is the automation of algorithms construction and their mapping on the architecture of a super-computer, aimed at a significant increase in the programming productivity. More specifically, this part of the activity is the development of the functional content (models, methods and technologies) of BSM. The second direction and purpose of ICE is the automated design of the high-performance applied software packages or complexes with high-quality execution characteristics comparable to professional compilers or operating systems.

The creation of scientific ICE places high demands on the level of intelligence of the project, and the concept of its integration actually means the transition from artisan to industrial design and implementation of large applications, whose continued existence implies an active support, development and operation, which also involves a variety of user-friendly interfaces. Note that a number of intellectual issues of the methodology of mathematical modeling and creation of a new type of software for it are considered in [10,11].

This paper is constructed as follows. Paragraph 2 describes the tasks and approaches to solving the problem of intellectualization of the main technological stages of modeling. The third section contains the analysis of various methodologies and tools for of implementation of cognitive and ontological principles in the framework of ICE, and in conclusion discusses the current open issues of cognitive processes in basic research and optimal control in applied fields.

2 Features of Intellectualization of Technological Stages of Modeling

With all the variety of problems of mathematical knowledge mining, they are structurally decomposed in steps of fairly well-established methodologies.

2.1 Tasks of Geometric and Functional Modeling

The first stage of the computational experiment, of course, is statement of the task, preprocessing and analysis of the initial data. For a direct initial-boundary value problem, the description includes the equation to be solved, the computational domain, boundary and initial conditions:

$$Lu = f(x, t), \quad x \in \bar{\Omega} = \Omega \bigcup \Gamma, \quad 0 < t \le T < \infty, \tag{1}$$

$$lu = g(x, t), \quad x \in \Gamma, \quad u(x, 0) = u^0(x). \tag{2}$$

Here, the unknown solution u is a vector function, L is a differential and/or an integral operator (possibly of the matrix type) defined in the computational domain Ω with the boundary Γ, x and t – spatial and temporal independent variables, l is the operator of boundary conditions, and given functions $f(x, t)$ and $g(x, t)$ can also depend on the original solution in a nonlinear way. The computational domain (bounded or unbounded) can consist of various subdomains Ω_j with the corresponding inner or outer boundary segments Γ_j^i, Γ_j^e:

$$\bar{\Omega} = \bigcup \bar{\Omega}_j, \ \Gamma = \Gamma^e \bigcup \Gamma^i, \ \Gamma^i = \bigcup \Gamma_{j, k}^i = \bigcup (\bar{\Omega}_j \bigcap \bar{\Omega}_k). \tag{3}$$

It is important to note that different types of equations can be solved in different subdomains, and different boundary conditions can be set on different surface segments.

Formal descriptions (1)–(3) cover a huge class of mathematical modeling problems, including systems of Maxwell's equations for electromagnetism, the Navier-Stokes equations – for hydro-gasdynamics, the Lame equations – for elasticity, Darcy equations – for the filtration problems, etc. In addition, initial statements can be given in classical or generalized (variational) formulations.

On the other hand, similar mathematical concepts may relate to completely different application areas or industry sectors: energy, engineering, biology, geophysics, chemistry, ecology, medicine, agriculture, etc.

In real cases the ultimate goal of the research consists in solving not direct but inverse problems, which means, for example, the identification of the model parameters, the optimization of some processes, etc. The universal optimization approach to solving the inverse problems is formulated as minimization of the objective functional

$$\Phi_0(u(x, t, p_{opt})) = \min_{p} \Phi_0(u(x, t, p)), \tag{4}$$

which depends on the solution u and on some vector parameter p which is included in the input data of the direct problem. The constrained optimization is carried out under the linear conditions

$$p_k^{min} \leq p_k \leq p_k^{max}, \quad k = 1, \ldots, m_1, \tag{5}$$

and/or under the functional inequalities

$$\Phi_l u(x, t, p) \leq \delta_l, \quad l = 1, \ldots, m_2, \quad p = \{p_k\} \in \mathcal{R}^m, \quad m = m_1 + m_2. \tag{6}$$

There are two main kinds of the optimization problems. The first one consists in the local minimization. This means that we look for a single minimum of the objective function in the vicinity of the initial guess $p^0 = (p_1^0, \ldots, p_m^0)$. The second problem presents the global minimization, i. e. the search for all extremal points of $\Phi_0(p)$, which requires the solution of many direct problems.

In the recent decades, such a scientific direction has been developed dramatically fast in many applications, based on the so-called surrogate optimization (see [12] and the literature therein). The last mentioned approach corresponds to the situation, when the run time for computing one value of the objective function is too expensive and requires several hours or more. In such a case, the design, or planning of numerical experiments is very important, as well as using special methods for approximation of the investigated functionals.

As can be seen even at first glance at formulas (1)–(6), the mathematical formulation of high-tech problem is a complex logical structure. The initial information is divided into the two main groups - functional and geometric. The first one includes the types of equations to be solved, representations of their coefficients, boundary and initial conditions, descriptions of minimized functionals and constraints for inverse problems, etc. The geometric data must uniquely describe the computational domain, including its subdomains, boundary fragments, edges (surface intersections), and nodes that are the intersection points of the edges.

The initial information should first of all be tested for its completeness and consistency, for example, to meet the conditions of existence, uniqueness and correctness of the solutions, as well as for the presence of any features or singularities that must be taken into account when using numerical algorithms.

It is obvious that the in-depth study of specific processes and phenomena is an important experimental study with multiple calculations and variation of the initial data of the problem. This gives rise to various problems of geometric modeling of functional objects. In particular, the relevant areas of analysis arise in the inverse problems related to the optimization of geometric and logical configurations, metric transformation, and discrete exterior differential forms, isogeometric analysis, etc., see [13, 14]. Note that the end result of this stage should be interconnected geometric and functional data structures (GDS and FDS), completely and unambiguously determining the mathematical problem and specific source data for its solution.

2.2   The Intellectialization of the Grid Generation

Based on geometric and functional data structures we can realize the grid generation, which presents an important and resources-consuming stage of the numerical solution of the multi-dimensional problems. In the world software market, there are many available (free of charge) and expensive commercial codes, but the problem of constructing optimal or even "good" 3-D grids in the complicated computational domain is far enough from its final solution. Moreover, it is not easy to define the concept of an optimal or a good mesh, and there are many different quantitative characteristics of the grid quality.

Formally, the mesh data structure is similar to the GDS and includes the following objects: the grid computational domain $\bar{\Omega}^h = \Omega^h \bigcup \Gamma^h$ with the boundary Γ^h, the grid subdomains $\bar{\Omega}_k^h = \Omega_k^h \bigcup \Gamma_k^h$ with the corresponding faces Γ_k^h, the grid edges E_p^h and the nodes P_q^h. The conventional approach to the discretization of the computational domain consists in constructing an adaptive grid. This means that the vertices P_q, the edges E_p and the surfaces Γ_k of the computational domain Ω should coincide with the corresponding grid nodes P_q^h, the grid edges E_p^h and the faces Γ_k^h.

There are many kinds of the grids with different types of finite elements, with various distributions of the meshsteps h, local refinement and multi-grid approaches included. Also, there are a lot of algorithms for the mesh generation, which are based on the frontal principles, on conformal or quasi-conformal transformations on the differential geometry and various metrics, see review in [15]. In general, the grid computational domain consists of the grid subdomains which can have different types of the finite volumes, and grids in different subdomains can be constructed by different algorithms.

In a sense, the grids considered present a two-level hyper-graph at the macro- and micro-, or mesh, levels. In the technological sense, the final result of the grid generator should be the mesh data structure (MDS) with full mapping of the input geometric and functional data onto the micro (mesh) level. In particular, all inter-connections between grid objects should be strictly defined. Also, the affiliation of each finite volume T_j^h, grid face Γ_k^h into the corresponding subdomains Ω_k and the boundary surface segment Γ_p must be given.

The principles of constructing the library DELAUNAY are described in [16]. In fact, it presents the integrated instrumental media for supporting a considered class of problems, based on original algorithms, as well as on re-using the external codes (there are popular free available mesh generators NETGEN, GMESH, TETGEN, for example). In the world "grid developer community", there are several popular grid formats, and the subsystem DELAUNAY should include the corresponding data converters with the MDS. At this stage one of important operations includes the decomposition of the grid computational domain into grid subdomains, when the number of mesh points is too large.

There are many numerical approaches to construct the qualitative or optimal grids, but, in general, these mathematical questions are open yet. Also, we do not consider here resource-consuming problems of generating the dynamic meshes which are changed during the computational process.

Formally, the grid can be presented as an indirect graph, and many useful software tools for graph transformation (METIS or its parallel version parMETIS, for example) can be used efficiently for mesh generation and its improvement.

As can be seen from the above algorithmic aspects, the generator of "good" grids must solve many highly intelligent problems. The quality criteria for the discretization of the computational domain have many quantitative characteristics, on which the accuracy, reliability, resource consuming and efficiency of modeling largely depend. An important property is the adaptability of the grid to the geometric and material features of the mathematical formulation. In this case, the points-vertices of the boundary must be nodes in the mesh, and macro-edges and macro-facets of the subdomain should be well approximated by the relevant grid objects. Of great importance is the refinement of the grid in the vicinity of the singularity of the solution associated with the features of the boundary of the domains or coefficients of the original equation, whose nature can be determined based on a priori or a posteriori analysis.

2.3   Automation of Approximation Procedures

It can be said that this stage carries the greatest theoretical load, since it is here where the orders of accuracy of the approximate structures and spectral properties of the resulting systems of algebraic equations are laid, which basically determine the efficiency and the robustness of a constructed computational model. The original data for the approximation of the initial boundary value problem is the interconnected grid, geometric and functional data structures (MSD, GSD, FSD) formed at the previous stages.

The most popular approaches are finite difference, finite volume, finite element, and discontinuity Galerkin methods (FDM, FVM, FEM, and DGM, see [9] and reference therein for example). The advanced theoretical and applied mathematical results have profound foundations and technologies for constructing and justification of high order accuracy numerical schemes for complicated IBVPs with real data. The implementation of such algorithms on the non-structured grids is not simple, and the tools for automatic construction of the scheme are very useful for such problems (so called computer algebra tools are implemented in the program package FEniCS [3] and the language PYTHON, for example). A very powerful approach here is based on the element technology with computing the local matrices and assembling the global matrix, which provide the "natural" parallelization and easy programming of the algorithms.

The concept of the integrated operating environment for the methods of approximation of the multi-dimensional IBVP is presented in the library CHEBYSHEV [17] based on original algorithms and re-using the external software. The end result of this subsystem consists in the algebraic data structure (ADS) which presents the original problem to be solved at a discrete level. To provide the necessary accuracy the obtained systems of linear algebraic equations (SLAEs) should have very large dimensions (10^8 and more) and sparse matrices. To save such systems in the memory, the conventional compressed formats are used, Compressed Sparse Row (CSR), for example. For the big degrees of freedom, the distributed versions of the CSR are used, i.e. a matrix is divided into block rows, and each one is placed in the corresponding MPI-process.

The concept of the library "approximators" as a universal tool environment for different types of original equations for different types of grids and methods of construction of discrete approximations, unlike other computational stages, has no analogues and allows the use of modern intelligent tools for automation of analytical tools with complex formula transformations to build algorithms.

2.4   Automatic Construction of the Algebraic Algorithms

The most resource-consuming stage of mathematical modeling is a numerical solution of large sparse SLAEs, because the volume of arithmetic operations grows nonlinearly, when the number of unknowns increases. Fortunately, the computational algebra is one of the most progressive parts of numerical mathematics, both in algorithmic and in technological senses (see [18–20] and the literature, cited therein). In particular, there are many applied software packages and libraries with algebraic solvers which are free accessible (with parallel algorithms in PETSc and PARMS included). The main approaches to solve large sparse SLAEs are based on the preconditioned iterative methods in the Krylov subspaces. The scalable parallelism is provided in the framework of the two-level iterative domain decomposition methods (DDM) by means of hybrid programming with using MPI tools for the distributed memory of the heterogeneous cluster MPS, multi-thread computing on the shared memory of the multi-core CPUs, vectorization of operations by means of the AVX system, as well as fast computation on the graphic accelerators (GPGPU or Intel Phi).

The grid computational domain is decomposed into grid subdomains with parametrized overlapping and different interface conditions which realize some Poincare - Steklov operators on the interior boundaries. Algebraically, the external iterative process presents the multi-preconditioned generalized minimal residual (GMRES) or a semi-conjugate residual (SCR) algorithm, based on the parallel block Schwarz - Jacobi method, coarse grid correction, deflation and/or augmentation procedures, restarted least squares approaches, and an advanced low-rank approximation of the original matrix. At each external iteration, solving the auxiliary SLAEs in subdomains is implemented synchronously by means of direct or iterative algorithms, with various internal preconditioning matrices (for example, defined by incomplete LU - factorization, Alternating Direction Implicit Schemes, Cimmino method, etc.). Here, it is very important to provide the balancing domain decomposition and minimization of the communication time, by means of buffering data to be transfered between subdomains.

The described parallel methods are realized in the framework of the library KRYLOV [19] which presents the integrated algebraic environment, based on the original algorithms and efficient re-using the external products. The robust matrix-vector operations and other algebraic tools from the library MKL Intel are applied in KRYLOV in a productive manner.

If the original continuous problem is nonlinear, then after its discretization we will have a system of nonlinear algebraic equations (SNLAEs). In these cases, the quasi-linearization process is applied, based on the Newtonian type of iterations, and at each of such steps the linear equations are solved.

Of course, the high performance and scalable parallelism are the most important for very resource consuming tasks which are presented by interdisciplinary inverse problems which require the multiply solutions of large direct problems. Some technological approaches for this issues are presented in [21].

As can be seen from the presented review of the modeling stages, the computational process is a complex scheme, since in general, the calculations include multiple nested cycles with modification of the initial data, with reconstruction of grids by recalculation of approximations, with numerical integration by time steps for non-stationary problems, with the solution of systems of nonlinear and linear algebraic equations. Therefore, the planning and control of a machine experiment is also an intellectual problem, which is based on the analysis of the preliminary results of the calculation.

As for parallel post-processing and visualization of the numerical results, this resource consuming stage can be realized by means of existing power tools (the cluster version of PARAVIEW [22], for example).

3   Methods and Tools of Artificial Intelligence for Mathematical Modeling

Recent decades have been marked by major scientific and practical achievements in the field of artificial intelligence. Well-known a success means in computer chess, the game of go and in other games, in robotics, in neural networks, in pattern recognition, in machine translation of texts, etc. Against this background, there are almost no breakthroughs in programming methods for modeling, despite the fact that computers were originally invented specifically for large calculations. Although the algorithmic languages of programming and compilers, operating systems, various instrumental tools, numerous applied developments are actively implemented, they are mainly focused on achieving the high code performance on the MPS. As a result, with a rapid growth of computer performance, there appears a global programming crisis, when the growth of developers' productivity is far behind the computer evolution rate. Obviously, this situation requires a change in the programming paradigm, primarily through the integration of development and intellectualization of technologies.

To date, there are quite many published works on semantic modeling [23] based on the apparatus of mathematical logic, and on the ontology of designing [24–27] based on cognitive principles, on the methodology of active knowledge [28] and on many aspects of deep machine learning and intelligent technologies that could become the foundation for creating a knowledge base on mathematical models and algorithms within an integrated computing environment, which will allow, according to the figurative expression by Kleppe [29], moving from "paleo-informatics" to "neo-informatics" in mathematical modeling.

Note that the methodology of creating the integrated instrumental environments for cloud technologies has been actively developed in the Irkutsk scientific school of programming for many years, see [30]. A large amount of basic mathematical knowledge, including symbolic calculations, is incorporated in the well-known Mathematica and Maple systems, as well as in the Python [31] language and in the multi-user Matlab [32] tools. The use of meta-programming components with C^{++} [33] templates, as well as "factories" of problem-oriented languages for scientific research studies (Domestic Specific Languages, [29]) can significantly increase productivity. As for the extremely relevant mathematical knowledge base for the mathematical models, computational methods and technologies, here a good information and methodological basis is the project ALGO-WIKI [34].

The intellectualization of the ICE seems to be non-alternative and the highest priority software for a new generation of mathematical modeling on supercomputers. We emphasize that the project of the type MegaScience does not cancel the individual programming and provides a comfortable environment with numerous tools, which greatly increases the professional specialization and avoids duplication of works. No less important is another focus of the intelligent ICE, namely, on the formation of friendly interfaces for the end users, which can be divided into the following categories: research scientists and production engineers. The first can be attributed to both theorists and experimenters. The supercomputer modeling becomes an indispensable tool for obtaining the new fundamental or applied knowledge from any scientific field. As for practitioners, they ideally get virtual, or digital twins for their objects of activities, with which they can carry out or optimization of design, or planning, or operating of their processes. In fact, in such a symbiosis, a person receives an indispensable and reliable assistant for decision making, but not a competitor or rival as some futurologists write about it. And what is very important in the social sense, we will obtain a wide class of the new professions with high supercomputer skills.

To make such a picture of the world a reality, the computing community will have to perform a huge amount of work that should unite specialists of the widest profile on the foundation of mathematization and artificial intelligence.

From the professional point of view, the intelligent software components of ICE can be divided into the three parts. The first one is oriented to mathematicians and application programmers who are responsible for the performance and automatic construction of algorithms on the supercomputer architectures. The second part would provide the flexible internal and external interfaces to interact between subsystems of ICE and other products (CAD, CAE, CAM systems included), as well as arrangement for the users with various skills. The last but the least intelligent tool concern the supports the own life cycle which requires of different system components to maintenance and further development of the integrated computational environment for the above considered stages of mathematical modeling.

4   Conclusion

In our paper, we consider the problems of artificial intelligence and mathematical modeling, which are separately studied quite actively, but have not yet become objects of the joint targeted research. Together with the trends in the use of the ICE for mathematical modeling, this leads to a project of a national scale that requires serious organizational decisions, infrastructure and appropriate investments, see [35]. But this is the case when the goal justifies the means. We must say that not every country can form such a comprehensive mega-science project, but the Russian surviving scientific schools can make such a breakthrough. It is important to note that the predicted revolutionary technological progress in the world will lead to a widening the gap between the advanced and developing countries, and therefore our historical mission is to take a place in the business class of the new Noah's ark departing for the future.

We just discuss the problem statement and the main technological ideas on the creating the intelligent instrumental media for the modern supercomputer simulation. Here many architecture principles, the structure solutions, integration problems, and the implementation issues still present the open questions and the best topics for future research.

References

1. IESP. www.exascale.org/iesp
2. ANSYS. www.ansys.com
3. FEniCS. http://fenicsproject.org
4. Netlib. http://netlib.org
5. Intel R Mathematical Kernel Library. http://software.intel.com/en-us/intel-mkl
6. DUNE. http://www.dune-project.org
7. INMOST: A toolkit for distributed mathematical modeling. www.inmost.org
8. Il'in, V.P.: The conception, requirements and structure of the integrated computational environment. In: Voevodin, V., Sobolev, S. (eds.) RuSCDays 2018. CCIS, vol. 965, pp. 653–665. Springer, Cham (2019). https://doi.org/10.1007/978-3-030-05807-4_56
9. Il'in, V.P.: Mathematical Modelling, Part I: Continuous and Discrete Models. SBRAS Publ., Novosibirsk (2017). (in Russian)
10. Il'in, V.P.: Fundamental issues of mathematical modeling. Her. Russ. Acad. Sci. **86**(2), 118–126 (2016)
11. Il'in, V.P.: Mathematical modeling and the philosophy of science. Her. Russ. Acad. Sci. **88**(1), 81–88 (2018)
12. Forrester, A., Sobester, A., Keane, A.: Engineering Design via Surrogate Modeling: A Practical Guide. Wiley, New York (2008)
13. Delfour, M., Zolesio, J.-P.: Shape and Geometries: Metrics, Analysis, Differential Calculus, and Optimization. SIAM Publ., Philadelphia (2011)
14. Cottrell, J., Hughes, T., Bazilevs, Y.: Isogeometric Analysis: Towards Integration of CAD and FEA. Wiley, Singapore (2009)
15. Liseikin, V.D.: Grid Generation Methods. Springer, Berlin (2010). https://doi.org/10.1007/978-90-481-2912-6

16. Il'in, V.P.: DELAUNAY: technological environment for grid generation. Sib. J. Ind. Math. **16**, 83–97 (2013). (in Russian)

17. Butyugin, D.S., Il'in, V.P.: CHEBYSHEV: the principles of automatical constructions of algorithms for grid approximations of initial-boundary value problems. In: Proceeding of International Conference on PCT-2014, pp. 42–50. SUSU Publ., Chelyabinsk (2014). (in Russian)

18. Dongarra, J.: List of freely available software for linear algebra on the web (2006). http://netlib.org/utk/people/JackDongarra/la-sw.html

19. Butyugin, D.S., Gurieva, Y.L., Il'in, V.P., Perevozkin, D.V., Petukhov, A.V.: Functionality and algebraic solvers technologies in Krylov library. Vestnik YuUrGU. Ser. Comput. Math. Inform. **2**(3), 92–105 (2013). (in Russian)

20. Il'in, V.P.: Problems of parallel solution of large systems of linear algebraic equations. J. Math. Sci. **216**(6), 795–804 (2016)

21. Il'in, V.P.: On the numerical solution of the direct and inverse electromagnetic problems in geoprospecting. Sib. J. Num. Math. **6**(4), 381–394 (2003). (in Russian)

22. PARAVIEW. https://www.paraview.org

23. Goncharov, S.S., Sviridenko, D.I.: Logical language of description of polynomial computing. Dokl. Math. **99**(2), 1–4 (2019). ISSN 1064–5624

24. Valkman, Y.R., Tarasov, V.B.: From ontologies of cognitive semiotics. Ontol. Des. **f8**(1(27)), 8–34 (2018). (in Russian)

25. Mikony, S.V.: Formalization of the cognitive process using the basis of models. Ontol. Des. **8**(1(27)), 35–48 (2018). (in Russian)

26. Borgest, N.M.: Key tems the ontology of designing: review, analysis, generalization. Ontol. Des. **3**(3(9)), 9–341 (2013). (in Russian)

27. Zagorulko, Y.A., Borovikova, O.I.: An approach for realization of the content patterns in implementation of the scientific domains. Syst. Inform. **12**, 27–39 (2018). (in Russian)

28. Malyshkin, V.E.: Literacy for oncoming centuries. In: Proceedings of the 13th International Conference on Intelligent Software Methodologies, Tools, and Techniques (SoMeT). Frontiers in Artificial Intelligence and Applications, vol. 246, pp. 899–905. IOS Press (2014)

29. Kleppe, A.: Software Language Enginneering: Creating Domain-Specific Language Using Metamodels. Addison-Wesley, New York (2008)

30. Feoktistov, A., Kostromin, R., Sidorov, I.A., Gorsky, S.A.: Development of distributed subject-oriented applications for cloud computing through the integration of conceptual and modular programming. In: Proceedings of the 41st International Conference on Information and Communication Technology, Electronics and Microelectronics, pp. 251–256. IEEE (2018)

31. Python Language. http://www.python.org

32. MATLAB. https://www.mathworks.com/products/matlab.html

33. Krasnov, M.M.: $C++$ template metaprogramming in the mathematical physics problems. Keldysh IAM RAS, Moscow, preprint (2017)

34. ALGOWIKI. https://algowiki-project.org

35. Il'in, V.P.: How to reorganize computer science and technologies? Vestnik RAS **89**(3), 232–242 (2019). Moscow. (in Russian)

Aspect-Oriented Set@l Language
for Architecture-Independent Programming
of High-Performance Computer Systems

Ilya I. Levin[1] ⓘ, Alexey I. Dordopulo[2] ⓘ, Ivan V. Pisarenko[2(✉)] ⓘ,
and Andrey K. Melnikov[3]

[1] Academy for Engineering and Technology, Institute of Computer
Technologies and Information Security, Southern Federal University,
Taganrog, Russia
iilevin@sfedu.ru
[2] Supercomputers and Neurocomputers Research Center, Taganrog, Russia
{dordopulo,pisarenko}@superevm.ru
[3] "InformInvestGroup" CJSC, Moscow, Russia
ak@iigroup.ru

Abstract. State-of-the-art programming languages for high-performance computer systems require a significant code revision for the porting of the same algorithm between different architectures. To solve this problem, we propose an architecture-independent Set@l programming language, which develops the main concepts of the COLAMO and SETL programming languages. Set@l represents the solution of a computational problem as sets with various attributes and relations between them. Furthermore, the Set@l language is based on the paradigm of aspect-oriented programming and describes an algorithm and features of its implementation as separate modules of a program. The Set@l syntax supports the classification of collections by various criteria, such as the type of parallelism, definiteness and optional user's attributes. To deal with the indefinite collections emerging in the case of the algorithm modification, the Vopenka's classification of collections by definiteness of their elements is introduced into the syntax of the Set@l programming language. In this paper, we consider the example of the Set@l application for the coding of lower-upper decomposition. The code shows that aspects can adapt the parallelizing of the basic algorithm to the implementation on computer systems with reconfigurable and multiprocessor architectures.

Keywords: Architecture-independent programming · Set@l programming
language · Aspect-oriented programming paradigm · Alternative set theory of
Vopenka · Algorithm parallelization

1 Introduction

The design of heterogeneous and reconfigurable computer systems, which contain both processors and field-programmable gate arrays (FPGAs) [1], is an urgent research direction in the field of supercomputer engineering. The variety of architectures used in

© Springer Nature Switzerland AG 2019
V. Voevodin and S. Sobolev (Eds.): RuSCDays 2019, CCIS 1129, pp. 517–528, 2019.
https://doi.org/10.1007/978-3-030-36592-9_42

hybrid computer systems and lack of efficient methods and tools for architecture-independent parallel programming considerably complicate the process of software porting. In the conventional programming languages, the algorithm for the solution of a computational problem and features of its implementation are described by indivisible code fragments. As a result, the change of parallelizing method caused by the porting of a program between computer systems with different architectures requires the development of a new code. Traditional approaches to the solution of the inter-architecture porting problem have significant disadvantages: they are based on the specialized translation algorithms (e.g. the Pyfagor language of functional programming [2]) or fix the procedural parallelization model (e.g. the OpenCL (Open Computing Language) standard [3]).

The high-level programming language COLAMO (Common-Oriented Language for Architecture of Multi-Objects) [4] solves the majority of problems related to the programming of FPGA-based reconfigurable computer systems. In COLAMO, the parallelization of an algorithm is described implicitly by the declaration of access types for arrays and indexing of their elements. However, COLAMO is aimed at the structural and procedural organization of calculations, and the porting of a parallel application in COLAMO to computer systems with different architectures seems to be very problematic.

To solve the aforementioned problem, we propose an architecture-independent Set@l programming language that develops the essential ideas of COLAMO and the set-theory-based programming language SETL (SET Language) [5]. Set@l is based on a paradigm of aspect-oriented programming (AOP) [6] and describes an algorithm and its implementation features as separate program modules. A program in the Set@l language represents the information graph of a computational problem as sets and relations between them. The decomposition and typing of collections define different variants of parallelization and other aspects of the algorithm implementation. In contrast to other set-theory-based programming languages (e.g. SETL), Set@l classifies sets by various criteria and operates with indefinite collections according to the alternative set theory (AST) of Vopenka [7].

2   Aspect-Oriented Approach to Programming of Computer Systems

Within the traditional methods of parallel programming, the descriptions of an algorithm and its realization features are divided into several fragments and distributed all over the source code. This factor considerably complicates the porting of software between computer systems with different architectures. In spite of the invariability of the algorithm's mathematical sense, the inter-architecture porting of a parallel application requires the development of a new code.

It is possible to solve the porting problem using the AOP paradigm [6]. According to the aspect-oriented approach, cross-cutting concerns, which cause the negative effects of code scattering and tangling, are described as separate program modules (aspects). A source code defines the main functionality of a program and contains a special marking that determines its interaction with aspects during translation or execution. The translator-preprocessor analyzes user's marking and generates a new executable program, in which cross-cutting concerns are weaved into the code. Owing to the AOP technology, it is possible to simplify the development and further support of software and increase the adaptability of programs to various modifications.

The available AOP languages (AspectJ, Spring AOP, AspectC++, etc.) are the extensions of general-purpose procedural programming languages (Java, C++, etc.) aimed at the further advancement of the object-oriented approach, but not at the solution of computational problems. Architecture-independent parallel programming of high-performance computer systems requires a fundamentally new declarative programming language. It should provide the aspect-oriented decomposition of algorithms and describe the features of its implementation on various architectures as separate program modules.

Set@1 is an aspect-oriented language intended for the architecture-independent programming of computer systems. It applies the set-theoretic code representation and relation calculus for the independent specification of an algorithm and its realization features (parallelism, usage of memory, updating, etc.). In contrast to the COLAMO programming language for reconfigurable computers [4], Set@1 represents the information graph of an applied problem as sets and relations between them, but not as operation vertices and data arrays with various types of access and storage. To define the parallelization method and other features of the algorithm implementation, Set@1 uses attributes which provide the classification of collections according to various criteria. This feature is a key distinction between Set@1 and other set-theory-based programming languages (e.g. SETL [5]). Making different combinations of sets, their attributes and partitions, one can describe multiple variants of the algorithm's execution and provide fast switching between them.

According to the AOP principles, a typical program in the Set@1 language consists of the architecture-independent source code (`program`) of the problem's solution and the system of aspects (`aspect`), which adapt the algorithm to the architecture and configuration of a computer system. Syntax elements used for the description of modules and sections of the Set@1 program are given in Table 1.

Table 1. Syntax elements used for description of modules and sections of program in Set@1

Unit/ section	Source code	Aspects	Interface section	Other sections

Format	`program(c1):`
	`  c=a+b;`
	`end(c1);`
		`aspect(a1):`
		`  type(a)='par';`
		`end(a1);`
			`interface::`
			`  c: input(c1);`
			`  k: output(a1);`
			`  d: extern;`
			`end(interface);`
				`block1::`
				`  v=c+b*k;`
				`end(block1);`

The Set@1 program can contain an arbitrary number of aspects defining different partitions and classifications of the algorithm's basic collections. The modules of the program are divided into sections declared with the headers separated by a symbol ":: " (Table 1). To specify connections between the source code and its aspects, each program module is supplemented with an interface section (`interface`), where input (`input`), output (`output`) and undefined (`extern`) parameters and references to source and target modules are declared. Other sections of the program are declared analogously to the interface one, but they do not contain parameter lists and can have various names. For example, in the source code it is reasonable to allocate the sections of data preparation and algorithm description.

Figure 1 shows the aspect-oriented structure of the Set@1 program designed for the solution of linear algebra problems, where d_1, d_2, ..., d_N are the input vertices of the information graph, o_1, o_2, o_3, o_j, o_{j+1} are the operation vertices, b, b_L are the output vertices.

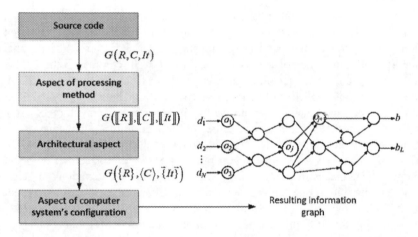

Fig. 1. The aspect-oriented structure of the Set@1 program intended for the solution of linear algebra problems

Within the source code, the algorithm is defined as a relation G between the collections of matrix rows R and columns C and set of processing iterations It (see Fig. 1). At this stage, we consider collections R, C and It as generalized objects of indefinite type, and they are characterized only by unique names. The aspect of processing method describes the sets of rows, columns and iterations as collections with undefined types of parallelism $[[R]]$, $[[C]]$, $[[It]]$ and specifies the logic of their partitioning into subsets. The features of decomposition determine various methods of matrix processing (e.g. by rows, columns, cells or iterations). In some special cases, the aspect of processing method can modify the algorithm for more efficient implementation on some supercomputer architectures. The aspect of architecture defines the typing of sets R, C and It and connects the decomposition options with the parameters of the computer system configuration. The aspect of computer system's configuration substitutes numerical values of parameters into parallelized collections $\{R\}$, $\langle C \rangle$ and $\overrightarrow{\{It\}}$ (different types of brackets correspond to different types of parallelism). As a result, the information graph of a computational problem is adapted to the architecture and configuration of a certain computer system.

3   Description of Algorithm Parallelization in Set@1

For the implicit declaration the algorithm parallelization, the classification of collections according to the parallelism of their elements during processing is introduced into the Set@1 programming language. The basic parallelism types of collections and format of their description in Set@1 are given in Table 2.

Table 2. Key types of collections classified by parallelism and formats of their description in Set@1

Type of collection	Processing type	Symbolic notation	Format of description
Tuple	Sequential	$[1, 2, ..., p]$	seq(1...p)
Pipeline tuple	Pipeline	$\langle 1, 2, ..., p \rangle$	pipe(1...p)
Set	Parallel-independent	$\{1, 2, ..., p\}$	par(1...p)
Set of processing by iterations	Parallel-dependent	$\overrightarrow{\{1, 2, ..., p\}}$	conc(1...p)
Implicit collection	Type is defined in other aspect	$[[1, 2, ..., p]]$	imp(1...p)

If the method for the parallelizing of collection's elements is clearly defined, the following types are used: "tuple" (seq – sequential processing), "pipeline tuple" (pipe – pipeline processing), "set" (par – parallel-independent processing) and "set of processing by iterations" (conc – parallel-dependent processing).

However, in some aspects (e.g. the aspect of processing method in Fig. 1) it is impossible to specify the exact type of collections by parallelism because any information about the architecture of computer system is not available. In this case, a special type imp (implicit or undefined) is applied. The typing of imp collections is defined in the architectural aspect by means of the following syntax structure:

```
type(<name of collection>)='<type of collection>';
```

Each collection of the Set@1 program has the only attribute of parallelism, but one can change it during the passing from one abstraction level to another.

The proposed classification of collections by parallelism provides the architectural independence of the source code in Set@1 and allows to describe various parallelizing methods for an algorithm as an entire program. To switch between implementations, user activates the corresponding architectural aspect, while the source code of an algorithm remains unchanged.

4 Indefinite Collections in Set@1

If aspects do not modify an algorithm during its architectural adaptation, the solution of a computational problem can be described within the Cantor-Bolzano set theory [8]. However, the functionality of aspects is not limited to the parallelization of algorithms. In some cases, it is reasonable to modify an algorithm according to the architectural features of the computer system used for calculations. Then some collections are indefinite and are not sets; so, it is impossible to describe them using the concepts of the traditional set theory.

The architecture-independent Set@1 programming language for high-performance computer systems describes various implementations of an algorithm in a unified aspect-oriented program. For this purpose, the classification of collections by the definiteness of their elements is introduced into Set@1 (see Table 3). In the Set@1 programming language, indefinite collections are described by the special mathematical objects (classes and semisets). The concepts of a class and semiset were proposed by Vopenka within the AST [7].

Table 3. Collections' classification by definiteness of their elements in Set@1

Type of collection	Description	Symbolic notation	Keyword
Set	Sharply defined collection of elements	{ }	set
Semiset	Indefinite collection of elements	{ ? ? } {? ¿}	sm
Class	Collection with the type that is not defined unambiguously	? ¿	cls

The type "set" (set) describes a sharply defined and definite collection of certain objects. For a set, we always exactly know if one or another object belongs to it or not. In Set@1, a set can be specified using the direct enumeration of its elements or by means of the relation calculus. Relational structures have the following format:

```
<name of set>=<type>(<variable>|<predicate>);
```

Sets of numbers forming a numerical sequence with the fixed step size are defined as follows:

```
<name>=<type>(<1st element>,<2nd element>,…,<last element>);
```

If the step size equals to 1, only the first and the last elements of a numerical sequence are mentioned:

```
<name of set>=<type>(<1st element>...<last element>);
```

The type "semiset" (sm) indicates a collection whose indefiniteness is a fundamental characteristic and can not be eliminated by the aspects of a program. The relation of inclusion usually connects a semiset with some sharply defined set. Therefore, to specify a semiset as an object of the Set@l program, it is necessary to form a suitable superset and declare the appropriate relation of inclusion. If the algorithm for the solution of the system of linear algebraic equations (SLAE) by the Jacobi method is implemented with one verification of the termination condition after several computational iterations, the collection of iterations represents the example of a semiset [9].

A class (cls) is the most common and multipurpose type of collections in the Set@l programming language. If the type and structure of a collection are not sharply defined on the current level of abstraction, it is declared as a class and is used in code analogously to standard sets. Owing to the extension of the class definition in the aspects of a program, it is possible to specialize the type and partition of the collection during translation. The application of classes provides the unification of objects' names in all units of an aspect-oriented program in Set@l. The indefiniteness of collections by parallelism denoted by imp attribute (see Table 2) can also be described with the help of classes. To specify a collection as a class in the Set@l program, one has to assign cls attribute to this collection and give its possible attributes using the following syntax construction:

```
cls(<name of class>);
typing(<name of class>):'<type 1>' or '<type 2>';
```

The collections of rows, columns and iterations *R*, *C*, and *It* (see Fig. 1) are the examples of classes because in the source code they are considered as objects with unknown types and decompositions.

Using classes, sets and semisets, one can describe various modifications methods for an algorithm in a unified aspect-oriented Set@l program. The application features of AST objects in Set@l programs are thoroughly considered in paper [9].

5 Program of Lower-Upper Decomposition in Set@l

Lower-upper (LU) decomposition is a well-known computational algorithm, which represents a $n \times n$ matrix as the product of a lower and an upper triangular matrices.

The source code of the LU-decomposition program in Set@l declares the problem's information graph G and describes its operational vertices in terms of collections, attributes and relations between them:

```
int(n)=<size of matrix>;
K=set(1…n-1);           // set of iteration numbers;
I=set(1…n);             // set of row numbers;
J=set(1…n);             // set of column numbers;
set(a);                 // matrix;
{graph,imp}(G);         // information graph;
(forall i in I and j in J):
  a(1,i,j)=a_init(i,j);// loading of initial matrix;
end(forall);

// Attribute of LU iteration:
attribute LU_iter(element(k),set(s1),set(s2)):
  (forall i in s1 and j in s2 | i<=k or (i>k and j<k)):
    a(k+1,i,j)=a(k,i,j);          // transit elements;
  end(forall);
  (forall i in s1 | i>k):          // recalculated elements;
    a(k+1,i,k)=a(k,i,k)/a(k,k,k);
    (forall j in s2 | j>k):
      a(k+1,i,j)=a(k,i,j)-a(k+1,i,k)*a(k,k,j);
    end(forall);
  end(forall);
end(LU_iter);

// Graph description:
(forall k in K):                   // for all iterations;
  G(k)=LU_iter(k,I,J);             // attribute assignment;
end(forall);
```

The previous Set@l program of the Gaussian elimination [10] used the partition and typing of the sets of row (I), column (J) and iteration (K) numbers for the specification of the algorithm parallelism. By contrast, the aforementioned code operates with special collection G that includes operational vertices of the information graph. This approach allows to consider the membership relations between sets and their elements in the traditional mathematical sense.

Within the source code, the parallelism type and partition of set G are unknown. Therefore, the special type imp (implicit) is applied.

The aspect of processing method for the LU-decomposition program in Set@l determines the partitions of the initial information graph G into subgraphs described by subsets with unknown type of parallelism:

```
(forall k in K):                    // decomposition by rows;
  R(k,i)=(G(k,i,j)|j in J);         // i-th row at k-th iteration;
  RB(k,p)=imp(R(k,i)|i in ((p-1)*s+1...p*s)); //p-th row subset;
  GR(k)=imp(RB(k,p)|p in (1...N));       // row-built subgraph;
end(forall);

(forall k in K):                    // decomposition by columns;
  C(k,j)=(G(k,i,j)|i in I);         // j-th column at k-th iteration;
  CB(k,q)=imp(C(k,j)|j in ((q-1)*c+1...q*c)); // column subset;
  GC(k)=imp(CB(k,q)|q in (1...M));     // column-built subgraph;
end(forall);

// Decomposition by iterations:
It(k)=(G(k,i,j)|i in I and j in J);          // k-th iteration;
IB(l)=imp(It(k)|k in ((l-1)*ni+1...l*ni));  // iteration subset;
G=imp(IB(l)|l in (1...T));            // iteration-built graph;
```

The aspect of processing method defines the partition of collection G into the row (RB(k,p)), column (CB(k,q)) and iteration (IB(l)) blocks with implicit type of parallelism. Each block consists of rows R(k,i), columns C(k,j) or iterations It (k). These partitions allows to describe the processing methods by rows, columns, cells and iterations [10] applied for the parallelizing of the linear algebra algorithms. The values of decomposition parameters s, N, c, M, ni and T depend on the architecture of a computer system and are declared in the aspect of configuration.

The aspect of architecture for the LU-decomposition program in Set@1 specifies the parallelism types of the basic set G and its subsets GR(k), GC(k), RB(k,p), CB(k, q) and IB(l). The code of the architectural aspect for the reconfigurable architecture of computer system is given below:

```
// Rows:
s=n;                    // number of rows in subset RB(k,p);
N=1;                    // number of row subsets;
type(RB(k,p))='pipe';   // pipeline processing of rows;
type(GR(k))='pipe';

// Columns:
c=n;                    // number of columns in subset CB(k,q);
M=1;                    // number of column subsets;
type(CB(k,q))='pipe';// pipeline processing of columns;
type(GC(k))='pipe';

// Iterations:
ni=floor(R/R0);         // number of iterations in subset IB(l);
T=(n-1)/ni;             // number of iteration subsets;
type(IB(l))='conc';     // parallel-dependent processing of
                        // iterations in each subset;
type(G)='pipe';         // G typing;
```

According to the code represented above, the algorithm of LU-decomposition is parallelized by iterations in the case of implementation on a reconfigurable computer system. In the architectural aspect, the characteristics of set partitions are calculated using the parameters of configuration (R and R0) and the size of processing matrix (n).

If the algorithm of LU-decomposition is realized on a multiprocessor computer system, the architectural aspect is given as follows:

```
// Rows:
s=q1;                    // number of rows in subset RB(k,p);
N=n/s;                   // number of row subsets;
type(RB(k,p))='par';     // parallel-independent processing of rows
                         // in each subset;
type(GR(k))='seq';       // sequential processing of subsets;

// Columns:
c=q2;                    // number of columns in subset CB(k,q);
M=n/c;                   // number of column subsets;
type(CB(k,q))='par';     // parallel-independent processing of
                         // columns in each subset;
type(GC(k))='seq';       // sequential processing of subsets;
// Iterations:
ni=n-1;                  // number of iterations in subset BI(k);
T=1;                     // number of iteration subsets;
type(IB(l))='seq';       // sequential processing of iterations;
type(G)='seq';           // G typing;
```

In contrast to a reconfigurable computer system, the implementation of the LU-decomposition algorithm on a multiprocessor supercomputer assumes the parallelization by cells. Analogously to the previous version of the architectural aspect, the decomposition of sets depends on the configuration parameters (q1 and q2) and the matrix size (n).

The aspect of computer system's configuration substitutes the specific values of configuration parameters into other modules of the program and completes the forming of set G:

```
// Reconfigurable architecture:
R=<available computing resource>;
R0=<resource of basic subgraph>;

// Multiprocessor architecture:
q1=<number of processors by rows>;
q2=<number of processors by columns>;
```

Owing to the parallelism typing of collections in the Set@l programming language, it is possible to describe different variants of the algorithm parallelizing in a single aspect-oriented program. To switch the method of implementation during the inter-architecture porting, one should change the architectural aspect of a program, but the source code remains unchanged.

6 Conclusions

The Set@l programming language applies the AOP paradigm, AST and relation calculus in order to represent the algorithm for the problem solution as the architecture-independent source code and to separate it from the description of implementation features, which are defined in aspects by means of the partition and classification of sets. Using the aspects of processing method, architecture and configuration, one can provide the efficient porting of parallel applications between computer systems with different architectures and adapt programs to various modifications of hardware resources.

Application of the Set@l language gives fundamentally new possibilities for efficient porting of software to various architectures of computer systems, including heterogeneous and reconfigurable ones. This paper summarizes the development of theoretical principles of Set@l: the distinctive features of the language are thoroughly considered, and the fundamental syntax elements are given. Currently, we are working at the development of translator for the Set@l programming language.

References

1. Mittal, S., Vetter, J.: A survey of CPU-GPU heterogeneous computing techniques. ACM Comput. Surv., **47**(4) (2015). https://doi.org/10.1145/2788396. Article No. 69
2. Legalov, A.I.: Functional language for creation of architecture-independent parallel programs. Comput. Technol. **10**(1), 71–89 (2005). (in Russian)
3. OpenCL: the open standard for parallel programming of heterogeneous systems. https://www.khronos.org/opencl/
4. Dordopulo, A.I., Levin, I.I., Kalyaev, I.A., Gudkov, V.A., Gulenok, A.A.: Programming of hybrid computer systems in the programming language COLAMO. Izv. SFedU. Eng. Sci. (11), 39–54 (2016). https://doi.org/10.18522/2311-3103-2016-11-3954. (in Russian)
5. Dewar, R.: SETL and the evolution of programming. In: Davis, M., Schonberg, E. (eds.) From Linear Operators to Computational Biology. Springer, London (2013). https://doi.org/10.1007/978-1-4471-4282-9_4
6. Dessi, M.: Spring 2.5 Aspect-Oriented Programming. Packt Publishing Ltd., Birmingham (2009)
7. Vopenka, P.: Introduction to Mathematics in Alternative Set Theory. Alfa, Bratislava (1989). (in Czech)

8. Haggarty, R.: Descrete Mathematics for Computing. Pearson Education, Harlow (2002)
9. Levin, I.I., Dordopulo, A.I., Pisarenko, I.V., Melnikov, A.K.: Description of Jacobi algorithm for solution of linear equation system in architecture-independent Set@l programming language. Izv. SFedU. Eng. Sci., (5), 34–48 (2018). https://doi.org/10.23683/2311-3103-2018-5-34-48. (in Russian)
10. Levin, I.I., Dordopulo, A.I., Pisarenko, I.V., Melnikov, A.K.: Approach to architecture-independent programming of computer systems in aspect-oriented Set@l language. Izv. SFedU. Eng. Sci., (3), 46–58 (2018). https://doi.org/10.23683/2311-3103-2018-3-46-58. (in Russian)

Bridging the Gap Between Applications and Supercomputing: A New Master's Program in Computational Science

Iosif Meyerov$^{(\boxtimes)}$, Alexander Sysoyev, Anna Pirova,
Natalia Shestakova, and Mikhail Ivanchenko

Lobachevsky State University of Nizhni Novgorod, Nizhni Novgorod, Russia
meerov@vmk.unn.ru, {alexander.sysoyev,anna.pirova,
natalia.shestakova,mikhail.ivanchenko}@itmm.unn.ru

Abstract. Modern applied science is becoming increasingly interdisciplinary, creating a priority demand for highly qualified scientists and engineers capable of generating new ideas and transferring advanced scientific developments to the industry. Often, breakthrough results arise at the interface of sciences as a result of the coordinated work of specialists from different subject areas. The training of scientists and engineers capable of such activities requires the development of new educational approaches. The article describes a new Master's program in computational science that meets the challenge. The program bridges the gap between computational mathematics and cutting-edge supercomputing technologies, offering an appropriate range of general courses, as well as the set of electives with the possibility of building an individual educational trajectory. The article formulates the main ideas underlying the program, describes the structure of the curriculum, emphasizes the main disciplines, and summarizes the results of training over four years of the program implementation at the Lobachevsky State University of Nizhni Novgorod.

Keywords: Interdisciplinary science · Master program · Computational science · Parallel computing · High performance computing · Education

1 Introduction

In the 21st century, supercomputers play a significant role in obtaining breakthrough results in applied physics, chemistry, biology, biomedicine, and other problem domains. It has become possible owing to the prominent progress achieved in the development of hardware, mathematical models, computational methods, and technologies for parallel computing, numerous software libraries, tools for development, debugging, and profiling of supercomputing software. A significant contribution has been made by the development of educational programs that combine supercomputing related topics with the branches of fundamental and applied mathematics, physics, etc.

This paper describes the experience of building and implementing a new Master's program in Computational science. The main goal of this program is to prepare broadminded applied mathematicians, able to work in emerging subject areas, understand the models used in those areas, and develop and use software for supercomputing

V. Voevodin and S. Sobolev (Eds.): RuSCDays 2019, CCIS 1129, pp. 529–541, 2019.
https://doi.org/10.1007/978-3-030-36592-9_43

simulation. Our long-term practice of teaching applied mathematicians and conducting interdisciplinary projects at the Lobachevsky State University of Nizhni Novgorod (UNN) confirms that the training of such professionals is not trivial. On the one hand, by the time they start Master's education, students should have a good mathematical background. On the other hand, they should understand many aspects of computer science such as algorithms and data structures, system programming, parallel programming, and modern software development tools. The Master's program should enable students to significantly deepen their knowledge and develop their skills, to gain experience of real work in projects in science or high-tech industry.

The article is organized as follows. Section 2 provides an overview of similar Master's programs at leading universities. In Sect. 3, the main ideas underlying the considered Master's program are emphasized. Section 4 discusses the structure of the curriculum, highlights the main and elective courses, gives their classification and formulates possible educational trajectories. Section 5 provides a brief description of the main courses. Section 6 describes the program implementation experience and the results achieved. Section 7 concludes the paper.

2   Related Work

Modern science and industry need specialists who are able to enter a new problem area, understand and make use of its mathematical models and numerical methods, and effectively implement them on a supercomputer. Training specialists in Computational Science is a priority area, as evidenced by the large number of such Master's programs at leading universities over the world. Many master's programs in computational sciences are focused on particular problem areas (computational physics, computational biology, computational biomedicine, computational finance), a number of programs in accordance with the current demand also contain an impressive set of courses in data science. The set of mandatory courses is often very limited, so that electives prevail, giving students an opportunity to choose their specialization. In many universities besides preparing master thesis, students must complete a practical project or take part in scientific seminars. Below we briefly overview several Master's programs, a detailed list of US and European programs is available on the SIAM website [1].

The Master's program Computation for Design and Optimization at the Massachusetts Institute of Technology [2] aims at educating on advanced computational methods and their applications in science and engineering. Students must attend three of four core courses: numerical simulation, numerical methods, numerical methods for PDEs, and optimization methods. Then students have to take two courses from a wide list of electives. Course topics cover numerical methods in different areas of natural science, data analysis, discrete and continuous optimization.

The Master's program Computational Science and Engineering at ETH Zurich [3] prepares specialists on computer simulation. The graduates are able to use numerical methods and simulation to solve scientific problems. The program offers specialization in natural science and some related areas: physics, astrophysics, physics of the atmosphere, chemistry, fluid dynamics, electromagnetics, geophysics, biology, control theory, robotics, and computational finance. The core courses of the program are advanced numerical methods and computational statistics.

The Master's program Computational Science at the University of Oslo [4] is designed in a multidisciplinary way and involves studying mathematical approximation theory, computer science and application modeling. The graduates have both theoretical and practical skills required to solve modern scientific and engineering problems. The program has ten specializations: astrophysics, bioinformatics, bioscience, chemistry, geoscience, imaging and biomedical computing, materials science, mechanics and physics. The program includes numerical analysis and applied data analysis and machine learning as mandatory courses. The set of recommended elective courses depends on the specialization.

The Master's program Modelling for Science and Engineering at the Autonomous University of Barcelona [5] focuses on modeling and numerical simulation of systems in different scientific domains. The program has four specializations: complex systems modelling, mathematical modeling, modeling for engineering and data science. Parallel programming and research and innovation are mandatory courses. Elective courses include applied stochastic processes, deterministic modelling, partial differential equations, mathematics and big data, optimization, parallel and distributed systems, data visualization and modelling.

The Master's program Computational Science and Engineering (CSE) at the Technical University of Munich [6] focuses on studying methods and tools for numerical simulation on modern computers. It provides students the skills required for a full simulation cycle from constructing mathematical model to validation and visualization of numerical results. In comparison with the other programs, the program pays a great deal of attention to computer science part. The mandatory courses of the program are advanced programming, parallel programming, numerical programming, parallel numerics and scientific computing. Elective courses involve additional modules in computer science, in applications, methods and techniques of CSE.

The Master's program in Computational Science and Engineering at the Swiss Federal Institute of Technology in Lausanne (EPFL) [7] prepares specialists in high-performance computing (HPC) with deep knowledge in mathematical modeling, numerical algorithms and data analysis. The program contains eleven core courses, including advanced numerical analysis, algorithms, computational physics, image processing, parallel and high-performance computing. There are four groups of elective courses: computational modeling based on differential equations; computational modeling based on discrete systems; numerical methods, algorithms, high performance systems, and numerical methods, algorithms; data science.

Several such Master's programs are open in Russian universities, in particular, the Master's programs in Supercomputers and Applications [8] and Computational Technologies and Simulation [9] at the Moscow State University. The former puts emphasis on Supercomputing technologies, and the latter on mathematical modeling, choosing appropriate numerical methods, and their implementation for modern computers. Both programs are based on scientific expertise in the relevant problem areas, accumulated at the Moscow State University (MSU) and research institutes of the Russian Academy of Sciences.

In general, Master's programs in computational science involve selected topics of mathematical modeling, applied mathematics, computer science, and data science. Most programs are interdisciplinary and problem-solving oriented, covering applications from various scientific areas. In this paper we describe the new Master's program in Computational Science based on our interdisciplinary research experience and fifteen years of educational background in parallel and distributed computing. Courses on supercomputing were originally developed as part of the "Supercomputing Education" project (supported by the Government of the Russian Federation) [11, 13] and the NSF TCPP program for parallel and distributed computing [10, 12].

3 Main Principles

The following main ideas formed the basis of the developed Master's program.

1. This Master's program prepares students for work in interdisciplinary teams and, in itself, is an interdisciplinary project. In this regard, several departments of the institute participated in the development and implementation of the program: the Department of Software and Supercomputer Technologies, the Department of Applied Mathematics, and the Department of Algebra, Geometry and Discrete Mathematics. As a result, the program is not localized in one of the departments and its working group includes specialists from different subject areas.
2. The set of mandatory disciplines is designed to acquaint students with the latest advances in machine learning, algorithms and data structures, statistics, numerical methods, parallel programming and software development. At the same time, the main attention is paid to applied aspects, that is, forming the competence of practical application of the knowledge and skills in science and the high-tech industry.
3. The set of elective disciplines allows students to choose an individual trajectory, e.g. focusing on the development and implementation of numerical methods for solving problems in computational sciences; on algorithmic issues and problems of efficient implementation of algorithms on modern computing systems; data analysis issues in applications, etc.
4. Supervision of Master's thesis is assisted by scientists and specialists from the academy and industry. The best students not only follow the cutting-edge research projects, but also become their active participants. The results of their work are published in recognized scientific journals and reported at conferences. The last semester is exempt from classes to complete the diplomas.
5. The Master program is kept developing; new elective courses are added according to emerging research projects and direction. For example, a block of disciplines in computational biology is currently under development.

4   Curriculum Structure

The curriculum covers four academic semesters. In accordance with the educational standards established in the Russian Federation, the fourth semester is exempt from studies so that students can concentrate on preparing Master's thesis. The first three semesters, on the contrary, are quite saturated. All three semesters are organized according to the following scheme (Fig. 1). Compulsory courses, basically, have the same time, two academic hours of lectures and two hours of practical training. These courses fall into three categories: mathematics, computer science and humanities. The choice of mathematical courses is determined both by the availability of appropriate expertise in the UNN, and by the needs of research areas actively developing at the university. In this regard, the curriculum includes courses on data analysis and machine learning (machine learning and deep learning), applied mathematical statistics, various aspects of numerical methods and optimization theory. The set of compulsory courses in computer science is designed so that students acquire the knowledge and skills necessary to complete the thesis and useful for subsequent professional career. In particular, it contains an advanced course on algorithms and data structures, on the theory and practice of parallel computing, and the agile software development methodology. As a rule, an exam is required for a mandatory course at the end of the semester.

In addition, the curriculum involves a large number of elective courses. Like mandatory courses, elective courses are devoted to the study of various fields of applied mathematics and computer science. In each of the three semesters, the study of two courses is compulsory, and attending a larger number of courses is highly encouraged. Some elective courses complement the mandatory courses, allowing students to delve into relevant areas of knowledge according to their personal preferences. In particular, reinforcement learning course continues the compulsory course machine learning; courses string algorithms, algorithms on graphs, bioinformatics algorithms, quantum computing, continue the course advanced algorithms and data structures, a set of courses on various aspects of parallel computing and other examples. Importantly, the curriculum offers a wide variety of elective courses, which allows students to form an individual educational trajectory. The provisional trajectories form competences for analysts who prefer to focus on the development and implementation of algorithms and data structures, for future data analysis engineers, for specialists in the effective implementation of numerical methods on modern supercomputers. Note that the courses support and reinforce each other. Figure 2 exemplifies a fragment of the curriculum that contains courses on algorithms and their effective implementation for state-of-the-art computing systems. Similar diagrams can be constructed for numerical methods and for data analysis.

The program is constantly evolving, currently, additional courses in computational physics and computational biology, a course in scientific programming in Python are prepared.

TERM I	Applied Statistics	2-2	Math	**Mandatory**
	Machine Learning	2-2	Math	
	Advanced Data Structures	2-2	CS	
	Professional Practice	1-1	H	
	Discrete Optimization	1-1	Math	**Elective**
	Decision Theory	1-1	Math	
	Computer Graphics	1-1	CS	
	Performance Engineering	1-1	CS	
	Bioinformatics Algorithms	1-1	CS	
TERM II	Parallel Numerical Methods	2-2	Math	**Mandatory**
	Nonlinear Dynamics	2-2	Math	
	Parallel Computing	2-2	CS	
	English	0-2	H	
	Polytopes and Optimization	1-1	Math	**Elective**
	Reinforcement Learning	1-1	Math	
	Stochastic Differential Equations	1-1	Math	
	String Algorithms	1-1	CS	
	Computational Graphics	1-1	CS	
	Parallel Programming Technologies	1-1	CS	
	Python Automation and Testing	1-1	CS	
TERM III	Deep Learning	1-1	Math	**Mandatory**
	Agile Software Development	1-1	CS	
	Philosophy	2-2	H	
	English	0-2	H	
	Finite Element Method	1-1	Math	**Elective**
	Algorithms on Graphs	1-1	CS	
	Quantum Computing	1-1	CS	
	GPU Programming	1-1	CS	
	Advanced Parallel Algorithms	1-1	CS	
	Advanced Parallel Programming	1-1	CS	

Fig. 1. The structure and contents of the curriculum. The set of mandatory and elective courses by semester is listed. Courses (column 1), class hours (lectures-practical lessons; column 2), subject area (mathematics, computer science, humanities; column 3) are shown.

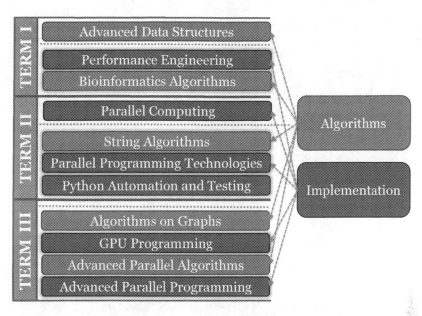

Fig. 2. The part of the curriculum representing the courses on algorithms and their high performance implementation for state-of-the-art computational infrastructure.

5 Courses Description

In this section we shortly overview the contents of the mandatory courses from mathematics and computer science problem areas.

5.1 Term I

Applied Statistics. The course is designed to familiarize students with the basic methods and problems of mathematical statistics and numerical applied data analysis. The main topics are as follows:

- Introduction to R. Types of data. Pseudorandom numbers generation with different probability distributions. Monte-Carlo method.
- Empirical probability distribution and sample statistics. Kernel density estimators.
- Statistical hypotheses and types of errors. Goodness-of-fit tests. Normality tests and tests for exponential distribution.
- Confidence intervals. Methods of obtaining point estimators.
- Tests on distribution parameters. The Neymann–Pearson lemma.
- t-distribution and F-distribution.
- Nonparametric tests for homogeneity and independence. Rank tests.
- Regression analysis.
- One-way analysis of variance.

Machine Learning. The goal of the course is the study of algorithms and methods of machine learning, the foundations of the statistical theory of Vapnik and Chervonenkis, formation of skills and abilities in solving practical problems using methods of machine learning. The main topics are as follows:

- Machine learning examples and taxonomy.
- Probabilistic formulation of learning problems.
- Assessing the quality of learning.
- Principal component analysis.
- The least squares method for solving the regression problem.
- Overfitting in regression problems and how to prevent it (ridge regression, lasso and other methods).
- Nearest neighbors methods.
- Naive Bayes classifier.
- Linear and quadratic discriminant analysis.
- Neural networks. Introduction to deep learning.
- Support Vector Machine.
- Decision Trees.
- Ensembles of decision trees. Bagging and boosting (Random Forests, AdaBoost, Gradient Boosting, XGBoost).
- Preprocessing, working with categorical features, with missing values, balancing datasets.
- Clustering (k-means, k-medoids, DBSCAN, hierarchical clustering).
- Fundamentals of the Vapnik–Chervonenkis theory.

Advanced Data Structures. The goal of the course is the study of advanced data structures and algorithms, the understanding of methods for estimating the complexity of algorithms. Main topics are as follows:

- Complexity analysis.
- Priority queues and their applications.
- Disjoint-sets and their applications.
- Search trees and their applications.

5.2   Term II

Parallel Computing. The purpose of the discipline is to study mathematical models, methods and technologies of parallel programming for supercomputers. The stated set of knowledge and skills constitutes the theoretical basis for methods of developing complex programs. The course is supported by advanced laboratory practice.

The main sections of the course include:

- Introduction to parallel data processing. Parallelism and concurrency.
- Overview of modern parallel computing systems. Classification and performance evaluation.

- The concepts of multicore and multiprocessor computing systems with shared and distributed memory.
- Performance metrics of parallel computing: speedup, efficiency, scalability. The computation model in the form of a graph "operations-operands".
- Analysis of the computation model: determination of the execution time of the parallel algorithm, estimation of the maximum achievable speedup, selection of a computational load distribution method, methods for evaluating the scaling efficiency of parallel algorithms.
- Introduction to MPI.
- Data transfer in MPI. Point-to-point and collective operations. Reductions.
- Types of send/receive operations. Collection and distribution of data. The organization of asynchronous schemes of calculations.
- MPI data types. Virtual topologies.
- Parallel programming in shared memory systems. Introduction to OpenMP.

Parallel Numerical Methods. The objectives of the course are to study basic numerical algorithms, as well as to discuss methods of their parallelization. The course includes the study of the following main topics:

- Elements of floating point arithmetic.
- Direct methods for solving SLAEs and their parallelization.
- Iterative methods for solving SLAEs and their parallelization.
- Methods for solving ordinary differential equations and their parallelization.
- Methods for solving partial differential equations and their parallelization.
- Parallel Monte Carlo methods.

Nonlinear Dynamics. The goal of the course is the study of computational methods and approaches that are often used in solving applied problems of physics and mathematical biology. The course includes the study of the following main topics:

- Steady states and stability theory.
- Bifurcations.
- Numerical integration of dynamic systems.
- Floquet analysis of linear nonautonomous conservative systems.
- Chaotic dynamics.

5.3   Term III

Deep Learning. The content of the discipline is aimed at the study of modern methods of data analysis and the formation of skills in solving related state-of-the-art problems. The course includes the following main topics:

- Introduction to deep learning.
- Multi-layer fully connected neural networks.
- Overview of deep learning software libraries. Neural network development, logistic regression. The problem of recognizing handwritten numbers.

- Convolutional neural networks.
- Visualization of filters/outputs on intermediate network layers.
- Recurrent neural networks.
- Unsupervised learning.
- Transfer learning of deep neural networks.

Agile Software Development. The objectives of the course are the study of software design and development techniques, as well as the organization of software projects under conditions of unclear or rapidly changing requirements. The course includes the study of the following main topics:

- Introduction to agile software development. Definition, manifest and the main features of the agile methodologies.
- Writing and maintaining a clean code. Key concepts of a code quality.
- Refactoring.
- Test-Driven Development. The concept, the development cycle.
- The Scrum methodology. Sprint diagram. The role of a Scrum master and a product owner. Scrum artifacts and practices.
- Design of the presentation layer (The Model-View-ViewModel pattern). Typical problems with a user interface. The MVVM and MVP diagram.
- The Extreme Programming (XP) methodology. XP values and practices. Pair programming. Benefits. Management strategy. Coding strategy.
- Principles of object-oriented programming. The SOLID principles. The Demeter's law. C++ programming standards.
- The Domain-Driven Design (DDD) pattern and diagram. Application of DDD.
- Design of a Data Access layer. Typical architecture problems in the absence of the Data Access layer. How to organize the Data Access layer. Benefits.
- The Kanban methodology. The roots of the methodology in the industry. Basic principles. Comparison with Scrum. Benefits.

6   Implementation

The discussed Master's program is one of four programs in the field applied mathematics and computer science at the Lobachevsky State University of Nizhni Novgorod. After admission, the enrolled students meet with potential scientific advisors and become familiar with the possible topics of work. Students, who had previously studied at the Institute of Information Technologies, Mathematics and Mechanics, often continue their scientific work previously started at the undergraduate degree level.

Most of the diploma projects of students belong to one of the three areas, approximately in equal shares. Thus, the first group is related to computational biomedicine. Diploma projects on this subject combine the use of algorithms and methods of computational mathematics and computational biology, computer graphics and scientific visualization, analysis of large heterogeneous datasets, and parallel computations. Research in this area is conducted in close cooperation with other universities and medical institutions (City Clinical Hospital No. 5, Specialized Cardiac Surgery

Clinical Hospital and others). Anonymous medical data is received from there for analysis, visualization and classification, the expertise of the obtained results is also provided.

The second group of diploma projects addresses problems of computational physics, in particular, supercomputer modeling of laser plasma, non-equilibrium quantum systems and in other fields. These diplomas are carried out in close cooperation with colleagues from UNN, Institute of Applied Physics RAS, Institute for Physics of Microstructures RAS, Chalmers University of Technology, Augsburg University and other research centers. Students prepare their theses in interdisciplinary research groups. Physicists are engaged in the formulation of problems, the choice of research methods and the interpretation of results. Students together with supervisors use their expertise in numerical methods and the use of parallel computing technologies for designing, developing and application of supercomputer software. Such an interaction, with the proper organization of work, has repeatedly proved its effectiveness and led to the obtaining of new physical results.

The third direction for the implementation of graduation projects combines work on the development of parallel algorithms for solving global optimization problems, the sparse algebra and others. Within this direction, students develop new parallel algorithms, learn to develop software tools that effectively utilize modern supercomputing systems. Computational experiments are performed using supercomputers "Lomonosov" (Moscow State University) [14], "MVS-10P" (JSCC RAS) and "Lobachevsky" (UNN). The best students are actively publishing and participate in international conferences on supercomputing and computational science. Some of them achieve significant success by completing theses on applied topics developed in leading IT companies, whose offices are located in the Nizhny Novgorod region. Employment statistics after graduation shows that about 20% of students work in universities and research centers, other students work as engineers in software development in deep learning, computer vision, computer-aided design and other problem areas in Yandex, Intel, Intellivision and other high-tech companies.

7 Conclusion

The Master program in Computational Science has been implemented at the Institute of Information Technologies, Mathematics and Mechanics of the UNN since 2015. Most of the students are enrolled in the program having obtained the bachelor degree in Applied Mathematics or Fundamental Informatics and Information Technologies. A significant role in the attractiveness of the program is played by a large number of elective courses, which provides the opportunity to choose an individual educational trajectory. This allows us to attract students with sufficiently good background in mathematics and programming. Students enrolled in the program over the past three years have demonstrated good progress in terms of their successful participation in scientific and industrial projects at the UNN and big high-tech companies. The authors of the program believe that attracting students to research projects throughout their education plays a key role in their professional development.

One of the promising areas of further development of this master program is the organization of a new educational trajectory in computational biology. This work is planned in the megagrant "Digital personalized medicine of healthy aging (CPM-aging): network analysis of Large multi-ohm data to search for new diagnostic, predictive and therapeutic goals" that is being implemented in the UNN. It is expected that the collection of elective courses will be expanded with new disciplines according to the goals of the ongoing project.

Acknowledgements. I.M. and M.I. acknowledge support of Ministry of Science and Higher Education of the Russian Federation agreement No. 074-02-2018-330. The authors thank A. Zorine and N. Zolotykh for useful discussions.

References

1. SIAM. Graduate and Undergraduate Programs in Computational Science. https://www.siam.org/Students-Education/Resources/For-Graduate-Students/Detail/graduate-and-undergraduate-programs-in-computational-science. Accessed 01 Mar 2019
2. MIT. MIT's Master of Science Program in Computation for Design and Optimization. https://computationalengineering.mit.edu/cdo. Accessed 01 Mar 2019
3. ETH Zurich. The Master Program in Computational Science and Engineering. https://www.ethz.ch/content/specialinterest/study-programme-websites/master-comp-science-and-engineering/en/the-programme/master.html. Accessed 01 Mar 2019
4. UiO. Study programs in English. Computational Science. https://www.uio.no/english/studies/programmes/computational-science-master. Accessed 01 Mar 2019
5. UAB. Official Master's Degree in Modelling for Science and Engineering. https://www.uab.cat/web/estudiar/official-master-s-degrees/general-information/modelling-for-science-and-engineering-1096480962610.html?param1=1307112830469. Accessed 01 Mar 2019
6. TUM. Computational Science and Engineering (M.Sc.). https://www.in.tum.de/en/for-prospective-students/masters-programs/computational-science-and-engineering. Accessed 01 Mar 2019
7. EPFL. Master's Programs. Computational Science and Engineering. https://www.epfl.ch/education/master/programs/computational-science-and-engineering. Accessed 01 Mar 2019
8. MSU. The Master's program Supercomputers and Applications. http://master.cmc.msu.ru/?q=node/2536. Accessed 01 Mar 2019
9. MSU. The Master's program Computational Technologies and Simulation. http://master.cmc.msu.ru/?q=node/2517. Accessed 01 Mar 2019
10. Prasad, S.K., et al.: NSF/IEEE-TCPP curriculum initiative on parallel and distributed Computing – core topics for undergraduates, Version I (2012). https://grid.cs.gsu.edu/~tcpp/curriculum/?q=home. Accessed 01 Mar 2019
11. Voevodin, V., Gergel, V., Popova, N.: Challenges of a systematic approach to parallel computing and supercomputing education. In: Hunold, Sascha, et al. (eds.) Euro-Par 2015. LNCS, vol. 9523, pp. 90–101. Springer, Cham (2015). https://doi.org/10.1007/978-3-319-27308-2_8
12. Gergel, V., Liniov, A., Meyerov, I., Sysoyev, A.: NSF/IEEE-TCPP curriculum implementation at University of Nizhni Novgorod. In: Proceedings of Fourth NSF/TCPP Workshop on Parallel and Distributed Computing Education, pp. 1079–1084. IEEE (2014)
13. Meyerov, I., Bastrakov, S., Sysoyev, A., Gergel, V.: Comprehensive Collection of Time-Consuming Problems for Intensive Training on High Performance Computing. In:

Voevodin, V., Sobolev, S. (eds.) RuSCDays 2018. CCIS, vol. 965, pp. 523–530. Springer, Cham (2019). https://doi.org/10.1007/978-3-030-05807-4_44

14. Voevodin. V.V., et al.: Supercomputer Lomonosov-2: large scale, deep monitoring and fine analytics for the user community. In: Supercomputing Frontiers and Innovations, V. 6, #2, pp. 4–11 (2019)

DLI: Deep Learning Inference Benchmark

Valentina Kustikova[1]([✉]), Evgenii Vasiliev[1], Alexander Khvatov[1],
Pavel Kumbrasiev[1], Roman Rybkin[1], and Nadezhda Kogteva[2]

[1] Lobachevsky State University of Nizhni Novgorod, Nizhny Novgorod, Russia
`valentina.kustikova@gmail.com`, `eugene.unn@gmail.com`,
`khvatov.alexander@gmail.com`, `pavel.kumbrasev@gmail.com`,
`roma-roma97@mail.ru`
[2] Intel Corporation, Nizhny Novgorod, Russia
`nadezhda.kogteva@intel.com`

Abstract. We examine the problem of performance evaluation for deep
neural networks. We develop a software, which, unlike the existing ones,
is focused on evaluating the performance of deep models' inference on
CPUs, integrated graphics and embedded devices. The implementation
is open source and free available on GitHub: https://github.com/itlab-
vision/openvino-dl-benchmark. The software is verified using the example of the well-known classification model ResNet-152 and the Inference
Engine component of the OpenVINO toolkit which is distributed by
Intel. The primarily advantage of the OpenVINO toolkit is the absence
of restrictions on the choice of a library for model training, since the
toolkit contains an utility for converting models into its own intermediate format. We analyze the performance of ResNet-152 in synchronous
and asynchronous inference modes on the Intel CPUs and Intel Processor
Graphics. We provide recommendations on the selection of the optimal
execution parameters. Inference performance results for more than 20
well-known deep models on the available hardware are posted on the
project web page: http://hpc-education.unn.ru/dli.

Keywords: Deep learning · Inference engine · Performance evaluation

1 Introduction

Deep learning is applied in various areas such as computer vision and image
processing [1–3], physics [4,5], bioinformatics and biomedicine [6,7], and other
problem areas [8]. The use of deep models involves the development of a neural
network topology, *training* a model on a training dataset, network *inference*,
and analyzing the quality of the trained model on a test dataset. The model
deployment is preceded by the inference performance evaluation on the target
hardware. If the obtained performance is acceptable, then this stage is followed
by the model compression, as well as a repeated loop of training and quality
evaluation.

© Springer Nature Switzerland AG 2019
V. Voevodin and S. Sobolev (Eds.): RuSCDays 2019, CCIS 1129, pp. 542–553, 2019.
https://doi.org/10.1007/978-3-030-36592-9_44

Currently, there are many neural networks that provide solutions to classical computing problems from different areas of knowledge. Collections of pre-trained models are accumulated in the format of various software tools (model zoos) [9–15]. *Transfer learning* allows usage of existing models for effective solution to new practically important tasks. In this case, models are used directly, or modified and re-trained in accordance with the problem statement. Deep neural network training is a computationally intensive and time-consuming process that is carried out in offline mode. The training is performed on powerful computing servers, which require discrete GPUs [16] and specialized network equipment [17]. The use of trained models implies *inference* execution (testing). Inference, in contrast to the network training, should be carried out in real time to quickly obtain a practical task solution [18]. Performance analysis of a deep neural network is an important step in the development of real-world applications. This step allows to estimate the inference time and depending on this step subsequent model compression could be performed.

The goal of this research is to develop a software to automatically evaluate the inference performance of the well-known neural network models on various hardware. The main advantage of this software from the existing ones is that along with the open source code the inference results for a large number of deep models on various hardware are provided (Intel CPUs and Intel Processor Graphics, Intel Movidius Vision Processing Unit is currently planed). The software sources are available on GitHub [21], it provides the possibility to carry out experiments on testing models of interest on preferred hardware. We publish performance results that allow anyone to estimate the perspective for the practical application of models.

The paper is structured as follows. First, an overview of the existing software for evaluation of deep models' performance is given. Further, the architecture of the developed software, its execution scheme and the implementation details are provided. Hereafter we analyze inference performance for the ResNet-152 model [19] on various hardware using the Inference Engine component of the OpenVINO toolkit which is distributed by Intel [20]. We give recommendations on the selection of the optimal execution parameters in synchronous and asynchronous inference modes on the Intel CPUs and Intel Processor Graphics.

2   Related Work

In recent years, there has been an increased interest in the issue of evaluating the performance of deep neural networks. DeepBench [22] is one of the first proposed benchmarking software. The goal of its development is to estimate the performance of basic operations that are used in deep learning algorithms (dense matrix multiplication, convolution, etc.). This software provides low-level information on the execution time of separate operations, but it does not allow to evaluate the training and testing time of a deep model.

Developers of the software represented in [23] offer a solution for assessing training and testing performance of deep models on different GPUs, taking into account the possibilities of half-precision. The limitations of this software are a few number of models and the fixed versions of deep learning tools. Currently the software is not supported.

DAWNBench [24] is an infrastructure where anyone can post the performance results described in a specific format. At the same time, information about the hardware and software configuration, the source code of the model training and testing, the achieved accuracy after each epoch, performance measurements and the cost of model training in the cloud are published. The main disadvantages are the lack of guarantees of the experimental conditions correctness and the experiments' reproducibility. Therefore, the performance comparison is not pure from the benchmarking point of view.

DLBS from Hewlett Packard Enterprise [25] solves the issue with the purity of the experiments. DLBS is a command-line toolkit for consistent and reproducible experiments on various hardware and software platforms. Developers provide a significant amount of functionality for evaluating the performance of a large number of deep learning tools. This software is positioned as a recommender one when choosing hardware for inference of deep neural networks. Carrying out experiments involves the presence of user hardware. The lack of available performance results is a significant drawback.

Deep500 [26] is one of the newest software. The authors try to combine the positive aspects of the existing software analogs. A distinctive feature is the ability to evaluate the performance of procedures related to the individual operators, the entire neural network, the training methods and the distributed training algorithms. The system is being actively developed. By the moment, there are no examples of the performance results of training and testing the models on various hardware.

The proposed software, unlike the existing ones listed above, is focused on automatic evaluation of the deep models' inference performance on CPUs, integrated graphics, embedded devices. The software is based on the Intel Distribution of OpenVINO toolkit [20]. The OpenVINO toolkit provides an ability to convert models from TensorFlow [32], Caffe [33], MXNet [28] and ONNX [34] formats to its intermediate format. The user takes an opportunity to evaluate the model performance and to determine the perspectives of its practical appliance, regardless of the training framework choice. The software is published in open source which allows its unlimited usage by anyone on their own environment. Performance results are provided which gives a possibility to estimate capabilities of the benchmarked hardware.

3   Benchmark Architecture

The proposed software for inference performance analysis consists of the several components (Fig. 1).

1. **Target Hardware** is a target computer for model inference. It is assumed that the required software is installed on this computer and a set of models for benchmarking are prepared.

2. **FTP server** stores test configurations for each target hardware and performance results.
3. **Integrator** is a component intended for the performance results gathering which could be accessed online through the project web page [31].

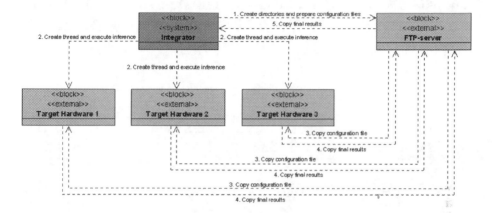

Fig. 1. The software architecture

The loop of benchmarking includes the following steps.

1. **Integrator** creates a directory structure on the **FTP server** and generates configuration files for the deep models' inference for each **Target Hardware**.
2. **Integrator** executes a performance analysis on each **Target Hardware**. Performance analysis involves obtaining a configuration of the deep models inference from the **FTP server** and consistently executing tests for each model in separate process. Performance measurements are collected during tests.
3. When the tests are completed, the performance results are copied from the **Target Hardware** to the **FTP server**.
4. Once benchmark completes all tests on each hardware, obtained results are saved in the form of a csv-table, which is automatically converted into a html-page and published on the Internet.

4   Implementation

The software is developed in the Python 3 programming language. The Intel Distribution of OpenVINO toolkit [20] is used for inference of deep neural networks. The developed software is free and sources are available on GitHub [21]. The complete inference performance results for the well-known deep models on the available hardware are posted on the project web page [31].

5   Experiments

5.1   Hardware and Software

For the developed software verification, several hardware and software configurations are used, their parameters are given below (Table 1). We use both servers and laptops. We installed identical versions of the OpenVINO toolkit. Processor frequency is not fixed. Each inference experiment is repeated many times. The iterations number of the test loop is set to 1000 when analyzing the inference performance of the test model.

Table 1. Hardware and software

	Hardware and software
1	CPU: Intel® Core™ i5-8600K CPU 3.60GHz; RAM: 32 GB; OS: Ubuntu 16.04
	GPU: Intel® UHD Graphics 630, Coffee Lake GT2, 24 shaders, 128 bit bus width
	Software: Compiler gcc 5.4.0, Intel Distribution of OpenVINO toolkit R5, Python 3.5.2
2	CPU: Intel® Core™ i3-7100 CPU 3.90GHz; RAM: 8 GB; OS: Windows 10
	GPU: Intel® HD Graphics 630, Coffee Lake GT2, 24 shaders, 128 bit bus width
	Software: Compiler MSVC 19.16.27025.1, Intel Distribution of OpenVINO toolkit R5, Python 3.6.0
3	CPU: Intel® Core™ i5-7700K CPU 4.20GHz; RAM: 16 GB; OS: Windows 10
	GPU: Intel® HD Graphics 630, Coffee Lake GT2, 24 shaders, 128 bit bus width
	Software: Compiler MSVC 19.16.27026.1, Intel Distribution of OpenVINO toolkit R5, Python 3.6.5
4	CPU: Intel® Core™ i5-8300H CPU 2.30GHz; RAM: 8 GB; OS: Windows 10
	GPU: Intel® UHD Graphics 630, Coffee Lake GT2, 24 shaders, 64 bit bus width
	Software: Compiler MSVC 19.16.27026.1, Intel Distribution of OpenVINO toolkit R5, Python 3.6.5

5.2   Models

During the software verification, inference performance results for more than 20 well-known models are collected. In this paper we present the performance analysis for the ResNet-152 network [19] chosen to demonstrate common performance effects. ResNet-152 classifies images with 1000 classes on the ImageNet dataset [29]. In 2015, the model demonstrated the best quality in the ImageNet Large Scale Visual Recognition Competition (ILSVRC), reaching 3.57% classification error [30]. ResNet-152 is a deep residual network proposed to prevent the gradient degradation problem while training the model. The model contains 50 residual blocks. The number of 152 in the network name shows the total number of convolutional layers. The input image resolution is 224×224 pixels. The model description and trained weights are public available in the original Caffe format [35].

5.3 Datasets

Neural network performance was evaluated on a subset of the dataset images, the training samples of which were used to train this model. The ImageNet dataset [29] was used for the ResNet-152 model. 16 images from the ImageNet validation dataset were selected to verify the correctness of the network inference implementation based on the OpenVINO toolkit and to measure inference performance. This subset contains images of different classes of wildlife and human-created objects, which are recognized by the model with the accuracy of more than 90%. The computational complexity of the neural network inference does not depend on the scene in the image.

5.4 Experiment Types

Deep neural networks inference using the Inference Engine of the Intel Distribution of OpenVINO toolkit [20] is supported by various devices: Intel CPUs, Intel Processor Graphics, Intel VPUs and Intel FPGAs. We present the experiments for a number of CPUs and integrated GPUs. Parameters of the computational nodes are shown in the Table 1. Further we denote the test configuration as "{computer identifier}({device})", where {computer identifier} corresponds to the computer number in the Table 1, and {device} is the computational device used for the inference (takes values of CPU or GPU), for example, 3(GPU).

The OpenVINO toolkit provides two modes of deep models' inference.

1. **Synchronous mode.** Involves creating and executing a single request to infer the model on the selected device. The next inference request is created at the end of the previous one. During performance analysis, the number of generated requests is determined by the iterations number of the model test loop.
2. **Asynchronous mode.** Involves creating a set of requests to infer the neural network on the selected device. The order of requests completion in the simplest case corresponds to the sequence of their creation, but for some tasks it is determined by the neural network topology and the input image complexity. The number of generated request sets is determined by the number of iterations of the model test loop.

One inference request corresponds to the forward propagation of the neural network for a *batch* of images. The required execution parameters are a batch size, a number of iterations, a number of requests created in asynchronous mode. Inference can be executed in multi-threading mode. A number of threads could be set as a model execution parameter. Moreover, for asynchronous mode there is a possibility to execute requests in parallel using streams. A number of streams is an asynchronous mode parameter.

5.5   Measurements

Due to the fact that OpenVINO toolkit provides two inference APIs performance measurements are taken for each mode. When evaluating inference performance for **the synchronous mode**, requests are executed sequentially. The next request is performed after the completion of the previous one. For each request, its duration time is measured. The standard deviation is calculated on the set of obtained durations and the ones that goes beyond three standard deviations relative to the mean inference time are discarded. The resulting set of times is used to compute the performance metrics for the synchronous mode.

– **Latency** is a median of execution times.
– **Average time of a single pass** is the ratio of the total execution time of all iterations to the number of iterations.
– **FPS** is the ratio of the batch size to the latency.

For **the asynchronous mode**, performance metrics are different and provided below.

– **Average time of a single pass** is the ratio of the execution time of all requests sets to the iterations number of the test loop. It is the execution time of a set of simultaneously created requests on the device.
– **FPS** is the ratio of the product of the batch size and the iterations number to the execution time of all requests.

5.6   Performance Analysis

The performance of the ResNet-152 model has been measured on the available hardware for synchronous and asynchronous modes with various parameters. First, consider the features of the synchronous mode on CPUs (Fig. 2). Note that the FPS depends on the processor performance when the batch size and the number of threads are fixed.

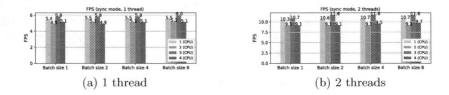

(a) 1 thread   (b) 2 threads

Fig. 2. FPS for the synchronous inference mode on the CPUs

Further we consider the experimental results on the first hardware configuration (Intel® Core™ i5-8600K CPU 3.60GHz, 32 GB, 6 cores). The following conclusions are valid for the other systems represented in the Table 1.

It is interesting to analyze synchronous inference performance scaling with various number of CPU threads. Note that with an increase in the threads number, a decrease in the average time of a single network pass is observed for each fixed batch size (Fig. 3, a). Speedup (Fig. 3, b) grows almost linearly, multithreading implementation of the synchronous inference is highly scalable. For 4 threads the speedup is ~ 3.4, for 6 threads it is ~ 4.7. Moreover, the speedups for the fixed threads number are approximately equal (Fig. 3, b) for batch sizes larger than 2 images. Thus, it is advisable to set threads number equal the number of physical cores and submit more than two images to the model input in the synchronous mode. The maximum batch size is limited by the available RAM.

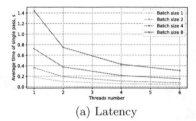
(a) Latency

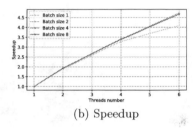
(b) Speedup

Fig. 3. Average time of a single pass and speedup depending on the threads number for different batch sizes (synchronous mode, 1(CPU))

Using the specified number of threads and batch size, FPS exceeds 25 frames per second (Table 2). It means that the inference is executed in real time.

Table 2. The dependence of FPS on the threads number and batch size (synchronous inference mode, 1(CPU))

Batch size	Threads number			
	1	2	4	6
1	5.4	10.3	18.0	21.7
2	5.5	10.6	18.7	**25.9**
4	5.5	10.7	18.9	**26.1**
8	5.5	10.7	18.8	**26.1**

Asynchronous mode is an alternative to synchronous one. The advantage of the asynchronous mode can be seen in the situations where it is necessary to optimize not the time of a single pass, but the throughput of the model. An example is the processing video frames using deep neural networks. Frames are received sequentially, and a queue of inference requests can be formed. In this case, a small batch of frames is supplied to the input of the model in each request. The goal of the asynchronous mode is the effective execution of multiple inference requests in parallel by creating independent streams. Let we fix the threads number by default and the requests number equal to 6 (by the number of physical cores in the system) and analyze the changes of FPS depending on the streams number on the first hardware (Intel® Core™ i5-8600K CPU 3.60GHz, 32 GB, 6 cores). Obtained results (Fig. 4) show that in the case of a single stream, we observe a sequential execution of requests, and the throughput is minimal. When choosing the streams number equal to 4 for 6 requests, the first four requests are executed in parallel, and upon their completion the remaining two requests are executed. When choosing the streams number equal to the requests number (6 requests), parallel execution of inference requests is provided and the maximum throughput is achieved. The inference is executed in real time, and FPS is about 25. Therefore, the parameter configuration in which the number of streams and requests coincides is the most effective in terms of throughput.

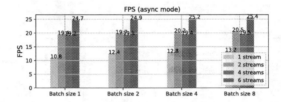

Fig. 4. The dependence of FPS on the number of streams (asynchronous mode, 1(CPU), requests number is 6, threads number is set by default)

It is necessary to determine the optimal batch size of images on the same hardware configuration. Table 3 shows the FPS values obtained for various batch sizes and streams number. The maximum batch size provides the greatest throughput.

Table 3. The dependence of FPS on the batch size and streams number (asynchronous inference mode, 1(CPU), threads number is set by default)

Streams number	Batch size			
	1	2	4	8
1	21.3	24.7	24.9	**25.4**
2	25.1	25.7	25.9	**26.3**
4	19.2	19.3	**19.4**	**19.4**
6	24.6	24.9	25.2	**25.5**

CPU is one of the most critical resources and distribution of load between other devices is often considered on practice. It is interesting to compare the efficiency of the synchronous inference mode on Intel CPUs and Intel Processor Graphics using the example of the first hardware configuration. Figure 5 shows the performance obtained for the batch size of 8 images. Note that the CPU version can be executed in multi-threading mode. From the presented histograms one can see that the average time of a single pass and FPS on the available GPU are comparable with the corresponding ones obtained for a two-threading synchronous inference on the CPU (Fig. 5, dark bins). Performance on the GPU in asynchronous mode is also comparable to the two-streams CPU version. Therefore, Intel Processor Graphics can be considered a good alternative to the inference execution device.

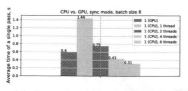
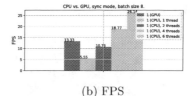

(a) Average time of a single pass   (b) FPS

Fig. 5. Performance in synchronous mode (Intel® Core™ i5-8600K CPU 3.60GHz; 32 GB; Intel® UHD Graphics 630, Coffee Lake GT2, 24 Unified shaders, 128 bit Bus width; Ubuntu 16.04). CPU performance measured in multi-threading mode with batch size equal 8

To summarize, we give the following general guidelines for effective inference using the OpenVINO toolkit.

- Synchronous mode should be used in applications where the inference time is important. It is highly recommended to use default multi-threading mode. The batch size is limited by the size of RAM.
- Asynchronous mode should be used when throughput is most important. An efficient parallel scheme of asynchronous inference assumes that the requests being created are executed in parallel, i.e. the number of inference requests is the same as the streams number.
- Intel Processor Graphics are promising devices for deep models' inference.

Notice that the specific values of the performance measurements depend on the model topology.

6   Conclusion

Software that focuses on evaluating the inference performance of deep models on wide range of devices (CPUs, integrated GPUs, embedded devices) has been developed. An open source implementation is available on GitHub [21], it is based on the OpenVINO toolkit [20]. Comprehensive performance results for the well-known models on the available hardware, providing for the presence of the Intel CPUs and Intel Processor Graphics, are published on the project web page [31].

In the future, we plan to increase the number of software and hardware platforms. We will analyse performance for the inference implementations based on the well-known deep learning frameworks, in particular, Caffe2 [27] and MXNet [28]. Further we will compare inference performance using various deep learning tools.

Acknowledgements. The research was supported by the Intel Corporation. The authors thank company's employees for their help and attention to the research.

References

1. Howard A.G., et al.: MobileNets: efficient convolutional neural networks for mobile vision applications. In: NIPS 2016 Proceedings of the 30th International Conference on Neural Information Processing Systems, pp. 379–387 (2017)
2. Redmon J., Farhadi A.: YOLOv3: An Incremental Improvement (2018). https://arxiv.org/abs/1804.02767
3. Chen, L.-C., et al.: DeepLab: semantic image segmentation with deep convolutional nets, atrous convolution, and fully connected CRFs. IEEE Trans. Pattern Anal. Mach. Intell. **40**(2018), 834–848 (2018)
4. George, D., Huerta, E.A.: Deep learning for real-time gravitational wave detection and parameter estimation: results with advanced LIGO data. Phys. Lett. B **778**(2018), 64–70 (2017)
5. Mehta, P., et al.: A high-bias, low-variance introduction to Machine Learning for physicists (2018). https://arxiv.org/abs/1803.08823
6. Yoon, S.: lncRNAnet: long non-coding RNA identification using deep learning. Bioinformatics **34**(22), 3889–3897 (2018)
7. Yu, T.: A graph-embedded deep feedforward network for disease outcome classification and feature selection using gene expression data. Bioinformatics **34**(21), 3727–3737 (2018)
8. Nemirovsky, D., et al.: A general guide to applying machine learning to computer architecture. Supercomput. Front. Innov. **5**(1), 95–115 (2018)
9. Model Zoo: Discover open source deep learning code and pretrained models. https://modelzoo.co
10. Caffe Model Zoo. https://github.com/BVLC/caffe/wiki/Model-Zoo
11. Models and examples built with TensorFlow. https://github.com/tensorflow/models
12. The models subpackage TORCHVISION.MODELS. https://pytorch.org/docs/stable/torchvision/models.html
13. Keras Applications: Available models. https://keras.io/applications
14. Cognitive Toolkit: Model gallery. https://www.microsoft.com/en-us/cognitive-toolkit/features/model-gallery
15. OpenVINO Toolkit - Open Model Zoo repository. https://github.com/opencv/open_model_zoo
16. Deep Learning Workstation Solutions: Unlock high-performance AI supercomputing from your desktop. https://www.nvidia.com/en-us/deep-learning-ai/solutions/workstation
17. Mellanox Enables the Most Efficient Machine Learning Platforms. Allowing AI to Perform Critical & Real Time Decisions to Enhance Competitive Advantages. http://www.mellanox.com/solutions/machine-learning

18. Intel AI: Hardware. https://ai.intel.com/hardware
19. He, K., Zhang, X., Ren, S., Sun, J.: Deep residual learning for image recognition. In: The IEEE Conference on Computer Vision and Pattern Recognition (CVPR), pp. 770–778 (2016). https://arxiv.org/abs/1512.03385
20. Intel Distribution of OpenVINO toolkit. https://software.intel.com/en-us/openvino-toolkit
21. Deep learning benchmark based on Intel Deep Learning Deployment Toolkit. https://github.com/itlab-vision/openvino-dl-benchmark
22. DeepBench: Benchmarking Deep Learning operations on different hardware. https://github.com/baidu-research/DeepBench
23. Deep Learning Benchmark for comparing the performance of DL frameworks, GPUs, and single vs half precision. https://github.com/u39kun/deep-learning-benchmark
24. DAWNBench: An End-to-End Deep Learning Benchmark and Competition. https://dawn.cs.stanford.edu/benchmark, https://cs.stanford.edu/~deepakn/assets/papers/dawnbench-sosp17.pdf
25. Deep Learning Benchmarking Suite (DLBS). https://hewlettpackard.github.io/dlcookbook-dlbs/. https://github.com/HewlettPackard/dlcookbook-dlbs
26. Deep500: A Deep Learning Meta-Framework and HPC Benchmarking Library. https://github.com/deep500/deep500. https://arxiv.org/pdf/1901.10183.pdf
27. Caffe2: A New Lightweight, Modular, and Scalable Deep Learning Framework. https://caffe2.ai
28. Apache MXNet (Incubating): A flexible and efficient library for deep learning. mxnet.incubator.apache.org
29. ImageNET. http://www.image-net.org
30. ImageNet Large Scale Visual Recognition Competition (ILSVRC). http://www.image-net.org/challenges/LSVRC
31. DLI: Deep Learning Inference Benchmark (in English). http://hpc-education.unn.ru/dli-ru (In Russian). http://hpc-education.unn.ru/dli
32. TensorFlow. https://www.tensorflow.org
33. Caffe: Deep learning framework. http://caffe.berkeleyvision.org
34. ONNX: Open Neural Network Exchange Format. https://onnx.ai
35. The ResNet-152 model (.prototxt and.caffemodel files). https://onedrive.live.com/download?cid=4006CBB8476FF777&resid=4006CBB8476FF777%2117893&authkey=AAFW2-FVoxeVRck. https://onedrive.live.com/download?cid=4006CBB8476FF777&resid=4006CBB8476FF777%2117897&authkey=AAFW2-FVoxeVRck

Educational Course "Introduction to Deep Learning Using the Intel neon Framework"

Valentina Kustikova$^{(\boxtimes)}$, Nikolay Zolotykh, and Maxim Zhiltsov

Lobachevsky State University of Nizhni Novgorod, Nizhny Novgorod, Russia
valentina.kustikova@gmail.com, Nikolai.Zolotykh@gmail.com,
zhiltsov.max35@gmail.com

Abstract. The interest of researchers in deep learning is constantly increasing. Deep learning methods penetrate physics, biology and other problem areas. Often, scientists and engineers consider a deep model as a "black box", allowing them to solve a problem on a specific dataset. However, there are typical schemes for the application of deep learning methods and standard recommendations for the pragmatic use of various deep models. In this paper, we present a new training course that provides a minimal theoretical basis and creates practical experience in applying deep learning for solving computer vision problems using the Intel neon Framework. The course studies the biological basis of artificial neurons, provides a classification of deep models, discusses constructing deep topologies and training methods of fully-connected, convolutional and recurrent neural networks, describes methods of unsupervised learning. The issues of efficient utilization of computational resources of modern clusters for training and testing deep models are also discussed. A distinctive feature of the course is the independence from a deep learning framework. All materials can be easily modified to use another framework. The paper formulates the main ideas of the course, describes its structure and provides the results of training over two years at the Lobachevsky State University of Nizhni Novgorod. Course materials (in Russian and English) are publicly available under Apache 2.0 license.

Keywords: Deep learning · Educational course · Intel neon Framework

1 Introduction

Importance of deep learning is increasingly growing. Deep learning is applied in various areas, from video and audio analysis to physics, biology and biomedicine [1–7]. A large number of software tools has been developed, zoos of deep models have been collected, which allow solving classical problems of computer vision, natural language processing, sound processing, etc. A significant contribution has been made by the development of educational courses which describe theoretical fundamentals and applied aspects of deep learning.

© Springer Nature Switzerland AG 2019
V. Voevodin and S. Sobolev (Eds.): RuSCDays 2019, CCIS 1129, pp. 554–562, 2019.
https://doi.org/10.1007/978-3-030-36592-9_45

This paper describes the experience of building and implementing a new educational course on deep learning. The main goal of this course is to train specialists who understand the general scheme of solving applied problems using deep learning and have the minimum necessary theoretical basis in order to apply their knowledge in the field of their specialization. The course implies that students have both good mathematical knowledge (in algebra, optimization methods, probability theory), as programming skills in Python. The practice of teaching the course demonstrated a high interest of students, especially those whose work is concerned with data analysis.

The article is organized as follows. Section 2 provides an overview of similar educational courses. In Sect. 3, the main principles underlying the proposed course are emphasized. Section 4 discusses the course structure, describes the theoretical topics and practical classes. Section 5 describes the course implementation experience and the achieved results. Section 6 concludes the paper.

2   Related Work

An overview showed that publicly available educational courses can be divided into three groups.

1. Courses focused on the training and applying fully-connected neural networks, understanding the key parameters in a neural network's architecture, as well as on the developing effective implementations [8,9].
2. Courses that study various types of deep models [10,12–14].
3. Courses oriented on solving tasks in specific problem areas (usually, computer vision or natural language processing) [15–17].

The first group of educational courses is a theoretical one. These courses cover the basics of linear algebra, gradient descent, backpropagation algorithm for training fully-connected neural networks. They require strong mathematical knowledge in order to deeply understand the basics of constructing and training fully-connected neural networks. Courses of this group are usually supported by the practical task of implementing the training of the certain fully-connected network.

The second group of courses studies specific deep models. The Google AI's course [10] focuses on convolutional neural networks and its implementation using TensorFlow [11]. Intel offers the course [13] oriented on solving practical problems of self-driving cars, speech interfaces, genomic sequence analysis and algorithmic trading using convolutional and recurrent networks. Authors also consider the issues of distributed training. The MIT course [14] covers all existing deep models (fully-connected neural networks, convolutional neural networks, recurrent neural networks, autoencoders, generative adversarial networks), considers the topic of deep reinforcement learning.

The goal of the third group of courses is to introduce students into a specific problem area and study state-of-the-art deep models that allow solving classical tasks in this area. The course [15] considers models for image classification and annotation, object recognition and image search, various object detection techniques, motion estimation, object tracking in video, human action recognition, and finally image stylization, editing and new image generation. The program of the Stanford course [16] covers both the general principles of neural networks and their training, as well as the main types of neural networks. The course is a complete theoretical and practical guide to solving visual recognition problems. Practice involves the implementation of a course project. The course is focused on the academic community and has a high threshold of entry. The Stanford course [17] is analogous to the previous one, but it is focused on problems of natural language processing.

We develop the educational course that provide a "quick start" in practical deep learning. The theoretical part of the course is similar to the MIT course [14]. There is a difference in several topics. The course studies the biological basis of artificial neurons, provides a classification of deep models, discusses constructing deep topologies and training methods of fully-connected, convolutional and recurrent neural networks, describes methods of unsupervised learning. The issues of efficient utilization of computational resources for training and testing deep models are also discussed. The practice involves solving a certain computer vision problem using various deep models. A distinctive feature of our course is its independence from a deep learning framework. All materials can be easily modified to use another framework.

3   Main Principles

The basis of the educational course consists of the following principles.

1. The minimum of theory necessary to understand the methods of constructing deep neural networks, the methods and parameters of their training, the quality measurements of training convergence and the quality indicators of solving the problem.
2. Maximum practical tasks that allow you to go through the entire loop of solving the applied problem using deep learning: preparing train and test data, selecting quality indicators for a specific problem, developing a neural network topology, training a constructed model on the train dataset, evaluating the model quality on the test data, topology modification.
3. No restrictions on the choice of problem and deep learning tool. The course materials provide a basic theory and an example of applying the described approaches to solving a certain problem using the Intel neon Framework.

4   Course Structure

4.1   Course Description

The course examines the construction and the performance analysis of deep neural networks using the Intel neon Framework. The following topics are covered:

1. Introduction to deep learning.
2. Multilayered fully-connected neural networks.
3. Introduction to the Intel neon Framework.
4. Convolutional neural networks. Deep residual networks.
5. Transfer learning of deep neural networks.
6. Unsupervised learning: autoencoders, restricted Boltzmann machines. Deconvolutional networks.
7. Recurrent neural networks.
8. Introduction to the Intel nGraph.

The course is practice oriented. There are 8 lectures (2 h each) and 5 individual consultations in groups of 2–3 people (for each group). Lectures are held in plain lecture or master class (tutorial) form. The presentation of the theoretical material in most lectures/master classes is supported by examples of developing a deep neural network topology using the Intel neon Framework. The problem for which deep models are constructed is comprehensive and covers the entire lecture part, with the exception of an introductory lecture of a survey nature. The practice of the course is structured as follows. Students are divided into the groups of 2–3 people. Each group chooses a specific problem and tries to achieve the maximum quality by constructing different types of deep topologies and modifying their internal structure or training parameters. Students follow the provided tutorials that represent step-by-step deep model development using the Intel neon Framework. The final control of knowledge assumes presentation of the developed project with demonstration of quality/performance measurements of the proposed deep neural networks.

The course is aimed at engineers, teachers and researchers, as well as postgraduate students and students of higher educational institutions.

Students should have basic programming skills in the scripting programming language Python. The course also requires theoretical knowledge in optimization methods, probability theory, image processing and computer vision.

The course schedule is as follows (Table 1). We published all materials [18] under Apache 2.0 license [19].

4.2   Course Theory

The theory of the course includes 8 lectures (Table 1). First, the concept of deep learning is introduced, examples of deep models' use in natural language processing and computer vision are given, a classification of deep models is given (Lecture 1). Further, the biological fundamentals of artificial neurons is considered, fully-connected neural networks are introduced, the training scheme of this model type and the main parameters of the training method are considered (Lecture 2). Lecture 3 gives an overview of the Intel neon Framework and the general scheme of training/testing deep models using this framework.

The following lectures consistently describe methods for constructing convolutional neural networks (Lecture 4), transfer learning as one of the quick approaches for obtaining the first solution of a practical problem (Lecture 5),

Table 1. The course structure

Topic	Hours
Introduction to deep learning **(LECTURE 1)** The notion of deep learning. Biological fundamentals of deep learning. Examples of practical problems. Classification of deep models.	2
Multilayered fully-connected neural networks **(LECTURE 2)** The structure of fully-connected neural networks (FCNN), types of activation functions. Training problem of FCNN, loss function. Backpropagation method.	2
Preprocessing and converting data to HDF5 format for the Intel neon Framework **(PRACTICAL CLASS 0)** Preliminary practice to prepare dataset for the subsequent practical classes.	4
Introduction to the Intel neon Framework **(LECTURE 3)** Introduction to the Intel neon Framework. Installation. The structure of application for training/testing of the single-layer fully-connected neural network using the Intel neon Framework.	2
The development of fully-connected neural networks using the Intel neon Framework **(PRACTICAL CLASS 1)** Problem statement for the practice. Developing topologies of fully-connected neural networks with different number of hidden layers and number of hidden elements on each layer. Developing scripts for training/testing the proposed topologies. Carrying out experiments, collecting performance measurements.	4
Convolutional neural networks. Deep residual networks **(LECTURE 4)** The structure of a convolutional layer and network. Example of training/testing a single-layer convolutional network using the Intel neon Framework. Deep residual networks, a typical structural block, an example of a residual network.	2
The development of convolutional neural networks using the Intel neon Framework **(PRACTICAL CLASS 2)** Development of convolutional network topologies with different number of hidden layers and filter parameters on each layer. Developing scripts for training/testing the proposed topologies. Carrying out experiments, collecting performance measurements.	4
Transfer learning of deep neural networks **(LECTURE 5)** Description of the general approach underlying the transfer learning of deep neural networks. An example of transfer learning application using the Intel neon Framework.	2
Application of transfer learning to solve a given problem using the Intel neon Framework **(PRACTICAL CLASS 3)** Selection of the original problem (connected with a given problem) and a corresponded trained model. Modification of the network topology for a given problem. Complete training of the parameters of all network layers with arbitrary initialization. Training parameters of all layers with initialization, obtained as a result of training the model to solve the original problem. Learning only the last layers (modified) of the network with initialization, obtained as a result of training the model to solve the original problem.	4
Unsupervised learning: autoencoders, restricted Boltzmann machine. Deconvolutional networks **(LECTURE 6)** Unsupervised learning methods. The concept of an autoencoder, a stack of autoencoders, deconvolutional networks.	2

(continued).

Table 1. (*continued*)

Initial pretraining the weights of the most perspective architectures of fully-connected networks for the subsequent solution of a given problem in supervised manner using the Intel neon Framework **(PRACTICAL CLASS 4)** Selection of several fully-connected neural networks. Developing a stack of autoencoders. Training of the developed architectures. Application of the obtained initial weights for training the network in supervised manner to solve a given problem.	4
Recurrent neural networks **(LECTURE 7)** The general structure of the model. Deploying a recurrent neural network in time. Recurrent networks training. Long short-term memory network. An example of training/testing a simple recurrent network using the Intel neon Framework.	2
The development of recurrent neural networks using the Intel neon Framework **(PRACTICAL CLASS 5)** Development of topologies of recurrent neural networks with different number of hidden layers and number of hidden elements on each layer. Developing scripts for training/testing the proposed topologies. Carrying out experiments, collecting performance measurements.	4
Efficient execution of neural networks. The Intel nGraph overview **(LECTURE 8)** Introduction to the Intel nGraph. The neon frontend to the Intel nGraph.	2

unsupervised learning for pretraining the weights of deep models (Lecture 6), recurrent neural networks (Lecture 7). At the end of the course, an overview of the Intel nGraph (Lecture 8) [21] is given. nGraph compiler aims to accelerate developing AI workloads using any deep learning framework and deploying to a variety of hardware targets [21].

4.3 Course Practice

We provide tutorials for practical classes represented in the Table 1: a case study in source code that demonstrates the implementation of practical tasks, and a step-by-step description [18]. We use the IMDB-WIKI dataset [20] (Fig. 1) to demonstrate the implementation of the practical tasks on the problem of person's gender classification by a photo.

Fig. 1. The IMDB-WIKI dataset [20]

The tutorial consists of the following sections.

1. **Introduction**. In this section we give a short description of the practice.
2. **Guidelines**. Here goals and tasks are discussed as well as a recommended study sequence.
3. **Manual**. This section provides technical information necessary for working with a specific type of deep models, gives a step-by-step description of the implementation of a certain model, its training and testing, discusses the execution parameters of the implementation.

Let us consider the Practical class 2. This practice is aimed at studying convolutional neural networks and developing topologies of the specified model type using the Intel neon Framework to solve a practical problem. To achieve this goal, it is necessary to solve the following tasks.

1. Study the scheme of constructing convolutional neural networks.
2. Study the tools of the Intel neon Framework for working with convolutional networks.
3. Develop a script for training and testing of deep models to solve the problem.
4. Develop various topologies of convolutional neural networks using the Intel neon Framework.
5. Train the proposed models and evaluate the classification quality.

The tutorial provides a step-by-step description for solving each of these tasks for the problem of person's gender classification by a photo. As an example of topology development, a convolutional network consisting of a single layer is given.

The practice is assessed according to the several criteria.

1. Topologies of convolutional networks to solve the problem are developed. The models vary the number of convolutional layers, the convolutions parameters, activation functions; residual connections are applied. The transition from one model to another is explained experimentally or theoretically.
2. The constructed models are trained and tested, the source code for training and testing is free available on GitHub.
3. A brief report is prepared. The report contains a description of the developed topologies, as well as quality and performance analysis of the proposed models.

We offer a list of practical computer vision problems (single-image, multi-class classification problems); nevertheless, students can find their own task and dataset. There are some examples of the suggested tasks below, the full list is available in the course materials [18].

1. Image classification with a large number of categories. The Cifar-10 dataset https://www.kaggle.com/c/cifar-10.
2. Digit recognition. The Street View House Numbers (SVHN) dataset http://ufldl.stanford.edu/housenumbers.
3. Fashion classification. The Fashion MNIST dataset https://www.kaggle.com/zalando-research/fashionmnist.

5 Implementation

The developed course is read in the form of a compulsory course of the variable part of the master programs "Computer graphics and modeling of living and technical systems" and "Computational methods and supercomputer technologies" of the Institute of Information Technology, Mathematics and Mechanics at the Lobachevsky State University of Nizhni Novgorod. Classes are held in the first semester of the second year of study. First, the theory is recited in the form of lectures and master classes. As the necessary theoretical base will be available, the practical assignments are stated. Students are divided into groups, choose an applied problem and a dataset to solve it. Motivated students, as a rule, select the problems of interests and use their own labeled datasets. The area of interest is associated with research conducted by students in the course of their diplomas, or with their professional activities. In this case, the problem is consistent with the teacher to assess the feasibility of practical assignments. Further, students choose deep learning framework and implement practical tasks. The source code of programs for preparing data, training and testing deep models are published to their repository on GitHub. Each practice involves preparing a brief report that is attached to the source code. Examples of repositories can be found on the links https://github.com/ViktorRoy94/deep_learning, https://github.com/Fznamznon/Deep-Learning (in Russian).

6 Conclusion

The educational course "Introduction to deep learning using the Intel neon Framework" has been read at the Institute of Information Technology, Mathematics and Mechanics of the UNN since 2017. Currently, deep learning is an integral part of the specialist qualification in the field of information technologies. The developed course allows to get the basic knowledge necessary for a quick start in the applying of deep learning. The widespread use of deep learning confirms the relevance of the course.

There are several possible ways for further development of the course: increasing the set of typical deep models, and considering the specific deep topologies proposed for solving well-known applied problems.

Acknowledgements. This research financially supported by Intel Corporation.

References

1. Redmon J., Farhadi A.: YOLOv3: an incremental improvement (2018). https://arxiv.org/abs/1804.02767
2. Chen, L.-C., et al.: DeepLab: semantic image segmentation with deep convolutional nets, atrous convolution, and fully connected CRFs. IEEE Trans. Pattern Anal. Mach. Intell. **40**(4), 834–848 (2018)

3. George, D., Huerta, E.A.: Deep Learning for real-time gravitational wave detection and parameter estimation: results with Advanced LIGO data. Phys. Lett. B **778**(2018), 64–70 (2017)

4. Mehta, P., et al.: A high-bias, low-variance introduction to Machine Learning for physicists. https://arxiv.org/abs/1803.08823 (2018)

5. Yoon, S.: LncRNAnet: long non-coding RNA identification using deep learning. Bioinformatics **34**(22), 3889–3897 (2018)

6. Yu, T.: A graph-embedded deep feedforward network for disease outcome classification and feature selection using gene expression data. Bioinformatics **34**(21), 3727–3737 (2018)

7. Nemirovsky, D., et al.: A general guide to applying machine learning to computer architecture. Supercomput. Front. Innovations **5**(1), 95–115 (2018)

8. Ng, A., et al.: Neural networks and deep learning. https://www.coursera.org/learn/neural-networks-deep-learning. (in English)

9. Moskvichev, A., et al.: Neural networks. https://stepik.org/course/401/promo. (in Russian)

10. Moroney, L.: Introduction to tensorflow for artificial intelligence, machine learning, and deep learning. https://www.coursera.org/learn/introduction-tensorflow. (in English)

11. TensorFlow: an end-to-end open source machine learning platform. https://www.tensorflow.org

12. Sokolov, E., et al.: Introduction to deep learning. https://www.coursera.org/learn/intro-to-deep-learning. (in English)

13. Rodriguez, A., et al.: An introduction to practical deep learning. https://www.coursera.org/learn/intro-practical-deep-learning. (in English)

14. Fridman, L.: MIT deep learning basics: introduction and overview with tensorflow. https://medium.com/tensorflow/mit-deep-learning-basics-introduction-and-overview-with-tensorflow-355bcd26baf0. (in English)

15. Konushin, A., et al.: Deep learning in computer vision. https://www.coursera.org/learn/deep-learning-in-computer-vision. (in English)

16. Li, F.-F., et al.: Convolutional neural networks for visual recognition. http://cs231n.stanford.edu. (in English)

17. Manning, C., et al.: Natural language processing with deep learning. http://web.stanford.edu/class/cs224n. (in English)

18. Kustikova, V., et al.: Educational course "Introduction to deep learning using the Intel neon Framework". http://hpc-education.unn.ru/%D0%BE%D0%B1%D1%83%D1%87%D0%B5%D0%BD%D0%B8%D0%B5/%D0%BA%D1%83%D1%80%D1%81%D1%8B/intel-neon-framework (in Russian). http://hpc-education.unn.ru/en/trainings/collection-of-courses/introduction-to-deep-learning-using-the-intel-neon-framework (in English)

19. Apache 2.0 license. http://www.apache.org/licenses/LICENSE-2.0.txt

20. IMDB-WIKI dataset. https://data.vision.ee.ethz.ch/cvl/rrothe/imdb-wiki

21. nGraph is an open source C++ library, compiler and runtime for Deep Learning frameworks. https://github.com/NervanaSystems/ngraph. https://ngraph.nervanasys.com/docs/latest

Evaluation of Intel Memory Drive Technology Performance for Computational Astrophysics

Igor Chernykh[1]([⊠]), Vladimir Mironov[2], Andrey Kudryavtsev[3], and Igor Kulikov[1]

[1] Institute of Computational Mathematics and Mathematical Geophysics
SB RAS, 630090 Novosibirsk, Russia
{chernykh, kulikov}@ssd.sscc.ru
[2] Lomonosov Moscow State University, 119991 Moscow, Russia
vmironov@lcc.chem.msu.ru
[3] Intel Corporation, Folsom, CA 95630, USA
andrey.o.kudryavtsev@intel.com

Abstract. In this paper, we present a new version of the AstroPhi code for the numerical simulation of relativistic astrophysics. We provide benchmark data for Intel Memory Drive Technology (IMDT), which was used as an extension of DDR4 memory on the computational node. We used this new generation of Software-defined Memory (SDM) based on Intel ScaleMP collaboration and using 3D XPointTM based Intel Solid-State Drives (SSDs) called Optane for numerical simulation of astrophysical problems. Modern astrophysical problems such as a variety of dynamic and general relativistic phenomena (mergers of binary neutron stars and black hole-neutron star binaries or stellar collapse and explosion) require a large amount of memory as well as a large number of computational nodes. IMDT gave the possibility of extending DRAM memory or extending the scratch drive for an operating system defined by the user. To put the performance of IMDT in comparison, we used two systems: DRAM and DRAM+IMDT nodes. The performance was measured as a percentage of used memory and analyzed in detail.

Keywords: Computational astrophysics · High-performance computing · Hybrid memory systems

1 Introduction

For most of Top500 HPC systems, we can divide the amount of memory by amount of cores and we can see that most of the systems have 1–2 GB memory per core. If we analyze prices for the last 2–3 years, we can see that memory can contribute up to 90% to the cost of the servers. In addition, HPC integrators saying that there is a problem to buy fast a large amount of memory because there is a big queue to the memory solutions companies. Recently, Intel announced [1] a new SSD product based on novel 3D XPointTM technology under the name Intel Optane®. It was developed to overcome the drawbacks of NAND-technology: block-based memory addressing and limited write endurance. To be more specific, with 3D XPoint each memory cell can be

© Springer Nature Switzerland AG 2019
V. Voevodin and S. Sobolev (Eds.): RuSCDays 2019, CCIS 1129, pp. 563–572, 2019.
https://doi.org/10.1007/978-3-030-36592-9_46

addressed individually and write endurance of 3D XPoint memory is significantly higher than NAND SSD. A novel IMDT allows using Intel Optane drives as system memory. Another important advantage of 3D XPoint compared to DRAM is that it has a high density of memory cells, which allows building compact systems with massive memory banks. The disadvantage of this technology is the lifetime limit on reading and writing to flash memory in comparison with DRAM. At this moment, we have some statistics of Optanes usage as a part of a real computational node in Siberian Supercomputer Center. We have reached 30% of the max read/write cycles for the last year with a 90% load of this node. The main idea of this paper is to extend one paragraph of AstroPhi [2, 3] Optane tests in [4] and to show the efficiency comparison between two Intel Optane SSD generations.

2 Intel Memory Drive Technology (IMDT)

Intel® Memory Drive Technology is a result of the software development over a decade to bring new memory hierarchy to the system design. It's a software product, which relies on the specific hardware configuration. With such, it's only for Intel® Optane™ SSDs, due to their unique differentiating features. Originally released in 2017, Intel Optane P4800X SSDs are based in new media class 3D XPoint™ Technology and NVMe specifications which make them plug and play into existing systems. While the specification ensures system compatibility, the main differentiation is coming from a media. Those SSDs are designed with up to 10x smaller response time due to reduced latency, balanced read/write operations and extremely high endurance of 60DWPD based on JEDEC219 specifications. Such performance characteristics make them ideal for memory extension scenarios, where a data directly resides and is processed from a drive. Classic implementations of mmap() and OS paging are definitely experience performance improvements of a new product class, however they still have significant software overhead due to multi-layer design implementations, dependent on a driver, block layer, file system and realized differently in Linux kernels.

Intel Memory Drive Technology (IMDT) solves that problem. It's still considered a paging technology, however it's designed to be abstracted from the OS. It's running in the hypervisor layer, being effectively memory hypervisor. OS runs the in the VM layer, de-facto is the only VM. With such approach a memory range that OS sees is provided by IMDT and is different from the hardware layout. This allows to run original OS in the most transparent way on new hybrid memory. No changes required to the OS for the functionality and it sees hybrid memory as normal system memory not differentiating DRAM and Optane SSDs. Inside hypervisor layer IMDT does effective paging scenarios not possible with standard implementations such as OS Swap. One of those is data location management. DRAM and Optane SSDs are considered exclusive tiers, where user sees the capacity as a combination of two minus some software managed area. On every write to the memory it's placed to the DRAM first. Then if required it's aggregated and moved to Optane SSDs. This provides write latencies close to the DRAM. On a read operations, if data is in DRAM tier user will see it with DRAM-like latency. If it's not in a DRAM then performance will be based on 10us Optane latency.

The advantage of IMDT is hiding those 10us latency which are critical for application performance. That's done in multiple ways in parallel. One of them is active data movement for read prefetch. Analyzing workload pattern in real-time, IMDT AI engine is capable of creating an estimation for next memory location to be requested, so the data is moved ahead in spare CPU cycles. This allows to identify complex data structures in memory and effectively use read ahead for them. Another technology of masking Optane SSD latency is managing high concurrency. With more parallel threads running in the system, IMDT while hitting Optane tier submits asynchronous I/O and puts that core on a pause, while keep others running. This effectively helps to avoid system locks while delivering data outside of DRAM tier. Finally IMDT benefits of multiple Optane SSDs and scales bandwidth with more drives. That's done in combination with NUMA-aware data placement, where data from DRAM is moved to locally attached SSDs if possible and also in parallel I/O to multiple of them at the same time.

3 Mathematical Model and Numerical Method

A relativistic description of fluid dynamics should be used for solving astrophysical problems where the local velocity of the flow is close to the light speed in vacuum c or in case of the local internal energy density is comparable (or larger) than the local rest–mass density of the fluid.

3.1 Mathematical Model

For our problem, the speed of light in a vacuum $c \equiv 1$. The relativistic hydrodynamic equations in the form of conservation laws can be written [5] as:

$$\frac{\partial D}{\partial t} + \frac{\partial (Dv_k)}{\partial x_k} = 0 \tag{1}$$

$$\frac{\partial M_j}{\partial t} + \frac{\partial \left(M_j v_k + p\delta_{jk}\right)}{\partial x_k} = 0 \tag{2}$$

$$\frac{\partial E}{\partial t} + \frac{\partial (E+p)v_k}{\partial x_k} = 0 \tag{3}$$

Or it can be written in a more compact vector form in 3D space:

$$\frac{\partial U}{\partial t} + \sum_{k=1}^{3} \frac{\partial F_k}{\partial x_k} = 0 \tag{4}$$

where the vector of conservative variables and the vectors of flows are given as:

$$U = \begin{pmatrix} D \\ M_j \\ E \end{pmatrix} = \begin{pmatrix} \Gamma\rho \\ \Gamma^2\rho h v_j \\ \Gamma^2\rho h - p \end{pmatrix} \quad F_k = \begin{pmatrix} \rho\Gamma v_k \\ \rho h\Gamma^2 v_j v_k + p\delta_{jk} \\ \rho h\Gamma^2 v_k \end{pmatrix}, \text{ where } \rho \text{ - density,}$$

V_k - components of speed vector, δ_{jk} - Kronecker symbol, p – pressure, h – special enthalpy:

$$h = 1 + \frac{\gamma}{\gamma - 1}\frac{p}{\rho}, \tag{5}$$

γ - adiabatic index. Lorentz factor Γ determined by

$$\Gamma = \frac{1}{\sqrt{1 - v^2}}. \tag{6}$$

Sound speed can be evaluated by

$$c_s^2 = \gamma\frac{p}{\rho h} \tag{7}$$

Note that in the numerical method, calculations are performed in conservative variables D, M_j, E. We need to take into account that the nonlinear dependence between conservative variables and primitive ρ, v, p requires the special procedure for their recovery. This procedure is based on scheme from [6]. This scheme is very well parallelizable, because the recovery procedure goes independently in each cell.

3.2   Numerical Method

We will consider the area with uniform rectangular grid with step h. A fractional index will be used for cell numbering; an integer index will be used for node numbering. We write the one-dimensional analogue of the Godunov scheme for Eq. (4):

$$\frac{U_{i+1/2}^{n+1} - U_{i+1/2}^n}{\tau} + \frac{F_{i+1}^{n+1/2} - F_i^{n+1/2}}{h} = 0 \tag{8}$$

where $F_i^{n+1/2}$ - solution of the linearized Riemann problem for special relativistic hydrodynamics. Let us consider in detail the procedure for solving the linearized Riemann problem written for primitive variables:

$$\frac{\partial}{\partial t}\begin{pmatrix} \rho \\ v_x \\ v_y \\ v_z \\ p \end{pmatrix} + A\frac{\partial}{\partial x}\begin{pmatrix} \rho \\ v_x \\ v_y \\ v_z \\ p \end{pmatrix} = 0 \tag{9}$$

The matrix A can be decomposed as $A = R\Lambda L$, where R and L - matrix of right and left eigenvectors, Λ - diagonal matrix of eigenvalues. The Eq. (9) can be written as:

$$\frac{\partial w}{\partial t} + R\Lambda L \frac{\partial w}{\partial x} = 0, \tag{10}$$

where $w = (\rho, v_x, v_y, v_z, p)^T$. Let multiply the equations on the matrix L. We got the time-independent transport Eq. (11) by making replace $q = Lw$ using equality $LR = I$.

$$\frac{\partial q}{\partial t} + \Lambda \frac{\partial q}{\partial x} = 0 \tag{11}$$

The solution of the last equation depends on the sign of the eigenvalue. In case of $\lambda > 0$

$$q_L(-\lambda\tau) = q_i^R - \frac{\lambda\tau}{2h}\left(\Delta q_i - q_i^6\left(1 - \frac{2\lambda\tau}{3h}\right)\right) \tag{12}$$

otherwise

$$q_R(\lambda\tau) = q_i^L + \frac{\lambda\tau}{2h}\left(\Delta q_i + q_i^6\left(1 - \frac{2\lambda\tau}{3h}\right)\right) \tag{13}$$

We present a detailed procedure for constructing a parabola and parameters, $q_i^R, q_i^L, \Delta q_i, q_i^6$. For definiteness, we will construct a piecewise parabolic function of an arbitrary parameter $q(x)$ on a regular grid with a step h, on the interval $\left[x_{i-1/2}, x_{i+1/2}\right]$. In general, a parabola can be written as:

$q(x) = q_i^L + \xi\left(\Delta q_i + q_i^{(6)}(1 - \xi)\right)$, where q_i — cell center value, $\xi = (x - x_{i-1/2})h^{-1}, \Delta q_i = q_i^L - q_i^R. q_i^{(6)} = 6\left(q_i - 1/2(q_i^L + q_i^R)\right)$ in case of

$$q_i = h^{-1} \int_{x_{i-1/2}}^{x_{i+1/2}} q(x)dx \tag{14}$$

To construct the values $q_i^R = q_{i+1}^L = q_{i+1/2}$ we will use the fourth-order interpolation function:

$$q_{i+1/2} = 1/2(q_i + q_{i+1}) - 1/6(\delta q_{i+1} - \delta q_i) \tag{15}$$

where $\delta q_i = 1/2(q_{i+1} - q_{i-1})$. Next, we describe the algorithm for obtaining a local parabola. The input of the algorithm is the values in the points of the cells q_i. At the output of the algorithm, all parameters of piecewise parabolic functions are determined at all intervals $\left[x_{i-1/2}, x_{i+1/2}\right]$.

Step 1: In the first step, we construct the values $\delta q_i = 1/2(q_{i+1} - q_{i-1})$. To do this, we only need the knowledge of neighboring cells $q_{i+1}, qi-1$. To avoid extremums of functions, we use the modification of the last formula for δq_i as:

$$\delta_m q_i = \begin{cases} min(|\delta q_i|, 2|q_{i+1} - q_i|, 2|q_i - q_{i-1}|)sign(\delta q_i) \\ (q_{i+1} - q_i)(q_i - q_{i-1}) > 0 \\ 0, (q_{i+1} - q_i)(q_i - q_{i-1}) \le 0 \end{cases}$$

For the parallel implementation we need to make exchanges of a single overlap layer of the computational domain by MPI tools. Then we recalculate the values on the bound by the fourth order interpolant:

$$q_i^R = q_{i+1}^L = q_{i+1/2} = 1/2(q_i + q_{i+1}) - 1/6(\delta_m q_{i+1} - \delta_m q_i)$$

Step 2: At the second step of the algorithm, we begin to construct the local parabola using the formulas:

$$\Delta q_i = q_i^L - q_i^R \tag{16}$$

$$q_i^{(6)} = 6(q_i - 1/2(q_i^L + q_i^R)) \tag{17}$$

In the case of non-monotonicity of a local parabola, we rearrange the values at the cells interface q_i^L, q_i^R by next formulas:

$$q_i^L = q_i, q_i^R = q_i, (q_i^L - q_i)(q_i - q_i^R) \le 0 \tag{18}$$

$$q_i^L = 3q_i - 2q_i^R, \Delta q_i q_i^{(6)} > (\Delta q_i)^2 \tag{19}$$

$$q_i^R = 3q_i - 2q_i^L, \Delta q_i q_i^{(6)} < -(\Delta q_i)^2 \tag{20}$$

Thus, the boundary values satisfy the conditions of monotonicity.

Step 3: At this step, we rebuild the parameters of the parabola, taking into account the new values at the cells interface:

$$\Delta q_i = q_i^L - q_i^R$$
$$q_i^{(6)} = 6(q_i - 1/2(q_i^L + q_i^R))$$

As the result, we got the local parabolas in each cell. $[x_{i-1/2}, x_{i+1/2}]$. It should be noted that parabolas may have a discontinuity on the cells interfaces. In the case of using the classical piecewise parabolic method (PPM), the Riemann problem should be solved for parabolas. In our case, local parabolas are used as part of the Riemann problem. The solution of the Riemann problem can be recovered by $w = Rq$. It is obvious that the one-dimensional scheme is generalized to the multidimensional case.

Thus, the Godunov method and the piecewise-parabolic on a local stencil (PPML) method are used to solve the relativistic hydrodynamic equations. The calculation of flows across the cells interfaces occurs independently for each cell of the computational domain using the information only about neighboring cells. This fact is very important for the parallel realization of this method. Independent calculation of flows gives more than 80% parallel code efficiency in terms of weak scalability on 50K + cores systems. Calculation of flows occurs in primitive variables (density, velocity, pressure). The Newton method is used for recovering primitive variables from conservative. Detailed performance analysis of parallel realization of this methods can be found in [7–11]. We considered some optimization ideas from [12–14].

4   Hardware and Software Configuration

In this study, we used dual-socket Intel Broadwell (Xeon E5 2699 v4, 22 cores, 2.2 GHz) node. We have used two memory configurations for this node. In the first configuration, it was equipped with 256 GB DDR4 registered ECC memory (16 × 16 ~ GB Kingston 2133 ~ MHz DDR4) and four Intel Optane® SSDs P4800X (320 ~ GB memory mode). We used Intel Memory Drive Technology 8.2 to expand system memory up to approximately 1,500 GB. In the second configuration, the node was exclusively equipped by 1,536 GB of DDR4 registered ECC memory (24 × 64 ~ GB Micron 2666 ~ MHz DDR4). In both configurations we used a stripe of four 400 GB Intel DC P3700 SSD drives as a local storage. We also use dual-socket Intel Xeon Gold 6154 (2 × 18 cores, 3.0 GHz) with 192 GB ECC DDR4 and 8x Intel Optane 4801X for the same tests. Intel Parallel Studio XE 2017 (update 4) was used to compile the code for all benchmarks. In current study we used BigMPI wrapper library for addressing arrays larger than 32 GB [15]. Hardware counters on non-IMDT setup were collected using Intel® Performance Counter Monitor [16].

5   Benchmarking

The main ideas of tests were to show how our code working on the DRAM-configured node, DRAM+IMDT node (only DRAM usage), DRAM+IMDT node (mixed memory usage). Table 1 shows memory usage for different problem sizes. We tried to adapt the computational grid size for existing hardware. In addition, it was interesting to test a non-standard grid size. This is why we used 2304^3 and 2000^3 grid sizes. The benchmarking results for our code is shown in Fig. 1. Non-standard grid size did not affect the benchmarking result.

Table 1. Memory usage and grid size.

Grid size	Memory usage
1024 × 1024 × 1024	138 GB
1512 × 1512 × 1512	443 GB
1768 × 1768 × 1768	638 GB
2000 × 2000 × 2000	965 GB
2304 × 2304 × 2304	1470 GB

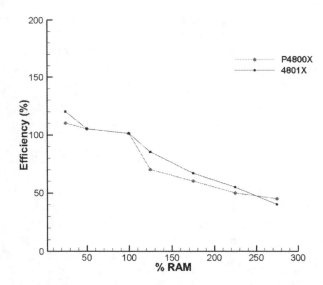

Fig. 1. IMDT efficiency plots for our code. Higher efficiency is better. 100% efficiency corresponds to DRAM performance. Red line is the efficiency for Intel Optane P4800X, black line is for Intel Optane 4801X. We achieve 10–15% better efficiency for 4801X model with M.2 interface than for PCIex version of 4800X model. (Color figure online)

When a benchmark requests memory smaller than the amount of available DRAM, the application performance on the IMDT-configured node is typically higher than for DRAM-configured node. At a certain threshold, which is typically a multiple of DRAM size, the IMDT efficiency declines based on the CPU Flop/S and memory bandwidth requirements. On the figure, we can see a slow decrease in efficiency down to ≈50% when the data does not fit into DRAM cache of IMDT.

6 Conclusion

High-Performance Computing is the use of computing to solve challenging problems that require significant computing resources [17]. For the last 5 years, top HPC systems became 7–10 times faster. However, the progress of memory growth is not so impressive. The problem is in the high cost of DRAM. Recently, Intel announced a new SSD product based on novel 3D XPoint™ technology under the name Intel Optane®. It was developed to overcome the drawbacks of NAND-technology: block-based memory addressing and limited write endurance. One of the major IMDT advantages is the high density of memory. It will be feasible in the near future to build systems with many terabytes of Optane memory. In fact, the bottleneck will not be the amount of Optane memory, but the amount of available DRAM cache for IMDT. It is currently possible to build an IMDT system with 24 TB of addressable memory (with 3 TB DRAM cache), which is not possible to build with DRAM. IMDT is not a panacea for all kind of algorithms. For example, it cannot help in situations when an application has random memory access patterns across a large number of memory pages with a low degree of application parallelism. This is another challenge for the scientific community. We should test and optimize our applications for new hardware. In this work, we presented a numerical method and its software realization for solving relativistic astrophysical problems. We achieved suitable performance (only 50% efficiency drop) for our code on the hybrid DRAM+IMDT system. The applications with random memory access patterns can significantly slow down (by 8 times) the performance on IMDT systems in comparison with DRAM-configured systems due to the IMDT specifications. In the future, we continue to test our code for finding the best ratio between DRAM and IMDT amount of memory for the computational node.

Acknowledgments. This work was supported by Russian Science Foundation (project no. 18-11-00044). We would like to thank Siberian Supercomputer Center for providing access to HPC facilities.

References

1. Intel Memory Drive Technology. https://www.intel.com/content/www/us/en/software/intel-memory-drive-technology.html
2. Kulikov, I.M., Chernykh, I.G., Snytnikov, A.V., Glinskiy, B.M., Tutukov, A.V.: AstroPhi: a code for complex simulation of dynamics of astrophysical objects using hybrid supercomputers. Comput. Phys. Commun. **186**, 71–80 (2015)
3. Kulikov, I., Chernykh, I., Glinsky, B.: Numerical simulations of astrophysical problems on massively parallel supercomputers. In: AIP Conference Proceedings, vol. 1776 (2016). 090006
4. Mironov, V., Moskovsky, A., Kudryavtsev, A., Alexeev, Y., Kulikov, I., Chernykh, I.: Evaluation of Intel memory drive technology performance for scientific applications In: ACM International Conference Proceeding Series, MCHPC 2018 Proceedings, pp. 14–21 (2018)
5. Kulikov, I., Glinsky, B., Chernykh, I., Nenashev, V., Shmelev, A.: Numerical simulations of astrophysical problems on massively parallel supercomputer. In: Proceedings of 11th International Forum on Strategic Technology, IFOST 2016, pp. 320–323 (2017). 090006
6. Landau, L.D., Lifshitz, E.M.: The Classical Theory of Fields, vol. 2, 4th edn. Butterworth-Heinemann, Oxford (1975)
7. la Nunez-de Rosa, J., Munz, C.: XTROEM-FV: a new code for computational astrophysics based on very high order finite-volume methods – II. Relativistic hydro- and magnetohydrodynamics. Monthly Not. R. Astron. Soc. **460**(1), 535–559 (2016)
8. Chernykh, I., Kulikov, I., Glinsky, B., Vshivkov, V., Vshivkova, L., Prigarin, V.: Advanced vectorization of PPML method for Intel® Xeon® scalable processors. In: Voevodin, V., Sobolev, S. (eds.) RuSCDays 2018. CCIS, vol. 965, pp. 465–471. Springer, Cham (2019). https://doi.org/10.1007/978-3-030-05807-4_39
9. Kulikov, I.M., Chernykh, I.G., Glinskiy, B.M., Protasov, V.A.: An efficient optimization of HII method for the second generation of Intel Xeon Phi Processor. Lobachevskii J. Math. **39**(4), 543–551 (2018)
10. Kulikov, I.M., Chernykh, I.G., Tutukov, A.V.: A new parallel Intel Xeon Phi hydrodynamics code for massively parallel supercomputers. Lobachevskii J. Math. **39**(9), 1207–1216 (2018)

11. Kulikov, I., Vorobyov, E.: Using the PPML approach for constructing a low-dissipation, operator-splitting scheme for numerical simulations of hydrodynamic flows. J. Comp. Phys. **317**, 318–346 (2016)
12. Khoperskov, S., Venichenko, Yu., Khrapov, S., Vasiliev, E.: High performance computing of magnetized galactic disks. Supercomputing Frontiers Innov. **5**(4), 103–106 (2018)
13. Yamaguchi, K., et al.: Performance evaluation of different implementation schemes of an iterative flow solver on modern vector machines. Supercomputing Frontiers Innov. **6**(1), 36–47 (2019)
14. Kulikov, I., Chernykh, I., Vshivkov, V., Prigarin, V., Mironov, V., Tutukov, A.: The parallel hydrodynamic code for astrophysical flow with stellar equations of state. In: Voevodin, V., Sobolev, S. (eds.) RuSCDays 2018. CCIS, vol. 965, pp. 414–426. Springer, Cham (2019). https://doi.org/10.1007/978-3-030-05807-4_35
15. BigMPI (2019). https://github.com/jeffhammond/BigMPI
16. Intel Performance Counter Monitor - A better way to measure CPU utilization (2018). www.intel.com/software/pcm
17. Gropp, W.: Challenges in high performance computing. In: Cyberbridge 2013 Workshop Presentation (2013)

Extended Routing Table Generation Algorithm for the Angara Interconnect

Anatoly Mukosey[1], Alexey Simonov[1], and Alexander Semenov[1,2(✉)]

[1] JSC "NICEVT", Moscow, Russia
{mukosey,simonov,semenov}@nicevt.ru
[2] National Research University Higher School of Economics, Moscow, Russia

Abstract. In this paper we describe the extended routing rules in the low-latency high-bandwidth Angara interconnect with torus topology. The Angara interconnect supports 4D torus topology with routing based on the direction order routing (DOR) implemented using direction bits and additional first and last steps. To avoid deadlocks in a ring bubble flow control is used. Implementation of the First and Last Steps method allows to violate the DOR rule. We propose an algorithm for generation and analysis of routing tables that guarantees no deadlocks in the Angara interconnect. The proposed algorithm increases the number of different routable systems and improves fault tolerance.

Keywords: Angara interconnect · Torus topology · Deadlock free · Channel dependency graph · Routing · Fault tolerance · Direction order

1 Introduction

JSC NICEVT has developed the Angara high-speed interconnect [19] with multi-dimensional torus topology. The Angara-C1 cluster [2] and the Desmos cluster [21] are based on the Angara interconnect. Many authors have obtained results with use of the Angara interconnect [10,14,16,22,23].

The Angara interconnect router implements deterministic routing based on the bubble flow control [17] and direction ordered routing (DOR) [1,18] rules and direction bits [18]. The Angara chip also supports non standard First Step/Last Step [18] for bypassing failed nodes and links.

The direction order rule allows to avoid deadlocks in network. In the paper [13] we have proposed an algorithm of routing table generation when non standard the first and last (FS/LS) steps preserve the direction order rule. But there are no hardware limitations in the Angara chip for setting the first and last steps according to the direction order rules, but a deadlock can be arised, because the direction order rule can be violated.

Channel dependency graph (CDG) is a fundamental technique for a deadlock-freedom analysis of the interconnect routing rules [6,7]. Dally et al. [6] postulate a theorem that routing rules are deadlock free if and only if there are no cycles in the corresponding channel dependency graph. Channel dependency graph is

© Springer Nature Switzerland AG 2019
V. Voevodin and S. Sobolev (Eds.): RuSCDays 2019, CCIS 1129, pp. 573–583, 2019.
https://doi.org/10.1007/978-3-030-36592-9_47

used in many different papers for network analysis and routing table and path generation, e.g. [7,20].

However, CDG does not allow to analyze an interconnect packet path history, which is needed to support the dirbit Angara routing rule. For Angara routing table generation is offered a special graph of paths (PG) [13], path graph vertices represent the history of a possible packet path. This technique is needed to support the dirbit rule and represent the paths in the network. The idea of the graph of paths is to store the history of a packet path we found only in [3], in which the authors solve a problem of message latency minimization in delay tolerant networks [8].

There are many multi-dimensional torus routing rules based on turn model [4,9,11,12,15]. The model involves the dimensional directions analysis in which packets can turn in the network and the cycles that the turns can form. It prohibits just enough turns to break all of the cycles. Routing algorithms that employ the remaining turns are deadlock free. In this paper we use the technique of prohibiting certain turns and apply the channel dependency graph technique for deadlock analysis.

In this paper we describe the Angara routing rules that allow to increase the number of different routable subsystems in a system. We propose an extended algorithm for generation and analysis of routing tables that guarantees no deadlocks in the Angara interconnect. The extended routing table generation algorithm is based on the previously proposed algorithm and involves the prohibiting certain turns and the channel dependency graph technique for deadlock analysis. We evaluate the proposed algorithm and show that it allows to increase the number of different routable systems and to improve fault tolerance.

2   Preliminaries

In this section we introduce some formal definitions that will be used in this work.

The n-dimensional torus has $d_1 \times d_2 \times \cdots \times d_n$ nodes, with d_i nodes along each dimension i, where $d_i \geq 2$ for $1 \leq i \leq n$. Each node $u \in N$ is identified by n coordinates $(u_1, u_2, ..., u_n)$, where $0 \leq u_i < d_i$ for $1 \leq i \leq n$.

The direction D_j is a vector $(0, ..., \underbrace{\pm 1}_{j \bmod n}, ..., 0)$, where each coordinate is zero except one on the position $j \bmod n$ and it is equal $+1$ if $1 \leq j \leq n$ or -1 if $n + 1 \leq j \leq 2n$. Direction D_j is *positive* when $1 \leq j \leq n$, and is *negative* when $n + 1 \leq j \leq 2n$.

Two nodes $u = (u_1, u_2, ..., u_n)$ and v are neighbors in direction D_j if $v = u + D_j = (u_1, ..., (u_{j \bmod n} \pm 1) \bmod d_{j \bmod n}, ..., u_n), 1 \leq j \leq 2n$. Set of all directions is denoted by $\mathcal{D} = \{D_j\}_{j=\overline{1,2n}}$. On the set of directions $\mathcal{D}$, we introduce the order: $D_i < D_j$ if $i < j$.

Definition 1. *Communication channel (link) is* α_{u, D_i}, *where* $u \in N$ *and* $D_i \in \mathcal{D}$. *The set of all communication channels is denoted by* $\mathcal{E} = N \times \mathcal{D}$.

Definition 2. *Each node can be transit or active. Active nodes inject and eject data into a network and can serve as transit nodes. Transit nodes only redirect data from nodes to another nodes, they do not inject data to the network. Active nodes is denoted by a "a" index and transit nodes by a "t" index.*

Definition 3. *Path $\mathcal{P}$ from node u^0 to u^l is described by a sequence $u^0, s_1, u^1, s_2, ..., s_l, u^l$, where $u^i \in N$ and $s_i \in D$ is a direction from the node u^{i-1} to the node u^i. l is a length of the path. Nodes $u^1, ..., u^{l-1}$ are transit nodes of the path. The transit nodes of the path can be obtained from corresponding steps, thus a path can be written as $u^0, s_1, s_2, ..., s_l$.*

Definition 4. *Set of nodes $M_{a,t} = M_a \cup M_t$ is routable (connected) if for each nodes $u, v \in M_a$ there is a path from u to v and transit nodes of the path belong to $M_{a,t}$. M_a is an active node set and M_t is a transit node set.*

Definition 5. *Routing table of nodes $M_{a,t}$ is a set of paths such that for all $u, v \in M_a$ there is a path from u to v and transit nodes of the path belong to $M_{a,t}$.*

3   Angara Interconnect Routing

3.1   Direction-Order Routing and Dirbit Routing

Among the routing algorithms for multidimensional torus topology, it can be distinguished a class of algorithms based on a *direction order* rule [5]. All directions in a path are used in a predetermined order. Direction order algorithms have a property of absence of mutual locks between the rings of torus topology with any number of simultaneous requests for data transmission over the network.

Definition 6. *Path $\mathcal{P} = u, s_1, ..., s_l$ from node u to node v matches the direction order rule if $s_{i-1} \leq s_i$ for $2 \leq i \leq l$, where l is a length of the path, $s_i \in D$.*

Path $\mathcal{P} = u, s_1, ..., s_l$ from node u to node v matches the direction order rule can be written as $u, S_1, ..., S_{2n}$ where S_j is a set of steps in the $D_j \in D$ direction. The set S_j can be empty. Length of a path can be obtained as $l = \sum_{i=j}^{2n} |S_j|$, where $|S_j|$ is a number of steps in set S_j.

Definition 7. *Path $\mathcal{P} = u, S_1, ..., S_{2n}$ from node u to node v matches the direction bit rule if one $|S_i| > 0$ or the other $|S_{i+n}| > 0$ but not both, or $|S_{i+n}| = |S_i| = 0$ for $1 \leq i \leq n$.*

$\mathcal{P}_{dirbit}$ denotes a path that matches the direction bit rule and $\mathcal{D}_{dirbit}$ denotes a set of directions matches the direction bit rule.

Angara interconnect routing between directions in the torus topology is based on the direction bit rule. To avoid deadlocks in a ring (movement without changing a direction) the bubble routing rule is used [17].

3.2 First Step/Last Step

The First Step/Last Step (FS/LS) method [18] is used in the Angara inter-connect as a mechanism for bypassing failed nodes. FS/LS method provides a possibility of a first positive and/or a last negative non-standard steps in a path.

Path with FS/LS can be written as $u, D_{FS}, D_{dirbit}, D_{LS}$, where D_{FS} is a positive step, D_{LS} is a negative step. Note that set of directions $D_{FS}, D_{dirbit}, D_{LS}$ can violate the direction bit and the direction order rules.

4 Extended Direction Order Routing

There are no hardware limitations in the Angara interconnect for setting the FS/LS according to the direction order rules. However, following these rules eliminates situations of mutual resource locks (deadlock). The direction-order rule and the direction bit rule allow to present paths between two any nodes in a torus topology without failed nodes or links. But if there are broken nodes or links, it can be exist two disconnected nodes in a torus system. FS/LS can assist to fix connectivity, but a deadlock can be arised, because the direction order rule can be violated. In this section, we consider the possibility of violating the direction order rule that guarantees no resource locks.

For analysis of mutual resource locks we use a channel dependency graph [6].

Definition 8. *The channel dependency graph (CDG) for a given network is defined as a directed graph $G(C, E)$, whose node set consists of the communications channels $\mathcal{E}$. The edge set E is induced by a routing rules and consists of channel pairs $(\cdot, \cdot)$, i.e. $(\alpha_{v,s_v}, \alpha_{u,s_u}) \in E$, where $\alpha_{v,s_v}, \alpha_{u,s_u} \in C$, $s_v, s_u \in \mathcal{D}$, and $\exists u : u = v + s_v$.*

Note that for the DOR routing each edge $(\alpha_{v,s_v}, \alpha_{u,s_u})$ must satisfy $s_u \geq s_v$. Dally et al. [6] postulate the following theorem:

Theorem 1. *Routing rules are deadlock free if and only if there are no cycles in the corresponding channel dependency graph.*

Figure 1 shows 2-dimensional mesh with 4 nodes 2×2. In Fig. 2 is shown corresponding channel dependency graph for this system topology. For convenience the vertex in the graph is denoted as 2 system nodes, a link and a direction over the link. There are 8 vertices and 4 edges in the CDG. Solid lines show all edges corresponding to the direction order rule (DOR) with $+x+y-x-y$ order directions.

In Fig. 3 is shown the 2-dimensional system topology with 5 nodes. In Fig. 4 is shown corresponding channel dependency graph for this system topology. Solid lines show all edges corresponding to the direction order rule (DOR) with $+x+y-x-y$ order directions. Dotted line shows an additional edge. CDG this system has cycle in a ring by x measurement: $\alpha_{1,+x} \longrightarrow \alpha_{2,+x} \longrightarrow \alpha_{3,+x} \longrightarrow \alpha_{1,+x}$. This case is solved in the Angara interconnect using the bubble flow control [17]. In CDG we can see that there is no path from node 5 to node 3 and from

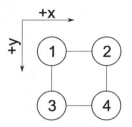

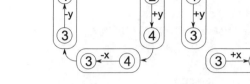

Fig. 1. Example of 2-dimensional mesh with 4 nodes.

Fig. 2. Example of channel dependency graph (CDG) for 2-dimensional mesh (Fig. 1) with 4 nodes.

node 4 to node 3 with the direction order rule. We can add an additional edge $\alpha_{5,-y} \longrightarrow \alpha_{2,-x}$ to resolve this issue. This edge breaks the DOR rule, but we this edge does not create cycles in CDG.

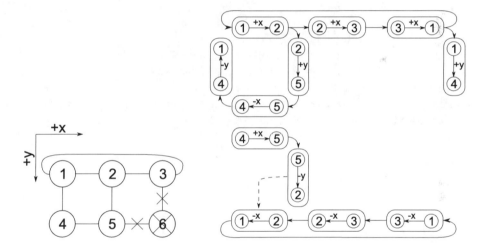

Fig. 3. Example of 2-dimensional torus with 5 nodes.

Fig. 4. Example of CDG for 2-dimensional torus with 5 nodes from Fig. 3. Solid lines show all the edges corresponding to the direction order rule (DOR). Dotted line shows an additional edge.

To evaluate the possibility of making steps with violation of the deadlock-freedom rules, we build for each vertex of channel dependency graph the *used direction set* in the paths from this vertex:

Definition 9. *Used direction set $B(\alpha_{u,s_u})$ is a set of directions $s_1, ..., s_k, s_i \in D$ $\forall i\ 1 \leq i \leq k$, which can be used in all possible paths in channel dependency graph started from vertex $\alpha_{u,s_u} \in C$.*

For CDG presented in the Fig. 4 and the vertex $\alpha_{2,+x}$ used direction set $B(\alpha_{2,+x}) = +x, +y, -x, -y$.

Theorem 2. *Additional edge* $(\alpha_{u_j,s_j}, \alpha_{u_k,s_k})$, *where* $s_j > s_k$ *and* $u_k = u_j + s_j$ *in the channel dependency graph does not create cycles in the graph if* $s_j \notin B(\alpha_{u_k,s_k})$.

Proof. We add edge $(\alpha_{u_j,s_j}, \alpha_{u_k,s_k})$ to the CDG and suppose there is a path in the CDG that creates a cycle. Then there is a path from α_{u_k,s_k} to α_{u_j,s_j}, then direction $s_j \in B(\alpha_{u_k,s_k})$, it is in conflict with the theorem condition.

For CDG presented in the Fig. 4 we can add edge $\alpha_{5,-y} \longrightarrow \alpha_{2,-x}$ because $-y \notin B(\alpha_{2,-x})$, where $B(\alpha_{2,-x}) = -x$.

Algorithm for adding additional edges (see Algorithm 1) can be divided into the two stages. In the first stage the breadth-first search (BFS) algorithm is used to build the used direction set for each CDG vertex. BFS starts from each vertex and stores all directions from the reachable vertices.

In the second stage it is necessary to find possible edges satisfying the Theorem 2. For each vertex α_{v_1,s_1} we consider all the vertices α_{v_2,s_2} are neighbors in the system topology and if s_1 is not in the used direction set of α_{v_2,s_2} vertex then we add the edge to the CDG.

Then we rebuild the used direction set for each CDG vertex from which there is a path to vertex α_{v_1,s_1}. After adding the edge to the channel dependency graph CDG we start BFS from node α_{v_1,s_1} in CDG with the reverted edges $\bar{E}$ and add directions from $B(\alpha_{v_2,s_2})$ to all reachable vertices. The second stage are performed until all possible edges are constructed.

Algorithm 1. Adding edges to CDG.

Input   : $CDG(C, E)$ – channel dependency graph for a system topology with direction order routing,

  min_dir – directions, which are less than this will not be considered

Output: CDG with added edges

// build the used direction sets

foreach $v \in C$ **do**

  $\mid$ $B(v) = \{s_i : \alpha_{u_i,s_i} \in BFS(CDG(C,E), v)\}$

end

foreach $\alpha_{v_1,s_1}, \alpha_{v_2,s_2} \in C : v_2 = v_1 + s_1, (\alpha_{v_1,s_1}, \alpha_{v_2,s_2}) \notin E, s_1 \geq min\_dir$

  do

end

if $s_1 \notin B(\alpha_{v_2,s_2})$ **then**

  add $(\alpha_{v_1,s_1}, \alpha_{v_2,s_2})$ to E

  // rebuild used direction set for α_{v_1,s_1}

  foreach $v \in BFS(CDG(C, \bar{E}), \alpha_{v_1,s_1})$ **do**

    $\mid$ $B(v) = B(v) \cup B(\alpha_{v_2,s_2})$

  end

end

It is found that it is better to build additional edges for vertices α_{v,s_v}, where s_v is a negative direction and next for other vertices. Therefore for the Angara 4-dimensional torus interconnect we firstly run Algorithm 1 with $min\_dir = -x$ and secondly with $min\_dir = +x$.

4.1 Routing Table Generation Algorithm

Channel dependency graph is not suitable for building paths in Angara interconnect because it does not support the Angara direction bit routing rule: CDG does not allow to analyze an interconnect packet path history, which is needed to control the absence in the packet path of simultaneous using of the positive and the negative direction of a dimension.

For Angara routing table generation is offered a special graph of paths (PG) [13]. The idea of the graph of paths is to store the history of a possible packet path. This technique is needed to represent the paths in the network.

In the graph of paths vertex set of the PG is a set $\{U^i_{begin}, U^i_{FS_j}, U^i_{dirbit_j},$ $U^i_{LS_j}, U^i_{end}\}$ for each network node $u_i \in N$:

1. U^i_{begin} is a vertex from which a path is started (injection to the network);
2. U^i_{FS} is a vertex that can be reached by completing the first step $FS \in \mathcal{D}$ and FS is a positive direction;
3. $U^i_{dirbit_k}$ is a vertex that can be reached by completing steps in the $dirbit_k$ ordered direction list. The ordered direction list $dirbit_k$ satisfies the direction bit rule.
4. U^i_{LS} is a vertex that can be reached by completing the last step $LS \in \mathcal{D}$ and FS is a negative direction.
5. U^i_{end} is a vertex in which the path is finished (ejection from the network).

Vertices of the PG are connected in such a manner that a movement from a vertex to another vertex corresponds to packet paths through the corresponding network nodes and satisfies the direction bit rule.

The our previous version of the routing table generation algorithm (PGA) preserves the DOR rule [13]. In more detail, for the first step each vertex U^i_{FS} is connected with a vertex $U^j_{dirbit_k}$ if and only if $u^i + FS = u^j$, the length of the $dirbit_k$ set is one and a direction FS and a direction from the $dirbit_k$ set satisfy the DOR rule. Similarly for the last step each vertex $U^i_{dirbit_k}$ is connected with a vertex U^j_{LS} if and only if a last direction from the $dirbit_k$ ordered set and a direction LS satisfy the DOR rule, and $u^i + LS = u^j$.

In the current work we relax the DOR rule for the routing table generation algorithm by augmenting the edge set of PG by adding the additional edges of the channel dependency graph for a given system topology.

For a given torus topology we construct a base PG and a base CDG. Then we add all possible additional edges to the CDG by the developed Algorithm 1. After CDG analysis we need to augment the PG. For each U^i_{FS} and $U^j_{dirbit_k}$ PG vertices we test the $(\alpha_{u^i,FS}, \alpha_{u^j,dirbit_k})$ edge of the CDG. Similarly for last direction in $dirbit_k$ for each $U^i_{dirbit_k}$ and U^j_{FS} PG vertices we test the $(\alpha_{u^i,dirbit_k}, \alpha_{u^j,FS})$

edge of CDG. If the CDG edge exist then we add the corresponding edge to PG. New algorithm is denoted by PGA+.

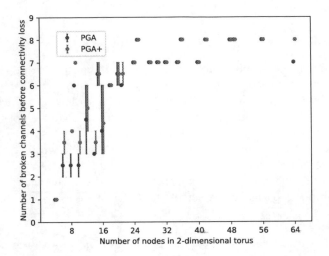

Fig. 5. Evaluation of the routing table generation algorithms for the all considered 2-dimensional systems.

5   Algorithm Evaluation

Algorithm evaluation is performed on different topology systems with up to 128 nodes. For each number of nodes all possible n-dimensional torus topology systems with $2 \leq d_i \leq 8$, $2 \leq n \leq 4$ were constructed.

For each system communication channels are randomly broken. The number of broken channels are increased as long as it is possible to generate a routing table for the whole system. For each number of broken channels we conduct 100 attempts to construct the routing table. For the system we obtain a maximum number of broken channels before the system loses connectivity.

In Fig. 5 is shown connectivity evaluation for the all considered 2-dimensional systems. The Y axis represents the number of broken communication channels before a system loses connectivity for all systems for a given node number. In figure is shown the maximum, minimum and average (a circle) value of the broken channels for all system. The proposed PGA+ algorithm shows better fault tolerance. Similarly in Figs. 6 and 7 we present evaluation results for the 3-dimensional and the 4-dimensional torus topology systems.

On average for all the 2-dimensional systems the proposed extended routing method increases the number of broken links by 4.91%, and for the 3-dimensional systems by 8.17% and 34.05% – for the 4-dimensional torus topology systems.

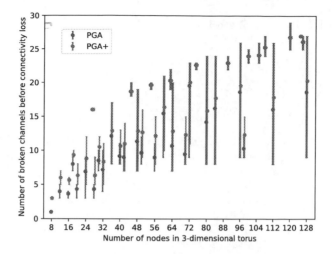

Fig. 6. Evaluation of the routing table generation algorithms for the all considered 3-dimensional systems.

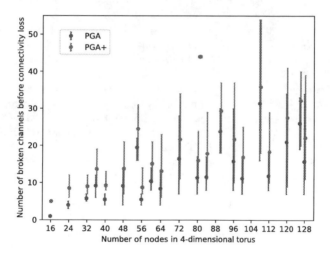

Fig. 7. Evaluation of the routing table generation algorithms for the all considered 4-dimensional systems.

6   Conclusion

This paper introduces the extended routing table generation algorithm for the the low-latency high-bandwidth Angara interconnect with torus topology. The proposed algorithm based on the previously developed path graph and analysis of channel dependency graph increases the number of different routable systems and improves fault tolerance. The algorithm evaluation shows that on average for all the 2-dimensional systems the proposed extended routing algorithm increases the number of broken links before a system loses connectivity by 4.91%, and for the 3-dimensional systems by 8.17% and 34.05% – for the 4-dimensional torus topology systems.

References

1. Adiga, N.R., et al.: Blue Gene/L torus interconnection network. IBM J. Res. Dev. **49**(2.3), 265–276 (2005)
2. Agarkov, A., Ismagilov, T., Makagon, D., Semenov, A., Simonov, A.: Performance evaluation of the Angara interconnect. In: Proceedings of the International Conference on Russian Supercomputing Days, Moscow, Russia, pp. 626–639 (2016)
3. Bulut, E., Geyik, S.C., Szymanski, B.K.: Conditional shortest path routing in delay tolerant networks. In: International Symposium on World of Wireless Mobile and Multimedia Networks (WoWMoM), pp. 1–6. IEEE (2010)
4. Chiu, G.M.: The odd-even turn model for adaptive routing. IEEE Trans. Parallel Distrib. Sys. **11**(7), 729–738 (2000)
5. Dally, W.J., Seitz, C.L.: The torus routing chip. Distrib. Comput. **1**(4), 187–196 (1986)
6. Dally, W.J., Seitz, C.L.: Deadlock-free message routing in multiprocessor interconnection networks (1988)
7. Domke, J., Hoefler, T., Matsuoka, S.: Routing on the dependency graph: a new approach to deadlock-free high-performance routing. In: Proceedings of the 25th ACM International Symposium on High-Performance Parallel and Distributed Computing, pp. 3–14. ACM (2016)
8. Fall, K.: A delay-tolerant network architecture for challenged internets. In: Proceedings of the 2003 Conference on Applications, Technologies, Architectures, and Protocols for Computer Communications, pp. 27–34. ACM (2003)
9. Glass, C.J., Ni, L.M.: The turn model for adaptive routing. ACM SIGARCH Comput. Archit. News **20**(2), 278–287 (1992)
10. Khalilov, M., Timofeev, A.: Optimization of MPI-process mapping for clusters with Angara interconnect. Lobachevskii J. Math. **39**(9), 1188–1198 (2018)
11. Kim, J.H., Liu, Z., Chien, A.A.: Compressionless routing: a framework for adaptive and fault-tolerant routing. In: ACM SIGARCH Computer Architecture News, vol. 22, pp. 289–300. IEEE Computer Society Press (1994)
12. Mohapatra, P.: Wormhole routing techniques for directly connected multicomputer systems. ACM Comput. Surv. (CSUR) **30**(3), 374–410 (1998)
13. Mukosey, A.V., Semenov, A.S.: An approximate algorithm for choosing the optimal subset of nodes in the Angara interconnect with failures. Vychislitel'nye Metody i Programmirovanie **18**(1), 53–64 (2017)
14. Ostroumova, G., Orekhov, N., Stegailov, V.: Reactive molecular-dynamics study of onion-like carbon nanoparticle formation. Diam. Relat. Mater. **94**, 14–20 (2019)
15. Palesi, M., Holsmark, R., Kumar, S., Catania, V.: Application specific routing algorithms for networks on chip. IEEE Trans. Parallel Distrib. Sys. **20**(3), 316–330 (2008)
16. Polyakov, S., Podryga, V., Puzyrkov, D.: High performance computing in multiscale problems of gas dynamics. Lobachevskii J. Math. **39**(9), 1239–1250 (2018)
17. Puente, V., Beivide, R., Gregorio, J.A., Prellezo, J., Duato, J., Izu, C.: Adaptive bubble router: a design to improve performance in torus networks. In: Proceedings of the 1999 International Conference on Parallel Processing, pp. 58–67. IEEE (1999)

18. Scott, S.L., et al.: The Cray T3E network: adaptive routing in a high performance 3D torus (1996)
19. Simonov, A., Makagon, D., Zhabin, I., Shcherbak, A., Syromyatnikov, E., Polyakov, D.: Pervoye pokoleniye vysokoskorostnoy kommunikatsionnoy seti ≪Angara≫ (the first generation of Angara high-speed interconnect). Naukoyemkiye tekhnologii (Sci. Technol.) **15**(1), 21–28 (2014)
20. Skeie, T., Lysne, O., Theiss, I.: Layered shortest path (lash) routing in irregular system area networks. In: Proceedings of the 16th International Parallel and Distributed Processing Symposium, IPDPS 2002, pp. 194–201. IEEE Computer Society, Washington, DC (2002). http://dl.acm.org/citation.cfm?id=645610.661560
21. Stegailov, V., et al.: Angara interconnect makes GPU-based Desmos supercomputer an efficient tool for molecular dynamics calculations. Int. J. High Perform. Comput. Appl. **33**, 507–521 (2019)
22. Stegailov, V., Smirnov, G., Vecher, V.: VASP hits the memory wall: processors efficiency comparison. Concurrency Comput. Pract. Exp. **31**, e5136 (2019). https://doi.org/10.1002/cpe.5136
23. Tolstykh, M., Goyman, G., Fadeev, R., Shashkin, V.: Structure and algorithms of SLAV atmosphere model parallel program complex. Lobachevskii J. Math. **39**(4), 587–595 (2018)

High-Performance Solution of the Two-Class SVM Problem for Big Data Sets by the Mean Decision Rule Method

Mikhail Kurbakov, Alexandra Makarova, and Valentina Sulimova[✉]

Tula State University, Tula, Russia
muwsik@mail.ru, aleksarova@gmail.ru,
vsulimova@yandex.ru

Abstract. Support Vector Machines (SVM) is one of the most convenient and reliable tools for solving the two-class recognition problem. But it has very high computational complexity in the case of large training sets. In our previous paper we proposed a simple approach, named Mean Decision Rule (MDR) method, that allows to quickly enough find an approximate (but not very different from the exact) solution of the SVM problem in linear feature space for single computer even for large enough training sets. In this paper we propose a parallel version of MDR method. Experiments with real data sets show, that it has quasilinear acceleration of training stage and jointly with the proposed optimized data strategy allows to additionally increase the computation performance.

Keywords: Two-class SVM · Linear feature space · Big data sets · Parallel realization · Distributed computing · High-performance computation

1 Introduction

The two-class recognition problem [1] is one of the most popular one in the data analysis. Mass sources of applied problems of such kind are molecular biology, medical and video surveillance systems, marketing and many others.

The solution of the two-class recognition problem consists of two stages: learning and recognition. The learning stage is based on the analysis of some available training set of objects $\Omega^* = \{\omega_j, j = 1, \ldots, N\} \in \Omega$, tagged by labels $y_j = y(\omega_j) \in \{+1; -1\}$, that determine their class memberships. The result of learning is the decision rule function $\hat{y}(\omega) : \Omega \to \{+1; -1\}$ that defines a class label for any object $\omega \in \Omega$ (including those which didn't participate in the training) arriving at its input. The recognition stage consists in applying the constructed decision rule to new objects to define their classes.

One of the most convenient and accurate methods for solving two-class recognition problems is Support Vector Machines (SVM) method proposed by Vapnik [1].

SVM learning leads to a quadratic programming optimization problem. It has a unique solution, which in case of a small dimension of a feature space and a small number of objects, can be easily found by classical optimization methods.

© Springer Nature Switzerland AG 2019
V. Voevodin and S. Sobolev (Eds.): RuSCDays 2019, CCIS 1129, pp. 584–596, 2019.
https://doi.org/10.1007/978-3-030-36592-9_48

However, an important feature of modern data analysis is the need for training in the conditions of a large number of objects. A training set can contain tens and hundreds of thousands, and in some cases millions of objects. In this case, the learning process turns out to be very laborious - the construction of one decision rule can take dozens of minutes, hours, or even days. In this regard, recently, a lot of works has appeared, aimed at improving the performance of the solution of the SVM problem.

In particular, for training in conditions where there are a lot of objects, but they can be placed in the memory of one computer or there is a flow of data, some methods have been proposed that reduce the amount of required memory and speed up calculations on one computer, among which there are two groups: (1) increment and decrement methods, including the stochastic gradient descent method (SGD) [2] and (2) methods based on decomposition, such as chunking [3], Sequential Minimal Optimization (SMO) [4] and others. The decomposition methods form the basis of such popular libraries for solving the SVM problem as LIBSVM [5, 6] and SVMLight [7, 8].

In addition, a whole series of papers try to adopt learning methods to the conditions of distributed processing of a large number of objects: in particular, parallel implementations of stochastic gradient descent (SGD) with synchronous [9] and asynchronous [10–12] interaction of processes; parallel implementations of coordinate descent in solving the dual task of SVM learning [11–13]; methods for approximating the kernel function matrix [14], caching it's values and shrinking [7] to reduce the required memory and a network traffic; methods that take into account the sparseness of features [15]. Also there are known attempts to express the learning process in terms of the MapReduce paradigm for distributed processing of big data sets [16, 17], etc.

The papers [18, 19] provide the detailed comparison of most popular open access realizations of SVM and show, that despite the massive nature of research in this area, a universal tool for solving the SVM problem has not yet been found. Each of the approaches and its implementations has its advantages and disadvantages.

In this connection in our previous paper [19] we presented a new method, named Mean Decision Rule (MDR) method, that is able to quickly enough find an approximate (but not very different from the exact) solution of the SVM problem in the conditions of big training sets. It is economical in memory (which would ensure its application for training on a single computer), but is expressed in no iterative manner, what opens the possibility to effective parallel implementation.

The paper [19] shows advantages of the proposed MDR method in contrast to existing open access implementations of SVM for a single computer. In this paper we propose a parallel version of MDR method. Experiments with real data sets show, that it has quasilinear acceleration of the training stage and jointly with proposed optimized data load schemes allows to additionally increase the computation performance and give the possibility to train in any amount of objects.

2 Mean Decision Rule (MDR) Method

2.1 The Main Idea of the MDR Method

The main idea of the MDR method is to form a set of random small subsamples from the training set, independent learning separately for each of the subsamples and the subsequent averaging them to obtain one general decision rule.

The role of a basic learning method for each of the subsamples can be played by any approach that allows finding a solution to the SVM learning problem with the required accuracy, for example, SMO [4], that is implemented in the LibSVM library [5, 6].

In the framework of this work, only training in linear feature space is considered.

The rationale for averaging the decision rules can be the following reasoning.

Let $[X, Y]$, $X = [\mathbf{x}_j, j = 1, \ldots, N]$, $\mathbf{x}_j \in R^m$, $Y = [y_j, j = 1, \ldots, N]$, $y_j \in \{-1; 1\}$ be initial training set and $[X, Y]^{(i)} \in [X, Y], i = 1, \ldots, k$ – sets of random subsamples from it.

In accordance with SVM the result of training for each random subsample $[X, Y]^{(i)}$, $i = 1, \ldots, k$ is an estimate of two parameters – the guiding vector of the optimal separating hyperplane $\hat{\mathbf{a}}^{(i)} = \hat{\mathbf{a}}([X, Y]^{(i)})$ and the displacement $\hat{\mathbf{b}}^{(i)} = \hat{\mathbf{b}}([X, Y]^{(i)})$. Obviously, these estimates will depend on which sets of objects fall into the corresponding subsamples.

In this case, since the formation of subsamples is random, the set of pairs of estimates $[\hat{\mathbf{a}}^{(i)}, \hat{b}^{(i)}]$, $i = 1, \ldots, k$ can be viewed as a set of equally distributed random variables with finite mathematical expectation m and variance d.

The averaged estimate of the parameters of the decision rule $[\hat{\mathbf{a}}, \hat{b}]$, where $\hat{\mathbf{a}} = \frac{1}{k}\sum_{i=1}^{k} \hat{\mathbf{a}}^{(i)}$ and $\hat{b} = \frac{1}{k}\sum_{i=1}^{k} \hat{b}^{(i)}$, also is a random variable with mathematical expectation but its variance, according to the properties of the numerical characteristics of random variables will be equal $D[\hat{\mathbf{a}}, \hat{b}] = \frac{d}{k}$, i.e. with an increase in the number of subsamples, the variance of estimates of decision rules tends to decrease.

Moreover, according to the law of large numbers, the averaged estimate of the parameters of the decision rule converges in probability to the mathematical expectation of the corresponding random variable:

$$\lim_{k \to \infty} P\left\{ \left| \frac{1}{k}\sum_{i=1}^{k} [\hat{\mathbf{a}}^{(i)}, \hat{b}^{(i)}] - m \right| < \varepsilon \right\} = 1, \quad \forall\, \varepsilon > 0.$$

Thus, as the number of subsamples increases, the average estimate should stabilize and stop behaving like a random variable. This effect is visually demonstrated in [19] for model data.

However, it should be noted that the value of the mathematical expectation m, to which the averaged decision rule should tend, does not have to coincide with the exact solution of the SVM problem over the entire training set (in this sense, the resulting solution is approximate), but experiments with the model and real data show [19] that the averaging may provide a solution that has a greater generalization ability compared to the traditional approach.

2.2   Sequential MDR Algorithm

The simplest sequential MDR algorithm uses as parameters the number of subsamples k, the size of one subsample (ss_size), and the entire training set $[X, Y]$. Such algorithm performs a fixed number of iterations, each of which is trained on a separate i-th subsample $i = 1, .., k$. Then the training results from all iterations are averaged to obtain the final decision rule. More detailed description of this and some other possible variants of sequential MDR algorithms are presented in [19].

2.3   Parallel MDR Algorithm

The described in the Sect. 2.2. algorithm is not the best for sequential implementation because it is very expensive in using memory. However, at the same time, all its iterations are independent and can be performed in parallel.

The model of the respective parallel algorithm for fixed number of subsamples k of fixed size (ss_size) and infinite number of processors is presented in Fig. 1 in the form of an "operations-operands" graph. Its vertices correspond to the operations being performed and the edges - to the operands. At that the vertices that do not have input edges correspond to the receipt of input data. Vertices with no output edges determine the result of the calculations.

As can be seen from the Fig. 1, the algorithm contains very few data dependencies. The need for interprocess communication arises only once, at the very last stage of combining individual decision rules.

This algorithm can be easily modified for the limited number p of processors. The main difference consists in that, each processor constructs about k/p decision rules and find its personal mean decision rule. Then all particular mean decision rules are joined by the main process to obtain the final mean decision rule.

As a result, this version of MDR algorithm can be effectively implemented using parallel and distributed programming technologies for systems with shared and distributed memory.

From a theoretical point of view, the proposed approach has no restrictions on the number of objects. Moreover, it has a significant advantage over traditional methods for solving the SVM problem, since it does not require simultaneous storage of the entire training set in memory, which can be a problem for big data sets. However, the performance of the method is largely determined by the efficiency of working with data, and therefore this issue requires special consideration.

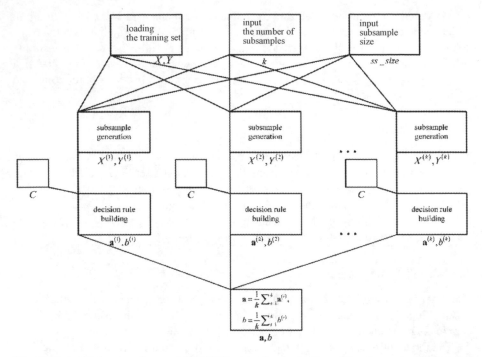

Fig. 1. A parallel computing model of MDR algorithm in the form of an "operations-operands" graph

3   Loading Data Optimization

3.1   The Input Data Format

For initial data representation, we use such popular format of input data as libsvm one that is used by many open access implementations of SVM, in particularly by LibSVM library.

The libsvm data file contains a number of rows. Each row corresponds to the information about one object in the next form:

$<$ class label $>$ $<$ number of feature $>$: $<$ value $>$ ... $<$ number of feature $>$: $<$ value $>$

The peculiarity of this format is that if the data is sparse (contain many zero values of features), it allows you to store information in a compressed form, indicating the values of only those features whose values are non-zero. It helps to use less disk space for sparse data, what is actual for big data sets.

But from the other hand, libsvm file has rows of different lengths. This feature requires applying special strategies for working with data to fully use advantages of the proposed method.

3.2   Data Strategies

Traditionally one-time download of all data in RAM is used. When training in small learning sets using traditional algorithms, such a data strategy is the most optimal.

But in the case of big data sets, all the data may not fit in the RAM together with the training task. Even more, the problem is aggravated when parallel implementations are used and each process or thread loads its own copy of the data in the memory.

Splitting the data into blocks, described in [20] takes a lot of time of the preliminary work and is not convenient.

In this regard, this strategy has significant limitations in the application.

In our previous paper [21] we proposed a number of data strategies that allow to essentially improve efficiency of MDR method by optimization of the process of working with big data sets on a single computer. But all of them are fundamentally sequential. So, their use reduces the effect of applying the parallel version of MDR.

In this connection in this paper we propose a new strategy for working with big data sets in libsvm format, that allows an effective parallel and distributed implementation.

The proposed data strategy is implemented in two main stages: (1) the stage of data preparation and (2) the stage of direct use of data for training.

The Data Preparation Stage. The aim of the first stage is to increase the speed of random access to objects in the libsvm file, which is required in accordance to the proposed MDR method. Special preparation in this case is need because of different length of rows in libsvm file, that makes impossible the strict computation of object's start positions.

First of all, we propose performing a logical partitioning of a libsvm file into z approximately equal parts and finding arrays of numbers of objects of positive $\mathbf{n}^{+1} = \left(n_j^{+1}, j = 1, \ldots, z \right)$ and negative $\mathbf{n}^{-1} = \left(n_i^{-1}, i = 1, \ldots, z \right)$ classes that are contained in each part $j = 1, \ldots, z$ of the file.

On the basis of $\mathbf{n}^{+1}$ and $\mathbf{n}^{-1}$ we find first and last numbers of objects in each part:

$$\mathbf{m}^{+1} = \left(\begin{bmatrix} m_{i,first}^{+1} \\ m_{i,last}^{+1} \end{bmatrix}, j = 1, \ldots, z \right), \quad \mathbf{m}^{-1} = \left(\begin{bmatrix} m_{j,first}^{-1} \\ m_{j,last}^{-1} \end{bmatrix}, j = 1, \ldots, z \right), \quad (1)$$

where $m_{j,first}^{\pm 1} = \sum_{t=1}^{j-1} n_j^{\pm 1} + 1$ is the number of the first object of the positive (negative) class in the j-th part of the file, $m_{j,last}^{\pm 1} = \sum_{t=1}^{j} n_t^{\pm 1}$ is the number of the last object of the positive (negative) class in the j-th part of the file.

To make an access to parts of the file faster we use the mechanism of operating system, named "mapping files into memory" [22], that allows us to fast obtain data from any part of the file without its traditional reading.

A parallel computing model of the data preparation stage in the form of an "operations-operands" graph for an infinite number of processors is presented at the Fig. 2. It should be noted, operations that take longest time (i.e. finding numbers of

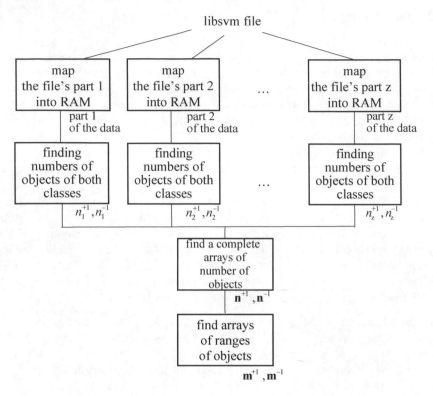

Fig. 2. The parallel computing model of the data preparation stage in the form of an "operations-operands" graph

objects of both classes) can be performed in parallel and the sequential part is small enough.

For multiprocessing implementation such data strategy requires data exchange between processes of "all-to-all" type. The amount of data of each process is defined by the number of data parts z and is constant and small for each part.

The Stage of Forming Random Subsets of Objects for Training. To obtain an object of known class type ($+1$ or -1) by its number n to form the i-th random subsample of the training set, this stage consists in 4 steps:

(1) to find the data part in which the given object falls $\mathbf{m}^{\pm 1}(n, \pm 1) \rightarrow j$;
(2) to map $j - th$ data part into RAM;
(3) to find the respective object in the data part;
(4) to add the object to the training subsample.

It should be noted, the execution time of this stage essentially depends on the number of data parts z. The execution time grows while z decreases due to increasing the time of step 3. So, z is an important parameter of the proposed method. But from the other hand, as soon as all subsamples are formed independently, this process can be effectively parallelized.

4   Experimental Setup

4.1   Data Description

In all experiments of this paper, we use the data set kddcup99 [23] that contains 4898430 objects for training and 145253 objects for tests. Each object if represented by 122 real valued features.

4.2   Study of the Parallel MDR with the Traditional Data Strategy

In our previous paper [19] the detailed comparative study of the sequential MDR method for a number of model and real data sets is presented. Experiments showed that even sequential implementation of MDR essentially outperforms such popular open access implementations of SVM as libSVM [5, 6], SVMlight [7, 8] and π SVM [26], while an accuracy is approximately the same and, moreover, in a number of cases it exceeds an accuracy of libSVM. Such SVM library as liblinear [24] and its parallel implementation mpiliblinear [25] that developed specially for sparse data sets and are extremely fast for them, but in a number of cases they have significantly lower accuracy in contrast to libSVM and MDR, as well as SGD [2, 27].

The main aim of experiments of this paper is to study the performance of the parallel implementation of MDR. The Table 1 presents times (in seconds) of performing different stages of the parallel MDR with the traditional data strategy (preliminary reading the full training set in the RAM) for different number of random subsets and different number of processors. The number of objects in each subset for all experiments of this section is 300. All times are averaged through 5 runs.

Table 1.   Mean times (sec) for stages of the Parallel MDR with the traditional data strategy.

Stages of the Parallel MDR	Number of random subsets							
	256				1024			
	Number of processes							
	1	8	16	32	1	8	16	32
1. Reading the training set	12,559	12,791	12,831	13,345	12,580	12,778	12,810	13,591
2. Forming random subsets	0,166	0,022	0,011	0,006	0,599	0,077	0,039	0,022
3. Training	0,154	0,027	0,021	0,019	0,576	0,073	0,036	0,019
Full working time	12,878	12,840	12,863	13,370	13,761	12,936	12,896	13,645

All experiments of this paper are performed using the equipment of the shared research facilities of HPC computing resources at Lomonosov Moscow State University [28]. The characteristics of each computational unit are: Intel Xeon X5570 (2.93 GHz), 8 cores, 8 Gb RAM.

Figure 3 shows the dependence of the mean time for training with forming sub-sequences (stages 2 + 3) (left) and the dependence of the acceleration (right) on the number of processes.

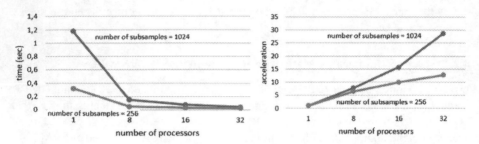

Fig. 3. The dependence of the mean time for training with forming subsequences (stages 2 + 3) (left) and the dependence of the acceleration (right) on the number of processes

As we can see from the Table 1 and the Fig. 3, we have near to ideal the acceleration of the training stage (approximately equal to the number of processes) for the number of subsamples equal to 1024. However, at the same time, the traditional preliminary reading the full training set into the RAM takes long time in contrast to the training time of MDR. As a results, the full working time is big enough and practically independent on the number of processes. And this effect is further aggravated by the growth of the training set.

Moreover, it should be noted that in practice we usually need to solve SVM problem tens, hundreds or even thousand times because of necessity to choose optimal values of parameters. So, each second of a single run actually turns into about 15 min.

So, we need to further increase the computational performance and we can do it by optimizing the data strategy in accordance with the Sect. 3.2 and parallelizing the data preparation stage.

4.3   Study of the Parallel MDR with the Optimized Data Strategy

The main aim of this experiment is to show the effect of applying the proposed data strategy. For this purpose, we repeated experiments of the previous section, replacing the only data strategy.

The resulting times (in seconds) are presented in the Table 2. The number of objects in each subsample is 300 and the number of data parts is 25600. All times are averaged through 5 runs.

Figure 4 shows the dependence of the mean full working time (left) and the dependence of the acceleration (right) on the number of processes.

Table 2. Mean times (sec) for stages of the Parallel MDR with the optimized data strategy.

Stages of the Parallel MDR	Number of random subsets							
	256				1024			
	Number of processes							
	1	8	16	32	1	8	16	32
1. Data preparation	3,757	0,770	0,418	0,211	3,663	0,766	0,381	0,206
2. Forming random subsets	9,733	1,523	1,056	0,902	3,852	6,109	3,457	2,064
3. Training	0,134	0,019	0,014	0,012	0,502	0,071	0,041	0,024
Full working time	13,625	2,312	1,488	1,125	42,680	6,946	3,879	2,294

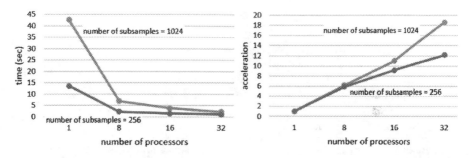

Fig. 4. The dependence of the mean full working time (left) and the dependence of the acceleration (right) on the number of processes

As we can see from the Table 2 and the Fig. 4, the acceleration of the whole procedure is smaller in contrast to the acceleration of the only training stage due to the presence of a sequential computing in the data preparation stage. But it is evident, that the proposed data strategy allows us to additionally reduce the full working time.

4.4 Influence of Parameters of the Parallel MDR on Its Performance and Accuracy

The Table 3 presents mean full working times (in seconds), computed on the basis of 5 runs, accompanied by standard deviations from the mean and the respective mean accuracy values, obtained for different values of the parameters of the Parallel MDR: the number of data parts, the number of random subsamples, the number of objects in each subsample and the number of processes, that are used for computation.

The obtained results confirm the theoretical properties of the Parallel MDR.

First of all, an increase in the number of parts of the full training data set can significantly reduce the computation time for the same number of processors without reducing the accuracy.

Table 3. Mean times (sec) and accuracy of the Parallel MDR for different values of parameters.

Number of data parts	Number of subsamples	Number of objects in a subsample: 300					
			Number of processes				
			1	8	16	32	64
2560	1024	Acc.	91,70 ± 0,04	91,68 ± 0,03	91,69 ± 0,04	91,68 ± 0,04	91,70 ± 0,03
		Time	127,0 ± 3,50	31,27 ± 0,90	15,46 ± 0,60	8,469 ± 0,33	4,018 ± 0,12
25600	256	Acc.	91,69 ± 0,10	91,68 ± 0,10	91,66 ± 0,13	91,69 ± 0,17	91,68 ± 0,08
		Time	13,62 ± 0,51	2,312 ± 0,08	1,488 ± 0,08	1,125 ± 0,07	1,235 ± 0,05
	512	Acc.	91,70 ± 0,08	91,69 ± 0,09	91,67 ± 0,08	91,67 ± 0,07	91,68 ± 0,08
		Time	27,29 ± 0,88	4,421 ± 0,15	2,270 ± 0,09	1,528 ± 0,06	1,458 ± 0,05
	1024	Acc.	91,69 ± 0,05	91,71 ± 0,04	91,70 ± 0,04	91,69 ± 0,03	91,71 ± 0,03
		Time	42,68 ± 0,74	6,946 ± 0,42	3,879 ± 0,17	2,294 ± 0,08	1,975 ± 0,06
	2048	Acc.	91,68 ± 0,04	91,69 ± 0,04	91,69 ± 0,03	91,69 ± 0,03	91,69 ± 0,03
		Time	97,54 ± 0,87	15,87 ± 0,40	8,808 ± 0,21	3,841 ± 0,13	3,087 ± 0,07

			Number of processes: 128				
			Number of objects in a subsample				
			300	500	700	1000	2000
25600	1024	Acc.	91,68 ± 0,05	91,72 ± 0,06	91,72 ± 0,03	91,74 ± 0,04	91,77 ± 0,01
		Time	2,139 ± 0,08	2,829 ± 0,21	3,098 ± 0,24	3,239 ± 0,34	4,676 ± 0,26

Secondly, an increase in the number of random subsamples of the training set to a certain value leads to a stabilization of the solution, reducing the dispersion of accuracy obtained with different runs. Of course, such an increase leads to growing the mean full working time due to growing computation at the stage of forming subsamples and at the stage of training. But, from the other side, we can reduce the computation time by increasing the number of processors till seconds.

The most significant influence on an accuracy the number of objects in random subsamples makes. But of course, according to the above, it only makes sense in combination with a suitable value of the number of random subsamples. It should be noted, that an appropriate value of this parameter has the connection with the size of the full training set. So, for data sets of the moderate size (up to tens and hundreds of thousands of objects) in accordance with our previous results [19] it is enough to use subsamples of about 300 objects to obtain an accuracy, that is near enough to the value, obtained via the libSVM. For bigger data sets, that contain some millions of objects, like one, that is used in this study, the more appropriate value is 1000 or 2000.

So the proposed method jointly with the proposed optimized data strategy allows to train SVM for some millions of objects and to reduce the computation time till few seconds. It should be noted, that such popular implementations of SVM as libSVM, SVMlight and π SVM can't solve the respective SVM training problem during hours.

5   Conclusions

In this paper we propose a parallel version of the Mean Decision Rule method, that allows to quickly enough find an approximate (but not very different from the exact) solution of the SVM problem in a linear feature space.

Experiments with the real data set, that contains some millions of objects shows, that it has quasilinear acceleration of training stage and jointly with the proposed optimized data strategy allows to additionally increase the computation performance and to reduce the computation time till few seconds.

The proposed method has no theoretical and practical restrictions for the number of training objects and doesn't require large amount of the RAM.

Acknowledgements. The work is supported by the RFBR, project №18-07-01087.

The research is carried out using the equipment of the shared research facilities of HPC computing resources at Lomonosov Moscow State University [28].

References

1. Vapnik, V.: Statistical Learning Theory. Wiley, Hoboken (1998)
2. Bottou, L.: Stochastic learning. In: Bousquet, O., von Luxburg, U., Rätsch, G. (eds.) ML - 2003. LNCS (LNAI), vol. 3176, pp. 146–168. Springer, Heidelberg (2004). https://doi.org/10.1007/978-3-540-28650-9_7
3. Boser, B.E., Guyon, I.M., Vapnik, V.: A training algorithm for optimal margin classifiers. In: Fifth Annual Workshop on Computational Learning Theory. ACM (1992)
4. Platt, J.: Sequential minimal optimization: a fast algorithm for training support vector machines. Technical report, MSR-TR-98-14. Microsoft Research (1998)
5. Chang, C.-C., Lin, C.-J.: LIBSVM: a library for support vector machines (2001). http://www.csie.ntu.edu.tw/cjlin/libsvm
6. LIBSVM - A Library for SVM. https://www.csie.ntu.edu.tw/~cjlin/libsvm/
7. Joachims, T.: Making large-scale support vector machine learning practical. In: Advances in Kernel Methods: Support Vector Learning, pp. 169–184. MIT Press, Cambridge (1999)
8. SVMLight Support Vector Machine. http://svmlight.joachims.org
9. Dekel, O., Gilad-Bachrach, R., Shamir, O., Xiao, L.: Optimal distributed online prediction using mini-batches. J. Mach. Learn. Res. **13**(1), 165–202 (2012)
10. Agarwal, A., Duchi, J.C.: Distributed delayed stochastic optimization. In: Advances in Neural Information Processing Systems, pp. 873–881 (2011)
11. Jaggi, M., et al.: Communication-efficient distributed dual coordinate ascent. In: Advances in Neural Information Processing Systems, pp. 3068–3076 (2014)
12. Ma, C., Smith, V., Jaggi, M., Jordan, M.I., Richtárik, P., Takáč, M.: Adding vs. averaging in distributed primal-dual optimization. arXiv preprint arXiv:1502.03508 (2015)
13. Yang, T.: Trading computation for communication: distributed stochastic dual coordinate ascent. In: Advances in Neural Information Processing Systems, pp. 629–637 (2013)
14. Chang, E.Y., et al.: PSVM: parallelizing support vector machines on distributed computers. In: NIPS, vol. 20 (2007)
15. Joachims, T.: Training linear SVMs in linear time. In: ACM KDD, pp. 217–226 (2006)
16. Chu, C.-T., et al.: Map reduce for machine learning on multicore. In: NIPS (2006)

17. Zhao, H.X., Magoules, F.: Parallel support vector machines on multi-core and multipro-cessor systems. In: Fox, R. (ed.) 11th International Conference on Artificial Intelligence and Applications (2011)
18. Makarova, A.I., Sulimova, V.V.: Comparative analysis of SVM implementations for two-class pattern recognition learning for large number of objects. Tidings of the Tula State University. Natural Sciences, no. 10, pp. 164–175 (2018). (in Russian)
19. Makarova, A.I., Sulimova, V.V.: Fast approximate two-class SVM learning for large training sets. In: Proceedings of International Conference Information Technology and Nanotech-nology ITNT-2019 (2019). (in Russian)
20. Li, C.: Training and Predicting Criteo's Terascale Data Set on a Machine with 128 GB RAM, October 2017. https://www.csie.ntu.edu.tw/ ~ cjlin/libsvmtools/dtasets/docs/criteo_tb/criteo_tb_document.pdf
21. Kurbakov, M.Y., Makarova, A.I., Sulimova, V.V.: Data load optimization for solving SVM problem via averaging decision rules method for big training sets. In: Proceedings of the International Conference on Information Technology and Nanotechnology ITNT-2019 (2019). (in Russian)
22. Tanenbaum, A.S.: Modern Operating Systems, 3rd edn. Prentice Hall (2008)
23. KDD Cup 1999 Data. http://kdd.ics.uci.edu/databases/kddcup99/kddcup99.html
24. Liblinear Support Vector Machine. https://www.csie.ntu.edu.tw/ ~ cjlin/liblinear/
25. Mpiliblinear Support Vector Machine. https://www.csie.ntu.edu.tw/ ~ cjlin/libsvmtools/distributed–liblinear/
26. PiSvMSoftware. http://pisvm.source-forge.net
27. Stochastic Gradient Descent SVM classifier. https://github.com/joa-ofaro/SVMSGD
28. Sadovnichy, V., Tikhonravov, A., Voevodin, V., Opanasenko, V.: "Lomonosov": super-computing at Moscow State University. In: Contemporary High Performance Computing: From Petascale Toward Exascale, pp. 283–307. Chapman & Hall/CRC Computational Science, Boca Raton; CRC Press (2013)

Performance and Scalability of Materials Science and Machine Learning Codes on the State-of-Art Hybrid Supercomputer Architecture

Nikolay Kondratyuk[1,2,3], Grigory Smirnov[1,2,3], Alexander Agarkov[4], Anton Osokin[1], Vsevolod Nikolskiy[1,2], Alexander Semenov[1,4], and Vladimir Stegailov[1,2,3(✉)]

[1] National Research University Higher School of Economics, Moscow, Russia
v.stegailov@hse.ru
[2] Joint Institute for High Temperatures of RAS, Moscow, Russia
[3] Moscow Institute of Physics and Technology, Dolgoprudny, Russia
[4] JSC NICEVT, Moscow, Russia

Abstract. 8 of top 10 supercomputers of Top500 list published in November 2018 consist of computing nodes with hybrid architectures that require special programming techniques. 5 systems among these are based on Nvidia GPUs. In this paper, we consider the benchmark results of the brand new hybrid supercomputer installed in March 2019 in NRU HSE. This system gives us the possibility to estimate the performance of several widely used material science and machine learning codes that we discuss in this work within the framework of the results available for older HPC systems.

Keywords: MPI latency · MPI bandwidth · Gromacs · CP2K · VASP · Machine learning

1 Introduction

Rapid development of parallel computational methods and supercomputer hardware provide great benefits both for mathematical modelling and machine learning. There are two main ways of hardware acceleration for nearly all types of algorithms.

The first possibility consists in the increase of the computing capabilities of individual nodes of MPP systems. Multi-CPU and multi-core shared-memory node architectures provide essential acceleration. However, the scalability of shared memory systems is limited by their cost and speed limitations of DRAM access for multi-socket and/or multi-core nodes. It is the development of GPGPU that boosts the performance of shared-memory systems.

The Nvidia CUDA technology was introduced in 2007 and provided a convenient technique for GPU programming. Many algorithms have been rewritten

ⓒ Springer Nature Switzerland AG 2019
V. Voevodin and S. Sobolev (Eds.): RuSCDays 2019, CCIS 1129, pp. 597–609, 2019.
https://doi.org/10.1007/978-3-030-36592-9_49

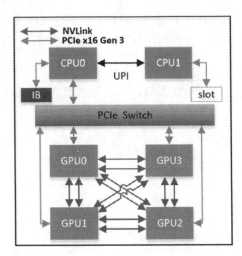

Fig. 1. The scheme of the supercomputer node.

and thoroughly optimized to use the GPU capabilities. However, the majority of them deploy only a fraction of the GPU theoretical performance even after careful tuning, e.g. see [10,11,14]. The sustained performance is usually limited by the memory-bound nature of the algorithms.

There are other ways to increase performance of individual nodes: using GPU accelerators with OpenCL, using Intel Xeon Phi accelerators or even using custom built chips like MDGRAPE [6] or ANTON [8].

The second possibility for MD calculations acceleration is the use of distributed memory massively-parallel programming (MPP) systems. For example, for MD calculations, domain decomposition is a natural technique to distribute both computational load and data across nodes of MPP systems [1].

Modern MPP systems can unite up to 10^5 nodes for solving one computational problem. For this purpose, MPI is the most widely used programming model. The architecture of the individual nodes can differ significantly and is usually selected (co-designed) for the main type of MPP system deployment. The most important component of MPP systems is the interconnect that properties stand behind the scalability of any MPI-based parallel algorithm.

In this work we evaluate the Infiniband EDR interconnect of the new supercomputer installed in NRU HSE and compare the results with the benchmark data for the Infiniband FDR based cluster (Fisher) and Angara interconnects installed in Desmos [12]. The bechmarks of Gromacs, CP2K, VASP codes as well as a typical machine learning code are discussed. The results for VASP are embedded in the wide set of recently published benchmark data [13].

2   New Supercomputer in NRU HSE

The new supercomputer of the National Research University Higher School of Economics (NRU HSE) is a hybrid system with 26 nodes connected with dual-rail Infiniband EDR interconnect. Each node is a DELL PowerEdge C4140 server with two Intel Xeon Gold 6152 CPUs and four Nvidia Tesla V100 GPUs with 32 Gb of memory. The scheme of such a node is shown on Fig. 1.

Performance studies reported here have been carried out using the standard HPC software stack based on CentOS Linux release 7.6.1810, GNU compilers, OpenMPI, Intel MKL 2019 and the CUDA driver ver. 410.79.

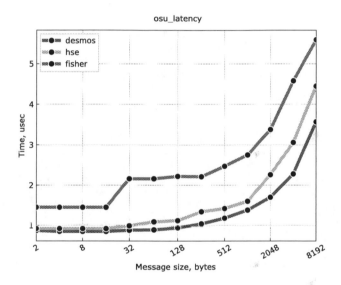

Fig. 2. Performance of osu_latency benchmark on two nodes, one process per node.

3   Interconnect Benchmarks

The Fig. 2 shows the message latency results between two nodes depending on the message size obtained by the OSU Micro-Benchmarks test. For different clusters minimum latencies are: for the Desmos cluster – 0.85 usec; for the HSE cluster – 0.92 usec; for the Fisher cluster – 1.43 usec. The Desmos latency is better than the corresponding values for the other clusters due to the Angara interconnect. The Angara interconnect hardware implementation is optimized for high performance computing applications, the latency of a hop (the router latency and the link latency) is extremely low (129 ns). This fact and high frequency of CPUs of the Desmos cluster lead to the impressive results. The dual AMD processor node of the Fischer cluster consists of 8 4-core NUMA blocks and the Infiniband adapter is connected to the 6th NUMA block. With osu_latency default running we obtain 1.93 usec latency result on two Fisher

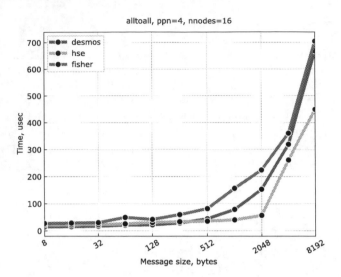

Fig. 3. Times for IMB MPI_Alltoall benchmark on 16 nodes for small messages: from 8 to 8192 bytes.

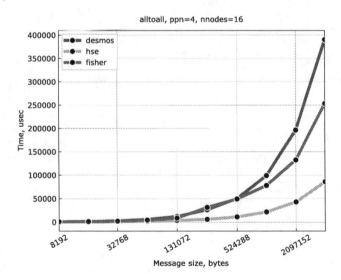

Fig. 4. Times for IMB MPI_Alltoall benchmark on 16 nodes for large messages: from 8 Kbytes to 2 Mbytes.

nodes, and with process binding to the 6th NUMA block we obtain 1.43 usec. But this result is rather poor for the 4× FDR Infiniband interconnect, this is a subject for further analysis.

We use Intel MPI Benchmarks to evaluate MPI_Alltoall operation time for different number of cluster nodes. MPI_Alltoall performance results are obtained for 4 processes per node. MPI_Alltoall times for small messages (Fig. 3)

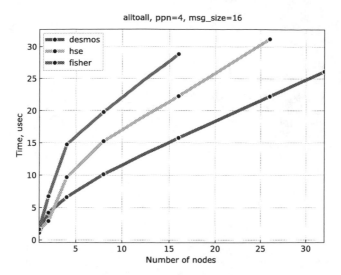

Fig. 5. Times for IMB MPI_Alltoall benchmark on 16 bytes messages depending on the number of nodes.

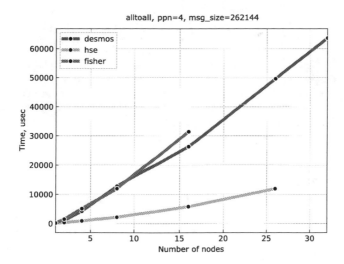

Fig. 6. Times for IMB MPI_Alltoall benchmark for 256 Kbyte message size depending on the number of nodes.

correlate with latency results performance on small messages. But when message size exceeds 1 Kbyte, bandwidth of PCIe interface of the HSE cluster allow to inject to network greater number of messages than the Angara interconnect. The processor interface is a bottleneck of the Angara interconnect for large messages (Figs. 4 and 6), the Desmos cluster MPI_Alltoall results are worse than on the Fisher and HSE clusters. Additionally, another algorithm of the alltoall collective operation can solve the problem on the Angara interconnect. But for very small 16-byte message size the Desmos cluster outperforms the other clusters on different number of nodes (Fig. 5).

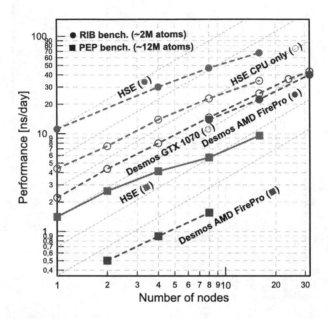

Fig. 7. The results of the RIB and PEP benchmarks in ns/day of physical time that can be simulated. Blue color shows the performance of the Desmos supercomputer [12]. Red color corresponds to the data obtained on the HSE supercomputer. Filled circles and squares are the results of RIB and PEP benchmarks correspondingly. Grey lines show 2× increase of the performance. (Color figure online)

4   Molecular Dynamics Benchmarks with Gromacs

Classical molecular dynamics (MD) is an important modern scientific tool. Nowadays, MD simulations can be performed on the large number of different GPU-based architectures since they can be carried out in the partial use of single precision (e.g. [2]).

Kutzner et al. in 2015 [3] gave the comprehensive instructions on which hardware (CPU+GPU) should be used to get the best performance in the MD case using GROMACS software. For this purpose, they developed a set of benchmarks: protein in membrane surrounded by water (MEM), ribosome in water (RIB) and peptides in water (PEP). These benchmarks differ by the number of atoms which determine the complexity of the MD simulation. We decide to use RIB (2M of atoms) and PEP (12M of atoms) to test the performance of supercomputers under study.

Figure 7 depicts the results of the benchmarks in ns/day of physical time that can be simulated. Blue color shows the performance of the Desmos supercomputer [12]. Red color corresponds to the data obtained on the HSE supercomputer. Filled circles and squares are the results of RIB and MEM benchmarks correspondingly. Grey lines show 2× increase of the performance. For the tests on upgraded Desmos with AMD FirePro S9150 GPUs installed, we use versions of GROMACS that are higher than 5.×.× since they have the option to run multiple MPI processes per GPU. We do not find any sufficient degradation of performance between the GROMACS versions in other cases.

The RIB benchmark is launched for 20000 MD steps, cycle counts are reset at 5000 MD step. The non-bonded calculations are performed on GPUs. All the processes are pinned to the physical cores. The global communication parameter *gcom* is set to 100. The numbers of *omp* processes per node are varied to get the best performance on each node count.

Desmos with AMD FirePro S9150 GPUs installed shows almost the same results for the RIB model as with Nvidia GTX 1070 GPUs. It can be explained by the fact that these two GPUs have similar single precision peak performance (5070 GFlops vs. 5783 GFlops correspondingly).

The HSE supercomputer (red filled circles) gives about $3 \div 5$ higher performances on RIB on the same number of nodes than the Desmos cluster (blue open circles). However the HSE supercomputer values are lower than expected. We think that superiority of the HSE supercomputer over Desmos machine should be close to ×10 by comparing the peak performances of the nodes. The performance loss because of the communication between 16 nodes is much higher on the HSE machine (62%) than on Desmos (26%). The simulations without GPUs (red open circles) show better scalability for the HSE supercomputer. Such degradation of the HSE supercomputer performance on 16 nodes could be caused by the relatively small number of atoms per node in RIB model that is not enough to saturate Tesla V100 GPUs.

The performances of the HSE supercomputer and Desmos are also evaluated using the PEP model. For this test, Desmos is inferior to the HSE machine performance 3.7 times on 8 nodes. This result matches the trend that is observed for the RIB case. Due to the bigger model size, the degradation of the HSE supercomputer performance is lower on 16 nodes (57%). Moreover, Desmos demonstrates better scalability.

5   Electronic Structure Calculations Benchmarks with CP2K

Electronic structure calculations methods and ab initio molecular dynamics are extremely popular computational tools to study systems in physics, chemistry and biology. Many commercial and free codes are available for end-users.

CP2K is a software package for ab-initio electronic structure calculations, which is optimized for the mixed Gaussian Plane-Wave approach based on pseudopotentials. It is written in Fortran 2008 language and can be efficiently run in parallel using MPI and OpenMP. Some parts of the code support CUDA acceleration, but the speedup is usually low. Three different models were used to test the scalability of the MPI version of the CP2K. The first model is ab initio molecular dynamics simulation of the 512 water molecules. Time per one MD step is shown in Fig. 8. On the large number of cores performance decreases as the fraction of MPI exchanges becomes dominant.

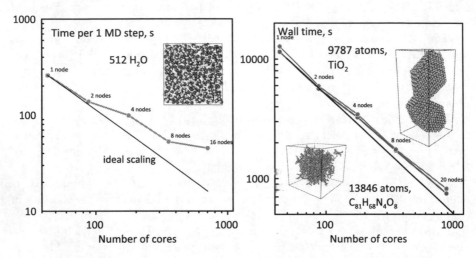

Fig. 8. (left) Scalability of the DFT model with 512 water molecules in CP2K (black line is ideal scaling). (right) Scalability of the linear scaling DFT in CP2K. Red line is amorphous system of 86 $C_{81}H_{68}N_4O_8$ molecules and blue line is the TiO_2 nanoparticle. (Color figure online)

The second and the third models are the linear scaling DFT calculations (LS DFT). The regular DFT methods scale as $O(N^3)$ with the number of atoms and they are applicable only to small systems. LS DFT methods scale as $O(N)$, but with a larger prefactor, that is they are less efficient for small systems and very effective for big systems. The second model is the TiO_2 nanoparticle with 9787 atoms and the third model is amorphous system of 86 $C_{81}H_{68}N_4O_8$ molecules (13846 atoms in total). The total run time versus the number of cores is shown in Fig. 8. Scalability of the system is almost ideal up to the maximum number of cores on the cluster.

Table 1. The selected best time-to-solution values (NCORE=1, KPAR=4). The number of MPI processes per socket is given together with the number of OpenMP threads per one MPI process. The new data are shown together with the data from [13]

PE type	LREAL=TRUE		LREAL=FALSE	
	τ_{iter} (sec)	Options	τ_{iter} (sec)	Options
2 × Xeon E5-1650v3	36	6 MPI	66	2 MPI × 3 OMP
2 × Xeon E5-2660v4	25	14 MPI	66	4 MPI × 3 OMP
2 × Xeon E5-2698v4	24	20 MPI	59	4 MPI × 4 OMP
			59	8 MPI × 2 OMP
2 × Epyc 7301	20	16 MPI	39	8 MPI × 2 OMP
2 × Epyc 7551	13	32 MPI	33	8 MPI × 4 OMP
2 × Xeon Gold 6152	12	22 MPI	17	22 MPI
1 × Tesla P100 (IBM)	12	NSIM=8	n/a	
2 × Tesla P100 (IBM)	7.5	NSIM=8	n/a	
2 × Tesla P100 (DGX-1)	7.5	NSIM=8	n/a	
4 × Tesla P100 (DGX-1)	5.5	NSIM=8	n/a	
1 × Tesla V100 (HSE)	15	NSIM=32	n/a	
2 × Tesla V100 (HSE)	10	NSIM=32	n/a	
4 × Tesla V100 (HSE)	7.5	NSIM=32	n/a	

6 Electronic Structure Calculations Benchmarks with VASP

The performance studies of VASP on the HSE supercomputer follows the approach reported recently in [13].

The VASP code is an implementation of the DFT approach for calculation of atomic structure of materials that is represented (i) by electron wave functions in the plane wave basis and (ii) by effective PAW models (pseudopotentials) that imitate valence electrons interaction with nuclear Coulomb potentials screened by frozen electronic cores. Following the DFT approach, the electronic density that minimizes the energy of the system is found in VASP by iterative optimization algorithms. VASP is known to be both a memory-bound and a compute-bound code. Generally speaking, the main part of the VASP execution time is dominated by the back and forth FFTs (from/to the real space to/from the reciprocal Fourier space) and zgemm/dgemm calls.

One of the important choices in VASP that governs both calculation speed and accuracy is the calculation method for the non-local part of the pseudopotential. The corresponding projection operators can be evaluated either in reciprocal or real space (the LREAL tag).

The model corresponds to a crystal of GaAs with 80 atoms in the supercell. The mesh of 4×4×1 k-points is used in this model that gives possibility to deploy parallelization over k-points available in VASP. The calculation protocol corresponds to the iterative electron density optimization via the blocked-Davidson

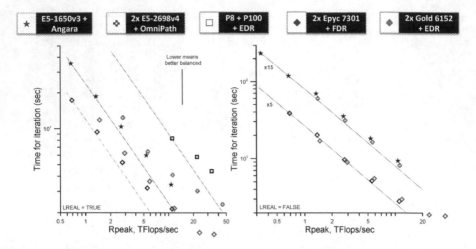

Fig. 9. Parallel scalability of the GaAs test. The time for the first iteration τ_{iter} is shown for different systems considered. The data are shown in the following representations: the plots show the dependencies on the total double precision floating-point peak performance for the nodes deployed)

scheme. The time for the first iteration τ_{iter} during this optimization is used as a target parameter of the performance metric.

Figure 9 shows that the results for the Intel Xeon Gold 6152 CPUs with 22 cores per CPU in the LREAL=FALSE case demonstrate the same level of balance as the results for AMD Epyc CPUs [13]. Still for the LREAL=TRUE case AMD Epyc CPUs give slightly better time-to-solution values for the same amount of total peak Flops/sec. It can be explained by higher total memory bandwidth (there are only 6 memory channels in Intel Xeon Scalable CPUs versus 8 channels in AMD Epyc CPUs).

Table 1 summarizes the absolute values of τ_{iter} for CPU and GPU variants of VASP. In the LREAL=FALSE case we see a very small τ_{iter} value for a dual-socket node of the HSE supercomputer. The results for the GPU version running on Tesla V100 GPU are not better that the results for Tesla P100 GPUs of the IBM Minsky servers or DGX-1 servers [13]. This fact can be explained by the

Table 2. Comparison of the ML performance for difference GPU architectures

GPU model	Architecture	1 GPU	4 GPUs
Tesla V100	Volta (2017)	2 days, 12 h	17 h
GTX 1080Ti	Pascal (2016)	3 days, 18 h	1 day, 3 h
Tesla M60	Maxwell (2015)	9 days, 6 h	2 days, 13 h
Tesla K80	Kepler (2014)	18 days, 17 h	4 days, 19 h

limited PCIe bandwidth of a PowerEdge C4140 node that uses only 16 PCIe lanes with a PCIe switch to feed data to all 4 GPUs inside one node (see Fig. 1).

7 Machine Learning: Performance and Collocation Effects

To benchmark the GPU performance, we have used the training procedure of the Faster R-CNN object detector [9] with ResNet-101 backbone. We used the implementation of maskrcnn-benchmark implementation [5] based on the PyTorch library [7] and trained it on the COCO dataset, version 2017 [4] (http://cocodataset.org/).[1] To adapt the learning schedules to different number of GPUs, we've used the rules for the learning rate schedules and number of iterations suggested he library[2].

We have tested the training of the network on both 1 and 4 GPU configurations on the HSE cluster and compared it against 3 other GPU solutions: regular deep learning server with GeForce GTX 1080 Ti (solutions of the medium budget for 2018) and two types of machines available in the Microsoft Azure cloud: NV24 (4× Tesla M60) and NC24 (2× Tesla K80 = 4× Tesla K40, Tesla K80 are also available for free for limited time in Google Colab https://colab.research. google.com). The used GPUs cover 4 generations of micro-architectures: Volta, Pascal, Maxwell and Kepler, respectively. In Table 2, we provide the training times on both 1-GPU and 4-GPU training runs for all the 4 machines we used.

Table 3. The illustration of the influence on time-to-solution values (in sec) for the benchmark runs that have been accompanied with the simultaneous machine-learning workload on 8 CPU cores and 4 GPUs in each node of the HSE supercomputer (VASP runs correspond to LREAL=TRUE, the number of MPI processes per socket is shown)

N_{nodes}:	1	2	4
22 MPI per CPU w/o ML	11.8	6.2	3.6
16 MPI per CPU w/o ML	14.5 (−23%)	8.5 (−37%)	4.7 (−30%)
16 MPI per CPU w/ ML	16.5 (−40%)	9.0 (−45%)	5.2 (−44%)

The task-scheduling policy (e.g. in SLURM) on such a hybrid system as the HSE supercomputer should maximize the utilization of the nodes. To reach this goal it would be beneficial if CPU-only jobs could share nodes with GPU-oriented jobs such as ML applications. The only shared recourse for these two types of jobs is the memory subsystem. Sharing memory bandwidth can result is certain performance degradation.

---

[1] Full config files are available here: https://github.com/facebookresearch/maskrcnn-benchmark/blob/master/configs/e2e_faster_rcnn_R_101_FPN_1x.yaml.

[2] https://github.com/facebookresearch/Detectron/blob/master/configs/getting_started/tutorial_1gpu_e2e_faster_rcnn_R-50-FPN.yaml#L14-L30.

In order to quantify this effect we performed the benchmarks when CPU-only VASP calculations on 1, 2 and 4 nodes using 16 cores per socket share the allocated nodes with ML applications running on 4 CPU cores per socket and 4 GPUs. The benchmark results presented in Table 3 shows that the slowdown for VASP that stems from this collocation is about 40–45%. Despite such a significant reduction of performance, it could be still reasonable to allow node-sharing for CPU-only and ML GPU applications for maximization of total supercomputer utilization level.

8   Conclusions

In this work we present the comparison of the MPI latency and bandwidth related tests for the new HSE supercomputer based on dual-rail Infiniband EDR. The perfomance and scalability of Gromacs, CP2K and VASP is described using typical benchmark models. It is shown that the limited CPU-GPU PCIe bandwidth of nodes prevents Gromacs to reach the performance level proportional to the peak performance of the Tesla V100 GPUs deployed in this system. Performance of CPU-version of VASP on Intel Xeon Gold CPUs has been compared with novel AMD Epyc CPUs and showed comparable level of balance between computational and memory subsystems. Performance increase of Nvidia GPUs for machine learning calculations for different subsequent architectures has been illustrated. It was shown that collocation of CPU-only and machine learning GPU jobs sharing node of such a hybrid supercomputer results in the performance degradation about 40–45% for CPU applications.

References

1. Begau, C., Sutmann, G.: Adaptive dynamic load-balancing with irregular domain decomposition for particle simulations. Comput. Phys. Commun. **190**, 51–61 (2015). https://doi.org/10.1016/j.cpc.2015.01.009. http://www.sciencedirect.com/science/article/pii/S0010465515000181
2. Höhnerbach, M., Ismail, A.E., Bientinesi, P.: The vectorization of the tersoff multi-body potential: an exercise in performance portability. In: Proceedings of the International Conference for High Performance Computing, Networking, Storage and Analysis, SC 2016, pp. 7:1–7:13. IEEE Press, Piscataway (2016). http://dl.acm.org/citation.cfm?id=3014904.3014914
3. Kutzner, C., Páll, S., Fechner, M., Esztermann, A., de Groot, B.L., Grubmüller, H.: Best bang for your buck: GPU nodes for gromacs biomolecular simulations. J. Comput. Chem. **36**(26), 1990–2008 (2015)
4. Lin, T.-Y., et al.: Microsoft COCO: common objects in context. In: Fleet, D., Pajdla, T., Schiele, B., Tuytelaars, T. (eds.) ECCV 2014, Part V. LNCS, vol. 8693, pp. 740–755. Springer, Cham (2014). https://doi.org/10.1007/978-3-319-10602-1_48
5. Massa, F., Girshick, R.: maskrcnn-benchmark: Fast, modular reference implementation of Instance Segmentation and Object Detection algorithms in PyTorch (2018). https://github.com/facebookresearch/maskrcnn-benchmark

6. Ohmura, I., Morimoto, G., Ohno, Y., Hasegawa, A., Taiji, M.: MDGRAPE-4: a special-purpose computer system for molecular dynamics simulations. Philos. Trans. R. Soc. London A: Math. Phys. Eng. Sci. **372**(2021) (2014). https://doi.org/ 10.1098/rsta.2013.0387, http://rsta.royalsocietypublishing.org/content/372/2021/ 20130387
7. Paszke, A., et al.: Automatic differentiation in pytorch. In: NIPS-W (2017)
8. Piana, S., Klepeis, J.L., Shaw, D.E.: Assessing the accuracy of physical models used in protein-folding simulations: quantitative evidence from long molecular dynamics simulations. Curr. Opin. Struct. Biol. **24**, 98–105 (2014). https://doi.org/10.1016/ j.sbi.2013.12.006
9. Ren, S., He, K., Girshick, R., Sun, J.: Faster R-CNN: Towards real-time object detection with region proposal networks. In: Advances in Neural Information Processing Systems (NIPS) (2015)
10. Rojek, K., Wyrzykowski, R., Kuczynski, L.: Systematic adaptation of stencil-based 3D MPDATA to GPU architectures. Concurr. Comput. Pract. Exp. (2016). https://doi.org/10.1002/cpe.3970, https://doi.org/10.1002/cpe.3970
11. Smirnov, G.S., Stegailov, V.V.: Efficiency of classical molecular dynamics algorithms on supercomputers. Math. Models Comput. Simul. **8**(6), 734–743 (2016). https://doi.org/10.1134/S2070048216060156
12. Stegailov, V., et al.: Angara interconnect makes GPU-based desmos supercomputer an efficient tool for molecular dynamics calculations. Int. J. High Perform. Comput. Appl. **33**(3), 507–521 (2019)
13. Stegailov, V., Smirnov, G., Vecher, V.: VASP hits the memory wall: processors efficiency comparison. Concurr. Comput. Pract. Exp. e5136. https://doi.org/10. 1002/cpe.5136, https://doi.org/10.1002/cpe.5136, e5136 cpe.5136
14. Stegailov, V.V., Orekhov, N.D., Smirnov, G.S.: HPC hardware efficiency for quantum and classical molecular dynamics. In: Malyshkin, V. (ed.) PaCT 2015. LNCS, vol. 9251, pp. 469–473. Springer, Cham (2015). https://doi.org/10.1007/978-3-319-21909-7_45

Performance of the Particle-in-Cell Method with the Intel (Broadwell, KNL) and IBM Power9 Architectures

Evgeny Berendeev, Alexey Snytnikov, and Anna Efimova[✉]

Institute of Computational Mathematics and Mathematical Geophysics SB RAS, Novosibirsk, Russia
anna.an.efimova@gmail.com

Abstract. The particle-in-cell method is one of the efficient methods of plasma simulation. But the principal limitation of the method is its resource intensity. As the motion computation of a large number of model particles can be performed using the parallel algorithms, the computational node architecture is very important. In this paper comparison is made of the performance of the particle-in-cell method between the classic Intel Broadwell architecture, Intel Xeon Phi accelerators, and IBM Power9 processor. As the number of computing operations per one particle depends on its form-factor, in the given paper comparison has been made of the form-factors from the first to the fourth order. The computational experiments have shown that the IBM and Intel Broadwell nodes are similar in performance, and the use of Intel KNL in case of higher-order form-factors can promote essential performance growth. Moreover, in order to effectively use the modern processors it is necessary to take into account their key features such as the memory access, vector instructions, etc.

Keywords: High performance computing · Particles-in-cell method · Code optimization

1 Introduction

The particle-in-cell method is widely used to solve the problems of the simulation of plasma dynamics [1]. The authors are associated with the scientists from the Budker Institute of Nuclear Physics (INP) of the Siberian Branch of the Russian Academy of Sciences (SB RAS) and the Institute of Laser Physics (ILP) of the SB RAS. They jointly develop the code meant to simulate the effect of generating the high-power terahertz radiation in the opposing wakefields that are established in the plasma by the femtosecond laser pulses. This program complex will be used both for the interpretation of the laboratory experiments and for the search of optimal parameters of the physical installation. According to the preliminary estimates a full-scale three-dimensional description of the considered physical effect will require a large spacial grid ($>10^9$) and quite a few model particles

© Springer Nature Switzerland AG 2019
V. Voevodin and S. Sobolev (Eds.): RuSCDays 2019, CCIS 1129, pp. 610–624, 2019.
https://doi.org/10.1007/978-3-030-36592-9_50

($>10^{10}$), with the laboratory experiments having the typical parameters in the ILP of the SB RAS. In order to solve the problem it is necessary to use modern high-performance systems and to develop advanced parallel algorithms for them. The present paper considers the effectiveness of the particle-in-cell code created by the authors for the computational nodes equipped with different types of processors such as Intel (Broadwell, KNL) and IBM Power9. The approaches to the optimization of computations are also described.

The three-dimensional basic code for the full-scale simulation of physical experiments is reported in the paper. The two-dimentional cylindrical code is also presented which can be used to perform computations in order to find the optimal system parameters at the axially symmetrical approximation.

Today, there are a lot of implementations of the particle-in-cell method both in different programming languages and in different architectures (primarily, they are x86 and Nvidia). In Russia such implementations have been done at Keldysh Applied Mathematics Institute (by Andrianov and Efimkin) [2], at Lobachevsky State University of Nizhny Novgorod (the PICADOR code) [3], at Moscow Institute of Physics and Technology (the KARAT code) [4], at the Institute of Computational Mathematics and Mathematical Geophysics of the SB RAS (the UMKA code and others) [5, 6].

In other countries they are the following codes OSIRIS [7], SMILEI [8], FBPIC [9], SHARP [10] and WARP [11].

The abundance of numerical codes and models on the basis of the particle-in-cell method is related to the fact that in order to solve a certain problem it is necessary to modify the standard algorithms, to change the boundary conditions, and to take into account various physical effects. However, the use of the consistent solution for a wide range of problems is inefficient from the computational point of view. The OSIRIS code is the most universal and highly-productive. It is designed for both the cylindrical geometry and the Cartesian geometry. It has a wide range of tools for the neutralization of computational drawbacks of the particle-in-cell method. But this code is inaccessible. However, many general recommendations on the improvements of computational performance can be made. They are storing the particles in cells, collecting the values of electromagnetic fields before the interpolation, vectorizing the code, and grouping the computation of the current. The effectiveness of these approaches is widely covered in the literature [3, 12]. Moreover, as it is shown further, the use of such optimizations is of crucial importance for the achievement of a high performance of modern processors. In the paper we are going to generalize the recommendations for the 2D and 3D code being developed. We shall also try to test its performance with the Intel Broadwell, Intel KNL and IBM Power9 architectures and for the different form-factors of particles. The form-factor order is not only important for the elimination of numerical noises in the particle-in-cell method and in smoothing the solution but also in the algorithm performance. When the sizes of model particles are different (1 cell for the first-order form-factor and 2,5 cells for the fourth-order form-factor), it is needed to process different quantities of the grid nodes both for the interpolation of electromagnetic fields to the particle and the computation of the current density. It may seem that enhancing the form-factor order will increase the computation time substantially as the particle-in-cell method is a memory-bounded algorithm. But, as it is shown further, the properly arranged memory access can diminish this difference.

2   The Particle-in-Cell Method. The Main Features of Algorithms

Let us consider the algorithm of the particle-in-cell method in more detail and note the key features that affect the performance of computations. The main idea of the particle-in-cell method is that the plasma is presented as a set of quite a large number of model particles, each particle being a carrier of some characteristics of the medium, such as mass, velocity, temperature, etc. In this case the distribution function of point particles $f(\overrightarrow{r}, \overrightarrow{v}, t)$ is replaced by the distribution function of model particles $\tilde{f}(\overrightarrow{r}, \overrightarrow{v}, t)$, which possess particular sizes (it is determined by the form factor of the particle core $S(\overrightarrow{r}, \overrightarrow{r}')$) and are able to go through each other easily.

$$\tilde{f}(\overrightarrow{r}, \overrightarrow{v}, t) = \int f(\overrightarrow{r}', \overrightarrow{v}, t) S(\overrightarrow{r}, \overrightarrow{r}') d\overrightarrow{r}' = \sum_j S(\overrightarrow{r}, \overrightarrow{r}_j(t)) \delta(\overrightarrow{v} - \overrightarrow{v_j}(t)) \quad (1)$$

Thus, the input Vlasov equation for the distribution function of real particles in the collisionless plasma is replaced by a similar equation for the distribution function of model particles.

$$\frac{\partial f_\alpha}{\partial t} + \overrightarrow{v} \frac{\partial f_\alpha}{\partial \overrightarrow{r}} + q_\alpha \left(\overrightarrow{E} + \frac{1}{c}[\overrightarrow{v}, \overrightarrow{B}] \right) \frac{\partial f_\alpha}{\partial \overrightarrow{p}} = 0, \quad (2)$$

$$\frac{\partial \tilde{f}_\alpha}{\partial t} + \overrightarrow{v} \frac{\partial \tilde{f}_\alpha}{\partial \overrightarrow{r}} + q_\alpha \left(\overrightarrow{E} + \frac{1}{c}[\overrightarrow{v}, \overrightarrow{B}] \right) \frac{\partial \tilde{f}_\alpha}{\partial \overrightarrow{p}} = 0, \quad (3)$$

Here, the α index denotes the types of particles (ions and electrons of plasma, electrons of beams), $\overrightarrow{p} = m\gamma\overrightarrow{v}$ is the relativistic momentum of particles, and q is the charge of particles. The characteristics of the equation describe the motion of particles:

$$\frac{d\overrightarrow{p_j}(t)}{dt} = q_j(\overrightarrow{E_j} + \frac{1}{c}[\overrightarrow{v_j}, \overrightarrow{B_j}]), \quad \frac{d\overrightarrow{r_j}(t)}{dt} = \overrightarrow{v_j}. \quad (4)$$

where

$$\overrightarrow{B_j} = \int S(\overrightarrow{r}, \overrightarrow{r_j}(t)) \overrightarrow{B}(\overrightarrow{r}) d\overrightarrow{r}, \quad \overrightarrow{E_j} = \int S(\overrightarrow{r}, \overrightarrow{r_j}(t)) \overrightarrow{E}(\overrightarrow{r}) d\overrightarrow{r}. \quad (5)$$

are the values of electromagnetic fields affecting particle j. To solve these equations we shall use the well known Boris scheme (6–7) [13]:

$$\frac{\overrightarrow{p}_j^{m+1/2} - \overrightarrow{p}_j^{m-1/2}}{\tau} = q_j \left(\overrightarrow{E}_j^m + \frac{1}{c} \left[\frac{\overrightarrow{v}_j^{m+1/2} + \overrightarrow{v}_j^{m-1/2}}{2}, \overrightarrow{B}_j^m \right] \right) \quad (6)$$

$$\frac{\vec{r}_j^{\,m+1} - \vec{r}_j^{\,m}}{\tau} = \vec{v}_j^{\,m+1/2} \tag{7}$$

The current density and the charge density of the model particle are calculated according to the formula:

$$\tilde{\rho}(\vec{r},t) = \sum_j q_j S(\vec{r}, \vec{r}_j(t)), \quad \vec{\tilde{j}}(\vec{r},t) = \sum_j q_j \vec{v}_j S(\vec{r}, \vec{r}_j(t)) \tag{8}$$

These values of the current density and the charge density appear in the Maxwell equation for electromagnetic fields (9–11):

$$\mathrm{rot}\,\vec{B} = \frac{4\pi}{c}\vec{\tilde{j}} + \frac{1}{c}\frac{\partial \vec{E}}{\partial t}, \quad \mathrm{rot}\,\vec{E} = -\frac{1}{c}\frac{\partial \vec{B}}{\partial t}, \tag{9}$$

$$\mathrm{div}\,\vec{E} = 4\pi\tilde{\rho}, \tag{10}$$

$$\mathrm{div}\,\vec{B} = 0, \tag{11}$$

which complete the system of equations for the dynamics of particles in the self-consistent electromagnetic fields. Different order for form-factor S can be used:

$$S(y) = \frac{1}{\Delta x} \begin{cases} 1 - |y|, & 0 \le |y| < 1, \\ 0, & otherwise, \end{cases} \tag{12}$$

$$S(y) = \frac{1}{\Delta x} \begin{cases} 3/4 - y^2, & 0 \le |y| < 1/2, \\ 1/8(3 - 2|y|)^2, & 1/2 \le |y| < 3/2, \\ 0, & otherwise, \end{cases} \tag{13}$$

$$S(y) = \frac{1}{\Delta x} \begin{cases} 2/3 - y^2 + \frac{|y|^3}{2}, & 0 \le |y| < 1, \\ 1/6(2 - |y|)^3, & 1 \le |y| < 2, \\ 0, & otherwise, \end{cases} \tag{14}$$

$$S(y) = \frac{1}{\Delta x} \begin{cases} 115/192 - \frac{5y^2}{8} + \frac{y^4}{4}, & 0 \le |y| < 1/2, \\ 1/96(55 + 20|y| - 120y^2 + 80|y|^3 - 16y^4), & 1/2 \le |y| < 3/2, \\ 1/384(5 - 2|y|)^4, & 3/2 \le |y| < 5/2, \\ 0, & otherwise, \end{cases} \tag{15}$$

(12) is the PIC form-factor. The Maxwell equations are usually solved using the grid. This is done either explicitly, for example, by using the FDTD method [14], or in the k-space in order to prevent a number of numerical instabilities [9]. In this paper we apply the FDTD scheme. Thus, the generic computational loop is as follows. The first stage includes the calculation of electromagnetic fields affecting

the particle and the computation of the particle motion according to the scheme (6–7). This stage incorporates the calculation of the current density on the basis of (8). In the given paper we deal with the method of calculating the current according to the formulae by Zigzag [15] for the 3D code and by Esirkepov [16] for the 2D code, since this method allows one to use almost any form-factors of the particle. The second stage includes the solution of the Maxwell equations (9–11) according to the FDTD scheme with the aim of determining some new values of electromagnetic fields:

$$\frac{\vec{B}^{m+1/2} - \vec{B}^{m-1/2}}{\tau} = -c \operatorname{rot}_h \vec{E}^m, \tag{16}$$

$$\frac{\vec{E}^{m+1} - \vec{E}^m}{\tau} = -4\pi j^{m+1/2} + c \operatorname{rot}_h \vec{B}^{m+1/2}. \tag{17}$$

At the same time, the two remaining equations:

$\operatorname{div}_h \vec{B}^{m+1/2} = 0$

$\operatorname{div}_h \vec{E}^m = 4\pi \rho^m$

are fulfilled automatically if they are correct at the time zero.

It should be noted that the first stage of the algorithm described above is much more cumbersome as compared to the second stage. This is because the calculations involve more particles than grid nodes. That is why we pay special attention to the performance of the 1st stage in this paper. The principal directions of the performance improvement are the use of the data locality and the code vectorization. It is necessary to note that the organization of data in the memory has a strong effect on the performance. The model particles are located within the computation domain in a random manner. Even if the model particles are situated next to each other in the array where their coordinates are stored, the values of coordinates themselves will only be closely adjacent at the beginning. The particles having closely adjacent values of coordinates stay in the neighboring cells or even in the same cell. Later the model particles move within the computation domain unpredictably, thus they stop being in the neighboring cells. It means that the access to the three-dimensional or two-dimensional arrays containing electric and magnetic fields are orderless. If the particle j has to have access to a cell of the three-dimensional grid (three-dimensional array) with the indices of (i, l, k), the particle $j + 1$, most probably, will have to have access to a cell which is far removed within the computation domain but not to a cell with the indices of $(i, l, k - 1)$ or $(i, l, k + 1)$, i.e. to the neighboring cell.

Thus, it is convenient to arrange the particles into cells in order to use the cache effectively. It is possible to use the local array of fields here, the array containing the values of the nodes that influence the particles of the given cell. Interestingly, the node values are put into the array in advance. A similar approach is described in [3]. The size of such an array in each direction is equal to four elements for the form-factors of the first and second orders, and it is equal to six elements for the form-factors of the third and fourth orders. Similar arrays of the same size are used to calculate the contribution to the current density. In case of the three-dimensional code the number of particles in a cell is fewer than in case of the two-dimensional code. This is due to the necessity to use a much larger number of particles. Therefore, when applying the three-dimensional code we are going to use only the form-factors of the first order. We shall also use the zigzag scheme to calculate the current density, since in this case it works much faster than the Esirkepov scheme.

3   Code Optimization

3.1   General Remarks

The primary way of the optimization of computations for the particle-in-cell method is the appliance of the locality of data. The use of cache would be much more efficient if the particles were arranged in order. Then the field values brought into memory when computing the motion of a particle could be used once again for the next particle if it is closely located. It is sufficient to attach the particles to cells, that is, to store the particles in some way together in a cell. It means that full-scale sorting of the array of particles is not necessary as from a cache perspective the order of particles inside a cell is not important. Model particles located in some cell can be stored in the form of a linked list or an array. The advantages of the list are apparent: the number of particles is not limited and a simple addition and removal is possible. But there also is a disadvantage: a greater access time in comparison with the array. If the particles of a cell are stored in the form of an array (a static array), then, for a three-dimensional simulation, it will result in a four-dimensional array just for one coordinate X of all the particles. Three components locate the cell in the three-dimensional space and one component locates the particle in the cell. It is worth reminding here that a model particle is characterized by six attributes. The storage of the electromagnetic field values can be optimized in the same way. When calculating six three-dimensional arrays are used: three components of an electric field and three components of a magnetic field. In order to use cache more effectively it would be appropriate to use a 4D array for storing the field. In this array the first three indices signify the number of the grid cell, and the fourth index signifies a field component (from 0 to 5). The main problem in case of a static array is the maximal number of particles in a cell. It means that it can not be known in advance what size should the array be in order to store all the particles in every cell. For this purpose it is necessary to take an oversized array. This will substantially increase the used RAM depending on the problem solved. If the dynamic arrays are used for this purpose, the problem of memory overuse can be handled. However, it makes another problem: the necessity to have its own effective manager of the dynamic memory inside the program. This problem may be solvable but it can hardly result in the substantial decrease of the program execution time. Therefore, a compromise version was implemented. The decision was taken to store the numbers of particles located in the given cell at the given moment for all sorts of particles in each cell of the integer array with the length of 4N. The number sets the particle position in big real arrays (around 100 million elements), the arrays storing the coordinates and impulses of model particles. Thus, when the particle is transferred from one cell to another (it is mandatory that the cell is a neighboring one - it is due to the stability of the particle-in-cell method), the particle number is only transferred. The particle number is removed from the array of numbers, describing the active cell and is added to the array of numbers of one of the neighboring cells. The particles never move inside the coordinate arrays and impulse arrays themselves. The version was also implemented involving the storage of particles from each cell as a linked list. In this situation there is a 4D array of pointers defining the first element of the list in each cell, but there are no big arrays as all the information about the particles is only stored in lists. In both versions six small arrays are applied to the input of the particle pusher. The size of arrays cannot be bigger that 4N. The arrays store the coordinates and impulses of particles for a particular cell. The arrays are created either on the basis of the list of particles or on the basis of the array of particle numbers of the cell.

3.2 Optimization Options

Thus, there are the following variants of particle organization in the program:

1. original non-optimized variant;
2. storage of the field values in a 4D array;
3. sorting the particles with the use of arrays of numbers;
4. sorting the particles with the use of a linked list.

The code considered in this article is implemented in C++ with parallelizing loops using OpenMP technology. Depending on the optimization and data storage option, paralleling was carried out either at the level of cell processing loops (with the processing of the ejected or deleted particles), or simply by particles. In the field loop, parallelization is performed along one direction. For communication between computational nodes, the MPI is used with decomposition of the computational domain, but in this paper this part of the computations is not considered, since only computational nodes are compared. When the current density is calculated there is a principal problem on OpenMP to be overcome. It is a simultaneous record of the current density contribution in one and the same node from the particles processed by different threads having shared memory. To prevent this, parallelization is carried out into the cells with interleaving and with the predefined increment value. For example, the first thread processes the first cell along the given direction, the second thread processes the 10-th cell, the third thread processes the 30-th cell, etc. Then the first thread processes the second cell, the second thread processes the 11-th cell, etc. The interleaving step depends on the total number of the threads applied and on the size of the model particle. The second important stage is the transfer of particles between cells. In order to remove the conditional statements from the particle processing loop some optional buffers are introduced. All the particles arriving at the cell are recorded into these buffers. The synchronization is only performed after all the particles have been processed. The code vectorization can be performed either along the field components or along the nodes of the local array for the fields/currents. The first approach is used in [3], for example. However, for the Esirkepov scheme, the vectorization of loops when computing the contributions of fields from the local array is more natural. So it is this version that is considered for the 2D code. We shall take the problem of dynamic simulation of plasma in a long narrow channel in the 3D geometry as a test computation. In the computation domain having the form of a rectangular there is some plasma, the plasma being constrained by the vacuum from two sides (along the directions R and Z). The plasma is being kept by a strong longitudinal magnetic field. Along the Z direction open boundaries are used [17]. Through the boundaries either an electron beam or some laser impulses can penetrate.

3.3   Tests of 3D Code

We shall now consider the results of tests showing the effectiveness of the optimization performed. The test computations were made using the work station AMD Phenom (Phenom II X6 1055T), (peak performance 6 cores 2,8 Ghz × 4 double FLOP/per tact = 67,2 GFLOP/s, 6 Mb L3 cache, 8Gb DDR2 SDRAM), and using the cluster at Novosibirsk State University, equipped with the processors Intel Xeon E5540 (peak performance 4 cores 2,53 Ghz × 4 double FLOP/per tact = 40,5 GFLOP/s, 8 Mb L3 cache, 8 Gb DDR3 SDRAM). In both cases the grid of such size was chosen that even one 3D array containing, for example, one of the field components definitely cannot be placed in cache. The grid size is of $64 \times 32 \times 32$ nodes, 150 particles in a cell, 9.8 million particles in all. The PIC form-factor 12 was used in all experiments. As there are 440 double-precision operations per one particle, it is possible to work out the performance in units of FLOPS/s.

$$FLOP = FP \times NP/\Delta t$$

Here:

FP - number of operations per one model particle, $FP = 440$;

NP - number of model particles per node (9.8 million particles as mentioned above);

To measure time, we used the function "gettimeofday". The measurement results were averaged out of 100 program launches with 1000 time steps each run. Δt - time step length, sec.

It can be seen from Table 1 that the maximal performance can be obtained by using the local storage of fields and the storage of particles with the help of arrays of numbers. AMD Phenom is more powerful than Intel Xeon but it has a slower memory - DDR2 and less L3 cache size - 6Mb vs 8Mb. If we try to arrange the particles somehow, it will give no substantial growth. At the same time using Intel Xeon we can double the computations if we apply the optimizations considered. Also, access time to the next item in the linked list was too long, and this optimization (No.4) is inefficient. The given tests were carried out using rather out-of-date processors that are only capable to process 4 double per one tact. On such processors, using the considered optimizations, we managed to achieve no more than 25% of the peak performance. At the same time, modern processors

Table 1. Calculation time, in seconds, and performance, GFLOP/s.

No	Variant of optimization	Time Phenom	Time Xeon	Performance Phenom	Performance Xeon
1	Original non-optimized version	1,325	0,762	3,25	5,7
2	Using a local array of fields	0,88	0,672	4,9	6,4
3	Ordering particles using arrays of numbers	1,251	0,567	3,4	7,6
4	Particle ordering using the linked list	1,05	1,03	4,1	4,2
5	The combination of options 2 and 3	1,092	0,367	3,9	11,7

with a similar clock frequency can process more elements per clock. Let us consider now how we can improve the performance using modern processors with the Intel Broadwell architecture. To make comparisons we used the cluster of Peter the Great St. Petersburg Polytechnic University "Polytechnic" (processor Intel Xeon 2697v3, 36 Mb L3 cache, 64 Gb DDR4 SDRAM) and "Lomonosov" [19,20], the main section (the out-of-date processor Intel Xeon 5570, 8 Mb L3 cache, 8 Gb DDR3 SDRAM). The PIC form-factor was used in all experiments. Comparative performance of some processor elements is shown in Table 2.

Table 2. Comparative performance of some processor elements.

Processors	Performance, GFLOP/s	Peak performance
Intel Xeon 2697v3	209,02	14 cores $\times$ 16 FLOP $\times$ 2,6 GHz = 582,4 GFLOP/s
Intel Xeon 5570	11,39	4 cores $\times$ 4 FLOP $\times$ 2,93 Ghz = 46,9 GFLOP/s

Therefore, the use of a more productive processor with the Intel Broadwell architecture allows us to obtain almost twenty-fold acceleration. But the peak performance of Intel Broadwell is almost 10 times higher. This is not only due to the fact that the number of processor cores is greater but also because the FMA and SSE-2 instructions are used, which allow performing 16 DP operations per tact in one core. Moreover, the DDR4 SD RAM also plays a role in promoting the acceleration. In the same way, if on the processors of the old generation we could have reached only 25% of the peak performance, then for Intel Broadwell we have already reached more than 35% of the peak power. The use of vectorization and of storing the particles in cells allows us to improve the given result with the help of the new generation processors. Similar performance indicators have been achieved for code on an Intel Xeon Platinum 8160, 2.1 GHz (Skylake) processor with 96 GB of RAM [18] - 740 million particles per second per processor and PICADOR code on processors Intel Xeon 2697v3 - 128 million particles per second [21] and on processor Intel Xeon E5-2660 processor - 72 million particles per second per processor [3]. Our result based on Table 2 was 470 million particles per second.

4 Performance Tests of the 2D Code with the Intel and IBM Architectures

Since the architecture which is used to make computations is of great importance, it is worth considering a few major trends being developed by both the Intel and the IBM [22]. To test the performance we are going to use various form-factors of particles. That is why we shall only have to employ the 2D code. This will allow us to make computations with a large amount of particles in one cell within the reasonable amount of time. It will also be possible for the form-factors of higher orders. We use optimization option 2 and 3 from the section above which provide the local storage of data and the vectorization.

We are going to consider the following architectures - Intel Broadwell, Intel KNL, IBM Power9. These architectures were set up at one cluster NKS-1p. The Siberian Branch of the Russian Academy of Sciences (SB RAS) Siberian Supercomputer Center is great fully acknowledged for providing supercomputer facilities.

The description of nodes:

- The cluster node (section Broadwell):
  $2 \times$ Xeon E5-2697A v4, 16 cores 2.6 (3.6) GHz (128 Gb DDR4 or Intel Optane memory), 1331.2 GFLOP/s peak performance
- The cluster node (section KNL):
  $1 \times$ Xeon Phi 7290, 72 cores 1.5 (1.7) GHz (KNL), 72 nodes 16 GB memory MCDRAM (cache) + 96 Gb DDR4 SDRAM, 3456 GFLOP/s peak performance
- The cluster node (IBM):
  $2 \times$ 12-core 2.7 (3.8) GHz IBM POWER9 Processor, 32 Gb DDR4 Memory. Peak performance 1037 GFLOP/s

The Intel Broadwell and IBM Power9 architectures have an advantage: they have rather a large cache L3–40 MB and 120 MB per chip, respectively. It is much faster than in case of the MCDRAM KNL. But the KNL permits the use of a maximally large amount of cores - 72 cores (versus 16 cores in Intel Broadwell and 12 cores in IBM Power9). Each core can processing of 32 DP numbers per tact (versus 16 per core in Broadwell and Power9). That is why the vectorization of computations with the use of the Intel KNL is supposed to give a gain in productivity by all means. For the Intel Broadwell node the memory was tested with the help of Intel Optane technique. As it will be demonstrated further it is possible to gain high performance by employing the locality of storing and processing the particles.

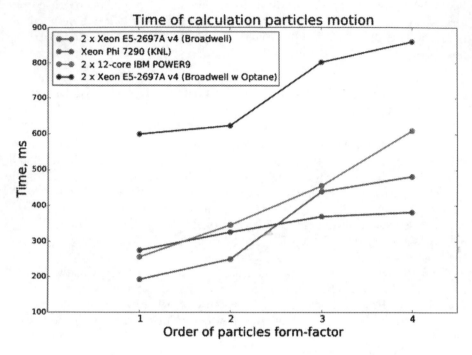

Fig. 1. The computation time of the particle motion for different architectures and form-factors.

Computational parameters are the following: the number of model particles is $4 * 10^7$, the grid is 1024×1024 nodes. Figure 1 shows the computation time of the particle motion for different architectures and form-factors.

The figure shows that the Intel KNL performance alone is only affected by the order of the used form-factor to a small extent. The figure indicates that the least time for the form-factor of the first order can be obtained using the Intel Broadwell node. The use of Intel Optane technology slows down the performance 3-fold. The more productive Intel KNL node works 1,42 times slower. This is due to the fact that vectorization does not work to the full extent as the sizes of local arrays for the fields are very small. However, the Intel KNL node operates 1,19 and 1,26 times faster than the Intel Broadwell node for the form-factors of the third and fourth order. For the Intel Broadwell nodes the shift from the form-factor of the second order to the form-factor of the third order results in a substantial decrease of performance. This is because this shift causes the enhancement of the sizes of local arrays for the fields. This is especially noticeable when using Optane, the difference between the form-factors of the 1st and 2nd, 2nd and 3rd, 3rd and 4th orders is equal to 1,04, 1,28 and 1,07 times, respectively.

The IBM nodes are not so sensitive to the increase of the form-factor as they do not use the vector operations so extensively. The difference in performance between the Intel Broadwell and IBM nodes is 1,3. This is the difference between the peak performances of the nodes. The performance of the Intel KNL node acts absolutely differently. The differences between various form-factors are almost uniform and they are mainly associated with the number of operations per one core. This is due to the vectorization.

We are going to consider the performance the code. Number of operations per one model particle for 1st order of form-factor - 400, 2st - 470, 3-st - 550, 4-st - 620. Table 3 shows the performance in units of GFLOPS/s for different nodes and order of form-factors.

Table 3. The performance in units of GFLOPS/s for different nodes and different order of form factors.

	Intel Broadwell, 1331.2 GFLOP/s peak	Intel KNL, 3456 GFLOP/s peak	IBM Power9, 1037 GFLOP/s peak	Intel Broadwell + Optane, 1331.2 GFLOP/s peak
Order 1	414	291	312	133
Order 2	376	288	250	150
Order 3	250	297	241	137
Order 4	257	324	203	144

The table shows that code provide about 20–30% performance Intel Broadwell (10% with Optane), 10% Intel KNL, 20–30% IBM Power9.

Thus, it can be concluded that the basic principles of optimization that uses the local storage of data and the vectorization make it possible to effectively use modern computational nodes of different architectures.

5   Scalability of Computations

Another parameter characterizing the effectiveness of the parallel code implementation is its scalability. Figure 2 shows the plot of scalability of the same problem as in the previous section for different processing cores of Broadwell, KNL and IBM. We used the same parallelization technology with the same optimizations as in the previous section.

By efficiency we basically mean the E value = real acceleration when using N threads/N (ideal acceleration). The figure shows that the computational efficiency is rather high in all cases, and it only begins to decrease when a larger amount of physical cores of the processor is used than it really has. It indicates that the parallel implementation of computations used is also rather efficient.

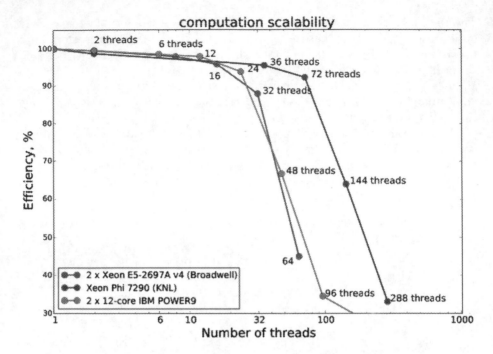

Fig. 2. Scalability of the code at different architectures.

However, for all architectures, scalability on a large number of threads, exceeding the physical number of cores, is more than 30%. This means that the physical cores are not sufficiently loaded and there is a reserve for increasing the performance of the code - by these 30–50%. For comparison, the non-optimized version of the code has a parallelization efficiency of about 50–70% - that is, just by increasing the number of threads you can achieve acceleration, although the total calculation time in this way can not be significantly reduced.

6   Conclusion

The state of the art computational nodes provide opportunities for the substantial increase of the computational performance. In order to obtain that it is necessary to use such special features of the architecture as FMA and AVX-512, cache, etc. To the contrary, if the data are not stored properly, it is impossible to obtain a substantial acceleration as compared to the 10 years old processors. Thus, the approaches to the optimization of computations described in the paper are correct not only for the 2D and 3D codes but also for different architectures. Computational experiments have indicated that the IBM and Broadwell nodes have similar performance, while the use of the Intel KNL with the cores of higher orders can substantially increase the performance due to the vectorization of computations. For the Intel Broadwell and IBM Power9 nodes the performance is the lowest when the shift happens from the form-factor of the 2nd order to the form-factor of the 3rd order. This is because in this case the size of the local arrays of fields needed for the computation of the force affecting the particles. As the Intel KNL deals with the longer vectors, it does not have such drawback.

Acknowledgements. The work is supported by the RFBR under Grant No. 19-07-00446 and 18-07-00364 and the state errand No. 0315-2019-0009 for ICMMG SB RAS.

References

1. Birdsall, C.K., Langdon, A.B.: Plasma Physics via Computer Simulation. Institute of Physics Publishing, Bristol (1991)
2. Andrianov, A.N., Efimkin, K.N.: Particles in cell method: accounting in a parallel implementation the particles interaction. Keldysh Inst. Prepr. **071**, 16 (2016)
3. Bastrakov, S., Surmin, I., Efimenko, E., Gonoskov, A., Meyerov, I.: Performance aspects of collocated and staggered grids for particle-in-cell plasma simulation. In: Malyshkin, V. (ed.) PaCT 2017. LNCS, vol. 10421, pp. 94–100. Springer, Cham (2017). https://doi.org/10.1007/978-3-319-62932-2_8
4. Aplin, K.L., Tarakanov, V.P.: Modelling studies of charged particle interactions for a space application. Inst. Phys. Conf. Ser. **178**, 221–226 (2003)
5. Bulanov, S.V., Naumova, N.M., Vshivkov, V.A., Dudnikova, G.I., Pegoraro, F., Pogorelsky, I.V.: Laser acceleration of charged particles in inhomogeneous plasmas. In: Plasma Physics Reports, vol. 23, no. 4, pp. 259–269 (1997)
6. Berendeev, E., Dudnikova, G., Efimova, A., Vshivkov, V.: Computer simulation of plasma dynamics in open plasma trap. In: Dimov, I., Faragó, I., Vulkov, L. (eds.) NAA 2016. LNCS, vol. 10187, pp. 227–234. Springer, Cham (2017). https://doi.org/10.1007/978-3-319-57099-0_23
7. Davidson, A., Tableman, W.: An implementation of a hybrid particle code with a PIC description in r-z and a gridless description in ϕ into OSIRIS. J. Comput. Phys. **281**, 1063–1077 (2015)
8. Derouillat, J., et al.: SMILEI: A collaborative, open-source, multi-purpose particle-in-cell code for plasma simulation. Comput. Phys. Commun. **222**, 351–373 (2018)
9. Lehe, R., et al.: A spectral, quasi-cylindrical and dispersion-free Particle-In-Cell algorithm. Comput. Phys. Commun. **203**, 66–82 (2016)
10. Shalaby, M., et al.: SHARP: a spatially higher-order, relativistic Particle-in-Cell Code. Astrophys. J. **841**(1), 52 (2017)
11. http://warp.lbl.gov/
12. Wen, M., Chen, M., Lin, J.: Optimizing a particle-in-cell code on Intel knights landing. In: HPC Asia 2018 Proceedings of Workshops of HPC Asia, pp. 71–74 (2018)
13. Boris, J.P.: Relativistic plasma simulation - optimization of a hybrid code. In: Fourth Conference on numerical Simulation of Plasmas, Washington, pp. 3–67 (1970)
14. Taflove, A.: Computational Electrodynamics: The Finite-Difference Time-Domain Method, p. 611. Artech House Publishers, Boston (1995)
15. Umeda, T., Omura, Y., Tominaga, T., Matsumoto, H.: A new charge conservation method in electromagnetic particle-in-cell simulations. Comput. Phys. Commun. **156**(1), 73–85 (2003)

16. Esirkepov, T.Z.: Exact charge conservation scheme for Particle-in-Cell simulation with an arbitrary form-factor. Comput. Phys. Commun. **135**(2), 144–153 (2001)
17. Timofeev, I.V., Berendeev, E.A., Dudnikova, G.I.: Simulations of a beam-driven plasma antenna in the regime of plasma transparency. Phys. Plasmas **24**(9), 093114 (2017). (1–7)
18. Barsamian, Y., Charguéraud, A., Hirstoaga, S.A., Mehrenberger, M.: Efficient strict-binning particle-in-cell algorithm for multi-core SIMD processors. In: Aldinucci, M., Padovani, L., Torquati, M. (eds.) Euro-Par 2018. LNCS, vol. 11014, pp. 749–763. Springer, Cham (2018). https://doi.org/10.1007/978-3-319-96983-1_53
19. Voevodin, V.V., Zhumatiy, S.A., et al.: Supercomputer Lomonosov-2: large scale, deep monitoring and fine analytics for the user community. Supercomput. Front. Innovations **6**(2), 4–11 (2019)
20. Nikitenko, D.A., Voevodin, V.V., Zhumatiy, S.A.: Deep analysis of job state statistics on Lomonosov-2 Supercomputer. Supercomput. Front. Innovations **5**(2), 4–10 (2018)
21. Surmin, I., Bastrakov, S., Matveev, Z., Efimenko, E., Gonoskov, A., Meyerov, I.: Co-design of a particle-in-cell plasma simulation code for Intel Xeon Phi: a first look at Knights Landing. In: Carretero, J., et al. (eds.) ICA3PP 2016. LNCS, vol. 10049, pp. 319–329. Springer, Cham (2016). https://doi.org/10.1007/978-3-319-49956-7_25
22. Glinskiy, B.M., Kulikov, I.M., Snytnikov, A.V., Romanenko, A.A., Chernykh, I.G., Vshivkov, V.A.: Co-design of parallel numerical methods for plasma physics and astrophysics. Supercomput. Front. Innovations **1**(3), 88–98 (2015)

Software Development Tools for FPGA-Based Reconfigurable Systems Programming

Ilya Levin[1,2] ⓘ, Alexey Dordopulo[2](✉) ⓘ, Vyacheslav Gudkov[1,2],
Andrey Gulenok[2], Alexander Bovkun[2], Georgyi Yevstafiyev[1,2],
and Kirill Alekseev[1,2]

[1] Academy for Engineering and Technology, Institute of Computer
Technologies and Information Security, Southern Federal University,
Taganrog, Russia
{iilevin, VGudkov}@sfedu.ru
[2] Scientific Research Centre of Supercomputers and Neurocomputers,
Taganrog, Russia
{levin, dordopulo, gudkov, gulenok, bovkun,
evstafiev, alekseev}@superevm.ru

Abstract. In the paper we consider an architecture and principles of functioning of software development tools for translation of sequential C-programs into FPGA configuration files. The software development tools, which consist of the separate translators "Angel", "Mermaid", and "Procrustes", transform a sequential C-program (the ISO/IEC 9899:1999 standard) of the compiler gcc into an information graph, described in the programming language COLAMO. Then, the information graph is translated by the COLAMO-translator into FPGA configuration files for the specified reconfigurable computer resource. The distinctive feature of the software development tools is scalability of calculations in the case of reduction of available hardware resource. Scaling is performed by a special translator "Nutcracker", which automatically reduces not only the number of basic subgraphs of the task, but also the number of operations of the basic subgraph and the capacity of processed data.

Keywords: Resource-independent parallel programming · High-level programming language COLAMO · Reconfigurable computer system · FPGA · C-to-VHDL translator

1 Introduction

Reconfigurable computer systems (RCS) [1, 2], which contain computational fields of large logical capacity FPGAs as principal computational resource become more and more required for implementation of computationally expensive tasks in different fields of science and technology [3] owing to considerable gain in real performance and power efficiency in comparison with cluster multiprocessor computer systems.

In contrast to automatic parallelizing compilers such as Polaris [3], SUIF [4], VAST/Parallel [5], Intel/OpenMP [6], etc., used in shared memory systems, and ParaWise [7], Parallel Studio [8], SAPFOR [9, 10], ORS [11], etc., used in distributed

© Springer Nature Switzerland AG 2019
V. Voevodin and S. Sobolev (Eds.): RuSCDays 2019, CCIS 1129, pp. 625–640, 2019.
https://doi.org/10.1007/978-3-030-36592-9_51

memory systems, for creation of a parallel program in RCS we use an approach which is an alternative to parallelization of a sequential program. For RCS the task is initially represented in an absolutely parallel form of an information graph which reflects natural parallelism and pipelining of operations [1]. The graph can be adapted to the current configuration of the computer system with the help of methods of computer system performance scaling (induction and reduction). The information graph can be scaled not only by data but also by iterations, and, as a result, the number of used memory (or input/output) channels is being reduced.

For 17 years, an original suite of RCS software tools [1, 12] has been developed by the scientific team of the Scientific-Research Centre of Supercomputers and Neuro-computers (Taganrog), the leading Russian vendor of high-performance RCSs. The developed software suite includes the translator of high-level programming language COLAMO and synthesizer Fire!Constructor for multichip VHDL-solution generation. The distinctive features of the developed suit is programming of multichip RCS in a high-level programming language with automatic synchronization of all task fragments placed in separate FPGAs.

2 Software Development Tools for Next-Generation Reconfigurable Computer Systems

Since 2017, in Scientific-Research Centre of supercomputers and neurocomputers a new suit of application development tools is being developed. The suit is used for translation of the source C-program into a COLAMO-program with further adaptation to the RCS architecture and synthesis of FPGA bit-stream files. The suit structure and flow-chart is shown in Fig. 1.

The software development tools for programming RCS and hybrid computer systems in the high-level language COLAMO with the help of resource-independent programming methods contain:

- a converter "Angel" which transforms a C-program (ISO/IEC 9899:1999) into an absolutely parallel COLAMO -program;
- a converter "Mermaid" which transforms an absolutely parallel COLAMO-program into a resource-independent (scalable) COLAMO-program;
- a tool "Procrustes" which adapts parameters of a resource-independent COLAMO-program to the RCS architecture;
- a converter "Nutcracker" which reduces the performance of the resource-independent program in the case of lack of hardware resource;
- an integrated development environment;
- a translator of the high-programming language COLAMO;
- a synthesizer of scalable computing structures Fire!Constructor;
- RCS descriptions (passports) and a library of IP-cores;
- tools for diagnostics and monitoring;
- tools of soft-architecture description and a synthesizer Steam!Constructor;
- a control C-application.

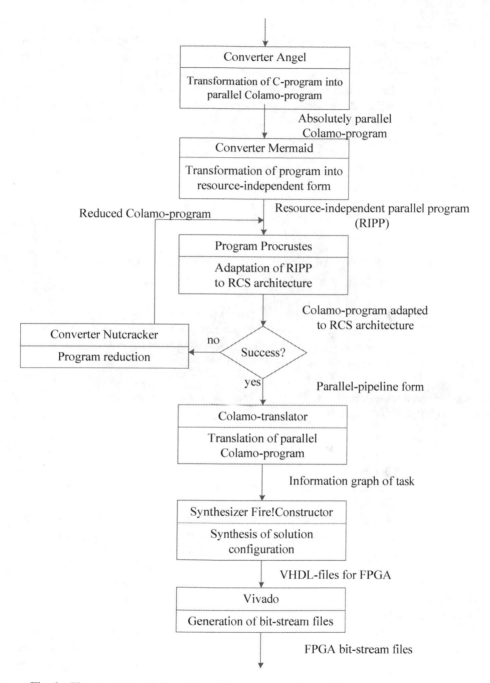

Fig. 1. The structure and flow-chart of the next generation software development tools

In contrast to the majority of well-known translators of the C-language into FPGA bit-stream files (the translators C-to-RTL, MitrionC, CatapultC, etc.), the considered software development tools do not synthesize a special-purpose calculator based on an automata model or a processor paradigm; it maps a sequential program into the absolutely parallel form and adapts this form to available hardware resource of some RCS or hybrid RCS, taking into account data dependency. In contrast to its most close analogue Xilinx Vivado HLS (High-Level Synthesis), the tools provide support of multichip solutions with automatic synchronization of data and control signals, but have much in common with it, concerning operation capabilities.

Functioning of the software development tools is based on a methodology of transformation of a sequential C-program into a parallel COLAMO-program, which is transformed into bit-stream files for FPGAs of some RCS or HRCS by the COLAMO-translator and the synthesizer Fire!Constructor.

3   The Methodology of Transformation of a Sequential C-Program into a Parallel COLAMO-Program

The input program is a sequential C-program developed according to ISO/IEC 9899:1999 with a GNU-extension for the gcc compiler. The methodology of transformation of a sequential C-program into a COLAMO-program contains 6 main steps (see the detailed description in Sects. 3.1–3.6).

3.1   Transformation of a C-Program into an Absolutely Parallel COLAMO-Program

The first step of transformations is performed by the translator "Angel" (see Fig. 1).

Transformation of the C-program into the canonical form (expansion of conditional compilation directives, ternary operations, #pragma directives, pointer-to-array conversion and other auxiliary transformations) to simplify mapping of the program into the absolutely parallel form.

The source C-program is transformed into the absolutely parallel COLAMO-form by the converter "Angel" with marking of memory variables from the basic subgraph. Memory variables are variables and data arrays stored in RCS distributed memory. Distributed memory controllers (DMC) supply memory variables (data flows) into the computing structure. As a rule, DMCs in the RCS are in small quantity – 8-16 DMC channels. Quantity of DMCs is defined by the RCS architecture. For this reason, quantity of memory variables in any parallel COLAMO-program is limited.

All arrays, initialized in the C-program (the ones used for data read and write) become memory arrays with parallel access (vector in all dimensions) in the COLAMO-program. The array description **int** M [R][C] in a sequential C-program is translated into the array description **Var** M : **Array Integer** [R : **Vector**, C : **Vector**] **Mem** in a parallel COLAMO-program.

Memory arrays are used only for reading or writing of input/result data according to the rules of the COLAMO programming language such as the single substitution rule and the single assignment rule.

According to the COLAMO language, for each memory array a corresponding switching array is declared. It has the same number of vector dimensions and the same size, as the one used in the basic subgraph:

Var MCom : **Array Integer** [R : **Vector,** C : **Vector**] **Com;**

The switching array occupies no cells of distributed memory and, in fact, is a connection name. Any operations with switching arrays (increasing of the number of dimensions or the size of any dimension) require no additional hardware resource. Switching arrays-copies are used instead of the memory ones in descriptions of calculations to fulfil the single substitution rule and the single assignment rule.

Switching arrays, used as data sources for calculations, are initialized by the values of memory arrays with the help of slice operations (MCom[*,*] := M [*,*]) or in loops.

In the text of the COLAMO-program all memory arrays are replaced with switching arrays.

Besides, in this step, computation expressions in conditional operators are being combined for reducing the number of multiplexers, operators which are the same in the main and the alternative branches of conditional operators are taken out, etc.

The result of the first step is an absolutely parallel COLAMO-program which requires for its implementation a large quantity of DMC channels. Reducing of the quantity of used DMC channels is one of the main problems of the third step of transformation of a sequential program.

3.2   Analysis of Information Dependences of the Source Program, Splitting of Scalar Variables and Stretching of Arrays by Iterations

The second step of transformations is also performed by the translator "Angel" (see Fig. 1), which performs one of the most complicated parts of the methodology – transformation of the variable with an arbitrary memory access in the sequential program to the variables of the parallel program, which uses data flows and provides information equivalence of computational results. In this case, it is necessary, keeping data connections of the source sequential program, to fulfil the single substitution rule and the single assignment rule in the parallel program by analysis of information dependences of variables and arrays of the source program.

The information dependence of data arrays and scalar variables in the source program is declared as a dependence of a current value from one or several previous values. Any information dependence, when data are processed cyclically, is an iterative dependence and can be pipelined for efficient stream processing. There are two different kinds - explicitly and implicitly declared information dependences.

An explicitly declared information dependence for a loop on i is described by the expression

$$x[i] := f(x[i-k]),$$

where the current value of an array item in the i-th iteration depends on the previous value in the $(i-k)$-th iteration (for example, $x_i=x_{i-3}+a*y_j$), i.e. **the next array item of the data array (or the dataflow)** depends on one or several **previous items of the data array (or the data flow)** of the current loop.

The implicitly declared information dependence for a scalar variable is described by the expression $a := f(a)$. For a loop on $i - x[i] := f(x[i])$ – the current value in the iteration i depends on the previous value of the same item. All items $x[i]$ can be independent one from another and can be calculated concurrently. This is a pseudo iterative dependence, which requires splitting for scalar variables and stretching for arrays to fulfil the single assignment rule of data flow languages. The implicitly declared information dependence is frequently used in sequential C-programs for intermediate scalar variables used for accumulation of values in such expressions as $A := A +B[i]$.

Independent calculations are declared by the expression $x[i] := f(k[i])$, i.e. all items $x[i]$ do not depend on their previous values and on values of other items of the same array; all of them are independent of others and can be calculated concurrently.

Analysis of information dependences between variables of a sequential program is required for array parallelization method detection (by layers or by iterations) in a data processing operator.

Parallelization by layers is applied for independent calculations. In this case, each independently implemented basic subgraph requires separate DMC channels; so, in the best case the maximum degree of parallelization by layers is equal to the number of DMCs on the board (for the majority of boards it is 16). Loops, in which arrays can be parallelized by layers, are called layerwise.

Parallelization by iterations is applied for explicitly and implicitly declared information dependences. Besides, it provides decreasing of the task solution time, if additional computational resource is used for implementation of several iterations with data flows transfer directly into the next iteration, without writing results into memory. So, the number of occupied DMC channels is reduced. Loops, in which arrays can be parallelized by iterations, are called iterative.

During loop processing, **each array or data flow** (not the whole expression or operator!) has **information dependences** separately. Therefore one and the same loop for different arrays (data flows) can be different – a layerwise one for one array and an iterative one for another array.

To detect layerwise and iterative loops in the source program, all loops of arrays (data flows) and indexing of array items are analysed. The loop type (layerwise or iterative) is detected for each array, used in a loop. For this purpose the following criterion is used: if a variable has no information dependence within the analysed loop, then it is considered layerwise; if there is an explicitly or implicitly declared information dependence, then the loop is considered iterative for this variable.

The notions "explicitly or implicitly declared information dependence", "layerwise/iterative loop" are applied only to variables and arrays, which are being written (or read and written) in loops. These notions are not applicable for those variables, which are only being read in loops.

By default, all loops in an absolutely parallel program, written in the programming language COLAMO, are considered iterative for all arrays and variables. During analysis of information dependences of the source program, the following features of an iterative loop are checked for each variable (array), used in this iterative loop, and for each loop:

- if within the loop data is only being written (no reading operations) into an array, indexed by the loop variable, then the loop is considered layerwise;
- if within the loop data is being read and written from/into an array, indexed by the loop variable, then the loop is considered:
  - layerwise in the case of implicitly declared information dependence;
  - iterative in the case of explicitly declared information dependence.

By default, the outermost loop is considered iterative, if its loop variable is not used for array indexing in the nested loops, and not used as a constant in each iteration of some nested loop.

Analysis of information dependences is performed for all loops, including nested ones, and for all variables used in loops (both arrays and scalar variables).

If not all loop variables are used for access to a data array with explicit information dependence, those loops, whose loop variables are not used for access to the data array (flow), are iterative for this data array (as a rule, iterations involve the innermost loop).

In this case, in each iteration of the iterative loop data will be written into the same items of the switching array; it will break the single assignment rule. Therefore, it is necessary to perform **stretching of a switching array by iterations** (the initial memory array remains unchanged). Stretching of a switching array by iterations is performed as follows (see Fig. 2):

Source program fragment	Stretching of a switching array by iterations

`for i = 1 to n do`
`    for j = 1 to m do`
`        x[j] = a*x[j-1] + y[i];`
	`Var xCom : Array Integer [n: Vector,`
	`                           n+1: Vector] Com;`
	`...`
	`xCom[0,1] = x[0];`
	`for i = 1 to n do`
	`  begin`
	`    for j = 1 to m do`
	`        xCom[j,i+1] = a*xCom[j-1,i] + y[i];`
	`// rewriting data for`
	`// next iteration on i`
	`    xCom[0, i+1] = xCom[0, i];`
	`  end;`

Fig. 2. An example of stretching of a switching array by iterations

(1) In the description of the switching array a new dimension is added; its size is equal to the size of the iterative loop (it is an external loop: array indices do not depend on it explicitly, but it defines the number of processing iterations).

(2) The initial data are copied into the switching array from the memory array. The added dimension is initialized by initial data (for example, MCom[*,0] := M [*]). The initial value of added dimension is equal to the initial value of the iterative loop.

(3) In the program text all invocations to the stretched array in expressions of data processing are corrected according to the added dimension which contains the current index of the iterative loop.

(4) When the nested loop is finished, the data which remains unmodified in the current iteration, are being rewritten for the next iteration.

In this example, in the source program fragment, the information dependence by the loop j for the variable x[j] is declared explicitly; so, the loop on j is iterative for this variable. The loop variable i is not used for access to the variable x[j], therefore the loop on i for the variable x[j] is also iterative. The variable y[i] in the loop on j is used only for reading, the loop variable j is not used for access and does not modify its value, therefore for the loop on j the variable y[i] is a constant. The loop on i for the variable y[i] is layerwise, because there is no information dependence between the variable y[i] and the loop variable i.

If there is several iterative loops (see Fig. 3-a), then stretching of the switching array by iterations is performed for all loops. In this case, it is necessary to calculate the index of the current iteration access to switching variable according to the expression

$$x[j, k*N+i] = a*x[j-1, k*N+i] + y[i].$$

An alternative to re-calculation of the index is combination of iterative loops into one for code optimization (see Fig. 3-b). Then stretching of the switching array is performed according to steps 1–4 for the united iterative loop (Fig. 3).

Source program fragment	Combination of iterative loops for a switching array
	```Var xCom : Array Integer [m: Vector, n*L+1: Vector] Com;``` ...
```for k = 1 to L do``` ```for i = 1 to n do``` ``` for j = 1 to m do``` ``` x[j] = a*x[j-1] + y[i];```	``` xCom[0,1] := x[0];``` ``` for ki = 1 to n*L do``` ``` begin``` ``` for j = 1 to n do``` ``` xCom[j, ki] = a*xCom[j-1, ki] +``` ``` y[ki mod L];``` ```// rewriting of data for``` ```// the next iteration on ki``` ``` xCom[0, ki+1] = xCom[0, ki];``` ``` end;```
a)	b)

Fig. 3. An example of loops combination during stretching of a switching array by iterations

In the given example the information dependence by the loop j for the variable x[j] is declared explicitly. Therefore, the loop on j is iterative for this variable. The loops on i and k for the variable x[j] are iterative, because none of them is used for access to the variable x[j]. Therefore, the loops on i and k for the variable x[j] can be united into a single loop on a united variable ki with the number of iterations, equal to the production $n*L$ of the upper boundaries of the combined loops. For the loop on j, the variable y[i] is a constant; the loop on i is layerwise for it, and the loop on k is iterative. Since the variable y[i] is used only for data reading, its value is the same for all iterations of the loop k. Therefore, "mod" operation is used for access to y[i] in the iteration loop on k using united loop variable ki.

It is the second approach with combination of iterative loops, which is used in the software development tool of the next generation.

Implicit information dependence is described by an expression $x_i = f(x_i)$, which is traditional for procedural programming languages: **a new value of an item of a data array (flow)** depends on **the previous value of the same item of this data array (flow)**. For implicitly declared information dependence the single substitution rule is violated. This rule is a special case of the single assignment rule; it is violated when reading and writing access to one and the same channel occurs at the same time. Implicitly declared information dependence is a pseudo iterative dependence. In this case, it is necessary to perform **stretching of the switching array by iterations** (the initial memory array remains unchanged). Stretching of the switching array by iterations for a pseudo iterative dependence is performed as follows:

(1) In the description of the switching array a new dimension is added; its size is greater by unity than the size of the iterative loop (it is an external loop: array indices do not depend on it explicitly, but which defines the number of processing iterations).

(2) The operator, which initializes the added dimension of the switching array with the initial memory array values (for example, MCom[*,*,0] := M [*,*]).

(3) In data processing expressions all invocations to the stretched array are corrected according to the added dimension: if the array is being read, then the current index of the iterative loop is used; if data is being written into the array, then the next index of the iterative loop is used (index +1) (see Fig. 4).

Source program fragment	Stretching for implicit information dependence

```for i = 1 to n do```
``` for j = 1 to m do```
```   x[j] = a*x[j] + y[i];```
	```xCom[*,1] := x[*];```
	```for i = 1 to n do```
	``` for j = 1 to m do```
	``` xCom[j,i+1] = a*xCom[j,i] + y[i];```

Fig. 4. An example of stretching of a switching array by iterations for an implicit information dependence

In the given example, in contrast to the previous ones, the information dependence by the loop j for the variable x[j] is declared implicitly: the current value of the variable x[j] depends on its previous value, but not on other items of the array. Therefore, the information dependence by the loop j, declared for the variable x[j], is pseudo iterative. And the loop on i for it is iterative as in all previous examples. So, that is why the array x[j] is stretched by iterations.

For the variable y[i], as in the previous example, the variable j is not used for access and does not modify its value; therefore, y[i] is a constant for the loop on j. The loop on i is layerwise for the variable y[i], because there is no information dependence between the variable y[i] and the loop variable i.

If there are several iterative loops, then, before stretching of the switching array by iterations, the loops are to be combined into one general loop (if possible), and steps 1–3 for the iteration loop variable of the switching array are to be performed.

Stretching by iterations is performed only for switching arrays, because they are used in all computing operations of the program, and memory arrays only supply data from distributed memory controllers into the computing structure.

Splitting of a scalar is a well-known transformation [13], which is very much alike the described stretching of the switching array, but it is used for implicit information dependence of scalar variables. In the case, when the implicit information dependence a:= f(a) is declared for a scalar variable (not for an array):

- is this expression is used without any loops, then the scalar variable is split into a data vector of size 2 and the expression is corrected as a[1]:= f(a[0]);
- is this expression is used in a loop, then the scalar is split into a switching array of (size +1) of the iterative loop. The order of transformations corresponds to steps 1–3.

Stretching and splitting are not performed simultaneously, because they are performed on different kinds of variables!

In order not to violate the single assignment rule, transfer of data flows between iterations is performed as follows: an array is copied to the next iteration with the help of slice operators:

$$\texttt{XCom[*, i+1] = XCom[*, i];}$$

If variables are being stretched and must be initialized with the values of memory arrays, the single assignment rule is often violated due to concurrent writing into array during its initialization and during calculations (Fig. 5).

In the considered example, data is being written into the variable xCom[*,1] during its initialization and in the first iteration if the loop on i. Then, in each iteration of the loop on i, the operator xCom [*, i+1] = xCom[*, i] transfers the calculated data to the next iteration, in which the operator xCom[j,i]=a*xCom[j-1,i] + y[i] writes data into the same memory cells.

Source program fragment	Violation of single assignment rule

`for i = 1 to n do`
`  for j = 1 to m do`
`    x[j]  =  a*x[j-1]  +`
`      y[i];`
	`xCom[*,1] = x [*];`
	`for i = 1 to n do`
	`  begin`
	`    for j = 1 to m do`
	`      xCom [j, i] = a*xCom[j-1, i] + y[i];`
	
	`    xCom[*, i+1] = xCom[*, i];`
	`  end;`

Fig. 5. An example of violation of the single assignment rule

To formally fulfil the single assignment rule, it is possible to use declaration of additional switching variables (XCom1, XCom2, etc.) for each iteration, and rewrite their values in each iteration. Such method is rather complex and leads to use of numerous intermediate switching arrays in the COLAMO-program. An alternative method, which provides formal fulfilment of the single assignment rule is declaration of an additional dimension of the switching variable xCom with the size equal to (the number of writing operations of the switching variable + 1). As a rule, for the majority of cases, when one and the same array is being read and written in each iteration, a dimension of size 2 is added to the declaration of the array (Fig. 6).

Source program fragment	Fulfilment of the single assignment rule

`for i = 1 to n do`
`  for j = 1 to m do`
`    x[j]=a*x[j-1]+y[i];`
	`xCom[*,1, 0] = x [*];`
	`for i = 1 to n do`
	`  begin`
	`    for j = 1 to m do`
	`      xCom[j,i,1]=a*xCom[j-1,i,0] + y[i];`
	
	`    xCom[*,i+1,0] = xCom[*,i,1];`
	`  end;`

Fig. 6. An example of fulfilment of the single assignment rule with the help of additional dimension into the switching array

After all transformations (analysis of information dependences, stretching of switching arrays, and splitting of scalars, transfer of data flows between iterations) of the source code of the absolutely parallel program, performed by the converter "Angel", a well-formed (without violations of the single assignment rule and the single substitution rule) COLAMO program in the absolutely parallel form is generated.

3.3 Conversion into the Parallel-Pipeline Form, Separation of Arrays and Loops into Vector and Stream Components

The third step is transformation of the task information graph and the parallel COLAMO-program from the absolutely parallel form into the parallel-pipeline form. This transformation is performed by the processor "Mermaid" (see Fig. 1).

Each dimension of any array (memory or switching one) is separated into 2 components – vector and stream, with parallel and sequential access, respectively. The scheme of separation is as follows: the stream component size is declared as R, the vector component size is declared as (the initial size of the array dimension +R-1)/R)). The vector component must be integer, i.e. the initial size of the array dimension must be **divisible without a reminder** by R. For keeping equity of the generated parallel-pipeline program and the source absolutely parallel program, the stream size is by default equal to 1:

```
const rows = (Integer) 100 ; const columns = (Integer) 90 ;
const R1 = 1; const R2 = 1;
Var matrix : Array Integer [(rows+ R1-1)/R1:Vector, R1:Stream,
                (columns+ R2-1)/R2:Vector, R2: Stream] Mem;
```

All vector dimensions of each and every array (memory and switching ones) are scaled by separate scaling parameters of the vector component. For arrays like X[n][n+1] for each dimension (for n and n+1) is used its own stream size.

According to the new dimensions, use of memory and switching variables in the program code is corrected. In the case, when declarations of switching arrays, loops boundaries or indices contain the expression (N+1 или N-1), which depends on the initial size of the array, only the initial size N is divided by the scaling parameter (i.e. ((N+R-1)/R + 1 or (N+R-1)/R - 1).

All basic loops of the program are separated into 2 parts: a vector part (with a prefix v for the loop variable) and a stream part (with a prefix s for the loop variable). To define the boundaries of the vector loop, both boundaries of the initial (basic) loop of the absolutely parallel COLAMO-program are divided by the stream component R with rounding downward. The stream loop is declared from 0 to (R-1), and its upper boundary is **always** equal to (R-1):

```
(For vi:= 0 to rows/R1 - 1 Step 1 Do
     For si:= 0 to R1 - 1 Step 1 Do
          For vj:= 0 to columns/R2 - 1 Step 1 Do
               For sj:= 0 to R2 - 1 Step 1 Do
                         tmpMass[vi, si, vj + 1, sj]   := tmpMass[vi, si,
vj, sj] + matrixCom[vi, si, vj , sj] * vector_RENCom[vj , sj] ;
                    end;
               end;
```

In the case, when the counter of a nested loop depends on the counter of an upper level loop, separation is performed only for the boundary which does not depend on the upper level loop counter (i.e. only for the vector part).

```
(For vi:= 0 to rows/R1- 1 Step 1 Do
     For si:= 0 to R1 - 1 Step 1 Do
          For vj:= vi+1 to columns/R2 -1 Step 1 Do
               For sj:= 0 to R2 - 1 Step 1 Do
                    tmpMass[vi, si, vj + 1, sj]   := tmpMass[vi, si, vj, sj]
+ matrixCom[vi,si,vj,sj]*vector_RENCom[vj,sj] ;
                    end;
               end;
```

As a result of this transformation, the absolutely parallel COLAMO-program turns into a parallel-pipeline one, in which it is possible to control parallelism, varying the size of the stream component from 1 to the initial array size, and the program will always be well-formed (no violation of the single assignment rule and the single substitution rule).

3.4 Feedback Implementation

The fourth step of transformations is performed by the processor "Procrustes" (see Fig. 1).

In tasks, the information dependence declared explicitly is marked as an index offset within one and the same array ($A[i+1]$:= $A[i]$ $+D[i]$). Besides, it is necessary to distinguish information dependence by data (according to the task structure) and information dependence by iterations, which occurs when variables are being split by iterations due to violence of the single assignment rule. The difference is the following: information dependence by iterations does not cause feedback occurrence in contrast to information dependence by data. That is why it is necessary to separate loops for array dimensions into iteration dependence and data dependence.

To implement feedback, when the task structure contains data dependence, the number of data processing units is calculated the number of data processing IP-cores which can be expanded by iterations, and feedback is implemented with the help of the index of stream parameter of the type StreamNumber. In each iteration of the stream loop, the current index or the index from the feedback loop is used.

```
if (vj = 0) then
   begin
     it_v := (N3 - 1 + 1);
     if (N4 - 1 > 0) then
       it_s := sj  - 1;   // it_s := sj  - |( vj + 1 - vj)|;
     else
       it_s := sj;
   end
else
   begin
     it_v := vj;
     it_s := sj;
   end;
```

As a rule, feedback occurs at parallel-pipeline or pipeline implementation of the applied task, when RCS hardware resource is not enough for absolutely parallel implementation of the task.

3.5   Transformation into the Scalable Parallel-Pipeline Form

The fifth step of transformations is also performed by the processor "Procrustes" (see Fig. 1).

Matching of the scaling parameter R for a selected board is performed as follows.

The number of DMCs, required for implementation of the basic subgraph, is calculated with the help of the sum of vector dimensions for memory arrays $\kappa_{DMCtask}$. As a result, we obtain the minimum number of memory channels (DMC) $K = \frac{K_{DMCCM}}{K_{DMCtask}}$, required for the task.

If $K < 1$, then DMC resource is not sufficient for implementation of the basic subgraph; it is necessary to perform reduction of the program [14]. If $2 > K \geq 1$, then scaling of the basic subgraph by channels is impossible and the parallel-pipeline form remains unchanged. If $K \geq 2$, then scaling is performed.

The obtained scaling coefficient determines parallelism of each dimension of the array. We define the stream part as $R = \frac{N}{K}$, and the vector part as N/R, and set all required values in scaling constants. The obtained coefficient K is not always a final one, because initial data size N should be divide without a remainder by K. If N is not divisible without a reminder by K, then K is being decreased by unity until the remainder is equal to zero.

Matching of the scaling coefficient for the selected board according to available hardware resource.

In the same way hardware resource (LUTs, DSPs, Flip-Flops and other FPGA resource), required for implementation of the basic subgraph, and the scaling resource coefficient Q is calculated.

If $Q < 1$, then hardware resource is not sufficient for implementation of the basic subgraph; it is necessary to perform reduction of the program by functional cores. If $2 > Q \geq 1$, then scaling of the basic subgraph by hardware resource is impossible, and the parallel-pipeline form remains unchanged. If $Q \geq 2$, then scaling by iterations (increase the number of units in the feedback chain) can be performed, if it is possible.

3.6   Generation of a Computing Structure

The sixth step of transformations is also performed by the processor "Procrustes" (see Fig. 1).

In the case, when hardware resource (channels or FPGA cells) is not sufficient for implementation of all iterations of the program algorithm, it is necessary to implement the task as a single-structure with 2 procedural cadres [1] on the base of structural-procedural realization of calculations.

It is necessary to calculate the number of iterations, which can be structurally implement on available hardware resource, to declare the developed computing structure by LET-operator, and to organize structural-procedural processing with the help of 2 procedural cadres, where data sources and targets swap places [1].

Owing to the described methodology, it is possible to synthesize a resource-independent parallel application, which can adapt to available computational resource by changing of several constants in automatic mode without any considerable modification of the program source code. As a result, after all six steps of transformations, a scalable COLAMO-application is generated. This application is transformed into FPGA configuration files for multichip RCS with the help of the COLAMO-translator, the synthesizer Fire!Constructor, and other 4-th generation development tools.

4   Translation Results of Several Application Tasks

At present we have developed the prototype of the software development tools of the next generation, which contains all tools and converters shown in Fig. 1. Using this prototype, we have successfully translated several sequential C-programs into COLAMO-programs, and then into FPGA bit-stream files for various problem areas. So, we have successfully translated applications of mathematical physics such as SLAE solution with the help of the Gauss method, SLAE solution with the help of the Jacobi method, SLAE solution with the help of LU-decomposition (lower and upper triangle matrices). We have solved 6 applied tasks for the symbolic processing problem area. The applications, translated with the help of the software development tools of the next generation provide high efficiency: not less than 85% in comparison with those developed by application developers in the COLAMO language, and not less than 70% in comparison with application solutions designed by circuit engineers. The translation time of sequential C-programs into COLAMO-programs and FPGA configuration files (without synthesis of bit-stream files) does not exceed 30 min (the basic translation time of the Xilinx Vivado design environment).

5   Conclusion

FPGAs as principal components of reconfigurable supercomputers provide stable, ramping performance of RCS, and give new perspectives for design of supercomputers with petaflops performance. The created software development tools of the next generation will considerably reduce the programming time of multichip RCS owing to translation of the source sequential C-program into FPGA bit-stream files.

For efficient programming of RCS and hybrid reconfigurable computer systems we have developed the methodology, which provides translation of a sequential C-program into a COLAMO-program, and then into FPGA bit-stream files.

References

1. Guzik, V.F., Kalyaev, I.A., Levin, I.I.: Reconfigurable Computer Systems, p. 472. SfedU Publishing, Taganrog (2016)
2. Design for Xilinx FPGAs with the help of high-level languages in Vivado HLS. Components and Technologies, №12 (2013). https://www.kit-e.ru/preview/pre_40_12_13_VHLS_Xilinx.php. Accessed 15 Feb 2019

3. Polaris Developer's Document. http://polaris.cs.uiuc.edu/polaris/polaris_developer/polaris_developer.html. Accessed 15 Feb 2019
4. The Stanford SUIF Compiler Group. http://suif.stanford.edu/. Accessed 15 Feb 2019
5. VAST/Parallel. http://www.crescentbaysoftware.com/vast_parallel.html. Accessed 15 Feb 2019
6. Intel OpenMP. http://www.intel.com/software/products/compilers/flin/docs/main_for/mergedprojects/copts_for/common_options/option_openmp.htm. Accessed 15 Feb 2019
7. System ParaWise. http://www.parallelsp.com. Accessed 15 Feb 2019
8. Intel Parallel Studio. https://software.intel.com/en-us/parallel-studio-xe. Accessed 15 Feb 2019
9. System SAPFOR. http://www.keldysh.ru/dvm/SAPFOR/. Accessed 15 Feb 2019
10. Bakhtin, V.A., et al.: Automatization of parallelizing of software complexes. In: Scientific Service in Internet: Proceedings of the XVIIIth All-Russian Scientific Conference (19–24 September 2016, Hovorossiysk). Keldysh IPM, Moscow, pp. 76–85. https://doi.org/10.20948/abrau-2016-31
11. Open parallelizing system. http://www.ops.rsu.ru. Accessed 15 Feb 2019
12. Gulenok, A.A., Dordopulo, A.I., Levin, I.I., Gudkov, V.A.: Hybrid computer system programming technology with adaptation and scaling of calculations. Bulletin of the South Ural State University. Computational Mathematics and Software Engineering, vol. 6, no. 1, pp. 73–86 (2017). https://doi.org/10.14529/cmse170105
13. Shteinberg, B.Y.: Mathematical Methods of Parallelization of Recurrent Program Loops on Supercomputers with Parallel-Access Memory, p. 192. Publishing of Rostov University, Rostov-on-Don (2004)
14. Sorokin, D.A., Dordopulo, A.I., Levin, I.I., Melnikov, A.K.: The decision of tasks with substantially-variable rate of data rate on reconfigured computing systems. The bulletin of computer and information technologies. Mechanical engineering, Moscow, no. 2, pp. 49–56 (2012). https://doi.org/10.14489/issn.1810-7206

Software Q-system for the Research of the Resource of Numerical Algorithms Parallelism

Valentina Aleeva$^{(\boxtimes)}$, Ekaterina Bogatyreva, Artem Skleznev,
Mikhail Sokolov, and Artemii Shuppa

South Ural State University (National Research University), Chelyabinsk, Russia
aleevavn@susu.ru, kate_215@mail.ru, skleznew@bk.ru, michael-0801@yandex.ru,
artem.shuppa@gmail.com

Abstract. The paper describes software Q-system for research of the resource of numerical algorithms parallelism. The theoretical basis of the Q-system is the concept of Q-determinant where Q is the set of operations used by the algorithm. The Q-determinant consists of Q-terms. Their number is equal to the number of output data items. Each Q-term describes all possible ways to calculate one of the output data items based on the input data. Any numerical algorithm has a Q-determinant and can be represented in the form of a Q-determinant. Such a representation is a universal description of numerical algorithms. It makes the algorithm transparent in terms of structure and implementation. The software Q-system enables to calculate the parallelism resource of any numerical algorithm, and also to compare the parallelism resources of two algorithms that solve the same algorithmic problem. In the paper we show the application of the Q-system on the example of numerical algorithms with different structures of Q-determinants. Among them, we have the matrix multiplication algorithm, methods of Gauss–Jordan, Jacobi, Gauss–Seidel for solving systems of linear equations, and other algorithms. The paper continues the research begun in the previous papers of the authors. The results of the research can be used to increase the efficiency of implementing numerical algorithms on parallel computing systems.

Keywords: Q-term of algorithm · Q-determinant of algorithm ·
Representation of the algorithm in the form of Q-determinant ·
Q-effective implementation of algorithm · Parallelism resource of
algorithm · Height of the algorithm · Width of the algorithm · Software
Q-system · Parallel computing system · Parallel program · Q-effective
program

1 Introduction

One of the ways to improve the performance of parallel computing systems is the efficient implementation of algorithms by using their internal parallelism

© Springer Nature Switzerland AG 2019
V. Voevodin and S. Sobolev (Eds.): RuSCDays 2019, CCIS 1129, pp. 641–652, 2019.
https://doi.org/10.1007/978-3-030-36592-9_52

resource completely. In the book [1, p. 207] it is noted that the use of internal parallelism has an obvious advantage as it doesn't need to study the computational properties of newly created algorithms, but it is necessary to determine and investigate graphs of algorithms. Also it is necessary to replace that algorithm to another unless its internal parallelism is adequate to effective use of specific parallel computer. However, it isn't easy to implement, since we should know the parallel structure of the algorithms, but it is unknown.

There are many approaches to the research of the parallelism resource of numerical algorithms and its implementation. We give a brief overview of some of them. A very important and developed field of research of the parallel structure of algorithms and programs for the aim of their implementation on parallel computing systems is the field, the bases of which are set forth in [1,2]. The open encyclopedia AlgoWiki [3,4] uses the researches in this field. The graphs of specific algorithms are defined and investigated there. However, software for the study of the resource parallelism of algorithms is not considered in this field.

Various approaches to the development of parallel programs were proposed. The development of parallel computing led to the creation of dozens of parallel programming languages and many different tools. T-system [5] is one such development. It provides a programming environment with support for automatic dynamic parallelization of programs. However, it can't be asserted that the creation of parallel programs with the help of a T-system completely use the parallelism resource of algorithm. The parallel program synthesis is another approach to creating parallel programs. This approach is to construct new parallel algorithms using the knowledge base of parallel algorithms for solving more complex problems. The technology of fragmented programming, its implementing language, and programming system LuNA are developed on the base of parallel programs synthesis method [6]. This approach doesn't solve the problem of research and use of the algorithm parallelism resource, despite the fact that it is universal. To overcome resource limitations, the author of paper [7] suggests methods of constructing parallel programs using a functional programming language independent of computer architecture. This approach is developing also. However, there is not shown that the created programs use the entire parallelism resource of algorithms.

There are many studies of the development of parallel programs take into account the specific nature of algorithms and the architecture of parallel computing systems. Examples of such studies are [8–11]. These studies improve the efficiency of the implementation of specific algorithms or the implementation of algorithms on parallel computing systems of certain architecture. However, they do not provide general universal approach.

It seems to remain relevant the problem of defining and research graphs of algorithms with the aim of using their internal parallelism, posed in [1]. Some approach to solving this problem is proposed in given paper. The purpose of the research described in the paper is to develop a software system (named Q-system) for research of the resource of numerical algorithms parallelism.

2   Theoretical Foundation of Q-system

The theoretical basis for creating a Q-system is the concept of Q-determinant. It was first described in [12] and summarized briefly in [13–15].

Let $\mathcal{A}$ be an algorithm for solving an algorithmic problems $\bar{y} = F(N, B)$, where $N = \{n_1, \ldots, n_k\}$ is a set of dimension parameters of the problem, B is a set of input data, $\bar{y} = (y_1, \ldots, y_m)$ is a set of output data items. Let $I = \{1, \ldots, m\}$. Suppose that the algorithm $\mathcal{A}$ is that the Q-terms f_i must be computed to determine y_i $(i \in I)$. Then the set of Q-terms f_i $(i \in I)$ is called a Q-determinant of algorithm $\mathcal{A}$ and representation of algorithm in the form $y_i = f_i$ $(i \in I)$ is called a representation of the algorithm in the form of Q-determinant. More exactly, we have the partition $I = I_1 \cup I_2 \cup I_3$. One or two subsets I_i $(i = 1, 2, 3)$ may be empty. Then we have

1. f_{i_1} $(i_1 \in I_1)$ is an unconditional Q-term, $f_{i_1} = w^{i_1}$;   (QA)

2. f_{i_2} $(i_2 \in I_2)$ is conditional Q-term, $f_{i_2} = \left\{ \left(u_j^{i_2}, w_j^{i_2} \right) \right\}_{j=1,\ldots,l_{i_2}}$,

   l_{i_2} is either constant or computable function of N for $N \neq \varnothing$;

3. f_{i_3} $(i_3 \in I_3)$ is a conditional infinite Q-term, $f_{i_3} = \left\{ \left(u_j^{i_3}, w_j^{i_3} \right) \right\}_{j=1,2,\ldots}$.

For example, representation of the Gauss–Seidel method for solving a system of linear equations in the form of Q-determinant is written in [15] as

$$x_i = \{(||\bar{x}^1 - \bar{x}^0|| < \epsilon, x_i^1), \ldots, (||\bar{x}^k - \bar{x}^{k-1}|| < \epsilon, x_i^k), \ldots\} \, (i = 1, \ldots, n).$$

Q-determinant of the Gauss–Seidel method consists of n conditional infinite Q-terms. The concept of a Q-determinant makes it possible to use the following methods for studying the resources of parallelism of numerical algorithms.

2.1   Method of Constructing of Q-determinant of Algorithm

Here we will construct the Q-determinants of the algorithms using their flowcharts. We select the following blocks of allowed flowchart blocks: data; process (it displays the data processing function); decision (it displays a switching type function that has one input and a few alternative outputs, one and only one of which can be activated after calculating the condition defined in the block); terminal (it displays the input from the external environment or output to the external environment). There are some limitations and clarifications of the used flowcharts. The flowchart has two terminal blocks, one of which "Start" means the beginning of the algorithm, and the other "End" is the end of the algorithm. The "Start" block has one outgoing flowline and has no incoming flowline. The "End" block has one incoming flowline and no outgoing flowline. The "decision" block has two outgoing flowlines, one of which corresponds to the transfer of control if the block condition is true, and the other if it is false. The condition uses one comparison operation. Its operands don't contain operations. The "process" block contains one assignment of a value to a variable. There is no more than one operation to the right of the assignment sign. So, block chains are used for groups of operations. We divide the blocks "data" into blocks "Input data" and "Output data".

To construct the Q-determinant of the algorithm, we will analyze the flowchart for fixed values of the dimension parameters of the algorithmic problem $\bar{N} = \{\bar{n}_1, \ldots, \bar{n}_k\}$. We investigated the features of the algorithms whose Q-determinants contain various types of Q-terms.

If Q-determinant of algorithm has unconditional Q-terms then the pass on the flowchart should be carried out sequentially in accordance with the execution algorithm. The expressions $w^{i_1}(\bar{N})\,(i_1 \in I_1)$ will be obtained as the values of unconditional Q-terms $f_{i_1}\,(i_1 \in I_1)$ (cf. (QA)). They are formed using the contents of the "process" blocks involved in the calculation of $y_{i_1}\,(i_1 \in I_1)$.

If the Q-determinant contains conditional Q-terms then the pass on the block "decision" with the condition on the input data generates a branching. Then each branch is processed separately. As the result of processing one branch, we obtain for $j \in \{1, \ldots, l_{i_2}\}$ the pairs of expressions $(u_j^{i_2}(\bar{N}), w_j^{i_2}(\bar{N}))\,(i_2 \in I_2)$. The expressions $u_j^{i_2}(\bar{N})$ are obtained by the conditions of the "decision" blocks that contain the input data. The expressions $w_j^{i_2}(\bar{N})$ are formed using the contents of the "process" blocks. As soon as first branch is processed, the handler of the flowchart returns to the nearest block where the branching occurred and continues processing with the opposite condition. After all branches are processed, all pairs of expressions $(u_j^{i_2}(\bar{N}), w_j^{i_2}(\bar{N}))\,(i_2 \in I_2, j = 1, \ldots, l_{i_2})$ will be obtained for conditional Q-terms (cf. (QA)).

Conditional infinite Q-terms are included in the Q-determinants of iterative numerical algorithms. By limiting the number of iterations, we can reduce the case of the Q-determinant with conditional infinite Q-terms to the case of the Q-determinant with conditional Q-terms.

2.2   Method of Obtaining of Q-effective Implementation of Algorithm

The Q-effective implementation of the algorithm is understood as the computation of the expressions in

$$W(\bar{N}) = \{w^{i_1}(\bar{N})\,(i_1 \in I_1);\, u_j^{i_2}(\bar{N}), w_j^{i_2}(\bar{N})\,(i_2 \in I_2, j = 1, \ldots, l_{i_2}); \qquad \text{(QEI)}$$
$$u_j^{i_3}(\bar{N}), w_j^{i_3}(\bar{N})\,(i_3 \in I_3, j = 1, 2, \ldots)\}$$

is performed simultaneously and the operations are performed as soon as their operands are calculated. The method of obtaining the Q-effective implementation of the algorithm consists in calculating the nesting levels of operations included in the expressions $W(\bar{N})$.

2.3   Method of Calculating Characteristics of a Parallel Complexity of Q-effective Implementation of Algorithm

We will introduce characteristics of parallel complexity of realizable Q-effective implementation of the algorithm. Let it be $W(\bar{N})$ as (QEI).

1. Let $T^{w(\bar{N})}$ be an expression nesting level $w(\bar{N}) \in W(\bar{N})$.
   Then *the height of the algorithm* is called

$$D(\bar{N}) = \max_{w(\bar{N}) \in W(\bar{N})} T^{w(\bar{N})}. \tag{HA}$$

2. Let $O_r^{w(\bar{N})}$ be the number of operations of the nesting level r of the expression $w(\bar{N}) \in W(\bar{N})$. Then *the width of the algorithm* is called

$$P(\bar{N}) = \max_{1 \leq r \leq D(\bar{N})} \sum_{w(\bar{N}) \in W(\bar{N})} O_r^{w(\bar{N})}. \tag{WA}$$

$D(\bar{N})$ characterizes the execution time of the Q-effective implementation of the algorithm and $P(\bar{N})$ characterizes the number of processors required to execute the Q-effective implementation. In fact, we use a finite length of Q-term of f_{i_3} ($i_3 \in I_3$) that is sufficient for its calculation. So, the characteristics of parallel complexity of specific numerical algorithm are determined correctly.

2.4 Method of Comparing the Characteristics of the Parallel Complexity of Q-effective Implementations of Algorithms

Also, we create the database for storage of obtained results. More exactly, the database contains for every studied algorithm the following data: the unique identifier, the name, the text description of the algorithm, its Q-determinants for different values of $\bar{N}$, the number of iterations and the corresponding characteristics of $D(\bar{N})$ and $P(\bar{N})$.

If we have two algorithms for solving the same algorithmic problem then we can compares the characteristics of $D(\bar{N})$ and $P(\bar{N})$ for the same values of $\bar{N}$ and the number of iterations. This makes it possible to determine the algorithm with the best characteristic either $D(\bar{N})$, or $P(\bar{N})$.

3 Program Realization of Software Q-system

The Q-system consists of two subsystems: the creation of Q-determinants of numerical algorithms and the calculation of the resource of numerical algorithms parallelism. The first subsystem realizes the method of constructing of the Q-determinants of the algorithms using their flowcharts. The remaining methods for research of the resource of numerical algorithms parallelism are realized in the second subsystem.

3.1 Subsystem for the Creation of Q-determinants of Numerical Algorithms

This subsystem is .NET application in object-oriented programming language C#. Microsoft Visual Studio was used as the development environment. Data-interchange format JSON was used to describe the input and output data of the subsystem.

The flowchart of the algorithm is a description of the Vertices blocks and the Edges connections under JSON. The Vertices blocks are identified by the number Id, the type Type and the text content Content. Type values of blocks Vertices: 0 is block "Start"; 1 is block "End"; 2 is block "process"; 3 is block "decision"; 4 is block "Input data"; 5 is block "Output data". The Edges connectors are determined by the numbers of the starting From and ending To blocks and the type of connector Type. The Type values of connectors Edges are the following: 0 is pass by condition "no"; 1 is pass by condition "yes"; 2 is normal connection. On the Fig. 1 there is the flowchart of the Gauss–Seidel method for solving systems of linear equations in JSON format. We use the following notation in this flowchart: A is the coefficient matrix of the system of linear equations, B is the column of the constant terms, $X0$ is the initial approximation, e is the accuracy of calculations, iterations is the restriction on the number of iterations.

```
{"vertices":[
    {"Id":1,"Type":0,"Content":"Start"},
    {"Id":2,"Type":4,"Content":"A[n,n]"},
    {"Id":3,"Type":4,"Content":"B[n]"},
    {"Id":4,"Type":4,"Content":"X0[n]"},
    {"Id":5,"Type":4,"Content":"e"},
    {"Id":6,"Type":4,"Content":"iterations"},
    {"Id":7,"Type":2,"Content":"it=1"},
    {"Id":8,"Type":2,"Content":"i=1"},
    {"Id":9,"Type":3,"Content":"i<=n"},
    {"Id":10,"Type":2,"Content":"X(i)=X0(i)"},
    {"Id":11,"Type":2,"Content":"i=i+1"},
    {"Id":12,"Type":2,"Content":"i=1"},
    {"Id":13,"Type":3,"Content":"i<=n"},
    {"Id":14,"Type":2,"Content":"newX(i)=B(i)"},
    {"Id":15,"Type":2,"Content":"j=1"},
    {"Id":16,"Type":3,"Content":"j<=n"},
    {"Id":17,"Type":3,"Content":"i!=j"},
    {"Id":18,"Type":3,"Content":"j<i"},
    {"Id":19,"Type":2,"Content":"D=A(i,j)*newX(j)"},
    {"Id":20,"Type":2,"Content":"D=A(i,j)*X(j)"},
    {"Id":21,"Type":2,"Content":"newX(i)=newX(i)-D"},
    {"Id":22,"Type":2,"Content":"j=j+1"},
    {"Id":23,"Type":2,"Content":"newX(i)=newX(i)/A(i,i)"},
    {"Id":24,"Type":2,"Content":"i=i+1"},
    {"Id":25,"Type":2,"Content":"i=1"},
    {"Id":26,"Type":2,"Content":"D=X(i)-newX(i)"},
    {"Id":27,"Type":2,"Content":"norm=abs(D)"},
    {"Id":28,"Type":2,"Content":"X(i)=newX(i)"},
    {"Id":29,"Type":2,"Content":"i=i+1"},
    {"Id":30,"Type":3,"Content":"i<=n"},
    {"Id":31,"Type":2,"Content":"D=X(i)-newX(i)"},
    {"Id":32,"Type":2,"Content":"D=abs(D)"},
    {"Id":33,"Type":2,"Content":"norm=norm+D"},
    {"Id":34,"Type":3,"Content":"norm<e"},
    {"Id":35,"Type":2,"Content":"it=it+1"},
    {"Id":36,"Type":3,"Content":"it<=iterations"},
    {"Id":37,"Type":5,"Content":"X[n]"},
    {"Id":38,"Type":1,"Content":"End"}],
"Edges":[
    {"From":1,"To":2,"Type":2},      {"From":2,"To":3,"Type":2},
    {"From":3,"To":4,"Type":2},      {"From":4,"To":5,"Type":2},
    {"From":5,"To":6,"Type":2},      {"From":6,"To":7,"Type":2},
    {"From":7,"To":8,"Type":2},      {"From":8,"To":9,"Type":2},
    {"From":9,"To":10,"Type":1},     {"From":9,"To":12,"Type":0},
    {"From":10,"To":11,"Type":2},    {"From":11,"To":9,"Type":2},
    {"From":12,"To":13,"Type":2},    {"From":13,"To":14,"Type":1},
    {"From":13,"To":25,"Type":0},    {"From":14,"To":15,"Type":2},
    {"From":15,"To":16,"Type":2},    {"From":16,"To":17,"Type":1},
    {"From":16,"To":23,"Type":0},    {"From":17,"To":18,"Type":1},
    {"From":17,"To":22,"Type":0},    {"From":18,"To":19,"Type":1},
    {"From":18,"To":20,"Type":0},    {"From":19,"To":21,"Type":2},
    {"From":20,"To":21,"Type":2},    {"From":21,"To":22,"Type":2},
    {"From":22,"To":16,"Type":2},    {"From":23,"To":24,"Type":2},
    {"From":24,"To":13,"Type":2},    {"From":25,"To":26,"Type":2},
    {"From":26,"To":27,"Type":2},    {"From":27,"To":28,"Type":2},
    {"From":28,"To":29,"Type":2},    {"From":29,"To":30,"Type":2},
    {"From":30,"To":31,"Type":1},    {"From":30,"To":34,"Type":0},
    {"From":31,"To":32,"Type":2},    {"From":32,"To":33,"Type":2},
    {"From":33,"To":28,"Type":2},    {"From":34,"To":37,"Type":1},
    {"From":34,"To":35,"Type":0},    {"From":35,"To":36,"Type":1},
    {"From":36,"To":12,"Type":1},    {"From":36,"To":37,"Type":0},
    {"From":37,"To":38,"Type":2}]}
```

Fig. 1. The flowchart of the Gauss–Seidel method in JSON format

We describe the structure of the output file of this subsystem. Each conditional Q-term determines l lines of the file where l is the length of Q-term. Each of these lines contains the identifier of the output variable calculated using this Q-term, an equality sign and one pair of expressions $(u_i(\bar{N}), w_i(\bar{N}))$ $(i = 1, \ldots, l)$ (cf. (QA)). Here u_i is an unconditional logical Q-term and w_i is an unconditional Q-term for every $i = 1, \ldots, l$. The expressions $u_i(\bar{N})$ and $w_i(\bar{N})$ are described in JSON format and separated by a semicolon. Each unconditional Q-term w determines one line of the file. In this case, there is no logical Q-term u, so a space is used instead. Thus, the output file contains the representation of the algorithm in the form of a Q-determinant for fixed parameters of dimension N of an algorithmic problem and a limited number of iterations. On the Fig. 2 there is the output file for one iteration of the Gauss–Seidel method if the matrix A is of order 2. The following notation is used for description of unconditional Q-terms in JSON format: op is an operation, fO is the first operand (firstOperand), sO is the second operand (secondOperand), od is the operand.

X(1)={"op":"<","fO":{"op":"+","fO":{"op":"abs","od":{"op":"-","fO":"X0(1)","sO":{"op":"/","fO":{"op":"-","fO":"B
(1)","sO":{"op":"*","fO":"A(1,2)","sO":"X0(2)"}},"sO":"A(1,1)"}}},"sO":{"op":"abs","od":{"op":"-","fO":"X0
(2)","sO":{"op":"/","fO":{"op":"-","fO":"B(2)","sO":{"op":"*","fO":"A(2,1)","sO":{"op":"/","fO":
{"op":"-","fO":"B(1)","sO":{"op":"*","fO":"A(1,2)","sO":"X0(2)"}},"sO":"A(1,1)"}}},"sO":"A(2,2)"}}}},"sO":"e"};
{"op":"/","fO":{"op":"-","fO":"B(1)","sO":{"op":"*","fO":"A(1,2)","sO":"X0(2)"}},"sO":"A(1,1)"}
X(2)={"op":"<","fO":{"op":"+","fO":{"op":"abs","od":{"op":"-","fO":"X0(1)","sO":{"op":"/","fO":{"op":"-","fO":"B
(1)","sO":{"op":"*","fO":"A(1,2)","sO":"X0(2)"}},"sO":"A(1,1)"}}},"sO":{"op":"abs","od":{"op":"-","fO":"X0
(2)","sO":{"op":"/","fO":{"op":"-","fO":"B(2)","sO":{"op":"*","fO":"A(2,1)","sO":{"op":"/","fO":
{"op":"-","fO":"B(1)","sO":{"op":"*","fO":"A(1,2)","sO":"X0(2)"}},"sO":"A(1,1)"}}},"sO":"A(2,2)"}}}},"sO":"e"};
{"op":"/","fO":{"op":"-","fO":"B(2)","sO":{"op":"*","fO":"A(2,1)","sO":{"op":"/","fO":{"op":"-","fO":"B
(1)","sO":{"op":"*","fO":"A(1,2)","sO":"X0(2)"}},"sO":"A(1,1)"}}},"sO":"A(2,2)"}

Fig. 2. The output file of the subsystem for the creation of Q-determinants of numerical algorithms for the Gauss–Seidel method

All variables in the flowchart are divided into four categories: dimension parameters of an algorithmic problem, input, output, and internal variables that don't belong to the first three categories. For example, we have the following categories for the flowchart on Fig. 1: the first category includes n, the second category is the variables $A(i, j)$ $(i, j = 1, \ldots, n)$, $B(i)$ $(i = 1, \ldots, n)$, $X0(i)$ $(i = 1, \ldots, n)$, e, iterations, to the third category variables $X(i)$ $(i = 1, \ldots, n)$, to the fourth category variables it, i, $newX(i)$ $(i = 1, \ldots, n)$, j, D, $norm$.

The values of the variables of the first category are entered by the user at the request of the program. All variables of the second category, with the exception of the variable iterations, have no values, because the program constructs the Q-determinant depending on the identifiers of the input variables. The variable iterations is used to limit the number of iterations and its value is entered by the user at the request of the program. The entered value is assigned to the *static int iterations* variable. The values of the variables of the third and fourth categories change during the processing of the flowchart.

Each variable category is stored in its own collection. The collection of dimension parameters stores the pairs of identifiers of dimension parameters and their values. The input variable collection contains input variable identifiers. The output and internal variable collections store pairs of variable identifiers and their values.

The processing of the flowchart begins with a search for blocks with type 4. In these blocks, the identifiers of the input variables and the parameters of the algorithmic problem dimension are indicated. They are enclosed in brackets and separated by a comma. The identifiers of dimension parameters are extracted from type 4 blocks and the user is prompted to enter their values. The dimension parameter identifier and the entered value are written to the dimension parameters collection. Also the input variable identifiers are extracted from type 4 blocks and indexes are added to them. The resulting input variables are written to the collection of input variables. If the identifier is iterations, then the user is prompted to enter the number of iterations. The identifiers of output variables are extracted from blocks with type 5 and indexes are added to them. The resulting output variables and their values 0 of type *string* are written to the output variable collection. For example, suppose that when processing a Gauss–Seidel flowchart the user entered the value of the dimension parameter $n = 2$. Then a pair of $(n, 2)$ will be written to the collection of dimension parameters. The variables $A(i, j)$ $(i, j = 1, 2)$, $B(i)$ $(i = 1, 2)$, $X0(i)$ $(i = 1, 2)$, e, iterations will be written to the collection of input variables. The $(X(1), 0)$ and $(X(2), 0)$ pairs will be written to the collection of output variables.

After that we pass through the flowchart from the block with type 0 to the block with type 1. The order of passage of the blocks is determined by the description of the flowchart. The blocks of types 2 and 3 are processed during the passage.

When processing a block with type 2 it is analyzed that to the right of the assignment operator. The following options are possible: number, variable of any category without indices or with indices, unary or binary operation. If there is an operation, then the operands are analyzed. The following options are possible for operands: number, variable of any category without indices or with indices. We calculate the values of all found indices. Then the index values of the variable to the left of the assignment operator, if they exist, and the category of the variable are determined. A variable can be either output or internal, or not fall into any category. In the last case we set it as a new internal variable. The result of the analysis of a block with type 2 is the calculation of the value to the right of the assignment operator and its recording to the directory as the value of the variable to the left of the assignment operator. If the value to the right of the assignment operator depends on the input variables, then it is formed as an expression in the JSON format. After passing through the flowchart, the output variable identifiers and the corresponding unconditional Q-terms will be in the output variables catalog.

When processing a block with type 3, a comparison operation and each operand are determined. The following options for operands are possible: number, variable of any category with or without indices. We calculate the values of all found indices. If the condition has no input variables, then it is calculated and control is transferred to the next block depending on the calculated value of 1 (true) or 0 (false). If the condition contains input variables, then control is transferred to the next block by the value 1, if we have first pass through the block and by the value 0, if we have second pass. Suppose that the input variable iterations is missing. Then, depending on the transfer of control over 1 or 0, the condition or its inversion is added as a logical factor to the logical Q-term being formed. If the input variable iterations exists, then the logical Q-term is formed only from the condition of the last type 3 block containing the input variables.

If there are blocks with type 3 whose conditions contain input variables, a branching appears. Only one branch is processed once in the flowchart. After processing the branches, the identifiers of the output variables and the corresponding pairs of logical and unconditional Q-terms are written to the output file, as shown in Fig. 2. The experience shows there is necessary to cancel the output in the output file of the processing branch results sometimes. To implement this feature, the internal variable empout is used. By default, the value of the empout variable is set to 1, and it is assigned the value 0 in case if it is necessary to cancel the output to the output file.

We describe the exhaustion procedure of the branches. A branch is defined by a sequence of blocks with type 3, the conditions of which contain input variables, as well as ways of exiting the blocks by the value 1 or 0. The branch collection stores information about processed branches. After the processing of the next branch is completed, the collection stores the sequence of pairs consisting of Id numbers of branch blocks and output values from blocks 1 or 0. The pairs in the collection are followed in order of processing the blocks. During the first pass through the flowchart, information about the first branch being processed is recorded in a collection of branches. We are looking for pairs with a block output of 0. Suppose that the last pair is such one. Then, we delete such pairs with 0 starting with the last one up to the pair with 1. Deletion ends when there are either no such pairs, or a block with an output value of 1 is found. If all pairs are deleted, it means that all branches are processed. In this case, the processing of the flowchart is completed. If the collection is not empty, then the last pair has the block with an output value of 1. We change this value to 0 and get a new pair P. Now the new branch appears as a subsequence of pairs of the processed branch, ending in P and its extension according to the flowchart. As a result, new items will be written to the branch collection.

3.2 Subsystem for the Calculating of the Resource of Numerical Algorithms Parallelism

The subsystem includes a database, server and client applications. We used PostgreSQL database management system for database development. The database contains the entities Algorithms and Determinants. Attributes of the Algorithms entity are the following: primary key, algorithm name, algorithm description, number of Q-determinants loaded into the database, which correspond to different values of dimension parameters and number of iterations. Attributes of the Determinants entity are the following: primary key, unique algorithm identifier, dimension parameter values, Q-determinant, $D(\bar{N})$ value (cf. (HA)), $P(\bar{N})$ value (cf. (WA)), number of iterations.

A server application has been developed for interacting with database entities. The server application implements the following methods: recording a new algorithm, updating the algorithm information, obtaining a list of algorithms with complete information about them, comparing the characteristics of the parallel complexity of two algorithms with an indication of the compared attribute $D(\bar{N})$ or $P(\bar{N})$, deletion of the algorithm along with its Q-determinants, loading of a new Q-determinant and calculated characteristics of parallel complexity of Q-effective implementation, obtaining a list of Q-determinants, downloading Q-determinant, removal of Q-determinant. The Q-determinant of the algorithm is written to the database as a set of $W(\bar{N})$ expressions in the JSON format. In this regard, software has been developed for converting the description of the representation of the algorithm, obtained using the subsystem to form Q-determinants, into the format of the description of the Q-determinant for the database. To obtain the Q-effective implementation of the algorithm and calculate the characteristics of $D(\bar{N})$ and $P(\bar{N})$, an original algorithm was developed and implemented. Also, we develop and realize the original algorithm comparing the characteristics of $D(\bar{N})$ and $P(\bar{N})$ of two algorithms. The Q-system is open for viewing information. Therefore, the identification and the authentication were used to prevent unauthorized access to editing information.

The client application manages the database by calling the server application methods. The main page of the client application contains a table with the results of the query of all algorithms recorded in the database and the interface elements for logging in authorized users to add, edit, delete and compare algorithms. Interface elements allow any user to select algorithms for comparison and get the result of their comparison. In addition, the main page shows the number of Q-determinants written to the database for each algorithm. From the main page, you can go to the page containing the results of querying all Q-determinants for the selected algorithm. For each Q-determinant, it contains the dimension parameters, the number of iterations, the characteristics of parallel complexity $D(\bar{N})$ and $P(\bar{N})$. Interface elements allow any user to download any Q-determinant to a file. Also, authorized users can also add and remove Q-determinants by interface. We developed the Q-system functionality for interpolation and extrapolation of characteristics of parallel complexity $D(\bar{N})$ and $P(\bar{N})$. Also we test and study the functionality of the Q-system for graphical representation of the characteristics of parallel complexity.

4 Results of Trial Operation of the Q-system

The Q-system is available at

$$\text{https://qclient.herokuapp.com}$$

The database contains several numerical algorithms and their Q-determinants. For example, among such algorithms, Gauss–Jordan, Gauss–Seidel, Jacobi methods for solving a system of linear equations, an algorithm for calculating the scalar product of vectors, matrix multiplication algorithm, algorithm for finding the maximum element in a sequence of numbers, and others. If the algorithm has no dimension parameters and iterations, then for it one Q-determinant was written to the database. An example of such an algorithm is an algorithm for solving a quadratic equation. In other cases, for each algorithm, several Q-determinants were written to the database for different values of the dimension parameters and the number of iterations.

More exactly, if we want to write the Q-determinant of algorithm in our database we should make the following steps. First we will create a flowchart of this algorithm in JSON format. Then we get a representation of the algorithm in the form of Q-determinant for specific values of the dimension parameters and number of iterations by the subsystem for the creation of Q-determinants from the flowchart. Next, we convert the received Q-determinant into a format for storing the Q-determinant in a database and write it there.

Under trial operation we detect that the Q-system generates correct data.

5 Conclusion

We described the software Q-system for the research of the resource of numerical algorithms parallelism that based on the concept of Q-determinant. This system has the following subsystems: the creation of Q-determinants of numerical algorithms, the calculating of the resource of numerical algorithms parallelism. It allows the user to calculate the parallelism resource of any numerical algorithm and compare the parallelism resources of two numerical algorithms, solving the same algorithmic problem. As a result, using the Q-system, from several algorithms you can choose an algorithm with the best parallelism resource. Then, for the selected algorithm, we can design Q-effective program using the algorithm's parallelism resource completely [14].

The subsystem for the creation of Q-determinants of numerical algorithms forms algorithm representation as Q-determinant. This representation contains all the machine-independent properties of the algorithm. So, we plan to create a new database and its applications for storing and processing representations of algorithms in the form of Q-determinants, and not just Q-terms of algorithms. Thus, we will enable to investigate the machine-independent properties of numerical algorithms in an automated mode.

In addition, the possibility of software formation of the representation of numerical algorithms in the form of a Q-determinant using the Q-system opens up prospects for computer-aided design Q-effective programs.

Acknowledgements. The reported study was funded by RFBR according to the research project № 17-07-00865 a. The work was supported by Act 211 Government of the Russian Federation, contract № 02.A03.21.0011.

References

1. Voevodin, V.V., Voevodin, V.V.: Parallel Computing. BHV-Petersburg, St. Petersburg (2002). (in Russian)
2. Voevodin, V.V., Voevodin, V.V.: The V-Ray technology of optimizing programs to parallel computers. In: Vulkov, L., Waśniewski, J., Yalamov, P. (eds.) WNAA 1996. LNCS, vol. 1196, pp. 546–556. Springer, Heidelberg (1997). https://doi.org/10.1007/3-540-62598-4_136

3. Open Encyclopedia of Parallel Algorithmic Features. http://algowiki-project.org/en/Open_Encyclopedia_of_Parallel_Algorithmic_Features
4. Antonov, A.S., Dongarra, J., Voevodin, V.: AlgoWiki project as an extension of the Top500 methodology. In: Supercomputing Frontiers and Innovations, vol. 5, no. 1, pp. 4–10. Publishing Center of South Ural State University, Chelyabinsk (2018). https://doi.org/10.14529/jsfi180101
5. Abramov, S.M., Vasenin, V.A., Mamchits, E.E., Roganov, V.A., Slepukhin, A.F.: Dynamic parallelization of programs based on parallel graph reduction. A software architecture of new T-system version. In: Proceedings Book of MIPHI Scientific Session, Moscow, 22–26 January 2001, vol. 2 (2001). (in Russian)
6. Malyshkin, V.E., Perepelkin, V.A., Schukin, G.A.: Distributed algorithm of data allocation in the fragmented programming system LuNA. In: Malyshkin, V. (ed.) PaCT 2015. LNCS, vol. 9251, pp. 80–85. Springer, Cham (2015). https://doi.org/10.1007/978-3-319-21909-7_8
7. Legalov, A.I.: Functional language for creating architecturally independent parallel programs. Comput. Technol. 1(10), 71–89 (2005). (in Russian)
8. Wang, Q., Liu, J., Tang, X., Wang, F., Fu, G., Xing, Z.: Accelerating embarrassingly parallel algorithm on Intel MIC. In: IEEE International Conference on Progress in Informatics and Computing, pp. 213–218 (2014). https://doi.org/10.1109/PIC.2014.6972327
9. Li, Y., Dou, W., Yang, K., Miao, S.: Optimized data I/O strategy of the algorithm of parallel digital terrain analysis. In: 13th International Symposium on Distributed Computing and Applications to Business, Engineering and Science, pp. 34–37 (2014). https://doi.org/10.1109/DCABES.2014.10
10. Matveev, S.A., Zagidullin, R.R., Smirnov, A.P., Tyrtyshnikov, E.E.: Parallel numerical algorithm for solving advection equation for coagulating particles. In: Supercomputing Frontiers and Innovations, vol. 5, No. 2, pp. 43–54. Publishing Center of South Ural State University, Chelyabinsk (2018). https://doi.org/10.14529/jsfi180204
11. Setukha, A.V., Aparinov, V.A., Aparinov A.A.: Supercomputer modeling of parachute flight dynamics. In: Supercomputing Frontiers and Innovations, vol. 5, No. 3, pp. 121–125. Publishing Center of South Ural State University, Chelyabinsk (2018). https://doi.org/10.14529/jsfi180323
12. Aleeva, V.N.: Analysis of parallel numerical algorithms: Preprint No. 590. Novosibirsk, Computing Center of the Siberian Branch of the Academy of Sciences of the USSR (1985)
13. Aleeva, V.N., Sharabura, I.S., Suleymanov, D.E.: Software system for maximal parallelization of algorithms on the base of the conception of Q-determinant. In: Malyshkin, V. (ed.) PaCT 2015. LNCS, vol. 9251, pp. 3–9. Springer, Cham (2015). https://doi.org/10.1007/978-3-319-21909-7_1
14. Aleeva, V.: Designing a parallel programs on the base of the conception of Q-determinant. In: Voevodin, V., Sobolev, S. (eds.) RuSCDays 2018. CCIS, vol. 965, pp. 565–577. Springer, Cham (2019). https://doi.org/10.1007/978-3-030-05807-4_48
15. Aleeva, V.N., Aleev, R.Zh.: High-performance computing using the application of the Q-determinant of numerical algorithms. In: Proceedings - 2018 Global Smart Industry Conference, GloSIC 2018. Article number 8570160, 8 p. IEEE (2018). https://doi.org/10.1109/GloSIC.2018.8570160

The Role of Student Projects in Teaching Machine Learning and High Performance Computing

Andrey Sozykin[1,2(✉)], Anton Koshelev[1], and Dmitry Ustalov[3]

[1] Ural Federal University, Ekaterinburg, Russia
{Andrey.Sozykin,Anton.Koshelev}@urfu.ru
[2] Krasovskii Institute of Mathematics and Mechanics, Ekaterinburg, Russia
[3] University of Mannheim, Mannheim, Germany
dmitry@informatik.uni-mannheim.de

Abstract. We describe an approach to teaching Machine Learning and High-Performance Computing classes for Master students at Ural Federal University. In addition to the theoretical classes, the students participate in the projects in collaboration with the partner companies and research laboratories of the university and institutes of the Russian Academy of Sciences. The partners provide not only project topics, but also the experienced mentors to assist the students in project work. We discuss the structure of the Project Workshop class that was designed to include the project-based learning into the curriculum. As a result, during the Master studies, the students not only learn the theoretical basis but also gain experience solving real world problems, which has a positive effect on employment.

Keywords: Machine learning · Parallel computing · Teaching · Project-based learning

1 Introduction

More and more organizations around the globe use the data-driven paradigm to tackle the problems that they were not able to solve in the past. However the progress in data driven economy is impeded by the lack of machine learning specialists and data scientists. Despite the wide availability of machine learning educational programs, most of them do not provide the students with necessary skills to answer real-world questions with data. Teaching machine learning is mostly devoted to studying various machine learning methods, which are illustrated using the clean datasets that are suitable for those methods [1]. As a result, the students are not able to solve the real-world problems when they have to deal with messy data, choose appropriate machine learning method and adapt to the changing requirements. In addition, the students have very vague understanding of how their machine learning solutions will be applied in business.

V. Voevodin and S. Sobolev (Eds.): RuSCDays 2019, CCIS 1129, pp. 653–663, 2019.
https://doi.org/10.1007/978-3-030-36592-9_53

In order to answer the real-world questions with data, the students should not only study machine learning and programming, but also acquire the soft skills, such as problem solving, collaboration, communication, system thinking, project management and so on. Song *et al.* [2] proposed that the data science programs should teach Chief Data Officers and include courses that develop such soft skills. However, the authors acknowledged that it is very hard to include all those courses into one program.

An alternative approach to practice-oriented education and soft skills development is the project-based learning when the students have to implement some project in the teams instead of attending lectures. Project-based learning have been successfully used to teach software development [3] and machine learning [4].

We present the project-based learning approach to teaching machine learning for Master students at Ural Federal University. In addition to the theoretical classes, the students participate in the projects in collaboration with the industry partners and research laboratories of the university and institutes of the Russian Academy of Sciences. We describe the structure of the Machine Learning Master program at Ural Federal University, the Project Workshop course that have been designed to include the student projects into the curriculum, and some examples of successfully implemented projects. In addition, we pay attention to important aspects of the inevitable convergence of machine learning, high performance computing and internet of things that arises in the complex projects. This convergence should be taken into account during the design of educational programs.

2   Related Work

Germany has a special type of educational programs, which are called integrated degree programs, that combine the university education and working at the company. For example, the Scientific Programming Bachelor integrated program [5] is implemented by the Aachen University of Applied Science in cooperation with the IT companies. The university provide the theoretical part of the program and the companies provide the practical part of the vocational training. In contrast to traditional programs, the lectures and tutorials are held two days a week. During other three days the students work in real-world projects at the companies. The students are paid for their work and feel better prepared for working life because they already have a working experience. Over 70% of the Scientific Programming integrated program graduates stay in the company where they had vocational training. The companies benefit from the program because there is no training period for the program graduates who are already familiar with the company.

The Harvard professors in the paper [1] presented an approach to teaching data science by developing the three important skills: *computing, connecting,* and *creating*. The data scientists should be able to not only develop the new machine learning methods, but also to implement them in code (*computing*). In addition to teaching the machine learning methods and techniques, the students should be taught how to *connect* the real-world questions with the appropriate methods, tools and datasets. The current approach implicitly teaches students to be passive and wait for the customer to come and ask questions. In practice, however, the data scientists are expected to be active: *create* and formulate questions to solve. In order to develop those three skills, the authors suggested to organize the data science course around a set of diverse case studies instead of machine learning methods, and to structure the course activities to realistically mimic a data scientist's experience.

3   The Structure of the Master Program

We have designed the Machine Learning Master program at Ural Federal University using the project-based learning approach. The program consists of three main parts (Fig. 1): the mandatory courses, the project workshop, and the elective courses. The purpose of the mandatory courses is to teach the students the foundation of machine learning and research work. The students apply acquired knowledge to implement projects during the project workshop. In addition, the students have to select two elective courses per semester, which should be relevant to the topic of their projects.

1st semester	2nd semester	3rd semester	4th semester
Machine Learning	Machine Learning	Natural Language Processing	
Python Programming	Computer Vision	Time Series Analysis	
Research Seminar	Research Seminar	Research Seminar	Master Thesis
Project Workshop	Project Workshop	Project Workshop	
Elective Course 1	Elective Course 1	Elective Course 1	
Elective Course 2	Elective Course 2	Elective Course 2	

Fig. 1. The curriculum of the Master Program in Machine Learning at Ural Federal University

The Project Workshop is a special type of course designed to include the project-based learning into the curriculum. The course has significantly big workloads of 9 ECTS, which allows the students to implement non-trivial projects. The course is described in further detail in Sect. 4.

The project topics for Machine Learning Master program are proposed by the partner companies and the research laboratories of Ural Federal University and institutes of the Russian Academy of Sciences. The topics are directly related to the problems that the companies and labs are working on [6–8]. Hence, the students are able to gain the real work experience while implementing the projects.

The projects are implemented in the team of 2 to 4 students (Fig. 2). It helps students to develop soft skills: communication, work distribution, time management and so on. In addition, such an approach allows to find the leaders among the students, who take responsibility for organization of work in the teams.

In addition to projects topics, the companies and the research laboratories provide the experienced mentors who help the students to implement the project. The mentors provide the students with necessary background on the company and the task of the project, help them to get required data and choose appropriate machine learning method for data analysis.

The university also provides the mentors for the project. In contrast to mentors from companies and research laboratories, the university mentors help students to organize their work properly in order to successfully implement the project in time. The university mentors also advise the students on choosing elective courses, which will be helpful in their project work.

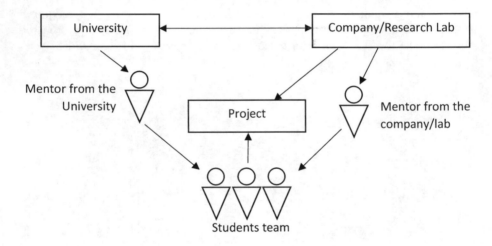

Fig. 2. The structure of the project

4 Project Workshop

In projects the student teams work on real-world tasks for which the solution is not known in advance. The students must find the appropriate solution by themselves. Hence, the students face a large amount of uncertainty: which machine learning methods should be used, how to prepare the data properly for the chosen method, how to measure the quality of developed machine learning model and how to use the model in practice. The students cannot cope with this amount of uncertainty on their own due to lack of experience. According to our experience, it is essential to design the Project Workshop course in a way that helps students to overcome uncertainty. Otherwise, many student teams will fail their projects. In this chapter we describe our approach to conduct the Project Workshop course that helps students to make the important project decisions as quickly and efficiently as possible. As a result, most of the student teams are able to successfully implement the projects. The Project Workshop course uses the agile methodology, the students work is divided into two weeks iterations. Each semester consists of the four main parts, presented in Table 1.

Table 1. The project workshop steps

Step name	Step duration
1. Project topics presentations	1 iteration
2. Projects selection and planing	1 iteration
3. Projects implementation	5–6 iterations
4. Projects defense	1 iteration

The first step of the Project Workshop is introducing the students to the partner companies and research laboratories. During two weeks the representatives of the companies and laboratories give presentation to the students. The presentations describe the company or laboratory in general, the topics of the projects, why they are interesting and important both for the company and for the students. In addition, the possible problems and challenges in projects are discussed.

The next step is the project selection and planning. The students select the project topics, which are interesting for them, and create the teams of 2–4 people. After that, the student teams meet with project mentors from the company of research lab. During the meetings, the mentors describe the projects in more details, students get acquainted with the goals and objectives of the project. Together with the mentors, the student teams define the expected result of the project, which they will present by the end of the semester, and develop the plan that contains the milestones for each iteration of the project. Then the student teams give the presentations of their projects that must include the following topics:

- **Project Goal.** What problem will be solved during the project, why is it important for the company or laboratory? What research should be done to solve the problem? What is the state-of-the-art in the area?
- **Project Deliverables.** What results should be achieved in order to solve the problem stated in the project goal? The results should include clearly described solution, which can be implemented in the allotted time.
- **Definition of Done.** How the achievement of the project goal could be verified? For machine learning model, the team can provide a demonstration of the model, for example, in the Jupyter notebook, and analysis of model quality. For research project, the team give a presentation about the research

with numerical characteristics of the expected results. For example, five types of classificators will be considered, for each type the accuracy and performance will be measured. Another possible output is a ready to use application. In such a case, the team should provide the demonstration of the application and describe some application metrics related to project goals that will be measured.

After reaching the agreement between the student team, the university mentor and the company mentor on the project goal and expected results, the students proceed to the project planing. For each iteration of the project they define the goal, the expected outcomes and the definition of done in the same way, as they do for the entire project. In addition, the role for each student in the team is defined. At the end of the step, the teams give the presentation about the project plan and role distributions.

During the next step, the student teams work on the project implementation. The students work by themselves, but present their progress once per two weeks, at the end of each iteration. For those teams, which were not able to achieve the results stated in the plan, the detailed analysis of impediments is performed by the university mentor. The problems may be caused by the unrealistic planning, when the students misjudged the amount of work. Another possible reason is unforeseen situations, for example, when experiments or literature review provide the unexpected results. In such a case, the team together with the university mentor modifies the project plan and the expected deliverables for each subsequent iteration. However, if the iteration goal was not met because the team did not allocate enough time to work on the project, the plan is not modified and the team lose points.

The university mentor provides feedback not only on the project progress, but also on the quality of the presentations. The students get recommendations which topics are most important and should be described in details and what can be skipped in order not to waste the listeners' time. In addition, the mentor helps the team to clearly describe a contribution of each student.

During the implementation step, the student teams regularly meet with the company mentors. The students demonstrate the achieved results and ask questions. As a result, the students get different prospective on the same problem from the university and company mentors. The company mentors can provide the additional expertise, which the university mentors do not have. Moreover, the company mentors are able to decrease the quality requirements of the expected solution, so the students will consider the task achievable.

The last step of the Project Workshop course is a project defence. The student teams present their projects to the mentors and other representatives from the university, companies and research laboratories. The students give presentations about their research and demonstrate prototypes or ready to use applications. For each solution the quality metrics are presented and the role of each student in the team is emphasized. The teams are assessed by the achieved project results and the quality of the presentation.

The Machine Learning Master program curriculum include the Project Workshop course in first three semesters. The students can work on the same project during all three semesters and write the master thesis using the results of the project. However, the students are able to change the project topic at the start of each semester. In addition, the company may refuse to continue working on the project with the student or entire student team if the company is not satisfied with the previous results.

5   Examples of the Student Projects

5.1   The Tenants Requests Classification System

The company League of Housing and Utilities, which provides housing and communal services at Yekaterinburg, Russia, needed a system for classification of the tenants requests. The system should automatically redirect the requests to the appropriate specialist of the company. The manual distribution of the requests required a lot of time, which slowed down the requests processing and significantly hampered the business growing.

The company provided the dataset with the texts of the requests and the labels of true classes. The dataset included 2000 requests belonging to 30 classes. The student team developed the classification model using the Catboost library [9]. The requests text preprocessing included removing of stop words, words normalization using pymorphy2 library [10] and vectorization with the help of Scikit-learn [11] library. Such an approach allowed to achieve the mean classification accuracy of 92%. However, for several underrepresented classes the accuracy was much lower. As a result, the creation of fully automated classification system was not possible.

The project team negotiated with the customer and they jointly decided to use semi-automated processing. The tenants requests were classified by the model, but assigning the requests to the specialist was performed by the manager. The manager had the ability to change the request class in case of classification error. The semi-automated approach made it possible to put the system into production in a short time, significantly decreased the amount of manual labor for request classification and allowed to automatically collect the data for additional training of the classification model.

5.2   Obscenity Detection

One of the leading providers of service desk solutions for Government and Enterprises in Russia, the Naumen company, proposed a case for obscenity detection in service requests. The users of service desk portals for police and other security agencies often use obscene language, which is prohibited by law. In addition, bad language in the requests demotivates police officers to help people.

In order to solve the problem, the company planned to develop the system for automatic detection of rude words. When the system detects such words, it should reject the submission of the request and show the message about the indecent behavior. However, the company did not provided clear rules about which words should be considered rude and lead to request rejection.

The student team discussed the problem with the customer and proposed the pilot project, which was focused only on detection of filthy language. The students found several dictionaries of filthy language and developed a detector of filthy words using dictionary search. However, the quality of the detector was low. To improve the quality, the team suggested to use the character level classification. The probability of being a filthy language was computed not for words, but for every character in the text. The accuracy of the suggested solution was 75%, which was sufficient for the customer. The company provided a positive feedback on the non-standard approach, suggested by the students.

5.3   Prediction of the Government Procurement Results

In Russia all government purchasing must be carried out on a centralized website [12]. The government procurement data in Russia are in open access. The procurement participants want to know in advance whether the purchase will be successful and how many suppliers will participate.

The big Russian provider of cloud services for business and accounting, the SKB Kontur company, proposed a project for the students in the area of government procurement predictions. The student team was required to develop two models: the regression model for predicting the number of a government tender participants and the classification model to predict whether the tender be successful or not. The company provided preprocessed data about government purchasing for several years.

The student team tried various machine learning algorithms and feature engineering techniques during several months. The best results were achieved using the Catboost library [9]. The quality was measured using the coefficient of determination R^2 for the regression model and the F1-score for classification model. The quality was sufficient for the customer and the company allowed the students to provide open access for their software and models [13].

6   On the Convergence of Machine Learning and High Performance Computing in the Projects

Project-based learning make possible the convergence of multiple topics including machine learning, parallel computing, internet of things and so on. The students often have to deal with several of such topics during the projects.

Training real-world machine learning models requires big computational resources. In addition, to solve the problems with the data, the students have to train several models and choose the best one. Often it is not possible to train all required models using the laptops and personal computers. Hence, the students have to use the parallel computational clusters of Ural Federal University for model training. To further improve the training speed, the students are able to use cluster nodes with GPUs.

The convergence also occurs inside some project topics. For example, the industrial company has proposed a project to analyze data from the sensors on the industrial equipment in order to predict the failure of the equipment. To implement this project, the students should be able to use not only machine learning, but also internet of thing. Another example of multidisciplinary project is developing new materials using machine learning, which is carried out in cooperation with several research laboratories of Ural Federal University [14]. To find new material with desired properties, the researchers need to conduct the series of simulations or experiments with various values of material parameters. When the parameter space to search is very large, the simulation is computationally expensive and requires a long time, it is very hard to obtain the results in a reasonable time. Machine learning can help to find appropriate values of parameters that allow to create the material with desired properties by approximation of the dependency of functional properties on the parameters using limited number of simulation or experiments [15]. In addition, the existing databases with material properties can be used. Hence, this type of projects require the knowledge of parallel computing, big data, and material science.

Although the mandatory courses on High Performance Computing, GPU Programming, Internet of Things and Big Data are not included in the Machine Learning Master program curriculum, the students are able to take them as electives. The elective course on Linux, which is used on the parallel computing cluster, is also popular among the students. Furthermore, the students are able to choose electives taught by other departments of the university (e.g. Material Science, Material Informatics or Chemoinformatics) if the courses will help them to implement the projects.

7   Discussion

The participation in real-world projects allowed the students to understand the current state of the industry. On their own experience the students learned which problems company and research laboratories face today and how machine learning is used to solve such problems. In addition, they learned which knowledge and skills are in demand and which are obsolete.

An important skill, acquired by the students, is communication with the customer. The students learned the importance of negotiating of the project results and defining the clear metrics for results evaluation in advance. The teams with vague definition of expected results often struggle during the project defence, because their solutions are not able to solve the customer problems.

We require that the projects must be implemented in teams, hence, the students acquired the soft skills required for teamwork: how to plan the work in the project, how to distribute the work among the team members according to their roles in the projects. They also learned how to communicate in the team efficiently to ensure that every member of the team knows the current status of the project and what he or she must do next. The teamwork allowed the students with good management skills to take a leadership position in their teams.

During the projects the students have chances to face the challenges that happen in real work. For example, the customer of the project does not know exactly what he really wants and cannot set the clear goals for students. In such a case, the students must not only create a solution, but also prove to the customer that the proposed solution is what he needs. Another frequently occurring problem is when in the middle of the project the team realize that their solution was wrong and they have to start from scratch. The students learned how to find the ways to overcome all the difficulties and to present some results at the end of the semester.

The companies and research laboratories provided the positive feedback. They were able to evaluate the students during the project work and hired only those graduates who had sufficient skills and were suitable for the company culture. In addition, the newly hired graduates did not need the adaptation period because they already knew the company.

8 Conclusion

We presented an approach to teach machine learning specialists who are able to solve the real-world problems with data. To learn how to do it, the students participate in real projects while studying at the university. The projects are implemented in partnership with the companies and the research laboratories.

The developed Machine Learning Master program provides benefits for the students, companies and university. The real-world project experience positively affects the student employment. The companies are able to hire the employees who are already familiar with their business and ready to make contribution from the first day. The university becomes a hub that brings together the companies and builds the ecosystem for data driven economy in the region.

References

1. Hicks, S.C., Irizarry, R.A.: A guide to teaching data science. Am. Stat. **72**(4), 382–391 (2018). https://doi.org/10.1080/00031305.2017.1356747
2. Song, I.Y., Zhu, Y.: Big data and data science: what should we teach? Expert Syst. **33**, 364–373 (2016). https://doi.org/10.1111/exsy.12130
3. Sababha, B., Alqudah, Y., Abualbasal, A., AlQaralleh, E.: Project-based learning to enhance teaching embedded systems. Eurasia J. Math. Sci. Technol. Educ. **12**(9), 2575–2585 (2016). https://doi.org/10.12973/eurasia.2016.1267a
4. Russell, I., Markov, Z., Neller, T.: Teaching AI through machine learning projects. SIGCSE Bull. **38**(3), 323–323 (2006). https://doi.org/10.1145/1140123.1140230
5. Kuppers, B., Dondorf, T., Willemsen, B., et al.: The scientific programming integrated degree program - a pioneering approach to join theory and practice. Procedia Comput. Sci. **80**, 1957–1967 (2016). https://doi.org/10.1016/j.procs.2016.05.516

6. Borodin, A., Mirvoda, S., Porshnev, S., Bakhterev, M.: Improving penalty function of R-tree over generalized index search tree possible way to advance performance of PostgreSQL cube extension. In: IEEE 2nd International Conference on Big Data Analysis (ICBDA), pp. 130–133 (2017). https://doi.org/10.1109/ICBDA.2017.8078791

7. Rubinchik, M., Shur, A.M.: EERTREE: an efficient data structure for processing palindromes in strings. In: Lipták, Z., Smyth, W.F. (eds.) IWOCA 2015. LNCS, vol. 9538, pp. 321–333. Springer, Cham (2016). https://doi.org/10.1007/978-3-319-29516-9_27

8. Kumkov, S.S., Le Ménec, S., Patsko, V.S.: Zero-sum pursuit-evasion differential games with many objects: survey of publications. Dyn. Games Appl. **7**(4), 609–633 (2016). https://doi.org/10.1007/s13235-016-0209-z

9. Prokhorenkova, L., Gusev, G., Vorobev, A., et al.: Catboost: unbiased boosting with categorical features. In: Advances in Neural Information Processing Systems, pp. 6638–6648 (2018)

10. Korobov, M.: Morphological analyzer and generator for Russian and Ukrainian languages. In: Khachay, M.Y., Konstantinova, N., Panchenko, A., Ignatov, D.I., Labunets, V.G. (eds.) AIST 2015. CCIS, vol. 542, pp. 320–332. Springer, Cham (2015). https://doi.org/10.1007/978-3-319-26123-2_31

11. Pedregosa, F., Varoquaux, G., Gramfort, A., et al.: Scikit-learn: machine learning in python. J. Mach. Learn. Res. **12**, 2825–2830 (2011)

12. Government Procurement System of Russian Federation (in Russian). http://www.zakupki.gov.ru

13. Prediction of the Government Procurement Results (in Russian). https://github.com/zakoopkee/zakupki

14. Sotnikov, O.M., Mazurenko, V.V., Iakovlev, I.A.: Supervised learning approach for recognizing magnetic skyrmion phases. Phys. Rev. B **98**(17), 174411 (2018). https://doi.org/10.1103/PhysRevB.98.174411

15. Hill, J., Mulholland, G., Persson, K., Seshadri, R., Wolverton, C., Meredig, B.: Materials science with large-scale data and informatics: unlocking new opportunities. MRS Bull. **41**(5), 399–409 (2016). https://doi.org/10.1557/mrs.2016.93

Distributed and Cloud Computing

Budget and Cost-Aware Resources Selection Strategy in Cloud Computing Environments

Victor Toporkov[1($\boxtimes$)], Andrei Tchernykh[2], and Dmitry Yemelyanov[1]

[1] National Research University "MPEI", Moscow, Russia
{ToporkovVV, YemelyanovDM}@mpei.ru
[2] Computer Science Department, CICESE Research Center, Ensenada, Mexico
chernykh@cicese.mx

Abstract. In this work, we introduce algorithms for resource selection in heterogeneous cloud computing environments. Cloud resources are represented as virtual machine instances ready to start with characteristics including performance, RAM, storage, bandwidth, and usage price. User request contains requirements that can be satisfied by different bundles of the virtual machines. We propose and analyze algorithms and scenarios for efficient resources selection and compare them with known approaches. The novelty of the proposed approach is in multiobjective selection of cloud resource bundles according to the specified limited budget.

Keywords: Cloud computing · Optimization · Resources selection · CloudSim · Virtual machine · Economic scheduling · Budget and cost-aware strategies

1 Introduction

Two of the most important problems in high performance and cloud computing are efficient resources utilization and compliance with the terms of the services quality agreements. Cloud and hybrid computing services are often used not only to solve large scientific and practical computationally complex problems but also for a large number of commercial applications [1, 2].

Computing system services support interfaces between users and providers of computing resources and data storages, for instance, in datacenters. Preferences of main stakeholders are usually contradictive. Users are interested in total expenses minimization while obtaining the best service conditions: low response times, higher hardware specifications, 24/7/365 service, etc. Service providers and administrators are interested in profits maximization based on efficient resources usage, energy consumption and system management costs reduction. The challenges of system management can lead to inefficient resources usage in some commercial and corporate cloud systems.

The most common problem is resources overprovisioning. Resources selection optimization of one or several criteria can increase the computing system capacity and reduce operational cost. On the other hand, providing a certain level of pricing, QoS

© Springer Nature Switzerland AG 2019
V. Voevodin and S. Sobolev (Eds.): RuSCDays 2019, CCIS 1129, pp. 667–677, 2019.
https://doi.org/10.1007/978-3-030-36592-9_54

and users' private preferences fulfillment remain important factors for an efficient operation [1–3].

There is a tendency for hybridization of cloud services and platforms with distributed technologies [2, 4, 20]. Formation and maintenance of scalable computing systems and cloud services (Amazon EC2, IBM Cloud, VMware vCloud, Microsoft Azure, Everest, etc.) are based on the use of meta-schedulers, brokers and job-flow management systems.

Local scheduling systems and resource brokers are responsible for efficient selection of heterogeneous resources considering both system and user criteria. The resource brokers usually perform job-flow optimization in accordance with market mechanisms [1–4]. Centralized and hierarchical meta-scheduling systems, on the contrary, optimize characteristics of the computing environment.

Execution of user requests or a bag of tasks requires selection and co-allocation of a requested number of resources, for example, virtual machines or hard drives. User request includes both desired values for the resources characteristics (such as CPU performance, RAM and storage volumes, system architecture, etc.) as well as the limit for their usage prices [1–6]. Thus, to fulfill user and datacenter's resources utilization policies, the broker and meta-scheduling modules require algorithms performing resources selection based on the specified criteria.

Implementation of the fair scheduling policies [5, 6] in cloud systems requires coordination with environment-specific computing and scheduling features. For instance, cloud services should provide resources on demand with as a low response time and price as possible. The concept of fairness is often used for resource management and distribution in high performance computing. In addition to the transparent free-market relations between user and resource providers, the fair scheduling should provide mechanisms for resources selection control based on private preferences and corporate rules [6].

In this paper, we propose algorithms for resources bundle selection for user request considering several criteria and the limited budget. The general form of the target criterion allows us to implement and study different resources selection scenarios.

The paper is organized as follows. Section 2 formalizes the problem definition. Section 3 briefly reviews related work on VM selection and scheduling. Section 4 introduces a general scheme for the criterion-based resource bundle selection. Section 5 contains simulation results analysis and comparison of proposed and the state of the art algorithm. Section 6 summarizes the paper and describes further research directions.

2 Problem Definition

We address the problem of VM selection based on the user resource request with a limited budget. The request contains the number n of VMs, maximum budget C, and minimal requirements values $f_{j\min}$ of the characteristics $[p, m, d, b, c]$ of VMs: performance p_i (MIPS), RAM m_i (Gb), storage volume d_i (Gb), bandwidth b_i (Gbps), and usage price c_i. Here, $j \in J$ represents the index of VM characteristics.

n is a hard constraint for the resources selection representing parallelism require-ments for user's computational job. The job processing time is unknown until the job has completed its execution (non-clairvoyant case) and all VMs must be provided at the same time 0.

We consider resource $r_i \in R$, from the set R of available VMs, with price c_i and characteristics f_{ij}. The set of selected admissible VMs must satisfy $f_{ji} \geq f_{j\min}$, for each i and j.

An optimization criterion $Z(S_{select})$ consists of a set of the user preferences. It includes one or several characteristics of the selected VMs set $S_{select} = \{p, m, d, b, c\}$. The objective of the function $Z(S_{select})$ is to optimize one or several criteria such as performance p_{max}, RAM m_{max}, storage volume d_{max}, bandwidth b_{max}, and price c_{min}.

A good selection algorithm should satisfy various user demands in an equitable fashion. VM selection algorithm involves multiple objectives and may use multi-criteria decision support, for instance, based on the Pareto optimality. However, it is very difficult to achieve fast solutions needed for VM selection by using the Pareto dominance. So, the problem is very often simplified to a single objective problem.

There are various ways to model preferences, for instance, they can be given explicitly by users to specify an importance of every criterion or a relative importance between criteria. We perform a joint analysis of five metrics assuming equal importance of each VM characteristic. The goal is to find a robust and well performing strategy under all test cases, with the expectation that it will also perform well under other conditions, e.g., with different VM configurations and user requests. In our algorithm, the aggregated multi-criteria optimization function may be represented as a linear combination of VM characteristics, for example: $h_i = (p_i + m_i + d_i + b_i)$.

3 Related Works

The scheduling problem in heterogeneous computing environments is NP-hard due to its combinatorial nature. Many heuristic-based solutions are proposed for resources selection and parallel jobs scheduling. The simplest one is the First Fit (FF) strategy, where first available suitable resource instances are selected [7, 8]. Many algorithms do not take into account such features of distributed or cloud computing environments as resources heterogeneity, dynamic resource load, economic relations, specific resources characteristics. Algorithms presented in [9–11] use an exhaustive search, based on a linear integer programming [9, 10] or mixed-integer programming [11].

In [3], heuristic algorithms for slot selection, based on user-defined utility func-tions, are introduced. NWIRE system [3] performs resources selection with the user defined criterion under the maximum total execution cost constraint.

However, the optimization occurs only on the stage of the best found offer selec-tion. Moab scheduler [12] implements the backfilling algorithm. However, it does not take into account additional constraints such as the minimum required storage volume or the maximum allowed total allocation cost.

Modern distributed and cloud computing simulators such as GridSim and Cloud-Sim [13, 14] provide tools for jobs execution and co-allocation of simultaneously available computing resources. Basic CloudSim simulator performs First Fit selection algorithms.

CloudAuction extension [14] of CloudSim supports a double auction to distribute resources between a job flow with a fair allocation policy. All these algorithms consider price constraints on individual nodes and not on a total allocation cost. However, as we showed in [15], algorithms with a total cost constraint can perform the search among a wider set of resources and increase the overall scheduling efficiency. The authors of [16] extends CloudSim to support dynamic VoIP calls arrival and bin packing based scheduling depending on the actual VMs utilization, startup delays, and call requests. The algorithm presented in [17] minimizes the job response and finish time but does not take into account constraints on a total budget.

The algorithm presented in [18] performs the search on a list of available resources sorted by their response time. It implements window shifting and finish performance maximization, but does not support other optimization criteria and the overall job execution cost constraint.

AEP algorithm [15, 19] performs window search with the constraint on a total resources allocation cost. It implements optimization according to a number of criteria but does not support a general case optimization.

In this paper, we study algorithms and scenarios for effective cloud resources selection based on user-defined criteria. The novelty of the proposed approach consists in implementing a dynamic programming scheme to allocate a set of simultaneously available virtual machines taking into account a variety of heterogeneous hardware and cost metrics.

4 Resource Selection Algorithm

4.1 CloudAuction

CloudAuction (CA) [14] implements an economic model of scheduling and resources selection based on a double auction procedure. At the beginning of the scheduling cycle, datacenters and users send their resource provisioning and demand bids to the auctioneer scheduler. The resources assignment is performed based on a heuristic density function, unifying bid prices and performance characteristics. User and data-center bids are ordered by the density values in descending and ascending order, respectively, to prioritize user requests processing as well as datacenter resources selection.

An important feature of the resource selection and reservation in CA is the determination of the resource transaction price. When a resource r_i with price c_i is selected for user bid with maximum declared price c for one VM $\geq c_i$, the transaction price is calculated as $c_t = \frac{(c + c_i)}{2}$. That is, the auctioneer closes a deal with an average price value between the user and the resource owner expectations. Such a formula, coupled with the monotonous function for determining the auction winners (density function depends on the bid price), approaches to the equilibrium in true prices [14]. However, it does not guarantee an exact equilibrium solution.

4.2   Resource Selection Procedure

We propose the following two-step algorithm named VMOfferFinder (VF) for selection of n VMs based on the user request. The proposed approach has the following features.

The first step is the filtration of R that determines a subset of admissible resources that meet requirements of the minimum characteristics values $f_{j\min}$. The algorithm passes through the list of all available resource types and extracts admissible instances i for which $f_{ji} \geq f_{j\min}$ is satisfied for each j.

A computation complexity of this step is linear to the number of resources and characteristic types: $O(|R| * |J|)$.

Also, at this step, estimated prices are calculated for each admissible resource types based on the following equilibria equation:

$$c_{ti} = \max(c_i, \frac{1}{2}(C/n + c_i)).$$

Thus, if some resource price is higher than the value allocated by the user for a single VM in the bundle $(C/n \leq c_i)$, then the transaction price is equal to the resource price: $c_{ti} = c_i$. That is, the price cannot be less than that offered by the resource owner. Otherwise, the formula for true prices equilibrium solution is used.

As a result of this step, a subset R_f of admissible resources and their prices are selected. Each resource from R_f can be used for the user request fulfillment.

The second step selects n VMs from R_f with the total price less than the budget $\sum_{i=1}^{n} c_{ti} \leq C$ and optimizes the target criterion Z.

In this work, we consider additive separable functions for Z. We assume that in a general scenario, Z maximization is required. Then the optimization problem may be formulated as follows:

$$Z = \sum_{i=1}^{|R_f|} x_i z_i \rightarrow \max, \tag{1}$$

with restrictions:

$$Z = \sum_{i=1}^{|R_f|} x_i c_{ti} \leq C,$$
$$\sum_{i=1}^{|R_f|} x_i = n,$$
$$x_i \in \{0, 1\}, \ i = 1 \dots |R_f|.$$

Here, x_i is a decision variable determining whether to select i-th VM instance $(x_i = 1)$ or not $(x_i = 0)$ for the user request.

This problem relates to the class of integer linear programming problems, which imposes obvious limitations on the practical methods solving. However, we use the 0–1 knapsack problem as a base for our implementation. Indeed, the classical 0–1 knapsack problem with a total weight C and items (VMs) with weights c_{ti} and values z_i has the same formal model (1) except for the extra restriction on the number of items required: $x_1 + x_2 + \cdots + x_m = n$.

To take this into account, we implement the following dynamic programming recurrent scheme:

$$f_i(C_l, n_k) = \max\{f_{i-1}(C_l, n_k), f_{i-1}(C_l - c_{ti}, n_k - 1) + z_i\}, \tag{2}$$

$$i = 1, .., |R_f|, l = 1, .., C, k = 1, .., n,$$

where $f_i(C_l, n_k)$ defines the maximum Z criterion value for n_k-size VM bundle selected out of first i VMs from R_f for a budget C_l.

After the forward induction procedure (2) is finished the maximum value $Z_{\max} = f_{|R_f|}(C, n)$. x_i is then obtained by a backward induction procedure.

As an algorithm result, n-size VMs bundle satisfying user requirements for the resources characteristics $f_{j\min}$ and total price C is selected from R_f to maximize user criterion $Z = \sum_{i=1}^{n} z_i$.

z_i can be represented by any additive-separable function over VM instances. Thus, z_i can take values of individual resources characteristics f_j, for example, maximizing total bundle performance ($p_s \rightarrow \max$), as well as their linear combinations. As an example of such a combination, we consider the problem of maximizing a total value for a set of k target characteristics: $z_i = \sum_{j=1}^{k} f_{ij}$.

Unlike the FF approach, CA resource selection procedure, and other greedy algorithms, the proposed algorithm considers resources-candidates with a price higher than C/n. This extends parameters space for the problem solution, while restrictions of the problem (1) guarantee user requirements.

The pricing mechanisms are consistent with CA models to provide approximate equilibrium in true prices. Moreover, they allow to correctly comparing the scheduling results obtained by both approaches.

The computational complexity of VF is determined by the complexity of the most time-consuming VMs subset selection step: $O(|R_f| * n * C)$. That is, n times higher than the complexity of the original 0–1 knapsack problem.

5   Experimental Analysis

5.1   Experimental Setup

Although the presented algorithm may be used as a resource selection step in a more complex job-flow scheduling procedure, in this work, we restrict our study for the resource selection for a single user request.

We assume that the VM prices represent usage costs for one hour. Similarly, user budget is a maximum available cost for the whole VMs bundle for one hour. We do not take into account actual jobs execution time. However, the maximum execution time may be estimated based on the minimum requested performance value p_{min} of a single VM.

To obtain valuable statistical results, we perform 35000 independent experiments. Each experiment includes resource generation (datacenters and VMs) and resource selection for a single user request.

The user requirements remained unchanged between the experiments: allocate 8 VMs with performance ≥ 2048 MIPS, RAM ≥ 2 Gb, disc space ≥ 30 Gb, network bandwidth ≥ 8 Gb/s, and budget: $8 * 35 = 280$ cost units. The generation of 100 VM types implied availability of resources both deficient and superior characteristics with a price sufficient to fulfill the request. VM characteristics are generated randomly with uniform distribution on the following intervals that correspond to the Amazon instances: $p_i \in [1024; 4096]$, $m_i \in [1024; 8192]$, $d_i \in [10; 100]$, $b_i \in [1024; 16384]$, and $c_i \in [20; 40]$. VM configurations with even higher performance characteristics were not considered as infeasible for the user request fulfillment.

A *hardware index* parameter is used to provide a correlation between hardware and price characteristics. VMs with the higher performance tend to have higher hardware characteristics that correspond to a higher resource tier in a pricing plan. For example, VM with 0.5 hardware index provided $p = 2740$ and $d = 58000$ for price $c = 30.1$, while another VM with 0.99 hardware index was generated with $p = 3767$, $d = 89000$ and $c = 39.7$.

In 5000 simulations, we perform scheduling with the CA algorithm. In the rest 30000 simulations, the resources selection is performed by six VFs.

Different optimization criteria and corresponding versions of the VF algorithm are used. Objective of VF_p is the total performance maximization (p_{max}), VF_m is the total RAM maximization (m_{max}), VF_d is the total disc space maximization (d_{max}), VF_b is the network bandwidth maximization (b_{max}), VF_c is the total usage cost minimization (c_{min}), and VF_h is the maximization of aggregated metric (h_{max}).

5.2 Simulation System

CloudSim [13] is a well-known framework for modeling and simulation of cloud computing infrastructures. It implements event-based simulation and main component entities (brokers, datacenters, schedulers, etc.). The event queue may contain events for resources creation, release, reservation, cloudlets processing, simulation management, etc.

Basic CloudSim provides general cloud computing architecture, as well as realistic resources functioning model including cloudlets, virtual machines, computing nodes, datacenters.

The resource management and scheduling are implemented on a first-come-first-serve basis: for each request, the first available suitable nodes are allocated (as a rule, they are sorted by a unique entity identifier).

More specific scheduling and resource management solutions are implemented as CloudSim extensions (http://www.cloudbus.org/cloudsim/).

5.3 Experimental Results

The obtained average values for the considered resources characteristics are given in Table 1.

During the experiment we decreased user budget for strategies VF_p, VF_m, VF_d, VF_b and VF_h from 280 to 270 so the resulting average price of selected resources coincides with CA solution. This adjustment allows direct comparison of VMs characteristics allocated for the same price by different algorithms.

Table 1. Average optimization criteria values of the resources selection.

Characteristic	CA	VF_p	VF_m	VF_d	VF_b	VF_h	VF_c
Price	33,2	33,2	33,2	33,2	33,2	33,2	**32,3**
Performance	2946	**3143**	2980	2981	2979	3013	2507
RAM	5112	5592	**5968**	5593	5587	5756	4485
Storage	61352	67343	67363	**72112**	67276	70028	53419
Bandwidth	9875	10829	10827	10825	**11629**	11050	8731

The best values obtained for each metric are highlighted in bold in Table 1. As expected, that these values are generally provided by VF with the corresponding optimization criterion. CA provides comparable resources performance, but loses on the other characteristics. The difference reaches 10% in absolute values of metrics and 80% relative to the interval (minimum and maximum) of possible values of other strategies (Fig. 1).

As expected, VF_c provides the lowest obtained user price but the worst VMs hardware characteristics. VF_h obtains high values for all considered characteristics but do not provide the best value for any criterion.

Figure 1 shows histograms of the parameters obtained during resource selections by CA and different VF optimization strategies.

For convenience, the characteristics values are normalized according to the min-max method in percent. The values are relative to an interval between the minimum and maximum average values obtained for each metric during the simulation:

$$\gamma = \frac{strategy\ metric\ value - worst\ metric\ value}{(best\ metric\ value - worst\ metric\ value)} * 100,$$

where γ is in the range [0, 100], where 0 presents worst and 100 best results.

For example, with the minimum performance value 2507 MIPS provided by VF_c and maximum value 3143 provided by VF_p, the value 2946 by CA is represented as 69% in Fig. 1(a)–(e).

We are interested in maximizing γ value for each VM characteristic presented in Fig. 1: performance, RAM, disc storage volumes, and channel bandwidth.

The smallest values are provided by VF_c strategy, while the maximum values are provided by the corresponding VF strategies: VF_p, VF_m, VF_d, VF_b.

In Fig. 1(a), VF_c strategy is represented as a pentagon at 0% level indicating the minimum hardware and price characteristics values. CA histogram in Fig. 1 has a shift towards the performance optimization, which may be explained by the density function used for bids in the selection algorithm [14].

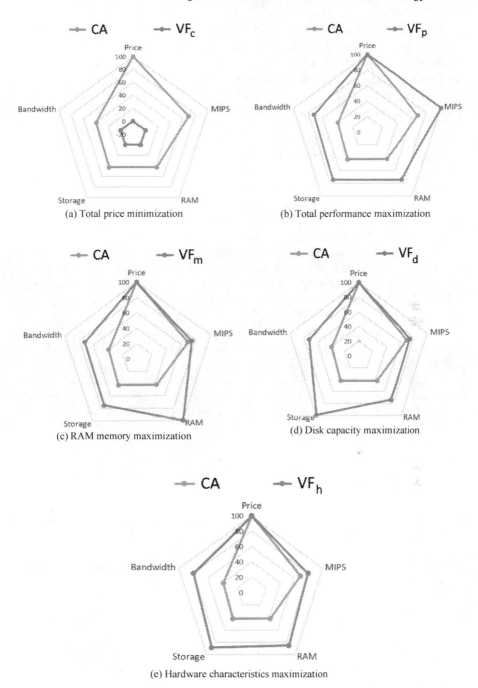

(a) Total price minimization

(b) Total performance maximization

(c) RAM memory maximization

(d) Disk capacity maximization

(e) Hardware characteristics maximization

Fig. 1. Resources section provided by CA and VF

Figure 1(b)–(d) show VF_p, VF_m, and VF_d strategies. They demonstrate histograms shifted towards the corresponding optimized characteristic.

Finally, Fig. 1(e) shows VF_h strategy represented as a pentagon with a 10%–20% characteristics values degradation relatively to the best values.

We see that VF algorithms outperform CA considering all metrics (including non-targeted ones, for example, higher RAM volume during performance maximization).

6   Conclusion and Future Work

In this work, we address the problem of resource selection for user requests in cloud computing environments with heterogeneous resources. General two-steps algorithm VMOfferFinder for VM selection is proposed and analyzed. An admissible subset selection algorithm supports a general case optimization problem.

The presented results show the efficiency of VF algorithm for a single request in a heterogeneous cloud environment based on five user-defined criteria: performance, RAM, disc capacity, bandwidth, and price. It can be implemented as an intermediate API of resource brokers or centralized scheduling systems for a single or aggregated optimization of user defined criteria.

However, further study is required to assess its actual efficiency and effectiveness in real systems. This will be the subject of future work providing a comprehensive experimental study of multi-objective optimization with real cloud providers.

A drawback of the general case algorithm is a relatively high computational complexity, especially compared to the First Fit approach. We will refine a general resource selection scheme to decrease its computational complexity in the further work.

Acknowledgments. This work was partially supported by the Council on Grants of the President of the Russian Federation for State Support of Young Scientists (YPhD- 2979.2019.9), RFBR (grants 18-07-00456 and 18-07-00534) and by the Ministry on Education and Science of the Russian Federation (project no. 2.9606.2017/8.9).

References

1. Lee, Y.C., Wang, C., Zomaya, A.Y., Zhou, B.B.: Profit-driven scheduling for cloud services with data access awareness. J. Parallel Distrib. Comput. **72**(4), 591–602 (2012)
2. Netto, M., Calheiros, R., Rodrigues, E., Cunha, R., Buyya, R.: HPC cloud for scientific and business applications: taxonomy, vision, and research challenges. ACM Comput. Surv. (CSUR) **51**(1), 8 (2018)
3. Ernemann, C., Hamscher, V., Yahyapour, R.: Economic scheduling in grid computing. In: Feitelson, D.G., Rudolph, L., Schwiegelshohn, U. (eds.) JSSPP 2002. LNCS, vol. 2537, pp. 128–152. Springer, Heidelberg (2002). https://doi.org/10.1007/3-540-36180-4_8
4. Jatoth, C., Gangadharan, G., Fiore, U., Buyya, R.: SELCLOUD: a hybrid multi-criteria decision-making model for selection of cloud services. J. Soft Comput. 1–15 (2018). https://doi.org/10.1007/s00500-018-3120-2

5. Carroll, T., Grosu, D.: Divisible load scheduling: an approach using coalitional games. In Proceedings of the Sixth International Symposium on Parallel and Distributed Computing, ISPDC, p. 36 (2007)
6. Toporkov, V., Yemelyanov, D.., Bobchenkov,, A, Potekhin, P.: Fair resource allocation and metascheduling in grid with VO stakeholders preferences. In. Proceedings of 45th International Conference on Parallel Processing Workshops, pp. 375–384. IEEE (2016)
7. Aida, K., Casanova, H.: Scheduling mixed-parallel applications with advance reservations. In: 17th IEEE International Symposium on HPDC, pp. 65–74. IEEE CS Press, New York (2008)
8. Elmroth, E., Tordsson, J.: A standards-based grid resource brokering service supporting advance reservations, co-allocation and cross-grid interoperability. J. Concurr. Comput. Pract. Exp. **25**(18), 2298–2335 (2009)
9. Garg, S.K., Konugurthi, P., Buyya, R.: A linear programming-driven genetic algorithm for meta-scheduling on utility grids. Int. J. Parallel Emergent Distrib. Syst. **26**, 493–517 (2011)
10. Takefusa, A., Nakada, H., Kudoh, T., Tanaka, Y.: An advance reservation-based co-allocation algorithm for distributed computers and network bandwidth on QoS-guaranteed grids. In: Frachtenberg, E., Schwiegelshohn, U. (eds.) JSSPP 2010. LNCS, vol. 6253, pp. 16–34. Springer, Heidelberg (2010). https://doi.org/10.1007/978-3-642-16505-4_2
11. Blanco, H., Guirado, F., Lérida, J.L., Albornoz, V.M.: MIP model scheduling for multi-clusters. In: Caragiannis, I., et al. (eds.) Euro-Par 2012. LNCS, vol. 7640, pp. 196–206. Springer, Heidelberg (2013). https://doi.org/10.1007/978-3-642-36949-0_22
12. Moab Adaptive Computing Suite. http://www.adaptivecomputing.com
13. Calheiros, R.N., Ranjan, R., Beloglazov, A., De Rose, C.A.F., Buyya, R.: CloudSim: a toolkit for modeling and simulation of cloud computing environments and evaluation of resource provisioning algorithms. J. Softw. Pract. Exp. **41**(1), 23–50 (2011)
14. Samimi, P., Teimouri, Y., Mukhtar, M.: A combinatorial double auction resource allocation model in cloud computing. J. Inf. Sci. **357**(C), 201–216 (2016)
15. Toporkov, V., Toporkova, A., Bobchenkov, A., Yemelyanov, D.: Resource selection algorithms for economic scheduling in distributed systems. In: Proceedings of International Conference on Computational Science, ICCS 2011, Singapore, 1–3 June 2011 (2011). Procedia Computer Science. Elsevier, vol. 4, pp. 2267–2276
16. Cortés-Mendoza, J.M., Tchernykh, A., Armenta-Cano, F., Bouvry, P., Drozdov, A., Didelot, L.: Biobjective VoIP service management in cloud infrastructure. J. Sci. Program. 1–14 (2016). https://doi.org/10.1155/2016/5706790. Article ID5706790
17. Makhlouf, S., Yagoubi, B.: Resources co-allocation strategies in grid computing. In: CIIA. CEUR Workshop Proceedings, vol. 825 (2011)
18. Netto, M.A.S., Buyya, R.: A flexible resource co-allocation model based on advance reservations with rescheduling support. Technical report, GRIDSTR-2007–17, Grid Computing and Distributed Systems Laboratory, The University of Melbourne, Australia, 9 October 2007
19. Toporkov, V., Toporkova, A., Tselishchev, A., Yemelyanov, D.: Slot selection algorithms for economic scheduling in distributed computing with high QoS rates. In: Zamojski, W., Mazurkiewicz, J., Sugier, J., Walkowiak, T., Kacprzyk, J. (eds.) New Results in Dependability and Computer Systems. AISC, vol. 224, pp. 459–468. Springer, Heidelberg (2013). https://doi.org/10.1007/978-3-319-00945-2_42
20. Schwiegelshohn, U., Tchernykh, A.: Online scheduling for cloud computing and different service levels. In: IEEE 26th International Parallel and Distributed Processing Symposium Workshops and PhD Forum, IPDPS 2012, pp. 1067–1074 (2012)

Building an Algorithmic Skeleton for Block Data Processing on Enterprise Desktop Grids

Sergei Vostokin$^{(\boxtimes)}$ (iD) and Irina Bobyleva (iD)

Samara National Research University, Samara, Russia
easts@mail.ru, ikazakova90@gmail.com

Abstract. The paper presents a method for building an algorithmic skeleton and automation of the pairwise processing of block data on enterprise desktop grid computing environment. The automation is based on the principle of the round-robin (each with each) tournament. The semantics of calculations and decomposition of the algorithmic skeleton into sequential subprograms using the model of actors is given. A graphical notation explaining the relationship between the elements of the algorithmic skeleton is introduced. The applicability of the method was studied on block sorting of a large data set.

Keywords: Actor model · Enterprise desktop grid · Round-robin tournament · Block sort · Algorithmic skeleton

1 Introduction

The desktop computer grids have long and successful history of usage in the field of scientific computing, both on the Internet and on the scale of enterprises. The main reason why the desktop grids are in wide use is the radical reduction of the computational cost. The grids built on desktop computers (broadly, on any personal computing systems: smartphones, tablets, laptops, etc.) make it possible to use a large amount of devices on the Internet for your computations with a consent of the devices owners. In many cases, that is more convenient and cheaper than using cluster or supercomputer. The use of temporarily idle (for example at night hours) equipment of the enterprise is another alternative solution for cheaper computations.

While hardware costs are reduced, programming costs begin to play an important role in the overall cost of grid computing. The costs remain low, while desktop grids are used to implement simple search or brute force strategies with massive parallelism. This is due to the fact that such problems are native to desktop grids. The problems are easy to program with the desktop grid APIs. Also there are ready to use algorithmic skeletons [1] of the MAP type (when an operation is applied to all elements of data set in parallel) in which the general management of calculations is already implemented [2]. The researcher only needs to define algorithms for the tasks to be solved on the desktop computer grid.

However, as communication and computing equipment improves, the use of desktop grid systems for solving computational problems with more complex control

Supported by the Ministry of Education and Science of the Russian Federation in the framework of the State Assignments program (#9.1616.2017/4.6).

V. Voevodin and S. Sobolev (Eds.): RuSCDays 2019, CCIS 1129, pp. 678–689, 2019.
https://doi.org/10.1007/978-3-030-36592-9_55

(compared to massively parallel control) becomes relevant. For example, these may be complex data analysis tasks. An enterprise can accumulate data during the day and process it on idle computers at night.

In the research we propose a method and apply it to build an algorithmic skeleton for automation of calculations on desktop grid systems. The skeleton is designed to simplify the programming of pairwise processing of data blocks. This processing is similar to the round-robin sport tournament, where teams play with each other. This type of processing can be used for sorting, constructing frequency distributions, and solving similar problems.

The article has the following structure. Firstly, based on the model of actors and a special graphical notation, generalized description of the parallel computing semantics in the desktop grid is created. The description follows the principles of top-bottom decomposition of algorithms for the grid systems and allows one to define data types and sequential procedures for a specific parallel algorithm. Secondly, we specify the description of the data types and procedures by defining the well known algorithmic skeleton called *bag of tasks*. In turn, we present a new skeleton called *asynchronous round-robin tournament*. The skeleton is built on the basis of the bag of tasks skeleton. Finally, the applicability of the asynchronous round-robin tournament skeleton is studied experimentally. Using a cluster model of enterprise's desktop grid environment, we implement and test block sorting application for large data arrays and make a conclusion about possible speedup of data processing in real enterprise grid systems.

2   Related Work

The most common systems for distributing calculations across the desktop grid are Condor [3], BOINC [4], XtremWeb [5], OurGrid [6]. These systems can be implemented at various scales, ranging from office or laboratory to all the world [7]. The characteristics and classification of desktop computer grids are given in [8, 9].

The desktop computer grids can be used not only in the interests of science, but also in the interests of various enterprises. Not all grid systems can really be effectively applied within the local network of an enterprise, since some of them can solve only a narrow class of problems and require a high-speed and uninterrupted connection between elements of the system, which is not always possible. But the solution of this issue and systems capable of working in the network of an enterprise are considered in [10]. Task scheduling techniques can also be used to minimize server load and optimize the desktop grid efficiency [11].

The model presented in the paper is based on the actor model—a model of parallel computation proposed by Carl Hewitt in 1973. Since its inception, it has been actively explored and applied to solve various problems. In the article [12], the authors described in detail all the basic properties of the model of actors, as well as the entire history of its changes over the past time. We also use the bag of tasks model of computations. The authors set forth in detail the bag of tasks model and presented the results of a number of experiments on its application in [13].

In experimental research, we considered a cluster as a model for the desktop grid. The use of a computing cluster as a desktop grid was also studied in [14, 15].

In the article we provide a point of view on actor model and its application in the context of building algorithmic skeletons [1] for the desktop grids controlled by Everest platform [16] which we consider relevant.

3   The Actor Model of Algorithmic Skeletons for Desktop Grid Applications

From a general point of view, the desktop grid calculations are organized according to the master-workers scheme. The master process coordinates the work of connected worker processes. The master and workers processes form communication graph with a star topology. Let's build an actor model of the master-workers scheme. For this, we use a special graphical notation for the actor's semantics of execution.

The *master* class is shown in Fig. 1a. The master process simulates the work of the controlling process or the orchestrator of the desktop grid.

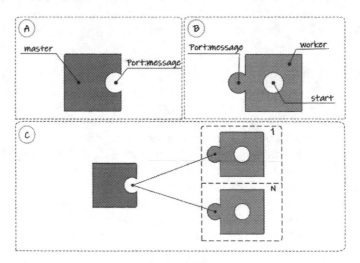

Fig. 1. The master and the worker: (a) the master; (b) the worker; (c) the interaction of master and workers.

Figure 1a means that objects of type *master* can receive messages of type *message* in the *port*. In C++ programming language, this can be encoded as follows: *struct message{..}; struct master{void port_handler(message&m){..}..}.*

The class of *worker* processes is shown in Fig. 1a. This class simulates the work of a desktop computer connected to the grid.

The notation in Fig. 1b is interpreted according to the following description. The worker process can receive messages of type *message* on port named *port*. Additionally, an instance of the *message* type is associated with each *worker* instance. The circle inside the worker process symbol means a handler with the name *worker::start*. This is a system message handler. The message arrives at the beginning of the calculation. In C++, this can be encoded as follows: *struct worker{void port_handler(message&m) {..}; message port; void start(){..}..}.*

The behavior of message objects and the order of calls to message handlers **_handler* is based on the actor's semantics of execution. The message object can be in two states: (a) in the state of interconnection with some actor object; (b) in the state of delivery to port of some actor object. At the time of delivery, the message handler **_handler* is activated. The actor may have a special message handler named *start*. The *start* handler is activated at the beginning of the calculations.

There are rules for accessing actor variables and messages from message handlers. Access to variables of the actor object for which the handler is called is allowed. Access to variables of the message object being in the state of interconnection with the actor to which the handler is called is also allowed.

Two primitive operations are available for managing messages in the context of the ** _handler* and *start* handlers: *access()* and *send()*. The access operation is used to check the availability of the message. Checking the availability of a message means asking the runtime system whether the message is in a state of interconnection with the actor object or not. The *m.send()* operation is used to send a message *m* to a port of some actor. The *m.send()* call is allowed if you have an access to the message *m* (the *access(m)* call returns *true*). After the execution of *m.send()* the access is lost until the completion of the current handler. When the handler is activated, the message *m* transmitted as a handler *void *_handler(message&m)* parameter is available (the *access(m)* call returns *true*). The runtime ensures that the message *m* is eventually delivered after the execution of *m.send()* operation, but no assumptions are made about the message delivery sequence.

A message object is used for communication between a pair of actor objects. For this purpose the links between two actor's ports are established. The links are shown on Fig. 1c. In the model of calculations on the desktop grid, one master actor is associated with N instances of the worker actors. In C++, links are encoded as follows: *struct master{void port(message&){..}..}; struct worker{message port;..}; master a_master; worker a_worker; a_master.port(a_worker.port).*

At the initial moment, the message is available in the actor where the message was declared. In Fig. 1c, these are actors of *worker* type. The message is then used to request the port of another associated actor. In Fig. 1c, this is a *master* actor. After processing, the same message object is used for the response. The interaction can be repeated many times. Thus, the client-server interaction between actors is implemented.

Our goal is to develop an algorithmic skeleton, which is a specialization of the model in Fig. 1c. Therefore, we will further need to define the following types: *message*, *master*, and *worker*. Also we will need to define a message handlers *master::-port_handler*, *worker::port_handler*, and *worker::start* associated with the listed types. The definition is given in the next two sections.

4 Specification of Bag-of-Tasks Skeleton

Let's further clarify the computation model for the desktop grid system. To solve an applied problem, the user defines the following parts of the code. He defines the state of the master process – *struct bag{..}*; the state of a task – *struct task{..}*; the function that tests for the presence of a task – *bool test(bag&)*; the function that gets a new task – *void get(task&, bag&){..}*; the function that processes a task – *void proc(task&){..}*; the function that puts the results of calculations in the state of the master process – *void put (task&, bag&)*. The interaction of the listed functions can be described in the form of sequential C++ code as follows: *bag b; task t; while(test(b)){get(t,b); proc(t); put(t,b);}*.

The algorithmic skeleton that takes the listed types and functions as parameters is usually called the bag of tasks. Having a previously defined general model of computations on the desktop grid, now we can define the bag of tasks skeleton.

The bag will be a part of the master actor state: *struct master{bag b;..}*; the task will be a part of the message state: *struct message{task t;..}*. When processing a message, it is necessary to determine whether the result of the previous calculation is delivered in it. To do this, we introduce the flag: *struct message{bool is_first;..}*. When sending messages from a worker to the master at the beginning of calculations, the flag of the first message is set to *true*: *void worker::start(){port.is_first=true; port.send();}*. When a response is received from the master, the task transferred to the worker is processed: *void worker::port_handler(message&m){proc(m.t); m.send();}*. The result of the processing is sent in a reply message. This is where the worker description is complete.

To describe the behavior of the master process, it is required to keep a list of pointers to messages from workers waiting for the task: *struct master{list<message*>wait;..}*. The message processing method in the master process is performed in 3 consecutive steps: *void master::port_handler(message&m){Step_1; Step_2; Step_3;}*.

Step 1. We put the results of processing the message (*m*) into the state (*b*) of the bag, and the pointer to the message into the wait queue: *if(m.is_first) m.is_first=false; else put(m.t, b); wait.push_back(&m);*. Notice that the first message from the worker does not contain the result of task calculation and is not processed in the *put()*.

Step 2. We issue tasks from the bag for processing by the waiting workers: *while(!wait.empty() && test(b)){message*m=wait.back(); wait.pop_back(); get(m->t, b); m->send();}*.

Step 3. We check the completion of calculations: *if(wait.size()==N) stop();*. Calculations are completed if all workers are waiting for tasks. *N* is the number of worker processes in Fig. 1c.

Thus, we defined the semantics of the algorithmic skeleton called BOT (bag of tasks) as a higher order function on types and ordinary functions: *BOT<struct bag; struct task; bool test(bag&); void get(task&, bag&); void proc(task&); void put(task&, bag&)>*.

5   Specification of Asynchronous Round-Robin Tournament Skeleton

Having the definition of the bag of task skeleton, we can define more specialized skeleton for pairwise processing of data blocks. We call this skeleton the asynchronous round-robin tournament: *ART<void prepare(int team); void play(int team_i, int team_j)>*. The functionality of the skeleton can be represented as the organization of a sports circular tournament, in which M teams participate. Each team plays with each other team. In this case, the total number of games played is $M(M-1)/2$. You cannot simultaneously assign a team to play with more than one rival team. Additional restrictions with the required properties of the tournament may be imposed. However, we expect that these restrictions do not change in time depending on the results of already played games.

For example, a plan of a tournament in the form of a sequence of games can be written as a program in C++:

$$
\begin{aligned}
&\text{for (int } i = 0; \ i < M; \ i{++}\text{) prepare (i);}\\
&\text{for (int } i = 1; \ i < M; \ i{++}\text{) for (int } j = 0; j < i; j{++}\text{) play(j, i);}
\end{aligned}
\tag{1}
$$

For an asynchronous parallel tournament plan, a directed acyclic graph (DAG) is required. This graph determines for every game after which games this game is played. It can be shown that it is enough to track only two games preceding the *play(i, j)* of the game: namely a game in which i^{th} team played, and a game in which j^{th} team played. Then the rules of an asynchronous tournament in the form of an oriented acyclic dependency graph of its tasks can be encoded with the two matrices of size $M \times M$ (*int I1[M][M]; int I2[M][M];*) as shown in Fig. 2.

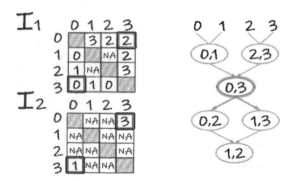

Fig. 2. Coding the task dependencies of an asynchronous round-robin tournament.

Game plays for which the *play(i, j)* is the previous one can be defined as *play(I1[j] [i], I1[i][j])* and *play (I2[j][i], I2[i][j])*, where *I1* and *I2* are matrices of size $M \times M$. If the *play(i, j)* of a game (i, j) does not have dependent games or has only one such game, then the unused elements of the matrices *I1* and *I2* contain special value: *const int NA* = -1.

Using the matrices *I1* and *I2*, the auxiliary matrix *int S[M][2]* is calculated. This matrix encodes the *play(S[i][0], S[i][1])*, immediately following the preparation *prepare(i)* of the ith command.

Let's consider the variables needed to track the current state of the tournament. The *int D[M][M]* matrix stores the number of unplayed games *D[i][j]* preceding the *play(i, j)* directly. The *list<pair<int, int>>games;* contains games (play operations) or preparations to the games (prepare operations) that are not yet assigned to run. To distinguish the preparation from the play in the list of games, a special value *NA* is recorded in the second element of the *pair<int, int>*.

The above description of the state and methods of BOT skeleton from Sect. 4 allow us to determine the state and methods of the ART skeleton (asynchronous round-robin tournament) as follows.

The bag state is supplemented by the following data fields: *struct bag{int D[M][M]; list<pair<int, int>> games; int I1[M][M]; int I2[M][M]; int S[M][2];}*. Matrices *I1, I2*, and *S* are filled at the beginning and do not change during the calculations. The matrix *S* is trivially calculated from the matrices *I1* and *I2*. The list of games is initially filled according to the C++ code: *for(int i = 0; i < M; i++) {pair<int, int> p(i, NA); games.push_back(p);}*. The task state is defined as *struct task{int i; int j;}*. Data fields of the structure correspond to *play(i, j)* for $j \neq NA$ and *prepare(i)* for $j = NA$.

The code for checking whether a task is present in the current state of the bag is *bool test(bag&b){return !b.games.empty();}*.There are tasks for the processing if the games list is not empty.

The task retrieval code is *void get(task&t, bag&b){pair<int, int>p=b.games.back(); b.games.pop_back(); t.i=p.first; t.j=p.second;}*. It means taking the last element of the list of games as a task.

The task processing code is *void proc(task&t){if(t.j == NA) prepare(i); else play(t.i, t.j);}*. It means performing a user-defined prepare or play procedure.

The code for calculating the next tasks at completion of the task *t* implements the following idea of adding tasks to the games list. When a prepare task has completed, it affects the launch of one play task. When a play task has completed, it can affect the launch of one or two play tasks. The tasks that can be performed at the completion of a current task are found by the matrices *I1, I2, S*. The value of the counter *D* decreases for the tasks that can be potentially performed. If the counter has reached zero, then the task stop waiting for the completion of the previous tasks and is planned by adding on the games list.

The procedure of getting the matrices *I1* and *I2* for a tournament with given properties is not discussed in detail here. We only note that in the experimental study described below we used the following procedure. First, a sequence of tournament games was formed, for example, using the algorithm (1). Then this sequence was parallelized. At the end, the resulting dependency graph of the tournament games was encoded with matrices *I1* and *I2*.

Thus, we defined the semantics of the algorithmic skeleton named asynchronous round-robin tournament as the higher order function: *ART<void prepare(int i); void play(int i, int j)>*.

6   Experimental Study of Asynchronous Round-Robin Tournament Skeleton

The asynchronous round-robin tournament skeleton was used to build the orchestrator program that controls task submission to the enterprise desktop grids. The prepare and play parameters of the skeleton are algorithms for processing tasks on the desktop grid system. Testing was performed on a typical problem of sorting a large data set. The data set was divided into several files. The *prepare*(i) algorithm implemented the sorting of a single file identified by the block number i in the data set. As a result of the *play*(i, j) algorithm, the numbers in the pre-sorted files i and j were ordered so that the concatenation of files i and j formed an ordered sequence of numbers. The overall processing result was a sorted set of M files with identifiers 0, 1, 2, ..., $M - 1$. Sequential concatenation of 0, 1, 2, ..., $M - 1$ files formed an ordered sequence of numbers at the end of processing. At the beginning of processing the files were filled with random numbers.

In the experiments we studied: the rate of issuing prepare/play tasks in the implementation of the orchestrator according to the scheme in Fig. 1c; the sorting speedup when prepare/play tasks are calculated in distributed computing environment; the setting of the orchestrator to work in the Everest platform. For all experiments, the orchestrator was implemented in C++ language using Visual Studio 2015 compiler for the desktop system and GCC 4.1.2 compiler for the cluster system. We used x86_64 optimal performance compilation mode.

The rate of task submission and the correctness of the algorithm that implements the ART skeleton was tested on Intel(R) Core(TM) i3-3220T CPU @ 2.80 GHz computer with 4 GB of RAM on board. We used stubs of the prepare/play algorithms and 4 worker processes ($N = 4$ in Fig. 1c). Blocks containing only one integer number were processed in the prepare/play stubs. The data set was stored in RAM. The number of data elements varied from 100 to 1000 in increments of 100. The maximum number of tasks in the experiment was 1000 prepare tasks and $1000 \times (1000 - 1)/2$ play tasks, that was 500,500 tasks in total. Two types of tournaments were tested: the TRIV sort tournament constructed by parallelizing the algorithm (1); the OPTIM sort tournament with a smaller DAG diameter compared to the TRIV sort. The test results are shown in Table 1.

The experiment showed that sequential actor implementation with message exchange is suitable for controlling distributed processing in the desktop grid even in the case of a large number of short tasks. One task requires two messages (see Fig. 1c). It results in sending 1,001,000 messages between actors, when the number of blocks is equal to 1000. But the processing time still remains less when 0.5 s on a processor with relatively low performance. Also it can be seen that different tournaments (differing in matrices *I1* and *I2*) are almost the same in terms of execution time.

In the second series of experiments, the possibility of obtaining a speedup when processing a large set of data on the enterprise desktop grid was investigated. As a model of enterprise desktop grid environment, we used Sergey Korolev cluster system. Sergey Korolev cluster is installed at the Samara University. The cluster configuration is presented on the *hpc.ssau.ru* website. In the tested MPI program, the control process (rank = 0) served as the orchestrator, the remaining worker processes (rank > 0) processed tasks from the orchestrator. The files being sorted were available in all MPI-processes using the IBM GPFS distributed file system.

Table 1. Total submission time of all tournament tasks depending on the number of blocks in the data set.

Number of blocks	OPTIM sort, s	TRIV sort, s
100	0.00260576	0.00328716
200	0.0131043	0.013965
300	0.0362816	0.0354059
400	0.0487192	0.0705439
500	0.0654783	0.0765974
600	0.142984	0.122198
700	0.215872	0.185085
800	0.199767	0.319882
900	0.277575	0.260136
1000	0.390505	0.420731

The sorting was applied to a data set of size from 10 to 100 files in increments of 10. Each file in the set contained 189,000,000 four-byte integers ($\sim$720 MB). The test results are shown in Table 2. For a given number of files, only the best result is shown among the results with different distribution of worker processes on the nodes of the cluster (in Table 2 *nnode* is the number of nodes, *ppn* is the number of simultaneously running tasks on one node). The number of nodes ranged from 2 to 19, while the number of processes per node was fixed to 2. This cluster configuration corresponds to a small enterprise desktop grid. The speedup was estimated based on the average execution time of prepare task (55.7468 s) and play task (6.70886 s) when sorting a set of 20 files in the configuration $nnode = 1$, $ppn = 1$. Thus, the sequential execution time in seconds for processing M files was estimated by the formula $55.7468 \times M + 6.70886 \times M \times (M - 1)/2$.

Experiments show that it is possible to achieve significant speedup while sorting sets of 30 files. The best result was $\sim$5 times speedup and $\sim$1 h reduction of computing time. As the number of files increases, the network was overloaded and the speedup dropped. However, we sorted 100 files with the speedup of 3.23. Due to the longer sorting time, the absolute reduction in time reached $\sim$7 h, which is a significant result.

We conducted a simulation experiment to assess how fast sorting could be performed with our ART skeleton, if we have no loss of performance due to the network overload. In the experiment the time of *prepare* task was also taken to be 55.7468 s, and the time of *play* task was taken to be 6.70886 s of model time. Simulations were computed with required number of workers (for example, 50 workers for 100 files) for the OPTIM sort tournament. The speedup was evaluated similarly to the experiments presented in Table 2. The results of the simulation experiment are shown in Table 3.

Table 2. The dependence of the sorting time on the number of files.

Number of files	Nnode	ppn	Sorting time, s	Speedup
10	2	2	288.434	2.97
20	4	2	457.772	5.22
30	7	2	911.613	5.03
40	7	2	1679.97	4.44
50	13	2	2974.02	3.70
60	11	2	3962.42	3.84
70	13	2	5605.15	3.58
80	15	2	7368.07	3.48
90	17	2	9548.26	3.33
100	19	2	12000.3	3.23

Table 3. The dependence of the sorting time on the number of files (simulation experiment).

Number of files	Sorting time, s	Speedup
10	149.671	5.74171
20	250.304	9.54688
30	350.937	13.0814
40	451.57	16.5263
50	552.202	19.9305
60	652.835	23.3129
70	760.177	26.4467
80	854.101	30.043
90	961.443	33.1649
100	1055.37	36.7489

From Table 3 it can be seen that for a small data sets up to 30 files, the actual speedup (in Table 2) is only 2 .. 2.5 times less than theoretical speedup (in Table 3), but for larger data sets the difference reaches 10 times or even more. This suggests that there is a room for further optimization. For example, one can use caching and/or direct file transfer between worker processes.

We also set up a testbed for testing the orchestrator application in the desktop grid running the Everest platform. The tuning and testing of its functionality was carried out similarly to [17], except that the ART skeleton with the OPTIM sort tournament was used in the orchestrator.

7   Discussion

Let's discuss some particularities of our approach. The article presents a sorting method that resembles bubble sorting (see the algorithm (1)), except that it uses blocks and is parallel. This similarity leads to some loss of performance, but makes sorting applicable to desktop grids.

Both the TRIV and OPTIM sorting algorithms correspond to the ART skeleton. They differ only in DAG diameters. The OPTIM sorting has less diameter, thus potentially more parallel. The advantage of TRIV sorting over OPTIM sorting is that it takes up less memory. The TRIV sorting has linear memory complexity by block number (see [17] for details).

The difference between our work and [18] is that the All Pairs skeleton implies task independence and is performance oriented. For example, the ART skeleton prohibits simultaneous submission of (1, 2) and (2, 3) tasks, (1, 2) and (1, 3) tasks, etc. The problem of performance optimization, solved in AllPairs, is also of interest to our skeleton, but is not covered in this article.

The scope of application of our method includes the scope of the AllPairs skeleton. In addition, the method can be used to solve problems in which the processing of a pair implies write access to the data area associated with the element of the pair. For example, we plan to use Everest platform to determine the frequency of words in Twitter on an enterprise desktop grid during periods of it inactivity.

The MapReduce [19] skeleton is beyond the scope of our work because it is based on peer-to-peer communication between compute nodes. On the contrary, desktop grid systems, namely systems built on the Everest platform, support the star topology.

There are a number of grid systems that use static DAGs of tasks, for example DAGman meta scheduler in the HTCondor (https://research.cs.wisc.edu/htcondor/). Using dynamic tasks helps us to manage larger graphs potentially with millions of tasks. This feature was demonstrated in the experiments and shown in Table 1.

8   Conclusions

A method for the development of algorithmic skeletons for automating computations in enterprise desktop grids based on a variant of the actor model of calculations is proposed. The method was successfully applied to the development of the skeleton called asynchronous round-robin tournament. The practical use of the asynchronous round-robin tournament skeleton to build the orchestrator of a grid system was demonstrated in solving the block sorting problem.

References

1. González-Vélez, H., Leyton, M.: A survey of algorithmic skeleton frameworks: high-level structured parallel programming enablers. Softw.: Pract. Exp. **40**(12), 1135–1160 (2010)
2. Volkov, S., Sukhoroslov, O.: Running parameter sweep applications on everest cloud platform. In: Computer Research and Modeling, vol. 7, no. 3, pp. 601–606. Institute of Computer Science, Izhevsk (2015)
3. Schlinker, B., Mysore, R.N.: Condor: better topologies through declarative design. In: Schlinker, B., Mysore, R.N. (eds.) Proceedings of the 2015 ACM Conference on Special Interest Group on Data Communication, SIGCOMM 2015, pp. 449–463. Association for Computing Machinery, Inc., London (2015)

4. Anderson, D.P.: BOINC: a system for public-resource computing and storage. In: Proceedings - IEEE/ACM International Workshop on Grid Computing, pp. 4–10. IEEE, Pittsburgh (2004)

5. Fedak, G., Germain, C., Neri, V., Cappello, F.: XtremWeb: a generic global computing system. In: Proceedings - 1st IEEE/ACM International Symposium on Cluster Computing and the Grid, CCGrid 2001, no. 923246, pp. 582–587. IEEE, Brisbane (2001)

6. Andrade, N., Cirne, W., Brasileiro, F., Roisenberg, P.: OurGrid: an approach to easily assemble grids with equitable resource sharing. In: Feitelson, D., Rudolph, L., Schwiegelshohn, U. (eds.) JSSPP 2003. LNCS, vol. 2862, pp. 61–86. Springer, Heidelberg (2003). https://doi.org/10.1007/10968987_4

7. Afanasyev, A.P., Lovas, R.: Increasing the computing power of distributed systems with the help of grid systems from personal computers. In: Afanasyev, A.P., Lovas, R. (eds.) Proceedings of the Conference "Parallel Computational Technologies (PCT 2011)", pp. 6–14. Publishing Centre NRU, Chelyabinsk (2011)

8. Cérin, C., Fedak, G.: Desktop Grid Computing. CRC Press, Paris (2012)

9. Choi, S., Kim, H.: Characterizing and classifying desktop grid. In: Choi, S., Kim, H., (eds.) Proceedings - Seventh IEEE International Symposium on Cluster Computing and the Grid, CCGrid, no. 4215446, pp. 743–748. IEEE, Rio De Janeiro (2007)

10. Ivashko, E.: Enterprise desktop grids. In: CEUR Workshop Proceedings, vol. 1502, pp. 16–21. CEUR-WS, Dubna (2015)

11. Mazalov, V.V., Nikitina, N.N., Ivashko, E.E.: Task scheduling in a desktop grid to minimize the server load. In: Malyshkin, V. (ed.) PaCT 2015. LNCS, vol. 9251, pp. 273–278. Springer, Cham (2015). https://doi.org/10.1007/978-3-319-21909-7_27

12. De Koster, J., Van Cutsem, T., De Meuter, W.: 43 years of actors: a taxonomy of actor models and their key properties. In: Proceedings of the 6th International Workshop on Programming Based on Actors, Agents, and Decentralized Control, co-located with SPLASH, AGERE 2016, pp. 31–40. Association for Computing Machinery, Inc., New York (2016)

13. Senger, H., da Silva, F.A.B.: Bounds on the scalability of bag-of-tasks applications running on master-slave platforms. Parallel Process. Lett. **22**(2), 1250004 (2012)

14. Farkas, Z., Kacsuk, P., Balaton, Z., Gombás, G.: Interoperability of BOINC and EGEE. Future Gener. Comput. Syst. **26**(8), 1092–1103 (2010)

15. Afanasiev, A.P., Bychkov, I.V., Zaikin, O.S.: Concept of a multitask grid system with a flexible allocation of idle computational resources of supercomputers. J. Comput. Syst. Sci. Int. **56**(4), 701–707 (2017). https://doi.org/10.1134/s1064230717040025

16. Sukhoroslov, O., Volkov, S., Afanasiev, A.A.: Web-based platform for publication and distributed execution of computing applications. In: 14th International Symposium on Parallel and Distributed Computing (ISPDC), pp. 175–184. IEEE (2015)

17. Vostokin, S.V., Sukhoroslov, O.V., Bobyleva, I.V., Popov, S.N.: Implementing computations with dynamic task dependencies in the desktop grid environment using Everest and Templet Web. In: CEUR Workshop Proceedings, vol. 2267, pp. 271–275. CEUR-WS, Dubna (2018)

18. Moretti, C., Bulosan, J., Thain, D., Flynn, P.J.: All-pairs: an abstraction for data-intensive cloud computing. In: 2008 IEEE International Symposium on Parallel and Distributed Processing, pp. 1–11. IEEE (2008)

19. Dean, J., Ghemawat, S.: MapReduce: simplified data processing on large clusters. Commun. ACM **51**(1), 107–113 (2008)

Roadmap for Improving Volunteer Distributed Computing Project Performance

Vladimir Yakimets[1,2] and Ilya Kurochkin[1(✉)]

[1] Institute for Information Transmission Problems of Russian Academy
of Sciences, Moscow, Russia
iakimets@mail.ru, kurochkin@iitp.ru
[2] The Russian Presidential Academy of National Economy
and Public Administration, Moscow, Russia

Abstract. The methodology for improving activities of distributed computing projects with the participation of volunteers based on the results of multiparameter and index estimates is considered. Such project estimates provide a strategy for improving the work of a voluntary distributed computing project to streamline the process of building the appropriate road map. The concept of "target reference point" is introduced, with the help of which the project team, taking into account its specificity and available resource capabilities, in all parameters forms a vector of target values that are going to be achieved within a given time. Four options for selecting "targets" that set the direction of the roadmap for the development of the project of voluntary distributed computing are proposed. The results of a survey of the volunteer community on multiparameter evaluation of projects for 2016–2018 are described. The example of the Gerasim@home project shows how to improve its activities for the selected version of the targets. The results of changes in the project activities are discussed.

Keywords: Voluntary distributed computing (VDC) · The VDC project · Volunteers · Evaluation index of the VDC project · Characteristics for assessing the quality of VDC projects · Project targets · Road map for improving project performance

1 Introduction

The use of desktop grid systems (desktop grid) for solving scientific computing problems gained popularity in the late twentieth century. With the lack of computing power of multiprocessor computing systems for a certain type of tasks, divided by data (bag of tasks) [1] began to use a variety of distributed computing systems. The idea of using idle resources of personal computers and other personal devices in scientific computing experiments has become particularly popular, both in terms of efficient use of resources, and in terms of creating distributed computing systems based on available computing resources.

There was software for the organization of distributed computing systems, for example, Legion [2], HTCondor [3], Oracle Grid Engine [4], BOINC [5]. With the help

© Springer Nature Switzerland AG 2019
V. Voevodin and S. Sobolev (Eds.): RuSCDays 2019, CCIS 1129, pp. 690–700, 2019.
https://doi.org/10.1007/978-3-030-36592-9_56

of this software, it was possible to quickly and easily deploy grid computing systems, which used the computing power of both educational and scientific organizations, and the power of volunteers. Grid systems deployed to solve a single scientific problem or to conduct a series of similar experiments can be called distributed computing projects. If the computing power of volunteers was used, then the projects of voluntary distributed computing (VDC projects). As a rule, the organizers of the VDC projects were groups of scientists who were interested, first of all, in carrying out large computational experiments. In addition to attracting the computing power of volunteers, the organizers of the VDC projects could use the VDC project to promote both their research and science in General.

The volunteers community at the moment is several million people from around the world, and the total power of already connected computing devices to the VDC projects only on the BOINC platform is comparable to the most powerful supercomputers from the top500 rating [6].

One of the largest projects on the BOINC platform is the world Community Grid project of IBM Corporation, in which more than 700 thousand users participate and more than 5 million computing devices (personal computers, servers, smartphones, etc.) are connected [7]. This umbrella [8] project brings together several medical subprojects on topical issues: mapping cancer markers, the search for drugs for Zika virus, microbiome immunity project, etc. Or, for example, the first successful Russian project of voluntary distributed computing SAT@home to solve problems using the SAT-approach [9].

Within the framework of scientific projects of distributed computing, volunteers not only provide their computing resources, but also process images and other data obtained, conduct observations of birds, insects and the starry sky. For example, a project to classify different types of galaxies Zooniverse [10]. Or group of projects of the ornithological laboratory of the Cornell University [11].

The use of volunteers in research projects is denoted by the term citizen science and is a type of crowdsourcing [12]. As a rule, volunteers are given fairly simple tasks: to process the photo according to a certain algorithm, to find differences in two similar images, to find and highlight certain objects in satellite images. Interaction with the community of volunteers in solving certain scientific problems can increase the scale of research and free scientists from routine unskilled work. Improving mutual understanding with individual volunteers and the community as a whole will improve the effectiveness of the project [13]. It will be difficult to reach an understanding without feedback from the volunteer community, so tools to generate different assessments are needed to effectively support the project using volunteers.

As part of the tasks of forecasting, managing the development of different areas of knowledge, technology, products, etc. Recently, the method of constructing roadmaps has been widely used [14–16].

Most often, it is associated with the use of forecasting methods based on the use of the foresight concept which are able to have a maximum impact on the economy and society in the medium and long-term perspectives [14].

There is a wide variety of definitions of the concept of a roadmap and approaches to their construction.

Bearing in mind these and other similar definitions, let us consider the option of constructing a roadmap taking into account the specifics of the object of our research – voluntary distributed computing projects (VDC). By roadmap we mean the chosen development (or improvement) of the VDC project, corresponding to the group opinion of the representatives of the distributed team of project participants, describing and visualizing the desired state of the VDC project, taking into account the capabilities and resources of the project team.

In relation to the VDC projects, the roadmap is a detailed vision of the future in the content-specific direction of this project, and this vision is based on collective knowledge and assessments of scientists and specialists working in this field of activity.

Earlier, for a set of studied projects, a common methodology was developed for constructing a multiparameter portrait obtained as a result of processing individual assessments by specialists of the current state of projects on previously selected scales [17]. Based on the averaged group estimates of each of the VDC projects, differences in multiparameter portraits were identified. Some projects revealed a group of parameters with group estimates below the average, others had a subset of parameters with relatively high ratings, and the third dominated average ratings.

The task naturally arose as to how and what can be offered to project teams in order to improve the portraits of projects, based on the capabilities and limitations of the teams.

2 Additional Tasks for Desktop Grid

The organizers of the VDC projects in addition to solving scientific problems impose additional responsibilities:

1. Deployment and maintenance of the VDC project;
2. Increasing the computing power of the VDC project technical methods (fine-tuning desktop grid);
3. The increasing computing ability of the VDC project by bringing the resources of volunteers;
4. Hold the computational resources of volunteers in the VDC project.

If the team of organizers of the VDC project consists of one or several people, the solution of these problems is carried out on the residual principle. But the need for a method of determining the most important directions of development of the VDC project is very high.

3   Roadmap for VDC Project

The development of a roadmap for the development of our facility is necessary and justified if the management and team of the VDC project, having studied the multi-parameter assessment of the project, thinks about the possibility of competitive development and seeks to consider the existing ways of forming a strategic plan for making changes in the activities of the VDC project.

It is known that a well-designed roadmap should contain the following important components:

1. Project objective;
2. List of important tasks (activities) with identification of persons responsible for their implementation;
3. Significant requirements for the results of activities (works), for the implementation of which certain members of the VDC project team are responsible;
4. Estimate the time spent on each activity;
5. Possible options for different ways of project implementation and control points at each stage of its implementation.

In our case, the aim of the project is to form a set of possible strategies for the development of individual VDC projects, based on multiparameter assessments of their status, and choose an acceptable version of the strategy that improves the status of the VDC project, taking into account the capabilities and limitations of the team.

We will not deal here with a detailed review of the work on components 2–4 of the roadmap, but will focus on component 5.

Below are several alternative options for constructing additional maps to improve the status of VDC projects aimed at achieving targets for a predetermined project team subset of parameters.

We introduce the concept of a target point (hereinafter TP) when creating a road map. Co is the desired and achievable value of a single parameter of the VDC project, the size of which the team has a consensus (in the form of a qualified or simple majority). The value of TP for each negotiated parameter is chosen in the interval [0–1] and the upper is marked with an asterisk. For example, 0.75*.

There are 4 scenarios for the TP, which specifies the formation of possible strategies for improving the activity of VDC project:

A. TP not equivalent for all parameters: the orientation on the achievement by the project team of the vector are not equal, but desirable and achievable TP for all parameters with the command.

B. Setting the co for the selected subset of parameters: focus on the achievement of the project team vector desired and achievable co on the selected parameters, taking into account the specifics of the project.

C. co for the selected subset of priority parameters (with high values of significance coefficients): the orientation of the team to increase the values of the subset of the most significant parameters of evaluation of VDC projects.

D. co for the selected subset of parameters for which the project received low estimates.

Building a road map for each VDC project using these options consists of the following steps:

1. The project team chooses one or all 4 approaches.
2. For each selected approach, the TP are set according to the specified number of parameters. The rule of consensus or majority shall apply. Thus, the vector tp = {tp (1), tp(2), …, tp(m)} is formed. Here m is the number of parameters selected by the project team within approaches B, C and D. In case of option A, the vector includes all n parameters.
3. The values of the YaK-index are calculated using the co vector.
4. After calculating the values of the YaK-index by the values of the co for each of the 4 approaches, they are compared and, taking into account the capabilities of the team, a decision is made on choosing an acceptable strategy for improving the performance of the VDC project.
5. A set of tasks and actions that must be implemented to achieve the set values of the co (components 2–4 of roadmap).

4 Methods of Obtaining Data for Multivariate Assessment of VDC Projects

4.1 Questionnaire for Multiparameter Assessment of VDC Projects

In 2016–2018, a survey of the international community of volunteers was conducted to determine a weighted multiparameter assessment of the VDC projects in which volunteers participate. The multiparameter assessment consisted of the following 9 characteristics of the VDC project:

1. Clear design intent;
2. Scientific component of the project;
3. Quality of scientific and popular scientific publications on the project topic;
4. The design of the project (website, certificate screensaver);
5. Informative materials on the project website;
6. Visualization of project results (photo, video, infographics);
7. Organization of feedback (forums, chats, etc.);
8. Promotion of volunteers' participation in the project (competitions, scoring system, prizes);
9. Easy to join the project (no barriers and organizational and technical difficulties).

Each characteristic had not only a score from −2 to 2, but also its weight from 0 to 10.

In 2016, Russian and English versions of the questionnaire were formed. In 2018, the German and French versions of the questionnaire were added. A total of 402 questionnaires were collected (see Table 1).

Table 1. Distribution of questionnaires by VDC projects

VDC project	Number of questionnaires
SAT@home	56
SETI@home	32
Einstein@home	29
Gerasim@home	29
Rosetta@home	28
Asteroids@home	21
LHC@home	20
RakeSearch	18
MilkyWay@home	18
PrimeGrid	18
Folding@home	14
POGS@home	14
Collatz Conjecture	13
World Community Grid	13
Acoustics@home	8
Other projects	71
Total	**402**

Since information about the questionnaire was mainly distributed on the Russian-language volunteer sites, and in the preamble to the 2018 questionnaire there was a recommendation to evaluate first of all the projects of the Russian origin, the following distribution of the number of questionnaires by language was obtained (see Table 2).

Table 2. Distribution of questionnaires by language

VDC project	Number of questionnaires
Russian	252
English	133
French	9
German	8

4.2   Weights of Characteristics

To increase the information content, the characteristics were sorted in descending order of weight. In this case, a radar chart with averaged weights for all projects will look like Fig. 1.

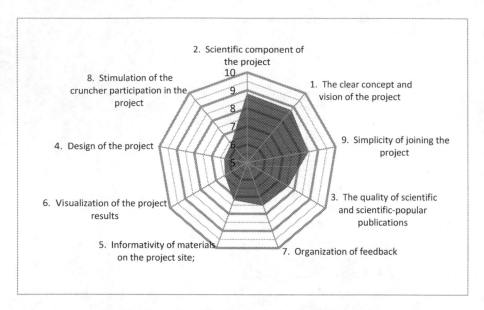

Fig. 1. Average weight characteristics of the VDC project

The values of the average weights of the project characteristics for the period from 2016 to 2018 have changed slightly (see Fig. 2).

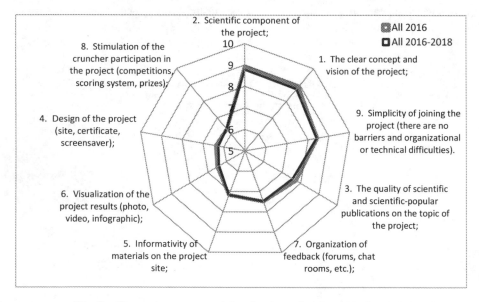

Fig. 2. Change in average weights for the period from 2016 to 2018

Therefore, the average data for the entire period 2016–2018 will be taken as the average estimate and the average weights.

4.3   Multiparameter Evaluation of Gerasim@home VDC Project in 2016

When analyzing the materials of multiparameter evaluation of Gerasim@home project in 2016 (Fig. 3 and Table 3), found that five of the nine characteristics of this VDC project had low scores from 3 to 4 points on a five-point scale, including:

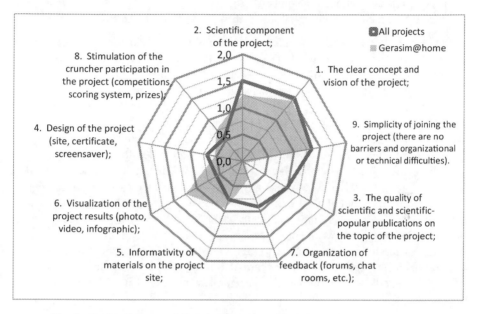

Fig. 3. Radar diagram of Gerasim@home project by questionnaires for 2016

Table 3. Weight and evaluation of characteristics for the project Gerasim@home in 2016

#	Characteristics	Weight for all project	Weight for Gerasim@home	Evaluation of characteristics
1	The clear concept and vision of the project	8.89	8.94	1.47
2	Scientific component of the project	8.94	8.06	1.24
3	The quality of scientific and scientific-popular publications about project	7.75	6.35	0.06
4	Design of the project (site, certificate, screensaver)	6.37	7.35	0.53
5	Informativity of materials on the project site	7.17	6.59	0.94
6	Visualization of the project results (photo, video, infographic)	6.49	8.71	1.24
7	Organization of feedback (forums, chat rooms, etc.)	7.49	7.18	0.35
8	Stimulation of the cruncher participation (competitions, scoring, prizes)	6.31	8.00	0.76
9	Simplicity of joining the project	8.44	8.35	1.35

- the quality of scientific and popular scientific publications on the project – just above 3 points (0.06 in our scale from −2 to +2 points);
- organization of feedback (forums, chats, etc.) – about 3.3 points (0.35);
- project design (website, certificate, screensaver) – just above 3.5 points (0.53);
- promotion of Cruncher's participation in the project (competitions, points accrual system, prizes) – about 3.7 points (0.76);
- Informative materials on the project website – 3.9 points (0.94).

The project team decided to make efforts to improve the situation on these aspects of the work, using the approach D to the construction and implementation of the roadmap to improve their project. At the same time, the values of the targets (co) for the five selected characteristics were set to 1 point (on a scale from −2 to +2 points). The justification for this choice of co values was justified by the fact that the capabilities of the project team were taken into account, on the one hand, and a strategy was laid to "bring" the values of these characteristics to the level of estimates for all projects (Fig. 3) in parallel, achieving higher values of the YaK-index for your project.

Almost two years of purposeful work of The Gerasim@home project team bore fruit. For four of the five selected characteristics, the targets were exceeded (see Fig. 1) (4). Comparing the data of Tables 3 and 4, we see that only one characteristic failed to achieve (slightly) co – is "the quality of scientific and popular publications on the project." Here the score was about 3.9 points (0.93).

At the same time, in the course of improving the activities of the project, the staff thought about the need for a clearer formulation of the idea and the scientific component. (see the two most significant characteristics #2 and #1 in Fig. 4 and Table 4).

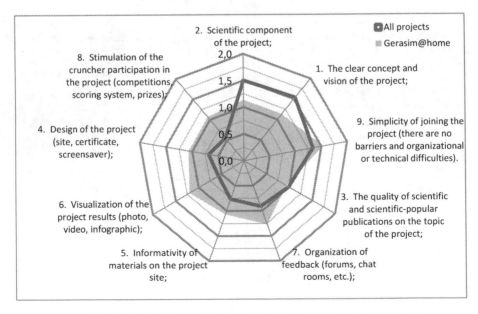

Fig. 4. Radar diagram for the project Gerasim@home in 2018

Table 4. Weight and evaluation of characteristics for the project Gerasim@home in 2018

#	Characteristics	Weight for all project	Weight for Gerasim@home	Evaluation of characteristics
1	The clear concept and vision of the project	8.89	7.73	1.13
2	Scientific component of the project	8.94	7.73	1.13
3	The quality of scientific and scientific-popular publications about project	7.75	7.60	0.93
4	Design of the project (site, certificate, screensaver)	6.37	7.60	1.07
5	Informativity of materials on the project site	7.17	8.07	1.07
6	Visualization of the project results (photo, video, infographic)	6.49	7.93	1.20
7	Organization of feedback (forums, chat rooms, etc.)	7.49	8.53	1.27
8	Stimulation of the cruncher participation (competitions, scoring, prizes)	6.31	7.53	1.07
9	Simplicity of joining the project	8.44	8.53	1.53

4.4   Multiparameter Evaluation of Gerasim@home VDC Project in 2018

Note that the YaK-index of the Gerasim@home project in 2016 was equal to 0.589, and in 2018 the values of this index for the Gerasim@home project grew to 0.628.

5   Conclusions

The proposed approaches to improve the VDC project for the community of volunteers allow the organizing team to minimize the efforts to support the VDC projects and concentrate on the most important targets for them. The collected data in the framework of the survey on evaluating the VDC projects make it possible not only to assess the dynamics of the multiparameter assessment of the VDC project, but also to compare the current project performance indicators with other VDC projects.

The proposed approaches can be applied not only in VDC projects, but also in other projects in which it is necessary to interact with the community of volunteers.

Acknowledgements. This work was funded by Russian Science Foundation (№16-11-10352).

References

1. Benoit, A., et al.: Scheduling concurrent bag-of-tasks applications on heterogeneous platforms. IEEE Trans. Comput. **59**(2), 202–217 (2010)
2. Grimshaw, A.S., Wulf, W.A.: The Legion vision of a worldwide virtual computer. Commun. ACM **40**(1), 39–45 (1997)

3. Litzkow, M.J., Livny, M., Mutka, M.W.: Condor-a hunter of idle workstations. Distrib. Comput. Syst. (1988)
4. Gentzsch, W.: Sun grid engine: towards creating a compute power grid. In: Proceedings First IEEE/ACM International Symposium on Cluster Computing and the Grid, pp. 35–36. IEEE, May 2001
5. Anderson, D.P.: BOINC: a system for public-resource computing and storage. Grid Comput. (2004)
6. The server of statistics of voluntary distributed computing projects on the BOINC platform. http://boincstats.com. Accessed 14 Apr 2019
7. Site of World Community Grid project. http://www.worldcommunitygrid.org. Accessed 14 Apr 2019
8. Kurochkin, I.I.: The umbrella project of volunteer distributed computing Optima@ home. In: CEUR Workshop Proceedings, vol. 1973, pp. 35–42 (2017)
9. Posypkin, M., Semenov, A., Zaikin, O.: Using BOINC desktop grid to solve large scale SAT problems. Comput. Sci. **13**(1), 25–34 (2012)
10. Simpson, R., Page, K.R., De Roure, D.: Zooniverse: observing the world's largest citizen science platform. In: Proceedings of the 23rd International Conference on World Wide Web, pp. 1049–1054. ACM (2014)
11. Bonney, R., et al.: Citizen science: a developing tool for expanding science knowledge and scientific literacy. BioScience **59**(11), 977–984 (2009)
12. Wynn, J.: Citizen Science in the Digital Age: Rhetoric, Science, and Public Engagement. University of Alabama Press (2017)
13. Jennett, C., et al.: Motivations, learning and creativity in online citizen science. J. Sci. Commun. **15**(3) (2016)
14. Manchulyantsev, O.A., Pavlycheva, E.Yu., Krasova, E.N., Tkacheva, A.V.: Roadmaps of Russian Business: Analytical Report on the Study. Open Innovation Inc, Moscow (2012)
15. Karasyov, O.I., Doroshenko, M.E.: Use of a method of road maps for formation of perspective vision of development of mega-regulation of financial sector in Russia. Bull. Moscow State Univ. (Econ. Ser.) **6**(4), 75–98 (2015)
16. Willyard, C.H., McClees, C.W.: Motorola's Technology Roadmap Process. Research Management, pp. 13–19 (1987)
17. Yakimets, V.N., Kurochkin, I.I.: Analysis of results of the rating of volunteer distributed computing projects. In: Voevodin, V., Sobolev, S. (eds.) RuSCDays 2018. CCIS, vol. 965, pp. 472–486. Springer, Cham (2019). https://doi.org/10.1007/978-3-030-05807-4_40

SAT-Based Cryptanalysis: From Parallel Computing to Volunteer Computing

Oleg Zaikin[✉][ID]

ISDCT SB RAS, Irkutsk, Russia
zaikin.icc@gmail.com

Abstract. Volunteer computing is a powerful tool for solving hard problems by the divide-and-conquer approach. During the last decade, several hard cryptanalysis problems were solved in the volunteer computing project SAT@home. In this study, the preliminary stage of these experiments are described: how SAT-based cryptanalysis problems are chosen; how these problems are studied on a computing cluster using state-of-the-art multithreaded SAT solvers; how decompositions of the chosen SAT problems are constructed using a Monte Carlo method; how server and client software are prepared for the corresponding experiments in SAT@home. These issues are described in application to several stream ciphers, for which it is planned to launch experiments in SAT@home.

Keywords: Volunteer computing · BOINC · SAT · Cryptanalysis

1 Introduction

Nowadays a lot of hard scientific problems satisfy the following two conditions. First, such problems can be decomposed into independent subinstances (i.e. they are embarrassingly parallel [1]). Second, their solving requires the necessity to involve plenty of computational resources for months or even years. Such problems appear, for example, in the following areas: astronomy, medicine, cryptography, combinatorics. Scientific problems of the mentioned kind are not well-suited for computing clusters. First, computing clusters are designed for solving problems in which the fine-grained (or, at least, the coarse-grained) parallelism [2] is used. It means that experiments based on the embarrassing parallelism surely can be run on a cluster, but its fast interconnect (that is quite expensive) will be almost idle. Second, as a rule, any computing task can be run on a cluster for limited amount of time (usually not more than a week). In order to overcome this restriction, an initial embarrassingly parallel problem should be divided into a family of tasks, each of which must be run manually one after another. Intermediate results should be saved in this case.

In opposite to the cluster computing (that is a special case of the parallel computing), the volunteer computing [3] is a quite cheap and natural method to solve embarassingly parallel computationally hard problems. Volunteer computing is a type of distributed computing that is based on using computers of

© Springer Nature Switzerland AG 2019
V. Voevodin and S. Sobolev (Eds.): RuSCDays 2019, CCIS 1129, pp. 701–712, 2019.
https://doi.org/10.1007/978-3-030-36592-9_57

private persons, which are called volunteers. Each volunteer computing project is designed to solve one or several hard problems. If authors of a volunteer project take into account volunteers' feedback, the project can can attract quite large computational resources [4].

During the last two decades, a number of important and challenging problems from the aforementioned areas were successfully solved in volunteer computing projects. Most of such projects are based on the BOINC platform [5] that was developed in Berkeley in 2002. Note, that BOINC can be also used to create non-volunteer desktop grids [6].

In 2011, the BOINC-based volunteer computing project SAT@home was launched [7]. It is aimed at solving computationally hard problems that can be reduced to the Boolean satisfiability problem [8].

According to SAT-based cryptanalsysis, an initial problem is reduced to SAT and solved using SAT solvers [9]. It is in fact is a special type of the algebraic cryptanalysis [10]. In the last decade, SAT-based cryptanalysis have been applied to the following stream ciphers and keystream generators: Crypto-1 [11]; Hitag-2 [11,12]; Bivium [11,13–16]; Trivium [15–18]; A5/1 [14,16,19]; alternating step generator [15,20]; Grain_v1, Mickey and Rabbit [18]; ZUC [21]; stream ciphers from the CAESAR competition [22].

A number of SAT-based cryptanalsysis problems were solved in SAT@home. The corresponding results were published in, e.g., [14]. However, the preliminary stage of the corresponding computational experiments has not been described in detail yet. This study is aimed at filling this gap. The contribution of this paper is as follows.

1. It is described how cryptanalysis problems are chosen for SAT@home.
2. It is shown how the hardness of the chosen problems is studied on a computing cluster using state-of-the-art multithreaded SAT solvers.
3. It is discussed how decompositions of the chosen problems are constructed using a Monte Carlo method and why some of the problems are discarded for further study in SAT@home.

All these issues are described for four keystream generators, for three of which it is planned to launch experiments in SAT@home in the nearest future.

Let us give a brief outline of the paper. In the next section, SAT@home is discussed, as well as SAT-based cryptanalsysis problems solved in it. Section 3 describes SAT-based cryptanalysis problems considered in the present study. In Sect. 4, a preliminary computational study of these problems is presented. Also, details of a computational experiment prepared for launching in SAT@home are discussed. Finally, conclusions are drawn.

2   Cryptanalysis Problems Solved in SAT@home

Problems from various areas (verification, cryptography, combinatorics, bioinformatics, etc.) can be effectively reduced to the Boolean satisfiability problem (SAT) [8]. SAT problems are usually considered as the problems of search for solutions of Boolean equations in the form of CNF = 1, where CNF stands for Conjunctive Normal Form. All known SAT solving algorithms are exponential in the worst case since SAT itself is NP-hard. Nevertheless, modern SAT solvers successfully cope with many classes of benchmarks based on the problems from the areas mentioned above.

In [23] and [24], SAT has been solved in parallel using non-public BOINC-based desktop grids. In 2011 the public BOINC-based volunteer computing project SAT@home [7] was started. It is aimed at solving hard SAT instances.

While SAT-based cryptanalysis problems are usually quite hard, it makes sense to solve them in parallel. There are two main approaches to parallel SAT solving: the Divide-and-Conquer and the Portfolio [25]. According to the Portfolio approach [26], many different sequential SAT solvers solve the same original SAT instance simultaneously. In the Divide-and-Conquer approach [27], the original instance is decomposed into a family of simpler subinstances that are solved separately by sequential solvers. In SAT@home, the following variant of the Divide-and-Conquer approach is used (see [14]): for a given CNF, a set of Boolean variables is chosen (it is called *decomposition set*) and all possible values of this variables are varied. As a result, a family of simpler subinstances is formed, in each of which values of the decomposition set are known.

In SAT@home, SAT-based cryptanalysis of several keystream generators was studied. Keystream generator is a discrete function that given a quite short binary sequence (secret key) produces a binary sequence (keystream) of any required size. By secret key for a keystream generator it is meant a state of the generator's registers before the producing of the first keystream bit. Hereinafter we consider a plaintext attack on keystream generators in the following formulation: based on the known fragment of keystream, it is required to find a secret key that was used to produce the fragment. Keystream generators are used as cryptographic primitives in stream ciphers [28]. That is why it is very important to study the cryptographic resistance of keystream generators.

In SAT@home, SAT-based cryptanalysis of two keystream generators was performed: A5/1 and Bivium. The corresponding results are briefly described below. The A5/1 keystream generator uses 3 linear feedback shift registers (LFSRs, see [28]) of sizes 19, 22 and 23 bits [29]. Thus, this generator has a secret key of 64 bits. An experiment aimed at solving 10 cryptanalysis instances of A5/1 was held in SAT@home from December 2011 to May 2012. Keystream fragments of size 144 were used. Each SAT instance was decomposed using the decomposition set S_1 from [14] (31 variables). Thus, for each instances at most 2^{31} subinstances should have been solved. All 10 instances constructed this way were successfully solved in SAT@home (i.e. the corresponding secret keys were found) in about 5 months. The second experiment on the cryptanalysis of A5/1 was launched in SAT@home in May 2014. The decomposition set S_3 was used [14]. Its size was 32 variables. All 10 instances from this experiment were solved within 4 months.

Bivium uses two shift registers [30]. The first register contains 93 cells, the second one contains 84 cells. Thus, Bivium has a secret key of size 177. Here we followed [13] and set the keystream fragment size to 200 bits. SAT-based cryptanalysis of Bivium turned out to be very hard [14], that is why we decided to solve several weakened cryptanalysis instances of this generator. Below we use the notation *BiviumK* to denote a weakened problem for Bivium with known values of K variables encoding the last K cells of the second shift register. Five instances of *Bivium9* were solved in SAT@home in 2014. In the corresponding experiment, the decomposition set from [14] was used (43 variables).

In 2016, another approach to solving weakened Bivium instances was tried [31]. On the first stage, a SAT instance was processed on a computing cluster by running the parallel SAT solver PDSAT [14] in the solving mode (using a decomposition set). During this process, the time limit of 0.1 s for every subinstance was used. By writing to a file, PDSAT collected all subinstances which could not be solved within the time limit. It turned out, that this approach allowed to solve 2 out of 3 instances of *Bivium10* on a cluster. It means that, despite the time limit, PDSAT found a satisfying assignments for these 2 instances. Solving the remaining cryptanalysis instance was performed in SAT@home based on the files collected by PDSAT.

3   New SAT-Based Cryptanalysis Problems

SAT@home is inactive since autumn 2016. However, it is planned to restart it soon. In this paper, details of the future experiments are given.

In the present study, SAT-based cryptanalysis of the following keystream generators is considered: Grain_v1 [32]; Mickey [33]; shrinking [34]; self-shrinking [35]. The shrinking and self-shrinking generators were chosen because they have not been analyzed by SAT-based cryptanalysis yet. As for Grain_v1 and Mickey, weakened SAT-based cryptanalysis problems have not been solved for them before.

Grain_v1 and Mickey are the finalists of the eSTREAM project [36]. Grain_v1 uses two shift registers, each of size 80 bits. The first of them is a non-linear feedback shift register, the second one is an LFSR. Mickey uses two shift registers, each of size 100 bits. Registers, as well as output functions of Grain_v1 and Mickey are described in [32] and [33] respectively.

The shrinking generator uses two LFSRs, where the first one controls the second one [34]. In the present study, two variants of the shrinking generator were analyzed: with 64-bit and 72-bit secret keys. They are denoted as SHRINKING-SC64 and SHRINKING-SC72 respectively. SHRINKING-SC64 uses LFSRs defined by the following polynomials:

1. LFSR 1 (31-bit): $X^{31} + X^7 + 1$;
2. LFSR 2 (33-bit): $X^{33} + X^{16} + X^4 + X + 1$.

Note, that in fact the first and the third LFSRs from A5/1 were used [29]. SHRINKING-SC72 uses LFSRs defined by the following polynomials:

1. LFSR 1 (35-bit): $X^{35} + X^{33} + 1$;
2. LFSR 2 (37-bit): $X^{37} + X^5 + X^4 + X^3 + X^2 + X + 1$.

The self-shrinking generator uses one LFSR [35]. In the present study, variants with 64-bit and 72-bit secret keys were analyzed. They are denoted as SELF-SHRINKING-SC64 and SELF-SHRINKING-SC72 respectively. They use LFSRs defined by the following polynomials: $X^{64} + X^{63} + X^{61} + X^{60} + 1$; $X^{72} + X^{66} + X^{25} + X^{19} + 1$.

The characteristics of the considered keystream generators are presented in Table 1.

Table 1. Characteristics of the keystream generators. Sizes are presented in bits.

Generator	Secret key size	Analyzed keystream size
Grain_v1	160	200
Mickey	200	250
SHRINKING-SC64	64	96
SHRINKING-SC72	72	108
SELF-SHRINKING-SC64	64	96
SELF-SHRINKING-SC72	72	108

SAT encodings of Grain_v1 and Mickey were taken from [18]. In order to construct SAT encodings of the shrinking and the self-shrinking generators, the TRANSALG tool was employed [37]. The characteristics of the SAT encodings are presented in Table 2.

Table 2. Characteristics of the SAT encodings.

Generator	Variables	Clauses	Size (Mb)
Grain_v1	2 425	47 702	1.4
Mickey	72 078	586 080	15.3
SHRINKING-SC64	121 017	396 003	7.5
SHRINKING-SC72	147 849	498 319	10.1
SELF-SHRINKING-SC64	148 554	481 990	9.3
SELF-SHRINKING-SC72	182 718	592 898	11.6

While Grain_v1 and Mickey are very resistant to any known type of cryptanalysis, two weakened cryptanalysis problems are considered for both of them. For Grain_v1, in the first (second) variant only the first 64 (72) bits of the secret key are unknown, while all remaining 96 (88) bits out of 160 are known (i.e. correct values of these variables are assigned in a CNF). As for Mickey, only the first 64 (72) bits out of 200 are unknown. The corresponding crypt-analysis problems are denoted as GRAIN-V1-SC-FIRST64, GRAIN-V1-SC-FIRST72, MICKEY-SC-FIRST64, and MICKEY-SC-FIRST72 respectively.

4   Preparation of Experiment for SAT@home

In this section, 8 SAT-based cryptanalysis problems are studied (see Sect. 3). For each of these problems 3 instances were constructed by randomly generating secret keys. Thus, 24 SAT instances were constructed in total.

In Subsect. 4.1, these 24 SAT instances are studied by state-of-the-art multithreaded SAT solvers. On the one hand, this stage is required to check which instances are simple enough to be solved by such solvers in reasonable time. On the other hand, hard instances, which have not been solved by any of considered solvers in reasonable time, can be considered as good candidates for a BOINC-based project. In Subsect. 4.2, decomposition sets for the hard instances are found. In Subsect. 4.3, details of the future experiments in SAT@home are given, which are based on the found decompositions sets.

4.1   Analysis via Multithreaded Solvers

Three multithreaded SAT solvers were chosen to study the considered 24 SAT instances: PLINGELING2018 [38], PAINLESS-MCOMSPS [25], ABCDSAT-P18 [39]. They are the top-3 solvers from the Parallel track of SAT Competition 2018. The experiments were conducted on the "Academician V.M. Matrosov" computing cluster [40]. Each computing node of this cluster is equipped with 2×18-core Intel Xeon E5-2695 CPUs and 128 Gb RAM. Each solver was launched on one node, so 36 CPU cores were used. The time limit was 1 day (86–400 s). The results are shown at cactus plot, depicted in Fig. 1.

It turned out, that no solver coped with any of 12 72-bit instances. As for 64-bit instances, PLINGELING2018 showed the best results: it coped with 7 instances out of 12. On GRAIN-V1-SC-FIRST64, MICKEY-SC-FIRST64, and SHRINKING-SC64, the best results were achieved by PLINGELING2018: all three instances of GRAIN-V1-SC-FIRST64 were solved with the average runtime 12 423 s; all instances of MICKEY-SC-FIRST64 were solved with the average runtime 3 083 s; 1 instance of SHRINKING-SC64 (out of 3) was solved within 53 960 s. As for SELF-SHRINKING-SC64, the best solver is PAINLESS-MCOMPSPS: all 3 instances were solved with the average runtime 31 711 s. Thus, the considered 64-bit instances are quite simple – they can be solved on a powerful computer by a multithreaded solver in reasonable time. However, all 72-bit instances are hard.

4.2   Finding Decompositions Sets for Hard Instances

SAT-based cryptanalysis problems for SHRINKING-SC-72, SELF-SHRINKING-SC72, GRAIN-V1-SC-FIRST72 and MICKEY-SC-FIRST72 are quite hard, so they were additionally studied. In particular, a decomposition set (see Sect. 2) for

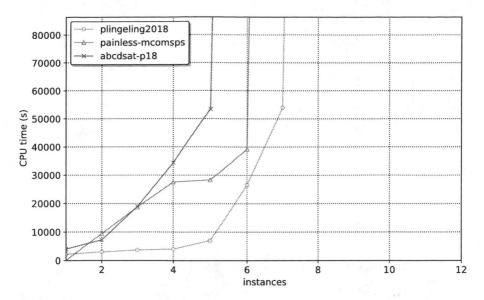

Fig. 1. Results of the top-3 multithreaded SAT solvers from SAT Competition 2018 on the considered instances.

each of them was constructed. The ALIAS tool [41] was used for this purpose. In ALIAS, the $(1+1)$ evolutionary algorithm [42] (a black-box optimization algorithm) and the SAT solver ROKK [43] were used.

ALIAS was launched for 1 day on the first instance of each of 4 problems on 1 cluster's node. In all cases as a start decomposition set all variables which encode a secret key were used. Details of four found decomposition sets are shown in Table 3. The details of the corresponding optimization processes are shown in Figs. 2 and 3.

Table 3. Details on found decomposition sets for the considered generators with 72-bit secret keys. Estimations are presented for 1 CPU core.

Generator	Decomposition set size (out of 72)	Estimation (seconds)
MICKEY-SC-FIRST72	26	6.21e+06
GRAIN-V1-SC-FIRST72	28	5.02e+07
SHRINKING-SC72	30	6.66e+08
SELF-SHRINKING-SC72	67	1.05e+20

From the table it follows, that SELF-SHRINKING-SC72 does not suit for the employed type of the Divide-and-Conquer approach: the found estimation is too high, and the size of the found decomposition set (67) is too close to the secret key size (72). Thus, SELF-SHRINKING-SC72 is not considered further. As

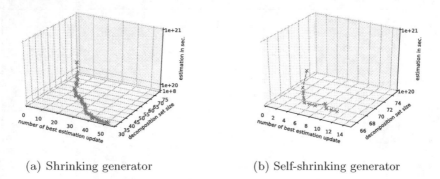

(a) Shrinking generator   (b) Self-shrinking generator

Fig. 2. Searching for decomposition sets with low runtime estimation: the shrinking and self-shrinking generators

for other three problems, the following decompositions sets were found for them (enumeration from 1):

- MICKEY-SC-FIRST72: 7 21 22 25 33 36 44 45 46 48 49 50 51 52 54 57 58 60 61 63 66 68 69 70 71 72;
- GRAIN-V1-SC-FIRST72: 10 14 17 19 20 21 22 23 25 26 27 29 30 34 39 40 42 43 47 48 51 52 60 63 64 65 67 71;
- SHRINKING-SC72: 2 3 4 5 6 7 8 9 10 11 12 13 14 15 16 17 18 19 20 22 23 24 26 27 28 30 32 33 34 35.

4.3   Details of Future SAT@home Experiments

It is assumed, that SAT@home's performance will quickly return on its high level after restart, and as a result a performance comparable to 500 CPU cores will be achieved. Note, that it is planned to use the CluBORun tool [44] to increase SAT@home's computational performance by resources of computing clusters. In Table 4, estimations on solving one instance of each considered problem in SAT@home are presented. Note, that these estimations hold true for the worst case – when all subinstances are solved. In practice, it is enough to solve about a half of subinstances, because all considered SAT instances are satisfiable.

It turned out, that MICKEY-SC-FIRST72 is way too simple for launching it SAT@home, so it is better so solve the corresponding instances on a computing cluster. GRAIN-V1-SC-FIRST72 and SHRINKING-SC72 suit well for launching in SAT@home, so the experiments on solving 3 instances for each of two problems will be conducted in the future.

For GRAIN-V1-SC-FIRST72, using the found decomposition set (see Subsect. 4.2), each subinstance is solved within 0.19 s on average. It is planned to vary the first 14 variables (out of 28) from the decomposition set on the project's server. The remaining 14 variables will be varied by a client application. As a

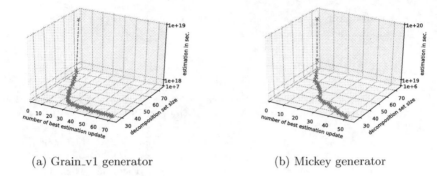

(a) Grain_v1 generator   (b) Mickey generator

Fig. 3. Searching for decomposition sets with low runtime estimation: the Grain_v1 and Mickey generators

Table 4. Estimations on solving instances in SAT@home.

Generator	Decomposition set size	Estimation, SAT@home
MICKEY-SC-FIRST72	26	3 h 27 min
GRAIN-V1-SC-FIRST72	28	1 d 4 h
SHRINKING-SC72	30	15 d 10 h

result, for one instance of GRAIN-V1-SC-FIRST72, 16 384 workunits will be created. To calculate a task of one such workunit, it would take about 52 min on a volunteer's host. For SHRINKING-SC72, using the found decomposition set, each subinstance is solved in 0.62 s on average. It is planned to vary the first 18 variables (out of 30) from the decomposition set on the project's server. The remaining 12 variables will be varied by a client application. As a result, for one instance of SHRINKING-SC72, 262 144 workunits will be created. To calculate a task of one such workunit, it would take about 42 min on a volunteer's host. According to the estimations, It should take about 25 days to solve all six SAT instances in SAT@home.

5 Conclusions

In the present paper, it was shown that solving SAT-based cryptanalysis problems in a BOINC-based volunteer computing project is in fact a final step of a long path. All preliminary steps are described in detail on examples of four keystream generators: Grain_v1, Mickey, Shrinking and Self-shrinking. It turned out, that cryptanalysis of only two of them (Grain_v1 and shrinking) suit well for SAT@home. The corresponding experiments are planned to be launched in SAT@home in the nearest future.

Acknowledgements. The research was partially supported by Council for Grants of the President of the Russian Federation (grant no. MK-4155.2018.9) and by Russian Foundation for Basic Research (grant no. 19-07-00746-a). The author thanks all

SAT@home participants for their computational resources, Stepan Kochemazov for fruitful discussions and Ilya Kurochkin for maintaining the project's server.

References

1. Foster, I.: Designing and Building Parallel Programs: Concepts and Tools for Parallel Software Engineering. Addison-Wesley Longman Publishing Co. Inc., Boston (1995)
2. Hwang, K.: Advanced Computer Architecture: Parallelism, Scalability, Programmability, 1st edn. McGraw-Hill Higher Education, New York (1992)
3. Anderson, D.P., Fedak, G.: The computational and storage potential of volunteer computing. In: Sixth IEEE International Symposium on Cluster Computing and the Grid (CCGrid 2006), 16–19 May 2006, Singapore, pp. 73–80. IEEE Computer Society (2006)
4. Yakimets, V.N., Kurochkin, I.I.: Analysis of results of the rating of volunteer distributed computing projects. In: Voevodin, V., Sobolev, S. (eds.) RuSCDays 2018. CCIS, vol. 965, pp. 472–486. Springer, Cham (2019). https://doi.org/10.1007/978-3-030-05807-4_40
5. Anderson, D.P.: BOINC: a system for public-resource computing and storage. In: Buyya, R. (ed.) 5th International Workshop on Grid Computing (GRID 2004), 8 November 2004, Pittsburgh, PA, USA, Proceedings, pp. 4–10. IEEE Computer Society (2004)
6. Ivashko, E., Chernov, I., Nikitina, N.: A survey of desktop grid scheduling. IEEE Trans. Parallel Distrib. Syst. 29(12), 2882–2895 (2018)
7. Posypkin, M., Semenov, A.A., Zaikin, O.: Using BOINC desktop grid to solve large scale SAT problems. Comput. Sci. (AGH) 13(1), 25–34 (2012)
8. Biere, A., Heule, M.J.H., van Maaren, H., Walsh, T. (eds.): Handbook of Satisfiability, Frontiers in Artificial Intelligence and Applications, vol. 185. IOS Press, Amsterdam (2009)
9. Massacci, F., Marraro, L.: Logical cryptanalysis as a SAT problem. J. Autom. Reason. 24(1/2), 165–203 (2000)
10. Bard, G.V.: Algebraic Cryptanalysis, 1st edn. Springer, Heidelberg (2009). https://doi.org/10.1007/978-0-387-88757-9. Incorporated
11. Soos, M., Nohl, K., Castelluccia, C.: Extending SAT solvers to cryptographic problems. In: Kullmann, O. (ed.) SAT 2009. LNCS, vol. 5584, pp. 244–257. Springer, Heidelberg (2009). https://doi.org/10.1007/978-3-642-02777-2_24
12. Courtois, N.T., O'Neil, S., Quisquater, J.-J.: Practical algebraic attacks on the Hitag2 stream Cipher. In: Samarati, P., Yung, M., Martinelli, F., Ardagna, C.A. (eds.) ISC 2009. LNCS, vol. 5735, pp. 167–176. Springer, Heidelberg (2009). https://doi.org/10.1007/978-3-642-04474-8_14
13. Eibach, T., Pilz, E., Völkel, G.: Attacking bivium using SAT solvers. In: Kleine Büning, H., Zhao, X. (eds.) SAT 2008. LNCS, vol. 4996, pp. 63–76. Springer, Heidelberg (2008). https://doi.org/10.1007/978-3-540-79719-7_7
14. Semenov, A., Zaikin, O.: Algorithm for finding partitionings of hard variants of boolean satisfiability problem with application to inversion of some cryptographic functions. SpringerPlus 5(1), 1–16 (2016)
15. Pavlenko, A., Semenov, A., Ulyantsev, V.: Evolutionary computation techniques for constructing SAT-based attacks in algebraic cryptanalysis. In: Kaufmann, P., Castillo, P.A. (eds.) EvoApplications 2019. LNCS, vol. 11454, pp. 237–253. Springer, Cham (2019). https://doi.org/10.1007/978-3-030-16692-2_16

16. Pavlenko, A., Buzdalov, M., Ulyantsev, V.: Fitness comparison by statistical testing in construction of SAT-based guess-and-determine cryptographic attacks. In: Auger, A., Stützle, T. (eds.) Proceedings of the Genetic and Evolutionary Computation Conference, GECCO 2019, Prague, Czech Republic, 13–17 July 2019. pp. 312–320. ACM (2019). https://doi.org/10.1145/3321707.3321847

17. Semenov, A., Zaikin, O., Otpuschennikov, I., Kochemazov, S., Ignatiev, A.: On cryptographic attacks using backdoors for SAT. In: AAAI 2018, pp. 6641–6648 (2018)

18. Zaikin, O., Kochemazov, S.: Pseudo-Boolean black-box optimization methods in the context of divide-and-conquer approach to solving hard SAT instances. In: OPTIMA 2018 (Volume), pp. 76–87. DEStech Publications, Inc. (2018)

19. Semenov, A., Zaikin, O., Bespalov, D., Posypkin, M.: Parallel logical cryptanalysis of the generator A5/1 in BNB-grid system. In: Malyshkin, V. (ed.) PaCT 2011. LNCS, vol. 6873, pp. 473–483. Springer, Heidelberg (2011). https://doi.org/10.1007/978-3-642-23178-0_43

20. Zaikin, O., Kochemazov, S.: An improved SAT-based guess-and-determine attack on the alternating step generator. In: Nguyen, P., Zhou, J. (eds.) ISC 2017. LNCS, vol. 10599, pp. 21–38. Springer, Heidelberg (2017). https://doi.org/10.1007/978-3-319-69659-1_2

21. Lafitte, F., Markowitch, O., Heule, D.V.: SAT based analysis of LTE stream cipher ZUC. J. Inf. Secur. Appl. **22**, 54–65 (2015). Special Issue on Security of Information and Networks

22. Dwivedi, A.D., Kloucek, M., Morawiecki, P., Nikolic, I., Pieprzyk, J., Wójtowicz, S.: SAT-based cryptanalysis of authenticated ciphers from the CAESAR competition. In: Samarati, P., Obaidat, M.S., Cabello, E. (eds.) Proceedings of the 14th International Joint Conference on e-Business and Telecommunications (ICETE 2017) - Volume 4: SECRYPT, Madrid, Spain, 24–26 July 2017, pp. 237–246. SciTePress (2017)

23. Black, M., Bard, G.: SAT over BOINC: an application-independent volunteer grid project. In: Jha, S., gentschen Felde, N., Buyya, R., Fedak, G. (eds.) 12th IEEE/ACM International Conference on Grid Computing, GRID 2011, Lyon, France, 21–23 September 2011, pp. 226–227. IEEE Computer Society (2011)

24. Biró, C., Kovásznai, G., Biere, A., Kusper, G., Geda, G.: Cube-and-Conquer approach for SAT solving on grids. Ann. Math. Inform. **42**, 9–21 (2013)

25. Le Frioux, L., Baarir, S., Sopena, J., Kordon, F.: PaInleSS: a framework for parallel SAT solving. In: Gaspers, S., Walsh, T. (eds.) SAT 2017. LNCS, vol. 10491, pp. 233–250. Springer, Cham (2017). https://doi.org/10.1007/978-3-319-66263-3_15

26. Hamadi, Y., Jabbour, S., Sais, L.: ManySAT: a parallel SAT solver. JSAT **6**(4), 245–262 (2009)

27. Zhang, H., Bonacina, M.P., Hsiang, J.: PSATO: a distributed propositional prover and its application to quasigroup problems. J. Symb. Comput. **21**(4), 543–560 (1996)

28. Menezes, A.J., Vanstone, S.A., Oorschot, P.C.V.: Handbook of Applied Cryptography, 1st edn. CRC Press Inc., Boca Raton (1996)

29. Golić, J.D.: Cryptanalysis of alleged A5 stream cipher. In: Fumy, W. (ed.) EUROCRYPT 1997. LNCS, vol. 1233, pp. 239–255. Springer, Heidelberg (1997). https://doi.org/10.1007/3-540-69053-0_17

30. Cannière, C.: TRIVIUM: a stream cipher construction inspired by block cipher design principles. In: Katsikas, S.K., López, J., Backes, M., Gritzalis, S., Preneel, B. (eds.) ISC 2006. LNCS, vol. 4176, pp. 171–186. Springer, Heidelberg (2006). https://doi.org/10.1007/11836810_13

31. Zaikin, O., Manzyuk, M., Kochemazov, S., Bychkov, I., Semenov, A.: A volunteer-computing-based grid architecture incorporating idle resources of computational clusters. In: Dimov, I., Faragó, I., Vulkov, L. (eds.) Proceedings of the Sixth Conference on Numerical Analysis and Applications (NAA 2016). Lecture Notes in Computer Sciences, vol. 10187, pp. 735–742. Springer, Heidelberg (2016). https://doi.org/10.1007/978-3-319-57099-0_89

32. Hell, M., Johansson, T., Maximov, A., Meier, W.: The grain family of stream ciphers. In: Robshaw and Billet [36], pp. 179–190

33. Babbage, S., Dodd, M.: The MICKEY stream ciphers. In: Robshaw and Billet [36], pp. 191–209

34. Coppersmith, D., Krawczyk, H., Mansour, Y.: The shrinking generator. In: Stinson, D.R. (ed.) CRYPTO 1993. LNCS, vol. 773, pp. 22–39. Springer, Heidelberg (1994). https://doi.org/10.1007/3-540-48329-2_3

35. Meier, W., Staffelbach, O.: The self-shrinking generator. In: De Santis, A. (ed.) EUROCRYPT 1994. LNCS, vol. 950, pp. 205–214. Springer, Heidelberg (1995). https://doi.org/10.1007/BFb0053436

36. Robshaw, M., Billet, O. (eds.): New Stream Cipher Designs. LNCS, vol. 4986. Springer, Heidelberg (2008). https://doi.org/10.1007/978-3-540-68351-3

37. Otpuschennikov, I., Semenov, A., Gribanova, I., Zaikin, O., Kochemazov, S.: Encoding cryptographic functions to SAT using TRANSALG system. In: ECAI 2016–22nd European Conference on Artificial Intelligence. Frontiers in Artificial Intelligence and Applications, vol. 285, pp. 1594–1595. IOS Press (2016)

38. Biere, A.: CaDiCaL, Lingeling, Plingeling, Treengeling and YalSAT entering the SAT competition 2018. In: Heule, M., Järvisalo, M., Suda, M. (eds.) Proceedings of SAT Competition 2018 - Solver and Benchmark Descriptions. Department of Computer Science Series of Publications B, vol. B-2018-1, pp. 13–14. University of Helsinki (2018)

39. Chen, J.: AbcdSAT and glucose hack: various simplifications and optimizations for CDCL SAT solvers. In: Heule, M., Järvisalo, M., Suda, M. (eds.) Proceedings of SAT Competition 2018 - Solver and Benchmark Descriptions. Department of Computer Science Series of Publications B, vol. B-2018-1, pp. 10–12. University of Helsinki (2018)

40. Irkutsk supercomputer center of SB RAS. http://hpc.icc.ru

41. Kochemazov, S., Zaikin, O.: ALIAS: a modular tool for finding backdoors for SAT. In: Beyersdorff, O., Wintersteiger, C.M. (eds.) SAT 2018. LNCS, vol. 10929, pp. 419–427. Springer, Cham (2018). https://doi.org/10.1007/978-3-319-94144-8_25

42. Droste, S., Jansen, T., Wegener, I.: On the analysis of the $(1+1)$ evolutionary algorithm. Theor. Comput. Sci. **276**(1–2), 51–81 (2002). https://doi.org/10.1016/S0304-3975(01)00182-7

43. Yasumoto, T., Okuwaga, T.: Rokk 1.0.1. In: Belov, A., Diepold, D., Heule, M., Järvisalo, M. (eds.) SAT Competition 2014, p. 70 (2014)

44. Afanasiev, A., Bychkov, I., Manzyuk, M., Posypkin, M., Semenov, A., Zaikin, O.: Technology for integrating idle computing cluster resources into volunteer computing projects. In: Proceedings of the 5th International Workshop on Computer Science and Engineering, Moscow, Russia, pp. 109–114 (2015)

Supporting Efficient Execution
of Workflows on Everest Platform

Oleg Sukhoroslov[✉]

Institute for Information Transmission Problems of the Russian Academy
of Sciences, Moscow, Russia
sukhoroslov@iitp.ru

Abstract. Workflows is an important class of parallel applications consisting of multiple tasks with control or data dependencies between them. Such applications are widely used for automation of computational and data processing pipelines in science and technology. The paper considers the execution of workflows on Everest, a web-based distributed computing platform. Two different approaches for workflow description and execution are presented and compared. The proposed solutions and optimizations address common problems related to the efficient execution of workflows on distributed computing resources. The results of experimental study demonstrate the effectiveness of proposed optimizations.

Keywords: Distributed computing · Workflows · Scheduling · Web services · Platform as a service

1 Introduction

Workflows is an important class of loosely coupled parallel applications that consist of multiple tasks with control or data dependencies. Such applications, commonly referred as scientific workflows [18], are often created for automation of complex computational and data processing pipelines in science and technology. The workflow tasks correspond to the execution of various standalone applications and tools. Therefore the tasks are usually run independently by exchanging data only through their input and output files. Workflows are often modeled as directed acyclic graphs (DAG) where the vertices represent the tasks and the edges correspond to the dependencies between tasks.

Many workflow managements systems (WMS) [4,6–9,17,24] have been developed to provide integrated environments for designing and execution of workflows on distributed infrastructures. The majority of WMSes are implemented as a standalone application with a graphical workflow editor. More recent web-based environments [3,10,11] implement a hosted multi-user WMS with a web user interface for designing and running workflows. The execution of workflow tasks on remote computing resources is achieved by direct job submission via native interfaces or by employing resource brokers such as HTCondor.

© Springer Nature Switzerland AG 2019
V. Voevodin and S. Sobolev (Eds.): RuSCDays 2019, CCIS 1129, pp. 713–724, 2019.
https://doi.org/10.1007/978-3-030-36592-9_58

This paper considers the execution of workflows on Everest, a web-based distributed computing platform. A distinguishing feature of Everest is the ability to serve multiple distinct groups of users and projects by implementing the Platform as a Service (PaaS) cloud computing model. In contrast to the mentioned web-based WMSes, the platform is not tied to some computing infrastructure and allows the users to attach their resources and bind them to the applications hosted by the platform. These features make it possible to use the publicly available platform instance without having to install it on-premises. The use of Everest enables convenient access to computing resources by means of domain-specific computational web services. It also allows one to seamlessly combine multiple resources of different types for running distributed computations.

Two different approaches for execution of workflows on Everest platform are presented and compared. The initial approach, based on external orchestration using a scripting language, is more flexible by supporting arbitrary workflows with complex logic. The new approach, based on a general-purpose service integrated into the platform and the use of a declarative workflow description, is more convenient for workflows with a static structure and allows several important optimizations. The results of experimental study demonstrate that the introduced optimizations can significantly improve the workflow execution time.

While the major contributions of the paper are related to the specific distributed computing platform, the presented solutions address common problems related to the description and efficient execution of workflows in distributed systems. Some of proposed solutions, such as the use of a general-purpose programming language for describing and running workflows, or the use of profiling and static scheduling algorithms to optimize the execution of repetitive workflows, are uncommon among the modern scientific WMSes and can be reused.

The paper is structured as follows. Section 2 provides an overview of the Everest platform and its relevant features. Section 3 describes the initial approach for workflow execution in Everest based on external orchestration via Everest API. Section 4 presents a new approach based on a general-purpose service integrated into the platform. Section 5 presents the results of experimental evaluation of the new approach. Section 6 concludes and discusses future work.

2   Everest Platform

Everest [1,13] is a web-based distributed computing platform. It provides users with tools to publish and share computing applications as web services. The platform also manages the execution of applications on external computing resources attached by the users. In contrast to traditional distributed computing platforms, Everest implements the PaaS model by providing its functionality via remote interfaces. A single instance of the platform can be accessed by many users in order to create, run and share applications with each other. Each application is published as a RESTful web service. This enables programmatic access to applications, integration with third-party tools and composition of applications. The platform also implements a convenient web user interface.

Everest supports the development and execution of applications based on the following model. An application has a number of *inputs* that constitute a request to the application and a number of *outputs* that constitute a result of computations corresponding to some request. Upon each request Everest creates a new *job* consisting of one or more *tasks* generated by the application from the job inputs. The task specification includes the command to be executed, input and output files, and resource requirements. The tasks are executed by the platform on computing resources specified by a user. The results of completed tasks are passed to the application and are used to produce the job outputs or new tasks if needed. The job is completed when all its tasks are completed. The described model is generic enough to support a wide range of application cases.

Everest provides a universal template for publishing single-task applications, which can be easily configured for a specific application purpose. This approach makes it possible to avoid programming while adding applications to Everest. The template supports both sequential and parallel applications, the only limitation is that the application should be executed with a single command. Everest also includes a general-purpose service for execution of bag-of-tasks applications consisting of a large number of independent tasks such as parameter sweeps [20]. At the core of the service is a declarative format for describing parametrized computations, which contains parameter definitions and other directives that together define the rules for generation of tasks and processing of their results. Again, this approach allows to minimize or completely avoid programming work.

Everest provides several mechanisms for execution of more complex many-task applications [16]. The low level *raw job* interface allows platform clients to dynamically manage a set of tasks within a job by sending commands (e.g., submit or cancel a task) and receiving notifications (e.g., change of a task state). To support applications which require cooperation between their tasks, a lightweight coordination and publish-subscribe mechanism is implemented based on the notion of shared variables [22]. The description and execution of workflows consisting of multiple tasks with dependencies is discussed in the following sections.

Instead of using a dedicated computing infrastructure, Everest performs the execution of application tasks on external resources attached by users. The platform implements integration with standalone machines and clusters through a developed *agent* [12]. The agent runs on a resource and acts as a mediator between it and Everest enabling the platform to submit and manage tasks on the resource. The agent performs routine actions related to staging of input files, submitting a task, monitoring a task state and collecting the task results. The platform also supports integration with grid infrastructures [12], desktop grids [14] and clouds [21]. Everest users can flexibly bind the attached resources to applications. In particular, a user can specify multiple resources, possibly of different type, for running an application [12]. In this case the platform performs dynamic scheduling of application tasks across the specified resource pool.

3   Workflow Execution via Everest Client Library

The most natural way of implementing workflows with Everest is by means of orchestration of Everest applications. In this case, the steps of workflow correspond to invocations of individual applications, i.e. Everest jobs. This approach aligns well with the service-oriented architecture of Everest where both applications and workflows can be represented as services, supporting the reuse and composition of loosely-coupled applications. An alternative approach, where the workflow is implemented as a standalone application orchestrating its internal tasks, i.e. with the raw job mechanism, is not discussed in this paper.

In this section, the initial approach for workflow execution in Everest introduced in [13] is discussed. This approach is based on external orchestration of Everest applications by means of Everest API. To execute the workflow a user should write and run a program called *workflow driver* that submits jobs via Everest API and passes data between the jobs according to the workflow logic.

To support automation of repetitive tasks, application composition and integration, Everest implements a REST API. It can be used to access Everest applications from any programming language that can speak HTTP protocol and parse JSON format. However REST API is too low level for most of users, so it is convenient to have ready-to-use client libraries built on top of it. For this purpose a Python client library [2] was implemented.

The Python client library implements the nonblocking semantics similar to the dataflow paradigm, which makes it simple to describe workflows without requiring a user to implement the boilerplate code dealing with waiting for tasks and passing data between them. This approach also implicitly supports parallel execution of independent tasks. Finally, the use of a general-purpose programming language instead of a declarative workflow description language provides maximum flexibility by enabling users to embed any additional processing logic.

Figure 1 contains an example of program using Python API. It implements the depicted diamond-shaped workflow that consists of running four different applications. Note that the *App.run()* method does not block the program execution until the job is done and its results are available. Instead the library allows the program to continue its execution after the job is created by performing the job submission and monitoring in the background thread.

The workflow driver implemented in Python using the client library can be executed on the user machine or published on Everest as a new application. In the latter case, the platform automatically passes the credentials for accessing the required applications on behalf of the user submitted the workflow to the driver. This enables reuse and sharing of workflows as applications among Everest users.

While the described approach allows to describe and execute arbitrary workflows with complex logic, it has a number of drawbacks. First, using a scripting language for describing workflows with a static structure can be more complex and verbose in comparison to using a declarative format. Second, the user should provide a machine for execution of a workflow driver, which can not run inside the platform. Third, since the management of workflow execution is decoupled from the platform, it is not possible to implement and provide important

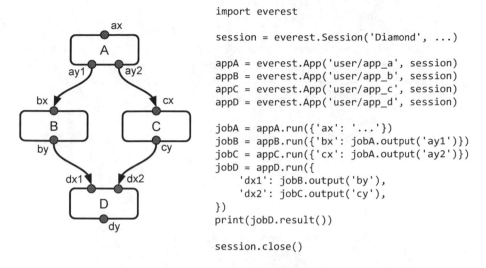

```
import everest

session = everest.Session('Diamond', ...)

appA = everest.App('user/app_a', session)
appB = everest.App('user/app_b', session)
appC = everest.App('user/app_c', session)
appD = everest.App('user/app_d', session)

jobA = appA.run({'ax': '...'})
jobB = appB.run({'bx': jobA.output('ay1')})
jobC = appC.run({'cx': jobA.output('ay2')})
jobD = appD.run({
    'dx1': jobB.output('by'),
    'dx2': jobC.output('cy'),
})
print(jobD.result())

session.close()
```

Fig. 1. Example of workflow described using Everest Python API.

optimizations for efficient workflow execution on the platform level. For example, this approach does not allow passing the complete job graph to the platform to enable scheduling optimizations, since only the jobs ready to run are dynamically submitted to Everest. It is also not possible to centrally manage and optimize the execution of multiple workflows by different users.

The described drawbacks motivated the development of a new mechanism for workflow execution based on the declarative workflow description and implemented inside the platform as a general-purpose service.

4   Workflow Runner Service

In this section, a new approach for workflow execution in Everest based on internal orchestration of applications is described. This approach addresses the shortcomings of the external API-based approach described in the previous section as follows. Instead of a scripting language, it uses a simple declarative format for workflow description. The workflow execution is managed internally inside the platform, avoiding the need for running an external driver program. Several optimizations are implemented to support the efficient execution of workflows on the platform level, such as local data transfers and static scheduling.

The presented approach is implemented as a special Everest application called *Workflow Runner* which provides a general-purpose service for workflow execution. This application is available to all platform users and allows to run arbitrary workflows on specified computing resources. Conceptually, it shares many similarities with the previously developed service for execution of parameter sweep computations [20]. The user prepares the workflow description and then submits it along with input files to the *Workflow Runner* service, specifying resources which should be used for the workflow execution. The service parses the workflow description into an internal DAG representation and manages the workflow execution by creating, scheduling, submitting and monitoring the workflow jobs. After the workflow execution is completed, the service returns the workflow results as a set of output files to the user.

4.1 Workflow Description

At the core of the developed service is a declarative format for describing a workflow based on YAML, a human friendly data serialization standard. Listing 41 contains an example with description of the diamond-shaped workflow with four jobs depicted on Fig. 1.

Listing 41. Example of workflow description

```
name:  Diamond
description:  A diamond-shaped  workflow  with  four  jobs
inputs:
  - name:  data
outputs:
  - name:  result
jobs:
  - name:  A
    app:  user/app_a
    inputs:
      ax:  ${data}
  - name:  B
    app:  user/app_b
    inputs:
      bx:  ${A.ay1}
  - name:  C
    app:  user/app_c
    inputs:
      cx:  ${A.ay2}
  - name:  D
    app:  user/app_d
    inputs:
      dx1:  ${B.by}
      dx2:  ${C.cy}
    outputs:
      dy:  result
```

The workflow description consists of four main parts: metadata, inputs, outputs and jobs. Metadata includes a general information about the workflow, such as name, description, keywords, author, etc. The *inputs* section includes a list of workflow inputs, which should be provided for workflow execution. Each input should have a unique name and can have optional metadata, such as description. Similarly, the *outputs* section includes a list of workflow outputs. The *jobs* section includes a list of workflow jobs. The job specification includes unique name, identifier of invoked Everest application, jobs inputs and output mappings. Job inputs can reference the workflow inputs using the $\${input\}$ syntax, or outputs of other jobs using the $\${job.output\}$ syntax. Output mappings are used to link a job output to a workflow output. Note that other job outputs are omitted from the description.

The described format is compact, human readable and easy to learn.

4.2 Workflow Execution

When a user submits a request including the workflow description and input files, a new Everest job is created and the job processing is delegated to the *Workflow Runner* application. In contrast to regular Everest applications, it does not generate compute tasks. Instead, it parses and validates the workflow description, collects workflow inputs, and then spawns a new *driver* object, which is responsible for management of workflow jobs.

The driver assigns ready jobs to resources using an internal *scheduler* instance, submits the scheduled jobs, and monitors their execution. The workflow jobs are executed by Everest as usual, i.e. by generating tasks via corresponding applications, execution of tasks on specified resources and saving job outputs created by applications. Upon a job completion, the driver collects the job outputs and copies them to the inputs of dependent jobs according to the workflow description. When all job inputs are defined, the job is marked as ready and is subject to scheduling. When all workflow jobs are successfully completed, the driver is terminated, the workflow outputs are produced and the main Everest job is marked as completed.

By default, the scheduling of workflow jobs is performed using a simple dynamic strategy. Ready jobs, sorted in the order of their definition in the workflow, are scheduled to the idle slots of resources, sorted in the order specified during the workflow submission. This strategy does not use any a priori information about the job execution times and resource performance. An optimized static scheduling strategy is described in the end of this section.

The current implementation handles the failures of workflow jobs as follows. When a job fails, the driver tries to resubmit it several times, and if the job still fails the driver terminates the workflow execution and the main job is marked as failed. Advanced failure handling strategies can be implemented in the future.

4.3 Data Transfer Optimizations

Before the development of the described service, task output files were always uploaded from the resource to Everest after the task execution. While this is natural for execution of standalone applications or parameter sweeps, this could lead to performance degradation and unnecessary load on the platform when executing workflows. Indeed, many jobs comprising a workflow, i.e. their tasks, produce intermediate results that are used only by subsequent jobs and are not considered as the workflow outputs that should be returned to the user. Transferring such data back and forth between the resource and the platform is wasteful and can significantly degrade a workflow execution time, especially for data-intensive workflows with large working data sets.

To address this issue, the support for storing and accessing the results of completed tasks has been implemented in the Everest agent. Upon the task submission, the platform can specify which output files should be uploaded back and which ones should be stored locally. When reporting the task results, the agent provides a URI for each locally stored output file. This URI can be used for downloading the file from the agent. When the task results are no longer needed, the platform can request their deletion from the agent.

The described mechanism is used in the *Workflow Runner* service to avoid the unnecessary data transfers. During the workflow execution, the intermediate results are stored locally on resources where they were produced, and the URIs of results are passed to the subsequent jobs. When an agent downloads task input files, it checks if the URI corresponds to a locally stored file and if so skips downloading. Otherwise, the file is downloaded from the platform or other agent. When running a workflow across multiple resources, the corresponding agents should be able to directly access each other. This can be problematic when an agent runs behind a firewall or NAT. We plan to address this issue in the future by switching to transferring the data via the platform in such cases.

As a related optimization, the Everest agent implements the caching of downloaded files (identified by the SHA1 digest of file content), which can greatly reduce data transfer overheads for common files used by many workflow jobs. Also, when a certain input file is concurrently requested by many tasks submitted to the agent, the file is downloaded only once to further reduce the data transfers.

4.4   Scheduling Optimization

The default scheduling strategy is simple and robust when running a workflow in a dynamic environment without a priori information about jobs, such as task execution times, input and output data sizes. However, when using a stable dedicated execution environment, such information can be collected and used to improve the subsequent workflow executions. Indeed, there is a large body of research on workflow scheduling algorithms [25, 26] that employ various heuristics taking into account the workflow topology and characteristics of individual jobs. Such algorithms are known to outperform simple dynamic strategies when given an accurate information about the workflow and the execution environment [15, 23].

The use of advanced scheduling algorithms can be beneficial for workflows which are executed many times with a similar execution profile in a stable environment. To enable this optimization, the collection of profiling information is added to the *Workflow Runner* service. The workflow profile includes information about each job, such as the job submission and completion times, task execution time, input and output data sizes, data transfer times. This information is collected by the workflow driver and is returned to the user as a YAML file. The profile file can also be created manually by the user. Having a workflow profile, the user can pass it to the *Workflow Runner* service when submitting the workflow. In such case, the workflow driver switches to using a new scheduler implementation, which is based on HEFT algorithm.

Heterogeneous Earliest Finish Time (HEFT) [19] is a well-known static workflow scheduling algorithm that employs the following list scheduling heuristics. The workflow tasks are scheduled in descending order of their rank computed as

$$rank(t_i) = \overline{w_i} + \max_{t_j \in children(t_i)} \left(\overline{c_{i,j}} + rank(t_j) \right),$$

where $\overline{w_i}$ is the average execution time of task t_i and $\overline{c_{i,j}}$ is the average communication time between tasks t_i and t_j. The averages are computed by considering all, possibly heterogeneous, resources of the target system. Each task is scheduled to a resource with a minimum earliest finish time for the task.

HEFT algorithm requires estimates of execution times of each task on all resources and data transfer times between all pairs of resources. However, the workflow profile collected by the service includes only information about actual executions and transfers. Thus, the current implementation targets only a homogeneous execution environment where such times can be assumed the same across all resources, for example a cluster of identical machines. The support for heterogeneous environments is planned to be implemented in the future by combining empirical results and analytical performance modes.

5   Experimental Evaluation

The presented *Workflow Runner* service has been evaluated by executing several workflows based on real-world scientific applications [5]:

- *Montage*: stitches together multiple images of the sky to create large-scale custom mosaics;
- *Inspiral*: analyses and filters the time-frequency data from the Laser Interferometer Gravitational Wave Observatory experiment;
- *Epigenomics*: automates various genome sequencing operations;
- *CyberShake*: characterizes earthquake hazards in a region;

The characteristics of the used workflows are presented in Table 1. The real workflow jobs are replaced by synthetic ones using the special Everest application *Synthetic* which simulates the execution of a real job given its input files, run time and the sizes of output files. Each workflow job is corresponded to a single task submitted to a resource.

The experiments were run on a dedicated testbed environment consisted of four machines with identical configuration connected with Gigabit Ethernet. Each machine hosted an Everest agent configured with four slots for task

Table 1. Workflow characteristics

Workflow	Jobs	Compute time (s)	Input/Intermediate/Output data (MB)
Montage	100	4533	68/426/1
Inspiral	100	10511	380/19/1
Epigenomics	100	4034	1084/64/12
CyberShake	100	4473	4086/58/1

execution. Thus, the testbed is consisted of four resources capable for parallel execution of 16 tasks in total. No other tasks or background activities were run on these resources during the experiments. The network connection between the testbed and Everest had the following characteristics: bandwidth - 100 MB/sec, latency - 2 ms.

Table 2 contains the measured workflow execution times on the testbed for three different configurations - baseline (no optimizations, similar to running a workflow via Everest API), data transfer optimizations, and both scheduling and data transfer optimizations. The obtained results confirm that the introduced optimizations can significantly improve the workflow execution efficiency resulting in up to 36% reduction of the execution time in comparison to the baseline. The data transfer optimization makes the greatest contribution for data-instensive workflows (up to 33% for CyberShake), while the impact of the scheduling optimization depends on the workflow structure ranging from 1% for Insprial to 26% for Montage. As can be seen, both optimizations are equally important for improving the workflow execution efficiency.

Table 2. Workflow execution times (seconds)

Workflow	Baseline	Transfer	Scheduling+Transfer
Montage	495	464 (94%)	338 (68%)
Inspiral	877	844 (96%)	834 (95%)
Epigenomics	728	595 (82%)	536 (74%)
CyberShake	1454	981 (67%)	929 (64%)

6   Conclusion and Future Work

Workflows represent an important class of computing applications which should be supported by any distributed computing platform. In this paper, two different approaches for execution of workflows on Everest platform are presented and compared. The initial approach, based on external orchestration and the use of a scripting language, is more flexible by supporting arbitrary workflows with complex logic. The new approach, based on a general-purpose service integrated into the platform and the use of a declarative workflow description, is more convenient for workflows with a static structure and allows several important optimizations. In particular, the storage of intermediate results on computing resources avoids redundant data transfers, which is important for data-intensive workflows. At the same time, the use of advanced scheduling algorithms can be beneficial for workflows which are executed many times with a similar execution profile in a stable environment. The results of experimental study demonstrate that the introduced optimizations can indeed significantly improve the workflow execution time.

It is planned to continue supporting both of these approaches in Everest, since each one has its advantages and limitations. Future work will focus on improving the presented *Workflow Runner* service, e.g. implementing the advanced scheduling and data transfers in heterogeneous environments, extending the workflow description language and supporting custom failure handling.

Acknowledgments. This work is supported by the Russian Foundation for Basic Research (grant 18-07-00956).

References

1. Everest. http://everest.distcomp.org/
2. Everest Python API. https://gitlab.com/everest/python-api
3. Afanasiev, A., Sukhoroslov, O., Voloshinov, V.: MathCloud: publication and reuse of scientific applications as RESTful web services. In: Malyshkin, V. (ed.) PaCT 2013. LNCS, vol. 7979, pp. 394–408. Springer, Heidelberg (2013). https://doi.org/10.1007/978-3-642-39958-9_36
4. Albrecht, M., Donnelly, P., Bui, P., Thain, D.: Makeflow: a portable abstraction for data intensive computing on clusters, clouds, and grids. In: Proceedings of the 1st ACM SIGMOD Workshop on Scalable Workflow Execution Engines and Technologies, p. 1. ACM (2012)
5. Bharathi, S., Chervenak, A., Deelman, E., Mehta, G., Su, M.H., Vahi, K.: Characterization of scientific workflows. In: 2008 Third Workshop on Workflows in Support of Large-Scale Science, pp. 1–10, November 2008
6. Deelman, E., Gannon, D., Shields, M., Taylor, I.: Workflows and e-science: an overview of workflow system features and capabilities. Futur. Gener. Comput. Syst. **25**(5), 528–540 (2009)
7. Deelman, E., et al.: Pegasus, a workflow management system for science automation. Futur. Gener. Comput. Syst. **46**, 17–35 (2015)
8. Fahringer, T., et al.: ASKALON: a grid application development and computing environment. In: The 6th IEEE/ACM International Workshop on Grid Computing, pp. 10–pp. IEEE (2005)
9. Glatard, T., Montagnat, J., Lingrand, D., Pennec, X.: Flexible and efficient workflow deployment of data-intensive applications on grids with moteur. Int. J. High Perform. Comput. Appl. **22**(3), 347–360 (2008)
10. Goecks, J., Nekrutenko, A., Taylor, J.: Galaxy: a comprehensive approach for supporting accessible, reproducible, and transparent computational research in the life sciences. Genome Biol. **11**(8), R86 (2010)

11. Kacsuk, P., et al.: WS-PGRADE/gUSE generic DCI gateway framework for a large variety of user communities. J. Grid Comput. **10**(4), 601–630 (2012)
12. Smirnov, S., Sukhoroslov, O., Volkov, S.: Integration and combined use of distributed computing resources with Everest. J. Grid Comput. **101**, 359–368 (2016)
13. Sukhoroslov, O., Volkov, S., Afanasiev, A.: A web-based platform for publication and distributed execution of computing applications. In: 2015 14th International Symposium on Parallel and Distributed Computing (ISPDC), pp. 175–184, June 2015
14. Sukhoroslov, O.: Integration of Everest platform with BOINC-based desktop grids. In: Ivashko, E., Rumyantsev, A. (eds.) Proceedings of the Third International Conference BOINC: FAST 2017, Petrozavodsk, Russia, pp. 102–107 (2017)
15. Sukhoroslov, O., Nazarenko, A., Aleksandrov, R.: An experimental study of scheduling algorithms for many-task applications. J. Supercomput. **75**, 7857–7871 (2018). https://doi.org/10.1007/s11227-018-2553-9
16. Sukhoroslov, O.: Supporting efficient execution of many-task applications with Everest. In: Proceedings of the VIII International Conference "Distributed Computing and Grid-Technologies in Science and Education" (GRID 2018), pp. 266–270 (2018)
17. Taylor, I., Shields, M., Wang, I., Harrison, A.: The Triana workflow environment: architecture and applications. In: Taylor, I.J., Deelman, E., Gannon, D.B., Shields, M. (eds.) Workflows for e-Science, pp. 320–339. Springer, Heidelberg (2007). https://doi.org/10.1007/978-1-84628-757-2_20
18. Taylor, I.J., Deelman, E., Gannon, D.B., Shields, M.: Workflows for e-Science: sCientific Workflows for Grids. Springer, Heidelberg (2014). https://doi.org/10.1007/978-1-84628-757-2. Incorporated
19. Topcuoglu, H., Hariri, S., Wu, M.Y.: Performance-effective and low-complexity task scheduling for heterogeneous computing. IEEE Trans. Parallel Distrib. Syst. **13**(3), 260–274 (2002)
20. Volkov, S., Sukhoroslov, O.: A generic web service for running parameter sweep experiments in distributed computing environment. Procedia Comput. Sci. **66**, 477–486 (2015)
21. Volkov, S., Sukhoroslov, O.: Simplifying the use of clouds for scientific computing with Everest. Procedia Comput. Sci. **119**, 112–120 (2017)
22. Voloshinov, V., Smirnov, S., Sukhoroslov, O.: Implementation and use of coarse-grained parallel branch-and-bound in Everest distributed environment. Procedia Comput. Sci. **108**, 1532–1541 (2017)
23. Wieczorek, M., Prodan, R., Fahringer, T.: Scheduling of scientific workflows in the askalon grid environment. ACM SIGMOD Rec. **34**(3), 56–62 (2005)
24. Wolstencroft, K., et al.: The Taverna workflow suite: designing and executing workflows of web services on the desktop, web or in the cloud. Nucl. Acids Res. **41**(W1), W557–W561 (2013)
25. Wu, F., Wu, Q., Tan, Y.: Workflow scheduling in cloud: a survey. J. Supercomput. **71**(9), 3373–3418 (2015)
26. Yu, J., Buyya, R., Ramamohanarao, K.: Workflow scheduling algorithms for grid computing. In: Xhafa, F., Abraham, A. (eds.) Metaheuristics for Scheduling in Distributed Computing Environments, pp. 173–214. Springer, Heidelberg (2008). https://doi.org/10.1007/978-3-540-69277-5_7

Start-up and the Results of the Volunteer Computing Project RakeSearch

Maxim Manzyuk[1], Natalia Nikitina[2(✉)], and Eduard Vatutin[3]

[1] Internet portal BOINC.ru, Moscow, Russia
hoarfrost@rambler.ru
[2] Institute of Applied Mathematical Research, Karelian Research Center
of the Russian Academy of Sciences, Petrozavodsk, Russia
nikitina@krc.karelia.ru
[3] Southwest State University, Kursk, Russia
evatutin@rambler.ru

Abstract. In this paper we describe the experience of setting up a computational infrastructure based on BOINC middleware and running a volunteer computing project on its basis. The project is aimed at characterizing the space of diagonal Latin squares of order 9 in the form of an ensemble of orthogonality graphs, previously not addressed. We implement the search for row-permutational squares orthogonal to an initial one, which allows to reconstruct the full graphs. We provide the developed application to search for orthogonal pairs of the squares and describe the obtained results. The results prove the efficiency of volunteer computing in unveiling the structure of the space of diagonal Latin squares.

Keywords: Desktop Grid · Volunteer computing · BOINC · Orthogonal diagonal Latin squares · Orthogonality graph

1 Introduction

1.1 Orthogonal Diagonal Latin Squares

A Latin square (further LS) of order N is an $N \times N$ array filled with elements from a finite set of size N in such a way that all elements within a single row or single column are distinct. A Latin square is called diagonal (further DLS) if all elements in both its main diagonal and main back-diagonal are distinct.

Two diagonal Latin squares $A = \{a_{ij}\}$ and $B = \{b_{ij}\}$ are called orthogonal mates (further ODLSs) or Graeco-Latin squares if all ordered pairs (a_{ij}, b_{ij}), $1 \leq i, j \leq N$, are distinct. A DLS is called normalized if the elements of its first row are sorted in ascending order (see Fig. 1). It is easy to show that by means of a bijective mapping of the elements one can normalize any correct DLS, and the corresponding set of DLSs forms an equivalence class of $N!$ of them. For a number of problems, the squares within the equivalence class do not differ, since

© Springer Nature Switzerland AG 2019
V. Voevodin and S. Sobolev (Eds.): RuSCDays 2019, CCIS 1129, pp. 725–734, 2019.
https://doi.org/10.1007/978-3-030-36592-9_59

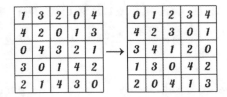

Fig. 1. Normalization of a DLS

they all possess the same properties (existence/absence of an orthogonal mate, the number of transversals etc.), which allows to significantly reduce the runtime in any corresponding computational experiment.

Latin squares find their applications in different areas [1]: in graph theory [2], the design of experiments [3], tournament scheduling [4], cryptography [5], encoding methods with error control for information transmission [6]. In theoretical combinatorics, a known unsolved mathematical problem is to find a triple of mutually orthogonal DLSs of order 10 or to prove that it does not exist [7].

In applications, it is important to know the structures of ODLSs subsets. However, the spaces of DLSs of order 9 or more have not been explicitly enumerated or described due to their large size. The presented work is aimed at directed research of the space of DLSs of order 9 using volunteer computing.

The systems of DLSs of order 9 connected by orthogonality relation have not been described before, excepting the case when all squares of a set are mutually orthogonal. Construction of ODLSs of orders 7 and 8 showed that row-permutational ODLSs can constitute parts of such systems. In the proposed work, the search is performed among the subset of such squares that can be obtained by rows permutations (with fixed first row) and are orthogonal to the initial square.

1.2   Desktop Grids

Desktop Grid is a distributed computing system that gathers together desktop computers, servers and/or other heterogeneous computational resources connected by the Internet or a local network and working for the Desktop Grid in their idle time. Traditional high-performance computing systems can be integrated into Desktop Grids as well [8]. The BOINC middleware [9] is often considered a de-facto standard for organizing Desktop Grids, as it is being actively developed and has been successfully used in many computational projects since 1997.

The BOINC system has a server-client architecture: a server distributes independent tasks to the nodes which perform computations and return the results to the server for further processing. Such division of a large resource-demanding computational problem into many independent tasks allows to solve it efficiently in a shorter time.

1.3   Search for Orthogonal Diagonal Latin Squares Using Desktop Grids

There are plenty of works that have used computers for finding or enumerating combinatorial structures based on Latin squares [10–14], in particular BOINC-based Desktop Grids [15–18].

The problem of characterizing subsets of ODLSs (as well as DLSs and LSs) fits well for implementation in Desktop Grids. The volunteer computing project SAT@home [19] searches for the pairs of ODLSs of order 10 and their systems using SAT methods within solving the problems of cryptoanalysis. The volunteer computing project Gerasim@home [20] performs search for the systems of ODLSs of order 10 and estimate some characteristics of DLSs of small order such as the minimal and maximal numbers of their transversals, number of symmetric and double symmetric squares, etc.

At the same time, the systems of ODLSs of order 9 have not been described, excepting the case when all squares of a set are mutually orthogonal. In this work, we describe the volunteer computing project RakeSearch [21] aimed at finding and describing such systems. The project is implemented basing on BOINC middleware within the grid segment of the Center for Collective Use of Karelian Research Center of the Russian Academy of Sciences [22]. The experience of building the computational infrastructure and porting the developed search application to it are described in [23].

In the rest of the paper we describe the details of implementing the volunteer computing project and the obtained results.

2   Setup of the BOINC-Based Desktop Grid

2.1   Server Infrastructure

At the moment, the project server works in a virtual machine which has 40 Gb hard drive and 8 Gb RAM. It is more than sufficient for supporting its work. On the average, 120 thousand of workunits are being processed every day; the average real performance of the project fluctuates within the range from 125 to 175 TeraFLOPS.

2.2   An Approach to Fast Discovery of Orthogonal Diagonal Mates

The total number of Latin squares of order 9 is 377 597 570 964 258 816 [24]. A classical method to search for ODLSs is the Euler-Parker approach which results in relatively slow discovery rate (about 2000 DLSs per second for order 9). It was noticed that the search among row-permutational squares (the ones obtained from an initial square by permutations of its rows) allows to find ODLSs much faster, resulting in the rate about 44–92 thousand DLSs per second depending on the optimization level. Such approach became the basis for the RakeSearch project. Figure 2 shows an example of row-permutational ODLSs of order 9.

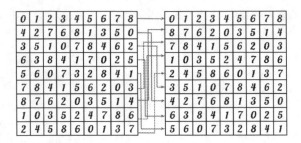

Fig. 2. Example of a pair of row-permutational ODLSs

2.3   Algorithm of Search for Row-Permutational ODLSs

Each instance of a workunit sent to a participant of the project is defined by a mask of a DLS with pre-filled first row, main and secondary diagonals and the first element of the second row (Fig. 3).

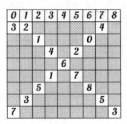

Fig. 3. Example of an input file for the workunit: the mask of a DLS

The overview of the computational algorithm is as follows:

1. Launch;
2. Verify the existence of the checkpoint file and the input parameters file;
3. Set the state of the computational process basing by the content of either the checkpoint file or the input parameters file (if the former is absent);
4. Search for row-permutational DLSs.

The input data are:

- `newSquare`—a matrix of a partially filled DLS;
- `path[l][2]`—two-dimensional array of length l, where l is the count of square cells to be filled, and (`path[i][0]`, `path[i][1]`) are the coordinates of a square cell to be filled according to the i-th position in the bypass path of the square. When bypassing the square, we can return to the same `path[i]` but with different values;
- `keyRowId`, `keyColumnId`, `keyValue`—coordinates of the "key cell" and its value indicating the end of search.

The variables of search are:

- `cellId`—the number of a cell in `path` according to which we are filling one of the square cells;
- `columns[n][n]`, `rows[n][n]`, `primary[n]`, `secondary[n]`—flag arrays indicating the use of cell values in columns, rows and diagonals;
- `cellsHistory[n][n][n]`—flag arrays indicating the previous use of cell values in the process of square filling (history of the cell values).

Bypass the matrix `newSquare` according to the path until the value in the key cell reaches the given one;

4.1. Fill the next cell of `newSquare`:
   Look through the possible values of the cell, from 1 to `n`. If we managed to find such `i`-th value that has not been used in these row and column and has not been written in the history of cell values, then remember it and:
   (a) Write the found value into the square;
      (1) If the square cell already contains a value, remember it;
      (2) Write the found value into the square matrix;
      (3) Write the fact of using the value into the flag arrays;
      (4) Unset the flags of using the previous value of the cell in the flag arrays, but not in the history of the cell values!
      (5) Step forward on the bypass path of the square (`path`);
      (6) If we have reached the path end, then the square is filled, a DLS is formed; call the row-permutational search for ODLSs for the obtained DLS.
   Otherwise:
   (b) Due to inability to fill the current cell with a new value, return to the previous cell:
      (1) For the value written into the current cell, unset the flags of its usage;
      (2) Write into the current cell an "empty value";
      (3) Clear the history of values for the current cell;
      (4) Step backward on the bypass path of the square (`path`).

The algorithm of search for orthogonal diagonal mates by rows permutations does permute the rows using the similar flag arrays, and after each permutation checks the resulting square for orthogonality to the initial one.

The search can be further optimized. The initial algorithm uses ordinary C++ arrays as the flag arrays. But if one replaces them with bit arrays and performs the search for the first free element using BSF instruction called by the functions `_BitScanForward` (in case of Visual C++) and `__builtin_ffs` (in case of GNU C++), then one can remove the corresponding loops of search from the program making it faster.

The program code is available online [25].

3   RakeSearch Project

The application was implemented for Linux 32- and 64-bit, Windows 32- and 64-bit and Android ARM. The average running time of a workunit was about 5 h for the default application and 30 min for the optimized application. Deadline was set to one week, the quorum was 2.

Orthogonal pairs of row-permutational DLSs have been found since the very first weeks of the project's work. Having assigned badges for their discovery, we attracted more volunteers to participate.

In December 2017, the first discovered graph of ODLSs was published on the project webpage. All discovered pairs of orthogonal DLSs are being published on the project website together with the workunit name and the names of the participants whose computers found them.

At the end of April 2018, the project experienced a peak load period during the first competition of BOINC teams. In July 2018, the Formula BOINC [26] sprint was held on the basis of the project, causing the highest load period ever. In Fig. 4 we provide the results receiving rate in a time interval including three days before the sprint start, the sprint itself and three days after the sprint end. Each bar on the diagram shows the number of results received during the corresponding hour. We see large spikes immediately after the race start and on the start of the last day of the competition. The results receiving rate was 10–15 times more than the average of the usual load. Such period of a high load revealed the bottleneck components of the server to be the database parameters for RAM caching, hard drive I/O performance and low parallelization of server daemons.

Basing on the results of the sprint, we optimized the MySQL instance serving the project database, and modified the algorithm of data archiving. These modifications will provide the basis for other periods of high load and improve the project scalability in general.

4   Results of the Project

At the time of June 2019, the RakeSearch project has been running for 22 months. With about 3000 active computational nodes belonging to more than 600 participants, its maximal daily average performance corresponded to the performance of a 100 TeraFLOPS cluster.

Such amount of available computational resources allowed to complete more than 23 million workunits in 22 months. The search results are represented in form of orthogonality graphs, where the vertices are DLSs of order 9, and there is an edge between two vertices if the corresponding squares are mutually orthogonal. Such graphs are undirected, without loops and multi-edges.

In total, 175 unique types of orthogonality graphs have been found in the project. Their sizes vary from 2 vertices and one edge to 649 728 vertices and 3 178 752 edges. We present 20 largest graphs in Table 1. One square per the each of graphs are presented in string representation (elements of the square are

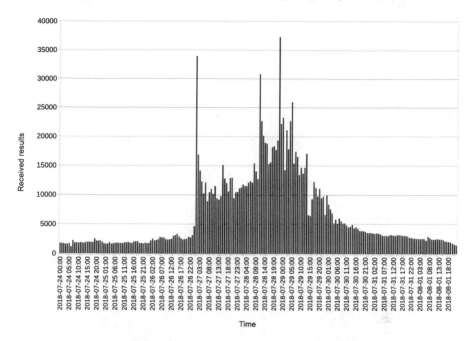

Fig. 4. Results receiving rate during the high server load

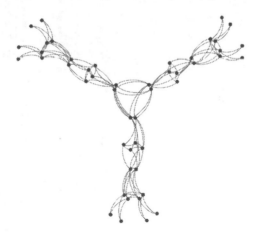

Fig. 5. The "Necklace" graph of orthogonal diagonal Latin squares of order 9

written from left to right in each row and from top to bottom row). In Fig. 5, we provide the first discovered graph which has 48 vertices and 123 edges.

Some graphs that were found earlier during investigating properties of central symmetry [27] of DLSs for this moment are not present in the list which means they do not contain row-permutational square pairs. Some graphs found within the project probably may have a coinciding number of vertices and edges,

Table 1. Largest graphs of orthogonal diagonal Latin squares of order 9 obtained in the RakeSearch project.

Graph no.	Vertices	Edges	Square
1	150	1194	012345678423076815781603542648532701154860237830457126267184350506721483375218064
2	154	1263	012345678427683510561824307736450182350268741148537026604712853875106234283071465
3	164	1383	012345678127850346861703524204671185374513806245628713038052641757306428163841270 5
4	176	912	012345678425681730563027481137456802348570216704168523680234157851702364276813045
5	181	1321	012345678523874016271480563160532784384761205756028431847106352635217840408653127
6	208	1412	012345678628134705831207564467582310504761283785413026243076851370658142156820437
7	210	1524	012345678526814037471683250763450821305168742284537106857206314640721583138072465
8	212	1104	012345678123857046451286730637412860557406328174013856286570132420867415338652041 7
9	224	1112	012345678124857306453786120701624853334657801286720153428513046753046278167801324 5
10	292	1882	012345678423076815781657816530426485327015048612378354071262671843501567204833702185 64
11	294	2234	012345678826057143481763025374681502540132867657208431235410786163874250708526314
12	368	1864	012345678628174305871203564446358271050486123738541702624703685173065814215672048 3
13	2388	7752	012345678627134805871603524380457162504861237735218046463582710248076351156720483
14	4048	6968	012345678828543176060385714245160238716827405374601823538472650123758041657016382 4
15	9056	45976	012345678128604537261758403873421056540863721654237810485170362307516284736082145
16	44160	231744	012345678728206835148412370564735028611547602833654781026870143252381567405068214 37
17	58368	546048	012345678728758013461637280534416720286053417604287135451672803870134562347560281
18	61824	374064	012345678428236187508517204637804531263758610426382075142675348015041862371460723 85
19	113616	675264	012345678421806537153280764508671342780453126834067215376128450645712083267534801
20	649728	3178752	012345678527186043631870524853421760745068132104237856280654317476503281368712405

however, they may not be isomorphic, which requires a separate study. All discovered graphs are visualized using the Gephi software [28] and published on the project website.

5 Conclusion

We have described the start-up of a volunteer computing project aimed at characterizing the space of diagonal Latin squares of order 9 and the experience of running it for 22 months. During this time, 175 unique types of orthogonality graphs have been found in the project. The obtained results prove the efficiency of distributed computing in unveiling the structure of the space of DLSs.

Acknowledgments. We would like to thank all volunteers who provided their computers to the project. We thank Daniel (BOINC@Poland team) for developing an optimized search application that allowed to save a lot of computational resources and time. Discussions and advice on the project forum were greatly appreciated too.

This work was supported by the Russian Foundation for Basic Research [grant numbers 18-07-00628_a, 18-37-00094_mol_a and 17-07-00317_a].

References

1. Colbourn, C.J., Dinitz, J.H.: Handbook of Combinatorial Designs, Second Edition (Discrete Mathematics and Its Applications). Chapman & Hall/CRC, Boca Raton (2006)
2. Bolshakova, N.S.: About one another application of Latin squares. Vestnik of MSTU **8**(1), 170–173 (2005). (in Russian)
3. Thomas, P.R., Morgan, J.P.: Modern experimental design. Stat. Theory Pract. **1**(3–4), 501–506 (2007)
4. Anderson, I.: Combinatorial Designs and Tournaments, vol. 6. Oxford University Press, Oxford (1997)
5. Cooper, J., Donovan, D., Seberry, J.: Secret sharing schemes arising from Latin squares. Bull. Inst. Comb. Appl. **12**, 33–43 (1994)
6. MacWilliams, F.J., Sloane, N.J.A.: The Theory of Error-Correcting Codes. North Holland Publishing Co., Amsterdam (1977)
7. Zaikin, O., Zhuravlev, A., Kochemazov, S., Vatutin, E.: On the construction of triples of diagonal Latin squares of order 10. Electron. Notes Discrete Math. **54**, 307–312 (2016)
8. Afanasiev, A.P., Bychkov, I.V., Manzyuk, M.O., Posypkin, M.A., Semenov, A.A., Zaikin, O.S.: Technology for integrating idle computing cluster resources into volunteer computing projects. In: Proceedings of the 5th International Workshop on Computer Science and Engineering, Moscow, Russia, pp. 109–114 (2015)
9. Anderson, D.P.: BOINC: a platform for volunteer computing. J Grid Computing (2019)
10. Parker, E.T.: Computer investigation of orthogonal Latin squares of order ten. In: Proceeding of Symposia in Applied Mathematics, vol. 15, pp. 73–81 (1963)
11. McKay, B.D., Rogoyski, E.: Latin squares of order 10. Electron. J. Comb. **2**(3), 1–4 (1995)

12. McKay, B.D., Wanless, I.M.: On the number of Latin squares. Ann. Comb. **9**(3), 335–344 (2005)
13. McKay, B.D., Meynert, A., Myrvold, W.: Small Latin squares, quasigroups, and loops. J. Comb. Des. **15**(2), 98–119 (2007)
14. Egan, J., Wanless, I.: Enumeration of MOLS of small order. Math. Comput. **85**(298), 799–824 (2016)
15. Lin, H.-H., Wu, I-C.: Solving the minimum sudoku poblem. In: 2010 International Conference on Technologies and Applications of Artificial Intelligence, pp. 456–461. IEEE (2010)
16. Vatutin, E.I., Zaikin, O.S., Kochemazov, S.E., Valyaev, S.Y.: Using volunteer computing to study some features of diagonal Latin squares. Open Eng. **7**(1), 453–460 (2017)
17. Vatutin, E.I., Kochemazov, S.E., Zaikin, O.S.: Applying volunteer and parallel computing for enumerating diagonal Latin squares of order 9. In: Sokolinsky, L., Zymbler, M. (eds.) PCT 2017. CCIS, vol. 753, pp. 114–129. Springer, Cham (2017). https://doi.org/10.1007/978-3-319-67035-5_9
18. Vatutin, E., Belyshev, A., Kochemazov, S., Zaikin, O., Nikitina, N.: Enumeration of isotopy classes of diagonal Latin squares of small order using volunteer computing. In: Voevodin, V., Sobolev, S. (eds.) RuSCDays 2018. CCIS, vol. 965, pp. 578–586. Springer, Cham (2019). https://doi.org/10.1007/978-3-030-05807-4_49
19. Zaikin, O., Kochemazov, S.: The search for systems of diagonal Latin squares using the SAT@home project. Int. J. Open Inf. Technol. **3**(11), 4–9 (2015)
20. Vatutin, E., Zaikin, O., Kochemazov, S., Valyaev, S.: Using volunteer computing to study some features of diagonal Latin square. Open Eng. **7**, 453–460 (2017)
21. RakeSearch. https://rake.boincfast.ru/rakesearch. Accessed 23 June 2019
22. Center for Collective Use of Karelian Research Center of the Russian Academy of Sciences. http://cluster.krc.karelia.ru/index.php?plang=e. Accessed 23 June 2019
23. Nikitina, N.N., Manzyuk, M.O., Vatutin, E.I.: Employment of distributed computing to search and explore orthogonal diagonal Latin squares of rank 9. In: Proceedings of the XI(1) All-Russian Research and Practice Conference on Digital Technologies in Education, Science, Society, pp. 97–100, November 2017. (in Russian)
24. Bammel, S.E., Rothstein, J.: The number of 9 × 9 Latin squares. Discrete Math. **11**(1), 93–95 (1975)
25. GitHub - Nevecie/RakeSearch: Rake search of Diagonal Latin Squares. https://github.com/Nevecie/RakeSearch. Accessed 23 June 2019
26. Formula BOINC. http://formula-boinc.org/. Accessed 23 June 2019
27. Vatutin, E.I., Kochemazov, S.E., Zaikin, O.S., Manzuk, M.O., Nikitina, N.N., Titov, V.S.: Properties of central symmetry for diagonal Latin squares (in Russian). High-Perform. Comput. Syst. Technol. **8**, 74–78 (2018)
28. Bastian, M., Heymann, S., Jacomy, M.: Gephi: an open source software for exploring and manipulating networks. In: International AAAI Conference on Weblogs and Social Media, pp. 1–2 (2009)

Use of a Desktop Grid to Effectively Discover Hits in Virtual Drug Screening

Evgeny Ivashko[1,2] and Natalia Nikitina[1]

[1] Institute of Applied Mathematical Research,
Karelian Research Centre of the RAS, Petrozavodsk, Russia
{ivashko,nikitina}@krc.karelia.ru
[2] Petrozavodsk State University, Petrozavodsk, Russia

Abstract. In this paper, we propose an efficient computational scheme for virtual drug screening using a Desktop Grid. The scheme is based on a game-theoretical mathematical model, more precisely a crowding game. The proposed scheme provides needed balance between the results quality and the search scope.

Keywords: High-throughput computing · Desktop Grid · BOINC · Task scheduling · Virtual screening · Game theory · Nash equilibrium

1 Introduction

High-performance computing plays today a significant role in implementing fundamental and applied research, developing new materials, new medicines, new types of industrial products etc. In particular, many fundamental and applied problems require execution of a large number of loosely-coupled computational tasks which is referred to as high-throughput computing (HTC). Aside from the common types of dedicated systems such as computational clusters, commercial clouds and Grids, the paradigm of Desktop Grid computing is also being applied for solving resource-demanding computational problems.

The term of Desktop Grid stands for a distributed HTC system which uses idle time of non-dedicated geographically distributed computing nodes connected over a low-speed regular network, as opposed to the supercomputer interconnect. In common case, the nodes are personal computers of volunteers connected over the Internet (volunteer computing) or organization desktop computers connected over local area network (Enterprise Desktop Grid). Desktop Grids can also be integrated into computational clusters or Grid systems – see [1,2] for examples.

In this paper we consider the applied problem of virtual drug screening using Desktop Grid. Overall, the creation of new medicines is a time-consuming process with high costs of research and development. Virtual drug screening [3] (further VS) allows to bring *in silico* the first stage of drug development process, namely the identification of a set of chemical compounds called *hits* with predicted desired biochemical activity. Hits are identified among a set of *ligands*,

© Springer Nature Switzerland AG 2019
V. Voevodin and S. Sobolev (Eds.): RuSCDays 2019, CCIS 1129, pp. 735–743, 2019.
https://doi.org/10.1007/978-3-030-36592-9_60

low-molecular compounds able to form a biochemical complex with a protein molecule responsible for disease progression, called *a target*.

VS methods can base on the knowledge about either the structures of known ligands (ligand-based VS) or the structure of the target protein (structure-based VS). In this work we will further restrict ourselves to the latter case.

In the course of structure-based VS, one performs molecular docking – computer modelling of the interaction of the candidate ligands with the target – and scores the resulting molecular complexes. The ligands with highest scores become hits. At the next stages of research, hits with proven biological activity become *leads*.

VS has recently assisted drug discovery [4,5] and development of new materials [6,7]. A review on the latest achievements and current state of VS lists more than a hundred successful examples of ligand discoveries in silico [8].

The problem of VS implementation is the need of substantial computational and temporal resources to estimate potential pharmacological properties of a set of molecules and to identify most prospective ligands. VS is not restricted by existing libraries of synthesised molecules, but can also be applied to estimate the prospectivity of chemical compounds that have not yet been synthesised or of molecule fragments.

Consequently, the large sizes of the libraries of ligands and target structure models bring up the necessity to involve the HPC/HTC tools for the VS, although the modelling of the interaction between a separate ligand and the given target is performed relatively quickly. The examples of such tools are supercomputers [9] and clouds [10]. Desktop Grids are instrumental for implementing VS as well [11–14].

The main factors of structure-based VS progress for the following years are believed to be the discovery of novel chemotypes, the improvement of molecular docking methods, quality of the molecule libraries and methods of target selection [8].

The problem of the discovery of novel chemotypes is closely connected with the problem of the fastest retrieval of the mostly chemically diverse hits for their testing in a laboratory [15]. At the same time, the desired set of hits for testing in the laboratory should be maximally diverse in terms of chemical properties, even if each distinct cluster of similar molecules contains only a few elements [16]. This increases the likelihood of finding lead compounds and reduces the number of false negative errors in the initial stages of the search.

To summarise, in the course of VS there is a need to balance between the hits discovery rate and their chemical diversity, or the chemical space coverage. The aim can be reached by special task scheduling when a ligand is selected for molecular docking in such a way that it has a high probability of being a hit and, at the same time, it differs from the already found hits.

Such a balance between the number and the diversity of hits can be formulated by means of a mathematical model for task scheduling in an HTC system.

In this paper, we propose a computational scheme for achieving the balance between the results retrieval rate and the search space coverage when performing

VS in a BOINC-based Desktop Grid with asynchronous task distribution and decentralised data sharing.

The rest of the paper has the following structure. In Sect. 2, we overview the existing works on task scheduling in Desktop Grids and task scheduling for VS. In Sect. 3, we describe a game-theoretical mathematical model of task scheduling for VS in Desktop Grids. In Sect. 4, we provide the task scheduling algorithm and computational process for a BOINC-based Desktop Grid which are based on the previously described mathematical model. Finally, in Sect. 5, we conclude the paper with result discussion and directions of future work.

2 Related Work

Apart from fundamental biological issues, preparation of target and ligands libraries and post-processing the VS results, one solves many tasks when organising VS. Let us divide them into three groups:

1. Efficiency of the molecular docking;
2. Efficiency of leveraging the HPC/HTC resources;
3. Efficiency of organising the search process in a chemical space.

The first task can be formulated as search for the compromise between speed and accuracy of molecular docking. The accuracy is usually increased by transmitting most computationally demanding parts of the modelling onto computing nodes or co-processors of increased performance: for instance, GPU [17] and Intel processors with MIC architecture [18]. Heuristics, such as gradually increasing the accuracy with reduction of the ligands set, are used as well [4,5].

The second task is being solved by optimisation of the computational system. In work [19], the authors consider VS in a multi-user environment. They compare various scheduling algorithms and address such efficiency criteria as fairness and user response time together with the overall system throughput.

The efficiency of a Desktop Grid configuration is being estimated by a certain set of characteristics, which most often include the total execution time of a set of tasks [20,21], the average system throughput [22,23], the error probability or the expected proportion of erroneous results [21,24], the number of overhead costs [24,25].

When modelling the Desktop Grid systems, game-theoretic methods can be used [24,26,27]. In 2015, a thesis [28] was defended on the topic of task scheduling in distributed computing systems based on optimisation methods and game theory. It presents methods for fair distribution of resources between heterogeneous computing nodes in order to optimise the throughput and average task execution time. The current state of research in the field of task scheduling in the Desktop Grid is described in the paper [29].

The third task is related to filtering the ligands space so as to concentrate on the most representative and chemically diverse compounds that can show required biological activity. The problem of fast retrieval of the most diverse hits is being solved, for example, using genetic algorithms and heuristics [30]. In work [31], the authors solve the problem of fast retrieval of the most prospective ligands at early stages of VS using the method of dividing the search space into classes by given molecular properties (including the estimation of the energy of binding with the target) and calculating the Bayesian probability of new ligands to fall into one or another class.

In paper [32], a congestion game was first proposed to provide a balance between the chemical diversity of results and the chemical space coverage. In work [33], this model was applied for developing a BOINC-based Enterprise Desktop Grid for VS. Further, in [34], the proposed model was modified so as to enable dynamic adjustment of the balance between the results quality and the search scope. The models allow to investigate the system's behaviour and reach the balance between the quality of results and the search scope. Yet, they have a drawback of the necessity to solve the optimisation problem by the project server that negatively influences its performance. Another drawback is the discretisation of the moments of task distribution so that the endings of all computations performed by all nodes must be synchronised.

The proposed in the present paper approach is free from these drawbacks. Deployment of a specific procedure of information exchange between the nodes (not present in BOINC by default) allows using a shared file resource in order to transfer the necessity of decision making to the computing nodes themselves. With such enrichment, the solution of the optimisation problem is simplified, the form of utility functions allows to get rid of discretisation and the necessity of synchronisation of the computing nodes. At the same time, the server keeps the capability of dynamic balance between the number of useful results and the search scope.

3   Mathematical Model

We propose to model the computational process using a crowding game, which is a singleton congestion game with player-specific payoffs [35]. More specifically, a crowding game is a non-cooperative game of N agents in strategic form (1) where a strategy of each player i is to choose exactly one resource r from a finite set of resources $\mathcal{R} = \{1, \ldots, R\}$ shared by all players, while his payoff function S_{ir} is non-increasing by the number of players n_r who have chosen the same resource.

$$\Gamma = \langle \mathcal{N}, (S_i)_{i \in \mathcal{N}}, (U_i)_{i \in \mathcal{N}} \rangle = \langle \mathcal{N}, \mathcal{R}, (U_i)_{i \in \mathcal{N}} \rangle \tag{1}$$

The motivation of a player to choose a task block r is the expected number of hits he would find and their value. The hit value depends on the number of previously found hits in the same block: it is preferable to discover one of the few. Also, it depends on the fraction size of the block to investigate: the more molecules the block has, the more diverse they potentially are.

Each report of results to the server marks an update of the progress of virtual screening. The progress is reflected by the following variables: n_r—the number of finished tasks in block r, h_r—the number of discovered hits in block r, σ_r—the observed fraction of hits considering an apriori estimate. The initial number of tasks in block r is N_r.

A hit may have different value depending not only on its uniqueness but also on the overall progress of the block. We assume that the larger is the remaining part of the block, the more diverse are potential hits. On the contrary, if the block is nearly empty, the likelihood to find anything unique is small. Under such assumptions, we define the hit value in block r as follows:

$$c_r = F_c(n_r, h_r). \tag{2}$$

With heterogeneous nodes, each node may receive different amount of work. More precisely, the node C_i will receive w_i tasks. The total number of tasks taken by all players who selected block r will constitute w_r. Then the current hit value in a block will depend on block congestion together with the overall progress of the block,

$$\delta_r = F_\delta(N_r, n_r, w_r, h_r, \sigma_r). \tag{3}$$

Under such assumptions, the utility of node C_i that chooses block r takes the following form:

$$U_{ir} = w_i\left(\alpha\delta_r + (1-\alpha)\sigma_r\right). \tag{4}$$

Here, $\alpha \in [0, 1]$ is the coefficient to express the type of a player: does he tend to be a "digger" ($\alpha = 0$) or an "explorer" ($\alpha = 1$).

Each player maximizes its own utility U_{ir} using formula (4) and chooses the corresponding block $r_i^\star$:

$$r^\star = \arg\max_r U_{ir}. \tag{5}$$

A strategy profile $\bar{s} = (s_1, \ldots, s_N) \in \mathcal{R}^N$ is a Nash equilibrium in game $\Gamma \iff \forall i \in \mathcal{N}, \forall t \in \mathcal{R}, U_{is_i}(\bar{s}) \geq U_{it}(t, \bar{s}_{-i})$. It means that the equilibrium action s_i of player i is his best response against the actions of other players.

4   Computational Process

The described above mathematical model provides to each computing node a task which is the most valuable from the point of view of balance between the number of hits and their diversity. The task assignment algorithm and the corresponding computational process can be centralised or decentralised.

Using the centralised algorithm, a server holds the actual values of parameters (n_r—the number of finished tasks in block r, h_r—the number of discovered hits in block r, σ_r—the observed fraction of hits considering an apriori estimate, α, δ); it also solves the optimisation problem (4) to find out the block from which to assign tasks. In this case computational nodes do not make any decisions, just perform computations. Finishing the computations, a computing node transfer the results to the server, which put them into a database, and when recalculate the values of parameters and solves the optimisation problem again. This approach corresponds to the regular use of a Desktop Grid and to the computational process of BOINC. Pseudo code of the algorithm is presented below.

Server

0. Input data: apriori values of δ_j, σ_j, α; generated tasks.
1. If a client i asks for a task, solve equation (5), send a task from the block $r^\star$.
2. Update $w_r^\star$.
   Update α if necessary.
3. If a client sends a result, receive it and update δ_j, σ, $n_r^\star$ $h_r^\star$.
   Update α if necessary.

Client

0. Set resources for the project.
1. Ask for tasks.
2. Perform computations.
3. Send the result to the server.

Using the decentralised algorithm, one de-facto substitutes the server of a Desktop Grid by a shared file resource. This file resource stores all the tasks partitioned to the blocks, a database of the computations results, and the actual values of the parameters. A computing node reads the values of the parameters and solves the optimisation problem (4), then grabs tasks of the corresponding block and updates the parameters. Finishing the computations, the computing node writes data to the shared database and updates the parameters. This approach reduces the load of the server of a Desktop Grid (consequently, increases the number of served computing nodes) or eliminates it at all, but needs appropriate efforts to support parallel handling of the file resources by multiple computing nodes. Pseudo code of the algorithm is presented below.

Server

0. Input data: apriori values of δ_j, σ_j, α; generated tasks.
   Shared file resources: tasks, database of the results, parameters.

Client

0. Set resources for the project.
1. Select the task block j that maximises the utility (4). Ask the server for a task of block j. If success, update c_j and n_j.
2. Execute the task.
3. Send the result to the server.

In both cases the parameter α can be changed during the computational process.

5 Conclusion

Virtual drug screening is one of the major stages of drug development. At this stage, one needs to filter a huge space of potentially active chemical compounds using specific computer models to discover compounds with desired properties.

Despite the employment of HPC technologies, this stage of drug development remains quite long due to a large number of potentially active chemical compounds to check. However, the proper organisation of virtual screening allows solving the problem of the fastest acquisition of hit compounds.

In this paper, we propose a mathematical model that develops our previous works in this area. The model describes a game-theoretical setup or, more precisely, the crowding game enabling the balance between the number of hit compounds and the search scope. In contrast with our previous works, the proposed model is better adapted to a computational process in a Desktop Grid. Specifically, the task distribution between the nodes is performed asynchronically, and the data for an optimal choice of tasks is shared avoiding the involvement of the computational server. We describe a centralised and decentralised approaches to the computational process implementation. We describe the corresponding computational procedure and the algorithm of task distribution between the nodes.

The proposed mathematical model, the corresponding computational process and the algorithm of task distribution between the nodes can serve as a basis for creating a specialised Enterprise Desktop Grid for virtual drug screening.

Acknowledgements. This work was supported by the Russian Foundation of Basic Research, projects 18-07-00628 and 18-37-00094.

References

1. Afanasiev, A.P., Bychkov, I.V., Zaikin, O.S., Manzyuk, M.O., Posypkin, M.A., Semenov, A.A.: Concept of a multitask grid system with a flexible allocation of idle computational resources of supercomputers. J. Comput. Syst. Sci. Int. **56**(4), 701–707 (2017)
2. Kovács, J., Marosi, A.C., Visegrádi, Á., Farkas, Z., Kacsuk, P., Lovas, R.: Boosting gLite with cloud augmented volunteer computing. Future Gener. Comput. Syst. **43–44**, 12–23 (2015)
3. Bielska, E., Lucas, X., Czerwoniec, A., Kasprzak, J.M., Kaminska, K.H., Bujnicki, J.M.: Virtual screening strategies in drug design – methods and applications. J. Biotechnol. Comput. Biol. Bionanotechnol. **92**(3), 249–264 (2011)
4. Pandey, R.K., et al.: Exploring dual inhibitory role of febrifugine analogues against plasmodium utilizing structure-based virtual screening and molecular dynamic simulation. J. Biomol. Struct. Dyn. **35**(4), 791–804 (2017)
5. Mirza, S.B., Salmas, R.E., Fatmi, M.Q., Durdagi, S.: Virtual screening of eighteen million compounds against dengue virus: combined molecular docking and molecular dynamics simulations study. J. Mol. Graph. Model. **66**, 99–107 (2016)
6. Gómez-Bombarelli, R., et al.: Design of efficient molecular organic light-emitting diodes by a high-throughput virtual screening and experimental approach. Nat. Mater. **15**, 1120–1127 (2016)

7. Husch, T., Yilmazer, N.D., Balducci, A., Korth, M.: Large-scale virtual high-throughput screening for the identification of new battery electrolyte solvents: computing infrastructure and collective properties. Phys. Chem. Chem. Phys. **17**(5), 3394–3401 (2015)
8. Irwin, J.J., Shoichet, B.K.: Docking screens for novel ligands conferring new biology. J. Med. Chem. **59**(9), 4103–4120 (2016)
9. Luo, C., et al.: Applying high-performance computing in drug discovery and molecular simulation. Nat. Sci. Rev. **3**(1), 49–63 (2016)
10. Olğaç, A., Türe, A., Olğaç, S., Möller, S.: Cloud-based high throughput virtual screening in novel drug discovery. In: Kołodziej, J., González-Vélez, H. (eds.) High-Performance Modelling and Simulation for Big Data Applications. LNCS, vol. 11400, pp. 250–278. Springer, Cham (2019). https://doi.org/10.1007/978-3-030-16272-6_9
11. Xia, J., et al.: Massive-scale binding free energy simulations of HIV integrase complexes using asynchronous replica exchange framework implemented on the IBM WCG distributed network. J. Chem. Inf. Model. **59**(4), 1382–1397 (2019). PMID: 30758197
12. Ochoa, R., Watowich, S.J., Flórez, A., Mesa, C.V., Robledo, S.M., Muskus, C.: Drug search for leishmaniasis: a virtual screening approach by grid computing. J. Comput.-Aided Mol. Des. **30**(7), 541–552 (2016)
13. Perryman, A.L., et al.: A virtual screen discovers novel, fragment-sized inhibitors of mycobacterium tuberculosis inha. J. Chem. Inf. Model. **55**(3), 645–659 (2015). PMID: 25636146
14. Nakamura, Y., et al.: Identification of novel candidate compounds targeting TrkB to induce apoptosis in neuroblastoma. Cancer Med. **3**(1), 25–35 (2014)
15. Harper, G., Pickett, S.D., Green, D.V.: Design of a compound screening collection for use in high throughput screening. Comb. Chem. High Throughput Screening **7**(1), 63–70 (2004)
16. Lionta, E., Spyrou, G., Vassilatis, D.K., Cournia, Z.: Structure-based virtual screening for drug discovery: principles, applications and recent advances. Curr. Top. Med. Chem. **14**(16), 1923–1938 (2014)
17. Imbernón, B., Cecilia, J.M., Pérez-Sánchez, H., Giménez, D.: METADOCK: a parallel metaheuristic schema for virtual screening methods. Int. J. High Perform. Comput. Appl. **32**(6), 789–803 (2018)
18. Cheng, Q., Peng, S., Lu, Y., Zhu, W., Xu, Z., Zhang, X.: MD3DOCKxb: an ultra-scalable CPU-MIC coordinated virtual screening framework. In: Proceedings of the 17th IEEE/ACM International Symposium on Cluster, Cloud and Grid Computing, pp. 671–676. IEEE Press (2017)
19. Kim, J.-S., et al.: Towards effective scheduling policies for many-task applications: practice and experience based on HTCaaS. Concurr. Comput. Pract. Exp. **29**(21), e4242 (2017)
20. Moca, M., Litan, C., Silaghi, G.C., Fedak, G.: Multi-criteria and satisfaction oriented scheduling for hybrid distributed computing infrastructures. Future Gener. Comput. Syst. **55**, 428–443 (2016)
21. Ochi, K., Fukushi, M.: A group-based job scheduling method for parallel volunteer computing. In: 2015 Third International Symposium on Computing and Networking (CANDAR), pp. 571–575. IEEE (2015)
22. Yasuda, S., Nogami, Y., Fukushi, M.: A dynamic job scheduling method for reliable and high-performance volunteer computing. In: 2015 2nd International Conference on Information Science and Security (ICISS), pp. 1–4. IEEE (2015)

23. Atlas, J., Estrada, T., Decker, K., Taufer, M.: Balancing scientist needs and volunteer preferences in volunteer computing using constraint optimization. In: Allen, G., Nabrzyski, J., Seidel, E., van Albada, G.D., Dongarra, J., Sloot, P.M.A. (eds.) ICCS 2009. LNCS, vol. 5544, pp. 143–152. Springer, Heidelberg (2009). https://doi.org/10.1007/978-3-642-01970-8_15

24. Wang, Y., Wei, J., Ren, S., Shen, Y.: Toward integrity assurance of outsourced computing—a game theoretic perspective. Future Gener. Comput. Syst. **55**, 87–100 (2016)

25. Chmaj, G., Walkowiak, K., Tarnawski, M., Kucharzak, M.: Heuristic algorithms for optimization of task allocation and result distribution in peer-to-peer computing systems. Int. J. Appl. Math. Comput. Sci. **22**(3), 733–748 (2012)

26. Anta, A.F., Georgiou, C., Mosteiro, M.A., Pareja, D.: Multi-round master-worker computing: a repeated game approach. In: 2016 IEEE 35th Symposium on Reliable Distributed Systems (SRDS), pp. 31–40. IEEE (2016)

27. Donassolo, B., Legrand, A., Geyer, C.: Non-cooperative scheduling considered harmful in collaborative volunteer computing environments. In: Proceedings of the 2011 11th IEEE/ACM International Symposium on Cluster, Cloud and Grid Computing, pp. 144–153. IEEE Computer Society (2011)

28. Legrand, A.: Scheduling for large scale distributed computing systems: approaches and performance evaluation issues. Ph.D. thesis. Université Grenoble Alpes (2015)

29. Ivashko, E., Chernov, I., Nikitina, N.: A survey of desktop grid scheduling. IEEE Trans. Parallel Distrib. Syst. **29**(12), 2882–2895 (2018)

30. Rupakheti, C., Virshup, A., Yang, W., Beratan, D.N.: Strategy to discover diverse optimal molecules in the small molecule universe. J. Chem. Inf. Model. **55**(3), 529–537 (2015)

31. Pradeep, P., Struble, C., Neumann, T., Sem, D.S., Merrill, S.J.: A novel scoring based distributed protein docking application to improve enrichment. IEEE/ACM Trans. Comput. Biol. Bioinf. **12**(6), 1464–1469 (2015)

32. Nikitina, N., Ivashko, E., Tchernykh, A.: Congestion game scheduling for virtual drug screening optimization. J. Comput. Aided Mol. Des. **32**, 363 (2018)

33. Nikitina, N., Ivashko, E., Tchernykh, A.: Congestion game scheduling implementation for high-throughput virtual drug screening using BOINC-based desktop grid. In: Malyshkin, V. (ed.) PaCT 2017. LNCS, vol. 10421, pp. 480–491. Springer, Cham (2017). https://doi.org/10.1007/978-3-319-62932-2_46

34. Nikitina, N., Ivashko, E.: Adaptive scheduling for adjusting retrieval process in BOINC-based virtual screening. In: Voevodin, V., Sobolev, S. (eds.) RuSCDays 2018. CCIS, vol. 965, pp. 453–464. Springer, Cham (2019). https://doi.org/10.1007/978-3-030-05807-4_38

35. Milchtaich, I.: Congestion games with player-specific payoff functions. Games Econ. Behav. **13**, 111–124 (1996)

Author Index

Printed in the United States
By Bookmasters